The Squadrons
of the
Royal Air Force

James J Halley

An AIR-BRITAIN Publication

FOUNDED
1948

Published in Great Britain by
Air-Britain (Historians) Ltd
1 East Street, Tonbridge, Kent, England

ISBN 0 85130 083 9

Printed by Kingprint Ltd
Orchard Road, Richmond, Surrey TW9 4PD

Worldwide distribution by
Midland Counties Publications
24 The Hollow, Earl Shilton
Leicester, LE9 7NA

Venom NF.3 night fighters of No.23 Squadron over the Norfolk coast.

Foreword

In 1969, Air-Britain produced two volumes entitled *Royal Air Force Unit Histories 1918–1968*. This was the first time that brief histories of all Royal Air Force squadrons had been collected together as a single work. Since then many changes have taken place and new facts unearthed.

This volume has expanded on the earlier edition by the inclusion of movement and equipment tables. The former details the exact dates of squadron moves as far as possible while the latter gives the months of re-equipment, the mark numbers of each type and a representative serial number for the benefit, mainly, of modellers looking for an appropriate marking for a particular type and unit.

For the first time, an order of battle for RAF squadrons can now be compiled for any date to show the location, role and equipment of each squadron. While we are making no claim to total omniscience, especially in view of the workings of the Public Records Act which denies access to documents with a closing date more recent than thirty years, we believe the end-result is about 99% complete and awaiting the final one per cent would place a severe strain on the author s longevity. A bird in the hand is perhaps worth 1.01 in the bush.

It goes without saying that the compilation of this book owes much to a large number of organisations and individuals who have made material available for research. First and foremost, our gratitude to the staff of the Air Historical Branch of the Ministry of Defence who, over the past twenty years, have produced literally tons of records for perusal and continue to be unfailingly helpful despite the manifold demands of importunate historians.

We would also like to express our thanks to historians in numerous squadrons who have delved into their records to fill gaps and to the staff of the Public Record Office and Imperial War Museum, both indispensable sources to the historian.

Our thanks are also due to those individual members of Air-Britain who have contributed information and photographs over a very long period for the Association's various publications, some of which has been incorporated in this volume, especially Squadron Leader C. G. Jefford for helping to reduce a lengthy list of queries to reasonable proportions.

Finally, mention must be made of he who started it all. More years ago than either of us like to remember, John D. R. Rawlings proved to the author that it was possible to reconstruct the histories of Royal Air Force squadrons even without recourse to official records (then closed to the public) when he took on the task of being Air-Britain's first specialist on RAF squadron histories. Since then he has become an acknowledged authority on the subject as has his counterpart in the field of RAF stations and airfields, Peter M. Corbell, whose aid is also gratefully acknowledged.

J. J. Halley
Shepperton, England
September 1979

Buccaneer S.2s of No.12 Squadron and Phantom FGR.2s of No.54 Squadron on the apron at Luqa, Malta, during exercises in the Mediterranean.

D.H.2s of No.29 Squadron at Abeele, near Ypres in 1916.

Introduction

Throughout the history of the Royal Air Force, there have been many formations of varying sizes. The Royal Flying Corps began as a small group of squadrons and a flying school but, with the expansion brought about by World War One, the service was divided into Brigades and Wings. After the formation of the Royal Air Force on 1 April 1918, Groups and Areas were formed in the British Isles. In 1936, Areas became Commands and later autonomous Air Forces were set up overseas. The order of Air Force, Command, Group and Wing continued after World War Two.

The basic unit which made up all of these larger formations was the Squadron. Squadrons were of varying size and had individual functions. Each consisted of two or three Flights and the latter were frequently formed as independent units for purposes requiring formations smaller than squadrons. The lives of independent flights were usually short.

Four squadrons, with the Central Flying School, made up the original Royal Flying Corps and more squadrons were formed as it expanded. The size of these early squadrons varied according to the availability of aircraft but during World War One the intention was to maintain two flights of six aircraft each for operations with additional reserve aircraft when available. These numbers were sometimes augmented for special operations or depleted by losses or lack of replacement aircraft. About twenty pilots (and a corresponding number of observers where appropriate) were kept on strength to allow for sickness, leave, training and other reasons.

The original, and sole, role of RFC squadrons was reconnaissance but the development of armed single-seaters resulted in some squadrons becoming fighter units while others specialized in bombing, leaving reconnaissance and artillery direction to corps reconnaissance units. Later were added night bomber, coastal patrol, night fighter and home defence squadrons.

From the small force of aircraft which accompanied the British Expeditionary Force to France in August 1914, the RFC and RAF grew into a far-flung organization with squadrons not only in France and the British Isles but also in Italy, Greece, the Near East, Mesopotamia (now Iraq), East Africa and India while smaller units were based at Gibraltar, Malta, Crete, Aden and in the Aegean. On aerodromes around Nancy in eastern France were gathered the squadrons of the Independent Force, the world's first strategic bomber force and as the war ended a new group of four-engined heavy bombers was forming in Norfolk. At the time of the Armistice, the RAF had a strength of 291,170 men, about 25,000 women, 22,647 aircraft and 675 aerodromes and seaplane stations.

By the end of 1920, the bulk of this vast force had been dispersed. There were few squadrons left and most of these were in the Middle East and India. In place of the traditional punitive expeditions that had maintained a tenuous peace on the North-West Frontier of India, a new concept of air policing was developed, similar tasks being given to the RAF in Iraq, Transjordan and the Sudan. Replacing vulnerable columns of ground troops, a small number of RAF squadrons cooperated with local forces to restrain the more warlike tribes from preying on towns and villages in the more settled regions. In the course of these operations, the RAF found itself controlling its own armoured car squadrons and local levies, the former creating a precedent for the formation of the Royal Air Force Regiment on 12 February 1942 to man anti-aircraft defences and provide guards for airfields.

At home, the RAF's operational forces were divided between the Fighting Area, primarily for the defence of London, the Wessex Bombing Area controlling the bomber squadrons and Coastal Area, for maritime work. In keeping with the contemporary theory that offence was the best means of defence, bomber squadrons outnumbered fighter units but the former had few heavy bombers, the bulk of the squadron's equipment being single-engined light bombers of short range. Coastal Area consisted of a handful of flying boats and disembarked Fleet Air Arm aircraft. Its expansion began in 1929 with several squadrons being formed from coastal reconnaissance flights while the establishment of a Far East Flight resulted in the nucleus of a Far East command based on Singapore.

A turning point for the RAF came in 1935. An expansion scheme began and the Italian invasion of Ethiopia resulted in a sizeable portion of the home-based RAF being deployed to the Mediterranean and Middle East. During the next four years, the bulk of the RAF's equipment changed from the traditional biplanes to a new range of monoplanes for all tasks. By the outbreak of World War Two, most squadrons had modern equipment, the breathing space given by the Munich agreement having given time for the introduction of vital Hurricanes and Spitfires into Fighter Command squadrons. In September 1939, the RAF had 10,208 aircraft in service, approximately 3,500 being in operational units. Of the latter number, about half were modern.

Two groups of squadrons were despatched to France on the outbreak of war. One was the Advanced Air Striking Force and consisted of ten squadrons of Fairey Battles and two Hurricane squadrons. Based on airfields around Reims, the AASF was positioned to allow its short-range aircraft to operate over Germany. Conversion to Blenheims was in progress when the German invasion came in May 1940 and most of the AASF's obsolescent Battles were destroyed in the ensuing few weeks.

The second force to go to France was the Air Component of the British Expeditionary Force, consisting of five squadrons of Lysanders for army cooperation and four of Hurricanes. Its airfields were overrun in the early stages of the German attack and its squadrons retired to bases in southern England.

Fighter Command remained the essential air defence of the United Kingdom throughout the war but was forced to detach squadrons for operations over France in May and June 1940. Operating outside the Command's vital air defence radar network and ground control centres, these also suffered heavily but were back at full strength by the beginning of the Battle of Britain.

Bomber Command's home-based squadrons had not been employed in bombing during the early months of the war to prevent reprisals but after April 1940 it opened a night bomber offensive against German industry and a variety of tactical and naval targets. It lacked the navigational and target identification aids to be fully effective but had several successes despite this fact. Day bombing had been abandoned in the first months of the war when medium

Bristol Fighters of No. 20 Squadron at Risalpur in 1929 with Wapitis of No. 11 Squadron in the background.

Valentias of No.31 Squadron operating from the dusty airstrip at Drosh on the North West Frontier of India.

bombers were found to lack the armament and protection to face enemy fighters. Thereafter, the bulk of daylight bombing was undertaken by No.2 Group's light and medium bombers.

Coastal Command's tasks were two-fold. Enemy shipping had to be located and, if possible, attacked, both in the North Sea and English Channel and, should an enemy ship break out into the Atlantic, anywhere within range of Coastal's bases. Secondly, air escort had to be provided for convoys and naval forces. This was either close escort in the proximity of ships or by means of sweeps over the areas into which they were sailing in order to locate and attack U-boats lying in wait. Eventually, long-range fighters were provided for air defence of convoys and fleet units.

In the Middle East, hostilities did not begin until June 1940 when Italy entered the war. The bulk of the RAF was concentrated in the Western Desert to meet an attack on Egypt from Libya. A small force of fighters defended Malta and was later supplemented by reconnaissance units. Reinforcements arrived from India which also sent aircraft to the Far East. With a critical situation in Europe, modern aircraft were few and far between and many of the RAF's pre-war biplanes equipped the thin line of squadrons in Africa, where Australian, South African and Rhodesian squadrons had reinforced the RAF units.

After the defeat of the Luftwaffe in the Battle of Britain in 1940, Fighter Command grew in strength despite having to divert many squadrons to the Middle and Far East. Offensive operations began at the end of the year and

became a major task for the next three and a half years. In the summer of 1943, a substantial number of squadrons was transferred to the new Second Tactical Air Force, formed to support an Allied invasion of the Continent. In June 1944, these covered the landings in Normandy, moving to France as soon as airstrips had been prepared and made secure. The defence of the United Kingdom was left to a revived Air Defence of Great Britain — a title first used in the 1920s — but this later reverted to the name of Fighter Command.

Bomber Command concentrated on night bombing, mainly against German industrial targets, for the rest of the war. Four-engined bombers came into service in increasing numbers from 1941 while light bombers of No.2 Group engaged in daylight operations were transferred to Second Tactical Air Force in June 1943.

Coastal Command's long-range flying boats were gradually supplemented by landplanes but these were converted bombers wrung from a reluctant Bomber Command. However, supplies of Liberators from a neutral USA provided a welcome reinforcement with their long range and Catalinas replaced the last of the biplane flying boats. Attacks on enemy shipping along the long enemy-held coastline of Europe increased and specialized strike wings were set up for this purpose. Enemy surface ships rarely ventured into the Atlantic after the destruction of the *Bismarck* in May 1941 and most of Coastal's efforts were expended in combatting the menace of the U-boats. A major effort over the Bay of Biscay — through which the majority of U-boats had to sail to reach the safety of their bomb-proof shelters on the French coast — and long-range patrols by Liberators, Sunderlands and Catalinas over the convoy routes in the Atlantic resulted in a large increase in U-boat sinkings in 1943 which, added to the toll taken by naval ships, turned the tide in the Battle of the Atlantic and enabled the men and supplies required for the invasion of Europe to be transported safely to the British Isles.

Originally a small organization concerned with ferrying US- and Canadian-built aircraft across the Atlantic, Ferry Command became Transport Command on 25 March 1943. It built up a force of Dakotas, Stirlings, Halifaxes and Albemarles to carry an airborne division to Normandy in June 1944 and later provided an airlift for landings in the Netherlands and Germany. Other squadrons were engaged in flying passengers and urgent freight between the UK and overseas commands.

After the Japanese invasion of Malaya and Burma, the small number of squadrons available were forced out of these territories. The remnants of the Malayan squadrons were evacuated to Sumatra and Java and few aircraft survived, many of their ground personnel being withdrawn to India and Ceylon to man new units. In Burma, the British forces withdrew to the Indian frontier and their air component was gradually built up into a large tactical air force (Third TAF) despite shortages of aircraft and supplies. Ceylon became a base for strike and patrol squadrons.

Supplementing the tactical combat aircraft in South-East Asia were transport squadrons, mainly flying Dakotas, which provided a supply line in the sky for the Fourteenth Army deep in the jungles of Burma. Without airborne supplies, the destruction of the Japanese army in Burma could not have been accomplished.

The Western Desert Air Force moved westwards after the Battle of El Alamein in October 1942 and was joined by tactical squadrons from the UK which arrived in Algeria with the Allied invasion forces in November. United in Tunisia, these tactical air forces accompanied the Allied armies through Sicily to Italy, still under the title of Desert Air Force. They also covered landings in southern France in August 1944, returning to Italy when Allied forces from Normandy linked up with those from the south.

Second Tactical Air Force provided fighter-bomber support for the 21st Army Group throughout the campaign in north-west Europe and became the air component of the occupation forces in 1945 as British Air Forces of Occupation (BAFO). After the German surrender, home commands contracted to a peace-time level after an initial flurry of preparation for the transfer of a heavy bomber force to the Far East under the title of 'Tiger Force'. Squadrons in the Mediterranean returned to their pre-war stations and in the Far East the Japanese surrender resulted in Singapore again becoming the RAF's main base. The air forces in India were engaged in transferring control to the Royal Indian Air Force and the newly-formed Royal Pakistan Air Force. A large number of squadrons in all commands were disbanded and their personnel released to civil life.

The most obvious change in RAF strategy was brought about by the existence of nuclear weapons. To replace the wartime piston-engined heavy bombers, the RAF received first Canberra light bombers and, later, Valiant, Victor and Vulcan four-jet bombers. The three V-bombers formed the backbone of Britain's nuclear deterrent force until relieved by Polaris-armed nuclear submarines. Fighter Command received jet fighters in quantity soon after the end of the war but in the absence of the 100 per cent interception rate

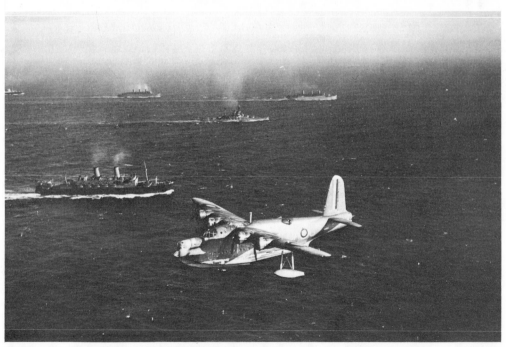

A Sunderland I of No.210 Squadron flies escort to a convoy of troopships in the Atlantic.

necessary against nuclear bombers, had to restrict itself to defending V-bomber bases, aided by squadrons of ground-to-air missiles. A force of intermediate-range ballistic missile squadrons was formed in the UK to supplement the V-bomber force.

Since the late 1960s, the RAF's overseas commands have contracted and all but one have vanished. The Far East Air Force disbanded on 1 November 1971. Air Forces Gulf, responsible for security in the Gulf area, was withdrawn by the end of the year, leaving the defence of the Trucial states to a number of small independent air forces in each country. Air Forces Near East, based on Cyprus, covered the area of the Eastern Mediterranean with squadrons in Malta, the last of which left in 1978. The remaining overseas force is RAF Germany, a component of Second Allied Tactical Air Force consisting of fighter, ground-attack and reconnaissance squadrons.

Despite the vast changes undergone by the RAF since its inception, many of its original squadrons remain in service. Bomber Command and Fighter Command merged to become Strike Command on 30 April 1968, to be joined by Coastal Command on 28 November 1969. Air Support Command, formed from Transport Command on 1 August 1967, was also merged with Strike Command on 1 September 1972, to provide the RAF with a single unified operational command in the UK, leaving Training and Maintenance Commands to cover non-operational tasks and later to merge as Support Command.

During the 1970s, a major re-equipment programme resulted in squadrons receiving Harriers, Jaguars, Buccaneers, Phantoms and Nimrods. These were capable of long-range deployment and partly made up for the reduction in overseas-based squadrons, only one helicopter squadron in Hong Kong and another in Cyprus remaining at the end of the decade.

Hurricane IIC night intruders of No.247 Squadron over Portreath, Cornwall.

Squadron Numbering

The numbers allotted to squadrons fall into the following groups:

Nos.1 to 200	Regular RAF squadrons, many originally ex-RFC
Nos.201 to 299	Regular RAF squadrons, many originally ex-RNAS
Nos.300 to 399	Allied squadrons (Polish, Czechoslovak, Dutch, French, Norwegian, Greek, Belgian and Yugoslav). Not all used and a few numbers used for RAF squadrons in India.
Nos.400 to 499	Article XV squadrons of the Royal Canadian Air Force, Royal Australian Air Force and Royal New Zealand Air Force. Not all used and outside the scope of this volume.
Nos.500 to 599	Originally intended for Special Reserve squadrons but many numbers used for wartime units.
Nos.600 to 699	Originally intended for Auxiliary Air Force squadrons but later numbers used for wartime units.
Nos.700 to 799	Fleet Air Arm second-line and catapult squadrons outside the scope of this volume.
Nos.800 to 899	Fleet Air Arm first-line squadrons outside the scope of this volume
Nos.900 to 999	Barrage balloon squadrons.

The above framework was not rigidly adhered to. The first 200 numbers were not all used by the RFC and unused numbers were appropriated for new RAF squadrons formed after 1 April 1918, while some remained unused until World War Two. Existing RNAS squadrons on 1 April 1918 were allocated 200-series numbers by adding 200 to their current RNAS squadron number (e.g. No.1 Squadron RNAS became No.201 Squadron RAF). Other unnumbered units administered by former RNAS stations were allotted numbers in the 200-series during August 1918 but the full range was not used in World War One. Allocation of 200-series numbers during World War Two had, in the majority of cases, no connection with the original intention and were used as necessary.

Less than half the 300-series was used. In addition to Allied squadrons, a batch from 352 to 358 was allotted to squadrons formed in India. Nos.360 and 361 were allocated to new squadrons in 1966 which were combined RAF and RN units.

There has occasionally been confusion in various accounts between the RAF and other air forces of the Commonwealth. Permanent squadrons of Commonwealth air forces often duplicated RAF numbers. Home-based RCAF squadrons, which also operated in Alaska, were renumbered in the 400-series if transferred to RAF commands but Canadian-based maritime reconnaissance squadrons could be confused with RAF units (e.g. No.162 Squadron RCAF over the North Atlantic). RAAF squadrons were often found in RAF commands alongside similarly-numbered South African and Indian Air Force units. RNZAF squadrons operating in the South Pacific were seldom in contact with RAF units, all those operating in Europe and Africa being numbered in the 400-series. No.1 Squadron, Southern Rhodesian Air Force, became No.237 Squadron to avoid confusion with No.1 Squadron SAAF, also flying in East Africa.

It should be borne in mind that during both world wars, large numbers of Commonwealth personnel served in RAF squadrons and many RAF men in Commonwealth squadrons. The same applied to Allied squadrons and personnel.

The 400-series consisted of squadrons of the RCAF, RAAF and RNZAF. Article XV of the British Empire Air Training Scheme agreement catered for the provision of a certain number of squadrons manned by Canadian, Australian and New Zealand personnel to RAF Commands. These were squadrons of the RCAF, RAAF and RNZAF and so have been omitted from this volume of RAF squadrons. In addition to these 400-series squadrons, each air force had other squadrons numbered in its permanent air force series which duplicated RAF numbers. The South African Air Force did not participate in Article XV and numbered its squadrons from 1 onwards.

The Special Reserve was set up in 1925 to provided cadre units which could become operational in a very short time, having a nucleus flight of regular personnel on permanent service. Only five Special Reserve squadrons were formed and many 500-series numbers were allocated to new squadrons during World War Two when the 1 to 299 series of numbers was exhausted — with the exception of No.188 which, for some reason, was never used again.

The Auxiliary Air Force (Royal Auxiliary Air Force from 16 December 1947) was a territorial force manned by volunteers as a spare time service. A small regular nucleus administered the squadrons and maintained their aircraft but aircrews and many of the ground personnel were civilians. After No.616, numbers were allocated as necessary to new units formed during World War Two.

The 700- and 800-series numbers were naval squadrons and are not dealt with in this volume. Although part of the RAF for many years, such squadrons fall more naturally into a record of Royal Navy squadrons which would also include RNAS squadrons from 1914 to 1918.

Balloon squadrons numbered from 900 onwards were responsible for manning the balloon barrages during World War Two. There were also Royal Navy squadrons in the 1700 and 1800 ranges, these being overflows from the exhausted 700 and 800 series. One exception to the rule was No.1435 Squadron which adopted the number of a disbanded RAF Flight and was designated a squadron when it expanded beyond the maximum strength of a flight.

A Hastings Met.1 of No.202 Squadron used for long-range meteorological flights over the North Atlantic.

Meteor F.8s of Nos. 600 and 615 Squadrons.

Squadron Roles

The roles allocated to each squadron are given in the text of the squadron narratives. The following is a brief explanation of the tasks coming under the various role headings.

Corps Reconnaissance/Army Cooperation

Primary task of all the early squadrons, reconnaissance was frequently combined with other tasks. Armed scouts developed into fighters, the occasional bombing raids became more frequent and certain squadrons concentrated on this role, some confining their activities to night flying. The remaining squadrons developed special operational techniques in support of the army and were known as corps reconnaissance units.

These squadrons were expected to undertake artillery observation, tactical reconnaissance, photography, message and supply dropping and, if required, light bombing and ground attack. A two-seat, single-engined aircraft became standard in this role and remained in service until the outbreak of World War Two, the term 'corps reconnaissance' being changed to 'army cooperation' soon after World War One. Rapid development of fighters in the late 1930s made the survival of slower and more bulky aircraft difficult and within two years of the outbreak of World War Two, re-equipment was in hand with two types — a single-seat fighter, often equipped with cameras, and a light air observation post developed from pre-war civil light aircraft. The tasks were now divided between fighter-reconnaissance, photographic reconnaissance and air observation post (see below).

Fighter-Reconnaissance

Using single-seat fighters adapted to carry cameras, FR squadrons normally operated at low altitudes securing photographs of enemy positions and targets and depended on speed and surprise to evade interception. As a last resort, they were sufficiently fast and well-armed to fight their way out. Some early FR aircraft suffered from a shortage of cameras and conversion facilities and relied on visual reconnaissance. This basic role continues to the present and is now normally combined with a ground-attack capability.

Photographic Reconnaissance

Photographic reconnaissance is usually considered as strategic reconnaissance, the aircraft involved operating over long distances and without armament. Strategic reconnaissance was a task laid at first to bomber squadrons as only they possessed aircraft with adequate range but early in World War Two specially modified aircraft became available to the Photographic Reconnaissance Unit from which several squadrons were formed. Stripped Spitfires operating at high altitude successfully evaded interception on the majority of sorties and were later joined by Mosquitos. After World War Two, photographic reconnaissance became a major task and developments in radar provided more flexible all-weather equipment to supplement purely photographic methods of acquiring information.

11

Air Observation Post

To provide local air observation, developments of pre-war light aircraft were put into service with AOP squadrons to act as observers for artillery, cooperate with ground forces by locating enemy positions and provide liaison aircraft for transporting senior officers. By using simple light aircraft, these units could operate from small fields without the back-up necessary for the more complicated types. All AOP squadrons were transferred to the Army Air Corps on its formation and throughout their existence these squadrons had been manned by army personnel.

Fighters

Fighter squadrons were first formed in 1951 to meet the threat of formations of German aircraft armed with machine-guns which were making life hazardous for the crews of slow reconnaissance aircraft of the RFC. Their basic equipment was single-seat fast scouts which were the only aircraft suitable for arming which were capable of meeting German fighters on approximately equal terms. Specially-designed fighters began arriving in 1916 and fighter design remained wedded to the single-engined biplane until 1938 when the first eight-gun monoplanes came into service with the RAF.

Variants were developed over the years. Night fighting was carried out by an *ad hoc* collection of training and reconnaissance types until the advent of squadrons of night-fighting Sopwith Camels in 1918. The two-seat fighter enjoyed a relatively brief career over two periods, one during World War One when the presence of a gunner to defend the tails of Bristol Fighters did not detract from their ability to be flown in the style of single-seat fighters. Lapsing after the armistice, the class was revived in the Hawker Demon as a variant of the fast Hart bomber but its replacement in the shape of the Boulton-Paul Defiant was to prove a failure. The weight of a gunner and his power-operated turret resulted in a serious performance gap between the Defiant and single-seat fighters. Future two-seater fighters carried radar operators or navigators and the type in its original form became extinct.

Radar-equipped fighters began as night fighters during World War Two and developed into all-weather fighters, the Gloster Javelin being the best known. With the addition of radar, single-seat fighters could also operate in all weather conditions and the all-weather fighter became the standard.

To provide escorts for bombers and naval forces, the long-range fighter was developed. Originally Blenheims and Beaufighters carried out this task but the design of droppable fuel tanks capable of fitment to existing single-seat fighters removed much of the need for a single-role type.

From the earliest days, fighters could carry light bombs but it was not until World War Two that substantial bomb loads began to be fitted to single-seat fighters. Their ability to engage the enemy on equal terms after a bombing attack meant the eventual replacement of the vulnerable light bomber. Rockets supplemented bombs within a few years and the fighter-bomber was eventually reclassed as 'Fighter/Ground Attack'. In the current Harrier and Phantom squadrons, the ground-attack role is often combined with that of reconnaissance.

The Hastings was the backbone of Transport Command's fleet during the 1950s. A Hastings C.1 of No.36 Squadron is seen over the Solent.

Flanked by a pair of Swift FR.5s of No.79 Squadron are Hunters of Nos.14 and 26 Squadrons flying over the Mohne Dam.

Bombers

The gradual diversion of certain squadrons to bombing meant that the first bombers were identical with corps reconnaissance aircraft but specially-designed day bombers were not long in appearing. For the next twenty years, the standard type was a two-seat biplane but before World War Two, these had been replaced by single-engined, three-seat Fairey Battles and twin-engined Bristol Blenheims, both monoplanes. Although light bombers operated throughout the war, the existence of smaller and faster fighter-bombers after 1941 meant their eventual withdrawal. Their jet-powered equivalent, the Canberra, came to be used for both day and night bombing and a variety of other tasks.

Night bombing was based on the F.E.2B two-seat fighter withdrawn from fighter squadrons in the absence of more suitable types but the first true night bomber was the big Handley Page 0/100 (and its development the 0/400) designed for the RNAS. This type set a pattern for the next two decades in its twin-engined biplane design. Monoplane bombers arrived shortly before World War Two and the first generation of twin-engined aircraft was replaced from 1941 by four-engined heavy bombers. The advent of nuclear bombs resulted in their replacement in the mid-1950s by jet bombers capable of carrying nuclear weapons.

A specialised type of bomber squadron was that equipped with torpedo-bombers. RAF torpedo-bomber squadrons were formed in the late 1920s for coast defence duties and were in use for most of World War Two until the torpedo was replaced by the rocket projectile.

General and Maritime Reconnaissance

An increasing threat from submarines brought into being reconnaissance units for use over the sea. Flying-boats and seaplanes flew long-range sorties while squadrons of modified trainers patrolled the coastline. After World War One, flying-boats became the RAF's sole maritime reconnaissance equipment but in 1936 new coastal reconnaissance squadrons were formed with Ansons and designated General Reconnaissance units. The term was changed to Maritime Reconnaissance after the end of World War Two. Flying-boats were gradually replaced by landplanes until the end of the 1950s. Tasks undertaken by GR/MR squadrons included anti-submarine patrols, shipping reconnaissance and air-sea rescue.

Transport

The RAF's involvement in India and the Middle East over areas lacking in adequate ground communications led to the use of bomber-transport units with a dual role between the wars. During World War Two, the bomber requirement was dropped and transport squadrons equipped mainly with unarmed aircraft, the militarized DC-3 airliner being the most famous as the Dakota. The transport of airborne troops became a major task while in the Far East whole divisions were maintained by airborne supplies. In addition, communications between various theatres of war relied on air transport.

After the war, transport squadrons concentrated on two main aspects. Heavy transports maintained regular routes to overseas commands while tactical transports cooperated with the ground forces using helicopters and aircraft capable of operating from unprepared fields.

Miscellaneous Tasks

At various times, the RAF has included squadrons given special roles. These have been described in the text but the main tasks which have fallen to such units include the following:

Air-Sea Rescue squadrons were formed in 1941 to rescue airmen from the sea. At first they used Lysanders for spotting and Walrus amphibians for picking up survivors but a large variety of types was later added, including larger aircraft capable of carrying airborne lifeboats. After the war, air-sea rescue duties were handed over to the existing maritime reconnaissance units but later helicopter squadrons were formed for search and rescue purposes over both land and sea.

Anti-aircraft Cooperation was a prosaic but essential task carried out by squadrons formed from a number of individual flights from 1942 onwards. Targets were towed for anti-aircraft batteries, aircraft simulated attacks for gunlaying practice and some squadrons were engaged in calibrating radar stations and equipment.

Radio Countermeasures (RCM) units used electronic equipment to disrupt enemy radar and provided diversions to assist the main bomber force. Special Duties squadrons dropped supplies and personnel to resistance forces and landed in enemy territory to pick up agents.

The trio of V-bombers which formed the Royal Air Force's nuclear deterrant force; Victor B.1 of No.55 Squadron, Valiant B.1 of No.90 Squadron and Vulcan B.1 of No.101 Squadron.

Notes

The activities of the squadrons of the Royal Air Force cover a vast canvas. In this volume can be accommodated only the basic facts of each squadron's contribution to the history of the whole Service. For this reason, details of individual operations have been omitted with the exception of certain transport squadrons which, to date, have lacked any detailed account of their contributions to the major airborne operations of World War Two.

The intention is to provide information on the following basic items:

    dates of formation and disbandment;

    dates of moves;

    types of aircraft flown and period of use;

    tasks undertaken.

To this end, a certain amount of simplification has been adopted.

The basis of the narratives and tables has been the contemporary record books maintained in various forms throughout the history of each squadron in varying degrees. Much depended on the ability, or lack of it, of the recording officers to set down the essential points. Many documents have failed to survive through loss or destruction and the current Forms 540 and 541 did not come into use until shortly before World War Two. Certain copies of these failed to reach the Air Ministry, notably those lost in France in 1940 and in Singapore in 1942. In the absence of these primary documents, recourse has been made to personal accounts of the periods and the records of other formations.

Access to official documents is available only up to 1948 in the case of this volume, a lapse of thirty years being laid down in the Public Records Act. Details of the post-war activities of squadrons are derived from published

A Nimrod MR.1 over Valetta, Malta.

histories, information summaries supplied by the Air Ministry and Ministry of Defence and other published sources. While every attempt has been made to cross-check such information, it should be remembered that the official records on which earlier facts have been based were not available when this book was closed in order to go to press.

Where exact details of re-equipment are not available from the squadron records, the aircraft movement cards have been analysed. The exact date of re-equipment with, and withdrawal from service of, a type is often imprecise. While a complete re-equipment with a new type or mark of aircraft has taken place in a single day, at other times new aircraft arrived over a period of months and some of the replaced aircraft have remained on charge after re-equipment. For this reason, many of the dates given for periods of service of certain types overlap.

Movement dates for each squadron have been quoted where known. Although most of these can be identified, some cannot be ascertained exactly. This is especially true where transport and other squadrons with large aircraft used them on a shuttle service to move personnel and stores from one base to another. In such cases, the letter (P), denoting a period move, has been placed against the movement date. Where this does not appear against an incomplete date, it implies that the exact date has yet to be ascertained. During wartime, the date given is that on which the bulk of the squadron's aircraft changed base; in peacetime, it is the official date of the move but squadrons normally sent advance parties ahead of the main body to prepare the way and left rear parties to close down their former premises. This causes discrepancies between squadron and station records.

In the Western Desert, the highly-mobile Desert Air Force normally kept operating by dividing into two parties, one of which remained operational while the other changed base. Detachments have been shown where significant and marked (D). A case where ground and air echelons moved on different dates is indicated by the suffixes (A) and (G); (C) denotes a date when a move was completed, various detachments having arrived over a period.

With the advent of flight-refuelling, long-range detachments became common. Consequently, no record of detachments has been attempted for the last twenty years, only the permanent base of the squadron being shown. This also applies to the occasional transfer of aircraft to a nearby airfield while the squadron's parent airfield's runways were resurfaced or rebuilt.

On some occasions, especially with general reconnaissance squadrons in the Far East, aircraft were operating in small detachments from a number of bases and it has proved difficult to identify the main base of the squadron. Squadron headquarters could be at a location devoid of squadron aircraft for much of the time.

Although large quantities of pre-war documents have been perused, a few movement dates remain unlocated and any addition from original sources would be welcome. We specify 'original sources' since, over many years, inaccurate dates have appeared (even in official records) and we have no wish to reinstate them.

Fury Is, No.1 Squadron

Harrier GR.1s, No.1 Squadron

No. 1 Squadron

Badge: The numeral 'I' winged
Motto: In omnibus princeps
(First in all things)

No.1 Squadron was one of the first four squadrons of the Royal Flying Corps when it was formed on 13 May, 1912, and took over the operation of its balloons, airships and kites from No.1 Airship Company, Air Battalion, Royal Engineers. When airships became the responsibility of the Naval Wing on 1 January, 1914, the squadron continued to operate at Farnborough until it was redesignated the Airship Detachment, RFC on 1 May, 1914. On the same day, a cadre No.1 Squadron was formed at Brooklands but the outbreak of war in August resulted in its aircraft being taken over by the other active squadron destined to accompany the British Expeditionary Force to France.

Resuming training with whatever aircraft were to hand, the squadron completed training in February 1915 and early in March moved to France as a reconnaissance unit, beginning operations on 10 March. A few single-seat scouts were received during 1915 and the first true single-seat fighters (Nieuport 17s) arrived in March 1916 and were flown in small numbers. In January 1917, No.1 completely equipped with Nieuports and became a fighter squadron, converting to S.E.5As in January, 1918. For the remainder of the war, it was engaged in fighter patrols and ground attack duties over the Western Front. In February 1919, it was reduced to a cadre and in March returned to the UK where it was disbanded on 20 January 1920.

On 21 January 1920, No.1 Squadron was reformed at Risalpur on the North-West Frontier of India initially designated B Squadron with Snipe but in May 1921 was moved to Iraq to join the RAF force policing the desert area where it remained until disbanded on 1 November 1926. On 1 February 1927, it reformed at Tangmere with Siskins as part of the fighter defence of the UK and in February 1932, re-equipped with Furies which it flew until they were replaced by Hurricanes in October 1938. On the outbreak of World War Two, No.1 moved to France as one of the two fighter squadrons with the Advanced Air Striking Force. The German offensive in May 1940 soon forced the squadron to withdraw westwards and after covering the evacuation of British forces from the Biscay ports it returned to the UK to re-equip.

After taking part in the first half of the Battle of Britain, No.1 was withdrawn to Wittering where it remained until December when the squadron moved south again and began taking part in sweeps over northern France. Night fighter missions became frequent in the spring of 1941 and continued for a year. Early in 1942 the Hurricanes began to be used for intruder sorties over German bomber airfields in France and lasted until July when No.1 moved to Northumberland to convert to Typhoons. Despite teething troubles, the new type's speed made it the RAF's best counter to enemy fighter-bomber raids and the squadron moved south in February 1943 for this role. Cross-Channel sweeps were resumed in January 1944 and in April the squadron converted to Spitfire IXs. Carrying 500-lb bombs, it flew fighter-bomber missions over Brittany until the opening of the flying bomb attacks brought it back to south-east England for defensive duties.

After the capture of the V.1 launching sites in northern France, the flying bomb offensive waned and No.1 became a long-range escort squadron, working with the Lancasters and Halifaxes of Bomber Command on their daylight raids over Germany. As the war ended, it re-equipped with Spitfire F.21s which were replaced by Meteors in October

1946. In August 1947, however, these were taken away when No.1 became No.11 Group's instrument training unit for which duties Oxfords and Harvards were used until June 1948 when the squadron once more became a first-line unit with Meteors. In October 1955, conversion to Hunters was completed but the squadron disbanded on 23 June 1958.

No.263 Squadron at Stradishall with Hunters was renumbered 1 Squadron on 1 July, 1958. In March 1960 ground-attack Hunters began to arrive as the first step in the movement from Fighter to Transport Command. A new air support organisation had been set up to provide tactical support for the army with helicopters, tactical transports and ground-attack fighters and No.1 was, with No.54, to form the ground-attack wing of No.38 Group. In July 1969, the squadron moved to Wittering to become the first operational vertical take-off fighter squadron in the world, with an ability to operate away from fixed airfields and from relatively short distances behind the battle area with Harrier ground-attack and reconnaissance fighters.

Squadron bases

Farnborough	13 May 1912	Berry-au-Bac	10 May 1940
Brooklands	Aug 1914	Condé-Vraux	17 May 1940
Netheravon	Nov 1914	Anglure	18 May 1940
St. Omer	7 Mar 1915	Chateaudun	3 Jun 1940
Bailleul	29 Mar 1915	Nantes/Chateau Bougon	
Ste. Marie Cappel	29 Mar 1918		14 Jun 1940
Clairmarais South	13 Apr 1918	St. Nazaire	17 Jun 1940
Fienvillers	5 Aug 1918	Northolt	18 Jun 1940
Senlis	6 Oct 1918	Tangmere	23 Jun 1940
Bouvincourt	26 Oct 1918	Northolt	1 Aug 1940
Izel-le-Hameau	18 Nov 1918	Wittering	9 Sep 1940
London Colney	1 Mar 1919	Northolt	15 Dec 1940
Uxbridge	Oct 1919	Kenley	5 Jan 1941
	to 20 Jan 1920	Croydon	7 Apr 1941
Risalpur	21 Jan 1920	Redhill	1 May 1941
Bangalore	11 May 1920	Kenley	1 Jun 1941
Hinaidi	1 May 1921	Redhill	14 Jun 1941
	to 1 Nov 1926	Tangmere	1 Jul 1941
Tangmere	1 Feb 1927	Acklington	8 Jul 1942
Northolt	7 Aug 1928	Biggin Hill	9 Feb 1943
Tangmere	17 Aug 1928	Lympne	15 Mar 1943
Octeville	9 Sep 1939	Martlesham Heath	15 Feb 1944
Norrent Fontes	29 Sep 1939	North Weald	3 Apr 1944
Vassincourt	9 Oct 1939	Ayr	22 Apr 1944
Berry-au-Bac	11 Apr 1940	Predannack	29 Apr 1944
Vassincourt	19 Apr 1940	Harrowbeer	20 Jun 1944
Detling	22 Jun 1944	Tangmere	30 Apr 1946
Lympne	11 Jul 1944	Akrotiri	7 Aug 1956
Detling	10 Aug 1944	Nicosia	1 Sep 1956
Manston	18 Dec 1944	Tangmere	24 Dec 1956
Coltishall	8 Apr 1945		to 23 Jun 1958
Ludham	14 May 1945	Stradishall	1 Jul 1958
Hutton Cranswick	23 Jul 1945	Waterbeach	7 Nov 1961
Hawkinge	24 Sep 1945	West Raynham	13 Aug 1963
Hutton Cranswick	22 Oct 1945	Wittering	18 Jul 1969

Aircraft Equipment	Period of service	Representative Serial
Lighter-than-air	May 1912 – Apr 1914	'Delta'
Misc.training types	May 1914 – Mar 1915	
Avro 504	Mar 1915 – Sep 1915	2859
B.E.8	Mar 1915 – Jun 1915	2130
Bristol Scout	Apr 1915 – Oct 1915	4672
Caudron G-III	Mar 1915 – Sep 1915	5038
Martinsyde S.1	Jun 1915 – Jul 1915	748
Morane Parasol	Mar 1915 – Jan 1917	5006
Nieuport 12 and 14	Jul 1916 – Jan 1917	5171
Morane Biplane	Jan 1916 – Jan 1917	5160
Nieuport 17	Mar 1916 – Aug 1916	A130
	Jan 1917 – Dec 1917	
Nieuport 27	Aug 1917 – Jan 1918	N3481
S.E.5A	Jan 1918 – Mar 1919	C8846 (M)
Snipe	Jan 1920 – Nov 1926	H4866
Nighthawk	Jan 1920 – Apr 1921	HR8544
Siskin IIIA	Feb 1927 – Feb 1932	J8635
Fury I	Feb 1932 – Nov 1938	K2881 (E)
Hurricane I	Oct 1938 – Feb 1941	P3395 (JX-B)
Hurricane IIA	Feb 1941 – Jun 1941	Z2502
Hurricane IIB	Apr 1941 – Jan 1942	Z3496
	Jun 1942 – Sep 1942	
Hurricane IIC	Jul 1941 – Sep 1942	BE215 (JX-I)
Typhoon IB	Jul 1942 – Apr 1944	EJ974 (JX-T)
Spitfire IXB	Apr 1944 – May 1945	MK997 (JX-F)
Spitfire F.21	May 1945 – Oct 1946	LA217 (JX-G)
Meteor F.III	Oct 1946 – Aug 1947	EE458 (JX-B)
Harvard T.2B	Aug 1947 – Jun 1948	FX411 (JX-F)
Oxford T.2	Aug 1947 – Jun 1948	LX132 (JX-N)
Meteor F.4	Jun 1948 – Sep 1950	VW270 (JX-D)
Meteor F.8	Sep 1950 – Oct 1955	WF642 (T)
Hunter F.5	Sep 1955 – Jun 1958	WP119 (T)
Hunter F.6	Jul 1958 – Jun 1960	XE623 (G)
Hunter FGA.9	Mar 1960 – Jul 1969	XG229 (K)
Harrier GR.1, GR.1A, GR.3	Jul 1969 – date	XV749 (K)

No. 2 Squadron

Badge: Three concentric circles over all a Wake Knot
Motto: Hereward

No.2 Squadron was formed on 13 May 1912 as one of the original squadrons of the Royal Flying Corps. It flew a variety of types of aircraft during the formative years of the new service at Farnborough and Montrose and on the outbreak of World War One moved to France with the British Expeditionary Force with a mixed complement of reconnaissance aircraft. When the Western Front settled down to a fixed line, tactical reconnaissance and artillery spotting became the squadron's main tasks. Standardisation became possible in 1915 when B.E.s formed the bulk of No.2's aircraft and bombing raids were added to its other duties. For the rest of the war, No.2 was a corps reconnaissance unit and in April 1917, re-equipped with F.K.8s. In

February 1919, it was reduced to a cadre and returned to the UK disbanding on 20 January 1920.

On 1 February 1920, No.2 reformed at Oranmore to co-operate with the army in Ireland. Equipped with Bristol Fighters, it moved to England in February 1922, but returned to Ireland at the end of May in case of trouble in Ulster. No.2 moved its headquarters to Farnborough in September 1922, but left a detachment in Ulster until February 1923. In April 1927, the squadron left for Shanghai, where disturbances in China were threatening the International Settlement. It left for Manston in September 1927, and re-equipped with Atlases at the end of 1929. Until the outbreak of World War Two, No.2 was engaged in army-co-operation training in southern England, moving to France in October 1939, with Lysanders as part of the Air Component of the BEF. In May 1940, the squadron's landing grounds were soon over-run by the German invasion and within ten days it was back in the UK carrying out bombing and supply-dropping flights over Northern France. Coastal patrols began in June to check at first light whether there had been any enemy landings during the night. Exercises occupied most of the squadron's time and in August 1941 it received some Tomahawks for low-level tactical reconnaissance. Lysanders remained in service until April 1942, when the squadron converted to Mustangs. These began operations on 14 November 1942, and tactical reconnaissance missions

Jaguar T.2, No.2 Squadron

over France and the Low Countries became normal. The French coastal defences were photographed in preparation for the Allied invasion and on D-Day, No.2 undertook spotting for the naval bombardment force. At the end of July, the squadron moved to Normandy and remained with the 21st Army Group during its advance to the Netherlands. In November 1944, Spitfires began to replace the Mustangs which flew their final missions on 17 January 1945. After the end of the war, No.2 remained in Germany as a fighter-reconnaissance unit of BAFO. In December 1950, Meteors began to replace Spitfires and were flown until the first Swifts arrived in March 1956. These were replaced by Hunters in March 1961 which served the squadron for ten years. On 7 December, 1970, No.2 (Phantom) Squadron formed at Bruggen with Phantom FGR.2s, while No.2 (Hunter) Squadron carried on with Hunters at Gutersloh until the end of March 1971. On 1 April 1971, the re-equipped No.2 Squadron took up its operational base at Laarbruch. Conversion to Jaguars began in March 1976 and the squadron became fully operational on the type in September.

Squadron bases

Farnborough	13 May 1912	Berlaiment	24 Aug 1914
Montrose	15 Jan 1913	Le Cateau	25 Aug 1914
Farnborough	13 Jun 1914	Juilly	1 Sep 1914
Amiens	13 Aug 1914	Serris	2 Sep 1914
Maubeuge	16 Aug 1914	Pezarches	3 Sep 1914
		Melun	3 Sep 1914

Pezarches	7 Sep 1914	Gravesend	16 Jul 1943
Coulommiers	9 Sep 1914	Odiham	10 Aug 1943
Fere-en-Tardenois	12 Sep 1914	North Weald	22 Jan 1944
Vieul Aroy	20 Sep 1914	Sawbridgworth	29 Feb 1944
Merville	Nov 1914	Dundonald	11 Mar 1944
Hesdigneul	30 Jun 1915	Sawbridgworth	24 Mar 1944
Floringhem	9 Jun 1918	Gatwick	4 Apr 1944
Mazingarbe	20 Jun 1918	B.10 Plumetot	30 Jul 1944
Genech	26 Oct 1918	B.4 Beny-sur-Mer	14 Aug 1944
Bicester	12 Feb 1919	B.27 Boisney	3 Sep 1944
Weston-on-the-Green		B.31 Fresnoy Folney	
	Sep 1919 to 20 Jan 1920		6 Sep 1944
Oranmore	1 Feb 1920	B.43 Fort Rouge	11 Sep 1944
Digby	Feb 1922	B.61 St. Denis Westrem	
Aldergrove	31 May 1922		27 Sep 1944
Farnborough	Sep 1922	B.70 Deurne	11 Oct 1944
Andover	17 Sep 1923	B.77 Gilze-Rijen	23 Oct 1944
Manston	31 Mar 1924	B.89 Mill	9 Mar 1945
Left for China	20 Apr 1927	B.106 Twente	18 Apr 1945
Shanghai Racecourse		B.116 Celle	30 May 1945
	31 May 1927	B.150 Hustedt	18 Jun 1945
Left for UK	13 Sep 1927	Warmwell	6 Jul 1945
Manston	27 Oct 1927	B. 150 Hustedt	20 Jul 1945
Hawkinge	3 Nov 1935	Celle	17 Sep 1945
Abbeville/Drucat	6 Oct 1939	Wunstorf	15 Apr 1947
Lympne	19 May 1940	Buckeburg	29 Jun 1950
Bekesbourne & Croydon		Gutersloh	15 May 1952
	20 May 1940	Wahn	1 Jul 1953
Bekesbourne	21 May 1940	Geilenkirchen	28 Oct 1955
Hatfield	8 Jun 1940	Jever	10 Oct 1957
Sawbridgworth	24 Oct 1940	Gutersloh	9 Sep 1961
Bottisham	3 Feb 1943	Bruggen	7 Dec 1970*
Fowlmere	20 Mar 1943	Laarbruch	1 Apr 1971
Sawbridgworth	27 Apr 1943	* Phantom element only	

Aircraft Equipment	Period of Service	Representative Serial and Code
Various e.g. B.E.1 (201); Breguet (211); Henry Farman F.20 (352); Maurice Farman S.7 (207); B.E.2 (205); B.E.2a (217); B.E.2b (667); R.E.1; B.E.8 (209); Bleriot XI (221); R.E.5 (660); between May 1912 - Sep 1914.		
B.E.2c, B.E.2d, B.E.2e	Sep 1914 — Apr 1917	C7086
Bristol Scout	Jul 1915	4667
F.K.8	Apr 1917 — Feb 1919	B246 (13)
Bristol F.2b	Feb 1920 — Jan 1930	J5592
Atlas	Dec 1929 — Sep 1934	J9958
Audax	Sep 1934 — Nov 1937	K3086
Hector	Nov 1937 — Sep 1938	K9738
Lysander I, II	Sep 1938 — Apr 1942	N1203 (KO-M)

Aircraft Equipment	Period of service	Representative Serial and Code
Tomahawk I, IIA	Aug 1941 — Apr 1942	AH916 (XV-U)
Mustang I, Ia	Apr 1942 — May 1944	AG620 (XV-A)
Mustang II	May 1944 — Jan 1945	FR922
Spitfire XIV	Nov 1944 — Jan 1951	TZ164 (OI-A)
Spitfire XI	Sep 1945 — Jan 1946	PM132
Spitfire XIX	Jan 1946 — Mar 1951	PM549 (OI-F)
Meteor FR.9	Dec 1950 — May 1956	VZ602 (B-A)
Meteor PR.10	Mar 1951 — Jun 1951	VZ974
Swift FR.5	Mar 1956 — Mar 1961	XD912 (C)
Hunter FR.10	Mar 1961 — Mar 1971	XE556 (W)
Phantom FGR.2	Dec 1970 — Sep 1976	XW470 (V)
Jaguar GR.1	Mar 1976 — date	XZ105 (Y)

Woodcock IIs, No.3 Squadron

No. 3 Squadron

Badge: On a monolith, a cockatrice
Motto: Tertius primus erit (The Third shall be first)

No.3 Squadron was formed as one of the original squadrons of the Royal Flying Corps at Larkhill on 13 May 1912 and for the next two years flew a variety of types for training purposes. On the outbreak of war, it took its most effective aircraft to France with the British Expeditionary Force and was engaged mainly in reconnaissance duties for the first three years of the conflict. The squadron had finally standardised on Morane Parasols early in 1916 which it used for artillery spotting duties but in September 1917 No.3 became a fighter unit with Camels. For the rest of the war, the squadron was engaged in fighter and ground attack duties, being reduced to a cadre in February 1919 on returning to the UK where it was disbanded on 27 October 1919.

On 1 April 1920, No.3 reformed at Bangalore, India, from A Squadron with Snipes as a fighter squadron but was again disbanded on 30 September 1921. On the next day, the Mobile Flight of No.205 Squadron at Leuchars was re-designated No.3 Squadron. Equipped initially with D.H.9As, it was allocated to Fleet co-operation duties and in January 1922 began to re-equip with Walruses. On 1 April 1923, the squadron was divided into Nos.421 and 422 Flights which became independent units.

No.3 reformed as a fighter squadron at Manston on 1 April 1924 equipped with Snipes and moved a few weeks later to Upavon, its base for the next ten years. Over this period, the squadron flew Snipes, Woodcocks, Gamecocks and Bulldogs in succession and in October 1935 took the last-named to the Sudan during the Abyssinian crisis. In August 1936, it returned to the UK and in March 1938 conversion to Hurricanes began but in July the squadron reverted to Gladiators while Kenley was extended to cope with monoplane fighters. A move to Biggin Hill in May 1939 coincided with the return of Hurricanes and after the outbreak of World War Two these were flown on defensive patrols over southern England. When the German army attacked through the Low Countries in May 1940, No.3 was sent to reinforce the fighter squadrons covering the BEF in France but after ten days had to retire to British bases as the enemy occupied many of the RAF's airfields in Northern France.

The squadron was sent to the North of Scotland to re-equip and train new pilots, having lost the equivalent of its flying establishment in France. B Flight was detached on 21 July 1940 to form No.232 Squadron and No.3 remained in the area for the defence of Scapa Flow until April 1941. Convoy patrols were flown and the squadron began to concentrate on night fighting, fruitless sorties being flown in co-operation with Turbinlite aircraft. Intruder operations were also flown over Northern France and in February 1943 the first Typhoon was received though it was May before the last Hurricane was replaced.

Fighter-bomber raids on shipping and targets in France and the Low Countries began in June 1943 and some night intruder missions flown. In March 1944, No.3 became one

Hurricane IICs, No.3 Squadron

of the first Tempest squadrons which it used to combat flying bombs when the Germans began using these in June. In September their launching sites were captured and the squadron resumed armed reconnaissance sweeps, moving at the end of the month to join Second TAF on the Continent for the rest of the war. It remained in Germany with the occupation forces after the war, converting to Vampires in April 1948. These were replaced by Sabres in May 1953 which were, in turn, supplanted by Hunters in May 1956. With the reduction in the German-based day fighter forces, the squadron was disbanded on 15 June 1957.

On 21 January 1959, No.96 Squadron at Geilenkirchen was renumbered 3 Squadron. Equipped with Javelins, it formed part of the all-weather defence force in Germany until disbanded on 31 December 1960. No.59 Squadron, also based at Geilenkirchen, was renumbered 3 Squadron on 1 January 1961 and flew Canberras for eleven years before converting to Harriers for tactical reconnaissance and ground attack duties.

Castletown	10 Feb 1941	B.160 Kastrup	21 Jun 1945
Martlesham Heath	3 Apr 1941	B.156 Luneburg	18 Jul 1945
Debden	3 May 1941	B.158 Lubeck	8 Aug 1945
Martlesham Heath	13 May 1941	B.155 Dedelstorf	5 Sep 1945
Stapleford Tawney	23 Jun 1941	B.170 Sylt	6 Oct 1945
Hunsdon	9 Aug 1941	B.152 Fassberg	27 Oct 1945
Shoreham	14 Aug 1942	Wunstorf	23 Jan 1946
Hunsdon	21 Aug 1942	Gatow	27 Mar 1946
West Malling	14 May 1943	Dedelstorf	6 May 1946
Manston	11 Jun 1943	Manston	1 Jun 1946
Swanton Morley	28 Dec 1943	Dedelstorf	12 Jun 1946
Manston	14 Feb 1944	Wunstorf	21 Sep 1946
Bradwell Bay	6 Mar 1944	Gutersloh	25 Jun 1948
Ayr	6 Apr 1944	Wildenrath	31 Mar 1952
Bradwell Bay	14 Apr 1944	Geilenkirchen	21 Jul 1953
Newchurch	28 Apr 1944		to 15 Jun 1957
Matlask	21 Sep 1944	Geilenkirchen	21 Jan 1959
B.60 Grimbergen	28 Sep 1944		to 31 Dec 1960
B.80 Volkel	1 Oct 1944	Geilenkirchen	1 Jan 1961
Warmwell	2 Apr 1945	Laarbruch	15 Jan 1968
B.112 Hopsten	17 Apr 1945	Wildenrath	1 Jan 1972
B.152 Fassberg	26 Apr 1945	Gutersloh	Mar 1977

Squadron bases

Larkhill	13 May 1912	Wye	Feb 1919
Netheravon	16 Jun 1913	Dover	June 1919
Amiens	13 Aug 1914		to 27 Oct 1919
Maubeuge	16 Aug 1914	Bangalore	1 Apr 1920
Le Cateau	23 Aug 1914	Ambala	1 Apr 1921
St. Quentin	25 Aug 1914		to 30 Sep 1921
La Fère	26 Aug 1914	Leuchars	1 Oct 1921
Compiegne	28 Aug 1914	Gosport	Oct 1922
Senlis	30 Aug 1914		to 1 Apr 1923
Juilly	31 Aug 1914	Manston	1 Apr 1924
Serris	2 Sep 1914	Upavon	30 Apr 1924
Pezearches	3 Sep 1914	Kenley	10 May 1934
Melun	4 Sep 1914	Left for Middle East	
Le Touquin	7 Sep 1914		4 Oct 1935
Coulommiers	10 Sep 1914	Khartoum	18 Oct 1935 (A)
Fère-en-Tardenois			22 Oct 1935 (G)
	12 Sep 1914	Port Sudan	20 Jan 1936
Amiens	6 Oct 1914	Left for U.K.	14 Aug 1936
Abbeville	8 Oct 1914	Kenley	28 Aug 1936
Bienfay	9 Oct 1914	Biggin Hill	2 May 1939
St. Omer	12 Oct 1914	Croydon	2 Sep 1939
Houges	24 Nov 1914	Manston	10 Sep 1939
Auchel	1 Jun 1915	Croydon	17 Sep 1939
Bruay	15 Mar 1916	Hawkinge (D)	17 Dec 1939
Bertangles	1 Apr 1916		to 10 Feb 1940
La Houssoye	10 Apr 1916	Merville	10 May 1940
Lavieville	23 Jan 1917	Kenley	20 May 1940
Longavesnes	15 Jul 1917	Wick	23 May 1940
Lechelle	26 Aug 1917	Castletown	2 Sep 1940
Warloy Baillon	10 Oct 1917	Turnhouse	14 Sep 1940
Vert Galand	25 Mar 1918	Dyce	9 Oct 1940
Valhereux	26 Mar 1918	Castletown	12 Oct 1940
Lechelle	15 Oct 1918	Sumburgh (D)	2 Jan 1941
Inchy	4 Nov 1918		to 29 Mar 1941
		Skeabrae	7 Jan 1941

Aircraft

Equipment	Period of service	Representative Serial and Code
Various (e.g. Bleriot XI (260), Deperdussin, Farman, Tabloid, B.E.2, B.E.2a (220), B.E.3, B.E.4, B.E.8 (209), Avro 500 (285), Avro 504, Bristol Boxkite, S.E.2 (609), Bristol Scout (648) etc.) May 1912 – Dec 1915		
Morane Parasol	Dec 1915 – Sep 1917	A6607
Morane BB	Dec 1915 – 1916	
Camel	Sep 1917 – Feb 1919	B6234 (A)
Snipe	Apr 1920 – Oct 1921	H4883
	Apr 1924 – Oct 1925	
D.H.9A	Oct 1921 – Oct 1922	H3518
Walrus	Jan 1922 – Apr 1923	N9332
Woodcock II	Jul 1925 – Sep 1928	J7725
Gamecock I	Aug 1928 – Jul 1929	J9571
Bulldog II	May 1929 – Dec 1932	J9579
Bulldog IIA	Feb 1931 – Jan 1932	K2220
	Dec 1932 – Jun 1937	
Gladiator I	Mar 1937 – Mar 1938	K7958 (OP-Q)
	Jul 1938 – Jul 1939	
Hurricane I	Mar 1938 – Jul 1938	L1934 (OP-D)
	Jul 1939 – Apr 1941	
Hurricane IIA, IIB	Apr 1941 – Nov 1941	Z2891 (QO-R)
Hurricane IIC	Apr 1941 – May 1943	BD867 (QO-Y)
Typhoon IB	Feb 1943 – Apr 1944	DN623 (QO-H)
Tempest V	Feb 1944 – Apr 1948	SN330 (J5-H)
Vampire F.1	Apr 1948 – May 1949	VF279 (J5-T)
Vampire FB.5	May 1949 – May 1953	VV445 (A-T)
Sabre F.1/F.4	May 1953 – Jun 1956	XB913 (L)
Hunter F.4	May 1956 – Jun 1957	XF975 (W)
Javelin FAW.4	Jan 1959 – Dec 1960	XA750 (A)
Canberra B(I).8	Jan 1961 – Jan 1972	XH204 (A)
Harrier GR.1A, GR.3	Jan 1972 – date	XW766 (E)

Atlas Is, No.4 Squadron

No. 4 Squadron

Badge: A sun in splendour divided per bend by a flash of lightning
Motto: In futurum videre

No.4 Squadron was formed at Farnborough in August 1912 from No.2 Flight, No.2 Squadron and flew a variety of types until the outbreak of World War One. After flying patrols over the Straits of Dover and the Thames Estuary for two weeks, the squadron moved to France on 16 August 1914 with a mixed collection of the more serviceable aircraft available to the RFC to provide air reconnaissance for the British Expeditionary Force. As the opposing armies settled into static defence lines at the end of 1914, No.4 began the tasks which were to occupy it for the rest of the war, artillery observation, reconnaissance and photography. Early in 1916 the squadron standardised on B.E.s, replacing these with R.E.8s in May 1917 and A Flight became No.4A Squadron in January 1918 for two months while attached to the Portuguese Corps. In February 1919, No.4 returned to the UK as a cadre but was brought up to strength on 30 April 1920 at Farnborough with Bristol Fighters.

A Flight was detached to Ireland to co-operate with security forces there between November 1920 and January 1922 and in September 1922 No.4 was sent to Turkey during the Chanak crisis. It returned a year later and re-equipped with Atlases in October 1929 which were replaced by Audaxes in December 1931. In May 1937 Hectors were received (but not operated until July) and in January 1939 No.4 converted to the last of the traditional multi-role army

co-operation types, the Lysander. These it took to France on the outbreak of World War Two in support of the BEF but during the German invasion in May 1940 was forced out of its airfields and was withdrawn to the UK. Coastal patrols were flown along the East Coast and later detachments of Lysanders were provided for air-sea rescue duties. Some Tomahawks and Mustangs were received in April 1942 which replaced the last Lysanders in August and in October the squadron standardised on Mustangs for tactical reconnaissance duties.

Operations began on 14 October 1942 and in addition to reconnaissance flights along the French coast, the Mustangs were used occasionally for defensive patrols. No.4 joined No.130 Airfield of Second TAF in August 1943 and in January 1944 re-equipped with Spitfires and Mosquitos for photographic reconnaissance missions over enemy communications and bases in France. The last Mosquito sortie was made on 20 May and thereafter the squadron operated Spitfires, supplemented by a small number of Typhoons for low-level missions in October. Reconnaissance occupied the squadron for the rest of the war and on 31 August 1945 it disbanded in Germany.

On 1 September 1945 No.605 Squadron at Celle was renumbered 4 Squadron. It flew Mosquitos as part of BAFO until re-equipped with Vampire fighter-bombers in 1950. In 1953 the squadron received Sabres and became a day fighter unit replacing these with Hunters in 1955. Disbandment came on 31 December 1960 but on the next day No.79 Squadron at Gutersloh was renumbered 4 Squadron. Hunter fighter-reconnaissance aircraft were flown until May 1970, the Hunter FGA.9s of No.54 Squadron joining No.4 on 1 September 1969 as its UK Echelon. After converting to Harriers at Wittering, this detachment became No.4 Squadron on 28 May 1970, the section of the squadron at Gutersloh then disbanding. In June 1970 the re-equipped squadron rejoined RAF Germany at Wildenrath.

Mohawk IV, No.5 Squadron

Squadron bases

Farnborough	26 Jul 1913	Kohat	22 Jan 1925
Fère-en-Tardenois	17 Sep 1914	Risalpur	15 Oct 1925
Abbeville	8 Oct 1914	Quetta	15 Dec 1928
Moyenville	9 Oct 1914	Kohat	16 May 1930
St. Omer	12 Oct 1914	Quetta	15 Mar 1931
Bailleul	23 Oct 1914	Risalpur	9 Jul 1935
Abeele	27 Apr 1915	Chaklala	15 Oct 1935
Droglandt	11 Mar 1916	Miramshah	14 Apr 1936
Marieux	2 Oct 1916	Risalpur	20 Apr 1937
La Gorgue	24 Mar 1917	Miramshah	14 Aug 1937
Savy	7 Apr 1917	Risalpur	21 Apr 1938
Ascq	2 June 1917	Arawali	14 May 1938
Le Hameau	25 May 1918	Risalpur	10 Jun 1938
Bovelles	4 Aug 1918	Fort Sandeman	4 Oct 1939
Izel-le-Hameau	24 Aug 1918	Lahore	10 Jun 1940
Pronville	14 Oct 1918	Risalpur	18 Feb 1941
Enerchicourt	24 Oct 1918	Dum Dum	11 Dec 1941
Aulney	10 Nov 1918	Dinjan	5 May 1942
Pecq	16 Nov 1918	Feni	29 Sep 1942
Cognelée	27 Nov 1918	Alipore	1 Oct 1942
Elsenborn	7 Dec 1918	Agartala	6 Oct 1942
Hangelar	20 Dec 1918	Khargpur	1 Jun 1943
Bicester	8 Sep 1919	Sapam	7 Dec 1943
	to 20 Jan 1920	Wangjing	24 Mar 1944
Quetta	1 Apr 1920	Lanka	31 Mar 1944
Ambala	26 Oct 1922	Dergaon	6 Jun 1944
Dardoni	10 Mar 1924	Vizagapatam	22 Jun 1944
		Cholavarum	24 Oct 1944
Kajamalai	29 Oct 1944	Bhopal	17 Feb 1946
St. Thomas Mount	2 Dec 1944	Poona	1 Jun 1946
Nazir	12 Dec 1944	Risalpur (D)	26 Nov 1946
Cox's Bazaar	19 Apr 1945		to 23 Jan 1947
Kyaukpyu	28 Apr 1945	Peshawar	22 Jan 1947
Vizagapatam	10 Jun 1945	Mauripur	3 Jul 1947
Bobbili	14 Jun 1945 (G)		to 1 Aug 1947
	24 Jun 1945 (A)	Pembrey	11 Feb 1949
Vizagapatam	30 Aug 1945	Chivenor	25 Oct 1949
Baigachi	12 Sep 1945		to 25 Sep 1951
Zayatkwin	25 Sep 1945	Wunstorf	1 Mar 1952
Baigachi	30 Sep 1945		to 12 Oct 1957
Bobbili	2 Oct 1945	Laarbruch	20 Jan 1959
Vizagapatam	2 Nov 1945		to 7 Oct 1965
Baigachi	5 Dec 1945	Binbrook	8 Oct 1965

Aircraft Equipment	Period of service	Representative Serial
Various e.g. Avro 500, 504 (637); B.E.8; S.E.2; Henry Farman (341); B.E.2a (383); Bleriot (576); Voisin; Caudron G.III; S.E.2a (609); Bristol Scout (633); F.E.8; Vickers F.B.5 (1637); D.H.2 (4732) between Jul 1913 and Apr 1917		
B.E.2c, B.E.2e	Mar 1916 — May 1917	1784
R.E.8	May 1917 — Sep 1919	C2731 (1)
Bristol F.2b	Mar 1919 — Sep 1919 Apr 1920 — May 1931	F4320 (D)
Wapiti IIA	May 1931 — Jun 1940	J9509 (C)
Hart	Jun 1940 — Feb 1941	K4380
Audax	Feb 1941 — Sep 1942	K7333
Mohawk IV	Dec 1941 — Jun 1943	AR690
Hurricane IIC, IID	Jun 1943 — Sep 1944	KW865 (Q)
Thunderbolt I, II	Sep 1944 — Feb 1946	FL749 (R)
Tempest F.2	Mar 1946 — Aug 1947	PR559 (OQ-R)
Spitfire LF.16E	Feb 1949 — Sep 1951	SL600 (E)
Martinet TT.1	Feb 1949 — Sep 1951	RG897
Oxford T.1	Feb 1949 — Sep 1951	PH318 (7B-T)
Beaufighter TT.10	Jan 1950 — Sep 1951	RD577 (P)
Vampire F.3	Aug 1950 — Sep 1951	VG697
Vampire FB.5	Mar 1952 — Dec 1952	WG843 (B-C)
Venom FB.1	Dec 1952 — Jul 1955	WE329 (B-X)
Venom FB.4	Jul 1955 — Oct 1957	WR470
Meteor NF.11	Jan 1959 — Aug 1960	WD663 (C)
Javelin FAW.5	Jan 1960 — Nov 1962	XA649 (D)
Javelin FAW.9	Nov 1962 — Oct 1965	XH756 (Z)
Lightning F.3, F.6	Oct 1965 — date	XR764 (L)

No. 6 Squadron

Badge: An eagle, wings elevated, preying on a serpent
Motto: Oculi exercitus (The eyes of the army)

No.6 Squadron was formed at Farnborough on 31 January, 1914, but did not move to France with the other squadrons of the RFC in August 1914, having transferred most of its aircraft to the expeditionary force. After building up its strength, the squadron moved to Belgium on 7 October but after a week had retired over the French frontier as the trench lines took shape in Flanders. Corps reconnaissance duties began and remained No.6's main role for the rest of the war. Artillery spotting and tactical reconnaissance over the Western Front formed the bulk of the squadron's operations but bombing raids were occasionally mounted. Soon after the Armistice, No.6 was transferred to the Middle East and arrived in Iraq in July 1919. There it undertook patrol duties, initially against Turkish-backed rebels in Northern Iraq and later policed large areas of desert to protect towns against marauding bands of raiders. In October 1929, the squadron left Iraq for Egypt where in 1931 it changed its title from 'Army Cooperation' to 'Bomber' and replaced its Bristol Fighters with Gordons. These were exchanged for Harts in October 1935, one flight being equipped with Demon two-seat fighters for a short period before these were passed to No.29 Squadron in January 1936.

Tension between Arabs and Jews in Palestine brought No.6 to the region to cooperate with the police and army. Early in 1938, Harts were replaced by general-purpose Hardys, supplemented in 1939 by Gauntlets and Lysanders. On the outbreak of the Second World War, the squadron remained in Palestine and it was not until September 1940 that its first operations were flown against the Italians in the Western Desert. By now completely equipped with Lysanders, No.6 provided tactical reconnaissance for the army but its headquarters remained in Palestine until February 1941. As the Lysander was not suited to reconnaissance in the face of enemy fighters, one flight was converted to Hurricanes and these replaced Lysanders completely in June 1941. Within a few weeks, however, the squadron was withdrawn and its aircraft transferred to other units.

During August 1941, No.6 was re-equipped with Lysanders and Gladiators, later augmented by a few Blenheims and Hurricanes. In January 1942, these were taken away and the squadron allocated to maintenance duties until April when Hurricane IIDs were received. These were equipped with a pair of 40mm anti-tank cannon and were taken into action in June against the Afrika Korps. In December, the squadron was withdrawn to Egypt for shipping protection duties but returned to the desert in February, 1943, once more in an anti-tank role. After moving westwards into Tunisia, No.6 returned to Egypt in September 1943 to convert to rocket-firing Hurricanes which it took to Italy in February 1944 for operations over the Adriatic and the Balkans. Ground-attack and anti-shipping missions were flown until the end of the war and in July 1945 the squadron moved back to Palestine.

Some Spitfires were received in December 1945 but it was a year before the last Hurricanes departed, No.6 having operated the type for some time after every other Hurricane squadron had re-equipped or disbanded. Tempests were received soon after the squadron moved to Cyprus and were taken to the Sudan in November 1947. In May 1948, No.6 arrived in Egypt where it converted to Vampires in 1949, later re-equipping with Venoms. After a period of moving around the Middle East, the squadron took up residence in Cyprus in April 1956 where it received Canberras in July 1957. These were flown until No.6 disbanded on 13 January 1969 for the first time in fifty-five years.

On 7 May, 1969, No.6 reformed at Coningsby as the first Phantom squadron, becoming operational in August for tactical reconnaissance and ground-attack duties. The squadron disbanded on 1 October, 1974, but was reformed the following day at Lossiemouth with Jaguars for ground-attack duties. In November 1974, it moved to its operational base at Coltishall.

Squadron bases

Farnborough	31 Jan 1914	Bailleul	18 Nov 1914		
Dover	6 Oct 1914	Abeele	24 Apr 1915		
Bruges	7 Oct 1914	Droglandt	2 Oct 1916		
Ostend	8 Oct 1914	Abeele	3 Nov 1916		
St. Pol	13 Oct 1914	Bertangles	12 Nov 1917		
St.Omer	21 Oct 1914	St. Andre	23 Mar 1918		

Le Crotoy	26 Mar 1918	LG.89	29 Jul 1942
Fienvillers	17 Jul 1918	LG.172	6 Nov 1942
Bovelles	5 Aug 1918	Idku	9 Dec 1942
Auxi-le-Chateau	17 Aug 1918	Bu Amud	2 Feb 1942
Ascq	27 Aug 1918	Castel Benito	2 Mar 1943
Moislans	27 Sep 1918	Sorman	7 Mar 1943
Longavesnes	6 Oct 1918	Senom	14 Mar 1943
Bertry	19 Oct 1918	Gabes	4 Apr 1943
Maretz	20 Oct 1918	Sfax/El Maou	31 Apr 1943
Gondecourt	9 Nov 1918	Bou Goubrine	16 Apr 1943
Recq	16 Nov 1918	Ben Gardane	2 Jun 1943
Gerpinnes	6 Dec 1918	Heliopolis	8 Sep 1943
Sart	19 Mar 1919	Fayid	22 Sep 1943
Left for Iraq	14 Apr 1919	Grottaglie	24 Feb 1944
Baghdad West	18 Jul 1919	Foggia	4 Jul 1944
Hinaidi	9 Oct 1922	Canne	14 Aug 1944
Mosul	19 May 1924	Prkos	9 Apr 1945
Hinaidi	20 Oct 1926	(Det. from 8 Feb 1945)	
Ismailia	28 Oct 1929	Canne	18 May 1945
Ramleh (D)	28 Oct 1929	Left for Palestine	7 Jul 1945
	to 29 May 1936	Megiddo	13 Jul 1945 (G)
Ramleh	29 May 1936		30 Jul 1945 (A)
Ismailia	19 Nov 1936	Petah Tiqva	3 Sep 1945
Ramleh (D)	19 Nov 1936	Ein Shemer	4 Jun 1946
	to 22 Nov 1937	Nicosia	3 Oct 1946
Ramleh	22 Nov 1937	Khartoum	26 Nov 1947
Qasaba (D)	19 Sep 1940	Fayid	5 May 1948
	to 1 Feb 1941	Deversoir	1 Sep 1948
Tobruk (D)	1 Feb 1941	Habbaniya	7 Jan 1950
	to 17 Feb 1941	Deversoir	9 Feb 1950
Aqir	17 Feb 1941	Mafraq	1 Jun 1950
Barce	24 Feb 1941	Deversoir	29 Jun 1950
Maraua	4 Apr 1941	Habbaniya	22 Nov 1950
El Adem	6 Apr 1941	Shaibah	18 Jun 1951
El Gubbi	8 Apr 1941	Habbaniya	19 Sep 1951
Tobruk West	9 Apr 1941	Abu Sueir	13 Nov 1951
Qasaba	23 Apr 1941	Habbaniya	27 Nov 1951
Tel Aviv	1 Jul 1941	Abu Sueir	28 Jan 1952
Wadi Halfa	18 Aug 1941	Nicosia	31 May 1952
Kufra (D)	28 Aug 1941	Abu Sueir	28 Jul 1952
	to 12 Jan 1942	Sharjah	17 Sep 1952
Helwan	12 Feb 1942	Habbaniya	1 Oct 1952
Kilo 26	22 Feb 1942	Akrotiri	6 Apr 1956
Shandur	28 Apr 1942		to 13 Jan 1969
Gambut	4 Jun 1942	Coningsby	7 May 1969
Sidi Haneish	17 Jun 1942		to 1 Oct 1974
LG.106	28 Jun 1942	Lossiemouth	2 Oct 1974
LG.91	29 Jun 1942	Coltishall	6 Nov 1974

Gordon I, No.6 Squadron

Demon I, No.6 Squadron

Aircraft Equipment	Period of service	Representative Serial	Aircraft Equipment	Period of service	Representative Serial and Code
B.E.2, B.E.2a, B.E.2b, B.E.8, Maurice Farman F.20			Hurricane I	Mar 1941 – Jun 1941	V7777
Bleriot XI	Jul 1914 – Oct 1914			Sep 1941 – Jan 1942	
R.E.5	Aug 1914 – Oct 1914	659	Gladiator II	Aug 1941 – Jan 1942	N5830
R.E.7	Oct 1914		Blenheim IV	Nov 1941 – Jan 1942	P4863
B.E.2c	Oct 1914 – Oct 1916	7341	Hurricane IIC	Dec 1942 – Feb 1943	HM118
Martinsyde S.1	Mar 1915 – Sep 1915		Hurricane IID	Apr 1942 – Dec 1942	HV669 (JV-E)
Bristol Scout	Apr 1915 – Jun 1916	5311		Feb 1943 – Jul 1943	
B.E.2d	Jun 1916 – Apr 1917	5767	Hurricane IV	Jul 1943 – Dec 1946	LE400 (D)
B.E.2e	Oct 1916 – May 1917	6278	Spitfire IX	Dec 1945 – Dec 1946	PT470 (JV-C)
R.E.8	May 1917 – Jul 1920	B5013	Tempest F.6	Dec 1946 – Dec 1949	NX191 (JV-H)
Bristol F.2B	Feb 1919 – Apr 1919	FR4744	Vampire FB.5	Oct 1949 – Feb 1954	VX981 (K)
	Jul 1920 – Jun 1932		Vampire FB.9	Feb 1952 – May 1954	WX222
Gordon	Jun 1931 – Oct 1935	K2722	Venom FB.1	Feb 1954 – Jul 1955	WE454 (D)
Hart	Oct 1935 – Mar 1938	K4415	Venom FB.4	Jun 1955 – Sep 1957	WR501
Demon	Oct 1935 – Jan 1936	K4514	Canberra B.2	Jul 1957 – Jan 1960	WH885
Hardy	Jan 1938 – Apr 1940	K4070	Canberra B.6	Dec 1959 – Dec 1962	WJ778
Gauntlet II	Aug 1939 – Apr 1940	K4088	Canberra B.16	Jan 1962 – Jan 1969	WJ780
Lysander I, II	Sep 1939 – Dec 1939		Phantom FGR.2	May 1969 – Sep 1974	XV480 (M)
	Feb 1940 – Jun 1941	L6857 (JV-P)	Jaguar GR.1	Oct 1974 – date	XX738
	Aug 1941 – Jan 1942				

Hurricane IVs, No.6 Squadron

No. 7 Squadron

Badge: On a hurt, seven mullets of six points forming a representation of the constellation Ursa Major

Motto: Per diem, per noctem (By day and by night)

No.7 Squadron was formed at Farnborough on 1 May 1914, the last of the RFC squadrons to be formed before the outbreak of World War One. Until April 1915, it was engaged in experimental flying and many of its personnel were lost to the active squadrons but it finally reached France on 8 April 1915 to undertake reconnaissance and artillery spotting duties. After using a mixture of types, it standardised on B.E.2cs by the summer of 1916 and in July 1917 received R.E.8s, its equipment for the rest of the war. As a corps reconnaissance unit, No.7 directed artillery fire and undertook tactical reconnaissance over the Western Front until the Armistice. In September 1919, it returned to the UK and disbanded on 31 December 1919.

On 1 June 1923, No.7 reformed at Bircham Newton with Vimys as a bomber squadron, initially with a single flight but on 5 July 1923, D Flight of 100 Squadron was added.

In April 1927, it re-equipped with Virginias which were flown until April 1935, when Heyfords replaced them. In April 1937, some Wellesleys arrived to re-equip B Flight which was detached to form No.76 Squadron on 12 April and at the end of November 1938, the first Whitleys were collected. In April 1939, conversion to Hampdens took place but the squadron was allotted a training role on 1 June 1939, which continued after the outbreak of World War Two and on 4 April 1940, No.7 merged with No.76 Squadron to form No.16 Operational Training Unit. On 30 April a new No.7 began to reform with Hampdens but was disbanded again on 20 May 1940.

On 1 August 1940, No.7 reformed at Leeming as the first Stirling squadron and after training with these flew its first operation on 10 February 1941 In October 1942 it was transferred to the Pathfinder Force and flew its last missions with Stirlings on 28 June 1943, before converting to Lancasters. For the rest of the war, No.7 spearheaded the night bomber force in its attacks on Germany and remained as part of the post-war Bomber Command, re-equipping with Lincolns in August 1949. In 1954, detachments were sent to Malaya to assist in attacks on terrorist camps in the jungle and on 1 January 1956, the squadron was disbanded.

On 1 November 1956, No.7 reformed at Honington with Valiants as part of the V-bomber force, being disbanded again on 1 September 1962. On 1 May 1970, it reformed at St. Mawgan with Canberras as a target facilities unit.

Virginia III, No.7 Squadron

Heyford III, No.7 Squadron

Squadron bases

Base	Date	Base	Date
Farnborough	1 May 1914	Eastleigh	10 Sep 1919
Netheravon	22 Oct 1914	Farnborough	19 Nov 1919
St. Omer	8 Apr 1915		to 31 Dec 1919
Boulogne (D)	19 Apr 1915	Bircham Newton	1 Jun 1923
	to 26 May 1915	Worthy Down	7 Apr 1927
Droglandt	11 Sep 1915	Finningley	3 Sep 1936
Bailleul	12 Dec 1915	Doncaster	1 Sep 1939
Warloy Baillon	30 Jul 1916	Finningley	15 Sep 1939
Moreuil	6 Feb 1917	Upper Heyford	23 Sep 1939
Matigny	15 Mar 1917		to 4 Apr 1940
Proven East	23 May 1917	Finningley	30 Apr 1940
Droglandt	13 Apr 1918		to 20 May 1940
Proven	3 Sep 1918	Leeming	1 Aug 1940
Bisseghem	22 Oct 1918	Oakington	29 Oct 1940
Staceghem	1 Nov 1918	Mepal	24 Jul 1945
Peronne	25 Nov 1918	Upwood	29 Jul 1946
Cognelee	26 Nov 1918		to 1 Jan 1956
Elsenborn	7 Dec 1918	Honington	1 Nov 1956
Bickendorf	15 Dec 1918	Wittering	1 Sep 1960
Spich	20 Dec 1918		to 30 Sep 1962
Buckheim	Jul 1919	St Mawgan	1 May 1970

Aircraft

Equipment	Period of service	Representative Serial	
Maurice Farman, B.E.8,			
Tabloid, Voisin, R.E.5,			
Bristol Scout	May 1914 – Jun 1916	–	
B.E.2c	Jul 1915 – Jul 1916	2108	
B.E.2d, B.E.2e	May 1916 – Jul 1917	5750	
R.E.8	Jul 1917 – Dec 1919	A4381	
Vimy	Jun 1923 – Apr 1927	F8631	
Virginia I, VIII, X	Apr 1927 – Jun 1935	J8328	(J)
Heyford II	Apr 1935 – Apr 1938	K4865	
Heyford III	Apr 1936 – Apr 1938	K6873	
Wellesley I	Apr 1937	K7714	
Whitley II	Mar 1938 – Dec 1938	K7233	
Whitley III	Nov 1938 – May 1939	K8964	
Anson I	Mar 1939 – Apr 1940	N5015	
Hampden I	Apr 1939 – May 1940	L4170	
Stirling I	Aug 1940 – Jul 1943	N3642	(MG-E)
Stirling III	Mar 1943 – Jul 1943	EF361	(MG-B2)
Lancaster I, III	Jul 1943 – Aug 1949	PB623	(MG-L)
Lincoln B.2	Aug 1949 – Dec 1955	RE340	(MG-D)
Valiant B.1	Dec 1956 – Sep 1962	XD826	
Canberra TT.18	May 1970 – date	WK122	
Canberra B.2	May 1970 – date	WJ611	

D.H.9As and Nighthawk, No.8 Squadron

No. 8 Squadron

Badge: An Arabian dagger sheathed
Motto: Uspiam et passim (Everywhere unbounded)

No.8 Squadron was formed at Brooklands on 1 January 1915 and moved to France in April 1915 with B.E.2cs. Reconnaissance and bombing missions were flown over the Western Front until squadrons became specialised, No.8 becoming a corps reconnaissance unit. Artillery spotting and tactical reconnaissance duties occupied the squadron for the rest of the war, its B.E.s being replaced by R.E.8s in August 1917. A few weeks after the Armistice, Bristol Fighters were received and in July No.8 returned to the UK where it was disbanded on 20 January 1920.

On 18 October 1920, No.8 was reformed at Helwan with D.H.9As and in February 1921 was transferred from Egypt to Iraq for patrol duties when the RAF was given responsibility for the security of the new country. In February 1927 the squadron was moved to Aden for similar tasks, remaining there until the end of World War Two. Fairey IIIFs were received in January 1928 and were replaced by Vincents in April 1935. These remained in service until 1942 but Blenheims began to arrive in April 1939 and were used for attacks on bases in Italian East Africa after Italy entered the war in June 1940. A flight of Free French Marylands was attached in August 1940 for reconnaissance duties but left for the Middle East in January 1941. After the capture of the Italian colonies in East Africa, the squadron undertook anti-submarine patrols and internal security, basing detachments at various times along the Arabian coast and in Somaliland. A flight of Hudsons began operations on 10 March 1943 and in December 1943 Wellingtons began to replace other types by the end of January 1944. These were flown on patrols until the squadron disbanded on 1 May 1945.

On 15 May 1945, No.200 Squadron at Jessore was re-numbered 8 Squadron and within a few days began to move its Liberators to Ceylon for special duties. Supply-dropping flights to guerilla forces in Malaya were made until the Japanese surrender and on 15 November 1945 the squadron again disbanded. On 1 September 1946, No.114 Squadron in Aden was renumbered 8 Squadron and remained in Aden until the base was closed down in 1967. Equipped initially with Mosquito fighter-bombers, the squadron converted to Tempests in April 1947 and in July 1949 received Brigands. These were replaced by Vampires and Venoms in turn while at times the squadron also had Meteor and Hunter fighter-reconnaissance aircraft on strength. On 1 August 1959, C Flight operating Meteors became the Arabian Peninsula Reconnaissance Flight but rejoined No.8 in August 1960. Meteors were replaced by Hunter FR.10s in April 1961, the remainder of the squadron having converted to Hunter FGA.9s in January 1960. These were frequently in action against incursions from the Yemen across the ill-defined frontier of the Aden Protectorate. The reconnaissance flight became No.1417 (Fighter-reconnaissance) Flight in May 1963, returning to No.8 in September 1967 when the squadron moved to Bahrain. In September 1971, a move was made to Sharjah before the squadron disbanded on 15 December 1971.

On 8 January 1972, No.8 reformed at Kinloss to fly Shackleton AEW aircraft. Maritime Shackletons were flown for the first few months pending the arrival of Shackleton AEW.2s in the Spring on 1972.

Squadron bases

Brooklands	1 Jan 1915	Malincourt	18 Oct 1918
Gosport	6 Jan 1915	Bellevue	16 Nov 1918
St. Omer	15 Apr 1915	Sart	11 May 1919
Abeele	1 May 1915	Duxford	28 Jul 1919
Oxelaere	May 1915		to 20 Jan 1920
Marieux	24 Jul 1915	Helwan	18 Oct 1920
Bellevue	20 Feb 1916	Suez	Dec 1920
Soncamp	3 Feb 1917	Basra	23 Feb 1921
Boiry St. Martin	9 May 1917	Baghdad West	4 Mar 1931
Longavesnes	18 Oct 1917	Hinaidi	29 Dec 1921
Mons-en-Chaussée	29 Oct 1917	Khormaksar	Feb 1927
Templeux	11 Mar 1918		to 1 May 1945
Chipilly	22 Mar 1918	Jessore	15 May 1945
Poulainville	24 Mar 1918	Minneriya	21 May 1945
Vert Galand	28 Mar 1918		to 15 Nov 1945
Auxi-le-Chateau	6 Apr 1918	Khormaksar	1 Sep 1946
Vignacourt	10 Jul 1918	Muharraq	Sep 1967 (P)
Bellevue	15 Aug 1918		Det. to 28 Nov 1967
Poucaucourt	11 Sep 1918	Sharjah	Sep 1971 (P)
Estrée-en-Chaussée			to 15 Dec 1971
	22 Sep 1918	Kinloss	8 Jan 1972
Hervilly	8 Oct 1918	Lossiemouth	17 Aug 1973

Aircraft Equipment	Period of service	Representative Serial and Code
B.E.2c	Jan 1915 — Aug 1917	
B.E.2e	Feb 1917 — Aug 1917	
R.E.8	Aug 1917 — Dec 1918	
Bristol F.2b	Dec 1918 — Jan 1920	D7901
D.H.9A	Oct 1920 — Jan 1928	H24 (E)
Fairey IIIF	Jan 1928 — Apr 1935	J9134 (D)
Vincent	Apr 1935 — Mar 1942	K4132 (B)
Blenheim I	Apr 1939 — Mar 1942	L1520
Blenheim IV	Aug 1941 — Apr 1943	Z9750
Blenheim V	Sep 1942 — Jan 1944	BA927
Maryland I	Aug 1940 — Jan 1941	M167 No. 102
Hudson VI	Feb 1943 — Jan 1944	FK625
Wellington XIII	Dec 1943 — May 1945	JA271 (A)
Liberator VI	May 1945 — Nov 1945	KH144 (U)
Mosquito FB.6	Sep 1946 — Apr 1947	
Tempest F.6	Apr 1947 — Jul 1949	NX237 (F)
Brigand B.1	Jul 1949 — Feb 1953	VS815 (F)
Vampire FB.9	Dec 1952 — Dec 1955	WL607 (B)
Venom FB.1	Jun 1955 — Oct 1955	WR337 (C)
Venom FB.4	Oct 1955 — Feb 1960	WR548 (F)
Meteor FR.9	Jan 1958 — Aug 1959	VZ603
	Aug 1960 — Apr 1961	
Hunter FGA.9	Jan 1960 — Dec 1971	XE435 (E)
Hunter FR.10	Apr 1961 — May 1963	XE589 (V)
	Sep 1967 — Dec 1971	
Shackleton MR.2c, AEW.2		
	Jan 1972 — date	WL747 (47)

No. 9 Squadron

Badge: A bat
Motto: Per noctum volamus
(Through the night we fly)

No.9 Squadron was formed on 8 December 1914 at St. Omer from the HQ Wireless Unit as the Royal Flying Corps first operational squadron equipped with radio for artillery spotting. A decision that existing artillery observation squadrons should have a wireless flight each resulted in No.9 being dispersed. A Flight went to No.6 Squadron and B Flight to No.2 Squadron on 9 February 1915, while C Flight was split, half going to No.5 Squadron with its Bleriots on 1 March and the other half to No.16 Squadron on 22 March 1915, when the squadron was disbanded.

On 1 April 1915, No.9 reformed at Brooklands as a radio training unit with B.E.s, Farmans and Bleriots and in July moved to Dover to add coastal defence to its training role. In November 1915, it was ordered to France and, equipped with B.E.2cs, moved there during December, starting operational flights on 29 December 1915. Bombing and reconnaissance were the squadron's main tasks until the end of 1916 when it began to concentrate on corps reconnaissance duties and in May 1917, it began to re-equip with R.E.8s for this role. Until the end of the war, it was engaged in artillery spotting and tactical reconnaissance but also took part in bombing raids from June 1918 during the Allied counter-

Heyford III, No.9 Squadron

offensive which eventually led to the Armistice. A few Bristol Fighters had been received during this period but re-equipment with this type did not begin until February 1919, and by May it was fully converted. On 30 July 1919, No.9 was reduced to a cadre unit and returned to the UK, disbanding at Castle Bromwich on 31 December 1919.

On 1 April 1924, the squadron reformed as a night bomber unit at Upavon with Vimys, moving at the end of the month to Manston. In January 1925, the first of the Virginias arrived, a type which was to equip No.9 in various marks until May 1936. This enabled a second flight to be formed in June 1925. In March 1936, Heyfords began to replace the Virginias and in October the squadron took up its new base at Scampton, moving in March 1938 to Stradishall where, in February 1939, it converted to Wellingtons. On the outbreak of World War Two the squadron flew anti-shipping sweeps over the North Sea until one of these, on 18 December 1939 lost five aircraft to enemy fighters and daylight operations were restricted. When the Germans invaded Norway, aircraft were detached to Lossiemouth to attack enemy shipping and captured airfields there and night bombing became No.9's main role. Attacks on enemy targets in Germany and the occupied countries increased in number and at the end of July 1942, the last Wellington was flown and the squadron converted to Lancasters which were used for strategic bombing until the end of the war. Attacks with 12,000 lb. bombs on the *Tirpitz* resulted in the sinking of this battleship at Tromso on 12 November 1944.

With the end of the war in Europe, No.9 was allotted to Tiger Force scheduled to bomb Japan but before this could begin the Japanese surrendered though the squadron arrived in India in January 1946, for photographic survey duties, returning to the UK in April. The last Lancaster flight took place on 3 July 1946, and ten days later five Lincolns arrived as replacements. The type was operated until May 1952, when conversion to Canberras took place. In March 1956, these were taken to Malaya for three months for bombing attacks on terrorist camps in the jungle and in October 1956, the Canberras moved to Malta for attacks on Egyptian airfields during the Suez operation, returning during November. On 13 July 1961, the squadron was disbanded.

No.9 reformed at Coningsby on 1 March 1962, and received Vulcans during the following month as part of the nuclear deterrent force. In January 1969, it was posted to the Near East Air Force in Cyprus, where, with No.35 Squadron, it replaced a Canberra wing at Akrotiri, returning to the UK during the rundown of RAF bases in the Near East.

Squadron bases

St. Omer	8 Dec 1914 to 22 Mar 1915	Bertangles	24 Dec 1915
		Allonville	26 Mar 1916
Brooklands	1 Apr 1915	Chipilly	15 Jul 1916
Dover	23 Jul 1915	Morlancourt	3 Sep 1916
St. Omer	12 Dec 1915	Mons-en-Chaussée (D)	14 Apr 1917 to 27 Apr 1917
Nurlu	27 Apr 1917	Aldergrove	15 Jan 1936
Estree-en-Chaussée		Scampton	1 Oct 1936
	16 May 1917	Stradishall	10 Mar 1938
Proven	10 Jun 1917	Honington	15 Jul 1939
Calais	11 Apr 1918	Waddington	7 Aug 1942
Agenvillers	6 Jun 1918	Bardney	14 Apr 1943
Quevenvillers	17 Jul 1918	Waddington	6 Jul 1945
Amiens	15 Aug 1918	Left for India	26 Nov 1945 (G)
Proyart	7 Sep 1918		1 Jan 1946 (A)
Athies	15 Sep 1918	Salbani	19 Jan 1946
Montigny Farm	6 Oct 1918	Binbrook	19 Apr 1946
Premont	18 Oct 1918	Butterworth (D)	18 Mar 1956
Tarcienne	29 Nov 1918		to 23 Jun 1956
Fort de Cognelee	11 Dec 1918	Hal Far (D)	30 Oct 1956
Ludendorf	3 Jan 1919		to 17 Nov 1956
Castle Bromwich	31 Jul 1919 to 31 Dec 1919	Coningsby	2 Jun 1959 to 13 Jul 1961
Upavon	1 Apr 1924	Coningsby	1 Mar 1962
Manston	30 Apr 1924	Cottesmore	10 Nov 1964
Boscombe Down	26 Nov 1930	Akrotiri	26 Feb 1969
Andover	15 Oct 1935	Waddington	Jan 1975

Aircraft Equipment	Period of service	Representative Serial and Code	
B.E.2a	Sep 1914 – Mar 1915	317	
B.E.2b	Jan 1915 – Feb 1915	733	
Bleriot XI	Dec 1914 – Mar 1915	1825	
Maurice Farman S.7, S.11	Oct 1914 – Mar 1915	1841	
Avro 504, 504A	Mar 1915		
	Jul 1915 – Nov 1915	772	
B.E.8a	Jul 1915 – Nov 1915	348	
Martinsyde S.1	Jul 1915 – Nov 1915		
R.E.5	Nov 1915	688	
R.E.7	Nov 1915	2351	
Bristol Scout	Dec 1915 – Jun 1916	5297	
B.E.2c	Jan 1915 – Feb 1915	2653	
	Nov 1915 – Oct 1916		
B.E.2d	Jun 1916 – Aug 1916	5817	
B.E.2e	Aug 1916 – May 1917	A2880	
R.E.8	May 1917 – May 1919	A4366	(21)
Bristol F.2b	Jul 1918 – Oct 1918	E9588	
	Feb 1919 – Dec 1919		
Vimy	Apr 1924 – Jun 1925	F8631	
Virginia V, VI	Jan 1925 – Apr 1927	J7562	
Virginia VII	May 1926 – Jun 1930	J7706	
Virginia VIII	Mar 1927 – May 1927	J6856	
Virginia IX	Jul 1928 – Jul 1931	J7711	(Y)
Virginia X	May 1930 – May 1936	J7716	(U)
Heyford III	Mar 1936 – Feb 1939	K6906	
Wellington I	Feb 1939 – Sep 1939	L4274	(KA-K)
Wellington IA	Sep 1939 – Mar 1940	N2964	(WS-D)
Wellington IC	Mar 1940 – Sep 1941	T2619	(WS-T)
Wellington III	Sep 1941 – Aug 1942	BJ606	(WS-R)
Lancaster I, III	Aug 1942 – Nov 1945	JA711	(WS-A)
	Apr 1946 – Jul 1946		
Lancaster VII	Nov 1945 – Apr 1946	NX678	(WS-S)
Lincoln B.2	Jul 1946 – May 1952	SX977	(WS-F)
Canberra B.2	May 1952 – Jun 1956	WF908	
	Jun 1957 – Nov 1958		
Canberra B.6	Sep 1955 – Jul 1961	WJ756	
Vulcan B.2	Apr 1962 – date	XL385	

Wellington I, No.9 Squadron

Virginia I, No.9 Squadron

V.C.10 C.1, No.10 Squadron

No. 10 Squadron

Badge: A winged arrow
Motto: Rem acu tangere (To hit
the mark)

No. 10 Squadron was formed on 1 January 1915, at Farn-borough from a nucleus supplied by No.1 Reserve Squadron and flew a mixed collection of training types until it moved to France on 25 July 1915, its aircraft flying over three days later. It was fully equipped with B.E. variants, the RFC's standard corps reconnaissance aircraft and for the rest of the war was engaged in artillery observation, tactical recon-naissance and light bombing duties. In September 1917, its B.E.s were replaced by Armstrong Whitworth F.K.8s which were flown until January 1919, the squadron being reduced to a cadre on 8 February for return to the UK and was formally disbanded on 31 December 1919.

On 3 January 1928, No.10 reformed at Upper Heyford as a night bomber squadron with Hyderabads, the first three of which arrived on 25 January. In December 1930, these began to be replaced by Hinaidis, an improved version of the Hyderabad, and when the squadron moved to Boscombe Down in April 1931, it was fully re-equipped. In September 1932, conversion to Virginias began but two years later these venerable aircraft began to be replaced by Heyfords. In January 1937, No.10 moved to the new airfield at Dish-forth and in March began to receive Whitleys, the type with which it was destined to go to war. The expansion of the

RAF had already resulted in the squadron detaching a flight to form the nucleus of a new squadron twice, B Flight to form No.97 Squadron on 16 September 1935, and again to form No.78 Squadron on 1 November 1936.

On 8 September 1939, No.10 flew its first operation, a leaflet-dropping flight over Germany and these continued until the opening of the German offensive in the Spring of 1940. Whitleys took part in night raids until replaced by Halifaxes in December 1941. In June 1942, a detachment was sent to the Middle East to form a heavy bomber element there and this joined No.462 Squadron on 7 September 1942. The remainder of the squadron was brought up to strength again and formed part of the main force of Bomber Command for the rest of the war. As the war ended, No.10 was transferred to Transport Command on 7 May 1945, and converted to Dakotas in August, taking these to India in October for transport duties until disbanded on 20 December 1947.

On 5 November 1948, No.238 Squadron at Oakington was renumbered 10 Squadron and flew Dakotas until dis-banded on 20 February 1950, after taking part in the Berlin Airlift. On 15 January 1953, No.10 was again reformed, this time as a Canberra light bomber squadron at Scampton. In October 1956, it was detached to Cyprus for the Suez oper-ation, returning a month later and being disbanded on 15 January 1957.

On 15 April 1958, No.10 reformed as a Victor squadron at Cottesmore and formed part of the V-bomber force of nuclear bombers in the UK until disbanded on 1 March 1964. On 1 July 1966, it reformed at Brize Norton to fly the RAF's VC.10s on the trunk routes of Transport Command, begin-ning scheduled operations in April 1967. On completion of handling facilities at the Command's main base at Brize Norton in 1967, the squadron transferred its aircraft to that station from Fairford.

No. 11 Squadron

Squadron bases

Farnborough	1 Jan 1915	Dishforth	25 Jan 1937
Brooklands	8 Jan 1915	Leeming	8 Jul 1940
Hounslow	1 Apr 1915	Melbourne	19 Aug 1942
Netheravon	7 Apr 1915	Broadwell	6 Aug 1945
St. Omer	25 Jul 1915	St. Mawgan	28 Aug 1945
Aire	30 Jul 1915	Bilaspur	5 Oct 1946
Chocques	7 Aug 1915	Poona	May 1947 (P)
Abeele	17 Nov 1917		to 20 Dec 1947
Droglandt	12 Apr 1918	Oakington	5 Nov 1948
Abeele	21 Sep 1918		to 20 Feb 1950
Menin	21 Oct 1918	Scampton	15 Jan 1953
Staceghem	5 Nov 1918	Honington	16 May 1955
Menin	19 Nov 1918		to 15 Jan 1957
Reckem	1 Dec 1918	Cottesmore	15 Apr 1958
Ford	17 Feb 1919		to 1 Mar 1964
	to 31 Dec 1919	Fairford	1 Jul 1966 (A)
Upper Heyford	3 Jan 1928	Brize Norton	1 Jul 1966 (G)
Boscombe Down	1 Apr 1931		23 May 1967 (A)

Aircraft

Equipment	Period of service	Representative Serial	
B.E.2c, B.E.2d, B.E.2e, B.E.2f			
B.E.2g	Jan 1915 – Sep 1917	7194	
Farman			
Bleriot	Jan 1915 – Jul 1915	–	
Martinsyde S.1			
Bristol Scout	1915 – May 1916	4667	
B.E.12	Aug 1915 – Apr 1917		
B.E.2e	Apr 1917 – Sep 1917	A2956	
F.K.8	Sep 1917 – Jan 1919	B271	
Hyderabad	Jan 1928 – Mar 1931	J8810	(E)
Hinaidi	Dec 1930 – Sep 1932	K1919	(H)
Virginia X	Sep 1932 – Nov 1934	K2332	
Heyford IA, III	Aug 1934 – Jun 1937	K4027	(A)
Whitley I	Mar 1937 – May 1939	K7192	(C)
Whitley IV	May 1939 – May 1940	K9034	(ZA-S)
Whitley V	Mar 1940 – Dec 1941	T4143	(ZA-J)
Halifax II	Dec 1941 – Mar 1944	HX190	(ZA-E)
Halifax III	Mar 1944 – Aug 1945	RG426	(ZA-X)
Dakota III, IV	Aug 1945 – Dec 1947	KN678	
Dakota C.4	Nov 1948 – Feb 1950	KN514	
Canberra B.2	Jan 1953 – Jan 1957	WH667	
Victor B.1	Apr 1958 – Mar 1964	XA929	
VC.10 C.1	Jul 1966 – date	XR808	

Canberrra B.2, No. 10 Squadron

Badge: Two eagles volant in pale
Motto: Ociores acrierosque
aquilis (Swifter and
keener than eagles)

The formation of No.11 Squadron was sanctioned on 28 November 1914, and a nucleus supplied by No.7 Squadron became independent at Netheravon on 14 February 1915, where it received Vickers F.B.5 Gunbuses before moving to France on 25 July 1915. Operating as a fighter unit, it flew patrols over the Western Front and in June 1916, re-equipped with F.E.2b two-seat fighters. These were used for reconnaissance missions behind the German lines for a year before the squadron received Bristol Fighters and once more became primarily a fighter unit for the rest of the war. After spending a short time in Germany, the squadron returned to the UK in September 1919 and disbanded on 31 December 1919.

On 13 January 1923, No.11 reformed at Andover from personnel of the Air Pilotage School and pending the arrival of its service aircraft it looked after those used for Group communications duties at Andover. In September 1923, it moved to Bircham Newton and received D.H.9As on a single-flight basis, a second flight forming on 1 June 1924, on the move of the squadron to Netheravon with Fawns. In November 1926, the latter began to be replaced by Horsleys which were passed to No.100 Squadron in November 1928, when No.11 was ordered to India. In preparation for this, two Wapitis were received for training before the squadron embarked on 29 December 1928. On 22 January 1929, it arrived at Risalpur and built up its strength until it was fully equipped by the end of March 1929. Patrol and army co-operation duties were relieved by occasional punitive raids on marauding tribesmen in the North-West Frontier district and in February 1932, Harts began to

replace the Wapitis, re-equipment being completed in August. In January 1935, the squadron provided twelve aircraft for a trial reinforcement flight to Singapore and back, repeating this in January 1937. In April 1938, a similar flight was made to Egypt and in July 1939, Blenheims began to arrive. These were taken to Singapore in August 1939, but in May 1940, the squadron moved to Egypt while the ground echelon arrived in Aden in June whence the squadron aircraft were recalled to take part in bombing raids on Italian bases and airfields in Eritrea and Ethiopia. In June 1940, it moved to Egypt and in January 1941, was sent to Greece where it carried out raids and reconnaissance missions over Albania until the German invasion. The squadron arrived back in Egypt at the end of April and in May moved to Palestine where it took part in the occupation of Syria and in August moved to Iraq to support the occupation of Iran before returning to bombing operations in the Western Desert.

In March 1942, No.11 moved to Ceylon just in time to take part in attacks on the Japanese carrier force which attacked the island in April. No further action by the Japanese took place but the squadron remained on guard until January 1943, when it began moving to the Burma front where it carried out raids on Japanese bases and communications until withdrawn for re-equipment with Hurricanes in August 1943. In December 1943, these returned to operations in support of the 14th Army. In March 1944, it moved to the Imphal battle area for close support missions, many of which took place close to the squadron base. No.11 remained with the 14th Army throughout its offensive that cleared Burma by June 1945, and it then moved to southern India to re-equip with Spitfires in preparation for the invasion of Malaya. The Japanese surrender forestalled this operation and on 9 September 1945, the squadron was flown off HMS *Trumpeter* to Kelanang. It remained in Malaya as a fighter-reconnaissance unit until May 1946, when it moved to Japan as part of the Commonwealth occupation forces. On 23 February 1948, it disbanded at Miho.

On 4 October 1948, No.107 Squadron at Wahn was renumbered 11 Squadron which then became a Mosquito fighter-bomber unit in Germany. In August 1950 conversion

to Vampires took place and these were in turn replaced by Venoms in August 1952, No.11 being the first to receive this type. On 15 November, 1957, the squadron disbanded.

On 21 January, 1959, No.256 Squadron at Geilenkirchen was renumbered 11 Squadron. Its Meteor night-fighters began to be replaced by Javelins in November 1959 and in December 1962, it re-equipped with Javelin FAW.9s from No.25 Squadron on the latter's disbandment, many of No.25's crews also joining No.11. On 12 January, 1966, the squadron was again disbanded.

On 1 April, 1967, No.11 reformed at Leuchars as a Lightning squadron for the defence of the UK.

Squadron bases

Netheravon	28 Nov 1914	Sheikh Othman	
St. Omer	25 Jul 1915		10 Jun 1940 (G)
Villers-Brettoneux	29 Jul 1915		16 Jun 1940 (A)
Bertangles	Nov 1915	Helwan	1 Dec 1940 (A)
Izel-le-Hameau	31 Aug 1916		9 Dec 1940 (G)
La Bellevue	1 Jun 1917	Eleusis	24 Jan 1941
Fienvillers	27 Mar 1918	Larissa	28 Jan 1941
Remaisnil	16 Apr 1918	Paramythia	23 Feb 1941
Le Quesnoy	Jul 1918	Larissa	26 Feb 1941
Vert Galand	19 Sep 1918	Almyros	16 Mar 1941
Mory	15 Oct 1918	Menidi	16 Apr 1941
Bettoncourt	1 Nov 1918	Heraklion	22 Apr 1941 (A)
Aulnoy	18 Nov 1918	Heliopolis	23 Apr 1941 (A)
Nivelles	19 Dec 1918	Suda Bay	26 Apr 1941 (G)
Spich	20 May 1919	Ramleh	2 May 1941
Scopwick	3 Sep 1919	Aqir	24 May 1941
	to 31 Dec 1919	Habbaniya	7 Aug 1941 (A)
Andover	13 Jan 1923		9 Aug 1941 (A)
Bircham Newton	16 Sep 1923	LG.09	27 Sep 1941
Netheravon	31 May 1924	LG.104	9 Oct 1941
	to 29 Dec 1928	'LG.116	25 Oct 1941
Risalpur	22 Jan 1929	Bu Amud	30 Dec 1941
Tengah	5 Aug 1939	LG.116	27 Jan 1942
Kallang	9 Sep 1939	Helwan	20 Feb 1942
Lahore	20 Apr 1940 (A)	Ratmalana	28 Feb 1941 (A)
Ismailia	9 May 1940 (A)	Embarked for Ceylon	
			3 Mar 1942 (G)

Blenheim I, No.11 Squadron

Colombo Racecourse		Madura	8 Aug 1945 (A)
	18 Mar 1942 (G)		17 Aug 1945 (G)
	2 Apr 1942 (A)	'Trumpeter'	1 Sep 1945 (A)
Baigachi	7 Jan 1943 (A)	Kelanang	9 Sep 1945 (A)
	17 Jan 1943 (G)		18 Sep 1945 (G)
Feni	14 Feb 1943	Kuala Lumpur	21 Sep 1945
Ranchi	11 Aug 1943	Tengah	23 Sep 1945
Cholavarum	15 Oct 1943	Seletar	25 Sep 1945 (A)
Lalmai	2 Dec 1943		4 Oct 1945 (G)
Ramu	25 Jan 1944	Kuala Lumpur	7 Jan 1946
Sapam	2 Mar 1944	Iwakuni	1 May 1946
Tulihal	5 Mar 1944	Miho	7 May 1946
Lanka	12 Apr 1944		to 23 Feb 1948
Dimapur	30 Jun 1944	Wahn	4 Oct 1948
Imphal	3 Oct 1944	Celle	17 Sep 1949
Tamu	5 Nov 1944	Wunstorf	14 Aug 1950
Kan	26 Jan 1945	Fassberg	27 Sep 1955
Sinthe	9 Feb 1945	Wunstorf	11 Oct 1955
Magwe	30 Apr 1945		to 15 Nov 1957
Feni	19 May 1945	Geilenkirchen	21 Jan 1959
Chettinad	22 May 1945		to 12 Jan 1966
Tanjore	31 May 1945	Leuchars	1 Apr 1967
Chettinad	7 Jun 1945	Binbrook	22 Mar 1972

Fawn II, No.11 Squadron

Aircraft Equipment	Period of service	Representative Serial and Code	Aircraft Equipment	Period of service	Representative Serial and Code
Vickers F.B.5	Jun 1915 – Jun 1916	2878	Blenheim IV	Jan 1941 – Sep 1943	T2177 (V)
Bristol Scout	May 1915 – Jul 1916		Hurricane IIC	Sep 1943 – Jun 1945	LF197 (S)
Nieuport 13	Mar 1915 – Jul 1916	A134	Spitfire XIV, XVIII	Jun 1945 – Feb 1948	NH875 (G)
F.E.2b	Jun 1916 – Jun 1917		Mosquito FB.6	Oct 1948 – Aug 1950	TA581
Bristol F.2b	Jun 1917 – Sep 1919	A7131 (S)	Vampire FB.5	Aug 1950 – Aug 1952	WA190 (EX-M)
D.H.9A	Sep 1923 – Apr 1924		Venom FB.1	Aug 1952 – Aug 1955	WE309 (L-P)
Fawn III	Apr 1924 – Dec 1926	J7205	Venom FB.4	Aug 1955 – Nov 1957	WR499
Horsley	Nov 1926 – Nov 1928	J7996	Meteor NF.11	Jan 1959 – Mar 1960	WD771 (E)
Wapiti I	Oct 1928 – Nov 1928	J9748	Javelin FAW.4	Oct 1959 – Mar 1962	XA724 (F)
Wapiti IIA	Feb 1929 – Aug 1932	K1304	Javelin FAW.5	Jan 1962 – Dec 1962	XA650
Hart	Feb 1932 – Jul 1939	K2121	Javelin FAW.9	Dec 1962 – Jan 1966	XH881 (M)
Blenheim I	Jul 1939 – Jan 1941	L4919	Lightning F.3, F.6	Apr 1967 – date	XS928 (D)

Fox I, No.12 Squadron

No. 12 Squadron

Badge: A fox's mask
Motto: Leads the Field

No.12 Squadron was formed at Netheravon on 14 February 1915 and moved to France in September 1915 equipped with a variety of types of aircraft. Reconnaissance and bombing duties formed the bulk of the squadron's work during the first few months on the Western Front but early in 1916 it standardised on B.E.s and became a corps reconnaissance unit. For the rest of the war No.12 was engaged in artillery spotting and reconnaissance duties, re-equipping with R.E.8s in August 1917. After the Armistice, the squadron moved to Germany and remained with the army of occupation until disbanded on 27 July 1922.

On 1 April 1923 No.12 reformed at Northolt as a day bomber squadron. Its D.H.9As were soon replaced by Fawns and in June 1926 the squadron began to receive Foxes, being the only unit to fly this type. In January 1931, No.12 converted to Harts which were taken to Aden in October 1935 during the Abyssinian crisis. Returning to the UK in August 1936, the squadron re-equipped with Hinds which were replaced by Battles in February 1938. As part of the AASF, No.12 moved to France on the outbreak of World

War Two and during the German offensive in May 1940 lost most of its aircraft, being evacuated to the UK to re-arm. After taking part in night attacks on enemy invasion craft in the French Channel ports, the squadron converted to Wellingtons for night bombing. Lancasters were received in November 1942 and for most of the war No.12 formed part of the main force of Bomber Command. Retained in the post-war bomber force, it converted to Lincolns in August 1946 which were flown until the arrival of Canberras in April 1952. During the Suez campaign, the squadron operated from Malta and was disbanded on 13 July 1961.

On 1 July 1962, No.12 reformed with Vulcans at Coningsby as part of the V-bomber force. In November 1964, it moved to Cottesmore where the squadron was disbanded on 31 December 1967. Reformed on 1 October 1969 at Honington, No.12 is equipped with Buccaneer strike aircraft and has a mainly maritime role.

Squadron bases

Netheravon	14 Feb 1915	Bickendorf	17 Nov 1920
St. Omer	6 Sep 1915		to 27 Jul 1922
Vert Galand	28 Feb 1916	Northolt	1 Apr 1923
Avesnes-le-Comte	3 Mar 1916	Andover	23 Mar 1924
Wagonlieu	9 May 1917	Left for Aden	4 Oct 1935
Ablainzeville	7 Jul 1917	Khormaksar	20 Oct 1935
Courcelles-le-Comte	Aug 1917	Robat	25 Nov 1935
Boiry St. Martin	16 Dec 1917	Khormaksar	23 Mar 1936
Soncamp	22 Mar 1918	Robat	18 May 1936
Mory	17 Sep 1918	Left for UK	11 Aug 1936
Estourmel	14 Oct 1918	Andover	29 Aug 1936
Gerpinnes	29 Nov 1918	Bicester	9 May 1939
Clavier	6 Dec 1918	Berry-au-Bac	2 Sep 1939
Duren	19 Dec 1918	Amifontaine	8 Dec 1939
Heumar	5 May 1919	Echemines	16 May 1940

Souge	8 Jun 1940	Binbrook	14 Mar 1948
Finningley	16 Jun 1940	Butterworth	31 Oct 1955
Binbrook	3 Jul 1940	Binbrook	24 Mar 1956
Thorney Island	7 Aug 1940	Hal Far	25 Sep 1956
Eastchurch	12 Aug 1940	Binbrook	1 Dec 1956
Binbrook	7 Sep 1940	Coningsby	2 Jul 1959
Wickenby	25 Sep 1942		to 13 Jul 1961
Binbrook	24 Sep 1945	Coningsby	1 Jul 1962
Waddington	26 Jul 1946	Cottesmore	17 Nov 1964
Binbrook	18 Sep 1946		to 31 Dec 1967
Hemswell	12 Jan 1948	Honington	1 Oct 1969

B.E.2C, No.12 Squadron

Aircraft Equipment	Period of service	Representative Serial and Code	
Avro 504	May 1915 – Sep 1915	794	
B.E.2c	Jun 1915 – Feb 1917	2506	
B.E.2d	Jul 1916 – Jan 1917	6229	
B.E.2e	Dec 1916 – Aug 1917	A2807	
Bristol Scout	Sep 1915 – May 1916	5298	
Voisin	Sep 1915 – Nov 1915	5001	
R.E.5	Sep 1915 – Feb 1916	2458	
R.E.7	Sep 1915 – Jan 1916	2287	
F.E.2b	Feb 1916	6340	
R.E.8	Aug 1917 – Jul 1919	C2783	
Bristol F.2b	Mar 1918 – Jul 1922	F4429	(A4)
D.H.9A	Apr 1923 – Apr 1924		
Fawn II, III	Mar 1924 – Dec 1926	J7980	
Fox I	Jun 1926 – Jan 1931	J7944	
Fox IA	Jan 1929 – Jan 1931	J9028	
Hart	Jan 1931 – Oct 1936	K2425	
Hind	Oct 1936 – Feb 1938	K5549	
Battle	Feb 1938 – Nov 1940	L5227	(PH-J)
Wellington II	Oct 1940 – Nov 1942	Z8328	(PH-R)
Wellington III	Aug 1942 – Nov 1942	BJ653	(PH-H)
Lancaster I, III	Nov 1942 – Aug 1946	PB243	(PH-D)
Lincoln B.2	Aug 1946 – Mar 1952	RF390	(PH-K)
Canberra B.2	Apr 1952 – Mar 1959	WD990	
Canberra B.6	May 1955 – Jul 1961	WH968	
Vulcan B.2	Jul 1962 – Dec 1967	XM602	
Buccaneer S.2, S.2b	Oct 1969 – date	XV155	

No. 13 Squadron

Badge: In front of a dagger, a lynx's head affrontée
Motto: Adjuvamus tuendo (We assist by watching)

No.13 Squadron was formed at Gosport on 10 January 1915 and moved to France in October as a corps reconnaissance unit equipped with B.E.2cs. Artillery observation and photographic reconnaissance remained the squadron's main tasks throughout World War One, the B.E.s being replaced by R.E.8s in April 1917. In March 1919, it returned to the UK and disbanded on 31 December 1919.

On 1 April 1924, No.13 reformed at Kenley as an army co-operation squadron equipped with Bristol Fighters. The squadron played a large part in the development of co-operation between land and air forces, flying Atlases and Audaxes. In May 1937, it received Hectors which were replaced by Lysanders in January 1939. After the outbreak of World War Two, No.13 went to France with the BEF where it attempted to carry out tactical reconnaissance missions in the face of strong enemy fighter forces during the German invasion in May 1940. By the end of the month, the remnants of the squadron were back in the UK.

Patrols began along the coasts of Lancashire and North Wales on 17 June and training with the army occupied the squadron until it re-equipped with Blenheims in the summer of 1941. Co-operation with ground forces still formed a large part of the training programme, low-level bombing, gas spraying and laying smokescreens being practiced. It took part in the first 'Thousand Bomber Raid' in May 1942 and laid a smokescreen for landing craft during the Dieppe raid in August. Equipped with Blenheim Vs, No.13 moved to Algeria soon after the Allied landing in November 1942. Day and night raids on enemy bases in Tunisia began three days

Audax Is, No.13 Squadron

after arrival but after heavy losses were sustained by No.18 Squadron, Blenheims were restricted to night attacks only. After the capture of the last Axis footholds in Africa, the squadron carried out anti-submarine patrols and convoy escort missions, converting to Venturas in November. In December, the squadron left for Egypt to become a Baltimore unit. In February 1944, it arrived in Italy to join No.3 (SAAF) Wing, aircraft arriving during March and becoming operational on 1 April. Formation attacks on enemy communications were undertaken for the first month, after which the squadron was switched to night interdiction missions. In October 1944, Bostons replaced Baltimores for the rest of the war. In September 1945, No.13 moved to Greece where it disbanded on 19 April 1946.

On 1 September 1946, No.680 Squadron at Ein Shemer was renumbered 13 Squadron. Its photographic reconnaissance Mosquitos moved from Palestine to Egypt in December and were replaced by Meteors in January 1952. In January 1956, the squadron moved to Cyprus where it converted to Canberras in 1956. These it took to Malta in November 1956, where it became the resident photo-reconnaissance unit, until it returned to the UK in October 1978.

Squadron bases

Gosport	10 Jan 1915	Kenley	1 Apr 1924
St. Omer	19 Oct 1915	Andover	30 Jun 1924
Vert Galand	21 Oct 1915	Netheravon	23 Sep 1929
Izel-le-Hameau	12 Mar 1916	Old Sarum	3 May 1935
Savy	18 Mar 1916	Odiham	16 Feb 1937
Etrun	9 May 1917	Mons-en-Chaussée	2 Oct 1939
Izel-le-Hameau	22 Mar 1918	Douai	11 May 1940
Mory	22 Sep 1918	Abbeville	22 May 1940
Carnières	19 Oct 1918	Emb. for UK	29 May 1940 (G)
Vert Galand	1 Dec 1918	Hooton Park	1 Jun 1940
St. Omer	19 Jan 1919	Speke	17 Jun 1940
Sedgeford	27 Mar 1919	Hooton Park	13 Jul 1940
	to 31 Dec 1919	Odiham	14 Jul 1941
		Macmerry	1 Aug 1942

Emb. for N. Africa		Iesi	27 Oct 1944 (G)
	10 Nov 1942 (G)	Marcianise	31 Oct 1944 (A)
Gibraltar	17 Nov 1942 (A)	Falconara	28 Dec 1944
Blida	18 Nov 1942 (A)	Forli	7 Mar 1945
	25 Nov 1942 (G)	Aviano	12 May 1945
Canrobert	5 Dec 1942	Hassani	14 Sep 1945
Oulmene	8 Feb 1943		to 19 Apr 1946
Blida	22 May 1943	Ein Shemer	1 Sep 1946
Protville II	4 Sep 1943	Kabrit	14 Dec 1946
Sidi Ahmed	12 Oct 1943	Fayid	5 Feb 1951
Sidi Amor	26 Oct 1943	Abu Sueir	1 Jan 1955
Kabrit	19 Dec 1943	Akrotiri	1 Feb 1956
Biferno	23 Feb 1944 (G)	Luqa	1 Sep 1965
	21 Mar 1944 (A)	Akrotiri	6 Jan 1972
Regina	2 May 1944		12 Jan 1972 (C)
Tarquinia	22 Jun 1944	Luqa	10 Oct 1972
Cecina	18 Jul 1944		17 Oct 1972 (C)
Perugia	16 Oct 1944	Wyton	3 Oct 1978

Aircraft

Equipment	Period of service	Representative Serial and Code	
B.E.2c, B.E.2d, B.E.2e	Jan 1915 — Apr 1917	2017	
R.E.8	Apr 1917 — Mar 1919	B5070	
Bristol F.2b	Apr 1924 — Jan 1928	J7660	
Atlas	Aug 1927 — Jul 1932	J9046	
Audax	Jul 1932 — May 1937	K2015	
Hector	May 1937 — Feb 1939	K9759	
Lysander I, II	Jan 1939 — May 1941	L4762	
Lysander III, IIIA	May 1941 — Sep 1941	T1429	(OO-C)
Blenheim IV	Jul 1941 — Sep 1942	N3545	
Blenheim V	Sep 1942 — Dec 1943	BB176	(D)
Ventura V	Oct 1943 — Dec 1943	FP553	(D)
Baltimore IV, V	Jan 1944 — Oct 1944	FW567	(S)
Boston IV, V	Oct 1944 — Apr 1946	BZ656	(S)
Mosquito PR.34	Sep 1946 — Feb 1952	RG298	(F)
Meteor PR.10	Jan 1952 — Aug 1956	WH569	
Canberra PR.7	May 1956 — Aug 1961	WE137	
Canberra PR.9	Aug 1961 — date	XH130	

Hector Is, No.13 Squadron

No. 14 Squadron

Badge: A winged plate charged
with a cross throughout
and shoulder pieces of a
suit of armour.

Motto: I spread my wings and
keep my promise (Arabic
script)

No.14 Squadron was formed at Shoreham on 3 February 1915 and after a period of training left for the Middle East in November. From its bases in Egypt, it provided detachments of B.E.s for co-operation with the army in Egypt, Palestine, the Western Desert and Arabia for the rest of the war. During the advance into Palestine, the squadron was engaged in bombing and corps reconnaissance duties, having acquired a number of single-seat fighters in May 1917 for protective purposes. When No.111 Squadron was formed in August 1917 it took over the fighter tasks and No.14 concentrated on army co-operation duties for the rest of the campaign. In October 1918 the squadron left for Greece and, later, for the UK where it disbanded on 4 February 1919.

On 1 February 1920, No.111 Squadron was renumbered 14 Squadron at Ramleh and was engaged in patrol duties in Palestine and Transjordan for the next twenty years. For most of the time, the squadron was divided between Ramleh and Amman, flying Bristol Fighters, D.H.9As, Fairey IIIFs, Gordons and Wellesleys, the last-named arriving in March 1938. On the outbreak of World War Two, No.14 moved to Egypt but returned after a few months to Amman. The imminent entry of Italy into the war sent the squadron south to the Sudan where bombing raids began on Italian bases in Eritrea on 11 June. In September 1940, a flight of Gladiators

was attached and conversion to Blenheims began. In April 1941, these were taken to Egypt for bombing operations over the Western Desert for three months, followed by a period in Palestine and Iraq. The squadron returned to the desert in November 1941 for day and night raids and in August 1942 began converting to Marauders, Blenheims flying their last operations on 2 August. Bombing, minelaying and shipping reconnaissance missions began on 28 October and in March 1943 No.14 moved to Algeria for anti-submarine patrols. Detachments operated from Italy and Sardinia, a move being made to the island in June. During September 1944, parties began leaving for the UK, No.14's last Marauder mission being flown on 21 September.

The squadron began to re-assemble at Chivenor on 24 October 1944 and during November began to receive Wellingtons for anti-submarine patrols. The first of these was flown on 2 February 1945 and they continued until the end of the war, No.14 being disbanded on 1 June 1945. On the same day, No.143 Squadron at Banff was renumbered 14 Squadron and flew Mosquitos until disbanded on 31 March 1946.

On 1 April 1946, No.128 Squadron at Wahn was renumbered 14 Squadron. Mosquitos were flown with the occupation forces in Germany until replaced by Vampires in February 1951. The squadron converted to Venoms in May 1953 and became a day fighter unit in 1955 when Hunters were received. On 17 December, 1962, No.14 was disbanded.

Simultaneously No.88 Squadron at Wildenrath was renumbered 14 Squadron and flew Canberras until disbanded on 30 June 1970. A new No.14 Squadron at Bruggen took over on the same day and operated Phantom fighter-reconnaissance and ground-attack aircraft in Germany. Conversion to Jaguars began when the squadron reformed at Bruggen on 9 April 1975, re-equipment being completed in November.

Wellesley Is, No.14 Squadron

Jaguar GR.1, No. 14 Squadron

Squadron bases				Aircraft Equipment	Period of service	Representative Serial and Code
Shoreham	3 Feb 1915	(Note: There were numerous detachments during the above period in the Middle East)		Maurice Farman	Feb 1915 — May 1915	
Hounslow	May 1915			Martinsyde S.1	Mar 1915 — May 1915	
Gosport	Aug 1915	LG.116	8 Feb 1942	B.E.2c	May 1915 — Nov 1917	4395
Left for Egypt	7 Nov 1915	El Firdan	2 May 1942	B.E.2d, B.E.2e	Nov 1915 — Nov 1917	
Ismailia	23 Nov 1915	LG.116	2 Jun 1942	B.E.12a	Apr 1916	A566
Heliopolis	9 Dec 1915	Qassassin	Jun 1942	D.H.2	May 1917 — Aug 1917	
Ismailia	29 Jan 1916	LG.224	10 Aug 1942	Vickers F.B.19	May 1917 — Aug 1917	
Kilo 143	20 Jan 1917	Berka III	17 Feb 1943	Bristol Scout	May 1917 — Aug 1917	4688
Rafa	25 Mar 1917	Telergma	2 Mar 1943	Bristol M.1c	May 1917 — Aug 1917	
Deir el Belah	27 Apr 1917	Blida	12 Mar 1943	R.E.8	Nov 1917 — Nov 1918	B6604
Julis	20 Nov 1917	Protville	7 Jun 1943	Nieuport 17	Nov 1917 — Dec 1917	
Junction Station	30 Nov 1917	Grottaglie (D)	1 Oct 1943 to 26 Jul 1944	Bristol F.2b	Feb 1920 — Jan 1926	
Qantara	24 Oct 1918			D.H.9A	Aug 1924 — Dec 1929	J7254
Salonika	2 Nov 1918	Blida	20 Nov 1943	Fairey IIIF	Dec 1929 — Sep 1932	J9793 (R)
Tangmere	1 Jan 1919 to 4 Feb 1919	Alghero	1 Dec 1943 (D) 29 Jun 1944 (C) to Sep 1944	Gordon	Sep 1932 — Jun 1938	KR2637(N)
Ramleh & Amman	1 Feb 1920			Wellesley	Mar 1938 — Dec 1940	L2676 (D)
Ismailia	24 Aug 1939	Chivenor	24 Oct 1944 to 1 Jun 1945	Gladiator I	Sep 1940	
Amman	19 Dec 1939			Blenheim IV	Sep 1940 — Sep 1942	Z6436 (F)
Port Sudan	19 May 1940	Banff	1 Jun 1945 to 31 Mar 1946	Marauder I	Aug 1942 — Sep 1944	FK151 (O)
Heliopolis	12 Apr 1941			Wellington XIV	Nov 1944 — Jun 1945	NB909 (CX-K)
LG.21	1 May 1941	Wahn	1 Apr 1946	Mosquito VI	Jun 1945 — Mar 1946	TA593
Petah Tiqva	7 Jul 1941	Celle	19 Sep 1949	Mosquito FB.16	Apr 1946 — Jul 1948	PF612 (CX-G)
Habbaniya	10 Aug 1941	Fassberg	Nov 1950	Mosquito B.35	Dec 1947 — Feb 1951	RS704 (B)
Qaiyara	24 Aug 1941	Oldenburg	May 1955	Vampire FB.5	Feb 1951 — May 1953	VZ344 (T)
Habbaniya	8 Oct 1941	Ahlhorn	Sep 1957	Venom FB.1	May 1953 — Jun 1955	WE363 (B-A)
Lydda	26 Oct 1941	Gutersloh	15 Sep 1958 to 17 Dec 1962	Hunter F.4	May 1955 — Dec 1962	XG274 (P)
LG.15	4 Nov 1941			Canberra B(I).8	Dec 1962 — Jun 1970	XM273
LG.75	18 Nov 1941	Wildenrath	17 Dec 1962 to 30 Jun 1970	Phantom FGR.2	Jun 1970 — Nov 1975	XV463 (463)
Gambut	18 Dec 1941			Jaguar GR.1	Apr 1975 — date	XX756
Bu Amud	27 Jan 1942	Bruggen	30 Jun 1970			

Washington B.1, No.15 Squadron

No. 15 Squadron

Badge: A hind's head affrontée
erased at the neck between
wings elevated and
conjoined in base
Motto: Aim sure

No.15 Squadron was formed at Farnborough on 1 March 1915, from a nucleus supplied by No.1 Reserve squadron and after training moved to France in December with B.E.2cs as a reconnaissance unit. Artillery spotting and photography occupied the squadron for the rest of the war, the obsolete B.E.s being replaced by R.E.8s in June 1917. During the German offensive of March 1918, No.15 was pressed into ground-attack missions against the advancing enemy troops but resumed its corps reconnaissance role after the crisis had passed. In February 1919, the squadron returned to the UK and disbanded on 31 December 1919.

On 24 March 1924 No.15 reformed at Martlesham Heath as an armament testing squadron of the Aeroplane and Armament Experimental Establishment. This phase ended when it handed over its aircraft to the A&AEE and reformed at Abingdon on 1 June 1934 as a day bomber squadron equipped with Harts. These carried the squadrons 'XV' marking which became the traditional usage for the squadron's number. In June 1938, it converted to Battles which it took

to France in September 1939, with the Advanced Air Striking Force. In December 1939, it returned to the UK to re-equip with Blenheims and when the German attack began on 10 May 1940 No.15 began bombing raids on enemy columns in the Low Countries. Night raids on enemy airfields and barges in the Channel ports began in August and in November the squadron converted to Wellingtons.

In April 1941 No.15 became the second squadron to receive Stirlings and began bombing raids with these at the end of the month. Between June and August, daylight attacks were undertaken on targets in northern France, these missions being flown under strong fighter escort in an effort to lure enemy fighters into the air. The Stirling's size made it a large target for enemy flak and they were eventually withdrawn from daylight raids and replaced by light bombers. During 1942, minelaying became the squadron's main task and continued until Stirlings were replaced by Lancasters at the end on 1943. For the rest of the war, No.15 carried out raids on Germany as part of the strategic air offensive.

Retained as a unit of the post-war air force, No.15 re-equipped with Lincolns in February 1947, replacing these with Washingtons in January 1951. Canberras were received in May 1953, and were detached to Cyprus during the Suez landings in October 1956. On 15 April 1957, the squadron was disbanded.

Reformed as the second Victor squadron on 1 September 1958, No.15 was based at Cottesmore until disbanded on 31 October 1964. On 1 October 1970, it reformed at Honington with Buccaneers, moving to Laarbruch in January 1971 to take up its operational base.

Squadron bases			
Farnborough	1 Mar 1915	Fowlmere	15 Feb 1919
Hounslow	13 Apr 1915		to 31 Dec 1919
Dover	11 May 1915	Martlesham Heath	20 Mar 1924
St.Omer	28 Dec 1915	Abingdon	1 Jun 1934
Droglandt	5 Jan 1916	Betheniville	2 Sep 1939
Vert Galand	8 Mar 1916	Conde-Vraux	12 Sep 1939
Marieux	27 Mar 1916	Wyton	10 Dec 1939
Lealvilliers	2 Oct 1916	Alconbury	14 Apr 1940
Courcelles-le-Comte	6 Jun 1917	Wyton	15 May 1940
La Gorgue	7 Jul 1917	Bourn	13 Aug 1942
Savy	8 Aug 1917	Mildenhall	14 Apr 1943
Longavesnes	21 Aug 1917	Wyton	Aug 1946
Lechelle	8 Oct 1917	Marham	Nov 1950
Lavieville	22 Mar 1918	Coningsby	Feb 1951
Le Houssoye	25 Mar 1918	Cottesmore	22 May 1954
Fienvillers	26 Mar 1918	Honington	15 Feb 1955
Vert Galand	10 Apr 1918		to 15 Apr 1957
Senlis	14 Sep 1918	Cottesmore	1 Sep 1958
Lechelle	2 Oct 1918		to 31 Oct 1964
Selvigny	15 Oct 1918	Honington	2 Oct 1970
Vignacourt	3 Dec 1918	Laarbruch	11 Jan 1971 (A)
			15 Jan 1971 (G)

Aircraft Equipment	Period of service	Representative Serial and Code	
B.E.2c	Mar 1915 – Jul 1917	2120	
Bristol Scout	Mar 1916 – Oct 1916		
B.E.2d	Oct 1916 – Jun 1917		
B.E.2e	Oct 1916 – Jun 1917		
R.E.8	Jun 1917 – Dec 1919	B836	(15)
Various	Mar 1924 – May 1934		
Hart	Jun 1934 – Mar 1936	K3900	
Hind	Mar 1936 – Jun 1938	K5460	
Battle	Jun 1938 – Dec 1939	K9300	
Blenheim IV	Dec 1939 – Nov 1940	R3777	(LS-W)
Wellington IC	Nov 1940 – May 1941	T2806	(LS-N)
Stirling I	Apr 1941 – Jan 1943	N3656	(LS-H)
Stirling III	Jan 1943 – Dec 1943	EF333	(LS-X)
Lancaster I, III	Dec 1943 – Mar 1947	HK619	(LS-Y)
Lincoln B.2	Feb 1947 – Oct 1950	RF514	(LS-B)
Washington B.1	Jan 1951 – Mar 1953	WF498	(LS-B)
Canberra B.2	May 1953 – Apr 1957	WJ974	
Victor B.1	Sep 1958 – Oct 1964	XH588	
Buccaneer S.2B	Oct 1970 – date	XW526	

Canberra B(I).8, No.16 Squadron

No. 16 Squadron

Badge: Two keys in saltire, the wards upwards and outwards

Motto: Operta aperta (Hidden things are revealed)

No.16 Squadron was formed on 10 February 1915, at St. Omer from detached flights of Nos.2, 5 and 6 Squadrons. A variety of types of aircraft was flown on reconnaissance duties for the first year before B.E.s became standard equipment. Tactical reconnaissance, artillery observation and photography were the squadron's main tasks throughout World War One, R.E.8s being received in May 1917. In February 1919 No.16 was reduced to a cadre and returned to the UK, disbanding on 31 December 1919.

On 1 April 1924, No.16 reformed at Old Sarum as an army co-operation squadron equipped with Bristol Fighters, primarily to co-operate with artillery. In January 1931, it re-equipped with Atlases which were replaced by Audaxes in December 1933. For the first ten years, the squadron was attached to the School of Army Co-operation based at Old Sarum and was carried on the latter's establishment but on 1 June 1934, it became an independent unit. In June 1938, it became the first Lysander squadron, a type which was to prove to be the last of a long line of multi-purpose army co-operation aircraft. Trials were carried out with Ansons, Oxfords and Battles as potential replacements but all were, fortunately, rejected. No.16 remained in the UK until April 1940 when it moved to France for training. The German attack during May resulted in a few days operational flying before the aircraft were withdrawn to Lympne where they flew occasional reconnaissance and supply-dropping missions. Coastal patrols began at the end of June, first off East Anglia and, from August, along the coasts of Devon and Cornwall. These patrols continued until March 1941, being additional to normal army training exercises. In April 1942, a replacement for the outmoded Lysanders arrived in the shape of Mustang tactical reconnaissance fighters, but Lysanders continued to serve the squadron till May 1943. Shipping reconnaissance missions began on 10 October 1942 and in June 1943 the low-level Mustangs were given the task of intercepting German fighter-bombers attacking coastal towns. In September 1943, conversion to Spitfires began and these were used for photographic reconnaissance missions at both high and low levels in preparation for the invasion of Europe. In September 1944, No.16 joined Second TAF in Belgium for the rest of the war, and from June 1945 operated a fast mail service for the occupation forces for three months. On 17 September 1945 No.16 was divided into three flights which were transferred to Nos.2, 26 and 268 Squadrons. A few days later, ground personnel returned to the UK and the squadron disbanded on 20 October 1945.

Despite the existence of No.16's ground echelon at Dunsfold, two more No.16 Squadrons sprang into being. No.487 Squadron was informed that with effect from 19 September 1945, it was No.16 Squadron; so, unfortunately, was No.268 Squadron. The confusion was eventually resolved by No.487 Squadron being retrospectively numbered 268 Squadron while No.268 Squadron had its date of renumbering to 16 Squadron amended to 20 October 1945. Based at Celle, it flew fighter-reconnaissance Spitfires until disbanded on 31 March 1946.

On 1 April 1946, No.56 Squadron was renumbered 16 Squadron at Fassberg and flew Tempests until converting to Vampires in December 1948. In January 1954 it re-equipped with Venoms and disbanded in June 1957. On 1 March 1958, the squadron reformed at Laarbruch as an interdictor unit with Canberras which were flown until 6 June 1972 when No.16 was reformed at Laarbruch with Buccaneers.

Squadron bases			
St. Omer	10 Feb 1915	Lympne	23 Nov 1941
Chocques	1 Jun 1915	Weston Zoyland	27 Nov 1941
Merville	18 Jul 1915	Andover	2 Jan 1943
La Gorgue	12 Dec 1915	Middle Wallop	1 Jun 1943
Bruay	1 Sep 1916	Hartfordbridge	29 Jun 1943
Complain l'Abbé	25 May 1917	Northolt	7 Apr 1944
La Brayelle	21 Oct 1918	A.12 Balleroy	4 Sep 1944
Auchy	25 Oct 1918	B.48. Amiens/Glisy	9 Sep 1944
Fowlmere	12 Feb 1919	B.48 Melsbroek	27 Sep 1944
	to 31 Dec 1919	B.78 Eindhoven	15 Apr 1945
Old Sarum	1 Apr 1924	Dunsfold	22 Sep 1945
Hawkinge	16 Feb 1940		to 20 Oct 1945
Bertangles	14 Apr 1940	Celle	20 Oct 1945
Lympne	19 May 1940		to 31 Mar 1946
Redhill	2 Jun 1940	Fassberg	1 Apr 1946
Cambridge	29 Jun 1940	Gutersloh	1 Dec 1947
Okehampton	3 Aug 1940	Celle	2 Nov 1950
Weston Zoyland	14 Aug 1940		to Jun 1957
Thruxton	25 Sep 1941	Laarbruch	1 Mar 1958
Weston Zoyland	3 Oct 1941		to 6 Jun 1972
		Laarbruch	6 Jun 1972

Aircraft Equipment	Period of service	Representative Serial and Code
Maurice Farman, Voisin, Bleriot XI, R.E.5, Vickers F.B.5, Martinsyde S.1, Bristol Scout	Feb 1915 – May 1915	–
B.E.2a, B.E.2b, B.E.2c, B.E.2d, B.E.2e	Feb 1915 – May 1917	A2815
R.E.8	May 1917 – Feb 1919	B5010 (17)
Bristol F.2b	Apr 1924 – Jan 1931	F4513
Atlas	Jan 1931 – Dec 1933	K1511
Audax	Dec 1933 – Jun 1938	K3688
Lysander I	Jun 1938 – Apr 1939	L4801 (KJ-Y)
Lysander II	Apr 1939 – Oct 1940	P9077
Lysander III, IIIA	Oct 1940 – May 1943	T1705
Mustang	Apr 1942 – Nov 1943	AL996
Tomahawk I	Feb 1943 – Apr 1943	AH746
Spitfire XI	Sep 1943 – Sep 1944	PA849
Spitfire XIX	Mar 1945 – Sep 1945 Oct 1945 – Mar 1946	PS853 (KY-C)
Spitfire XIV	Oct 1945 – Mar 1946	NH807
Spitfire XVI	Dec 1945 – Mar 1946	
Tempest V	Apr 1946 – Apr 1947	SN135 (EG-R)
Tempest F.2	Apr 1947 – Dec 1948	PR736 (EG-M)
Vampire FB.5	Nov 1948 – Jan 1954	VV557 (EG-H)
Venom FB.1	Jan 1954 – Jun 1957	WK399 (F)
Canberra B(I).8	Mar 1958 – Jun 1972	XM268 (A)
Buccaneer S.2	Jun 1972 – date	XW536

No. 17 Squadron

Badge: A gauntlet
Motto: Excellere contende (Strive to excel)

No.17 Squadron was formed at Gosport on 1 February 1915 and after a period of training embarked for Egypt in November. On 24 December, it began to make reconnaissance flights over the Turkish lines in Sinai, also flying in support of troops engaged with Turkish bands in the Western Desert. Detachments were also to be found in Arabia until July 1916, when the squadron was sent to Salonika as a mixed unit of twelve B.E.2cs for reconnaissance and a scout component of two D.H.2s and three Bristol Scouts. At first it was the only RFC unit in Macedonia but was later joined by others and in April 1918, handed over its fighters to a newly-formed No.150 Squadron. For the rest of the war, it was engaged in tactical reconnaissance and artillery spotting on the Bulgarian border. In December 1918, the squadron re-equipped with twelve D.H.9s and six Camels, sending A Flight to Batum to support the White Russian forces and B and C Flights to Constantinople in January 1919. On 14 November 1919 No.17 disbanded.

Reforming at Hawkinge on 1 April 1924, with Snipes, No.17 formed part of the fighter defence of the UK until the outbreak of World War Two. Successively equipped with Woodcocks, Siskins, Bulldogs and Gauntlets, the squadron remained in the UK during the Abyssinian crisis but lost most of its Bulldogs as reinforcements for squadrons moving to the Middle East and had to fly Harts for a period. In June 1939, Hurricanes were received and flew defensive patrols until the German attack on France in May 1940. Fighter sweeps were then flown over Holland and Belgium and French airfields used to cover the retreat of Allied troops.

In June, the squadron moved to Brittany as the remnants of the BEF and RAF units in France were evacuated, retiring to the Channel Islands two days before returning to the UK. No.17 flew over southern England throughout the Battle of Britain, being moved to northern Scotland in April 1941. In November 1941, the squadron sailed for the Far East where war broke out in December. Diverted to Burma, it arrived in January 1942, as Japanese troops neared Rangoon. Defensive patrols were flown until the Rangoon airfields were overrun and No.17 moved north, eventually being cut off from India while operating from Lashio. The surviving aircraft were flown out and ground personnel made their way across Burma to the Indian border. By the end of May, the squadron had re-assembled at Calcutta and in June received aircraft again for the defence of the area. Ground attack missions began in February 1943 and continued till August when the squadron moved to Ceylon. Spitfires began to arrive in March 1944 and were taken back to the Burma front in November to fly escort and ground-attack missions. In June 1945, it was withdrawn to prepare for the invasion of Malaya and was taken by carrier to the landing beaches near Penang in early September soon after the Japanese capitulation. In April 1946, it arrived in Japan to form part of the Commonwealth occupation force until disbanded on 23 February 1948.

On 11 February 1949 No.691 Squadron based at Chivenor for anti-aircraft co-operation duties was renumbered No.17 Squadron, being disbanded on 13 March 1951. No.17 reformed at Wahn on 1 June 1956 as a Canberra photographic reconnaissance squadron in Germany, disbanding on 12 June 1969. On 16 October 1970 the squadron reformed at Bruggen with Phantoms, which were flown until December 1975, No.17 having begun conversion to Jaguars in July.

Squadron bases			
Gosport	1 Feb 1915	Upavon	14 Oct 1926
Emb. for Egypt	22 Nov 1915	Kenley	10 May 1934
Heliopolis	18 Dec 1915	North Weald	23 May 1939
Mikra Bay	7 Jul 1916	Croydon	2 Sep 1939
Amber-Koj	22 Sep 1918	Debden	9 Sep 1939
San Stephano	28 Jan 1919	frequent detachments to	
	to 14 Nov 1919	Martlesham Heath until	
Hawkinge	1 Apr 1924		Apr 1940

Hawkinge	17 Apr 1940	Alipore	16 Apr 1943	
Debden	21 May 1940	Agartala	29 May 1943	
Kenley	24 May 1940	China Bay	17 Aug 1943	
Hawkinge	6 Jun 1940	Minneriya	13 Jan 1944	
Le Mans	8 Jun 1940	Vavuniya	30 Jun 1944	
Jersey & Guernsey	17 Jun 1940	Sapam	20 Nov 1944	
		Palel	30 Nov 1944	
Debden	19 Jun 1940	Taukkyan	17 Dec 1944	
Tangmere	19 Aug 1940	Tabingaung	19 Jan 1945	
Debden	2 Sep 1940	Ywadon	2 Feb 1945	
Martlesham Heath	8 Oct 1940	Meiktila Main	9 Apr 1945	
Croydon	28 Feb 1941	Thedaw	18 Apr 1945	
Martlesham Heath	31 Mar 1941	Tennant	26 Apr 1945	
Castletown	4 Apr 1941	Thedaw	10 May 1945	
Elgin	29 Jul 1941	Madura	17 Jun 1945	
Tain	16 Sep 1941	HMS Trumpeter	1 Sep 1945	
Catterick	31 Oct 1941	Kelanang	9 Sep 1945	
Left for Middle East but		Seletar	25 Sep 1945	
diverted to Far East		Kuala Lumpur	8 Jan 1946	
	12 Nov 1941	Iwakuni	30 Apr 1946	
Mingaladon	16 Jan 1942		to 23 Feb 1948	
Magwe	Feb 1942	Chivenor	11 Feb 1949	
Lashio	Mar 1942		to 13 Mar 1951	
Pankham Fort	Mar 1942	Wahn	1 Jun 1956	
	to Apr 1942	Wildenrath	3 Apr 1957	
Jessore	May 1942		to 12 Dec 1969	
Alipore	23 Aug 1942	Bruggen	16 Oct 1970	
Red Road	4 Sep 1942			
Kalyanpur	6 Mar 1943			

Aircraft Equipment	Period of service	Representative Serial and Code	
B.E.2c, B.E.2d, B.E.2e	Feb 1915 – Jun 1918	4124	
Bristol Scout	Jul 1916 – Sep 1916		
D.H.2	Jul 1916		
B.E.12, B.E.12A	Nov 1916 – Jun 1918	A4006	
Nieuport 17	Aug 1917 – Apr 1918	A3284	
Spad S.VII	Jul 1917 – Dec 1917	A8806	
S.E.5A	Dec 1917 – Apr 1918	B690	
F.K.8	Mar 1918 – Dec 1918	B3353	
D.H.9	Dec 1918 – Nov 1919		
Camel	Dec 1918 – Nov 1919	E5170	
Snipe	Apr 1924 – Mar 1926	E6544	
Woodcock II	Mar 1926 – Jan 1928	J8311	
Gamecock	Jan 1928 – Sep 1928	J8408	
Siskin IIIA	Sep 1928 – Oct 1929	J8880	
Bulldog II, IIA	Oct 1928 – Aug 1936	K2153	
Hart Special	Oct 1935 – Mar 1936	K4424	
Gauntlet II	Aug 1936 – Jun 1939	K5348	(UV-B)
Hurricane I	Jun 1939 – Feb 1941		
	Apr 1941 – Sep 1941	V7311	(YB-P)
Hurricane IIA	Feb 1941 – Apr 1941	Z2799	(YB-P)
	Jan 1942 – Apr 1942		
Hurricane IIB	Jul 1941 – Nov 1941	BD741	
	Jun 1942 – Aug 1942		
Hurricane IIC	Aug 1942 – Jun 1944	HV798	
Spitfire VIII	Mar 1944 – Jun 1945	LV643	
Spitfire XIVE	Jun 1945 – Feb 1948	RN150	(YB-W)
Spitfire LF.16E	Feb 1949 – Mar 1951	SM406	(UT-H)
Oxford T.2	Feb 1949 – Apr 1951	PH318	
Beaufighter TT.10	May 1949 – Mar 1951	RD751	
Canberra PR.7	Jun 1956 – Dec 1969	WH801	(X)
Phantom FGR.2	Oct 1970 – Dec 1975	XV462	(H)
Jaguar GR.1	Jul 1975 – date	XX819	

Bulldog IIA, No.17 Squadron

Wessex HC.2, No.18 Squadron

No. 18 Squadron

Badge: A Pegasus rampant
Motto: Animo et fide (With courage and faith)
Badge: 'Burma'

No.18 Squadron was formed on 11 May 1915, at Northolt from a nucleus supplied by No.4 Reserve Squadron and moved to France in November 1915 as a fighter-reconnaissance unit equipped with Vickers Gunbuses. These were replaced by F.E.2bs in April 1916, in time for the Battle of the Somme when the squadron flew tactical reconnaissance missions and contacts for the Cavalry Corps. In May 1917, it began to re-equip with D.H.4s for day bombing, a task it retained until the end of the war. Shortly before the Armistice, it received D.H.9As and in September 1919, the squadron returned to the UK and disbanded on 31 December 1919.

On 20 October 1931, No.18 reformed at Upper Heyford as a light bomber squadron with Harts. On 10 February 1936, C Flight was detached to form No.49 Squadron and in April, Hinds were received. May 1939 saw conversion to Blenheims which the squadron took to France on the outbreak of World War Two as part of the Air Component. During the German attack in May 1940, No.18 carried out bombing and reconnaissance missions over the battle area, the survivors being withdrawn to the UK ten days after the invasion of the Low Countries. Barges in the Channel ports and coastal shipping became the squadron's main targets until the end of the year, inland installations being later bombed under strong fighter escort. In October 1941, No.18's aircraft

flew out to Malta to attack enemy shipping and ports in the Mediterranean. In January 1941 its remaining Blenheims were withdrawn to Egypt where the detachment was disbanded on 21 March 1942 and the five surviving Blenheims handed over.

A ground echelon had remained in the UK and on 12 March 1942, the first three new crews joined to begin a build-up to operational strength. Bombing raids were resumed on 26 April. In September Blenheim Vs were received for the forthcoming operations in North Africa, the squadron flying out to Algeria in November. After a series of daylight raids on German bases in Tunisia, the squadron met heavy fighter opposition early in December and the resulting losses caused the Blenheim squadrons to be switched to night bombing for the rest of the campaign. Bostons began to arrive in March 1943 and were taken to Sicily in August 1943. In October, its base was changed to Italy and for the rest of the war it was engaged in interdiction bombing of enemy communications in northern Italy and the Balkans and also in attacks on coastal shipping. In September 1945, No.18 moved to Greece where it disbanded on 31 March 1946.

On 1 September 1946, No.621 Squadron which was flying Lancaster maritime reconnaissance aircraft from Ein Shemer was renumbered 18 Squadron but disbanded on 15 September 1946. On 15 March 1947 the squadron reformed from No.1300 Flight at Butterworth for meteorological duties in South East Asia until disbanded on 15 November 1947.

On 8 December 1947, No.18 reformed at Waterbeach with Dakotas and took part in the Berlin Airlift before disbanding again on 20 February 1950. On 1 August 1953, it reformed at Scampton with Canberra light bombers, disbanding on 1 February 1957. On 16 December 1958, C Flight of No.199 Squadron was redesignated No.18 Squadron and flew Valiants until disbanded on 31 March 1963.

The Wessex Trials Unit at Odiham became No.18 Squadron on 27 January 1964, which provides tactical transport in the UK and Germany.

D.H.4, No.18 Squadron

Squadron bases

Northolt	11 May 1915
Mousehold	16 Aug 1915
St. Omer	19 Nov 1915
Treizennes	25 Nov 1915
Auchel	12 Feb 1916
Bruay	1 Apr 1916
Treizennes	22 Jul 1916
Bruay	2 Aug 1916
Lavieville	6 Sep 1916
St. Leger	10 Dec 1916
Bertangles	7 Jan 1917
Baizieux	25 May 1917
La Bellevue	10 Jul 1917
Auchel	11 Oct 1917
Treizennes	2 Feb 1918
Serny	9 Apr 1918
Maisoncelle	17 Aug 1918
Izel-le-Hameau	18 Oct 1918
La Brayelle	27 Oct 1918
Maubeuge	28 Nov 1918
Bickendorf	24 Jan 1919
Merheim	1 May 1919
Weston-on-the-Green	
	2 Sep 1919
	to 31 Dec 1919
Upper Heyford	20 Oct 1931
Bircham Newton	7 Jan 1936
Old Sarum	14 Aug 1936
Upper Heyford	12 Sep 1936
Beauvraignes	30 Sep 1939
Meharicourt	16 Oct 1939 (A)
	18 Oct 1939 (G)
Poix	17 May 1940
Crecy & Abbeville	18 May 1940

Watton	20 May 1940
Gatwick	26 May 1940
West Raynham	12 Jun 1940
Great Massingham	8 Sep 1940
Oulton	3 Apr 1941
Horsham St. Faith	13 Jul 1941
Manston	16 Aug 1941
Horsham St. Faith	27 Aug 1941
Left for Malta	12 Oct 1941
detached until	21 Mar 1942
Oulton	5 Nov 1941 (G)
Horsham St. Faith	
	5 Dec 1941 (G)
Wattisham	9 Dec 1941 (G)
Helwan	10 Jan 1942 (A)
LG.05	5 Feb 1942 (A)
Fuka	14 Feb 1942 (A)
	to 21 Mar 1942
Dundonald	13 May 1942
Ayr	15 May 1942
Wattisham	20 May 1942
West Raynham	23 Aug 1942
Blida	11 Nov 1942
Canrobert	30 Nov 1942
Setif	5 Dec 1942
Canrobert	17 Dec 1942
Oulmene	7 Mar 1943
Souk el Arba	17 Apr 1943
Grombalia	7 Jun 1943
Gela West	3 Aug 1943
Comiso	9 Aug 1943
Gerbini	24 Aug 1943
Brindisi	7 Oct 1943
Foggia No.1	30 Oct 1943
Marcianise	16 Feb 1944

Nettuno/La Blanca	
	14 Jun 1944
Tarquinia	25 Jun 1944
Cecina	18 Jul 1944
Falconara	13 Oct 1944 (G)
	18 Oct 1944 (A)
Forli	7 Mar 1945
Aviano	13 May 1945
Hassani	12 Sep 1945
	to 31 Mar 1946
Ein Shemer	1 Sep 1946
	to 15 Sep 1946
Butterworth	15 Mar 1947
Mingaladon	16 Apr 1947

Butterworth	1 Oct 1947
	to 15 Nov 1947
Waterbeach	8 Dec 1947
	to 20 Feb 1950
Scampton	1 Aug 1953
Upwood	22 May 1955
	to 1 Feb 1957
Finningley	16 Dec 1958
	to 31 Mar 1963
Odiham	27 Jan 1964
Gutersloh	1 Jan 1965
Acklington	5 Jan 1968
Odiham	4 Aug 1969
Gutersloh	31 Aug 1970

Aircraft

Equipment	Period of service	Representative Serial and Code	
Vickers F.B.5	May 1915 – Apr 1916		
F.E.2b	Apr 1916 – Jun 1917		
D.H.4	May 1917 – Oct 1918	B2066	
D.H.9A	Oct 1918 – Sep 1919	F1042	
Hart	Nov 1931 – May 1936	K2451	
Hind	Apr 1936 – May 1939	K5473	
Blenheim I	May 1939 – Feb 1940	L1444	
Blenheim IV	Feb 1940 – Sep 1942	V6197	(WV-D)
Blenheim V	Sep 1942 – Apr 1943	BB181	(R)
Boston III, IIIA	Mar 1943 – Jul 1944	AL700	(T)
Boston IV, V	Jul 1944 – Mar 1946	BZ511	(M)
Lancaster GR.3	Sep 1946	RF313	(F)
Mosquito Met.6	Mar 1947 – Nov 1947	RF822	(F)
Dakota C.4	Dec 1947 – Feb 1950	KN499	
Canberra B.2	Aug 1953 – Feb 1957	WJ733	
Valiant B.1	Dec 1958 – Mar 1963	WZ372	
Wessex HC.2	Jan 1964 – date	XR506	(H)

No. 19 Squadron

Badge: Between wings elevated and conjoined in base, a dolphin head downwards
Motto: Possunt quia posse videntur (They can because they think they can)

No.19 was formed at Castle Bromwich on 1 September 1915, from a nucleus supplied by No.5 Reserve Squadron and for the rest of the year it trained on various types of aircraft. In December, R.E.7s were received for operational use but the move to France was postponed and when it took place in July 1916, the squadron was equipped with B.E.12s. Unsuit-

able as this type was as a fighter, No.19 carried out patrols over the Western Front for the rest of the year before replacing it with Spads. These were used for fighter and ground-attack missions until replaced by Dolphins in January 1918 which were flown until the Armistice. In February 1919, the squadron returned to the UK as a cadre and disbanded on 31 December 1919.

On 1 April 1923, No.19 reformed at Duxford, the home of No.2 Flying Training School, as a single flight of Snipes for training single-seat fighter pilots and was brought up to full strength on 1 June. At the end of June, No.2 FTS moved and No.19 became an independent fighter squadron, re-equipping with Grebes in December. After flying Siskins, Bulldogs and Gauntlets in turn, the squadron became the first to receive Spitfires in August 1938. It remained on defensive duties at Duxford for the opening months of World War Two but at the end of May 1940, took part in covering the

Lightning F.2A, No.19 Squadron

evacuation of the BEF from Dunkirk and was active throughout the Battle of Britain. For a short period during the battle it was equipped with Spitfires armed with two 20mm cannon but these were beset by stoppages and were withdrawn after a short time.

In March 1941, it began taking part in sweeps over Northern France and also put up night patrols. The squadron joined Second TAF on its formation and continued operations in preparation for the invasion, also providing escorts for day bombers. In February 1944, conversion to Mustangs took place and from D-Day onwards these provided close support for the army, attacking enemy communications and positions in the battle area. In September, No.19 returned to undertake long-range escort missions from East Anglia, moving to Scotland in February 1945, to provide similar support to strike wings operating off Norway until the end of the war.

In March 1946, the Mustangs were replaced by Spitfires which were flown for a short time before No.19 became a twin-engined fighter squadron, receiving Hornets in October 1946 which were used as escort and intruder fighters and were replaced by Meteors in January 1951. These were in turn replaced by Hunters and Lightnings and the latter were taken to Germany in September 1965, for fighter defence duties.

Conversion to Phantoms began in July 1976 when a Phantom element of No.19 formed at Coningsby. This moved to Wildenrath on 1 October and became the full squadron when No.19's Lightning element disbanded on 31 December 1976.

Squadron bases

Castle Bromwich	1 Sep 1915	Abscon	24 Oct 1918
Netheravon	Jan 1916	Genech	9 Feb 1919
Filton	4 Apr 1916	Ternhill	17 Feb 1919
St. Omer	30 Jul 1916		to 31 Dec 1919
Fienvillers	1 Aug 1916	Duxford	1 Apr 1923
Vert Galand	2 Apr 1917	Henlow	11 Jun 1935
Lièttres	31 May 1917	Duxford	20 Jul 1935
Poperinghe	14 Aug 1917	Horsham St. Faith	17 Apr 1940
Bailleul	5 Sep 1917	Duxford	16 May 1940
Ste Marie Cappel	25 Dec 1917	Hornchurch	25 May 1940
Bailleul	13 Feb 1918	Duxford	5 Jun 1940
Ste Marie Cappel	23 Mar 1918	Fowlmere	25 Jun 1940
Savy	31 Mar 1918	Duxford	3 Jul 1940
Capelle	17 Aug 1918	Fowlmere	24 Jul 1940
Savy	23 Sep 1918	Duxford	30 Oct 1940
		Fowlmere	6 Feb 1941

Matlask	16 Aug 1941
Ludham	1 Dec 1941
Hutton Cranswick	4 Apr 1942
Perranporth	6 May 1942
Warmwell	1 Jun 1942
Perranporth	14 Jun 1942
Biggin Hill	1 Jul 1942
Perranporth	7 Jul 1942
Colerne	23 Jul 1942
Perranporth	31 Jul 1942
Rochford	16 Aug 1942
Perranporth	20 Aug 1942
Middle Wallop	1 Mar 1943
Membury	10 Mar 1943
Middle Wallop	13 Mar 1943
Fairlop	5 Apr 1943
Digby	18 May 1943
Matlask	4 Jun 1943
Gravesend	20 Jun 1943
Bognor	26 Jun 1943
Newchurch	2 Jul 1943
Kingsnorth	18 Aug 1943
Weston Zoyland	30 Sep 1943
Gatwick	15 Oct 1943
Gravesend	24 Oct 1943
Ford	15 Apr 1944
Southend	12 May 1944
Funtington	20 May 1944
Ford	15 Jun 1944
B.7 Martragny	25 Jun 1944
B.12 Ellon	15 Jul 1944
B.24 St. André de l'Eure	2 Sep 1944
B.40 Nivillers	3 Sep 1944
B.60 Grimbergen	9 Sep 1944
Matlask	28 Sep 1944
Andrews Field	14 Oct 1944
Peterhead	13 Feb 1945
Acklington	23 May 1945
Bradwell Bay	13 Aug 1945
Molesworth	7 Sep 1945
Wittering	22 Jun 1946
Church Fenton	23 Apr 1947
Leconfield	29 Jun 1959
Gutersloh	23 Sep 1965

Aircraft

Equipment	Period of service	Representative Serial and Code	
Maurice Farman, Avro 504, Caudron G.III, B.E.2c	Sep 1915 – Dec 1915		
R.E.7	Dec 1915 – Jun 1916		
B.E.12	Jun 1916 – Feb 1917		
Spad S.VII	Dec 1916 – Jun 1917	B3520	(A)
Spad S.XIII	Jun 1917 – Jan 1918	A8794	
Dolphin	Jan 1918 – Feb 1919	E4514	(E)
Snipe	Apr 1923 – Dec 1924	E8245	
Grebe	Dec 1924 – Mar 1928	J7417	
Siskin IIIA	Mar 1928 – Sep 1931	J8886	
Bulldog IIA	Sep 1931 – May 1935	K2159	
Gauntlet I	May 1935 – Dec 1938	K4104	
Spitfire I	Aug 1938 – Sep 1940	X4474	(QV-I)
Spitfire IIA	Sep 1940 – Oct 1941	P7423	(QV-Y)
Spitfire VB, VC	Oct 1941 – Aug 1943	AA764	
Spitfire IX	Aug 1943 – Feb 1944	MH616	(QV-P)
Mustang III, IV	Feb 1944 – Mar 1946	FB113	(QV-H)
Spitfire LF.16E	Mar 1946 – Oct 1946	TE470	(QV-B)
Hornet F.1	Oct 1946 – May 1948	PX246	(QV-A)
Hornet F.3	May 1948 – Jan 1951	PX332	(QV-D)
Meteor F.4	Jan 1951 – Apr 1951	EE598	
Meteor F.8	Apr 1951 – Oct 1956	WE870	(G)
Hunter F.6	Oct 1956 – Nov 1962	XE583	(D)
Lightning F.2, F.2A	Nov 1962 – Dec 1976	XN781	(B)
Phantom FGR.2	Jul 1976 – date	XV412	(J)

No. 20 Squadron

Badge: In front of a rising sun, an eagle, wings elevated and perched on a sword
Motto: Facta non verba (Deeds not words)

No.20 Squadron was formed on 1 September 1915 at Netheravon and in January 1916 moved to France with F.E.2bs for fighter-reconnaissance duties. In August 1917, the squadron re-equipped with Bristol Fighters which it flew for the rest of the war. Instead of being returned to the UK, No.20 was posted to India, arriving at Bombay on 6 June 1919 to reinforce the handful of B.E.s patrolling the North-West Frontier. Between the wars, the squadron was engaged in policing the borders, replacing its Bristol Fighters with Wapitis in 1932. At the end of 1935, Audaxes were received, to be replaced on the outbreak of war in the Far East with Lysanders. In July 1942 the squadron began operations against the Japanese, flying tactical reconnaissance and liaison missions in support of a Chinese ground force. Moving to the Arakan in October, No.20's operational detachment used its Lysanders for army co-operation until the arrival of some Hurricanes in February 1943. By the end of May, the squadron was completely equipped with Hurricane IID anti-tank aircraft and, after a short period of weapon training, began operations on 23 December. Shortage of 40mm ammunition and suitable armoured targets restricted the use of the squadron on ground-attack duties, but tactical reconnaissance tasks were also given to No.20. Operations ended on 10 August 1944 to permit the squadron to be withdrawn

Harrier GR.1, No.20 Squadron

to India for re-equipment with rocket-firing Hurricanes while some Hurricanes were equipped for anti-mosquito spraying. Ground-attack sorties were resumed in December and continued until 18 May 1945 when the squadron was again withdrawn for re-equipment. In September 1945, No.20 received Spitfires and moved to Thailand soon after the Japanese surrender. Next year it converted to Tempests in India but disbanded on 1 August 1947.

On 11 February 1949 No.631 Squadron at Llanbedr was renumbered 20 Squadron. A variety of types was used for anti-aircraft co-operation duties until disbandment on 16 October 1951. On 1 July 1952 No.20 reformed at Jever as a fighter-bomber squadron in Germany. Its Vampires were replaced by Sabres in 1953 and Hunters were received at the end of 1955. The squadron was a day fighter unit for seven years, disbanding again on 30 December 1960.

On 3 July 1961, No.20 reformed at Tengah with Hunters for ground-attack duties in the Far East. From May to November 1962 it was detached to Thailand as part of a SEATO deployment to counter Communist activity in the Thai/Laos border areas. In 1969 a flight of Pioneers was added for forward air control duties as a result of the disbandment of No.209 Squadron and on 13 February 1970 the squadron itself disbanded. On 1 December 1970, No.20 reformed at Wildenrath as a Harrier squadron in Germany, but transferred these to Nos.3 and 4 Squadrons to reform on 1 March 1977 at Bruggen with Jaguars.

Squadron bases			
Netheravon	1 Sep 1915	Boisdinghem	13 Apr 1918
Filton	Dec 1915	Vignacourt	26 Aug 1918
St. Omer	16 Jan 1916	Suzanne	16 Sep 1918
Clairmarais	23 Jan 1916	Proyart	24 Sep 1918
Boisdinghem	19 Jan 1917	Moislains	7 Oct 1918
Ste. Marie Cappel	15 Apr 1917	Clary/Iris Farm	25 Oct 1918
		Ossogne	3 Dec 1918

Left for India	30 May 1919	Chiringa	25 May 1944
Risalpur	16 Jun 1919	Kajamalai	23 Jul 1944
Parachinar	21 Jul 1919	St. Thomas Mount	20 Sep 1944
Bannu	22 Sep 1919	Sapam	20 Dec 1944 (A)
Parachinar	18 Jul 1920		28 Dec 1944 (G)
Tank	5 Nov 1920	Thazi	16 Jan 1945
Parachinar	11 Apr 1921	Monywa	13 Feb 1945
Ambala	17 Oct 1921	Thedaw	13 Apr 1945
Quetta	24 Oct 1922	Toungoo/Tennant	28 Apr 1944
Peshawar	5 Jan 1925	Thedaw	8 May 1945
Kohat	22 May 1925	Chettinad	Jun 1945
Peshawar	12 Oct 1925	St. Thomas Mount	Jun 1945
Miramshah	2 Dec 1936	Amarda Road	27 Aug 1945
Peshawar	24 Dec 1936	Don Muang	Sep 1945
Miramshah	7 Jan 1937	Baigachi	1946
Peshawar	16 Jan 1937	Mingaladon	1946
Miramshah	16 Apr 1937	Agra	May 1946
Peshawar	Dec 1937		to 1 Aug 1947
Miramshah	13 May 1938	Llanbedr	11 Feb 1949
Peshawar	21 May 1938	Valley	19 Jul 1949
Miramshah	29 Aug 1939		to 16 Oct 1951
Peshawar	30 Oct 1939	Jever	1 Jul 1952
Kohat	8 Apr 1940	Oldenburg	28 Jul 1952
Secunderabad/Begumpet		Gutersloh	1 Sep 1958
	10 Jun 1941		to 30 Dec 1960
Peshawar	2 Mar 1942	Tengah	3 Jul 1961
Jamshedpur	1 May 1942		to 13 Feb 1970
Chharra	11 Dec 1942	Wildenrath	1 Dec 1970
Kalyanpur	16 May 1943		to 28 Feb 1977
Nidania	30 Nov 1943	Bruggen	1 Mar 1977
Madhaibunia	25 May 1944		

Aircraft Equipment	Period of service	Representative Serial
Various	Sep 1915 – Dec 1915	–
F.E.2b	Dec 1915 – Jun 1916	6336
F.E.2d	Jun 1916 – Sep 1917	A6480
Bristol F.2b	Aug 1917 – Mar 1932	H1508 (P)
Wapiti IIA	Jan 1932 – Dec 1935	J9731
Audax	Dec 1935 – Dec 1941	K4854
Blenheim I	Jun 1941 – Dec 1941	
Lysander II	Dec 1941 – May 1943	L4776 (A)
Hurricane IIB	Feb 1943 – May 1943	BN135
Hurricane IID, IV	Feb 1943 – Sep 1945	KX229 (H)
Spitfire VIII	Sep 1945 – Dec 1945	MD377
Spitfire XIV	Dec 1945 – 1946	SM888 (B)
Tempest F.2	Jun 1946 – Aug 1947	PR602 (HN-D)
Spitfire LF.16E	Feb 1949	TE399 (B)
Beaufighter TT.10	Feb 1949 – Oct 1951	RD783
Oxford T.2	Feb 1949 – Oct 1951	PH467
Martinet TT.1	Feb 1949 – Oct 1951	HN885
Harvard T.2B	Feb 1949 – Oct 1951	
Vampire F.1. F.3	Jul 1949 – Nov 1950	VF283
Vampire FB.9	Jul 1952 – Oct 1953	WR177 (G)
Sabre F.2, F.4	Oct 1953 – Nov 1955	XB731 (J)
Hunter F.4	Nov 1955 – Oct 1957	WV401 (T)
Hunter F.6	Aug 1957 – Dec 1960	XJ680 (A)
Hunter FGA.9	Aug 1961 – Feb 1970	XG265 (K)
Pioneer CC.1	Jan 1969 – Jan 1970	XL666
Harrier GR.1	Dec 1970 – Feb 1977	XV779 (Q)
Jaguar GR.1	Mar 1977 – date	XZ374 (CA)

No. 21 Squadron

Badge: A hand erased at the wrist, holding a dumbell
Motto: Viribus vincimus (By strength we conquer)

No.21 Squadron was formed at Netheravon on 23 July 1915, and moved to France in January 1916, equipped with R.E.7s. Reconnaissance flights over the Western Front were the main occupation of the squadron but bombing raids were also carried out on enemy bases. In the face of increasing enemy fighter strength, additional fighter squadrons were required and No.21 was re-equipped with single-seat B.E.12s in August 1916. These were almost useless as fighters and were used more effectively as bombers until February 1917, when they were replaced by R.E.8s. No.21 became a corps reconnaissance squadron and flew artillery spotting missions for the rest of the war. In February 1919 it returned to the UK and disbanded on 1 October 1919.

On 3 December 1935 No.21 reformed at Bircham Newton as a light bomber squadron with Hinds. In August 1938 it re-equipped with Blenheims. Apart from a few reconnaissance missions and shipping searches, the squadron saw little action until the German attack on the Low Countries which resulted in attacks on the advancing enemy columns. In June 1940 No.21 moved to Lossiemouth for anti-shipping operations off the Norwegian and Danish coasts, returning to East Anglia in October for attacks on coastal targets. In December 1941 the squadron flew out to Malta to attack enemy convoys and ports in Italy and Libya and on 14 March 1942 it was disbanded.

Reformed the same day at Bodney, No.21 took over No.82 Squadron's Blenheims and in May began to receive Venturas.

Training continued for the rest of the year and it was 6 December before the first operation took place, seventeen aircraft being sent on a daylight raid to the Philips works at Eindhoven. Venturas were obsolescent for day bombing before they arrived in service and in September 1943 were replaced by Mosquitos. These took part in several daylight precision attacks in addition to their normal night raids. In February 1945 the squadron moved to France and carried out intruder raids over Germany for the rest of the war. It remained in Germany until disbanded on 7 November 1947.

On 21 September 1953 No.21 reformed at Scampton as part of the home-based Canberra force, disbanding on 30 June 1957. On 1 October 1958, No.542 Squadron at Upwood was renumbered 21 Squadron. Most of the squadron was detached to Laverton, Australia in connection with nuclear weapons trials until the beginning of 1959, but the squadron was again disbanded on 15 January 1959.

On 1 May 1959 No.21 reformed at Benson as the first Twin Pioneer squadron, moving to Kenya in September as a light transport unit. In June 1965 it moved to Aden to support army operations in the Radfan until disbanded on 15 September 1967. On 3 February 1969 the Western Communications Squadron at Andover was redesignated No.21 Squadron, which disbanded on 31 March 1976.

Mosquito B.6, No.21 Squadron

Squadron bases

Netheravon	23 Jul 1915	Watton & Bodney	29 Oct 1940
Boisdinghem	23 Jan 1916	Lossiemouth	27 May 1941
St André-au-Bois	2 Apr 1916	Watton	14 Jun 1941
Fienvillers	19 Jun 1916	Manston	17 Jul 1941
Boisdinghem	28 Jul 1916	Watton	25 Jul 1941
Bertangles	25 Aug 1916	Lossiemouth	7 Sep 1941
Boisdinghem	10 Feb 1917	Watton	21 Sep 1941
Droglandt	24 Mar 1917	Luqa	26 Dec 1941
La Lovie	19 Mar 1917		to 14 Mar 1942
St. Inglevert	13 Apr 1918	Bodney	15 Mar 1942
Floringhem	22 Apr 1918	Methwold	30 Oct 1942
Hesdigneul	19 Oct 1918	Exeter	21 Mar 1943
Seclin	26 Oct 1918	Methwold	24 Mar 1943
Froidmont	11 Nov 1918	Oulton	1 Apr 1943
Sweveghem	16 Nov 1918	Sculthorpe	27 Sep 1943
Coucou	18 Dec 1918	Hunsdon	31 Dec 1943
Fowlmere	18 Feb 1919	Gravesend	17 Apr 1944
	to 1 Oct 1919	Thorney Island	18 Jun 1944
Bircham Newton	3 Dec 1935	B.57 Rosières-en-Santerre	
Abbotsinch	22 Jul 1936		6 Feb 1945
Lympne	3 Nov 1936	B.58 Melsbroek	17 Apr 1945
Eastchurch	15 Aug 1938	Y.99 Gutersloh	3 Nov 1945
Watton	2 Mar 1939	T.94 Munster/Handorf	
Lossiemouth	24 Jun 1940		23 Jun 1946

Y.99 Gutersloh	9 Aug 1946	Benson	1 May 1959
	to 7 Nov 1947	Eastleigh	15 Sep 1959
Scampton	21 Sep 1953	Khormaksar	1 Jun 1965
Waddington	28 May 1955		to 15 Sep 1967
	to 30 Jun 1957	Andover	3 Feb 1969
Upwood	1 Oct 1958		to 31 Mar 1976
	to 15 Jan 1959		

Aircraft

Equipment	Period of service	Representative Serial
R.E.7	Jul 1915 – Aug 1916	2351
B.E.2c, B.E.2e	Apr 1916 – Aug 1916	
B.E.12	Aug 1916 – Feb 1917	
R.E.8	Feb 1917 – Feb 1919	A4351 (B)
Hind	Jan 1936 – Aug 1938	K5373
Blenheim I	Aug 1938 – Sep 1939	L1400
Blenheim IV	Sep 1939 – Jul 1942	V6254 (YH-N)
Ventura I, II	May 1942 – Sep 1943	AE717 (YH-O)
Mosquito VI	Sep 1943 – Oct 1947	RS532 (YH-E)
Canberra B.2	Sep 1953 – Jun 1957	WJ609
	Oct 1958 – Jan 1959	
Canberra B.6	Oct 1958 – Jan 1959	WH946
Twin Pioneer CC.1	May 1959 – Sep 1967	XM961
Dakota C.4	Aug 1965 – Sep 1967	KN452
Andover C.2	– Sep 1967	XS793
Pembroke C.1	Feb 1969 – Mar 1976	WV746

Twin Pioneer CC.1, No.21 Squadron

Beaufort Is, No.22 Squadron

No. 22 Squadron

Badge: On a torteau, a Maltese
cross throughout. Over all
a 'pi' fimbriated
Motto: Preux et audacieux
(Valiant and brave)

No.22 Squadron was formed at Gosport on 1 September 1916 and after training moved to France on 1 April 1916 as a reconnaissance unit equipped with F.E.2bs. The squadron's task was the location and surveillance of enemy dumps, rail-heads and camps behind the Western Front in the course of which it met considerable opposition from enemy aircraft and in July 1917, re-equipped with Bristol Fighters. These were flown both on reconnaissance and fighter missions, the latter becoming the squadron's major role for the rest of the war. After a short period in Germany after the Armistice, No.22 returned to the UK in September 1919, and disbanded on 31 December 1919

On 24 July 1923, the squadron reformed at Martlesham Heath as part of the Aeroplane and Armament Experimental Establishment and was engaged in testing duties until disbanded on 1 May 1934. On the same day, No.22 reformed at Donibristle with six Vildebeests as a torpedo-bomber squadron. In October 1935 it moved to Malta during the Abyssinian crisis, returning to the UK in August 1936 and moving to Thorney Island in March 1938. On the outbreak of war the squadron was still equipped with Vildebeests but Beauforts began to arrive in November 1939, though the last Vildebeest did not leave till February 1940, having flown anti-submarine patrols since the beginning of October 1939. On 15 April 1940, the Beauforts flew their first operations which consisted mainly of minelaying except when units of the German fleet were located at sea. In August, C Flight received Marylands for crew-training, the trained crews

ese carrier attacks were never repeated and the squadron was engaged on convoy escort and anti-submarine patrols until re-equipped with Beaufighters in June 1944. Rockets now became the main means of attack though torpedos could still be carried and in December 1944, the squadron moved to the Burma front where it undertook ground-attack and air-sea rescue missions until 1945. On 30 September 1945, the squadron was disbanded.

On 1 May 1946, No.89 Squadron at Seletar was renumbered 22 Squadron and flew Mosquito fighter-bombers until disbanded on 15 August 1946. On 15 February 1955, No.22 reformed as a search and rescue squadron at Thorney Island and maintained detachments in southern England for this purpose at various airfields.

Squadron bases

Gosport	1 Sep 1915	Donibristle	1 May 1934
Vert Galand	1 Apr 1916	Hal Far	10 Oct 1935
Bertangles	16 Apr 1916	Donibristle	29 Aug 1936
Chipilly	27 Jan 1917	Thorney Island	10 Mar 1938
Flez (D)	1 May 1917	North Coates	8 Apr 1940
Flez	1 Jul 1917	Thorney Island	25 Jun 1941
Warloy Baillon	3 Jul 1917	St. Eval	28 Oct 1941
Izel-le-Hameau	5 Jul 1917	Emb. for Far East	
Boisdinghem	14 Aug 1917		16 Feb 1942 (G)
Estree Blanche	10 Sep 1917	Left for Far East	
Auchel	22 Jan 1918		18 Mar 1942 (A)
Treizennes	2 Feb 1918	Ratmalana	28 Apr 1942
Serny	21 Mar 1918	Minneriya	30 Sep 1942
Vert Galand	23 Mar 1918	Vavuniya	15 Feb 1943
Serny	10 Apr 1918	Ratmalana	21 Apr 1944
Maisoncelle	30 Jul 1918	Vavuniya	7 Jul 1944
Izel-le-Hameau	22 Oct 1918	Kumbhirgram	23 Dec 1944
Aniche	26 Oct 1918	Joari	26 Jan 1945
Aulnoye	17 Nov 1918	Chiringa	18 Apr 1945
Witheries	22 Nov 1918	Gannavaram	21 Jun 1945
Nivelles	20 Dec 1918		to 30 Sep 1945
Spich	21 May 1919	Seletar	1 May 1946
Ford	1 Sep 1919		to 15 Aug 1946
	to 31 Dec 1919	Thorney Island	15 Feb 1955
Martlesham Heath	24 Jul 1923	St. Mawgan	4 Jun 1956
	to 1 May 1934		

Aircraft

Equipment	Period of service	Representative Serial and Code
Various	Sep 1915 – Mar 1916	—
F.E.2b	Mar 1916 – Jul 1917	A5216

Vampire NF.10s, No.23 Squadron

No. 23 Squadron

Badge: An eagle preying on a
                falcon
Motto: Semper aggressus (Always
                having attacked)

No.23 Squadron was formed at Gosport on 1 September
1915 and during training supplied aircraft to defend London
against air attack. In March 1916, the squadron moved to
France with F.E.2b fighters and flew patrols and reconnaissance missions over the Western Front until re-equipped with
Spads in February 1917. Ground-attack missions began to
be flown against enemy troops and transport behind the front
line which were continued after conversion to Dolphins in

the squadron was fully equipped with these aircraft now
named Demons. In September 1935 many squadrons were
moved to the Middle East during the Abyssinian crisis and
No.23 lost most of its aircraft as reinforcements during the
next six months before it began to be brought up to strength
again. In December 1938 conversion to Blenheims took place
and these were given a night fighter role when war broke out.
After defensive duties during the early stages of the German
attacks, No.23 began intruder missions over enemy airfields
in December 1940. In March 1941 Havocs began to replace
the Blenheims and intruder duties remained the squadron's
role after conversion to Mosquitos in July 1942. These it
took to Malta in December for operations over Sicily, Italy,
and Tunisia. In December 1943, No.23 moved to Sardinia
whence its aircraft ranged over southern France and northern
Italy until May 1944 when the squadron returned to the UK.

On 1 Jun 1944, No.23 joined No.100 Group at Little
Snoring and began operations as an intruder squadron in
support of Bomber Command's heavy bombers. These continued until the end of the war and on 25 September 1945

Squadron bases			
Gosport	1 Sep 1915	Manston	6 Aug 1942
Fienvillers	16 Mar 1916	Bradwell Bay	14 Aug 1942
Izel-le-Hameau	18 Mar 1916	Manston	21 Aug 1942
Fienvillers	1 Sep 1916	Bradwell Bay	13 Oct 1942
Vert Galand	5 Sep 1916	Left for Malta	11 Dec 1942 (G)
Baizieux	5 Mar 1917	Portreath	21 Dec 1942 (A)
Auchel	23 May 1917	Gibraltar	23 Dec 1942 (A)
Bruay	29 May 1917	Luqa	27 Dec 1942 (A)
La Lovie	13 Jun 1917	Sigonella (D)	3 Sep 1943
Matigny	16 Feb 1918		to 5 Oct 1943
Moreuil	22 Mar 1918	Gerbini Main (D)	5 Oct 1943
Bertangles	28 Mar 1918		to 1 Nov 1943
St Omer	29 Apr 1918	Pomigliano (D)	1 Nov 1943
Bertangles	16 May 1918		to 7 Dec 1943
Cappy	13 Sep 1918	Alghero	7 Dec 1943
Hancourt	11 Oct 1918	Blida	8 May 1944 (A)
Bertry East	25 Oct 1918	Left for UK	19 May 1944
Clermont	3 Dec 1918	Little Snoring	2 Jun 1944
Waddington	Mar 1919		to 25 Sep 1945
	to 31 Dec 1919	Wittering	11 Sep 1946
Henlow	1 Jul 1925	Coltishall	23 Jan 1947
Kenley	6 Feb 1927	Church Fenton	19 Nov 1949
Biggin Hill	17 Sep 1932	Coltishall	22 Sep 1950
Northolt	21 Dec 1936	Horsham St. Faith	12 Oct 1956
Wittering	16 May 1938	Coltishall	28 May 1957
Collyweston	31 May 1940	Leuchars	9 Mar 1963
Ford	12 Sep 1940		21 Mar 1963 (C)
Middle Wallop (D)	12 Sep 1940		to 31 Oct 1975
	to 25 Sep 1940	Coningsby	1 Dec 1975
		Wattisham	25 Feb 1976

Aircraft Equipment	Period of service	Representative Serial and Code	
Avro 504A	Sep 1915 – Mar 1916	4024	
Bleriot XI	Sep 1915 – Oct 1915	574	
Caudron G.III	Sep 1915 – Dec 1915	5270	
Maurice Farman	Sep 1915 – Jan 1916	2947	
Martinsyde S.1	Oct 1915 – Mar 1916	4251	
B.E.2c	Oct 1915 – Mar 1916	2048	
F.E.2b	Jan 1916 – Feb 1917	5215	
Spad S.VII	Feb 1917 – Mar 1918	B3479	(M)
Spad S.XIII	Dec 1917 – Apr 1918	B6842	
Dolphin	Mar 1918 – Mar 1919	E4729	(P)
Snipe	Jul 1925 – May 1926	E6615	
Gamecock	Apr 1926 – Sep 1931	J8040	
Bulldog IIA	Apr 1931 – Apr 1933	K2151	
Hart/Demon	Jul 1931 – Dec 1938	K5698	
Blenheim IF	Dec 1938 – Apr 1941	L8617	(YP-K)
Havoc I	Mar 1941 – Aug 1942	BD124	(YP-D)
Boston III	Feb 1942 – Aug 1942	W8374	
Mosquito II	Jul 1942 – Sep 1943	DD798	(YP-S)
Mosquito VI	May 1943 – Sep 1945	HX896	(YP-D)
Mosquito NF.30	Aug 1945 – Sep 1945 Sep 1946 – Feb 1947	RL145	(C)
Mosquito NF.36	Feb 1947 – May 1952	RL141	(YP-B)
Vampire NF.10	Sep 1951 – Jan 1954	WP248	(B)
Venom NF.2	Nov 1953 – Mar 1956	WR779	(G)
Venom NF.3	Oct 1955 – May 1957	WX843	(P)
Javelin FAW.4	Apr 1957 – Jul 1959	XA737	
Javelin FAW.7	Apr 1959 – Jul 1960	XH960	(N)
Javelin FAW.9	Apr 1960 – Sep 1964	XH890	(M)
Lightning F.3	Aug 1964 – Nov 1967	XP760	(K)
Lightning F.6	May 1967 – Oct 1975	XR763	(G)
Phantom FGR.2	Dec 1975 – date	XV484	(F)

Javelin FAW.7s, No.23 Squadron

No. 24 Squadron

Badge: A blackcock
Motto: In omnia parati (Ready in all things)
Name: 'Commonwealth'

the squadron re-equipped with D.H.5s which were in turn replaced by S.E.5As in December 1917. For the rest of the war, No.24 flew fighter and ground-attack missions and in February 1919 returned to the UK as a cadre, being attached to No.41 Training Depot Station at London Colney for the rest of the year. On 1 February 1920, the squadron was disbanded.

No.24 was reformed on 1 April 1920 at Kenley as a communications and training squadron. Initially equipped with

Hart (Communications), No.24 Squadron

D.H.89A, No.24 Squadron

been carried out in service and training aircraft. A D.H.89A was then received for VIP flights, being supplemented by a D.H.86B in October 1937. To replace the variety of types on hand, it was planned to equip the squadron with twenty Miles Mentors but World War Two broke out before this could be done and No.24 acquired an even larger miscellany of types, many being impressed civil aircraft. Until the German occupation of France, communications and mail flights across the Channel were frequent but after June 1940 all but a few flights were within the UK.

In April 1942, the squadron was transferred to Ferry Command and began flights to Malta with mail and passengers. Dakotas were received in April 1943 and next month the first VIP York arrived. No.512 Squadron took over many of the squadrons personnel and short-range aircraft in August 1943 while No.24 concentrated on longer-ranged services. In October 1944, the squadron standardised on Dakotas and Ansons and in February 1946 it moved to Bassingbourn where it was joined by the Yorks and Lancasters of No.1359 (VIP) Flight. Yorks became standard equipment and in April 1947 the squadron became No.24 (Commonwealth) Squadron. Hastings began to arrive in December 1950 and equipped the squadron fully in November 1951. VIP flights continued but general transport duties increased over the years. In January 1957, No.24 moved to Colerne to become part of a transport wing and flew Hastings until January 1968 when conversion to Hercules took place.

Squadron bases			
Hounslow Heath	1 Sep 1915	Baizieux	10 Jul 1917
St. Omer	7 Feb 1916	Teteghem	23 Sep 1917
Bertangles	10 Feb 1916	Marieux	24 Nov 1917
Chipilly	17 Dec 1916	Villers-Bretonneux	1 Jan 1918
Flez	19 Apr 1917	Matigny	28 Jan 1918
		Moreuil	22 Mar 1918

Bertangles	26 Mar 1918		to 1 Feb 1920
Conteville	28 Mar 1918	Kenley	1 Apr 1920
Bertangles	14 Aug 1918	Northolt	15 Jan 1927
Cappy	8 Sep 1918	Hendon	9 Jul 1933
Athies	6 Oct 1918	Bassingbourn	25 Feb 1946
Busigny	27 Oct 1918	Waterbeach	11 Jun 1949
Bissighem	10 Nov 1918	Lyneham	29 Nov 1950
Ennetières	16 Nov 1918	Topcliffe	9 Feb 1951
Bissighem	11 Dec 1918	Abingdon	7 May 1953
London Colney	12 Feb 1919	Colerne	1 Jan 1957
Uxbridge	Nov 1919	Lyneham	9 Feb 1968

Aircraft Equipment	Period of service	Representative Serial and Code
Various (e.g. Curtiss J.N.4, Avro 504A, B.E.2c, Bleriot XI, Maurice Farman, Henry Farman, Bristol Scout, Martinsyde Scout)		
	Sep 1915 – Jan 1916	–
Vickers FB.5	Nov 1915 – Jan 1916	–
D.H.2	Dec 1915 – Apr 1917	5967 (A)
D.H.5	Apr 1917 – Dec 1917	A9435 (E)
S.E.5A	Dec 1917 – Jan 1919	B891 (7)
Various communications types e.g. Bristol F.2b (J8430), Wapiti (J9096), Fairey IIIF (K1118), Cirrus Moth (J9104), Tomtit (K1782), Tutor (K1234), Bulldog (K2209), Audax (K2008), Hart (K2455), Tiger Moth (K2570), DH.89A (K5070), D.H.86B (L7596), Nighthawk (L6846), Vega Gull (P1749), Magister (L5931), Anson I (K6290), Mentor (L4440), Flamingo (R2764), Percival Q6 (P5636), Lockheed 10A (W9106), Lockheed 12A (LA619), D.H.84 Dragon (G-ACIV), Hornet Moth (W9390), Oxford II (P8832), Envoy (L7270), Fokker F-22 (HM159), Warferry (HM497), Hudson I (N9375), Proctor I (P6129), Ensign (G-ADST), DC 3 (OO-AUI), Savoia-Marchetti S-73 (OO-AGX), Curtiss SBC-4 Cleveland (AS468), Roc (L3120), Hind (K6814), Wellington XVI (N2990), Dakota I, III, IV (KN648-NQ-V).		
York C.1	May 1943 – Nov 1951	LV633 'Ascalon'
Lancastrian II	Jun 1946 – Oct 1949	VL980
Hastings C.1, C.2	Dec 1950 – Jan 1968	WD487
Hercules C.1	Jan 1968 – date	XV191

Hastings C.2s, No.24 Squadron

Javelin FAW.7s, No.25 Squadron

No. 25 Squadron

Badge: On a gauntlet a hawk
rising affrontée
Motto: Ferines tego (Striking I
defend)

No.25 Squadron was formed on 25 September 1915 at Montrose from a nucleus supplied by No.6 Reserve Squadron and after a period of training moved to France in February 1916 equipped with F.E.2bs. It was engaged in fighter and reconnaissance missions over the Western Front before the increasing obsolescence of the F.E.s resulted in re-equipment with D.H.4 day bombers in June 1917. These were flown in attacks on enemy bases behind the lines and on reconnaissance missions for the rest of the war. The squadron was scheduled to convert to D.H.9As when the war ended but retained D.H.4s until the end of 1919 when it moved to Scopwick as a cadre and disbanded on 31 January 1920.

No.25 began to reform at Hawkinge on 1 February 1920 and this was completed on 26 April. Equipped with Snipes, the squadron was one of the few fighter units existing at this time. At the end of September 1922, No.25 was sent to Turkey for a period, returning in October 1923. In October 1924, the squadron converted to Grebes which were replaced by Siskins in May 1929. Furies were received in February 1932 and were flown until No.25 became a two-seat fighter squadron with the arrival of Demons in October 1937. A reversion to single-seaters came in June 1938 but Blenheims began to arrive in December 1938 and on the outbreak of World War Two were used for night patrols. Conversion to Beaufighters was completed by January 1941

and these were flown for two years until replaced by Mosquitos. Intruder missions began to be flown on 16 February 1943 and in addition to defensive patrols, the squadron flew bomber support sorties over Germany against enemy night fighters. After the end of the war, No.25 was retained as a permanent night fighter unit, flying Mosquitos until converted to Vampires in 1951. In April 1954, these were replaced by Meteor night fighters which were flown until disbandment on 23 June 1958.

On 1 July 1958, No.153 Squadron at Waterbeach was renumbered 25 Squadron. Equipped again with Meteor night fighters, the squadron converted to Javelins in March 1959 and flew this type until disbanded on 30 November 1962. On 1 October 1962, No.25 was reformed at North Coates as a Bloodhound surface-to-air guided missile unit, moving to Germany in 1971.

Squadron bases

Montrose	25 Sep 1915	Northolt	4 Oct 1939
Thetford	31 Dec 1915	North Weald	16 Jan 1940
St. Omer	20 Feb 1916	Martlesham Heath	19 Jun 1940
Auchel	1 Apr 1916	North Weald	1 Sep 1940
Boisdinghem	11 Oct 1917	Debden	8 Oct 1940
Villers-Brettoneux	6 Mar 1918	Wittering	27 Nov 1940
Beauvois	24 Mar 1918	Ballyhalbert	24 Jan 1942
Ruisseauville	29 Mar 1918	Church Fenton	16 May 1942
La Brayelle	27 Oct 1918	Acklington	19 Dec 1943
Maubeuge	29 Nov 1918	Coltishall	5 Feb 1944
Bickendorf	26 May 1919	Castle Camps	27 Oct 1944
Merheim	7 Jul 1919	Boxted	Jan 1946
South Carlton	6 Sep 1919	West Malling	Sep 1946
Scopwick	Dec 1919	Tangmere	30 Sep 1957
	to 31 Jan 1920		to 23 Jun 1958
Hawkinge	1 Feb 1920	Waterbeach	1 Jul 1958
Left for Turkey	28 Sep 1922	Leuchars	23 Oct 1961
San Stephano	11 Oct 1922		to 30 Nov 1962
Left for UK	22 Sep 1923	North Coates	1 Oct 1963
Hawkinge	3 Oct 1923	Laarbruch (D)	22 Apr 1970
Northolt	12 Sep 1938		to date
Hawkinge	10 Oct 1938	Bruggen	7 Aug 1970
Northolt	22 Aug 1939	Wildenrath (D)	1 Feb 1971
Filton	15 Sep 1939		to date

Aircraft Equipment	Period of service	Representative Serial and Code	
Various (e.g. Maurice Farman, Caudron G.III, B.E.2c, Avro 504, Martinsyde G.100, Curtiss JN.4)			
	Sep 1915 – Jan 1916	–	
F.E.2b	Jan 1916 – May 1917	A784	
F.E.2d	Mar 1917 – Jun 1917	A6401	
D.H.4	Jun 1917 – Dec 1919	A7442	(B)
D.H.9A	Nov 1918 – Sep 1919	E9705	
Snipe	Feb 1920 – Nov 1924	F2485	
Grebe II	Oct 1924 – Jun 1929	J7372	
Siskin IIIA	May 1929 – Mar 1932	J9325	
Fury I	Feb 1932 – Nov 1936	K2057	
Fury II	Nov 1936 – Oct 1937	K7279	
Demon	Oct 1937 – Jun 1938	K4538	
Gladiator II	Jun 1938 – Jun 1939	K6149	
Blenheim IF	Dec 1938 – Jan 1941	L1200	(ZK-H)
Blenheim IVF	Aug 1939 – Nov 1939	N6194	
Beaufighter I	Oct 1940 – Jan 1943	X7587	(ZK-O)
Havoc I	Jul 1941 – Sep 1941	BD120	
Mosquito II	Oct 1942 – Feb 1944	DD782	
Mosquito VI	Sep 1943 – Feb 1945	PZ200	(ZK-A)
Mosquito XVII	Dec 1943 – Nov 1944	HK256	
Mosquito 30	Dec 1944 – Sep 1946	NT425	(ZK-H)
Mosquito NF.36	Sep 1946 – Nov 1951	RL123	(ZK-F)
Vampire FB.5	Feb 1951 – May 1952	VV678	
Vampire NF.10	Jul 1951 – Apr 1954	WP234	(B)
Meteor NF.12	Mar 1954 – Mar 1959	WS699	(C)
Meteor NF.14	Apr 1954 – Mar 1959	WS776	(K)
Javelin FAW.7	Mar 1959 – Jan 1961	XH909	(E)
Javelin FAW.9	Dec 1959 – Nov 1962	XH884	(C)
Bloodhound 1 and 2	Oct 1963 – date	–	

Blenheim IF, No.25 Squadron

No. 26 Squadron

Badge: A springbok's head couped
Motto: 'N Wagter in die Lug (A guard in the sky)

No.26 Squadron was formed at Netheravon on 8 October 1915 from personnel of the South African Flying Unit which had earlier been operating against the Germans in South West Africa. Equipped with B.E.s and Farmans, it left for East Africa in December 1915, arriving at Mombasa at the end of 1916. German forces based in Tanganyika posed a threat to British East Africa and No.26 had been sent to co-operate with Imperial troops in dispersing the enemy and occupying the German East African colonies. In February 1918, the need for the squadron had declined sufficiently for it to be despatched to the UK via Cape Town. On arrival at Blandford Camp in July 1918, the squadron was disbanded. Reforming was scheduled to take place at Chingford on 14 November 1918 but the Armistice forestalled this.

On 11 October 1927, No.26 reformed at Catterick as a single flight of Atlas army co-operation aircraft, a second flight being added on 1 September 1928. Audaxes were received in July 1933 which were, in turn, replaced by Hectors in August 1937. Re-equipment with Lysanders had been completed before the outbreak of World War Two and early in October 1939 the squadron moved to France as part of the Air Component of the BEF. Soon after the German invasion of Belgium in May 1940, the squadron was forced to evacuate its bases and moved to Lympne where it flew reconnaissance, bombing and supply missions over northern France. Coastal patrols began in June and training with the army occupied most of the squadron's time for the next

few years. Tomahawks began to arrive in February 1941 and Mustangs in January 1942, both types being intended to replace the obsolete Lysanders for tactical reconnaissance missions, the last Lysander leaving in May 1942. In October 1941, Tomahawks had begun to fly low-level ground-attack sorties over northern France but they lacked the performance required for operations of this nature and were replaced by Mustangs in January 1942.

Tactical reconnaissance and day intruder missions continued until July 1943, when the squadron moved first to Yorkshire and then in March 1944 to Scotland, a detachment being based in Ulster. In preparation for the landings in Normandy, No.26 trained in spotting for naval guns, a task it carried out on and after D-Day. For this role it had re-equipped with Spitfires but reverted to Mustangs in January 1945 for reconnaissance sorties over the Netherlands. In April, the squadron spent two weeks spotting for French warships bombarding German pockets of resistance near Bordeaux. No.26 was transferred to Germany in August 1945 where it was disbanded on 1 April 1946.

On the same day, No.41 Squadron at Wunstorf was re-numbered 26 Squadron and flew Spitfires and Tempests until re-equipped with Vampires in April 1949. In November 1953, the squadron converted to Sabres and remained a day fighter unit until disbanded on 15 September 1957. On 1 September 1958, No.26 was reformed with Hunters at Gutersloh as part of No.121 Wing but disbanded again on 30 December 1960.

Reformed at Odiham on 1 June 1962, No.26 became a helicopter squadron with Belvederes. Moving to Aden in 1963, it provided transport support for the army in the Radfan until the end of November 1965 when it was transferred to Singapore, being merged with No.66 Squadron at Seletar on 30 November 1965. On 3 February 1969, the Northern Communication Squadron detachment at Wyton was redesignated No.26 Squadron and provided communications aircraft for Training Command, until disbanded on 1 April 1976.

Squadron bases

Netheravon	8 Oct 1915	Gatwick	22 Jul 1941
Left for East Africa		Manston	22 Nov 1941
	23 Dec 1915	Gatwick	30 Nov 1941
Mombasa	31 Jan 1916	Weston Zoyland	7 Feb 1942
Mbuyini	1 Feb 1916	Gatwick	23 Feb 1942
Taveta	23 Mar 1916	Detling	12 Jan 1943
Mbuyini	28 Mar 1916	Stoney Cross	27 Feb 1943
Kahe	22 May 1916	East Manton	10 Mar 1943
Marago Opuni	27 May 1916	Red Barn	11 Mar 1943
Old Lassiti	29 May 1916	Stoney Cross	13 Mar 1943
Kwa Lokua	2 Jun 1916	Gatwick	7 Apr 1943
Mbagui	18 Jun 1916	Detling	21 Jun 1943
Dakawa	18 Aug 1916	Martlesham Heath	11 Jul 1943
Morogoro	31 Aug 1916	Detling	16 Jul 1943
Tulo	5 Oct 1916	Ballyhalbert (D)	19 Jul 1943
Kilwa	19 Dec 1916		to 3 Mar 1944
Songea	16 Mar 1917	Church Fenton	21 Jul 1943
Likuju	16 May 1917	Hutton Cranswick	28 Dec 1943
Mtua	13 Oct 1917	Scorton	12 Feb 1944
Dar-es-Salaam	Jan 1918	Hutton Cranswick	28 Feb 1944
Left for South Africa		Peterhead	30 Mar 1944
	8 Feb 1918	Dundonald	10 Apr 1944
Cape Town	4 Mar 1918	Ayr	21 Apr 1944
Left for UK	Jun 1918	Hutton Cranswick	26 Apr 1944
Blandford	8 Jul 1918	Lee-on-Solent	28 Apr 1944
Catterick	11 Oct 1927	Hawkinge	6 Oct 1944
Abbeville/Drucat	8 Oct 1939	Tangmere	10 Oct 1944
Dieppe	Apr 1940	Manston	1 Nov 1944
Authie	15 May 1940	Tangmere	4 Nov 1944
Lympne	19 May 1940	Exeter	8 Dec 1944
West Malling	8 Jun 1940	Harrowbeer	14 Jan 1945
Gatwick	3 Sep 1940	North Weald	21 Jan 1945
Weston Zoyland	14 Jul 1941	Harrowbeer	3 Apr 1945
Leconfield	18 Jul 1941	Cognac	13 Apr 1945

Atlas I, No.26 Squadron

Harrowbeer	1 May 1945	Gutersloh	19 Nov 1947
Chilbolton	23 May 1945	Wunstorf	7 Jan 1950
Brussels	18 Aug 1945	Oldenburg	Aug 1952
B.164 Schleswig	20 Aug 1945		to 15 Sep 1957
B.158 Lubeck	7 Sep 1945	Gutersloh	1 Sep 1958
B.170 Sylt	8 Dec 1945		to 30 Dec 1960
B.158 Lubeck	24 Dec 1945	Odiham	1 Jun 1962
	to 1 Apr 1946	Khormaksar	Feb 1963
Wunstorf	1 Apr 1946	Left for Far East	Nov 1965
Fassberg	13 Apr 1946	Absorbed	30 Nov 1965
Chivenor	Sep 1946	Wyton	3 Feb 1969
Fassberg	Nov 1946		to 1 Apr 1976

Aircraft

Equipment	Period of service	Representative Serial and Code
B.E.2c, B.E.2e	Feb 1916 – Jan 1918	8424
Henry Farman	Feb 1916 – Jan 1918	3619
Atlas	Oct 1927 – Sep 1933	J9043
Audax	Jul 1933 – Sep 1937	K3091
Hector	Aug 1937 – May 1939	K9730
Lysander I,II	Feb 1939 – May 1942	L4775
Tomahawk IIA	Feb 1941 – Jan 1943	AH791 (RM-E)
Mustang I	Jan 1942 – Mar 1944	AM171
	Dec 1944 – Jun 1945	
Spitfire VA, VB, VC	Mar 1944 – Jan 1945	W3432
Spitfire XI	Oct 1945 – Apr 1946	PL892
Spitfire XIV	Jun 1945 – Jan 1947	NH747
Tempest F.2	Jan 1947 – Apr 1949	PR782 (XC-Q)
Vampire FB.5	Apr 1949 – Aug 1952	VV531 (XC-N)
Vampire FB.9	Jun 1952 – Nov 1953	WR157
Sabre F.1/F.4	Nov 1953 – Jun 1955	XB767 (Y)
Hunter F.4	Jun 1955 – Sep 1957	WT769 (B)
Hunter F.6	Jun 1958 – Dec 1960	XE535 (F)
Belvedere HC.1	Jun 1962 – Nov 1965	XG458 (E)
Basset CC.1	Feb 1969 – Apr 1976	XS768

Tomahawk Is, No.26 Squadron

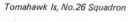

No. 27 Squadron

Badge: An elephant
Motto: Quam celerrime ad astra
(With all speed to the
stars)

No.27 Squadron was formed on 5 November 1915 at Hounslow Heath as a scout squadron and moved to France in March 1916 with Martinsyde Elephants. As these proved to lack agility the squadron began to use this type for bombing and reconnaissance behind the enemy lines and in the autumn of 1917 re-equipped with D.H.4s. These were used for the rest of the war but replacement by D.H.9s began in September. In March 1919 the squadron returned to the UK and disbanded on 22 January 1920.

On 1 April 1920, No.99 Squadron at Mianwali was renumbered 27 Squadron which then flew D.H.9As on patrols over the North-West Frontier of India. Wapitis were received as replacements in May 1930 and were in service until the outbreak of World War Two. The squadron was then designated a training unit and received Harts and Tiger Moths for this role, being brought to operational status again on 21 October 1940 with Blenheim fighters. These it took to Malaya in February 1941 where it lost most of its aircraft on the ground during the Japanese invasion. After withdrawing to Sumatra in January 1942, it became dispersed during further Japanese landings and ceased to exist early in February.

On 19 September 1942, No.27 reformed at Amarda Road as a Beaufighter squadron, receiving its first aircraft in November. Attacks on general targets in Burma began on 25 December and continued until the squadron converted to Mosquitos at the end of 1943. This was not completed before No.27 was allotted rocket-armed Beaufighters as part of a strike wing consisting of Nos.27 and 47 Squadrons. As there were few suitable maritime targets by this time, the squadron returned to ground-attack duties over Burma in November 1944. In April 1945 it was diverted to air-jungle rescue, a similar task to that of the air-sea rescue units except that No.27's searches were over the jungles of South-East Asia. On 1 February 1946, the squadron was disbanded.

On 24 November 1947, No.27 reformed at Oakington as a transport squadron, flying Dakotas as part of No.46 Group during the Berlin Airlift before disbanding on 10 November 1950.

The squadron was again reformed, this time as a Canberra unit at Scampton on 15 June 1953. After taking part in the Suez campaign from Cyprus, No.27 disbanded on 31 December 1956. On 1 April 1961 it reformed at Scampton with Vulcans as part of the first wing to use Blue Steel stand-off bombs, being disbanded on 29 March 1972.

On 1 November 1973, No.27 reformed at Waddington for strategic reconnaissance duties with Vulcans.

Squadron bases			
Hounslow Heath	5 Nov 1915	Kallang	17 Feb 1941
Dover	Dec 1915	Butterworth	17 May 1941
St. Omer	1 Mar 1916	Sungei Patani	21 Aug 1941
Treizennes	2 Mar 1916	Butterworth	10 Dec 1941
St André-aux-Bois	7 Jun 1916	Kallang	12 Dec 1941
Fienvillers	19 Jun 1916	Palembang	23 Jan 1942
Clairmarais	31 May 1917		to Feb 1942
Serny	12 Oct 1917	Amarda Road	19 Sep 1942
Villers-Brettoneux	7 Mar 1918	Kanchrapara	9 Jan 1943
Beauvois	24 May 1918	Agartala	11 Feb 1943
Ruisseauville	29 Mar 1918	Parashuram	9 Feb 1944
Fourneuil	3 Jun 1918	Cholavarum	30 Mar 1944
Ruisseauville	21 Jun 1918	Ranchi	23 Sep 1944
Chailly	15 Jul 1918	Agartala	21 Oct 1944
Beauvois	6 Aug 1918	Dohazari	5 Nov 1944
Villers-lez-Cagnicourt		Chiringa	19 Nov 1944
	29 Oct 1918	Akyab	19 Jun 1945
Bavay	28 Nov 1918	Mingaladon	12 Oct 1945
Shotwick	Mar 1919		to 1 Feb 1946
	to 22 Jan 1920	Oakington	24 Nov 1947
Mianwali	1 Apr 1920	Wunstorf	9 Jul 1948
Risalpur	15 Apr 1920	Fassberg	19 Jul 1948
Dardoni	14 Dec 1922	Oakington	1 Sep 1948
Risalpur	20 Apr 1923	Netheravon	10 Jun 1950
Peshawar	26 May 1925		to 1 Nov 1950
Risalpur	12 Oct 1925	Scampton	15 Jun 1953
Kohat	17 Dec 1928	Waddington	26 May 1955
Tengah	31 Jan 1937		to 31 Dec 1956
Kohat	14 Feb 1937	Scampton	1 Apr 1961
Risalpur	25 Sep 1939		to 29 Mar 1972
		Waddington	1 Nov 1973

Aircraft Equipment	Period of service	Representative Serial and Code
Martinsyde G.100	Dec 1915 – Nov 1917	A6263 (A5)
D.H.4	Sep 1917 – Nov 1918	A7842 (E)
D.H.9	May 1918 – Mar 1919	D3163
D.H.9A	Apr 1920 – May 1930	J7057 (K)
Wapiti IIA	May 1930 – Oct 1940	K1299 (A)
Hart	Oct 1939 – Oct 1940	K2085
Tiger Moth	Oct 1939 – Oct 1940	T1778
Blenheim IF	Nov 1940 – Jan 1942	L8507
Beaufighter VI	Nov 1942 – Mar 1944	EL449 (C)
Beaufighter X	Mar 1944 – Feb 1946	KW404 (T)
Mosquito II	Apr 1943 – Mar 1944	DZ695 (V)
Mosquito VI	Dec 1943 – Mar 1944	HJ811 (J)
Dakota C.4	Nov 1947 – Nov 1950	KN361 (D)
Canberra B.2	Jun 1953 – Dec 1956	WH733
Vulcan B.2	Apr 1961 – Mar 1972	XL445
Vulcan SR.2	Nov 1973 – date	XH537

No. 28 Squadron

Badge: In front of a demi-pegasus, a fasces
Motto: Quicquid agas age
(Whatsoever you may do, do)

No.28 Squadron was formed at Gosport on 7 November 1915, where it spent eighteen months as a training unit. In September 1917 it was mobilised as a fighter squadron and moved to France with Camels in October. Before it could begin operations over the Western Front, however, it was sent

Lysander II, No.28 Squadron

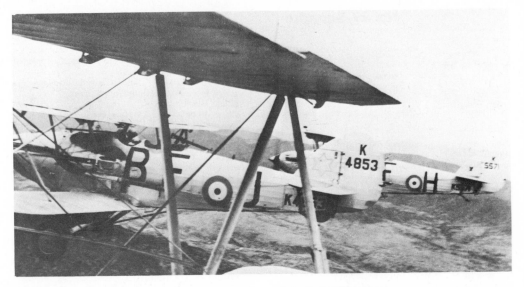

to Italy as part of an Anglo-French ground and air force despatched to aid the Italians after the Battle of Caporetto. For the rest of the war, it flew offensive patrols over the front in north-east Italy before the Austro-Hungarian Empire collapsed. In February 1919, it returned to the UK and disbanded on 20 January 1920.

On 1 April 1920, No.114 Squadron at Ambala became No.28 and flew Bristol Fighters on internal security duties on the North-West Frontier. These continued until the outbreak of war, Wapitis being received in September 1931 and Audaxes in June 1936. In September 1941 the squadron began to re-equip with Lysanders which it took to Burma when the Japanese attacked in December 1941. Bombing raids and army co-operation missions were carried out in the face of strong enemy opposition until Burma was over-run. Reforming at Lahore in March 1942, No.28 took part in army exercises until December 1942, when it converted to Hurricanes for tactical reconnaissance duties. Operations over Burma began in January 1943 and continued until the Japanese surrender, re-equipment with Spitfires beginning in July 1945. In November 1945, No.28 moved to Malaya and in May 1949, to Hong Kong to strengthen its defences in view of the civil war in China. Vampires were received in January 1951 and these were replaced by Venoms in February 1956. Ground-attack Hunters arrived in July 1962 and were flown until the squadron disbanded on 2 January 1967.

On 1 April 1968 No.28 reformed at Kai Tak from a detachment of Whirlwind helicopters of No.103 Squadron for transport support and search and rescue duties at Hong Kong.

Squadron bases			
Gosport	7 Nov 1915	Ambala	1 Apr 1920
Yatesbury	23 Jul 1917	Kohat	15 Oct 1921
St. Omer	8 Oct 1917	Parachinar	15 Apr 1922
Droglandt	10 Oct 1917	Kohat	10 Oct 1922
Milan	9 Nov 1917	Dardoni	12 Dec 1922
Brescia/Ghedi	17 Nov 1917	Tank	17 Mar 1923
Verona	22 Nov 1917	Peshawar	19 Apr 1923
Grossa	28 Nov 1917	Quetta	5 Jan 1925
Sarcedo	20 Aug 1918	Ambala	15 Dec 1926
Treviso	22 Oct 1918	Kohat	27 Feb 1939
Sarcedo	5 Nov 1918	Lashio	28 Jan 1942
Yatesbury	Feb 1919	Magwe	8 Feb 1942
Leighterton	Jun 1919	Asansol	6 Mar 1942
Eastleigh	Oct 1919	Lahore	7 Mar 1942
	to 20 Jan 1920	Ranchi	3 Apr 1942
		Kohat	17 Apr 1942

Audax Is, No.28 Squadron

Ranchi	31 Aug 1942	Penang	Nov 1945
Dets. on Burma front		Kuala Lumpur	Apr 1946
	7 Jan 1943	Tengah	Feb 1947
	to 29 Oct 1943	Sembawang	26 Jan 1948
Imphal	29 Oct 1943	Kai Tak	11 May 1949
Dalbhumgarh	17 Jun 1944	Sek Kong	1 May 1950
Ranchi	2 Aug 1944	Kai Tak	Oct 1950
Dalbhumgarh	2 Oct 1944	Sek Kong	Mar 1951
Tamu	9 Dec 1944	Kai Tak	15 Aug 1955
Kaleymo	11 Jan 1945	Sek Kong	5 Dec 1955
Ye-U	29 Jan 1945	Kai Tak	Jun 1957
Sadaung	11 Feb 1945		to 31 Dec 1966
Meiktila	8 Apr 1945	Kai Tak	1 Apr 1968
Mingaladon	22 May 1945	Sek Kong	30 Jun 1978

Aircraft Equipment	Period of service	Representative Serial and Code
F.E.2b	Nov 1915 – Sep 1917	
Camel	Sep 1917 – Feb 1919	D8239 (R)
Bristol F.2b	Apr 1920 – Sep 1931	F4630
Wapiti IIA	Sep 1931 – Jun 1936	K1272 (S)
Audax	Jun 1936 – Jan 1942	K5210
Lysander II	Sep 1941 – Dec 1942	R2026
Hurricane IIB	Dec 1942 – Dec 1944	BW938
Hurricane IIC	Mar 1944 – Oct 1945	LD172
Spitfire IX	Jul 1945 – Oct 1945	
Spitfire VIII	Oct 1945 – Oct 1945	
Spitfire XIV	Oct 1945 – Feb 1947	SM888 (B)
Spitfire FR.18	Feb 1947 – Feb 1951	TP423 (A)
Vampire FB.5	Feb 1951 – Apr 1952	WA252
Vampire FB.9	Feb 1952 – Jul 1956	WP990 (A)
Venom FB.1	Feb 1956 – Nov 1959	WR299 (A)
Venom FB.4	Nov 1959 – Jul 1962	WR540 (E)
Hunter FGA.9	May 1962 – Jan 1967	XE535 (C)
Whirlwind HAR.10	Apr 1968 – Aug 1972	XP363 (D)
Wessex HC.2	Jan 1972 – date	XR500 (A)

Venom FB.4, No.28 Squadron

S.E.5As, No.29 Squadron

No. 29 Squadron

Badge: An eagle in flight, preying on a buzzard

Motto: Impiger et acer (Energetic and keen)

No.29 Squadron was formed at Gosport on 7 November 1915 from a nucleus supplied by No.23 Squadron and after training moved to France in March 1916 as the third squadron to be fully equipped with fighters. Its D.H.2s were engaged in escort duties to protect the slow and vulnerable reconnaissance aircraft over the Western Front and in March 1917, it re-equipped with Nieuport Scouts. In April 1918 these were replaced by S.E.5As which were used for the rest of the war on fighter and ground attack missions. After a short period in Germany, the squadron was reduced to a cadre and returned to the UK in August 1919 where it was disbanded on 31 December 1919.

On 1 April 1923, No.29 reformed as a fighter squadron at Duxford with Snipes, re-equipping with Grebes in January 1925. In turn, these were replaced by Siskins in March 1928 and Bulldogs in June 1932. In March 1935 No.29 became a two-seat fighter squadron with the arrival of Demons which it took in October to Egypt during the Abyssinian crisis, a few Gordons being used for night patrols at this time. Returning to the UK a year later, it converted to Blenheims in December 1938. On the outbreak of World War Two these were used for patrols over shipping and early trials with airborne radar. When German night bombers began operating in strength in June 1940 No.29 became fully involved in night fighting, beginning to receive Beaufighters in November though it was February 1941 before the squadron was fully equipped. Its defensive role remained after conversion to Mosquitos in May 1943 but in May 1944 intruder missions began to be flown which continued until February 1945. Conversion to Mosquito 30s began but few operations were flown before the end of the war. In October 1945 the squadron moved to West Malling to become part of the peace-time night fighter force in the UK.

The Mosquitos continued to serve until replaced by Meteors in August 1951 at Tangmere. In January 1957 the squadron moved north, first to Northumberland and in July

Phantom FGR.2, No.29 Squadron

1958 to Scotland, conversion to Javelins taking place in November 1957. In February 1963 No.29 was moved to Cyprus and in December 1965 went to Zambia for nine months on detachment. In May 1967 the squadron returned to the UK to become a Lightning squadron, disbanding on 19 July 1974. No.29 reformed at Coningsby as a Phantom squadron on 31 December 1974.

Squadron bases			
Gosport	7 Nov 1915	North Weald	12 Sep 1936
St. Omer	25 Mar 1916	Debden	22 Nov 1937
Abeele	15 Apr 1916	Drem	4 Apr 1940
Izel-le-Hameau	23 Oct 1916	Debden	10 May 1940
Poperinghe	5 Jul 1917	Digby	Jun 1940
La Lovie	16 Feb 1918	Wellingore	8 Jul 1940
Teteghem	11 Apr 1918	West Malling	27 Apr 1941
St. Omer	22 Apr 1918	Bradwell Bay	13 May 1943
Vignacourt	11 Jun 1918	Ford	3 Sep 1943
St. Omer	22 Jul 1918	Drem	29 Feb 1944
Hoog Huis	1 Aug 1918	West Malling	1 May 1944
La Lovie	25 Sep 1918	Hunsdon	19 Jun 1944
Hoog Huis	5 Oct 1918	Colerne	22 Feb 1945
Marcke	23 Oct 1918	Manston	11 May 1945
Nivelles	26 Nov 1918	West Malling	29 Oct 1945
Bickendorf	19 Dec 1918	Tangmere	30 Nov 1950
Spittlegate	10 Aug 1919	Acklington	14 Jan 1957
	to 31 Dec 1919	Leuchars	22 Jul 1958
Duxford	1 Apr 1923	Nicosia	28 Feb 1963
North Weald	1 Apr 1928	Akrotiri	16 Mar 1964
Left for Egypt	4 Oct 1935	Ndola	3 Dec 1965
Amriya	31 Oct 1935	Akrotiri	1 Sep 1966
Helwan	20 Jul 1936	Wattisham	10 May 1967
Aboukir	6 Aug 1936		to 19 Jul 1974
		Coningsby	31 Dec 1974

Aircraft Equipment	Period of service	Representative Serial and Code	
Maurice Farman	Nov 1915 – Mar 1916	2947	
Avro 504A	Nov 1915 – Mar 1916	4768	
Caudron G.III	Nov 1915 – Mar 1916		
B.E.2b	Feb 1916 – Mar 1916	2886	
B.E.2c	Dec 1915 – Mar 1916	2065	
D.H.2	Mar 1916 – Mar 1917	A2614	
F.E.8	Jun 1916 – Aug 1916	6383	
Nieuport 17 and 27	Mar 1917 – Apr 1918	B1515	
S.E.5A	Apr 1918 – Aug 1919	F899	(C)
Snipe	Apr 1923 – Jan 1925		
Grebe II	Jan 1925 – Mar 1928	J7390	
Siskin IIIA	Mar 1928 – Jun 1932	J8946	
Bulldog IIA	Jun 1932 – Apr 1935	K2866	
Demon	Mar 1935 – Aug 1936	K5898	
	Oct 1936 – Dec 1938		
Gordon	Mar 1936 – Aug 1936		
Blenheim IF	Dec 1938 – Feb 1941	L1503	(YB–E)
Hurricane I	Aug 1940 – Dec 1940	P3201	
Beaufighter I	Nov 1940 – Jun 1943	T4646	(RO-G)
Beaufighter VI	Mar 1943 – May 1943	V8324	(RO-B)
Mosquito XII	May 1943 – Apr 1944	HK129	(RO-G)
Mosquito XIII	Oct 1943 – Feb 1945	MM463	(RO-J)
Mosquito VI	Jul 1943 – Aug 1943	HP852	
Mosquito NF.30	Feb 1945 – Aug 1946	MT490	(RO-O)
	Oct 1950 – Aug 1951	NT609	(RO-S)
Mosquito NF.36	Aug 1946 – Oct 1950	RL175	(RO-P)
Meteor NF.11	Aug 1951 – Nov 1957	WD722	(E)
Meteor NF.12	Feb 1958 – Jul 1958	WS593	
Javelin FAW.6	Nov 1957 – May 1961	XA825	(K)
Javelin FAW.9	Apr 1961 – May 1967	XH848	(L)
Lightning F.3	May 1967 – Jul 1974	XP707	(H)
Phantom FGR.2	Dec 1974 – date	XV420	(H)

No. 30 Squadron

Badge: A date palm tree
Motto: Ventre a terre (All out)

Hardy Is, No.30 Squadron

No.30 Squadron was formed at Farnborough during October 1914 in preparation for service in Egypt but did not adopt its number until 24 March 1915. After arrival, the unit flew reconnaissance flights along the Suez canal which was being threatened by Turkish forces and during April 1915 a second flight was formed at Bombay to defend the oil pipeline from Abadan to Basra. As British and Indian forces built up in Mesopotamia, this detachment provided reconnaissance aircraft and was joined by the remainder of the squadron from Egypt at the beginning of 1916, having become part of No.30 on 5 August 1915. During April 1916, the squadron flew one of the first air supply operations when it dropped supplies to the besieged garrison of Kut-el-Amara. Reconnaissance and bombing occupied No.30 for the rest of the war, small numbers of fighters and bombers supplementing the squadron's B.E.s until the Turkish surrender and in April 1919 it was reduced to a cadre at Baghdad.

Responsibility for the security of the new kingdom of Iraq was given to the RAF and on 1 February 1920 No.30 was brought up to strength and became one of the permanent squadrons in Iraq. D.H.9As were flown until 1929 when they were replaced by Wapitis. Hardys began to arrive in April 1935 and Blenheims in January 1938, the latter being taken to Egypt a few days before the outbreak of World War Two. When Italy entered the war in June 1940, the Blenheims

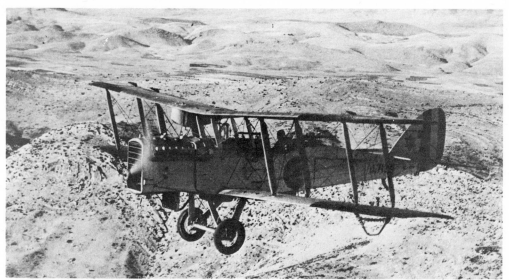
D.H.9A, No.30 Squadron

were fitted with gun-trays and flew escort missions over the Western Desert and provided air defence for Alexandria. After the Italian invasion of Greece, No.30 moved there and attacked enemy bases in Albania, being officially designated a fighter squadron in March 1941. After a short period in Crete in April, the squadron was forced to retire to Egypt where it re-equipped with Hurricanes. These were used for night air defence of Alexandria until December when operations in the Western Desert began.

The squadron was embarked on the carrier *Indomitable* and flown off to reinforce Ceylon early in March 1942 in time to counter Japanese carrier-borne air attacks on Colombo and Trincomalee but no further raids took place and No.30 remained on air defence duties until February 1944. It was then transferred to the Burma front and flew escort and ground-attack missions until May when it was withdrawn for re-equipment with Thunderbolts. Operations were resumed on 15 October and continued until 13 May 1945, the squadron being withdrawn for rest. When the Japanese surrendered, No.30 remained in India and converted to Tempests in June 1946, disbanding on 1 December 1946.

On 24 November 1947, No.30 was reformed at Oakington as a transport squadron. Its Dakotas took part in the Berlin Airlift before being replaced by Valettas in November 1950. Beverleys were received in April 1957 and were taken to Kenya in November 1959, before moving to Bahrain in 1964. On 6 September 1967, the squadron was disbanded. No.30 reformed at Fairford on 10 June 1968 as a Hercules squadron in Air Support Command.

Squadron bases

Farnborough	Oct 1914	Hinaidi	3 Dec 1922
Left for Egypt	4 Nov 1914	Kirkuk	19 May 1924 (A)
Ismailia	20 Nov 1914	Hinaidi	Nov 1927
		Mosul	25 Oct 1929
LG.05	16 Nov 1941	Vizagapatam	3 Jul 1945
LG.121	23 Jan 1942	Zayatkwin	24 Sep 1945 (A)
Emb. in Indomitable		Vizagapatam	29 Sep 1945
	25 Feb 1942	Baigachi	4 Dec 1945
Ratmalana	6 Mar 1942	Bhopal	Mar 1946
Dambulla	31 Aug 1942	Agra	Jun 1946
Colombo	15 Feb 1943		to 1 Dec 1946
Dambulla	3 Aug 1943	Oakington	24 Nov 1947
Feni	23 Jan 1944	Abingdon	21 Nov 1950
Fazilpur	12 Feb 1944		15 Dec 1950 (C)
Comilla	9 Apr 1944	Benson	2 May 1952
Yelahanka	25 Apr 1944	Dishforth	Apr 1953 (P)
Arkonam	13 Sep 1944	Eastleigh	15 Nov 1959
Chittagong	5 Oct 1944	Muharraq	1 Sep 1964
Jumchar	10 Dec 1944		to 6 Sep 1967
Akyab Main	24 Apr 1945	Fairford	10 Jun 1968
Chakulia	18 May 1945	Lyneham	24 Sep 1971 (C)

Aircraft Equipment	Period of service	Representative Serial and Code
Maurice Farman	Nov 1914 – Oct 1916	712
Henry Farman	Nov 1914 – May 1917	
B.E.2a	Nov 1914 – 1915	
B.E.2c	Dec 1914 – Feb 1918	4500
B.E.2e	May 1917 – Feb 1918	
Voisin	May 1915 – Nov 1916	8523
Martinsyde S.1	Sep 1916 – Nov 1917	4244
Bristol Scout	May 1917 – Oct 1917	
Spad VII	Sep 1917 – May 1918	A8806
R.E.8	Oct 1917 – Apr 1919	A4357
Vickers F.B.19	Nov 1917	
D.H.4	Dec 1917 – Jan 1918	A7621
Martinsyde G.100	Dec 1918 – Feb 1919	7467
S.E.5A	Jan 1919 – Feb 1919	
R.E.8	Feb 1920 – Jan 1921	
D.H.9A	Jan 1921 – Sep 1929	E8512
Wapiti IIA	Apr 1929 – Aug 1935	J9409
Hardy	Apr 1935 – Jan 1938	K4054
Blenheim I, IF	Jan 1938 – May 1941	K7178 (P)

Bristol F.2B, No.31 Squadron

No. 31 Squadron

Badge: In front of a wreath of laurel, a mullet
Motto: In caelum indicum primus (First into Indian skies)

No.31 Squadron was formed at Farnborough on 11 October 1915 and was intended for service in India. A Flight left on 27 November and arrived at Risalpur on 26 December. Two more flights were formed at Gosport in January and April 1916 and by the end of May the squadron was complete. For the rest of the war, No.31 co-operated with the Indian Army on the North-West Frontier of India and in 1919 re-equipped with Bristol Fighters. These remained in service until replaced by Wapitis in February 1931 and in July 1935 No.31 received Vincents. On 1 April 1939, the squadron's role was changed from army co-operation to bomber-transport, the Bomber-Transport Flight, India, being absorbed. Conversion to Valentias had begun in January and these were replaced by DC-2s during 1941, both types being used to carry troops during the Iraqi uprising. During the Japanese invasion of Burma, the squadron evacuated casualties and flew supplies to the small army force retreating to the Indian frontier and in April 1942 Dakotas began to replace the older DC-2s. In May 1943 No.31 was fully equipped with Dakotas and for the rest of the war was engaged in

India occupied the squadron until it was again disbanded on 31 December 1947. On 19 July 1948, the Metropolitan Communications Squadron at Hendon was redesignated 31 Squadron but reverted to its former title on 1 March 1955. On the same day, the squadron reformed at Laarbruch with Canberras for photographic reconnaissance duties in Germany, disbanding on 31 March 1971. No.31 reformed at Bruggen with Phantoms on 7 October 1971 and became operational with Jaguars on 1 July 1976.

Squadron bases

Farnborough	11 Oct 1915	Khargpur	21 May 1943
Left for India	27 Nov 1915	Agartala	12 Feb 1944
Nowshera	29 Dec 1915	Basal	11 Jul 1944
Risalpur	1 Mar 1916	Agartala	1 Nov 1944
Murree	29 Jul 1916	Comilla	1 Jan 1945
Risalpur	5 Oct 1916	Hathazari	6 Feb 1945
Mhow	15 Apr 1920	Kyaukpyu	15 May 1945
Cawnpore	26 Nov 1920	Mingaladon	Aug 1945 (P)
Peshawar	19 Oct 1921	Kallang	1 Oct 1945
Dardoni	17 Apr 1923	Kemajoran	1 Nov 1945
Ambala	13 Mar 1924		to 30 Sep 1946
Quetta	15 Dec 1926	Mauripur	1 Nov 1946
Drigh Road	8 Jun 1935	Palam	1 Sep 1947
Lahore	27 Oct 1938	Mauripur	6 Nov 1947
Peshawar	Dec 1939		to 31 Dec 1947
Lahore	Feb 1941	Hendon	19 Jul 1948
Drigh Road	26 Mar 1941		to 1 Mar 1955
Lahore	Sep 1941	Laarbruch	1 Mar 1955
Dhubalia	18 Feb 1943		to 31 Mar 1971
		Bruggen	7 Oct 1971

Aircraft Equipment

	Period of service	Representative Serial and Code
B.E.2c, B.E.2e	Jan 1916 − Feb 1920	4131 (B2)
Henry Farman	Jan 1916 − 1918	
Bristol F.2b	1919 − Apr 1931	E2297
Wapiti IIA	Feb 1931 − Aug 1939	J9388
Valentia	Apr 1939 − Sep 1941	K3612
DC-2X	Apr 1941 − May 1943	LR252 (E)

Siskin IIIA, No.32 Squadron

Bulldog IIA, No.32 Squadron

No. 32 Squadron

Badge: A hunting horn stringed
Motto: Adeste comites (Rally round, comrades)

No.32 Squadron was formed on 12 January 1916 at Netheravon and moved to France as a fighter squadron in May 1916. Equipped with D.H.2s, it flew patrols over the Western Front for a year before beginning to re-equip with D.H.5s. These in turn began to be replaced by S.E.5As in December 1917 which were flown for the rest of the war on fighter and ground-attack missions. In March 1919, the squadron returned to the UK as a cadre and disbanded on 29 December 1919.

No.32 reformed on 1 April 1923 at Kenley as a single flight of Snipe fighters. A second flight was formed on 10 December 1923 and a third brought the squadron up to strength on 1 June 1924. Grebes were received at the end of 1924 and were replaced by Gamecocks two years later. Equipped in succession with Siskins, Bulldogs and Gauntlets, No.32 received Hurricanes in October 1938 and these were flown on defensive patrols when World War Two broke out. In May 1940, the squadron flew patrols over northern France

and took part in the defence of south-east England during the opening weeks of the Battle of Britain before moving to northern England at the end of August 1940. Returning south in December No.32 flew defensive missions until beginning night training in May 1942. Intruder sorties began in July but in September the squadron became non-operational for the invasion of North Africa. Arriving in Algeria in December 1942, it flew covering patrols over coastal convoys and ports until the end of the campaign. Conversion to Spitfires was completed in August 1943 and these were taken to Italy in October for a short period, returning to North Africa until January 1944 when the squadron again moved to Italy. Fighter-bomber and escort missions occupied No.32 until October 1944 when it moved to Greece in the wake of the German withdrawal. In February 1945, the squadron was transferred to Palestine, remaining in the Middle East after the end of the war.

In May 1948, No.32 moved to Cyprus and converted to Vampires in March 1949, returning to Egypt in January 1951. Re-equipment with Venoms was completed in January 1955 when the squadron moved to the Persian Gulf for nine months before being transferred to Malta. After a short period in Jordan, No.32 converted to Canberras at Weston Zoyland in January 1957 and flew these from Cyprus until disbanded on 3 February 1969. On the same day, the Metropolitan Communications Squadron at Northolt was redesignated No.32 Squadron. Equipped with light transports and helicopters, it is engaged in communications duties.

Canberra B.2, No.32 Squadron

Squadron bases

Netheravon	12 Jan 1916	West Malling	4 May 1942	Amman	Aug 1956
St. Omer	28 May 1916	Friston	14 Jun 1942	Mafraq	Oct 1956
Auchel	4 Jun 1916	West Malling	7 Jul 1942	Nicosia	Feb 1957
Treizennes	7 Jun 1916	Friston	14 Aug 1942		
Vert Galand	21 Jul 1916	West Malling	20 Aug 1942		
Lealvilliers	25 Oct 1916	Honiley	9 Sep 1942		
Abeele	3 Jul 1917	Baginton	18 Oct 1942		
Droglandt	8 Jul 1917	Left for N. Africa			
Bailleul	5 Mar 1918		25 Nov 1942		
Bellevue Farm	27 Mar 1918	Philippeville	7 Dec 1942 (G)		
Beauvois	29 Mar 1918	Maison Blanche			
Fouquerolles	3 Jun 1918		17 Dec 1942 (A)		
Ruisseauville	21 Jun 1918		10 Feb 1943 (G)		
Le Touquin	14 Jul 1918	Tingley	25 May 1943		
La Bellevue	3 Aug 1918	La Sebala	19 Aug 1943		
Bronville	27 Oct 1918	Montecorvino	1 Oct 1943 (D)		
La Brayelle	1 Nov 1918		28 Oct 1943 (C)		
Izel-le-Hameau	16 Nov 1918	Reghaia	20 Nov 1943		
Serny	18 Jan 1919	Foggia Main	31 Jan 1944		
Tangmere	4 Mar 1919	Canne	14 Jul 1944		
Croydon	Oct 1919	Brindisi	23 Sep 1944		
	to 29 Dec 1919	Araxos (D)	2 Oct 1944		
Kenley	1 Apr 1923		to 17 Oct 1944		
Bircham Newton	30 Jun 1924	San Pancrazio	15 Oct 1944		
Kenley	5 Aug 1924	Kalamaki	17 Oct 1944		
Biggin Hill	21 Sep 1932	Salonika/Sedes	9 Nov 1944		
Gravesend	3 Jan 1940	Ramat David	25 Feb 1945 (A)		
Manston	8 Mar 1940		12 Mar 1945 (G)		
Gravesend	22 Mar 1940	Petah Tiqva	27 Sep 1945		
Biggin Hill	27 Mar 1940	Aqir	Mar 1946		
Wittering	26 May 1940	Ramat David	Jun 1946		
Biggin Hill	4 Jun 1940	Ein Shemer	Oct 1946		
Acklington	28 Aug 1940	Nicosia	25 May 1948		
Middle Wallop	15 Dec 1940	Shallufa	Jan 1951		
Ibsley	16 Feb 1941	Deversoir	27 Jan 1952		
Pembrey	17 Apr 1941	Kabrit	15 Sep 1954		
Angle	1 Jun 1941	Shaibah	14 Jan 1955		
Manston	26 Nov 1941	Takali	15 Oct 1955		

Amman	Aug 1956	Akrotiri	10 Mar 1957 to 3 Feb 1969
Mafraq	Oct 1956		
Nicosia	Feb 1957	Northolt	3 Feb 1969

Aircraft Equipment

Aircraft	Period of service	Representative Serial
Henry Farman	Jan 1916 – May 1916	
Vickers F.B.5	Jan 1916 – May 1916	
D.H.2	Feb 1916 – Jul 1917	6015
D.H.5	May 1917 – Mar 1918	A9258 (B2)
S.E.5A	Dec 1917 – Mar 1919	B166 (A)
Snipe	Apr 1923 – Dec 1924	E6268
Grebe II	Nov 1924 – Feb 1927	J7399
Gamecock II	Sep 1926 – Apr 1928	J8081
Siskin IIIA	Apr 1928 – Jan 1931	J9338
Bulldog IIA	Sep 1930 – Jul 1936	K1623
Gauntlet II	Jul 1936 – Oct 1938	K5321
Hurricane I	Oct 1938 – Jul 1941	L1699 (KT-G)
Hurricane IIB	Jul 1941 – Nov 1942	BE213
Hurricane IIC	Nov 1941 – Aug 1943	HL859 (GZ-F)
Spitfire VC	Apr 1943 – Nov 1943 / May 1944 – Sep 1945	JK193
Spitfire IX	Jun 1943 – Jul 1944 / Nov 1944 – Jun 1947	MA802 (GZ-D)
Spitfire VIII	Dec 1943 – Jul 1944	JF566
Spitfire F.18	Jun 1947 – May 1949	TP373 (GZ-C)
Vampire F.3	Mar 1949 – Jan 1951	VT859 (X)
Vampire FB.5	Jan 1951 – Sep 1954	VZ234 (S)
Vampire FB.9	Apr 1952 – Jan 1955	WL583 (T)
Venom FB.1	Sep 1954 – Jan 1957	WR276 (G)
Canberra B.2	Jan 1957 – Mar 1962	WK111
Canberra B.15	Jul 1961 – Feb 1969	WH947
Basset CC.1	Feb 1969 – Jan 1975	XS769
Sycamore HC.14	Feb 1969 – Aug 1972	XJ918
Andover CC.2	Feb 1969 – date	XS794
Whirlwind HCC.12, HC.10	Jan 1970 – date	XR486
HS.125 CC.1	Mar 1971 – date	XX508

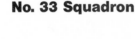

No. 33 Squadron

Badge: A hart's head affrontee, couped at the neck
Motto: Loyalty

No.33 Squadron was formed at Filton on 12 January 1916, from a nucleus left behind when No.12 Squadron moved to France. In March it moved to Yorkshire as a home defence unit to defend the industrial areas of the North Midlands against attacks by enemy airships. For the first three months, No.33 was also committed to training pilots by day but was relieved of this task by No.57 Squadron and for the rest of the war was engaged in night patrols. The slow B.E.s were replaced by more suitable F.E.s in November 1916 and when the home defence squadrons were modernised in 1918, No.33 received some Bristol Fighters in June and, in August, Avro 504Ks adapted as night fighters. Despite numerous patrols, no successful interceptions were made and the squadron disbanded on 13 June 1919.

attacking settlements. When Italy entered the war in June 1940, No.33's Gladiators flew fighter patrols over the desert before conversion to Hurricanes began in September, the last Gladiator departing on 26 October. Ground-attack sorties were flown until January 1941 when the squadron was withdrawn for transfer to Greece. In February it began flying bomber escort missions over Albania but the German attack from Bulgaria outflanked the Greek army and resulted in the evacuation of Commonwealth troops from Greece. At the end of April the squadron's last four Hurricanes left for Crete after covering convoys leaving Greece and amalgamated with the remnants of No.80 squadron to form an improvised fighter defence. A German airborne invasion of the island supported by large numbers of fighters and bombers soon made the Cretan airfields untenable and on 19 May No.33's last Hurricane was flown to Egypt. Its ground crews were captured with the airfields but succeeded in escaping during the battle and were evacuated from the south coast to Egypt.

During June the squadron became operational again over the Western Desert and Egypt, first on defensive duties and later on escort missions and fighter sweeps. Conversion to Tomahawks began in February 1942 but was soon suspended and the squadron re-equipped with Hurricane IIBs. For the rest of 1942 it flew fighter patrols over the Western Desert during the major battles but after the rout

Horsley IIs, No.33 Squadron

Hart I, No.33 Squadron

May with Spitfire IXs, also undertaking some fighter-bombing sorties before D-Day. By the end of August the squadron had moved to Normandy and flew ground-attack missions in support of the army until December, when it returned to the UK to convert to Tempests. In February 1945, No.33 rejoined Second TAF and flew fighter sweeps over Germany until the end of the war. It remained in Germany until July 1949 when it was transferred to Malaya to fly ground-attack missions against the camps of the Communist guerilla forces in the jungle, first with Tempests and later with Hornets. On 31 March 1955, No.33 Squadron was merged with No.45 Squadron and ceased to exist.

On 15 October 1955 No.33 reformed at Driffield as a night fighter squadron with Venoms, flying these until disbanded on 3 June 1957. On 30 September 1957 No.264 Squadron was renumbered 33 Squadron which now flew Meteor night fighters from Leeming. In July 1958 it converted to Javelins which it flew until disbanded on 17 November 1962.

Reformed as a surface-to-air guided missile unit on 1 March 1965, No.33 was based in Malaysia for air defence duties until disbanded on 30 January 1970. On 14 June 1971 it reformed at Odiham as the first Puma squadron to provide additional helicopter strength in No.38 Group.

Squadron bases

Filton	12 Jan 1916	Eleusis	19 Feb 1941
Coal Aston		Larissa	Mar 1941
Bramham Moor	18 Mar 1916	Eleusis	18 Apr 1941
Beverley		Maleme	27 Apr 1941 (A)
Gainsborough (HQ only)		Amriya	1 Jun 1941 (G)
	Dec 1916	Gerawla	13 Jun 1941
Kirton Lindsey	Jun 1918	Amriya	19 Jun 1941
	to 13 Jun 1919	Gamil	6 Jul 1941
Netheravon	1 Mar 1929	Amriya	11 Jul 1941
Eastchurch	14 Sep 1929	Fuka	24 Aug 1941
Bicester	5 Nov 1930	Amriya	25 Aug 1941
Upper Heyford	27 Nov 1934	Sidi Haneish	1 Sep 1941
Left for Middle East		Gerawla	10 Sep 1941
	4 Oct 1935	Giarabub	8 Nov 1941
Aboukir	14 Oct 1935	LG.125	20 Nov 1941
Mersa Matruh	25 Oct 1935	Msus	1 Jan 1942
Amman	11 Jul 1936	Antelat	13 Jan 1942
Gaza	10 Aug 1936	Msus	21 Jan 1942
Ismailia	6 Nov 1936	Mechili	24 Jan 1942
Heliopolis	28 Sep 1938	Gazala No.1	28 Jan 1942
Ismailia	3 Oct 1938	Gambut	3 Feb 1942
Ramleh	21 Oct 1938	Sidi Azeiz	17 Jun 1942
Lydda	9 Dec 1938	LG.75	18 Jun 1942
Ramleh	24 Mar 1939	LG.76	20 Jun 1942
Helwan	24 Apr 1939	LG.12	23 Jun 1942
Ismailia	25 May 1939	LG.154	27 Jun 1942
Qasaba	5 Aug 1939	LG.85	27 Jul 1942
Mersa Matruh	1 Sep 1939	Idku	5 Aug 1942
Qasaba	23 Oct 1939	LG.85	31 Aug 1942
Mersa Matruh	28 Oct 1939	LG.154	2 Oct 1942
Qasaba	17 Jun 1940	LG.172	23 Oct 1942
Gerawla	22 Jun 1940	LG.101	11 Nov 1942
Helwan	25 Jun 1940	El Adem	18 Nov 1942
Fuka	22 Sep 1940	Benina	28 Nov 1942
Amriya	15 Jan 1941	Bersis	11 Feb 1943
		Misurata West	24 Jun 1943

Bersis	9 Sep 1943	B.155 Dedelstorf	19 Jun 1945
Mersa Matruh	17 Jan 1944	B.106 Twente	14 Sep 1945
Left for UK	1 Apr 1944	Sylt	17 Sep 1945
North Weald	23 Apr 1944	Dedelstorf	6 Oct 1945
Lympne	17 May 1944	Fassberg	23 Oct 1945
Tangmere	3 Jul 1944	Gutersloh	1 Dec 1947
Funtington	17 Jul 1944	Left for Far East	2 Jul 1949
Selsey	6 Aug 1944	Changi	Aug 1949
Fairwood Common		Butterworth	Sep 1949
	12 Aug 1944	Changi	Oct 1949
Selsey	18 Aug 1944	Kuala Lumpur	Apr 1950
B.10 Plumetot	20 Aug 1944	Butterworth	Jun 1950
Tangmere	20 Aug 1944	Kuala Lumpur	Sep 1950
B.17 Carpiquet	31 Aug 1944		to 31 Mar 1955
Lympne	7 Sep 1944	Driffield	15 Oct 1955
B.35 Le Treport	10 Sep 1944		to 3 Jun 1957
B.51 Merville	12 Sep 1944	Leeming	30 Sep 1957
B.65 Maldeghem	2 Nov 1944	Middleton St. George	
Predannack	15 Dec 1944		30 Sep 1958
B.77 Gilze-Rijen	20 Feb 1945		to 17 Nov 1962
B.91 Kluis	7 Apr 1945	Butterworth	1 Mar 1965
B.109 Quackenbruck			to 30 Jan 1970
	20 Apr 1945	Odiham	14 Jun 1971

Aircraft

Equipment	Period of service	Representative Serial and Code
B.E.2c, B.E.2d	Jan 1916 – Nov 1916	
F.E.2b, F.E.2d	Nov 1916 – Aug 1918	B1884
Bristol F.2b	Jun 1918 – Aug 1918	
Avro 504K	Aug 1918 – Jun 1919	
Horsley II	Mar 1929 – May 1930	J8605
Hart	Feb 1930 – Mar 1938	J9945
Gladiator I, II	Feb 1938 – Oct 1940	L7620 (SO-O)
Gauntlet II	Feb 1940 – Apr 1940	K5316
Hurricane I	Sep 1940 – Feb 1942	Z4107
Hurricane IIB	Feb 1942 – Jun 1942	BE173 (M)
Hurricane IIC	Jun 1942 – Dec 1943	HL627
Spitfire VB, VC	Jan 1943 – Jun 1943	JG880
	Dec 1943 – Mar 1944	
Spitfire IXE	Apr 1944 – Dec 1944	BS239 (5R-E)
Tempest V	Dec 1944 – Nov 1945	SN315 (5R-Y)
Spitfire XVIE	Nov 1945 – Oct 1946	NH425
Tempest F.2	Oct 1946 – Jun 1951	PR753 (5R-E)
Hornet F.3	Apr 1951 – Mar 1955	WB871 (5R-P)
Venom NF.2	Oct 1955 – Jun 1957	WR785 (D)
Meteor NF.14	Sep 1957 – Jul 1958	WS810 (V)
Javelin FAW.7	Jul 1958 – Jan 1961	XH897 (W)
Javelin FAW.9	Oct 1960 – Nov 1962	XH758 (R)
Puma HC.1	Jun 1971 – date	XW209 (CF)

Gladiator I, No.33 Squadron

Beverley C.1, No.34 Squadron

No. 34 Squadron

Badge: In front of an increscent, a wolf passant
Motto: Lupus vult, lupus volat (Wolf wishes, wolf flies)

No.34 Squadron was formed at Castle Bromwich on 7 January 1916 from a nucleus supplied by No.19 Squadron. In July 1916 it moved to France with B.E.2es as a corps reconnaissance unit, re-equipping with R.E.8s in January 1917. After Austrian successes in north-east Italy, an Anglo-French force was sent to reinforce the Italian line and No.34 was one of the squadrons which accompanied it. For the rest of the war it flew reconnaissance and bomber missions in Italy, returning to the UK in May 1919 and disbanding on 25 September 1919.

On 3 December 1935 No.34 reformed at Bircham Newton from a detachment supplied by No.18 Squadron. Equipped initially with Hinds, it converted to Blenheims in July 1938. A few weeks before the outbreak of war, No.34 was sent to Singapore. It remained there until Japan entered the war in December 1941. In the ensuing two months, continuous action in Malaya, Sumatra and Java reduced the squadron strength to a point where it could no longer operate and its ground echelon was evacuated to India.

On 1 April 1942, No.34 reformed at Chakrata and during the month received Blenheim IVs. After a detachment had been sent to the North-West Frontier in July and August to help quell a tribal uprising, the squadron began bombing raids on Japanese bases in Burma which continued until April 1943. Conversion to Hurricanes began and fighter-bomber operations were resumed at the beginning of November. In March 1945 the squadron re-equipped with Thunderbolts which were used mainly for ground-attack missions for the rest of the war. On 15 October 1945 No.34 Squadron was disbanded.

On 1 August 1946, No.681 Squadron at Palam was re-numbered 34 Squadron and flew photo-reconnaissance Spitfires until disbanded on 31 July 1947. On 11 February 1949 No.695 Squadron at Horsham St. Faith was renumbered 34 Squadron. It was engaged on anti-aircraft co-operation duties with Beaufighters and Spitfires until disbanded on 20 July 1951.

No.34 next reformed at Tangmere as a fighter squadron with Meteors on 1 August 1954. In February 1956, the squadron converted to Hunters which it flew until disbanded on 10 January 1958. In October 1956 it had been detached to Cyprus to take part in the Suez operation, flying defensive patrols over the island.

On 1 October 1960 No.34 reformed at Seletar as a transport squadron equipped with Beverleys which it flew on supply missions until disbanded on 31 December 1967.

Squadron bases

Castle Bromwich	7 Jan 1916	Tengah	10 Sep 1939
Beverley	Mar 1916	Palembang	18 Jan 1942
Lilbourne	Jun 1916	Lahat	Feb 1942
Allonville	10 Jul 1916	Batavia	Feb 1942
Villers Brettoneux	31 Jan 1917		to 20 Feb 1942
Nurlu	16 May 1917	Chakrata	1 Apr 1942
Nesle	23 May 1917	Allahabad	15 Apr 1942
Nurlu	1 Jun 1917	Ondal	17 Jun 1942
Estree-en-Chaussée		Jessore	30 Jan 1943
	12 Jun 1917	Silchar	7 Mar 1943
Bray Dunes	2 Jul 1917	Kumbhirgram	18 Mar 1943
Candas	31 Oct 1917	St. Thomas Mount	3 May 1943
Milan	13 Nov 1917	Cholavarum	15 Sep 1943
Montichiari	17 Nov 1917	Alipore	15 Oct 1943
Verona	22 Nov 1917	Palel	1 Nov 1943
Grossa	28 Nov 1917	Dergaon	10 Apr 1944
Istrana	3 Dec 1917	Palel	15 Jul 1944
Marcon	14 Feb 1918	Yazagyo	20 Dec 1944
Istrana	12 Mar 1918	Onbauk	23 Jan 1945
Villaverla	30 Mar 1918	Ondaw	15 Mar 1945
Santa Luca	23 Oct 1918	Kwetnge	20 Apr 1945
Villaverla	16 Nov 1918	Kinmagan	1 Jun 1945
Caldiero	Feb 1919	Meiktila	1 Jul 1945
Old Sarum	May 1919	Zayatkwin	18 Aug 1945
	to 25 Sep 1919		to 15 Oct 1945
Bircham Newton	3 Dec 1935	Palam	1 Aug 1946
Abbotsinch	30 Jul 1936		to 31 Jul 1947
Lympne	3 Nov 1936	Horsham St. Faith	11 Feb 1949
Upper Heyford	11 Jul 1938		to 20 Jul 1951
Watton	2 Mar 1939	Tangmere	1 Aug 1954
Left for Singapore			to 10 Jan 1958
	12 Aug 1939 (G)	Seletar	1 Oct 1960
	16 Aug 1939 (A)		to 31 Dec 1967

Aircraft

Equipment	Period of service	Representative Serial and Code	
B.E.2c	Jan 1916 – May 1916		
B.E.2e	May 1916 – Jan 1917		
R.E.8	Jan 1917 – May 1919	E130	
Bristol F.2b	Mar 1918 – Jul 1918		
Hind	Jan 1936 – Jul 1938	K6689	
Blenheim I	Jul 1938 – Nov 1941	L1252	(LB-H)
Blenheim IV	Nov 1941 – Feb 1942	Z9583	
	Apr 1942 – Jan 1943		
Blenheim V	Jan 1943 – Aug 1943	BA207	
Hurricane IIC	Aug 1943 – Mar 1945	LB935	(C)
Thunderbolt II	Mar 1945 – Oct 1945	KJ356	(E)
Spitfire PR.19	Aug 1946 – Jul 1947	PM552	
Beaufighter TT.10	Feb 1949 – Jul 1951	RD767	
Oxford T.2	Feb 1949 – Jul 1951	PH146	
Spitfire LF.16E	Feb 1949 – Mar 1951	TE450	(8Q-R)
Meteor F.8	Aug 1954 – Feb 1956	WL175	(B)
Hunter F.5	Feb 1956 – Jan 1958	WP133	(L)
Beverley C.1	Oct 1960 – Dec 1967	XM104	(P)

Vulcan B.2, No.35 Squadron

No. 35 Squadron

Badge: A horse's head winged
Motto: Uno animo agimus (We
act with one accord)
Name: 'Madras Presidency'

No.35 Squadron was formed on 1 February 1916, at Thetford as a corps reconnaissance unit and after training moved to France in January 1917 with F.K.8s. Artillery observation and photographic missions occupied the squadron throughout its period of service on the Western Front though it had been trained for co-operation with the Cavalry Corps. By March 1918 it had become apparent that the possibilities of a cavalry breakthrough were remote and No.35 became a general purpose unit. Bristol Fighters began to replace the slow F.K.8s in October 1918 but the war ended before re-equipment was complete. In March 1919 the squadron returned to the UK and disbanded on 26 June 1919.

On 1 March, 1929, No.35 reformed at Bircham Newton as a day bomber squadron equipped initially with D.H.9As. By January 1930 these had been replaced by Fairey IIIFs and in 1932 Gordons were received. The Abyssinian crisis in 1935 resulted in the squadron taking its Gordons to the Sudan where it arrived in October, returning to the UK in August 1936. In July 1937, conversion to Wellesleys began but No.35 began to replace them with Battles in April 1938. In July 1939 some Ansons were received to provide for the squadron's training commitment and on the outbreak of World War Two No.35 did not go with most of the other Battle squadrons to France but remained in the UK as a crew training unit, forming with No.207 Squadron No.1 Group Pool on 1 October 1939. Training with Battles, Blenheims and Ansons continued until the combined unit became No.17 Operational Training Unit on 8 April 1940.

On 5 November 1940, No.35 was reformed as the first Halifax squadron and introduced the type into operational service, flying its first night raid on 10 March 1941. After taking part in raids on Germany and Italy, the squadron was transferred to the Pathfinder Force on its formation in August 1942. In March 1944 it converted to Lancasters which were flown for the rest of the war. In July and August 1946, the squadron carried out a goodwill tour round the U.S.A. and in September 1949 converted to Lincolns which it flew until disbanded on 23 February 1950.

On 1 September 1951, No.35 reformed at Marham with Washingtons which were flown as interim equipment until the arrival in service of jet bombers. In April 1954 the squadron re-equipped with Canberras which were detached to Cyprus in October 1956 during the Suez crisis. On 11 September 1961, the squadron was disbanded again.

When reformed at Coningsby on 1 December 1962 No.35 became part of the V-bomber force with Vulcan B.2s. For six years it was a unit of the nuclear deterrent force but in January 1969 was transferred to Cyprus as part of the Near East Air Force for a period.

Squadron bases

Thetford	1 Feb 1916	St. André	4 Feb 1917
Narborough	16 Jun 1916	Savy	28 Mar 1917
St. Omer	25 Jan 1917	Villers Brettoneux	13 May 1917
		Mons-en-Chaussée	23 May 1917

Savy 13 Jul 1917
La Gorgue 19 Aug 1917
La Lovie 5 Oct 1917
Bruay 17 Oct 1917
Estree-en-Chaussée 7 Nov 1917
Chipilly 22 Mar 1918
Poulainville 24 Mar 1918
Abbeville 28 Mar 1918
Poulainville 5 Apr 1918
Villers Bocage 2 May 1918
Suzanne 7 Sep 1918
Moislains 13 Sep 1918
Longavesnes 6 Oct 1918
Elincourt 17 Oct 1918
Flaumont 10 Nov 1918
La Grand Fayt 11 Nov 1918
Elincourt 13 Nov 1918
La Bellevue 29 Nov 1918
Ste. Marie Cappel 19 Jan 1919
Netheravon Mar 1919
 to 26 Jun 1919
Bircham Newton 1 Mar 1929
Left for Sudan 4 Oct 1935

Ed Damer 17 Oct 1935
Gebeit 6 Apr 1936
Left for UK 14 Aug 1936
Worthy Down 20 Aug 1936
Cottesmore 20 Apr 1938
Cranfield 25 Aug 1939
Bassingbourn 7 Dec 1939
Upwood 1 Feb 1940
 to 8 Apr 1940
Boscombe Down 5 Nov 1940
Leeming 20 Nov 1940
Linton-on-Ouse 5 Dec 1940
Graveley 15 Aug 1942
Stradishall 10 Sep 1946
Mildenhall 10 Feb 1949
 to 23 Feb 1950
Marham 1 Sep 1951
Upwood 16 Jul 1956
 to 11 Sep 1961
Coningsby 1 Dec 1962
Cottesmore 7 Nov 1964
Akrotiri 15 Jan 1969
Scampton Jan 1975

Aircraft Equipment	Period of service	Representative Serial or Code
Various	Feb 1916 – Jan 1917	–
F.K.8	Jan 1917 – Mar 1919	
Bristol F.2b	Oct 1918 – Mar 1919	
D.H.9A	Mar 1929 – Jan 1930	J7316
Fairey IIIF	Nov 1929 – Sep 1932	J9787
Gordon	Jul 1932 – Aug 1936 Nov 1936 – Aug 1937	K2620 (4)
Wellesley	Jul 1937 – Jun 1938	K8530 (35-G)
Battle	Aug 1938 – Feb 1940	K9471 (WT-M)
Anson I	Jul 1939 – Apr 1940	N5191
Blenheim IV	Nov 1939 – Apr 1940	L8845
Halifax I	Nov 1940 – Feb 1942	L9579 (TL-P)
Halifax II	Jan 1942 – Mar 1944	JP123 (TL-F)
Halifax III	Dec 1943 – Mar 1944	LV818 (TL-L)
Lancaster I, III	Mar 1944 – Oct 1949	RF183 (TL-H)
Lincoln B.2	Sep 1949 – Feb 1950	SX983 (TL-S)
Washington B.1	Sep 1951 – Apr 1954	WF572 (N)
Canberra B.2	Apr 1954 – Sep 1961	WK133
Vulcan B.2	Jan 1963 – date	XM604

Horsley IIIs, No.36 Squadron

No. 36 Squadron

Badge: An eagle, wings elevated, perched on a torpedo
Motto: Rajawali raja langit (Malay) (Eagle King of the sky)

No.36 Squadron was formed on 18 March 1916 from the Home Defence Flight at Cramlington, Northumberland for the defence of the coast between Newcastle and Whitby and was the first squadron specifically formed for this purpose. In November 1916, one of its aircraft destroyed Zeppelin L.34 over the Durham coast but this was the only one caught during sporadic airship raids. With the withdrawal of airships from bombing, the squadron undertook training duties until the end of the war and disbanded on 13 June 1919.

On 1 October 1928 the Coast Defence Torpedo Flight was re-designated No.36 Squadron at Donibristle and until it left for Singapore in October 1930, it flew Horsleys and took part in exercises with naval units from Rosyth. On 14 October 1930 the squadron embarked in the *Lancashire* at Liverpool and arrived at Seletar on 14 November. The Horsleys had been shipped to Karachi where they were erected and flown through India, Burma and Malaya to Singapore in December. In July 1935 the squadron re-equipped with

Vildebeests which were still in service when the war broke out in the Far East in December 1941. During the Japanese landings in Malaya, the squadron lost the bulk of its aircraft and combined with No.100 Squadron which had also lost most of its Vildebeests. The remaining aircraft were evacuated to Java and Sumatra and when the last two were lost on 7 March 1942, the squadron ceased to exist on the following day.

On 22 October 1942 No.36 reformed in India while personnel were in transit to Tanjore where they arrived on 24 October. In mid-December the first Wellingtons arrived and patrols off Madras began on 13 January 1943. Lack of Japanese submarine activity off India resulted in the squadron being moved to Algeria, the first aircraft arriving on 7 June 1943 at Blida where the ground echelon joined them on 30 July. Detachments operated from various bases on anti-submarine patrols and in September 1944 a further move was made when the squadron's Wellingtons flew to Chivenor for similar duties. In March 1945, it moved to Benbecula where it disbanded on 4 June 1945.

On 1 October 1946 No.248 Squadron at Thorney Island was renumbered 36 Squadron and flew Mosquitos as part of a strike wing until disbanded on 15 October 1947. On 1 July 1953 it reformed at Topcliffe with Neptunes for maritime reconnaissance duties, disbanding again on 28 February 1957. On 1 September 1958 No.36 again reformed, this time as a transport unit with Hastings at Colerne moving to Lyneham to re-equip with Hercules in August 1967, becoming operational on 26 September 1967. The squadron disbanded on 3 November 1975.

Hastings C.1s, No.36 Squadron

Squadron bases			
Cramlington	18 Mar 1916	Tjikampeh	15 Feb 1942
Seaton Carew &		Tjikamber	1 Mar 1942
Cramlington	May 1916		to 8 Mar 1942
Newcastle	1 Jul 1918	Tanjore	24 Oct 1942
Flts. at		Dhubalia	Mar 1943 (P)
Seaton Carew		Blida	7 Jun 1943 (A)
Hylton			30 Jul 1943 (G)
Ashington		Reghaia	30 Apr 1944
Usworth	Nov 1918	Tarquinia	18 Sep 1944
Flts. at	to 13 Jun 1919	Chivenor	26 Sep 1944 (A)
Seaton Carew			21 Oct 1944 (G)
Ashington (D)		Benbecula	9 Mar 1945
Donibristle	1 Oct 1928		to 4 Jun 1945
Kenley	12 Jun 1930	Thorney Island	1 Oct 1946
Donibristle	28 Jun 1930		to 15 Oct 1947
Left for Singapore	14 Oct 1930	Topcliffe	1 Jul 1953
Seletar	14 Nov 1930		to 28 Feb 1957
Kuantan	3 Aug 1941	Colerne	1 Sep 1958
Seletar	17 Aug 1941	Lyneham	1 Aug 1967
Kalidjati	1 Feb 1942		to 3 Nov 1975

Aircraft Equipment	Period of service	Representative Serial	
Various, e.g.			
Bristol Scout, B.E.2c			
B.E.2c, B.E.12	Feb 1916 — Jun 1918	—	
F.K.8, F.E.2b			
Avro 504K. Pup			
Bristol F.2b	Apr 1918 — Jun 1919		
Horsley I	Oct 1928 — Aug 1930	S1245	
Horsley III	Aug 1930 — Jul 1935	S1420	
Vildebeest III	Jul 1935 — Mar 1942	K4175	(V)
Wellington Ic	Dec 1942 — Nov 1943	HE114	(RW-C)
Wellington VIII	Jan 1943 — Nov 1943	LB123	(RW-A)
Wellington X	Jun 1943 — Nov 1943	MP651	(RW-K)
Wellington XI	Jun 1943 — Nov 1943	HZ274	
Wellington XII	Jul 1943 — Nov 1943	MP690	(RW-Y)
Wellington XIII	Jun 1943 — Nov 1943	MP704	(RW-A)
Wellington XIV	Sep 1943 — Jun 1945	HF310	(RW-E)
Mosquito FB.6	Oct 1946 — Oct 1947	RS564	
Neptune MR.1	Jul 1953 — Feb 1957	WX545	(T-C)
Hastings C.1	Sep 1958 — Jul 1967	TG620	
Hercules C.1	Aug 1967 — Nov 1975	XV190	

No. 37 Squadron

Badge: A hawk hooded, belled
and fessed, wings elevated
and addorsed
Motto: Wise without eyes

No.37 Squadron was formed on 15 April 1916 at Orfordness as an experimental unit but was merged with the main experimental station there during the following month. On 15 September 1916 it was reformed as a home defence unit with its headquarters at Woodham Mortimer, Essex and its aircraft were based on landing grounds at Stow Maries, Goldhanger and Rochford. In common with the other home defence squadrons, No.37 had a variety of types on strength as the units in France enjoyed first priority in the supply of aircraft. On the night of 16/17 June 1917 one of the squadron's B.E.12s destroyed Zeppelin L.48 over Suffolk. Around this time, the main menace ceased to be Zeppelins and became the Belgian-based Gothas so some Pups and Sopwith 1½-strutters were added. In June 1918 squadron headquarters moved to Stow Maries airfield but a detachment remained at Goldhanger, Rochford having been given

up in August 1917 to make way for night flying training units. In October 1918 the squadron received Camels in preparation for a possible increase in enemy bomber activity but the war ended a few weeks later. In March 1919, No.37 moved to Biggin Hill where it flew some Snipes before being renumbered 39 Squadron on 1 July 1919.

On 26 April 1937, B Flight of No.214 Squadron was re-designated 37 Squadron at Feltwell as a heavy bomber unit, flying Harrows until re-equipped with Wellingtons in May 1939. On the outbreak of war, No.37 flew its first operation only seven hours after the British ultimatum to Germany expired when it provided six aircraft for a sweep over Heligoland Bight. Losses on this type of mission resulted in Bomber Command's squadrons turning to night bombing and this was to be No.37's role for the rest of the war. After taking part in attacks on enemy targets in Europe, the squadron was ordered to the Middle East in November 1940, six aircraft leaving for Malta in November (one of which returned with engine trouble) and another seven on 12 November. After flying a few sorties from Malta the first aircraft arrived in Egypt on 14 November where they were joined by the ground echelon on 30 November. Attacks on enemy ports and bases in Libya began and in March 1941 it sent a large detachment to Greece for operations over Albania. In April 1941, after the German attack on Greece began, missions were flown over Bulgaria but the bombers had to be evacuated on 18 April in view of the enemy air

69

superiority over Greece. In May 1941, the squadron took part in suppressing the Iraqi uprising but until the rout of the Afrika Korps at El Alamein, its main targets were in Libya, Sicily and southern Italy. In February 1943 the squadron moved to Libya in the wake of the 8th Army thus increased its radius of action over Italy and in May moved to Tunisia. In December 1943, No.37 moved to Italy where it was based for the rest of the war. At the end of October 1944, the first Liberators were received and the last Wellington mission was flown on 13 December, Liberators having started operations on 3 December. For the rest of the war, the squadron took part in bombing raids over Italy, Yugoslavia, Hungary, Bulgaria and Albania, one of its regular tasks being to drop mines in the Danube to hamper enemy shipping. In addition, the squadron's Liberators carried out supply drops to Yugoslav partisan forces. On 2 October 1945, a move to Palestine began and in December No.37 returned to Egypt where it disbanded on 31 March 1946.

On 15 April 1946, No.214 Squadron at Fayid was renumbered 37 Squadron which flew Lancasters until it again was disbanded on 1 April 1947. On 14 September 1947, No.37 reformed at Ein Shemer in Palestine as a maritime reconnaissance unit with Lancasters and until May 1948, when it left Palestine finally, its patrols were mainly directed towards locating illegal immigrant ships. In April 1948, the squadron headquarters began operating in Malta, a detachment remaining in Palestine until 19 May. In August 1953 it converted to Shackletons and in August 1957 moved to Aden where it flew patrols until disbanded in September 1967.

Squadron bases		
Orfordness	15 Apr 1916	
Woodham Mortimer		
	15 Sep 1916 (HQ)	
Goldhanger (D)		
Stow Maries (D)		
Rochford (D)		
Stow Maries	Jun 1918	
Biggin Hill	17 Mar 1919	
	to 1 Jul 1919	
Feltwell	26 Apr 1937	
Fayid	30 Nov 1940	
Shallufa	17 Dec 1940	
LG.09	25 Apr 1942	
LG.224	27 Jun 1942	
Abu Sueir	29 Jun 1942	
LG.224	6 Nov 1942	
LG.106	13 Nov 1942	
LG.140	30 Nov 1942	
El Magrun	23 Jan 1943	

Snipe, No.37 Squadron

Gardabia East	14 Feb 1943		to 31 Mar 1946
Gardabia West	25 Feb 1943	Fayid	15 Apr 1946
Kairouan/Temmar		Kabrit	26 Aug 1946
	30 May 1943	Shallufa	16 Sep 1946
Djedeida	15 Nov 1943		to 1 Apr 1947
Cerignola	14 Dec 1943	Ein Shemer	14 Sep 1947
Tortorella	29 Dec 1943	Luqa	1 Apr 1948
Aqir	2 Oct 1945	Khormaksar	21 Aug 1957
Shallufa	12 Dec 1945		to Sep 1967

Aircraft Equipment	Period of service	Representative Serial
B.E.2c, B.E.2d B.E.12, B.E.12a R.E.7, R.E.8, Sopwith 1½-strutter	Sep 1916 – Oct 1918	–
Camel	Oct 1918 – Jul 1919	
Snipe	Apr 1919 – Jul 1919	F2390
Harrow II	Apr 1937 – May 1939	K7001 (S)
Wellington I	May 1939 – Nov 1939	L4352
Wellington IA	Sep 1939 – Oct 1940	L7779 (P)
Wellington IC	Oct 1940 – Mar 1943	ES980 (K)
Wellington III	Mar 1943 – Apr 1943	DF680
Wellington X	Mar 1943 – Dec 1944	HE660 (S)
Liberator VI	Oct 1944 – Mar 1946	KH270 (S)
Lancaster III	Apr 1946 – Jun 1946	RF298 (T)
Lancaster VII	Jun 1946 – Apr 1947	NX792
Lancaster MR.3	Sep 1947 – Aug 1953	TX270
Shackleton MR.2	Aug 1953 – Sep 1967	WL785

No. 38 Squadron

Badge: A heron volant
Motto: Ante lucem
(Before the dawn)

No.38 Squadron was formed at Thetford on 1 April 1916 but was redesignated No.25 (Reserve) Squadron on 22 May 1916. Formation was resumed on 14 July 1916 at Castle Bromwich as a home defence squadron and in October the squadron's headquarters were established at Melton Mowbray with its three flights dispersed to Stamford, Buckminster and Leadenham. From these, it maintained anti-Zeppelin patrols to defend the Midlands. In September 1916 the squadron received F.E.2bs and was also engaged in night flying training until sent to France as a night bomber unit at the end of May 1918, leaving behind a nucleus that became No.90 Squadron. Bombing raids began on 13 June and continued until August when No.38 was moved back to re-equip with Handley-Page O/400s. These were not received however and the squadron returned to night bombing with F.E.2bs for the rest of the war. In February 1919, No.38

returned to the UK and disbanded on 4 July 1919.

On 16 September 1935, No.38 reformed from B Flight of No.99 Squadron at Mildenhall as a heavy bomber squadron. Equipped with Heyfords, it became the only squadron to receive Hendons in November 1936, replacing these with Wellingtons at the end of 1938. Apart from a few sweeps over the North Sea, no operations were flown until the German invasion of the Low Countries in May 1940, bombing raids beginning on 11 May. These continued until early in November when the squadron was ordered overseas. By the end of the month, No.38's aircraft had been deployed to Egypt for attacks on enemy bases in Libya, Italy and the Balkans. In January 1942, the squadron began training for night torpedo attacks in No.201 Group and began anti-shipping missions in March. Minelaying and torpedo-bombing were the squadron's main tasks during 1942. After the rout of the Afrika Korps in October 1942, trans-Mediterranean shipping in the Eastern Mediterranean ceased and the Wellingtons flew further afield to find their targets along the Balkan and Italian coasts. Torpedo-bombing ended in January 1943, minelaying, bombing reconnaissance and anti-submarine patrols being flown thereafter. In November 1944, No.38 moved to Greece for a month before basing itself in southern Italy with No.334 Wing. After some supply-dropping flights over Yugoslavia, the squadron re-equipped with Wellington XIVs and was engaged in attacks on enemy coastal shipping off the coasts of northern

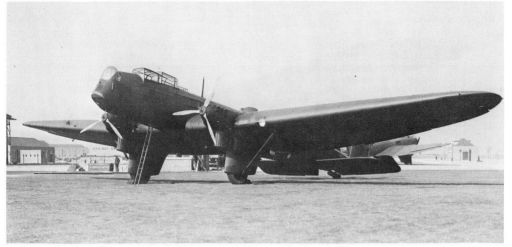

Hendon I, No.38 Squadron

Italy for the rest of the war. In July 1945 it moved to Malta and became operational with Warwicks on 23 August for air-sea rescue duties, detachments being based in Sardinia and Libya for a year. After converting to Lancasters, No.38 moved to Palestine where for eighteen months it was engaged in maritime reconnaissance before returning to Malta. Re-equipped with Shackletons in 1954, the squadron remained at Luqa until disbanded on 31 March 1967.

Squadron bases

Thetford	1 Apr 1916		22 Nov 1940 (A)
	to 22 May 1916	Ismailia	24 Nov 1940 (A)
Castle Bromwich	14 Jul 1916	Fayid	30 Nov 1940 (G)
Melton Mowbray	1 Oct 1916		7 Dec 1940 (A)
Capelle	31 May 1918	Shallufa	18 Dec 1940
Beauregard	24 Aug 1918	Gambut	1 Apr 1941
St. Pol	29 Sep 1918	Shallufa	12 Apr 1941
Harlebeke	26 Oct 1918	Luqa (D)	9 Aug 1941
Serny	16 Dec 1918		to 26 Oct 1941
Hawkinge	14 Feb 1919	LG.226 Gianaclis (D)	
	to 4 Jul 1919		1 Aug 1942
Mildenhall	16 Sep 1935		to 18 Nov 1942
Marham	5 May 1937	Gambut (D)	18 Nov 1942
Left for Middle East			to 1 Mar 1943
	12 Nov 1940 (G)	Berka III	1 Mar 1943

Kalamaki/Hassani		Luqa	11 Jul 1945
	11 Nov 1944	Ein Shemer	Sep 1946 (P)
Grottaglie	10 Dec 1944	Luqa	1 Apr 1948 (P)
Foggia Main	2 Feb 1945		to 31 Mar 1967
Falconara	21 Apr 1945		

Aircraft Equipment	Period of service	Representative Serial
B.E.2c, B.E.2e	Apr 1916 – May 1916	
	Jul 1916 – Jul 1917	
B.E.12	Jul 1916 – Jul 1917	
R.E.7	1916 – 1916	
F.E.2b	Sep 1916 – Jan 1919	B422
Heyford I, Ia, III	Sep 1935 – Jun 1937	K6862
Hendon	Nov 1936 – Jan 1939	K5087 (E)
Wellington I	Nov 1938 – Dec 1939	L4235 (NH-R)
Wellington IA, IC	Sep 1939 – Jan 1942	N2756 (HD-U)
Wellington III	Jan 1942 – Oct 1943	AD597 (N)
Wellington X	May 1942 – Oct 1943	HZ308 (A)
Wellington VIII	Jun 1943 – Oct 1943	LA975 (D)
Wellington XI	Oct 1943 – May 1944	HZ394 (S)
Wellington XIII	Oct 1943 – Jan 1945	HZ881 (F)
Wellington XIV	Jan 1945 – Jun 1946	NC771 (C)
Warwick I	Jul 1945 – Sep 1946	BV437 (Y)
Lancaster ASR.3, GR.3	Jul 1946 – Dec 1954	RF323 (RL-C)
Shackleton MR.2	Sep 1953 – Mar 1967	WL787 (38-S)

No. 39 Squadron

Badge: A winged bomb
Motto: Die noctuque
(By day and night)

No.39 Squadron was formed at Hounslow on 15 April 1916 as a home defence unit. Flights of B.E.s were detached to Suttons Farm, Hornchurch and nearby Hainault Farm to guard the eastern approaches to London and in August the squadron headquarters were moved to Woodford, Essex and a further detachment was based at North Weald. When the Germans replaced their Zeppelin attacks by formations of Gotha bombers, No.39 replaced its inadequate B.E.s with Bristol Fighters and in November 1918 moved to France. Five days later the Armistice came and the squadron was disbanded on 16 November 1918.

On 1 July 1919 No.37 Squadron at Biggin Hill was renumbered 39 Squadron and remained a cadre until moved to Spittlegate in February 1923 to be equipped with D.H.9As as a day bomber unit. In December 1928 the squadron left for India and began patrol duties on the North-West Frontier with Wapitis in February 1929. Harts were received in November 1931 and were replaced by Blenheims in 1939 before No.39 moved to Singapore shortly before the outbreak of World War Two. In April 1940 it returned to India en route for the Middle East but was diverted to Aden when Italy's entry into the war became imminent. Bombing raids were made on targets in Italian East Africa until November when No.39 moved to Egypt. Converting to Marylands in January 1941, the squadron began strategic reconnaissance missions in April. In August some Beauforts were received for anti-shipping operations which began on 17 September but Marylands continued reconnaissance flights until January 1942. Torpedo-bomber missions against enemy convoys were mounted from advanced bases in Egypt and Libya while a detachment was

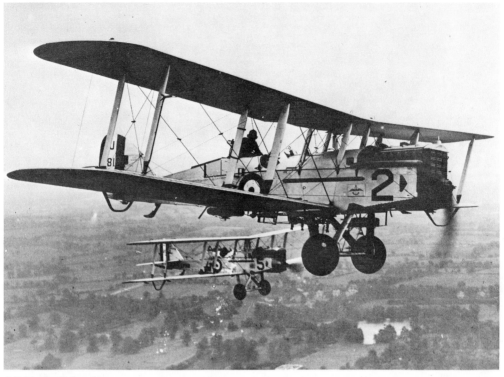

D.H.9As, No.39 Squadron

based in Malta. On 20 August 1942, this detachment joined others of Nos.86 and 217 Squadron to become No.39 Squadron, the residue of No.39 in Egypt joining No.47 Squadron.

Anti-shipping and minelaying operations with Beauforts continued until they were replaced by Beaufighters in June 1943. Sorties ranged over the Central Mediterranean, first from North Africa and later from Sardinia. Night intruder missions over northern Italy supplemented shipping strikes along the French and Italian coasts and a move in July 1944 to Italy extended these activities to the Balkans but in December the squadron began to receive Marauders. Operations with these began on 7 February 1945 and in October No.39 moved to the Sudan where it began to re-equip with Mosquitos. On 8 September 1946, the squadron disbanded.

On 1 April 1948, No.39 reformed at Nairobi as a Tempest squadron but disbanded again on 28 February 1949. On 1 March 1949, it reformed at Fayid with Mosquito night fighters for the defence of the Suez Canal. In March 1953, it re-equipped with Meteors and moved to Malta in January 1955 where it was disbanded on 30 June 1958.

No.69 Squadron at Luqa was renumbered 39 Squadron on 1 July 1958 and its Canberras were engaged on photographic reconnaissance duties attached to NATO until September 1970 when the squadron moved to the UK.

Squadron bases

Hounslow	15 Apr 1916	Left for India	29 Dec 1928
Woodford	Aug 1916	Risalpur	22 Jan 1929
North Weald	Dec 1917	Seletar	16 Jan 1938
Bavichove	6 Nov 1918	Tengah	28 Jan 1938
	to 16 Nov 1918	Risalpur	25 Feb 1938
Biggin Hill	1 Jul 1919	Tengah	12 Aug 1939
Kenley	18 Jan 1922	Kallang	9 Sep 1939
Spittlegate	8 Feb 1923	Lahore	19 Apr 1940
Bircham Newton	21 Jan 1928	Heliopolis	7 May 1940

Sheikh Othman		Protville I	17 Oct 1943
	31 May 1940 (A)	Sidi Amor	21 Oct 1943
	10 Jun 1940 (G)	Reghaia	20 Nov 1943
Helwan	1 Dec 1940	Alghero	19 Feb 1944
Heliopolis	23 Jan 1941	Biferno	13 Jul 1944
Shandur	21 Mar 1941	Hassani (D)	16 Dec 1944
Wadi Natrun	May 1941		to 18 Jan 1945
Ikingi Maryut	10 Oct 1941	Rivolto	Jun 1945
LG.86	27 Dec 1941	Khartoum	Oct 1945 (P)
Shandur	1 Jul 1942		to 8 Sep 1946
Luqa	20 Aug 1942	Nairobi/Eastleigh	1 Apr 1948
Shallufa	9 Dec 1942		to 28 Feb 1949
Luqa	21 Jan 1943	Fayid	1 Mar 1949
Gianaclis (D)	27 Feb 1943	Luqa	Jan 1955 (P)
	to 20 Jun 1943		to 30 Jun 1958
Protville II	1 Jun 1943	Luqa	1 Jul 1958
LG.224	3 Jun 1943	Wyton	30 Sep 1970
Protville II	11 Jun 1943		

Aircraft

Equipment	Period of service	Representative Serial
B.E.2c, B.E.2e	Apr 1916 – Sep 1917	B4482
B.E.12, B.E.12a	Aug 1916 – Sep 1917	A6326
Bristol F.2b	Sep 1917 – Nov 1918	B1350 (3)
D.H.9A	Feb 1929 – Dec 1931	J7819 (5)
Wapiti IIA	Feb 1929 – Dec 1931	J9393
Hart	Nov 1931 – Jul 1939	K2096 (2)
Blenheim I	Aug 1939 – Jan 1941	L4920
Blenheim IV	Dec 1940 – Jan 1941	
Maryland I	Jan 1941 – Jan 1942	AX689
Beaufort I	Aug 1941 – Jun 1943	AW290 (S)
Beaufighter X	Jun 1943 – Feb 1945	JM387 (M)
Marauder III	Feb 1945 – Sep 1946	HD607 (F)
Mosquito VI	Feb 1946 – Sep 1946	TE662
Tempest F.6	Apr 1948 – Feb 1949	NX172
Mosquito NF.30, NF.36	Mar 1949 – Mar 1953	RL233 (G)
Meteor NF.13	Mar 1953 – Jan 1958	WM363 (H)
Canberra PR.3	Jul 1959 – Nov 1962	WE137 (A)
Canberra PR.9	Oct 1962 – date	XH171 (M)
Canberra PR.7	Oct 1970 – Mar 1972	WJ825

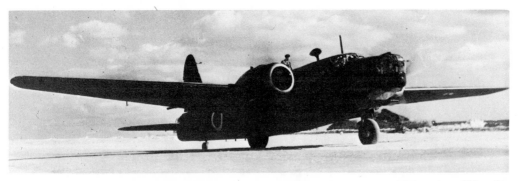

Wellington IC, No.40 Squadron

No. 40 Squadron

Badge: A broom
Motto: Hostem coelo expellere
(To drive the enemy from
the sky)

No.40 Squadron was formed on 26 February 1916 at Gosport and after training moved to France with F.E.8 fighters in August. Fighter patrols over the Western Front began but the squadron's pusher scouts were obsolete within a short time and were completely outclassed by enemy fighters. In March 1917 a complete patrol of nine F.E.8s was shot down over the lines and the squadron re-equipped with Nieuports immediately to start a successful period with effective fighters. In October 1917, No.40 received S.E.5As which it flew for the rest of the war. After the German offensive in March 1918, the squadron was engaged in low-level attacks on enemy troops and transport. In February, 1919, it returned to the UK where it disbanded on 30 June 1919, though the Air Ministry ruled that the official date was 4 July 1919.

On 1 April 1931, No.40 reformed as a day bomber squadron at Upper Heyford, moving with its Gordons to Abingdon in October 1932. In November 1935 it re-equipped with Harts and on 7 January 1936 detached C Flight to form No.104 Squadron which became an independent unit on 1 July. In March 1936, Hinds were received and in July 1938 conversion to Battles began. On the outbreak of war, the squadron moved to France with the Advanced Air Striking Force but returned in December to re-equip with Blenheims. Attacks on advancing German columns began on 10 May 1940 as the enemy flooded into the Low Countries and continued throughout the Battle of France. Invasion barges gathering in the Channel ports were the next target and in November the squadron became a night bomber unit with Wellingtons. For a year it took part in night raids until in October 1941 it began to fly its aircraft out to Malta for attacks on targets in Italy and North Africa. The remainder of the squadron continued to operate from the UK until it became No.156 Squadron on 14 February 1942.

The detachment in Malta had suffered from its exposed position and a few surviving aircraft were withdrawn to Egypt where the squadron was rebuilt to full strength. From bases near the Suez Canal, it carried out bombing raids on North African ports until early in 1943 when it moved to

newly-captured airfields in Tunisia and Cyrenaica. In December 1943 a move was made to Italy which brought the Balkans and northern Italy into bombing range. In March 1945 it converted to Liberators which were moved to Egypt in October. In January 1946 these were replaced by Lancasters which were flown until the squadron disbanded on 1 April 1947.

On 1 December 1947 No.40 reformed as a transport squadron at Abingdon. Its Yorks played their part during the Berlin airlift in bringing supplies to the beleaguered city. On 15 March 1950 the squadron disbanded but reformed on 28 October 1953 as a Canberra light bomber unit at Coningsby. On 15 December 1956, No.40 merged with No.50 Squadron which, from 1 February 1957 was designated No.50/40 Squadron.

Squadron bases			
Gosport	26 Feb 1916	LG.222A	7 Nov 1942
St. Omer	1 Aug 1916	LG.104	12 Nov 1942
Treizennes	2 Aug 1916	Luqa	25 Nov 1942
Auchel	25 Apr 1917	LG.237	20 Jan 1943
Bruay	29 Apr 1917	Gardabia East	15 Feb 1943
Bryas	4 Jun 1918	Gardabia South	13 Mar 1943
Aniche	24 Oct 1918	Kairouan/Cheria	26 May 1943
Orcq	29 Dec 1918	Hani West	25 Jun 1943
Tangmere	13 Feb 1919	Oudna 1	18 Nov 1943
	to 4 Jul 1919	Left for Italy	4 Dec 1943 (G)
Upper Heyford	1 Apr 1931	Cerignola	16 Dec 1943
Abingdon	8 Oct 1932	Foggia Main	30 Dec 1943
Betheniville	2 Sep 1939	Abu Sueir	21 Oct 1945
Wyton	2 Dec 1939	Shallufa	17 Sep 1946
Alconbury	2 Feb 1941		to 1 Apr 1947
	to 14 Feb 1941	Abingdon	1 Dec 1947
Luqa	31 Oct 1941	Bassingbourn	25 Jun 1949
	to May 1942		to 15 Mar 1950
Abu Sueir	May 1942	Coningsby	28 Oct 1953
Shallufa	Jun 1942	Wittering	24 Feb 1954
Kabrit	20 Aug 1942	Upwood	1 Nov 1956
			to 15 Dec 1956

Aircraft Equipment	Period of service	Representative Serial
Various	Feb 1916 – Jul 1916	–
F.E.8	Jul 1916 – Mar 1917	7607
Nieuport 17	Mar 1917 – Oct 1917	B1551 (K)
S.E.5A	Oct 1917 – Jun 1919	C1071 (Y)
Gordon	Apr 1931 – Nov 1935	K2625 (C3)
Hart (Special)	Nov 1935 – Mar 1936	K4416
Hind	Mar 1936 – Sep 1938	K5465
Battle	Jul 1938 – Dec 1939	K9360
Blenheim IV	Dec 1939 – Nov 1940	N3592 (BL-C)
Wellington IC	Nov 1940 – May 1942	X9630 (BL-J)
Wellington III	May 1942 – Jul 1943	HZ125 (BL-Q)
Wellington X	May 1943 – Mar 1945	ME313 (U)
Liberator VI	Mar 1945 – Jan 1946	KK313 (F)
Lancaster VII	Jan 1946 – Apr 1947	NX683 (BL-G)
York C.1	Dec 1947 – Mar 1950	MW193
Canberra B.2	Oct 1953 – Dec 1956	WJ605

No. 41 Squadron

Badge: A double armed cross
Motto: Seek and destroy

No.41 Squadron was formed on 14 July 1916 at Gosport, an earlier nucleus during the previous month having been re-designated No.27 Reserve Squadron. Equipped with F.E.8 fighters, it moved to France in October 1916 for patrols over the Western Front. Despite the F.E.8's deficiencies as a fighter, the squadron flew this type until re-equipped with D.H.5s in July 1917 and four months later received S.E.5As. These the squadron flew for the rest of the war, ground-attack missions being added to its normal fighter and escort tasks. In January 1919, No.41 was reduced to a cadre and returned to the UK where it disbanded on 31 December 1919.

On 1 April 1923, No.41 reformed at Northolt as a single flight equipped with Snipes, being increased to two flights in April 1924 and re-equipped with Siskins. A third flight was added a year later and in October 1931 the squadron converted to Bulldogs. No.41 became a two-seat fighter unit in July 1934 when Demons arrived and these were taken to Aden in October 1935 during the Abyssinian crisis. Returning to the UK in August 1936, the squadron reverted to single-seaters and flew Furies until it converted to Spitfires in January 1939. After flying defensive patrols during the first months of World War Two, No.41 moved south at the end of May 1940 to fly covering operations over the Dunkirk beaches, alternating between Yorkshire and south-east England during the Battle of Britain. In July 1941, sweeps over northern France began and continued until August 1942 when the squadron moved north for patrols over the Irish Sea. Re-equipped with new Spitfire XIIs, No.41 returned to the south-east in April 1943 to combat

low-level fighter-bomber attacks on coastal targets and fly shipping reconnaissance and bomber escort missions. In April 1944, the squadron moved to south-west England for sweeps over Brittany, being recalled in June when flying bombs began to arrive over the Kent coast. Sweeps and escort missions were resumed in August and on 5 October 1944 No.41 joined Second TAF, moving to Belgium in December to become part of No.125 Wing. Armed reconnaissance sweeps over Germany were flown for the rest of the war and on 1 April 1946, the squadron was renumbered 26 Squadron at Wunstorf.

On 1 April 1946, No.122 Squadron at Dalcross was renumbered 41 Squadron and two weeks later moved south to Wittering. Initially equipped with Spitfire F.21s, the squadron was nominated as No.12 Group's instrument flying training unit in August 1947 and received Oxfords and Harvards. In June 1948 it was relieved of this task and re-equipped with Hornets, flying these until converting to Meteors early in 1951 before moving to Biggin Hill. Hunters arrived in August 1955 and were flown until the squadron was disbanded on 31 January 1958.

On 1 February 1958, No.141 Squadron at Coltishall was renumbered 41 Squadron, Javelin all-weather fighters being flown until disbandment on 6 December 1963. The squadron reformed at West Raynham on 1 September 1965 as a Bloodhound surface-to-air missile unit, disbanding on 18 September 1970. On 1 April 1972, No.41 reformed at Coningsby with Phantoms for fighter-reconnaissance and ground-attack duties in No.38 Group. In August 1976, a Jaguar element began conversion at Coltishall and the squadron disbanded on 31 March 1977, this element becoming a reformed 41 Squadron next day.

Squadron bases			
Gosport	14 Jul 1916	Savy	9 Apr 1918
St. Omer	15 Oct 1916	Serny	11 Apr 1918
Abeele	21 Oct 1916	Estrée Blanche	19 May 1918
Hondschoote	24 May 1917	Conteville	1 Jun 1918
Abeele	15 Jun 1917	St. Omer	14 Aug 1918
Lealvilliers	3 Jul 1917	Droglandt	20 Sep 1918
Marieux	22 Mar 1918	Halluin	23 Oct 1918
Fienvillers	27 Mar 1918	Tangmere	7 Feb 1919
Alquines	29 Mar 1918	Croydon	Oct 1919
			to 31 Dec 1919

					Aircraft Equipment	Period of service	Representative Serial
Northolt	1 Apr 1923	Southend	6 Feb 1944		Vickers F.B.5	Jul 1916 – Oct 1916	
Left for Aden	4 Oct 1935	Tangmere	20 Feb 1944		D.H.2	Jul 1916 – Oct 1916	
Khormaksar	20 Oct 1935	Friston	11 Mar 1944		F.E.8	Sep 1916 – Jul 1917	7616 (2)
Sheikh Othman	18 Mar 1936	Bolt Head	29 Apr 1944		D.H.5	Jul 1917 – Nov 1917	B340
Left for UK	11 Aug 1936	Fairwood Common	16 May 1944		S.E.5A	Nov 1917 – Jan 1919	F5547 (Y)
Catterick	25 Sep 1936	Bolt Head	24 May 1944		Snipe	Apr 1923 – May 1924	
Wick	19 Oct 1939	West Malling	19 Jun 1944		Siskin III	May 1924 – Mar 1927	J7764
Catterick	25 Oct 1939	Westhampnett	28 Jun 1944		Siskin IIIa	Mar 1927 – Nov 1931	J8657 (O)
Hornchurch	28 May 1940	Friston	2 Jul 1944		Bulldog IIa	Oct 1931 – Aug 1934	K2184 (K)
Catterick	8 Jun 1940	Lympne	11 Jul 1944		Demon	Jul 1934 – Aug 1936	K3772 (G)
Hornchurch	26 Jul 1940	B.64 Diest/Schaffen	5 Dec 1944			Nov 1936 – Oct 1937	
Catterick	8 Aug 1940	Y.32 As/Ophoven	30 Dec 1944		Fury II	Oct 1937 – Jan 1939	K8238
Hornchurch	3 Sep 1940	B.80 Volkel	27 Jan 1945		Spitfire I	Jan 1939 – Nov 1940	X4178 (EB-K)
Catterick	23 Feb 1941	Warmwell	7 Mar 1945			Mar 1941 – Apr 1941	
Merston	28 Jul 1941	B.78 Eindhoven	18 Mar 1945		Spitfire IIA	Oct 1940 – Aug 1941	P7666 (EB-Z)
Westhampnett	16 Dec 1941	B.106 Twente	7 Apr 1945		Spitfire VB	Aug 1941 – Mar 1943	AD504 (EB-W)
Merston	1 Apr 1942	B.118 Celle	16 Apr 1945		Spitfire XII	Feb 1943 – Sep 1944	MB798 (EB-U)
Martlesham Heath	15 Jun 1942	B.160 Kastrup	9 May 1945		Spitfire XIV	Sep 1944 – Apr 1946	RM913 (EB-P)
Hawkinge	30 Jun 1942	B.158 Lubeck	11 Jul 1945		Spitfire F.21	Apr 1946 – Aug 1947	LA226 (EB-F)
Debden	8 Jul 1942	B.116 Wunstorf	30 Jan 1946		Oxford T.2	Aug 1947 – Jul 1948	PH509
Longtown	4 Aug 1942		to 1 Apr 1946		Harvard T.2B	Aug 1947 – Jun 1948	KF128
Llanbedr	9 Aug 1942	Dalcross	1 Apr 1946		Hornet F.1	Jun 1948 – Aug 1948	PX277 (EB-W)
Tangmere	16 Aug 1942	Wittering	15 Apr 1946		Hornet F.3	Jul 1948 – Feb 1951	PX314 (EB-F)
Llanbedr	20 Aug 1942	Church Fenton	16 Apr 1947		Meteor F.4	Jan 1951 – Apr 1951	VZ415
Eglinton	22 Sep 1942	Biggin Hill	29 Mar 1951		Meteor F.8	Apr 1951 – Aug 1955	WE867 (S)
Andreas	29 Sep 1942		to 31 Jan 1958		Hunter F.5	Aug 1955 – Jan 1958	WP187 (R)
Llanbedr	30 Sep 1942	Coltishall	1 Feb 1958		Javelin FAW.4	Feb 1958 – Feb 1960	XA758 (S)
Tangmere	5 Oct 1942	Wattisham	3 Jul 1958		Javelin FAW.5	Aug 1958 – Feb 1960	XA707
Llanbedr	11 Oct 1942		to 6 Dec 1963		Javelin FAW.8	Nov 1959 – Dec 1963	XJ129 (A)
High Ercall	25 Mar 1943	West Raynham	1 Sep 1965		Bloodhound SAM.2	Sep 1965 – Sep 1970	
Hawkinge	13 Apr 1943		to 18 Sep 1970		Phantom FGR.2	Apr 1972 – Mar 1977	XV401
Biggin Hill	21 May 1943	Coningsby	1 Apr 1972		Jaguar GR.1	Aug 1976 – date	XZ117 (E)
Friston	27 May 1943		to 31 Mar 1977				
Westhampnett	21 Jun 1943	Coltishall	1 Apr 1977				
Tangmere	4 Oct 1943						

No. 42 Squadron

Badge: On a terrestrial globe, a figure of Perseus

Motto: Fortiter in re (Bravely in action)

No.42 Squadron was formed at Filton on 1 April 1916 and after training moved to France in August as a corps reconnaissance unit. Equipped with B.E.2es, it flew artillery spotting and tactical reconnaisance missions over the Western Front for fifteen months before being transferred to northern Italy. R.E.8s had replaced the B.E.s in April 1917 and were taken to the Austro-Italian Front for three months before the squadron returned to France in mid-March 1918 during the German offensive. Soon after the Armistice, No.42 returned to the UK where it disbanded on 26 June 1919.

On 14 December 1936, No.42 reformed at Donibristle from B Flight of No.22 Squadron. Equipped with Vildebeest torpedo-bombers, the squadron was one of the only two strike units in the UK and it was April 1940 before it received Beauforts to replace its obsolete biplanes. On 5 June 1940, operations with Beauforts began and anti-shipping and minelaying missions along the coasts of northern Europe continued until June 1942 when the squadron left for the Far East. No.42's aircraft flew out via the Mediterranean where they were attached to No.47 Squadron for attacks on enemy shipping before and after the Battle of El Alamein. It was December before the squadron was established in Ceylon and in February 1943

Beaufort I. No.42 Squadron

it converted to Blenheims which were taken into action over Burma for the first time on 16 March 1943. In August, bombing operations ended to permit conversion to Hurricanes to begin. Ground-attack mission began on 22 December 1943 and continued until May 1945. The squadron was disbanded on 30 June 1945 but on the following day No.146 Squadron was renumbered 42 Squadron and flew Thunderbolts until disbanded on 30 December 1945.

On 1 October 1946, No.254 Squadron at Thorney Island was renumbered 42 Squadron. Beaufighters were flown on strike duties in Coastal Command until the squadron was again disbanded on 15 October 1947. On 28 June 1952, No.42 was reformed at St. Eval as a maritime reconnaissance squadron equipped with Shackletons. In October 1958, it moved to St. Mawgan and later provided detachments in the Persian Gulf and Madagascar, converting to Nimrods in April 1971.

Squadron bases

Base	Date	Base	Date
Filton	1 Apr 1916	Rely	25 Apr 1918
St. Omer	8 Aug 1916	Chocques	13 Oct 1918
La Gorgue	14 Aug 1916	Ascq	22 Oct 1918
Bailleul	1 Sep 1916	Marquain	Nov 1918
Fienvillers	16 Nov 1917	Aulnoy	28 Nov 1918
Left for Italy	17 Nov 1917	Saultain	11 Dec 1918
Santa Pelagio	2 Dec 1917	Abscon	30 Dec 1918
Istrana	7 Dec 1917	Netheravon	17 Feb 1919
Grossa	17 Dec 1917		to 26 Jun 1919
Santa Luca	19 Feb 1918	Donibristle	14 Dec 1936
Poggia Renatico	10 Mar 1918	Gosport	30 May 1937
Fienvillers	14 Mar 1918	Boscombe Down	14 Jun 1937
Chocques	22 Mar 1918	Exeter	13 Jul 1937
Treizennes	9 Apr 1918	Donibristle	17 Jul 1937
Catfoss	28 Aug 1937	Palel	Oct 1943 (G)
Eastleigh	17 Sep 1937	St.Thomas Mount	10 Nov 1943
Donibristle	28 Oct 1937	Palel	7 Dec 1943
Gosport	13 Jan 1938	Kangla	2 May 1944
Donibristle	30 Jan 1938	Tulihal	5 Jul 1944
Thorney Island	11 Mar 1938	Kangla	15 Nov 1944
Bircham Newton	12 Aug 1939	Onbauk	16 Jan 1945
Thorney Island	27 Apr 1940	Ondaw	14 Mar 1945
Wick	19 Jun 1940	Magwe/Maida Vale	30 Apr 1945
Leuchars	1 Mar 1941	Chakulia	18 May 1945
Left for Middle East		Dalbhumgarh	22 May 1945
	18 Jun 1942		to 30 Jun 1945
Ratmalana	14 Oct 1942 (G)	Meiktila	1 Jul 1945
Jalahalli	10 Nov 1942 (G)		to 30 Dec 1945
Yelahanka	7 Dec 1942	Thorney Island	1 Oct 1946
Rajyeswarpur	12 Mar 1943		to 15 Oct 1947
Kumbhirgram	1 May 1943	St. Eval	28 Jun 1952
Yelahanka	Oct 1943 (A)	St. Mawgan	8 Oct 1958

Aircraft Equipment	Period of service	Representative Serial
B.E.2d, B.E.2e	Apr 1916 – Apr 1917	
R.E.8	Apr 1917 – Feb 1919	
Vildebeest III	Dec 1937 – Jun 1937	K4598
	Sep 1939 – Apr 1940	
Vildebeest IV	Mar 1937 – Apr 1940	K6411
Beaufort I	Apr 1940 – Feb 1943	L9890 (AW-L)
Blenheim V	Feb 1943 – Oct 1943	BA851 (R)
Hurricane IIC	Oct 1943 – Jan 1945	LD294 (AW-X)
Hurricane IV	Nov 1944 – Jun 1945	LD101 (AW-D)
Thunderbolt II	Jul 1945 – Dec 1945	HK316 (AW-Y)
Beaufighter X	Oct 1946 – Oct 1947	RD687
Shackleton MR.1	Jun 1952 – Jul 1954	WG510 (A-F)
Shackleton MR.2	Apr 1954 – Apr 1966	WR952 (E)
Shackleton MR.3	Dec 1965 – Sep 1971	XF706 (E)
Nimrod MR.1	Apr 1971 – date	XV252 (52)

No. 43 Squadron

Badge: A Game Cock
Motto: Gloria finis (Glory is the end)

No.43 was formed at Stirling on 15 April 1916 and moved to France in January 1917 with Sopwith 1½-strutters for fighter and reconnaissance duties. In addition some bombing raids were carried out behind the German lines before the squadron re-equipped with Camels in September 1917. Fighter patrols and ground-attack missions occupied the squadron for the rest of the war, Snipes beginning to arrive in August. Conversion was completed only a few weeks before the Armistice and after a short period in Germany

No.43 returned to the UK and disbanded on 31 December 1919.

On 1 July 1923, No.43 reformed at Henlow as a fighter squadron equipped with Snipes. These were replaced by Gamecocks in 1926 which were in turn superceded by Siskins in 1928. Furies arrived in May 1931 and were flown until the squadron converted to Hurricanes at the end of 1938. Soon after the outbreak of World War Two, No.43 moved north for defensive duties, returning to Tangmere at the end of May 1940 for patrols over the Dunkirk beaches. After taking part in the first half of the Battle of Britain, the squadron was withdrawn to northern England to re-equip, moving to Scotland in December to act as a training unit in addition to its defensive role. It did not return south until June 1942 when it began to take part in sweeps over France and flew night intruder missions. In September, the squadron was withdrawn in preparation for a move overseas, arriving in Gibraltar in November. After the Allied landings in North Africa, No.43 flew into newly-captured airfields in Algeria to provide cover for the 1st Army and its supply

Gamecock I, No.43 Squadron

Meteor F.8, No.43 Squadron

Phantom FG.1s, No.43 Squadron

ports. Conversion to Spitfires took place in February 1943 and in June the squadron moved to Malta to cover the landings in Sicily. After a short time in Sicily, No.43 moved to Italy in September to fly fighter patrols. In July 1944, it was transferred to Corsica to provide fighter cover for the landings in southern France and after six weeks in France returned to Italy for fighter-bomber duties for the rest of the war. After a period with the occupation forces in Austria and northern Italy, the squadron disbanded on 16 May 1947.

On 11 February 1949, No.266 Squadron at Tangmere was renumbered 43 Squadron. Meteors were flown until replaced by Hunters in 1954, a move to Scotland being made in October 1950. In June 1961, the squadron moved to Cyprus for ground-attack duties, being transferred to Aden in March 1963 to provide air support for the Army. On 14 October 1967, it was disbanded.

No.43 reformed on 1 September 1969 at Leuchars with Phantoms for fighter and ground-attack duties in Strike Command.

Squadron bases

Stirling	15 Apr 1916	Henlow	1 July 1925
Netheravon	30 Aug 1916	Tangmere	7 Dec 1926 (G)
Northolt	8 Dec 1916		12 Dec 1926 (A)
St. Omer	17 Jan 1917	Acklington	18 Nov 1939
Treizennes	28 Jan 1917	Wick	26 Feb 1940
Auchel	30 May 1917	Tangmere	31 May 1940
La Gorgue	15 Jan 1918	Northolt (D)	23 Jul 1940
Avesnes-le-Comte	22 Mar 1918		to 1 Aug 1940
Fouquerolles	3 Jun 1918	Usworth	8 Sep 1940
Liettres	21 Jun 1918	Drem	12 Dec 1940
Le Touquin	14 Jul 1918	Crail	22 Feb 1941
Fienvillers	3 Aug 1918	Drem	1 Mar 1941
Senlis	6 Oct 1918	Acklington	4 Oct 1941
Bouvincourt	31 Oct 1918	Tangmere	16 Jun 1942
Bisseghem	15 Nov 1918	Kirton-in-Lindsey	1 Sep 1942
Fort de Cognelée	26 Nov 1918	Left for Gibraltar	28 Oct 1942
Bickendorf	19 Dec 1918	Gibraltar	5 Nov 1942
Eil	12 Aug 1919	Maison Blanche	8 Nov 1942
Spittlegate	25 Aug 1919	Jemappes	13 Mar 1943
	to 31 Dec 1919	Tingley	19 Apr 1943
		Nefza	2 May 1943

Mateur	26 May 1943	Sisteron	25 Aug 1944
Hal Far	9 Jun 1943 (G)	Lyon/Bron	7 Sep 1944
	11 Jun 1943 (A)	La Jasse	27 Sep 1944
Comiso	14 Jul 1943	Peretola	2 Oct 1944 (A)
Pachino	30 Jul 1943		13 Oct 1944 (G)
Panebianco	29 Aug 1943	Rimini	16 Nov 1944
Catania	30 Aug 1943	Ravenna	17 Feb 1945
Cassala	2 Sep 1943	Rivolto	5 May 1945
Falcone	6 Sep 1943	Klagenfurt	11 May 1945
Tusciano	16 Sep 1943	Zeltweg	10 Sep 1945
Capodichino	11 Oct 1943	Tissano	23 Sep 1946
Lago	16 Jan 1944	Treviso	15 Jan 1947
Nettuno	21 May 1944		to 16 May 1947
Tre Cancelli	5 Jun 1944	Tangmere	11 Feb 1949
Tarquinia	14 Jun 1944	Leuchars	Nov 1950
Grossetto	25 Jun 1944	Nicosia	21 Jun 1961
Piombino	5 Jul 1944	Khormaksar	2 Mar 1963
Calvi Main	20 Jul 1944		to 14 Oct 1967
Ramatuelle	20 Aug 1944	Leuchars	1 Sep 1969

Aircraft Equipment

Equipment	Period of service	Representative Serial	
Various (e.g. B.E.2e, Avro 504K)	Apr 1916 – Dec 1916		
Sopwith 1½-strutter	Dec 1916 – Sep 1917	A1100	(C5)
Camel	Sep 1917 – Oct 1918	B2510	(A)
Snipe	Aug 1918 – Sep 1919	E8064	(F)
	Apr 1925 – May 1926		
Gamecock I	Mar 1926 – Jun 1926	J7905	
Siskin IIIA	Jun 1928 – Jul 1926	J9318	-
Fury I	May 1931 – Feb 1939	K5675	
Hurricane I	Nov 1938 – Apr 1941		
	Sep 1942 – Nov 1942	L1847	(NQ-J)
Hurricane IIA, IIB	Apr 1941 – Aug 1942	BD715	(FT-M)
Hurricane IIC	Dec 1941 – Aug 1942		
	Nov 1942 – Mar 1943	HV817	(FT-C)
Spitfire VB, VC	Feb 1943 – Jan 1944	JG936	(FT-C)
Spitfire VIII	Aug 1944 – Nov 1944	MT680	(FT-E)
Spitfire IX	Aug 1943 – May 1947	MH711	(FT-G)
Meteor F.4	Feb 1949 – Sep 1950	VT257	(SW-T)
Meteor F.8	Sep 1950 – Sep 1954	WH466	(R)
Hunter F.1	Aug 1954 – Aug 1956	WT641	(T)
Hunter F.4	Mar 1956 – Dec 1956	WV663	(V)
Hunter F.6	Dec 1956 – 1960	XF456	(A)
Hunter FGA.9	1960 – Oct 1967	XJ684	(D)
Phantom FG.1	Sep 1969 – date	XT875	(K)

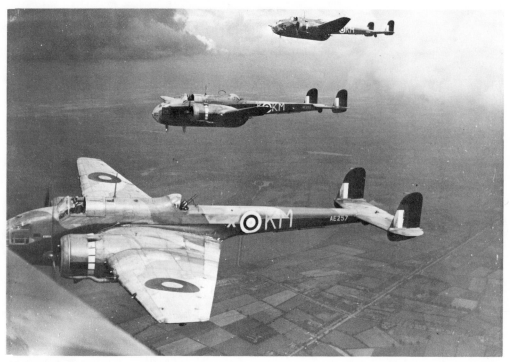

Hampden Is, No.44 Squadron

No. 44 Squadron

Badge: On a mount, an elephant
Motto: Fulmina regis justa (The
King's thunderbolts are
righteous)
Name: 'Rhodesia'

No.44 Squadron was formed at Hainault Farm, Essex, on 24 July 1917 as a home defence unit. Intended for the defence of the London area, the squadron was equipped with Camels to combat enemy bombers which had begun to replace the Zeppelin as a means of air attack on south-east England. Despite the difficult handling qualities of the Camel, the squadron began night patrols with some success. With the end of the war, No.44 was disbanded on 31 December 1919.

The squadron was reformed at Wyton on 8 March 1937 with Hind light bombers, replacing these with Blenheims at the end of the year. Early in 1939, it received Hampdens and Ansons and was given the task of converting No.5 Group pilots from single- to twin-engined aircraft. On 1 June the Ansons were transferred to No.76 Squadron and No.44 reverted to being an operational unit. During the first months of World War Two, the squadron flew some sweeps over the North Sea and was later engaged in leaflet dropping but it was not until the German invasion of Norway that bombing operations began. At the end of 1941, the Hampdens were withdrawn to permit No.44 to become the first Lancaster squadron. On 3 March 1942 the first Lancaster mission was flown and this type remained the squadron's equipment for the rest of the war as part of the main force of Bomber Command.

Retained as a peace-time unit, No.44 re-equipped with Lincolns over a period in 1946-47 and converted to Washingtons in January 1951. These, in turn, were replaced by Canberras which the squadron flew over Egypt from Cyprus during the Suez operation. On 16 July 1957 a reduction in the bomber force resulted in disbandment.

No.44 reformed at Waddington on 10 August 1960 with Vulcans received from No.83 Squadron, replacing these with Vulcan B.2s in November 1967.

Squadron bases			
Hainault Farm	24 Jul 1917	Mepal	21 Jul 1945
North Weald	1 Jul 1919	Mildenhall	25 Aug 1945
	to 31 Dec 1919	Wyton	29 Aug 1946
		Marham	11 Jan 1951
Wyton	8 Mar 1937	Coningsby	9 Apr 1951
Andover	18 Mar 1937	Cottesmore	20 May 1954
Waddington	16 Jun 1937	Honington	20 Feb 1955
Dunholme Lodge	31 May 1943		to 16 Jul 1957
Spilsby	30 Sep 1944	Waddington	10 Aug 1960

Aircraft Equipment	Period of service	Representative Serial
Sopwith 1½-strutter	Jul 1917 — Aug 1917	
Camel	Aug 1917 — Dec 1919	B5402 (2)
Hind	Mar 1937 — Jan 1938	K5401
Blenheim I	Dec 1937 — Feb 1939	K7133 (44-L)
Hampden I	Feb 1939 — Dec 1941	AE257 (KM-X)
Anson I	Feb 1939 — Jun 1939	N5000
Lancaster I, III	Dec 1941 — May 1947	R5556 (KM-C)
Lincoln B.2	Oct 1945 — May 1946	
	Dec 1946 — Mar 1947	RF423 (KM-K)
	May 1947 — Jan 1951	
Washington B.1	Jan 1951 — Apr 1953	WF509
Canberra B.2	Apr 1953 — Jul 1957	WD965
Vulcan B.1, B.1A	Aug 1960 — Nov 1967	XH498
Vulcan B.2	Nov 1967 — date	XM606

Vengeance IA, No.45 Squadron

No. 45 Squadron

Badge: A winged camel
Motto: Per ardue surge (Through difficulties I arise)

No.45 was formed at Gosport on 1 March 1916 and after a training period moved to France in October 1916 as a fighter squadron. For the first nine months it flew fighter patrols over the Western Front with Sopwith 1½-strutters and Nieuport 12s before re-equipping with Camels. In November 1917, the squadron moved to northern Italy for operations on the Austrian front as part of an Anglo-French ground and air force sent to reinforce the Italian line. In September 1918, it returned to France and joined the Independent Force for bomber escort duties for the rest of the war. In February 1919, No.45 returned to the UK as a cadre and disbanded on 31 December 1919.

On 1 April 1921, the squadron reformed at Helwan, receiving Vimys by the end of the year. With these it pioneered air routes in the Middle East and in March 1922 re-equipped with Vernons on being transferred to Iraq for bomber-transport duties. On 1 November 1926, No.45 was reduced to single-flight basis and on 17 January 1927 was absorbed by No.47 Squadron.

Reformed at Heliopolis on 25 April 1927 with D.H.9As, the squadron was engaged in patrol duties in Egypt and Palestine for many years. Fairey IIIFs were received in September 1929 and began to be replaced by Harts in September 1935 but the sole flight re-equipped was transferred to No.6 Squadron on 1 January 1936. Vincents finally replaced IIIFs in December 1935. B Flight was detached to Nairobi on 25 September 1935 and received Gordons in January 1936 before becoming No.223 Squadron on 15 December 1936.

Wellesleys began to arrive in November 1937 and were flown until replaced by Blenheims in June 1939. Bombing operations began on the day after Italy entered the war and in July a detachment was sent to the Sudan for attacks on Italian East Africa. The whole squadron moved there in September for three months before returning to Egypt, taking part in the Syrian campaign in June 1941. After a further period of bombing operations in the Western Desert, No.45 was despatched to Burma in February 1942. Arriving as the Allied forces were withdrawing from that country, the squadron became dispersed and reassembled in India during March. Attacks on Japanese bases and communications were resumed on 27 June 1943 after No.45 had converted to Vengeance dive-bombers and had spent a lengthy training period with the new type. After six months, the squadron was withdrawn for conversion to Mosquitos but difficulties with these wooden aircraft prevented any operations until 28 September 1944. On 12 May 1945, the squadron flew its last mission in World War Two and moved to India. Transferred to Ceylon in May 1946, No.45 received Beaufighters for strike duties in December 1945 and in May 1949 supplemented these with three Brigands for meteorological duties for a month before passing them on to No.1301 Flight when posted to Malaya. A detachment had begun operating against Communist guerillas in Malaya in August 1948 and conversion to Brigand B.1s was under way at the end of 1949. These were flown on strike and patrol duties until replaced by Hornets in 1952. In May 1955, No.45 re-equipped with Vampires and in December received Venoms. The squadron converted to Canberras at Coningsby in November 1957 and these were flown until disbandment on 13 January 1970.

On 1 August 1972, No.45 reformed at West Raynham for ground-attack training duties with Hunters, moving to Wittering in September of the same year. On 4 June 1976, the squadron disbanded.

Squadron bases			
Gosport	1 Mar 1916	Left for France	12 Sep 1918
Thetford	3 May 1916	Bettoncourt	22 Sep 1918
St. Omer	12 Oct 1916	Izel-le-Hameau	21 Nov 1918
Fienvillers	15 Oct 1916	Rendcombe	Feb 1919
Boisdinghem	4 Nov 1916	Eastleigh	Nov 1919
Ste. Marie Cappel	4 Dec 1916		to 31 Dec 1919
Fienvillers	16 Nov 1917	Helwan	1 Apr 1921
Left for Italy	12 Dec 1917	Almaza	11 Jul 1921
Padova	20 Dec 1917	Basra	14 Mar 1922
Scata Pelagio	18 Dec 1917	Hinaidi	16 May 1922
Istrana	26 Dec 1917		to 17 Jan 1927
Grossa	17 Mar 1918	Heliopolis	25 Apr 1927
		Helwan	21 Oct 1927

Nairobi (D)	25 Sep 1935 to 15 Dec 1936	Asansol (D)	28 May 1942 to 16 Aug 1942
Ismailia	16 Jan 1939	Asansol	16 Aug 1942
Fuka	4 Aug 1939	Cholavarum	8 Nov 1942
Helwan	20 Jun 1940	Asansol	12 Mar 1943
Erkoweit (D)	29 Jul 1940 to 13 Aug 1940	Digri	17 May 1943 (A) 20 May 1943 (G)
Wadi Gazouza	27 Sep 1940	Kumbhirgram	11 Oct 1943
Helwan	4 Dec 1940	Yelahanka	11 Feb 1944
Qotafiya	8 Dec 1940	Dalbhumgarh	26 May 1944
LG.81	30 Dec 1940	Ranchi	27 Aug 1944
Menastir	31 Dec 1940	Kumbhirgram	29 Sep 1944
Helwan	9 Feb 1941	Joari	27 Apr 1945
Gambut	7 Apr 1941	Cholavarum	4 Jun 1945
Fuka	10 Apr 1941	St. Thomas Mount	
Wadi Natrun	1 Jun 1941		12 Oct 1945
Aqir	22 Jun 1941	Negombo	May 1946
Habbaniya	10 Aug 1941	Kuala Lumpur	1 May 1949
LG.16	27 Sep 1941	Tengah	5 Dec 1949
LG.75	14 Nov 1941	Butterworth	Mar 1955 to 1 Nov 1957
Gambut	19 Dec 1941	Coningsby	1 Nov 1957 (D)
Helwan	3 Jan 1942	Tengah	Nov 1957 (P) to 13 Jan 1970
Left for Burma	17 Feb 1942 (G)	West Raynham	1 Aug 1972
Magwe	Feb 1942 (A)	Wittering	29 Sep 1972 to 4 Jun 1976
Lashio	23 Mar 1942 (A)		
Dum Dum	18 Mar 1942 (G)		

Aircraft Equipment	Period of service	Representative Serial	
Sopwith 1½-strutter	Mar 1916 — Apr 1917	B2583	
Nieuport 12	Apr 1917 — Jul 1917		
Camel	Jul 1917 — Jan 1919	B2321	(S)
Snipe	Nov 1918 — Jan 1919		
Vimy	Nov 1921 — Mar 1922	J6869	
Vernon	Mar 1922 — Jan 1927	J7134	'Valkyrie'
D.H.9A	Apr 1927 — Sep 1929	J7832	(1)
Fairey IIIF	Sep 1929 — Dec 1935	SR1174	(N1)
Hart	Sep 1935 — Jan 1936	K4460	
Vincent	Nov 1935 — Dec 1937	K4671	
Gordon	Jan 1936 — Dec 1936	K1728	
Wellesley	Nov 1937 — Jun 1939	K7781	(L)
Blenheim I	Jun 1939 — Mar 1941	L6663	
Blenheim IV	Mar 1941 — Aug 1942	Z9609	
Vengeance IA, II	Dec 1942 — Feb 1944	AN711	(Q)
Mosquito VI	Feb 1944 — May 1946	HR371	
Beaufighter X	Dec 1945 — Feb 1950	RD805	
Brigand Met.1, B.1	May 1949 — Jun 1949	VS854	
	Nov 1949 — Feb 1952		
Hornet F.3	Jan 1951 — May 1955	WB898	(OB-A)
Vampire FB.9	May 1955 — Mar 1956	WL554	
Venom FB.1	Dec 1955 — Nov 1957	WR312	(D)
Canberra B.2, B.15	Nov 1957 — Jan 1970	WH853	
Hunter FGA.9	Aug 1972 — Jun 1976	XG130	(61)

No. 46 Squadron

Badge: Two arrow heads surmounted by a third, all in bend
Motto: We rise to conquer
Name: 'Uganda'

No.46 Squadron was formed at Wyton on 19 April 1916 from a nucleus supplied by No.2 Reserve Squadron and trained as a reconnaissance unit. In October it moved to France with Nieuport two-seaters to undertake artillery observations and photographic missions over the Western Front. In April 1917 it re-equipped with Pups to become a fighter squadron as a result of increasing strength of German fighter units over the Front. In July 1917 No.46 returned to the UK for defensive duties after a heavy German air raid on London but returned to France in August without seeing action. The squadron re-equipped with Camels in November 1917 and ground-attack missions became common, especially during the German offensive in March 1918. As the Germans retreated during the last months of the war, attacks were made on communications and dumps behind the front line. In January 1919 the squadron was reduced to a cadre and returned to the UK in February, disbanding on 31 December 1919.

On 3 September 1936 B Flight of No.17 Squadron became No.46 Squadron at Kenley with Gauntlets. It was the end of February 1937 before a full complement of aircraft was in service and in February 1939 conversion to Hurricanes took place. For the first months of World War Two defensive patrols were flown covering convoys off the East Coast. With the German invasion of Norway in April 1940 preparations were put in hand for the transfer of the squadron to northern Norway to augment the handful of Gladiators operating from improvised airfields. On May 14, No.46's Hurricanes left the Clyde in HMS *Glorious* for an airfield near Harstad but had to return with the carrier to Scapa Flow when the landing ground was found to be unusable. On 26 May ten aircraft were flown off to Skaanland

Dakota C.4, No.46 Squadron

but due to the soft surface two crashed on landing and the remainder were diverted to Bardufoss, sixty miles further north. After providing fighter cover for the Narvik area, the situation in France resulted in the evacuation of all forces from Norway and on 7 June, the squadron flew its Hurricanes on to the deck of *Glorious* despite their lack of arrester hooks. Ground crews embarked in other ships and reassembled at Digby but *Glorious* and her destroyer escort encountered German battle-cruisers en route and were sunk.

By the end of June, No.46 was operational again and early in September moved south to relieve a squadron depleted by continuous action during the first stages of the Battle of Britain. It remained until after the Battle, moving to Yorkshire at the end of February 1941 for day and night offensive patrols. In May the squadron embarked for the Middle East but the ground crews found no aircraft waiting for them and acted as a maintenance unit until May 1942. No.46's pilots in the meantime were flying from Malta against heavy enemy raids and were absorbed by No.261 Squadron a few weeks later. On 8 May 1942, the squadron moved to Idku where it absorbed a detachment of No.89 Squadron's Beaufighters and began reforming as a night fighter unit. Patrols began immediately and cover was provided over Egypt and coastal shipping by both day and night. In August 1943 intruder missions over the Greek islands

began and detachments were based around the Eastern Mediterranean to provide fighter defence for the area. In July 1944 some Mosquitos were received but in December the squadron left for the UK, reforming at Stoney Cross on 9 January 1945 as a transport unit with Stirlings. On 1 April trooping flights to India began and at the beginning of 1946 Dakotas replaced the Stirlings. During 1946, the squadron's routes were mainly in Europe. When the Russian blockade of Berlin began in July 1948, No.46's Dakotas started operating flights carrying food and coal which lasted for a year until the blockade was lifted. Though based at Oakington, No.46's aircraft operated from Wunstorf, Fassberg and Lubeck. On 20 February 1950 the squadron disbanded.

No.46 Squadron reformed at Odiham on 15 August 1954 equipped with Meteor night fighters. In March 1956 it became the first Javelin squadron, flying this type until disbanded on 30 June 1961. On 1 December 1966, the squadron reformed at Abingdon as a tactical transport unit equipped with Andovers, disbanding on 31 August 1975.

Squadron bases

Wyton	19 Apr 1916	Busigny	27 Oct 1918
St. Omer	20 Oct 1916	Baizieux	16 Nov 1918
Droglandt	26 Oct 1916	Rendcombe	8 Feb 1919
Boisdinghem	25 Apr 1917		to 31 Dec 1919
La Gorgue	12 May 1917	Kenley	3 Sep 1936
Bruay	6 Jul 1917	Digby	15 Nov 1937
Suttons Farm	10 Jul 1917	Acklington	9 Dec 1939
Ste Marie Cappel	30 Aug 1917	Digby	17 Jan 1940
Filescamp	7 Sep 1917	Emb. in 'Glorious'	9 May 1940
Liettres	16 May 1918	Skaanland & Bardufoss	
Serny	17 June 1918		26 May 1940
Poulainville	14 Aug 1918	Bardufoss	27 May 1940
Cappy	8 Sep 1918	Emb. in 'Glorious'	8 Jun 1940
Athies	6 Oct 1918		to 9 Jun 1940 (A)
		Digby	13 Jun 1940

Andover C.1, No.46 Squadron

Duxford	18 Aug 1940	Dets. in Libya, Egypt, Palestine	
Digby	19 Aug 1940	and Cyprus	
Stapleford Tawney	1 Sep 1940	Left for UK	13 Dec 1944
North Weald	8 Nov 1940	Stoney Cross	9 Jan 1945
Digby	14 Dec 1940	Manston	11 Oct 1946
Church Fenton	28 Feb 1941	Abingdon	16 Dec 1946
Sherburn-in-Elmet	1 Mar 1941	Oakington	Nov 1947
Left for Middle East			to 20 Feb 1950
	20 May 1941 (G)	Odiham	15 Aug 1954
Kasfareet	10 Jul 1941	Waterbeach	15 Jul 1959
Abu Sueir	16 Jul 1941		to 30 Jun 1961
Kilo 17	9 Sep 1941	Abingdon	1 Dec 1966
Idku	8 May 1942	Thorney Island	Sep 1970 (P)
El Khanka	2 Jul 1942		to 31 Aug 1975
Idku	19 Jul 1942		

Aircraft Equipment	Period of service	Representative Serial	
Nieuport 12	Apr 1916 – Apr 1917	A3274	
B.E.2c	Nov 1916 – Apr 1917	5773	
B.E.2e	Feb 1917 – Apr 1917	7060	
Pup	Apr 1917 – Nov 1917	A677	(C)
Camel	Nov 1917 – Feb 1919	F1977	
Gauntlet II	Sep 1936 – Feb 1939	K7794	
Hurricane I	Feb 1939 – Dec 1940	V7442	
Hurricane IIA	Dec 1940 – May 1941		
Hurricane IIC	May 1941 – Jun 1941		
Beaufighter I	May 1942 – Jul 1942	V8317	(C)
Beaufighter VI	May 1942 – Dec 1944	MM875	(N)
Beaufighter X	Apr 1944 – Jul 1944	LZ846	(R)
Mosquito XII	Jul 1944 – Dec 1944	HJ671	
Stirling V	Feb 1945 – Feb 1946	PJ952	(XK-F)
Dakota III, IV	Feb 1946 – Feb 1950	KN241	(XK-K)
Meteor NF.12	Aug 1954 – Mar 1956	WS607	(A)
Meteor NF.14	Aug 1954 – Mar 1956	WS830	(H)
Javelin FAW.1	Mar 1956 – Nov 1957	XA626	(Q)
Javelin FAW.2	Aug 1957 – Jun 1961	WA777	(R)
Javelin FAW.6	May 1958 – Jun 1961	XA812	(B)
Andover C.1	Dec 1966 – Aug 1975	XS604	

No. 47 Squadron

Badge: In front of a fountain, a
demoiselle crane's head
erased

Motto: Nili nomen roboris omen
(The name of the Nile is
an omen of our strength)

No.47 Squadron was formed on 1 March 1916 at Beverley
and in September left for Greece, arriving at Salonika on
20 September to join a British, French and Serbian force
holding an area of Macedonia against the Bulgarian and
Austro-Hungarian armies. Two flights operated reconnaissance aircraft and one flight fighters until April 1918, when
the fighter flight was transferred to No.150 Squadron.
As normal on fronts remote from France, the squadron used
a variety of aircraft until the last months of the war. When
the Bulgarian army finally retreated, the squadron was
engaged in bombing raids on its escape routes until Bulgaria
signed an Armistice. In April 1919 No.47 moved to south
Russia to aid the White Russian forces with Camels and
D.H.9s, becoming A Squadron, RAF Mission on 7 October
1919.

On 1 February 1920, No.206 Squadron at Helwan was
renumbered 47 Squadron. Initially equipped with D.H.9s,
it received D.H.9As in 1921 and stationed a detachment at
Khartoum to co-operate with the ground forces in the Sudan.
This detachment was joined by the rest of the squadron in
October 1927, and until Italy entered the war in June 1940,

Gordon I, No.47 Squadron

No.47 co-operated with the Sudan Defence Force in policing
the desert areas. From February 1929 a floatplane flight
operated from the Nile over the river's upper reaches and
along the Red Sea coast until 1939. Wellesleys arrived in
June 1939 to replace Gordons and Vincents, but a flight
of the latter remained for army co-operation duties until
July 1940.

On the day after war came to East Africa, No.47 began
bombing raids on Italian airfields and bases in Eritrea and
Ethiopia despite its obsolete aircraft. These continued
throughout the campaign and it moved to Asmara after the
Italian forces in Eritrea surrendered. In December 1941 the
squadron moved to the Middle East and began anti-submarine
patrols in April 1942 along the Egyptian coast, still flying
Wellesleys. Conversion to Beaufort torpedo-bombers began
in July but the Wellesley flight continued to fly patrols
until disbanded on 3 March 1943. On 8 October 1942,
No.47 flew its first anti-shipping operations with Beauforts
against convoys supplying the Axis armies in Libya. In June
1943, the squadron moved to Tunisia, at the same time
re-equipping with Beaufighters which began shipping strikes
off the coasts of Sicily, Italy and Sardinia as both torpedo-
carriers and escort fighters. In October it moved to Libya
for operations over the Aegean and Greek coast, being
transferred to India in March 1944 to form part of a strike
wing. In October No.47 converted to Mosquitos but early
examples suffered structural problems in the tropical heat
and humidity and Beaufighters returned in November. In
January 1945 these began ground-attack missions over
Burma with rockets but in February Mosquitos again arrived
to begin operations on 1 March. Until August, low-level

Beverley C.1s, No.47 Squadron

attacks were made on enemy transport and bases in Burma and in November 1945 a detachment was sent to Java where nationalist forces had began attacking Allied troops landed to disarm the Japanese. Ground-attack sorties against marauding bands and escort flights over road convoys occupied the detachment until the squadron disbanded on 21 March 1946.

On 1 September 1946, No.644 Squadron at Qastina was renumbered 47 Squadron and flew its Halifax transports back to the UK at the end of the month. Exercises with airborne forces were undertaken until September 1948, when it moved to Dishforth to become the first Hastings squadron. These it flew on the Berlin Airlift from November until the blockade was lifted, carrying mainly coal to keep the city's industries going. In March 1956, it became the first squadron to receive Beverley heavy transports and flew these until disbanded on 31 October 1967.

On 25 February 1968, No.47 Squadron reformed at Fairford with Hercules transports.

Squadron bases

Beverley	1 Mar 1916	Left for Egypt 9 Dec 1941 (G)	
Left for Greece	6 Sep 1916	Burg el Arab	25 Jan 1942
Salonika	20 Sep 1916	LG.87	9 Feb 1942
Janes	27 Oct 1916	Kasfareet	18 Mar 1942 (G)
Salonika	3 Nov 1918	LG.89	16 Apr 1942 (A)
Amberkoj	16 Feb 1919	St. Jean	16 Jul 1942 (A)
Ekaterinodar*	May 1919	Shandur	8 Sep 1942
	to 7 Oct 1919	Gianaclis	29 Jan 1943
Helwan	1 Feb 1920	Misurata West	3 Mar 1943
Khartoum	21 Oct 1927	Protville No.2	16 Jun 1943
Erkowit	28 May 1940	Sidi Amor	16 Oct 1943
Carthago	7 Jul 1940	El Adem	22 Oct 1943 (A)
Sennar	27 Nov 1940		13 Nov 1943 (G)
Gordon's Tree	14 Dec 1940	Gambut III	24 Nov 1943
Asmara	29 May 1941	Amriya South	15 Mar 1944
		Left for India	25 Mar 1944

Cholavarum	30 Mar 1944 (A)	Fairford	30 Sep 1946
	20 Apr 1944 (G)	Dishforth	14 Sep 1948
Yelahanka	7 Oct 1944	Schleswigland (A)	1 Nov 1948
Ranchi	12 Nov 1944		to May 1949
Kumbhirgram	10 Jan 1945	Topcliffe	22 Aug 1949
Kinmagon	26 Apr 1945	Abingdon	13 May 1953
Hmawbi	16 Aug 1945		to 31 Oct 1967
Butterworth	15 Jan 1946	Fairford	25 Feb 1968
	to 21 Mar 1946	Lyneham	Sep 1971
Qastina	1 Sep 1946		

*Squadron headquarters; detachments operated from many locations during this period.

Aircraft

Equipment	Period of service	Representative Serial
F.K.3	Mar 1916 – Apr 1916	5508
B.E.12, B.E.12a	Mar 1916 – Apr 1918	A4022
B.E.2c, B.E.2d	Apr 1916 – Mar 1918	A8691
Bristol Scout	Sep 1916 – Feb 1917	5323
D.H.2	Feb 1917 – Dec 1917	A4772
Vickers F.B.19	Jun 1917 – Feb 1918	A5226
S.E.5A	Nov 1917 – Apr 1918	B695
Bristol M.1c	Feb 1918 – Apr 1918	C4926
F.K.8	Feb 1917 – Jun 1919	C3557
D.H.9	Aug 1918 – Oct 1919 Feb 1920 – 1921	C6236
Camel	Apr 1919 – Oct 1919	F6396
D.H.9A	1921 – Apr 1928	E959 (BII)
Fairey IIIF	Dec 1927 – Jan 1933	SR1143
Gordon	Jan 1933 – Jun 1939	KR2603 (Z)
Vincent	Jul 1936 – Jul 1940	K4707
Wellesley	Jun 1939 – Mar 1943	L2652 (KU-O)
Beaufort I	Jul 1942 – Jun 1943	DE118 (S)
Beaufighter X	Jun 1943 – Oct 1944 Nov 1944 – Apr 1945	NE502 (H)
Mosquito VI	Oct 1944 – Nov 1944 Feb 1945 – Mar 1946	RF763 (B)
Halifax A.7, A.9	Sep 1946 – Sep 1948	RT922
Hastings C.1, C.2	Sep 1948 – Mar 1956	TG601
Beverley C.1	Mar 1956 – Oct 1967	XB287 (T)
Hercules C.1	Feb 1968 – date	XV290

No. 48 Squadron

Badge: On an equilateral triangle
a Petrel's head erased
Motto: Forte et fidele

No.48 Squadron was formed on 15 April 1916 at Netheravon and moved to France in March 1917 as the first Bristol Fighter squadron. After overcoming its teething troubles, this type settled down to become one of the most successful fighters of the First World War. After flying fighter and escort missions over the Western Front until the Armistice, No.48 was transferred to India in June 1919 where it was renumbered 5 Squadron on 1 April 1920.

On 25 November 1935, No.48 reformed at Bicester from personnel supplied by C Flight, No.101 Squadron and in December moved to Manston where it helped to form the School of Air Navigation. B Flight, Calshot, joined the squadron in January 1936, bringing with it Saro Cloud amphibians but these were not very suitable for navigation training and in March were replaced by Ansons. The RAF Expansion Scheme required large numbers of aircrew and No.48 was enlarged during 1936 to an establishment of eighty pupils. In September 1938, the squadron moved to Eastchurch to become a general reconnaissance unit and handed over its training commitments to the School of Air Navigation. Moving to Thorney Island a few days before the outbreak of the Second World War, No.48 began flying anti-submarine patrols, stationing detachments at various points around the Channel coasts. During the evacuation from Dunkirk, the squadron's Ansons joined with No.500 in maintaining anti-E-boat patrols off the beaches. Also in May 1940, Beauforts began to arrive but were not flown operationally by the squadron due to development problems with the Taurus engines. The type was flown at St. Eval where all aircraft and converted crews were transferred to No.217 Squadron in November.

In July 1940, the squadron moved to Merseyside to carry out patrols over the approaches to the Clyde and Irish Sea. In December a detachment was sent to the Shetlands and was joined by the remainder of the squadron in July 1941. Conversion to Hudsons had started a month earlier but it was October before the last Anson was withdrawn. By the end of October, shipping patrols and strikes on enemy craft off the Norwegian coast began. In August 1942, anti-submarine patrols were resumed between Scotland and

Iceland and in December No.48 moved to Gibraltar for patrols over the approaches to the Mediterranean. These ended in February 1944 when the squadron returned to the UK and re-equipped with Dakotas on being transferred to Transport Command. On D-Day, No.48 provided thirty aircraft to drop paratroops before dawn, following up with twenty-two glider-towing sorties. At Arnhem in September, the squadron lost a third of its strength flying re-supply missions in the face of intense flak after successfully towing forty-nine gliders in the first two days of the airborne landings. After taking part in the crossing of the Rhine, No.48 was sent to India in August 1945 but the Japanese surrender resulted in its disbandment on 16 January 1946.

On 15 February 1946, No.215 Squadron at Seletar, Singapore, was renumbered 48 Squadron and undertook transport duties in Malaya with Dakotas, Valettas and Hastings until disbanded on 3 March 1967, having played a large part in keeping anti-terrorist forces supplied in the jungle during the Emergency.

On 1 October 1967, No.48 reformed at Changi, Singapore with Hercules transports and in September 1971 returned to the UK where it was disbanded on 7 January 1976.

Squadron bases

Netheravon	15 Apr 1916	Skitten	20 Oct 1941
Rendcombe	Jun 1916	Wick	6 Jan 1942
Bertangles	8 Mar 1917	Sumburgh	23 Sep 1942
Bellevue	Mar 1917	Gosport	19 Nov 1942
Leffrinckhoucke	Sep 1917	Gibraltar	23 Dec 1942
Flez	Dec 1917	Bircham Newton	21 Feb 1944
Bertangles	Aug 1918	Down Ampney	24 Feb 1944
Ste. Marie Cappel	Sep 1918	Patenga	Aug 1945 (P)
Reckem	Oct 1918		to 16 Jan 1946
Left for India	26 May 1919	Kallang	15 Feb 1946
Arrived in India	22 Jun 1919	Changi	24 Apr 1946
Quetta	12 Jul 1919	Kuala Lumpur	1 Jun 1949
	to 1 Apr 1920	Changi	12 Dec 1949
Bicester	25 Nov 1935		to 3 Mar 1967
Manston	16 Dec 1935	Kuala Lumpur (D)	Jan 1951
Eastchurch	1 Sep 1938		to May 1951
Thorney Island	25 Aug 1939	Changi	1 Oct 1967
Hooton Park	16 Jul 1940	Lyneham	1 Sep 1971
Stornoway	24 Jul 1941		to 7 Jan 1976

Aircraft Equipment

Aircraft Equipment	Period of service	Representative Serial	
B.E.12	Apr 1916 – Mar 1917		
Bristol F.2B	Mar 1917 – Feb 1920	C814	(12)
Cloud	Feb 1936 – Jun 1936	K4302	
Anson I	Mar 1936 – Oct 1941	L7047	
Beaufort I	May 1940 – Nov 1940	L9868	
Hudson III	Jun 1941 – Oct 1941	T9426	(ZS-P)
Hudson V	Jun 1941 – Nov 1942	AM567	
Hudson VI	Feb 1942 – Feb 1944	EW893	(ZS-O)
Dakota III, IV	Feb 1944 – Jan 1946	KG337	(ZS-UC)
Dakota C.4	Feb 1946 – May 1951	KJ887	
Valetta C.1	May 1951 – Aug 1957	VW198	
Hastings C.1, C.2	Aug 1957 – Mar 1967	TG425	
Hercules C.1	Oct 1967 – Jan 1976	XV203	

Cloud I, No.48 Squadron

Anson I, No.48 Squadron

No. 49 Squadron

Badge: A greyhound courant
Motto: Cave canem (Beware of the dog)

No.49 Squadron was formed at Dover on 15 April 1916 and undertook training duties with B.E.2cs and R.E.7s for the first eighteen months of its career. In November 1917 it moved to France with D.H.4s for day bombing and reconnaissance. During the German offensive in March 1918 the squadron took part in low-level attacks on enemy troops and transport before re-equipping with D.H.9s. Low bombing of tactical objectives was supplemented by high-altitude raids on communications centres behind the front until the end of the war. After a period with the occupation forces, No.49 disbanded in Germany on 18 July 1919.

On 10 February 1936 C Flight of No.18 Squadron became No.49 Squadron at Bircham Newton with Hind light bombers. In September 1938 conversion to Hampdens began, No.49 being the first unit equipped with the type. Reconnaissance, minelaying and leaflet dropping occupied the opening period of World War Two but on 11 May 1940 bombing attacks on Germany began. In April 1942 re-equipping with Manchesters began but the type was unsuccesful and the squadron received Lancasters in July. These were flown as part of the main force of Bomber Command for the rest of the war and No.49 remained in being as part of the post-war RAF, receiving Lincolns in

October 1949. In November 1953 it was detached to Kenya for reconnaissance and bombing missions during the Mau Mau uprising, returning in February 1954 and disbanding on 1 August 1955.

On 1 May 1956 No.49 reformed at Wittering with Valiants and took part in nuclear bomb trials at Christmas Island in 1956/57, a squadron aircraft dropping the first British hydrogen bomb during these. With the grounding of the Valiant force, the squadron disbanded on 1 May 1965.

Squadron bases			
Dover	15 Apr 1916	Bircham Newton	10 Feb 1936
La Bellevue	12 Nov 1917	Worthy Down	8 Aug 1936
Zeauvis	27 Mar 1918	Scampton	14 Mar 1938
Boisdinghem	29 Mar 1918	Fiskerton	2 Jan 1943
Petite Synthe	30 Mar 1918	Fulbeck	16 Oct 1944
Conteville	3 May 1918	Syerston	22 Apr 1945
Fourneuil	2 Jun 1918	Mepal	28 Sep 1945
Beauvois	21 Jun 1918	Upwood	Jul 1946
Rozoy-en-Brie	14 Jul 1918	Waddington	25 Jun 1952
Beauvois	4 Aug 1918	Wittering	Aug 1953
Villers-lez-Cagnicourt		Eastleigh	Nov 1953
	30 Oct 1918	Upwood	Feb 1954
Bavai	24 Nov 1918		to 1 Aug 1955
Bickendorf	29 May 1919	Wittering	1 May 1956
	to 18 Jul 1919	Marham	26 Jun 1961
			to 1 May 1965

Aircraft Equipment	Period of service	Representative Serial
B.E.2c	Apr 1916 — Nov 1917	
R.E.7	Dec 1916 — Nov 1917	
D.H.4	Apr 1917 — Apr 1918	A7694 (6)
D.H.9	Apr 1918 — Jul 1919	C6114 (M)
Hind	Feb 1936 — Dec 1938	K5412
Hampden I	Sep 1938 — Apr 1942	P1333 (EA-F)
Manchester I	Apr 1942 — Jul 1942	L7453 (EA-T)
Lancaster I, III	Jul 1942 — Oct 1949	DV238 (EA-D)
Lincoln B.2	Oct 1949 — Aug 1955	RF349
Valiant B.1	May 1956 — Dec 1964	WZ366

B.E.12, No.50 Squadron

No. 50 Squadron

Badge: A sword in bend severing a mantle palewise
Motto: From defence to attack

No.50 Squadron was formed on 15 May 1916 at Dover as a home defence unit. Equipped with B.E. variants, it carried out defensive patrols from airfields in Kent until the end of the war, receiving Camels in February 1918 to combat enemy bombers based in Belgium. The squadron disbanded on 13 June 1919.

On 3 May 1937 No.50 reformed at Waddington with Hinds and converted to Hampdens at the end of 1938. On the outbreak of war the squadron began bombing raids on 19 March 1940 and continued until the end of the war as part of the main force of Bomber Command. Conversion to Lancasters began in May 1942 and this type served the squadron until replaced by Lincolns in 1946. On 31 January 1951 the squadron was disbanded.

On 15 August 1952 No.50 reformed at Binbrook with Canberras which were flown until disbandment on 1 October 1959. On 1 August 1961 it reformed at Waddington as a V-bomber squadron equipped with Vulcans.

Squadron bases			
Dover	15 May 1916	Skellingthorpe	26 Nov 1941
Harrietsham	Oct 1916 (P)	Swinderby	20 Jun 1942
Flights at Detling,		Skellingthorpe	17 Oct 1942
Bekesbourne,		Sturgate	15 Jun 1945
Throwley		Waddington	25 Jan 1946
Bekesbourne	8 Feb 1918		to 31 Jan 1951
	to 13 Jun 1919	Binbrook	15 Aug 1952
Waddington	3 May 1937	Upwood	9 Jan 1956
Lindholme	10 Jul 1940		to 1 Oct 1959
Swinderby	19 Jul 1941	Waddington	1 Aug 1961

Aircraft Equipment	Period of service	Representative Serial
B.E.2c, B.E.2d, B.E.2e	May 1916 — Feb 1918	2699
B.E.12a, B.E.12b,		
F.K.8, R.E.8, Pup	May 1916 — Feb 1918	
Camel	Feb 1918 — Nov 1918	
S.E.5A	Nov 1918 — Jun 1919	
Hind	May 1937 — Jan 1939	K6812
Hampden I	Dec 1938 — May 1942	AE370 (VN-P)
Manchester I	Apr 1942 — Jun 1942	L7471
Lancaster I, III	May 1942 — Nov 1946	DV197 (VN-T)
Lincoln B.2	Jul 1946 — Jan 1951	RF384 (VN-H)
Canberra B.2	Aug 1952 — Oct 1959	WK133
Vulcan B.1, B.1A	Aug 1961 — Nov 1966	XH498
Vulcan B.2	Dec 1965 — date	XM572

No. 51 Squadron

Badge: A goose volant
Motto: Swift and sure

No.51 Squadron was formed at Thetford on 15 May 1916 as a home defence unit using airfields in East Anglia for anti-Zeppelin patrols. For the rest of the war, it was deployed to defend both the Midlands and London from enemy raiders approaching their targets via The Wash, thus out-flanking the defences of London and avoiding long overland flights to reach the Midlands. In May 1919 the squadron moved to the London area and disbanded on 13 June 1919.

On 5 March 1937 B Flight of No.58 Squadron became No.51 Squadron at Driffield and flew Virginias and Ansons until the arrival of Whitleys in February 1938. On the outbreak of World War Two, the squadron carried out leaflet raids until the German invasion of France and the Low Countries in May 1940 resulted in bombing operations being started. In February 1942, No.51 carried paratroops on their first raid on France and in May the squadron was transferred to Coastal Command for patrols over the Bay of Biscay. In October 1942 it returned to Bomber Command and re-equipped with Halifaxes, resuming bombing raids on 9 January 1943. Halifaxes were flown for the rest of the war and on 8 May 1945 No.51 was transferred to Transport Command and converted to Stirlings. Trooping flights to India and the Middle East began in July and continued till the end of the year. In February 1946, the squadron converted to Yorks and flew these on the Berlin Airlift before being disbanded on 30 October 1950.

On 21 August 1958 No.192 Squadron at Watton was renumbered 51 Squadron. Flying Canberras and Comets on long-range calibration duties, the squadron was transferred to Bomber Command in March 1963, and moved to Wyton.

Comet T.2, No.51 Squadron

Squadron bases

Thetford	15 May 1916	Dishforth	9 Dec 1939
Hingham	23 Sep 1916	Chivenor	6 May 1942
Marham	Aug 1917	Snaith	27 Oct 1942
dets at:		Leconfield	20 Apr 1945
Marham		Stradishall	21 Aug 1945
Mattishall		Waterbeach	20 Aug 1946
Tydd St. Mary		Abingdon	8 Dec 1947
Suttons Farm	14 May 1919	Bassingbourn	25 Jun 1948
	to 13 Jun 1919		to 30 Oct 1950
Driffield	15 Mar 1937	Watton	21 Aug 1958
Boscombe Down	24 Mar 1937	Wyton	31 Mar 1961
Linton-on-Ouse	20 Apr 1938	Honington	23 Mar 1970
		Wyton	30 Sep 1970

Aircraft Equipment

Equipment	Period of service		Representative Serial
B.E.2e, B.E.2d, B.E.2e, B.E.12b	May 1916 –	1917	A1882
F.E.2b, F.E.2d	Jun 1917 –	1918	A6531
Martinsyde G.100	1917 –	1918	A4002 (8)
Avro 504K	Jan 1918 – Jun 1919		A9785
Camel	1918 – Jun 1919		
Virginia X	Mar 1937 – Feb 1938		K2669
Anson I	Mar 1937 – Feb 1938		K6277 (51-T)
Whitley II	Feb 1938 – Dec 1939		K7261
Whitley III	Aug 1938 – Dec 1939		K9008 (MH-J)
Whitley IV	Nov 1939 – May 1940		K9043 (MH-G)
Whitley V	May 1940 – Nov 1942		Z9274 (MH-O)
Halifax II	Nov 1942 – Jan 1944		LW287 (MH-C)
Halifax III	Jan 1944 – Jun 1945		NR255 (C6-H)
Stirling V	Jun 1945 – Dec 1947		PJ883 (MH-A)
York C.1	Feb 1946 – Oct 1950		MW250
Canberra B.2	Aug 1958 – date		WJ640
Comet C.2, R.2	Aug 1958 – Nov 1974		XK695
Nimrod R.1	Jul 1971 – date		XW664

Stirling V, No.51 Squadron

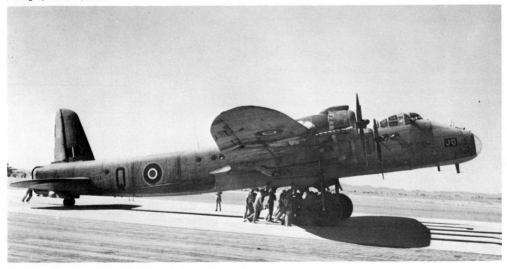

Battle I, No.52 Squadron

No. 52 Squadron

Badge: A lion rampant guardant holding in the forepaws a flash of lightning.
Motto: Sudore quam sanguine (By sweat other than through blood)

No.52 Squadron was formed on 15 May 1916 at Hounslow Heath and moved to France as a corps reconnaissance unit in November. Equipped at first with R.E.8s, the squadron handed these over to No.34 Squadron in February 1917 and flew B.E.2es for three months before reverting to R.E.8s. It was engaged in artillery spotting, tactical reconnaissance and light bombing duties for the rest of the war. Returning to the UK as a cadre in February 1919, the squadron was disbanded on 23 October 1919.

On 18 January 1937, No.52 was reformed at Abingdon from a nucleus supplied by No.15 Squadron. By the end of the year it had replaced its Hinds with Battles and in February 1939 was given a training role, receiving five Ansons as additional equipment. On the outbreak of war, the squadron remained on training duties and became part of No.12 OTU on 8 April 1940.

No.52 was reformed at Habbaniya on 1 July 1941 as a maintenance unit. Although it had no aircrew on strength, it was equipped with twenty-one Audaxes which were occasionally used for a local reconnaissance flown by No.31 Squadron pilots. In December the squadron disposed of its aircraft and its personnel were attached to other units. Aircrews allotted to No.52 operated Blenheims in the Western Desert while attached to other squadrons and it was not until October 1942 that the ground echelon received any aircraft. Blenheims carried out some survey flights over Iraq before the squadron left for Egypt in February 1943, there to convert to Baltimores. In June No.52 moved to Tunisia for shipping reconnaissance and convoy escort duties before being transferred to Italy in November. In February 1944, the squadron moved to Gibraltar where it was disbanded on 31 March 1944.

On 1 July 1944, C and D Flights of No.353 Squadron at Dum Dum, Calcutta, were redesignated No.52 Squadron. Equipped with Dakotas, the squadron was engaged in general transport duties in India for the rest of the war. For a period it also flew Expediter light transports and Tiger Moths modified as ambulance aircraft. A series of scheduled services was begun after the Japanese surrender to Burma, China and Malaya and in 1947 the squadron moved to Singapore. During the emergency in Malaya, No.52 was engaged in supply-dropping to security forces in the jungle, Valettas replacing Dakotas in June 1951. These were flown until disbandment on 25 April 1966.

On 1 December 1966, No.52 reformed at Seletar with Andovers for transport support duties in the Far East Air Force, being disbanded again on 31 December 1969.

Squadron bases			
Hounslow Heath	15 May 1916	Lopcombe Corner	Aug 1919
Bertangles	18 Nov 1916		to 23 Oct 1919
Chippilly	15 Dec 1916	Abingdon	18 Jan 1937
Citadel	26 Jan 1917	Upwood	1 Mar 1937
Longavesnes	29 Mar 1917	Alconbury	1 Sep 1939
Bray Dunes	15 Jun 1917	Upwood	7 Sep 1939
Izel-le-Hameau	7 Dec 1917	Kidlington	9 Sep 1939
La Houssoye	6 Jan 1918	Benson	18 Sep 1939
Matigny	12 Jan 1918		to 8 Apr 1940
Bonneuil	23 Jan 1918	Habbaniya	1 Jul 1941
Catigny	22 Mar 1918	Mosul	17 Aug 1942
La Houssoye	24 Mar 1918	Kasfareet	11 Feb 1943
Poulainville	25 Mar 1918	LG.91	22 Feb 1943
Abbeville	28 Mar 1918	Protville I	4 Jun 1943
Serches	3 May 1918	Borizzo	1 Nov 1943
Fismes	5 May 1918	Gibraltar	20 Feb 1944
Cramaille	27 May 1918		to 31 Mar 1944
Anthenay	28 May 1918	Dum Dum	1 Jul 1944
Trecon	29 May 1918	Changi	1 Aug 1947
Auxi-le-Chateau	30 Jun 1918	Kuala Lumpur	21 Nov 1948
Izel-le-Hameau	4 Aug 1918	Seletar	31 May 1949
Savy	24 Aug 1918	Changi	27 Aug 1949
Bourlon	19 Oct 1918	Kuala Lumpur	Jul 1950
Avesnes-le-Sec	25 Oct 1918	Changi	Jan 1951
Aulnoye	10 Nov 1918	Kuala Lumpur	Jul 1959
Linselles	16 Nov 1918	Butterworth	Sep 1960
Aulnoye	23 Nov 1918		to 25 Apr 1966
Netheravon	17 Feb 1919	Seletar	1 Dec 1966
			to 31 Dec 1969

Aircraft Equipment	Period of service	Representative Serial
B.E.2c	May 1916 -- Oct 1916	
R.E.8	Oct 1916 — Feb 1917	
	May 1917 — Feb 1919	A4417 (15)
B.E.2e	Feb 1917 — May 1917	
Hind	Jan 1937 -- Dec 1937	K5556
Battle I	Nov 1937 — Apr 1940	K7602 (52-B)
Anson I	Feb 1939 — Apr 1940	N5027
Audax	Jul 1941　Jan 1942	K3111
Blenheim IV	Oct 1942 — Feb 1943	Z7784
Baltimore IIIa, IV	Jan 1943 — Feb 1943	
	Mar 1943 -- Mar 1944	AG861
Dakota III, IV	Jul 1944 — Jun 1951	KN341 (TYW)
Expediter I	Apr 1945 — Jun 1945	
Tiger Moth	Mar 1945 — Jul 1945	DG456
Valetta C.1	Jun 1951 — Apr 1966	VX512
Andover C.1	Dec 1966 — Dec 1969	XS612

No. 53 Squadron

Badge: In front of a saltire, a
thistle slipped and leaved
Motto: United in effort

Belfast C.1, No.53 Squadron

No.53 Squadron was formed at Catterick on 15 May 1916 as a training unit but in December was mobilised and sent to France. Equipped with B.E.2es, it was based in Flanders for artillery observation and tactical reconnaissance duties until April 1917 when it re-equipped with R.E.8s. These it flew over the Western Front for the rest of the war and in April 1919 the squadron returned to the UK and disbanded on 25 October 1919.

On 28 June 1937 No.53 reformed at Farnborough with Hectors as an army co-operation unit, specialising in night reconnaissance. In April 1938 it received a Valentia for troop-carrying exercises which transported 5,160 men in the next four months. In January 1939 Blenheims were received, the squadron being fully converted in June. Soon after the outbreak of World War Two, the squadron moved to France for strategic reconniassance duties, beginning operations on 28 September. It returned to the UK ten days after the German attack began in May 1940 to fly reconnaissance missions from south-east England and began night bombing sorties in July. In February 1941 No.53 moved to Cornwall for patrols and anti-shipping operations off the French coast and in July converted to Hudsons. Anti-submarine patrols were its main task but shipping strikes were flown from North Coates in the spring of 1942, before the squadron moved to the United States early in July. Anti-submarine patrols from Rhode Island began on 23 July to supplement the meagre and inexperienced sea defences of North America which had suddenly faced soon after America entered the war by a swarm of German U-boats switching their attacks to the almost undefended

Eastern seaboard of the USA. Increasing activity in the Caribbean resulted in the squadron moving to Trinidad in August. At the end of November, the squadron left for the UK and re-assembled at Davidstowe Moor on 31 December 1942. During January 1943, aircraft returned to England and in February Whitleys were received. Patrols from East Anglia began on 10 April but only nine were flown before No.53 moved to Thorney Island and conversion to Liberators began. These began anti-submarine patrols on 25 June over the Bay of Biscay and the Western Approaches, the squadron moving to Iceland in September 1944 where it spent the rest of the war flying patrols over the North Atlantic. In June 1945 No.53 returned to the UK and joined Transport Command on 25 June, beginning trooping flights to India in August. On 15 June 1946 the squadron was disbanded.

On 1 November 1946 No.53 reformed at Netheravon with Dakotas and flew these on the Berlin Airlift in 1948-49, being disbanded on 31 July 1949. On 1 August 1949, the squadron reformed at Topcliffe with Hastings, re-equipping with Beverleys in February 1957. It formed part of the UK-based transport force until merged with No.47 Squadron on 28 June 1963.

On 1 November 1965 No.53 reformed at Fairford and received its first Belfast in January 1966. As the only operator of the ten Belfasts built for the RAF, the squadron flew heavy equipment world-wide until disbanded on 14 September 1976.

Squadron bases			
Catterick	15 May 1916	Seclin	16 Nov 1918
Farnborough	11 Dec 1916	Reumont	24 Nov 1918
St. Omer	26 Dec 1916	Raneffe	28 Nov 1918
Bailleul	4 Jan 1917	Old Sarum	17 Mar 1919
Abeele	1 Feb 1918		to 25 Oct 1919
Villeseneux	21 Feb 1918	Farnborough	28 Jun 1937
Allonville	22 Mar 1918	Odiham	8 Apr 1938
Fienvillers	24 Mar 1918	Plivot	18 Sep 1939
Boisdinghem	25 Mar 1918	Poix	11 Oct 1939
Abeele	7 Apr 1918	Crecy	19 May 1940
Clairmarais	13 Apr 1918	Lympne	19 May 1940
Abeele	11 Sep 1918	Andover	20 May 1940
Coucou	21 Oct 1918	Eastchurch	1 Jun 1940
Sweveghem	5 Nov 1918	Gatwick	13 Jun 1940
		Detling	3 Jul 1940

Thorney Island	20 Nov 1940	Beaulieu	25 Sep 1943			
Bircham Newton	10 Feb 1941	St. Eval	3 Jan 1944			
St. Eval	23 Feb 1941	Reykjavik	13 Sep 1944			
Bircham Newton	2 Jul 1941	St. David's	1 Jun 1945			
St. Eval	19 Oct 1941	Merryfield	17 Sep 1945			
Limavady	17 Dec 1941	Gransden Lodge	3 Dec 1945			
North Coates	18 Feb 1942		to 15 Jun 1946			
St. Eval	16 May 1942	Netheravon	1 Nov 1946			
Left for USA	5 Jul 1942	Waterbeach	Nov 1947 (P)			
Quonset Point, RI	Jul 1942 (P)		to 31 Jul 1949			
Wheeler Field,		Schleswigland	1 Aug 1949 (A)			
Trinidad	5 Aug 1942	Topcliffe	22 Aug 1949			
Edinburgh Field,		Wunstorf	7 Oct 1949 (A)			
Trinidad	22 Aug 1942	Topcliffe	13 Dec 1949			
Moved to UK	23 Nov 1942	Lyneham	9 Feb 1951			
Davidstowe Moor		Abingdon	1 Jan 1957			
	31 Dec 1942 (G)		to 28 Jun 1963			
Docking	17 Feb 1943	Fairford	1 Nov 1965			
Bircham Newton	17 Mar 1943	Brize Norton	May 1967 (P)			
Thorney Island	28 Apr 1943		to 14 Sep 1976			

Aircraft Equipment	Period of service	Representative Serial
F.K.3	May 1916 – Dec 1916	
Avro 504	May 1916 – Dec 1916	
B.E.2e	Dec 1916 – Apr 1917	6323
R.E.8	Feb 1917 – Oct 1919	D6801
Hector	Jun 1937 – Jun 1939	K8096
Blenheim IV	Jan 1939 – Jul 1941	L4870 (TE-Q)
Hudson V	Jul 1941 – Jul 1942	AE639
Hudson III	Jul 1942 – Feb 1943	V9232 (PZ-A)
Whitley VII	Feb 1943 – May 1943	EB331
Liberator V, Va	May 1943 – Mar 1945	BZ720 (PH-N)
Liberator VI	Jun 1944 – Mar 1945	EW302 (PH-G)
	Aug 1945 – Jun 1946	
Liberator VIII	Jan 1945 – Jun 1946	KH388 (PH-B)
Dakota C.4	Nov 1946 – Jul 1949	KN434 (PU-U)
Hastings C.1	Aug 1949 – Dec 1956	WD332 (GAY)
Beverley C.1	Feb 1957 – Jun 1963	XM105 (E)
Belfast C.1	Jan 1966 – Sep 1976	XR365 'Hector'

Spitfire VC, No.54 Squadron

No. 54 Squadron

Badge: A lion rampant semée de Lys
Motto: Audax omnia perpeti (Boldness to endure anything)

No.54 was formed on 16 May 1916 at Castle Bromwich and moved to France as a fighter squadron in December with Pups. A year later, these were replaced by Camels which, in addition to normal fighter and escort missions, were engaged in low-level attacks on troops and transport behind the enemy lines until the end of the war. In January 1919 the squadron handed over its aircraft to No.151 Squadron and returned to the UK in February where it remained a cadre unit until disbanded on 25 October 1919.

On 15 January 1930 No.54 was reformed at Hornchurch as a fighter squadron, flying Siskin two-seaters until the arrival of its Bulldogs between April and October. In September 1936 Gauntlets were received and in May 1937, Gladiators. Spitfires began to arrive in March 1939 and on the outbreak of World War Two were flown on defensive duties from Hornchurch. During the evacuation from Dunkirk in May 1940, the squadron flew patrols over the Belgian coast to intercept German raids on the port and beaches. After being heavily engaged in the first half of the Battle of Britain, No.54 was moved to Yorkshire early in September, returning south in February 1941 to take part in sweeps over the French coast until November 1941 when it moved to northern Scotland.

In June 1942 the squadron embarked for Australia as part of a Spitfire wing allocated to the defence of north-west Australia, then under attack from Japanese aircraft based on captured bases in the Dutch East Indies. Due to diversion of aircraft to the Middle East, it was not until January 1943 that the wing took up its station and by the end of July enemy raids had ceased. There was little activity for the rest of the war and in September 1945 the squadron disposed of its aircraft and by the end of October its personnel had embarked for the UK, the squadron disbanding on 31 October 1945.

On 15 November 1945 No.183 Squadron at Chilbolton was renumbered 54 Squadron. Equipped with Tempest IIs, it moved to Odiham in June 1946 to convert to Vampires in July. In April 1952 these were replaced by Meteors and in March 1955 Hunters were received. After nearly thirteen years at Odiham, the squadron moved to Stradishall in July 1959 where it received ground-attack Hunters in March 1960. With the formation of a ground-attack wing in Transport Command, No.54 joined No.1 Squadron as its component units and moved to West Raynham in August 1963. When No.1 began converting to Harriers, No.54 was scheduled to follow but on 1 September 1969 was disbanded, its remaining Hunters and pilots being transferred to No.4 Squadron though remaining in Britain as its UK echelon.

On the same day, a new No.54 Squadron was formed at Coningsby as a Phantom unit of Air Support Command, disbanding on 23 April 1974. On 29 March 1974, No.54 had formed at Lossiemouth with Jaguar GR.1s as a ground-attack and tactical reconnaissance unit to replace the Phantom echelon.

Squadron bases

Castle Bromwich	15 May 1916	Liettres	30 Jun 1918
London Colney	22 Dec 1916	Le Touquin	14 Jul 1918
St. Omer	24 Dec 1916	Fienvillers	4 Aug 1918
Bertangles	26 Dec 1916	Avesnes-le-Compte	25 Aug 1918
Flez	23 Apr 1917	Rely	17 Oct 1918
Bray Dunes	18 Jun 1917	Merchin	24 Oct 1918
Leffrinckoucke	16 Jul 1917	Yatesbury	17 Feb 1919
Teteghem	8 Sep 1917		to 25 Oct 1919
Bruay	6 Dec 1917	Hornchurch	15 Jan 1930
La Houssoye	18 Dec 1917	Upavon	28 May 1931
Flez	1 Jan 1918	Hornchurch	20 Jun 1931
Champien	22 Mar 1918	(frequent dets to Rochford	
Bertangles	24 Mar 1918	October 1939 to March 1940)	
Conteville	28 Mar 1918	Catterick	28 May 1940
Clairmarais	7 Apr 1918	Hornchurch	4 Jun 1940
Caffiers	29 Apr 1918	Rochford	25 Jun 1940
St. Omer	1 Jun 1918	Hornchurch	24 Jul 1940
Vignacourt	11 Jun 1918	Catterick	28 Jul 1940
Boisdinghem	16 Jun 1918	Hornchurch	8 Aug 1940
Catterick	3 Sep 1940	Darwin	21 Oct 1944
Hornchurch	23 Feb 1941	Melbourne	23 Sep 1945
Southend	31 Mar 1941		to 31 Oct 1945
Hornchurch	20 May 1941	Chilbolton	15 Nov 1945
Debden	11 Jun 1941	Odiham	28 Jun 1946
Hornchurch	13 Jun 1941	Molesworth	5 Sep 1946
Martlesham Heath	4 Aug 1941	Odiham	30 Sep 1946
Castletown	17 Nov 1941	Stradishall	13 Jul 1959
Wellingore	1 Jun 1942	Waterbeach	20 Nov 1961
Left for Australia		West Raynham	14 Aug 1963
	18 Jun 1942		to 1 Sep 1969
Richmond	24 Aug 1942	Coningsby	1 Sep 1969
Darwin	17 Jan 1943 (A)	Lossiemouth	29 Mar 1974
	25 Jan 1943 (G)	Coltishall	8 Aug 1974
Livingstone	8 Jun 1944		

Aircraft Equipment	Period of service	Representative Serial	
B.E.2c	Aug 1916 – Dec 1916		
Avro 504	Sep 1916 – Dec 1916		
Pup	Sep 1916 – Dec 1917	A6211	
Camel	Dec 1917 – Feb 1919	B7320	(P)
Siskin IIIDC	Jan 1930 – Dec 1930	J7156	
Bulldog IIA	Apr 1930 – Sep 1936	K1611	
Gauntlet II	Sep 1936 – May 1937	K5313	
Gladiator I	Apr 1937 – Apr 1939	K8014	
Spitfire I	Mar 1939 – Feb 1941	K9883	(DL-T)
Spitfire IIA	Feb 1941 – May 1941 Aug 1941	P7618	(KL-Z)
Spitfire IIB	Nov 1941 – Mar 1942	P8697	
Spitfire VA	May 1941 – Aug 1941	R7279	(KL-S)
Spitfire VB	Jun 1941 – Nov 1941 Mar 1942 – May 1942	AA761	
Spitfire VC	Sep 1942 – May 1944	BR536	(DL-H)
Spitfire VIII	Mar 1944 – Sep 1945	A58-498	(D)
Tempest II	Nov 1945 – Oct 1946	MW774	(HF-X)
Vampire F.1	Oct 1946 – Aug 1948	TG298	(HF-F)
Vampire FB.5	Oct 1949 – Apr 1952	VV630	
Vampire F.3	Apr 1948 – Nov 1949	VT864	(H)
Meteor F.8	Apr 1952 – Mar 1955	WK669	(X)
Hunter F.1	Mar 1955 – Oct 1955	WW641	(B)
Hunter F.4	Sep 1955 – Jan 1957	WV281	(M)
Hunter F.6	Jan 1957 – Mar 1960	XE645	(P)
Hunter FGA.9	Mar 1960 – Sep 1969	XF517	(V)
Phantom FGR.2	Sep 1969 – Mar 1974	XV477	(477)
Jaguar GR.1	Mar 1974 – date	XX725	

Hunter F.1s, No.54 Squadron

Wapiti IIAs, No.55 Squadron

No. 55 Squadron

Badge: A cubit arm, the arm
grasping a spear
Motto: Nil nos tremefacit
(Nothing shakes us)

No.55 Squadron was formed at Castle Bromwich on 27 April 1916 as a training unit and became the first unit to be equipped with D.H.4s in January 1917. It took these to France in March for bombing and reconnaissance duties, attacking enemy airfields, communications and bases behind the Western Front. With the formation of the Independent Force in June 1918, the squadron was attached to No.41 Wing for strategic raids on German targets. After a short period carrying mail to the occupation forces, the squadron was reduced to a cadre in January 1919, on its return to the UK and it disbanded on 22 January 1920.

On 1 February 1920, No.142 Squadron at Suez was re-numbered 55 Squadron with D.H.9s, soon replaced by D.H.9As which it took to Turkey in July as part of Q Force, returning in September to be based in Iraq. In February 1930, re-equipment with Wapitis began and in February 1937 No.55 received Vincents. For nineteen years, the squadron formed part of the peace-keeping force in Iraq, taking part in various operations against raiding tribesmen.

In March 1939 Blenheims began to arrive and in August these were taken to Egypt as war approached. Italy's entry into the war in June 1940 began a series of bombing attacks on enemy airfields, ports and bases in Libya which continued for a year. In March 1941 No.55 was the only day bomber squadron left in the Western Desert, the rest having gone to Greece. After a period of rest and training, the squadron resumed operations on 12 September 1941, flying anti-shipping sweeps until withdrawn to Egypt in March 1942. In May it converted to Baltimores and first flew these on operations on 2 July and after the rout of the Afrika Korps at El Alamein in October, the squadron began moving forward to keep within bombing range of the enemy until it reached Tunisia where it attacked enemy bases and airfields until the Axis forces surrendered.

From bases in Tunisia, attacks began on Sicily in preparation for the Allied landings in July 1943, and once airfields were ready there the squadron moved in August. The capture of bases in southern Italy resulted in a further move forward at the end of September and for the rest of the war the squadron was engaged in attacks on enemy communications and tactical targets in support of the Allied Armies in Italy.

In September 1945, No.55 moved to Greece where, in June 1946, conversion to Mosquitos began and these were flown until disbandment came on 1 November 1946.

On 1 September 1960, No.55 reformed at Honington as a Victor unit of the V-bomber Force. In May 1965 it became a flight-refuelling unit at Marham and provided tanker aircraft for long-range moves by RAF aircraft.

Squadron bases

Castle Bromwich	27 Apr 1916	Helwan	2 Jun 1941
Lilbourne	10 Jun 1916	LG.100 Wadi Natrun	1 Jul 1941
Fienvillers	6 Mar 1917	Aqir	9 Aug 1941
Boisdinghem	31 May 1917	Fuka	21 Sep 1941
Ochey	11 Oct 1917	Bu Amud	8 Jan 1942
Tantonville	7 Nov 1917	Benina	12 Jan 1942
Azelot	5 Jun 1918	Berka Main	20 Jan 1942
Le Planay	16 Nov 1918	El Gubba	26 Jan 1942
St. André-aux-Bois	7 Dec 1918	Gambut	31 Jan 1942
Renfrew	30 Jan 1919	Fuka	3 Feb 1942
Shotwick	30 Dec 1919	Helwan	25 Mar 1942
	to 22 Jan 1920	Luxor	3 Apr 1942
Suez	1 Feb 1920	LG.99 Amriya	10 May 1942
Maltepe	Jul 1920	Ismailia	1 Jul 1942
Baghdad West	4 Sep 1920	LG.98	16 Jul 1942
Mosul	Mar 1921	LG.86	28 Aug 1942
Hinaidi	19 May 1924	El Sirtan	7 Mar 1943
Habbaniya	Sep 1937 (P)	Marsa Gardane	13 Mar 1943
Ismailia	25 Aug 1939	Medenine Main	4 Apr 1943
Fuka	11 Jun 1940	La Fauconnerie South	
LG.79	10 Jun 1941		15 Apr 1943
Amseat	16 Jan 1941	Enfidaville	1 Jun 1943
Bu Amud	4 Feb 1941	Reyville	21 Jun 1943
Heliopolis	15 Feb 1941	Gela West	9 Aug 1943
Maraua	10 Mar 1941	Gerbini 3/Sigonella	
Derna	4 Apr 1941		22 Aug 1943
Gazala North	6 Apr 1941	Brindisi	27 Sep 1943
Great Gambut	6 Apr 1941	Foggia 1/Celone	28 Oct 1943
Maaten Bagush	9 Apr 1941	Kabrit	4 Jan 1944
LG.95	2 May 1941	Biferno	24 Mar 1944
San Severo	2 May 1944		2 Nov 1944 (HQ)
Tarquinia	23 Jun 1944	Falconara	10 Dec 1944
Cecina	18 Jul 1944	Forli	7 Mar 1945
Perugia	18 Oct 1944 (A)	Aviano	12 May 1945
Marcianise	29 Oct 1944 (A)	Hassani	20 Sep 1945
	to 11 Jan 1945		to 1 Nov 1946
Ancona	25 Oct 1944 (HQ)	Honington	1 Sep 1960
Porto Potenzo		Marham	24 May 1965

Aircraft

Equipment	Period of service	Representative Serial and Code
Various incl. B.E.2c, B.E.2e, F.K.8, Avro 504	Apr 1916 – Jan 1917	
D.H.4	Jan 1917 – Jan 1920	A2159
D.H.9	Feb 1920 – Sep 1920	
D.H.9A	Jun 1920 – Feb 1931	E8512 (B4)
Wapiti IIA	Feb 1930 – Mar 1937	J9628 (A1)
Vincent	Feb 1937 – May 1939	K6331
Blenheim I	Mar 1939 – Dec 1940	L8557
Blenheim IV	Dec 1940 – Apr 1942	R3883 (Y)
Baltimore I, II, III	May 1942 – Mar 1943	AG767 (G)
Baltimore IIIA	Mar 1943 – Oct 1943	FA316 (T)
Baltimore IV	Jun 1943 – May 1944	FA657 (V)
Baltimore V	Jan 1944 – Oct 1944	FW370 (B)
Boston IV	Oct 1944 – Jul 1946	BZ564 (Y)
Boston V	Feb 1945 – Jul 1946	BZ617 (B)
Mosquito FB.26	Jun 1946 – Nov 1946	KA309
Victor B.1A	Oct 1960 – Mar 1967	XH614
Victor K.1A, K.2	Dec 1966 – date	XH620

No. 56 Squadron

Badge: A phoenix
Motto: Quid si coelum ruat
(What if heaven falls?)
Name: 'Punjab'

No.56 Squadron was formed on 9 June 1916 at Gosport from a nucleus supplied by No.28 Squadron and moved early in July to London Colney where it trained with a variety of aircraft until March 1917 when it received S.E.5s, the first squadron to do so. Early in April, it moved to France where it flew patrols over the Western Front for the rest of the war, apart from two weeks at the end of June 1917 when it returned to the UK for defensive duties after enemy air attacks. During the final German offensive and subsequent withdrawal, No.56 took part in ground-attack missions against enemy troops and transport and in February 1919 returned to the UK where it disbanded on 22 January 1920.

On 1 February 1920 No.80 Squadron at Aboukir was renumbered 56 Squadron and Snipes were flown until 23 September 1922 when the squadron disbanded. A detachment of No.56 attached to No.208 Squadron at Constantinople continued to use the number until August 1923 despite the fact that No.56 had been reformed at Hawkinge on 1 November 1922 as a fighter squadron, also with Snipes. In September 1924, Grebes were received, being replaced in September 1927 by Siskins. Bulldogs arrived in October 1932 and were succeeded by Gauntlets in May 1936 and Gladiators in July 1937. The Hurricanes with which the squadron entered World War Two arrived in May 1938 and were used for defensive patrols until required to give fighter cover for the beaches at Dunkirk in May 1940. Flights operated for short periods from French airfields during the Battle of France. No.56 was based in southern England

Gauntlet II, No.56 Squadron

throughout the Battle of Britain and in September 1941 began to re-equip with Typhoons. Unfortunately, this type had to be rushed into service and No.56 was the first to be equipped. Teething troubles kept the squadron non-operational until 30 May 1942 when it finally flew its first operational sortie with a Typhoon. Ground-attack and anti-shipping missions interspersed patrols to catch enemy fighter-bombers at low altitude but the Typhoon continued to have problems until well into 1943. In November 1943, the squadron began carrying bombs for attacks on enemy airfields and bases in northern France and in February 1944 it changed to rockets as its means of offence. In April however, conversion to Spitfires took place but after flying some escort and shipping reconnaissance missions it received Tempests at the end of June. It used its fast new fighters against flying bombs over southern England until the end of September when it moved to the Low Countries to join Second Tactical Air Force. For the rest of the war, it was engaged in armed reconnaissance sweeps over Germany and on 31 March 1946 was renumbered 16 Squadron.

On the following day, No.124 Squadron at Bentwaters was renumbered 56 Squadron which now flew Meteors as part of the peace-time fighter defence of the UK. In February 1954 Swifts were received to replace Meteors but the type was unsuccessful as an interceptor and was replaced by Hunters in May 1955. These served with the squadron until the arrival of Lightnings in January 1961. In 1967, No.56 moved to Cyprus to form the fighter component of the Near East Air Force. With the rundown of British forces in the Near East, it returned to the UK.

On 22 March 1976, a Phantom element was formed at Coningsby which, on 29 June 1976, became No.56 Squadron, replacing the Lightning echelon at Wattisham.

Squadron bases

Base	Date	Base	Date
Gosport	9 Jun 1916	Wittering	3 Jun 1940
London Colney	4 Jul 1916	North Weald	4 Jun 1940
St. Omer	7 Apr 1917	Boscombe Down	1 Sep 1940
Vert Galand	20 Apr 1917	Middle Wallop	29 Nov 1940
Liettres	31 May 1917	North Weald	17 Dec 1940
Bekesbourne	21 Jun 1917	Martlesham Heath	23 Jun 1941
Estrée Blanche	5 Jul 1917	Duxford	26 Jun 1941
Lavieville	20 Nov 1917	Snailwell	30 Mar 1942
Baizieux	21 Jan 1918	Matlask	24 Aug 1942
Valheureux	25 Mar 1918	Manston	22 Jul 1943
Lechelle	15 Oct 1918	Martlesham Heath	6 Aug 1943
Esnes	17 Oct 1918	Manston	15 Aug 1943
La Targette	29 Oct 1918	Bradwell Bay	23 Aug 1943
Bethencourt	22 Nov 1918	Martlesham Heath	4 Oct 1943
Narborough	15 Feb 1919	Scorton	15 Feb 1944
Bircham Newton	30 Dec 1919	Acklington	23 Feb 1944
	to 22 Jan 1920	Scorton	7 Mar 1944
Aboukir	1 Feb 1920	Ayr	30 Apr 1944 (G)
	to 23 Sep 1922		7 Apr 1944 (A)
San Stephano (D)	26 Sep 1922	Newchurch	28 Apr 1944
	to Aug 1923	Matlask	23 Sep 1944
Hawkinge	1 Nov 1922	B.60 Grimbergen	28 Sep 1944
Biggin Hill	7 May 1923	B.80 Volkel	1 Oct 1944
North Weald	12 Oct 1927	B.112 Rheine-Hopsten	
Martlesham Heath	22 Oct 1939		11 Apr 1945
North Weald	28 Feb 1940	B.152 Fassberg	26 Apr 1945
Gravesend	10 May 1940	Warmwell	8 May 1945
North Weald	12 May 1940	B.152 Fassberg	23 May 1945
Digby	31 May 1940	B.160 Kastrup	22 Jun 1945
		B.164 Schleswig	22 Aug 1945
B.155 Dedelstorf	5 Sep 1945	Lubeck	2 Oct 1947
B.152 Fassberg	23 Oct 1945	Duxford	31 Nov 1947
B.170 Sylt	31 Dec 1945	Thorney Island	2 Feb 1948
B.152 Fassberg	22 Jan 1946	Waterbeach	10 May 1950
Gatow	22 Feb 1946	Wymeswold	2 Jun 1954
Fassberg	25 Mar 1946	Waterbeach	16 Jul 1954
	to 31 Mar 1946	Wattisham	10 Jul 1959
Bentwaters	1 Apr 1946	Nicosia	6 Aug 1959
Boxted	16 Sep 1946	Wattisham	15 Oct 1959
Acklington	5 Nov 1946	Akrotiri	Jan 1967
Wattisham	20 Dec 1946	Coningsby (D)	22 Mar 1976
Duxford	17 Apr 1947	Wattisham	8 Jul 1976

Aircraft Equipment

Equipment	Period of service	Representative Serial and Code
Various	Aug 1916 – Mar 1917	
S.E.5	Mar 1917 – Aug 1917	A8903
S.E.5A	Jun 1917 – Jan 1920	B4863 (G)
Snipe	Jan 1920 – Sep 1922	E7522
	Nov 1922 – Nov 1924	
Grebe II	Sep 1924 – Sep 1927	J7535
Siskin IIIA	Sep 1927 – Oct 1932	J8832
Bulldog IIA	Oct 1932 – May 1936	K2215
Gauntlet II	May 1936 – Jul 1937	K5296 (F)
Gladiator II	Jul 1937 – May 1938	K7991
Hurricane I	May 1938 – Feb 1941	L1800 (LR-R)
Hurricane IIB	Feb 1941 – Jan 1942	Z3442 (US-M)
Typhoon IA	Sep 1941 – Dec 1942	R7588 (US-X)
Typhoon IB	Mar 1942 – May 1944	JR503 (US-K)
Spitfire IX	Apr 1944 – Jun 1944	ML189 (US-H)
Tempest V	Jun 1944 – Mar 1946	EJ742 (US-T)
Meteor F.3	Apr 1946 – Sep 1948	EE365 (ON-N)
Meteor F.4	Aug 1948 – Dec 1950	RA434 (US-Q)
Meteor F.8	Dec 1950 – Feb 1954	WF643 (P)
Swift F.1	Feb 1954 – May 1955	WK207 (N)
Swift F.2	Aug 1954 – May 1955	WK245 (H)
Hunter F.5	May 1955 – Nov 1958	WP116 (W)
Hunter F.6	Nov 1958 – Jan 1961	XG157 (H)
Lightning F.1A	Jan 1961 – 1965	XM179 (F)
Lightning F.3	1965 – Sep 1971	XR719 (D)
Lightning F.6	Sep 1971 – Jun 1976	XR759 (P)
Phantom FGR.2	Mar 1976 – date	XV470 (C)

Hunter F.6, No.56 Squadron

No. 57 Squadron

Badge: Issuant from two logs fessewise in saltire, a phoenix
Motto: Corpus non animum muto (I change my body not my spirit)

No.57 Squadron was formed at Copmanthorpe on 8 June 1916 from a nucleus supplied by No.33 Squadron and until October was engaged in flying training. It then began to mobilise, moving to France in December with F.E.2ds for fighter duties. As this type of pusher fighter was obsolescent, it was flown for only five months before being replaced by D.H.4s. Bombing and reconnaissance missions were flown for the rest of the war and in May 1919 the squadron was re-equipped with D.H.9As for mail-carrying before returning to the UK in August where it disbanded on 31 December 1919.

On 20 October 1931, No.57 reformed at Netheravon as a light bomber squadron with Harts. These were replaced by Hinds in May 1936 and at the end of March 1938 Blenheims began to arrive. The squadron moved to France with the Air Component in September 1939 for strategic reconnaissance duties. During May 1940, No.57's Blenheims were engaged in locating and bombing enemy columns

Hart Is, No.57 Squadron

invading Belgium and France and after eight days it was forced to evacuate its remaining aircraft to England where it continued to fly reconnaissance missions until June. In July the squadron moved to Scotland for anti-shipping operations over the North Sea, returning south in November to convert to Wellingtons. Night bombing began on 13 January 1941 and continued for the rest of the war. The squadron re-equipped with Lancasters in September 1942 which formed part of the main force of Bomber Command until the end of the war. A few Lincolns were received for trials in August 1945 but the squadron was disbanded on 25 November 1945.

On the following day, No.103 Squadron's Lincoln Flight at Elsham Wolds was redesignated No.57 Squadron. Washingtons replaced Lincolns in May 1951 and were in turn superceded by Canberras in May 1953. These were flown until disbandment on 9 December 1957. On 1 January 1959 the squadron was reformed at Honington as a Victor unit of the V-bomber Force. In June 1966, No.57 became a tanker squadron at Marham.

Squadron bases

Copmanthorpe	8 Jun 1916	Mory	22 Oct 1918
Tadcaster	20 Aug 1916	Bethencourt	9 Nov 1918
St. André-aux-Bois	16 Dec 1916	Vert Galand	23 Nov 1918
Fienvillers	22 Jan 1917	Bruyeres	24 Nov 1918
Droglandt	12 Jun 1917	Spy	12 Dec 1918
Boisdinghem	27 Jun 1917	Morville	7 Jan 1919
Ste. Marie Cappel	23 Nov 1917	South Carlton	2 Aug 1919
Le Quesnoy	29 Mar 1918		to 31 Dec 1919
Vert Galand	19 Sep 1918	Netheravon	20 Oct 1931

Upper Heyford	5 Sep 1932	Scampton	4 Sep 1942
Roye/Amy	24 Sep 1939	East Kirby	28 Aug 1943
Rosières-en-Santerre			to 25 Nov 1945
	18 Oct 1939	Elsham Wolds	26 Nov 1945
Poix	17 May 1940	Scampton	2 Dec 1945
Crécy-en-Ponthieu	19 May 1940	Lindholme	1 May 1946
Wyton	21 May 1940	Waddington	7 Oct 1946
Gatwick	27 May 1940	Coningsby	Apr 1952
Wyton	11 Jun 1940	Cottesmore	22 May 1954
Lossiemouth	24 Jun 1940	Honington	15 Feb 1955
Elgin	13 Aug 1940	Coningsby	15 Nov 1956
Wyton	1 Nov 1940		to 9 Dec 1957
Feltwell	20 Nov 1940	Honington	1 Jan 1959
Methwold	5 Jan 1942	Marham	1 Dec 1965

Aircraft Equipment	Period of service	Representative Serial
Avro 504A, B.E.2c	Jun 1916 – Dec 1916	
F.E.2d	Nov 1916 – May 1917	A22
D.H.4	May 1917 – May 1919	H5290
D.H.9A	May 1919 – Aug 1919	J577
Hart	Oct 1931 – May 1936	K3034
Hind	May 1936 – May 1938	K6713
Blenheim I	Mar 1938 – Mar 1940	L1171 (57-K)
Blenheim IV	Mar 1940 – Nov 1940	R3751
Wellington IC	Nov 1940 – Feb 1942	Z8794 (DX-H)
Wellington II	Jul 1941 – Feb 1942	W5434 (DX-Y)
Wellington III	Feb 1942 – Sep 1942	Z1565
Lancaster I, III	Sep 1942 – May 1946	NG398 (DX-N)
Lincoln B.2	Aug 1945 – Apr 1951	RF517 (DX-X)
Washington B.1	May 1951 – May 1953	WF555 (DX-H)
Canberra B.2	May 1953 – Dec 1957	WJ972
Victor B.1, B.1A	Mar 1959 – Jun 1966	XH649
Victor K.1A, K.2	Jun 1966 – date	XH650

Victor K.1, No.57 Squadron

No. 58 Squadron

Virginia X, No.58 Squadron

Badge: On a branch, an owl
Motto: Alis nocturnis (On the
wings of the night)

No.58 Squadron was formed on 8 June 1916 at Cramlington from a nucleus supplied by No.36 Squadron and was initially employed on advancd training duties. In December 1917 it was mobilised at Dover and received F.E.2bs which it took to France on 10 January 1918. The first night raid by the squadron was flown on 2 February 1918, and attacks on enemy bases and communications behind the lines continued for the rest of the war, re-equipment with Handley Page O/400s starting in September. In May 1919 No.58 began flying its H.P.s out to Egypt while other crews collected Vimys from the UK and brought them out later in the year though complete re-equipment had not taken place before the squadron was renumbered 70 Squadron on 1 February 1920.

On 1 April 1924, No.58 reformed as a bomber squadron at Worthy Down on a single-flight basis, a second being added on 1 January 1925. The Vimys were supplemented and eventually replaced by Virginias which remained the squadron equipment until the end of 1937. To give personnel experience in more modern types, some Ansons were added in February 1937, and in October the first Whitleys arrived. The original Whitley IIs suffered from teething troubles and at first had no turrets; to remedy the shortage of serviceable aircraft, nine Heyfords were loaned from Leconfield for a few weeks in April 1939 but in May No.7 Squadron passed on its Whitley IIIs to No.58 and it

Canberra PR.9s, No.58 Squadron

was with this type that the squadron went to war. On the first day of the war, seven of the squadron's Whitleys went leaflet-dropping over the Ruhr but the tacit truce in bombing that developed meant that No.58 could be transferred to Coastal Command in October, beginning convoy escort patrols on 10 October. In February 1940, the squadron returned to Bomber Command and converted to Whitley Vs and with the German invasion of Norway bombing attacks began on 17 April and continued until 8 April 1942, when the squadron was again transferred to Coastal Command and began anti-submarine patrols from St. Eval on 19 April. In August it moved to the Hebrides but came south to Holmsley South in December to convert to Halifaxes. The first anti-submarine patrols over the Western Approaches with these took place on 23 February 1943, and were continued from Stornoway when the squadron moved to the Hebrides in August 1944. In October, attacks on enemy shipping off the Norwegian coast and in the Skaggerak began and continued until the end of the war. After a final patrol on 23 May 1945, the squadron disbanded on 25 May 1945.

On 1 October 1946, No.58 reformed at Benson as a photographic-reconnaissance squadron. Mosquitos and Ansons were used for survey work in addition to its oper-

ational commitments, No.58 carried out overseas surveys including a major survey of the Caribbean completed in 1966. On 30 September 1970, the squadron was disbanded while temporarily based at Honington.

On 1 August 1973, No.58 was reformed at Wittering from No.45 Squadron. Equipped with Hunters, the squadron's task was operational training for Jaguar ground-attack pilots. It disbanded on 4 June 1976.

Squadron bases

Cramlington	8 Jun 1916	Boscombe Down	6 Oct 1939
Dover	22 Dec 1917	Linton-on-Ouse	14 Feb 1940
St. Omer	10 Jan 1918	St. Eval	8 Apr 1942
Treizennes	12 Jan 1918	Wick (D)	28 Jul 1942
Clairmarais	1 Feb 1918		to 11 Aug 1942
Izel-le-Hameau	25 Mar 1918	Stornoway	30 Aug 1942
Auchel	31 Mar 1918	Holmsley South	2 Dec 1942
Fauquembergues	23 Apr 1918	St. David's	6 Dec 1943
Proven	27 Oct 1918	Stornoway	28 Aug 1944
Heliopolis	2 May 1919		to 25 May 1945
	to 1 Feb 1920	Benson	1 Oct 1946
Worthy Down	1 Apr 1924	Wyton	Mar 1953
Upper Heyford	13 Jan 1936	Honington	23 Mar 1970
Driffield	31 Aug 1936		to 30 Sep 1970
Boscombe Down	24 Mar 1937	Wittering	1 Aug 1973
Linton-on-Ouse	20 Apr 1938		to 4 Jun 1976

Aircraft Equipment	Period of service	Representative Serial	
B.E.2c, B.E.2e	Jun 1916 – Dec 1917	–	
F.E.2b	Dec 1917 – Sep 1918	C9811	
Handley Page O/400	Sep 1918 – Feb 1920	D4595	
Vimy	Jul 1919 – Feb 1920	F3184	
	Apr 1924 – Mar 1925		
Virginia V, VII, IX, X	Dec 1924 – Dec 1937	K2675	(V)
Anson I	Feb 1937 – Dec 1937	K6271	
Heyford III	Apr 1939	on loan	
Whitley I	Oct 1937 – Dec 1937	K7211	
Whitley II	Oct 1937 – May 1939	K7260	
Whitley III	May 1939 – Mar 1940	K8964	(GE-R)
Whitley V	Mar 1940 – Dec 1942	N1470	(GE-J)
Whitley VII	Nov 1942 – Dec 1942	BD568	(GE-W)
Halifax II	Dec 1942 – Mar 1945	DT665	(BY-K)
Halifax III	Mar 1945 – May 1945	NA235	(BY-F)
Mosquito PR.34	Oct 1946 – Nov 1947	RG180	
	Jan 1949 – 1953		
Mosquito PR.35	1952 – 1953	VL619	
Anson C.19	Oct 1946 – Mar 1952	TX215	
Lincoln B.2	May 1951 – Oct 1951	SX991	
Canberra PR.3	1953 – Oct 1955	WH802	
Canberra PR.7	Dec 1955 – Sep 1970	WT512	
Canberra PR.9	Jan 1960 – Mar 1963	XH168	
Hunter FGA.9	Aug 1973 – Jun 1976	XJ694	(94)

No. 59 Squadron

Badge: A broken wheel
Motto: Ab uno disce omnes
(From one learn all)

No.59 Squadron was formed on 1 August 1916 at Narborough as a corps reconnaissance unit and moved to France on 13 February 1917 equipped with R.E.8s. For the remainder of World War One, the squadron was engaged in artillery spotting and tactical reconnaissance duties and after a short period with the Army of Occupation in Germany was disbanded on 4 August 1919.

The squadron reformed at Old Sarum on 28 June 1937 as an army co-operation unit in No.22 Group. Equipped with Hectors, it specialised initially in night reconnaissance and began to convert to Blenheims in May 1939. One flight retained Hectors for night flying until September when the squadron was allotted a strategic reconnaissance role, moving to France in October. After the German attack in May 1940, No.59 was engaged in reconnaissance missions over northern France and Belgium until forced out of its airfields in France. Withdrawn to southern England, it continued to operate over France from the British bases. In July, bombing raids on the Channel ports and anti-submarine patrols were added to the squadron's tasks and from October 1940 its reconnaissance flights were mostly taken over by the Photographic Reconnaissance Unit. Night attacks on enemy ports and airfields continued through the winter and 1 April 1941 it was redesignated a general reconnaissance squadron. Anti-shipping strikes began using Blenheims but in July No.59 re-equipped with Hudsons, the last Blenheim sortie being flown on 30 August. On 18 December, the squadron became non-operational for a period as eighteen crews were detached to fly Hudsons out to the Far East where the Japanese had opened their attack on Malaya.

After training new crews, the squadron resumed operations in March 1942 with anti-shipping patrols off the

Dutch coast. During August, conversion to Liberators began, the last Hudson mission being flown on 19 August. Anti-submarine patrols with Liberators began on 24 October but during December these were replaced by Fortresses which flew their first patrol on 23 January 1943. The type did not serve with No.59 for long, Liberator flying being resumed in March. In May 1943 the squadron moved to Northern Ireland and flew patrols over the Atlantic for the rest of the war. In common with many other Liberator squadrons, No.59 was transferred to Transport Command and moved to Waterbeach in September 1945 to commence trooping flights to India in 1 October. These continued until the squadron was disbanded on 15 June 1946.

On 1 December 1947, No.59 was reformed at Abingdon as a transport squadron equipped with Yorks, flying these on the Berlin Airlift before disbanding on 31 October 1950. On 20 August 1956, No.102 Squadron, a Canberra-equipped interdiction unit based at Gutersloh, was renumbered 59 Squadron as part of 2nd ATAF. On 4 January 1961, it was renumbered 3 Squadron.

Squadron bases

Narborough	1 Aug 1916	Odiham	9 Jun 1940
St. Omer	13 Feb 1917	Thorney Island	3 Jul 1940
La Bellevue	23 Feb 1917	Manston	1 Feb 1941
Izel-le-Hameau	1 Jun 1917	Bircham Newton (D)	1 Mar 1941
Longavesnes	15 Jun 1917		to 2 Jun 1941
Mons-en-Chaussée	15 Jul 1917	Thorney Island	15 Mar 1941
Longavesnes	29 Oct 1917	Detling	23 Jun 1941
Estree-en-Chaussée		(Det to 31 Aug 1941)	
	30 Nov 1917	Thorney Island	22 Jul 1941
Courcelles-le-Comte		Bircham Newton (D)	
	16 Dec 1917		20 Oct 1941
Lealvilliers	22 Mar 1918		to 18 Dec 1941
Vert Galand	12 Apr 1918	North Coates	17 Jan 1942
Beugnatre	17 Sep 1918	Thorney Island	28 Aug 1942
Caudry	14 Oct 1918	Chivenor	6 Feb 1943
Gerpinnes	29 Nov 1918	Thorney Island	27 Mar 1943
Bickendorf	14 Mar 1919	Aldergrove	11 May 1943
Duren	3 May 1919	Ballykelly	14 Sep 1943
	to 4 Aug 1919	Waterbeach	14 Sep 1945
Old Sarum	28 Jun 1937		to 15 Jun 1946
Aldergrove	2 Mar 1939	Abingdon	1 Dec 1947
Old Sarum	1 Apr 1939	Bassingbourn	25 Jun 1949
Andover	11 May 1939		to 31 Oct 1950
Poix	12 Oct 1939	Gutersloh	20 Aug 1956
Crécy-en-Ponthieu	19 May 1940	Geilenkirchen	25 Nov 1957
Lympne	20 May 1940		to 4 Feb 1961
Andover	21 May 1940		

Aircraft Equipment	Period of service	Representative Serial	Aircraft Equipment	Period of service	Representative Serial and Code
R.E.8	Jun 1916 — Aug 1919	B5106 (A1)	Liberator V	Mar 1943 — Mar 1944	BZ717 (X)
Hector	Jun 1937 — Sep 1939	K9732	Liberator VIII	Mar 1944 — Jun 1946	KK322 (BY-Q)
Blenheim IV	May 1939 — Sep 1941	L8791 (PJ-Y)	York C.1	Dec 1947 — Oct 1950	MW260
Hudson III	Jul 1941 — Aug 1942	AM524 (PJ-V)	Canberra B.2	Aug 1956 — Mar 1957	WJ612
Liberator III	Aug 1942 — Dec 1942	FL922 (PJ-M)	Canberra B(I).8	Feb 1957 — Jan 1961	XH204
Fortress IIa	Dec 1942 — Mar 1943	FK198 (M)			

D.H.10As, No.60 Squadron

No. 60 Squadron

Badge: A markhor's head
affrontée

Motto: Per ardue ad aethera
tendo (I strive through
difficulties to the sky).

No.60 Squadron was formed on 30 April 1916 at Gosport and moved to France in May equipped with Moranes. During the early stages of the Battle of the Somme, the squadron suffered heavy losses to its obsolescent equipment and in August re-equipped with Nieuport single-seat fighters. These it flew until July 1917 when it received S.E.5s for fighter and ground-attack duties for the rest of the war. In February 1919, the squadron returned to the UK and disbanded on 22 January 1920.

On 1 April 1920, No.97 Squadron at Lahore was re-numbered 60 Squadron and moved a few weeks later to Risalpur. Equipped with D.H.10s, the squadron was engaged in supporting the army and police on the North-West Frontier in India. D.H.9As were received in 1923 and were replaced by Wapitis in 1930. Shortly before the outbreak of World War Two No.60 converted to Blenheims which were used on coastal patrol duties by detached flights based at Karachi, Bombay, Madras and Calcutta. In February 1941, the squadron moved to Burma and in July received Buffalo

fighters which were passed on to No.67 Squadron in October. When Japan attacked Malaya in December 1941, most of the squadron's aircraft were based in Singapore and took part in attacks on enemy shipping and airfields. The remainder of the squadron was evacuated to India and reformed as an operational unit at Asansol on 1 March 1942 with Blenheim IVs. Bombing raids on Japanese bases in Burma were begun and continued until the last Blenheim mission was flown on 13 May 1943. No.60 then moved to southern India to convert to Hurricanes which began ground attack and escort sorties on 10 November. The squadron supported the 14th Army throughout the Burma campaign, flying its last mission on 16 May 1945 before being withdrawn for conversion to Thunderbolts. In September it moved to Malaya and in October to Java for the rest of the year in support of Allied ground forces. During December 1946 the squadron converted to Spitfires with the aid of No.28 Squadron's FR.14s before receiving Mark 18s equipped as fighter-bombers and with their cameras replaced by extra fuel tanks. During the emergency in Malaya, No.60 carried out attacks on guerilla camps and was engaged in reconnaissance over the jungle, having inherited some Spitfire PR.19s from No.81 Squadron in 1950. In December 1950, conversion to Vampires began, these being replaced by Venoms from April 1955. Transferred to an all-weather role by the arrival of Meteor night fighters in October 1959, No.60 re-equipped with Javelins in 1961 and was disbanded on 30 April 1968.

On 3 February 1969, the RAF Germany Communications Squadron was numbered 60 Squadron to fly light transports from Wildenrath.

Squadron bases

Gosport	30 Apr 1916	Drigh Road from	
St. Omer	28 May 1916	9 Nov 1939 (H later W Flt)	
Boisdinghem	31 May 1916	Lahore	19 Sep 1940
Vert Galand	16 Jun 1916	Mingaladon	14 Feb 1941
St. André-aux-Bois	3 Aug 1916	Det. to Kuantan and	
Izel-le-Hameau	23 Aug 1916	Tengah	Nov 1941
Savy	1 Sep 1916		to Jan 1942
Filescamp	18 Jan 1917	Dispersed	Feb 1942
Ste. Marie Cappel	7 Sep 1917	Asansol	1 Mar 1942
Bailleul	8 Mar 1918	Jessore	20 Dec 1942
La Bellevue	23 Mar 1918	Dohazari	22 Jan 1943
Fienvillers	27 Mar 1918	Yelahanka	14 May 1943
Boffles	12 Apr 1918	St. Thomas Mount	7 Jul 1943
Baizieux	17 Sep 1918	Yelahanka	31 Jul 1943
Beugnatre	14 Oct 1918	St. Thomas Mount	1 Sep 1943
Quievy	31 Oct 1918	Cholavarum	2 Oct 1943
Inchy	23 Nov 1918	Agartala	6 Nov 1943
Narborough	28 Feb 1919	Silchar West	20 Mar 1944
Bircham Newton	30 Dec 1919	Dergaon	4 May 1944
	to 22 Jan 1920	Kumbhirgram	2 Jul 1944
Risalpur	1 Apr 1920	Kangla	20 Sep 1944
Peshawar	28 May 1925	Taukkyan	5 Jan 1945
Kohat	15 Oct 1925	Monywa	10 Feb 1945
Ambala	2 Mar 1939	Thedaw	11 Apr 1945
Dets at Dum Dum from		Kalewa	28 Apr 1945
28 Aug 1916 (Z Flight)		Mingaladon	18 May 1945
St. Thomas Mount from		Thedaw	26 May 1945
3 Sep 1929 (Y Flight)		Tanjore	30 Jun 1945
Juhu from		Kuala Lumpur	2 Oct 1945
24 Oct 1939 (V Flight)		Kemajoran	21 Oct 1945

Soerabaja (D)	9 Nov 1945	Kuala Lumpur	6 Dec 1949
	to 14 Dec 1945	Tengah	31 Jan 1950
Tengah	1 Dec 1946		to 30 Apr 1968
Sembawang	24 Jan 1948	Wildenrath	3 Feb 1969
Tengah	30 Aug 1949		

Aircraft

Equipment	Period of service	Representative Serial	
Morane Parasol Type LA	May 1916 — Aug 1916		
Morane Type I, V	Aug 1916 — Oct 1916	A198	
Morane Type BB	May 1916 — Aug 1916		
Nieuport 17	Aug 1916 — Jul 1917	A200	(6A)
S.E.5, S.E.5A	Jul 1917 — Feb 1919	B533	(A)
D.H.10A	Apr 1920 — Apr 1923	E5453	
D.H.9A	Apr 1923 — Jul 1930	E785	(Q)
Wapiti IIA	Jul 1930 — Aug 1939	J9717	(Q)
Blenheim I	Jun 1939 — Feb 1942	L8609	(MU-X)
Blenheim IV	Mar 1942 — Aug 1943	Z7318	
Buffalo I	Jul 1941 — Oct 1941	AN192	
Hurricane IIC	Aug 1943 — Jul 1945	LD346	(MU-T)
Thunderbolt II	Jul 1945 — Dec 1946	KL187	(MU-M)
Spitfire FB.18	Jan 1947 — Jan 1951	SM943	(B)
Spitfire PR.19	Mar 1950 — Nov 1950		
Vampire FB.5	Dec 1950 — Apr 1952	WA240	
Vampire FB.9	Feb 1952 — Aug 1955	WG882	(D)
Venom FB.1	Apr 1955 — Sep 1958	WR372	(E)
Venom FB.4	Apr 1957 — Nov 1959	WR553	(D)
Meteor NF.14	Oct 1959 — Sep 1961	WA810	(F)
Javelin FAW.9	Jul 1961 — Apr 1968	XH841	(D)
Pembroke C.1	Feb 1969 — date	XL931	
Heron C.4	Feb 1969 — Jul 1972	XR391	

Meteor NF.14s, No.60 Squadron

No. 61 Squadron

Badge: The Lincoln Imp
Motto: Per purum tonantes
(Thundering through the clear sky)

No.61 Squadron was formed on 24 July 1917 at Rochford as a home defence unit guarding the approaches to London. Initially equipped with Pups, it re-equipped with S.E.5As to combat German bomber raids from bases in Belgium. Shortly before the end of the war, Camels were received and the squadron disbanded on 13 June 1919.

On 8 March 1937, No.61 reformed at Hemswell as a bomber squadron. Equipped initially with Audaxes, it received Ansons within a few weeks in preparation for more modern equipment. Blenheims arrived in January 1938 and were replaced by Hampdens from February 1939. Operations over Germany began on 24 February 1940 and night raids with Hampdens continued until 10 October 1941. Manchesters had begun to replace Hampdens in July 1941 but teething troubles with the type delayed full equipment for several months. In April 1942, the first Lancasters were received and were flown for the rest of the war, the squadron forming part of the main force of Bomber Command. Conversion to Lincolns began in May 1946 and in December 1950 No.61 moved to Malaya for a few months to operate against the Communist guerillas and in March 1954 undertook a similar role against the Mau Mau in Kenya. In August 1954, Canberras were received which were taken to Cyprus in October 1956 during the Suez operation. On 31 March 1958 the squadron disbanded.

Squadron bases

Rochford	24 Jul 1917	Coningsby	1 Feb 1944
	to 13 Jun 1919	Skellingthorpe	15 Apr 1944
Hemswell	8 Mar 1937	Sturgate	16 Jun 1945
North Luffenham	17 Jul 1941	Waddington	25 Jan 1946
Woolfox Lodge	Nov 1941 (P)	Wittering	6 Aug 1953
Syerston	5 May 1942	Upwood	3 Jul 1955
Skellingthorpe	16 Nov 1943		to 31 Mar 1958

Aircraft

Equipment	Period of service	Representative Serial	
Pup	Aug 1917 — Jan 1918		
S.E.5A	Jan 1918 — Oct 1918	C8711	
Camel	Oct 1918 — Jun 1919		
Audax	Mar 1937 — Apr 1937	K7428	
Anson I	Mar 1937 — Jan 1938	K6306	(61-P)
Blenheim I	Jan 1938 — Mar 1939	K7170	(61-V)
Hampden I	Feb 1939 — Oct 1941	AE256	
Manchester I	Jul 1941 — Jun 1942	R5789	
Lancaster I, III	Jun 1942 — May 1946	LM359	(QR-B)
Lancaster II	Oct 1942 —	DS604	(QR-W)
Lincoln B.2	May 1946 — Aug 1954	RF576	(QR-O)
Canberra B.2	Aug 1954 — Mar 1958	WJ751	

Anson I, No.61 Squadron

Lancaster II, No.61 Squadron

No. 62 Squadron

Badge: A meteor
Motto: Inseperato (Unexpectedly)

No.62 Squadron was formed at Filton on 8 August 1916 from a nucleus supplied by No.7 Training Squadron and spent nearly a year on training duties before beginning to mobilise. Bristol Fighters were received in May 1917 and were taken to France in January 1918. Fighter patrols over the Western Front occupied the squadron until the Armistice and after a short period with the occupation forces it was disbanded on 31 July 1919.

On 3 May 1937, No.62 reformed from B Flight on No.40 Squadron at Abingdon. Flying Hind light bombers until re-equipped with Blenheims in the spring on 1938, the squadron left for the Far East a few days before the outbreak of World War Two. Based in Singapore, it flew coastal patrols between training missions until Japan entered the war in December 1941. No.62 was based in northern Malaya at this time and carried out attacks on Japanese shipping engaged in landing troops in southern Thailand but lost most of its aircraft in air attacks on its airfields. While the remaining Blenheims were engaged in raids on Japanese airfields, the squadron re-equipped with Hudsons and withdrew to Sumatra. After Japanese landings near its airfields, No.62 moved to Burma where the enemy

was rapidly overrunning the country. The remnants of No.139 Squadron were absorbed and attacks on Japanese shipping and airfields continued, reconnaissance missions also being flown to locate possible enemy naval forces in the Bay of Bengal. These continued until May 1943 when No.62 was withdrawn to convert to Dakotas. Supply-dropping flights over the 14th Army front in Burma began on 7 January 1944 and continued in all weathers for the rest of the campaign. After the Japanese surrender, the squadron was engaged in general transport duties in south-east Asia until disbanded on 15 March 1946.

On 1 September 1946 No.76 Squadron at Mingaladon, Rangoon, was renumbered 62 Squadron and flew Dakotas. In March 1947 the squadron moved to India as a cadre, being brought up to strength in June before being disbanded on 10 August 1947. On 8 December 1947, No.62 was reformed at Waterbeach and flew Dakotas on the Berlin Airlift until disbanded again on 1 June 1949. Reformed at Woolfox Lodge on 1 February 1960, the squadron was a ground-to-air missile unit until disbanded on 31 January 1963.

Squadron bases

Filton	8 Aug 1916	Spich	2 May 1919
Rendcombe	17 Jul 1917		to 31 Jul 1919
St. Omer	29 Jan 1918	Abingdon	3 May 1937
Serny	1 Feb 1918	Cranfield	12 Jul 1937
Cachy	8 Mar 1918	Left for Far East	
Remaisnil	24 Mar 1918		12 Aug 1939 (G)
Planques	29 Mar 1918		23 Aug 1939 (A)
Croisette	7 Aug 1918	Tengah	22 Sep 1939 (A1)
La Bellevue	26 Sep 1918		25 Sep 1939 (G)
Villers-lez-Cagnicourt		Alor Star	10 Feb 1941
	29 Oct 1918	Butterworth	8 Dec 1941
Aulnoye	18 Nov 1918	Tengah	24 Dec 1941
Bouge	14 Dec 1918	Palembang	27 Jan 1942

Blenheim I, No.62 Squadron

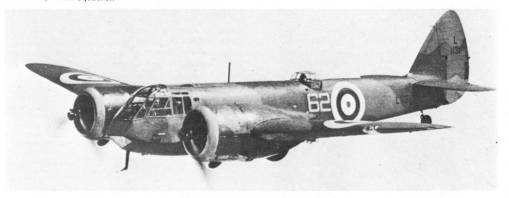

Semplak	16 Feb 1942	Basal	8 Aug 1944	
Dispersed	18 Feb 1942	Agartala	3 Nov 1944	
Akyab	26 Feb 1942	Comilla	30 Dec 1944	
Dum Dum	Mar 1942 (P)	Maunubyin	21 Mar 1945	
Cuttack	14 Jun 1942	Mingaladon	18 Sep 1945	
Asansol	13 Dec 1942		to 15 Mar 1946	
Cuttack	16 Dec 1942	Mingaladon	1 Sep 1946	
Dhubalia	20 Jan 1943	Palam	1 Mar 1947	
Jessore	Feb 1943 (P)		to 10 Aug 1947	
Chaklala	24 May 1943	Waterbeach	8 Dec 1947	
Comilla	3 Jan 1944		to 1 Jun 1949	
Chandina	30 Apr 1944	Woolfox Lodge	1 Feb 1960	
Agartala	12 Jul 1944		to 31 Jan 1963	

Aircraft Equipment	Period of service	Representative Serial
B.E.2c, B.E.2d, B.E.2e, R.E.7, Avro 504A	Aug 1916 — May 1917	
Bristol F.2b	May 1917 — Jul 1919	C4630 (J)
Hind	May 1937 — Mar 1938	K6772
Blenheim I	Feb 1938 — Jan 1942	L6667 (PT-D)
Hudson III, VI	Jan 1942 — Dec 1943	FH290 (P)
Dakota III	Jul 1943 — Mar 1946	FL602 (X)
Dakota C.4	Sep 1946 — Aug 1947 Dec 1947 — Jun 1949	KK181
Bloodhound	Feb 1960 — Jan 1963	—

Meteor F.8s, No.63 Squadron

No. 63 Squadron

Badge: A dexter arm in bend couped below the elbow grasping in the hand a battle axe

Motto: Pone nos ad hostem (Follow us to find the enemy)

No.63 Squadron was formed at Stirling on 31 August 1916 and was originally intended to train as a light bomber unit for the Western Front but in June 1917, its destination was changed to Mesopotamia and it arrived at Basra on 13 August. Disease and intense heat made the assembly of aircraft and equipment difficult and it was 10 September before the first two aircraft were ready to fly. From its base at Samarra, the squadron was attached to the First Indian Corps during its advance on Kirkuk and Mosul and when the Turks surrendered the squadron moved to the latter place. Aircraft had been detached from squadron headquarters throughout the campaign but in February 1920 it assembled as a complete unit as Baghdad where it was disbanded on 29 February 1920.

On 15 February 1937, No.63 reformed at Andover from B Flight of No.12 Squadron with Hinds as a light bomber squadron but replaced these with Audaxes during March on moving up to Upwood. In May it became the first squadron to receive Battles and flew this type until the outbreak of war, being designated a training squadron on 17 March 1939, and supplementing its Battles with some Ansons. When World War Two broke out, No.63 was transferred to Abingdon to join No.6 Group but moved later in the month to Benson where it was engaged in training Battle crews until redesignated No.12 Operational Training Unit on 8 April 1940.

On 15 June 1942, a detachment a No.239 Squadron was redesignated No.63 Squadron at Gatwick. Its Mustangs were used mainly in exercises with the army but on 11 January 1943 it flew its first operations from Odiham, staging through that airfield from its Scottish base. In November 1943, the squadron moved to southern England to join No.123 Airfield for tactical reconnaissance duties but returned to Scotland in January 1944, where it re-equipped with Hurricanes in March and took part in training for bombardment spotting with the navy. In May 1944, it received Spitfires and during the invasion of Normandy provided spotting aircraft for the naval forces supporting the landings. There followed a period of defensive duties until it was again called to undertake spotting for the warships at the Walcheren landings. After a few escort missions from North Weald, the squadron handed over its aircraft to No.41 OTU and disbanded on 30 January 1945.

On 1 September 1946, No.164 Squadron at Middle Wallop was renumbered 63 Squadron. Its Spitfires formed part of the fighter defence of the UK until replaced by Meteors in April 1948 at Thorney Island, where it had moved in December 1947. In May 1950, the squadron moved to Waterbeach where it remained until disbanded on 31 October 1958, having converted to Hunters for the last two years.

Squadron bases			
Stirling	31 Aug 1916	West Freugh	24 Oct 1937
Cramlington	31 Oct 1916	Upwood	25 Nov 1937
Sailed for Mesopotamia		West Freugh	29 Aug 1938
	23 Jun 1917	Upwood	26 Sep 1938
Basra	13 Aug 1917	Warmwell	30 Jan 1939
Samarra	5 Sep 1918	Upwood	17 Feb 1939
Mosul	Nov 1918	Abingdon	7 Sep 1939
Baghdad	17 Feb 1919	Benson	17 Sep 1939
	to 29 Feb 1920		to 8 Apr 1940
Andover	15 Feb 1937	Gatwick	15 Jun 1942
Upwood	3 Mar 1937	Catterick	16 Jul 1942
		Weston Zoyland	6 Nov 1942

Catterick	13 Nov 1942	Peterhead (D)	29 Mar 1944
Macmerry	20 Nov 1942		to 31 Mar 1944
Lossiemouth (D)	6 Dec 1942	Dundonald (D)	9 Apr 1944
	to 17 Dec 1942		to 21 Apr 1944
Odiham (D)	31 Dec 1942	Woodvale (D)	27 Apr 1944
	to 19 Feb 1943		to 26 May 1944
Dalcross (D)	6 Jun 1943	Ballyhalbert (D)	26 Apr 1944
	to 14 Jun 1943		to 25 May 1944
Acklington (D)	21 Jun 1943	Lee-on-Solent	28 May 1944
	to 28 Jun 1943	Woodvale	3 Jul 1944
Turnhouse	26 Jul 1943	Ballyhalbert (D)	4 Jul 1944
Thruxton	8 Nov 1943		to 29 Aug 1944
Sawbridgworth	12 Nov 1943	Lee-on-Solent	30 Aug 1944
North Weald	30 Nov 1943	North Weald	19 Sep 1944
Benson (D)	10 Dec 1943	Manston	1 Nov 1944
	to 21 Jan 1944	North Weald	4 Nov 1944
Turnhouse	16 Jan 1944		to 30 Jan 1945
Peterhead (D)	14 Feb 1944	Middle Wallop	1 Sep 1946
	to 16 Feb 1944	Thorney Island	5 Jan 1948
Tealing (D)	29 Mar 1944	Waterbeach	10 May 1950
	to 31 Mar 1944		to 31 Oct 1958

Aircraft

Equipment	Period of service	Representative Serial
B.E.2c, B.E.2d, Martinsyde G.100	Sep 1916 – Jun 1917	
R.E.8	Aug 1917 – Feb 1920	A4346
Bristol Scout	Aug 1917 – 1918	
Spad S.VII	Aug 1917 – 1918	
D.H.4	Aug 1917 – Nov 1918	
Hind	Feb 1937 – Mar 1937	K6674
Audax	Mar 1937 – Jun 1937	K7464
Battle	May 1937 – Apr 1940	K7650 (63-M)
Anson I	Mar 1939 – Apr 1940	N5071
Mustang I, IA	Jun 1942 – May 1944	AL965
Hurricane IIC, IV	Mar 1944 – May 1944	Z4967 (O)
Spitfire VC	May 1944 – Jan 1945	BM587
Spitfire LF.16E	Sep 1946 – Apr 1948	TE202 (UB-B)
Meteor F.3	Apr 1948 – Jun 1948	EE354 (UB-B)
Meteor F.4	Jun 1948 – Dec 1950	VT280 (UB-K)
Meteor F.8	Dec 1950 – 1956	WK720 (D)
Hunter F.6	1956 – Oct 1958	XE647 (E)

Hornet F.3, No.64 Squadron

No. 64 Squadron

Badge: A scarabee
Motto: Tenax propositi
(Firmness of purpose)

No.64 Squadron was formed at Sedgeford on 1 August 1916 as a training unit with F.E.2bs and Farmans but in June 1917, received fighter types in preparation for operations in France. In October 1917, the squadron moved to the Western Front for fighter patrols and ground-attack duties for the rest of the war. In February 1919, it returned to the UK and disbanded on 31 December 1919.

On 1 March 1936, No.64 reformed at Heliopolis though for political reasons it was announced as having formed at Henlow. Its Demons had already been sent out to Egypt where they formed D Flights in 6 and 208 Squadrons which were transferred during March to 64 Squadron. With the Abyssinian crisis still on, the squadron's duties were to carry out attacks on enemy airfields and act as cover for bombers being refuelled at advance landing grounds. In August 1936, the squadron embarked for the UK to form part of the fighter defences of London. In February 1938, Demons with turrets were received and by the end of the year these had been replaced by Blenheim fighters at Church Fenton. On the outbreak of war, the squadron was engaged in patrols off the East Coast and in December 1939 provided fighter defence for the fleet from Evanton for a month. In April 1940, conversion to Spitfires took place in time for the squadron to help cover the evacuation from Dunkirk and later to take part in the Battle of Britain. In May 1941, it moved to Scotland for air defence duties, returning south in November to begin taking part in sweeps over northern France until March 1943, when it moved back to Scotland. In August it resumed offensive operations from bases in southern England and in June 1944, moved to Cornwall before beginning long-range escort missions from East Anglia. In November 1944, it converted to Mustangs and flew these for the rest of the war in support of Bomber Command's daylight raids on Germany. In May 1946, No.64 received Hornet twin-engined fighters and moved to its peace-time base at Linton-on-Ouse in August. In April 1951 it converted to Meteors but in September 1956 began to replace its F.8s with night-fighter versions of the Meteor. In August 1951 the squadron had moved to Duxford where it remained for ten years and in September 1958 became a Javelin squadron. These it took to Singapore in 1964 where it provided all-weather defence for the island until disbanded on 16 June 1967.

Squadron bases

Sedgeford	1 Aug 1916		to 31 Dec 1919
St. Omer	14 Oct 1917	Heliopolis	1 Mar 1936
Izel-le-Hameau	15 Oct 1917	Ismailia	9 Apr 1936
Aniche	24 Oct 1918	Aboukir	1 Aug 1936
Saultain	22 Nov 1918	Emb. for UK	16 Aug 1936
Froidment	10 Dec 1918	Martlesham Heath	29 Aug 1936
Narborough	14 Feb 1919	North Weald	30 Jul 1937

Martlesham Heath	13 Aug 1937	Fairlop	8 Sep 1942			
Church Fenton	18 May 1938	Hornchurch	14 Nov 1942			
Evanton (D)	4 Dec 1939	Predannack	9 Dec 1942			
	to 8 Jan 1940	Fairlop	2 Jan 1943			
Catterick (D)	18 Apr 1940	Hornchurch	15 Mar 1943			
	to 11 May 1940	Ayr	28 Mar 1943			
Kenley	16 May 1940	Friston	7 Aug 1943			
Leconfield	19 Aug 1940	Gravesend	19 Aug 1943			
Biggin Hill	13 Oct 1940	West Malling	6 Sep 1943			
Coltishall	15 Oct 1940	Coltishall	25 Sep 1943			
Hornchurch	10 Nov 1940	Ayr	21 Jan 1944			
Southend	27 Jan 1941	Coltishall	3 Feb 1944			
Hornchurch	31 Mar 1941	Deanland	29 Apr 1944			
Martlesham Heath	8 May 1941	Harrowbeer	23 Jun 1944			
Hornchurch	14 May 1941	Bradwell Bay	30 Aug 1944			
Turnhouse	16 May 1941	Bentwaters	28 Dec 1944			
Drem	20 May 1941	Horsham St. Faith	18 Aug 1945			
Turnhouse	6 Aug 1941	Linton-on-Ouse	6 Aug 1946			
Drem	4 Oct 1941	Duxford	8 Aug 1951			
Hornchurch	17 Nov 1941	Waterbeach	17 Jul 1961			
Southend	31 Mar 1942	Binbrook	24 Aug 1962			
Hornchurch	1 May 1942	Tengah	1 Apr 1965 (P)			
Martlesham Heath	20 Jul 1942		to 16 Jun 1967			
Hornchurch	28 Jul 1942		(Dets from Dec 1963)			

Aircraft Equipment	Period of service	Representative Serial
F.E.2b, Henry Farman, Avro 504, Pup	Aug 1916 — Jun 1917	
D.H.5	Jun 1917 — Mar 1918	A9507 (E)
S.E.5A	Mar 1918 — Dec 1919	D6900
Demon	Mar 1936 — Dec 1938	K4516
Blenheim If	Dec 1938 — Apr 1940	L1472 (GR-L)
Spitfire I	Apr 1940 — Feb 1941	
Spitfire IIA, IIB	Feb 1941 — Nov 1941	P7747 (SH-K)
Spitfire VB	Nov 1941 — Jul 1942	AA907 (SH-S)
Spitfire VB, VC	Mar 1943 — Jul 1944	W3320 (SH-L)
Spitfire IX	Jul 1942 — Mar 1943	BR600 (SH-V)
	Jul 1944 — Nov 1944	MJ714 (SH-B)
Mustang III	Nov 1944 — May 1946	FZ169 (SH-C)
Mustang IV	Aug 1945 — May 1946	KM256 (SH-W)
Hornet F.1	May 1946 — May 1948	PX284 (SH-B)
Hornet F.3	Mar 1948 — Apr 1951	PX391 (SH-R)
Meteor F.8	Apr 1951 — Mar 1957	WE913 (F)
Meteor NF.12	Aug 1956 — Sep 1958	WS617 (A)
Meteor NF.14	Dec 1956 — Sep 1958	WS840 (S)
Javelin FAW.7	Sep 1958 — Jun 1960	XH747 (B)
Javelin FAW.9	Jun 1960 — Jun 1967	XH879 (D)

Hornet F.3, No.65 Squadron

No. 65 Squadron

Badge: In front of fifteen swords in pile, the hilts in base, a lion passant
Motto: Vi et armis (By force of arms)
Name: 'East India'

No.65 Squadron was formed at Wyton on 1 August 1916 from a nucleus flight supplied by Norwich training station and used a variety of types for training until it left for France with Camels in October 1917. It began flying defensive patrols over the Western Front and in February 1918 began ground-attack missions with light bombs on enemy troops and battlefield positions. In August 1918, it moved to the Belgian coastal sector and provided escorts for day bombers attacking enemy bases. During the last weeks of the war it covered the Allied advance into Belgium and returned to the UK in February 1919, where it disbanded on 25 October 1919.

On 1 August 1934, No.65 reformed at Hornchurch with Demons but in September 1935, it began losing its personnel to drafts being sent to the Middle East during the Abyssinian crisis and was reduced to a cadre, being brought up to strength from July 1936, at the same time as Gauntlets were received to replace the remaining Demons. In June 1937 it re-equipped with Gladiators, converting to Spitfires in March 1939. In June 1940, offensive patrols began to be flown over France and the Low Countries to cover the evacuation from Dunkirk, the squadron being moved to Lincolnshire to refit at the end of May. It returned south a week later and took part in the Battle of Britain until the end of August, when it moved to Scotland. In November 1940 it came south again and began offensive sweeps over France in January 1941, before a further move to Lincolnshire took place in February 1941, although several offensive operations were carried out later by staging through southern airfields. In October 1941, No.65 received Spitfire Vs which it used for low-level attacks on enemy transport and for shipping reconnaissance from bases in southern England until October 1942, when it moved to Scotland. In January 1943, the squadron carried out deck-landing training with Seafires in preparation for the future amphibious landing using the training carrier *Argus* in the Clyde and in March 1943, moved to Cornwall for fighter patrols and bomber escort missions. In May it joined Second TAF in preparation for the invasion of Europe, converting to Mustangs in December which it used as fighter-bombers during the months before the landings. By the end of June the squadron was based in Normandy where it provided ground-attack support for the army until September 1944, when it was moved to East Anglia to act as fighter escorts for the heavy bombers of Bomber Command in their daylight raids over Germany. In January 1945, it moved to northern Scotland to provide similar services to the strike wings of Coastal Command attacking enemy shipping off Norway and Denmark.

In May 1945, the squadron moved to East Anglia where it replaced its Mustangs with Spitfires and in July 1946 began to receive Hornets, moving during the following month to Yorkshire. In December 1950, it began to replace the Hornets with Meteor F.4s but these arrived slowly and in April, 1951, re-equipment was completed with Meteor F.8s. In August 1951 a move was made to Duxford where the squadron spent the next ten years. In December 1956 Hunters began to arrive and this became the squadron's equipment for the rest of its career as a fighter squadron, disbandment taking place on 31 March 1961.

Squadron bases

Wyton	1 Aug 1916	Bertangles	6 Apr 1918
La Lovie	27 Oct 1917	Capelle	12 Aug 1918
Bailleul	4 Nov 1917	Bray Dunes	16 Aug 1918
Poperinghe	17 Feb 1918	Petite Synthe	19 Sep 1918
Droglandt	21 Mar 1918	Bisseghem	25 Oct 1918
Clairmarais	24 Mar 1918	Yatesbury	12 Feb 1919
Conteville	28 Mar 1918		to 25 Oct 1919

Hornchurch	1 Aug 1934	Selsey	31 May 1943
Northolt	2 Oct 1939	Kingsnorth	1 Jul 1943
Hornchurch	28 Mar 1940	Ashford	5 Oct 1943
Kirton-in-Lindsey	29 May 1940	Gatwick	15 Oct 1943
Hornchurch	5 Jun 1940	Gravesend	24 Oct 1943
Turnhouse	28 Aug 1940	Ford	15 Apr 1944
Tangmere	29 Nov 1940	Funtington	14 May 1944
Kirton-in-Lindsey	26 Feb 1941	Ford	15 Jun 1944
Westhampnett	7 Oct 1941	B.7 Martagny	25 Jun 1944
Debden	22 Dec 1941	B.12 Ellon	17 Jul 1944
Great Sampford	14 Apr 1942	B.24 Beauvais	3 Sep 1944
Martlesham Heath	9 Jun 1942	B.60 Grimbergen	8 Sep 1944
Great Sampford	15 Jun 1942	Matlask	29 Sep 1944
Hawkinge	30 Jun 1942	Andrews Field	14 Oct 1944
Great Sampford	7 Jul 1942	Peterhead	16 Jan 1945
Gravesend	29 Jul 1942	Banff	21 Jan 1945
Eastchurch	14 Aug 1942	Peterhead	2 Feb 1945
Gravesend	20 Aug 1942	Andrews Field	6 May 1945
Drem	26 Sep 1942	Bentwaters	15 May 1945
Lympne	2 Oct 1942	Hethel	6 Sep 1945
Drem	11 Oct 1942	Spilsby	11 Feb 1946
Arbroath	29 Dec 1942	Horsham St. Faith	14 Mar 1946
Machrihanish	3 Jan 1943	Linton-on-Ouse	12 Aug 1946
Drem	10 Jan 1943	Duxford	15 Aug 1951
Perranporth	29 Mar 1943		to 31 Mar 1961
Fairlop	18 May 1943		

Aircraft

Equipment	Period of service	Representative Serial
Various (e.g. Shorthorn, Graham-White XV, Bristol Scout, Avro 504, Nieuport 12, D.H.5, Pup	Aug 1916 – Oct 1917	–
Camel	Oct 1917 – Oct 1919	H7007
Demon	Aug 1934 – Jul 1936	K3783
Gauntlet II	Jul 1936 – Jun 1937	K5333
Gladiator I	Jun 1937 – Apr 1939	K8040
Spitfire I	Mar 1939 – Mar 1941	K9909 (FZ-L)
Spitfire IIA, IIB	Mar 1941 – Oct 1941	P7850 (YT-C)
Spitfire VB, VC	Oct 1941 – Aug 1943	AB786 (YT-W)
Spitfire IX	Aug 1943 – Jan 1944	MH367 (YT-C)
Mustang III	Dec 1943 – Mar 1945	SR411
Mustang IV	Mar 1945 – May 1945	KM140 (YT-E)
Spitfire XVIE	May 1945 – Sep 1946	TD134 (YT-W)
Hornet F.1	Jul 1946 – Nov 1948	PX282 (YT-B)
Hornet F.3	Nov 1948 – Apr 1951	PX346 (YT-E)
Meteor F.4	Dec 1950 – Apr 1951	VW258
Meteor F.8	Apr 1951 – Feb 1957	WL116 (O)
Hunter F.6	Dec 1956 – Mar 1961	XF507 (A)

No. 66 Squadron

Badge: A rattlesnake
Motto: Cavete praemonui
(Beware, I have given
warning)

No.66 Squadron was formed at Filton on 30 June 1916 and moved to France in March 1917 as a fighter unit. Equipped with Pups, it flew patrols over the Western Front until October 1917 when it re-equipped with Camels and moved during the following month to northern Italy. Until the end of the war, it was engaged on the north-eastern front against the Austrians and in March 1919 returned to the UK as a cadre where it disbanded on 25 October 1919.

On 20 July 1936, No.66 reformed at Duxford from C Flight of No.19 Squadron. In November 1938 it replaced its Gauntlets with Spitfires which were flown on defensive duties after the outbreak of World War Two. In May 1940 the squadron flew covering patrols over Dunkirk and re-

mained in the south-east throughout the Battle of Britain. In February 1941, No.66 took part in a few sweeps over France before moving to south-west England for coastal patrols. For the next two years, it also provided escorts for day bombers over France before moving to the Orkneys for four months, returning south to join Second TAF's sweeps across the Channel. Fighter-bomber sorties began shortly before the landings in Normandy and five days after the invasion No.66 made use of airstrips in the beachhead for the first time. The squadron transferred its base to France in August and moved forward to Belgium and the Netherlands in September. After flying armed reconnaissance sweeps over Germany and the German-occupied part of the Netherlands until 27 April 1945, the squadron disbanded on 30 April 1945.

On 1 September 1946, No.66 reformed at Duxford with Spitfires, replacing these with Meteors in March 1947. In October 1949 it moved to Yorkshire where it converted to Sabres in December 1953. Hunters were received in March 1956 and were flown until disbandment on 30 September 1960. Reformed from the Belvedere Trials Unit on 15 September 1961, No.66 moved to Singapore in June 1962 where it provided transport support for the security forces in Malaya until disbanded on 20 March 1969.

Belvedere HC.1, No.66 Squadron

Squadron bases

Filton	30 Jun 1916	Ibsley	27 Apr 1942
Netheravon	2 Jul 1916	Tangmere	3 Jul 1942
Filton	30 Jul 1916	Ibsley	7 Jul 1942
Vert Galand	18 Mar 1917	Tangmere	16 Aug 1942
Estrée Blanche	31 May 1917	Ibsley	20 Aug 1942
Calais	20 Jun 1917	Zeals	24 Aug 1942
Estrée Blanche	6 Jul 1917	Predannack	26 Sep 1942
Suttons Farm	8 Jul 1917	Zeals	29 Sep 1942
Estrée Blanche	10 Jul 1917	Hawkinge	8 Oct 1942
Milan	22 Nov 1917	Zeals	9 Oct 1942
Verona	29 Nov 1917	Warmwell	1 Nov 1942
Grossa	4 Dec 1917	Zeals	14 Nov 1942
Treorso	18 Feb 1918	Ibsley	23 Dec 1942
San Pietro	10 Mar 1918	Skeabrae	9 Feb 1943
Arcade	1 Nov 1918	Churchstanton	28 Jun 1943
San Pietro	6 Nov 1918	Redhill	10 Aug 1943
Leighterton	10 Mar 1919	Kenley	13 Aug 1943
	to 25 Oct 1919	Perranporth	17 Sep 1943
Duxford	20 Jul 1936	Hornchurch	8 Nov 1943
Digby	12 Jul 1938	Southend	16 Nov 1943
Duxford	15 Jul 1938	Hornchurch	30 Nov 1943
Horsham St. Faith	16 May 1940	Llanbedr	23 Feb 1944
Coltishall	29 May 1940	North Weald	1 Mar 1944
Kenley	3 Sep 1940	Bognor	31 Mar 1944
Gravesend	11 Sep 1940	Southend	22 Apr 1944
West Malling	30 Oct 1940	Bognor	25 Apr 1944
Exeter	24 Feb 1941	Castletown	8 May 1944
Perranporth	27 Apr 1941	Bognor	14 May 1944
Portreath	14 Dec 1941	Tangmere	22 Jun 1944
Warmwell	8 Feb 1942	Funtington	6 Aug 1944
Portreath	22 Feb 1942	Ford	12 Aug 1944

B.16 Villons les Buissons	20 Aug 1944	B.105 Twente	18 Apr 1945
			to 30 Apr 1945
B.33 Camp Neuseville	6 Sep 1944	Duxford	1 Sep 1946
		Linton-on-Ouse	7 Oct 1949
B.57 Lille/Wambrechies	11 Sep 1944	Acklington	14 Feb 1957
			to 30 Sep 1960
B.60 Grimbergen	6 Oct 1944	Odiham	15 Sep 1961
B.79 Woensdrecht	22 Dec 1944	Left for Far East	1 Jun 1962
Fairwood Common	21 Feb 1945	Seletar	Jun 1962 (P)
B.85 Schijndel	17 Mar 1945		to 20 Mar 1969

Aircraft

Equipment	Period of service	Representative Serial	
Various e.g. B.E.2b, B.E.2c, B.E.2d, B.E.12, Avro 504A	Jul 1916 – Mar 1917		
Pup	Oct 1917 – Mar 1919	A634	(D)
Camel	Oct 1917 – Mar 1919	D9588	(O)
Gauntlet II	Jul 1936 – Dec 1938		
Spitfire I	Nov 1938 – Nov 1940	K9805	(RB-R)
Spitfire IIA	Nov 1940 – Feb 1942	P7735	(LZ-M)
Spitfire VA, VB, VC	Feb 1942 – Nov 1943	EE661	(LZ-R)
Spitfire IX	Nov 1943 – Nov 1944	PT529	(LZ-F)
Spitfire XVI	Nov 1944 – Apr 1945 Sep 1946 – Mar 1947	RK842	
Meteor F.3	Mar 1947 – May 1948	EE352	(HI-A)
Meteor F.4	May 1948 – Jan 1951	VT122	(LZ-B)
Meteor F.8	Jan 1951 – Dec 1953	WA988	(Q)
Sabre F.4	Dec 1953 – Mar 1956	XD715	(K)
Hunter F.4	Mar 1956 – Oct 1956	XE713	(E)
Hunter F.6	Oct 1956 – Sep 1960	XG266	(R)
Belvedere HC.1	Sep 1961 – Mar 1969	XG462	(H)

No. 67 Squadron

Badge: A drongo volant
Motto: No odds too great

No.67 Squadron was originally formed on 12 September 1916, when No.1 Squadron Australian Flying Corps, was renumbered at Heliopolis. It flew a variety of types for reconnaissance duties and included among these were a few fighters. By the end of the summer of 1917, No.67's equipment had become more standardised and before it reverted to the title of No.1 Squadron, AFC on 6 February 1918, it had started to acquire Bristol Fighters. It later became a specialised fighter squadron and disbanded on 5 March 1919.

On 12 March 1941 No.67 reformed at Kallang from a draft of five officers and 111 airmen which had arrived on the previous day at Singapore on the *Aquitania*. Buffalos began to arrive within a few days and the squadron was fully equipped by the end of May. On 8 October 1941, No.67 handed over its aircraft to No.488 Squadron, RNZAF and embarked the following day for Burma, taking over sixteen Buffaloes from 60 Squadron on arrival. When the Japanese attacked in December 1941 the squadron was engaged in the defence of the Rangoon area but attacks on its airfields and the inadequacy of the Buffalo resulted in their replacement by Hurricanes by February 1942. As Burma was rapidly being overrun, the squadron withdrew to India and became dispersed as detachments were sent to various airstrips in an attempt to cover the withdrawal of the small land force to the Indian border. By the end of March, the squadron ceased to be effective.

During May 1942 various parties of squadron personnel re-assembled at Alipore and No.67's Hurricanes formed part of the fighter defence of the Calcutta area. In June 1943, detachments began flying over Burma to escort Dakotas and provide fighter defence. In November it returned to the defence of Calcutta and converted to Spitfires in February 1944. In July 1944 No.67 returned to the front and began an intensive period of offensive patrols over Burma seeking out Japanese camps and transport and also provided tactical support for the army. 1945 opened with the squadron moving into a Burmese base for the first time since 1942 and attacks on Japanese troops and camps continued until May when offensive operations ceased. The squadron was ordered to

Buffalo Is, No.67 Squadron

Martinsyde G-100, No.67 Squadron

disband on 23 August 1945, but it was the end of the month before it disposed of its aircraft.

On 1 September 1950 No.67 reformed at Gutersloh as part of the RAF force in Germany and received Vampire fighter-bombers. In May 1952, it moved its base to Wildenrath and in May 1953 re-equipped with Sabres. In July 1955 it moved again to Bruggen where in January 1956 it began to receive Hunters. On 16 April 1957 the squadron disbanded.

Squadron bases

Heliopolis	12 Sep 1916	Alipore	30 Nov 1943
Mustabig	17 Dec 1916	Amarda Road	7 Mar 1944
Kilo 143	5 Jan 1917	Alipore	28 Mar 1944
El Arish	Jan 1917	Baigachi	12 Apr 1944
Rafa	Mar 1917	Comilla	5 Jul 1944
Deir el Belah	Jul 1917	Double Moorings	30 Nov 1944
Weli Sheikh Nuran	Sep 1917	Maunghnama	1 Jan 1945
Julis	Dec 1917	Dabaing 2	7 Feb 1945
	to 6 Feb 1918 (to 1 AFC)	Akyab Main	14 May 1945
Kallang	12 Mar 1941		to 31 Aug 1945
Mingaladon	13 Oct 1941	Gutersloh	1 Sep 1950
Toungoo, Magwe, Akyab		Duxford	21 Apr 1952
	Feb/Mar 1942	Wildenrath	5 May 1952
Alipore	May 1942	Bruggen	5 Jul 1955
Chittagong	24 Aug 1943		to 16 Apr 1957

Aircraft

Equipment	Period of service	Representative Serial
Various incl. B.E.2c, B.E.2e, D.H.6, Avro 504, Martinsyde S.1, Nieuport 17	Sep 1916 – Sep 1917 (approx)	
R.E.8	Sep 1917 – Feb 1918	
B.E.12A	Sep 1917 – Feb 1918	A6328
Martinsyde G.100/102	Oct 1917 – Feb 1918	A3955
Bristol F.2b	Jan 1918 – Feb 1918	A7188
Buffalo	Mar 1941 – Feb 1942	W8220 (RD-U)
Hurricane IIB	Feb 1942 – Mar 1942	BN476
Hurricane IIC	May 1942 – Feb 1944	HV640
Spitfire VIII	Feb 1944 – Aug 1945	MB966 (RD-R)
Vampire FB.5	Sep 1950 – May 1953	WA101
Sabre F.1	May 1953 – Mar 1956	XB586 (X)
Hunter F.4	Jan 1956 – Apr 1957	XE689 (W)

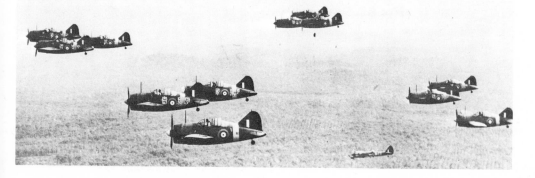

No. 68 Squadron

Badge: A tawny owl's head couped
Motto: Vzdy pripraven (Czech) (Always ready)

No.68 Squadron was formed on 30 January 1917, at Harlaxton as a fighter unit and moved to France in September 1917, equipped with D.H.5s. In January 1918 it re-equipped with S.E.5As and on 19 January 1918 was redesignated No.2 Squadron, Australian Flying Corps. It spent the rest of the war under this title, disbanding on 28 February 1919.

On 7 January 1941 No.68 reformed at Catterick as a night fighter squadron equipped with Blenheims and became operational on 7 April before moving to High Ercall for the defence of the Midlands. In May, conversion to Beaufighters took place and in March 1942, the squadron moved to East Anglia where it spent two years at Coltishall mainly on defensive tasks though some intruder missions were flown. In the first half of 1944, three months were spent in South Wales and in July No.68 re-equipped with Mosquitos for

intercepting flying bombs. With the capture of their launching sites the squadron turned its attention to enemy bombers used for carrying V-1s to a firing position over the North Sea as well as flying patrols to counter enemy intruder aircraft over the East Coast. On 20 April 1945 the squadron was disbanded.

On 1 January 1952, No.68 reformed as a night fighter squadron at Wahn and flew Meteors in Germany until renumbered 5 Squadron on 20 January 1959.

Squadron bases

Harlaxton	30 Jan 1917	Castle Camps	24 Jun 1944
Baizieux	21 Sep 1917	Coltishall	27 Oct 1944
	to 19 Jan 1918	Wittering	8 Feb 1945
Catterick	7 Jan 1941	Coltishall	27 Feb 1945
High Ercall	17 Apr 1941	Church Fenton	15 Mar 1945
Coltishall	8 Mar 1942		to 20 Apr 1945
Coleby Grange	5 Feb 1944	Wahn	1 Jan 1952
Fairwood Common	1 Mar 1944	Laarbruch	17 Jul 1957
			to 20 Jan 1959

Aircraft

Equipment	Period of service	Representative Serial
D.H.5	Sep 1917 – Jan 1918	A9449 (1)
S.E.5A	Jan 1918 – Feb 1919	C9539 (V)
Blenheim If	Jan 1941 – May 1941	L1513
Beaufighter I	May 1941 – Mar 1943	R2148
Beaufighter VI	Jan 1943 – Jul 1944	V8592 (WM-L)
Mosquito XVII, XIX	Jul 1944 – Feb 1945	HK250 (WM-Z)
Mosquito 30	Feb 1945 – Apr 1945	NT321 (WM-O)
Meteor NF.11	Mar 1952 – Jan 1959	WD677 (D)

D.H.5, No.68 Squadron

R.E.8, No.69 Squadron

No. 69 Squadron

Badge: In front of an anchor, a telescope
Motto: With vigilance we serve

No.69 Squadron was formed on 28 December 1916 at South Carlton on the arrival of a draft of Australian personnel from Egypt. In September 1917 it moved to France as a corps reconnaissance unit and on 19 January 1918 was redesignated No.3 Squadron, Australian Flying Corps.

On 10 January 1941 No.431 Flight was redesignated No.69 Squadron. Based on Malta, it carried out strategic reconnaissance missions over enemy ports and airfields in Sicily, Italy and Libya. Marylands formed a large part of its strength until May 1942 when Spitfires began to carry out all the reconnaissance tasks but were later supplemented by Baltimores for shipping reconnaissance and anti-submarine patrols and these were flown until April 1944. No.69 left for the UK during the month and re-assembled at Northolt on 5 May 1944 as part of No.34 Wing of Second TAF. Equipped with Wellingtons for night reconnaissance duties, it began operations on the eve of D-Day, using flares to locate enemy troop movements. In September, the squadron moved to France and Belgium and continued reconnaissance missions until 7 May 1945. After a period of survey work over Denmark and Norway, the squadron disbanded on 7 August 1945.

On 8 August 1945, No.613 Squadron at Cambrai was renumbered 69 Squadron and flew Mosquito fighter-bombers until disbanded on 31 March 1946. No.180 Squadron at Wahn became No.69 Squadron on 1 April 1946 which was equipped with Mosquito light bombers until again disbanded on 6 November 1947.

No.69 reformed on 5 May 1954 at Laarbruch as a Canberra reconnaissance squadron and remained in Germany until renumbered 39 Squadron on 1 July 1958.

Squadron bases		
South Carlton	28 Dec 1916	
Savy	9 Sep 1917	
Bailleul	Nov 1917	
	to 19 Jan 1918	
Luqa	10 Jan 1941	
Montecorvino	7 Feb 1944	
Left for UK	10 Apr 1944	
Northolt	5 May 1944	
A.12 Balleroy	4 Sep 1944	
B.48 Amiens-Glisy	11 Sep 1944	
B.58 Melsbroek	26 Sep 1944	
B.78 Eindhoven	15 Apr 1945	
	to 7 Aug 1945	
Aalborg West (D)	8 Jul 1945	
	to 9 Aug 1945	
Cambrai/Epinoy	8 Aug 1945	
	to 31 Mar 1946	
Wahn	1 Apr 1946	
Tangmere	18 Apr 1947	
Wahn	19 May 1947	
	to 6 Nov 1947	
Laarbruch	5 May 1954	
	to 1 Jul 1958	

Aircraft Equipment	Period of service	Representative Serial
Various	Dec 1916 – Sep 1917	–
R.E.8	Sep 1917 – Jan 1918	F6016 (K)
Maryland I	Jan 1941 – May 1942	BS762
Beaufighter I	Jan 1941 – Feb 1942	T4705
Hurricane IIA	Jan 1941 – Jan 1942	Z3123
Spitfire IV	Jan 1941 – Feb 1943	BP908
Mosquito I	Jan 1942 – Mar 1942	W4063
Baltimore I, II	Jun 1942 – Aug 1943	AG755 (B)
Baltimore III, IIIa, IV	Jun 1943 – Apr 1944	FA326 (D)
Wellington IC, VIII	Aug 1942 – Aug 1943	HX576 (Z)
Wellington XIII	May 1944 – Aug 1945	NC489
Mosquito VI	Aug 1945 – Mar 1946	PZ229
Mosquito XVI	Apr 1946 – Nov 1947	PF612
Canberra PR.3	May 1954 – Jul 1958	WE139

Maryland I, No.69 Squadron

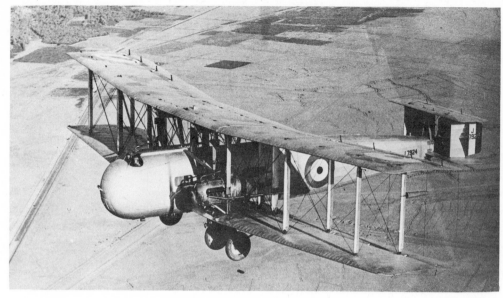

Victoria III, No.70 Squadron

No. 70 Squadron

Badge: A demi-winged lion erased
Motto: Usquam (Anywhere)

No.70 Squadron was formed at Farnborough on 22 April 1916 as a fighter unit and was equipped with the first British fighter to have a synchronised machine-gun as standard equipment, the two-seat Sopwith 1½-strutter. The absence of sufficient effective fighters on the Western Front resulted in the squadron being moved to France in sections, A Flight arriving on 21 May to be joined by the remaining flights at monthly intervals. In addition to fighter patrols, No.70 was also engaged in reconnaissance and bombing missions. In July 1917, it was the first squadron to re-equip with Camels which it used for fighter patrols and ground-attack duties for the rest of the war. In February 1919, No.70 was reduced to a cadre and returned to the UK where it disbanded on 22 January 1920.

On 1 February 1920, No.58 Squadron at Heliopolis was renumbered 70 Squadron as a bomber-transport unit equipped with Vimys. This type was in the process of replacing Handley Page O/400s and was in use until the arrival of its transport variant, the Vernon, in November 1922. In December 1921, the squadron moved to Iraq where it remained as the resident bomber-transport unit until the outbreak of World War Two. During this period, it provided air transport for RAF and Iraqi forces policing the remoter parts of the country and in 1928 evacuated over 500 British citizens caught up in a civil war in Afghanistan. Victorias began to arrive in August 1926 and their developments, the Valentias, were used until the squadron moved to Egypt in August 1939.

After Italy entered the war in June 1940, there was a need for heavy bombers in the Middle East. No.70 was con-

verted to Wellingtons and began operations on 18 September. Attacks were made by night on ports and bases in Libya, Italy and Greece to restrict supplies to the enemy during the campaign in the Western Desert. In 1941 some operations were flown over Iraq and Syria to support local campaigns. As the front line moved westwards, the squadron left Egypt for bases in Libya and, later, Tunisia. Its main targets were now in Italy and Sicily and in December 1943, No.70 moved to captured airfields around Foggia where it spent the rest of the war. Operations over northern Italy and the Balkans continued with Wellingtons until conversion to Liberators early in 1945. In addition to bombing raids, the squadron undertook minelaying in the Danube and dropped supplies to Yugoslav partisan forces. In October 1945, No.70 returned to the Middle East where it was disbanded on 31 March 1946.

On 15 April 1946 No.178 Squadron at Fayid was renumbered 70 Squadron and flew Lancasters in Egypt until disbanded on 1 April 1947. On 1 May 1948, No.215 Squadron at Kabrit became No.70 Squadron. Equipped with Dakotas, the squadron was engaged in transport duties in the Middle East, converting to Valettas in January 1950. In December 1955, a move was made to Cyprus to re-equip with Hastings and these were flown until replaced by Argosies in November 1967. During the Suez operation, No.70's Hastings dropped parachute troops on Port Said and one Hastings was retained as a VIP transport until July 1968. Conversion to the Hercules began in November 1970 but a few Argosies remained in service until 1973. With the rundown of British forces in the Near East, No.70 returned to the UK early in 1975.

Squadron bases

Farnborough	22 Apr 1916	Poperinghe	8 Aug 1917
Fienvillers	21 May 1916 (A)	Marieux	16 Mar 1918
	29 Jun 1916 (B)	Fienvillers	28 Mar 1918
	30 Jul 1916 (C)	Remaisnil	16 Apr 1918
Auchel	15 Dec 1916	Boisdinghem	8 Jul 1918
Vert Galant	4 Mar 1917	Esquerdes	1 Aug 1918
Fienvillers	2 Apr 1917	Droglandt	22 Sep 1918
Boisdinghem	14 May 1917	Menin	25 Oct 1918.
Estrée Blanche	27 Jun 1917	Namur	25 Nov 1918

Elsenborn	6 Dec 1918	LG.140	30 Nov 1942			
Bickendorf	13 Dec 1918	Benina	19 Jan 1943			
Spittlegate	3 Sep 1919	El Magrun	23 Jan 1943			
	to 22 Jan 1920	Gardabia East	10 Feb 1943			
Heliopolis	1 Feb 1920	Gardabia West	25 Feb 1943			
Baghdad West	17 Dec 1921 (G)	Kairouan/Temmar				
	16 Jan 1922 (A1)		25 May 1943			
Hinaidi	31 May 1922	Djedida	15 Nov 1943			
Habbaniya	16 Oct 1937	Cerignola	17 Dec 1943			
Helwan	30 Aug 1939	Aqir	Oct 1945 (P)			
Habbaniya (D)	30 Aug 1939	Shallufa	12 Dec 1945			
	to 5 Oct 1940		to 31 Mar 1946			
Heliopolis	10 Jun 1940	Fayid	15 Apr 1946			
Kabrit	9 Sep 1940	Kabrit	21 Aug 1946			
Tatoi (D)	6 Nov 1940	Shallufa	17 Sep 1946			
	to 24 Nov 1940		to 1 Apr 1947			
LG.75	12 Jan 1942	Kabrit	1 May 1948			
LG.104	15 Jan 1942	Nicosia	12 Dec 1955			
LG.224	26 Jun 1942	Akrotiri	12 Jul 1966			
Abu Sueir	29 Jun 1942	Lyneham	1 Feb 1975			
LG.224	6 Nov 1942					
LG.106	11 Nov 1942					

Aircraft Equipment	Period of service	Representative Serial
Sopwith 1½-strutter	Apr 1916 — Jul 1917	A1514
Camel	Jul 1917 — Feb 1919	B7320 (P)
Snipe	Dec 1918 — Feb 1919	E8057 (14)
Handley Page O/400	Feb 1920 — Apr 1920	
Vimy	Feb 1920 — Nov 1922	F8643
Vernon	Nov 1922 — Dec 1926	J7541
Victoria	Aug 1926 — Nov 1935	K1311 (B)
Valentia	Nov 1935 — Oct 1940	K3168 (K)
Wellington IC	Sep 1940 — Feb 1943	Z9023 (X)
Wellington III	Jan 1943 — Dec 1943	HF750 (L)
Wellington X	Jun 1943 — Feb 1945	NA720 (J)
Liberator VI	Jan 1945 — Mar 1946	KK315 (C)
Lancaster I	Apr 1946 — Apr 1947	NX727 (L)
Dakota C.4	May 1948 — Jan 1950	KN266
Valetta C.1	Jan 1950 — Dec 1955	WD157 (F)
Hastings C.1, C.2, C.4	Jan 1956 — Jul 1958	TG551 'Homer'
Argosy C.1	Nov 1967 — Feb 1972	XR107 'Jason'
Hercules C.1	Nov 1970 — date	XV305

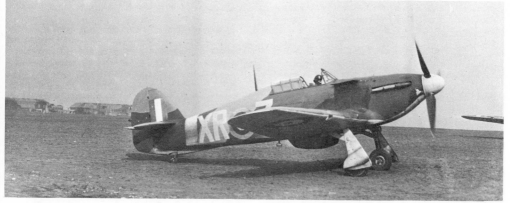

Hurricane I, No.71 Squadron

No. 71 Squadron

Badge: A bald-headed eagle displayed charged with three stars of nine points
Motto: First from the eyries
Name: 'Eagle'

No.71 Squadron was formed at Castle Bromwich on 27 March 1917 from a draft of Australian personnel arriving from Australia for service with the RFC. In December 1917 the squadron moved to France with Camels to fly fighter patrols over the Western Front but was redesignated No.4 Squadron, Australian Flying Corps, on 19 January 1918. Under this title, it served in France until the Armistice and after a short period with the occupation forces in Germany, disbanded on 28 February 1918.

On 19 September 1940, No.71 was reformed at Church Fenton as the first 'Eagle' squadron to be manned by American personnel. By the end of October a few Buffalos had been received but being completely obsolete by European standards these were used only for training and during November the squadron was equipped with Hurricanes. Becoming operational on defensive duties on 5 February 1941, No.71 converted to Spitfires in August and took part in sweeps over northern France. On 29 September 1942, the squadron was, in company with two other 'Eagle' squadrons, transferred to the 4th Pursuit Group, US Army Air Corps, as the 334th Pursuit Squadron and ceased to be a RAF unit.

On 1 October 1950, No.71 reformed at Gutersloh as a fighter-bomber squadron in Germany, receiving Vampires. These were replaced in 1953 by Sabres and the squadron remained a day fighter unit until disbanded on 30 April after a year equipped with Hunters.

Squadron bases

Castle Bromwich	27 Mar 1917	Debden	2 May 1942
St. Omer	18 Dec 1917	Gravesend	30 Jun 1942
Bruay	22 Dec 1917	Debden	7 Jul 1942
	to 19 Jan 1918	Gravesend	14 Aug 1942
Church Fenton	19 Sep 1940		to 29 Sep 1942
Kirton-in-Lindsey	23 Nov 1940	Gutersloh	1 Oct 1950
Martlesham Heath	9 Apr 1941	Wildenrath	11 Mar 1952
North Weald	23 Jun 1941	Bruggen	May 1956
Martlesham Heath	14 Dec 1941		to 31 Apr 1957

Aircraft Equipment	Period of service	Representative Serial
Various	Mar 1917 — Dec 1917	
Camel	Dec 1917 — Jan 1918	B7406 (W)
Buffalo I	Oct 1940 — Nov 1940	AS414
Hurricane I	Nov 1940 — May 1941	V7608 (XR-J)
Hurricane II	Apr 1941 — Aug 1941	Z3174 (XR-B)
Spitfire IIA	Aug 1941 — Sep 1941	P7308 (XR-D)
Spitfire VB	Sep 1941 — Sep 1942	W3801
Vampire FB.5	Oct 1950 — Oct 1953	WA223 (L-J)
Sabre F.1/F.4	Oct 1953 — May 1956	XB710 (J)
Hunter F.4	Apr 1956 — Apr 1957	XF313 (G)

No. 72 Squadron

Badge: A swift volant
Motto: Swift
Name: 'Basutoland'

Bristol M.1C, No.72 Squadron

No.72 Squadron was formed on 2 July 1917 from a nucleus supplied by the Central Flying School. In December it left for Mesopotamia split into several parties which assembled at Basra on 2 March 1918. Equipped with a variety of single-seat fighters, the squadron was divided into detached flights and allotted to different army formations for fighter protection and tactical reconnaissance duties. Soon after the end of the war, No.72 re-assembled at Baghdad where it was reduced to a cadre on 13 February 1919 on leaving for England where it was formally disbanded on 22 September 1919.

On 22 February 1937, No.72 reformed at Tangmere from a flight of No.1 Squadron as a fighter squadron with Gladiators. In April 1939, conversion to Spitfires took place and these were engaged in defensive duties until June 1940 when the squadron moved south to help cover the Dunkirk beaches for a few days. In August, it moved to the Biggin Hill sector during the Battle of Britain before returning north in November. Fighter sweeps over northern France began in July 1941 and in September 1942 the squadron became non-operational to prepare for a move overseas.

For the invasion of North Africa in November, No.72 operated from Gibraltar until airfields had been captured in Algeria. For the rest of the Tunisian campaign, the squadron was engaged in fighter patrols and bomber escort duties and in June 1943 moved to Malta for sweeps over Sicily. After Allied landings there in July, a move was made to newly-captured airfields on the island and in September No.72 arrived in Italy. In July 1944, it joined a force of Spitfire squadrons in Corsica to cover the landings in southern France during August, after which the squadron spent six

weeks in France before returning to the Italian front. Ground-attack missions and defensive patrols occupied the squadron until the end of the war and after a period in northern Italy and Austria, No.72 disbanded on 30 December 1946.

On 1 February 1947, No.130 Squadron at Odiham was renumbered 72 Squadron and flew Vampires until converted to Meteors in July 1952 as a day fighter unit. In February 1956, it was re-equipped with Meteor night fighters which were replaced by Javelins in 1959. These were flown until the squadron disbanded on 30 June 1961. On 15 November 1961, No.72 reformed at Odiham with Belvedere helicopters for transport support duties in No.38 Group, Transport Command. Belvederes were replaced by Wessexes in August 1964.

Squadron bases			
Upavon	2 Jul 1917	Church Fenton	13 Jan 1940
Netheravon	8 Jul 1917	Acklington	2 Mar 1940
Sedgeford	1 Nov 1917	Gravesend	1 Jun 1940
Left for Mesopotamia		Acklington	6 Jun 1940
	25 Dec 1917	Biggin Hill	31 Aug 1940
Basra	2 Mar 1918	Croydon	1 Sep 1940
Dets. to Samarra ('A' Flight)		Biggin Hill	14 Sep 1940
Baghdad & Kasvin ('B' Flt)		Coltishall	13 Oct 1940
Mirjana ('C' Flight)		Matlask	30 Oct 1940
Baghdad	25 Nov 1918	Coltishall	2 Nov 1940
Left for U.K.	13 Feb 1919	Leuchars	29 Nov 1940
Disbanded	22 Sep 1919	Acklington	19 Dec 1940
Tangmere	22 Feb 1937	Gravesend	8 Jul 1941
Church Fenton	1 Jun 1937	Biggin Hill	26 Jul 1941
Leconfield	15 Oct 1939	Gravesend	20 Oct 1941
Drem	28 Oct 1939	Biggin Hill	22 Mar 1942
Leconfield	12 Jan 1940	Martlesham Heath	22 Jun 1942
		Biggin Hill	29 Jun 1942

Gladiator Is, No.72 Squadron

Lympne	30 Jun 1942	Tre Cancelli	4 Jun 1944			
Biggin Hill	7 Jul 1942	Tarquinia	13 Jun 1944			
Duxford	2 Aug 1942	Grosseto	24 Jun 1944			
Morpeth	4 Aug 1942	Piombino	5 Jul 1944			
Ayr	13 Aug 1942	Calvi	20 Jul 1944			
Ouston	26 Sep 1942	Ramatuelle	18 Aug 1944			
Left for N. Africa		Sisteron	25 Aug 1944			
	8 Nov 1942 (G)	Lyon/Bron	7 Sep 1944			
Maison Blanche		Salon/La Jasse	26 Sep 1944			
	16 Nov 1942 (A)	Peretola	2 Oct 1944			
Bone	18 Nov 1942	Rimini	16 Nov 1944			
Souk el Arba	20 Nov 1942	Ravenna	17 Feb 1945			
Souk el Khemis	15 Jan 1943	Rivolto	4 May 1945			
La Sebala	13 May 1943	Klagenfurt	11 May 1945			
Mateur	24 May 1943	Zeltweg	8 Sep 1945			
Hal Far	10 Jun 1943	Campoformido	2 Oct 1945			
Comiso	17 Jul 1943	Zeltweg	22 Oct 1945			
Pachino	30 Jul 1943	Tissano	23 Sep 1946			
Pachino South	2 Aug 1943		to 30 Dec 1946			
Panebianco	29 Aug 1943	Odiham	1 Feb 1947			
Cassala	2 Sep 1943	North Weald	22 Mar 1950			
Falcone	4 Sep 1943	Church Fenton	11 May 1953			
Tusciano	12 Sep 1943	Leconfield	28 Jun 1959			
Capodichino	12 Oct 1943		to 30 Jun 1961			
Lago	15 Jan 1944	Odiham	15 Nov 1961			

Aircraft

Equipment	Period of service	Representative Serial
Various	Jul 1917 – Dec 1917	–
Spad S.VII	Mar 1918 – 1918	A8806
Martinsyde G.100	Mar 1918 – Nov 1918	
Bristol M.1c	Mar 1918 – Feb 1919	
S.E.5A	Mar 1918 – Feb 1919	
Gladiator I	Feb 1937 – May 1939	K6134
	Mar 1940	
Spitfire I	Apr 1939 – Apr 1941	K9934 (SD-K)
Spitfire IIA, IIB	Apr 1941 – Jul 1941	P7895 (RN-N)
Spitfire VB, VC	Jul 1941 – Jan 1944	AA945 (RN-C)
Spitfire IX	Jul 1942 – Aug 1942	
	Feb 1943 – Dec 1946	MA444 (RN-B)
Vampire F.1	Feb 1947 – Oct 1948	VF309 (FG-W)
Vampire F.3	Jun 1948 – Feb 1950	VV194 (FG-B)
Vampire FB.5	Nov 1949 – Jul 1952	VZ272 (D)
Meteor F.8	Jul 1952 – Feb 1956	VZ525 (N)
Meteor NF.12	Feb 1956 – Jun 1959	WS623 (Q)
Meteor NF.14	Feb 1956 – Jun 1959	WS808 (U)
Javelin FAW.4	Apr 1959 – Jun 1961	XA737 (K)
Javelin FAW.5	Jun 1959 – Jun 1961	XA667
Belvedere HC.1	Nov 1961 – Aug 1964	XG462 (H)
Wessex HC.2	Aug 1964 – date	XR524 (F)

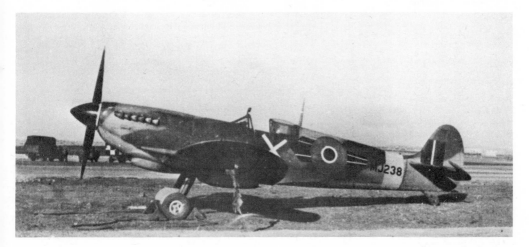

Spitfire IX, No.73 Squadron

No. 73 Squadron

Badge: A demi-talbot rampant,
charged on the shoulder
with a maple leaf.
Motto: Tutor et ultor
(Protector and avenger)

No.73 Squadron was formed on 1 July 1917 at Upavon as a fighter unit. Equipped with Camels, it moved to France in January 1918 to fly fighter patrols and bomber escort missions over the Western Front. In March, the German offensive resulted in the squadron undertaking large numbers of ground attack sorties and during the final Allied attack was engaged in low-level co-operation with armoured forces until the end of the war. In February 1919, No.73 returned to the UK and disbanded on 2 July 1919.

On 15 March 1937, No.73 reformed at Mildenhall as a fighter squadron with Furies. In June, these were replaced by

Gladiators which were flown until conversion to Hurricanes took place in July 1938 and the Gladiators transferred to No. 3 Squadron. On the outbreak of World War Two, it was one of the two Hurricane squadrons attached to the Advanced Air Striking Force and moved to France. After the German attack in May 1940, No.73 helped to cover Allied airfields and bases, falling back as its airfields were overrun by enemy columns. On 18 June, the squadron retired to England where it concentrated on night fighting during the Battle of Britain. Operations ceased on 20 October to allow No.73 to prepare for transfer to the Middle East. Its Hurricanes were taken in the carrier *Furious* to Takoradi in the Gold Coast and flown across Africa to Egypt where they were joined by ground crews brought through the Mediterranean by a cruiser. Defensive patrols over shipping on the supply route to Tobruk, night patrols and ground-attack missions occupied the squadron's Hurricanes throughout the campaign in the Western Desert and Tunisia. In June 1943, No.73 converted to Spitfires and in October the squadron moved to Italy for defensive patrols, becoming a fighter-bomber unit in April 1944. It retained this role for the rest of the war, operating mainly over the Balkans. In December 1944, a large detachment was sent to Greece during a Communist attempt to take over the country in the wake of the German evacuation, returning to Italy at the end of January 1945. In April the squadron was operating from Yugoslav soil until the end of the war and in July 1945 moved to Malta. Conversion to Vampires took place in Cyprus in 1948 and these were flown in the Mediterranean and Middle East until replaced by Venoms in November 1954. In March 1957, No.73 converted to Canberras in Cyprus and flew this type until disbanded on 3 February 1969.

Squadron bases

Upavon	1 Jul 1917	Villeneuve-les-Vertus	
Lilbourne	10 Jul 1917		16 May 1940
St. Omer	9 Jan 1918	Gaye	18 May 1940
Liettres	12 Jan 1918	Echemines	3 Jun 1940
Champien	5 Mar 1918	Raudin	7 Jun 1940
Cachy	23 Mar 1918	Nantes	15 Jun 1940
Remaisnil	24 Mar 1918	Church Fenton	18 Jun 1940
Beauvois	30 Mar 1918	Castle Camps	5 Sep 1940
Fouquerolles	3 Jun 1918	Left for Middle East	
Ruisseauville	21 Jun 1918		13 Nov 1940
Le Touquin	14 Jul 1918	Takoradi	27 Nov 1940 (A)
La Bellevue	4 Aug 1918	Heliopolis	30 Nov 1940 (G)
Foucaucourt	21 Sep 1918		6 Dec 1940 (A)
Estrée-en-Chausée		Sidi Haneish	30 Dec 1940
	23 Sep 1918	Gazala West	31 Jan 1941
Hervilly	8 Oct 1918	Bu Amud	10 Mar 1941
Malencourt	19 Oct 1918	El Gubbi	9 Apr 1941
Baizieux	16 Nov 1918	Sidi Haneish	27 Apr 1941
Yatesbury	8 Feb 1919	Amriya	1 Sep 1941
	to 2 Jul 1919	Port Said/Gamil	6 Sep 1941
Mildenhall	15 Mar 1937	Kilo 8 (D)	10 Oct 1941
Debden	12 Jun 1937		to 18 Dec 1941
Sutton Bridge	4 Oct 1937	Shandur (D)	18 Dec 1941
Denden	23 Oct 1937		to 3 Apr 1942
Digby	9 Nov 1937	El Adem	3 Feb 1942
Le Havre/Octeville		Gasr-el-Arid	18 Feb 1942
	9 Sep 1939	Gambut II	21 Feb 1942
Norrent Fontes	28 Sep 1939	Gasr-el-Arid	27 Feb 1942
Rouvres	9 Oct 1939	Gambut I	11 Mar 1942
Reims/Champagne		Gambut Main	17 Apr 1942
	11 Apr 1940	El Adem	20 May 1942
Rouvres	19 Apr 1940	Gambut Main	27 May 1942
Reims/Champagne		LG.115	17 Jun 1942
	10 May 1940	LG.76	20 Jun 1942
Rouvres	11 May 1940	Qasaba	23 Jun 1942
Reims/Champagne		El Daba	26 Jun 1942
	14 May 1940	Burg-el-Arab	28 Jun 1942

LG.89	2 Jul 1942	Gabes Main	8 Apr 1943
El Ballah	23 Jul 1942	Sfax/El Maou	12 Apr 1943
Shandur	30 Jul 1942	Kairouan/Alem	20 Apr 1943
LG.85	22 Aug 1942	Monastir	21 Apr 1943
LG.21	7 Nov 1942	La Sebala II	29 Apr 1943
LG.13	8 Nov 1942	Montecorvino	18 Oct 1943
LG.155	10 Nov 1942	Foggia Main	2 Dec 1943
Gambut West	12 Nov 1942	Canne	12 Sep 1944
El Adem	16 Nov 1942	Hassani (D)	8 Dec 1944
El Magrun	28 Nov 1942		to 21 Jan 1945
Merduma	23 Nov 1942	Prkos	2 Apr 1945
Alem el Chel	1 Jan 1943	Brindisi	15 May 1945
Tamet	11 Mar 1943	Hal Far	3 Jul 1945
Bir Dufan	22 Jan 1943	Takali	1946
Gasr Garabulli	4 Feb 1943	Habbaniya	May 1953
El Assa	15 Feb 1943	Akrotiri	2 May 1955
Nefatia South	21 Mar 1943		to 3 Feb 1969

Aircraft

Equipment	Period of service	Representative Serial
Camel	Jul 1917 – Feb 1919	D8164
Fury II	May 1937 – Jul 1937	K8277
Gladiator I	Jun 1937 – Jul 1938	K7965
Hurricane I	Jul 1938 – Jan 1942	N2358 (Z)
Hurricane IIA, IIB	Dec 1941 – Jun 1942	BD930 (R)
Hurricane IIC	Jun 1942 – Jul 1943	BN131 (P)
Tomahawk IIB	Sep 1941 – Nov 1941	AN301
Spitfire VC	Jun 1943 – Oct 1944	JK991 (E)
Spitfire VIII	Jul 1944 – Nov 1944	JF560
Spitfire IX	Oct 1943 – Nov 1947	MA630 (C)
Spitfire F.22	Nov 1947 – Oct 1948	PK518 (F)
Vampire F.3	Aug 1948 – Apr 1950	VT855 (B)
Vampire FB.5	Apr 1950 – May 1953	VZ318 (R)
Vampire FB.9	Nov 1951 – Dec 1954	WR214 (K)
Venom FB.1	Nov 1954 – Mar 1957	WR314 (W)
Canberra B.2	Mar 1957 – Aug 1962	WD988
Canberra B.15	Jun 1962 – Feb 1969	WH977

Canberra B.15, No.73 Squadron

No. 74 Squadron

Badge: A tiger's face
Motto: I fear no man
Name: 'Trinidad'

No.74 Squadron was formed on 1 July 1917 at Northolt and in March 1918 received S.E.5As before moving to France. Operations began on 12 April and fighter patrols continued till the Armistice, with low-level attacks on enemy troops being carried out in the closing months as the German army retreated towards Germany. In February 1919, the squadron returned to the UK where it disbanded on 3 July 1919.

On 3 September 1935 No.74 reformed aboard the transport *Neuralia* at Southampton and sailed for Malta where, on being disembarked, it was known only as 'Demon Flights, the number '74' not being advised until 14 November. This was for security purposes during the Abyssinian crisis which resulted in the movement of numerous RAF squadrons to the Middle East. In July 1936, the squadron's Demon two-seat fighters were dismantled for shipment and No.74 re-assembled at Hornchurch on 21 September. In April 1937 it re-equipped with Gauntlets and in February 1939 conversion to Spitfires began. During the opening months of World War Two the squadron flew defensive patrols before covering the evacuation fleet at Dunkirk in May 1940. After taking part in the first phase of the Battle of Britain, No.74 was withdrawn in mid-August for rest, returning south in mid-October. Sweeps over France began in January 1941 and continued till July when the squadron moved to northern England for defensive duties, carrying out the same task later in Wales and Northern Ireland.

In April 1942, the squadron embarked for the Middle East and arrived in Egypt early in June. Due to lack of aircraft, it acted as a maintenance unit in Palestine and Iran until Hurricanes were received in December. In May 1943 these were taken to Egypt for defensive and shipping patrols, conversion to Spitfires taking place in September. In October, No.74 operated over the Aegean islands during the abortive campaign to occupy certain of these and

Hunter F.6, No.74 Squadron

Lightning F.6, No.74 Squadron

remained in the Eastern Mediterranean until April 1944 when it embarked for the UK.

On 24 April 1944, No.74 re-assembled at North Weald with Spitfire IXs and began sweeps over France in May. After the landings in Normandy, the squadron was engaged in fighter-bomber missions and bomber escort duties. In August 1944 it moved to Normandy and flew ground-attack sorties in support of the 21st Army Group during its advance to the Netherlands and during the winter campaign. In April 1945 the squadron began operating from German bases but left a few days after the end of the war to convert to Meteors in the UK. In October 1946 it took up its peace-time station at Horsham St. Faith where it converted to Hunters in March 1957. These were replaced by Lightnings in July 1960 and in February 1964 the squadron moved to Scotland, remaining there until transferred to the Far East in June 1967. With the run-down of RAF units in the Far East, No.74 disbanded on 31 August 1971.

Squadron bases

Northolt	1 Jul 1917	Hornchurch	25 Jun 1940
London Colney	10 Jul 1917	Wittering	14 Aug 1940
Goldhanger	25 Mar 1918	Kirton-in-Lindsey	21 Aug 1940
St. Omer	30 Mar 1918	Coltishall	9 Sep 1940
Teteghem	1 Apr 1918	Biggin Hill	15 Oct 1940
La Lovie	9 Apr 1918	Manston	20 Feb 1941
Clairmarais	3 Oct 1918	Gravesend	1 May 1941
Marcke	23 Oct 1918	Acklington	9 Jul 1941
Cuerne	1 Nov 1918	Llanbedr	3 Oct 1941
Froidmont	17 Nov 1918	Long Kesh	24 Jan 1942
Hulluin	30 Nov 1918	Atcham	24 Mar 1942
Lopcombe Corner	10 Feb 1919	Emb. for Middle East	
	to 3 Jul 1919		10 Apr 1942
Aboard 'Neuralia'	3 Sep 1935	Geneifa	4 Jun 1942
Hal Far	11 Sep 1935	Helwan	21 Jun 1942
Hornchurch	21 Sep 1936	Ramat David	8 Jul 1942
(Frequent detachments to		Hadeira	4 Sep 1942
Rochford until	May 1940)	Doshan Tappeh	18 Oct 1942
Leconfield	27 May 1940	Mehrabad	1 Dec 1942
Rochford	6 Jun 1940		to 19 May 1943
		Abadan	24 Mar 1943

Shaibah	29 Mar 1943	Southend	24 Jul 1944
Habbaniya	17 May 1943	Tangmere	6 Aug 1944
Aqir	21 May 1943	B.8 Sommervieu	19 Aug 1944
LG.106	23 May 1943	B.29 Bernay	2 Sep 1944
Idku	26 Aug 1943	B.37 Gamaches	10 Sep 1944
Nicosia	19 Sep 1943	B.51 Lille-Vendeville	
Peristerona	11 Oct 1943		12 Sep 1944
Idku	23 Oct 1943	B.55 Wevelghem	17 Sep 1944
Dekheila	22 Nov 1943	B.70 Deurne	25 Sep 1944
Idku	12 Dec 1943	B.85 Schijndel	6 Feb 1945
Dekheila	13 Jan 1944	B.105 Drope	16 Apr 1945
Idku	4 Mar 1944	Colerne	11 May 1945
Emb. for U.K.	7 Apr 1944	Horsham St. Faith	14 Oct 1946
North Weald	24 Apr 1944	Coltishall	8 Jun 1959
Lympne	17 May 1944	Leuchars	Feb 1964 (P)
Tangmere	3 Jul 1944	Tengah	11 Jun 1967
Selsey	17 Jul 1944		to 31 Aug 1971

Aircraft Equipment	Period of service	Representative Serial
Avro 504K	Jul 1917 – Mar 1918	
S.E.5A	Mar 1918 – Jul 1919	D276 (A)
Demon	Sep 1935 – Apr 1937	K2906
Gauntlet II	Apr 1937 – Feb 1939	K7792
Spitfire I	Feb 1939 – Sep 1940	K9926 (JH-C)
Spitfire IIA	Sep 1940 – May 1941	P8018
	Jul 1941 – Jan 1942	
Spitfire VB	May 1941 – Jul 1941	W3171
	Nov 1941 – Apr 1942	
Hurricane IIB	Dec 1942 – Sep 1943	HV660
Spitfire VB, VC	Aug 1943 – Apr 1944	JG799
Spitfire IX	Oct 1943 – Apr 1944	MA455 (D)
Spitfire IXE	Apr 1944 – May 1945	PT999 (4D-T)
Spitfire XVIE	Mar 1945 – May 1945	TB675 (4D-V)
Meteor F.3	Jun 1945 – Mar 1948	EE318 (4D-Z)
Meteor F.4	Dec 1947 – Oct 1950	VT106 (4D-D)
Meteor F.8	Oct 1950 – Mar 1957	WF710 (J)
Hunter F.4	Mar 1957 – Jan 1958	XE683 (G)
Hunter F.6	Nov 1957 – Nov 1960	XE612 (M)
Lightning F.1	Jun 1960 – Apr 1964	XM142 (B)
Lightning F.3	Apr 1964 – Jan 1967	XP700 (A)
Lightning F.6	Nov 1966 – Aug 1971	XS897 (K)

No. 75 Squadron

Badge: In front of two mining hammers in saltire, a tiki
Motto: Ake ake kia kaha (Maori) (For ever and ever be strong)
Name: 'New Zealand'

No.75 Squadron was formed on 1 October 1916, at Goldington as a home defence unit with flights operating from landing grounds in Bedfordshire an anti-Zeppelin patrols. In September 1917 it moved to East Anglia to fly patrols in the area bounded by Colchester, Newmarket and Elmswell with B.E.12s. In May 1918, it moved to North Weald for the defence of London and used Camels and Bristol Fighters before disbanding on 13 June 1919.

On 15 March 1937, No.75 reformed at Driffield from B Flight of No.215 Squadron and while awaiting the arrival of Harrows trained on four Virginias and seven Ansons. During September, the last Virginia left and the first Harrows arrived, the squadron being fully equipped in November. In July 1938 it moved to Honington where, on 1 March 1939, it became a Group Pool Squadron engaged in training bomber crews, acquiring Ansons for this purpose. In July 1939 it moved to Stradishall where it partly re-equipped with Wellingtons in place of Harrows and on the outbreak of war transferred its activities to Harwell where, in October

1939, it transferred its Ansons to 148 Squadron. On 4 April 1940, the organisation of Operational Training Units resulted in No.75 being absorbed into No.15 OTU.

On the same day, the New Zealand Flight, which had formed on 1 June 1939 to train with Wellingtons in preparation for the delivery of this type to New Zealand, was redesignated No.75 Squadron at Feltwell and began operations soon afterwards. In August 1942 it moved to Mildenhall and in October began to convert to Stirlings flying its first operation with these on 20 November. In March 1944, Lancasters began to replace these and were flown until the end of the war. After the end of hostilities, the squadron flew prisoners-of-war back home and disbanded on 15 October 1945. The squadron number was perpetuated by its reformation as part of the Royal New Zealand Air Force.

Squadron bases

Goldington	1 Oct 1916	Elmswell	8 Sep 1917
dets at:		dets at	
Yelling		Harling Road,	
Old Weston		Hadleigh	
Therfield		North Weald	22 May 1918
			to 13 Jun 1919

Driffield	15 Mar 1937	Mildenhall	15 Aug 1940
Honington	11 Jul 1938	Newmarket	1 Nov 1942
Stradishall	13 Jul 1939	Mepal	28 Jun 1943
Harwell	4 Sep 1939	Spilsby	21 Jul 1945
	to 4 Apr 1940		to 15 Oct 1945
Feltwell	4 Apr 1940		

Aircraft Equipment	Period of service	Representative Serial
B.E.2c, B.E.2d, B.E.2e	Oct 1916 – Sep 1917	
B.E.12, B.E.12b	Sep 1917 – Jul 1918	C3094
Camel	1918 – 1918	
Avro 504K	Jul 1918 – Jun 1919	
Bristol F.2b	May 1918 – Jun 1919	
Virginia X	Mar 1937 – Sep 1937	K2672
Anson I	Mar 1937 – Nov 1937	K6299
	Mar 1939 – Oct 1939	
Harrow I, II	Sep 1937 – Jul 1939	K6947 (75-P)
Wellington I	Jul 1939 – Apr 1940	L4256
Wellington I, IA	Apr 1940 – Sep 1940	P9206 (AA-A)
Wellington IC	Apr 1940 – Jan 1942	R1117 (AA-F)
Wellington III	Jan 1942 – Oct 1942	X3595 (AA-K)
Stirling I	Oct 1942 – Aug 1943	R9283 (JN-K)
Stirling III	Feb 1943 – Apr 1944	LJ473 (AA-R)
Lancaster I, III	Mar 1944 – Oct 1945	HK600 (JN-K)
Lincoln II	Sep 1945 – Oct 1949	RF389 (AA-A)

Lincoln B.1, No.75 Squadron

No. 76 Squadron

Badge: In front of a rose, a lion passant guardant
Motto: Resolute

No.76 Squadron was formed at Ripon on 15 September 1916 as a home defence unit using landing grounds in Yorkshire to fly anti-Zeppelin patrols. On 13 June 1919, the squadron was disbanded.

On 12 April 1937, No.76 reformed at Finningley with Wellesleys from B Flight, No.7 Squadron. It converted to Hampdens in April 1939, but in June became a Group pool squadron and remained on training duties until it was merged with No.7 Squadron to form No.16 Operational Training Unit, ceasing to exist as a squadron on 22 April 1940. On 30 April it began to reform at West Raynham but disbanded again on 20 May 1940.

Reformed at Linton-on-Ouse on 1 May 1941, No.76 received Halifaxes and began bombing raids on 12 June. In July 1942, a detachment joined with No.454 Squadron in Palestine to form a heavy bomber force but on 12 August 1942, became No.462 Squadron. The home-based Halifaxes served for the rest of the war, playing their part in the strategic bomber offensive against Germany. On 8 May 1945, No.76 joined Transport Command and began to convert to Dakotas. In September, it moved to India for general transport duties and was renumbered 62 Squadron on 1 September 1946.

On 9 December 1953, No.76 reformed at Wittering as a light bomber squadron with Canberras, flying this type until disbanded on 31 December 1960. During nuclear weapons trials in 1956/57, the squadron supplied a detachment of Canberras for atomic cloud sampling over Australia and Christmas Island.

Squadron bases

Ripon	15 Sep 1916	det. Middle East	12 Jul 1942
dets at:			to 7 Sep 1942
Copmanthorpe		Linton-on-Ouse	17 Sep 1942
Helperby		Holme-in-Spalding Moor	
Catterick			16 Jun 1943
Tadcaster	3 Mar 1919	Broadwell	6 Aug 1945
	to 13 Jun 1919	Portreath	29 Aug 1945
Finningley	12 Apr 1937	Tilda	20 Sep 1945
Upper Heyford	23 Sep 1939	Poona	1 Nov 1945
	to 22 Apr 1940	Palam	25 May 1946
West Raynham	30 Apr 1940		to 1 Sep 1946
	to 20 May 1940	Wittering	9 Dec 1953
Linton-on-Ouse	1 May 1941	Weston Zoyland	15 Nov 1955
Middleton St. George		Hemswell	1 Apr 1957
	4 Jun 1941	Upwood	17 Jul 1958
			to 31 Dec 1960

Aircraft

Equipment	Period of service	Representative Serial
B.E.2c, B.E.2e, B.E.12, B.E.12a, B.E.12b	Sep 1916 — 1918	
Bristol F.2b	1918 — Jun 1919	
Wellesley	Apr 1937 — Apr 1939	K7748 (NM-H)
Hampden I	Mar 1939 — Apr 1940	P1269
Anson I	May 1939 — Apr 1940	N5000
Halifax I	May 1941 — Feb 1942	L9565 (MP-B)
Halifax II	Oct 1941 — Apr 1943	DT492 (MP-H)
Halifax V	Apr 1943 — Feb 1944	LK902 (MP-H)
Halifax III	Feb 1944 — Apr 1945	NR200 (MP-M)
Halifax VI	Mar 1945 — Aug 1945	TW796 (MP-Y)
Dakota IV	May 1945 — Sep 1946	KP257 (Y)
Canberra B.2, B.6	Dec 1953 — Dec 1960	WJ754

Whitley V, No.77 Squadron

No. 77 Squadron

Badge: A thistle
Motto: Esse potius quam videri
(To be, rather than seem)

No.77 Squadron was formed on 1 October 1916 at Edinburgh as a home defence unit, using airfields on the southeast coast of Scotland with headquarters in the city. In April 1917 the squadron concentrated at Turnhouse and for the rest of the war flew uneventful anti-Zeppelin patrols. On 13 June 1919, No.77 disbanded.

The squadron reformed at Finningley on 14 June 1937 from B Flight of No.102 Squadron, flying Audaxes until Wellesleys arrived in November 1937. In November 1938, it converted to Whitleys which were used for leaflet raids in the opening months of the Second World War. Bombing operations began in March 1940, and continued until May 1942, when it moved to Devon for anti-submarine patrols with Coastal Command. In October 1942, the squadron returned to Bomber Command and was equipped with Halifaxes which it flew on strategic bombing duties for the rest of the war. On 8 May 1945, No.77 joined Transport Command and re-equipped with Dakotas. In October, it moved to India where it was renumbered 31 Squadron on 1 November 1946.

On 1 December 1946, No.271 Squadron at Broadwell was renumbered 77 Squadron and flew Dakotas until 1 June 1949, when it disbanded at the end of a busy year on the Berlin Airlift. On 1 September 1958, the squadron reformed as a Thor intermediate range ballistic missile unit at Feltwell, disbanding on 10 July 1963.

Squadron bases

Edinburgh	1 Oct 1916	Topcliffe	5 Oct 1940
dets. at		Leeming	5 Sep 1941
Whiteburn		Chivenor	6 May 1942
New Haggerston		Elvington	5 Oct 1942
Penston		Full Sutton	15 May 1944
Turnhouse	13 Apr 1917	Broadwell	31 Aug 1945
Penston	Apr 1918	Kargi Road	1 Oct 1945
	to 13 Jun 1919	Mauripur	22 Oct 1945
Finningley	14 Jun 1937		to 1 Nov 1946
Honington	7 Jul 1937	Broadwell	1 Dec 1946
Driffield	25 Jul 1938	Manston	Sep 1947
Kinloss	15 Apr 1940	Waterbeach	Nov 1948
Driffield	4 May 1940		to 1 Jun 1949
Linton-on-Ouse	28 Aug 1940	Feltwell	1 Sep 1958
			to 10 Jul 1963

Aircraft

Equipment	Period of service	Representative Serial
B.E.2c, B.E.2e	Oct 1916 — Jan 1918	
B.E.12, B.E.12b	Oct 1916 — Feb 1918	
Avro 504K	Jan 1918 — Jun 1919	E3278
Audax	Jul 1937 — Nov 1937	K7454
Wellesley	Nov 1937 — Nov 1938	K8522
Whitley III	Nov 1938 — Oct 1939	K8977 (KN-P)
Whitley V	Sep 1939 — Oct 1942	BD195 (KN-M)
Halifax II	Oct 1942 — Nov 1942 Dec 1942 — May 1944	JB804 (KN-Q)
Halifax V	Nov 1942 — Dec 1944 Apr 1944 — Jun 1944	LL126 (KN-W)
Halifax III	May 1944 — Mar 1945	MZ715 (KN-Z)
Halifax VI	Mar 1945 — Aug 1945	RG536 (KN-Y)
Dakota III, IV	Jul 1945 — Nov 1946 Dec 1946 — Jun 1949	KP275 (L4)
Thor	Sep 1958 — Jul 1963	—

115

Twin Pioneer CC.1s, No.78 Squadron

No. 78 Squadron

Badge: A heradic tiger rampant
and double queued
Motto: Nemo non paratus
(Nobody unprepared)

No.78 was formed at Harrietsham on 1 November 1916 as a home defence unit and during December moved its headquarters to Hove. From there, it controlled three flights of B.E.s based at Telscombe Cliffs near Newhaven, Gosport near Portsmouth and Chiddingstone (later known as Penshurst) south of Maidstone. Anti-Zeppelin patrols were uneventful and in September 1917 the squadron moved to Suttons Farm (later to become Hornchurch) on the eastern approaches of London. Here it re-equipped with Sopwith 1½-strutters. These seldom managed to intercept the German Gothas which had now taken over the task of bombing London and in April 1918 some Camels supplemented them, the squadron converting fully to single-seaters in July. A few Snipes arrived at the time of the Armistice and the squadron was disbanded on 31 December 1919.

On 1 November 1936, No.78 reformed at Boscombe Down from B Flight, No.10 Squadron with Heyford night bombers. In February 1937 it moved to the new airfield at Dishforth where it began to convert to Whitleys in July 1937. By October, this was complete but on the outbreak of World War Two No.78 was designated a reserve squadron for training crews passed out of the Group Pool units. It was not until 19 July 1940 that the formation of operational training units enabled the squadron to begin night bombing missions over Germany. In March 1942 conversion to Halifaxes took place and these remained the squadron's operational type for the rest of the war. In May 1945 No.78 was transferred to Transport Command and converted to Dakotas for transport duties in the Mediterranean

and Middle East. In April 1950 it began to re-equip with Valettas which it flew until disbanded on 30 September 1954.

On 24 April 1956, No.78 reformed in Aden with Pioneers to provide support for the army in the Aden Protectorate. It re-equipped with the larger Twin Pioneers in October 1958 and in June 1965 converted to Wessex helicopters, its Twin Pioneers being passed to No.21 Squadron. In October 1967, the squadron moved to Sharjah for army support duties in the Trucial States, disbanding on 1 December 1971.

Squadron bases

Harrietsham	1 Nov 1916	Middleton St. George	
Hove	Dec 1916 (P)		7 Apr 1941
dets. at		Croft	20 Oct 1941
Telscombe Cliffs		Middleton St. George	
Chiddingstone	till Sep 1917		10 Jun 1942
Gosport	till Jul 1917	Linton-on-Ouse	16 Sep 1942
Suttons Farm	20 Sep 1917	Breighton	16 Jun 1943
	to 31 Dec 1919	Almaza	20 Sep 1945
Boscombe Down	1 Nov 1936	Kabrit	Sep 1946
Dishforth	1 Feb 1937	Fayid	Feb 1951
Ternhill	1 Sep 1939		to 30 Sep 1954
Dishforth	15 Sep 1939	Khormaksar	24 Apr 1956
Linton-on-Ouse	15 Oct 1939	Sharjah	17 Oct 1967
Dishforth	15 Jul 1940		to 1 Dec 1971

Aircraft

Equipment	Period of service	Representative Serial and Code
B.E.2c, B.E.2e	Nov 1916 − Oct 1917	
B.E.12, B.E.12a	Dec 1916 − Oct 1917	
Sopwith 1½-strutter	Oct 1917 − Jul 1918	B762
Camel	Apr 1918 − Dec 1919	B9287
Snipe	Nov 1918 − Sep 1919	E7580
Heyford II	Nov 1936 − Oct 1937	K4868
Heyford III	Nov 1936 − Oct 1937	K5194
Whitley I	Jul 1937 − Oct 1939	K7207 (78-R)
Whitley IV, IVA	Jun 1939 − Feb 1940	K9049
Whitley V	Sep 1939 − Mar 1942	T4209 (EY-Q)
Halifax II	Mar 1942 − Jan 1944	W1015 (EY-V)
Halifax III	Jan 1944 − Apr 1945	MZ361 (EY-D)
Halifax VI	Apr 1945 − Jul 1945	RG667
Dakota IV	Jul 1945 − Jul 1950	KP233
Valetta C.1	Apr 1950 − Sep 1954	VW812
Pioneer CC.2	Jun 1956 − Aug 1959	XL518
Twin Pioneer CC.1, CC.2	Oct 1958 − Jun 1965	XM289 (X)
Wessex HC.2	Jun 1965 − Dec 1971	XR500 (A)

No. 79 Squadron

Badge: A salamander salient
Motto: Nil nobis obstare potest
(Nothing can stop us)
Name 'Madras Presidency'

No.79 Squadron was formed at Gosport on 1 August 1918, and moved to France as a fighter unit in December. Until the end of the war it carried out fighter patrols and ground-attack missions with Dolphins and after the Armistice moved to Germany as part of the occupation forces, disbanding there on 15 July 1919.

On 22 March 1937 B Flight of No.32 Squadron at Biggin Hill became No.79 Squadron and flew Gauntlets until the arrival of Hurricanes at the end of 1938. After the outbreak of war, it flew defensive patrols and in May 1940, was sent to France for ten days when the German offensive opened. After taking part in the Battle of Britain, the squadron moved to South Wales until the end of 1941, when it began to prepare for a move to India. On 4 March 1942, it sailed for the Far East, arriving in India on 20 June. Until December, it flew defensive patrols before beginning to take part in sweeps over Burma. These continued until July 1943, and were resumed in December after a period of rest and refitting. In May 1944, No.79 was withdrawn for re-equipment with Thunderbolts which it took into action in September. Ground-attack and escort missions occupied the squadron until the end of to war and it disbanded on 30 December, 1945.

On 15 November, 1951, No.79 reformed at Gutersloh as a fighter-reconnaissance squadron in Germany. Swifts replaced the squadron's Meteors in the summer of 1956 and were flown until it was renumbered 4 Squadron on 1 January, 1961.

Squadron bases

Gosport	1 Aug 1917	Liettres	22 Feb 1918
Beaulieu	8 Aug 1917	Champien	5 Mar 1918
St. Omer	20 Feb 1918	Cachy	22 Mar 1918

Beauvais	24 Mar 1918	Baginton	27 Dec 1941
Ste. Marie Cappel	16 May 1918	Left for India	4 Mar 1942
Reckhem	22 Oct 1918	Arrived in India	20 Jun 1942
Nivelles	26 Nov 1918	Kanchrapara	27 Jun 1942
Bickendorf	20 Dec 1918	Dohazari	8 Jan 1943
	to 15 Jul 1919	Ramu	21 Jan 1943
Biggin Hill	22 Mar 1937	Comilla	25 May 1943
Manston	12 Nov 1939	Ranchi	20 Jul 1943
Biggin Hill	8 Mar 1940	Alipore	1 Oct 1943
Mons-en-Chaussée	10 May 1940	Chittagong	7 Dec 1943
Norrent Fontes	12 May 1940	Dohazari	28 Jan 1944
Merville	15 May 1940	Yelahanka	26 May 1944
Biggin Hill	20 May 1940	Arkonam	17 Sep 1944
Digby	27 May 1940	Manipur Road	19 Oct 1944
Biggin Hill	5 Jun 1940	Wangjing	19 Nov 1944
Hawkinge	2 Jul 1940	Myingyang North	19 Apr 1945
Sealand	11 Jul 1940	Meiktila	7 Jun 1945
Acklington	13 Jul 1940		to 30 Dec 1945
Biggin Hill	27 Aug 1940	Gutersloh	15 Nov 1951
Pembrey	8 Sep 1940	Buckeburg	Jul 1954
Fairwood Common	14 Jun 1941	Laarbruch	
Warmwell	5 Dec 1941	Gutersloh	15 Sep 1956
Fairwood Common	11 Dec 1941		to 1 Jan 1961

Aircraft

Equipment	Period of service	Representative Serial and Code	
Various	Aug 1917 – Jan 1918		
Dolphin	Dec 1917 – Jul 1919	C3944	(N)
Gauntlet II	Mar 1937 – Dec 1938	K7880	(AL-B)
Hurricane I	Nov 1938 – Jun 1941	L1710	(AL-D)
Hurricane IIB	Jun 1941 – Mar 1942	Z2674	(NV-M)
Hurricane IIC	Jun 1942 – Jul 1944	LB880	(NV-L)
Thunderbolt II	Jun 1944 – Dec 1945	KJ202	(NV-N)
Meteor FR.9	Nov 1951 – Aug 1956	WB122	(D)
Swift FR.5	Jun 1956 – Dec 1960	XD923	(E)
Hunter FR.10	– Dec 1960		

Swift FR.5, No.79 Squadron

Gladiator Is, No.80 Squadron

No. 80 Squadron

Badge: A bell
Motto: Strike true

No.80 Squadron was formed at Montrose on 1 August 1917, as a fighter squadron and took its Camels to France in January 1918. After the first few weeks of fighter patrols over the Western Front, the German offensive in March resulted in the squadron being mainly engaged in ground-attack duties and after the Allied offensive in August which brought the war to an end, it spent the last weeks of the war attacking enemy troops retreating back to Germany. In December 1918 it re-equipped with Snipes and at the end of May 1919, left for Egypt where it was renumbered 56 Squadron on 1 February 1920.

On 8 March 1937, No.80 reformed at Kenley with Gauntlets as a fighter squadron and replaced these with Gladiators within two months. At the end of April 1938, the squadron left for Egypt to become part of the air defences of the area. After the outbreak of war with Italy in June 1940, No.80 moved to the Libyan frontier for a period before being transferred to Greece in November when the Italians invaded that country. In February 1941, conversion to Hurricanes began but the German attack from Bulgaria resulted in the small British force in Greece being evacuated at the end of April. After a period of defensive duties in Syria, Palestine and Cyprus, the squadron returned to the Western Desert in October and flew patrols over the battle area until after the Battle of Alamein. With the retreat of the Afrika Korps, No.80 was given the task of providing air defence of the long lines of communication and coastal convoys supplying the 8th Army, a task which continued till January 1944, when it moved to Italy to fly offensive sweeps until April. It was then transferred to the UK to reinforce the fighter squadrons preparing for the invasion of Europe and, equipped with Spitfires, began flying sweeps and escort missions over France and the Low Countries. In August it converted to Tempests and took these to the Continent at the end of September to fly

armed reconnaissance missions for the rest of the war. It remained in Germany as part of the occupation forces until transferred to Hong Kong in August 1949, to reinforce the colony in the face of the threat from Communist forces which were taking over the Chinese mainland from the Nationalist Government at this time. In December 1951, the squadron re-equipped with Hornets which it flew until disbanded on 1 May 1955.

On 20 June 1955, No.80 reformed at Laarbruch with Canberras as a photographic reconnaissance squadron in Germany and formed part of 2nd ATAF until disbanded on 28 September 1969.

Squadron bases		Left for Middle East	
Montrose	1 Aug 1917		25 Apr 1941
Beverley	1 Nov 1917	Aqir	1 May 1941
Boisdinghem	22 Jan 1918	Nicosia (D)	3 Jun 1941
Champien	5 Mar 1918		to 20 Jul 1941
Cachy	22 Mar 1918	Haifa (D)	3 Jun 1941
Remaisnil	24 Mar 1918		to 19 Jul 1941
Wamin	29 Mar 1918	Nicosia	20 Jul 1941
Belleville Farm	30 Mar 1918	Aqir	14 Aug 1941
La Bellevue	4 Apr 1918	Rayak	9 Sep 1941
Fouquerolles	3 Jun 1918	Gaza	15 Oct 1941
Liettres	21 Jun 1918	LG.103	22 Oct 1941
Le Touquin	14 Jul 1918	LG.111	6 Nov 1941
Vignacourt	4 Aug 1918	LG.128	19 Nov 1941
Allonville	31 Aug 1918	El Gubbi	12 Dec 1941
Assevillers	8 Sep 1918	Gazala No.2	18 Dec 1941
Bouvincourt	8 Oct 1918	El Adem	27 Dec 1941
Bertry West	27 Oct 1918	LG.109	3 Feb 1942
Flaumont	10 Nov 1918	LG.102	11 Feb 1942
Grand Fayt	12 Nov 1918	Gambut	4 Mar 1942
Stree	3 Dec 1918	LG.121	30 May 1942
Clermont	Mar 1919	LG.18 Fuka Main	21 Jun 1942
Left for Middle East		LG.92	27 Jun 1942
	26 May 1919	El Bassa	21 Sep 1942
Aboukir	10 Jun 1919	LG.85	12 Oct 1942
	to 1 Feb 1920	LG.37	21 Oct 1942
Kenley	8 Mar 1937	LG.13	11 Nov 1942
Henlow	15 Mar 1937	Bu Amud	18 Nov 1942
Debden	9 Jun 1937	Idku	15 May 1943
Emb. for Middle East		Savoia	5 Jul 1943
	30 Apr 1938	St. Jean	12 Aug 1943
Ismailia	10 May 1938	Derna	1 Sep 1943
Amriya	24 Sep 1938	Kabrit	9 Nov 1943
Ismailia	10 Oct 1938	Madna	21 Jan 1944
Helwan	16 Jan 1939	Canne	23 Feb 1944
Amriya	21 Apr 1939	Trigno	13 Mar 1944
Sidi Haneish South		Emb. for U.K.	10 Apr 1944
	31 Aug 1940	Sawbridgworth	24 Apr 1944
Trikkala	19 Nov 1940	Hornchurch	6 May 1944
Larissa	4 Dec 1940	Detling	19 May 1944
Iannina	17 Jan 1941	Merston	22 Jun 1944
Eleusis	6 Mar 1941	Gatwick	27 Jun 1944
Argos	21 Apr 1941	West Malling	5 Jul 1944

Manston	29 Aug 1944	Thorney Island (D)	
Coltishall	20 Sep 1944		10 May 1948
Antwerp	29 Sep 1944		to 5 Jun 1948
B.82 Grave	1 Oct 1944	Gatow	22 Jun 1948
B.80 Volkel	7 Oct 1944	Gutersloh	14 Jul 1948
B.112 Hopsten	12 Apr 1945	Lubeck	23 Jul 1948
Warmwell	18 Apr 1945	Gutersloh	27 Aug 1948
Fassberg	7 May 1945	Left for Far East	2 Jul 1949
Kastrup	24 Jun 1945	Kai Tak	13 Aug 1949
Lubeck	6 Sep 1945	Sek Kong	3 Jan 1949
Wunstorf	31 Jan 1946	Kai Tak	1 Feb 1950
Gatow (D)	3 Jun 1947	Sek Kong	7 Mar 1950
	to 31 Jun 1947	Kai Tak	28 Apr 1950
Duxford (D)	2 Sep 1947		to 1 May 1955
	to 17 Sep 1947	Laarbruch	20 Jun 1955
Lubeck (D)	2 Apr 1948	Bruggen	11 Jun 1957
	to 29 Apr 1948		to 28 Sep 1969

Aircraft Equipment	Period of service	Representative Serial and Code
Camel	Aug 1917 – Dec 1918	C1581
Snipe	Dec 1918 – Feb 1920	
Gauntlet II	Mar 1937 – May 1937	K5355
Gladiator I, II	Mar 1937 – Apr 1941	K7900 (OD-S)
Hurricane I	Jun 1940 – Aug 1940	L1669
	Feb 1941 – Sep 1941	Z4162
Hurricane IIB, IIC	Sep 1941 – Apr 1943	HL841
Spitfire VC	Apr 1943 – Apr 1944	JG875
Spitfire IX	Jul 1943 – Nov 1943	MA504
	May 1944 – Aug 1944	MA828 (W2-B)
Tempest V	Aug 1944 – Jan 1948	SN209 (W2-E)
Spitfire F.24	Jan 1948 – Jan 1952	VN317 (W2-P)
Hornet F.3, F.4	Dec 1951 – May 1955	WF977 (B)
Canberra PR.7	Jun 1955 – Sep 1969	WH800

Hurricane IIB, No.81 Squadron

No. 81 Squadron

Badge: In front of a mullet, a
dagger erect

Motto: Non solum nobis (Not
for us alone)

No.81 Squadron was formed on 1 August 1917, at Scampton as a training unit but was not mobilised before disbanding on 4 July 1918. On 13 November 1918, it reformed as a fighter squadron at Wyton, being also designated No.1 Squadron, Canadian Air Force. It did not become operational and was disbanded on 1 February 1920.

On 1 December 1939, the Communications Squadron based at Mountjoie near Amiens was redesignated No.81 Squadron. It flew Tiger Moths on communications duties until the German invasion when the squadron returned to the UK and disbanded on 15 June 1940.

No.81 reformed at Leconfield on 29 July 1941, as a fighter squadron and in September flew its Hurricanes off HMS *Argus* to a North Russian airfield. After a few weeks of operations, the Hurricanes were handed over to the Russian Navy and the squadron returned to the UK in the cruiser *Kenya* at the end of November. Receiving Spitfires at Turnhouse, No.81 became operational again on 1 February 1942, on defensive duties, moving to southern England to begin offensive sweeps in May. At the end of October, the squadron left for Gibraltar to take part in the invasion of North Africa and on 8 November, nineteen of its Spitfires moved into the newly-captured airport at Algiers/Maison Blanche. Fighter cover for the 1st Army was provided throughout the campaign in Tunisia and in June 1943, the squadron moved to Malta to help cover the landings in Sicily. In September, it moved to Italy but was withdrawn early in November for transfer to India. The first aircraft arrived at Alipore on 4 December and the last on 8 December. Operations began in January 1944 and defensive and ground-attack missions were flown until No.81 was withdrawn to Ceylon in August 1944, where it remained until disbanded on 20 June 1945, its Spitfires being required to re-equip Indian Air Force squadrons.

On the same day, however, No.123 Squadron at Bobbili was renumbered 81 Squadron but its Thunderbolts did not become operational before the end of the war. In October, the squadron was sent to Java for tactical reconnaissance duties and to provide cover for Allied road convoys against nationalist guerillas. On 30 June 1946 the squadron was disbanded.

On 1 September 1946, No.684 Squadron at Seletar was renumbered 81 Squadron. Flying Mosquito photographic reconnaissance aircraft, the squadron added Spitfires in August 1947, from No.34 Squadron and remained the Far East Air Force's reconnaissance element for many years. On 9 July 1949, it flew its first mission during Operation 'Firedog' the RAF's contribution to countering the activities of Communist bands in the Malayan jungle. On 1 April 1954, No.81 flew the last operational Spitfire mission and on 15 December 1955, the last Mosquito mission. Some Pembrokes were used for survey work from January 1956 and the squadron converted to Canberras from Meteors in 1958. As the run-down of the Far East Air Force took effect, No.81 was disbanded on 16 January 1970.

Squadron bases			
Scampton	1 Aug 1917	Turnhouse	6 Dec 1941
	to 4 Jul 1918	Ouston	6 Jan 1942
Wyton	13 Nov 1918	Turnhouse	14 Feb 1942
Upper Heyford	20 Nov 1918	Ouston	14 Apr 1942
Shoreham	Mar 1919	Hornchurch	15 May 1942
	to 1 Feb 1920	Fairlop	17 Jul 1942
Amiens/Mountjoie	1 Dec 1939	Wellingore	1 Sep 1942
Andover	May 1940 (P)	Left for Gibraltar	30 Oct 1942
	to 15 Jun 1940	Maison Blanche	8 Nov 1942
Leconfield	29 Jul 1941	Bone/Tingley	16 Nov 1942
Vaenga	7 Sep 1941	Souk-el-Khemis	17 Mar 1943
	to 24 Nov 1941	Utique	19 May 1943
		Takali	4 Jun 1943

Lentini East	20 Jul 1943	Amarda Road	27 Apr 1945
Milazzo East	6 Sep 1943	Ratmalana	6 Jun 1945
Serretelle	23 Sep 1943		to 20 Jun 1945
Gioia del Colle	13 Oct 1943	Bobbili	20 Jun 1945
Left for India	3 Nov 1943	Vizagapatam	30 Aug 1945
Egypt (in transit)	Nov 1943	Baigachi	25 Sep 1945
Alipore	4 Dec 1943	Zayatkwin	30 Sep 1945
Imphal	5 Jan 1944	Kemajoran	21 Oct 1945
Tulihal	7 Jan 1944		to 30 Jun 1946
Ramu	9 Feb 1944	Seletar	1 Sep 1946
Tulihal	18 Feb 1944	Changi	1 Oct 1947
Kangla	28 Feb 1944	Tengah	1 Feb 1948
Tulihal	28 Mar 1944	Seletar	Mar 1950
Kumbhirgram	28 Apr 1944	Tengah	Mar 1958
Minneriya	10 Aug 1944		to 16 Jan 1970
Ratmalana	15 Dec 1944		

Aircraft Equipment	Period of service	Representative Serial an Code
Camel	Aug 1917 – Jul 1918	B7301
Dolphin	Nov 1918 –	E4864
S.E.5A	1919 – Jan 1920	E5755
Snipe	Nov 1918	
Tiger Moth	Dec 1939 – Jun 1940	N6801
Rota	Dec 1939 – Feb 1940	L7590
Hurricane IIB	Sep 1941 – Nov 1941	Z4006 (FV-54)
Spitfire VA	Jan 1942 – Apr 1942	
Spitfire VB	Apr 1942 – Oct 1942	BM423 (FL-B)
Spitfire VC	Nov 1942 – Nov 1943	
Spitfire IX	May 1942 – Jun 1942	
	Jan 1943 – Nov 1943	EN203 (FL-O)
Spitfire VIII	Nov 1943 – Jun 1945	JF698 (FL-J)
Thunderbolt II	Jun 1945 – Jun 1946	HD185 (FL-D)
Mosquito XVI	Sep 1946	
Mosquito PR.34	Sep 1946 – Dec 1955	RG239 (M)
Spitfire FR.18	Aug 1947 – 1949	TP407 (D)
Spitfire PR.19	1949 – Apr 1954	PM574 (B)
Meteor PR.10	Dec 1953 – Jul 1961	VS987
Canberra PR.7	1958 – Jan 1970	WH791
Pembroke C.(PR).1	Jan 1956 – Mar 1958	XF798

No. 82 Squadron

Badge: In front of a sun in splendour, a weathercock
Motto: Super omnia ubique (Over all things everywhere)
Name: 'United Provinces'

No.82 Squadron was formed on 7 January 1917 at Doncaster and after training moved to France in November with F.K.8s as a corps reconnaissance unit. Until the Armistice it was engaged in artillery spotting and tactical reconnaissance duties over the Western Front. In February 1919, the squadron returned to the UK and disbanded on 30 June 1919.

On 14 June 1937, No.82 reformed at Andover as a day bomber squadron equipped initially with Hinds from B Flight of No.142 Squadron. In March 1938, it converted to Blenheims which were used for attacks on enemy columns during the Battle of France. During the Battle of Britain, No.82 was engaged in night raids on invasion barges in the Channel Ports followed by anti-shipping missions. In June 1941, a large detachment of Blenheims was sent to Malta which was absorbed by other units and in March 1942 the squadron left for the Far East, arriving in May No.82 did not receive any aircraft until August when Vengeance dive-bombers came into service. Anti-submarine patrols began on 17 November but it was June 1943 before bombing raids began against Japanese targets in Burma. These continued for a year before the squadron was withdrawn

to equip with Mosquitos. Ground-attack sorties began in December and continued until 12 May 1945 after which No.82 was moved to India to prepare for the invasion of Malaya. After the Japanese surrender, the squadron disbanded on 15 March 1946.

On 1 October 1946, No.82 reformed at Benson from a flight of No.541 Squadron which at the time was engaged in survey duties in the Gold Coast. Equipped with Lancasters and Spitfires, the squadron undertook a survey of Nigeria, the Gold Coast, Sierra Leone and Gambia and in May 1947 moved to Kenya to continue this work in East Africa. By the end of 1952, No.82 was based in the UK and began a survey of West Germany, converting to Canberras in November 1953. A detachment was sent to the Far East before the squadron disbanded on 1 September 1956. On 22 July 1956, No.82 was reformed at Shepherds Grove as a Thor missile unit, disbanding on 10 July 1963.

Squadron bases			
Doncaster	7 Jan 1917	Shoreham	15 Feb 1919
Beverley	6 Feb 1917	Tangmere	May 1919
Waddington	30 Mar 1917		to 30 Jun 1919
St. Omer	17 Nov 1917	Andover	14 Jun 1937
Savy	20 Nov 1917	Cranfield	6 Jul 1937
Bonneuil	22 Jan 1918	Watton	25 Aug 1939
Catigny	22 Mar 1918	Bodney	1 Oct 1940
Allonville	24 Mar 1918	Lossiemouth	18 Apr 1941
Bertangles	27 Mar 1918	Bodney	3 May 1941
Argenvilliers	28 Mar 1918	Det. to Malta	11 Jun 1941
Quevenvillers	7 Jun 1918	Left for Far East	21 Mar 1942
Haussimont	15 Jul 1918	Karachi	24 May 1942
Quelmes	2 Aug 1918	Quetta	11 Jun 1942
Droglandt	3 Sep 1918	Cholavarum	6 Jul 1942
Proven	20 Sep 1918	Karachi (D)	2 Jul 1942
Bisseghem	22 Oct 1918		to 28 Oct 1942
Coucou	6 Nov 1918	Madhaigani (D)	26 Feb 1943
Bertangles	19 Nov 1918		to 5 Mar 1943
		Madhaiganj	5 Mar 1943

120

				Aircraft Equipment	Period of service	Representative Serial and Code
Asansol	12 Apr 1943	Kumbhirgram	19 Dec 1944	F.K.8	Jan 1917 – Feb 1919	
Salbani	23 May 1943	Joari	26 Apr 1945	Hind	Jun 1937 – Mar 1938	K6828
Chittagong (D)	31 May 1943	Cholavarum	4 Jun 1945	Blenheim I	Mar 1938 – Aug 1939	L1112 (OZ-A)
	to 29 Jun 1943	St.Thomas Mount	14 Oct 1945	Blenheim IV	Aug 1939 – Mar 1942	V5515 (UX-N)
Feni	8 Aug 1943 (A)		to 15 Mar 1946	Vengeance I, IA, II, III	Aug 1942 – Jul 1944	AN703 (X)
	13 Aug 1943 (G)	Benson	1 Oct 1946	Mosquito VI	Jul 1944 – Mar 1946	HR665 (UX-C)
Dohazari	21 Nov 1943	(det. Accra)		Lancaster I	Oct 1946 – Dec 1953	TW904 (E)
Jumchar	22 Jan 1944	Eastleigh &		Spitfire XIX	Oct 1946 –	PM612
Kumbhirgram (D)	20 Mar 1944	Takoradi	May 1947 (P)	Canberra PR.3	Nov 1953 – Feb 1955	WE167
	to 9 Apr 1944	Benson	30 Oct 1952	Canberra PR.7	Oct 1954 – Sep 1956	WH790
Kolar	25 May 1944 (A)	Wyton	31 Mar 1953	Thor	Jul 1959 – Jul 1963	–
	8 Jun 1944 (G)		to 1 Sep 1956			
Ranchi	5 Oct 1944	Shepherds Grove	22 Jul 1959			
Chharra	13 Dec 1944		to 10 Jul 1963			

No. 83 Squadron

Badge: An attire
Motto: Strike to defend

No.83 Squadron was formed at Montrose on 7 January 1917, and moved almost immediately to Spittlegate for training. In September 1917, it arrived at the mobilisation station at Wyton and received its operational equipment at the end of the year on moving to Narborough. On 6 March 1918, it arrived in France and was employed on night reconnaissance and night bombing duties for the rest of the war, attacking enemy bases and airfields behind the Western Front. The squadron returned to the UK as a cadre in February 1919, and disbanded on 31 December 1919.

On 4 August 1936, No.83 reformed at Turnhouse as a Hind day bomber squadron and by the end of the year was fully equipped. In March 1938, it moved south to Scampton and joined No.5 Group, collecting its first Hampden on 31 October, re-equipment being completed on 9 January 1939. On the outbreak of World War Two the squadron flew a sweep over the North Sea on the first day of war in the hope of catching enemy ships at sea and a few more were flown before bombing attacks began in earnest on 20 April 1940, after the German attack on Norway. Night raids with Hampdens continued until the Manchester arrived in service at the end of 1941, its first operation being 28 January 1942. This ill-fated type was soon replaced by Lancasters which the squadron flew for the rest of the war. In August 1942 No.83 moved to Wyton to join the Pathfinder Force and acted as a target-marking squadron for the main force of bombers until the German surrender in May 1945. In July 1946, it converted to Lincolns and moved to Hemswell in November 1946, where it remained until disbanded on 1 January 1956.

On 21 May 1957, No.83 reformed at Waddington as part of the nuclear-deterrant force and received Vulcans in July 1957. It handed over its Vulcan B.1s to No.44 Squadron in August 1960, and moved to Scampton in October where it received Vulcan B.2s in December 1960. These it flew until disbanded on 31 August 1969.

Squadron bases				Aircraft Equipment	Period of service	Representative Serial and Code
Montrose	7 Jan 1917	Turnhouse	to 31 Dec 1919 4 Aug 1936	Various	Jan 1917 – Dec 1917	
Spittlegate	Jan 1917	Scampton	14 Mar 1938	F.E.2b, F.E.2d	Dec 1917 – Feb 1919	B1887
Wyton	Sep 1917	Lossiemouth	21 Feb 1940	Hind	Sep 1938 – Jan 1939	L7198
Narborough	12 Dec 1917		to 20 Mar 1940 (D)	Hampden I	Nov 1938 – Jan 1942	P2125 (OL-L)
St. Omer	6 Mar 1918	Wyton	15 Aug 1942	Manchester I	Dec 1941 – May 1942	L7465 (OL-H)
Auchel	7 Mar 1918	Coningsby	18 Apr 1944	Lancaster I, III	May 1942 – Jul 1946	JA967 (OL-S)
Franqueville	2 May 1918	Hemswell	5 Nov 1946	Lincoln B.2	Jul 1946 – Dec 1955	RF369 (OL-G)
La Houssoye	10 Oct 1918		to 1 Jan 1956	Vulcan B.1	Jul 1957 – Aug 1960	XA902
Estrée-en-Chaussée	26 Oct 1918	Waddington	21 May 1957	Vulcan B.2	Dec 1960 – Aug 1969	XJ781
Serny	13 Dec 1918	Scampton	10 Oct 1960			
Hawkinge	14 Feb 1919		to 31 Aug 1969			

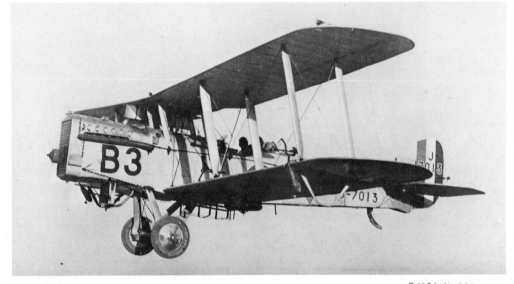

D.H.9A, No.84 Squadron

No. 84 Squadron

Badge: A scorpion
Motto: Scorpiones pungunt
(Scorpions sting)

No.84 Squadron was formed in January 1917 at Beaulieu and after training moved to France in September 1917 as a fighter squadron with S.E.5As. Fighter patrols and ground-attack duties occupied the squadron for the rest of the war and after a period with the occupation forces it returned to the UK as a cadre in August 1919 and disbanded on 30 January 1920.

On 13 August 1920, No.84 reformed at Baghdad and moved to Shaibah the following month for policing duties over the deserts of southern Iraq. It remained there throughout the inter-war years, flying successively D.H.9As, Wapitis, Vincents and Blenheims. In September 1940, the squadron was transferred to Egypt and was sent to Greece in November for operations against the Italians in Albania. Forced to evacuate by the German attack in April 1941, No.84 returned to Iraq for a period before resuming bombing raids in the Western Desert in November. In January 1942 the squadron

was transferred to the Far East, arriving in Sumatra at the end of January to join remnants of the Malayan-based units. Japanese landings in Sumatra and Java resulted in the squadron's ground echelon being evacuated by sea to India at the end of February and the remaining air and ground personnel were dispersed by the end of the month.

On arrival in India, the squadron was re-equipped with Blenheims but gave these up in June pending conversion to Vengeances. The latter type took a long time to become available for operational use and it was December before No.84 received any. After a lengthy period of dive-bombing training, the squadron began operations in Burma on 16 February 1944. These only lasted until 16 July after which No.84 was withdrawn for conversion to Mosquitos. The Vengeances were disposed of in October but difficulties in introducing the wooden Mosquitos to tropical conditions delayed their arrival until February 1945. When the Japanese surrender came in September No.84 was still training and moved forthwith to Singapore. In November, the squadron began providing support for Allied forces in Java and after returning to Singapore converted to Beaufighters at the end of 1946. In November 1948, No.84 returned to Iraq and received Brigands but was transferred back to Singapore in 1950 to take part in Operation *Firedog*, supporting security forces hunting Communist guerillas in the Malayan jungle. On 20 February 1953, the squadron was disbanded.

On the same day, No.204 Squadron at Fayid was renumbered 84 Squadron and flew Valettas on general transport

122

duties until the RAF moved out of its Egyptian bases. Transferred to Aden, the squadron provided transport support for the army, receiving Beverleys in June 1958. Valettas were retained until passed over to No.233 Squadron in August 1960. In August 1967, the squadron moved to Sharjah where it converted to Andovers and it remained in the Persian Gulf until disbanded on 31 October 1971.

On 17 January 1972, No.84 was reformed at Akrotiri from No.1563 Flight and a detachment of No.230 Squadron operating with the United Nations peace-keeping force in Cyprus. Equipped with Whirlwinds, the squadron also provides an air-sea rescue service for the island.

Cholavarum	28 Jan 1943	Kemajoran	1 Nov 1945 (D)
Ratmalana	11 Apr 1943		Jan 1946 (G)
Ranchi	29 Aug 1943	Kuala Lumpur	May 1946
Maharajpur	5 Dec 1943	Seletar	Sep 1946
Kumbhirgram	10 Feb 1944	Changi	1 Oct 1947
Quetta/Samungli		Tengah	1 Feb 1948
	22 Jul 1944 (A)	Habbaniya	11 Oct 1948
	28 Jul 1944 (G)	Tengah	Apr 1950
Yelahanka	28 Oct 1944		to 20 Feb 1953
Chharra	24 Apr 1945	Fayid	20 Feb 1953
St. Thomas Mount		Khormaksar	Jan 1957
	8 Jun 1945 (A)	Sharjah	Aug 1967
	26 Jun 1945 (G)	Muharraq	Dec 1970
Baigachi	1 Sep 1945 (A)		to 31 Oct 1971
Guindy	1 Sep 1945 (G)	Akrotiri	17 Jan 1972
Seletar	12 Sep 1945 (A)	det. Nicosia	
	18 Oct 1945 (G)		

Squadron bases

Beaulieu	Jan 1917	Shaibah	20 Sep 1920
Lilbourne	22 Mar 1917	Heliopolis	24 Sep 1940
Liettres	23 Sep 1917	Menidi	16 Nov 1940
Izel-le-Hameau	12 Nov 1917	Heraklion	Apr 1941
Flez	29 Dec 1917	Aqir	26 Apr 1941
Champien	22 Mar 1918	Habbaniya	12 May 1941
Vert Galand	23 Mar 1918	Mosul	7 Jun 1941
Conteville	28 Mar 1918	Habbaniya	Sep 1941
Bertangles	4 Apr 1918	Amriya	27 Oct 1941
Assevilliers	8 Sep 1918	LG.116	24 Nov 1941
Bouvincourt	8 Oct 1918	LG.75	26 Nov 1941
Bertry	25 Oct 1918	Gambut	18 Dec 1941
Thuilles	3 Dec 1918	Heliopolis	2 Jan 1942
Bickendorf	13 May 1919	Left for Far East	14 Jan 1942
Eil	6 Jul 1919	Palembang	23 Jan 1942
Tangmere	12 Aug 1919	Kalidjati	16 Feb 1942
Croydon	Dec 1919	Left for India	17 Feb 1942 (G)
Kenley	Jan 1920	Karachi	17 Mar 1942
	to 30 Jan 1920	Drigh Road	1 Apr 1942
Baghdad West	13 Aug 1920	Quetta	3 Jun 1942
		Vizagapatam	21 Nov 1942

Aircraft

Equipment	Period of service	Representative Serial and Code	
Various	Jan 1917 – Aug 1917	—	
S.E.5A	Aug 1917 – Aug 1919	H710	(P)
D.H.9A	Aug 1920 – Oct 1928	E803	
Wapiti IIA	Jul 1928 – Jan 1935	K1406	
Vincent	Jan 1935 – Jun 1939	K4120	
Blenheim I	Feb 1939 – Mar 1941	L1381	
Blenheim IV	Mar 1941 – Feb 1942 Apr 1942 – Jun 1942	V5443	
Vengeance I, IA, II, III	Dec 1942 – Oct 1944	FB941	(D)
Mosquito VI	Feb 1945 – Nov 1946	TA497	(X)
Beaufighter X	Nov 1946 – Mar 1949	RD801	
Brigand B.1	Feb 1949 – Feb 1953	RH776	(K)
Valetta C.1	Feb 1953 – Aug 1960	VX562	
Beverley C.1	Jun 1958 – Aug 1967	XL130	(Y)
Andover C.1	Aug 1967 – Oct 1971	XS611	
Whirlwind HAR.10	Jan 1972 – date	XJ764	

Hurricane Is, No.85 Squadron

No. 85 Squadron

Badge: On an ogress a hexagon voided

Motto: Noctu diuque venamur (We hunt by day and night)

No.85 Squadron was formed at Upavon on 1 August 1917, and after a period of training moved to France in May 1918. Equipped with S.E.5As, it flew fighter patrols and ground attack sorties over the Western Front until the Armistice. Returning to the UK in February 1919, the squadron disbanded on 3 July 1919.

On 1 June 1938, A Flight of No.87 Squadron was renumbered 85 Squadron at Debden and flew Gladiators until re-equipped with Hurricanes in September 1938. On the outbreak of war, the squadron moved to France as part of the Air Component of the BEF. When the German invasion came in May 1940, it gave fighter cover to the Allied armies until its bases were overrun and the four remaining aircraft retired to the UK. It re-equipped and resumed operations early in June. After taking part in the first half of the Battle of Britain over southern England, the squadron moved to Yorkshire in September and in October began night fighter patrols. In November, it returned south to fly night patrols but the Hurricane's lack of radar gave little chance of success. In January 1941, it began to receive Defiants but after only three sorties these were replaced by Havocs although Hurricanes continued to be flown till July. Mosquitos arrived in August 1942, and in March 1943, the squadron began flying intruder missions over France. Transferred to No.100 Group on 1 May 1944, No.85 flew bomber support missions, intruding over German night fighter airfieds and intercepting enemy fighters by accompanying the main bomber force. After the end of the war, No.85 remained as part of the post-war establishment of Fighter Command and converted to Meteors in September 1951. These it flew until disbanded on 31 October 1958.

On 30 November 1958, No.89 Squadron at Stradishall became No.85 and flew Javelin all-weather fighters until disbanded on 31 March 1963. On 1 April 1963, the Target Facilities Squadron at West Raynham was renumbered 85 Squadron and moved later in the month to Binbrook to provide aircraft for fighter interception training. On 19 December 1975, the squadron disbanded but reformed the same day at West Raynham as a Bloodhound missile unit.

Canberra T.11, No.85 Squadron

Squadron bases			
Upavon	1 Aug 1917	Church Fenton	5 Sep 1940
Norwich	10 Aug 1917	Kirton-in-Lindsey	23 Oct 1940
Hounslow	27 Nov 1917	Gravesend	23 Nov 1940
Marquise	22 May 1918	Debden	1 Jan 1941
Petite Synthe	25 May 1918	Hunsdon	3 May 1941
St. Omer	11 Jun 1918	West Malling	13 May 1943
Bertangles	13 Aug 1918	Swannington	1 May 1944
Savy	5 Sep 1918	West Malling	21 Jul 1944
Foucaucourt	23 Sep 1918	Swannington	29 Aug 1944
Estrée-en-Chaussée	9 Oct 1918	Castle Camps	27 Jun 1945
Escaucourt	27 Oct 1918	Tangmere	9 Oct 1945
Phalempin	9 Nov 1918	West Malling	16 Apr 1947
Ascq	7 Dec 1918	Church Fenton	23 Sep 1957
Lopcombe Corner	16 Feb 1919		to 31 Oct 1958
	to 3 Jul 1919	Stradishall	30 Nov 1958
Debden	1 Jun 1938	West Malling	5 Aug 1959
Rouen/Boos	9 Sep 1939	West Raynham	8 Sep 1960
Merville	29 Sep 1939		to 31 Mar 1963
Lille/Seclin	5 Nov 1939	West Raynham	1 Apr 1963
Mons-en-Chaussée	10 Apr 1940	Binbrook	25 Apr 1963
Lille/Seclin	26 Apr 1940	Scampton	30 Jul 1971
Debden	22 May 1940	Binbrook	16 Sep 1971
Croydon	19 Aug 1940	West Raynham	28 Jan 1972
Castle Camps	3 Sep 1940		to 19 Dec 1975
		West Raynham	19 Dec 1975

Aircraft Equipment	Period of service	Representative Serial and Code
S.E.5A	Aug 1917 – Feb 1919	F8953 (V)
Gladiator I	Jun 1938 – Sep 1938	K7969
Hurricane I	Sep 1938 – Jul 1941	P3854 (VY-Q)
Defiant I	Jan 1941 – Feb 1941	N3434
Havoc I, II	Feb 1941 – Sep 1942	AH514 (VY-D)
Mosquito II	Aug 1942 – Jul 1943	DD726
Mosquito XII	Mar 1943 – Nov 1944	HK119 (VY-S)
Mosquito XIII	Oct 1943 – May 1944	
Mosquito XV	Mar 1943 – Aug 1943	MP469
Mosquito XVII	Nov 1943 – May 1944	HK282 (VY-D)
Mosquito XXX	Nov 1944 – Jan 1946	MV546 (VY-P)
Mosquito NF.36	Jan 1946 – Nov 1951	RL213 (VY-F)
Meteor NF.11	Sep 1951 – Apr 1954	WD625 (R)
Meteor NF.12	May 1954 – Oct 1958	WS608 (Z)
Meteor NF.14	Apr 1954 – Oct 1958	WS777
Javelin FAW.2	Nov 1958 – Mar 1960	XA775 (N)
Javelin FAW.6	Nov 1958 – Jun 1960	XH702 (X)
Javelin FAW.8	Mar 1960 – Mar 1963	XJ122 (E)
Meteor F.8	Apr 1963 – Jul 1970	WH364 (U)
Canberra B.2, T.4, T.11, T.19	May 1963 – Dec 1975	WE113 (Q)
Bloodhound	Dec 1975 – date	–

No. 86 Squadron

Badge: A gull volant carrying in the beak a flash of lightning
Motto: Ad libertates volamus (We fly to freedom)

No.86 Squadron was formed on 1 September 1917 at Wye but did not become operational before being disbanded on 4 July 1918, to provide reinforcements for active units in France. It began to reform as a ground attack squadron on 30 October 1918, but this was suspended when the Armistice was signed two weeks later.

No.86 reformed on 6 December 1940 at Gosport and began convoy escort duties off the East Anglian coast on 28 March 1941. In June, re-equipment with Beauforts began and minelaying sorties started on 15 July. After flying

Beaufort Is, No.86 Squadron

reconnaissance and air-sea rescue missions for three months, the squadron's crews passed through a torpedo training course and anti-shipping strikes began on 11 November with the first torpedo-bomber operation taking place on 12 December. A detachment sent to St. Eval on 13 December was joined by the rest of the squadron in January 1942, and anti-shipping patrols were flown off the French coast until March, when the squadron moved to northern Scotland. Patrols and strikes off the Norwegian coast continued until July when No.86 sent its aircraft to the Middle East and moved to Thorney Island where it was reduced to a cadre on 26 August 1942. Fresh aircrews began arriving early in October, Liberators being received for the conversion training of No.160 Squadron. By the end of the month, No.86's own crews were converting and the squadron flew its first patrol on 16 February 1943, from St. Eval. In March, it moved to Northern Ireland to fly anti-submarine patrols for a year before moving to Iceland. In July 1944, the squadron returned to Scotland for the rest of the war and on 10 June

1945 No.86 joined Transport Command's No.301 Wing. Trooping flights to India began in October and continued until disbandment took place on 25 April 1946.

Squadron bases

Wye	1 Sep 1917	St. Eval	10 Jan 1942
	to 4 Jul 1918	Wick	9 Mar 1942
Brockworth	30 Oct 1918	Thorney Island	31 Jul 1942
	to Nov 1918	Aldergrove	19 Mar 1943
Gosport	6 Dec 1940	Ballykelly	3 Sep 1943
Leuchars	2 Feb 1941	Reykjavik	25 Mar 1944
Wattisham	3 Mar 1941	Tain	1 Jul 1944
North Coates	12 May 1941	Oakington	14 Aug 1945
			to 25 Apr 1946

Aircraft

Equipment	Period of service	Representative Serial and Code	
Salamander	Nov 1918		
Blenheim IV	Dec 1940 – Jul 1941	V5646	(BX-W)
Beaufort I	Jun 1941 – Jul 1942	W6471	(BX-Z)
Liberator IIIa	Oct 1942 – Aug 1944	FL916	(BX-N)
Liberator V	Mar 1943 – Feb 1945	BZ742	(BX-A)
Liberator VIII	Feb 1945 – Apr 1946	KH291	(BX-Y)

Hurricane IICs, No.87 Squadron

No. 87 Squadron

Badge: A serpent reversed, head reguardant and tail embowed

Motto: Maximus me metuit (The most powerful fear me)

Name: 'United Provinces'

No.87 Squadron was formed on 1 September 1917, from a nucleus supplied by D Squadron of the Central Flying School at Upavon. In April 1918, it moved to France with Dolphins to fly fighter and ground attack missions until the end of the war. In February 1919, it returned to the UK and disbanded on 24 June 1919.

On 15 March 1937, No.87 reformed at Tangmere with Furies and received Gladiators in June on moving to Debden. Conversion to Hurricanes began in July 1938 and these were taken to France on the outbreak of war as part of the Air Component of the BEF. When the German invasion came in May 1940, the squadron gave air cover on the Northern Front until its airfields were captured and after two weeks was evacuated to re-equip in Yorkshire. It moved to south-west England in July for day and night defensive patrols during the Battle of Britain and night fighting became its major task.

It remained in the area until the end of 1942, beginning intruder missions in March 1941. In November 1942, the squadron sent its aircraft to Gibraltar for the invasion of North Africa and provided fighter cover for the 1st Army throughout the Tunisian campaign. It remained in North Africa for defensive purposes until it moved to Sicily in September 1943 and in January 1944, began to take part in sweeps over the Balkans from Italy where detachments were based until the squadron moved completely in June. In August 1944, fighter-bomber missions began and continued until the end of the war. On 30 December 1946, the squadron was disbanded.

No.87 reformed on 1 January 1952, at Wahn as a night fighter squadron in Germany. Its Meteors were replaced by Javelins at the end of 1957 and on 3 January 1961, the squadron was disbanded.

Squadron bases

Upavon	1 Sep 1917	Rouen/Boos	9 Sep 1939
Sedgeford	14 Sep 1917	Merville	29 Sep 1939
Hounslow	19 Dec 1917	Lille/Seclin	5 Nov 1939
St. Omer	23 Apr 1918	Le Touquet	4 Apr 1940
Petite Synthe	27 Apr 1918	Amiens/Glisy	15 Apr 1940
Estrée-les-Crecy	27 May 1918	Senon	2 May 1940
Rougefay	29 Jun 1918	Lille/Marcq	10 May 1940
Soncamp	19 Sep 1918	Merville	20 May 1940
Boussières	4 Nov 1918	Debden	24 May 1940
Ternhill	9 Feb 1919	Church Fenton	26 May 1940
	to 24 Jun 1919	Exeter	5 Jul 1940
Tangmere	15 Mar 1937	Colerne	28 Nov 1940
Debden	7 Jun 1937	Charmy Down	11 Dec 1940

		Aircraft Equipment	Period of service	Representative Serial and Code
Colerne	6 Aug 1941			
Charmy Down	27 Jan 1942			
Left for North Africa				
	2 Nov 1942 (A)	Avro 504K	Sep 1917 – Apr 1918	
	24 Nov 1942 (G)	Pup	Sep 1917 – Apr 1918	
Phillipeville	7 Dec 1942 (G)	S.E.5A	Sep 1917 – Apr 1918	
	19 Dec 1942 (A)	Dolphin	Dec 1917 – Feb 1919	C4159 (C)
Djidjelli	22 Dec 1942	Fury II	Mar 1937 – Jun 1937	K8249
Setif and Taher	15 Feb 1943	Gladiator I	Jun 1937 – Jul 1938	K7980
Taher	4 Apr 1943	Hurricane I	Jul 1938 – Jun 1941	L1790 (LK-K)
Bone/Tingley	22 May 1943	Hurricane IIC	Jun 1941 – Jan 1944	Z3775 (LK-B)
Monastir	1 Jul 1943	Spitfire VB, VC	Apr 1943 – Aug 1944	JG866 (LK-J)
Tingley	21 Jul 1943	Spitfire VIII	Jan 1944 – Aug 1944	JF356
La Sebala I	13 Aug 1943	Spitfire IX	Jun 1943 – Dec 1946	NH346 (LK-M)
Palermo	30 Sep 1943	Meteor NF.11	Mar 1957 – Nov 1957	WM156 (G)
Borizzo	3 Oct 1943	Javelin FAW.1	Sep 1957 – Jan 1961	XA565 (K)
Palermo	6 Dec 1943	Javelin FAW.4	Dec 1959 – Jan 1961	XA761
Catania	3 Apr 1944	Javelin FAW.5	Sep 1958 – Nov 1960	XA645
Foggia	11 Jun 1944			
Perugia	23 Jul 1944			
Loreto	25 Aug 1944			
Fano	4 Sep 1944			
Borghetto	16 Sep 1944			
Fano	2 Oct 1944			
Perestola	17 Nov 1944			
Pontedera	1 Jan 1945			
Bologna	25 Apr 1945			
Verona/Villafranca	1 May 1945			
Campoformido	16 May 1945			
Treviso	22 Aug 1945			
Zeltweg	23 Sep 1946			
Tissano	2 Dec 1946			
	to 30 Dec 1946			
Wahn	1 Jan 1952			
Bruggen	2 Jul 1957			
	to 3 Jan 1961			

Boston IIIs, No.88 Squadron

No. 88 Squadron

Badge: A serpent gliding
Motto: En garde (French) (Be on your guard)
Name: 'Hong Kong'

No.88 Squadron was formed at Gosport on 24 July 1917 and moved to France in April 1918 with Bristol Fighters as a fighter-reconnaissance unit. It operated in the area south of Dunkirk for the period of its war service during which it claimed the destruction of 164 enemy aircraft. Ground attack missions were also undertaken and after the Armistice the squadron remained in Belgium until disbanded on 10 August 1919.

On 7 June 1937, No.88 reformed at Waddington as a light bomber squadron equipped with Hinds. In December these were replaced by Battles which the squadron took to France on the outbreak of the Second World War as part of the AASF. During the Battle of France most of the squadron's aircraft were lost during attacks on the advancing German armies and it was withdrawn to the UK in mid-June. Based in Northern Ireland, it carried out patrols for the next year before moving to East Anglia to re-equip with Bostons. In August it began operations with this type, taking part in No.2 Group's daylight attacks on enemy coastal targets and shipping. In preparation for the invasion of Europe, the squadron attacked enemy communications targets and airfields and on D-Day provided aircraft to lay a smokescreen for the initial waves of landing craft off the Normandy beaches. In October 1944 No.88 moved to France and for the rest of the war was engaged in tactical bombing in support of the Allied armies. On 4 April 1945 disbandment took place.

On 1 September 1946 No.1430 Flight at Kai Tak, Hong Kong was redesignated No.88 Squadron for transport duties with Sunderlands. Courier services between bases in the Far East were operated until it was redesignated a general reconnaissance unit and in July 1950 the outbreak of the Korean War resulted in detachments being sent to Iwakuni in Japan for patrols off the Korean coast. In June 1951 these were taken over by other squadrons as No.88 moved to Seletar where, on 1 October 1954, it was disbanded.

On 15 January 1956 No.88 reformed at Wildenrath as an interdiction squadron equipped with Canberras. On 17 December 1962 it was renumbered 14 Squadron.

Squadron bases			
Gosport	24 Jul 1917	Serny	2 Aug 1918
Harling Road	2 Aug 1917	Floringham	21 Oct 1918
Kenley	Apr 1918	Gondecourt	26 Oct 1918
Capelle	20 Apr 1918	Bersee	28 Oct 1918
Drionville	19 Jul 1918	Aulnoye	18 Nov 1918
		Dour	13 Dec 1918

126

Burdinne	14 Dec 1918	Swanton Morley	8 Jul 1941		
Nivelles	18 Dec 1918	Attlebridge	1 Aug 1941		
	to 10 Aug 1919	Oulton	29 Sep 1942		
Waddington	7 Jun 1937	Swanton Morley	30 Mar 1943		
Boscombe Down	17 Jul 1937	Hartfordbridge	19 Aug 1943		
Auberive	2 Sep 1939	Vitry-en-Artois	17 Oct 1944		
Mourmelon	12 Sep 1939		to 6 Apr 1945		
Les Grandes Chappelles		Kai Tak	1 Sep 1946		
	16 May 1940	Seletar	Jun 1951 (P)		
Moisy	3 Jun 1940		to 1 Oct 1954		
Driffield	14 Jun 1940	Wildenrath	15 Jan 1956		
Sydenham	23 Jun 1940		to 17 Dec 1962		

Aircraft

Equipment	Period of service	Representative Serial and Code
Bristol F.2B	Apr 1918 – Aug 1919	E2610 (4)
Hind	Jun 1937 – Jan 1938	K6844
Battle	Dec 1937 – Sep 1941	K9244 (RH-L)
Blenheim IV	Feb 1941 – Dec 1941	Z7427 (RH-K)
Boston I	Dec 1940 – Dec 1941	AW399
Boston III, IIIA	Sep 1941 – Apr 1945	Z2236 (RH-G)
Boston IV	Jun 1944 – Apr 1945	BZ449 (RH-P)
Sunderland GR.5	Sep 1946 – Oct 1954	NJ176 (F)
Canberra B(I).8	Jan 1956 – Dec 1962	XM270

Beaufighter VI, No.89 Squadron

No. 89 Squadron

Badge: A wivern pierced by a flash of lightning
Motto: Dei auxilio telis meis (By the help of God with my own weapons)

No.89 Squadron was formed on 1 September 1917 at Netheravon as a training unit and was disbanded on 4 July 1918 without being operational. It reformed at Wyton on 11 November 1918 but as the First World War ended that day, formation was immediately suspended, its proposed move to Chingford to receive Dolphins being cancelled.

On 25 September 1941, No.89 reformed at Colerne as a night fighter squadron. It flew its Beaufighters out to the Middle East in November and began night patrols in December. A detachment was sent to Malta in June 1942, which also flew intruder missions over Sicily. Detachments were based along the North African coast for night defence until October 1943, when the squadron moved to Ceylon. In September 1944, intruder flights over Burma began in addition to normal night fighter patrols. Conversion to Mosquitos took place early in 1945 and in September No.89 moved to Singapore where it lost its aircraft in March 1946.

It flew some Walruses on air-sea rescue duties until it was disbanded on 1 May 1946, a cadre being transferred to No.22 squadron.

On 15 September, 1955, No.89 reformed at Stradishall with Venom night fighters. In October it converted to Javelins which it flew until renumbered 85 Squadron on 30 November, 1958.

Squadron bases

Netheravon	1 Sep 1917	Bu Amud	9 Aug 1943
	to 4 Jul 1918	Idku	16 Sep 1943
Wyton	11 Nov 1918	Left for Ceylon	15 Oct 1943
Colerne	25 Sep 1941	Vavuniya	25 Oct 1943
Began leaving for		Minneriya	29 Mar 1944
Middle East	24 Nov 1941 (A)	Vavuniya	25 Jun 1944
Kilo 17	30 Nov 1941	Baigachi	13 Aug 1944
Abu Sueir	10 Dec 1941	Seletar	2 Sep 1945
Bersis	19 Jan 1943		to 1 May 1946
Castel Benito	8 Mar 1943	Stradishall	15 Dec 1955
			to 30 Nov 1958

Aircraft

Equipment	Period of service	Representative Serial and Code
Avro 504K, Pup, R.E.8, Camel	Sep 1917 – Jul 1918	–
Beaufighter I	Sep 1941 – Oct 1944	V8311 (T)
Beaufighter VI	Jul 1942 – Apr 1945	X8141 (X)
Mosquito VI	Feb 1945 – Apr 1945	
Mosquito XIX	Apr 1945 – Mar 1946	TA178
Walrus II	Mar 1946 – Apr 1946	
Venom NF.3	Dec 1955 – Nov 1957	WX930 (Q)
Javelin FAW.2	Oct 1957 – Nov 1958	XA774 (J)
Javelin FAW.6	Oct 1957 – Nov 1958	XH696 (H)

127

No. 90 Squadron

Badge: A hind salient
Motto: Celer (Swift)

No.90 Squadron was formed on 8 October 1917 at Shaw-bury as a fighter unit but was disbanded on 3 August 1918, without becoming operational and its personnel used as reinforcements for active units. On 14 August 1918, it reformed at Buckminster for home defence duties in the Midlands but saw no action before the Armistice and disbanded on 13 June 1919.

On 15 March 1937, No.90 reformed from A Flight of No.101 Squadron at Bicester with Hinds. In May, it converted to Blenheims and became a training squadron for No.6 Group on the outbreak of war. It trained Blenheim crews until it merged with No.35 Squadron to form No.17 Operational Training Unit on 4 April 1940.

On 7 May 1941 No.90 reformed at Watton to be the first Fortress squadron in Bomber Command. Daylight operations began on 8 July but the type proved inadequate for European conditions. In October 1941 a detachment of Fortresses was sent to the Middle East where it was absorbed by No.220 Squadron and No.90 flew Blenheims spasmodically until disbanded on 14 February 1942.

The squadron's fifth reformation was at last effective when it became a Stirling night bomber unit in No.3 Group at Bottesford on 7 November 1942. Bombing operations began on 8 January 1943 and continued until the end of the war, with considerable minelaying activity in addition. Stirlings flew their last sorties on 17 June 1944, and No.90 converted to Lancasters for the rest of the war. In May 1947, it re-equipped with Lincolns and these were flown until disbandment on 1 September 1950.

No.90 reformed at Marham on 4 October 1950, to fly Washingtons, the first arriving in December. In November 1953, replacement Canberras began to arrive and the last Washington left in March 1954. On 1 May 1956, the squadron was again disbanded but reformed at Honington on 1 January 1957, as a unit of the V-bomber force, receiving its Valiants in March 1957. With the grounding of the Valiant force, the squadron disbanded on 16 April 1965, having become operational as a flight-refuelling squadron in April 1962.

Squadron bases

Shawbury	8 Oct 1917	West Raynham	15 May 1941
Shotwick	5 Dec 1917	Polebrook	28 Jun 1941
Brockworth	5 Jul 1918		to 14 Feb 1942
	to 3 Aug 1918	Bottesford	7 Nov 1942
Buckminster	14 Aug 1918	Ridgewell	29 Dec 1942
	to 13 Jun 1919	Wratting Common	31 May 1943
Bicester	15 Mar 1937	Tuddenham	13 Oct 1943
West Raynham	10 May 1939	Wyton	31 May 1946
Weston-on-the-Green			to 1 Sep 1950
	7 Sep 1939	Marham	4 Oct 1950
Upwood	19 Sep 1939		to 1 May 1956
	to 4 Apr 1940	Honington	1 Jan 1957
Watton	7 May 1941		to 16 Apr 1965

Aircraft

Equipment	Period of service	Representative Serial and Code
Dolphin	Jul 1918 – Aug 1918	
F.E.2b	Oct 1917 – Aug 1918	
Avro 504K	Oct 1917 – Aug 1918	
	Aug 1918 – Jun 1919	
Hind	Mar 1937 – Jun 1937	K6740
Blenheim I	May 1937 – Apr 1940	K7054 (9O-F)
Blenheim IV	Mar 1939 – Apr 1940	L4875
	Oct 1941 – Feb 1942	
Fortress I	May 1941 – Feb 1942	AN535 (WP-O)
Stirling I	Dec 1942 – May 1943	R9306 (WP-J)
Stirling III	Feb 1943 – Jun 1944	BF410 (WP-E)
Lancaster I, III	May 1944 – Dec 1947	NE149/G (WP-A)
Lincoln B.2	May 1947 – Sep 1950	RR451 (WP-N)
Washington B.1	Dec 1950 – Mar 1954	WF442 (WP-P)
Canberra B.2	Nov 1954 – May 1956	WJ993
Valiant B.1, BK.1	Mar 1957 – Feb 1965	WZ377

No. 91 Squadron

Badge: In front of a fountain
two triangles interlaced
Motto: We seek alone
Name: 'Nigeria'

No.91 Squadron was formed on 1 September 1917, at Chattis Hill where it was engaged in wireless telegraphy training with various aircraft until disbanded on 4 July 1918. The number was transferred to a fighter squadron beginning to form at Kenley but it did not become operational before the end of the war and disbanded on 3 July 1919.

On 11 January 1941, No.421 (Reconnaissance) Flight at Hawkinge was renumbered 91 Squadron. The tasks undertaken by its Spitfires included shipping reconnaissance and reporting the movements, markings and tactics of enemy aircraft. By summer it had become a normal single-seat fighter squadron undertaking shipping patrols and weather reconnaissance to which were later added air-sea rescue sweeps until the new ASR squadrons could undertake these in their own aircraft.

In April 1943, the squadron moved to the Midlands to convert to Spitfire XIIs, returning south next month to undertake sweeps over northern France. In March 1944, it joined Second TAF and flew armed reconnaissance sweeps over the approaches to the invasion area in Normandy. Soon after D-Day, flying bomb attacks began and No.91 was engaged in destroying these until August 1944. In September it began flying long-range escort missions for day bombers and in April 1945, moved to East Anglia to carry out armed reconnaissance missions over the Netherlands and search for midget submarines off the coast of Holland and Belgium.

Based at Duxford after the end of the war, the squadron converted to Meteors in October 1946 which it flew until renumbered 92 Squadron on 31 January 1947.

Squadron bases

Chattis Hill	1 Sep 1917 to 4 Jul 1918	Hutton Cranswick	8 Feb 1944
Kenley	4 Jul 1918 to 3 Jul 1919	Tangmere	20 Feb 1944
		Castle Camps	29 Feb 1944
		Drem	8 Mar 1944
Hawkinge	11 Jan 1941	West Malling	23 Apr 1944
Lympne	23 Nov 1942	Deanland	21 Jul 1944
Hawkinge	11 Jan 1943	Biggin Hill	7 Oct 1944
Honiley	20 Apr 1943	Manston	29 Oct 1944
Kings Cliffe	9 May 1943	Ludham	8 Apr 1945
Hawkinge	21 May 1943	Duxford	Apr 1946
Westhampnett	28 Jun 1943	Debden	Nov 1946
Tangmere	4 Oct 1943	Acklington	Jan 1947 to 31 Jan 1947

Aircraft

Equipment	Period of service	Representative Serial and Code
B.E.2e, R.E.8, etc.	Nov 1917 — Jul 1918	—
Dolphin	Jul 1918 — Jul 1919	
Spitfire IIA	Jan 1941 — May 1941	P7836 (DL-K)
Spitfire VA, VB	Mar 1941 — Apr 1943	BL994 (DL-S)
Spitfire XII	Apr 1943 — Mar 1944	MB803
Spitfire XIV	Mar 1944 — Aug 1944	RB180 (DL-E)
Spitfire IXB	Aug 1944 — Apr 1945	PL271
Spitfire F.21	Apr 1945 — Oct 1946	LA260 (DL-D)
Meteor F.3	Oct 1946 — Jan 1947	EE409 (DL-F)
Meteor F.4	Jan 1947	EE461

Hunter F.6s, No.92 Squadron

No. 92 Squadron

Badge: A cobra entwining a sprig of maple
Motto: Aut pugna aut morere (Either fight or die)
Name: 'East India'

No.92 Squadron was formed at London Colney on 1 September 1917, as a fighter unit and moved to France in July 1918. It was engaged in fighter and ground-attack duties over the Western Front for the rest of the war and disbanded on 7 August 1919.

On 10 October 1939, No.92 reformed at Tangmere and received Blenheims. In March 1940, these were replaced by Spitfires which became operational on 9 May and flew patrols over France during May and June before being sent to South Wales for defensive duties. In September it was transferred to No.11 Group for the final phase of the Battle of Britain, beginning offensive operations at the end of the year. Withdrawn to Lincolnshire in October 1941 No.92 left for the Middle East in February 1942 only to find on arrival that lack of aircraft had delegated the squadron to maintenance duties. In August Spitfires arrived and were used for fighter sweeps and bomber escort missions over the desert during the defense of El Alamein and the subsequent rout of the Axis armies. Moving west behind the 8th Army, the squadron reached Tunisia and in June 1943, flew to Malta to cover the landings in Sicily. After moving into captured airfields there it arrived in Italy in September where it became a fighter-bomber unit in July 1944, for the rest of the war. The squadron disbanded in Austria on 30 December 1946.

On 31 January 1947, No.91 Squadron at Acklington was renumbered 92 Squadron and flew Meteors as part of the fighter defence of the UK until converted to Sabres in February 1954. These were replaced by Hunters in April 1956, which in turn gave place to Lightnings in April 1963. At the end of 1968 No.92 moved to Germany to reinforce Second ATAF. In January 1977, conversion to Phantoms began and on 31 March 1977, the squadron disbanded. On 1 April 1977, the Phantom element at Wildenrath became No.92 Squadron.

Wadi Sirru/Darragh	19 Jan 1943	Fabrica	17 Jun 1944
Castel Benito	15 Feb 1943	Perugia	3 Jul 1944
Hazbub	24 Feb 1943	Loreto	24 Aug 1944
Ben Gardane	1 Mar 1943	Fano	4 Sep 1944
Bou Grara	10 Mar 1943	Bellaria	4 Dec 1944
La Fauconnerie	11 Apr 1943	Treviso	3 May 1945
Bou Goubrine	15 Apr 1943	Zeltweg	23 Sep 1946
Hergla	5 May 1943		to 30 Dec 1946
Ben Gardane	20 May 1943	Acklington	31 Jan 1947
Luqa	14 Jun 1943	Duxford	15 Feb 1947
Pachino	13 Jul 1943	Linton-on-Ouse	7 Oct 1949
Cassibile	17 Jul 1943	Middleton St. George	
Lentini	26 Jul 1943		1 Mar 1957
Grottaglie	14 Sep 1943	Thornaby	30 Sep 1957
Gioia del Colle	23 Sep 1943	Middleton St. George	
Tortorella	5 Oct 1943		1 Oct 1958
Triolo	18 Oct 1943	Leconfield	25 May 1961
Canne	22 Nov 1943	Geilenkirchen	29 Dec 1965
Marcianise	17 Jan 1944	Gutersloh	22 Jan 1968
Venafro	23 Apr 1944		to 31 Mar 1977
Littorio	12 Jun 1944	Wildenrath	1 Apr 1977

Aircraft Equipment	Period of service	Representative Serial and Code
Spad S.VII	Sep 1917 — Mar 1918	
Pup	Sep 1917 — Mar 1918	
Avro 504K	Sep 1917 — Mar 1918	
S.E.5A	Jan 1917 — Aug 1919	E4024
Blenheim If	Nov 1939 — Mar 1940	L6776 (GR-R)
Spitfire I	Mar 1940 — Feb 1941	P9367 (QJ-A)
Spitfire VB	Feb 1941 — Feb 1942	R6919 (QJ-L)
Spitfire VB, VC	Aug 1942 — Sep 1943	BR466
Spitfire IX	Mar 1943 — Sep 1943 Jun 1946 — Dec 1946	TA808
Spitfire VIII	Jul 1943 — Dec 1946	JF413 (QJ-V)
Meteor F.3	Jan 1947 — May 1948	EE388 (DL-S)
Meteor F.4	May 1948 — Oct 1950	RA388 (DL-P)
Meteor F.8	Oct 1950 — Feb 1954	VZ546 (C)
Sabre F.4	Feb 1954 — Apr 1956	XD710 (B)
Hunter F.4	Apr 1956 — May 1957	XF324 (D)
Hunter F.6	Feb 1957 — Apr 1963	XG186 (J)
Lightning F.2, F.2A	Apr 1963 — Mar 1977	XN793 (K)
Phantom FGR.2	Jan 1977 — date	XV435 (O)

Squadron bases

London Colney	1 Sep 1917	Pembrey	18 Jun 1940
Chattis Hill	14 Sep 1917	Biggin Hill	8 Sep 1940
Tangmere	17 Mar 1918	Manston	9 Jan 1941
Bray Dunes	2 Jul 1918	Biggin Hill	20 Feb 1941
Drionville	19 Jul 1918	Gravesend	24 Sep 1941
Serny	2 Aug 1918	Digby	20 Oct 1941
Proyart	27 Sep 1918	Left for Middle East	
Estrée-en-Chaussée	9 Oct 1918		12 Feb 1942
Bertry	25 Oct 1918	Fayid	16 Apr 1942
Thuilles	3 Dec 1918	Heliopolis	30 Apr 1942
Eil-	Jun 1919	LG.173	4 Aug 1942
	to 7 Aug 1919	LG.21	7 Nov 1942
Tangmere	10 Oct 1939	Gambut West	14 Nov 1942
Croydon	30 Dec 1939	Msus	24 Nov 1942
Northolt	9 May 1940	El Hassiet	4 Dec 1942
Hornchurch	23 May 1940 (A)	El Nogra	9 Dec 1942
Duxford	25 May 1940 (A)	El Merduna	21 Dec 1942
Northolt	4 Jun 1940	El Chel	1 Jan 1943
Hornchurch	9 Jun 1940	Tamet	3 Jan 1943
		Hamraiet	9 Jan 1943

No. 93 Squadron

Badge: An escarabuncle
Motto: Ad arma parati (Ready for battle)

No.93 Squadron was formed at Chattis Hill on 1 September 1917, as a fighter unit with S.E.5As but did not become opetational and was disbanded on 14 October 1918. On the same day, a new No.93 Squadron was authorised but with the end of the war a few weeks later this was abandoned. It had been intended to form at Oxford with Dolphins.

On 7 December 1940, No.93 Squadron reformed from No.420 Flight at Middle Wallop, the latter having been itself formed on 29 September 1940. The squadron was equipped with Harrows modified to carry 'Pandora' aerial mines and some operational use was made of this weapon against enemy night bombers. From December 1940, Havocs began to arrive while Wellingtons later took over from the Harrows operationally though for a short period only. By June 1941, the squadron was fully equipped with Havocs but the aerial mines proved of little value. With the increasing number of radar-equipped night fighters coming into service the exper-

iment was abandoned and the squadron disbanded on 6 December 1941, its crews passing to No.1458 Flight.

On 1 June 1942, No.93 reformed at Andreas with Spitfires for convoy patrols over the Irish Sea. In September it became non-operational and its pilots moved to Gibraltar to await the beginning of Operation 'Torch', the invasion of North Africa. In November, it moved to Algeria where the ground crews rejoined later in the month and its Spitfires provided fighter cover for the First Army during its campaign in Algeria and Tunisia. After the surrender of the Axis forces in North Africa, the squadron moved to Malta to help cover the landings in Sicily and Italy, flying fighter patrols until July 1944 when it moved to Corsica. After providing fighter patrols over the Allied invasion beaches in southern France, No.93 moved to the liberated area to cover the forces pushing north to join up with the Allied armies from Normandy. In September 1944 these joined up and the squadron returned to Italy to take up fighter-bomber duties for the rest of the war. After a short period of occupation duties in Austria, the squadron disbanded on 5 September 1945.

On 1 January 1946, No.237 Squadron at Lavariano was renumbered 93 Squadron which flew Mustangs in northern Italy until disbanded on 30 December 1946. On 15 November 1950, No.93 reformed at Celle as a Vampire fighter-bomber squadron in Germany. In April 1954 it converted to Sabres which were replaced by Hunters in January 1956. These remained in service until the squadron was disbanded on 31 December 1960.

Squadron bases

Chattis Hill	1 Sep 1917	Falcone	6 Sep 1943	Tissano	24 Jan 1946	Oldenburg	Apr 1954
	to 14 Oct 1918	Battipaglia	28 Sep 1943	Treviso	20 Dec 1946	Jever	1955
Middle Wallop	29 Sep 1940	Capodichino	12 Oct 1943		to 30 Dec 1946		to 31 Dec 1960
	to 6 Dec 1941	Lago	15 Jan 1944	Celle	15 Nov 1950		
Andreas	1 Jun 1942	Tre Cancelli	5 Jun 1944				
Kings Cliffe	8 Sep 1942	Tarquinia	13 Jun 1944				
Gibraltar	6 Nov 1942 (A)	Grosseto	25 Jun 1944				
Maison Blanche		Piombino	5 Jul 1944				
	13 Nov 1942 (A)	Calvi	21 Jul 1944				
Souk-el-Arba	21 Nov 1942 (A)	Ramatuelle	20 Aug 1944				
	22 Nov 1942 (G)	Sisteron	26 Aug 1944				
Souk-el-Khemis	31 Dec 1942	Lyon-Bron	9 Sep 1944				
La Sebala	13 May 1943	La Jasse	27 Sep 1944				
Mateur	26 May 1943	Peretola	2 Oct 1944				
Hal Far	12 Jun 1943	Rimini	16 Nov 1944				
Comiso	14 Jul 1943	Ravenna	17 Feb 1945				
Pachino	30 Jul 1943	Rivolto	5 May 1945				
Panebianco	27 Aug 1943	Klagenfurt	16 May 1945				
Cassale	2 Sep 1943		to 5 Sep 1945				
		Lavariano	1 Jan 1946				

Aircraft

Equipment	Period of service	Representative Serial and Code	
S.E.5A	Sep 1917 – Oct 1918		
Harrow II	Dec 1940 – Jun 1941	K7005	
Havoc	Dec 1940 – Dec 1941	AX916	(HN-L)
Wellington IC	Mar 1941 – May 1941	T1370	
Spitfire VB, VC	Jun 1942 – Aug 1943	BM514	(HN-B)
Spitfire IX	Jul 1943 – Sep 1945	MA636	(HN-N)
Mustang III/IV	Jan 1946 – Dec 1946	KH798	
Vampire FB.5	Nov 1950 – Apr 1954	WA109	(A)
Vampire FB.9	Nov 1953 – Apr 1954	WR139	
Sabre F.4	Apr 1954 – Jan 1956	XB768	(Q)
Hunter F.4	Jan 1956 – Feb 1958	XE685	(B)
Hunter F.6	Feb 1958 – Dec 1960	XJ717	(Z)

Hurricane IICs, No.94 Squadron

No. 94 Squadron

Badge: A wolf's head erased
Motto: Avenge

No.94 Squadron was formed at Harling Road on 1 August 1917 as a training unit for Camel pilots but in May 1918 was mobilised as an active squadron. After training with S.E.5As, the squadron moved to France at the end of October. The imminent end of the war resulted in No.94 not becoming engaged in operational flying and it returned to the UK in February 1919, disbanding on 30 June 1919.

On 26 March 1939, No.94 reformed at Khormaksar as a fighter squadron for the defence of Aden. After Italy's entry into World War Two in June 1940 the squadron flew defensive patrols over Aden and British Somaliland. In April 1941 it handed over its Gladiators to the SAAF and moved to Egypt where it re-equipped with Hurricanes in May. After a period of day and night defensive patrols, the squadron began ground-attack missions over the Western Desert in November, re-equipping with Kittyhawks in February 1942. These it flew on fighter patrols over the desert until May when it was withdrawn and received Hurricanes for defensive duties. As the Eighth Army moved westwards after the Battle of El Alamein, No.94 covered coastal convoys supplying the army. In February 1944 it converted to Spitfires which were used on sweeps over Crete and in September a move was made to Greece to attack the retreating German army as it withdrew through Macedonia and Bulgaria. In December 1944 it provided air support for the army during an attempted Communist take-over of Greece and on 20 April 1945 was disbanded.

On 1 December 1950 No.94 reformed at Celle as a Vampire fighter-bomber squadron. In January 1954 it converted to Venoms and operated over Germany until disbanded on 15 September 1957. The squadron was reformed at Misson (near Finningley) on 1 October 1960, as a Bloodhound air defence missile unit, disbanding on 30 June 1963.

Squadron bases					
Harling Road	1 Aug 1917	El Adem	15 Feb 1942		
Senlis	31 Oct 1918	Gasr el Arid	17 Feb 1942		
Izel-le-Hameau	19 Nov 1918	LG.115	26 Feb 1942		
Tadcaster	3 Feb 1918	Gasr el Arid	17 Mar 1942		
	to 30 Jun 1919	Ikingi Maryut	16 May 1942		
Khormaksar	26 Mar 1939	El Gamil	25 May 1942		
Sheikh Othman	2 May 1939	Martuba	13 Jan 1943		
Left for Egypt	6 Apr 1941	Savoia	1 Apr 1943		
Ismailia	22 Apr 1941	Apollonia	25 May 1943		
El Ballah	29 Aug 1941	Savoia	19 Jun 1943		
LG.103	27 Oct 1941	El Adem	4 Nov 1943		
LG.109	7 Nov 1941	El Adem South (LG.809)			
LG.124	20 Nov 1941		29 Dec 1943		
Sidi Rezegh	12 Dec 1941	Bu Amud	7 Apr 1944		
Gazala No.2	18 Dec 1941	Savoia	15 Jul 1944		
Mechili	22 Dec 1941	Amriya	31 Aug 1944		
Msus	24 Dec 1941	Kalamaki/Hassani	19 Sep 1944		
Antelat	11 Jan 1942	Sedes	14 Feb 1945		
Msus	23 Jan 1942		to 20 Apr 1945		
Mechili	24 Jan 1942	Celle	1 Dec 1950		
LG.110	1 Feb 1942		to 15 Sep 1957		
Gambut	14 Feb 1942	Misson	1 Oct 1960		
			to 30 Jun 1963		

Aircraft Equipment	Period of service	Representative Serial and Code
Camel	Aug 1917 – Jun 1918	
S.E.5A	Jun 1918 – Jun 1919	
Gladiator I, II	Mar 1939 – Jun 1941	N7616
Hurricane I	May 1941 – Dec 1941	V7479 (U)
	May 1942 – Aug 1942	
Hurricane IIB	Dec 1941 – Jan 1942	BD919
Tomahawk IIB	Feb 1942	AN329
Kittyhawk I	Feb 1942 – May 1942	AK807
Hurricane IIC	May 1942 – Apr 1944	HW738 (GO-G)
Spitfire VC, VB	Mar 1944 – Feb 1945	JK435 (GO-D)
Spitfire IX	Feb 1944 – Aug 1944	MH703 (GO-B)
	Feb 1945 – Apr 1945	
Spitfire VIII	Feb 1945 – Apr 1945	
Vampire FB.5	Dec 1950 – Jan 1954	VV700 (A-C)
Venom FB.1	Jan 1954 – Sep 1957	WR284 (A-G)
Venom FB.4	Mar 1957 – Sep 1957	WR425
Bloodhound	Oct 1960 – Jun 1963	—

Sunderland I, No.95 Squadron

No. 95 Squadron

Badge: On a mount in waves of the sea in front of a palm tree, a crowned crane displayed

Motto: Trans mare exivi (I went out over the sea)

No.95 Squadron was formed on 1 September 1917 but before becoming operational was disbanded on 4 July 1918 to provide personnel for active units. It began to reform at Kenley on 1 October 1918 as a fighter squadron but formation was abandoned with the armistice a few weeks later before it received any of its intended Martinsyde F.4s.

On 16 January 1941 a detachment of three Sunderlands of No.210 Squadron at Pembroke Dock became No.95 Squadron and flew its first boat out to Gibraltar early in February. After flying patrols, the squadron began to arrive at its base at Freetown, Sierra Leone, on 17 March to begin anti-submarine patrols over the South Atlantic. In July 1941 activities by Vichy reconnaissance aircraft resulted in a flight of Hurricanes being added to the Squadron, this becoming No.128 Squadron on 7 October 1941. In March 1943, No.95 moved to Bathurst, Gambia, operating detachments from Sierra Leone, Dakar and Liberia for the rest of the war. On 30 June 1945 the squadron disbanded.

Squadron bases			
		Pembroke Dock	16 Jan 1941
Shotwick	1 Sep 1917	Freetown	17 Mar 1941
	to 4 Jul 1918	Jui	9 Apr 1942
Kenley	1 Oct 1918	Bathurst	7 Mar 1943
	to Nov 1918		to 30 Jun 1945

Aircraft Equipment	Period of service	Representative Serial and Code
Various	Sep 1917 – Jul 1918	
Sunderland I	Jan 1941 – Jan 1944	L2163 (DQ-G)
Sunderland III	Jul 1942 – Jun 1945	DW107 (DQ-R)
Hurricane I	Jul 1941 – Oct 1941	Z4257

No. 96 Squadron

Badge: A lion passant facing to
the sinister with ten stars
representing the constel-
lation of Leo
Motto: Nocturni obambulamus
(We prowl by night)

No.96 was formed at South Carlton on 28 September 1917 as a training unit but was disbanded on 4 July 1918 to provide personnel for operational units. It reformed at Wyton as a ground-attack squadron on 28 September 1918 and would have flown Salamanders but did not become operational before the Armistice caused its formation to be abandoned.

On 18 December 1940, No.422 Flight, a Hurricane night fighter unit at Cranage, was redesignated No.96 Squadron. In February 1941 it received Defiants as additional equipment and flew night patrols in defence of Merseyside and the Midlands. Beaufighters arrived in May 1942 to convert the squadron and in April 1943 it began to fly intruder missions from Ford as an advanced base. In June 1943, the squadron converted to Mosquitos and prepared for a move overseas but this was cancelled and No.96 resumed defensive operations in August 1943 from Church Fenton. In September it moved to Scotland for two months before coming south to Kent. After the Normandy landings, the squadron provided night fighter cover over the landing areas and soon afterwards was engaged in countering flying bombs launched against London at night. On 12 December 1944, the squadron was disbanded.

No.96 reformed at Leconfield on 30 December 1944 as a Halifax squadron in Transport Command but gave these up in March when it left for the Far East. Arriving in Egypt,

it collected Dakotas and flew these to India where it was engaged in parachute and glider training. Detachments were provided for operations over Burma and in September the squadron began general transport flights throughout South-East Asia Command. In April 1946 a move was made to Hong Kong where services were maintained to Malaya and China but on 15 June 1946 the squadron was re-numbered 110 Squadron.

On 1 October 1952 No.96 reformed as a Meteor night fighter squadron at Ahlhorn. As part of No.125 Wing, it provided night cover for Germany until renumbered 3 Squadron on 21 January 1959.

Squadron bases			
South Carlton	28 Sep 1917	Ford	20 Jun 1944
	to 4 Jul 1918	Odiham	24 Sep 1944
Wyton	28 Sep 1918		to 12 Dec 1944
	to Nov 1918	Leconfield	30 Dec 1944
Cranage	18 Dec 1940	Left for Far East	25 Mar 1945
Wrexham	21 Oct 1941	Cairo West	Mar 1945 (P)
Honiley	20 Oct 1942	Bilaspur	1 May 1945
Tangmere	4 Mar 1943	Hmawbi	4 Sep 1945
Honiley	12 Mar 1943	Kai Tak	16 Apr 1946
Church Fenton	4 Aug 1943		to 15 Jun 1946
Drem	3 Sep 1943	Ahlhorn	1 Oct 1952
West Malling	8 Nov 1943	Geilenkirchen	1958
			to 21 Jan 1959

Aircraft Equipment	Period of service	Representative Serial
B.E.2c	Sep 1917 – Jul 1918	
Salamander	Sep 1918 – Nov 1918	
Hurricane I	Dec 1940 – Aug 1941	P8813
Hurricane IIC	Jul 1941 – Mar 1942	W9172
Defiant I, Ia	Feb 1941 – Jun 1942	T4052 (ZJ-H)
Defiant II	Feb 1942 – Jun 1942	AA575
Beaufighter II	May 1942 – Jun 1943	T3009
Beaufighter VI	Sep 1942 – Aug 1943	X8025 (ZJ-B)
Mosquito XII	Jun 1943 – Aug 1943	
Mosquito XIII	Aug 1943 – Dec 1944	HK379 (ZJ-F)
Halifax III	Dec 1944 – Mar 1945	MZ464 (6H-Q)
Dakota III, IV	Mar 1945 – Jun 1946	KN119
Meteor NF.11	Oct 1952 – Jan 1959	WM144 (A)

No. 97 Squadron

Badge: An ogress pierced by an
arrow, point downwards
Motto: Achieve your aim
Name: 'Straits Settlements'

No.97 Squadron was formed on 1 December 1917, at Waddington as a training unit until the end of March 1918, when it moved to Netheravon to become an operational unit. In July it received Handley Page O/400s and took these to France in August to join the Independent Force for strategic bombing over Germany until the end of the war. In March 1919, it returned to the UK and re-equipped with D.H.10s, leaving for India in July where, on 1 April 1920 it was re-numbered 60 Squadron.

On 16 September 1935, No.97 reformed at Catfoss as a night bomber squadron with Heyfords, becoming a training squadron on 7 June 1938. In February 1939, it converted to Whitleys and on the outbreak of war moved to Abingdon to continue training duties until redesignated No.10 Operational Training Unit on 6 April 1940. Reforming began on 1 May 1940, but it disbanded again on 20 May without receiving any aircraft.

On 25 February 1941, No.97 reformed from a nucleus

supplied by No.207 Squadron at Waddington with Manchesters and flew these on its first operation on 8 April. Mechanical problems with Manchesters restricted their use and some Hampdens were used to bridge the gaps in operational strength but in January 1942 Lancasters began to arrive. This type was flown by the squadron for the rest of the war, at first with the main force and from April 1943, as a unit of the Pathfinder Force for a year. It remained in being as part of the post-war Bomber Command and re-equipped with Lincolns in July 1946 which it continued to fly until disbanded on 1 January 1956.

On 1 December 1959, No.97 reformed at Hemswell as a Thor intermediate range ballistic missile unit, being disbanded on 24 May 1963. On 25 May 1963, No.151 Squadron at Watton was renumbered 97 and flew Canberras and Varsities in Signals Command until disbanded on 2 January 1967.

Squadron bases			
Waddington	1 Dec 1917	Abingdon	17 Sep 1939
Stonehenge	21 Jan 1918		to 6 Apr 1940
Netheravon	31 Mar 1918	Driffield	1 May 1940
Xaffévillers	9 Aug 1918		to 20 May 1940
St. Inglevert	17 Nov 1918	Waddington	25 Feb 1941
Ford	4 Mar 1919	Coningsby	10 Mar 1941
Left for India	19 Jul 1919	Woodhall Spa	2 Mar 1942
Allahabad	13 Aug 1919	Bourn	18 Apr 1943
Lahore	15 Nov 1919	Coningsby	18 Apr 1944
Risalpur	28 Mar 1920	Hemswell	Nov 1946
	to 1 Apr 1920		to 1 Jan 1956
Catfoss	16 Sep 1935	Hemswell	1 Dec 1959
Boscombe Down	Sep 1935 (P)		to 24 May 1963
Leconfield	7 Jan 1937	Watton	25 May 1963
			to 2 Jan 1967

Aircraft Equipment	Period of service	Representative Serial and Code
D.H.4	Dec 1917 – Jul 1918	
O/400	Jul 1918 – Apr 1919	D8304
D.H.10	Apr 1919 – Apr 1920	E5484
Heyford I, IA, II, III	Sep 1935 – Feb 1939	K3493
Anson I	Feb 1939 – Apr 1940	N5004
Whitley II	Feb 1939 – Apr 1940	K7229 (OF-A)
Whitley III	Feb 1939 – Apr 1940	K9000
Manchester I, IA	Mar 1941 – Feb 1942	L7453 (OF-X)
Hampden I	Jul 1941 – Aug 1941	AE300
Lancaster I, III	Jan 1942 – Jul 1946	JA846 (OF-N)
Lincoln B.2	Jul 1946 – Dec 1955	RE305 (OF-N)
Thor	Dec 1959 – May 1963	–
Canberra B.2	May 1963 – Jan 1967	WH739
Varsity T.1	May 1963 – Jan 1967	WL690
Hastings C.2	May 1963 – Jan 1967	WJ338

Whitley I, No.97 Squadron

No. 98 Squadron

Badge: Cerberus
Motto: Never failing

Hind I, No.98 Squadron

No.98 Squadron was formed at Harlaxton on 30 August 1917, from a nucleus supplied by No.4 Training Squadron and moved the same day to Old Sarum to begin training as a day bomber unit. It moved to France with D.H.9s in April 1918, and began bombing missions on the 9th against troop concentrations, railways and enemy airfields in the area of the German offensive which was in full spate when the squadron arrived. In July No.98 moved south to meet another German attack, this time on the French in Champagne, returning north in August to take part in the British counter-offensive which eventually reached Belgium before the Armistice. In March 1919, it returned to the UK and disbanded on 24 July 1919.

On 17 February 1936, No.98 reformed at Abingdon from a detachment supplied by No.15 Squadron. Initially equipped with Hinds, it converted to Battles in June 1938, but remained a training unit when most of the other Battle squadrons left for France in September 1939. In April 1940, it moved to Nantes where it continued to receive crews for operational training before sending them to their squadrons. In June, No.98 was recalled due to the imminent collapse of the French front and many of the squadron personnel were lost when the liner *Lancastria* was sunk off St. Nazaire. After re-assembling at Gatwick, the need for a squadron to be sent to Iceland resulted in the transfer of No.98 in August for coastal patrol duties. In June 1941, Hurricanes were added but on 15 July 1941, the squadron was redesignated No.1423

Mitchell IIs, No.98 Squadron

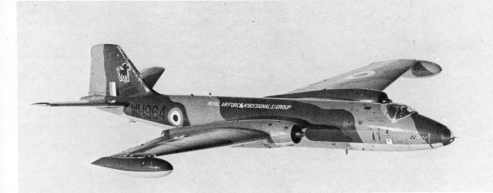

Canberra B.2, No.98 Squadron

Flight and reduced in size.

On 12 September 1942, No.98 reformed at West Raynham as a medium bomber squadron in No.2 Group. Equipped with Mitchells, it flew its first operation on 22 January 1943. Attacks on enemy communications centres and airfields formed part of the preparations for the invasion of Europe and when the landings took place in June 1944, the squadron became increasingly involved in tactical bombing in support of the Allied armies. In October 1944, it moved to Belgium to reduce the range and at the end of April 1945, to Germany. After the end of the war, No.98 converted to Mosquitos and remained with the occupation forces.

In February 1951, the squadron converted to Vampire fighter-bombers, replacing these with Venoms in August 1953. It became a day fighter unit in March 1955, on receiving Hunters, and disbanded on 15 July 1957.

On 1 August 1959, No.98 was reformed at Driffield as an intermediate range ballistic missile squadron with Thors, being disbanded again on 18 April 1963. On the following day, No.245 Squadron at Tangmere was renumbered 98 Squadron and in October moved its Canberras to Watton, Signals Command's main base. In April 1969, it moved to Cottesmore with No.90 (Signals) Group and disbanded on 27 February 1976.

Squadron bases

Harlaxton	30 Aug 1917	Coudekerque	25 May 1918
Old Sarum	31 Aug 1917	Ruisseauville	6 Jun 1918
Lympne	1 Mar 1918	Drionville	21 Jun 1918
St. Omer	1 Apr 1918	Chailly-en-Brie	14 Jul 1918
Clairmarais	3 Apr 1918	Blangermont	3 Aug 1918
Alquines	13 Apr 1918	Abscon	27 Oct 1918
		Marquain	27 Dec 1918

Alquines	19 Jan 1919	B.58 Melsbroek	18 Oct 1944
Shotwick	21 Mar 1919	B.110 Achmer	30 Apr 1945
	to 24 Jun 1919	B.58 Melsbroek	17 Sep 1945
Abingdon	17 Feb 1936	Wahn	15 Mar 1946
Hucknall	21 Aug 1936	Celle	17 Sep 1949
Scampton	2 Mar 1940	West Malling	27 Sep 1949
Finningley	19 Mar 1940	Celle	7 Oct 1949
Chateau Bougon	16 Apr 1940	West Malling	17 Apr 1950
Gatwick	8 Jun 1940 (G)	Celle	12 May 1950
	15 Jun 1940 (A)	Fassberg	1 Nov 1950
Newton	26 Jul 1940 (A)	Aston Down	10 Oct 1951
Left for Iceland	27 Jul 1940 (G)	Fassberg	19 Oct 1951
Kaldadarnes	31 Jul 1940 (G)	Jever	19 Mar 1955
	27 Aug 1940 (A)		to 15 Jul 1957
	to 15 Jul 1941	Driffield	1 Aug 1959
West Raynham	12 Sep 1942		to 18 Apr 1963
Foulsham	15 Oct 1942	Tangmere	19 Apr 1963
Dunsfold	18 Aug 1943	Watton	1 Oct 1963
Swanton Morley	27 Mar 1944	Cottesmore	17 Apr 1969
Dunsfold	10 Apr 1944		to 27 Feb 1976

Aircraft Equipment	Period of service	Representative Serial and Code
B.E.2c, B.E.2e, D.H.4, F.K.8, Avro 504K	Sep 1917 – Feb 1918	–
D.H.9	Feb 1918 – Jun 1919	D7224 (H)
Hind	Feb 1936 – Jun 1938	K6717
Battle	Jun 1938 – Jul 1941	K9212
Hurricane I	Jun 1940 – Jul 1941	Z4045
Mitchell II	Sep 1942 – Nov 1945	FL176 (VO-B)
Mitchell III	Sep 1944 – Nov 1945	HD371 (VO-J)
Mosquito XVI	Nov 1945 – Aug 1948	PF596 (VO-T)
Mosquito B.35	Aug 1948 – Feb 1951	TH995 (VO-Y)
Vampire FB.5	Feb 1951 – Aug 1953	WE841 (L-D)
Venom FB.1	Aug 1953 – Mar 1955	WK388 (L-H)
Hunter F.4	Mar 1955 – Jul 1957	WW649 (E)
Canberra B.2, E.15	Apr 1963 – Feb 1976	WJ603 (K)

No. 99 Squadron

Badge: A puma salient
Motto: Quisque tenax (Each tenacious)
Name: 'Madras Presidency'

No.99 Squadron was formed on 15 August 1917 at Yatesbury from a nucleus supplied by No.13 Training Squadron. In April 1918 it received D.H.9s and moved at the end of the

Aldershot Is, No.99 Squadron

135

Hinaidi I, No.99 Squadron

month to France as a day bomber squadron. As a unit of No.41 Wing, it became part of the Independent Force on its formation in June and took part in attacks on German industrial targets for the rest of the war. Re-equipment with D.H.9As began in September 1918 and these were taken to India in May 1919 where the squadron was renumbered 27 Squadron on 1 April 1920.

On 1 April 1924, No.99 reformed at Netheravon with Vimys, moving two months later to Bircham Newton where it re-equipped with Aldershots. These large single-engined bombers were replaced by Hyderabads at the end of 1925 and by its development, the Hinaidi, over a period of fifteen months from October 1929. Heyfords began to arrive in November 1933 and were flown until the squadron converted to Wellingtons in October 1938. Leaflet-dropping flights were made over Germany from September 1939 and bombing raids began with the German invasion of Norway in April 1940. These continued until 14 January 1942 when the squadron ceased operations in the UK and left for India. After being split up for a period, No.99 reassembled at Ambala on 6 June 1942 and began night bombing raids on Japanese bases in Burma in November. In September 1944, the squadron converted to Liberators for long-range attacks and in July 1945 moved to the Cocos Islands in preparation for the invasion of Malaya. After flying some anti-shipping strikes over the Dutch East Indies the squadron was disbanded

on 15 November 1945.

On 17 November 1945, No.99 reformed at Lyneham with Yorks as a transport squadron and re-equipped with Hastings in August 1949. During the Suez operations, the squadron dropped parachute troops on Port Said from bases in Cyprus and in the summer of 1959 it received Britannias. These were flown on the main routes of Transport Command and its successor, Air Support Command, around the world, until disbandment on 6 January 1976.

Squadron bases			
Yatesbury	15 Aug 1917	Elmdon	9 Sep 1939
Old Sarum	30 Aug 1917	Newmarket	15 Sep 1939
St. Omer	25 Apr 1918	Waterbeach	18 Mar 1941
Tantonville	3 May 1918	Left for India	Feb 1942 (P)
Azelet	5 Jun 1918	Ambala	6 Jun 1942 (G)
Auxi-le-Chateau	16 Nov 1918	Pandaveswar	19 Sep 1942
St. André-aux-Bois	Nov 1918	Digri	25 Oct 1942
Aulnoye	Dec 1918	Chaklala	12 Apr 1943
Left for India	May 1919	Jessore	23 May 1943
Ambala	15 Jun 1919	Dhubalia	26 Sep 1944
Mianwali	30 Sep 1919	Left for Cocos Is.	
	to 1 Apr 1920		14 Jul 1945 (G)
Netheravon	1 Apr 1924	Cocos Island	29 Jul 1945
Bircham Newton	31 May 1924		to 15 Nov 1945
Upper Heyford	5 Jan 1928	Lyneham	17 Nov 1947
Mildenhall	15 Nov 1934	Brize Norton	16 Jun 1970
			to 6 Jan 1976

Aircraft Equipment	Period of service	Representative Serial and Code
D.H.6	Aug 1917 – Apr 1918	
B.E.2e	Aug 1917 – Apr 1918	
D.H.9	Apr 1918 – Nov 1918	B9366 (Y)
D.H.9A	Sep 1918 – Apr 1920	E8560
Vimy	Apr 1924 – Dec 1924	
Aldershot	Aug 1924 – Dec 1925	J6956 (4)
Hyderabad	Dec 1925 – Jan 1931	J9032 (R)
Hinaidi	Oct 1929 – Mar 1934	K1075 (Y)
Andover	May 1926	J7263
Heyford I, IA, II, III	Nov 1933 – Oct 1938	K3494 (O)
Wellington I, IA, IC	Oct 1938 – Oct 1942	T2501 (LN-F)
Wellington III	Oct 1942 – Nov 1943	HD977
Wellington X	Jun 1943 – Sep 1944	JA467 (U)
Wellington XVI	Oct 1943 – Dec 1943	HZ400
Liberator VI	Sep 1944 – Nov 1945	KG976 (L)
York C.1	Nov 1947 – Aug 1949	MW294 (AF)
Hastings C.1, C.2	Aug 1949 – Jan 1959	WD476 (JAK)
Britannia C.1, C.2	Jun 1959 – Jan 1976	XL637 'Vega'

No. 100 Squadron

Badge: In front of two human bones in saltire, a skull
Motto: Sarang tebuan jangan dijolok (Malay) (Never stir up a hornet's nest)

No.100 Squadron was formed at Hingham on 23 February 1917 as a night bomber unit and moved to France with F.E.2bs in March. The squadron was engaged in night raids on German bases behind the lines until May 1918, when it moved to the Nancy area to begin strategic bombing. In August 1918, it re-equipped with Handley Page O/400s and as part of the Independent Force carried out attacks on enemy industrial targets in Germany for the rest of the war. In September 1919 No.100 returned to the UK as a cadre and on 31 January 1920, absorbed the cadres of Nos.117 and 141 Squadrons at Baldonnel to become operational as an army co-operation unit with the local security forces in Ireland. With the formation of the Irish Free State, the

squadron returned to the UK and became a day bomber squadron. In May 1924 it re-equipped with Fawns and in 1926 with Horsleys. In November 1930, No.100 moved to Scotland to become a torpedo-bomber squadron and began to receive Vildebeests in November 1932. A requirement for torpedo-bomber squadrons for the defence of Singapore resulted in No.100 leaving for the Far East in December 1933. Re-equipment with Australian-built Beauforts was scheduled for the end of 1941 but these failed to materialise before the Japanese attack on Malaya began in December 1941. After attacks on Japanese landing ships and columns, most of the squadron's aircraft had been lost by the time the remnants merged with No.36's Vildebeests in February 1942.

On 15 December 1942 No.100 reformed at Grimsby as a heavy bomber squadron in No.1 Group. Equipped with Lancasters, it took part in Bomber Command's strategic bombing offensive against Germany until the end of the war and was retained as part of the peace-time RAF. In May 1946 the squadron converted to Lincolns which were taken to Malaya in June 1950 to carry out attacks on terrorist camps in the jungle for six months. In January 1954 it arrived in Kenya for two months during the Mau Mau uprising and in April 1954, converted to Canberras which it flew until disbanded on 1 September 1959.

Vildebeest II, No.100 Squadron

On 1 May 1962 No.100 reformed at Wittering with Victors as part of the V-bomber force, disbanding on 30 September 1968. On 1 February 1972, the squadron reformed at West Raynham with Canberras for target facilities duties.

Squadron bases

Hingham	23 Feb 1917	Bicester	10 Jan 1928
Farnborough	Feb 1917	Weston Zoyland	14 Apr 1928
St. André-aux-Bois	Mar 1917	Bicester	19 May 1928
Izel-le-Hameau	21 Mar 1917	Donibristle	3 Nov 1930
Treizennes	10 May 1917	Gosport	3 Jun 1932
Ochey	11 Oct 1917	Catfoss	15 Jul 1932
Villeseneux	1 Apr 1918	Donibristle	27 Aug 1932
Ochey	9 May 1918	Gosport	8 Jun 1933
Xaffévillers	10 Aug 1918	Donibristle	30 Jun 1933
Ligescourt	18 Dec 1918	Left for Far East	7 Dec 1933
St. Inglevert	Jun 1918	Seletar	5 Jan 1934
To UK as cadre	Sep 1919		to Feb 1942
Baldonnel	31 Jan 1920	Grimsby	15 Dec 1942
Spittlegate	4 Feb 1922	Elsham Wolds	1 Apr 1945
Eastchurch	May 1924	Scampton	3 Dec 1945
Spittlegate	Jul 1924	Lindholme	May 1946
Weston Zoyland	17 Jun 1926	Hemswell	Oct 1946
Spittlegate	30 Aug 1926	Waddington	26 Mar 1950

Tengah	Jun 1950	Wittering	Mar 1954
Waddington	8 Dec 1950		to 1 Sep 1959
Shallufa	21 May 1952	Wittering	1 May 1962
Waddington	16 Aug 1952		to 30 Sep 1968
Wittering	1 Aug 1953	West Raynham	1 Feb 1972
Eastleigh	Jan 1954	Marham	Jan 1976

Aircraft

Equipment	Period of service	Representative Serial and Code	
F.E.2b, B.E.2d	Feb 1917 — Aug 1918	A852	
Handley Page O/400	Aug 1918 — Sep 1919	D8302	
Bristol F.2b	Jan 1920 — Mar 1922		
D.H.9A	Mar 1922 — May 1924	J7081	
Vimy	Mar 1922 — May 1924		
Fawn	May 1924 — Dec 1926	J7209	(3)
Horsley II, III	Sep 1926 — Apr 1933	J8003	(1)
Vildebeest I	Nov 1932 — Aug 1933	S1708	
Vildebeest II	Aug 1933 — Dec 1941	K4166	(S)
Vildebeest III	Jan 1934 — Feb 1942	K6384	(RA-T)
Lancaster I, III	Jan 1943 — May 1946	EE180	(HW-D)
Lincoln B.2	May 1946 — Apr 1954	RF472	(HW-B)
Canberra B.2	Apr 1954 — Sep 1959	WJ822	
Canberra B.6	Aug 1954 — Sep 1959	WH945	
Victor B.2	May 1962 — Sep 1968	XM717	
Canberra B.2, E.15, T.19			
	Feb 1972 — date	WH972	(X)

No. 101 Squadron

Badge: Issuant from the battlements of a tower, a demi-lion rampant guardant
Motto: Mens agitat molem (Mind over matter)

No.101 Squadron was formed on 12 July 1917 at Farnborough as a night bomber squadron, moving to France two weeks later. For the rest of the war, it took part in night raids on enemy camps, communications, dumps and airfields in northern France and Belgium. In March 1919 it was reduced to a cadre and returned to the UK where it was disbanded on 31 December 1919.

On 21 March 1928 No.101 reformed at Bircham Newton and after flying D.H.9As for a year began to receive Sidestrands. The squadron was for almost eight years the only squadron in the RAF operating twin-engined day bombers, being re-equipped with Overstrands in 1935. In June 1938 the squadron converted to Blenheims, re-equipment being complete by the end of August. After the outbreak of war, No.101 was engaged in training, its first bombing raid not being made until 4 July 1940. Targets were mainly barge concentrations in the Channel ports at night and in April 1941, the squadron received Wellingtons and began to take part in Bomber Command's night raids on Germany in June. In addition to bombing, No.101 was one of the squadrons engaged in counter-measures duties, in this case apparatus

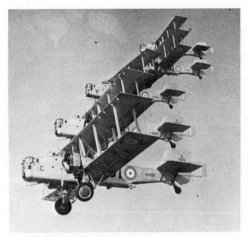

Overstrand Is, No.101 Squadron

the first RAF squadron to receive Canberras and these formed its equipment until disbandment on 1 February 1957.

On 15 October 1957 No.101 reformed at Finningley as a V-bomber squadron, receiving Vulcans in January 1958.

Squadron bases			
Farnborough	12 Jul 1917	Filton	16 Mar 1919
St. André-aux-Bois	25 Jul 1917		to 31 Dec 1919
Izel-le-Hameau	7 Aug 1917	Bircham Newton	21 Mar 1928
Clairmarais	31 Aug 1917	Andover	10 Oct 1929
Auchel	2 Feb 1918	Bicester	1 Dec 1934
Catigny	16 Feb 1918	West Raynham	6 May 1939
Fienvillers	24 Mar 1918	Oakington	1 Jul 1941
Haute Visée	25 Mar 1918	Bourn	11 Feb 1942
Famechon	7 Apr 1918	Stradishall	11 Aug 1942
La Houssoye	8 Oct 1918	Holme-in-Spalding Moor	
Proyart East	8 Oct 1918		29 Sep 1942
Hancourt	25 Oct 1918	Ludford Magna	15 Jun 1943
Catillon	12 Nov 1918	Binbrook	1 Oct 1945
Stree	29 Nov 1918		to 1 Feb 1957
Morville	13 Dec 1918	Finningley	15 Oct 1957
		Waddington	26 Jun 1961

Aircraft Equipment	Period of service	Representative Serial and Code	
F.E.2b, F.E.2d	Jul 1917 – Mar 1919	A5522	
D.H.9A	Nov 1928 – Jun 1929		
Sidestrand	Mar 1929 – Jul 1936	J9769	(101-G)
Overstrand	Jan 1935 – Aug 1938	K4561	(101-U)
Blenheim I	Jun 1938 – Apr 1939	L1118	
Blenheim IV	Apr 1939 – May 1941	V5493	(SR-G)
Wellington IC	Apr 1941 – Feb 1942	R1699	(SR-D)
Wellington III	Feb 1942 – Oct 1942	BJ590	(SR-H)
Lancaster I, III	Oct 1942 – Aug 1946	NG128	(SR-B)
Lincoln B.2	Aug 1946 – Jun 1951	RF362	(SR-D)
Canberra B.2	May 1951 – Jun 1954	WH948	
Canberra B.6	Jun 1954 – Feb 1957	WJ761	
Vulcan B.1, B.1A	Jan 1958 – Jan 1968	XA912	
Vulcan B.2	Jan 1968 – date	XM610	

being carried to jam enemy radio frequencies. German-speaking operators were carried in each crew to use this equipment (code-named 'ABC' or 'Airborne Cigar'). The peak of this activity came on D-Day when twenty-one aircraft were despatched to jam enemy radio signals and prevent interference by night fighters with the airborne assault. In October 1942 the squadron had converted to Lancasters which were flown for the rest of the war. They were replaced by Lincolns in August 1946. In May 1951 No.101 became

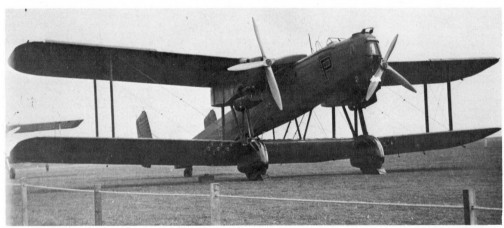

Heyford II, No.102 Squadron

No. 102 Squadron

Badge: On a demi-terrestrial globe a lion rampant guardant holding in the forepaws a bomb
Motto: Tentate et perficite (Attempt and achieve)
Name: 'Ceylon'

No.102 Squadron was formed at Hingham in August 1917 as a night bomber squadron with F.E.2bs and F.E.2ds and

in September moved to France where it began a series of night raids on enemy supply bases, railways and airfields behind the German front in northern France. In March 1919 the squadron returned to the UK and was disbanded on 3 July 1919.

On 1 October 1935, B Flight of No.7 Squadron at Worthy Down was renumbered 102 Squadron and on 13 March 1936 became an independent unit. In July 1936, the original batch of Heyford IIs was supplemented by Heyford IIIs and in September the squadron moved to its newly-built base at Finningley. On 14 June 1937, B Flight was detached to form No.77 Squadron and in October 1938 No.102 began to receive Whitleys which it took into action during the opening

138

years of World War Two. Leaflet-dropping raids over Germany began on the day after war was declared but it was not until the German invasion of Norway that bombing operations got under way. In September 1940 the squadron was loaned to Coastal Command for convoy escort duties from Prestwick for six weeks before resuming bombing raids and in December 1941 the first Halifaxes were received, the last Whitley operation being flown on 31 January 1942. Due to conversion problems and teething troubles with the Halifax, their first operations were not flown until 14 April 1942 and in May 1944 the Mark IIs were replaced by Mark IIIs which maintained the squadron's contribution to Bomber Command's strategic bomber offensive until the end of the war. On 8 May 1945, No.102 was transferred to Transport Command and in September moved to Bassingbourn to convert to Liberators for trooping duties to India which began in January 1946, but on 28 February 1946 the squadron was disbanded.

On 20 October 1954, No.102 reformed at Gutersloh with Canberras as a light bomber unit with Second Tactical Air Force in Germany and on 20 August 1956 was renumbered 59 Squadron. On 1 August 1959 the squadron's number was given to a Thor strategic missile unit at Full Sutton which was disbanded on 27 April 1963.

Canberra B.2, No.102 Squadron

Worthy Down	1 Oct 1935	Topcliffe	7 Jun 1942
Finningley	3 Sep 1936	Pocklington	7 Aug 1942
Honington	7 Jul 1937	Bassingbourn	8 Sep 1945
Driffield	11 Jul 1938	Upwood	15 Feb 1946
Leeming	25 Aug 1940	Gutersloh	20 Oct 1954
Prestwick	1 Sep 1940		to 20 Aug 1956
Linton-on-Ouse	10 Oct 1940	Full Sutton	1 Aug 1959
Topcliffe	15 Nov 1940		to 27 Apr 1963
Dalton	15 Nov 1941		

Aircraft

Equipment	Period of service	Representative Serial and Code
F.E.2b, F.E.2d	Aug 1917 – Jul 1919	B486
Heyford II, III	Oct 1935 – Oct 1938	K4870 (K)
Whitley III	Oct 1938 – Jan 1940	K8945 (V)
Whitley V	Nov 1939 – Feb 1942	N1370 (J)
Halifax II	Dec 1941 – May 1944	JD276 (Z)
Halifax III, IIIA	May 1944 – Sep 1945	MZ504 (Y)
Halifax VI	Jul 1945 – Sep 1945	RG502 (Q)
Liberator VI, VIII	Sep 1945 – Feb 1946	KN742
Canberra B.2	Oct 1954 – Aug 1956	WK146
Thor	Aug 1959 – Apr 1963	—

Squadron bases

Hingham	Aug 1917	Famechon	19 Sep 1918
St. André aux Bois	24 Sep 1917	Hurlebise Farm	19 Oct 1918
Izel-le-Hameau	28 Sep 1917	La Targette	23 Oct 1918
Treizennes	3 Oct 1917	Bevillers	27 Oct 1918
Izel-le-Hameau	5 Mar 1918	Serny	14 Dec 1918
Surcamps	10 Apr 1918	Lympne	Mar 1919
			to 3 Jul 1919

Whirlwind HC.10, No.103 Squadron

No. 103 Squadron

Badge: A swan, wings elevated and addorsed
Motto: Nili me tangere (Touch me not)

No.103 Squadron was formed at Beaulieu on 1 September 1917, as a day bomber unit and moved to France with D.H.9s in May 1919. For the remaining months of the war, it was engaged in bombing raids on enemy supply bases, airfields and communications behind the Western Front. In March 1919 it returned to the UK as a cadre and was disbanded on 1 October 1919.

On 10 August 1936, No.103 reformed at Andover with Hind light bombers and in February 1938 moved to Usworth where it received its first Battle on 18 July 1938, followed by its operational aircraft during August before transferring its base to Abingdon. Earmarked for the Advanced Air Striking Force, the squadron moved to its war base in France the day before the outbreak of World War Two, where it flew reconnaissance missions during the early days of the war. After the German invasion in May 1940, No.103 was forced to move back to central France, taking over No.218 Squadron's Battles on 21 May to bring its strength up to thirty-one aircraft. By the time it was withdrawn to Brittany only sixteen were left and only half that number flew back to the UK to reassemble at Honington, the ground crews being evacuated through Brest. For a few months, the squadron's Battles carried out night raids on invasion barges gathering in Channel ports before it re-equipped with Wellingtons and joining the night bombing attacks on Germany from 22 December 1940. In July 1942, conversion to Halifaxes took place but after three months of operations Lancasters were received. These were flown for the rest of the war as part of the main force of Bomber Command and on 26 November 1945 the squadron was re-numbered 57 Squadron.

On 30 November 1954, No.103 Squadron was reformed at Gutersloh as part of No.551 Wing in Germany but disbanded again on 1 August 1956. On 1 August 1959, No.284 Squadron at Nicosia was renumbered 103 Squadron for rescue and army support duties in Cyprus and Libya but became Nos.1563 and 1564 Flights on 31 July 1963.

On 1 August 1963, B Flight of No.110 Squadron was redesignated 103 Squadron at Seletar and its helicopters were engaged in search and rescue operations in addition to transport support for the ground forces in Malaya and Borneo until disbandment on 31 July 1975.

Squadron bases

Beaulieu	1 Sep 1917	Rheges/St. Lucien Ferme	16 May 1940
Old Sarum	8 Sep 1917	Ozouer-le-Doyen	4 Jun 1940
Serny	12 May 1918	Souge	14 Jun 1940
Floringham	21 Oct 1918	Abingdon	15 Jun 1940 (A)
Ronchin	26 Oct 1918	Honington	16 Jun 1940
Maisoncelle	25 Jan 1919	Newton	3 Jul 1940
Shotwick	26 Mar 1919	Elsham Wolds	11 Jul 1941
	to 1 Oct 1919		to 26 Nov 1945
Andover	10 Aug 1936	Gutersloh	30 Nov 1954
Usworth	26 Feb 1937		to 1 Aug 1956
Abingdon	2 Sep 1938	Nicosia	1 Aug 1959
Benson	1 Apr 1939		to 31 Jul 1963
Challerange	2 Sep 1939	Seletar	1 Aug 1963
Plivot	28 Nov 1939	Changi	Mar 1969
Betheniville	15 Feb 1940	Tengah	Oct 1971
			to 31 Jul 1975

Aircraft Equipment

	Period of service	Representative Serial and Code
Various	Sep 1917 – Dec 1917	–
D.H.9	Dec 1917 – Oct 1919	D3046
Hind	Aug 1936 – Aug 1938	K5557
Battle	Aug 1938 – Oct 1940	L5010 (PM-C)
Wellington IC	Oct 1940 – Jul 1942	R1234 (PM-A)
Halifax II	Jul 1942 – Nov 1942	W1212 (PM-P)
Lancaster I, III	Nov 1942 – Nov 1945	LM132 (PM-I)
Canberra B.2	Nov 1954 – Aug 1956	WJ677
Sycamore HR.14	Aug 1959 – Jul 1963	XL820
Whirlwind HAR.10	Aug 1963 – Nov 1972	XR482
Wessex HC.2	Nov 1972 – Jul 1975	XT680 (E)

No. 104 Squadron

Badge: A thunderbolt
Motto: Strike hard

Liberator VI, No 104 Squadron

No.104 Squadron was formed at Wyton on 4 September 1917, as a light bomber unit and moved to Andover soon afterwards for bombing training. In May 1918 it became operational and moved to France to join the Independent Force which had been formed for the purpose of attacking strategic targets in Germany. Most of the D.H.9's targets were in the Saar industrial area due to its relatively short range. At the end of the war the squadron was preparing to take twin-engined D.H.10s into action but the Armistice prevented this. In February 1919 it returned to the UK and disbanded on 30 June 1919.

On 7 January 1936, No.104 reformed at Abingdon from C Flight of No.40 Squadron and remained attached to the latter squadron until 1 July 1936, when it became independent. In May 1938, it moved to the new airfield at Bassingbourn and re-equipped with Blenheims but on the outbreak of war was designated a Group Training Squadron in No.6 Group and spent the next six months training Blenheim crews, including some for the Finnish Air Force. On 8 April 1940 the squadron merged with No.108 Squadron to form No.13 Operational Training Unit.

On 1 April 1941 No.104 reformed at Driffield as a night bomber squadron with Wellingtons and flew its first operation on 9 May. In mid-October, fifteen of the squadron's aircraft left for Malta where they carried out attacks on targets in Libya, Sicily and Italy before moving on to Egypt early in January 1942. The ground echelon arrived in Egypt later in the month and the squadron was notified that it was now No.158 Squadron but on 31 January it reverted to being

No.104 while the UK echelon still operating from Driffield became No.158 Squadron on 14 February 1942.

Night bombing attacks on enemy bases in support of the campaign in the Western Desert occupied the squadron until the German retreat to Tunisia when No.104 moved westwards to captured fields in Tripolitania and southern Tunisia. After the enemy surrender in North Africa, the Wellingtons continued to attack Italian targets from Tunisia until December 1943, when the squadron moved to southern Italy for the rest of the war, its raids ranging over the Balkans and northern Italy. In February 1945 conversion to Liberators began, the last Wellington operation being flown on 27 February. In October 1945 No.104 moved to Egypt where it re-equipped with Lancasters and flew these until disbanded on 1 April 1947.

On 15 March 1955 No.104 reformed at Gutersloh as a Canberra light bomber squadron in No.551 Wing but disbanded on 1 August 1956. It reformed on 22 July 1959 at Ludford Magna as a Thor strategic missile unit and disbanded on 24 May 1963.

Squadron bases

Wyton	4 Sep 1917	Hucknall	21 Aug 1936
Andover	16 Sep 1917	Bassingbourn	2 May 1938
St. Omer	19 May 1918	Bicester	18 Sep 1938
Azelot	20 May 1918		to 8 Apr 1940
Maisoncelle	20 Nov 1918	Driffield	1 Apr 1941
Turnhouse	1 Feb 1919		to 14 Feb 1942
Crail	3 Mar 1919	Luqa (D)	18 Oct 1941
	to 30 Jun 1919	Kabrit	3 Jan 1942 (A)
Abingdon	7 Jan 1936		14 Jan 1942 (G)
		LG.106	19 May 1942

Lancaster B.7, No.104 Squadron

Kabrit	26 Jun 1942	Oudna	18 Nov 1943
Luqa (D)	6 Nov 1942	Cerignola	14 Dec 1943 (G)
	to 21 Jan 1943		20 Dec 1943 (A)
LG.224	7 Nov 1942	Foggia Main	30 Dec 1943
LG.104	12 Nov 1942	Abu Sueir	20 Oct 1945
LG.237	27 Nov 1942	Shallufa	Jul 1946 (P)
Soluch	6 Feb 1943 (A)		to 1 Apr 1947
	12 Feb 1943 (G)	Gutersloh	15 Mar 1955
Gardabia Main	14 Feb 1943		to 1 Aug 1956
Kairouan/Cheria	27 May 1943	Ludford Magna	22 Jul 1959
Hani West	24 Jun 1943		to 24 May 1963

Aircraft Equipment	Period of service	Representative Serial and Code
D.H.9	Sep 1917 – Feb 1919	D487
D.H.10	Nov 1918 – Feb 1919	
Hind	Jan 1936 – May 1938	K4646
Blenheim I	May 1938 – Apr 1940	L1185
Blenheim IV	Oct 1939 – Apr 1940	P6921
Anson I	Sep 1939 – Apr 1940	N5114
Wellington II	Apr 1941 – Jul 1943	W5437 (Q)
Wellington X	Jul 1943 – Mar 1945	LN272 (Z)
Liberator VI	Feb 1945 – Nov 1945	KL373 (U)
Lancaster VII	Nov 1945 – Apr 1947	NX729 (P)
Canberra B.2	Mar 1955 – Aug 1956	WJ658
Thor	Jul 1959 – May 1963	–

No. 105 Squadron

Badge: A battle axe
Motto: Fortis in proeliis (Valiant
in battles)

No.105 Squadron was formed at Andover on 14 September 1917, as a day bomber unit but was later reclassified as a corps reconnaissance squadron and received R.E.8s in April 1918. Instead of moving to France, the squadron was sent to Ireland in May 1918 to support army units there. In December 1918 it re-equipped with Bristol Fighters and was disbanded on 1 February 1920.

On 12 April 1937, No.105 reformed from B Flight of No.18 Squadron at Upper Heyford with Audaxes as interim equipment. In August 1937 Battles began to arrive and these

Blenheim IV, No.105 Squadron

were taken to France in September 1939 as part of the Advanced Air Striking Force based around Reims. During the German offensive in May 1940, the squadron was engaged in attacking German ground forces until forced to withdraw to the UK. It re-equipped with Blenheims and began attacks on enemy-occupied ports and airfields in northern France and the Low Countries until July 1941, when No.105's Blenheims flew out to Malta to attack enemy ports and shipping. At the end of September, the remaining crews returned and in November the squadron received its first Mosquito, being the first unit to receive this type. After intensive training, operations began in May 1942, mainly low-level daylight attacks. In June 1943 it was transferred to No.8 Group for pathfinder duties using 'Oboe' radar to mark targets for the main force of Bomber Command. The squadron retained this role until the end of the war and disbanded on 1 February 1946.

On 21 February 1962 No.105 reformed at Benson with Argosy transports and flew these out to Aden in June to provide transport support for the army in the Aden Protectorate. In August 1967 it moved to Bahrain where it was disbanded on 20 January 1968.

Squadron bases			
Andover	14 Sep 1917	Watton	10 Jul 1940
Omagh	May 1918	Swanton Morley	31 Oct 1940
Oranmore	Jul 1919	Luqa (A)	28 Jul 1941
	to 1 Feb 1920		to 11 Oct 1942
Upper Heyford	12 Apr 1937	Horsham St. Faith	8 Dec 1941
Harwell	26 Apr 1937	Marham	28 Sep 1942
Reims/Champagne	3 Sep 1939	Bourn	23 Mar 1944
Villeneuve-les-Vertus		Upwood	29 Jun 1945
	12 Sep 1939		to 1 Feb 1946
Echemines	16 May 1940	Benson	21 Feb 1962
Nantes/Bougenais	22 May 1940	Khormaksar	17 Jun 1962
Honington	14 Jun 1940	Muharraq	6 Aug 1967
			to 20 Jan 1968

Aircraft Equipment	Period of service	Representative Serial and Code
D.H.6, B.E.2b, B.E.2d, D.H.9	Sep 1917 – Apr 1918	–
R.E.8	Apr 1918 – Dec 1918	
Bristol F.2b	Dec 1918 – Feb 1920	
Audax	Apr 1937 – Oct 1937	K7438
Battle	Aug 1937 – Jun 1940	K7578 (GB-F)
Blenheim IV	Jun 1940 – May 1942	V6014 (GB-J)
Mosquito IV	Nov 1941 – Mar 1944	DZ518 (GB-A)
Mosquito IX	Jul 1943 – Feb 1946	ML913 (GB-A)
Mosquito XVI	Mar 1944 – Feb 1946	MM134
Argosy C.1	Jun 1962 – Jan 1968	XP410

Hampden I, No.106 Squadron

No. 106 Squadron

Badge: A lion sejant rampant, holding a banner charged with an astral crown
Motto: Pro libertate (For Freedom)

No.106 Squadron was formed at Andover on 30 September 1917 as a corps reconnaissance unit equipped with R.E.8s. In May 1918 it moved to Ireland where it remained until disbanded on 8 October 1919.

No.106 reformed at Abingdon on 1 June 1938 from a flight of No.15 Squadron with Hinds and during July received Battles. By the end of September it was up to strength and in May 1939 converted to Hampdens. For the first year of World War Two the squadron was engaged in operational training but in September 1940, minelaying trips began and soon it was fully engaged in bombing raids on Germany. In February 1942 Manchesters began to arrive but were replaced by Lancasters in June and it was with the latter that No.106 continued its part in the strategic bomber offensive against Germany until the end of the war. In September 1945 it began transport duties, mainly to Italy, and was disbanded on 18 February 1946. On 22 July 1959 No.106 reformed at Bardney as a Thor unit, disbanding on 24 May 1963.

Squadron bases			
Andover	30 Sep 1917	Cottesmore	1 Sep 1939
Fermoy	20 May 1918	Finningley	6 Oct 1939
	to 8 Oct 1919	Coningsby	23 Feb 1941
Abingdon	1 Jun 1938	Syerston	1 Oct 1942
Thornaby	1 Sep 1938	Metheringham	11 Nov 1943
Grantham	26 Sep 1938		to 18 Feb 1946
Thornaby	14 Oct 1938	Bardney	22 Jul 1959
Evanton	19 Aug 1939		to 24 May 1963

Aircraft Equipment	Period of service	Representative Serial and Code
R.E.8	Sep 1917 – Oct 1919	
Hind	Jun 1938 – Jul 1939	K6760
Battle	Jul 1938 – Jun 1939	K7600
Hampden I	May 1939 – Mar 1942	P1320 ZM-B
Anson I	May 1939 – Sep 1939	N5165 XS-X
Manchester I	Feb 1942 – Jun 1942	L7417 ZM-V
Lancaster I, III	May 1942 – Feb 1946	NN726 ZM-D
Thor	Jul 1959 – May 1963	–

No. 107 Squadron

Badge: A double-headed eagle displayed, gorged with a collar of fleur-de-lys.
Motto: Nous y serons (French) (We shall be there)

No.107 Squadron was formed at Lake Down on 15 May 1918 as a day bomber squadron equipped with D.H.9s and moved to France early in June. Attacks on enemy communications, airfields and base areas began and continued till the end of the war. In March 1919 the squadron returned to the UK where it disbanded on 30 June 1919.

On 10 August 1936 it reformed at Andover as a light bomber squadron and received Hinds. These were replaced by Blenheims in August 1938 and on the day following the outbreak of World War Two No.107 took part in the first

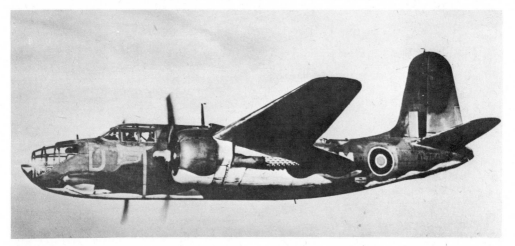

Boston III, No.107 Squadron

attack on German warships at Wilhelmshaven. In April 1940 it carried out attacks on German forces involved in the invasion of Norway and after the enemy assault on France and the Low Countries was engaged in raids on enemy columns and communications. Invasion barges in the Channel ports became the next target but in March 1941 the squadron was transferred to Coastal Command for two months to carry out anti-submarines patrols and attacks on enemy shipping from Scotland. Returning to Bomber Command, the squadron's aircraft flew out to Malta at the end of August 1941 for attacks on Italy, Sicily, North Africa and enemy shipping. These continued until 9 January 1942 when the detachment was withdrawn from operations and disbanded on 12 January.

The remaining ground personnel at Great Massingham were supplemented by Bostons and crews in January 1942 and in March attacks on airfields, railway yards and ports were resumed. In February 1944 Mosquitos were received. Night intruder missions became the squadron's main role and continued after a move to the Continent in November 1944. In November 1945 No.107 moved to Germany and formed part of the occupation forces until renumbered 11 Squadron on 4 October 1948.

On 22 July 1959, C Flight of No.77 Squadron was redesignated No.107 Squadron at the Thor intermediate range ballistic missile base at Tuddenham. On 10 July 1963 the squadron was disbanded.

Squadron bases		Moislains	26 Oct 1918
Lake Down	15 May 1918	Bavay	22 Nov 1918
Le Quesnoy	5 Jun 1918	Franc Waret	15 Dec 1918
Drionville	25 Jun 1918	Nivelles	21 Dec 1918
Le Quesnoy	2 Jul 1918	Maubeuge	8 Jan 1919
Chailly-en-Brie	15 Jul 1918	Hounslow	17 Mar 1919
Ecoivres	3 Aug 1918		to 30 Jun 1919

Andover	10 Aug 1936	Hartfordbridge	30 Oct 1944
Old Sarum	25 Feb 1937	A.75 Cambrai/Epinoy	
Harwell	14 Jun 1937		19 Nov 1944
Scampton	3 Aug 1938	Fersfield	3 Jul 1945
Harwell	8 Aug 1938	A.75 Cambrai/Epinoy	
Wattisham	11 May 1939		10 Jul 1945
Leuchars	3 Mar 1941	B.58 Melsbroek	19 Jul 1945
Great Massington	11 May 1941	Y.99 Gutersloh	3 Nov 1945
Luqa	20 Aug 1941	Wahn	13 Nov 1947
	to 12 Jan 1942 (A)		to 4 Oct 1948
Hartfordbridge	1 Aug 1943	Tuddenham	22 Jul 1959
Lasham	3 Feb 1944		to 10 Jul 1963

Aircraft Equipment	Period of service	Representative Serial and Code
D.H.9	May 1918 — Jun 1919	D1111
Hind	Sep 1936 — Sep 1938	K6692
Blenheim I	Aug 1938 — May 1939	L1290
Blenheim IV	May 1939 — Jan 1942	R3816 (OM-J)
Boston III, IIIa	Jan 1942 — Feb 1944	BZ371 (OM-S)
Mosquito VI	Feb 1944 — Oct 1948	MM411 (OM-V)
Thor	Jul 1959 — Jul 1963	—

Mosquito FB.6, No.107 Squadron

No. 108 Squadron

Badge: An oak leaf
Motto: Viribus contractis (With gathering strength)

No.108 Squadron was formed at Stonehenge on 11 November 1917 as a day bomber unit and moved to France in July 1918, equipped with D.H.9s. Operations began on 12 August and for the rest of the war the squadron was engaged in bombing enemy bases in Belgium. In February 1919, it returned to the UK and was disbanded on 3 July 1919.

On 4 January 1937 No.108 reformed at Upper Heyford from B Flight, No.57 Squadron. In June 1938, its Hinds were replaced by Blenheims but on the outbreak of war the squadron was allotted a training role and gave advanced

Liberator II, No.108 Squadron

training to aircrews for other No.2 Group squadrons until it joined No.104 Squadron to form No.13 OTU on 8 April 1940.

On 1 August 1941, No.108 reformed at Kabrit as a night bomber squadron. Its Wellingtons began bombing raids on 22 September, targets being ports on the Libyan coast and in Greece. In November it began to receive Liberators and these supplemented the Wellingtons until June 1942, when they were withdrawn after flying bombing and supply-dropping missions over the Balkans. In November 1942 all aircrews were posted to other Wellington squadrons and the remaining personnel operated the Liberators of the Special Operations (Liberator) Flight until reduced to a cadre on 18 December which disbanded on 25 December 1942.

On 15 March 1943 No.108 reformed at Shandur from a nucleus supplied by No.89 Squadron as a night fighter squadron. Its Beaufighters flew night patrols over Egypt, Libya and Malta and were supplemented by Mosquitos in February 1944. The latter were used for intruder missions until withdrawn in July while the Beaufighters moved back to Libya for intruder operations over Greece and the Aegean. The German retirement from Greece resulted in No.108 arriving there during October 1944, becoming involved in the attempted Communist take-over of the country in December. After taking part in attacks on rebel positions until the uprising was quelled, the squadron gave up its aircraft and sailed for Italy in March 1945, disbanding on 28 March 1945.

Squadron bases

Stonehenge	11 Nov 1917	Fayid	12 Sep 1941
Lake Down	2 Dec 1917	LG.105	20 May 1941
Kenley	14 Jun 1918	Kabrit	26 Jun 1942
Capelle	22 Jul 1918	LG.237	19 Aug 1942
Bisseghem	24 Oct 1918	LG.106	13 Nov 1942
Gondecourt	16 Nov 1918	LG.237	27 Nov 1942
Lympne	16 Feb 1919		to 25 Dec 1942
	to 3 Jul 1919	Shandur	15 Mar 1943
Upper Heyford	4 Jan 1937	Bersis	5 May 1943
Farnborough	19 Feb 1937	Luqa	3 Jun 1943
Cranfield	7 Jul 1937	Hal Far	1 Jul 1944
Bassingbourn	2 May 1938	Idku	27 Jul 1944
Bicester	17 Sep 1938	Hassani	22 Oct 1944
	to 7 Apr 1940	Left for Italy	2 Mar 1945
Kabrit	1 Aug 1941	Disbanded	28 Mar 1945

Aircraft Equipment

	Period of service	Representative Serial and Code
D.H.9	Nov 1917 – Feb 1919	D602
Hind	Jan 1937 – Jun 1938	K6775
Blenheim I	Jun 1938 – Apr 1940	L1202 (108-J)
Blenheim IV	Oct 1939 – Apr 1940	L8871
Anson I	May 1939 – Apr 1940	N5177
Wellington IC	Aug 1941 – Nov 1942	R1098 (U)
Liberator II	Nov 1941 – Jun 1942 Nov 1942 – Dec 1942	AL566 (P)
Beaufighter VI	Mar 1943 – Feb 1945	KV934 (A)
Mosquito XII	Feb 1944 – Jul 1944	HK178 (S)

No. 109 Squadron

Badge: A panther rampant incensed
Motto: Primi hastati (The first of the legion)

No.109 Squadron was formed as a day bomber squadron during the last year of World War One but remained a training nucleus and was probably one of the squadrons disbanded in July 1918. No records appear to have survived of its activities.

On 10 December 1940, The Wireless Intelligence Development Unit at Boscombe Down became No.109 Squadron. Equipped with Ansons and Wellingtons, it carried out various tasks including identifying enemy methods of using radio

beams and developing radar aids for use by the RAF. The squadron was dispersed in January 1942, its headquarters and the Wireless Development Flight going to Tempsford, the Wireless Reconnaissance Flight to Upper Heyford and the Wireless Investigation Flight remained at Boscombe Down. By April 1943, the squadron had re-assembled at Stradishall where its main pre-occupation was the development of 'Oboe', a navigation aid for use by Bomber Command. Moving to Wyton in August 1943, No.109 became one of the first units of No.8 Group, the Pathfinder Force, and received Mosquitos. Operational flights began on 20 December and on the last night of 1943 it used Oboe to drop target markers accurately on Dusseldorf for the main force of bombers, the first use of this bombing aid. Attacks on Germany continued for the rest of the war and on 30 September, 1945, the squadron was disbanded.

On 1 October, 1945, No.627 Squadron at Woodhall Spa was renumbered 109 Squadron and flew Mosquitos until converted to Canberras in August 1952. During the Suez Campaign, it was based in Cyprus and on 1 February, 1957, was disbanded.

Canberra B.6, No.109 Squadron

Squadron bases

Lake Down Probably	May 1918		to 30 Sep 1945
	to Jul 1918	Woodhall Spa	1 Oct 1945
Boscombe Down	10 Dec 1940	Wickenby	19 Oct 1945
Tempsford	19 Jan 1942	Hemswell	27 Nov 1945
Stradishall	6 Apr 1942	Coningsby	4 Nov 1946
Wyton	6 Aug 1942	Hemswell	Mar 1950
Marham	4 Jul 1943	Binbrook	1 Jan 1956
Little Staughton	2 Apr 1944		to 1 Feb 1957

Aircraft Equipment	Period of service	Representative Serial	
D.H.9	May 1918 — Jul 1918		
Whitley V	Dec 1940 — Jan 1941	P5047	
Anson I	Dec 1940 — Aug 1942	N4953	
Wellington IC	Jan 1941 — Aug 1942	P5047	(ZP-N)
Lancaster I	Aug 1942	R5485	
Mosquito IV	Aug 1942 — Jun 1944	DK331	(HS-D)
Mosquito IX	Jun 1943 — Sep 1945	LR511	(HS-Q)
Mosquito XVI	Mar 1944 — Sep 1945	PF408	(HS-B)
	Oct 1945 — Dec 1948		
Mosquito B.35	Apr 1948 — Jul 1952	VR792	
Canberra B.2	Aug 1952 — Dec 1954	WJ714	
Canberra B.6	Dec 1954 — Jan 1957	WT303	

Whirlwind HC.10s, No.110 Squadron

No. 110 Squadron

Badge: Issuant from an astral crown, a demi-tiger
Motto: Nec timeo nec sperno (I neither fear nor despise)
Name: 'Hyderabad'

No.110 Squadron was formed at Rendcombe on 1 November 1917, as a light bomber unit and spent the winter at Sedgeford in Norfolk, training with a variety of types. In July 1918 it received its operational aircraft, being the first squadron to be equipped with D.H.9As. On 1 September 1918 it arrived at its base in France to form part of the Independent Force and began a series of daylight raids on industrial targets in Germany, mainly in the Saar, which continued until the Armistice. On 27 August 1919 the squadron disbanded after a period of mail-carrying duties.

On 18 May 1937, No.110 reformed at Waddington with Hinds and in January 1938, re-equipped with Blenheims which it flew in the first RAF bombing attacks of World War Two on enemy warships in German ports. In April 1940 it spent a period at Lossiemouth attacking airfields during the German invasion of Norway and providing reconnaissance aircraft. When the Germans invaded the Low Countries the squadron took part in attacks on enemy troops and communications throughout the campaign in France and then began a series of raids on ports in the occupied countries harbouring invasion barges. With the defeat of the Luftwaffe in the Battle of Britain, the squadron turned to airfields and industrial targets for the next eighteen months and in July 1941 provided a detachment in Malta to attack ports and shipping.

In March 1942 the squadron left for India, the aircrew flying out Blenheims for use in South-East Asia. Arriving in mid-May, the squadron had to wait until October before Vengeances became available and it was March 1943 before these could be taken into action on the Burma front. Support for the 14th Army continued until May 1944, when No.110 was withdrawn for conversion to Mosquitos, the first of which arrived in November. In August 1944 a detachment of Vengeances was sent to the Gold Coast for mosquito-spraying experiments and this disbanded in December without rejoining the squadron. On 31 March 1945 the Mosquitos began operations and attacks were made on Japanese bases and communications until the end of the campaign in Burma. In September 1945 the squadron's aircraft moved to Singapore and in October and November it operated in Java. A detachment moved to Labuan in December which was joined by the remainder of the squadron in February but disbandment came soon afterwards on 15 April 1946.

On 15 June 1946, No.110 came into existence again when No.96 Squadron at Kai Tak was renumbered. The squadron's Dakotas were engaged in transport duties in the area till July 1947, when it became temporarily non-operational but in September 1947 it resumed transport missions from Singapore. During the emergency in Malaya, the squadron was engaged in supply-dropping to the army and police forces in the jungle where Communist guerilla forces had begun a major attempt to take over the country and these continued until the guerillas had been driven into jungle hide-outs over the Thai border. In October 1951 re-equipment with Valettas began and the last Dakotas were sent away in April 1952. Transport and courier services continued until the squadron disbanded on 31 December 1957. On 3 June 1959, No.110 was reformed by combining Nos.155 and 194 Squadrons at Kuala Lumpur and renumbering them. Initially the squadron flew Whirlwinds but in April 1960 added Sycamores which had been out of service for a period for technical reasons. It flew both types on supply and transport duties in Malaya and in April 1963 sent a detachment to Brunei which, as the Indonesian guerilla attacks on the Malaysian Federation grew, developed into the whole squadron being involved in operations in Borneo. These continued until November 1967 when the Indonesians gave up and the squadron returned to Singapore. On 15 February, 1971, No.110 was disbanded as part of the run-down of RAF units in the Far East.

Squadron bases

Rendcombe	1 Nov 1917		to 22 Sep 1943
Dover	12 Nov 1917	Kumbhirgram	15 Oct 1943
Sedgeford	Nov 1917	Allahabad (D)	1 Jun 1944
Kenley	15 Jun 1918		to 5 Jun 1944
Bettoncourt	1 Sep 1918	Kalyanpur	5 Jun 1944 (A)
Auxi-le-Chateau	20 Nov 1918	Takoradi (D)	24 Aug 1944
Maisoncelle	30 Nov 1918		to 7 Dec 1944
Marquise	3 Jul 1919	Kolar	6 Oct 1944
	to 27 Aug 1919	Yelahanka	26 Oct 1944
Waddington	18 May 1937	Joari	11 Mar 1945 (A)
Wattisham	11 May 1939		16 Mar 1945 (G)
Lossiemouth (D)	19 Apr 1940	Kinmagan	22 May 1945
	to 2 May 1940	Hmawbi	16 Aug 1945
Horsham St. Faith (D)		Kallang/Seletar (D)	10 Sep 1945
	16 Feb 1941		to Oct 1945
	to 15 Mar 1941	Seletar	Oct 1945
Manston (D)	26 May 1941	Kemajoran (D)	31 Oct 1945
	to 9 Jun 1941		to 22 Nov 1945
Luqa (D)	1 Jul 1941	Labuan	27 Feb 1946
	to 28 Jul 1941		to 15 Apr 1946
Lindholme (D)	15 Sep 1941	Kai Tak	15 Jun 1946
	to 20 Sep 1941	Changi	15 Sep 1947
Lossiemouth (D)	23 Dec 1941	Kuala Lumpur	27 Jun 1948
	to 28 Dec 1941	Changi	20 Nov 1948
Left for India	17 Mar 1942 (G)	Seletar	27 May 1949
Karachi	19 May 1942	Changi	27 Aug 1949
Quetta	5 Jun 1942	Kuala Lumpur	12 Dec 1949
Karachi (D)	6 Sep 1942	Changi (D)	26 May 1950
	to 10 Dec 1942		to 12 Jul 1950
Ondal	11 Oct 1942	Changi	12 Jul 1950
Pandaveswar	31 Oct 1942	Kuala Lumpur	Jul 1951
Madhaiganj	6 Dec 1942	Changi	Oct 1951
Dohazari (D)	17 Mar 1943		to 31 Dec 1957
	to 24 Mar 1943	Kuala Lumpur	3 Jun 1959
Chittagong (D)	12 May 1943	Butterworth	1 Sep 1959
	to 31 May 1943	Seletar	17 Jan 1964
Digri	13 Jun 1943	Kuching	2 Sep 1965
Ranchi (D)	24 Jul 1943	Simanggang	May 1966
	to 16 Aug 1943	Seletar	Nov 1967
Amarda Road (D)	27 Jul 1943	Changi	Mar 1969
			to 15 Feb 1971

Aircraft

Equipment	Period of service	Representative Serial and Code	
B.E.2d, B.E.2e, R.E.8, D.H.6,			
Martinsyde G.100	Nov 1917 − Jul 1918		
D.H.4	Jan 1918 − Jul 1918		
D.H.9	Feb 1918 − Jul 1918		
	Jul 1919 − Aug 1919		
D.H.9A	Jul 1918 − Aug 1919	F995	(E)
Hind	May 1937 − Jan 1938	K6812	
Blenheim I	Jan 1938 − Jun 1939	K7145	
Blenheim IV	Jun 1939 − Mar 1942	Z7285	(VE-U)
Vengeance I, Ia, II	Oct 1942 − Dec 1944	AN862	(B)
Vengeance III, IV	Jun 1944 − Jan 1945	FP686	(R)
Mosquito VI	Nov 1944 − Apr 1946	HR438	(A)
Dakota III, IV	Jun 1946 − Jul 1947	KN586	(L)
	Sep 1947 − Apr 1952	KK114	(R)
Valetta C.1	Oct 1951 − Dec 1957	VW835	
Whirlwind HC.4	Jun 1958 − Jul 1963	XJ410	
Sycamore HR.14	Apr 1960 − Oct 1964	XL822	
Whirlwind HC.10	Jul 1963 − Feb 1971	XR479	

Lightning F.1As, No.111 Squadron

No. 111 Squadron

Badge: In front of two swords in saltire, a cross potent quadrat, charged with three seaxes fessewise in pale

Motto: Adstantes (Standing by)

No.111 Squadron was formed at Deir-el-Belah in Palestine on 1 August 1917 as a fighter squadron to support the army in its offensive against the Turks in Palestine and Syria. Initially it used a variety of types but standardised on Nieuports and S.E.5As at the beginning of 1918, the latter becoming its standard equipment in July. In October the campaign came to an end and the squadron was withdrawn to Egypt where it re-equipped with Bristol Fighters in February 1919. On 1 February 1920 the squadron was re-numbered 14 Squadron.

On 1 October 1923 No.111 reformed at Duxford as a fighter squadron, initially with one flight of Grebes. On 1 April 1924 a second flight of Snipes was added and in January 1925 a third flight with Siskins, which became standard equipment soon afterwards. In January 1931 Bulldogs were received and were replaced in May 1936 with Gauntlets. No.111 became the RAF's first Hurricane squadron in January 1938 and was engaged in defensive duties during the first months of World War Two. During the German invasion of France in May 1940 the squadron operated across the Channel, occasionally using French airfields, followed by a short but busy period providing air cover for the evacuation fleet at Dunkirk. During the first

half of the Battle of Britain it took part in the defence of south-east England, being withdrawn in September to refit in Scotland. In July 1941 it came south again to take part in sweeps over France.

No.111 was allocated to a fighter force destined to accompany the Allied force which was to occupy French North Africa and in November 1942 it. arrived in Algeria to begin fighter patrols over the 1st Army. After the capitulation of the enemy in Tunisia, the squadron moved to Malta to cover the landings in Sicily and later occupied captured airfields there. In September 1943 it moved to Italy- and in July 1944 to Corsica where it provided cover for the Allied landings in southern France in August. Moving into captured airfields, No.111 moved northwards until October when it returned to Italy and was engaged in fighter-bomber missions for the rest of the war. In May 1945 it began occupation duties in Austria and northern Italy, being disbanded on 12 May 1947.

On 2 December 1953 No 111 reformed at North Weald as a fighter squadron with Meteors. In June 1955 these were replaced by Hunters with which the squadron gained international fame as an aerobatic display team. In April 1961 the squadron converted to Lightnings which were flown until the squadron disbanded on 30 September 1974.

On 1 July 1974, a Phantom element began conversion at Coningsby which became 111 Squadron on 1 October 1974.

Squadron bases			
Deir-el-Belah	1 Aug 1917	Hornchurch	1 Apr 1928
Julis	1 Dec 1917	Northolt	12 Jul 1934
Ramleh	29 Mar 1918	Acklington	27 Oct 1939
Kantara	20 Oct 1918	Drem	7 Dec 1939
Ramleh	6 Feb 1919	Wick	27 Feb 1939
	to 1 Feb 1920	Northolt	13 May 1940
Duxford	1 Oct 1923	Digby	21 May 1940
		North Weald	30 May 1940

Croydon 4 Jun 1940
Debden 19 Aug 1940
Croydon 3 Sep 1940
Drem 8 Sep 1940
Dyce 12 Oct 1940
Montrose (Det) 12 Oct 1940
  to 5 Apr 1941
North Weald 20 Jul 1941
Debden 1 Nov 1941
North Weald 15 Dec 1941
Debden 22 Dec 1941
Gravesend 30 Jun 1942
Debden 7 Jul 1942
Kenley 28 Jul 1942
Martlesham Heath 21 Sep 1942
Fowlmere 27 Sep 1942
Emb. for Gibraltar
  20 Oct 1942 (A)
Gibraltar 6 Nov 1942 (A)
Maison Blanche
  11 Nov 1942 (A)
Bone 14 Nov 1942 (A)
  30 Nov 1942 (G)
Souk-el-Arba 3 Dec 1942
Souk-el-Khemis 22 Dec 1942
Protville I 13 May 1943
Mateur 25 May 1943
Safi 10 Jun 1943
Comiso 15 Jul 1943
Pachino South 30 Jul 1943

Panebianco 29 Aug 1943
Cassala 2 Sep 1943
Falcone 6 Sep 1943
Montecorvino 23 Sep 1943
Battipaglia 28 Sep 1943
Capodichino 11 Oct 1943
Lago 15 Jan 1944
Tre Cancelli 5 Jun 1944
Tarquinia 14 Jun 1944
Grosseto 25 Jun 1944
Piombino 5 Jul 1944
Calvi 20 Jul 1944
Ramatuelle 20 Aug 1944
Sisteron 25 Aug 1944
Lyon/Bron 7 Sep 1944
La Jasse 26 Sep 1944
Peretola 2 Oct 1944
Rimini 13 Nov 1944
Ravenna 17 Feb 1945
Rivolto 4 May 1945
Klagenfurt 16 May 1945
Zeltweg 12 Sep 1945
Tissano 23 Sep 1946
Treviso 16 Jan 1947
  to 12 May 1947
North Weald 2 Dec 1953
Wattisham 18 Jun 1958
  to 30 Sep 1974
Coningsby 1 Oct 1974
Leuchars 3 Nov 1975

Aircraft Equipment	Period of service	Representative Serial and Code
Bristol Scout	Aug 1917 – Oct 1917	
Bristol M.1B	Aug 1917 – Jan 1918	A5142
D.H.2	Aug 1917 – Dec 1917	
Vickers F.B.19	Aug 1917 – Jan 1918	A5223 (4)
Bristol F.2b	Sep 1917 – Feb 1918	A7194
S.E.5A	Oct 1917 – Feb 1919	B52
Nieuport 17	Jan 1918 – Jul 1918	B3597
Bristol F.2b	Feb 1919 – Feb 1920	E2288
Grebe II	Oct 1923 – Jan 1925	
Snipe	Apr 1924 – Jan 1925	F2441
Siskin III	Jun 1924 – Nov 1926	J7152
Siskin IIIA	Sep 1926 – Feb 1931	J9193
Bulldog IIA	Jan 1931 – Jun 1936	K1683
Gauntlet II	May 1936 – Feb 1938	K7183
Hurricane I	Jan 1938 – Apr 1941	L1621 (TM-D)
Hurricane IIA	Mar 1941 – May 1941	W9117
Spitfire I	Apr 1941 – May 1941	N3100
Spitfire IIA	May 1941 – Sep 1941	P8428
Spitfire VB	Aug 1941 – Oct 1942	W3450
Spitfire VC	Nov 1942 – Jan 1944	JK329 (JU-S)
Spitfire IXC	Jun 1943 – May 1947	PL168 (JU-A)
Meteor F.8	Dec 1953 – Jun 1955	WL118 (L)
Hunter F.4	Jun 1955 – Nov 1956	WT808 (G)
Hunter F.6	Nov 1956 – Apr 1961	XG203 (H)
Lightning F.1A	Apr 1961 – Feb 1965	XM188 (F)
Lightning F.3	Dec 1964 – Sep 1974	XR713 (C)
Phantom FG.1, FGR.2	Jul 1974 – date	XT873 (A)

Kittyhawk IV, No.112 Squadron

No. 112 Squadron

Badge: A cat sejant
Motto: Swift in destruction

No.112 Squadron was formed on 30 July 1917 as a home defence unit at Throwley for the defence of the London area. Day and night interceptions were flown against enemy bombers operating from bases in Belgium until the end of the war. The squadron was disbanded on 13 June 1919.

On 16 May 1939 No.112 reformed aboard the aircraft carrier *Argus* at Southampton for transportation to the Middle East and arrived in Egypt ten days later. Gladiators were received in June and when Italy entered the war in June 1940, the squadron flew fighter patrols over the Western Desert while a detached flight (K Flight) was operating in the Sudan. The latter was absorbed by No.14 Squadron on 30 June 1940. In January 1941 No.112 moved to Greece to provide air defence and fly offensive patrols over Albania. When the Germans invaded Greece from Bulgaria, the squadron provided fighter cover for the Athens area until evacuated first to Crete and then back to Egypt. In July 1941 No.112 re-equipped with Tomahawks for fighter sweeps over the desert and in May 1942 began fighter-bomber missions. The squadron flew ground-attack operations in support of the 8th Army throughout the campaign in the Western Desert and after the rout of the Axis armies at El Alamein it moved westwards into Tunisia. In July 1943 it moved to Sicily and on to Italy in September. For the rest of the war, it provided air support for the Allied armies in Italy, converting to Mustangs in June 1944. After a period on occupation duties in northern Italy, the squadron disbanded on 30 December 1946.

On 12 May 1951, No.112 reformed at Fassberg as a Vampire fighter-bomber squadron in Germany. It replaced these with Sabres in January 1954, which were flown until Hunters arrived in May 1956. On 31 May 1957 the squadron disbanded.

On 1 August 1960 No.112 reformed at Church Fenton as a Bloodhound ground-to-air missile squadron, later moving to its operational base at Breighton and disbanding on 31 March 1964. On 2 November 1964, No.112 reformed at Woodhall Spa with Bloodhound 2s, moving to Cyprus in October 1967.

Squadron bases

Throwley	30 Jul 1917	Mechili	24 Jan 1942
	to 13 Jun 1919	Gazala	28 Jan 1942
HMS 'Argus'	16 May 1939	El Adem	2 Feb 1942
Helwan	26 May 1939	Gambut Main	17 Feb 1942
Maaten Gerawla	18 Jul 1940	Sidi Haneish	14 Mar 1942
Sidi Barrani	3 Sep 1940	Gambut No.1	14 Apr 1942
Sidi Haneish	7 Sep 1940	Sidi Azeiz	17 Jun 1942
LG.79	4 Dec 1940	Sidi Barrani	18 Jun 1942
Amriya	1 Jan 1941	El Daba	26 Jun 1942
Iannina	24 Jan 1941	Amriya (LG.91)	28 Jun 1942
Paramythia (D)	7 Mar 1941	Amriya (LG.175)	25 Aug 1942
Agrinion	15 Apr 1941	Sidi Haneish	6 Nov 1942
Hassani	16 Apr 1941	Gazala	15 Nov 1942
Heraklion	22 Apr 1941	Martuba	19 Nov 1942
Fayid	31 May 1941	Belandah	6 Dec 1942
Sidi Haneish	12 Sep 1941	Hamraiet	9 Jan 1943
Sidi Barrani	14 Nov 1941	Bir Dufan	19 Jan 1943
Maddalena	19 Nov 1941	Castel Benito	19 Jan 1943
El Adem	19 Dec 1941	El Assa	15 Feb 1943
Msus	21 Dec 1941	Nefatia	8 Mar 1943
Antelat	13 Jan 1942	Medenine	21 Mar 1943
Msus	21 Jan 1942	El Hammam	3 Apr 1943
		El Djem	14 Apr 1943
Kairouan	18 Apr 1943	Lavariano	19 May 1945
Zuara	21 May 1943	Tissano	1 Mar 1946
Safi	9 Jul 1943	Treviso	23 Sep 1946
Pachino	18 Jul 1943	Lavariano	11 Nov 1946
Agnone	2 Aug 1943	Treviso	18 Nov 1946
Grottaglie	15 Sep 1943		to 16 Jan 1947
Brindisi	20 Sep 1943	Fassberg	12 May 1951
Bari	23 Sep 1943	Jever	7 Mar 1952
Foggia	3 Oct 1943	Bruggen	6 Jul 1953
Mileni	26 Oct 1943		to 31 May 1957
Vasto	30 Jan 1944	Church Fenton	1 Aug 1960
San Angelo	23 May 1944	Breighton	7 Nov 1960
Guidonia	13 Jun 1944		to 31 Mar 1964
Falerium	24 Jun 1944	Woodhall Spa	2 Nov 1964
Crete	10 Jul 1944	Episkopi	Oct 1967 (P)
Iesi	25 Aug 1944		
Fano	18 Nov 1944		
Cervia	25 Feb 1945		

Aircraft Equipment

Equipment	Period of service		Representative Serial and Code
Pup	Jul 1917 —	1918	B5910
Camel	1918 —	Jul 1919	D6415
Gladiator I, II	Jun 1939 —	Jul 1941	N5774
Gauntlet II	Mar 1940 —	Jun 1940	K7792
Tomahawk IIb	Jul 1941 —	Dec 1941	AK402 (GA-F)
Kittyhawk I, Ia	Dec 1941 —	Oct 1942	AK700 (GA-B)
Kittyhawk III	Oct 1942 —	Apr 1944	FR115 (GA-W)
Kittyhawk IV	Apr 1944 —	Jun 1944	FT949 (GA-H)
Mustang III	Jun 1944 —	May 1945	KH579 (GA-L)
Mustang IV	Feb 1945 —	Dec 1946	KM107 (GA-M)
Vampire FB.5	May 1951 —	Jan 1954	VV687 (T-O)
Sabre F.4	Jan 1954 —	Apr 1956	XB934 (X)
Hunter F.4	Apr 1956 —	May 1957	XF937 (T)
Bloodhound I	Aug 1960 —	Mar 1964	—
Bloodhound II	Nov 1964 —	date	—

Blenheim Is, No.113 Squadron

No. 113 Squadron

Badge: In front of a cross
potent, between four
like crosses, two swords
in saltire, the points
uppermost.

Motto: Velox et vindex (Swift to
vengeance)

No.113 Squadron was formed on 1 August 1917 at Ismailia as a corps reconnaissance unit. In September it began tactical reconnaissance and artillery spotting missions in Palestine where it remained until the end of the war. Returning to Egypt in May 1919, it was renumbered 208 Squadron on 1 February 1920.

No.113 reformed at Upper Heyford on 18 May 1937 as a day bomber squadron with Hinds. In April 1938 it left for the Middle East, converting to Blenheims in June 1939. After Italy entered the war in June 1940, the squadron carried out bombing raids on Italian bases in Libya before moving to Greece in March 1941. There it was overtaken by the German invasion and lost all its aircraft, the personnel being evacuated to Crete and Egypt. Bombing operations were resumed in June but the outbreak of war in the Far East resulted in No.113 flying out to Burma where they attacked Japanese columns until its remnants were withdrawn to Calcutta in March 1942. From bases in Assam, the squadron bombed Japanese communications and airfields until it converted to Hurricanes in September 1943. These were used for ground-attack duties, being replaced by Thunderbolts in April 1945. On 15 October, 1945, the squadron was disbanded.

On 1 September, 1946, No.620 Squadron at Aqir was renumbered 113 Squadron and was engaged in transport duties until disbanded on 1 May 1947. On 1 May 1947, it reformed at Fairford with Dakotas, being disbanded again on 1 September, 1948.

No.113 reformed at Mepal on 22 July, 1959, as a Thor intermediate-range ballistic missile squadron and was disbanded on 10 July, 1963.

Squadron bases			
Ismailia	1 Aug 1917	Helwan	20 Dec 1941
Weli Sheikh Nuran	10 Oct 1917	Mingaladon	7 Jan 1942
Julis	23 Nov 1917	Toungoo	30 Jan 1942
Khirbet Deiran	5 Dec 1917	Magwe	6 Feb 1942
Sarona	11 Jan 1918	Dum Dum	12 Mar 1942
Kantara	18 Nov 1918	Fyzabad	6 Apr 1942
Ismailia	16 Feb 1919	Asansol	8 Apr 1942
	to 1 Feb 1920	Jessore	19 Dec 1942
Upper Heyford	18 May 1937	Feni	21 Jan 1943
Grantham	31 Aug 1937	Chandina	28 Feb 1943
Emb. for Middle East		Comilla Main	4 May 1943
	30 Apr 1938	Feni	27 Jun 1943
Heliopolis	11 May 1938	Kharagpur	28 Aug 1943
Amriya	27 Sep 1938	Yelahanka	Sep 1943
Mersa Matruh	29 Sep 1938	St. Thomas Mount	2 Oct 1943
Heliopolis	11 Oct 1938	Cholavarum	9 Nov 1943
El Daba	21 Apr 1939	Manipur Road	22 Dec 1943
Heliopolis	20 May 1939	Dimapur	31 Dec 1943
Maaten Bagush	10 Jun 1940	Tulihal	17 Mar 1944
Sidi Barrani	15 Jan 1941	Palel	25 May 1944
Gambut	4 Feb 1941	Yazagyo	19 Dec 1944
Kabrit	22 Feb 1941	Onbauk	22 Jan 1945
Menidi	23 Mar 1941	Ondaw	14 Mar 1945
Larissa	29 Mar 1941	Kwetnge	20 Apr 1945
Niamata	4 Apr 1941	Kinmagan	8 Jun 1945
Menidi	16 Apr 1941	Meiktila	30 Jun 1945
Argos	22 Apr 1941 (G)	Zayatkwin	17 Aug 1945
Suda Bay	24 Apr 1941 (G)		to 15 Oct 1945
Alexandria	12 May 1941 (G)	Aqir	1 Sep 1946
Ramleh	15 May 1941 (G)		to 1 Apr 1947
Maaten Bagush	1 Jun 1941	Fairford	1 May 1947
Giarabub	14 Nov 1941		to 1 Sep 1948
LG.116	30 Nov 1941	Mepal	22 Jul 1959
			to 10 Jul 1963

Aircraft Equipment	Period of service	Representative Serial and Code
B.E.2e	Aug 1917 — 1918	
R.E.8	Jan 1918 — Feb 1920	A4408
Hind	May 1937 — Jun 1939	K6734
Blenheim I	Jun 1939 — Mar 1940 Jun 1941 — Dec 1941	L1381 (VA-G)
Blenheim IV	Mar 1940 — Apr 1941 Jun 1941 — Oct 1942	Z7706 (A)
Blenheim V	Oct 1942 — Sep 1943	BA717
Hurricane IIC	Sep 1943 — Apr 1945	LA131 (E)
Thunderbolt I, II	Apr 1945 — Oct 1945	KL221 (AD-X)
Halifax C.8	Sep 1946 — Dec 1946	PP370
Halifax A.9	Sep 1946 — Apr 1947	RT883 (Y)
Dakota C.4	Sep 1946 — Sep 1948	KN485

No. 114 Squadron

Badge: A cobra's head
Motto: With speed I strike
Name: 'Hong Kong'

No.114 Squadron was formed at Lahore in September 1917 from a nucleus supplied by No.31 Squadron as an additional army co-operation unit for service with the Indian Army. Equipped with B.E.s, it was renumbered 28 Squadron on 1 April 1920.

On 1 December 1936 No.114 reformed at Wyton with Hind light bombers, receiving Blenheims in March 1937 to become the first Blenheim squadron. In December 1939 it took these to France to join the AASF and during the German invasion in May 1940 was engaged in low-level

Argosy C.1s, No.114 Squadron

attacks on enemy columns. After losing most of its aircraft, the squadron returned to the UK at the end of May. Attacks on invasion barges gathering in the French and Belgian coastal ports began and continued until March 1941 when the squadron was transferred to Coastal Command for patrols and anti-shipping stikes. In July it returned to Bomber Command and took part in raids on targets in occupied Europe. No.114 was allocated to the forces for the invasion of North Africa and flew its Blenheims Vs to Algeria in November 1942 where it was engaged in tactical bombing.

In April 1943 it converted to Bostons which it took to Sicily in August 1943. Moving to Italy in October, the squadron attacked enemy communications and airfields until the end of the war. In September 1945 it moved to Aden where it began to convert to Mosquitos but on 1 May 1946 was reduced to a cadre which was renumbered 8 Squadron on 1 September 1946.

On 1 August 1947, No.114 reformed as a transport squadron at Kabrit. Equipped initially with Dakotas, it replaced these by Valettas in September 1949. During March 1956 it moved base to Cyprus where disbandment took place on 31 December 1957.

On 20 November 1958 No.114 reformed at Hullavington with Chipmunks for security duties in Cyprus, moving there in December, but on 14 March 1959 it disbanded again. On 5 May 1959 the squadron reformed at Colerne with Hastings as a transport unit and flew the type until disbanded on 30 September 1961. Next day, it reformed at Benson to be the first Argosy squadron, receiving its first aircraft in February 1962. On 31 October 1971 the squadron disbanded.

Blida	15 Nov 1942	Forli	7 Mar 1945
Setif	5 Dec 1942	Aviano	12 May 1945
Canrobert	12 Feb 1943	Khormaksar	15 Sep 1945 (A)
Kings Cross	13 Apr 1943		23 Sep 1945 (G)
Grombalia	31 May 1943		to 1 Sep 1946
Gela	3 Aug 1943	Kabrit	1 Aug 1947
Comiso	8 Aug 1943	Nicosia	Mar 1956 (P)
Brindisi	7 Oct 1943		to 31 Dec 1957
Celone	30 Oct 1943	Hullavington	20 Nov 1958
Marcianise	1 May 1944	Nicosia	15 Dec 1958
Nettuno III	12 Jun 1944		to 14 Mar 1959
Tarquinia	25 Jun 1944	Colerne	5 May 1959
Cecina	18 Jul 1944		to 30 Sep 1961
Perugia	13 Oct 1944 (G)	Benson	1 Oct 1961
	18 Dec 1944 (A)		to 31 Oct 1971
Falconara	21 Oct 1944 (A)		

Aircraft Equipment	Period of service	Representative Serial and Code
B.E.2c, B.E.2e	Sep 1917 – Oct 1919	
Bristol F.2b	Oct 1919 – Apr 1920	E2543
Hind	Dec 1936 – Mar 1937	K5401
Audax	Mar 1937 – Apr 1937	K7410
Blenheim I	Mar 1937 – May 1939	K7045 (114-Z)
Blenheim IV	Apr 1939 – Sep 1942	N6155 (FD-F)
Blenheim V	Sep 1942 – Apr 1943	BA817
Boston III, IIIA	Mar 1943 – Jul 1944	W8287 (S)
Boston IV	Jul 1944 – May 1946	BZ461
Boston V	Jan 1945 – May 1946	BZ610
Mosquito VI	Nov 1945 – Sep 1946	TE702
Dakota C.4	Aug 1947 – Nov 1949	KN331
Valetta C.1	Sep 1949 – Dec 1957	VW803 (B)
Chipmunk T.10	Nov 1958 – Mar 1959	WK586
Hastings C.1	May 1959 – Sep 1961	TG524
Argosy C.1	Feb 1962 – Oct 1971	XP442

Squadron bases

Lahore	Sep 1917	Nantes/Chateau Bougon	
Quetta	26 Mar 1919		21 May 1940
Lahore	20 May 1919	Wattisham	31 May 1940
Quetta	16 Jun 1919	Horsham St. Faith	10 Jun 1940
Ambala	2 Oct 1919	Oulton	10 Aug 1940
	to 1 Apr 1920	Thornaby	2 Mar 1941
Wyton	1 Dec 1936	Leuchars	13 May 1941
Condé-Vraux	9 Dec 1939	West Raynham	19 Jul 1941

No. 115 Squadron

Badge: A dexter hand erased at the wrist holding a tiller.
Motto: Despite the elements.

No.115 Squadron was formed at Catterick on 1 December 1917 from a nucleus supplied by No.52 Training Squadron. After training with various types of aircraft, it received Handley Page O/400 night bombers at Castle Bromwich in July 1918 which it took to France in September to join the Independent Force for strategic bombing. After taking part in attacks on German industrial targets during the last two months of the war, the squadron returned to the UK in March 1919 and was disbanded on 18 October 1919.

On 15 June 1937 No.115 reformed at Marham from B Flight of No.38 Squadron, using a few of the latter's Hendons until the arrival of Harrows later in the month. Conversion to Wellingtons began in April 1939 and in April 1940 attacks began on enemy shipping off Norway and enemy-occupied airfields. When the German attack on France opened, the squadron began raids on targets in Germany and, later, occupied Europe. In March 1943, No.115 re-equipped with Lancasters which were flown for the rest of the war as part of the main force of Bomber Command. Remaining in being as part of the post-war RAF, conversion to Lincolns took place in September 1949 but the squadron was disbanded on 1 March 1950.

On 13 June 1950, No.115 reformed at Marham and received Washingtons in August which it flew until converted to Canberras in February 1954. On 1 June 1957 disbandment again took place. On 21 August 1958 No.116 Squadron at Watton was renumbered No.115, moving its Varsities a few days later to Tangmere for Signals Command duties. In October 1963 it returned to Watton where the Varsities were supplemented by Argosies during 1969 before it moved to Cottesmore. In August 1970 No.115 became fully equipped with Argosies, and converted to Andovers between 1976 and 1978.

Squadron bases

Catterick	1 Dec 1917	Graveley	28 Sep 1945
Netheravon	15 Apr 1918	Stradishall	27 Sep 1946
Castle Bromwich	17 Jul 1918	Mildenhall	15 Feb 1949
Roville-sur-Chenes	1 Sep 1918		to 1 Mar 1950
St. Inglevert	Nov 1918	Marham	13 Jun 1950
Ford	4 Mar 1919		to 1 Jun 1957
	to 18 Oct 1919	Watton	21 Aug 1958
Marham	15 Jun 1937	Tangmere	25 Aug 1958
Mildenhall	24 Sep 1942	Watton	1 Oct 1963
East Wretham	8 Nov 1942	Cottesmore	9 Apr 1969
Little Snoring	6 Aug 1943		18 Apr 1969 (C)
Witchford	26 Nov 1943	Brize Norton	Feb 1976

Aircraft Equipment	Period of service	Representative Serial
Various	Dec 1917 – Jul 1918	—
O/400	Jul 1917 – Oct 1919	C9745
Harrow II	Jun 1937 – Sep 1939	K6962 (115-M)
Wellington I	Apr 1939 – Nov 1939	L4317
Wellington IA	Sep 1939 – Aug 1940	N2988 (KO-Q)
Wellington IC	Apr 1940 – Mar 1942	P9299 (KO-O)
Wellington III	Nov 1941 – Mar 1943	BK362 (KO-P)
Lancaster II	Mar 1943 – May 1944	DS626 (KO-J)
Lancaster I, III	Mar 1944 – Sep 1949	ND720 (KO-D)
Lincoln B.2	Sep 1949 – Mar 1950	RE411
Washington B.1	Aug 1950 – Feb 1954	WF447 (KO-G)
Canberra B.2	Feb 1954 – Jun 1957	WJ751
Varsity T.1	Aug 1958 – Aug 1970	WJ940 (Q)
Valetta C.1	Oct 1963 – May 1964	VW200
Argosy E.1	Feb 1968 – Jan 1978	XN855
Andover C.1, E.3	Nov 1976 – date	XS641

No. 116 Squadron

Badge: In front of a flash of lightning, a pair of dividers.
Motto: Precision in defence.

No.116 Squadron was formed on 31 March 1918 at Andover and moved next day to Bicester to become a night bomber unit. It trained with F.E.2bs pending arrival of Handley Pages but did not become operational before the end of the war and was disbanded in November 1918.

The squadron reformed at Hatfield on 17 February 1941 from No.1 Anti-Aircraft Calibration Flight with Lysanders. Its main task was the calibration of predictors and AA radar used by the numerous AA batteries in the UK. Due to the wide dispersal of these batteries, No.116 was fragmented into numerous detachments based at convenient airfields. In November 1941 some Hurricanes were received for simulating dive-bombing and low-level attacks and in June 1942, a large number of Tiger Moths (initially thirty-four) were allotted for use in AA radar alignment checks. Oxfords

began to replace Lysanders and were supplemented by Ansons later which were used for the rest of the war, the squadron disbanding on 26 May 1945.

On 1 August 1952 the squadron reformed at Watton from the Calibration Squadron of the Central Signals Establishment. It flew Varsities, Lincolns and Ansons until renumbered 115 Squadron on 21 August 1958.

Squadron bases

Andover	31 Mar 1918	North Weald	2 Jul 1944
Bicester	1 Apr 1918	Gatwick	27 Aug 1944
	to Nov 1918	Redhill	5 Sep 1944
Hatfield	17 Feb 1941	Hornchurch	2 May 1945
Hendon	24 Apr 1941		to 26 May 1945
Heston	20 Apr 1942	Watton	1 Aug 1952
Croydon	12 Dec 1943		to 21 Aug 1958

Aircraft Equipment	Period of service	Representative Serial and Code
F.E.2b	Apr 1918 – Nov 1918	
Lysander III	Feb 1941 – Jan 1943	T1703
Hurricane I	Nov 1941 – 1942	AG205
Hurricane IIA	Jun 1942 – May 1945	
Tiger Moth	Jun 1942 – May 1945	DE564
Oxford I, II	Nov 1942 – May 1945	ED218
Anson I, XII	Mar 1945 – May 1945	N5145
Hornet Moth	Jun 1942 – Jan 1943	X9310
Lincoln B.2	Aug 1952 – Apr 1954	WD124
Anson C.19	Aug 1952 – Aug 1958	TX232
Varsity T.1	Jan 1954 – Aug 1958	WL691

No. 117 Squadron

Badge: A terrestrial globe
Motto: It shall be done

No.117 Squadron was formed at Beaulieu on 1 January 1918 as a day bomber unit but did not become operational before disbanding on 4 July 1918. In September 1918 it began to reform but lost its first draft of personnel on 6 October. On the following day it began to build up again and on moving to Wyton at the end of November received D.H.9s. In April 1919 the squadron moved to Ireland for internal security duties in co-operation with the army and on 31 January 1920, it merged with No.141 Squadron's cadre to form No.100 Squadron.

On 30 April 1941 No.117 reformed at Khartoum and incorporated the local communications flight. Four Bombays were acquired from No.216 Squadron for long-range flights and in May it added four Savoia-Marchetti S.79Ks. The main task of the squadron was to operate the route between Takoradi and Khartoum along which reinforcement aircraft for the Middle East were flown. Occasionally, aircraft were detached to supply desert outposts. Douglas DC-2s arrived in October and in November the squadron moved to Egypt, leaving its communications types behind and returning its Bombays to No.216 Squadron. Freight flights to airfields in the Western Desert began in December and in March 1942 a flight of D.H.86Bs was added. In April 1942 the DC-2s were transferred to No.31 Squadron in India and Lodestars acquired in May when the first DC-3 also arrived. In August the last-mentioned began operating freight and passenger services to Malta while Hudsons were used in North Africa, the squadron standardising on Hudsons in November. Until June 1943 it

flew freight and casualty evacuation flights from airfields captured by the advancing 8th Army and then began to convert to Dakotas. Routine services were flown around the Mediterranean until the squadron moved to India at the end of October. After parachute-dropping training, supply missions began in January 1944; in addition, the squadron flew Chindits behind the Japanese lines and kept them maintained in March and April. Withdrawn in November 1944 for rest, No.117 returned to the Burma front in December and flew supply-dropping missions for the rest of the war. On 17 December 1945, the squadron was disbanded.

Squadron bases

Beaulieu	1 Jan 1918	El Djem	23 Apr 1943
	to 4 Jul 1918	Castel Benito	23 May 1943
Norwich	1 Sep 1918	Catania	3 Sep 1943
	to 6 Oct 1919	Bari	2 Oct 1943
Norwich	7 Oct 1918	Cairo	26 Oct 1943
Wyton	30 Nov 1918	Karachi	31 Oct 1943
Hooton Park	28 Mar 1919	Dhamial	1 Nov 1943
Tallaght	22 Apr 1919	Lalmai	19 Jan 1944
Gormanstown	24 Apr 1919	Tulihal	4 Mar 1944
	to 31 Jan 1920	Sylhet	11 Mar 1944
Khartoum	30 Apr 1941	Agartala	28 Jun 1944
Bilbeis	3 Nov 1941	Risalpur	1 Nov 1944
Amriya	3 Nov 1941	Bikrum	25 Nov 1944
El Adem	19 Nov 1942	Hathazari	10 Dec 1944
Marble Arch	9 Jan 1943	Kyaukpyu	17 May 1945
Castel Benito	6 Mar 1943	Patenga	16 Jun 1945
Gabes	13 Apr 1943	Hmawbi	19 Aug 1945
			to 17 Dec 1945

Aircraft Equipment	Period of service	Representative Serial and Code
D.H.4	Jan 1918 – Jul 1918	
R.E.8	Jan 1918 – Jul 1918	
D.H.9	Dec 1918 – Jan 1920	C1176 (F)
Bombay	Apr 1941 – Nov 1941	L5811
S.79K	May 1941 – Nov 1941	AX705
Various Communications types, e.g. Proctor I (P6127), Wellesley (L2657), Gladiator I (K6143), Caproni Ca.148 (I-GOGG) Apr 1941 – Nov 1941		
DC-2K	Oct 1941 – Apr 1942	HK821
DH.86B	Mar 1942 – May 1942	HK844
Lodestar	May 1942 – Nov 1942	EW997
DC-3	May 1942 – Sep 1942	FJ709
Hudson VI	Jul 1942 – Sep 1943	FK390 (H)
Dakota III	Jun 1943 – Dec 1945	FZ590 (C)

No. 118 Squadron

Badge: On waves of the sea an
ancient ship in full sail in
flames
Motto: Occido redeoque (I kill
and return)

Spitfire VB, No.118 Squadron

No.118 Squadron was formed at Catterick on 1 January 1918 as a night bomber unit and moved to Bicester to receive Handley Page O/400s but did not become operational before the end of the war. Soon after the Armistice, the squadron was disbanded while awaiting Vimys.

On 20 February 1941 No.118 reformed at Filton as a fighter squadron equipped with Spitfires. On 28 March convoy patrols began and in June the squadron began to provide bomber escorts and took part in fighter sweeps over northern France. In January 1943 it moved to East Anglia and began sweeps over the Netherlands moving in September to northern Scotland on defensive duties. In January 1944 the squadron came south again to join Second TAF but returned to the Orkneys in March for four months. Sweeps and bomber escort missions were resumed in July 1944, and in January 1945 the squadron converted to Mustangs for long-range escort duties. These began on 1 February and continued till 3 May 1945. On 10 March 1946 the squadron was disbanded.

On 15 May 1951 No.118 reformed at Fassberg as a Vampire fighter-bomber squadron in Germany. Re-equipping with Venoms in November 1953, the squadron became a day fighter unit when it joined the Hunter-equipped No.121 Wing at Jever in March 1955 but was disbanded on 31 July 1957.

On 12 May 1960, the Sycamore Flight of No.228 Squadron at Aldergrove became No.118 Squadron in Transport Command. On 31 August 1962 the squadron was disbanded.

Squadron bases			
Catterick	1 Jan 1918	Peterhead	23 Jan 1944
Bicester	Jun 1918	Detling	5 Feb 1944
	to Nov 1918	Skeabrae	10 Mar 1944
Filton	20 Feb 1941	Detling	12 Jul 1944
Colerne	7 Apr 1941	Peterhead	9 Aug 1944
Warmwell	9 Apr 1941	Westhampnett	29 Aug 1944
Ibsley	18 Apr 1941	Manston	25 Sep 1944
Tangmere	16 Aug 1942	Bentwaters	15 Dec 1944
Zeals	24 Aug 1942	Fairwood Common	
Ibsley	23 Dec 1942		11 Aug 1945
Wittering	3 Jan 1943	Horsham St. Faith	7 Sep 1945
Coltishall	17 Jan 1943		to 10 Mar 1946
Westhampnett	15 Aug 1943	Fassberg	15 May 1951
Merston	24 Aug 1943	Jever	Mar 1955
Peterhead	20 Sep 1943		to 31 Jul 1957
Castletown	19 Oct 1943	Aldergrove	12 May 1960
Detling	20 Jan 1944		to 31 Aug 1962

Aircraft Equipment	Period of service	Representative Serial and Code
F.E.2b	Jan 1918 – Nov 1918	
Spitfire IIA	Mar 1941 – Sep 1941	P7913 (NK-H)
Spitfire VB	Sep 1941 – Jan 1944	AA744 (NK-N)
	Mar 1944 – Jul 1944	
Spitfire IX	Jan 1944 – Mar 1944	ML348 (NK-L)
	Jul 1944 – Jan 1945	
Mustang III	Jan 1945 – Mar 1946	KH476 (NK-B)
Mustang IV	Mar 1946	KM236
Vampire FB.5	May 1951 – Nov 1953	WA317 (A-T)
Venom FB.1	Nov 1953 – Mar 1955	WE388 (A-M)
Hunter F.4	Mar 1955 – Jul 1957	WW657 (G)
Sycamore HR.14	May 1960 – Aug 1962	XE502

No. 119 Squadron

Badge: A sword, the point downwards, and an anchor in
saltire.
Motto: By night and day

No.119 Squadron was formed at Andover on 1 March 1918, moving next month to Duxford to train as a day bomber unit. It did not become operational and was disbanded in November 1918.

On 13 March 1941, G Flight at Bowmore was redesignated 119 Squadron. G Flight had been formed on 21 September 1940 to operate the three Short S.26 flying boats built for BOAC as their G class. Fitted with turrets and bomb racks, the first patrol was carried out by *'Golden Fleece'* on 15 December. *'Golden Hind'* became operational on 2 February 1941, and *'Golden Horn'* joined the squadron on 10 April.

The C class boats *'Clio'* and *'Cordelia'* were also used but were withdrawn for transport duties by October. In August No.119 moved to Pembroke Dock and, bereft of aircraft, became non-operational until April 1942.

On 14 April 1942, No.119 began to reform as an operational unit at Lough Erne, Catalinas beginning to arrive during May. In August, eleven crews were sent to Canada to ferry Catalinas and by the time the last of these arrived on 15 September, the squadron had moved to Pembroke Dock and began to receive Sunderlands. These flew their first patrol on 20 November 1942, but the squadron disbanded on 17 April 1943.

On 19 July 1944 the Albacore Flight of No.415 Squadron RCAF became No.119 Squadron when the rest of the squadron was transferred to Bomber Command. Part of No.155 (GR) Wing, the squadron began anti-shipping patrols at night, their quarry being enemy E-boats and R-boats operating along the Dutch coast. In October 1944, it moved to Belgium, midget submarines being added to its targets and in January 1945 Swordfish replaced Albacores. Several small submarines were destroyed before the squadron flew its last patrol on 11 May and returned to the UK to disband on 25 May 1945.

153

Swordfish IIIs, No.119 Squadron

Squadron bases

Andover	1 Mar 1918		to 17 Apr 1943
Duxford	Apr 1918	Manston	19 Jul 1944
	to Nov 1918	Swingfield	9 Aug 1944
Bowmore	13 Mar 1941	Bircham Newton	2 Oct 1944
Pembroke Dock	4 Aug 1941	B.83 Knocke/Le Zoute	
	to Nov 1941		29 Oct 1944
Lough Erne	14 Apr 1942	Bircham Newton	22 May 1945
Pembroke Dock	6 Sep 1942		to 25 May 1945

Aircraft Equipment	Period of service	Representative Serial and Code
D.H.9	Apr 1918 – Nov 1918	D5611
Short S.26/M	Mar 1941 – Oct 1941	X8275 'Golden Hind'
Short S.23/M	Apr 1941 – Aug 1941	AX659 (W)
Catalina Ib	Jun 1941 – Jul 1941	W8419 (U)
Catalina IIIa	May 1942 – Sep 1942	FP533
Sunderland II	Sep 1942 – Apr 1943	W6002 (R)
Sunderland III	Sep 1942 – Apr 1943	DV962 (Q)
Albacore I	Jul 1944 – Jan 1945	BF730
Swordfish III	Jan 1945 – May 1945	NF340

No. 120 Squadron

Badge: Standing on a demi-terrestrial globe, a falcon close

Motto: Endurance

No.120 Squadron was formed at Lympne on 1 January 1918, as a day bomber unit and trained with D.H.9s before receiving D.H.9As for service with the Independent Force. Before the squadron could move to France and become operational, the Armistice intervened. In May 1919 it moved to Hawkinge to carry mail between the UK and France until August and on 21 October 1919 was disbanded.

On 2 June 1941 No.120 reformed at Nutts Corner as a maritime reconnaissance squadron with Liberators. Anti-submarine patrols began on 20 September and in April 1943 the squadron moved to Iceland. The Liberators' long-range capacity enabled them to fill a vital gap between the limits of patrols from Britain and Canada and nineteen U-boats were sunk and many others damaged. In March 1944 No.120 returned to Ireland and flew patrols until disbanded on 4 June 1945.

On 1 October 1946, No.160 Squadron was renumbered 120 Squadron and flew Lancasters from Scotland on maritime reconnaissance duties until it converted to Shackletons in April 1951. This type served the squadron for twenty years, being replaced by Nimrods in February 1971.

Squadron bases

Lympne	1 Jan 1918	Aldergrove	14 Feb 1943
Hawkinge	May 1919	Reykjavik	13 Apr 1943
	to 21 Oct 1919	Ballykelly	23 Mar 1944
Nutts Corner	2 Jun 1941		to 4 Jun 1945
Ballykelly	21 Jul 1942	Leuchars	1 Oct 1946
Reykjavik (D)	4 Sep 1942	Kinloss	Dec 1949
	to 13 Apr 1943	Aldergrove	1 Apr 1952
		Kinloss	1 Apr 1959

Liberator IIIs, No.120 Squadron

Aircraft Equipment	Period of service	Representative Code and Serial
D.H.9	Jan 1918 – Oct 1918	
D.H.9A	Oct 1918 – Oct 1919	
Liberator I	Jun 1941 – Feb 1943	AM913 (OH-X)
Liberator II	Dec 1941 – Dec 1942	LV342 (V)
Liberator III	Jun 1942 – Jan 1944	FK220 (K)
Liberator V	Dec 1943 – Jan 1945	BZ912

Aircraft Equipment	Period of service	Representative Serial and Code
Liberator VIII	Dec 1944 – Jun 1945 Oct 1946 – Jun 1947	KH133
Lancaster GR.3, ASR.3	Nov 1946 – Apr 1951	RE158 (BS-B)
Shackleton MR.1	Apr 1951 – Oct 1956	WB844 (F)
Shackleton MR.2	Mar 1953 – Nov 1958	WL745 (B)
Shackleton MR.3	Nov 1958 – Dec 1970	WR988 (C)
Nimrod MR.1	Feb 1971 – date	XV242 (42)

Shackleton MR.3s, No.120 Squadron

No. 121 Squadron

Badge: An Indian warrior's head with head dress
Motto: For Liberty
Name: 'Eagle'

Spitfire VBs, No. 121 Squadron

No.121 Squadron was formed at Narborough on 1 January 1918 as a light bomber unit but did not become operational before being disbanded on 17 August 1918. Reforming began at Bracebridge Heath on 14 October 1918+ but was abandoned with the Armistice a few weeks later.

On 14 May 1941 the squadron reformed at Kirton-in-Lindsey as the second Eagle squadron to be manned by American volunteers. Equipped with Hurricanes, it began defensive patrols in October but in November converted to Spitfires. These it took to North Weald in December 1941 and in February 1942 began to take part in fighter sweeps over northern France. These continued until the squadron was transferred to the US Army Air Force on 29 September 1942, becoming the 335th Fighter Squadron of the 4th Fighter Group at Debden.

+It was intended to train with D.H.10s at Sherburn-in-Elmet from 1 December 1918.

Squadron bases			
Narborough	1 Jan 1918	Digby	29 Sep 1941
	to 17 Aug 1918	Kirton-in-Lindsey	3 Oct 1941
Bracebridge Heath	14 Oct 1918	North Weald	16 Dec 1941
	to Nov 1918	Southend	3 Jun 1942
Kirton-in-Lindsey	14 May 1941	Debden	23 Sep 1942
			to 29 Sep 1942

Aircraft Equipment	Period of service	Representative Serial and Code
D.H.9	Jan 1918 – Aug 1918	
Hurricane I	May 1941 – Jul 1941	
Hurricane IIB	Jul 1941 – Nov 1941	Z3593 (AV-F)
Spitfire IIA	Oct 1941 – Nov 1941	P8133
Spitfire VB	Nov 1941 – Sep 1942	BM590 (AV-R)

No. 122 Squadron

Badge: In front of a mullet, a leopard rampant
Motto: Victuri volamus (We fly to conquer)
Name: 'Bombay'

No.122 Squadron was formed on 1 January 1918 at Sedgeford as a day bomber unit but did not become operational before disbanding on 17 August 1918. It reformed on 29 October 1918 at Upper Heyford to fly D.H.10s but the Armistice came two weeks later and formation was suspended.

On 1 May 1941 No.122 reformed at Turnhouse with Spitfires and began flying patrols on 6 June. In March 1942 the squadron moved to Hornchurch and began flying sweeps over northern France. Joining the Second TAF in June 1943, ground-attack and bomber escort missions were flown. In February 1944 No.122 converted to Mustangs and moved to Normandy three weeks after the initial landings. At the end of September 1944 the squadron returned to the UK to undertake bomber escort missions for the rest of the war. In August 1945 Spitfires replaced Mustangs and were flown in Scotland until the squadron was renumbered 41 Squadron on 1 April 1946.

Squadron bases			
Sedgeford	1 Jan 1918	Kingsnorth	16 Sep 1943
	to 17 Aug 1918	Ashford	5 Oct 1943
Upper Heyford	29 Oct 1918	Weston Zoyland	15 Oct 1943
	to Nov 1918	Gravesend	3 Nov 1943
Turnhouse	1 May 1941	Ford	15 Apr 1944
Ouston	26 Jun 1941	Funtington	14 May 1944
Catterick	31 Aug 1941	Southend	20 May 1944
Scorton	6 Oct 1941	Funtington	28 May 1944
Hornchurch	1 Apr 1942	Ford	15 Jun 1944
Fairlop	8 Jun 1942	B.7 Martagny	25 Jun 1944
Martlesham Heath	29 Jun 1942	B.12 Ellon	16 Jul 1944
Fairlop	6 Jul 1942	B.24 St. André de l'Eure	
Hornchurch	17 Jul 1942		16 Jul 1944
Martlesham Heath	29 Sep 1942	B.42 Beauvais/Tillé	3 Sep 1944
Hornchurch	3 Oct 1942	B.60 Grimbergen	9 Sep 1944
Fairlop	16 Nov 1942	Matlask	28 Sep 1944
Hornchurch	9 Dec 1942	Andrews Field	14 Oct 1944
Eastchurch	18 May 1943	Peterhead	1 May 1945
Bognor Regis	1 Jun 1943	Dyce	3 Jul 1945
Kingsnorth	1 Jul 1943	Wick	Oct 1945
Brenzett	14 Sep 1943	Dalcross	Jan 1946
			to 1 Apr 1946

Aircraft Equipment	Period of service	Representative Serial and Code
D.H.4 and/or D.H.9	Jan 1918 – Aug 1918	
Spitfire I	May 1941 – Oct 1941	R7115
Spitfire IIA, IIB	Oct 1941 – Feb 1942	P8390
Spitfire VB, VC	Feb 1942 – Oct 1942	BM252 (MT-E)
	May 1943 – Aug 1943	
Spitfire IX	Oct 1942 – May 1943	MA746
	Aug 1943 – Feb 1944	
Mustang III	Feb 1944 – May 1945	FB226 (MT-K)
Mustang IV	May 1945 – Aug 1945	KH642 (MT-M)
Spitfire IX	Aug 1945 – Feb 1946	TE233
Spitfire F.21	Feb 1946 – Apr 1946	LA194

No. 123 Squadron

Badge: In front of two claymores in saltire, the points uppermost a tiger's head couped
Motto: Swift to strike
Name: 'East India'

Squadron bases

Waddington	1 Mar 1918	Abadan	24 Jan 1943
Duxford	1 Mar 1918	Bu Amud	3 May 1943
	to 14 Oct 1918	Left for India	29 Oct 1943 (G)
Upper Heyford	3 Nov 1918		16 Nov 1943 (A)
	to 5 Feb 1920	Feni	25 Nov 1943 (A)
Turnhouse	10 May 1941		9 Dec 1943 (G)
Drem	5 Aug 1941	Patharkundi	4 Jan 1944
Castletown	21 Sep 1941	St. Thomas Mount	
Left for Middle East			14 May 1944
	11 Apr 1942	Yelahanka	20 Sep 1944
Aboukir	19 Jun 1942	Cholavarum	24 Oct 1944
Muqeibila	15 Jul 1942	Kajamalai	29 Oct 1944
Hadera	6 Sep 1942	Baigachi	3 Dec 1944
Habbaniya	4 Oct 1942	Nazir	18 Dec 1944
Abadan (D)	12 Oct 1942	Kyaukpyu	28 Apr 1945
	to 24 Jan 1943	Cox's Bazaar	6 Jun 1945
Doshan Tappeh	22 Oct 1942	Baigachi	10 Jun 1945
Mehrabad	23 Nov 1942		to 20 Jun 1945

Aircraft

Equipment	Period of service	Representative Serial and Code	
D.H.9	Mar 1918 – Oct 1918		
Dolphin	Nov 1918 – Feb 1920		
Spitfire I	May 1941 – Sep 1941	R7122	(XE-E)
Spitfire IIA	Sep 1941 – Jan 1942	P8437	(XE-K)
Spitfire VB	Jan 1942 – Apr 1942	AD571	
Gladiator II	Oct 1942 – Nov 1942	N5857	
Hurricane I	Nov 1942		
Hurricane IIC	Nov 1942 – Aug 1944	KZ126	(R)
Spitfire VC	May 1943 – Oct 1943	BP287	
Thunderbolt II	Sep 1944 – Jun 1945	KJ263	(XE-K)

No.123 Squadron was formed as a nucleus at Waddington on 1 March 1918, moving the same day to Duxford to train as a day bomber unit. It did not become operational and disbanded on 14 October 1918. On 3 November 1918 No.123 reformed at Upper Heyford as a Canadian-manned fighter squadron which became No.2 Squadron, Canadian Air Force but was disbanded on 5 February 1920. No.123 suffered from some confusion in November 1918. It was originally intended that it should form at Shoreham and in addition the Independent Force believed No.123 was to be a heavy bomber squadron to be formed on 20 November 1918 at Oxford with D.H.9As.

On 10 May 1941 No.123 reformed at Turnhouse as a fighter squadron and became operational on 8 June on defensive duties. In April 1942 it left for the Middle East, arriving in June to find that lack of aircraft had caused the squadron to be assigned to maintenance duties in Iraq and Iran. In October 1942, one flight formed with Gladiators at Abadan for army co-operation duties and next month Hurricanes were received for air defence. In May 1943 No.123 arrived in the Western Desert for local defensive patrols until November when it flew to India. Escort missions for transports and dive-bombers began on 19 December and continued until May 1944, when the squadron was withdrawn to southern India, there to convert to Thunderbolts in September 1944. The squadron then returned to Burma and began fighter-bomber missions on 27 December, continuing until it was renumbered 81 Squadron on 20 June 1945.

Hurricane I, No.123 Squadron

No. 124 Squadron

Badge: A mongoose passant
Motto: Danger is our oppurtunity
Name: 'Baroda'

No.124 Squadron was formed on 1 March 1918 at Old Sarum as a day bomber unit but before it could become operational it was disbanded on 17 August 1918, and its personnel allotted to other units.

On 10 May 1941 No.124 reformed at Castletown with eighteen Spitfire Is and became operational in defence of the naval base at Scapa Flow on 29 June. In October 1941 it converted to Spitfire IIBs and in mid-November left these behind on moving to Biggin Hill where it took over Spitfire Vs. It began convoy patrols and after taking part in the action resulting from the escape of the German battlecruisers from Brest through the Channel to German ports, it flew escort missions over France for the rest of the year. At the end of July 1942, it became operational with high-altitude Spitfire VIs and at the end of December moved to Drem for four weeks. No.124 returned south in January 1943 and absorbed the SS Flight at Northolt whose task had been the interception of high-altitude enemy reconnaissance aircraft (Ju86Ps), receiving Spitfire VIIs in March. Detachments were sent to airfields in the West Country for high-altitude interceptions and in March 1944 the squadron joined No.141 Airfield at Church Fenton as part of Second TAF and flew escort missions over France until the invasion. In July 1944 it converted to Spitfire IXs and in August returned to Fighter Command (currently known as ADGB) for escort duties from the UK. In February 1945 it began attacks on V-2 sites in the Netherlands supplemented by shipping reconnaissance missions, flying its last operation on 25 April 1945. During July 1945 No.124 began flying Meteors with No.1335 Conversion Unit and became operational on this type on 2 October, moving a few days later to Bentwaters where it was renumbered 56 Squadron on 1 April 1946.

Squadron bases

Fowlmere	1 Mar 1918 to 17 Aug 1918
Castletown	10 May 1941
Biggin Hill	18 Nov 1941
Gravesend	3 May 1942
Eastchurch	30 Jun 1942
Martlesham Heath	5 Jul 1942
Gravesend	13 Jul 1942
Debden	29 Jul 1942
Gravesend	14 Aug 1942
Debden	20 Aug 1942
Tangmere	25 Sep 1942
Westhampnett	29 Oct 1942
North Weald	7 Nov 1942
Martlesham Heath	7 Dec 1942
Drem	29 Dec 1942 (A only)
Martlesham Heath	21 Jan 1943
Croughton	1 Mar 1943
Duxford	5 Mar 1943
North Weald	12 Mar 1943
Colerne (D)	28 Apr 1943 to 13 May 1943
Exeter (D)	13 May 1943 to 22 Jun 1943
Ibsley (D)	22 Jun 1943 to 14 Jul 1943
Exeter (D)	14 Jul 1943 to 16 Jul 1943
Fairwood Common (D)	16 Jul 1943 to 20 Jul 1943
Exeter (D)	20 Jul 1943 to 26 Jul 1943
Northolt	26 Jul 1943
West Malling	20 Sep 1943
Church Fenton	18 Mar 1944
Bradwell Bay	23 Apr 1944
Detling	26 Jul 1944
Westhampnett	9 Aug 1944
Manston	25 Sep 1944
Coltishall	10 Feb 1945
Hawkinge	7 Apr 1945
Hutton Cranswick	27 Apr 1945
Bradwell Bay	13 Jun 1945
Hutton Cranswick	10 Jul 1945
Molesworth	15 Jul 1945
Bentwaters	5 Oct 1945
Fairwood Common	18 Feb 1946
Bentwaters	20 Mar 1946 to 1 Apr 1946

Aircraft Equipment	Period of service	Representative Serial and Code
D.H.4, D.H.9	Mar 1918 – Aug 1918	
Spitfire I	May 1941 – Oct 1941	R7131
Spitfire IIA	Oct 1941 – Nov 1941	P8535
Spitfire VB	Nov 1941 – Jul 1942	BL330 (ON-T)
Spitfire VI	Jul 1942 – Mar 1943	BR579 (ON-H)
Spitfire VII	Mar 1943 – Jul 1944	MB808 (ON-C)
Spitfire IX	Jul 1944 – Jul 1945	PL249 (ON-Q)
Meteor F.3	Jul 1945 – Apr 1946	EE389 (ON-Y)

No. 125 Squadron

Badge: On a mount, a caribou
Motto: Nunquam domandi (Never to be tamed)
Name: 'Newfoundland'

No.125 Squadron was formed on 1 February 1918 as a light bomber unit at Old Sarum but did not become operational and was disbanded on 1 August 1918, to provide reinforcements for other units.

On 16 June 1941 No.125 reformed at Colerne as a night fighter squadron with Defiants and became operational at the end of September, providing night defence for western England and South Wales. In February 1942 it began conversion to Beaufighters and became fully equipped in April although it also borrowed Defiants and Hurricanes to supplement its patrols at this time. In October 1942 a detachment of four aircraft was sent to the Shetlands to try to intercept enemy reconnaissance aircraft over the North Sea and this returned to base in December. In November 1943 the squadron moved to Valley for patrols over the Irish Sea, some of its aircraft being based at Ballyhalbert for this purpose. In February 1944 it converted to Mosquitos and took these south to Hurn to cover the invasion forces awaiting the landings in Normandy. After flying night patrols over the bridgehead and convoys, No.125 moved to Middle Wallop to help defend the London area against flying bombs while a number of patrols were flown from Bradwell Bay over the Low Countries until the squadron moved to Coltishall. Patrols against enemy intruders and flying-bomb carriers continued until the end of the war and shipping reconnaissance missions were undertaken to locate what was left of German shipping. At the end of the war, No.125 spent a period in Yorkshire but disbanded on 20 November 1945, its aircraft and personnel passing to No.264 Squadron.

On 31 March 1955 No.125 reformed at Stradishall with Meteor night fighters, beginning to replace these with Venoms in November 1955. The latter type was flown until the squadron disbanded on 10 May 1957.

Squadron bases

Old Sarum	1 Feb 1918 to 1 Aug 1918
Colerne	16 Jun 1941
Charmy Down	7 Aug 1941
Fairwood Common	24 Sep 1941
Colerne	25 Jan 1942
Fairwood Common (D)	25 Jan 1942 to 10 Feb 1942
Fairwood Common	14 May 1942
Sumburgh (D)	7 Oct 1942 to 17 Dec 1942
Exeter	15 Apr 1943
Valley	14 Nov 1943
Hurn	25 Mar 1944
Middle Wallop	30 Jul 1944
Coltishall	18 Oct 1944
Church Fenton	24 Apr 1945 to 20 Nov 1945
Stradishall	31 Mar 1955 to 10 May 1957

Aircraft Equipment	Period of service	Representative Serial
D.H.4/D.H.9 (probably both)	Feb 1918 – Aug 1918	
Defiant I	Jun 1941 – Apr 1942	AA404 (VA-P)
Beaufighter IIf	Feb 1942 – Sep 1942	T3149 (VA-M)
Beaufighter VI	Sep 1942 – Feb 1944	V8751 (VA-G)
Mosquito XVII	Feb 1944 – Mar 1945	HK355 (VA-T)
Mosquito 30	Feb 1945 – Nov 1945	NT450 (VA-B)
Meteor NF.11	Apr 1955 – Jan 1956	WD640 (W)
Venom NF.3	Nov 1955 – May 1957	WX913 (F)

No. 126 Squadron

Badge: On a hurt a Maltese Cross throughout, overall a wreath of laurel.
Motto: Foremost in attack.

No.126 Squadron was formed at Old Sarum on 1 March 1918 as a day bomber unit and after training with D.H.9s was disbanded on 17 August 1918, to provide reinforcements for squadrons in France.

On 28 June 1941 No.126 reformed at Takali with Hurricanes for the defence of Malta against enemy attacks from nearby Sicilian bases. It played a large part in repelling these and in March 1942 received Spitfires flown from carriers to reinforce the island's defences. With these it helped to preserve Malta's security as an offensive base interrupting enemy supply lines between Italy and Libya until the defeat of the Afrika Korps at the end of 1942 enabled the siege to be lifted and the squadron turned to the offensive, beginning sweeps over Sicily in February 1943. In August 1943 it acquired a flight of Spitfire IXs shortly before it moved to newly-captured airstrips in Sicily and in October moved on to Italy where it remained until 1 April 1944; it was then placed non-operational for transfer to the United Kingdom where it re-assembled at the beginning of May with Spitfire IXs. At the end of the month it began operations from south-west England, escorting fighter-bombers over north-western France and flying patrols over shipping assembled for the invasion. In August 1944 it moved to East Anglia for escort duties and converted to Mustangs in December for the same role. After the end of the war, it remained in East Anglia and re-equipped with Spitfire XVIs in February 1946, disbanding on 10 March, 1946.

Squadron bases

Old Sarum	1 Mar 1918	Safi	10 Jun 1943
	to 17 Aug 1918	Gerbini	23 Sep 1943
Takali	28 Jun 1941	Grottaglie	16 Oct 1943
Luqa	1 May 1942		to 1 Apr 1944

Sawbridgeworth	1 May 1944	Hethel	5 Sep 1945
Culmhead	22 May 1944	Bradwell Bay	15 Sep 1945
Harrowbeer	3 Jul 1944	Hethel	5 Oct 1945
Bradwell Bay	29 Aug 1944		to 10 Mar 1946
Bentwaters	30 Dec 1944		

Aircraft

Equipment	Period of service	Representative Serial and Code
D.H.9	Mar 1918 – Aug 1918	
Hurricane I	Jun 1941 – 1941	
Hurricane IIB	1941 – Mar 1942	Z3766
Spitfire VC	Mar 1942 – Apr 1944	BR226 (C)
Spitfire IX	Aug 1943 – Dec 1943	EN390 (K)
	May 1944 – Dec 1944	MH438 (5J-X)
Mustang III	Dec 1944 – Mar 1946	KH564 (5J-H)
Mustang IV	Aug 1945 – Mar 1946	KM114
Spitfire XVIE	Feb 1946 – Mar 1946	RW384

No. 127 Squadron

Badge: A tarantula
Motto: Eothen (Out of the East)

No.127 Squadron was formed on 1 January 1918 at Catterick as a day bomber unit but was disbanded on 4 July 1918 without becoming operational.

On 29 June 1941 a detachment of four Hurricanes and four Gladiators to be based at Haditha in Iraq was designated No.127 Squadron. During the occupation of Syria in July, it flew reconnaissance and fighter missions until renumbered 261 Squadron on 12 July 1941.

On 2 August 1941 No.127 was reformed at Kasfareet from a detachment of ground personnel on No.249 Squadron and acted as a servicing echelon until receiving Hurricanes in March 1942. In June the squadron moved to the Western Desert for fighter operations, being placed on air defence duties in Egypt in September. It remained in the Eastern Mediterranean after the front moved westwards through Libya, sending detachments to Cyprus and providing cover for operations in the Aegean in November. In April 1944 No.127 left for the UK and re-assembled at North Weald on 23 April. Operations with Spitfire fighter-bombers began on 19 May and in August 1944 the squadron moved

to France where it flew fighter-bomber sweeps until disbanded on 30 April 1945.

Squadron bases

Catterick	1 Jan 1918	Left for UK	4 Apr 1944
	to 4 Jul 1918	North Weald	23 Apr 1944
Haditha (K.3)	29 Jun 1941	Lympne	17 May 1944
T.1	30 Jun 1941	Tangmere	4 Jul 1944
Tahoune Guemac	6 Jul 1941	Southend	12 Jul 1944
	to 12 Jul 1941	Tangmere	23 Jul 1944
Kasfareet	2 Aug 1941	Funtington	6 Aug 1944
Hurghada	17 Sep 1941	Ford	12 Aug 1944
St. Jean	16 Feb 1942	B.16 Villons les Buissons	
Shandur	2 Jun 1942		20 Aug 1944
LG.92 Amriya	25 Jun 1942	B.33 Camp Neuseville	
LG.172	14 Jul 1942		6 Sep 1944
LG.88	20 Aug 1942	B.57 Lille/Wambrechies	
Kilo 8	9 Sep 1942		11 Sep 1944
LG.89	10 Oct 1942	B.60 Grimbergen	6 Oct 1944
LG.37	23 Oct 1942	B.79 Woensdrecht	
LG.20	9 Nov 1942		23 Dec 1944
LG.08	18 Nov 1942	Fairwood Common	
St. Jean	6 Jan 1943		21 Feb 1945
Ramal David	26 Jan 1943	B.85 Schijndel	17 Mar 1945
Paphos (D)	13 Nov 1943	B.106 Twente	21 Apr 1945
	to 20 Nov 1943		to 30 Apr 1945

Aircraft

Equipment	Period of service	Representative Serial and code
D.H.9	Jan 1918 – Jul 1918	
Gladiator II	Jun 1941 – Jul 1941	K8048
Hurricane I	Jun 1941 – Jul 1941	
	Mar 1942 – Jun 1942	Z4115
Hurricane IIB	Jun 1942 – Oct 1943	BN160
Hurricane IIC	Aug 1943 – Mar 1944	KZ113
Spitfire VC	Jan 1943 – Oct 1943	AB321
Spitfire IX	Mar 1944	
	Apr 1944 – Nov 1944	ML235
Spitfire XVI	Nov 1944 – Apr 1945	RR257 (9N-Y)

No. 128 Squadron

Badge: In front of an ogress a shuttle in hand
Motto: Fulminis instar (Like a thunderbolt)

No.128 Squadron was formed at Thetford on 1 February 1918 as a day bomber unit but did not become operational before being disbanded on 4 July 1918, to provide reinforcements for squadrons in France.

On 7 October 1941 the Fighter Flight attached to No.95 Squadron at Hastings, Sierra Leone, became No.128 Squadron and flew Hurricanes on air defence duties in the colony until disbanded on 8 March 1943, the invasion of French North Africa having resulted in French air forces based at Dakar joining the Allies.

On 5 September 1944* No.128 reformed at Wyton as a Mosquito squadron in No.8 Group. As part of the Light Night Striking Force, it carried out raids over Germany for the rest of the war. On 20 September 1945, the squadron was transferred to No.2 Group and moved in October to Belgium to join No.139 Wing at Melsbroek. In March 1946 it moved to Germany where it was renumbered 14 Squadron on 31 March 1946.

*Due to a typographical error in the squadron's operations record book, this date is often quoted as 15 September.

Squadron bases		Wyton	5 Sep 1944
Thetford	1 Feb 1918	Warboys	22 Jun 1945
	to 4 Jul 1918	B.58 Melsbroek	8 Oct 1945
Hastings	7 Oct 1941	B.119 Wahn	7 Mar 1946
	to 8 Mar 1943		to 31 Mar 1946

Aircraft Equipment	Period of service	Representative Serial and Code
D.H.9	Feb 1918 — Jul 1918	
Hurricane I	Oct 1941 — Jan 1943	Z4484 (WG-A)
Hurricane IIB	Nov 1942 — Mar 1943	BD776 (WG-F)
Mosquito XX	Sep 1944 — Nov 1944	KB221 (M5-B)
Mosquito XXV	Oct 1944 — Nov 1944	KB449 (M5-V)
Mosquito XVI	Nov 1944 — Apr 1946	PF411 (M5-B)

Hurricane I, No.128 Squadron

No. 129 Squadron

Badge: The Gunda Bherunda of Mysore
Motto: I will defend the right
Name: 'Mysore'

No.129 Squadron was formed on 1 March 1918 at Duxford as a day bomber unit but disbanded on 4 July 1918, before becoming operational.

On 16 June 1941 No.129 reformed at Leconfield as a fighter squadron and its Spitfires became operational on 24 July. In August it moved south to provide escorts for day bombers and in December began taking part in offensive operations over France. The squadron moved to the Orkneys in September 1942 for local air defence, returning in February 1943 to south coast airfields for escort and anti-shipping missions. In June 1943 No.129 joined Second TAF on its formation and converted to Mustangs in April 1944. After covering the landings on D-Day, the squadron was given the task of intercepting flying bombs in July for two months before moving to East Anglia to provide long-range escorts for Bomber Command's daylight raids. In June 1945 it moved to Norway with Spitfires, returning to the UK in November. On 1 September 1946 the squadron was renumbered 257 Squadron at Church Fenton.

Squadron bases			
Duxford	1 Mar 1918	Coolham	6 Apr 1944
	to 4 Jul 1918	Holmsley South	22 Jun 1944
Leconfield	16 Jun 1941	Brenzett	9 Jul 1944
Westhampnett	29 Aug 1941	Andrews Field	10 Oct 1944
Debden	1 Nov 1941	Bentwaters	12 Dec 1944
Westhampnett	23 Dec 1941	Dyce	26 May 1945
Thorney Island	30 Jul 1942	Sumburgh	17 Jun 1945
Grimsetter	23 Sep 1942	Vaernes	20 Jun 1945
Skeabrae	19 Jan 1943	Gardermoen	16 Jul 1945
Ibsley	13 Feb 1943	Molesworth	9 Nov 1945
Tangmere	28 Feb 1943	Hutton Cranswick	3 Dec 1945
Ibsley	13 Mar 1943	Spilsby	7 Jan 1946
Hornchurch	28 Jun 1943	Hutton Cranswick	9 Feb 1946
Peterhead	17 Jan 1944	Lubeck	3 May 1946
Heston	16 Mar 1944	Church Fenton	28 Jun 1946
Llanbedr	30 Mar 1944		to 1 Sep 1946

Aircraft Equipment	Period of service	Representative Serial and Code
D.H.9	Mar 1918 — Jul 1918	
Spitfire I	Jun 1941 — Aug 1941	X4251
Spitfire IIA	Aug 1941	P8381
Spitfire VB, VC	Aug 1941 — Jun 1943	EE602 (DV-V)
Spitfire VI	Dec 1942 — Jan 1943	BR577
Spitfire IX	Jun 1943 — Apr 1944 May 1945 — Sep 1946	RR185 (DV-Q)
Mustang III	Apr 1944 — May 1945	FX862 (DV-K)

Spitfire XIV, No.130 Squadron

No. 130 Squadron

Badge: An elephant's head
Motto: Strong to serve
Name: 'Punjab'

No.130 Squadron was formed at Wyton on 1 March 1918 and moved later in the month to Hucknall for training with D.H.9s but was disbanded on 4 July 1918, without becoming operational.

On 20th June 1941 it reformed at Portreath with Spitfires as a fighter squadron and became operational on 21 July. Sweeps over north-west France, convoy patrols off Cornwall and Devon and local air defence duties occupied the squadron until March 1943, when it moved to Scotland for a month before becoming based in Northern Ireland. In July it returned to England and resumed offensive operations on 19 August for a month, moving north again first to Yorkshire and later to Scotland and northern England. On 13 February 1944 the squadron was disbanded.

On 5 April 1944 No.186 Squadron at Lympne was renumbered 130 Squadron and its Spitfires continued their missions over northern France without interruption as part of the Second TAF. In August 1944 it converted to Spitfire XIVs which were used to counter the flying bomb attacks on southern England. At the end of September No.130 moved to the Low Countries for armed reconnaissance sweeps over Germany, the Mark XIV's speed being used to hunt the Me 262 jet fighters which were beginning to appear over the battle area. Attacks on enemy transport and airfields continued until the end of the war when the Mk.XIVs were changed for No.411 Squadron's Mark IXs. By the end of May 1945 the squadron was back in Scotland ready to move to Norway, eighteen aircraft flying across to Kjevik (near Kristiansand) on 20 June escorted by two Mosquitos. It returned to the UK early in November and took up its permanent base at Odiham in July 1946. In October 1946 it converted to Vampires but was renumbered 72 Squadron on 1 February 1947.

On 1 August 1953 No.130 Squadron reformed at Bruggen as part of No.135 Wing as a fighter unit in Germany and converted to Hunters in April 1956, disbanding during May 1957. On 1 December 1959 it reformed at Polebrook as a Thor strategic missile unit, disbanding on 23 August 1963.

Squadron bases

Wyton	1 Mar 1918
Hucknall	Mar 1918
	to 4 Jul 1918
Portreath	20 Jun 1941
Harrowbeer	25 Oct 1941
Warmwell	30 Nov 1941
Perranporth	5 Dec 1941
Warmwell	12 Jul 1942
Perranporth	16 Jul 1942
West Freugh	4 Aug 1942
Perranporth	11 Aug 1942
Thorney Island	16 Aug 1942
Perranporth	20 Aug 1942
Warmwell	21 Oct 1942
Perranporth	31 Oct 1942
Drem	30 Mar 1943
Ballyhalbert	30 Apr 1943
Honiley	5 Jul 1943
West Malling	4 Aug 1943
Catterick	18 Sep 1943
Scorton	10 Nov 1943
Acklington	22 Nov 1943
Scorton	4 Jan 1944
	to 13 Feb 1944
Lympne	5 Apr 1944
Horne	30 Apr 1944
Westhampnett	19 Jun 1944
Merston	27 Jun 1944
Tangmere	3 Aug 1944
Lympne	11 Aug 1944
B.70 Antwerp/Deurne	30 Sep 1944
B.82 Grave	1 Oct 1944
B.64 Diest/Schaffen	1 Nov 1944
Y.32 Ophoven	31 Dec 1944
B.78 Eindhoven	27 Jan 1945
Warmwell	3 Feb 1945
B.78 Eindhoven	21 Feb 1945
B.106 Twente	7 Apr 1945
B.118 Celle	17 Apr 1945
B.152 Fassberg	7 May 1945
North Weald	10 May 1945
Dyce	24 May 1945
Kjevik	20 Jun 1945
Sola	29 Jul 1945
Kjevik	31 Jul 1945
Gardermoen	13 Oct 1945
Manston	4 Nov 1945
Charterhall	1 Dec 1945
Acklington	24 Jan 1946
Manston	27 Jan 1946
Acklington	Jun 1946
Odiham	23 Jul 1946
	to 1 Feb 1947
Bruggen	1 Aug 1953
	to May 1957
Polebrook	1 Dec 1959
	to 23 Aug 1963

Aircraft Equipment

Aircraft Equipment	Period of service	Representative Serial and Code
D.H.9	Mar 1918 – Jul 1918	
Spitfire II	Jun 1941 – Oct 1941	P7904
Spitfire VA, VC, VC	Oct 1941 – Feb 1944	W3314 (PJ-F)
	Apr 1944 – Aug 1944	
Spitfire XIV	Aug 1944 – May 1945	RM699 (AP-S)
Spitfire IX	May 1945 – Oct 1946	TA804 (AP-K)
Vampire F.1	Oct 1946 – Jan 1947	TG949 (Z)
Sabre F.4	Aug 1953 – Apr 1956	XB949 (Z)
Hunter F.4	Apr 1956 – May 1957	XF321 (G)

Hunter F.4, No.130 Squadron

Spitfire VBs, No.131 Squadron

No. 131 Squadron

Badge: In front of an estoile of sixteen points, a horse forcene
Motto: Invicta (Unconquered)
Name: 'County of Kent'

No.131 Squadron was formed at Shawbury on 1 March 1918 as a bomber unit but did not become operational before being disbanded on 17 August 1918.

On 30 June 1941 it reformed at Ouston as a fighter squadron and received Spitfires which became operational on air defence duties at Atcham in September. In February 1942 the squadron moved to Wales to fly patrols over convoys in the Irish Sea and in May moved to southern England to begin offensive sweeps over northern France. These continued until January 1943, when No.131 moved to the north of Scotland to provide fighter protection for Scapa Flow. During its stay in Scotland deck-landing training was carried out on HMS *Argus* in the Clyde in preparation for possible amphibious operations. In June 1943 the squadron moved to south-west England and took part in sweeps over north-west France in addition to convoy patrols. In March 1944 high-altitude Mark VIIs arrived which were used for bomber escort duties and in August the squadron moved to Friston to provide escorts for Bomber Command daylight raids until the end of October when it became non-operational. In November the squadron began to move

No. 132 Squadron

Badge: A leopard rampant
Motto: Cave leopardum (Beware the leopard)
Name: 'Bombay'

No.132 Squadron was formed on 1 March 1918 at Ternhill as a day bomber unit but failed to become operational before being disbanded on 4 July 1918. In October 1918 it began to form at Castle Bromwich to fly D.H.9A day bombers but the Armistice a few weeks later resulted in its formation being abandoned.

to India and re-assembled at Amarda Road on 5 February 1945 to receive Spitfire VIIIs. It did not become operational, however, as its aircraft were required for re-equipping Royal Indian Air Force units and it was disbanded on 10 June 1945.

On 26 June 1945 No.134 Squadron at Ulundurpet was renumbered 131 Squadron and began training with Thunderbolts for the invasion of Malaya. The Japanese surrender forestalled this and in September the squadron moved to Kuala Lumpur where it disbanded on 31 December 1945.

Squadron bases			
Shawbury	1 Mar 1918	Exeter	26 Jun 1943
	to 17 Aug 1918	Redhill	16 Aug 1943
Ouston	30 Jun 1941	Churchstanton	17 Sep 1943
Catterick	9 Jul 1941	Colerne	10 Feb 1944
Ternhill	6 Aug 1941	Harrowbeer	24 Mar 1944
Atcham	27 Sep 1941	Culmhead	24 May 1944
Llanbedr	8 Feb 1942	Friston	28 Aug 1944
Valley	3 Mar 1942	Amarda Road	5 Feb 1945
Llanbedr	16 Apr 1942	Dalbhumgarh	28 Apr 1945
Merston	16 May 1942		to 10 Jun 1945
Ipswich	24 Aug 1942	Ulundurpet	26 Jun 1945
Tangmere	31 Aug 1942	Bobbili	20 Aug 1945
Thorney Island	24 Sep 1942	Baigachi	31 Aug 1945
Westhampnett	7 Nov 1942	Zayatkwin	11 Sep 1945
Castletown	18 Jan 1943	Kuala Lumpur	20 Sep 1945
			to 31 Dec 1945

Aircraft Equipment	Period of service	Representative Serial and Code
F.E.2b	Mar 1918 – Aug 1918	
Spitfire I	Jul 1941 – Sep 1941	X4662
Spitfire IIA	Sep 1941 – Dec 1941	P7698 (NX-P)
Spitfire VB, VC	Dec 1941 – Sep 1943	AD411 (NX-B)
Spitfire IX	Sep 1943 – Mar 1944	MA848 (NX-U)
Spitfire VII	Mar 1944 – Nov 1944	MD123
Spitfire VIII	Feb 1945 – Jun 1945	MV231
Thunderbolt II	Jun 1945 – Dec 1945	KL173

On 7 July 1941 No.132 reformed at Peterhead as a fighter squadron, becoming operational with Spitfires on 19 July on defensive duties. It remained in northern Scotland till September 1942, when it moved to southern England and began to fly sweeps over France. Returning north in January 1944, it rejoined Second TAF in March for fighter-bomber missions in preparation for the invasion of Europe. It provided cover over the landing beaches and moved to Normandy by the end of June. In September 1944 No.132 returned to England to fly escort missions until December, when it left for the Far East. On 20 January 1945 the squadron re-assembled at Vavuniya in Ceylon. Preparations for the invasion of Malaya began in June and in September the squadron was embarked in HMS *Smiter*. The Japanese having surrendered, the carrier took No.132 to Hong Kong where it began flying anti-piracy patrols. On 15 April 1946, the squadron disbanded.

Squadron bases

Ternhill	1 Mar 1918
	to 4 Jul 1918
Castle Bromwich	Oct 1918
	to Nov 1918
Peterhead	7 Jul 1941
Skeabrae	15 Feb 1942
Grimsetter	11 Jun 1942
Martlesham Heath	23 Sep 1942
Hornchurch	2 Oct 1942
Martlesham Heath	9 Oct 1942
Zeals	1 Mar 1943
Eastchurch	5 Apr 1943
Perranporth	18 May 1943
Gravesend	20 Jun 1943
Newchurch	2 Jul 1943
Detling	12 Oct 1943
Castletown	17 Jan 1944
Detling	11 Mar 1944
Fairwood Common	
	13 Mar 1944
Detling	19 Mar 1944
Ford	18 Apr 1944
B.14 Amblie	25 Jun 1944
B.11 Longues	13 Aug 1944
A.61 Beauvais/Tillé	4 Sep 1944
B.70 Antwerp/Deurne	
	17 Sep 1944
Hawkinge	30 Sep 1944
Left for Far East	
	14 Dec 1944
Bombay	11 Jan 1945
Vavuniya	20 Jan 1945
Madura	23 Jun 1945
HMS 'Smiter'	2 Sep 1945
Kai Tak	15 Sep 1945
	to 15 Apr 1946

Spitfire XIV, No.132 Squadron

Aircraft Equipment	Period of service	Representative Serial and Code
D.H.9	Mar 1918 – Jul 1918	
Spitfire I	Jul 1941 – Nov 1941	R7250 (FF-L)
Spitfire IIB	Sep 1941 – Apr 1942	P8234
Spitfire VB, VC	Mar 1942 – Sep 1943	BM129 (FF-S)
	Jan 1944 – Mar 1944	BM129 (FF-S)

Aircraft Equipment	Period of service	Representative Serial and Code
Spitfire IXB	Sep 1943 – Jan 1944	MH486 (FF-H)
	Mar 1944 – Jul 1944	MH486 (FF-H)
Spitfire IXE	Jul 1944 – Dec 1944	NH305 (FF-R)
Spitfire VIII	Jan 1945 – May 1945	JG568
Spitfire XIV	May 1945 – Apr 1946	RN143 (FF-A)

No. 133 Squadron

Badge: On a hurt semeé of mullets, an eagle deployed
Motto: Let us to the battle
Name: 'Eagle'

No.133 Squadron was formed on 1 March 1918 at Ternhill as a night bomber squadron and was intended to receive Handley Page O/400s but there is no evidence that it ever received any. F.E.2bs were used for training until it disbanded on 4 July 1918 to provide reinforcements for active squadrons. On 28 October 1918 it started to reform but the war ended two weeks later and formation was not pursued.

On 1 August 1941 No.133 reformed at Coltishall as the third Eagle squadron to be manned by American personnel. Equipped with Hurricanes, it became operational at the end of September. Next month it moved to Northern Ireland, returning to Lincolnshire at the end of the year. In April 1942 the squadron took part in its first fighter sweep over France and moved to Biggin Hill early in May. Sweeps continued until 29 September 1942 when the squadron was transferred to the USAAF as the 336th Fighter Squadron of the 4th Fighter Group.

Squadron bases

		Eglinton	8 Oct 1941
Ternhill	1 Mar 1918	Kirton-in-Lindsey	2 Jan 1942
	to 4 Jul 1918	Biggin Hill	3 May 1942
Feltham	28 Oct 1918	Gravesend	31 Jul 1942
	to Nov 1918	Martlesham Heath	22 Aug 1942
Coltishall	1 Aug 1941	Biggin Hill	30 Aug 1942
Duxford	15 Aug 1941	Great Sampford	23 Sep 1942
Fowlmere	3 Oct 1941		to 29 Sep 1942

Aircraft Equipment	Period of service	Representative Serial and Code
F.E.2b	Mar 1918 – Jul 1918	
Hurricane IIB	Aug 1941 – Dec 1941	Z4999 (MD-A)
Spitfire IIA	Oct 1941 – Jan 1942	P8191 (MD-G)
Spitfire VA	Jan 1942 – Mar 1942	P8074
Spitfire VB	Feb 1942 – Sep 1942	EN951 (MD-U)
Spitfire IXC	Sep 1942	BS296 (MD-S)

Hurricane IIBs, No.134 Squadron

No.134 Squadron

Badge: A gauntlet closed
Motto: Per ardua volabimus (We
shall fly through
hardships)

No.134 Squadron was formed at Ternhill on 1 March 1918 as a night bomber unit and was intended to receive Handley Page O/400 twin-engined bombers but it is not known whether any had been received before the squadron disbanded on 4 July 1918.

On 31 July 1941 No.134 reformed at Leconfield from a nucleus flight supplied by No.17 Squadron. As part of No.151 Wing, the ground crews embarked for Russia on 12 August while twelve Hurricanes were flown off HMS *Argus* to Vaenga near Murmansk on 7 September, becoming operational within a few days. After providing fighter cover for Russian bombers and flying defensive patrols, the squadron handed over its Hurricanes to the Russian Navy on 19 October and during November embarked in various naval vessels for return to the UK. On 7 December 1941 No.134 re-assembled at Catterick and received some Spitfires, moving to Northern Ireland early in January 1942, where some Hurricanes were also used. In April the squadron embarked for the Middle East, arriving in Egypt in June where the ground crews were used to service the aircraft of other units pending the receipt of their own aircraft. It was not until January 1943 that No.134 became operational on Hurricanes again and provided fighter defence for the ports and bases along the North African coast. In November 1943, the squadron was transferred to India and flew its aircraft to the Burmese frontier area, becoming operational on 3 December. Ground-attack missions against Japanese positions in Burma occupied the squadron till the end of May when it moved back to India to convert to Thunderbolts. The first of these arrived in August and No.134 returned to operations over Burma on 7 December. After covering the landings at Rangoon in April 1945, the squadron returned to India and on 10 June was renumbered 131 Squadron.

Squadron bases

Ternhill	1 Mar 1918	Sousse (D)	28 Apr 1943
	to 4 Jul 1918		to 16 May 1943
Leconfield	31 Jul 1941	Bu Amud	14 May 1943
Emb. for North Russia		Bersis	23 Jun 1943
	12 Aug 1941	Qassassin	26 Oct 1943
Vaenga	7 Sep 1941	Left for India	14 Nov 1943 (A)
Began to move to the UK		Comilla	3 Dec 1943
	16 Nov 1941	Parashuram	15 Dec 1943 (A)
Catterick	7 Dec 1941		10 Dec 1943 (G)
Eglinton	1 Jan 1942	Fazilpur	20 Jan 1944
Baginton	25 Mar 1942	Hay	26 Jan 1944
Left for Middle East		Ramu III	1 Apr 1944
	10 Apr 1942	Arkonam	23 May 1944
Kasfareet	4 Jun 1942	Cuttack (D)	13 Jun 1944
Helwan	9 Jun 1942		to 25 Jul 1944
Kasfareet	24 Jun 1942	Yelahanka	15 Aug 1944
Lydda	5 Jul 1942	Arkonam	6 Oct 1944
Helwan	11 Nov 1942	Baigachi	19 Nov 1944
LG.222	16 Nov 1942	Ratnap	26 Nov 1944
Shandur	21 Mar 1942	Kyaukpyu	28 Apr 1945
LG.121	6 Feb 1943	Ulundurpet	12 Jun 1945
LG.219	15 Apr 1943	(for transfer of aircraft to 131 Squadron)	

Aircraft

Equipment	Period of service	Representative Serial and Code
Hurricane IIA	Sep 1941 – Oct 1941	Z5159 (GV-33)
Spitfire VA	Dec 1941 – Apr 1942	AB198
Spitfire IIA	Jan 1942 – Feb 1942	P7563
Hurricane IIA	Jan 1942 – Feb 1942	Z3347
Hurricane IIB, IIC	Jan 1943 – Aug 1944	LB885 (GQ-V)
Spitfire VB, VC	Jun 1943 – Aug 1943	AB275 (F)
Thunderbolt I, II	Aug 1944 – Jun 1945	KJ275 (GQ-T)

164

Thunderbolt Is, No.135 Squadron

No. 135 Squadron

Badge: A peacock in its pride
Motto: Pennas ubique monstramus
(We show our wings
everywhere).

No.135 Squadron was formed at Hucknall on 1 April 1918 but did not become operational before being disbanded on 4 July 1918.

On 15 August 1941 No.135 reformed at Baginton with Hurricanes received from 605 Squadron and became operational on 3 October for a month. It was then posted to India and embarked on 10 November, arriving there early in January to be immediately rerouted to Rangoon where it began operations on 26 January 1942, against Japanese aircraft attacking the area. The Rangoon airfields being in imminent danger of being overrun, the squadron ground echelon was evacuated to Calcutta while the aircraft were almost entirely lost during the Japanese attack on Burma. Reformed at Calcutta, the squadron began flying convoy patrols and in January 1943 began sweeps over Burma and air defence duties which lasted until the squadron was withdrawn to southern India at the end of May. After acting as a conversion unit for Blenheim squadrons being re-equipped with Hurricanes, it provided air defence of the area until re-equipped with Thunderbolts, the first arriving in May 1944 and conversion being completed by the end of August. On 16 October, 1944, ground-attack missions were resumed over Burma and continued until May 1945, when No.135 was withdrawn from operations and renumbered 605 Squadron on 10 June, 1945.

Squadron bases			
Hucknall	1 Apr 1918	Dohazari	16 May 1943
	to 4 Jul 1918	St.Thomas Mount	22May1943
Baginton	15 Aug 1941	Yelahanka	1 Jul 1943
Honiley	4 Sep 1941	St.Thomas Mount	22Nov1943
Emb. for Far East		Minneriya	16 Jan 1944
	10 Nov 1941	Amarda Road (A)	25 Aug 1944
Zayatkwin	16 Jan 1942		to 16 Sep 1944
Mingaladon	28 Jan 1942	Chittagong	9 Oct 1944
Emb. for India	20 Feb 1942	Jumchar	9 Dec 1944
Dum Dum	27 Mar 1942	Cox's Bazaar	15 Apr 1945
'George'/'Hove'	23 Jan 1943	Akyab	24 Apr 1945
Ramu/'Reindeer'	13 May 1943	Chakulia	17 May 1945
			to 10 Jun 1945

Aircraft Equipment	Period of service	Representative Serial and Code
Hurricane IIA	Aug 1941 — Feb 1942	Z2821
Hurricane IIB, IIC	Jan 1942 — Sep 1944	BG994 (D)
Hurricane IIC	Nov 1941	LB618 (P)
Thunderbolt I	May 1944 — Jun 1945	HB975 (WK-L)

No. 136 Squadron

Badge: Upon the side of a stem
of tree erect, a green
woodpecker
Motto: Nihil fortius
(Nothing is stronger)

No.136 Squadron was formed at Lake Down on 1 April 1918 but does not appear to have received any aircraft before being disbanded on 4 July 1918, to provide reinforcements for operational squadrons. It reformed on 20 August 1941 at Kirton-in-Lindsey with Hurricanes and became operational on 28 September for a month before embarking for the Far East on 9 November. On arrival in India it was redirected to Burma where it arrived early in February 1942, during the Japanese invasion. By the end of the month it had been re-embarked and evacuated to India where it reformed as an

Spitfire VIIIs, No.136 Squadron

operational Hurricane squadron on 31 March 1942 for convoy patrol and air defence duties around Calcutta. Detachments began operating from Chittagong over the Burma front in mid-December and by the end of the year it was based there. In June 1943 it was withdrawn for rest and converted to Spitfires in October. Operations with these began on 3 December 1943 and No.136 provided fighter defence and escorts over Burma until withdrawn to Ceylon in July 1944. At the end of March 1945 the squadron ground echelon left for the Cocos Islands and its aircraft began flying on completion of the airstrip a month later. After the Japanese surrender, the squadron moved to Malaya and remained there until May 1946, when it embarked for India. En route to Bombay on 8 May 1946, the squadron was renumbered 152 Squadron.

Alipore	31 Mar 1942	Rumkhapalong	25 Jan 1944
Red Road	27 Jun 1942	Sapam	5 Mar 1944
Alipore	17 Aug 1942	Wangjing	11 Mar 1944
Vizagapatam (D)	19 Aug 1942	Chittagong	18 Apr 1944
	to 3 Sep 1942	Ratmalana	7 Jul 1944
Dum Dum	6 Sep 1942	Minneriya	15 Dec 1944
Chittagong (D)	10 Dec 1942	Emb. for Cocos Island	
	to 15 Dec 1942		27 Mar 1945 (G)
Chittagong	21 Dec 1942	Cocos Island	7 Apr 1945 (G)
Baigachi	21 Jun 1943		26 Apr 1945 (A)
Amarda Road	6 Nov 1943	Left for Malaya	14 Oct 1945
Baigachi	21 Nov 1943	Kuala Lumpur	24 Oct 1945
Ramu/'Lyons'	1 Dec 1943	Left for India	5 May 1946
Alipore	7 Dec 1943	Renumbered	8 May 1946
Ramu/'Lyons'	20 Dec 1943		

Squadron bases

Lake Down	1 Apr 1918	Left for Far East	9 Nov 1941
	to 4 Jul 1918	Rangoon	6 Feb 1942
Kirton-in-Lindsey		Left for India	20 Feb 1942
	20 Aug 1941	Dum Dum	26 Feb 1942
		Asansol	27 Feb 1942

Aircraft

Equipment	Period of service	Representative Serial and Code
Hurricane IIB	Aug 1941 – Nov 1941	Z3238 (P)
Hurricane IIB, IIC	Mar 1942 – Oct 1943	BM952
Spitfire VC	Oct 1943 – Mar 1944	
Spitfire VIII	Jan 1944 – Feb 1945	MT567 (HM-B)
	Apr 1945 – May 1946	
Spitfire XIV	Feb 1946 – May 1946	RN193 (HM-A)

No. 137 Squadron

Badge: A horse's head couped
Motto: Do right, fear naught

No.137 Squadron was formed at Shawbury on 1 April 1918 as a day bomber unit but did not become operational before being disbanded on 4 July 1918.

On 20 September 1941 No.137 reformed at Charmy Down, a satellite airfield of Colerne, with Whirlwind twin-engined fighter-bombers, the second and last squadron to receive this type. Operations across the Channel began on 24 October and in November it moved to East Anglia. The squadron continued to operate Whirlwinds until the middle of June 1943, when it converted to Hurricanes equipped with 40mm cannon and rockets. The first attack with cannon on enemy transport took place on 23 July but by the end of the year rockets had been found more effective for ground-attack work. In January 1944 conversion to Typhoons took place and No.137 became operational with these on 8 February in No.124 Wing. After taking part in anti-shipping strikes, the squadron covered the landings in Normandy before beginning anti-flying-bomb patrols during June and July. On 13 August 1944 it moved to Normandy to provide ground-attack support for the Allied armies and by the end of September had advanced into the Netherlands. Armed reconnaissance sweeps were carried out over Germany for the rest of the war and after a short period in Germany the squadron was renumbered 174 Squadron on 26 August 1945, while its air echelon was temporarily based at Warmwell for an air-firing course.

Whirlwind I, No.137 Squadron

Squadron bases

Shawbury	1 Apr 1918	Manston	1 Apr 1944	B.118 Celle	7 May 1945	B.158 Lubeck	11 Jul 1945
	to 4 Jul 1918	B.6 Coulombs	13 Aug 1944	B.160 Kastrup	9 May 1945	Warmwell (A)	20 Aug 1945
Charmy Down	20 Sep 1941	B.30 Creton	29 Aug 1944	B.172 Husum	21 Jun 1945		to 26 Aug 1945
Coltishall	8 Nov 1941	B.48 Amiens/Glisy	3 Sep 1944				
Matlask	1 Dec 1941	B.58 Melsbroek	6 Sep 1944				
Snailwell	24 Aug 1942	B.78 Eindhoven	22 Sep 1944				
Manston	17 Sep 1942	B.86 Helmond	13 Jan 1945				
Southend	12 Jun 1943	B.106 Twente	11 Apr 1945				
Manston	8 Aug 1943	B.112 Hopsten	13 Apr 1945				
Lympne	14 Dec 1943	B.120 Langenhagen					
Colerne	2 Jan 1944		17 Apr 1945				
Lympne	4 Feb 1944	B.156 Luneburg	30 Apr 1945				

Aircraft

Equipment	Period of service	Representative Serial and Code
D.H.9	Apr 1918 – Jul 1918	
Whirlwind I	Sep 1941 – Jun 1943	P6993 (SF-A)
Hurricane IV	Jun 1943 – Jan 1944	KZ661
Typhoon IB	Jan 1944 – Aug 1945	MN421 (SF-D)

No.138 Squadron

Badge: A sword in bend, the point uppermost, severing a reef knot

Motto: For freedom

No.138 Squadron was formed on 1 May 1918 as a nucleus but formation was suspended on 4 July 1918 to provide reinforcements for operational units. On 30 September 1918 it reformed at Chingford as a fighter-reconnaissance squadron but did not become operational before the Armistice and was disbanded on 1 February 1919.

On 25 August 1941 No.1419 (Special Duties) Flight at Newmarket became No.138 Squadron. Its main task was maintaining communications with resistance movements in occupied Europe. Whitleys dropped arms, supplies and agents while Lysanders made landings in enemy-occupied territory to deliver and pick-up agents, the first successful pick-up taking place in February 1942. On many supply flights bombs were carried for attacks on communications targets as cover for their clandestine operations. In October 1942 Halifaxes replaced Whitleys, the pick-up task having been taken over by No.161 Squadron. In September 1944 the Halifaxes were replaced by Stirlings and all three types made numerous hazardous flights to all parts of German-occupied territory, some as far away as Poland, Yugoslavia and Austria, one flight being manned by Polish airmen. As the frontiers of the Third Reich contracted, the need for special duties units decreased and No.138 transferred to Bomber Command on 9 March 1945 and took part in bombing raids with Lancasters for the rest of the war. It remained in Bomber Command after the war and converted to Lincolns in September 1947. On 1 September 1950 the squadron was disbanded.

On 1 January 1955 No.138 reformed at Gaydon as the first Valiant squadron. In October 1956 it took these to Malta during the Suez landings and on 1 April 1962 was disbanded.

Squadron bases

Not known	1 May 1918	Tuddenham	9 Mar 1945
	to 4 Jul 1918	Wyton	Nov 1946
Chingford	30 Sep 1918	Scampton	5 Jul 1948
	to 1 Feb 1919		to 1 Sep 1950
Newmarket	25 Aug 1941	Gaydon	1 Jan 1955
Stradishall	Jan 1942 (P)	Wittering	6 Jul 1955
Tempsford	11 Mar 1942		to 1 Apr 1962

Aircraft

Equipment	Period of service	Representative Serial
Bristol F.2b	Sep 1918 – Feb 1919	
Whitley V	Aug 1941 – Oct 1942	Z9159
Lysander IIIa	Aug 1941 – Feb 1942	T1508
Halifax I	Oct 1941 – Dec 1942	L9618
Halifax II	Oct 1942 – Aug 1944	W1002
Stirling IV	Jun 1944 – Mar 1945	LJ503
Lancaster I	Mar 1945 – Sep 1947	LM275 (AC-V)
Lincoln B.2	Sep 1947 – Sep 1950	RF440 (NF-X)
Valiant B.1	Feb 1955 – Apr 1962	XD875

Victor B.2, No.139 Squadron

No. 139 Squadron

Badge: In front of a crescent, a fasces
Motto: Si placet necamus (We destroy at will)
Name: 'Jamaica'

No.139 Squadron was formed on 3 July 1918 at Villaverla in northern Italy from Z Flight which had been attached to No.34 Squadron. Its Bristol Fighters were used for fighter patrols and reconnaissance over the Piave front until the end of the war and in February 1919, the squadron returned to the UK for disbandment on 7 March 1919.

On 3 September 1936 No.139 reformed at Wyton with Hinds as a day bomber squadron and began to convert to Blenheims in July 1939. With these it flew the first reconnaissance mission by the RAF during World War Two when N6215 provided information on the position of the German fleet in north German ports. In December 1939 the squadron replaced No.40 in France and during the German invasion lost the bulk of its aircraft in attacks on German columns during the first days of the offensive. It returned to the UK to re-equip and began attacks by day and night on enemy-occupied ports and airfields which lasted until the end of 1941, when the squadron was posted to the Far East as a Hudson unit. On arrival in Burma it became immediately involved in the Japanese invasion and on 30 April 1942 was absorbed by No.62 Squadron.

On 8 June 1942, No.139 reformed with Blenheim Vs at Horsham St. Faith but did not fly these operationally before converting to Mosquitos in September, a few missions being flown in Mosquitos borrowed from 105 Squadron in the meantime. Attacks on Germany began soon afterwards and continued for the rest of the war, No.139 joining No.8 Group in July 1943 as part of the Pathfinder Force. After the end of the war, the squadron was retained in Bomber Command and replaced its Mosquitos with Canberras in November 1953. On 31 December 1959 it disbanded.

On 1 February 1962, the Victor B.2 Intensive Trials Unit became No.139 Squadron at Wittering and formed part of the V-bomber Force until disbanded on 31 December 1968.

Squadron bases

Villaverla	3 Jul 1918	Oulton	5 Dec 1941
Grossa	10 Oct 1918	Emb. for Far East	Dec 1941
San Luca	26 Oct 1918	Akyab	Feb 1942
Arcade	2 Nov 1918	Chittagong	22 Mar 1942
Grossa	14 Nov 1918		to 30 Apr 1942
Blandford	25 Feb 1919	Horsham St. Faith	
	to 7 Mar 1919		8 Jun 1942
Wyton	3 Sep 1939	Oulton	15 Jun 1942
Alconbury	8 Nov 1939	Horsham St. Faith	
Wyton	17 Nov 1939		20 Jun 1942
Betheniville	2 Dec 1939	Marham	29 Sep 1942
Plivot	18 Feb 1940	Wyton	4 Jul 1943
West Raynham	30 May 1940	Upwood	1 Feb 1944
Horsham St. Faith		Hemswell	4 Feb 1946
	10 Jun 1940	Coningsby	4 Nov 1946
Luqa (D)	May 1941	East Kirkby (D)	Aug 1947
	to Jun 1941		to Feb 1948
Oulton	13 Jul 1941	Hemswell	1 Apr 1950
Manston (D)	27 Aug 1941	Binbrook	31 Dec 1955
	to 7 Sep 1941		to 31 Dec 1959
Horsham St. Faith		Wittering	1 Feb 1962
	23 Oct 1941		to 31 Dec 1968

Aircraft equipment

	Period of service	Representative Serial and Code
Bristol F.2b	Jul 1918 – Feb 1919	D8084 (S)
Camel	Jul 1918 – Oct 1918	B6313 (1 only)
Hind	Sep 1936 – Aug 1937	K5375
Blenheim I	Jul 1937 – Sep 1939	K7078 (139-J)
Blenheim IV	Sep 1939 – Dec 1941	L8756 (XD-E)
Hudson III	Dec 1941; Feb 1942 – Apr 1942	V9114
Blenheim V	Jun 1942 – Oct 1942	AZ970
Mosquito IV	Sep 1942 – Jul 1944	DZ464 (XD-C)
Mosquito IX	Sep 1943 – Sep 1944	ML909 (XD-S)
Mosquito XVI	Feb 1944 – 1948	MM200 (XD-E)
Mosquito XX	Nov 1943 – Sep 1945	KB192 (XD-S)
Mosquito 25	Sep 1944 – Sep 1945	KB434 (XD-V)
Mosquito B.35	Oct 1948 – Nov 1953	TK620 (XD-L)
Canberra B.2, B.6	Nov 1953 – Dec 1959	WJ971
Victor B.2	Feb 1962 – Dec 1968	XL190

No. 140 Squadron

Badge: An eyed hawk moth
Motto: Foresight

No.140 Squadron was formed at Biggin Hill on 1 May 1918 as a fighter unit for the defence of London and was equipped with Bristol Fighters. Due to the lack of German air raids at this time, the squadron did not go into action and was disbanded on 4 July 1918, to provide reinforcements for active units.

On 17 September 1941 No.1416 Flight at Benson was renumbered 140 Squadron and one of its Spitfires flew the first photographic sortie of the squadron on the same day. Blenheims were also used for night reconnaissance missions and the first of these was flown over Cherbourg on 15 November though the majority of work was done by Spitfires. Blenheim operations ceased in August 1942, but some were retained until early in 1943, when Venturas were received as replacements. Few missions were flown by these before the first Mosquitos were received in August. Spitfires continued to provide photographic coverage over large areas of occupied Europe until April 1944, when the last Spitfire sortie was flown on the 27th and No.140 became fully equipped with Mosquitos. Both day and night reconnaissance missions were flown for the rest of the war but in 1945 night missions were in the majority. In September 1944 the squadron moved to Belgium to shorten the distance to its operational areas for the rest of the war. In July 1945 it returned to the UK without aircraft and was disbanded on 10 November 1945.

Squadron bases

Biggin Hill	1 May 1918 to 4 Jul 1918	A.12 Lignerolles	3 Sep 1944
		B.48 Amiens/Glisy	8 Sep 1944
Benson	17 Sep 1941	B.58 Melsbroek	26 Sep 1944
Weston Zoyland	29 Oct 1941	B.78 Eindhoven	15 Apr 1945
Benson	4 Nov 1941	Fersfield	9 Jul 1945
Mount Farm	20 May 1942	Acklington	12 Jul 1945
Hartfordbridge	13 Mar 1943	Fersfield	19 Sep 1945
Northolt	7 Apr 1944		to 10 Nov 1945

Aircraft

Equipment	Period of service	Representative Serial and Code
Bristol F.2b	May 1918 – Jul 1918	
Spitfire IV	Sep 1941 – Jan 1944	X4784
Spitfire XI	Sep 1943 – Apr 1944	MB942
Blenheim IV	Sep 1941 – Aug 1943	L3825
Ventura I	Feb 1943 – Jan 1944	AE714
Mosquito IX	+Nov 1943 – Dec 1944	LR479
Mosquito XVI	Dec 1943 – Jul 1945	NS522

+Two Mosquitos had been received in August but effective reequipment did not take place till November.

Venom NF.3, No.141 Squadron

No. 141 Squadron

Badge: On an ogress, a leopard's face
Motto: Caedimus noctu (We slay by night)

No.141 Squadron was formed at Rochford on 1 January 1918 as a home defence unit for the London Area, moving to Biggin Hill in February and giving up its mixed collection of types in favour of Bristol Fighters during March. In March 1919 it moved to Ireland where it was disbanded on 1 February 1920.

On 4 October 1939 No.141 reformed at Turnhouse and by the end of the month had received some Gladiators followed shortly afterwards by Blenheims and these two types formed the training equipment of the squadron till the arrival of Defiants in April 1940. Becoming operational on this type on 3 June 1940, the first operational patrol was flown by No.141 on 29 June and in July it moved to West Malling. The maintenance flight was based at Biggin Hill while the Defiants used Hawkinge as an advanced airfield and it was from the latter that the squadron had its first and last daylight encounter with the enemy. Six out of nine aircraft were lost over the Channel to Bf 109s and the squadron was withdrawn to Prestwick two days later as the ineffectiveness of the Defiant against single-seat fighters became evident. In September a detachment was sent back to southern England but this time for night patrols and the whole squadron moved there in October. In April 1941 No.141 returned to Scotland where it converted to Beaufighters for the defence of central Scotland and north-east England. In June 1942 it moved to Tangmere for local defence and in February 1943 to south-west England where it began flying intruder missions over north-west France. At the end of April 1943, it was transferred to Wittering and began flying intruder sorties over German airfields in support of Bomber Command in June. Mosquitos began to replace the Beaufighters in October and in December the squadron joined No.100 Group, sending aircraft with Bomber Command's main force to attack enemy night fighters and their bases. This type of operation continued until the German surrender and on 7 September 1945 the squadron was disbanded.

On 17 June 1946 No.141 reformed at Wittering, again as a Mosquito night fighter squadron. In September 1951 it began to convert to Meteors and replaced these with Venoms in 1955. Javelins began to arrive in February 1957 and were flown until the squadron was renumbered 41 Squadron on 1 February 1958. On 1 April 1959 it was reformed as a Bloodhound anti-aircraft missile unit at Dunholme Lodge, disbanding in March 1964.

Squadron bases

Rochford	1 Jan 1918	Grangemouth	19 Oct 1939
Biggin Hill	8 Feb 1918	Turnhouse	28 Jun 1940
Tallaght	1 Mar 1919	West Malling	12 Jul 1940
Baldonnel	14 Dec 1919	Prestwick	21 Jul 1940
	to 1 Feb 1920	Dyce & Montrose (D)	
Turnhouse	4 Oct 1939		22 Aug 1940
		Turnhouse	30 Aug 1940
Biggin Hill (D)	13 Sep 1940	Predannack	18 Feb 1943
	to 18 Sep 1940	Wittering	30 Apr 1943
Gatwick (D)	18 Sep 1940	Drem (D)	12 May 1943
	to 22 Oct 1940		to 11 Jun 1943
Drem	15 Oct 1940	West Raynham	4 Dec 1943
Gatwick	22 Oct 1940 (G)	Little Snoring	3 Jul 1945
	24 Oct 1940 (A)		to 7 Sep 1945
Gravesend	3 Nov 1940	Wittering	17 Jun 1946
Ayr	29 Apr 1941	Coltishall	23 Jan 1947
Acklington (D)	1 May 1941	Church Fenton	21 Nov 1949
	to 7 Aug 1941	Coltishall	22 Sep 1950
Drem (D)	11 Oct 1941	Horsham St. Faith	12 Oct 1956
	to 23 Jan 1942	Coltishall	28 May 1957
Acklington	29 Jan 1942		to 31 Jan 1958
Tangmere	23 Jun 1942	Dunholme Lodge	1 Apr 1959
Ford	10 Aug 1942		to Mar 1964

Aircraft Equipment

Aircraft Equipment	Period of service	Representative Serial and Code
Dolphin	Jan 1918 – Mar 1918	C3862
B.E.2e	Feb 1918 – Mar 1918	B723
Pup	Feb 1918 – Mar 1918	
B.E.12	Feb 1918 – Mar 1918	
Vickers F.B.26	Feb 1918 – Mar 1918	
Bristol F.2b	Mar 1918 – Feb 1920	D2157
Gladiator I, II	Oct 1939 – Apr 1940	K7990
Blenheim If	Nov 1939 – May 1940	K7059
Battle I	Feb 1940 – May 1940	
Defiant I	Apr 1940 – Aug 1941	L7036 (TW-H)
Beaufighter I	Jun 1941 – Jun 1943	V8253 (TW-T)
Beaufighter VI	May 1943 – Feb 1944	V8673 (TW-K)
Mosquito II	Oct 1943 – Aug 1944	DD790 (TW-L)
Mosquito VI	Jul 1944 – Mar 1945	PZ165 (TW-S)
Mosquito 30	Mar 1945 – Sep 1945	NT507 (TW-F)
Mosquito NF.36	Jun 1946 – Oct 1951	RL154 (TW-E)
Meteor NF.3	Jun 1955 – May 1957	WX840 (L)
Javelin FAW.4	Feb 1957 – Jan 1958	XA751 (751)
Bloodhound I	Apr 1959 – Mar 1964	—

Battle I, No.142 Squadron

No. 142 Squadron

Badge: A winged sphinx
Motto: Determination

No.142 Squadron was formed at Ismailia on 2 February 1918 as a corps reconnaissance unit for co-operation with the Army in Egypt and Palestine and was engaged in tactical reconnaissance and artillery observation duties until the end of the war. After a short period in Egypt, it was renumbered 55 Squadron on 1 February 1920.

On 1 June 1934 No.142 reformed at Netheravon with Harts as a day bomber unit. Early in October 1935 it embarked for the Middle East during the Abyssinian crisis and by the end of the month was installed in the Western Desert near the Libyan frontier. In November 1936 it returned to the UK and re-equipped with Hinds in January 1937. In March 1938 it converted to Battles and on the outbreak of World War Two took these to France as part of the Advanced Air Striking Force. During the German offensive in May 1940, the squadron was engaged in attacks on enemy troop colomns until forced to evacuate its airfields and return to the UK in mid-June. From Binbrook attacks on enemy barge concentrations in the Channel Ports began, a move being made to Eastchurch in August to shorten the range. In November 1940 Wellingtons began to arrive and the squadron began training for night bombing, operations being resumed on 15 April 1941. Attacks on enemy targets continued until 27 January 1943 when the section of the squadron remaining in the UK merged with 150 Squadron to form No.166. On 18 December 1942 a detachment of thirteen Wellingtons had flown to Algeria where they were joined by a ground echelon and, on the renumbering of the UK-based formation, this became the full squadron strength. Night attacks were carried out on enemy bases in Tunisia, Sicily, Italy and Sardinia as part of No.330 Wing and in December 1943 the squadron moved to bases in southern Italy. Attacks on targets in northern Italy and the Balkans continued until the squadron was disbanded on 5 October 1944, dispersal of the aircraft and personnel being complete by the end of the month.

On 25 October 1944 No.142 reformed at Gransden Lodge as a Mosquito squadron in No.8 Group. It carried out attacks at night, flying Canadian-built aircraft, frequently acting as Pathfinders, for the rest of the war and disbanded again on 28 September 1945. On 1 February 1959 No.142 reformed at Eastleigh, Kenya, as a fighter-bomber squadron with Venoms but was renumbered 208 Squadron on 1 April 1959.

The squadron next reformed at Coleby Grange on 22 July 1959 as a Thor strategic missile unit, disbanding on 24 May 1963.

Squadron bases

Ismailia	2 Feb 1918	Ramleh	4 Oct 1918
Julis	13 Feb 1918	Haifa	12 Nov 1918
Ramleh	18 Apr 1918	Ramleh	20 Nov 1918
Sarona	18 Sep 1918	Kantara	25 Nov 1918
Afuleh	22 Sep 1918	Suez	17 Feb 1919
			to 1 Feb 1920

Netheravon	1 Jun 1934	Grimsby	26 Nov 1941
Andover	3 Jan 1935	Thruxton	7 Jun 1942
Emb. for Middle East		Grimsby	7 Jul 1942
	4 Oct 1935	Blida	19 Dec 1942 (D)
Aboukir	13 Oct 1935	Kirmington	19 Dec 1942
Mersa Matruh	21 Oct 1935		to 27 Jan 1943
Helwan	8 May 1936	Blida	27 Jan 1943
Mersa Matruh	6 Jun 1936	Fontaine Chaude	5 May 1943
Ismailia	29 Jul 1936	Kairouan	26 May 1943
Aboukir	3 Nov 1936	Oudna	15 Nov 1943
Emb. for UK	21 Nov 1936	Cerignola	16 Dec 1943 (G)
Andover	3 Dec 1936		20 Dec 1943 (A)
Bicester	9 May 1939	Amendola	14 Feb 1944
Berry-au-Bac	2 Sep 1939	Regina	3 Jul 1944
Plivot	12 Sep 1939		to 5 Oct 1944
Berry-au-Bac	Sep 1939	Gransden Lodge	25 Oct 1944
Faux-Villecerf	16 May 1940		to 28 Sep 1945
Villiers- Faux	6 Jun 1940	Eastleigh	1 Feb 1959
Waddington	15 Jun 1940		to 1 Apr 1959
Binbrook	3 Jul 1940	Coleby Grange	22 Jul 1959
Eastchurch	12 Aug 1940		to 24 May 1963
Binbrook	6 Sep 1940		

Aircraft

Equipment	Period of service	Representative Serial and Code
B.E.12a	Feb 1918 — May 1918	A6328
Martinsyde G.100	Mar 1918 — May 1918	A4000
B.E.2c, B.E.2d, B.E.2e	Feb 1918 — Feb 1919	
R.E.8	Apr 1918 — Apr 1919	B7710
F.K.8	May 1918 — Mar 1919	C3617
D.H.9	Jan 1919 — Feb 1920	D573
Hart	Jun 1934 — Jan 1937	K3959
Hind	Jan 1937 — Mar 1938	K6654
Battle	Mar 1938 — Jan 1941	P2246
Wellington II	Nov 1940 — Oct 1941	W5387 (QT-V)
Wellington IV	Oct 1941 — Oct 1942	Z1210 (QT-M)
Wellington III	Sep 1942 — Oct 1943	BK298 (QT-O)
Wellington X	Aug 1943 — Oct 1944	HE815 (QT-Z)
Mosquito XXV	Oct 1944 — Sep 1945	KB449 (4H-V)
Venom FB.4	Feb 1959 — Apr 1959	WR400
Thor	Jul 1959 — May 1963	—

Beaufighter X, No.143 Squadron

No. 143 Squadron

Badge: A gamecock attacking
Motto: Vincere est vivere (To conquer is to live)

No.143 Squadron was formed at Throwley on 1 February 1918 as part of the 53rd (Home Defence) Wing for the defence of London against enemy bombers based in Belgium. Based in northern Kent, it was well placed to intercept enemy formations flying up the Thames Estuary but the German raids ceased by the summer on 1918 and were not resumed. In 1919, Snipes began to replace the Camels but the squadron was disbanded on 31 October 1919.

On 15 June 1941 No.143 reformed at Aldergrove as a long-range fighter unit in Coastal Command and by absorbing part of No.252 Squadron became operational almost immediatley. Early in July the squadron moved first to northeast England and then to Scotland for convoy patrols along the East Coast. In December 1941 No.143 returned to Ireland and became non-operational, giving up its Beaufighters for Blenheims and becoming a training unit. In August 1942 the squadron moved to East Anglia for convoy patrols and air-sea rescue missions and in September once more began to re-equip with Beaufighters, becoming operational on anti-shipping raids in November. As part of a strike wing, it operated off the Dutch coast until August 1943, when it moved to Cornwall to provide fighter support for anti-submarine aircraft operating over the Bay of Biscay. In February 1944 it returned to North Coates to resume attacks on enemy shipping and in May moved to Manston to fly anti-E-boat patrols on the eastern flank of the invasion forces for two months. In October 1944 No.143 moved to northern Scotland where it converted to Mosquitos as part of the Banff strike wing for attacks on enemy shipping off Norway for the rest of the war. On 25 May 1945, the squadron was disbanded and its personnel transferred to No.14 Squadron.

Squadron bases

		Thorney Island	9 Jun 1942
Throwley	1 Feb 1918	Docking	27 Jul 1942
Detling	Mar 1918	North Coates	27 Aug 1942
	to 31 Oct 1919	St. Eval	27 Aug 1943
Aldergrove	15 Jun 1941	Portreath	16 Sep 1943
Thornaby	4 Jul 1941	North Coates	11 Feb 1944
Dyce	19 Jul 1941	Manston	23 May 1944
Sumburgh	29 Sep 1941	North Coates	9 Sep 1944
Aldergrove	14 Dec 1941	Banff	23 Oct 1944
Limavady	23 Apr 1942		to 25 May 1945

Aircraft Equipment	Period of service		Representative Serial and Code
Camel	1918 —	1919	
S.E.5A	1918 —	1918	
Snipe	1919 — Oct 1919		E6843
Beaufighter I	Jun 1941 — Dec 1941		T3322
Blenheim IV	Dec 1941 — Sep 1942		L9478 (HO-P)
Beaufighter II	Sep 1942 — Mar 1943		V8204 (HO-Z)
Beaufighter XI	Mar 1943 — Apr 1944		JL880 (HO-C)
Beaufighter X	Apr 1944 — Oct 1944		LX973 (HO-R)
Mosquito II	Oct 1944 — Jan 1945		DD682
Mosquito VI	Oct 1944 — May 1945		PZ413 (HO-Y)

No. 144 Squadron

Badge: In front of a decrescent, a boar's head erased
Motto: Who shall stop us

No.144 Squadron was formed at Port Said on 20 March 1918 as a corps reconnaissance unit for co-operation with the army in Palestine and Egypt. It took part in Allenby's drive into Syria before being transferred to Mudros in the Aegean for operations over the Dardanelles. The Turks surrendered a few days later however and the squadron was reduced to a cadre in December and returned to the UK where it disbanded on 4 February 1919.

On 11 January 1937 No.144 reformed at Bicester as a day bomber squadron, initially with four Overstrands from No.101 Squadron but by the end of the month it had received Ansons. Early in February, it moved to the new airfield at Hemswell in No.3 Group where it began to receive Blenheims in August 1938 and joined No.5 Group. In March 1939 conversion to Hampdens began and on the outbreak of war, these flew their first operation over the North Sea on 26 September 1939. Leaflet raids and patrols over enemy mineleaying bases lasted until the German invasion of Norway when bombing raids began to be flown. These continued until April 1942, when the squadron's role was changed to torpedo-bombing and it joined Coastal Command.

After torpedo-dropping training, the squadron was sent to North Russia to help protect the Arctic convoys in September 1942, but no enemy warships ventured out of their bases in northern Norway during No.144's stay and at the end of October the surviving aircraft were handed over to the Russians and the squadron sailed home in a cruiser to start anti-submarine patrols and shipping strikes from Leuchars. In January 1943 conversion to Beaufighters began and in June these were flown to North Africa for attacks on enemy shipping in the Mediterranean. The squadron returned to the UK early in August and resumed operations at the end of October. In May 1944 it moved to south-west England to cover the west flank of the invasion

of Normandy and after helping to destroy the German naval forces in western France, the squadron joined a strike wing in Lincolnshire for attacks on enemy convoys off the Dutch coast. In September it returned to Scotland for similar missions off Norway and in January 1945 gave up its torpedo-bomber role for that of an anti-flak unit in the strike wing, remaining as such until the end of the war and disbanding on 25 May 1945.

On 1 December 1959 No.144 was reformed at North Luffenham as an intermediate-range ballistic missile squadron with Thors and was disbanded again on 23 August 1963.

Squadron bases

		Tain	8 Apr 1943
Port Said	20 Mar 1918	Emb. for N. Africa	
Junction Station	14 Aug 1918		15 May 1943 (G)
Mudros	17 Oct 1918	Protville II	17 Jun 1943 (G)
Ford	15 Dec 1918		18 Jun 1943 (A)
	to 4 Feb 1919	Tain (D)	15 May 1943
Bicester	11 Jan 1937		to 9 Jul 1943
Hemswell	9 Feb 1937	Benson (D)	9 Jul 1943
North Coates	9 Apr 1938		to 9 Aug 1943
Hemswell	7 May 1938	Tain (D)	9 Aug 1943
Speke	6 Sep 1939		to 14 Aug 1943
Hemswell	9 Sep 1939	Left for UK	29 Jul 1943
North Luffenham	17 Jul 1941	Tain	14 Aug 1943
Leuchars	21 Apr 1942	Wick	20 Oct 1943
Wick (D)	17 Jul 1942	Davidstowe Moor	10 May 1944
	to 3 Aug 1942	Strubby	30 Jun 1944 (G)
Sumburgh (D)	2 Sep 1942		4 Jul 1944 (A)
	to 4 Sep 1942	Banff	3 Sep 1944
Afrikanda	4 Sep 1942	Dallachy	22 Oct 1944
Vaenga I	6 Sep 1942		to 25 May 1945
	to 22 Oct 1942	North Luffenham	1 Dec 1959
Leuchars	29 Oct 1942		to 23 Aug 1963

Aircraft Equipment	Period of service	Representative Serial
Martinsyde S.1	Jun 1918 — Aug 1918	A1600
B.E.12a	May 1918 — Aug 1918	A6347
B.E.2e	Apr 1918 — Jul 1918	B3683
R.E.8	Jul 1918	B6681
D.H.6	Jul 1918 — Aug 1918	C7615
D.H.9	Aug 1918 — Dec 1918	C6300
O/400	Oct 1918 — Nov 1918	
Overstrand	Jan 1937 — Feb 1937	K4564
Anson I	Jan 1937 — Dec 1937	K6267
Audax	Mar 1937 — Dec 1937	K8312
Blenheim I	Aug 1937 — Mar 1939	K7081
Hampden I	Mar 1939 — Jan 1943	L4122 (NV-A)
Beaufighter VI	Jan 1943 — May 1943	JL654 (PL-H)
Beaufighter X	May 1943 — May 1945	LZ220 (PL-M)

No. 145 Squadron

Badge: In front of a templar's cross, a sword in bend downwards.
Motto: Diu noctuque pugnamus (We fight by day and night)

No.145 Squadron was formed on 15 May 1918 at Aboukir as a half-strength fighter unit and moved to Palestine in August with S.E.5As to provide fighter cover for Allenby's final offensive against the Turks which ended the war in the Middle East. The squadron disbanded on 2 September 1919.

On 10 October 1939 No.145 reformed at Croydon as a fighter squadron, receiving Blenheims in November. In March 1940 it began to re-equip with Hurricanes and in May became operational over northern France. After covering the evacuation from Dunkirk, the squadron took part in the Battle of Britain until withdrawn to Scotland in mid-August. Returning south in October, it converted to Spitfires in February 1941 and cross-Channel sweeps began in April. In July 1941 No.145 moved to Yorkshire, leaving in February 1942 for the Middle East. In April the squadron arrived in Egypt and moved to the Western Desert at the end of May where it was engaged in fighter patrols and bomber escort duties throughout the campaign which culminated in the expulsion of the enemy from North Africa. In June 1943 No.145 moved to Malta to carry out offensive patrols over Sicily and, in July, cover the Allied landings. It moved to Sicilian airstrips soon after their occupation and followed the 8th Army into Italy in September 1943. In December, the lack of air opposition by the enemy resulted in the squadron's Spitfires being diverted to attacking ground targets and in June 1944 it became a fighter-bomber unit for the rest of the war. On 19 August 1945 it was disbanded in northern Italy.

On 1 March 1952, No.145 reformed at Celle as a Vampire fighter-bomber squadron in Germany. In April 1954 it replaced these with Venoms which it flew until disbanded on 15 October 1957.

Squadron bases

Aboukir	15 May 1918	El Chel	4 Jan 1943 (A)
Abu Sueir	2 Jun 1918	Hamraiet	9 Jan 1943
Kantara	25 Aug 1918	Wadi Sirru	24 Jan 1943
Ramleh	13 Sep 1918	Castel Benito	8 Feb 1943
Kantara	18 Nov 1918	Hazbub	26 Feb 1943
Suez	Apr 1919 to 2 Sep 1919	Ben Gardane	2 Mar 1943
		Bu Grara	11 Mar 1943
Croydon	10 Oct 1939	La Fauconnerie	11 Apr 1943
Tangmere	10 May 1940	Goubrine	15 Apr 1943
Westhampnett	31 Jul 1940	Hergla	6 May 1943
Drem	14 Aug 1940	Ben Gardane	20 May 1943
Dyce	31 Aug 1940	Luqa	14 Jun 1943
Tangmere	9 Oct 1940	Pachino	13 Jul 1943
Merston	7 May 1941	Cassibile	17 Jul 1943
Catterick	28 Jul 1941	Lentini West	26 Jul 1943
Left for Middle East		Gioia del Colle	24 Sep 1943
	11 Feb 1942	Tortorella	5 Oct 1943
Heliopolis	16 Apr 1942	Foggia/Triolo	18 Oct 1943
Helwan	30 Apr 1942	Canne	22 Nov 1943
Gambut	24 May 1942	Marcianise	17 Jan 1944
LG.155	17 Jun 1942	Venafro	23 Apr 1944
LG.76	20 Jun 1942	Lago	21 May 1944
LG.13	24 Jun 1942	Venafro	4 Jun 1944
LG.15	26 Jun 1942	Littorio	12 Jun 1944
LG.154	29 Jun 1942	Fabrica	17 Jun 1944
Idku	5 Aug 1942	Perugia	3 Jul 1944
LG.154	21 Aug 1942	Loreto	25 Aug 1944
LG.92	26 Sep 1942	Fano	5 Sep 1944
LG.173	7 Oct 1942	Bellaria	4 Dec 1944
LG.21	6 Nov 1942	Treviso	3 May 1945 to 19 Aug 1945
LG.155	12 Nov 1942		
Gambut West	13 Nov 1942	Celle	1 Mar 1952 to 15 Oct 1957
Msus	24 Nov 1942		

Aircraft

Equipment	Period of service	Representative Serial and Code
S.E.5A	Jun 1918 – Apr 1919	C1767
Blenheim IF	Nov 1939 – Apr 1940	K7159 (SO-N)
Hurricane I	Mar 1940 – Feb 1941	N2601 (SO-H)
Spitfire IIA, IIB	Feb 1941 – Feb 1942	P7605 (SO-N)
Spitfire VA, VB	Jul 1941	
	Nov 1941 – Feb 1942	AB502 (ZX-B)
	Apr 1942 – Aug 1943	
Spitfire VIII	Aug 1943 – Aug 1945	JF952 (ZX-M)
Spitfire IX	Jun 1943 – Aug 1945	
Vampire FB.5	Mar 1952 – Apr 1954	VV666 (B-G)
Venom FB.1	Apr 1954 – Oct 1957	WK497 (K)

No. 146 Squadron

Badge: A panther's head couped, facing to the sinister
Motto: Percutit insidians pardus (The watchful panther strikes)

No.146 Squadron was formed at Risalpur on 15 October 1941 with four Audaxes of B Flight of No.5 Squadron which were transferred five days later. A few days before the outbreak of war in the Far East it moved to Assam to provide air defence for the area. Fortunately, it was not required to take its elderly biplanes into action before beginning to receive Mohawks at the end of March 1942. After losing the initial batch to No.5 Squadron and having a few Buffaloes as interim equipment, No.146 was withdrawn to Calcutta early in May where it began to convert to Hurricanes. Some Audaxes were retained for communications work while the Hurricanes formed part of the fighter defences of Bengal until January 1943, when the squadron began to fly ground-attack missions over Burma from advanced bases. In April 1943, No.146 moved to the Burma Front where it flew both offensive and defensive operations until February 1944, when it was withdrawn to southern India to counter a rumoured Japanese carrier raid. This did not materialise and in June the squadron converted to Thunderbolts which it took into action over Burma in September. Until June 1945, No.146's aircraft were engaged in ground-attack sweeps against Japanese bases and communications. On 30 June 1945 the squadron was disbanded.

Squadron bases

Risalpur	15 Oct 1941	Baigachi	1 Dec 1943
Dum Dum	26 Nov 1941	St.Thomas Mount	27 Feb 1944
Dinjan	14 Dec 1941	Yelahanka	5 Jun 1944
Dum Dum	8 May 1942	Arkonam	13 Aug 1944
Alipore	6 Sep 1942	Kumbhirgram	5 Sep 1944
Chittagong	10 Apr 1943	Wangjing	21 Nov 1944
Feni	6 May 1943	Myingyan North	30 Apr 1945
Comilla	27 Jun 1943	Meiktila	7 Jun 1945 to 30 Jun 1945

Aircraft

Equipment	Period of service	Representative Serial and Code
Audax	Oct 1941 – Jul 1942	K7372
Mohawk IV	Mar 1942 – Apr 1942	
Buffalo I	Apr 1942 – May 1942	W8246
Hurricane IIB	May 1942 – Jun 1944	BM927 (D)
Hurricane IIC	Dec 1942 – Jun 1944	LB619
Thunderbolt I	Jun 1944 – Mar 1945	HD152 (X)
Thunderbolt II	Jun 1944 – Nov 1944 Mar 1945 – Jun 1945	KL168 (S)

No. 147 Squadron

Badge: In front of a staff, a
shuttle
Motto: Assidue portamus (We
carry with regularity)

No.147 Squadron was formed in Egypt on 1 May 1918 and was intended to be a fighter-reconnaissance unit but after flying training types for several months it failed to become operational before the Armistice and was disbanded in March 1919. During January 1942 personnel No.147 began to assemble at St. Jean, Palestine, as the basis of a Liberator squadron but due to the shortage of aircraft at that time it did not receive any before disbanding in February 1943.

On 5 September 1944 No.147 reformed at Croydon as a transport squadron in No.110 Wing and its Dakotas began passenger and freight services between the UK and newly-liberated cities in France and Belgium. These were extended to include Italy soon afterwards and a flight of Ansons was placed in service for short-range services. On 31 August 1946 the last scheduled service took place and as the civil airlines had become established on the main European routes the squadron was disbanded on 13 September 1946.

On 1 February 1953 No.1 Long Range Ferry Unit at Abingdon was renumbered 147 Squadron and soon afterwards moved to Benson. Initially it was mainly engaged in ferrying Sabres from Canada to Germany and the UK then Venoms to the Middle and Far East and finally Swifts and Hunters to Germany. On 15 September 1958, it amalgamated with No.167 Squadron to form the Ferry Squadron.

Squadron bases			to Feb 1943
Egypt	1 May 1918	Croydon	5 Sep 1944
	to Mar 1919		to 13 Sep 1946
St. Jean d'Acre	Jan 1942	Abingdon	1 Feb 1953
Aqir	Apr 1942	Benson	16 Apr 1953
Shandur	Sep 1942		to 15 Sep 1958

Aircraft Equipment	Period of service	Representative Serial and Code
Various	May 1918 – Mar 1919	
Dakota III, IV	Sep 1944 – Sep 1946	KG771
Anson XII	Sep 1944 – Sep 1945	PH669
Anson XIX	Apr 1946 – Sep 1946	TX238

Lysander IIIA, No.148 Squadron

No. 148 Squadron

Badge: Two battle axes in saltire
Motto: Trusty

No.148 Squadron was formed on 10 February 1918 at Andover as a night bomber unit and took its F.E.2b and 2d makeshift bombers to France in April 1918, at a time when the Allies were hard-pressed by the final German offensive of the war. It was immediately engaged in attacks on enemy bases, communications and airfields behind the front and these continued till the end of the war, no replacement for the F.E.s having arrived. In February 1919 the squadron returned to the UK and disbanded on 30 June 1919.

On 7 June 1937 No.148 was reformed at Scampton as a bomber squadron from a detachment supplied by No.9 Squadron. For the first few weeks it had Audaxes but these were soon replaced by Wellesleys and by the end of September it was up to strength. The Wellesley's long-range was off-set by its lack of defensive armament and in November 1938 it was withdrawn from the squadron and Heyfords from No.99 Squadron were received as interim equipment until March 1939, when Wellingtons replaced them. During April 1939 No.148 was designated a Group Pool Squadron and received eight Ansons to assist in producing its quota of twelve trained bomber crews every six weeks. On the outbreak of war it moved to Harwell to continue its training role and was redesignated No.15 Operational Training Unit on 4 April 1940. On 30 April 1940 it reformed at Stradishall with Wellingtons but was disbanded again on 23 May 1940.

On 14 December 1940 detachments of 38, 99 and 115 Squadrons at Luqa were combined to reform No.148 and its Wellingtons attacked ports and airfields in Italy, Sicily and Libya from Malta until March 1941, when the squadron moved to Egypt. It continued to use Malta as an advanced base until again disbanded on 14 December 1942. On 14 March 1943 the Special Liberator Flight (X Flight) at Gambut was redesignated No.148 Squadron for special duties. Its Liberators and Halifaxes were engaged in dropping arms and supplies to resistance forces in Greece, Albania and Yugoslavia and in January 1944 it moved to Italy and added a Lysander flight for pick-up missions. Halifaxes completely replaced Liberators at the same time and Poland and northern Italy became the main area of operations for the squadron, but as the Russians overran Poland, missions over the Balkans again formed the bulk of the squadron's work, the final effort over Poland being an attempt to supply the Polish resistance forces in Warsaw by long-range sorties from southern Italy. As the war drew to a close, trips were being made to northern Italy, Austria, Czechoslovakia and southern Germany and after a period of general transport duties in Italy, the squadron moved to Egypt where it was disbanded on 15 January, 1946.

On 4 November, 1946, No.148 reformed at Upwood with Lancasters as part of the post-war Bomber Command, converting to Lincolns in January 1950. It flew these until disbanded on 1 July, 1955. On 1 July, 1956, it reformed at Marham with Valiants as part of the V-bomber Force and in October 1956 was detached to Malta for attacks on

Egyptian airfields during the Suez operation. In April 1965 the squadron was disbanded after the grounding of the Valiants.

Squadron bases

Andover	10 Feb 1918	LG.106	11 May 1942
Ford	1 Mar 1918	Kabrit	26 Jun 1942
Auchel	25 Apr 1918	LG.237	19 Aug 1942
Sains-les-Pernes	3 May 1918	LG.09	14 Nov 1942
Camblain l'Abbe	22 Oct 1918	LG.167	1 Dec 1942
Erre	31 Oct 1918	Luqa	7 Dec 1942 (A)
Serny	9 Dec 1918		to 14 Dec 1942
Tangmere	17 Feb 1919	Gambut	14 Mar 1943
	to 30 Jun 1919	Derna	5 Apr 1943
Scampton	7 Jun 1937	Tocra	2 Sep 1943
Stradishall	10 Mar 1938	Brindisi	31 Jan 1944
Harwell	4 Sep 1939	Foggia	Jun 1945
	to 4 Apr 1940	Gianaclis	Nov 1945 (P)
Stradishall	30 Apr 1940		to 15 Jan 1946
	to 23 Jun 1940	Upwood	4 Nov 1946
Luqa	14 Dec 1940		to 1 Jul 1955
Kabrit	9 Mar 1941 (A)	Marham	1 Jul 1956
	26 Mar 1941 (G)		to Apr 1965

Aircraft

Equipment	Period of service	Representative Serial and Code	
F.E.2b, F.E.2d	Feb 1918 — Jun 1919	D9187	
Audax	Jun 1937 — Jul 1937	K7434	
Wellesley	Jun 1937 — Nov 1938	K7714	
Heyford III	Nov 1938 — Mar 1939	K6857	
Wellington I	Mar 1939 — Apr 1940	R3173	
Anson I	Apr 1939 — Apr 1940	N5084	
Wellington IC	Apr 1940 — May 1940		
	Dec 1940 — Nov 1941	DV646	(A)
	Apr 1942 — Dec 1942		
Wellington II	Sep 1941 — Apr 1942	Z8359	(H)
Liberator II, III	Mar 1943 — Jan 1944	AL506	(X)
Halifax II	Mar 1943 — Nov 1944	BB301	(B)
Halifax V	Aug 1944 — Jun 1945	EB154	(J)
Lysander IIIA	Feb 1944 — Jun 1945	T1750	(B)
Stirling IV	Nov 1944 — Dec 1944	LK176	
Liberator VI	Mar 1945 — Jan 1946	KL545	(FS-Z)
Lancaster B.1	Nov 1946 — Jan 1950	PA385	(AU-S)
Lincoln B.2	Jan 1950 — Jul 1955	SX976	(AU-V)
Valiant B.1	Jul 1956 — Apr 1965	XD814	

Stirling I, No.149 Squadron

No. 149 Squadron

Badge: A horse shoe and a flash of lightning interlaced
Motto: Fortis nocte (Strong by night)
Name: 'East India'

No.149 Squadron was formed at Ford on 3 March 1918 as a night bomber unit and moved to France in June equipped with F.E.2bs. For the rest of the war it carried out night raids on German bases in Belgium and northern France. In March 1919 it moved to Ireland and disbanded on 1 August 1919.

On 12 April 1937 B Flight of No.99 Squadron was re-designated No.149 Squadron at Mildenhall and flew Heyfords until the arrival of Wellingtons at the beginning of 1939. On the outbreak of World War Two the squadron took part in the first raids on the German fleet in its harbours and began night bombing in May 1940. In November 1941 conversion to Stirlings took place, these being replaced by Lancasters in August 1944. Strategic bombing continued until the end of the war and the squadron remained in the post-war Bomber Command, converting to Lincolns in October 1949. On 1 March 1950 No.149 was disbanded.

The squadron reformed at Marham on 14 August 1950 and received Washingtons in November, being the first to equip with the type. In March 1953 it re-equipped with Canberras which it took to Germany in August 1954 to join No.125 Wing. On 31 August 1956, the squadron disbanded.

Squadron bases			
Ford	3 Mar 1918	Lakenheath	6 Apr 1942
Marquise	2 Jun 1918	Methwold	15 May 1944
Quilen	4 Jun 1918	Tuddenham	Apr 1946
Alquines	16 Jun 1918	Stradishall	Nov 1946
Clairmarais	16 Sep 1918	Mildenhall	28 Feb 1949
Le Quesnoy	25 Oct 1918		to 1 Mar 1950
Fort de Cogneleé	26 Nov 1918	Marham	14 Aug 1950
Bickendorf	24 Dec 1918	Coningsby	17 Oct 1950
Tallaght	26 Mar 1919	Cottesmore	22 May 1954
	to 1 Aug 1919	Ahlhorn	24 Aug 1954
Mildenhall	12 Apr 1937	Gutersloh	17 Sep 1954
			to 31 Aug 1956

Aircraft Equipment	Period of service	Representative Serial and Code
F.E.2b, F.E.2d	Mar 1918 – Aug 1919	C9799
Heyford I, Ia, II	May 1937 – Mar 1939	K4025
Heyford III	Apr 1937 – May 1937	K5180
Wellington I, IA, IC	Jan 1939 – Dec 1941	X9817 (OJ-N)
Stirling I	Nov 1941 – Jun 1943	R9142 (OJ-B)
Stirling III	Feb 1943 – Sep 1944	EF192 (OJ-S)
Lancaster I, III	Aug 1944 – Nov 1949	PA166 (OJ-G)
Lincoln B.2	Oct 1949 – Mar 1950	SX975
Washington B.1	Nov 1950 – Mar 1953	WF491
Canberra B.2	Mar 1953 – Aug 1956	WJ570

No. 150 Squadron

Badge: In front of a cross voided, two arrows in saltire, the points uppermost
Motto: Always ahead (Greek script)

No.150 Squadron was formed on 1 April 1918 at Kirec in Macedonia from A Flight of Nos.17 and 47 Squadrons. These flew the fighter elements of the two squadrons and No.150 began operating as a fighter squadron over the front north of Salonika while a detachment was based at Salonika for air defence at the end of the war. After the Bulgarians collapsed, the squadron remained in Macedonia until disbanded on 18 September 1919.

On 8 August 1938 No.150 reformed at Boscombe Down with Battles and moved to France as part of the AASF the day before war broke out with Germany. During the opening weeks, it flew reconnaissance missions and night leaflet raids and when the German attack came in May 1940, was engaged in attacking enemy columns advancing through Belgium into France. It continued its attacks by night when heavy losses to the Battles made daylight operations too hazardous until mid-June when it was evacuated to the UK. In October 1940 No.150 re-equipped with Wellingtons and became a night bomber squadron for the rest of the war. It moved to Algeria in December 1942 to carry out attacks on enemy bases in Sicily and Italy, moving to the

Italian mainland in December 1943 and disbanding on 5 October, 1944.

On 1 November, 1944, No.150 reformed from C Flight of No.550 Squadron at Fiskerton, moving later in the month to Hemswell. It carried out attacks on Germany for the rest of the war and disbanded on 7 November, 1945. On 1 August, 1959, it reformed as a Thor intermediate ballistic missile squadron at Carnaby, disbanding again on 9 April, 1963.

Squadron bases			
Kirec	1 Apr 1918	Kirmington	Oct 1942 (P)
	to 18 Sep 1919	Blida	19 Dec 1942
Boscombe Down	8 Aug 1938	Fontaine Chaude	17 May 1943
Benson	3 Apr 1939	Kairouan West	26 May 1943
Challerange	2 Sep 1939 (A)	Oudna No.1	14 Nov 1943
Ecury-sur-Coole		Cerignola No.3	21 Dec 1943
	11 Sep 1939 (A)	Amendola	14 Feb 1944
	18 Sep 1939 (G)	Regina	3 Jul 1944
Pouan	15 May 1940		to 5 Oct 1944
Houssay	3 Jun 1940	Fiskerton	1 Nov 1944
Abingdon	15 Jun 1940	Hemswell	22 Nov 1944
Stradishall	19 Jun 1940		to 7 Nov 1945
Newton	3 Jul 1940	Carnaby	1 Aug 1959
Snaith	10 Jul 1941		to 9 Apr 1963

Aircraft Equipment	Period of service	Representative Serial and Code
S.E.5A	Apr 1918 – Dec 1918	
Bristol M.1c	Apr 1918 – Sep 1919	
Nieuport 17	Apr 1918 – Dec 1918	
Camel	May 1918 – Sep 1919	
F.K.8	Dec 1918 – Sep 1919	
Battle	Aug 1938 – Oct 1940	P2244
Wellington IC	Oct 1940 –	T2622 (JN-D)
Wellington III	– Aug 1943	X3448 (JN-N)
Wellington X	Jun 1943 – Oct 1944	LP207 (JN-J)
Lancaster I, III	Nov 1944 – Nov 1945	NN752 (IQ-R)
Thor	Aug 1959 – Apr 1963	–

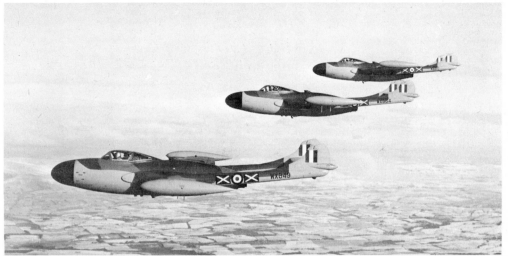

Venom NF.3, No.151 Squadron

No. 151 Squadron

Badge: On a hurt an owl affrontée, wings elevated alighting on a seax.

Motto: Foy pour devoir (French) (Fidelity unto duty)

No.151 Squadron was formed at Hainault Farm on 12 June 1918 as a night fighter squadron by combining one flight each from Nos.44, 78 and 112 Squadrons. Its purpose was to counter extensive enemy night attacks on British bases behind the Western Front and on 16 June the first flight crossed the Channel. By 26 June the squadron was installed at their base and began night flights on the following day. Several enemy night raiders were destroyed and for a short period the squadron pioneered the technique which was to become common in the Second World War by flying intruder missions over enemy airfields awaiting the return of the enemy night bombers. By the end of the war twenty-six enemy aircraft had been claimed destroyed by night with only primitive equipment and using Camels which, even in daylight, were tricky to fly. Returning to the UK in February 1919, the squadron disbanded on 10 September 1919.

On 4 August 1936, No.151 reformed at North Weald with Gauntlets from a detachment of No.56 Squadron. It began to receive Hurricanes in December 1938 and in February 1939 passed on its remaining thirteen Gauntlets to 602 Squadron. After defensive patrols for the opening months of World War Two, the squadron covered the evacuation fleet at Dunkirk and flew missions over northern France during May and June 1940, before taking part in the Battle of Britain. In November the squadron was transferred to night flying and received Defiants in addition to its Hurricanes for this purpose. The Defiants began operations in February 1941, and both types were flown until the arrival of Mosquitos in April 1942 when the Hurricanes were finally replaced, the Defiants following in July. In April 1943, the squadron moved to Colerne and began intruder patrols which continued after moving to Cornwall in March 1944. In October 1944, No.151 moved to East Anglia for bomber support duties which entailed intruder operations over enemy night fighter airfields and hunting their occupants in the air over Germany. These continued until the end of the war when the squadron was based in the south-west until disbanded on 10 October 1946.

On 15 September 1951 No.151 was reformed at Leuchars with Vampire night fighters for the defence of central Scotland, replacing these with Meteors in April 1953. In July 1955, the first Venoms began to arrive and two months later the squadron was fully equipped with these. Re-equipment with Javelins began in June 1957 and the squadron flew this type until disbanded on 19 September 1961.

On 1 January 1962, the Signals Command Development Squadron at Watton was redesignated 151 Squadron and was engaged in radar development and research work until renumbered 97 Squadron on 25 May 1963.

Meteor NF.11, No.151 Squadron

Lincoln B.2, No.151 Squadron

Squadron bases

Hainault Farm	12 Jun 1918	Wittering	22 Dec 1940
Marquise	16 Jun 1918	Coltishall (D)	22 Apr 1941
Fontaine-sur-Maye	21 Jun 1918		to 3 May 1941
Famechon	25 Jun 1918	Coltishall (D)	21 May 1941
Fontaine-sur-Maye	2 Jul 1918		to 2 Jun 1941
Vignacourt	8 Sep 1918	Coltishall (D)	Sep 1941
Bancourt	24 Oct 1918		to 25 Jan 1942
Liettres	5 Dec 1918	Colerne	30 Apr 1943
Gullane (Drem)	21 Feb 1919	Middle Wallop	16 Aug 1943
	to 10 Sep 1919	Predannack	24 Mar 1944
North Weald	4 Aug 1936	Castle Camps	7 Oct 1944
Martlesham Heath (D)		Hunsdon	19 Nov 1944
	28 Feb 1940	Bradwell Bay	1 Mar 1945
	to 12 May 1940	Predannack	17 May 1945
Martlesham Heath	13 May 1940	Exeter	Jun 1946
Manston	17 May 1940	Colerne	Sep 1946
Vitry-en-Artois	18 May 1940	Weston Zoyland	Sep 1946
North Weald	20 May 1940		to 10 Oct 1946
Stapleford Tawney	29 Aug 1940	Leuchars	15 Sep 1951
Digby	1 Sep 1940		to 19 Sep 1961
Bramcote	28 Nov 1940	Watton	1 Jan 1962
Wittering (D)	6 Dec 1940		to 25 May 1963
	to 22 Dec 1940		

Aircraft

Equipment	Period of service	Representative Serial
Camel	Jun 1918 – Sep 1919	B2458 (R)
Gauntlet II	Aug 1936 – Feb 1939	K5293
Hurricane I	Dec 1938 – Feb 1942	P3415 (DZ-V)
Hurricane IIB	Oct 1941 – Feb 1942	Z3467 (DZ-Y)
Defiant I	Dec 1940 – Apr 1942	N1793 (DZ-B)
Defiant II	Sep 1941 – Jul 1942	AA403
Mosquito II	Apr 1942 – Aug 1943	W4097 (DZ-N)
Mosquito VI	Aug 1943 – Oct 1943	PZ201
Mosquito XII	May 1943 – May 1944	HK183 (DZ-W)
Mosquito XIII	Nov 1943 – Nov 1944	MM450
Mosquito 30	Oct 1944 – Oct 1946	NT536 (DZ-F)
Vampire NF.10	Sep 1951 – Apr 1953	WM675 (K)
Meteor NF.11	Apr 1953 – Sep 1955	WD780 (R)
Venom NF.3	Jul 1955 – Jun 1957	WX805 (S)
Javelin FAW.5	Jun 1957 – Sep 1961	XH687 (G)
Lincoln B.2	Jan 1962 – May 1963	RA685 (M)
Hastings C.2	Jan 1962 – May 1963	WJ338
Varsity T.1	Jan 1962 – May 1963	WL686
Canberra B.2	Jan 1962 – May 1963	

No. 152 Squadron

Badge: The Dastar of H.E.H.
The Nizam of Hyderabad
Motto: Faithful ally
Name: 'Hyderabad'

Pembroke C.1, No.152 Squadron

No.152 Squadron was formed on 1 June 1918 at Rochford as a Camel night fighter unit and in mid-October moved to France to defend Allied bases against enemy night bombers. The war ended three weeks later and on 30 June 1919, the squadron disbanded.

On 1 October 1939, No.152 reformed at Acklington with Gladiators and became operational on 6 November. In January 1940, conversion to Spitfires began and after a period of defensive patrols in the north-east, the squadron moved to Warmwell to help defend southern England against attacks from the Luftwaffe forces now based in northern France. Throughout the Battle of Britain, No.152 defended this sector which included Portland naval base and finally left for Cornwall in April 1941, to fly convoy patrols. In August a further move to East Anglia took place for bomber escort missions and in January 1942, it was transferred to Northern Ireland. In August 1942, the squadron moved to Pembrokeshire for convoy patrols and at the end of September was ordered to prepare for overseas.

During November 1942, the ground crews sailed for North Africa as part of the invasion fleet for Operation 'Torch' while the squadron's Spitfires were taken to Gibraltar. On 14 November, the latter took off for Algeria to cover the Allied landings and subsequently defend newly-acquired bases from attacks by enemy aircraft. As the First Army advanced towards Tunisia, No.152 helped to provide air defence and escort for fighter-bombers supporting the army. In March 1943, it began fighter-bomber missions itself which continued until the enemy surrender in Tunisia. In June 1943, the squadron moved to Malta for sweeps over Sicily and to cover the Allied landings there in July. Soon afterwards, it moved to captured strips in Sicily and in September arrived in Italy.

The squadron was not destined to remain there long and in November it began to transfer to India, becoming operational over Burma on 19 December. Initially its Spitfire VIIIs were engaged in fighter patrols but at the end of April 1944, fighter-bomber operations were resumed. During the Battle of Imphal, No.152 operated from front-line strips around Imphal and supported the 14th Army during its final conquest of Burma. In September 1945 the squadron moved to Singapore after the Japanese surrender and was disbanded on 10 March 1946.

On 8 May 1946, No.136 Squadron was renumbered 152 Squadron while in transit to Worli and began flying Spitfires early in June pending the arrival of its Tempests. By early August, it had received these but the spares situation prevented much flying before the squadron was again disbanded on 15 January 1947, and handed its aircraft over to No.5 Squadron.

On 1 June, 1954, No.152 reformed at Wattisham with Meteor night fighters as part of the air defence of the UK It disbanded on 31 July, 1958. On 29 September, 1958, No.152 reformed once more, this time as a transport squadron from No.1417 flight for general transport and communications duties in the Persian Gulf area with Pembrokes and Twin Pioneers based at Bahrain. It was disbanded on 9 December, 1967, its duties being taken over by Air Forces Gulf Communications Squadron.

178

Squadron bases

Rochford	1 Jun 1918	Serretelle	24 Sep 1943		to 31 Jan 1947
Carvin	18 Oct 1918	Gioia del Colle	13 Oct 1943	Wattisham	1 Jun 1954
	to 30 Jun 1919	Baigachi	4 Dec 1943	Stradishall	11 Jun 1956
Acklington	1 Oct 1939	Double Moorings	21 Feb 1944	Wattisham	16 Jan 1957
Warmwell	12 Jul 1940	Chittagong	31 Mar 1944		
Portreath	9 Apr 1941	Rumkhapalong	17 Apr 1944	Stradishall	30 Aug 1957
Snailwell	25 Aug 1941	Comilla	1 May 1944		to 31 Jul 1958
Swanton Morley	31 Aug 1941	Palel	31 May 1944	Muharraq	29 Sep 1958
Coltishall	1 Dec 1941	Imphal	6 Jul 1944		to 9 Dec 1967
Eglinton	17 Jan 1942	Tulihal	6 Sep 1944		
Angle	16 Aug 1942	Tamu	29 Oct 1944		
Collyweston	27 Sep 1942	Kan	15 Jan 1945		
Wittering	30 Sep 1942	Sinthe	7 Feb 1945		
Emb. for North Africa		Magwe/Maida Vale			
	10 Nov 1942 (G)		30 Apr 1945		
Maison Blanche		Thedaw	25 May 1945		
	14 Nov 1942 (A)	Zayatkwin	20 Aug 1945		
Souk-el-Arba	24 Nov 1942	Penang	11 Sep 1945		
Constantine	31 Dec 1942	Kallang	12 Sep 1945		
Souk-el-Khemis	4 Feb 1943	Tengah	26 Sep 1945		
Protville	13 May 1943		to 10 Mar 1946		
Takali	6 Jun 1943	Worli	12 May 1946		
Lentini East	27 Jul 1943	Yelahanka	22 May 1946		
Milazzo East	6 Sep 1943	Risalpur	18 Jun 1946		
Asa	16 Sep 1943				

Aircraft Equipment	Period of service	Representative Serial and Code
Camel	Jun 1918 – Jun 1919	
Gladiator II	Oct 1939 – Feb 1940	N5640 (UM-M)
Spitfire I	Jan 1940 – Apr 1941	R6801 (UM-B)
Spitfire IIA	Apr 1941 – Feb 1942	P7996
Spitfire VB, VC	Feb 1942 – Nov 1943	LZ807 (UM-V)
Spitfire IX	Aug 1943 – Nov 1943	JL170 (UM-Q)
Spitfire VIII	Nov 1943 – Mar 1946	MD375 (UM-X)
	Jun 1946 – Jul 1946	
Spitfire XIV	Jan 1946 – Mar 1946	RM908 (UM-G)
	Jun 1946 – Jul 1946	
Tempest F.2	Jul 1946 – Jan 1947	PR541
Meteor NF.12	Jun 1954 – Jul 1958	WS674 (V)
Meteor NF.14	Jun 1954 – Jul 1958	WS805 (P)
Pembroke C.1	Sep 1958 – Dec 1967	WV747 (L)
Twin Pioneer CC.1	Dec 1958 – Sep 1967	XM289 (M)

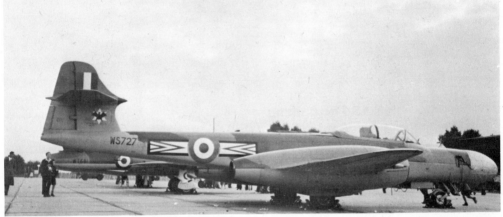

Meteor NF.14, No.153 Squadron

No. 153 Squadron

Badge: In front of a six-pointed star, a bat
Motto: Noctividus (Seeing by night)

No.153 Squadron was formed at Hainault Farm in November 1918, and was intended to be a night fighter unit but the war had ended as the squadron began to assemble. It did not become operational and probably did not receive any operational aircraft, being disbanded on 13 June 1919.

On 14 October 1941, A Flight of No.256 Squadron arrived at Ballyhalbert from Squires Gate to form 153 Squadron and began flying next day. On the official formation of No.153 on 24 October, the squadron was almost immediately operational with Defiants on night patrols. The arrival of a training Blenheim on 10 December heralded re-equipment and the first Beaufighter arrived on 29 January

1942. A Flight retained its Defiants until Beaufighters became operational in May. The squadron remained in Northern Ireland until December 1942, when sixteen Beaufighters flew out to Algeria via Gibraltar. Night patrols covering Allied bases were supplemented by convoy protection missions and detachments were based at several points along the Algerian coast. In July 1944, a detachment was sent to Sardinia for intruder missions over southern France and northern Italy which, in August, helped cover the Allied landings in southern France. In August 1944, a flight of Spitfires and Hurricanes was added for dawn patrols but the squadron disbanded on 5 September, 1944.

On 7 October, 1944, No.153 reformed at Kirmington with Lancasters and twenty-seven crews supplied by No.166 Squadron, beginning operations the same night. For the remaining months of the war, it carried out attacks on enemy targets as part of the main force of Bomber Command and after a short period of trooping flights to Italy was disbanded on 28 September, 1945.

On 28 February, 1955, No.153 reformed at West Malling as a night fighter squadron and in September received Meteor night fighters. On 2 July, 1958, the squadron disbanded.

Squadron bases

Hainault Farm	Nov 1918 to 13 Jun 1919	Reghaia	22 Jul 1943 to 5 Sep 1944
Ballyhalbert	24 Oct 1941 to 31 Jan 1943	Kirmington	7 Oct 1944
Left for North Africa		Scampton	15 Oct 1944 to 28 Sep 1945
	18 Dec 1942	West Malling	28 Feb 1955
Maison Blanche		Waterbeach	17 Sep 1957 to 2 Jul 1958
	19 Dec 1942 (A)		
	22 Dec 1942 (G)		

Aircraft

Equipment	Period of service	Representative Serial and Code
Defiant I	Oct 1941 – May 1942	V1178
Beaufighter I	Jan 1942 – Jan 1943	X7774 (TB-V)
Beaufighter VI	Aug 1942 – Sep 1944	V8895 (TB-F)
Spitfire VIII, IX	Aug 1944 – Sep 1944	MK950
Hurricane IIC	Aug 1944 – Sep 1944	LB677
Lancaster I, III	Oct 1944 – Sep 1945	NN803 (P4-O)
Meteor NF.12	Mar 1955 – Jul 1958	WS622 (K)
Meteor NF.14	Mar 1955 – Jun 1958	WS723 (T)

Spitfire VC, No.154 Squadron

No. 154 Squadron

Badge: In front of three arrows, one in pale and two in saltire, the points upwards, the 'Derestriction' road sign

Motto: His modus as victoriam
(By this means to victory)

No.154 Squadron began to form at Chingford during October 1918, but the end of the war a few weeks later resulted in its formation being suspended without any aircraft having been received. It reformed at Fowlmere on 17 November 1941, as a fighter squadron with Spitfire IIAs and became operational on 24 February 1942, with Spitfire Vs added to its strength for the first weeks before converting completely to the later mark. In May 1942, it left East Anglia for south-west England where it spent a month providing fighter cover for coastal convoys before moving to Hornchurch to take part in sweeps over northern France. The squadron flew its last operation in the UK on 30 August and began preparing for its move to North Africa as part of the forces engaged in Operation 'Torch'. The ground echelon embarked in the *Carmania* on 1 November and disembarked at Algiers on 13 November moving to Maison Blanche to join up with the squadron aircraft which had been operating from Gibraltar until airfields in Algeria had been captured. During the campaign in Tunisia, No.154 provided fighter cover and air defence for coastal shipping, ports and army installations. At the end of May 1943, the ground echelon left Sousse for Malta where the aircraft arrived on 4 June to undertake sweeps over Sicily, the next Allied target for invasion. After covering the landings on 10 July, the squad-

ron moved into newly-captured airfields in Sicily on the 18th to receive its aircraft two days later, at the same time adding some Spitfire IXs to its establishment. Soon after the Allied landings in Italy, No.154 moved there for defensive patrols until 9 December, when sixteen aircraft left to fly to Syria to provide air defence for the area, operating from airfields in Palestine and Cyprus in this role. On 2 April 1944, sixteen Spitfire IXs of the squadron left for Corsica, arriving two days later to begin sweeps over northern Italy and to supply escorts for bombing raids. On 15 August 1944, it covered the landings in southern France and on the 23rd moved to Frejus to cover the Allied armies' advance northwards to join up with forces from Normandy but on 19 September it passed its Spitfires to a French wing, receiving some Spitfire Vs in exchange for a few days before departing for Naples where it was dispersed and formally disbanded on 1 November 1944.

On 16 November 1944, No.154 reformed at Biggin Hill, taking over twenty-one Spitfire VIIs from No.131 Squadron. On 1 February 1945, it began flying escort missions over Germany for Bomber Command heavy bombers and later in the month began to receive Mustangs which were flown until the squadron again disbanded on 31 March 1945.

Squadron bases

Chingford	Oct 1918 to Nov 1918		1 Nov 1942 (G)
		Arr. in North Africa	
Fowlmere	17 Nov 1941		13 Nov 1942 (G)
Coltishall	12 Mar 1942	Djidjelli/Taher	21 Nov 1942 (R)
Fowlmere	5 Apr 1942	Bone	5 Jan 1943
Churchstanton	7 May 1942	Tingley	17 Jan 1943
Hornchurch	7 Jun 1942	Souk-el-Khemis	16 Mar 1943
Fairlop	27 Jul 1942	Protville	13 May 1943
Ipswich	10 Aug 1942	Takali	4 Jun 1943
Fairlop	15 Aug 1942	Lentini East	20 Jul 1943
Wellingore	1 Sep 1942	Milazzo East	7 Sep 1943
Left for North Africa		Serretelle	23 Sep 1943

180

Frejus	23 Aug 1944
Montelimar	5 Sep 1944
Le Vallon	19 Sep 1944
Left for Italy	28 Sep 1944
Naples	11 Oct 1944
	to 1 Nov 1944
Biggin Hill	16 Nov 1944
Hunsdon	1 Mar 1945
	to 31 Mar 1945

Gioia del Colle	13 Oct 1943
Minnick	13 Dec 1943 (A)
	23 Dec 1943 (G)
Ramat David	12 Feb 1944
Muqeibila	4 Mar 1944
Alto	4 Apr 1944 (A)
	11 Apr 1944 (G)
Poretta	19 Apr 1944
Calenzana	11 Jul 1944

Aircraft Equipment	**Period of service**	**Representative Serial and Code**
Spitfire IIA	Nov 1941 – Mar 1942	P7622
Spitfire VA, VB	Feb 1942 – Jan 1943	BM588 (HT-F)
Spitfire VC	Jan 1943 – Apr 1944	ER676 (HT-E)
Spitfire IX	Jul 1943 – Sep 1944	MA580 (HT-S)
Spitfire VIII	Nov 1944 – Feb 1945	MD134
Mustang IV	Feb 1945 – Mar 1945	KH697

Mohawk IVs, No.155 Squadron

No. 155 Squadron

Badge: A sword enfiled by a serpent nowed biting its tail
Motto: Eternal vigilance

No.155 Squadron was formed on 14 September 1918, at Feltham as a night fighter unit with Avro 504Js and Camels but the war ended a few weeks later and it did not become operational, disbanding on 7 December 1918.

On 1 April 1942 No.155 reformed at Peshawar as a fighter squadron but did not receive its first Mohawk until mid-August owing to the necessity to modify these aircraft for operational use. Air defence and convoy patrols began in September off Madras and in October the squadron moved to Bengal and detachments began operating over Burma. Reconnaissance, ground-attack and bomber escort missions occupied the squadron until January 1944, when it finally replaced its aged Mohawks with Spitfires. Initially these were used for air defence duties until the Japanese air force in Burma ceased to be a threat; ground-attack missions and escorts for transport aircraft then became the main tasks, the Spitfires carrying 500-lb. bombs during the last month of the campaign. In mid-September 1945, the squadron flew to Singapore soon after the Japanese surrender and in February 1946, moved to Sumatra to provide tactical support for the army units there until disbanded on 31 August 1946.

On 1 September 1954, No.155 reformed at Seletar with Whirlwind helicopters and provided transport and casualty evacuation support for the army and police in Malaya during their fight against Communist guerillas in the jungle. On 3 June 1959 it joined No.194 Squadron to form No.110 Squadron.

Squadron bases

Feltham	14 Sep 1918	Baigachi	27 Feb 1944	Zayatkwin	15 Aug 1945	to 31 Aug 1946
	to 7 Dec 1918	Kalyanpur	20 Mar 1944	Kallang	12 Sep 1945 Seletar	1 Sep 1954
Peshawar	1 Apr 1942	Baigachi	23 Apr 1944	Tengah	24 Sep 1945	to 3 Jun 1959
St. Thomas Mount	9 Jul 1942	Palel	14 Aug 1944	Medan	4 Feb 1946	
Alipore	18 Oct 1942	Sapam	30 Nov 1944			
Agartala	24 Nov 1942	Tulihal	8 Jan 1945			
Rajyeswarpur	29 Jan 1943	Tabingaung	12 Jan 1945			
Imphal	1 Feb 1943 (A)	Sadaung	11 Feb 1945			
	4 Mar 1943 (G)	Dwehla	6 Apr 1945			
Agartala	30 Jun 1943	Kwetnge	19 Apr 1945			
Imphal	2 Sep 1943	Toungoo/Tennant	28 Apr 1945			
Alipore	8 Jan 1944	Thedaw	9 May 1945			

Aircraft Equipment	Period of service	Representative Serial and Code
Avro 504 J	Sep 1918 – Dec 1918	
Camel	Oct 1918 – Dec 1918	
Mohawk IV	Aug 1942 – Jan 1944	BT470 (F)
Spitfire VIII	Jan 1944 – Aug 1946	JG181 (DG-M)
Whirlwind HC.4	Sep 1954 – Jun 1959	XJ410

Whirlwind HC.4s, No.155 Squadron

No. 156 Squadron

Badge: A figure of Mercury holding a torch
Motto: We light the way

No.156 Squadron was formed on 12 October 1918, as a D.H.9A unit, at Thetford but the end of World War One a month later resulted in its formation being abandoned in November 1918, before it had received any aircraft.

On 14 February 1942, No.156 reformed from a detachment supplied by No.40 Squadron at Alconbury as part of No.3 Group. Equipped with Wellingtons, it took part in Bomber Command's night offensive against enemy targets until August 1942, when it was transferred to the Pathfinder Force (No.8 Group). Initially, a squadron was transferred from each Group to form the basis of this force and each used the standard type of its former Group but in January 1943, No.156 converted to Lancasters. Until the end of the war, the squadron took part in the strategic bombing offensive, providing target identification for the main force of bombers. On 25 September 1945, the squadron was disbanded at Wyton after a short period repatriating prisoners-of-war and trooping.

Squadron bases			
Thetford	12 Oct 1918	Warboys	15 Aug 1942
	to Nov 1918	Upwood	5 Mar 1944
Alconbury	14 Feb 1942	Wyton	27 Jun 1945
			to 25 Sep 1945

Aircraft Equipment	Period of service	Representative Serial and Code
Wellington IC	Feb 1942 – Jan 1943	Z1114
Wellington III	Mar 1942 – Jan 1943	X3710 (GT-W)
Lancaster I, III	Jan 1943 – Sep 1945	ED919

No. 157 Squadron

Badge: A lion rampant chequy
Motto: Our cannon speak our thoughts

No.157 Squadron was formed at Upper Heyford in September 1918, to be a ground-attack unit equipped with Salamanders but did not become operational before the end of the war and was disbanded on 1 February 1919.

On 13 December 1941, No.157 reformed at Debden but moved four days later to Castle Camps where it received Mosquitos in January 1942, becoming the first Mosquito night fighter squadron. Patrols began on 27 April over East Anglia and in July 1943, some Mosquito VI fighter-bombers were added to the squadron strength to take part in intruder missions over France and the Low Countries. In November 1943, the squadron moved to Cornwall in a similar role and in March 1944 went north to Valley for defensive patrols over the Irish Sea. In May it returned to East Anglia to join No.100 Group and for the rest of the war provided support for the heavy bombers over Germany by flying sweeps in search of enemy night fighters. On 16 August 1945 the squadron disbanded.

Squadron bases			
Upper Heyford	Sep 1918	Predannack	9 Nov 1943
	to 1 Feb 1919	Valley	26 Mar 1944
Debden	13 Dec 1941	Swannington	7 May 1944
Castle Camps	17 Dec 1941	West Malling	21 Jul 1944
Bradwell Bay	15 Mar 1943	Swannington	28 Aug 1944
Hunsdon	13 May 1943		to 16 Aug 1945

Aircraft Equipment	Period of service	Representative Serial and Code
Various	Sep 1918 – Feb 1919	
Mosquito II	Jan 1942 – Jul 1944	W4079 (RS-F)
Mosquito VI	Jul 1943 – Apr 1944	TA482 (RS-F)
Mosquito XIX	May 1944 – Aug 1945	MM652 (RS-S)

Mosquito NF.30, No.157 Squadron

No. 158 Squadron

Badge: A circular chain of seven links
Motto: Strength in unity

No.158 Squadron was formed on 4 September 1918 at Upper Heyford but it did not become operational and was disbanded during November 1918, as the was ended. It had been nominated as a Salamander ground-attack unit.

On 14 February 1942 No.158 reformed from the home echelon of No.104 Squadron at Driffield. Equipped initially with Wellingtons, it flew these on night raids until re-equipped with Halifaxes in June 1942. Operations with Halifaxes began on 25 June and the squadron used various marks until

the end of the war on strategic bombing duties. On 7 January 1944, C Flight was detached to form No.640 Squadron and in May 1945, No.158 began handling its Halifaxes over to maintenance units, starting to receive Stirling V transports in June. Flights to India and the Middle East began in July but trooping flights by Stirlings ceased in December 1945, and the squadron disbanded on 31 December 1945.

Squadron bases			
Upper Heyford	4 Sep 1918	Rufforth	6 Jun 1942 (M)
	to Nov 1918	Lissett	6 Nov 1942
Driffield	14 Feb 1942	Stradishall	28 Feb 1943
East Moor	4 Jun 1942 (A)		Aug 1945 (P)
			to 31 Dec 1945

Aircraft Equipment	Period of service	Representative Serial and Code
Various	Sep 1918 – Nov 1918	
Wellington II	Feb 1942 – Jun 1942	Z8595 (NP-Q)
Halifax II	Jun 1942 – Jan 1944	W1157 (NP-A)
Halifax III	Jan 1944 – Jun 1945	HX331 (NP-L)
Halifax VI	Apr 1945 – Jul 1945	PP167 (NP-S)
Stirling V	Jun 1945 – Dec 1945	PJ950

No. 159 Squadron

Badge: In front of logs enflamed, a peacock's head erased, in the beak a woodman's axe.
Motto: Quo non, quando non (Whither not, when not?)

Liberator VI, No.159 Squadron

No.159 Squadron was formed on 1 June 1918, as a nucleus but was disbanded again on 4 July 1918, after formation had been suspended to provide reinforcements for France.

On 2 January 1942, No.159 reformed at Molesworth and its ground echelon left for the Middle East in February. After being employed on servicing duties, it was posted to India in May. The first group of No.159's Liberators were flown out to Palestine in July 1942, and carried out bombing raids on enemy bases in North Africa, Italy and Greece before flying on to India, the first arriving at Salbani on 30 September. Operations against the Japanese began on 17 November and long-range bombing and reconnaissance missions were undertaken for the rest of the war over targets in Burma, Siam, Malaya and the Dutch East Indies. After Japan surrendered, No.159 was engaged in transport and survey duties before disbanding on 1 June 1946.

Squadron bases			
Not known	1 Jun 1918	Chakrata	1 Jun 1942 (G)
	to 4 Jul 1918	St. Jean	Jul 1942 (A)
Molesworth	2 Jan 1942	Aqir	12 Aug 1942 (A)
Left for Middle East		Salbani	27 Sep 1942
	12 Feb 1942 (G)	Digri	23 Oct 1943
Fayid	15 Apr 1942 (G)	Dhubalia	6 Mar 1944
Left for India		Digri	15 Apr 1944
	10 May 1942 (G)	Salbani	Oct 1945 (P)
Deolali	24 May 1942 (G)		to 1 Jun 1946

Aircraft Equipment	Period of service	Representative Serial and Code
Liberator II	Jul 1942 – Aug 1943	AL550 (M)
Liberator III	Aug 1943 – Apr 1944	BZ906 (A)
Liberator VI	Mar 1944 – Jul 1945	KH257 (Q)
Liberator VIII	Jun 1945 – May 1946	KN762 (V)

Liberator II, No.160 Squadron

No. 160 Squadron

Badge: A Sinhalese lion rampant holding a Sinhalese sword
Motto: Api soya paragasamu (Sinhalese) (We seek and strike)

A nucleus of No.160 Squadron was formed on 1 June 1918, but existed for only a few weeks before being disbanded on 4 July 1918. On 16 January 1942, the squadron reformed at Thurleigh as a Liberator heavy bomber unit for the Middle East. The ground personnel left on 12 February but the aircrews remained in the UK for training and early in May moved to Nutts Corner for anti-submarine patrols over the Atlantic for a month. Early in June the squadron's Liberators began to fly out to Palestine where they began night bombing raids on enemy ports and bases in Libya and Crete. In the meantime the ground crews had arrived in India where they awaited the arrival of their aircraft but the situation in the Middle East resulted in these being retained there until after the Battle of El Alamein in October 1942. Liberators began leaving for India one by one until those remaining were merged with 178 Squadron on 15 January 1943. On 6 February 1943, the first patrols began to be flown over the Bay of Bengal and after a few weeks the bulk of the squadron moved to Ceylon. While mainly engaged in shipping protection, No.160 also used its long-range aircraft for photographic reconnaissance missions over Sumatra and the Nicobars and for minelaying. In June 1945, the squadron was transferred to special duties and began dropping agents and supplies to resistance groups in Malaya and Sumatra, some of the sorties lasting more than twenty-four hours. With the Japanese surrender, No.160 began transport duties between India, Ceylon and Malaya until June 1946 when its aircraft began to fly back to the UK At Leuchars it was reduced to six aircraft for general reconnaissance and air-sea rescue duties, the first of its replacement Lancasters arriving at the end of August. On 30 September 1946 the squadron was renumbered 120 Squadron.

Squadron bases

Not known	1 Jun 1918 to 4 Jul 1918	Salbani	22 Nov 1942
Thurleigh	16 Jan 1942	Ratmalana	19 Feb 1943
Left for India		Sigiriya	2 Aug 1943
	12 Feb 1942 (G)	Kankesanturai	1 Aug 1944
Nutts Corner	7 May 1942 (A)	Minneriya	7 Feb 1945
Drigh Road	4 Jun 1942 (G)		13 Feb 1945 (C)
Move to Middle East began		Kankesanturai	17 Oct 1945
	8 Jun 1942 (A)		22 Oct 1945 (C)
Aqir	11 Jun 1942 (A)	Left for UK	15 Jun 1946 (A1)
Shandur	8 Nov 1942 (A) to 15 Jan 1943		23 Jun 1946 (C)
		Leuchars	Jun 1946 (P) to 1 Oct 1946

Aircraft

Equipment	Period of service	Representative Serial and Code
Liberator II	May 1942 – Jan 1943	AL565 (BS-C)
Liberator III, IIIA	Nov 1942 – Jun 1946	BZ886 (R)
Liberator V	Jun 1944 – Jun 1946	FL911 (K)
Liberator VI	Jun 1944 – Jan 1945	KN777 (BS-A)
Liberator VIII	Oct 1945 – Oct 1946	KL544 (X)
Lancaster GR.3	Aug 1946 – Oct 1946	RE158 (BS-B)

No. 161 Squadron

Badge: An open fetterlock
Motto: Liberate

No.161 Squadron was formed as a nucleus of a day bomber unit on 1 June 1918, but was disbanded on 4 July 1918 to provide personnel for other units.

On 15 February 1942, No.161 reformed at Newmarket from a nucleus supplied by No.138 Squadron and the King's Flight. It joined with No.138 in dropping supplies and agents over occupied Europe and took over the landing and pick-up operations for which it used Lysanders, Havocs and Hudsons. Halifaxes were received in November 1942 and in September 1944, it began using Stirlings. Supply-dropping continued until the end of the war and on 2 June 1945 the squadron disbanded.

Lysander IIIA, No.161 Squadron

Squadron bases

Not known	1 Jun 1918 to 4 Jul 1918	Graveley Tempsford	Mar 1942 (P) 11 Apr 1942
Newmarket	15 Feb 1942		to 2 Jun 1945

Aircraft

Equipment	Period of service	Representative Serial
Lysander IIIa	Feb 1942 – Jun 1945	V9283
Whitley V	Feb 1942 – Dec 1942	Z9160
Havoc I	Feb 1942 – Dec 1943	AW399
Halifax V	Nov 1942 – Oct 1944	DG405
Hudson III, V	Oct 1943 – Jun 1945	T9439 (MA-R)
Stirling III, IV	Sep 1944 – Jun 1945	LK237

No. 162 Squadron

Badge: In front of a meteor, a bat's head erased
Motto: One time, one purpose

Blenheim V, No.162 Squadron

No.162 Squadron was formed as a nucleus on 1 June 1918, but was disbanded on 4 July 1918 before becoming effective. It reformed on 4 January 1942 at Kabrit from a detachment of Wellingtons of No.109 Squadron and for the first few weeks was referred to as the Signals Squadron until its number was advised. Its tasks included radar calibration, locating and identifying enemy radar stations and jamming enemy tank radios. To carry these out, small detachments of aircraft operated from many airfields in the Middle East, the bulk of the calibration work being carried out by Blenheims. On 24 May 1942, the squadron began bombing raids in support of the hard-pressed Eighth Army and during the attack on El Alamein its Wellingtons were engaged in jamming the radios of the enemy Panzer forces. After the rout of the Afrika Korps, bombing raids continued at intervals but the main task was calibration. In September 1943, Baltimores began to replace the Blenheims and in March 1944, the squadron took over the Wellington D.W.I. minesweepers of No.1 GRU and operated them until July.

On 25 September 1944 the squadron was disbanded and its calibration duties taken over by No.26 AACU.

On 18 December 1944 No.162 Squadron reformed at Bourn with Mosquitos as part of the Light Night Striking Force and carried out many night raids on Germany until the end of the war. In July 1945 it was transferred to Transport Command at Blackbushe to operate a mail service to the Continent, disbanding on 14 July 1946.

Squadron bases

Not known	1 Jun 1918 to 4 Jul 1918	LG.91 Idku	27 Aug 1943 20 Apr 1944
Kabrit	4 Jan 1942		to 25 Sep 1944
Shallufa	7 Jan 1942	Bourn	18 Dec 1944
Bilbeis	12 Apr 1942	Blackbushe	6 Jul 1945
Benina	4 Apr 1943		to 14 Jul 1946

Aircraft

Equipment	Period of service	Representative Serial and Code
Wellington IC	Jan 1942 – Sep 1944	Z9034 (Z)
Wellington III	Sep 1943 – Sep 1944	HF733 (L)
Wellington X	May 1944 – Sep 1944	HZ123
Blenheim IV	Mar 1942 – Jul 1942	V5508 (B)
Blenheim V	Jul 1942 – Mar 1944	EH434
Baltimore III	Sep 1943 – Sep 1944	AH134
Mosquito VI	Oct 1943 – Jan 1944	HJ671 (one only)
Mosquito 20, 25	Dec 1944 – Jul 1946	KB461 (CR-V)

No. 163 Squadron

No.163 Squadron was formed on 1 June 1918 at Waddington but was disbanded a few weeks later on 4 July 1918, without acquiring more than a small nucleus of personnel. On 10 July 1942, the squadron reformed at Suez for transport duties and embarked the same day for Massawa in Eritrea. On 15 July it disembarked and proceeded to Asmara where it began to receive Hudsons a week later. By the end of the month it was ready to start transport flights and on 1 September opened a mail service between Asmara and Khartoum, communications flying in Eritrea, Sudan and Ethiopia being extended by trips to Nigeria and Madagascar. On 18 December 1942 the squadron was reduced to a cadre which was finally disbanded on 16 June 1943.

On 25 January 1945 No.163 reformed at Wyton with Mosquitos in No.8 Group and began night raids on Germany three days later. These continued for the rest of the war and on 10 August 1945 the squadron was disbanded.

Squadron bases

Waddington	1 Jun 1918 to 4 Jul 1918	Asmara	15 Jul 1942 to 16 Jun 1943
En route	10 Jul 1942 to 15 Jul 1942	Wyton	25 Jan 1945 to 10 Aug 1945

Aircraft Equipment	Period of service	Representative Serial and Code
Hudson IIIA	Jul 1942 – Dec 1942	EW960
Hudson VI	Jul 1942 – Dec 1942	FK485
Mosquito 25	Jan 1945 – May 1945	KB510 (B)
Mosquito XVI	May 1945 – Aug 1945	PF405

Typhoon IB, No.164 Squadron

No. 164 Squadron

Badge: In front of a rising sun a lion passant guardant
Motto: Firmes volamos (Spanish) (Firmly we fly)
Name: 'Argentine-British'

No.164 Squadron was formed on 1 June 1918 but remained a nucleus without aircraft until disbanded on 4 July 1918. On 6 April 1942, it reformed at Peterhead as a fighter squadron and became operational with Spitfires early in May. In January 1943, it moved to South Wales where it received Hurricane fighter-bombers and began training as a ground-attack unit. Operations began in June against enemy shipping and coastal targets and continued till March 1944, when the Hurricanes were replaced by Typhoons. Using rockets, it attacked enemy communications, radar stations and transport in preparation for the invasion of Europe. After providing support for the landing forces from southern England, the squadron moved to France in July. During the Battle of Normandy, No.164 used its rockets against enemy armour in the battle area and after the breakout moved forward through northern France and Belgium in support of the 21st Army Group. For the remaining months of the war, the squadron was engaged in reconnaissance sweeps, attacking enemy transport and tanks and in April 1945 moved into its first German base. Soon after the end of the war it moved back to the UK and re-equipped with Spitfires. On 31 August 1946 the squadron was renumbered 63 Squadron.

Squadron bases

Peterhead	6 Apr 1942	B.7 Martragny	20 Jul 1944
Skeabrae	4 May 1942	B.23 Morainville	3 Sep 1944
Peterhead	10 Sep 1942	B.35 Baromesnil	6 Sep 1944
Tangmere	2 Oct 1942	B.53 Merville	13 Sep 1944
Peterhead	11 Oct 1942	B.67 Ursel	30 Oct 1944
Fairwood Common	29 Jan 1943	B.77 Gilze-Rijen	26 Nov 1944
Middle Wallop	8 Feb 1943	Fairwood Common	17 Dec 1944
Warmwell	19 Jun 1943	B.77 Gilze-Rijen	28 Dec 1944
Manston	5 Aug 1943	A.84 Chievres	1 Jan 1945
Fairlop	22 Sep 1943	B.77 Gilze-Rijen	19 Jan 1945
Twinwood Farm	4 Jan 1944	B.91 Kluis	21 Mar 1945
Fairlop	13 Jan 1944	B.103 Plantlunne	17 Apr 1945
Twinwood Farm	11 Feb 1944	B.116 Wunstorf	26 May 1945
Acklington	8 Mar 1944	Turnhouse	Jun 1945
Thorney Island	15 Mar 1944	Fairwood Common	19 Nov 1945
Llanbedr	11 Apr 1944		
Thorney Island	22 Apr 1944	Turnhouse	5 Jan 1946
Funtington	17 Jun 1944	Tangmere	25 Mar 1946
Hurn	21 Jun 1944	Middle Wallop	28 Apr 1946 to 31 Aug 1946
B.8 Sommervieu	17 Jul 1944		

Aircraft Equipment	Period of service	Representative Serial and Code
Spitfire VA	Apr 1942 – Sep 1942	R7267
Spitfire VB	Sep 1942 – Jan 1943	EP244
Hurricane IID	Feb 1943 – May 1943	
Hurricane IV	May 1943 – Mar 1944	KX561 (FJ-G)
Typhoon IB	Jan 1944 – Jun 1945	JP367 (FJ-J)
Spitfire IXE	Jun 1945 – Aug 1946	TB548
Spitfire XVIE	Jul 1946 – Aug 1946	TE342

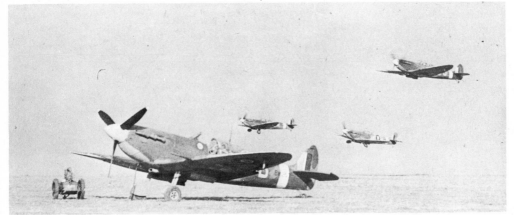

Spitfire VBs, No.165 Squadron

No. 165 Squadron

Badge: A double-headed dragon
affronteé, the necks
crossed spouting fire
Motto: Infensa virtuti invidia
(Envy is the foe of
honour)
Name: 'Ceylon'

No.165 Squadron was formed on 1 June 1918, as a nucleus but did not become effective before being disbanded again on 4 July 1918. It reformed on 6 April 1942 at Ayr with Spitfires as a fighter squadron and became operational on defensive duties on 1 May. In August, it moved to south-east England to take part in sweeps over northern France until returning to Scotland in March 1943. At the beginning of July it came south again and in August joined the Kenley Wing for bomber escort missions over the Continent for a month before transferring to the south-west. Escorts, convoy patrols, sweeps over north-west France and local air defence occupied No.165 until after the invasion, the squadron then moving to Kent to help combat flying-bomb attacks and provide escorts for bomber forces. In mid-December 1944, it moved to East Anglia where conversion to Mustangs was completed in February 1945, and long-range missions began. With the end of the war in Europe, the squadron moved to Dyce to re-equip with Spitfires and prepare for its transfer to Norway in mid-June. There it provided air defence for six months until the Royal Norwegian Air Force had re-organised after its return home from exile. Returning to the UK in January 1946, the squadron disbanded on 1 September 1946.

Squadron bases			
Ayr	6 Apr 1942	Predannack	3 Apr 1944
Gravesend	14 Aug 1942	Detling	22 Jun 1944
Tangmere	1 Nov 1942	Lympne	13 Jul 1944
Peterhead	29 Mar 1943	Detling	10 Aug 1944
Ibsley	1 Jul 1943	Bentwaters	16 Dec 1944
Exeter	30 Jul 1943	Dyce	30 May 1945
Kenley	8 Aug 1943	Vaernes	20 Jun 1945
Culmhead	17 Sep 1943	Charterhall	1 Jan 1946
Colerne	10 Feb 1944	Duxford	18 Jan 1946
			to 1 Sep 1946

Aircraft Equipment	Period of service	Representative Serial and Code
Spitfire VA, VB	Apr 1942 – Oct 1943	EP172 (SK-W)
Spitfire IX	Oct 1943 – Feb 1945	MK426 (SK-D)
Mustang III	Feb 1945 – Jun 1945	HB959 (SK-M)
Spitfire IX	Jun 1945 – Sep 1946	PL317 (SK-A)

No. 166 Squadron

Badge: A bulldog affrontee
Motto: Tenacity

No.166 Squadron was formed at Bircham Newton on 13 June 1918 as a night bomber squadron and in September became the first squadron of No.27 Group which had been set up to undertake bombing raids on Germany with Handley Page V/1500 four-engined bombers. Based in East Anglia, the Group's bombers were ready to make their first raid on Berlin when the Armistice intervened. On 31 May 1919 the squadron was disbanded.

No.166 reformed from A Flight No.97 Squadron at Boscombe Down on 1 November 1936. Equipped with Heyfords, it became a training unit in June 1938, and re-equipped with Whitleys in June 1939. On the outbreak of war, it moved to Abingdon and remained on training duties until merged with No.97 Squadron to form No.10 OTU on 6 April 1940.

On 27 January 1943, No.166 reformed from detachments of Nos.142 and 150 Squadrons at Kirmington and took part in night raids with Wellingtons until September 1943. It then re-equipped with Lancasters and formed part of the main force of Bomber Command until the end of the war, disbanding on 18 November 1945.

Squadron bases			
Bircham Newton	13 Jun 1918	Abingdon	17 Sep 1939
	to 31 May 1919		to 6 Apr 1940
Boscombe Down	1 Nov 1936	Kirmington	27 Jan 1943
Leconfield	20 Jan 1937		to 18 Nov 1945

Aircraft Equipment	Period of service	Representative Serial and Code	Aircraft Equipment	Period of service	Representative Serial and Code
F.E.2b	Jun 1918 – Oct 1918		Whitley III	Nov 1939 – Apr 1940	K8960
Handley Page V/1500	Oct 1918 – Mar 1919		Wellington III	Jan 1943 – Apr 1943	BK515 (AS-P)
Heyford III	Nov 1936 – Sep 1939	K6886	Wellington X	Feb 1943 – Sep 1943	HE752 (AS-W)
Whitley I	Jun 1939 – Apr 1940	K7185	Lancaster I, III	Sep 1943 – Nov 1945	DV220 (AS-J)

Heyford IIIs, No.166 Squadron

No. 167 Squadron

Badge: A woodpecker volant
Motto: Ubique sine mora (Everywhere without delay)
Name: 'Gold Coast'

No.167 Squadron was formed during November 1918, at Bircham Newton as the second heavy bomber squadron in No.27 Group. It was intended to operate Handley Page V/1500 four-engined bombers but the Armistice came before bombing raids on Germany could begin and the squadron disbanded on 21 May 1919.

On 6 April 1942, No.167 reformed at Scorton as a fighter squadron and became operational on 8 May. Next month it arrived in the North of Scotland to provide air defence for the fleet base at Scapa Flow and coastal convoys. In October 1942, the squadron moved to East Anglia for shipping reconnaissance and intruder missions over the Low Countries. Many of the pilots flying with No.167 were Dutch and it was decided to make the squadron a wholly Dutch formation. This took place on 12 June 1943, when it was renumbered 322 Squadron.

On 21 October 1944, No.167 reformed at Holmsley South as a transport squadron in No.110 Wing. Warwicks were received in November and began flying regular services to various Allied bases in Europe and West Africa. In May 1945, a flight of Ansons was operated on short-range routes and in July Warwicks were taken out of service for technical problems to be solved, crews in the meantime flying Dakotas with No.147 Squadron until Warwicks resumed operating in September. On 1 February 1946, the squadron was disbanded.

On 1 February 1953, No.3 (Long-range) Ferry Unit at Abingdon was redesignated No.167 Squadron. It was engaged in ferrying aircraft to units overseas until it merged with No.147 Squadron to form the Ferry Squadron on 15 September 1958.

Squadron bases			
Bircham Newton	Nov 1918	Ludham	13 Mar 1943
	to 21 May 1919	Digby	13 May 1943
Scorton	6 Apr 1942	Woodvale	12 Jun 1943
Acklington	23 May 1942	Holmsley South	21 Oct 1944
Castletown	1 Jun 1942	Blackbushe	27 Mar 1945
Ludham	14 Oct 1942		to 1 Feb 1946
Kidlington	1 Mar 1943	Abingdon	1 Feb 1953
Fowlmere	5 Mar 1943	Benson	16 Apr 1953
			to 15 Sep 1958

Aircraft Equipment	Period of service	Representative Serial and Code
Handley Page V/1500	Nov 1918 – May 1919	
Spitfire VC, VB	Apr 1942 – Jun 1943	EP350 (VL-F)
Warwick I	Nov 1944 – May 1945	BV252
Warwick III	Nov 1944 – Feb 1946	HG291
Anson XII	May 1945 – Feb 1946	PH672
Ferrying various types	Feb 1953 – Sep 1958	—

No. 168 Squadron

Badge: In front of a scroll, a flaming arrow, the point downwards
Motto: Rerum cognoscere causas (To know the cause of things)

No.168 Squadron was formed at Snailwell on 15 June 1942 as a tactical reconnaissance unit in Army Cooperation Command, a nucleus being supplied by No.268 Squadron. Initially Tomahawks were used but in November these were replaced by Mustangs which began attacks on shipping and coastal targets in December, which were exceptions to the normal training programme with the army. In July 1943 the squadron joined No.123 Airfield of the newly-formed Second Tactical Air Force and began reconnaissance duties in October in preparation for the coming invasion. In June

1944 No.168 moved to Normandy a few weeks after the landings and remained with the 21st Army Group during its movement into the Netherlands, providing tactical reconnaissnace support. In October 1944, it converted to Typhoons and spent the next four months flying armed reconnaissance sweeps over Germany and providing cover for day bombers. On 26 February 1945 the squadron was officially disbanded but operations continued for two more days before No.168 was grounded.

Squadron bases			
Snailwell	15 Jun 1942	Odiham	17 Mar 1943
Bottisham	13 Jul 1942	Hutton Cranswick	20 Sep 1943
Odiham	18 Nov 1942	Huggate	10 Oct 1943
Weston Zoyland	1 Mar 1943	Thruxton	15 Oct 1943
		Sawbridgeworth	12 Nov 1943

North Weald	30 Nov 1943	B.21 St. Honorine	14 Aug 1944
Llanbedr	21 Jan 1944	B.34 Avrilly	1 Sep 1944
North Weald	3 Feb 1944	B.66 Diest/Schaffen	
Gatwick	6 Mar 1944		20 Sep 1944
Odiham	31 Mar 1944	B.78 Eindhoven	2 Oct 1944
B.8 Sommervieu	29 Jun 1944		to 26 Feb 1945

Aircraft

Equipment	Period of service	Representative Serial and Code
Tomahawk IIA	Jun 1942 – Nov 1942	AH162
Mustang I	Nov 1942 – Aug 1943	AG510
Mustang Ia	Aug 1943 – Feb 1944	FD542
Mustang I	Feb 1944 – Oct 1944	AG474
Typhoon Ib	Sep 1944 – Feb 1945	JR244 (QC-S)

No. 169 Squadron

Badge: In front of a hurt, a hunting horn in bend
Motto: Hunt and destroy

No.169 Squadron was formed on 15 June 1942 at Twinwood Farm as a tactical reconnaissance unit of Army Cooperation Command. A nucleus of Mustangs was received from No.613 Squadron and after training with army units the squadron moved to Duxford in December to begin shipping reconnaissance and ground-attack missions. In July 1943 it was also employed in countering low-level attacks by enemy fighter-bombers on coastal towns but was disbanded on 30 September 1943.

On 1 October 1943, No.169 reformed at Ayr with a few Mosquitos and a Beaufighter to begin training with 'Gee'.

The squadron's former ground personnel were posted in from Middle Wallop and in December the squadron moved to Little Snoring. With Mosquito II night fighters, operations began on 20 January 1944 and consisted of providing intruder aircraft to attack enemy night fighters and clear the way for the heavy bomber force. This task continued until the end of the war, with occasional day missions being flown from October. On 10 August 1945 the squadron was disbanded.

Squadron bases			
Twinwood Farm	15 Jun 1942	Bottisham	10 Mar 1943
Doncaster	27 Jun 1942	Duxford	12 Mar 1943
Weston Zoyland	13 Oct 1942	Andover	25 Mar 1943
Doncaster	18 Oct 1942	Middle Wallop	21 Jun 1943
Clifton	15 Nov 1942		to 30 Sep 1943
Duxford	20 Dec 1942	Ayr	1 Oct 1943
Barford St. John	1 Mar 1943	Little Snoring	8 Dec 1943
Gransden Lodge	5 Mar 1943	Great Massingham	4 Jun 1944
			to 10 Aug 1945

Aircraft

Equipment	Period of service	Representative Serial and Code
Mustang I	Jun 1942 – Sep 1943	AL993
Mosquito III	Oct 1943 – Jan 1944	HJ870
Mosquito II	Jan 1944 – Jul 1944	DZ310 (VI-B)
Mosquito VI	Jun 1944 – Aug 1945	NS997 (VI-C)
Mosquito XIX	Jan 1945 – Aug 1945	MM644 (VI-G)

No. 170 Squadron

Badge: Issuant from a helmet affrontée, the vizor closed, a plume of three ostrich feathers
Motto: Videre non videri (To see and not to be seen)

No.170 Squadron was formed at Weston Zoyland on 15 June 1942, as a tactical reconnaissance unit equipped with Mustangs. After taking part in exercises with the army, it began reconnaissance missions on 4 January 1943. These continued throughout 1943, while other tasks included low-level defensive patrols to intercept enemy fighter-bombers attacking South Coast towns and intruder raids on communications targets in northern France. In July, the squadron

joined Second TAF but was disbanded on 15 January 1944.

On 15 October 1945, No.170 reformed at Kelstern from C Flight of No.625 Squadron and began night bombing with Lancasters on 19 October. These operations continued until the end of the war and on 14 November 1945, the squadron was disbanded.

Squadron bases			
Weston Zoyland	15 Jun 1942	Huggate	11 Oct 1943
Hurn	17 Jun 1942	Leconfield	14 Oct 1943
Thruxton	7 Oct 1942	Thruxton	16 Oct 1943
Andover	20 Oct 1942	Sawbridgeworth	12 Nov 1943
Ford	28 Feb 1943		to 15 Jan 1944
Andover	13 Mar 1943	Kelstern	15 Oct 1944
Snailwell	25 Mar 1943	Dunholme Lodge	22 Oct 1944
Odiham	26 Jun 1943	Hemswell	29 Nov 1944
Hutton Cranswick	20 Sep 1943		to 14 Nov 1945

Aircraft

Equipment	Period of service	Representative Serial and Code
Mustang I	Jun 1942 – Aug 1943	AM447
Mustang Ia	Aug 1943 – Jan 1944	FD496
Lancaster I, III	Oct 1944 – Nov 1945	ME320 (TC-L)

No. 171 Squadron

Badge: In front of an eagle displayed, a portcullis
Motto: Per dolum defendimus (Confound the enemy)

No.171 Squadron was formed at Gatwick on 15 June 1942 as a tactical reconnaissance unit of Army Co-operation Command. Equipped initially with Tomahawks it replaced these by Mustangs before beginning operations in October. Reconnaissance missions were flown along the French coast but on 31 December 1942 the squadron was disbanded and its equipment passed to No.430 Squadron, RCAF.

On 8 September 1944, C Flight of No.199 Squadron was detached and became No.171 Squadron at North Creake. Its Halifaxes and Stirlings were engaged in bomber support duties, dropping 'Window' to detract from the performance of enemy radar. In November, Stirlings ceased operations and the squadron continued to operate with Halifaxes only until the end of the war. On 27 July 1945 the squadron was disbanded.

Squadron bases			
Gatwick	15 Jun 1942	Gatwick	20 Sep 1942
Odiham	11 Jul 1942	Hartfordbridge	7 Dec 1942
Gatwick	25 Aug 1942		to 31 Dec 1942
Weston Zoyland	10 Sep 1942	North Creake	8 Sep 1944
			to 27 Jul 1945

Aircraft Equipment	Period of service	Representative Serial and Code
Tomahawk I, IIa	Jun 1942 – Dec 1942	AH831
Mustang Ia	Sep 1942 – Dec 1942	AG555
Stirling III	Sep 1944 – Jan 1945	LJ559 (6Y-J)
Halifax III	Sep 1944 – Jul 1945	NA110 (6Y-Z)

No. 172 Squadron

Badge: A gannet volant in front of a tower
Motto: Insidiantibus insidiamur (We ambush the ambushers)

Wellington VIII, No.172 Squadron

No.172 Squadron was formed at Chivenor on 4 April 1942 from the Leigh Light Flight which had formed on 8 March to operate Wellingtons equipped with airborne searchlights on anti-submarine patrols. The first operational night patrol was flown on 3 June during which two U-boats were located and attacked. In August, seven aircraft were detached to Wick for patrols over the North Sea and were the basis of No.179 Squadron when it formed on 14 September. Patrols over the Western Approaches and Bay of Biscay led to many sightings and in March 1943 the squadron's Wellingtons were fitted with ASV Mark III radar to guide the aircraft into a position where their searchlights could be exposed to reveal a U-boat. This method soon brought results, U-665 being sunk on 20 March and overall the squadron averaged one sighting for every four sorties. Between October 1943 and April 1944 detachments were based at Gibraltar and, later, in the Azores. In September 1944 No.172 moved to Northern Ireland and flew patrols over the Atlantic until disbanded on 4 June 1945.

Squadron bases			
			to 14 Sep 1942
Chivenor	8 Mar 1942	Limavady	1 Sep 1944
Skitten (D)	17 Aug 1942		to 4 Jun 1945

Aircraft Equipment	Period of service	Representative Serial and Code
Wellington VIII	Apr 1944 – Mar 1943	BB513 (OQ-B)
Wellington XII	Feb 1943 – Oct 1943	HX653 (OQ-L)
Wellington XIV	Aug 1943 – Jun 1945	HF130 (OQ-W)

No. 173 Squadron

Badge: A sword bentwise in its scabbard grasped beneath the hilt with an eagle's claw couped at the thigh in chief and a gauntlet likewise grasping the scabbard in base
Motto: Quocumque (Whithersoever)

No.173 Squadron was formed at Heliopolis on 9 July 1942, as a communications unit in No.216 Group. Initially A Flight operated Lodestars on passenger and freight services and B Flight flew an assortment of light aircraft on short-range communications. Numerous types were used and it was

September 1943 before reasonable standardisation was achieved, Ansons, Arguses and Proctors forming the short-range flight and Lodestars the medium-range. On 29 February 1944 the squadron became the Middle East Communications Squadron.

On 1 February 1953, No.4 (Home) Ferry Unit at Hawarden was renumbered 173 Squadron and was engaged in ferrying aircraft until disbanded on 1 September 1957. A proposal to allot the number to the Ferry Support Squadron at Benson does not appear to have been carried out.

Squadron bases			
Heliopolis	9 Jul 1942	Hawarden	1 Feb 1953
	to 29 Feb 1944		to 1 Sep 1957

Aircraft Equipment	Period of service	Representative Serial and Code
Lodestar	Jul 1942 – Feb 1944	EW996
Proctor I, III	Jul 1942 – Feb 1944	P6166
Argus I	Sep 1942 – Feb 1944	EV324
Anson I	Sep 1943 – Feb 1944	AW524

Various types in small numbers at various times, e.g. Scion Senior (HK868); Ju 52/3m (HK919); Oxford I (P1950); Lysander (P9191); Audax (K7525); Hurricane I (X4712); Blenheim IV (Z9715); Electra (AX700); Percival Q.6 (HK838); Gull (AX698); Magister (R1945); Hart (K6421); Boston III (Z2162); Moth Major (HK839); Dominie (HK864); Beaufighter I (V8344).

Lockheed 12A, No.173 Squadron

No. 174 Squadron

Badge: A winged Sambur deer springing
Motto: Attack
Name: 'Mauritius'

No.174 was formed at Manston on 3 March 1942, taking over seventeen Hurricanes and eight pilots from No.607 which enabled operations to be started on the same day. Fighter-bomber missions were flown against enemy shipping and coastal targets until December 1943 when it was withdrawn for army co-operation training in preparation for re-equipment with Typhoons. These arrived in February 1943, and No.174 joined the 2nd Tactical Air Force on its formation in June 1943. Ground-attack missions began in July and in January 1944, the squadron was equipped for rocket-firing and began attacking radar stations, flying bomb launching sites and communications targets in northern France. Soon after the landings in Normandy, the squadron moved into captured territory and provided close support for the army, attacking enemy tanks and transport in the field. By the end of September 1944 No.174 had moved forward to the Netherlands where it flew sweeps over Germany for the rest of the war, disbanding on 8 April

1945 with the end in sight.

On 26 August 1945, No.137 Squadron at Lubeck was renumbered 174 Squadron but disbanded on 6 September 1945. On 9 September 1945, No.274 Squadron, then on an air firing course at Warmwell, was renumbered 174 Squadron. Its Tempests were based in Germany until disbandment took place on 31 March 1946.

Squadron bases			
Manston	3 Mar 1942	B.2 Bazenville	19 Jun 1944
Fowlmere	9 Jul 1942	B.24 St. André	27 Aug 1944
Manston	12 Jul 1942	B.42 Beauvais-Tillé	1 Sep 1944
Warmwell	31 Aug 1942	B.50 Vitry-en-Artois	4 Sep 1944
Manston	21 Sep 1942	B.70 Deurne	17 Sep 1944
Odiham	6 Dec 1942	B.80 Volkel	30 Sep 1944
Chilbolton	1 Mar 1943	Warmwell	10 Nov 1944
Grove	11 Mar 1943	B.80 Volkel	21 Nov 1944
Zeals	12 Mar 1943	B.100 Goch	20 Mar 1945
Gravesend	5 Apr 1943		to 8 Apr 1945
Merston	12 Jun 1943	B.158 Lubeck	26 Aug 1945
Lydd	1 Jul 1943		to 6 Sep 1945
Westhampnett	10 Oct 1943	Warmwell	9 Sep 1945
Eastchurch	21 Jan 1944	Dedelstorf	19 Sep 1945
Westhampnett	4 Feb 1944	Gatow	19 Oct 1945
Holmsley South	1 Apr 1944	Fassberg	26 Nov 1945
			to 31 Mar 1946

Aircraft Equipment	Period of service	Representative Serial and Code
Hurricane IIB	Mar 1942 – Apr 1943	BE684 (XP-Y)
Typhoon IB	Apr 1943 – Apr 1945 Aug 1945 – Sep 1945	MN683 (XP-F)
Tempest V	Sep 1945 – Mar 1946	SN183

Hurricane IIBs, No.174 Squadron

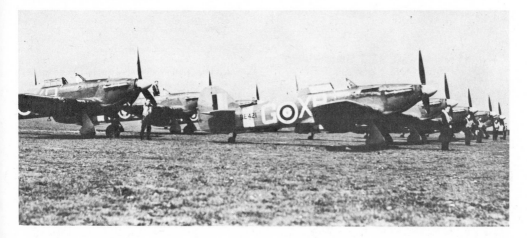

No. 175 Squadron

Badge: A bull's head couped fesswise
Motto: Stop at nothing

No.175 Squadron was formed at Warmwell on 3 March 1942, and took over the Hurricanes IIBs left behind by No.402 Squadron when it moved. It flew its first operation on 16 April 1942, when six Hurricanes attacked Maupertus airfield and for a period mixed attacks on enemy shipping with local and convoy protection patrols. In July, the squadron prepared to go overseas but this was cancelled and it resumed cross-Channel sweeps. In April 1943, Typhoons replaced the Hurricanes and operations with these began on 12 June as part of the newly-formed Second TAF. In February 1944, No.175 began training with rockets for army support duties and after helping to wreck enemy communications before the landing in Normandy, moved to the beachhead two weeks after the initial landings. It provided support for the 21st Army Group by attacking enemy bases and tanks in the battle area arriving in the Netherlands at the end of September. It continued its attacks on enemy communications and battlefield targets until the end of the war, moving into German bases from mid-March 1945. After a short period with the occupation forces, the squadron disbanded on 30 September 1945.

Squadron bases

Warmwell	3 Mar 1942	B.5 Le Fresney Camille	24 Jun 1944
Harrowbeer	10 Oct 1942	B.42 Beauvais-Tillé	2 Sep 1944
Gatwick	9 Dec 1942	B.50 Vitry-en-Artois	
Odiham	14 Jan 1943		4 Sep 1944
Stoney Cross	1 Mar 1943	B.70 Deurne	17 Sep 1944
Lasham	11 Mar 1943	B.80 Volkel	30 Sep 1944
Odiham	13 Mar 1943	Warmwell	21 Nov 1944
Stoney Cross	19 Mar 1943	B.80 Volkel	4 Dec 1944
Colerne	8 Apr 1943	B.100 Goch	21 Mar 1945
Lasham	24 May 1943	B.110 Achmer	11 Apr 1945
Appledram	2 Jun 1943	B.150 Hustedt	19 Apr 1945
Lydd	1 Jul 1943	Warmwell	28 May 1945
Westhampnett	9 Oct 1943	Manston	11 Jun 1945
Eastchurch	24 Feb 1944	B.164 Schleswig	16 Jun 1945
Westhampnett	8 Mar 1944	B.160 Kastrup	22 Aug 1945
Holmsley South	1 Apr 1944	B.164 Schleswig	5 Sep 1945
B.3 St. Croix	20 Jun 1944		to 30 Sep 1945

Aircraft Equipment	Period of service	Representative Serial and Code
Hurricane IIB	Mar 1942 – Apr 1943	BE482 (HH-T)
Typhoon IB	Apr 1943 – Sep 1945	EK455 (HH-H)

No. 176 Squadron

Badge: In front of a crescent, an eagle's claw holding an India dagger in bend, the point to the dexter
Motto: Nocte custodimus (We keep the night watch)

No.176 Squadron was formed on 14 January 1943, at Dum Dum, Calcutta, with the arrival of a detachment of No.89 Squadron in India from the Middle East. Equipped with eight Beaufighters, it became operational immediately, flying night patrols over the Calcutta area. In May 1943, a second flight was formed with AI-equipped Hurricanes which were replaced by Beaufighters in January 1944. In September 1943, a detachment was based in Ceylon to encounter Japanese reconnaissance aircraft and in January 1944, the squadron began operating over Burma from advanced bases. In August, No.176 moved to southern India but returned to the Burma front in April 1945. Conversion to Mosquitos began in June and the squadron disbanded on 31 May 1946.

Squadron bases

Dum Dum	14 Jan 1943	Minneriya	21 Aug 1944
Baigachi	6 Feb 1943	Baigachi	31 Mar 1945
			to 31 May 1946

Aircraft Equipment	Period of service	Representative Serial and Code
Beaufighter I	Jan 1943 – Dec 1943	X7776 (M)
Beaufighter VI	Jan 1943 – Jul 1945	KW189 (X)
Hurricane IIC	May 1943 – Jan 1944	KX754 (N)
Mosquito XVI	Jun 1945 – Jul 1945	
Mosquito XIX	Jul 1945 – May 1946	TA264

No. 177 Squadron

Badge: A cobra entwining two gun barrels in saltire
Motto: Silentur in medias res (Silently into the midst of things)

No.177 Squadron was formed on 28 November 1942, but at the time of formation the personnel of the squadron were still at sea en route from the UK. On 11 January 1943, it began to assemble at Amarda Road and moved to Allahabad in mid-March to join No.308 MU. Until aircraft were received, the aircrews were detached to No.27 Squadron. In May 1943, Beaufighters began to arrive and the first ground-attack mission was flown on 10 September 1943. Attacks on enemy shipping, railways and ports continued until May 1944 when the squadron was withdrawn to India. In August, it returned to operations over Burma, having added rockets to its armament and in May 1945, supported the landings at Rangoon before being withdrawn from operations and disbanded on 5 July 1945.

Squadron bases

Amarda Road	11 Jan 1943	Feni	21 Aug 1943
Allahabad	15 Mar 1943	Ranchi	28 May 1944
Phaphamau	6 May 1943	Chiringa	1 Aug 1944
Chittagong	13 Aug 1943	Hathazari	24 Jun 1945
			to 5 Jul 1945

Aircraft Equipment	Period of service	Representative Serial
Beaufighter VI	May 1943 – Aug 1944	EL354
Beaufighter X, XI	Nov 1943 – Jul 1945	LZ118 (H)

No. 178 Squadron

Badge: A demi lion erased holding a flash of lightning
Motto: Irae emissarii (Emissaries of wrath)

No.178 Squadron was formed at Shandur on 15 January 1943, from a detachment of No.160 Squadron and began bombing operations with Liberators on the same day. In March, the squadron moved to Libya to attack targets in North Africa, Italy and the Balkans, and carried out supply-dropping flights to partisans as far afield as northern Italy and Poland. In March 1944, No.178 moved to Italy where it remained for the rest of the war. In addition to Liberators, Halifaxes were used between May and September 1943, and on returning to Egypt in November 1945, the squadron converted to Lancasters. On 15 April 1946 it was renumbered 70 Squadron.

Squadron bases			
Shandur	15 Jan 1943	Celone	Mar 1944
Hosc Raui	4 Mar 1943	Amendola	Jul 1944
Terria	1 Oct 1943	Ein Shemer	25 Aug 1945
El Adem	Jan 1944	Fayid	5 Nov 1945
			to 15 Apr 1946

Aircraft Equipment	Period of service	Representative Serial and Code
Liberator II	Jan 1943 – Dec 1943	AL565 (C)
Liberator III	Sep 1943 – Dec 1943	BZ932 (Y)
Liberator VI	Dec 1943 – Nov 1945	KH248 (T)
Halifax II	May 1943 – Sep 1943	BB385 (Q)
Lancaster III	Nov 1945 – Apr 1946	RE202 (C)

No. 179 Squadron

Badge: In front of a harpoon, a lantern
Motto: Delentem deleo (I destroy the destroyer)

No.179 Squadron was formed on 1 September 1942, from a detached flight of No.172 Squadron. Equipped with Wellingtons fitted with Leigh Lights, it moved to Gibraltar for patrols over the approaches to the Mediterranean. It returned to England in April 1944, to fly anti-submarine patrols over the Bay of Biscay and the Western Approaches until the end of the war. Conversion to Warwicks took place in November 1944, and in February 1946, Lancasters began to arrive. While conversion was under way, the squadron was divided into two parts; No.179X converted to Lancasters while No.179Y remained operational with Warwicks. In May, the remaining Warwicks were disposed of and on 1 June, No.179Y Squadron was renumbered 210 Squadron and No.179X became simply No.179 Squadron. It was disbanded on 30 September 1946, and its aircraft and crews were transferred to No.210 Squadron.

Squadron bases			
Skitten	1 Sep 1942	Benbecula	21 Sep 1944
Gibraltar	18 Nov 1942	Chivenor	23 Oct 1944
Predannack	24 Apr 1944	St. Eval	1 Nov 1944
Chivenor	6 Sep 1944		to 30 Sep 1946

Aircraft Equipment	Period of service	Representative Serial and Code
Wellington VIII	Sep 1942 – Aug 1943	HX531 (OZ-M)
Wellington XIV	Aug 1943 – Nov 1944	MP772
Warwick V	Nov 1944 – May 1946	PN714
Lancaster ASR.3	Feb 1946 – Sep 1946	RF307

No. 180 Squadron

Badge: In front of two arrows in saltire, the points upwards, a velvet glove
Motto: Suaviter in modo fortiter in re (Agreeable in manner, forcible in act)

No.180 Squadron was formed at West Raynham on 13 September 1942, as a medium bomber unit in No.2 Group and received its first Mitchell by the end of the month. During October, it moved over a period to Foulsham and by the beginning of November it had twenty-two Mitchells based there. The first operation was flown on 22 January 1943, when two out of the six aircraft were lost on an attack on Ghent and there were no further bombing raids until May when attacks were resumed. On the formation of the Second Tactical Air Force, No.180 joined Nos.98 and 320 as part of No.139 Airfield (later Wing) at Dunsfold and began a long period of daylight tactical bombing missions in preparation for the invasion. Some night intruder raids were also flown during the Battle of Normandy and in October 1944, the squadron moved to Belgium and, in April 1945, to Germany, carrying out daylight attacks until the end of the war on German communications targets. In September 1945, the Mitchells were exchanged for Mosquitos and in March 1946, No.180 moved to Germany as part of the occupation forces and was renumbered 69 Squadron on 31 March 1946.

Squadron bases			
West Raynham	13 Sep 1942	B.58 Melsbroek	16 Oct 1944
Foulsham	19 Oct 1942	B.110 Achmer	29 Apr 1945
	1 Nov 1942 (C)	Fersfield	7 Jun 1945
Dunsfold	18 Aug 1943	B.110 Achmer	14 Jun 1945
Swanton Morley	12 Apr 1944	B.58 Melsbroek	17 Sep 1945
Dunsfold	26 Apr 1944	Wahn	8 Mar 1946
			to 31 Mar 1946

Aircraft Equipment	Period of service	Representative Serial and Code
Mitchell II	Sep 1942 – Sep 1945	FL198 (EV-P)
Mitchell III	Oct 1944 – Sep 1945	KJ705 (EV-T)
Mosquito XVI	Sep 1945 – Mar 1946	PF455

Mitchell IIs, No.180 Squadron

193

No. 181 Squadron

Badge: In front of two swords in saltire, an eagle's head erased

Motto: Irruimus vastatum (We rush in and destroy)

Typhoon IB, No.181 Squadron

No.181 Squadron was formed at Duxford on 1 September 1942, as a fighter unit and received its first Typhoon a week later. Despite teething troubles with the new fighter, defensive operations began on 28 November 1942, the Typhoon's speed being used to counter enemy fighter-bomber attacks on coastal towns. In February 1943, the squadron flew its first offensive sweep when it began attacks on enemy coastal shipping and later extended these to targets in northern France. In the summer of 1943, the Second Tactical Air Force was formed and No.181 became part of a fighter-bomber wing operating from advanced landing grounds in southern England. In January 1944, attacks began on flying bomb launching sites in northern France and in February the squadron adopted rockets for attacking enemy camps and communications in preparation for the invasion. Two weeks after the initial landings, No.181 began operating from fields in Normandy in support of the Allied armies and during the German retreat was engaged in attacks on enemy tanks and transport trying to escape from the battle area. By early September, it had reached the Low Countries where it spent the winter and during the final offensive moved into Germany with the Second Army. By the end of the war it had reached Lubeck on the Baltic, and on 30 September 1945 was disbanded.

Squadron bases

Duxford	1 Sep 1942	B.78 Eindhoven	23 Sep 1944
Snailwell	10 Dec 1942	Warmwell	12 Feb 1945
Cranfield	1 Mar 1943	B.86 Helmond	3 Mar 1945
Snailwell	8 Mar 1943	B.106 Enschede	11 Apr 1945
Gravesend	24 Mar 1943	B.112 Rheine/Hopsten	
Lasham	5 Apr 1943		13 Apr 1945
Appledram	2 Jun 1943	B.120 Langenhagen	
New Romney	2 Jul 1943		18 Apr 1945
Merston	8 Oct 1943	B.156 Luneberg	1 May 1945
Odiham	31 Dec 1943	B.158 Lubeck	7 May 1945
Merston	13 Jan 1944	B.160 Kastrup	6 Jul 1945
Eastchurch	6 Feb 1944	Manston	20 Jul 1945
Merston	21 Feb 1944	Warmwell	21 Jul 1945
Hurn	1 Apr 1944	B.160 Kastrup	3 Aug 1945
B.6 Coulombs	20 Jun 1944	B.166 Flensberg	5 Sep 1945
B.30 Creton	31 Aug 1944	B.164 Schleswig	8 Sep 1945
B.48 Amiens/Glisy	3 Sep 1944		to 30 Sep 1945
B.58 Melsbroek	6 Sep 1944		

Aircraft

Equipment	Period of service	Representative Serial and Code
Typhoon IB	Sep 1942 – Sep 1945	R8833 (EL-D)

Typhoon IB, No.182 Squadron

No. 182 Squadron

Badge: An airman's gauntlet grasping a sword in bend sinister thrusting to the dexter

Motto: Fearless I direct my flight

No.182 Squadron was formed on 25 August 1942, at Martlesham Heath and received Hurricanes for training in September, soon followed by Typhoons. Afer a single bombing mission over Belgium on 3 January 1943, the squadron took part in tactical training with the Army and in April began flying low-level patrols and intruder missions. Forming part of the newly-formed Second TAF, the squadron continued sweeps over France, attacking flying bomb launching sites from December 1943 and concentrating on communications targets in preparation for the invasion of Europe. Eight days after D-Day, No.182 began operating from airstrips in the beachhead each day, returning to Hurn overnight. Early in July, it moved to France and provided close support for the army during the Battle of Normandy. In September, the squadron moved forward to Belgium and the Netherlands and for the rest of the war flew armed reconnaissance missions against enemy transport and airfields. In April 1945 it occupied its first German airfield and disbanded on 30 September 1945.

Squadron bases

Martlesham Heath	25 Aug 1942	Holmsley South	22 Jun 1944
Sawbridgworth	7 Dec 1942	B.6 Coulombs	3 Jul 1944
Snailwell	17 Jan 1943	B.30 Creton	30 Aug 1944
Sawbridgworth	20 Jan 1943	B.48 Amiens-Glisy	3 Sep 1944
Martlesham Heath	30 Jan 1943	B.58 Melsbroek	6 Sep 1944
Middle Wallop	1 Mar 1943	B.78 Eindhoven	22 Sep 1944
Zeals	12 Mar 1943	B.86 Helmond	13 Jan 1945
Middle Wallop	13 Mar 1943	Warmwell	3 Feb 1945
Fairlop	5 Apr 1943	B.86 Helmond	21 Feb 1945
Lasham	29 Apr 1943	B.106 Enschede	11 Apr 1945
Appledram	2 Jun 1943	B.108 Rheine	13 Apr 1945
New Romney	2 Jul 1943	B.120 Langenhagen	
Wigtown	18 Sep 1943		17 Apr 1945
New Romney	22 Sep 1943	B.156 Luneberg	1 May 1945
Merston	12 Oct 1943	B.158 Lubeck	7 May 1945
Odiham	31 Dec 1943	B.160 Kastrup	11 Jul 1945
Eastchurch	5 Jan 1944	Warmwell	5 Aug 1945
Merston	21 Jan 1944	B.160 Kastrup	19 Aug 1945
Hurn	1 Apr 1944	B.166 Flensberg	5 Sep 1945
B.6 Coulombs	20 Jun 1944	B.164 Schleswig	8 Sep 1945
			to 30 Sep 1945

Aircraft

Equipment	Period of service	Representative Serial and Code
Hurricane I, X	Sep 1942 – Oct 1942	AG232 (XM-P)
Typhoon Ia	Sep 1942 – Oct 1942	R7624 (XM-D)
Typhoon Ib	Oct 1942 – Sep 1945	EJ952 (XM-S)

No. 183 Squadron

Badge: A demi-dragon rampant gorged with a chaplet of maple leaves, holding a rocket
Motto: Versatility
Name: 'Gold Coast'

No.183 Squadron was formed at Church Fenton on 1 November 1942, as a Typhoon squadron but due to early difficulties with this type it did not become operational until 5 April 1943, carrying out its first cross-Channel sweep on 19 April with fighter-bombers. Attacks on enemy shipping and airfields were continued from Cornwall when the squadron moved there in September and in November it began using rockets instead of bombs. In February 1944, No.183 returned to the south-east to begin a series of attacks on enemy communications and flying-bomb sites in northern France and soon after the landings in Normandy it moved to airstrips in the beachhead from which it supported the army by attacks on enemy tanks and transport in the battle area. By the end of November, it had moved forwards to the Netherlands and in January 1945, was based for several weeks at Chièvres to support the Americans during the German offensive in the Ardennes. In mid-April 1945, the squadron moved to Germany and continued to support the army until the end of the war by attacks on communications and battlefield targets. In June 1945, No.183 flew its Typhoons back to the UK and handed them over at Milfield before beginning to convert to Spitfires at Chilbolton. During August, however, it received Tempests and flew these until renumbered 54 Squadron on 15 November 1945.

Squadron bases

Church Fenton	1 Nov 1942
Cranfield	1 Mar 1943
Snailwell	8 Mar 1943
Church Fenton	12 Mar 1943
Colerne	26 Mar 1943
Gatwick	8 Apr 1943
Lasham	3 May 1943
Colerne	30 May 1943
Harrowbeer	5 Jun 1943
Tangmere	4 Aug 1943
Perranporth	18 Sep 1943
Predannack	13 Oct 1943
Tangmere	1 Feb 1944
Manston	15 Mar 1944
Thorney Island	1 Apr 1944
Funtington	18 Jun 1944
Hurn	22 Jun 1944
Eastchurch	14 Jul 1944
B.7 Martagny	25 Jul 1944
B.23 Morainville	3 Sep 1944
B.35 Baromesnil	6 Sep 1944
B.53 Merville	11 Sep 1944
B.67 Ursel	29 Oct 1944
B.77 Gilze-Rijen	25 Nov 1944
A.84 Chièvres	1 Jan 1945
B.77 Gilze-Rijen	19 Jan 1945
B.91 Kluis	21 Mar 1945
B.103 Plantlunne	17 Apr 1945
B.116 Wunstorf	27 Apr 1945
Milfield	16 Jun 1945
Chilbolton	17 Jun 1945
Fairwood Common	8 Oct 1945
	to 15 Nov 1945

Typhoon IB, No.183 Squadron

Aircraft Equipment	Period of service	Representative Serial and Code
Typhoon Ia, Ib	Nov 1942 – Jun 1945	JR260 (HF-J)
Spitfire IX	Jun 1945 – Aug 1945	
Tempest II	Aug 1945 – Nov 1945	MW811

No. 184 Squadron

Badge: A gun barrel in bend
Motto: Nihil impenetrabile (Nothing impenetrable)

No.184 Squadron was formed at Colerne on 1 December 1943, as a fighter-bomber unit equipped with Hurricanes. Initially, Mark IIDs with 40mm anti-tank cannon were received and the squadron trained with the army in ground-attack practice but the Hurricane IV, fitted with a wing capable of taking guns, bombs and rockets, replaced the IIDs and rockets became the main anti-tank weapon used by Second TAF. Attacks on enemy shipping began on 17 June 1943, and cross-Channel operations became No.184's main task. In October 1943, four Spitfires were received for conversion training but in December it was Typhoons which replaced the Hurricanes. With these, the squadron began a series of attacks on enemy communications in preparation for the invasion. On 27 June 1944, the squadron moved to Normandy and supported the 21st Army Group throughout the Battle of Normandy and the subsequent advance to the Netherlands by attacking enemy tanks and transport. After spending the winter in the Netherlands, it moved to Germany on 21 March 1945, claiming to be the first squadron to be based on German soil in World War Two. Attacks on enemy communications and airfields continued till the end of the war and after a short period with the occupation forces the squadron disbanded on 10 September 1945.

Squadron bases

Colerne	1 Dec 1942	Snailwell	15 Sep 1943
Milfield	3 Feb 1943	Newchurch	17 Sep 1943
Colerne	22 Feb 1943	Detling	12 Oct 1943
Chilbolton	1 Mar 1943	Odiham	6 Mar 1944
Grove	11 Mar 1943	Eastchurch	11 Mar 1944
Zeals	12 Mar 1943	Odiham	3 Apr 1944
Eastchurch	4 May 1943	Westhampnett	23 Apr 1944
Merston	31 May 1943	Holmsley South	13 May 1944
Manston	12 Jun 1943	Westhampnett	20 May 1944
Kingsnorth	14 Aug 1943	Holmsley South	17 Jun 1944
Newchurch	18 Aug 1943	B.10 Plumetot	27 Jun 1944

B.5 Le Fresney Camille	14 Jul 1944	B.100 Goch	21 Mar 1945
B.24 St. André de l'Eure		B.110 Achmer	11 Apr 1945
	28 Aug 1944	B.150 Hustedt	19 Apr 1945
B.42 Beauvais/Tille	2 Sep 1944	Warmwell	7 May 1945
B.50 Vitry-en-Artois		B.164 Schleswig	28 May 1945
	4 Sep 1944	B.160 Kastrup	2 Aug 1945
B.70 Deurne	17 Sep 1944	B.166 Flensburg	5 Sep 1945
B.80 Volkel	30 Sep 1944		to 10 Sep 1945

Aircraft Equipment

	Period of service	Representative Serial and Code
Hurricane IID, IV	Dec 1942 – Mar 1944	KX584 (BR-W)
Spitfire VB	Oct 1943 – Dec 1943	
Typhoon Ib	Dec 1943 – Sep 1945	MN301 (BR-Y)

Hurricane IIB, No.185 Squadron

No. 185 Squadron

Badge: In front of a Maltese cross, a griffin segreant
Motto: Ara fejn hu (Maltese) (Look where it is)

No.185 Squadron was formed on 21 October 1918, at East Fortune as a torpedo bomber unit for use on board HMS *Argus*. Its Cuckoos were intended for an attack on the German High Seas Fleet in its home ports but the war ended before this could be carried out and the squadron did not become operational. On 14 April 1919 it was disbanded.

On 1 March 1938, No. 185 reformed at Abingdon from B Flight of No.40 Squadron with Hinds, replacing these with Battles in June 1938. In June 1939, it converted to Hampdens but was designated a training squadron and did not take part in any operations before it was incorporated in No.14 Operational Training Unit on 5 April 1940. A new 185 Squadron began to form immediately but was disbanded on 17 May 1940.

On 27 April 1941, the squadron reformed in Malta with Hurricanes as part of the island's fighter defences. Early in 1942, these began to be replaced by Spitfires and until the defeat of the enemy in Libya the squadron was engaged in repelling enemy attacks from nearby bases in Sicily. In November 1942 it went over to the offensive, flying sweeps over Sicily and, in July 1943, covering the Allied landings there. A detachment went to Italy in February 1944 for air defence in the Taranto area and attacks across the Adriatic on enemy targets in Albania until August 1944, when the remainder of the squadron moved to the Italian front for fighter-bomber missions in support of the Allied armies until the end of the war. On 19 August 1945, the squadron was disbanded. On 15 September 1951, No.185 Squadron reformed at Takali with Vampires for air defence duties in Malta where it remained until disbanded finally on 1 May 1953.

Squadron bases

East Fortune	19 Oct 1918	Perugia	3 Aug 1944
	to 14 Apr 1918	Loreto	23 Aug 1943
Abingdon	1 Mar 1938	Fano	4 Sep 1944
Thornaby	1 Sep 1938	Borghetto	17 Sep 1944
Cottesmore	25 Aug 1939	Fano	7 Oct 1944
	to 17 May 1940	Peretola	17 Nov 1944
Takali & Hal Far	27 Apr 1941	Pontedera	1 Jan 1945
Qrendi	5 Jun 1943	Villafranca	30 Apr 1945
Hal Far	Oct 1943	Campoformido	16 May 1945
Grottaglie (D)	21 Feb 1944		to 19 Aug 1945
	to 2 Aug 1944	Takali	15 Sep 1951
			to 1 May 1953

Aircraft Equipment

	Period of service	Representative Serial and Code
Cuckoo	Oct 1918 – Apr 1919	
Hind	Mar 1938 – Jun 1938	K5426
Battle	Jun 1938 – Jun 1939	K7666
Hampden I	Jun 1939 – Apr 1940	L4204
Hereford I	Aug 1939 – Apr 1940	L6005
Hurricane I, IIA, IIB	Apr 1941 – Mar 1942	BE583 (T)
Spitfire VB, VC	Feb 1942 – Sep 1944	BR166 (GL-A)
Spitfire VIII	Aug 1944 – Sep 1944 Mar 1945 – Aug 1945	JF342 (GL-3)
Spitfire IX	Dec 1943 – Aug 1944 Sep 1944 – Aug 1945	RR192 (GL-A)
Vampire FB.5	Sep 1951 – May 1953	WA387
Vampire FB.9	May 1952 – May 1953	WR214

No. 186 Squadron

No.186 Squadron was formed at East Retford on 1 April 1918, as a night training unit for personnel of the home defence squadrons and the night fighter squadrons intended for the Western Front. In July 1919, it became a development squadron at Gosport for naval co-operation duties and was renumbered 210 Squadron on 1 February 1920.

On 27 April 1943, No.186 reformed at Drem as a fighter-bomber squadron but did not receive its first Hurricane until August by which time it had moved to Ayr. In November, it converted to Typhoons but in February 1944, these were replaced by Spitfire VBs with which the squadron flew its first cross-Channel sweep on 15 March. On 5 April 1944, however, the squadron was renumbered 130 Squadron. On 5 October 1944, the squadron reformed from C Flight of No.90 Squadron at Tuddenham as a Lancaster unit in Bomber Command. Its first raid was flown on 18 October and attacks on enemy targets continued for the rest of the war. After a short period of transport duties, mainly repatriating released prisoners-of-war, the squadron was disbanded on 17 July 1945.

Squadron bases		Tain	7 Jan 1944
East Retford	1 Apr 1918	Lympne	1 Mar 1944
Gosport	Jul 1919		to 5 Apr 1944
	to 1 Feb 1920	Tuddenham	5 Oct 1944
Drem	27 Apr 1943	Stradishall	17 Dec 1944
Ayr	3 Aug 1943		to 17 Jul 1945

Aircraft Equipment	Period of service	Representative Serial and Code
Avro 504J, 504K	Apr 1918 — 1919	E1830
D.H.9, Cuckoo, Bristol F.2b	Jul 1919 — Feb 1920	E8888 (D.H.9) C820 (F.2b)
Hurricane IV	Aug 1943 — Nov 1943	KZ222
Typhoon IB	Nov 1943 — Feb 1944	JR250
Spitfire VB	Feb 1944 — Apr 1944	
Lancaster I, III	Oct 1944 — Jul 1945	PB483 (AB-X)

No. 187 Squadron

Badge: A buzzard volant carrying in the claws a propellor
Motto: Versatile

No.187 Squadron was formed at East Retford on 1 April 1918, as a night training unit to provide night-flying experience for pilots destined to join home defence and night fighter squadrons. Early in 1919 the squadron was disbanded.

On 1 February 1945, No.187 reformed at Merryfield as a transport squadron equipped with Halifaxes but it was decided during the following month to equip the squadron with Dakotas for trooping to India. Flights began on 1 May 1945, and continued until suspended on 16 March 1946. In October 1945, shorter-range flights to the Continent began and in March 1946, became the squadron's main responsibility. In July 1946, ten Dakotas were detached to Bari and later, to Vienna, to provide support for the British occupation forces. On 1 November 1946, the squadron was renumbered 53 Squadron. On 1 February 1953, No.2 Home Ferry Unit at Aston Down was redesignated 187 Squadron and was engaged in ferrying aircraft in the UK and Germany before being disbanded again on 2 September 1957.

Squadron bases			
East Retford	1 Apr 1918	Netheravon	3 Oct 1946
	to 1919		to 1 Nov 1946
Merryfield	1 Feb 1945	Aston Down	1 Feb 1953
Membury	Oct 1945 (P)		to 2 Sep 1957

Aircraft Equipment	Period of service	Representative Serial and Code
Avro 504K, B.E.2e, Camel, Pup, D.H.6	Apr 1918 — 1919	—
Halifax III	Feb 1945 — Apr 1945	LW162
Dakota III, IV	Mar 1945 — Nov 1946	KK132

No. 188 Squadron

No.188 Squadron was formed at Throwley on 20 December 1917, as a training unit for night flying squadrons. Initially training was on Avro 504Ks, but in June 1918, the forming of squadrons of Camel night fighters resulted in No.188 being given the task of training pilots on this type. In March 1919, the squadron was disbanded. It was not reformed during World War Two.

Squadron bases	
Throwley	20 Dec 1917
	to 1 Mar 1919

Aircraft Equipment	Period of service	Representative Serial and Code
Avro 504K	Dec 1917 — Mar 1919	
Camel	Jun 1918 — Mar 1919	
Pup	Jun 1918 — Mar 1919	

Avro 504Ks, No.188 Squadron

No. 189 Squadron

No.189 Squadron was formed at Ripon on 20 December 1917, as a night-flying training unit, moving shortly afterwards to Sutton's Farm to continue this task until the end of the war. On 1 March 1919, the squadron was disbanded.

On 15 October 1944, No.189 reformed at Bardney as a Lancaster squadron in No.5 Group and began operations on 1 November. For the remaining months of the war it formed part of the main force of Bomber Command and after a few months of transport duties was disbanded on 20 November 1945.

Squadron bases

Ripon	20 Dec 1917	Fulbeck	2 Nov 1944
Sutton's Farm	Jan 1918	Bardney	8 Apr 1945
	to 1 Mar 1919	Metheringham	15 Oct 1945
Bardney	15 Oct 1944		to 20 Nov 1945

Aircraft

Equipment	Period of service	Representative Serial and Code
B.E.2c	Dec 1917 – Mar 1918	
Avro 504K	Dec 1917 – Mar 1919	
Pup	Dec 1917 – Jun 1918	
Camel	Jan 1918 – Mar 1919	
Lancaster I, III	Oct 1944 – Nov 1945	ME444 (CA-F)

Halifax III, No.190 Squadron

No. 190 Squadron

Badge: A cloak charged with a double-headed eagle displayed
Motto: Ex tenebris (Through darkness)

No.190 Squadron was formed at Newmarket on 24 October 1917, as a night training unit with B.E.2es and D.H.6s for basic training. In 1918, it moved to Upwood where it disbanded in January 1919.

On 1 March 1943, No.190 reformed at Sullom Voe with Catalinas and flew anti-submarine patrols over the North Atlantic until disbanded on 31 December 1943.

On 5 January 1944, No.190 reformed at Leicester East as an airborne forces squadron equipped with Stirlings. Flying began in March with glider-towing exercises and supply-dropping missions over France began in April. On D-Day, the squadron sent twenty-three aircraft with paratroops to the initial dropping zone, following up during the day with eighteen more towing gliders. During the first two days of the airborne landings at Arnhem, No.190 flew forty-six sorties, all but six towing gliders. Fifty-three supply flights were then made in the face of heavy anti-aircraft fire, losing eleven aircraft in three days. During the Rhine crossing in March 1945, thirty Stirlings towed gliders to the landing zone and in April the squadron was busy flying fuel for the army when divisions outran their supply lines. In May, army units were carried to Norway to disarm the German garrison and the squadron converted to Halifaxes. After a period of general transport duties, No.190 disbanded on 28 December 1945.

Squadron bases

			to 31 Dec 1943
Newmarket	24 Oct 1917	Leicester East	5 Jan 1944
Upwood	1918	Fairford	25 Mar 1944
	to Jan 1919	Great Dunmow	14 Oct 1944
Sullom Voe	1 Mar 1943		to 28 Dec 1945

Aircraft

Equipment	Period of service	Representative Serial and Code
B.E.2c, B.E.2e	Oct 1917 – Jan 1919	
D.H.6	Oct 1917 – Jan 1919	
Avro 504K	Jan 1918 – Jan 1919	
Catalina Ib	Mar 1943 – Dec 1943	FP215 (G5-E)
Catalina IV	Oct 1943 – Dec 1943	JX210 (G5-U)
Stirling IV	Jan 1944 – May 1945	LJ818 (L9-X)
Halifax III	May 1945 – Dec 1945	MZ976 (G5-V)
Halifax VII	May 1945 – Dec 1945	PN287 (G5-R)

No. 191 Squadron

Badge: A dolphin
Motto: Vidi, vici (I saw, I
conquered)

No.191 Squadron was formed at Marham on 6 November 1917, as a night training unit moving later to Upwood. Its role was to train pilots for night fighter and night bomber units and the squadron was disbanded in January 1919. On 17 May 1943, it began reforming at Korangi Creek, near Karachi as a general reconnaissance squadron equipped with Catalinas, flying its first patrol on 21 May. Until the end of the year, No.191's aircraft patrolled the Arabian Sea and Persian Gulf, detachments being sent to Bahrain and other bases to provide wider coverage. In 1944 the squadron's activities were concentrated off the East Coast of India and, apart from Addu Atoll, its Catalinas were based on flying-boat stations in southern India and Ceylon, maintenance being done at Korangi Creek until the squadron's base was moved to Madras in November 1944. At the end of April, it moved to Ceylon but was disbanded on 15 June 1945, due to the lack of enemy activity in the area.

Squadron bases

Marham	6 Nov 1917	Redhill's Lake	17 Nov 1944
Upwood	1918		30 Nov 1944 (P)
	to Jan 1919	Koggala	27 Apr 1945
Korangi Creek	17 May 1943		to 15 Jun 1945

Aircraft Equipment	Period of service	Representative Serial and Code
B.E.2c	Nov 1917 – 1918	
F.E.2b	Nov 1917 – Jan 1919	
Catalina Ib	May 1943 – Jun 1945	FP117 (U)
Catalina IVb	Sep 1944 – Jun 1945	JX369 (U)

No. 192 Squadron

Badge: In front of a flash of lightning, an owl's head affrontée
Motto: Dare to discover

No.192 Squadron was formed at Gainsborough on 5 September 1917, as an advanced night flying training unit to operate from Newmarket with F.E.2bs. It was engaged in training pilots for night bomber and home defence squadrons until the end of the war and disbanded in December 1918.

On 4 January 1943 No.192 reformed at Gransden Lodge from No.1474 Flight. The unit's role was radar countermeasures and this entailed the identification of enemy radar patterns and wavelengths. Initially Wellingtons, Mosquitos and Halifaxes were used although the last two types did not begin operations until June. Missions were flown mainly over Germany, France and the Low Countries but some were over the Bay of Biscay to check radar used against Coastal Command anti-submarine patrols. Between September 1944 and February 1945, USAAF two-seat Lightnings were attached to the squadron and in November 1944, much time was spent in searching for radio signals from V-2s, though these were later found to be uncontrolled. In January 1945, the Wellington flew its last operations and on 22 August 1945, the squadron disbanded to form the basis of the Central Signals Establishment.

On 15 July 1951, No.192 reformed at Watton in a similar role, using Lincolns, Washingtons and Canberras for countermeasures training until renumbered 51 Squadron on 21 August 1958.

Squadron bases

Newmarket	5 Sep 1917	Foulsham	25 Nov 1943
	to Dec 1918		to 22 Aug 1945
Gransden Lodge	4 Jan 1943	Watton	15 Jul 1951
Feltwell	5 Apr 1943		to 21 Aug 1958

Aircraft Equipment	Period of service	Representative Serial and Code
F.E.2b, 2d	Sep 1917 – Dec 1918	B404
Wellington IC	Jan 1943 – Feb 1943	N2272
Wellington III	Jan 1943 – Feb 1943	X3566
Wellington X	Jan 1943 – Mar 1945	HE229
Mosquito IV	Jan 1943 – Mar 1945	DZ377 (DT-L)
Mosquito XVI	Feb 1945 – Aug 1945	RF974 (DT-I)
Halifax II	Jan 1945 – Mar 1945	DT735
Halifax III	Mar 1944 – Aug 1945	LN398 (DT-A)
Halifax V	Aug 1943 – Nov 1943	DK246 (DT-R)
Oxford II	Aug 1945	
Anson I	Aug 1945	
Lincoln B.2	Jul 1951 – Mar 1953	WD130
Washington B.1	Apr 1952 – Feb 1958	WZ968
Canberra B.2	– Aug 1958	

Typhoon IB, No.193 Squadron

No. 193 Squadron

Badge: A Montagu's Harrier
volant carrying a grenade-
fired

Motto: Aera et terram imperare
(To govern the air and the
earth)

Name: 'Fellowship of the Bellows'

No.193 Squadron was formed at Harrowbeer on 18 December 1942 as a fighter squadron. Initially a few Hurricanes were received but in January 1943, it received its first operational equipment, Typhoons, and began operations on 1 April. The Typhoon's speed was used to catch enemy fighter-bombers attacking seaside towns and as escorts for fighter-bombers attacking enemy shipping. In January 1944, the squadron's aircraft began carrying 500-lb bombs in attacks on enemy communications, bases and flying-bomb launching sites in northern France, a move being made to south-east England in February. In April 1944, No.193 joined No.146 Wing for the invasion of Normandy and moved there in mid-July to provide fighter-bomber support for the Army during the breakout from the beachhead. By October it had reached Belgium and flew sweeps over Germany attacking transport targets and troops. During the final offensive, the squadron moved to Germany in April 1945 where it was disbanded on 31 August 1945.

Squadron bases

Harrowbeer	18 Dec 1942	Manston	8 Sep 1944
Gravesend	17 Aug 1943	B.51 Lille-Vendeville	
Harrowbeer	18 Sep 1943		11 Sep 1944
Fairlop	20 Feb 1944	Fairwood Common	
Thorney Island	15 Mar 1944		18 Sep 1944
Llanbedr	6 Apr 1944	B.70 Deurne	6 Oct 1944
Need's Oar Point	11 Apr 1944	B.89 Mill	8 Feb 1945
Hurn	3 Jul 1944	B.111 Ahlhorn	30 Apr 1945
B.15 Ryes	11 Jul 1944	R.16 Hildesheim	8 Jun 1945
B.3 St. Croix	15 Jul 1944		to 31 Aug 1945

Aircraft

Equipment	Period of service	Representative Serial and Code
Hurricane I, IIC	Jan 1943 – Feb 1943	AG705
Typhoon IB	Jan 1943 – Aug 1945	RB227 (DP-P)

No. 194 Squadron

Badge: A Malayan kris with a
dragonfly superimposed

Motto: Surrigere colligere (To
arise and to pick up)

No.194 Squadron was formed at Lahore on 14 October 1942 as a transport unit equipped with Hudsons. It maintained mail and passenger routes in India until it became an airborne forces squadron in September 1943. Dakotas had started to arrive in May and with the departure of the Hudsons, No.194 began paratroop training. In February 1944, supply-dropping flights to army units in Burma began and continued for the rest of the war. In January 1945, a casualty evacuation flight was attached to the squadron and Sentinels were used to pick up casualties from small jungle strips. After the end of the war, the squadron was engaged in general transport duties until disbanded on 15 February 1946.

On 1 February 1953, No.194 reformed at Sembawang with Dragonfly helicopters for co-operation with security forces in Malaya. Sycamores were received in October 1954. On 3 June 1959, the squadron merged with No.155 Squadron to reform No.110 Squadron.

Squadron bases

Lahore	14 Oct 1942	Imphal	10 Dec 1944
Palam	18 Feb 1943	Maunybyin	19 Mar 1945
Basal	18 Sep 1943	Akyab Main	May 1945 (P)
Comilla	8 Feb 1944	Mingaladon	21 Aug 1945
Agartala	9 Feb 1944		to 15 Feb 1946
Imphal	1 Sep 1944	Sembawang	1 Feb 1953
Basal	Nov 1944 (P)		to 3 Jun 1959

Aircraft

Equipment	Period of service	Representative Serial and Code
Hudson VI	Nov 1942 – Sep 1943	FK411
Dakota III	May 1943 – Feb 1946	KJ888 (H)
Sentinel	Jan 1945 – Sep 1945	KJ398
Dragonfly HC.2	Feb 1953 – Jun 1956	XB253
Sycamore HR.14	Oct 1954 – Jun 1959	XG504

No. 195 Squadron

Badge: A sabre-toothed tiger's
head erased

Motto: Velocitate fortis (Strong
by speed)

No.195 Squadron was formed at Duxford on 16 November 1942 and began to receive Typhoons later in the month. In February 1943 it moved to Lancashire for a period of training and in May arrived in East Anglia to begin flying sweeps and armed reconnaissance missions over France in preparation for the invasion of Europe. Before it could take part in that operation, however, the squadron was disbanded on 15 February 1944.

On 1 October 1944, No.195 reformed from C Flight of No.115 Squadron at Witchford as a Lancaster squadron in Bomber Command. It took part in raids over Germany for the rest of the war and after a short period of transport duties was disbanded on 14 August 1945.

Squadron bases

Duxford	16 Nov 1942	Fairlop	23 Sep 1943
Hutton Cranswick	21 Nov 1942		to 15 Feb 1944
Woodvale	12 Feb 1943	Witchford	1 Oct 1944
Ludham	13 May 1943	Wratting Common	
Matlask	31 Jul 1943		13 Nov 1944
Coltishall	21 Aug 1943		to 14 Aug 1945

Aircraft

Equipment	Period of service	Representative Serial and Code
Typhoon Ib	Nov 1942 – Feb 1944	JP407 (JE-L)
Hurricane I	Dec 1942 – Feb 1943	N1427
Lancaster I, III	Oct 1944 – Aug 1945	HK587 (A4-D)

No. 196 Squadron

Badge: A mailed fist holding a
dagger, hilt downwards
Motto: Sic fidem servamus (Thus
we keep faith)

No.196 Squadron was formed at Driffield on 7 November 1942 as a bomber unit and began to receive Wellingtons during December. On 1 February 1942, it was declared operational and began bombing raids on the 4th. The Wellingtons continued bombing and minelaying missions until the arrival of Stirlings in July when the crews converted at No.1651 HCU at Waterbeach, operations resuming at the end of August. In November 1943, the squadron was transferred to airborne support duties and began training in paratroop-dropping and glider-towing. In February 1944,

supply-dropping to resistance forces in France began and on D-Day twenty-three of the squadron's Stirlings carried troops to Normandy, followed later in the day by seventeen towing gliders. In September 1944, the squadron took part in the Arnhem landings and in February 1945, began tactical bombing raids in support of the army. In March, thirty aircraft were supplied for the Rhine crossing and fuel was carried to keep the advancing armies supplied. In May troops were taken to Norway and Denmark to disarm the German forces there, being followed by general transport duties. On 16 March 1946, the squadron was disbanded.

Squadron bases			
Driffield	7 Nov 1942	Tarrant Rushton	7 Jan 1944
Leconfield	22 Dec 1942	Keevil	14 Mar 1944
Witchford	19 Jul 1943	Wethersfield	9 Oct 1944
Leicester East	18 Nov 1943	Shepherd's Grove	26 Jan 1945
			to 16 Mar 1946

Aircraft Equipment	Period of service	Representative Serial and Code
Wellington X	Dec 1942 – Jul 1943	HE167 (ZO-A)
Stirling III	Jul 1943 – Feb 1944	EF468
Stirling IV	Feb 1944 – Mar 1946	LJ948 (7T-C)
Stirling V	Jan 1946 – Mar 1946	PJ887 (ZO-H)

Typhoon IB, No.197 Squadron

No. 197 Squadron

Badge: A lion's jamp holding a
sabre
Motto: Findimus caelum (We
cleave the sky)

No.197 Squadron was formed on 21 November 1942 at Turnhouse and received Typhoons during December, becoming operational on 27 January 1943. In March 1943 it moved to southern England for fighter patrols and bomber escort missions before becoming a fighter-bomber unit of the Second TAF in No.146 Wing. In preparation for the Allied landing in France, the squadron attacked enemy transport and troop concentrations with 500-lb bombs and moved

to Normandy in mid-July. With the army break-out, No.197 moved forward to provide support and by early October arrived in Belgium where it spent the winter. In February 1945 it moved to the Netherlands and flew armed reconnaissance missions over Germany until the end of the war. On 31 August 1945 the squadron disbanded.

Squadron bases			
Turnhouse	21 Nov 1942	B.70 Deurne	2 Oct 1944
Drem	25 Nov 1942	Fairwood Common	
Tangmere	28 Mar 1943		25 Nov 1944
Manston	15 Mar 1944	B.70 Deurne	11 Dec 1944
Tangmere	1 Apr 1944	B.89 Mill	8 Feb 1945
Need's Oar Point	10 Apr 1944	B.105 Drope	16 Apr 1945
Hurn	3 Jul 1944	B.111 Ahlhorn	30 Apr 1945
B.3 St. Croix	17 Jul 1944	R.16 Hildesheim	8 Jun 1945
Manston	2 Sep 1944		to 31 Aug 1945
B.51 Lille-Vendeville			
	11 Sep 1944		

Aircraft Equipment	Period of service	Representative Serial and Code
Typhoon Ib	Dec 1942 – Aug 1945	JR338 (OV-S)

Typhoon IB, No.198 Squadron

No. 198 Squadron

Badge: A phoenix holding in its
beak a sword
Motto: Igni renatus (Born again
in fire)

No.198 Squadron was formed on 1 June 1918 at Rochford from No.98 Depot Squadron as a night training squadron and was engaged, from June until September 1918, in elementary training duties followed by all-through training until the Armistice. In September 1919 it handed over its training responsibilities to Scampton and was disbanded.

On 8 December 1942, No.198 reformed at Digby with Typhoons as a night fighter squadron and flew defensive patrols over north-east England until March 1943, when it moved to Manston to help counter enemy fighter-bomber raids on coastal towns. In June, the squadron began ground-attack missions over France and at the beginning of 1944, adopted rockets as its main offensive weapon. Attacks on enemy communications, radar stations and coast defence works were a prelude to the invasion of France and on 1 July

1944 the squadron moved to Normandy. Ground-attack support for the army followed throughout the Battle of Normandy and the breakout from the beachhead as No.198 moved its bases forward to Belgium. In April 1945 it moved into Germany and remained there until disbanded on 15 September 1945.

Squadron bases			
Rochford	1 Jun 1917	B.5 and B.10	1 Jul 1944
	to Sep 1919	B.5 Camilly	9 Jul 1944
Digby	8 Dec 1942	B.10 Plumetot	11 Jul 1944
Ouston	23 Jan 1943	B.7 Martragny	29 Jul 1944
Acklington	9 Feb 1943	B.23 Morainville	3 Sep 1944
Manston	24 Mar 1943	B.35 Baromesnil	6 Sep 1944
Woodvale	15 May 1943	B.53 Merville	11 Sep 1944
Martlesham Heath	5 Jun 1943	B.67 Ursel	30 Oct 1944
Bradwell Bay	19 Aug 1943	Fairwood Common	
Manston	23 Aug 1943		6 Nov 1944
Tangmere	17 Mar 1944	B.67 Ursel	21 Nov 1944
Llanbedr	30 Mar 1944	B.77 Gilze-Rijen	26 Nov 1944
Thorney Island	6 Apr 1944	A.84 Chievres	31 Dec 1944
Llanbedr	22 Apr 1944	B.77 Gilze-Rijen	19 Jan 1945
Thorney Island	30 Apr 1944	B.91 Kluis	21 Mar 1945
Funtington	18 Jun 1944	B.103 Plantlunne	17 Apr 1945
Hurn	22 Jun 1944	B.116 Wunstorf	27 May 1945
			to 15 Sep 1945

Aircraft Equipment	Period of service	Representative Serial and Code
Avro 504K	Jun 1917 – Sep 1919	D9322
Camel	Jan 1918 – Jun 1918	
Typhoon IA, IB	Dec 1942 – Sep 1945	MN234 (TP-K)

No. 199 Squadron

Badge: In front of a fountain, two
swords palewise, one
point upwards and one
point downwards
Motto: Let tyrants tremble

No.199 Squadron was formed at Rochford on 1 June 1917 from No.99 (Depot) Squadron, as a training unit for pilots intended for service with the night bomber squadrons in France. Using F.E.2bs, it retained this task till the end of the war, moving to Harpswell in Lincolnshire in June 1918, where it disbanded in June 1919.

On 7 November 1942, No.199 reformed at Blyton with Wellingtons in Bomber Command and flew its first raid on 6 December 1942. After taking part in many attacks on enemy targets, the last Wellington sortie was flown on 13 June 1943 and the crews converted to Stirlings, resuming operations on 27 July. By the beginning of 1944 the Stirling had been withdrawn from the main attacking force of Bomber Command and was concentrating on minelaying and attacks on coastal targets. In May 1944, the squadron became non-operational and trained for counter-measures duties with No.100 Group. On D-Day the squadron put up a force of Stirlings equipped with various methods of radar jamming to simulate a large collection of ships and aircraft heading for the Pas-de-Calais area. This confused the enemy at a time when the main armada of invasion craft was heading for Normandy and resulted in enemy reserves being retained away from the battle area until too late to affect the landings. It continued to use these methods in support of the main

Stirling III, No.199 Squadron

bomber force by confusing enemy defensive radars until the end of the war, Halifaxes beginning to replace the Stirlings in April 1945. On 29 July 1945, the squadron disbanded.

No.199 reformed at Watton on 16 July 1951 as part of No.90 Group and again with a counter-measures role in addition to its normal bombing capability. Its Lincolns and Mosquitos were supplemented and eventually replaced by Canberras and Valiants and when the squadron disbanded on 15 December 1958, its Valiant flight formed the basis of a reformed No.18 Squadron.

Squadron bases

Rochford	1 Jun 1917	North Creake	1 May 1944
Harpswell	Jun 1918		to 19 Jul 1945
	to Jun 1919	Watton	16 Jul 1951
Blyton	7 Nov 1942	Hemswell	17 Apr 1952
Ingham	3 Feb 1943	Honington	1 Oct 1957
Lakenheath	20 Jun 1943		to 15 Dec 1958

Aircraft Equipment	Period of service	Representative Serial and Code
F.E.2b	Jun 1917 – Jun 1919	
Wellington III	Nov 1942 – May 1943	X3812 (EX-Q)
Wellington X	Mar 1943 – Jul 1943	LN406 (EX-G)
Stirling III	Jul 1943 – Mar 1945	EF450 (EX-N)
Halifax III	Feb 1945 – Jul 1945	NA275 (EX-W)
Lincoln B.2	Jul 1951 – Jun 1957	WD131
Mosquito NF.36	Dec 1951 – Mar 1954	RL189
Canberra B.2	Mar 1954 – Dec 1958	WJ616
Valiant B.1	Jun 1957 – Dec 1958	WP211

Canberra B.2, No.199 Squadron

No. 200 Squadron

Badge: In front of a fountain, a Pegasus
Motto: In loco parentis
(We act as guardians)

No.200 Squadron was formed at East Retford on 1 July 1917 as a night-flying training unit and retained this role until the end of World War One, disbanding soon after the Armistice.

On 25 May 1941 No.200 reformed at Bircham Newton from a nucleus supplied by No.206 Squadron and its ground echelon left a few days later for West Africa. Seven Hudsons left on 12 June to fly to Gambia and, on arrival at Gibraltar, four of these provided an escort for forty-eight Hurricanes flown off the carriers *Ark Royal* and *Victorious*

to Malta. The first five Hudsons arrived at Jeswang on 18 June and began anti-submarine patrols and convoy escort duties on 30 June. In July 1943 the squadron converted to Liberators, beginning patrols with these on 11 August. No.200 was transferred to India in March 1944, and began patrols from southern India on 28 April. In April 1945 the squadron was transferred to special duties and for a few weeks flew supply-dropping missions to guerilla bands in Burma before being renumbered 8 Squadron on 15 May 1945.

Squadron bases

East Retford	1 July 1917	Yundum	12 Mar 1943
	to Dec 1918	St. Thomas	29 Mar 1944
Bircham Newton	25 May 1941	Mount	11 Apr 1944 (C)
Jeswang	18 June 1941	Jessore	5 Apr 1945
			to 15 May 1945

Aircraft Equipment	Period of service	Representative Serial
F.E.2b	July 1917 – Dec 1918	
Hudson V	May 1941 – Sep 1943	FH255 (P1)
Liberator V	July 1943 – Nov 1944	BZ831 (C)
Liberator VI	Nov 1944 – May 1945	KH144 (U)

Sunderland MR.5s, No.201 Squadron

No. 201 Squadron

Badge: A seagull, wings elevated and addorsed
Motto: Hic et ubique
(Here and everywhere)

No.201 Squadron was formed on 1 April 1918 from No.1 Squadron, Royal Naval Air Service, at Fienvillers in northern France. In common with other squadrons of the RNAS absorbed on the formation of the Royal Air Force, No.1 (Naval) was renumbered by adding 200 to its squadron number. Equipped with Camels, it flew fighter patrols and ground attack missions over the Western Front until the Armistice. In February 1919, the squadron was reduced to a cadre and returned to the UK where it disbanded on 31 December 1919.

On 1 January 1929 No.480 (Coastal Reconnaissance) Flight at Calshot was redesignated No.201 Squadron and flew Southampton flying boats until the end of 1936. Re-equipment with Londons began in April 1936 and these were still in service at the outbreak of World War Two. Based in northern Scotland, the squadron flew patrols across the North Sea to the Norwegian coast to locate blockade runners, surface raiders and U-boats en route for the Atlantic. In April 1940 No.201 converted to Sunderlands and in October 1941 moved to Northern Ireland to carry out anti-submarine patrols over the North Atlantic. To prevent U-boats entering the English Channel during the landings in Normandy, the squadron moved to Pembroke

Dock in April 1944, returning to Ireland in November for the rest of the war. In August 1945, it took up its peacetime station at Pembroke Dock but moved in March 1946 to Calshot. There it became involved in the Berlin Airlift in 1948 before returning to Pembroke Dock to fly Sunderlands until disbanded on 28 February 1957.

On 1 October 1958, No.220 Squadron at St. Mawgan was renumbered 201 Squadron which flew Shackletons for the next twelve years. In March 1965, the squadron moved to Scotland where it converted to Nimrods in October 1970 for maritime reconnaissance duties.

Squadron bases			
Fienvillers	1 Apr 1918	Invergordon	29 Sep 1938
Noeux	12 Apr 1918	Calshot	7 Oct 1938
Ste. Marie		Sullom Voe	9 Aug 1939
Cappel	20 July 1918	Invergordon	6 Nov 1939
Poulainville	6 Aug 1918	Sullom Voe	26 May 1940
Noeux	14 Aug 1918	Castle Archdale	9 Oct 1941
Baisieux	19 Sep 1918	Pembroke Dock	8 Apr 1944
Beugnatre	14 Oct 1918	Castle Archdale	3 Nov 1944
La Targette	27 Oct 1918	Pembroke Dock	2 Aug 1945
Bethencourt	22 Nov 1918	Calshot	30 Mar 1946
Lake Down	15 Feb 1919	Pembroke Dock	18 Jan 1949
	to 31 Dec 1919		to 28 Feb 1957
Calshot	1 Jan 1929	St. Mawgan	1 Oct 1958
		Kinloss	14 Mar 1965

Aircraft Equipment	Period of service	Representative Serial	
Camel	Apr 1918 – Feb 1919	F5941	(E)
Snipe	Oct 1918	E8102	
Southampton	Jan 1929 – Dec 1936	S1645	
London I, II	Apr 1936 – Apr 1940	K5261	
Sunderland I	Apr 1940 – Jan 1942	N6138	(ZM-V)
Sunderland II	May 1941 – Mar 1944	T9077	(ZM-Y)
Sunderland III	Jan 1942 – Jun 1945	ML760	(NS-S)
Sunderland V	Feb 1945 – Feb 1957	VB881	(A)
Shackleton MR.3	Oct 1958 – Sep 1970	WR989	(K)
Nimrod MR.1	Oct 1970 – date	XV240	(40)

Fairey IIIFs, No.202 Squadron

No. 202 Squadron

Badge: A mallard alighting
Motto: Semper vigilate
(Be always vigilant)

No.202 Squadron was formed on 1 April 1918, from No.2 Squadron, RNAS at Bergues, near Dunkerque. Equipped with D.H.4s, it carried out bombing and reconnaissance missions over Belgium until the Armistice. In March 1919 it returned to the UK and disbanded on 22 January 1920. On 9 April 1920 No.202 was reformed at Alexandria as a naval co-operation unit but disbanded again on 16 May 1921.

On 1 January 1929, No. 481 Flight at Kalafrana, Malta, was redesignated No.202 Squadron with Fairey IIID seaplanes. Though officially numbered 202 (Flying Boat) Squadron, it flew seaplanes for six years, its original Fairey IIIDs being replaced by Fairey IIIFs in 1930. In May 1935 the first of its Scapas arrived and were replaced by Londons by the end of 1937. In September 1937 anti-submarine patrols had begun to protect neutral shipping from attacks by Italian submarines during the Spanish Civil War and a year later the squadron moved to Alexandria during the Munich crisis. On the outbreak of World War Two, No.202 took its Londons to Gibraltar to patrol the approaches to the Mediterranean and keep watch on German shipping bottled up in ports in southern Spain and Spanish Morocco. In September 1940 the Swordfish floatplanes of No.3 AACU were taken over for local patrols while Catalinas began to arrive in April 1941, to replace the elderly Londons. In December 1941 Sunderlands augmented the squadron's strength until September 1942 and in September 1944

No.202 moved to Northern Ireland for the rest of the war. After flying coastal patrols to counter U-boats operating close to the west coast, the squadron was disbanded on 12 June 1945.

On 1 October 1946 No.512 Squadron at Aldergrove was renumbered 202 Squadron. It flew Halifaxes on meteorological flights over the Atlantic until they were replaced by Hastings in October 1950. On 31 July 1964 the squadron was disbanded.

On 1 September 1964 No.228 Squadron at Leconfield was renumbered 202 Squadron which has since been engaged in search and rescue duties with Whirlwind helicopters over the northern half of the British Isles.

Squadron bases

Bergues	1 Apr 1918	Kalafrana	13 Oct 1938
Varssenaere	18 Nov 1918	Gibraltar	10 Sep 1929
Driffield	24 Mar 1919	Castle Archdale	3 Sep 1944
	to 22 Jan 1920		to 12 Jun 1945
Alexandria	9 Apr 1920	Aldergrove	1 Oct 1946
	to 16 May 1921		to 31 July 1964
Kalafrana	1 Jan 1929	Leconfield	1 Sep 1964
Alexandria	26 Sep 1938	Finningley	

Aircraft Equipment	Period of service	Representative Serial	
D.H.4	Apr 1918 – Mar 1919	F5706	(T)
D.H.9	May 1918 – Sep 1918	B7593	
Short 184	Apr 1920 – May 1921		
Fairey IIID	Jan 1929 – Sep 1930	S1078	
Fairey IIIF	July 1930 – Aug 1935	S1386	(5)
Scapa	May 1935 – Dec 1937	K4191	
London II	Sep 1937 – Jun 1941	K5264	(TQ-L)
Swordfish I	Sep 1940 – Jun 1941	K8354	(TQ-D)
Catalina Ib	Apr 1941 – Jan 1945	AJ160	(TQ-S)
Catalina IV	Oct 1944 – Jun 1945	JX242	(TQ-P)
Sunderland I, II	Dec 1941 – Sep 1942	W4024	(TQ-N)
Sunderland III	Mar 1942 – Sep 1942	DV962	
Halifax Met.6	Oct 1946 – May 1951	ST816	(TQ-Q)
Halifax A.9	Aug 1949 – Dec 1950	RT786	(TQ-A)
Hastings Met.1	Oct 1950 – July 1964	TG567	
Whirlwind HAR.10	Sep 1964 –	XJ414	
Sea King HAR.3	Aug 1978 – date	XZ596	

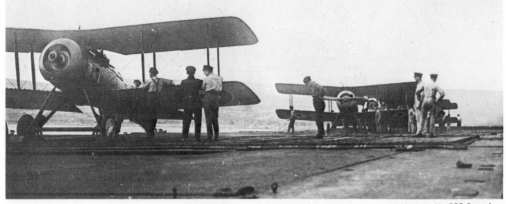

Nightjars, No.203 Squadron

No. 203 Squadron

Badge: A winged sea horse
Motto: Occidens oriensque
(West and East)

No.203 Squadron was formed on 1 April 1918 at Treizennes in northern France from No.3 Squadron RNAS on its absorption into the newly-formed Royal Air Force. Equipped with Camels, it flew fighter and ground-attack missions over the Western Front for the rest of the war. Reduced to a cadre in March 1919, it returned to the UK and disbanded on 21 January 1920. On 1 March 1920, No.203 was reformed at Leuchars as a fleet fighter squadron and flew Nightjars until redesignated No.402 Flight on 1 April 1923.

On 1 January 1929, No.482 (Coastal Reconnaissance) Flight at Mount Batten was redesignated No.203 Squadron and in February it left the UK with three Southampton flying boats, arriving at its new base in Iraq in mid-March. Patrols over the Persian Gulf were taken over by Rangoons in 1931 which were in turn replaced by Singapores in 1935. In September 1935, these were taken to Aden during the Abyssinian crisis and returned to Iraq in August 1936. The squadron returned to Aden on the outbreak of World War Two but began to convert to Blenheims in December 1939, receiving its own aircraft in March 1940. When Italy entered the war in June 1940, No.203's Blenheims flew reconnaissance and fighter patrols over the Red Sea until April 1941, when the squadron moved to Egypt and Palestine. After taking part in the Syrian campaign, it began reconnaissance missions over the Eastern Mediterranean and received some Marylands in February 1942. Baltimores were added in August 1942 and in November the squadron was fully equipped with the type. In November 1943, No.203 moved to India where it converted to Wellingtons for coastal patrol duties. These were replaced by Liberators in October 1944 and anti-shipping patrols began from Ceylon in February 1945. After a period of transport duties in South-East Asia, No.203 returned to the UK in May 1947 and converted to Lancasters. These were flown until the arrival of Neptunes in March 1953 which

were in service until the squadron disbanded on 1 September 1956.

On 1 November 1958, No.240 Squadron at Ballykelly was renumbered 203 Squadron and flew Shackletons on maritime patrol duties from Northern Ireland until the beginning of 1969, when the squadron moved to Malta. Early in 1972, difficulties arose over the use of Maltese bases and No.203 was transferred to the NATO base at Signonella in Sicily while converting to Nimrods, returning in April to Luqa. The squadron was disbanded on 31 December 1977.

Squadron bases

Treizennes	1 Apr 1918	Basra	24 Aug 1936
Liettres	9 Apr 1918	Aden/Isthmus	2 Sep 1939
Filescamp	16 May 1918	Sheikh Othman	15 Feb 1940
Allonville	14 Aug 1918	Khormaksar	18 May 1940
Filescamp	6 Sep 1918	Kabrit	16 Apr 1941
Izel-le-Hameau	23 Sep 1918	Heraklion	24 Apr 1941
Bruille	24 Oct 1918	Kabrit	30 Apr 1941
Auberchicourt	24 Nov 1918	LG.101	20 Jun 1941
Orcq	22 Dec 1918	Santa Cruz	15 Nov 1943
Boisdinghem	18 Jan 1919	Madura	9 Oct 1944
Waddington	Mar 1919	Kankesanturai	19 Feb 1945
Scopwick	Dec 1919	St. Eval	May 1947 (P)
	to 21 Jan 1920	Topcliffe	15 Aug 1952
Leuchars	1 Mar 1920		to 1 Sep 1956
	to 1 Apr 1923	Ballykelly	1 Nov 1958
Mount Batten	1 Jan 1929	Luqa	1 Feb 1969
Left for Iraq	28 Feb 1929	Sigonella	12 Jan 1972
Basra	14 Mar 1929	Luqa	23 Apr 1972
Aden	26 Sep 1935		to 31 Dec 1977

Aircraft

Equipment	Period of service	Representative Serial
Camel	Apr 1918 – Mar 1919	N6461
Nightjar	Mar 1920 – Apr 1923	J6938
Southampton II	Jan 1929 – Apr 1931	S1300
Fairey IIIF	Mar 1929 – Apr 1929	
Rangoon	Feb 1931 – Nov 1935	S1433
Singapore III	Sep 1935 – Mar 1940	K4583
Blenheim I	Mar 1940 – May 1940	L8545
Blenheim IV	May 1940 – Nov 1942	T1988 (Y)
Maryland I	Feb 1942 – Nov 1942	AH280 (Y)
Hudson III	Feb 1942	T9397
Baltimore I, II, IIIA, IV	Aug 1942 – Nov 1943	FA107 (F)
Wellington XIII	Nov 1943 – Oct 1944	HZ960
Liberator VI	Oct 1944 – Mar 1946	KG911 (D)
Liberator VIII	Jan 1946 – May 1947	KL517 (F)
Lancaster GR.3	May 1947 – Mar 1953	RF311
Neptune MR.1	Mar 1953 – Sep 1956	WX518 (B-J)
Shackleton MR.1	Nov 1958 – Sep 1959	WB860
Shackleton MR.2	July 1962 – Dec 1966	WL742 (H)
Shackleton MR.3	Dec 1958 – Jul 1962 Jun 1966 – Jan 1972	WR988 (E)
Nimrod MR.1	Oct 1971 – Dec 1977	XV257 (57)

Southampton I, No.204 Squadron

No. 204 Squadron

Badge: On water barry wavy,
a mooring buoy, theron a
cormorant displayed.
Motto: Praedam mari quaero
(I seek my prey in the sea)

No.204 Squadron was formed on 1 April 1918 at Bray
Dunes near Dunkerque from No.4 Squadron, RNAS. For
the remainder of the war it carried out fighter and ground-
attack missions over the Western Front and along the
Belgian coast. In February 1919 it was reduced to a cadre
and returned to the UK, disbanding on 31 December 1919.

On 1 February 1929 No.204 reformed at Mount Batten,
Plymouth, as a flying boat squadron equipped with five
Southamptons. It took these on a formation cruise to Malta
in August 1932 and, in August 1933, made a similar flight
around the Baltic. In August 1935 the first Scapa arrived to
re-equip the squadron and next month No.204 moved to
Egypt during the Abyssinian crisis, returning in August
1936. Two months later, Londons began to replace Scapas
and five were taken to Australia in December, returning to
the UK in May 1938. Conversion to Sunderlands began
in June 1939 and No.204 was fully equipped with eight
boats by the end of September. On the outbreak of war,
patrols began over the Channel and Western Approaches
and in April 1940 the squadron moved to the Shetlands for
patrols off Norway. A further move to Iceland took place
in April 1941, and in July No.204 moved to Gibraltar and
next month to Gambia. For the rest of the war, the squadron
flew anti-submarine patrols off the coasts of West Africa
and disbanded on 30 June 1945.

On 1 August 1947 No.204 reformed at Kabrit as a transport squadron in Egypt and flew Dakotas until these were
replaced by Valettas in 1949. On 20 February 1953 the
squadron was renumbered 84 Squadron. It was reformed at
Ballykelly on 1 January 1954, as a Shackleton maritime
reconnaissance squadron and sent a detachment to Australia
from August until November 1957, to support a nuclear
trials task force. The squadron ceased operations at Ballykelly on 31 March 1971, and became operational at Honington next day as a shipping surveillance and search and rescue
unit. On 28 April 1972 No.204 disbanded.

Squadron bases

Bray Dunes	1 Apr 1918	Mount Batten	29 May 1938
Teteghem	13 Apr 1918	Sullon Voe	2 Apr 1940
Cappelle	30 Apr 1918	Reykjavik	5 Apr 1941
Teteghem	9 May 1918	Gibraltar	15 July 1941
Heule	24 Oct 1918	Bathurst/Half Die	28 Aug 1941
Waddington	7 Feb 1919	Jui	28 Jan 1944
	to 31 Dec 1919	Bathurst	1 Apr 1944
Mount Batten	1 Feb 1929	Jui	8 Apr 1944
Aboukir	27 Sep 1935		to 30 Jun 1945
Alexandria	22 Oct 1935	Kabrit	1 Aug 1947
Mount Batten	5 Aug 1936	Fayid	22 Feb 1951
Left for Australia	2 Dec 1937		to 20 Feb 1953
Arrived in		Ballykelly	1 Jan 1954
Australia	25 Jan 1938	Honington	1 Apr 1971
Left for UK	4 Apr 1938		to 28 Apr 1972

Aircraft

Equipment	Period of service	Representative Serial
Camel	Apr 1918 – Feb 1919	C71
Southampton	Feb 1929 – Oct 1935	S1037
Scapa	Aug 1935 – Feb 1937	K4198
London I, II,	Oct 1936 – Aug 1939	K5911
Sunderland I	Jun 1939 – Sep 1943	L5800 (KG-J)
Sunderland II	Jun 1941 – Mar 1943	W3978
Sunderland III	Oct 1942 – Jun 1945	DD833 (KG-M)
Sunderland V	Apr 1945 – Jun 1945	ML872 (KG-B)
Dakota C.4	Aug 1947 – July 1949	KN654
Valetta C.1	May 1949 – Feb 1953	VW165 (D)
Shackleton MR.1A	Apr 1958 – Feb 1960	WB860 (L)
Shackleton MR.2	Jan 1954 – Apr 1972	WR966 (O)

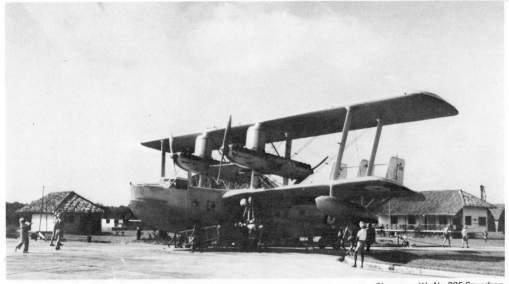

Singapore III, No.205 Squadron

No. 205 Squadron

Badge: A kris and a trident in
saltire
Motto: Pertamadi-Malaya
(Malay) (First in Malaya)

No.205 Squadron was formed on 1 April 1918, from No.5
Squadron RNAS at Bois de Roche in northern France.
Equipped with D.H.4s, it was engaged in bombing duties
over the Western Front for the rest of the war, returning to
the UK in March 1919, where it disbanded on 22 January
1920, after ten months as a cadre unit.

No.205 reformed at Leuchars on 15 April 1920, as a
Panther fighter-reconnaissance squadron in No.29 Group
for co-operation with the Navy and carrier operations but
on 1 April 1923 became No.441 Flight. On 8 January 1929
the Far East Flight which had flown out to Singapore
between October 1927 and February 1928 was redesignated
No.205 Squadron. As the first RAF squadron to be based
in the Far East, its flying boats carried out survey flights
with Southamptons until Singapores arrived to replace
them in April 1935, although it was February 1936 before
the last Southampton was withdrawn. By the end of May
1936 the squadron was fully equipped with six Singapores
and on the outbreak of was these flew patrols over the
approaches to Singapore and the Indian Ocean, using bases
in Ceylon and the Nicobar Islands as out-stations. In April
1941 No.205 received its first Catalina and by October the
last of its Singapores had been flown away by the RNZAF
for service in Fiji. With the coming of war to the Far East,
the squadron was engaged in trying to locate Japanese
naval forces on their way to invade Malaya and the Dutch
East Indies. After losing several boats on this task, it moved
to Java at the end of the year from its exposed base at
Seletar and when Japanese forces landed it retired to the

south coast of the island and in March 1942 to Australia
where it was disbanded on 31 March 1942. On 23 July
1942 No.205 reformed at Koggala in Ceylon from detachments supplied by Nos.202 and 240 Squadrons with eight
Catalinas. Anti-submarine and air-sea rescue patrols occupied
the squadron for the rest of the war. An additional task
was the operation of mail and passenger flights between
Ceylon and Australia. Conversion to Sunderlands began in
June 1945 and soon after the Japanese surrender, detachments moved back to Singapore. In October 1950 its
Sunderlands moved to Japan to fly patrols off the Korean
coast until May 1951. Conversion to Shackletons began
May 1958 at Changi and on 15 May 1959 the Sunderland
flew its last flight with the RAF and No.205 became fully
equipped with landplanes. It remained the RAF's maritime
reconnaissance force in the Far East until disbanded on
31 October 1971.

Squadron bases

Bois de Roche	1 Apr 1918	Oosthaven	2 Jan 1942
Bovelles	25 Aug 1918	Tjilatjap	Feb 1942 (P)
Proyart East	16 Sep 1918	Broome	1 Mar 1942
Moislains	7 Oct 1918		to 31 Mar 1942
Maubeuge	27 Nov 1918	Koggala	23 Jul 1942
La Louveterie	12 Jan 1919	Seletar	15 Sep 1949
Hucknall	18 Mar 1919	Iwakuni	28 Oct 1950
	to 22 Jan 1920	Seletar	10 Feb 1951
Leuchars	15 Apr 1920	Iwakuni	10 Apr 1951
	to 1 Apr 1923	Seletar	4 May 1951
Seletar	8 Jan 1929	Changi	15 May 1959
Batavia	31 Dec 1949		to 31 Oct 1971

Aircraft

Equipment	Period of service	Representative Serial	
D.H.4	Apr 1919 – Mar 1919	A7915	
D.H.9A	Aug 1918 – Mar 1919	E9707	
Panther	Apr 1920 – Apr 1923	N7509	
Southampton	Jan 1929 – Feb 1936	S1127	
Singapore III	Apr 1935 – Oct 1941	K6916	(FV-J)
Catalina I, Ib	Apr 1941 – Mar 1942		
	Jul 1942 – Mar 1945	Z2153	(FV-K)
Catalina IVb	May 1944 – Sep 1945	JX430	(FV-B)
Sunderland V	Jun 1945 – May 1959	RN289	(P)
Shackleton MR.1A	May 1958 – Nov 1962	WB818	(A)
Shackleton MR.2C	Apr 1962 – Oct 1971	WL745	(A)

No. 206 Squadron

Badge: An octopus
Motto: Nihil nos effugit
(Naught escapes us)

Hudson III, No.206 Squadron

No.206 Squadron was formed on 1 April 1918 from No.6 (Naval) Squadron at Ste. Marie Cappel with D.H.9s for bombing and reconnaissance duties. It operated over the Western Front until the end of the war and after spending a short time with the Army of Occupation in the Rhineland moved to the Middle East in June 1919. It was renumbered 47 Squadron on 1 February 1920.

On 15 June 1936, No.206 reformed at Manston from C Flight of No.48 Squadron. Equipped with Ansons, it began anti-submarine patrols on the outbreak of war and in March 1940 received its first Hudsons. These were used for reconnaissance and anti-shipping patrols off the German coast and over the Friesian Islands until May 1941, when the squadron moved to Cornwall for anti-submarine and shipping reconnaissance missions. In August 1941 No.206 moved to Northern Ireland and in June 1942 to Scotland, where it converted to Fortresses in August. These it took to the Azores in October 1943, when bases were acquired there and flew anti-submarine patrols over the Atlantic until March 1944. Returning to the UK, the squadron converted to Liberators, and after three months of patrols from Cornwall, moved to Scotland for the rest of the war to fly patrols off the Norwegian and Danish coasts. On 10 June 1945 No.206 was transferred to Transport Command and flew trooping flights until disbanded on 25 April 1946.

The squadron reformed at Lyneham on 17 November 1947, with Yorks and flew on the Berlin Airlift before disbanding on 20th February 1950.

No.206 reformed at St. Eval on 27 September 1952, as a Shackleton maritime reconnaissance squadron. In November 1971 it re-equipped with Nimrods.

Aircraft Equipment	Period of service	Representative Serial
DH.9	Apr 1918 – Feb 1920	C6170
Anson I	Jun 1936 – Jun 1940	K6179 (VX-A)
Hudson I, II, III	Mar 1940 – Aug 1942	AE617 (VX-R)
Fortress II, IIa	Aug 1942 – Apr 1944	FK213 (VX-C)
Liberator VI	Apr 1944 – Apr 1945	BZ984 (PQ-S)
Liberator VIII	Mar 1945 – Apr 1946	KK250 (PQ-T)
York C.1	Nov 1947 – Feb 1950	MW303
Shackleton MR.1	Sep 1952 – Apr 1958	WG528 (B-U)
Shackleton MR.2	Feb 1953 – Jul 1954	WL742 (B-Z)
Shackleton MR.3	Jan 1958 – Oct 1970	WR980 (B)
Nimrod MR.1	Nov 1970 – date	XV250

Shackleton MR.3, No.206 Squadron

Squadron bases

Ste. Marie Cappel	1 Apr 1918
Boisdinghem	11 Apr 1918
Alquines	15 Apr 1918
Boisdinghem	29 May 1918
Alquines	5 Jun 1918
Ste. Marie Cappel	5 Oct 1918
Linselles	24 Oct 1918
Nivelles	26 Nov 1918
Bickendorf	20 Dec 1918
Maubeuge	27 May 1919
Alexandria	19 Jun 1919
Heliopolis	24 Jun 1919
Helwan	27 Jun 1919
	to 1 Feb 1920
Manston	15 Jun 1936
Bircham Newton	30 Jul 1936
St. Eval	30 May 1941
Aldergrove	12 Aug 1941
Benbecula	30 Jun 1942
Lagens	8 Oct 1943 (G)
	18 Oct 1943 (A)
Davidstowe Moor	31 Mar 1944
St. Eval	12 Apr 1944
Leuchars	11 Jul 1944
Oakington	1 Aug 1945
	to 25 Apr 1946
Lyneham	17 Nov 1947
	to 20 Feb 1950
St. Eval	27 Sep 1952
St. Mawgan	14 Jan 1958
Kinloss	7 July 1965

Manchester I, No.207 Squadron

No. 207 Squadron

Badge: A winged lion statent
Motto: Semper paratus
(Always prepared)

No.207 Squadron was formed on 1 April 1918, from No.7 Squadron, RNAS at Coudekerque near Dunkerque. Equipped with Handley Page night bombers, the squadron carried out raids on German bases in Belgium and northern France for the rest of the war. After a period with the occupation forces in Germany, it was reduced to a cadre and returned to the UK in August 1919, where it disbanded on 20 January 1920.

On 1 February 1920, No.207 reformed at Bircham Newton from a nucleus of personnel supplied by No.274 Squadron and received D.H.9As for day bombing duties. In September 1922 the squadron was sent to Turkey during the Chanak crisis, returning to the UK in October 1923. In December 1927 Fairey IIIFs were received and these were replaced by Gordons in September 1932. During the Abyssinian crisis, No.207 was based in the Sudan between October 1935 and August 1936, converting to Wellesleys in September 1937. These it exchanged for Battles in April 1938 and supplemented them with Ansons on becoming a Group training squadron. It remained in the UK after the bulk of the Battle squadrons moved to France in September 1939, and trained crews until it became part of No.12 OTU on 8 April 1940.

On 1 November 1940, No. 207 reformed at Waddington with Manchesters as a night bomber squadron but incessant trouble with the type's engines made operations difficult. The squadron continued to fly Manchesters until March 1942, when it converted to Lancasters. For the rest of the war, it was engaged in bombing raids on Germany and remained in being as part of the post-war Bomber Command. In August 1949 conversion to Lincolns took place but the squadron disbanded on 1 March 1950.

On 29 May 1951 No.207 reformed at Marham with

Washingtons which it flew until converting to Canberras in March 1954. On 27 March 1956 the squadron again disbanded. It reformed at Marham on 1 April 1956 as a Valiant squadron and in October 1956, took these to Malta for operations during the Suez landings. At the end of 1964, Valiants were grounded and the squadron disbanded on 1 May 1965.

No.207 reformed at Northolt on 3 February 1969 as a communications unit, having previously been the Southern Communications Squadron.

Squadron bases			
Coudekerque	1 Apr 1918	Ed Damer	28 Oct 1935
Netheravon	22 Apr 1918	Gabeit	6 Apr 1936
Andover	May 1918	Worthy Down	29 Aug 1936
Ligescourt	7 June 1918	Cottesmore	20 Apr 1938
Estrée-en-		Cranfield	24 Aug 1939
Chaussée	26 Oct 1918	Waddington	1 Nov 1940
Carvin	1 Dec 1918	Bottesford	17 Nov 1941
Merheim	1 Jan 1919	Langar	20 Sep 1942
Hangelar	10 May 1919	Spilsby	12 Oct 1943
Tangmere	23 Aug 1919	Methwold	30 Oct 1945
Croydon	8 Oct 1919	Tuddenham	29 Apr 1946
Uxbridge	16 Jan 1920	Stradishall	8 Nov 1946
	to 20 Jan 1920	Mildenhall	1 Feb 1949
			to 1 Mar 1950
Bircham Newton	1 Feb 1920	Marham	29 May 1951
Left for Turkey	29 Sep 1922		to 27 Mar 1956
San Stephano	11 Oct 1922	Marham	1 Apr 1956
Eastchurch	3 Oct 1923		to 1 Nov 1965
Bircham Newton	7 Nov 1929	Northolt	3 Feb 1969

Aircraft Equipment	Period of service	Representative Serial	
Handley Page 0/100	Apr 1918	3118	
Handley Page 0/400	Apr 1918 – Aug 1919	B8811	(A2)
D.H.9A	Feb 1920 – Dec 1927	J7611	(C2)
Fairey IIIF	Dec 1927 – Sep 1932	J9136	(A1)
Gordon I	Sep 1932 – Apr 1936	K1167	(B2)
	Aug 1936 – Aug 1937		
Vincent I	Apr 1936 – Aug 1936	K4687	
Wellesley I	Aug 1937 – Apr 1938	K7766	
Battle I	Apr 1938 – Apr 1940	K9200	(207-Z)
Anson I	Jul 1939 – Apr 1940	N5265	
Manchester I	Nov 1940 – Mar 1942	L7488	(EM-Q)
Hampden I	Jul 1941 – Aug 1941	AE297	(EM-H)
Lancaster I, III	Mar 1942 – Aug 1949	PD217	(EM-Z)
Lincoln B.2	Aug 1949 – Mar 1950	RE324	(EM-C)
Washington B.1	Jul 1951 – Mar 1954	WF569	(V)
Canberra B.2	Mar 1954 – Mar 1956	WH906	
Valiant B.1	Jun 1956 – Feb 1965	WP219	
Devon C.1, C.2	Feb 1969 – date	VP968	
Bassett CC.1	Feb 1969 – Jul 1974	XS780	
Pembroke C.1	Feb 1969 – Mar 1977	XK884	

Bristol Fighters, No.208 Squadron

No. 208 Squadron

Badge: A sphinx affrontée
Motto: Vigilant

No.208 Squadron was formed on 1 April 1918 at Teteghem, near Dunkerque, from No.8 Squadron, RNAS which had been a fighter squadron on the Western Front since its formation on 25 October 1916. Equipped with Camels, it carried out fighter and ground-attack missions until the end of the war, re-equipment with Snipes being in progress at the time of the Armistice. After a period with the occupation forces in Germany, the squadron moved to the UK in September 1919, disbanding on 7 November 1919.

On 1 February 1920 No.113 Squadron at Ismailia was renumbered 208 Squadron and soon replaced its R.E.8s with Bristol Fighters for army co-operation duties. In September 1922 it was one of the squadrons sent to Turkey for a year during the Chanak crisis, returning to Egypt for a long period of co-operation with the Army. Atlases replaced Bristol Fighters in May 1930 and were in turn replaced by Audaxes in August 1935. Some Demon two-seat fighters were used by D Flight from September 1935 till it became the basis of No.64 Squadron on 16 March 1936. In January 1939 No.208 converted to Lysanders with which it began operations in the Western Desert in June 1940. Some Hurricanes were added in November 1940 for tactical reconnaissance duties and in April 1941, the squadron moved to Greece. The German invasion came a few days later and forced the evacuation of the RAF squadrons by the end of the month. After a period in Palestine, the squadron resumed

tactical reconnaissance missions in the Western Desert in October, which continued until December 1942 when No.208 moved to Iraq. In December 1943 it converted to Spitfires for air defence duties and in March 1944 moved to Italy where it flew fighter and ground-attack operations until the end of the war. Returning to Palestine in July 1945, No.208 remained a reconnaissance squadron in the Middle East, re-equipping with Meteors in March 1951. In January 1958 its air echelon took over No.34 Squadron's Hunters at Tangmere and flew them to Cyprus in March. On 30 March 1959 the squadron was disbanded.

No.142 Squadron at Eastleigh, Kenya, was renumbered 208 Squadron on 1 April 1959, and replaced its Venoms with Hunter ground-attack fighters in March 1960. In December 1961 the squadron moved to Aden and made a further move to Bahrain in June 1964 where it disbanded on 10 September 1971.

On 1 March 1974, No.208 reformed at Honington with Buccaneers for low level strike duties.

Squadron bases

Teteghem	1 Apr 1918	Qasaba	1 Sep 1939
La Gorgue	2 Apr 1918	Heliopolis	15 Nov 1939
Serny	9 Apr 1918	Qasaba	9 June 1940
Tramecourt	30 Jul 1918	Gambut	10 Jan 1941
Foucaucourt	23 Sep 1918	Barce	6 Feb 1941
Estrée-en-Chaussée	9 Oct 1918	Heliopolis	3 Mar 1941
Maretz	26 Oct 1918	Kazaklar	1 Apr 1941
Stree	3 Dec 1918	Elevsis	17 Apr 1941
Heumar	23 May 1919	Argos	22 Apr 1941
Eil	7 Aug 1919	Maleme	24 Apr 1941
Netheravon	9 Sep 1919	Gaza	1 May 1941
	to 7 Nov 1919	Ramleh	21 Jun 1941
Ismailia	1 Feb 1920	Aqir	29 Sep 1941
San Stephano	28 Sep 1922	Gerawla	13 Oct 1941
Ismailia	26 Sep 1923	El Gubbi	10 Dec 1941
Heliopolis	27 Oct 1927	Tmimi	19 Dec 1941
Mersa Matruh	24 Jan 1936	Acroma	3 Feb 1942
Heliopolis	18 Apr 1936	Sidi Azeiz	8 Feb 1942
Mersa Matruh	28 Sep 1936	Moascar	31 Mar 1942

Hunter FGA.9s, No.208 Squadron

Sidi Azeiz	15 May 1942	Ramat David	12 Jul 1945			
LG.103	18 Jun 1942	Petah Tiqva	13 Aug 1945	**Aircraft**		**Representative**
LG.100	28 Jun 1942	Aqir	12 Mar 1946	**Equipment**	**Period of service**	**Serial**
Heliopolis	1 Jul 1942	Ein Shemer	6 Jun 1946	Camel	Apr 1918 − Nov 1918	N6342
LG.100	12 Jul 1942	Nicosia	1 Apr 1948	Snipe	Nov 1918 − Sep 1919	E8270 (V)
Burg el Arab	18 Nov 1942	Fayid	17 Nov 1948	R.E.8	Feb 1920 − Nov 1920	
Aqsu	15 Jan 1943	Nicosia	9 Aug 1949	Bristol F.2b	Nov 1920 − May 1930	JR6788
K.1	12 Feb 1943	Fayid	13 Sep 1949	Atlas	May 1930 − Aug 1935	J9958
Rayak	1 Jul 1943	Khartoum	25 May 1950	Audax	Aug 1935 − Jan 1939	K3105
El Bassa	16 Nov 1943	Fayid	10 Aug 1950	Demon	Sep 1935 − Mar 1936	K4515
Megiddo	7 Jan 1944	Abu Sueir	18 Oct 1951	Lysander I, II	Jan 1939 − May 1942	L4680
Trigno	17 Mar 1944	Hal Far	17 Jan 1956	Hurricane I	Nov 1940 − Sep 1942	V7817
San Angelo	1 May 1944	Akrotiri	26 Mar 1956	Hurricane IIA, IIB	May 1942 − Dec 1943	Z2416
Venafro	1 Jun 1944	Takali	6 Aug 1956	Tomahawk IIb	May 1942 − Sep 1942	AN420
Aquino	4 Jun 1944	Tangmere	10 Jan 1958 (A)	Spitfire VC	Dec 1943 − Jul 1944	EE741
Osa	11 Jun 1944	Nicosia	21 Mar 1958	Spitfire VIII	Aug 1944 − Oct 1944	
Falerium North	15 Jun 1944		to 30 Mar 1959	Spitfire IX	Mar 1944 − Aug 1946	LZ935
Orvieto Main	23 Jun 1944	Eastleigh	1 Apr 1959	Spitfire FR.18	Aug 1946 − Mar 1951	TP295 (RG-M)
Castiglione	5 Jul 1944	Stradishall	29 Mar 1960 (A)	Meteor FR.9	Mar 1951 − Jan 1958	VZ589
Malignano	1 Aug 1944		to 3 Jun 1960	Hunter F.5	Jan 1958 − Feb 1958	WP111
Peretola	1 Oct 1944	Khormaksar	27 Nov 1961	Hunter F.6	Jan 1958 − Mar 1959	XG255 (E)
Bologna	2 Apr 1945	Muharraq	6 Jun 1964	Venom FB.4	Apr 1959 − Mar 1960	WR433 (F)
Villafranca	27 Apr 1945		to 10 Sep 1971	Hunter FGA.9	Mar 1960 − Sep 1971	XF421 (H)
Bari	26 Jun 1945	Honington	1 Jul 1974	Buccaneer S.2A	Oct 1974 − date	XV156

No. 209 Squadron

Badge: An eagle volant recursant descendant in pale, wings overture

Motto: Might and main

No.209 Squadron was formed on 1 April 1918, from No.9 Squadron, RNAS at Clairmarais. Equipped with Camels, it flew fighter and ground-attack missions over the Western Front for the rest of the war and was reduced to a cadre on 21 January 1919, returned to the UK and disbanded on 24 June 1919.

On 15 March 1930 No. 209 reformed at Mount Batten to fly Iris flying boats but as only four of the type were built, it was difficult to keep the squadron up to strength and other boats were used from time to time. In January 1934 replacement by Perths began but as only three were available, the same problem continued until July 1936,

when the squadron was at last fully equipped with Singapores. These it took to Malta in September 1937 for three months and in December 1938, began to convert to Stranraers. On the outbreak of World War Two No.209 moved to Invergordon to fly patrols over the North Sea between Scotland and Norway. In October 1939 it moved to Oban for patrols over the Atlantic and in December began to re-equip with Lerwicks. The type was not a success and after flying patrols from Wales and Scotland they were replaced by Catalinas in April 1941. From Lough Erne, anti-submarine patrols were flown over the Atlantic until August when the squadron moved to Iceland for two months. In March 1942, No.209 left for East Africa and flew patrols over the Indian Ocean for the rest of the war, using detached bases in South Africa, Madagascar, Oman and the Seychelles to extend its cover. In July 1945 the squadron moved to Ceylon with its recently-acquired Sunderlands and a detachment was sent to Rangoon to attack enemy coastal shipping along the Burmese and Malayan coasts. When Japan surrendered, a detachment was sent to Hong Kong in September which was joined by the rest of the squadron in October. In September 1946 the squadron moved to Singapore and in 1950/51 provided

Singapore III, No.209 Squadron

detachments in Japan for patrols off the Korean coast. On 1 January 1955 the squadron merged with No.205 Squadron.

No.267 Squadron at Kuala Lumpur was renumbered 209 Squadron on 1 November 1958, and flew Pioneers and Twin Pioneers on liaison and transport support duties in Malaysia until disbanded on 31 December 1968.

Squadron bases

Clairmarais	1 Apr 1918	Felixstowe	17 Dec 1937
Bertangles	7 Apr 1918	Invergordon	29 Sep 1938
Quelmes	20 Jul 1918	Felixstowe	8 Oct 1938
Bertangles	6 Aug 1918	Invergordon	27 Aug 1939
Izel-le-Hameau	14 Aug 1918	Oban	7 Oct 1939
Bruille	24 Oct 1918	Pembroke Dock	16 July 1940
Saultain	22 Nov 1918	Stranraer	9 Dec 1940
Froidmont	11 Dec 1918	Castle Archdale	26 Mar 1941
Scopwick	13 Feb 1919	Reykjavik	6 Aug 1941
	to 24 Jun 1919	Pembroke Dock	10 Oct 1941
Mount Batten	15 Jan 1930	Left for E. Africa	30 Mar 1942
Felixstowe	1 May 1935	Kipevu	15 Jun 1942
Kalafrana	19 Sep 1937	Koggala	12 Jul 1945

Kai Tak	27 Oct 1945	Kuala Lumpur	1 Nov 1958
Seletar	1 Sep 1946	Seletar	1 Oct 1959
	to 1 Jan 1955		to 31 Dec 1968

Aircraft Equipment	Period of service	Representative Serial	
Camel	Apr 1918 — Jan 1919	H6997	
Iris III, V	Feb 1930 — Jun 1934	S1593	
Saro A.7	Feb 1932 — Jul 1932	N240	
Singapore II	Aug 1932 — Nov 1932	N246	
Southampton	Feb 1933 — Jun 1934		
	Nov 1934 — Jul 1935	S1149	
	Jan 1936 — Jul 1936		
Perth	Jan 1934 — Jan 1936	K3582	
London I	Oct 1934 — Jan 1936	K3560	
Short R.24/41	Apr 1935 — Sep 1935	K5574	
Singapore III	Feb 1936 — Apr 1939	K6914	
Stranraer	Dec 1938 — Apr 1940	K7301	
Lerwick I	Dec 1939 — Apr 1941	L7263	(WQ-L)
Catalina Ib, II	Apr 1941 — Apr 1945	AH545	(WQ-Z)
Sunderland V	Feb 1945 — Dec 1954	PP103	(U)
Pioneer CC.1	Nov 1958 — Dec 1968	XJ465	
Twin Pioneer CC.1	Mar 1959 — Dec 1968	XP293	

Lerwick I, No.209 Squadron

No. 210 Squadron

Badge: A griffin segreant
Motto: Yn y nwyfre yn hedfan
(Welsh)
(Hovering in the Heavens)

Rangoon I, No.210 Squadron

No. 210 Squadron was formed on 1 April 1918, from No.10 (Naval) Squadron at Treizennes and was equipped with Camels. It had originally been formed at St. Pol on 12 February 1917, as part of the Royal Naval Air Service based in Flanders. During its first weeks as an RAF squadron, it was engaged in ground-attack duties helping to stop the German offensive and there followed for the rest of the war a period of offensive patrols and bomber escort missions over Belgium, fighter cover also being given to monitors off the Belgian coast. In February 1919, it returned to the UK and disbanded on 24 June 1919.

On 1 February 1920 No.210 was reformed at Gosport from No.186 Squadron as a torpedo bomber unit equipped with Cuckoos but disbanded again on 1 April 1923. It reformed on 1 March 1931 at Felixstowe as a flying boat squadron, receiving Southamptons in May. In June 1931 it moved to Pembroke Dock where a flying-boat base was being built which became the squadron's home base until the war. In August 1935 No.210 converted to Rangoons and moved next month to Gibraltar during the Ethiopian crisis, returning in August 1936 to re-equip with Singapores. In September 1937 it was detached to Algeria as part of an Anglo-French force assembled to counter the activities of submarines attacking neutral shipping during the Spanish Civil War, returning in December. In June 1938 the first Sunderlands arrived and by the end of the year No.210 was fully equipped. The first operational patrol with the type was flown on 3 September 1939, and in the following months detachments were positioned at Invergordon and Sullom Voe to fly patrols over the northern exits from the North Sea. In July 1940 the squadron moved to Oban to fly patrols over the Atlantic and in April 1941 converted to Catalinas. In February 1942 a move was made to the Shetlands and a detachment sent to Gibraltar in October when the rest of the squadron moved back to Pembroke Dock. In April 1943 a further move to Hamworthy took place and in December the Gibraltar detachment was transferred to No.202 Squadron and all the operational aircraft to No.302 Ferry Training Unit.

On 1 January 1944 No.190 Squadron was renumbered 210 Squadron and the latter's remaining detachment at Hamworthy was dispersed. Patrols from the Shetlands were flown for the rest of the war and on 4 June 1945 the squadron disbanded.

On 1 June 1946 No.179Y Squadron was redesignated No.210 at St. Eval and flew Lancasters on maritime patrols and air-sea rescue duties, the remainder of No.179 merging with 210 on 30 September. In October 1952, the squadron moved to Topcliffe and converted to Neptunes in February 1953, flying these until disbanded on 31 January 1957. On 1 December 1958, No.269 Squadron, a Shackleton unit at Ballykelly, was renumbered 210 Squadron and resumed the latter's maritime role. In November 1970, the squadron moved to the Persian Gulf where it was disbanded on 15 November 1971.

Squadron bases			
Treizennes	1 Apr 1918	Invergordon (D)	23 Oct 1939
Liettres	9 Apr 1918		to 6 Nov 1939
St. Omer	27 Apr 1918	Invergordon &	
Ste Marie Cappel	30 May 1918	Sullom Voe (D)	24 Nov 1939
Teteghem	8 Jul 1918		to 21 May 1940
Boussieres	23 Oct 1918	Oban	13 Jul 1940
Scopwick	Feb 1919	Sullom Voe	28 Feb 1942
	to 24 Jun 1919	Pembroke Dock	4 Oct 1942
Gosport	1 Feb 1920	Gibraltar (D)	25 Oct 1942
	to 1 Apr 1923		to 18 Dec 1943
Felixstowe	1 Mar 1931	Hamworthy	21 Apr 1943
Pembroke Dock	Jun 1931	Sullom Voe	1 Jan 1944
Gibraltar	28 Sep 1935		to 4 Jun 1945
Pembroke Dock	7 Aug 1936	St. Eval	1 Jun 1946
Arzeu	22 Sep 1937	Topcliffe	1 Oct 1952
Pembroke Dock	18 Dec 1937		to 31 Jan 1957
Tayport	29 Sep 1938	Ballykelly	1 Dec 1958
Pembroke Dock	8 Oct 1938	Sharjah	1 Nov 1970
			to 15 Nov 1971

Aircraft Equipment	Period of service	Representative Serial	
Camel	Apr 1918 – Jun 1919	B3925	(L)
Cuckoo	Feb 1920 – Apr 1923	N8003	
Southampton II	May 1931 – Jul 1935	S1421	
Singapore III	Jan 1935 – Apr 1935	K3594	
	Jul 1935 – Aug 1935	K4582	
	Sep 1936 – Nov 1936	K8565	
Rangoon	Aug 1935 – Sep 1936	S1433	
Stranraer I	Oct 1935 – Nov 1935	K3973	
London II	Oct 1935 – Nov 1935	K3560	
Sunderland I	Jun 1938 – Apr 1941	L2163	(DA-G)
Catalina I, Ib	Apr 1941 – Mar 1944	W8420	(DA-O)
Catalina IIa	Aug 1942 – Dec 1943	VA729	(DA-P)
Catalina IV	Mar 1944 – Jun 1945	JX268	(DA-J)
Lancaster GR.3, ASR.3	Jun 1946 – Feb 1953	SW370	(OZ-L)
Neptune MR.1	Feb 1953 – Jan 1957	WX514	(L-R)
Shackleton MR.2, MR.2c	Dec 1958 – Nov 1971	WL789	(H)

Neptune MR.1, No.210 Squadron

No. 211 Squadron

Badge: A lion disjointed, ducally crowned
Motto: Toujours a propos (French) (Always at the right moment)

No.211 Squadron was formed at Petite Synthe on 1 April 1918, from No.11 Squadron, RNAS. Equipped with D.H.4s and D.H.9s, it was engaged in bombing and reconnaissance duties over Flanders for the rest of the war, returning to the UK in March 1919 and disbanding on 24 June 1919.

On 24 June 1937 No.211 reformed as a day bomber squadron at Mildenhall, being equipped with Audaxes and Hinds until the arrival of Blenheims in May 1939. In April 1938 the squadron was transferred to the Middle East and on the outbreak of war with Italy in June 1940, began bombing operations over Libya. Soon after the Italian invasion of Greece, No.211 was sent to reinforce the Greek Air Force and carried out bombing attacks on Italian bases in Albania until forced to evacuate its airfields during the German attack from Bulgaria in April 1941. Next month it took part in the occupation of Syria before moving to the Sudan for operational training duties as part of No.72 OTU. At the end of the year, Japan's entry into the war caused No.211 to be despatched to Singapore but by the time it arrived, airfields in Malaya were under constant attack and most of the squadron's operations were flown from Sumatra. After withdrawing to Java in mid-February 1942, all surviving aircraft were passed to No.84 Squadron on 19 February 1942 and the squadron personnel were dispersed.

On 14 August 1943 No.211 reformed at Phaphamau, Allahabad, as a Beaufighter squadron, receiving its first aircraft in October. It became operational on the Burma front on 13 January 1944, attacking enemy river craft and communications with rockets and cannon. In May 1945, the squadron was withdrawn to India to re-equip with Mosquitos but did not take these into action in Burma as it was allocated to the invasion force in Malaya. The Japanese surrender forestalled this operation and in October the squadron moved to Bangkok where it disbanded on 15 March 1946.

Squadron bases

Petite Synthe	1 Apr 1918	Menidi	19 Apr 1941
Clary	24 Oct 1918	Heraklion	22 Apr 1941
Thuilles	3 Dec 1918	Heliopolis	23 Apr 1941
Wyton	15 Mar 1919	Ramleh	27 Apr 1941
	to 24 Jun 1919	Lydda	30 Apr 1941
Mildenhall	24 Jun 1937	Aqir	10 May 1941
Grantham	30 Aug 1937	Heliopolis	5 Jun 1941
Left for		Wadi Gazouza	22 Jun 1941
Middle East	30 Apr 1938	Left for Far East	Dec 1941
Helwan	10 May 1938	Palembang	23 Jan 1942
Ramleh	18 Jul 1938	Kalidjati	16 Feb 1942
Helwan	28 Sep 1938		to 19 Feb 1942
Ramleh	18 Jul 1938		
Helwan	28 Sep 1938	Phaphamau	14 Aug 1943
Ismailia	31 Jan 1939	Ranchi	8 Nov 1943
El Daba	20 Apr 1939	Silchar	29 Dec 1943
Ismailia	1 May 1939	Comilla/Bhatpara	26 Jan 1944
El Daba	10 Aug 1939	Feni	25 May 1944
Qotafiya	17 Jul 1940	Chiringa	9 Jul 1944
Ismailia	9 Nov 1940	Yelahanka	31 May 1945
Tatoi/Menidi	16 Nov 1940 (G)	St. Thomas Mount	11 Jul 1945
	22 Nov 1940 (A)	Left for	
Paramythia	9 Feb 1941	Siam	24 Sep 1945 (G)
	27 Feb 1941 (C)	Don Muang	18 Oct 1945 (G)
Agrinion	17 Apr 1941		6 Nov 1945 (A)
			to 15 Mar 1946

Aircraft Equipment	Period of service	Representative Serial
D.H.4	Apr 1918	B9499
D.H.9	Apr 1918 — Mar 1919	D2781 (M)
Audax	Jul 1937 — Oct 1937	K2011
Hind	Aug 1937 — May 1939	L7174
Blenheim I	May 1939 — May 1941	L1481
Blenheim IV	May 1941 — Feb 1942	Z6364
Beaufighter X	Oct 1943 — Jun 1945	LZ243
Mosquito VI	Jun 1945 — Mar 1946	RF779

No. 212 Squadron

Badge: Rising from water barry wavy, a flying fish
Motto: Amari ad astra (From the sea to the stars)

No.212 Squadron was formed in August 1918 from units based at the seaplane station at Great Yarmouth which had previously operated on a station basis. It carried out anti-submarine patrols for the rest of the war and disbanded on 9 February 1920.

On 10 February 1940 No.212 reformed at Heston to carry out strategic photographic reconnaissance duties in France, working closely with the Photographic Development Unit. It was intended to have three detachments each of three Spitfires but in the absence of sufficient camera-equipped Spitfires No.212 was equipped with Blenheims. After flying some operational missions, the detachment in France was forced to evacuate its base on 14 June 1940, and the squadron was absorbed by the Photographic Development Unit (which became the Photographic Reconnaissance Unit on 8 July) on 18 June 1940.

On 22 October 1942 No.212 reformed at Korangi Creek, Karachi, as a Catalina squadron but it was not until 30 November that it occupied its base, aircraft beginning to arrive during December. Patrols began on 20 December and detachments were sent to cover the Persian Gulf and Arabian Sea, mainly from Masirah. In October 1944 a detachment was based at Calcutta for air-sea rescue patrols along the Indo-Burmese coast and remained there until the squadron disbanded. In May 1945 No.212 moved to Madras where it was renumbered 240 Squadron on 1 July 1945.

Squadron bases

Great Yarmouth	Aug 1918	Dispersed	22 Oct 1942
	to 9 Feb 1920	Korangi Creek	30 Nov 1942
Heston	10 Feb 1940	Redhills Lake	1 May 1945
	to 18 Jun 1940		to 1 Jul 1945

Aircraft Equipment	Period of service	Representative Serial
D.H.4	Aug 1918 — Jan 1919	A8040
D.H.9	Aug 1918 — Feb 1920	D1081
D.H.9A	Aug 1918 — Feb 1920	
Blenheim IV	Feb 1940 — Jun 1940	
Spitfire I	Feb 1940 — Jun 1940	K9791
Catalina Ib	Dec 1942 — Oct 1944	FP165 (H)
	Feb 1945 — Jul 1945	
Catalina IV	Sep 1944 — Jul 1945	JX271 (F)

No. 213 Squadron

Badge: A hornet
Motto: Irritatus lacessit crabro
(The hornet attacks when
roused)

No.213 Squadron was formed on 1 April 1918, from No.13 (Naval) Squadron of the former Royal Naval Air Service, a Camel fighter squadron based at Bergues in Flanders. As part of No.61 Wing, it was engaged in fighter patrols and escort work with bombing and reconnaissance aircraft from the Dunkirk airfields until the end of the war. In March 1919 it returned to the UK where it disbanded on 31 December 1919.

On 8 March 1937 No.213 was reformed as a fighter squadron at Northolt with Gauntlets and moved to Yorkshire in July. In January 1938 Hurricanes began to arrive and the squadron was fully equipped by the beginning of March. On the outbreak of war, No.213 flew fighter patrols and in May 1940, sent a detachment to France to assist the hard-pressed squadrons of the Air Component of the BEF for a few days, the whole squadron moving south early in June. For the first part of the Battle of Britain, it was based in south-west England but moved to Tangmere early in September, remaining there until November when it returned to Yorkshire. In February 1941 it moved to the north of Scotland to provide fighter defence for Scapa Flow and in May became non-operational pending a move to the Middle East. On 21 May, the squadron was flown off HMS *Furious* to Malta and thence on the same day to Egypt. After aircraft had been attached to other squadrons for some weeks, No.213 began operations over Syria early in July, moving soon afterwards to Cyprus. In December 1941 it returned to Egypt for air defence duties and in June 1942 began

offensive sweeps over the Western Desert in support of the 8th Army. After the rout of the Afrika Korps at El Alamein the squadron moved into bases in Libya to cover coastal convoys and airfields, returning to Cyprus in November for two months before converting to Spitfires in Egypt in February 1944. In May 1944 conversion to Mustangs began and these were taken to Italy in July for operations with the Balkan Air Force. Sweeps over Yugoslavia and Albania occupied the squadron until the end of the war, the last weeks of which were spent in Yugoslavia.

In September 1945 No.213 moved to Palestine and a year later to Cyprus where it re-equipped with Tempests in January 1947. In September 1947, it moved to Egypt and at the end of September to the Sudan. In August 1948 a further move was made to Somaliland for two months and at the end of this period No.213 returned to Egypt to convert to Vampires which it flew as part of the defences of the Suez Canal Zone until disbanded on 30 September 1954. On 22 July 1955 No. 213 reformed at Ahlhorn but did not receive any aircraft until March 1956, when it became a Canberra interdictor unit at Bruggen, operating in Germany until disbanded on 5 December 1969.

Squadron bases

Bergues	1 Apr 1918		to 11 Dec 1941
Stahhille	27 Nov 1918	Idku (D)	23 Oct 1941
Scopwick	19 Mar 1919	Shandur (D)	11 Dec 1941
	to 31 Dec 1919		to 19 Dec 1941
Northolt	8 Mar 1937	LG.90	31 Dec 1941
Church Fenton	1 Jul 1937	Idku	12 Jan 1942
Wittering	18 May 1938	LG.12	31 May 1941
Merville (D)	17 May 1940	Gambut West	4 Jun 1942
	to 21 May 1940	Sidi Azeiz	17 Jun 1942
Biggin Hill	9 Jun 1940	LG.155	18 Jun 1942
Exeter	18 Jun 1940	LG.75	19 Jun 1942
Tangmere	7 Sep 1940	LG.76	20 Jun 1942
Leconfield	29 Nov 1940	LG.12	24 Jun 1942
Driffield	15 Jan 1941	LG.05	27 Jun 1942
Castletown	18 Feb 1941	LG.154	29 Jun 1942
'Furious'	11 May 1941	Kilo 8	5 Aug 1942
Abu Sueir	22 May 1941	LG.85	21 Aug 1942
Haifa	3 July 1941	LG.172	23 Oct 1942
Nicosia	19 Jul 1941	LG.20	8 Nov 1942
Ismailia (D)	22 Oct 1941	LG.101	13 Nov 1942

Leverano	9 Jul 1944	El Adem	17 Nov 1942	
Biferno	12 Jul 1944	Martuba	25 Nov 1942	
Prkos	26 Apr 1945	Misurata West	22 Jan 1943	
Biferno	16 May 1945	Idku	28 Jul 1943	
Brindisi	29 Jun 1945	Paphos (D)	8 Sep 1943	
Ramat David	13 Sep 1945		to 9 Nov 1943	
Nicosia	25 Sep 1946	Paphos	19 Nov 1943	
Shallufa	3 Sep 1947	Lakatamia	10 Jan 1944	
Khartoum	22 Oct 1947	Idku	2 Feb 1944	
Mogadishu	17 Aug 1948	Gamil	25 Feb 1944	
Deversoir	21 Oct 1948	Lakatamia (D)	1 Apr 1944	
	to 30 Sep 1954		to 14 May 1944	
Ahlhorn	22 Jul 1955	St. Jean (D)	1 Apr 1944	
Bruggen	22 Aug 1957		to 15 May 1944	
	to 5 Dec 1969	Idku	5 May 1944	

Aircraft Equipment	Period of service	Representative Serial	
Camel	Apr 1918 – Dec 1919	F3239	
Gauntlet II	Mar 1937 – Feb 1939	K5301	
Hurricane I	Jan 1939 – Feb 1942	Z4095	(AK-W)
Hurricane IIA, IIC	Aug 1941 – Mar 1944	BN286	(AK-O)
Spitfire VC	Feb 1944 – May 1944	JK712	
Spitfire IX	Feb 1944 – Jun 1944	MH676	(AK-K)
Mustang III	May 1944 – Feb 1947	FB337	(AK-A)
Mustang IV	Feb 1945 – Feb 1947	KM293	(AK-P)
Tempest F.6	Jan 1947 – Jan 1950	NX184	(AK-D)
Vampire FB.5	Nov 1949 – Apr 1952	VZ116	(E)
Vampire FB.9	Apr 1952 – Sep 1954	WX207	(F)
Canberra B(I).6	Mar 1956 – Dec 1969	WT325	

Stirling III, No.214 Squadron

No. 214 Squadron

Badge: A nightjar volant affrontée
Motto: Ulter in umbris
(Avenging in the shadows)
Name: 'Federated Malay States'

No.214 Squadron was formed on 1 April 1918, from No.14 (Naval) squadron at Coudekerque which had been in existence since 28 July 1917, first as No.7A Squadron and from 9 December 1917, as No.14 Squadron, Royal Naval Air Service. Equipped with Handley Page O/100 twin-engined bombers, it received the improved O/400s in June 1918, and spent the rest of the war attacking enemy bases and ports in Belgium and northern France. After the Armistice, it was transferred from France to Egypt in July 1919, where it disbanded on 1 February 1920.

On 16 September 1935, No.214 reformed at Boscombe Down from B flight of No.9 Squadron as a night bomber squadron with Virginias. After moving to its new base at Scampton in October 1936, it converted to Harrows in January 1937 and began to receive Wellingtons in May 1939.

The first operation was flown with these on 14 June 1940, and the squadron took part in Bomber Command attacks on Germany with Wellingtons until April 1942, when it converted to Stirlings. The last Stirling sortie was flown on 24 January 1944, while No.214 was converting to Fortresses for radar counter-measures duties in No.100 Group for the rest of the war. On 27 July 1945 the squadron disbanded.

On the same day, No.614 Squadron, a Liberator unit at Amendola, Italy, was renumbered 214 Squadron and moved to Palestine in August where it began to convert to Lancasters before being renumbered 37 Squadron on 15 April 1946. On 4 November 1946 No.214 reformed at Upwood as part of the post-war Bomber Command and re-equipped with Lincolns in February 1950. A detachment of these was based in Kenya during the Mau-Mau uprising and the squadron disbanded again on 30 December 1954.

On 21 January 1956 No.214 reformed at Marham to be a Valiant squadron of the V-bomber force and in September 1956 was detached to Malta for attacks on Egyptian airfields during the Suez campaign. In April 1962 it became a tanker squadron and was disbanded on 28 February 1965, with the grounding of the Valiant force.

On 1 July 1966 the squadron reformed at Marham with Victor tankers which were used for refuelling both fighters and bombers during long-range moves and in maintaining fighter patrols beyond their normal range. It disbanded on 28 January 1977.

Squadron bases				
Coudekerque	1 Apr 1918	Sculthorpe	16 Jan 1944	
St. Inglevert	29 Jun 1918	Oulton	16 May 1944	
Quilen	24 Oct 1918		to 27 Jul 1945	
Chemy	30 Oct 1918	Amendola	27 Jul 1945	
Left for Egypt	3 Jul 1919	Ein Shemer	24 Aug 1945	
Abu Sueir	Aug 1919 (P)	Fayid	7 Nov 1945	
	to 1 Feb 1920		to 15 Apr 1946	
Boscombe Down	16 Sep 1935	Upwood	4 Nov 1946	
Andover	15 Oct 1935		to 30 Dec 1954	
Scampton	6 Oct 1936	Eastleigh (D)	10 Jun 1954	
Feltwell	12 Apr 1937		to 30 Dec 1954	
Methwold	3 Sep 1939	Marham	21 Jan 1956	
Stradishall	12 Feb 1940		to 28 Feb 1965	
Honington	5 Jan 1942	Luqa (D)	Sep 1956	
Stradishall	12 Jan 1942		to Dec 1956	
Chedburgh	1 Oct 1942	Marham	1 July 1966	
Downham Market	10 Dec 1943		to 28 Jan 1977	

Aircraft Equipment	Period of service	Representative Serial
Handley-Page O/100	Apr 1918 – Jun 1918	3123
Handley-Page O/400	Jun 1918 – Feb 1920	C9666
Virginia X	Sep 1935 – Jan 1937	K2657
Harrow II	Jan 1937 – Jul 1939	K6988 (214-J)
Wellington I, IA, IC	May 1939 – Apr 1942	L4345 (UX-L)
Wellington II	Jun 1941 – Jan 1942	W5442 (BU-V)
Stirling I, III	Apr 1942 – Jan 1944	BF382 (BU-Q)
Fortress II	Jan 1944 – Nov 1944	SR382 (BU-B)
Fortress III	Nov 1944 – Jul 1945	HB800 (BU-V)
Liberator VIII	Jul 1945 – Dec 1945	
Lancaster I	Nov 1945 – Apr 1946	TW882 (BU-V)
	Nov 1946 – Feb 1950	
Lincoln B.2	Feb 1950 – Dec 1954	RE301 (CW)
Valiant B.1, BK.1	Jan 1956 – Feb 1965	XD812
Victor K.1, K.1A	Jul 1966 – Jan 1977	XA938

Liberator VI , No.215 Squadron

No. 215 Squadron

Badge: A porcupine
Motto: Surgite nox adest
(Arise, night is at hand)

No.215 Squadron was formed on 1 April 1918, from No.15 Squadron, RNAS which had itself only formed on 10 March 1918, at Coudekerque, near Dunkerque. Equipped with Handley Page O/100 night bombers for the first few weeks, it moved to the UK in April to re-equip with improved O/400s before returning to France in July. There it joined the newly-formed Independent Force for attacks on German industrial targets during the remaining months of the war. In February 1919 it returned to the UK and disbanded on 18 October 1919.

On 1 October 1935 A Flight of No.58 Squadron at Worthy Down became No.215 Squadron and initially flew Virginias. Ansons were added in February 1937 to provide some experience with modern aircraft and in August the squadron's Harrows began to arrive. By the end of the year, re-equipment was complete and the type was retained until after the outbreak of World War Two. Wellingtons had begun to replace Harrows in July 1939, but in September No.215 was designated a training unit and carried out bomber crew training until it became part of No.11 OTU on 8 April 1940.

On the same day, a new 215 Squadron began to form at Honington but was again absorbed by No.11 OTU on 22 May. When the squadron reformed at Newmarket on 9 December 1941, it was for overseas service and in February 1942 its personnel embarked for India where they arrived in April. No.215's air echelon was formed at Waterbeach on 21 February and after training with Wellingtons flew out to India at the end of March. At first it was engaged in supply-dropping flights during the aftermath of the retreat from Burma and in August coastal patrols began along the east coast of India. In October, airborne forces training began and it was March 1943 before the squadron undertook bombing missions over Burma. Wellingtons were withdrawn from operations on 23 June 1944, and No.215 moved back to Kolar for Liberator conversion training. Operations were resumed on 1 October by both day and night and in April the squadron's role was changed to transport duties, Liberators being replaced by Dakotas. Supply-dropping missions for the 14th Army continued while Burma was cleared of the Japanese and in October, the squadron moved to Malaya. Transport flights were undertaken in Malaya, Java and Hong Kong until the squadron was renumbered 48 Squadron on 15 February 1946.

On 1 August 1947, No.215 reformed at Kabrit as a transport squadron equippped with Dakotas. It was renumbered 70 Squadron on 1 May 1948. The squadron was reformed at Dishforth on 30 April 1956 with Pioneers for army support and communications duties, being renumbered 230 Squadron on 1 September 1958.

On 1 May 1963, No.215 reformed at Benson as an Argosy squadron and moved to Singapore in August to provide supply-dropping aircraft to support the army in Malaysia until disbanded on 31 December 1968.

Squadron bases					
Coudekerque	1 Apr 1918	Harwell	1 Mar 1942 (A)	Dishforth	30 Apr 1956
Netheravon	23 Apr 1918	Asansol	14 Apr 1942		to 1 Sep 1958
Andover	15 May 1918	Pandaveswar	17 Apr 1942	Benson	1 May 1963
Alquines	4 Jul 1918	St. Thomas		Changi	1 Aug 1963
Xaffévillers	19 Aug 1918	Mount	18 Aug 1942		to 31 Dec 1968
Alquines	21 Nov 1918	Chaklala	13 Oct 1942 (A)		
Ford	2 Feb 1919		1 Nov 1942 (G)		
	to 18 Oct 1919	Jessore	12 Mar 1943		
Worthy Down	1 Oct 1935	Digri	17 Sep 1944		
Upper Heyford	14 Jan 1936	Dhubalia	28 Dec 1944		
Driffield	3 Sep 1936	Tulihal	5 May 1945		
Honington	25 Jul 1938	Basal	1 June 1945 (1st)		
Bramcote	10 Sep 1939		22 Jun 1945 (C)		
Bassingbourn	24 Sep 1939	Patenga	9 Jul 1945		
	to 8 Apr 1940		17 Jul 1945 (C)		
Honington	8 Apr 1940	Hmawbi	19 Aug 1945		
Bassingbourn	18 May 1940	Kallang and	23 Oct 1945		
	to 22 May 1940	Kai Tak (D)	22 Nov 1945		
Newmarket	9 Dec 1941		to 15 Feb 1946		
Stradishall	5 Jan 1942	Kabrit	1 Aug 1947		
Left for India	12 Feb 1942 (G)	Aqir	31 Oct 1947		
Waterbeach	21 Feb 1942 (A)	Kabrit	23 Nov 1947		
			to 1 May 1948		

Aircraft Equipment	Period of service	Representative Serial	
Handley Page O/100	Apr 1918		
Handley Page O/400	Apr 1918 – Feb 1919	C9714	
Virginia X	Oct 1935 – Nov 1937	K2330	
Anson I	Feb 1937 – Nov 1937	N5030	
	Jan 1940 – Apr 1940		
Harrow II	Aug 1937 – Dec 1939	K6974	(215-G)
Wellington I, IA	Jul 1939 – Apr 1940	N2912	(LG-G)
Wellington IC	Feb 1942 – Sep 1943	ES985	(R)
Wellington X	Sep 1943 – Aug 1944	HE791	(T)
Liberator VI	Aug 1944 – Apr 1945	EW176	(K)
Liberator VIII	Aug 1944 – Apr 1945	KH372	(H)
Dakota III, IV	Apr 1945 – Feb 1946	KJ993	(R)
Dakota C.4	Aug 1947 – May 1948	KP277	
Pioneer CC.1	Apr 1956 – Sep 1958	XK369	
Argosy C.1	May 1963 – Dec 1968	XR107	

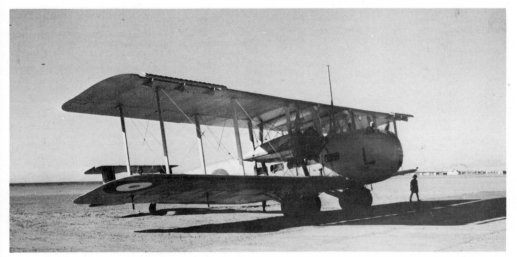

Valentia I, No.216 Squadron

No. 216 Squadron

Badge: An eagle, wings elevated, holding in the claws a bomb

Motto: CCXVI dona ferens (216 bearing gifts)

No.216 Squadron was formed on 1 April 1918, from No.16 Squadron, RNAS at Villeseneux and was equipped with Handley Page O/400 night bombers. It joined the Independent Force in May for strategic bombing duties for the rest of the war and in July 1919 began flying its aircraft out to Egypt. Until the outbreak of war in the Middle East in June 1940 the squadron was engaged in transport duties, being designated a bomber-transport unit on 2 April 1931. D.H.10s replaced O/400s over a period in 1920/21 and Vimys, Victorias and Valentias were flown until the arrival of Bombays in October 1939. These were used for night bombing raids from June 1940 but Valentias were retained for transport duties until September 1941. By the end of 1940, No.216's Bombays had been relieved by Wellingtons and devoted themselves to transport tasks, moving squadrons around the Middle East and Greece and keeping open the supply route across Africa to the Gold Coast for reinforcement aircraft being ferried to Egypt. Other flights were made to evacuate troops from Greece and supply Habbaniya and Tobruk when these bases were under siege. In July 1942 the squadron began to re-equip with Hudsons for supply and casualty evacuation duties. Dakotas began to arrive in March 1943, and in June the last Bombay left. In addition to regular services around the Mediterranean and Middle East, airborne forces were dropped on Aegean islands and a large detachment sent to Burma in April 1944, to help supply the 14th Army for two months. General transport duties continued after the war, Dakotas being replaced by Valettas in November 1949. In November 1955 the squadron returned to the UK and in June 1956 received Comets to become the first jet transport squadron in the world. In February 1962 it added larger Comet C.4s to its strength and after the withdrawal of Comet C.2s in

March 1967, continued to operate this mark on Air Support Command's routes around the world until disbandment on 30 June 1975.

Squadron bases			
Villeseneux	1 Apr 1918	Heliopolis	15 Apr 1921
Cramaille	20 Apr 1918	El Khanka	7 Oct 1941
Ochey	9 May 1918	Cairo West	4 Dec 1942
Autreville	12 Aug 1918	Agartala (D)	1 Apr 1944
Roville	28 Sep 1918		to 13 Jun 1944
Quilen	17 Nov 1918	Almaza	15 Jul 1945
Marquise	14 Dec 1918	Fayid	5 Sep 1946
Qantara	3 Jul 1919 (G)	Kabrit	14 Feb 1947
	19 Jul 1919 (A1)	Fayid	19 Feb 1951
Abu Sueir	Nov 1919 (P)	Lyneham	8 Nov 1955
			to 30 Jun 1975

Aircraft Equipment	Period of service	Representative Serial
Handley Page O/400	Apr 1918 – Oct 1921	C9680
D.H.10 Amiens	Dec 1919 – Jun 1922	E9090 'Cormorant'
Vimy	Jun 1922 – Jan 1926	H653
Victoria V	Jan 1926 – Sep 1936	J8926
Valentia	Sep 1935 – Oct 1941	K3605 (O)
Bombay I	Oct 1939 – Jun 1943	L5857 (SH-C)
D.H.86B	Dec 1942	AX672
Hudson III, VI	Jul 1942 – Apr 1943	FK387
Dakota I, II, III	Mar 1943 – Nov 1949	FD790
Valetta C.1	Nov 1949 – Nov 1955	VW205
Comet C.2	Jun 1956 – Mar 1967	XK671 'Aquila'
Comet C.4	Feb 1962 – Jun 1975	XR399

No. 217 Squadron

Badge: A demishark erased
Motto: Woe to the unwary

Beaufort I, No.217 Squadron

No.217 Squadron was formed on 1 April 1918, from No.17 (Naval) Squadron at Bergues, near Dunkerque, a formation which traced its ancestry back to the RNAS seaplane station formed at Dunkerque on 31 October 1914. Equipped with D.H.4s, it took part in daylight raids on enemy bases and airfields in Belgium until the end of the war, returning to the UK in March 1919, where it disbanded on 18 October 1919.

On 15 March 1937 No.217 reformed as a general reconnaissance squadron at Boscombe Down equipped with Ansons. On the outbreak of World War Two, it took up its war station and began flying patrols over the western approaches to the English Channel. For the next two years it was based at St. Eval which it occupied in an unfinished state in October 1939. In May 1940 No.217 began to receive Beauforts but teething troubles prevented these being used operationally until 25 September and the Ansons did not end their patrols till December. The Beauforts concentrated on attacks on enemy shipping and minelaying until transferred to the north of Scotland where only a few operations were flown before the squadron was transferred to Ceylon in May. The aircraft flew out via Gibraltar and Malta where they spent two months attacking enemy shipping in the Mediterranean. The ground echelon arrived in Ceylon in August where it received Hudsons for anti-submarine patrols, the Beauforts having been retained in the Middle East. New Beauforts began to arrive in April 1943, and by July the squadron had reverted to a strike unit, re-equipping with Beaufighters in July 1944. The Japanese made no further attempts to attack Ceylon and No.217 spent its time defensively until May 1945, when it was posted to Cocos Island to prepare for the invasion in Malaya. This was forestalled by the Japanese surrender and the squadron's aircraft never did get to Cocos, remaining in Ceylon until disbandment on 30 September 1945.

On 14 January 1952, No.217 reformed at St. Eval as a maritime reconnaissance squadron and received two Neptunes for trials. In April it moved to Kinloss where it equipped fully in July 1952, flying Neptunes until disbanded on 31 March 1957. On 1 February 1958 the squadron reformed from No.1360 Flight with Whirlwinds and moved to Christmas Island in February as part of a combined force of Shackletons, Canberras and Whirlwinds supporting the nuclear trials being carried out there. On 13 November 1959 the squadron was disbanded.

Neptune MR.1, No.217 Squadron

Warmwell	25 Aug 1939	Vavuniya	17 Feb 1943
St. Eval	2 Oct 1939	Ratmalana	29 Apr 1944
Thorney Island	28 Oct 1941	Vavuniya	10 Sep 1944
St Eval (D)	24 Dec 1941	Cocos Island	6 May 1945 (G)
	to 15 Feb 1942	Gannavaram	22 Jun 1945
Skitten	16 Feb 1942		to 30 Sep 1945
Leuchars	1 Mar 1942	St. Eval	14 Jan 1952
Left for		Kinloss	7 Apr 1952
overseas (G)	7 May 1942		to 31 Mar 1957
Luqa	10 Jun 1942 (A)	St. Mawgan	1 Feb 1958
	to 25 Aug 1942	Christmas Island	14 Feb 1958
Minneriya	8 Aug 1942		to 13 Nov 1959

Squadron bases

Bergues	1 Apr 1918	Boscombe Down	15 Mar 1937
Crochte	10 Jul 1918	Tangmere	7 Jun 1937
Varssenaere	23 Oct 1918	Bicester	16 Aug 1937
Driffield	28 Mar 1919	Tangmere	11 Sep 1937
	to 18 Oct 1919	Warmwell	26 Sep 1938
		Tangmere	5 Oct 1938

Aircraft

Equipment	Period of service	Representative Serial	
D.H.4	Apr 1918 – Oct 1919	D8393	
Anson I	Mar 1937 – Dec 1940	L9154	(MW-S)
Beaufort I	May 1940 – Nov 1941	L9807	(MW-A)
Beaufort II	Nov 1941 – Aug 1942	AW212	(MW-T)
Beaufort I	Apr 1943 – Aug 1944	DW949	(MW-G)
Hudson III, IIIA	Oct 1942 – Jun 1943	AE532	(MW-R)
Hudson VI	Oct 1942 – Jun 1943	FK483	(MW-T)
Beaufighter X	Jun 1944 – Sep 1945	NE662	
Neptune MR.1	Jan 1952 – Mar 1957	WX494	(A-B)
Whirlwind HAR.2	Feb 1958 – Nov 1959	XD164	

No. 218 Squadron

Badge: An hour-glass
Motto: In time
Name: 'Gold Coast'

Battle Is, No.218 Squadron

No.218 Squadron was formed at Dover on 24 April 1918 as a light bomber unit equipped with D.H.9s and moved to France a month later to join the former RNAS squadrons based around Dunkirk. Daylight raids were made on enemy bases and airfields in Belgium and around Lille until the end of the war, the squadron returning to the UK in February 1919, and disbanding on 24 June 1919.

On 16 March 1936 No.218 reformed from A Flight of No.57 Squadron at Upper Heyford with Hinds, re-equipping with Battles in January 1938. On the outbreak of war, the squadron moved to France as part of the Advanced Air Striking Force and when the German attack came in May 1940 suffered heavy casualties in attempts to halt the enemy columns. By early June no aircraft were left and the squadron personnel were evacuated to the UK where re-equipment with Blenheims took place. Operations began in July against enemy coastal targets and barge concentrations but in November No.218 was transferred to No.3 Group and converted to Wellingtons for night bombing. The squadron's first night raid was on 22 December and Wellingtons continued to operate until February 1942 when Stirlings replaced them. In August 1944 these were replaced by Lancasters which continued to take part in the strategic air offensive till the end of the war. On 10 August 1945, after a short period of transport duties, the squadron was disbanded.

On 1 December 1959 No.218 reformed at Harrington as a Thor strategic missile squadron, disbanding again on 23 August 1963.

Squadron bases				Aircraft		
Dover	24 Apr 1918	Moscou Ferme	May 1940	Equipment	Period of service	Representative Serial
Petite Synthe	23 May 1918	St. Lucien Ferme	May 1940			
Fretnum	7 Jul 1918	Chateau Bougon	May 1940	D.H.9	Apr 1918 – Jun 1919	D1750
Reumont	25 Oct 1918	Mildenhall	13 Jun 1940	Hind	Mar 1936 – Feb 1938	K6633
Vert Galand	16 Nov 1918	Oakington	18 Jul 1940	Battle I	Jan 1938 – Jun 1940	K7660 (218-L)
Hucknall	7 Feb 1919	Marham	25 Nov 1940	Blenheim IV	Jul 1940 – Nov 1940	R3666 (HA-J)
	to 24 June 1919	Downham Market	7 Jul 1942	Wellington IC	Nov 1940 – Feb 1942	R1448 (HA-L)
Upper Heyford	16 Mar 1936	Woolfox Lodge	7 Mar 1944	Wellington II	Mar 1941 – Dec 1941	W5448 (HA-Z)
Boscombe Down	22 Apr 1938	Methwold	4 Aug 1944	Stirling I	Jan 1942 – Apr 1943	N6129 (HA-X)
Auberive-sur-		Chedburgh	5 Dec 1944	Stirling III	Apr 1943 – Aug 1944	LK401 (HA-I)
Suippes	2 Sep 1939 (A)		to 10 Aug 1945	Lancaster I, III	Aug 1944 – Aug 1945	SW269 (HA-R)
	18 Sep 1939 (G)	Harrington	1 Dec 1959	Thor	Dec 1959 – Aug 1963	–
			to 23 Aug 1963			

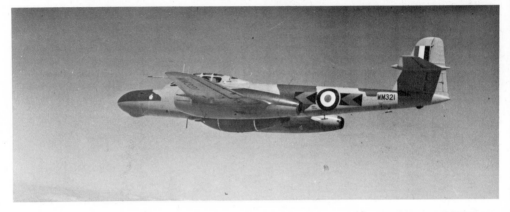

Meteor NF.13, No.219 Squadron

No. 219 Squadron

Badge: A Death's Head Hawk Moth
Motto: From dusk to dawn

No.219 Squadron was formed in August 1918 at Westgate from units of the seaplane station there and at nearby Manston. No.442 Flight flew seaplanes from Westgate while Nos.555 and 556 Flights and used D.H.9s at Manston, covered by No.470 Flight's Camels. On 7 February 1920 the squadron was disbanded.

On 4 October 1939 No.219 was reformed at Catterick with Blenheim fighters for shipping protection duties and became operational on 21 February 1940. It soon became fully employed on night patrols and based detachments at various points for night defence. In October 1940, the squadron moved south to protect London and began to convert to Beaufighters. It was June 1942 before it returned north where it remained until leaving for North Africa in May 1943. It stationed detachments to protect ports and bases in Algeria and Tunisia and in September sent aircraft to Sicily for local defence. In January 1944 No.219 left for the UK and joined Second TAF with Mosquitos. Intruder patrols were flown over France and the Low Countries and covered the Normandy beaches after D-day. In October 1944 the squadron moved to France for the rest of the war, returning to the UK in August 1945, where it disbanded on 1 September 1946.

No.219 reformed on 1 March 1951 at Kabrit as a night fighter squadron in Egypt. It replaced its Mosquitos by Meteors in March 1953 and disbanded on 1 September 1954, when its aircraft left for the UK. On 5 September 1955, No.219 reformed at Driffield with Venom NF.2 all-weather fighters, disbanding again on 31 July 1957.

Squadron bases			
Westgate & Manston	Aug 1918	Left for UK	29 Jan 1944
	to 7 Feb 1920	Woodvale	12 Feb 1944
Catterick	4 Oct 1939	Honiley	15 Mar 1944
Redhill	12 Oct 1940	Colerne	26 Mar 1944
Tangmere	10 Dec 1940	Bradwell Bay	1 Apr 1944
Acklington	23 Jun 1942	Hunsdon	28 Aug 1944
Scorton	21 Oct 1942	B.48 Amiens-Glisy	10 Oct 1944
Catterick	24 Apr 1943	B.77 Gilze-Rijen (D)	
Left for North			1 Feb 1945
Africa	14 May 1943 (G)		to 8 Jun 1945
	1 Jun 1943 (A)	B.106 Twente	8 Jun 1945
Casablanca/Cazes		Acklington	14 Aug 1945
	4 Jun 1943 (A)	Wittering	1 May 1946
Maison Blanche	8 Jun 1943 (A)		to 1 Sep 1946
Bone	14 Jun 1943 (G)	Kabrit	1 Mar 1951
	26 Jun 1943 (A)		to 1 Sep 1954
La Sebala	19 Aug 1943	Driffield	5 Sep 1955
			to 31 Jul 1957

Aircraft Equipment	Period of service	Representative Serial
Sopwith Baby	Aug 1918 – Oct 1918	N1962
Short 184	Aug 1918 – Feb 1920	N2807
Fairey IIIB	Oct 1918 – Feb 1920	
D.H.9	Aug 1918 – Feb 1920	
Camel	Aug 1918 – Feb 1920	
Blenheim IF	Oct 1939 – Dec 1940	L6709 (FK-P)
Beaufighter I	Oct 1940 – May 1943	R2204 (FK-J)
Beaufighter VI	May 1943 – Jan 1944	V8738 (FK-L)
Mosquito XVII	Feb 1944 – Dec 1944	HK315 (FK-N)
Mosquito 30	Jul 1944 – Sep 1946	MV522 (FK-F)
Mosquito NF.36	Mar 1952 – Apr 1953	RL205
Meteor NF.13	Apr 1953 – Sep 1954	WM321
Venom NF.2a	Sep 1955 – Jul 1957	WL872 (H)

Liberator VI, No.220 Squadron

No.220 Squadron

Badge: On a pellet, between two eight-pointed stars, a torch enflamed

Motto: We observe unseen (Greek script)

Aircraft Equipment	Period of service	Representative Serial	
Camel	Sep 1918 — Dec 1918	—	
Anson I	Aug 1936 — Nov 1939	K6209	(NR-O)
Hudson I, III, VI	Sep 1939 — Feb 1942	R4059	
Fortress I	Nov 1941 — Jul 1942	AN532	
Fortress II, IIa	Jul 1942 — Apr 1945	FK193	(H)
Fortress III	Jul 1944 — Apr 1945	HB791	(T)
Liberator VI	Dec 1944 — May 1946	KL687	(2-R)
Liberator VIII	Jul 1945 — May 1946	KH333	
Shackleton MR.1	Sep 1951 — Mar 1958	VP263	(T-D)
Shackleton MR.2	Apr 1953 — Oct 1958	WL745	(T-O)
Shackleton MR.3	Sep 1957 — Oct 1958	WR987	(R)
Thor	Jul 1959 — Jul 1963	—	

Squadron bases

Imbros	Sep 1918	Benbecula	13 Mar 1943
	to Dec 1918	Left for Azores	9 Oct 1943 (G)
Bircham Newton	17 Aug 1936	Lagens	18 Oct 1943 (A)
Thornaby	21 Aug 1939	St. Davids	30 May 1945 (A)
St. Eval (D)	6 Nov 1940	Waterbeach	22 Sep 1945
	to 28 Apr 1941		to 25 May 1946
Wick	1 Mar 1941 (D)	Kinloss	24 Sep 1951
	28 Apr 1941 (All)	St. Eval	14 Nov 1951
Nutts Corner	9 Jan 1942		to 1 Oct 1958
Ballykelly	20 Jun 1942	North Pickenham	22 Jul 1959
Aldergrove	14 Feb 1943		to 10 Jul 1963

No.220 Squadron was formed in September 1918 at Imbros from Nos.475, 476 and 477 Flights for fighter and reconnaissance duties in the Aegean. It flew Camels until disbanded in December 1918 as part of the No.62 Wing operating against the Turks.

On 17 August 1936 No.220 reformed at Bircham Newton as a general reconnaissance unit equipped with Ansons. On the outbreak of World War Two it began patrols from Thornaby and by November 1939 had converted to Hudsons. These it used for anti-shipping missions off Norway and the Dutch Coast from May 1940. In April 1941 the squadron moved to northern Scotland for attacks on coastal shipping and harbours in Norway and in November supplied a detachment to operate the surviving Fortresses of No.90 Squadron in the Middle East for two months. The home-based element of the squadron began conversion to Fortresses in January 1942 and became operational on 29 April from Northern Ireland. In March 1943 No.220 moved to Benbecula in the Outer Hebrides for seven months before being transferred to the Azores where it began to convert to Liberators in December 1944. For the rest of the war, it flew anti-submarine patrols over the South Atlantic, returning to the UK in June 1945, to join Transport Command. Trooping flights to India began in October and continued till the end of April 1946. On 25 May 1946 No.220 was disbanded.

On 24 September 1951 the squadron reformed at Kinloss as a maritime reconnaissance unit with Shackletons, being renumbered 201 Squadron on 1 October 1958. On 22 July 1959, it was reformed at North Pickenham as a Thor strategic missile squadron, disbanding on 10 July 1963.

Fortress II, No.220 Squadron

No. 221 Squadron

Badge: A flying fish
Motto: From sea to sea

D.H.9, No.221 Squadron

No.221 squadron was formed at Stavros on 1 April 1918 from D Squadron, RNAS for anti-submarine duties in the Aegean. Comprising Nos.552, 553 and 554 Flights, the squadron became mobile in October while based at Mudros and in December was taken by the seaplane carrier *Riviera* to South Russia to support the White Russian forces, disbanding there on 1 September 1919.

On 21 November 1940 No.221 reformed at Bircham Newton with Wellingtons and began convoy escort patrols on 23 February 1941. Next month it began shipping reconnaissance sweeps along the Dutch coast and in May moved to Northern Ireland for anti-submarine patrols. The squadron began to move to Iceland at the end of September, returning to the UK in December and in January 1941, was posted to the Middle East. No.221's Wellingtons flew out during January and February and were attached to No.47 Squadron until ground crews arrived by sea. Shipping search and strike missions began in March in addition to anti-submarine patrols while a detachment operated in Malta until absorbed by No.69 Squadron on 26 August 1942. A flight of Liberators was attached from No.120 Squadron in July and remained until 29 October. As well as locating and illuminating Axis convoys, the squadron was also equipped for night attacks with torpedo-carrying Wellingtons but as North Africa was cleared of the enemy, use of these weapons decreased and by May 1943 the squadron was mainly engaged in bombing ports in Italy and carrying out anti-submarine patrols. By September 1943 No.221 was fully occupied in patrol duties but after moving to Italy in March

1944, began shipping reconnaissance missions and attacks on enemy light craft in the Adriatic. After moving to Greece in October 1944, and taking part in bombing, anti-submarine and supply-dropping missions, the squadron returned to Egypt and disbanded on 25 August 1945.

Squadron bases		LG.39	8 Jan 1942 (A)
Stavros	1 Apr 1918	Luqa (D)	8 Jan 1942
Mudros	Oct 1918		to 26 Aug 1942
Petrovsk	19 Dec 1918	LG.89	5 Mar 1942 (G)
	to 1 Sep 1919		13 Mar 1942 (A)
Bircham Newton	21 Nov 1940	Shandur	30 Jun 1942
Limavady	2 May 1941	Shallufa	11 Aug 1942
Reykjavik	29 Sep 1941 (A)	Luqa	22 Jan 1943
	4 Oct 1941 (G)	Grottaglie	31 Mar 1944
Limavady	7 Dec 1941	Kalamaki/Hassani	
Docking	25 Dec 1941 (G)		23 Oct 1944
Left for Middle East		Idku	8 Apr 1945
	8 Jan 1942 (G)		to 25 Aug 1945

Aircraft Equipment	Period of service	Representative Serial
D.H.9	Apr 1918 – Sep 1919	D2854
D.H.9A	Dec 1918 – Sep 1919	E8765
Wellington IC	Dec 1940 – Jan 1942	T2979 (L)
Wellington VIII	Jan 1942 – Jan 1943	BB466 (B)
Wellington XI	Jan 1943 – Dec 1943	MP589
Wellington XIII	Dec 1943 – Aug 1945	JA179 (P)

Wellington VIII, No.221 Squadron

Hunter F.4s, No.222 Squadron

No. 222 Squadron

Badge: A wildebeest in full course
Motto: Pembili bo (Zulu)
(Go straight ahead)
Name: 'Natal'

No.222 Squadron was formed at Thasos on 1 April 1918, from A and Z Squadrons of the former No.2 Wing, RNAS when the Royal Air Force was formed. Renumbered No.62 Wing, the formation was given the task of maintaining raids on Turkish targets in Macedonia and Thrace operating from islands in the Northern Aegean and No.222 Squadron had fighters for escort and defensive purposes. With the end of the war, the squadron disbanded on 27 February 1919.

On 5 October 1939 No.222 reformed at Duxford as a shipping protection squadron and received Blenheims but in March 1940 it re-equipped with Spitfires as a day fighter unit. In May 1940 it moved to Essex to help cover the Dunkirk evacuation before returning to Lincolnshire and at the end of August again came back to the London area for the last part of the Battle of Britain. In November, 1940, it moved to East Anglia where it began to fly offensive operations early in 1941. In August 1942 it moved to Scotland, returning south for a few days during the Dieppe operation, and in March 1943 came back to Essex for more offensive duties, joining Second TAF in its preparation for the invasion of Europe. In April 1944 No.222 moved with No.135 Airfield to its advanced airstrip on Selsey Bill to provide fighter cover for the convoys and invasion beaches on D-Day and at the end of August moved to Normandy, moving forward behind the army until it was based in Belgium. In mid-December 1944 the squadron returned to the UK to convert to Tempests, taking these back to the Continent in February 1945 for the last months of the war. In June 1945 it moved back to the UK to re-equip with Meteors, beginning to receive these in October 1945. Various

marks of Meteor equipped the squadron until Hunters arrived in December 1954, and on 1 November 1957 No.222 was disbanded.

On 1 May 1960 No.222 became a Bloodhound SAM unit at Woodhall Spa and disbanded on 30 June 1964.

Squadron bases

Thasos	1 Apr 1918	Hornchurch	10 Mar 1944
	to 27 Feb 1919	Southend	4 Apr 1944
Duxford	5 Oct 1939	Selsey	11 Apr 1944
Digby	10 May 1940	Coolham	30 Jun 1944
Kirton-in-Lindsey		Funtington	4 Jul 1944
	23 May 1940	Selsey	6 Aug 1944
Hornchurch	28 May 1940	Tangmere	19 Aug 1944
Kirton-in-Lindsey	4 Jun 1940	B.17 Carpiquet	31 Aug 1944
Hornchurch	29 Aug 1940	B.35 Godelemesnil	10 Sep 1944
Coltishall	11 Nov 1940	B.53 Merville	12 Sep 1944
Matlask	6 June 1941	B.65 Maldegem	2 Nov 1944
Manston	1 Jul 1941	Predannack	17 Dec 1944
Southend	19 Jul 1941	B.77 Gilze-Rijen	21 Feb 1945
North Weald	18 Aug 1941	B.91 Kluis	7 Apr 1945
Manston	30 May 1942	B.109 Quackenbruck	
North Weald	7 Jul 1942		20 Apr 1945
Winfield	1 Aug 1942	Fairwood Common	4 Jun 1945
Drem	10 Aug 1942	Boxted	9 Jun 1945
Biggin Hill	16 Aug 1942	Exeter	12 Jun 1945
Drem	20 Aug 1942	Weston Zoyland	8 Jul 1946
Ayr	22 Oct 1942	Tangmere	1 Oct 1946
Southend	27 Mar 1943	Thorney Island	12 Jul 1948
Martlesham Heath	1 Apr 1943	Waterbeach	6 May 1950
Hornchurch	29 Apr 1943	Leuchars	15 May 1950
Woodvale	30 Dec 1943		to 1 Nov 1957
Catterick	14 Feb 1944	Woodhall Spa	1 May 1960
Acklington	25 Feb 1944		to 30 Jun 1964

Aircraft

Equipment	Period of service	Representative Serial
Camel	Apr 1918 – Feb 1919	
Blenheim If	Nov 1939 – Mar 1940	L8719 (ZD-C)
Spitfire I	Mar 1940 – Mar 1941	X4416 (ZD-J)
Spitfire IIA, IIB	Mar 1941 – Aug 1941	P7909 (ZD-P)
Spitfire VB	Aug 1941 – May 1943	BL619 (ZD-S)
Spitfire IX	May 1943 – Dec 1944	BS314 (ZD-A)
Tempest V	Dec 1944 – Oct 1945	NV939 (ZD-H)
Meteor F.3	Oct 1945 – Jun 1947	EE423 (ZD-L)
Meteor F.4	Jun 1947 – Sep 1950	VT184 (ZD-Q)
Meteor F.8	Sep 1950 – Dec 1954	WA925 (P)
Hunter F.1	Dec 1954 – Aug 1956	WT630 (T)
Hunter F.4	Aug 1956 – Nov 1957	WW650 (R)
Bloodhound SAM.1	May 1960 – Jun 1964	—

Baltimore IIIA, No.223 Squadron

No. 223 Squadron

Badge   A lion statant
Motto: Alae defendunt Africam
        (Wings defend Africa)

No.223 Squadron was formed on 1 April 1918 at Mitylene from B Squadron, RNAS for operations in the Aegean. It flew bombing and reconnaissance missions in the area until the end of the war, disbanding in May 1919.

On 15 December 1936, No.223 reformed at Nairobi from a detached flight of No.45 Squadron which had been based in Kenya since 25 September 1935. It remained as a single flight of Gordons and, from February 1937, Vincents until re-equipped with Wellesleys in June 1938. On the outbreak of war with Italy in June 1940, the squadron began bombing raids on Italian East Africa from the Sudan. With the main campaign almost over, No.223 moved to Egypt in May 1941, where it became a training unit for converting crews on to Blenheims, Marylands, Bostons and Baltimores. A detachment began operating Marylands in the Western Desert in October 1941 flying strategic reconnaissance missions until January 1942, when the squadron converted to Baltimores and resumed operations as a bomber unit in May. After moving westwards through Libya after the Battle of El Alamein, No.223 arrived in Tunisia in April 1943, and moved to Malta in July for attacks on tactical targets in Sicily. The ground echelon remained in North Africa until August, when the squadron became based in Sicily and by the end of September was operating from southern Italy. Until July 1944, it carried out interdiction raids on enemy communications in Italy and was renumbered 30 Squadron, South African Air Force, on 12 August 1944.

On 23 August 1944 No.223 reformed at Oulton in No.100 Group as a bomber support squadron. On 19 Sept-

ember it flew its first counter-measure missions with Liberators, adding some Fortresses in April 1945. On 29 July 1945 the squadron was disbanded. On 1 December 1959, No.223 reformed at Folkingham as a Thor strategic missile squadron, disbanding on 23 August 1963.

Squadron bases			
Mitylene	1 Apr 1918	Amriya	23 Jun 1942
Stavros	Aug 1918	Qassassin	30 Jun 1942
Mudros	Nov 1918	Amriya	2 Sep 1942
	to May 1919	Sirtan West	7 Mar 1943
Nairobi	15 Dec 1936	Sirtan North	10 Mar 1943
Summit	17 Sep 1939	Ben Gardane	13 Mar 1943
Khartoum	22 Jan 1940	Medenine Main	2 Apr 1943
Summit	18 May 1940	La Fauconnerie	15 Apr 1943
Aden (D)	13 Aug 1940	Enfidaville South	1 Jun 1943
	to 28 Aug 1940	Reyville	20 Jun 1943
Wadi Gazouza	1 Dec 1940	Luqa (D)	20 Jul 1943
Shandur	13 Apr 1941 (A)		to 10 Aug 1943
	17 Apr 1941 (G)	Monte Lungo	10 Aug 1943
Fuka (D)	12 Oct 1941	Gerbini 3	22 Aug 1943
	to 27 Dec 1941	Brindisi	27 Sep 1943
El Gubbi (D)	19 Dec 1941	Celone	29 Oct 1943
	to 5 Jan 1942	Biferno	14 Mar 1944
Tmimi (D)	5 Jan 1942	Pescara	26 Jun 1944
	to 29 Jan 1942		to 12 Aug 1944
Sidi Azeiz (D)	29 Jan 1942	Oulton	23 Aug 1944
	to Feb 1942		to 29 Jul 1945
Maaten Bagush	23 Apr 1942	Folkingham	1 Dec 1959
			to 23 Aug 1963

Aircraft Equipment	Period of service	Representative Serial
D.H.4	Apr 1918 – Nov 1918	
D.H.9	Apr 1918 – May 1919	
Gordon	Dec 1936 – Feb 1937	
Vincent	Feb 1937 – Jun 1938	K4709
Wellesley	Jun 1938 – Apr 1941	L2664
Maryland I	May 1941 – Feb 1942	AH349
Blenheim I	May 1941 – Jan 1942	L1533
Boston III	Oct 1941 – Jan 1942	
Baltimore I, II	Jan 1942 – Jun 1942	AG708
Baltimore III, IIA	Jun 1942 – Oct 1943	FA261 (J)
Baltimore IV	Jun 1943 – Feb 1944	FA403 (C)
Baltimore V	Feb 1944 – Aug 1944	FW284 (Q)
Liberator IV	Aug 1944 – Jul 1945	TS526 (6G-T)
Fortress II	Apr 1945 – Jul 1945	SR283 (6G-X)
Fortress III	Apr 1945 – Jul 1945	KL836 (6G-Z)
Thor	Nov 1959 – Aug 1963	–

Anson Is, No.224 Squadron

No. 224 Squadron

Badge: On a rock a tower
entwined by a serpent
drinking from a lamp
therein

Motto: Fedele all'amico (Italian)
(Faithful to a friend)

No.224 Squadron was formed on 1 April 1918 from a flight of No.6 Wing, RNAS based at Aliminni in southern Italy, the latter becoming No.66 Wing, RAF, on that date. Equipped with D.H.4s and, later, D.H.9s, it carried out raids on Austrian bases in Albania and Montenegro and during the last week of the war was engaged in attacking Austrian forces retreating up the Adriatic coast. In May 1919 the squadron was disbanded.

On 1 February 1937 No.224 reformed at Manston, personnel being supplied by No.48 Squadron. Ansons were received after moving to Boscombe Down two weeks later and in May 1939 were replaced by Hudsons. These became operational in August and the squadron moved to its war station at Leuchars to fly patrols over the North Sea in search of German ships. Convoy patrols were also flown and after the German invasion of Norway anti-shipping operations began. In April 1941 No.224 moved to Northern Ireland for anti-submarine patrols, a further move being made to Cornwall in December to fly patrols off Brest and attack shipping off the coast of Brittany. In February 1942 the squadron returned to Ulster for two months before moving on to Tiree where it converted to Liberators in July. These greatly increased the range of patrols over the Atlantic and were brought to southern England in September for anti-submarine operations over the Bay of Biscay and attacks on shipping off the French coast. With the capture of most

of France, No.224 was transferred to Scotland for attacks on U-boats and shipping off the Norwegian and Danish coasts which lasted till the end of the war. Returning to St. Eval in July, the squadron converted to Lancasters before disbanding on 10 November 1947.

On 1 March 1948 No.224 reformed at Aldergrove as a meteorological reconnaissance squadron equipped with Halifaxes. A detachment was based at Gibraltar which became the squadron's base in August 1951, the last meteorological flight having been made on 30 March 1951. At the same time as it moved, No.224 began to convert to Shackletons for maritime reconnaissance duties and was based at Gibraltar until disbandment on 31 October 1966.

Squadron bases			
Aliminni	1 Apr 1918	St. Eval	18 Dec 1941
Andrano	Jun 1918	Limavady	18 Feb 1942
Taranto	9 Dec 1918	Tiree	12 Apr 1942
	to May 1919	Beaulieu	9 Sep 1942
Manston	1 Feb 1937	St. Eval	25 Apr 1943
Boscombe Down	15 Feb 1937	Milltown	9 Sep 1944
Thornaby	9 Jul 1937	St. Eval	Jul 1945
Eastleigh	17 Jan 1938		to 10 Nov 1947
Thornaby	26 Mar 1938	Aldergrove	1 Mar 1948
Leuchars	30 Aug 1938	Gibraltar (D)	18 Oct 1948
Limavady	15 Apr 1941	Gibraltar	1 Aug 1951
			to 31 Oct 1966

Aircraft Equipment	Period of service	Representative Serial
D.H.4	Apr 1918 — Jul 1918	N6421
D.H.9	Jun 1918 — May 1919	D1661
Anson I	Feb 1937 — Aug 1939	K8786 (224-P)
Hudson I	May 1939 — Jul 1941	N7216 (QA-D)
Hudson V	May 1941 — Jul 1942	AM522 (QA-R)
Liberator II	Jul 1942 — Oct 1946	FL910 (XB-H)
Liberator V	Mar 1943 — Oct 1946	FL960 (XB-O)
Lancaster GR.3	Oct 1946 — Nov 1947	RF314 (XB-Q)
Halifax Met.6	May 1948 — Mar 1952	RG691 (XB-A)
Shackleton MR.1	Aug 1951 — Oct 1954	VP291 (B-C)
Shackleton MR.2	Sep 1952 — Oct 1966	WL741 (224-O)

No. 225 Squadron

Badge: In front of an anchor, two
swords in saltire, the
points uppermost

Motto: We guide the sword

No.225 Squadron was formed in August 1918 at Aliminni in southern Italy from units of the former RNAS air station at Otranto. Equipped with Camels, it flew escort missions across the Adriatic to protect bombers attacking targets in Albania until the end of the war. The squadron disbanded in December 1918.

On 3 October 1939 B Flight of No.614 Squadron was redesignated No.614A Squadron and became No.225 Squadron on 11 October 1939. Equipped with Lysanders, it was engaged in training exercises with the army for most of

Whirlwind HC.10, No.225 Squadron

the time but in June 1940 the squadron began flying coastal patrols along the coasts of Hampshire and the Isle of Wight and also provided detachments of Lysanders for air-sea rescue duties. In January 1942 it received some Hurricanes for tactical reconnaissance duties and in May began to convert to Mustangs. The squadron was allocated to the North African invasion force and moved there in November 1942, with a mixed complement of Mustangs and Hurricanes. After providing tactical reconnaissance support for the 1st Army throughout the Tunisian campaign, No.225 reequipped with Spitfires and moved to Sicily in August 1943. Next month, it arrived in Italy and in August 1944 accompanied the Allied invasion force to southern France. At the end of September, the squadron returned to Italy for the rest of the was and after a period of occupation duties disbanded on 7 January 1947.

On 1 January 1960, the Joint Experimental Helicopter Unit became No.225 Squadron at Andover and operated Sycamore and Whirlwind helicopter on tactical support duties. In May 1960, it moved to Odiham and in November 1963 detached to Malaysia to take part in operations against the Indonesian army there. On its return, the squadron was disbanded on 1 November 1965.

Squadron bases				
Aliminni	Aug 1918 to Dec 1918	Tilshead	1 Jul 1940
		Thruxton	4 Aug 1941
Odiham	11 Oct 1939	Abbotsinch	13 May 1942
Old Sarum	9 Jun 1940	Thruxton	21 May 1942
		Macmerry	1 Sep 1942

Left for			
North Africa	30 Oct 1942	Galoria	11 Jun 1944
Maison Blanche	13 Nov 1942	Tarquinia	19 Jun 1944
Bone	21 Nov 1942	Follonica	2 Jul 1944
Souk-el-Arba	22 Dec 1942	Ramatuelle	20 Aug 1944
Arjana	23 May 1942	Sisteron	27 Aug 1944
Bou Ficha	10 Jun 1943	Lyon/Satolas	5 Sep 1944
Francesco	22 Aug 1943	Salon-de-Provence	22 Sep 1944
Milazzo	2 Sep 1943	Peretola	28 Sep 1944
Salerno	10 Sep 1943 (A Flt)	Bologna	26 Apr 1945
Crotone/Izala		Villafranca	27 Apr 1945
	26 Sep 1943 (B Flt)	Tissano	15 May 1945
Serretelle	28 Sep 1943 (A Flt)	Lavariano	13 Aug 1945
Scanzano	28 Sep 1943 (B Flt)	Klagenfurt	18 Oct 1945
Palazzo	29 Sep 1943 (B Flt)	Tissano	11 Jun 1946
Capodichino		Campoformido	6 Jul 1946 to 7 Jan 1947
	6 Oct 1943 (A Flt)	Andover	1 Jan 1960
Foggia	6 Oct 1943 (B Flt)	Odiham	23 May 1960 to 1 Nov 1965
Lago	16 Jan 1944		
Tre Cancelli	3 Jun 1944		

Aircraft Equipment	Period of service	Representative Serial
Camel	Aug 1918 – Dec 1918	
Lysander II, III, IIIA	Oct 1939 – Jul 1942	N1256 (LX-M)
Hurricane I	Jan 1942 – Feb 1942	V6744
Hurricane IIC	Feb 1942 – Apr 1943	HL800
Mustang I, II	May 1942 – Aug 1943	AG361
Spitfire VC	Jan 1943 – Jan 1945	EF724 (X)
Spitfire IX	Jun 1944 – Jan 1947	JL132
Sycamore HR.14	Jan 1960 – Mar 1962	XJ919 (P)
Whirlwind HC.2, HC.4	Jan 1960 – Mar 1962	XK988 (G)
Whirlwind HAR.10	Mar 1962 – Nov 1965	XP393 (O)

No. 226 Squadron

Badge: On a fountain, a decrescent
Motto: Non sibi sed patriae (For country not for self)

No.226 Squadron was formed on 1 April 1918, at Pizzone from No.6 Wing of the former Royal Naval Air Service based at Taranto. Reconnaissance and bombing missions were flown over the Adriatic to Austrian bases in Albania and Montenegro and anti-submarine partols carried out, initially with D.H.4s and later with D.H.9s. In October 1918, the squadron moved to the Aegean for attacks on Turkish targets until the end of the war. Returning to southern Italy in November, it disbanded on 18 December 1918.

On 15 March 1937, No.226 reformed at Upper Heyford from B Flight of No.57 Squadron as a light bomber squadron. Its interim equipment of Audaxes was replaced by Battles in October 1937 and these were taken to France in September 1939 as part of the Advanced Air Striking Force. During the German invasion in May, 1940, the squadron was engaged in ground-attack missions in an attempt to halt the enemy columns but after withdrawing westwards it was evacuated from Brest on 16 June. It reassembled in Northern Ireland where it began to convert to Blenheims in February

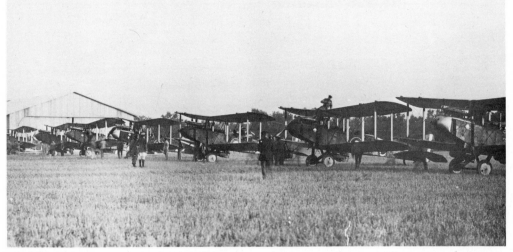

D.H.9s, No.226 Squadron

1941, moving in May to East Anglia to take part in daylight attacks on enemy ports and shipping across the North Sea. In November 1941 No.226 re-equipped with Bostons which were, in turn, replaced by Mitchells in May 1943. As part of Second TAF the squadron carried out daylight raids on enemy communications targets and airfields in preparation for the invasion of France. In October 1944, it moved to northern France and continued tactical bombing till the end of the war. In April it had moved to the Netherlands where it was disbanded on 20 September 1945.

On 1 August 1959, No.226 reformed at Catfoss with Thor intermediate range ballistic missiles, disbanding on 9 March 1963.

Squadron bases			
Pizzone	1 Apr 1918	Lemnos	8 Oct 1918
Otranto	May 1918	Taranto	Nov 1918
Taranto	Jun 1918		to 18 Dec 1918
		Upper Heyford	15 May 1937

Harwell	16 Apr 1937	Swanton Morley	9 Dec 1941
Reims/Champagne	2 Sep 1939	Hartfordbridge	13 Feb 1944
Faux-Villecerf	16 May 1940	B.50 Vitry-en-Artois	
Artins	Jun 1940		17 Oct 1944
Emb. for UK	16 Jun 1940 (G)	B.77 Gilze-Rijen	22 Apr 1945
Thirsk	18 Jun 1940		to 20 Sep 1945
Sydenham	27 Jun 1940	Catfoss	1 Aug 1959
Wattisham	26 May 1941		to 9 Mar 1963

Aircraft Equipment	Period of service	Representative Serial	
D.H.4	Apr 1918 – Jun 1918		
D.H.9	Jun 1918 – Dec 1918	D2906	
Audax	Mar 1937 – Oct 1937	K7403	
Battle	Oct 1937 – May 1941	K7597	(226-D)
Blenheim IV	Feb 1941 – Nov 1941	Z7358	(MQ-U)
Boston III, IIIA	Nov 1941 – May 1943	AL677	(MQ-P)
Mitchell II	May 1943 – Sep 1945	FV900	(MQ-F)
Mitchell III	Jan 1945 – Sep 1945	KJ561	(MQ-Y)

No. 227 Squadron

No.227 Squadron was formed on 18 April 1918 at Taranto as part of No.67 Wing. Its basis was Nos.499, 550 and 551 Flights of the Caproni Squadron established by the RNAS before it was absorbed by the RAF. Intended to become a day bomber unit, it did not become operational before the end of the war and was disbanded on 9 December 1918.

The number 227 appears to have been allotted to a detachment of Beaufighters in the Middle East whose air-crews were absorbed by No.272 Squadron on 27 June 1942. A ground echelon arrived at Aqir to service the Halifaxes of No.10 Squadron but on 7 September No.10's detachment amalgamated with those of Nos.76 and 462 Squadrons and the 227 Squadron ground echelon was dispersed.

On 20 August 1942, a detachment of Beaufighters of No.235 Squadron at Luqa, Malta was designated 227 Squadron and was operational immediately. After being engaged in escorting Beauforts and attacking enemy shipping from Malta, the squadron moved to Egypt and Libya for sweeps

over the Eastern Mediterranean in March 1943. In August 1944, it moved to Italy but was renumbered 19 Squadron, South African Air Force on 12 August 1944.

On 7 October 1944, the squadron was reformed at Bardney with Lancasters from A Flight of No.9 Squadron and B Flight of No.619. For the rest of the war, it took part in bombing raids on Germany and disbanded on 5 September 1945.

Squadron bases			
Taranto	18 Apr 1918	Limassol	16 Aug 1943
	to 9 Dec 1918	Lakatamia	23 Sep 1943
Luqa	20 Aug 1942	Berka III	31 Nov 1943
Takali	25 Nov 1942	Biferno	11 Aug 1944
Idku	1 Mar 1943		to 12 Aug 1944
Derna	5 May 1943	Bardney	7 Oct 1944
El Magrun North	24 Jun 1943	Balderton	21 Oct 1944
Gardabia West	8 Jul 1943	Strubby	5 Apr 1945
Derna	19 Jul 1943	Graveley	8 Jun 1945
			to 5 Sep 1945

Aircraft Equipment	Period of service	Representative Serial	
D.H.4, D.H.9	Apr 1918 – Dec 1918		
Beaufighter VI	Aug 1942 – Aug 1944	EL236	(Z)
Lancaster I, III	Oct 1944 – Sep 1945	RF131	(9J-B)

No. 228 Squadron

Badge: A winged helmet
Motto: Auxilium a caelo
(Help from the sky)

Scapa I, No.228 Squadron

No.228 Squadron was formed at Great Yarmouth on 20 August 1918 from flying boat flights based there during the re-organisation of the former RNAS stations into squadrons. It flew anti-submarine patrols over the North Sea and carried out reconnaissance flights to protect the Strait of Dover against possible incursions by enemy naval units. On 24 October it flew its last patrol and was disbanded on 30 June 1919.

On 15 December 1936 No.228 reformed at Pembroke Dock as a flying boat squadron and received its first boat on 4 February 1937. This was a Scapa due to delays in the delivery of the Stranraers which were scheduled to be the squadron's equipment and it was joined a few days later by a London. On 1 April its establishment included three Singapore IIIs and single examples of the Scapa, London and Stranraer. It was August 1938 before Stranraers were the sole equipment. Three months later Sunderlands began to arrive and during conversion some of these were delivered to No.230 Squadron in Singapore. At the end of May 1939, the squadron began moving to Alexandria where it remained until the outbreak of war brought the Sunderlands back to Pembroke Dock. Detachments were sent to Invergordon and Sullom Voe for patrols between Scotland and Norway but when Italy entered the war in June 1940 the squadron moved back to Egypt with a detachment operating from Gibraltar. In October its maintenance base moved from Pembroke Dock to Malta which then became the official base of No.228 until March 1941, when a move was made to a less-exposed position at Alexandria. Reconnaissance for the Fleet and anti-submarine patrols were the main

Stranraer Is, No.228 Squadron

tasks but during the evacuation of British and Commonwealth forces from Greece in April 1941, the Sunderlands were used to transport men and equipment back to Egypt. In June 1941 the squadron left for West Africa. The aircraft available numbered only two and after a few patrols they departed for the UK. The ground crews arriving by sea were redirected to Pembroke Dock but on arrival were sent to Stranraer where the squadron was once more made operational, moving to Oban in March 1942 to commence patrols. In December 1942 a move was made to Lough Erne and in May 1943, back to Pembroke Dock where the squadron remained for the rest of the war flying anti-submarine patrols, disbanding on 4 June 1945.

On 1 June 1946 No.224Y Squadron at St. Eval was redesignated No.228 Squadron and began passenger and freight services with Liberators to Iceland, Gibraltar, the Azores and Morocco. It also had reconnaissance, air-sea rescue and meteorological tasks until disbanded on 30 September 1946. On 1 July 1954 the squadron reformed at St. Eval with Shackletons as a maritime reconnaissance unit which it remained until disbanded again on 1 April 1959.

On 1 September 1959 No.275 Squadron at Leconfield was renumbered 228 Squadron and it flew Sycamores on air-sea rescue duties until they were passed to No.118 Squadron and replaced by Whirlwinds. On 1 September 1964 the squadron was renumbered 202 Squadron.

Squadron bases

Great Yarmouth	20 Aug 1918	
Killingholme	Jan 1919	
	to 30 Jun 1919	
Pembroke Dock	15 Dec 1936	
Invergordon	29 Sep 1938	
Pembroke Dock	9 Oct 1938	
Alexandria	5 Jun 1939	
Pembroke Dock	10 Sep 1939	
Kalafrana	Oct 1940	
Aboukir	25 Mar 1941	
Left for Gambia		
	16 Jun 1941 (G)	
	23 Jun 1941 (A)	
Half Die	1 Aug 1941 (A)	
Pembroke Dock		
	28 Aug 1941 (A)	
Stranraer	9 Oct 1941	
Oban	10 Mar 1942	
Castle Archdale	11 Dec 1942	
Pembroke Dock	4 May 1943	
	to 4 June 1945	
St. Eval	1 Jun 1946	
	to 30 Sep 1946	
St. Eval	1 Jul 1954	
St. Mawgan	29 Nov 1956	
St. Eval	14 Jan 1958	
	to 1 Apr 1959	
Leconfield	1 Sep 1959	
	to 1 Sep 1964	

Aircraft Equipment	Period of servcie	Representative Serial	
F.2A	Aug 1918 – Jun 1919	N4080	
Scapa	Feb 1937 – Aug 1938	K7306	
Singapore III	Apr 1937 – Sep 1937	K8856	
London I	Feb 1937 – Sep 1938	K5258	
Stranraer I	Apr 1937 – Apr 1939	K7287	(1)
Sunderland I	Nov 1938 – Aug 1942	L5803	(DG-T)
Sunderland II	Mar 1942 – Nov 1943	T9088	(DG-R)
Sunderland III	Mar 1942 – Jun 1945	JM678	(DG-V)
Sunderland V	Feb 1945 – Jun 1945	PP117	(DG-D)
Liberator VIII	Jun 1946 – Sep 1946	KK324	(A)
Shackleton MR.2	Jul 1954 – Mar1959	WR959	(L-O)
Sycamore HR.13, HR.14	Sep 1959 – Jan 1961	XG509	
Whirlwind HAR.2, HAR.4			
	Jan 1961 – May 1962	XJ412	
Whirlwind HAR.10	May 1962 – Sep 1964	XJ428	

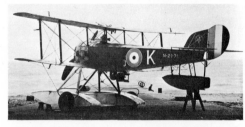

Sopwith Baby, No.229 Squadron

No. 229 Squadron

Badge: A boar's head erased,
pierced by a sword.
Motto: Be bold

No.229 Squadron was formed in August 1918 at Oudezeele in Flanders from units of the former RNAS station there. It flew coastal patrols until the end of the war and when the Dunkirk stations closed down moved to Great Yarmouth where it was disbanded on 31 December 1919.

On 6 October 1939 No.229 reformed at Digby as a fighter squadron. Equipped initially with Blenheims for shipping protection duties, it began convoy patrols on 21 December but also carried out night training and radar trials. In March 1940 the squadron was re-equipped with Hurricanes and soon after the German invasion of France in May 1940, sent one flight to reinforce the French-based fighter squadrons for eight days. After flying defensive patrols over the East Coast, No.229 moved to Northolt in September and remained there for the rest of the Battle of Britain. In December 1940 it moved to Merseyside and in May 1941 left for the Middle East. The squadron's pilots were embarked in *Furious* and flown off to Malta where, after refuelling, they moved on to Egypt, two separate detachments being conveyed fifteen days apart by the carrier. On arrival, the first detachment was attached to No.274 Squadron to cover the evacuation of Crete and the second detachment was divided between Nos.6, 208 and 213 Squadrons. A Flight was transferred from No.274 to No.73 Squadron on 11 June as the latter's C Flight and remained detached in Egypt at the end of July but it was September before the squadron began functioning as an independent unit. Fighter sweeps were flown over Libya until the end of March 1942, when the squadron was transferred to Malta to reinforce the island's fighter defences.On 29 April 1942 it ceased to function, its surviving aircraft and pilots being absorbed by other units.

On 3 August 1942 No.229 reformed at Qrendi, Malta, from No.603 Squadron and flew Spitfires in defence of Malta during the last months of the siege. In January 1943 the island's squadrons took to the offensive, flying sweeps over Sicily and in May No.229 began to operate fighter-bombers. After covering the landings in Sicily in July 1943, the squadron remained at Malta for defensive duties until January 1944, when it moved to Sicily. On 1 April 1944 it was withdrawn for transfer to the UK and re-assembled at Hornchurch on 24 April. After providing escorts for day bombers during the invasion period, No.229 moved to East Anglia for armed reconnaissance and escort missions over the Low Countries. Re-arming with Spitfire XVIs in December, it then flew fighter-bomber sweeps until renumbered 603 Squadron on 10 January 1945.

Squadron bases

Oudezeele	Aug 1918	
Great Yarmouth	Jan 1919	
	to 31 Dec 1919	
Digby	6 Oct 1939	
Wittering	26 June 1940	
Northolt	9 Sep 1940	
Wittering	15 Dec 1940	
Speke	22 Dec 1940	
Emb. in 'Furious'		
	10 May 1941 (A)	
Left for Middle East		
	20 May 1941 (G)	
Idku	22 May 1941 (A)	
	7 Jun 1941 (C)	
L.G.93	19 Jul 1941 (G)	
LG.12	14 Sep 1941	
LG.111	13 Nov 1941	
LG.123	21 Nov 1941	
LG.12	25 Nov 1941	
LG.123	26 Nov 1941	
Bu Amud	9 Dec 1941	
Gazala	16 Dec 1941	
Msus	27 Dec 1941	
Antelat	12 Jan 1942	
Gazala 3	20 Jan 1942	
LG.102	9 Feb 1942	
El Firdan	15 Feb 1942	
Gambut	26 Mar 1942	
Hal Far	28 Mar 1942	
	to 29 Apr 1942	
Takali	3 Aug 1942	
Qrendi	10 Dec 1942	
Hal Far	24 Sep 1943	
Catania	30 Jan 1944	
Left for UK	1 Apr 1944	
Hornchurch	24 Apr 1944	
Detling	19 May 1944	
Tangmere	22 Jun 1944	
Merston	24 Jun 1944	
Tangmere	27 Jun 1944	
Gatwick	28 Jun 1944	
Coltishall	1 Jul 1944	
Manston	25 Sep 1944	
Matlask	22 Oct 1944	
Swannington	20 Nov 1944	
Coltishall	2 Dec 1944	
	to 10 Jan 1945	

Aircraft Equipment	Period of service	Representative Serial	
Short 184	Aug 1918 – Dec 1919		
Sopwith Baby	Aug 1918 – Oct 1918		
Fairey IIIB, IIIC	Nov 1918 – Dec 1919		
Blenheim If	Nov 1939 – Mar 1940	K7181	(RE-P)
Hurricane I	Mar 1940 – Sep 1941	N2879	
Hurricane IIC	Sep 1941 – Apr 1942	Z4967	(HB-D)
Spitfire VC	Aug 1942 – Mar 1944	EP562	(HB-R)
Spitfire IX	Jan 1943 – Mar 1944	MH939	(9R-R)
	Apr 1944 – Dec 1944		
Spitfire XVI	Dec 1944 – Jan 1945	SM390	(9R-H)

Singapore IIIs, No.230 Squadron

No. 230 Squadron

Badge: In front of a palm tree
eradicated, a tiger passant
guardant
Motto: Kita chari jauh (Malay)
(We seek far)

No.230 Squadron was formed in August 1918 from units of
the seaplane station at Felixstowe. Nos.327 and 328 Flights
were equipped with F.2A flying boats for maritime reconnaissance while No.487 Flight flew Camels on escort duties
from nearby Butley airfield. At the end of the war, the
squadron was retained as one of the few coastal units in the
post-war RAF and moved to Calshot in May 1922 where on
1 April it was renumbered 480 Flight.

On 1 December 1934, No.230 reformed at Pembroke Dock
as a flying boat squadron, receiving its first Singapore III
in April 1935. In October 1935 the squadron moved to
Egypt during the Abyssinian crisis, returning during August
1936. Two months later, No.230's five Singapores left for
the Far East, seaborne personnel arriving at Seletar, Singapore,
in January 1937. In June 1938 the first Sunderlands began
to arrive and by the end of the year the squadron had been
fully equipped. On the outbreak of war, patrols over the
Indian Ocean and the approaches to Malaya and Singapore
began, a detachment being based in Ceylon from October.
This was augmented until in February 1940 it became the
entire squadron when the Singapore-based personnel were
transferred to No.205 Squadron. As it appeared probable
that Italy would enter the war, No.230 was transferred to
the Mediterranean in May where it flew reconnaissance
missions for the Mediterranean Fleet and carried out anti-
submarine patrols. In June 1941, the squadron administered
the Dornier Do.22s of No.2 (Yugoslav) Squadron which
had escaped from Yugoslavia after the German invasion, an
arrangement which lasted until February 1942, A move was
made to Dar-es-Salaam in Tanganyika in January 1943 for
patrols over the Indian Ocean and detachments were based
in Madagascar. In June 1943 other detachments were sent
to the Mediterranean for air-sea rescue and transport duties
and in February 1944 the squadron moved to Ceylon. In
February 1945 a detachment was sent to Calcutta to transport freight and casualties to and from a lake in Burma and
in April the squadron moved to Burma for attacks on
Japanese coastal shipping between Malaya and Burma. In
December 1945, the squadron returned to Singapore but
flew back to the UK during April 1946. In February 1949,
it moved to Pembroke Dock after taking part in the Berlin
Airlift and remained there until disbanded on 28 February
1957.

On 1 September 1958, No.215 Squadron at Dishforth
was renumbered 230 Squadron. Equipped with Pioneer
light transport and liaison aircraft, the squadron provided
transport support for army units. In January 1960 it augmented these with Twin Pioneers and both types were flown
until the end of 1962. In September 1960, A Flight was
detached to the Cameroons to supervise a change in status
of the territory, returning in September 1961. Whirlwinds
began to arrive in June 1962 and became the squadron's
standard equipment. In January 1963 No.230 moved to
Germany, returning to the UK in January 1965 before
being transferred to Borneo during the confrontation
between Indonesia and Malaysia. In January 1967 the
squadron returned to the UK and in November 1971 began
to convert to Pumas.

Pioneer CC.1, No.230 Squadron

Squadron bases

Felixstowe	Aug 1918	Colombo (D)	30 Oct 1939	Pembroke Dock	25 Feb 1949
Calshot	May 1922 (P)		to 23 Nov 1939		to 28 Feb 1957
	to 1 Apr 1923	Koggala (D)	23 Nov 1939	Dishforth	1 Sep 1958
Pembroke Dock	1 Dec 1934		to 13 Feb 1940	Upavon	1 May 1959
Left for Egypt	23 Sep 1935 (A)	Koggala	13 Feb 1940	Odiham	30 May 1960
	2 Oct 1935 (G)	Left for Egypt	2 May 1940 (A)	Mamfe (D)	Sep 1960
Aboukir	2 Oct 1935 (A)	Alexandria	6 May 1940		to Sep 1961
Alexandria	24 Oct 1935	Scaramanga (D)	12 Dec 1940		
Lake Timsah	25 Nov 1935		to 18 Apr 1941	Gutersloh	14 Jan 1963
Alexandria	1 Dec 1935	Aboukir	19 Jun 1941	Odiham	1 Jan 1965
Left for UK	30 Jul 1936 (A)	Kasfareet/Fanara	3 Jul 1942	Labuan	10 Mar 1965
	7 Aug 1936 (G)	Aboukir	28 Jul 1942	Left for UK	14 Nov 1966
Pembroke Dock		Dar-es-Salaam	9 Jan 1943	Odiham	9 Jan 1967
	3 Aug 1936 (A)	Dets. at Aboukir	1 Jun 1943	Wittering	10 Mar 1969
Left for Far East		and Bizerta	to 7 Nov 1943	Odiham	1 Jan 1972
	14 Oct 1936 (A)	Koggala	7 Feb 1944 (A1)		
Seletar	8 Jan 1937		1 Mar 1944 (C)		
Penang/Glugor (D)		Akyab	17 Apr 1945		
	15 Oct 1939	Rangoon	23 May 1945		
	to 27 Oct 1939	Redhills Lake	1 Aug 1945		
Trincomalee (D)	27 Oct 1939	Seletar	1 Dec 1945		
	to 30 Oct 1939	Calshot	Apr 1946 (P)		

Aircraft Equipment	Period of service	Representative Serial	
F.2A	Aug 1918 – c May 1922	4306	
F.5	1920 – Apr 1923	N4044	
Camel	Sep 1918 – Dec 1918		
Fairey IIIB, IIIC	Oct 1918 – Jun 1921		
Singapore III	Apr 1935 – May 1938	K4579	(4)
Sunderland I	Jun 1938 – Jan 1943	L2164	(Z)
Sunderland III	Apr 1942 – Mar 1945	JM659	(Q)
Sunderland V	Jan 1945 – Feb 1957	PP158	(T)
Pioneer CC.1	Sep 1958 – Dec 1962	XL665	(X)
Twin Pioneer CC.1	Jan 1960 – Dec 1961	XP295	
Whirlwind HC.10	Jun 1962 – Dec 1971	XP360	(O)
Puma HC.1	Nov 1971 – to date	XW218	(DB)

No. 231 Squadron

No.231 Squadron was formed from units of the seaplane station at Felixstowe in August 1918 and flew anti-submarine patrols for the remaining months of the war. On 7 July 1919 it was disbanded.

On 1 July 1940 No.231 reformed from No.416 Flight at Aldergrove as an army co-operation squadron equipped with Lysanders. In addition to taking part in exercises with the Army, it flew patrols along the border with Eire. In September 1941 conversion to Tomahawks began but a flight of Lysanders was retained until July 1943. In March 1943 the squadron moved to Yorkshire but left a detachment in Ulster until July and in April Mustangs began to arrive. By the time No.231 joined No.128 Airfield of Second TAF on 22 July 1943 it was fully equipped with Mustangs, this type having flown the squadron's first offensive operations on 4 July. Shipping and weather reconnaissance missions, defensive patrols and ground-attack sorties over northern France were flown until the squadron disbanded on 15 January 1944.

On 8 September 1944 No.231 reformed at Dorval, Canada, from No.45 Group Communications Squadron. The Group's main task was the ferrying of American and Canadian-built aircraft across the Atlantic. It also administered trans-Atlantic passenger and freight services and No.231's Coronado flying boats operated between North America, West Africa and the UK, using Largs as its British terminal. Other flights were flown with landplanes, using several types available in No.45 Group as required. In September 1945 the squadron moved to Bermuda where it disbanded on 15 January 1946. In January 1946 No.231 reformed for a short period at Full Sutton with Lancastrians, disbanding in July 1946.

Aircraft Equipment	Period of service	Representative Serial
F.2A	Aug 1918 – Jul 1919	N4307
F.5	Nov 1918 – Jul 1919	
Lysander II, III	Jul 1940 – Jul 1943	R9132
Tomahawk I, IIB	Sep 1941 – Jul 1943	AK100
Mustang I	Apr 1943 – Jan 1944	AP225
Coronado I	Sep 1944 – Jan 1946	JX501 'Bermuda'
Various transport types, e.g. Dakota III, IV; Liberator II (AL504 'Commando'); Skymaster I; Hudson VI (FK540); Liberator IX (JT983)	Sep 1944 – Jan 1946	
Lancastrian C.2	Jan 1946 – Jul 1946	VL972

Liberator IX, No.231 Squadron

Squadron bases			
Felixstowe	Aug 1918	Weston Zoyland	12 Jul 1943
	to 7 Jul 1919	Dunsfold	22 Jul 1943
Aldergrove	1 Jul 1949	Woodchurch	28 Jul 1943
Newtownards	15 Jul 1940	Redhill	15 Oct 1943
Long Kesh	11 Dec 1941		to 15 Jan 1944
Maghaberry	1 Feb 1942	Dorval	8 Sep 1944
Long Kesh	20 Nov 1942	Bermuda	Sep 1945 (P)
Nutts Corner	2 Jan 1943		to 15 Jan 1946
York	21 Mar 1943	Full Sutton	Jan 1946
Dunsfold	7 Jul 1943		to Jul 1946

No. 232 Squadron

Badge: A dragon-ship under sail, oars in action
Motto: Strike

No.232 Squadron was formed in August 1918 from units of the seaplane station at Felixstowe and was engaged in anti-submarine and reconnaissance patrols until the Armistice. The squadron disbanded on 5 January 1919.

On 17 July 1940 B Flight of No.3 Squadron at Sumburgh was redesignated No.232 Squadron. Hurricanes were flown on defensive duties in the north of Scotland and on 16 December it was brought up to full strength. In April 1941, the squadron became non-operational for transfer overseas, embarking on 10 May. No.232's pilots were at that time engaged in ferrying duties and its ground echelon remained afloat until disembarked on 6 June. Becoming operational again in north-east England, the squadron finally left for the Middle East in November. By the time the convoy arrived in South Africa, the Japanese had attacked in the Far East and No.232 was diverted to Singapore. On 13 January 1942, the ground echelon disembarked at Singapore but the squadron's pilots were embarked in HMS *Indomitable* two days later and flown off to Java on 27 January from a point 50 miles south of Christmas Island as the Singapore airfields had become untenable. Air and ground echelons were reunited at Palembang in Sumatra on 2 February but Japanese landings forced a withdrawal to Java on 15 February. No.232's Hurricanes were serviced by No.242 Squad-

ron until they were merged with the latter unit while the squadron's ground echelon was evacuated to Ceylon where it was dispersed among other units on arrival.

On 10 April 1942, No.232 reformed at Atcham with Spitfires and became operational on 30 May. Moving south in August, the squadron flew its first sweep over France on 17 August. In November, No.232 sailed for North Africa, being joined by its aircraft from Gibraltar at the end of December. Fighter patrols and ground-attack and escort missions occupied the squadron for the rest of the North African campaign and in June 1943 it moved to Malta to cover the landings in Sicily. Moving to captured airfields there, the squadron covered the Salerno landings before moving to Italy in September. In December, No.232 moved to the Lebanon for local air defence duties, and after re-equipping with Spitfire IXs arrived in Corsica in April 1944. After providing fighter cover for the landings in southern France, the squadron moved there behind the invasion force but early in October left for Naples where it was disbanded on 31 October 1944.

On 15 November 1944, No.232 reformed at Stoney Cross as a transport squadron with an establishment of twenty-five Wellington XVIs. On 6 January 1945, its aircrews were transferred to form Nos.243 Rear Echelon and No.1315 Flight and its Wellingtons passed to No.242 Squadron in February. In their place came Liberators which left for India on 14 February. These were supplemented by Skymasters for maintaining a Ceylon-Australia service while other transport flights were carried out in South-East Asia by Liberators. The Australian service terminating at Sydney began in August but the Skymasters were returned to the UK in February and March 1946, being replaced by Lancastrians. Conversion training was carried out in the UK while Liberators maintained services in India until the squadron disbanded on 15 August 1946, civil airlines having become established on the air routes in South-East Asia.

Lancastrian C.2, No.232 Squadron

Squadron bases

Felixstowe	Aug 1918 to 5 Jan 1919	Palembang II	30 Jan 1942 (A) 1 Feb 1942 (G)	Souk-el-Khemis	15 Mar 1943
Sumburgh	17 Jul 1940	Palembang I	2 Feb 1942	Protville	13 May 1943
Castletown	18 Sep 1940	Palembang II	14 Feb 1942	Takali	5 Jun 1943
Skitten	13 Oct 1940	Tjililitan	15 Feb 1942	Lentini East	18 Jul 1943
Drem	24 Oct 1940	Evacuated to Ceylon	26 Feb 1942	Asa	16 Sep 1943
Skitten	11 Nov 1940	Atcham	10 Apr 1942	Serretelle	23 Sep 1943
Elgin	4 Dec 1940	Llanbedr	15 May 1942	Gioia del Colle	17 Oct 1943
Montrose	29 Apr 1941+	Ayr	21 May 1942	Aleppo/Bab el Haoua	12 Dec 1943
Emb. at Gourock	10 May 1941 (G)	Merston	25 Jun 1942	Left for Corsica	20 Mar 1944 (G)
Disemb. to Selkirk	6 Jun 1941 (G)	Llanbedr	8 Jul 1942	Alto	5 Apr 1944
Abbotsinch	19 Jul 1941	Turnhouse	3 Aug 1942	Poretta	15 Apr 1944
Ouston	21 Jul 1941	Debden	11 Aug 1942	Calenzana	11 Jul 1944
Left for Middle East	11 Nov 1941	Gravesend	14 Aug 1942	Frejus	23 Aug 1944
Diverted to Far East	18 Dec 1941	Debden	20 Aug 1942	Left for Naples	2 Oct 1944
Seletar	13 Jan 1942 (G)	Turnhouse	1 Sep 1942	Disbanded	31 Oct 1944
Emb. in 'Indomitable'	15 Jan 1942 (A)	Left for N. Africa	25 Nov 1942 (G)	Stoney Cross	15 Nov 1944
Batavia	27 Jan 1942 (A)	Phillipville	8 Dec 1942 (G)	Left for India	14 Feb 1945
		Constantine	30 Dec 1942	Palam	Feb 1945 (P)
		Bone	7 Jan 1943	Poona	30 May 1946 to 15 Aug 1946
		Tingley	12 Feb 1943		

+ air echelon remained at Montrose

Aircraft

Equipment	Period of service	Representative Serial
F.2A, F.3	Aug 1918 – Jan 1919	
Hurricane I	Jul 1940 – Aug 1941	Z7075 (EF-T)
Hurricane IIB	Aug 1941 – Feb 1942	BE590
Spitfire VB	Apr 1942 – Feb 1944	BL520 (EF-D)
Spitfire IX	May 1943 – Oct 1944	MK137 (EF-G)
Wellington XVI	Nov 1944 – Feb 1945	DV704
Liberator III, VI, VIII	Feb 1945 – Aug 1946	KH408
Skymaster I	Jul 1945 – Mar 1946	KL985
Lancastrian C.2	Mar 1946 – Aug 1946	VM733

No. 233 Squadron

Badge: In front of a trident and sword in saltire, a star of eight points
Motto: Fortis et fidelis (Strong and faithful)

Anson I, No.233 Squadron

No.233 Squadron was formed at Dover in August 1918, from the former RNAS stations there and at Walmer which had been absorbed by the RAF on 1 April 1918. Nos.407 and 491 Flights at Dover flew anti-submarine patrols over the Strait of Dover while No.471 Flight at Walmer had Camels to protect patrolling aircraft from enemy fighters based in Belgium. On 15 May 1919 the squadron was disbanded.

On 18 May 1937 No.233 reformed at Tangmere as a general reconnaissance squadron with Ansons and in August 1939, moved to Scotland and began to convert to Hudsons. Patrols were carried out with both types for the first weeks of World War Two, the last by Ansons taking place on

Hudson I, No.233 Squadron

10 October. A flight of Blenheims was added at the end of October and flew patrols until January 1940, when it was detached to Bircham Newton to form the basis of a new squadron. Anti-shipping sweeps began after the Germans invaded Norway in April 1940 and continued till December 1940, when the squadron moved to Northern Ireland. In August 1941 No.233 moved to Cornwall to fly patrols over the Bay of Biscay and in December a detachment was sent to Gibraltar which was joined by the rest of the squadron in July 1942 where it remained until February 1944. A detachment was based in the Azores from October 1943 to February 1944 and after No.233 returned to the UK it was re-equipped with Dakotas for work with the airborne forces. On D-Day, thirty aircraft took gliders and paratroops to Normandy, followed later in the day by twenty-one more supply flights, four aircraft being lost. After carrying out casualty evacuation flights from the beach-head, it supplied thirty-seven sorties to the Arnhem airlift during the first two days, followed by thirty-five re-supply missions which lost three aircraft in the process. After general transport duties between the UK and Allied-occupied Europe, twenty-four Dakotas were provided for the last major airborne attack over the Rhine in March 1945 and in August the squadron began moving to India. By the time it had assembled, the Japanese had surrendered and after a period of general transport duties in South-East Asia, the squadron was merged with No.215 Squadron on

15 December 1945.

On 1 September 1960 the Valetta flight of No.84 Squadron was detached to form No.233 Squadron at Khormaksar. After providing transport support for the Army in Aden, the squadron was disbanded on 31 January 1964.

Squadron bases		Gibraltar	Jul 1942 (P)
Dover & Walmer	Aug 1918	Lagens	23 Oct 1943
	to 15 May 1919		to 24 Feb 1944
Tangmere	18 May 1937	Gosport	21 Feb 1944 (A)
Thornaby	9 Jul 1937		29 Feb 1944 (C)
Leuchars	1 Sep 1938	Bircham Newton	
Bircham Newton	Jun 1939		1 Mar 1944 (G)
Leuchars	Aug 1939	Blakehill Farm	5 Mar 1944
Aldergrove	3 Aug 1940	Odiham	8 Jun 1945
Leuchars	14 Sep 1940	Move to India began	
Aldergrove	8 Dec 1940		15 Aug 1945
St. Eval	8 Aug 1941	Tulihal	1 Sep 1945
Gibraltar (D)	1 Dec 1942		to 15 Dec 1945
	to Jul 1942	Khormaksar	1 Sep 1960
Thorney Island	Jan 1942 (P)		to 31 Jan 1964

Aircraft Equipment	Period of service	Representative Serial
Short 184	Aug 1918 – May 1919	
Camel	Aug 1918 – May 1919	
Anson I	May 1937 – Dec 1939	K6282 (QX-S)
Hudson I, III, VI	Aug 1939 – May 1944	AE606 (QX-M)
Dakota III	Mar 1944 – Dec 1945	KJ844 (5T-T)
Valetta C.1	Sep 1960 – Feb 1964	VW821

No. 234 Squadron

Badge: A dragon rampant, flames issuing from the mouth
Motto: Ignem mortemque despuimu
(We spit fire and death)
Name: 'Madras Presidency'

No.234 Squadron was formed in August 1918 from the seaplane station at Tresco, Isles of Scilly and flew anti-submarine patrols over the approaches to the English Channel until the Armistice, disbanding on 15 May 1919.

On 30 October 1939 No.234 reformed at Leconfield as a fighter squadron. Originally intended for shipping protection duties, it flew a mixture of Blenheims, Battles and Gauntlets until March 1940, when it began to receive Spitfires, becoming operational on 11 May. Throughout the Battle of Britain, it was based in southern England and in April 1941 began sweeps over northern France. These continued between defensive patrols until January 1943, when it moved to the Orkney Islands, returning south in June. After covering the invasion beaches in Normandy, No.234 converted to Mustangs and began long-range escort missions from East Anglia. A few days before the end of the war, the squadron moved to northern Scotland to escort strike wings operating along the Norwegian coast but returned to East Anglia in July to convert to Spitfires. These were flown until replaced by Meteors in February 1946 but on 1 September 1946 the squadron was renumbered 266 Squadron.

On 1 August 1952 No.234 reformed at Oldenburg as a Vampire ground-attack squadron in Germany. In November 1953 it received Sabres for day fighter duties and replaced these with Hunters in May 1956. On 15 July 1957 the squadron was disbanded.

Squadron bases

Tresco	Aug 1918 to 15 May 1919	Charmy Down	23 Aug 1942
Leconfield	30 Oct 1939	Portreath	29 Aug 1942
Church Fenton	22 May 1940	Perranporth	28 Oct 1942
St. Eval	18 Jun 1940	Portreath	26 Nov 1942
Middle Wallop	13 Aug 1940	Perranporth	26 Dec 1942
St. Eval	11 Sep 1940	Grimsetter &	
Warmwell	24 Feb 1941	Sumburgh (D)	22 Jan 1943
Ibsley	5 Nov 1941	Skeabrae	24 Apr 1943
Predannack	24 Dec 1941	Church Stanton	24 Jun 1943
Ibsley	31 Dec 1941	Honiley	8 Jul 1943
Warmwell	23 Mar 1942	West Malling	5 Aug 1943
Ibsley	4 Apr 1942	Rochford	16 Sep 1943
Portreath	27 Apr 1942	Hutton Cranswick	9 Oct 1943 (G)
Hutton Cranswick	15 Oct 1943 (A)	Dyce	3 Jul 1945
Church Fenton	28 Dec 1943	Bentwaters	24 Jul 1945
Coltishall	28 Jan 1944	Hawkinge	27 Aug 1945
Bolt Head	18 Mar 1944	Molesworth	12 Feb 1946
Deanland	29 Apr 1944	Boxted	28 Mar 1946 to 1 Sep 1946
Predannack	19 Jun 1944		
North Weald	28 Aug 1944	Oldenburg	1 Aug 1952
Bentwaters	17 Dec 1944	Geilenkirchen	8 Jan 1954 to 15 Jul 1957
Peterhead	1 May 1945		

Aircraft

Equipment	Period of service	Representative Serial
F.3	Aug 1918 — May 1919	N4241
Battle	Nov 1939 — Mar 1940	P5250
Blenheim If	Nov 1939 — Mar 1940	L1403
Gauntlet II	Nov 1939 — Dec 1939	On loan from 616 Squadron
Spitfire I	Mar 1940 — Nov 1940	P9363 (AZ-N)
Spitfire IIA	Nov 1920 — Sep 1941	P7925 (AZ-W)
Spitfire VB, VC	Sep 1941 — Sep 1944	BL325 (AZ-P)
Spitfire VI	Mar 1943 — May 1943	BS141
Mustang III	Sep 1944 — Aug 1945	FZ124 (AZ-N)
Mustang IV	Mar 1945 — Aug 1945	KM305 (AZ-X)
Spitfire IX	Aug 1945 — Feb 1946	TD310 (FX-C)
Meteor F.3	Feb 1946 — Sep 1946	EE449 (FX-N)
Vampire FB.5	Aug 1952 — Jan 1954	WA260 (W-D)
Vampire FB.9	Aug 1952 — Jan 1954	WR242 (W-B)
Sabre F.4	Nov 1953 — May 1956	XB727 (Y)
Hunter F.4	May 1956 — Jul 1957	XF943 (A)

No. 235 Squadron

Badge: A double Wyvern spouting fire
Motto: Jaculamur humi (We strike them to the ground)

No.235 Squadron was formed in August 1918 from the sea-plane station at Newlyn in Cornwall for anti-submarine patrols. It flew these till the Armistice and disbanded on 22 February 1919.

On 30 October 1939 No.235 reformed at Manston as a fighter squadron and received Battles for training purposes in December. In February 1940 it equipped with Blenheims and was transferred from Fighter to Coastal Command for fighter-reconnaissance duties. When the German invasion of the Low Countries began in May 1940, the squadron flew patrols over Holland and during the Battle of Britain was engaged in convoy protection and reconnaissance missions over the North Sea. Attacks on enemy shipping began in 1941 and the squadron moved to Scotland in June for operations along the Norwegian coast. In December 1941 conversion to Beaufighters took place and in May 1942, it moved to East Anglia for attacks off the Dutch coast returning to Scotland in January 1943. In August 1943 patrols over the Bay of Biscay began in support of anti-submarine aircraft operating there and in June 1944, the squadron

Blenheim IVFs, No.235 Squadron

237

re-equipped with Mosquitos. After moving to Banff in September, attacks on enemy shipping off Norway and Denmark occupied the squadron until the end of the war and on 10 July 1945 it disbanded.

Squadron bases

Newlyn	Aug 1918	Sumburgh	25 Mar 1942
	to 22 Feb 1919	Docking	31 May 1942
Manston	30 Oct 1939	Chivenor	16 Jul 1942
North Coates	27 Feb 1940	Leuchars	21 Jan 1943
Bircham Newton	25 Apr 1940	Portreath	29 Aug 1943
Detling	26 May 1940	St. Angelo	21 Feb 1944
Bircham Newton	24 Jun 1940	Portreath	27 Mar 1944
Dyce	4 Jun 1941	Banff	6 Sep 1944
			to 10 Jul 1945

Aircraft Equipment	Period of service	Representative Serial
Short 184	Aug 1918 – Feb 1919	N2958
Battle I	Dec 1939 – Feb 1940	L5413
Blenheim If	Feb 1940 – May 1940	K7120
Blenheim IVf	Feb 1940 – Dec 1941	T1807 (QY-E)
Beaufighter I	Dec 1941 – May 1942	T3240
Beaufighter VI	May 1942 – Oct 1943	EL242
Beaufighter X	Oct 1943 – May 1944	LX401
Beaufighter XI	Mar 1944 – Jun 1944	JM106
Mosquito VI	Jun 1944 – Jul 1945	HR114 (QY-R)

Beaufighter X, No.236 Squadron

No. 236 Squadron

Badge: In front of a fountain, a mailed fist grasping a winged sword.
Motto: Speculati nuntiate (Having watched, bring word)

No.236 Squadron was formed at Mullion in August 1918 as a coastal reconnaissance unit with D.H.6s and for the remaining months of the war flew anti-submarine patrols off south-west England. It disbanded on 15 May 1919.

On 31 October 1939 No.236 Squadron reformed at Stradishall in Fighter Command and received Blenheim fighters in December. It moved to Bircham Newton at the end of February 1940 to join Coastal Command but reverted to Fighter Command in April on arrival at Speke. During May and June the squadron flew defensive patrols over shipping in the English Channel and on 4 July rejoined Coastal Command for fighter and reconnaissance duties. A detachment was based in Northern Ireland from 18 September which became No.272 Squadron on 19 November but the bulk of the squadron's operations were flown from Cornwall and Pembrokeshire until 9 February 1942, when

it moved to East Anglia and became a cadre unit, its Beaufighters having been withdrawn for service with other squadrons. It became operational again on 15 March with Beaufighters which it used for escort and shipping reconnaissance missions. In July 1942 it began taking part in attacks on enemy shipping off the Dutch coast while detachments flew patrols over the Bay of Biscay to protect Coastal's anti-submarine aircraft from enemy fighters. In April 1943 a strike wing was formed at North Coates. No.236 joined it and remained an anti-shipping unit until the end of the war, disbanding on 25 May 1945.

Squadron bases

Mullion	Aug 1918	Middle Wallop	14 Jun 1940
	to 15 May 1919	Thorney Island	4 Jul 1940
Stradishall	31 Oct 1939	St. Eval	8 Aug 1940
Martlesham Heath	9 Dec 1939	Carew Cheriton	21 Mar 1941
North Coates	29 Feb 1940	Wattisham	9 Feb 1942
Speke	23 Apr 1940	Oulton	3 Jul 1942
Filton	25 May 1940	North Coates	19 Sep 1942
			to 25 May 1945

Aircraft Equipment	Period of service	Representative Serial
D.H.6	Aug 1918 – May 1919	C7645
Blenheim If	Dec 1939 – Jul 1940	L1299
Blenheim IVf	Jul 1940 – Mar 1942	L6797 (ND-Q)
Beaufighter I	Oct 1941 – Feb 1942 Mar 1942 – Mar 1943	T4800 (ND-C)
Beaufighter VI	Mar 1943 – Aug 1943	JL451 (ND-K)
Beaufighter X	Jun 1943 – May 1945	LX941 (ND-X)

238

Hurricane Is, No.237 Squadron

No. 237 Squadron

Badge: A lion passant guardant charged on the shoulder with an eagle's claw and holding in the fore paw an elephant's tusk
Motto: Primum agmen in caelo (The vanguard is in the sky)
Name: 'Rhodesia'

No.237 Squadron was formed in August 1918 from elements of the former RNAS seaplane station at Cattewater, Plymouth for anti-submarine patrols over the western part of the English Channel. It used Short seaplanes for this task until the end of the war, disbanding on 15 May 1919.

On 22 April 1940 No.1 Squadron, Southern Rhodesian Air Force, based at Nairobi was renumbered 237 (Rhodesia) Squadron. With Italy's entry into the war only a matter of time, the squadron's Audax, Hart and Hardy biplanes were distributed around landing grounds on the Kenyan border with Ethiopia for army co-operation and tactical reconnaissance duties. By September standardisation on Hardys had been carried out and the squadron moved to the Sudan to support the army in the conquest of Eritrea and Northern Ethiopia, receiving some Lysanders in November. Some Gladiators were also received for tactical reconnaissance duties in March 1941, and in the following month the old Hardys flew their last operational missions. At the end of May, it was withdrawn for transfer to Egypt and after local operations from Kufra Oasis handed its aircraft over to No.6 Squadron on 18 August and moved to the Western Desert where it received Hurricanes. Tactical reconnaissance missions with these began on 21 November and continued until the squadron was withdrawn from operations in February 1942. A few weeks later it moved to Iraq as part of the force based there to counter a possible German breakthrough from the Caucasus should Russian resistance collapse, moving to Iran in September. After the German defeat in Stalingrad, this danger was removed and No.237

moved to Egypt and Libya for air defence and convoy protection duties. In December 1943, conversion to Spitfires took place and the squadron moved to Corsica in April 1944 for operations over northern Italy and southern France. After the Allied invasion of southern France in August 1944, it moved to the newly-captured airfields there to support the army before moving to Italy early in October. For the rest of the war it flew sweeps over northern Italy and on 1 January 1946 the squadron was renumbered 93 Squadron.

Squadron bases

Cattewater	Aug 1918	Left for Iraq	23 Feb 1942 (G)
	to 15 May 1919	Mosul	8 Mar 1942
Nairobi	22 Apr 1940	Qaiyara	7 Jul 1942
Gordons Tree	18 Sep 1940	Kermanshah	10 Sep 1942
Umtali	31 Jan 1941	Kirkuk	29 Nov 1942
Barentu	9 Mar 1941	Shandur	6 Feb 1943
Umritsar	22 Mar 1941	LG.106	26 Feb 1943
Asmara	7 Apr 1941	Bersis	10 Jun 1943
Wadi Halfa	1 Jun 1941	Idku	9 Sep 1943
Kasfareet	24 Aug 1941	Savoia	7 Dec 1943
LG'Y'	21 Sep 1941	Sidi Barrani	31 Jan 1944
LG.10	30 Oct 1941	Left for Corsica	
LG.75	14 Nov 1941		21 Mar 1944 (G)
LG.128	22 Nov 1941	Poretta	19 Apr 1944 (A)
Gambut	13 Dec 1941	Serragia	23 May 1944
Tmimi	21 Dec 1941	St. Catharines	9 Jul 1944
Berka	30 Dec 1941	Cuers/Pierrefeu	
Tmimi	6 Jan 1942		25 Aug 1944
El Firdan	28 Jan 1942	Falconara	4 Oct 1944
Ismailia	6 Feb 1942	Rossignano	9 Feb 1945
			to 1 Jan 1946

Aircraft Equipment	Period of service	Representative Serial
Short 184	Aug 1918 – May 1919	N2959
Audax	Apr 1940 – Sep 1940	SR108
Hardy	Apr 1940 – Apr 1941	K4311
Hart	Jun 1940 – Sep 1940	SR103
Lysander I, II	Nov 1940 – Aug 1941	L4715
Gladiator II	Mar 1941 – Aug 1941	N5820
Hurricane I	Sep 1941 – Feb 1943	Z4055
Hurricane IIC	Feb 1943 – Dec 1943	BE338
Spitfire VC	Dec 1943 – Mar 1944	JK508
Spitfire IX	Mar 1944 – Dec 1945	MJ511

No. 238 Squadron

Badge: A three-headed hydra
Motto: Ad finem (To the end)

No.238 was formed in August 1918 from units at the sea-plane station at Cattewater, Plymouth and flew anti-sub-marine patrols until the end of the war, disbanding on 15 May 1919.

On 16 May 1940 No.238 reformed at Tangmere as a fighter squadron with Spitfires but in June these were replaced by Hurricanes. It became operational on 2 July and spent the period of the Battle of Britain in the Middle Wallop sector apart from four weeks in Cornwall. In May 1941 the squadron left for the Middle East, its aircraft being flown off HMS *Victorious* to Malta while the ground echelon sailed round the Cape of Good Hope. After refuelling in Malta, the Hurricanes flew on to the Western Desert where they were attached to No.274 Squadron pending the arrival of the squadron's own ground crews. By the end of July, No.238 was again operating as a complete unit, flying escort missions and fighter patrols throughout the campaign in the desert until after the Battle of El Alamein. It was then withdrawn to Egypt for air defence duties and converted to Spitfires in September 1943. In March 1944 the squadron moved to Corsica for sweeps over northern Italy and in August covered the Allied landings in southern France. After moving there for two months, it was withdrawn to Naples and disbanded on 31 October 1944.

On 1 December 1944 No.238 reformed at Merryfield as a transport squadron and was originally intended to fly Albemarles. In January 1945 it received Dakotas and on 14 February its first wave of ten aircraft left for India where they began supply-dropping and casualty evacuation missions over Burma. In June the squadron moved to Australia to provide transport support for the British Pacific Fleet, disbanding there on 27 December 1945. On 1 Dec-ember 1946, No.525 Squadron at Abingdon was renumbered 238 Squadron and flew Dakotas until renumbered 10 Squadron on 5 November 1948 during the Berlin Airlift.

Squadron bases			
Cattewater	Aug 1918	LG.76	20 Jun 1942
	to 15 May 1919	LG.07	23 Jun 1942
Tangmere	16 May 1940	LG.13	25 Jun 1942
Middle Wallop	20 Jun 1940	LG.15	26 Jun 1942
St. Eval	14 Aug 1940	LG.21	27 Jun 1942
Middle Wallop	10 Sep 1940	LG.105	27 Jun 1942
Chilbolton	30 Sep 1940	LG.92	29 Jun 1942
Pembrey	1 Apr 1941	LG.154	26 Sep 1942
Chilbolton	16 Apr 1941	LG.172	23 Oct 1942
'Victorious'	16 May 1941 (A)	LG.20	7 Nov 1942
Left for Middle East		LG.101	11 Nov 1942
	20 May 1941 (G)	El Adem	17 Nov 1942
Takali	14 Jun 1941 (A)	Martuba	28 Nov 1942
LG.07	15 Jun 1941 (A)	Gamil	12 Jan 1943
El Firdan	20 Jul 1941 (G)	LG.106	26 Jan 1944
LG.92	30 Jul 1941	Mersa Matruh	Feb 1944 (A)
LG.12	15 Sep 1941	Poretta	30 Mar 1944 (G)
LG.123	13 Nov 1941		28 Apr 1944 (A)
LG.12	25 Nov 1941	Serragia	1 May 1944
LG.123	26 Nov 1941	St. Catharines	8 Jul 1944
Bu Amud	12 Dec 1941	Cuers/Pierrefeu	31 Aug 1944
Gazala No.1	19 Dec 1941	Naples	8 Oct 1944 (G)
Msus	27 Dec 1941		to 31 Oct 1944
Antelat	30 Dec 1941	Merryfield	1 Dec 1944
El Gubbi	19 Jan 1942	Left for India	14 Feb 1945
Gambut	3 Feb 1942	Raipur	22 Feb 1945
LG.121	7 May 1942	Comilla	13 Mar 1945
Gambut West	1 Jun 1942	Parafield	2 Jul 1945 (1st)
Gambut No.2	16 Jun 1942		11 Jul 1945 (C)
Sidi Azeiz	17 Jun 1942		to 27 Dec 1945
LG.155	18 Jun 1942	Abingdon	1 Dec 1946
			to 5 Nov 1948

Aircraft Equipment	Period of service	Representative Serial
Short 184	Aug 1918 – May 1919	N1789
F.2A, F.3	Oct 1918 – May 1919	N4460
Spitfire I	May 1940 – Jun 1940	R6599
Hurricane I	Jun 1940 – Sep 1941	P3462 (VK-G)
	Jan 1942 – May 1942	
Hurricane IIB, IIC	Sep 1941 – Jan 1942	HL846 (X)
	May 1942 – Sep 1942	
Spitfire VB, VC	Jan 1943 – Apr 1944	EP953 (KC-G)
Spitfire IX	Sep 1943 – Oct 1944	MK486 (KC-M)
Spitfire VIII	Jun 1944 – Oct 1944	LV729 (KC-B)
Dakota III, IV	Jan 1945 – Dec 1945	KN298
	Dec 1946 – Nov 1948	

No. 239 Squadron

Badge: A winged star
Motto: Exploramus (We seek out)

No.239 Squadron was formed in August 1918 from the sea-plane station at Torquay and flew anti-submarine patrols until the Armistice, disbanding on 15 May 1919.

On 18 September 1940 No.239 was reformed as an army co-operation squadron by merging two flights from Nos.16 and 225 Squadrons. Equipped with Lysanders, the squadron took part in training exercises and in June 1941 acquired some Tomahawks for tactical reconnaissance duties. In January 1942 it became fully equipped with fighter-reconnaissance aircraft, having a mixed complement of Hurricanes and Tomahawks until converted to Mustangs in May 1942. Ground-attack and tactical reconnaissance missions over France began in June and the squadron joined Second TAF on its formation. In September 1943 it gave up its Mustangs and moved to Scotland for night fighter

training. In December No.239 received Mosquitos and moved to East Anglia to join No.100 Group for bomber support duties. For the rest of the war, it flew intruder missions over Germany to intercept and destroy enemy night fighters attempting to interfere with the heavy bombers and on 1 July 1945 the squadron was disbanded.

Squadron bases			
Torquay	Aug 1918	Odiham	18 Nov 1942
	to 15 May 1919	Hurn	6 Dec 1942
Hatfield	18 Sep 1940	Stoney Cross	25 Jan 1943
Gatwick	22 Jan 1941	Gatwick	7 Apr 1943
Abbotsinch	3 May 1942	Fairlop	21 Jun 1943
Gatwick	14 May 1942	Martlesham Heath	27 Jun 1943
Detling	19 May 1942	Fairlop	9 Jul 1943
Gatwick	31 May 1942	Hornchurch	14 Aug 1943
Twinwood Farm	30 Aug 1942	Ayr	Sep 1943
Cranfield	21 Oct 1942	West Raynham	9 Dec 1943
			to 31 Jul 1945

Aircraft Equipment	Period of service	Representative Serial	
Short 184	Aug 1918 — May 1919	N2962	
Lysander II, III	Sep 1940 — Jan 1942	L4786	(HB-U)
Tomahawk IIA	Jun 1941 — May 1942	AH793	
Hurricane I	Jan 1942 — May 1942	AG119	
Hurricane IIC	Jan 1942 — May 1942	BP397	(HB-J)
Mustang I	May 1942 — Sep 1943	AM238	(HB-V)
Mosquito II	Dec 1943 — Jan 1945	DZ270	
Mosquito VI	Sep 1944 — Jan 1945	PZ340	
Mosquito 30	Jan 1945 — Jul 1945	NT354	

Stranraer I, No.240 Squadron

No. 240 Squadron

Badge: In front of a hurt, a winged helmet
Motto: Sjo-Vordur Lopt-Vordur (Icelandic) (Guardian of the sea, guardian of the sky)

No.240 Squadron was formed in August 1918 at Calshot from Nos.345, 346 and 410 Flights, the former flying F.2a boats and No.410, Short seaplanes. After flying anti-submarine patrols over the English Channel until the end of the war, the squadron disbanded on 15 May 1919.

On 30 March 1937 No.240 reformed from C Flight of the Seaplane Training Squadron at Calshot. Equipped with Scapas, it was engaged in training duties until January 1939 when it became an operational unit. It had just replaced its Scapas with Singapores but reverted to a training role in

June 1939 and on receiving Londons became an operational unit again in July. Moving to its war station at Invergordon, No.240 began patrols over the North Sea when war broke out on 3 September. At the end of May 1940 the squadron moved to Pembroke Dock and began patrols over the Western Approaches with Stranraers, moving in July to Oban. Conversion to Catalinas began in March 1941, when the squadron's base changed to Lough Erne in Northern Ireland. After a year operating over the Atlantic, No.240 began to leave for India, its aircraft flying out in June to begin patrols over the Bay of Bengal and the Indian Ocean. In December 1944 it also began flying supplies and agents to the Dutch East Indies but was disbanded on 1 July 1945.

On the same day, No.212 Squadron also at Redhills Lake, was renumbered 240 Squadron and was joined by No.240's former Special Duties Flight. No.212 was in the course of converting from Catalinas to Sunderlands but after a few special duties and meteorological missions, the end of the war came. The squadron moved to Ceylon in January

1945 and disbanded on 31 March 1946.

On 1 May 1952 No.240 reformed at St. Eval as a maritime reconnaissance squadron equipped with Shackletons, moving in June 1952 to Northern Ireland where it was renumbered 203 Squadron on 1 November 1958. On 1 August 1959 it reformed at Breighton as a Thor strategic missile squadron, disbanding on 8 January 1963.

Aircraft

Equipment	Period of service	Representative Serial	
F.2a	Aug 1918 – May 1919		
Short 184	Aug 1918 – May 1919	N9176	
Scapa I	Mar 1937 – Dec 1938	K4194	
Singapore III	Nov 1938 – Jul 1939	K6920	
London II	Jul 1939 – Jun 1940	K5255	(BN-K)
Stranraer I	Jun 1940 – Mar 1941	K7295	(BN-L)
Catalina I, Ib, II	Mar 1941 – Dec 1945	AM265	(BN-A)
Catalina IV	May 1944 – Dec 1945	JX334	(C)
Sunderland V	Jul 1945 – Mar 1946	PP131	(J)
Shackleton MR.1a	May 1952 – Nov 1958	WB858	(L-A)
Thor	Aug 1959 – Jan 1963	–	

Squadron bases

Calshot	Aug 1918 to 15 May 1919
Calshot	30 Mar 1937
Invergordon	12 Aug 1939
Sullom Voe	4 Nov 1939
Invergordon	1 Apr 1940
Pembroke Dock	27 May 1940
Stranraer	30 Jul 1940
Killadeas	28 Mar 1941
Castle Archdale	25 Aug 1941
Left for Far East	29 Mar 1942 (G) 6 Jun 1942 (A)
Redhills Lake	4 Jul 1942 to 1 Jul 1945
Redhills Lake	1 Jul 1945
Koggala	10 Jan 1946 to 31 Mar 1946
St. Eval	1 May 1952
Ballykelly	Jun 1952 (P) to 1 Nov 1958
Breighton	1 Aug 1959 to 8 Jan 1963

Shackleton MR.1, No.240 Squadron

No. 241 Squadron

Badge: An eagle volant in front of two claymores in saltire

Motto: Find and forewarn

No.241 Squadron was formed in August 1918 from the former RNAS seaplane station at Portland and flew anti-submarine patrols over the English Channel for the remaining months of the war. On 18 June 1919 the squadron was disbanded.

On 25 September 1940 A Flight of No.614 Squadron was redesignated 241 Squadron at Inverness. Equipped with Lysanders, it took part in exercises and flew coastal patrols. During November, it had a few Rocs for divebombing demonstrations but it was not until March 1942 that it discarded its Lysanders. Some Tomahawks had been received for tactical reconnaissance training in July 1941, and in April 1942 it became fully equipped with Mustangs. In November 1942 the squadron moved to North Africa with Hurricanes and flew tactical reconnaissance and ground-attack missions for the rest of the Tunisian campaign. Converting to Spitfires in December 1943, No.241 moved

to Italy for tactical and shipping reconnaissance, escort and ground-attack duties. These continued until the end of the war and the squadron disbanded on 14 August 1945.

Squadron bases

Portland	Aug 1918 to 18 Jun 1919	Palata	29 Dec 1943 (G) 3 Jan 1944 (A)
Inverness	25 Sep 1940	Madna	20 Jan 1944
Bury St. Edmunds	15 Apr 1941	Canne	22 Feb 1944
Bottisham	1 Jul 1941	Trigno	7 Apr 1944
Weston Zoyland	8 Oct 1941	Sinello	1 Jun 1944
Bottisham	14 Oct 1941	San Vito	18 Jun 1944
Ayr	2 May 1942	Tortoretto	27 Jun 1944
Left for North Africa	12 Nov 1942	Fermio	1 Jul 1944
		Falconara	29 Jul 1944
Maison Blanche	25 Nov 1942 (G) 29 Nov 1942 (A)	Chiaravalle	24 Aug 1944
		Piagiolino	31 Aug 1944
		Cassandra	17 Sep 1944
Souk-el-Arba	21 Dec 1942	Rimini	28 Sep 1944
Souk-el-Khemis	16 Jan 1943	Fano	6 Nov 1944
Ariana	15 May 1943	Bellaria	4 Dec 1944
Bou Ficha	16 Jun 1943	Treviso	3 May 1945
Philippeville	25 Oct 1943		to 14 Aug 1945

Aircraft

Equipment	Period of service	Representative Serial	
Short 184	Aug 1918 – Jun 1919	N2965	
Lysander II, III	Sep 1940 – Mar 1942	V9707	(RZ-P)
Roc	Nov 1940 – Dec 1940	L3069	
Tomahawk II	Jul 1941 – Apr 1942	AK140	
Mustang I	Mar 1942 – Nov 1942	AM138	
Hurricane IIC	Nov 1942 – Dec 1943	HW144	
Spitfire VB	Feb 1943 – Mar 1943	ER945	
Spitfire IX	Dec 1943 – Aug 1945	SM425	(R)
Spitfire VIII	Jan 1944 – Aug 1945	JF403	

Stirling V, No.242 Squadron

No. 242 Squadron

Badge: A moose's head erased
Motto: Toujours pret
(Always ready)
Name: 'Canadian'

No.242 Squadron was formed in August 1918 from Nos.408, 409 and 514 Flights at the seaplane station at Newhaven and carried out anti-submarine patrols over the English Channel until the end of World War One. On 15 May 1919 the squadron was disbanded.

On 30 October 1939 No.242 reformed at Church Fenton as a fighter squadron and initially had a large number of Canadian personnel on strength. In December it received Blenheim fighters which were replaced in January 1940 by Hurricanes, the squadron becoming operational on 23 March. Operations over France began on 16 May, a detachment being based at French airfields until evacuated on 16 June. After taking part in the Battle of Britain, the squadron began offensive sweeps and bomber escort missions in December. These lasted until September 1941, when No.242 was withdrawn to North Wales for patrols over the Irish Sea shipping lanes. It became non-operational on 3 October to prepare for overseas and in December the squadron left for the Far East. It arrived in Singapore in January 1942, but the Japanese advance and air superiority forced a withdrawal to Sumatra and Java where it was dispersed at the end of February 1942.

On 10 April 1942 No.242 reformed at Turnhouse and after flying defensive patrols moved its Spitfires to North Africa in November to provide air cover for the 1st Army during the Tunisian campaign. In June 1943 the squadron moved to Malta to support the landings in Sicily, following

the army there for a period before moving to Italy in mid-September. In April 1944 No.242 was sent to Corsica to fly sweeps over northern Italy and covered Allied landings in southern France in August. After a month in France, the squadron disposed of its aircraft on 27 September and left for Naples a week later to be disbanded on 4 November 1944.

On 15 November 1944 No.242 reformed at Stoney Cross as a transport squadron and eighty crews were posted in for Nos.232 and 242 Squadrons. Training began on Wellington XVIs and in February 1945 Stirling Vs began to arrive. In April, the squadron's establishment of twenty-five Stirlings was amended to fifteen Yorks but in July Yorks were withdrawn and replaced by Stirlings for a short time. Yorks re-appeared in December and by January 1946 the squadron was fully equipped. It took part in the Berlin airlift and re-equipped with Hastings in 1949. On 1 May 1950 No.242 was disbanded.

Reformed at Marham on 1 October 1959 No.242 was a Bloodhound surface-to-air missile squadron until disbanded on 30 September 1964.

Squadron bases			
Newhaven	Aug 1918	Palembang	2 Feb 1942
	to 15 May 1919	Bandoeng	15 Feb 1942
Church Fenton	30 Dec 1939	Dispersed	10 Mar 1942+
Det. in France	16 May 1940	Turnhouse	10 Apr 1942
	to16 Jun 1940	Ouston	15 May 1942
Biggin Hill	21 May 1940	Drem	1 Jun 1942
Coltishall	18 Jun 1940	North Weald	11 Aug 1942
Duxford	26 Oct 1940	Manston	14 Aug 1942
Coltishall	30 Nov 1940	North Weald	20 Aug 1942
Martlesham Heath	16 Dec 1940	Digby	1 Sep 1942
Stapleford Tawney	9 Apr 1941	Left for North Africa	
North Weald	22 May 1941		30 Oct 1942
Manston	19 Jul 1941	Maison Blanche	8 Nov 1942 (A)
Valley	16 Sep 1941		12 Nov 1942 (G)
Left for Far East	5 Dec 1941	Djidjelli	14 Nov 1942
Seletar	13 Jan 1942	Bone	22 Nov 1942
		Constantine	5 Jan 1943

+ As the squadron lost aircraft and divided into detachments, its identity was lost. The date quoted is the last on which a detachment of the squadron existed as a formed unit.

Tingley	22 Jan 1943	Alto	8 Apr 1944	
Setif	29 Jan 1943	Poretta	19 Apr 1944	
Souk-el-Khemis	23 Feb 1943	Calenzana	11 Jul 1944	
Tingley	13 Mar 1943	Frejus	23 Aug 1944	
Marylebone	19 Apr 1943	Montelimar	4 Sep 1944	
Protville 3	13 May 1943	Le Vallon	21 Sep 1944	
Takali	5 Jun 1943	Left for Naples	6 Oct 1944	
Lentini East	22 Jul 1943	Disbanded	4 Nov 1944	
Milazzo East	6 Sep 1943	Stoney Cross	15 Nov 1944	
Asa	16 Sep 1943	Merryfield	9 Dec 1945	
Serretelle	24 Sep 1943	Oakington	2 May 1946	
Gioia del Colle	13 Oct 1943	Abingdon	1 Dec 1947	
Afisse North	Dec 1943	Lyneham	15 Jun 1949	
Ramat David	29 Jan 1944 (A)		to 1 May 1950	
Left for Corsica		Marham	1 Oct 1959	
	15 Feb 1944 (G)		to 30 Sep 1964	

Aircraft Equipment	Period of service	Representative Serial
Short 184	Aug 1918 – May 1919	N1244
Blenheim If	Dec 1939	K7122
Battle	Dec 1939 – Jan 1940	L5014
Hurricane I	Jan 1940 – Feb 1941	V6675 (LE-V)
Hurricane IIB	Feb 1941 – Feb 1942	Z2632 (LE-A)
Spitfire VB, VC	Apr 1942 – Apr 1944	JK260 (LE-K)
Spitfire IX	Jun 1943 – Oct 1944	JL230 (LE-B)
Wellington XVI	Jan 1945 – Feb 1945	DV738
Stirling V	Feb 1945 – Jan 1946	PJ908
Stirling IV	Sep 1945 – Dec 1945	LJ876
York C.1	Apr 1945 – Sep 1945	MW163
	Dec 1945 – Sep 1949	
Hastings C.1	Sep 1949 – May 1950	WJ337 (GAF)
Bloodhound 1	Oct 1959 – Sep 1964	–

No. 243 Squadron

Badge: A seahorse holding a sword erect
Motto: Swift in pursuit

Short 184, No.243 Squadron

No.243 Squadron was formed in August 1918 from the sea-plane station at Cherbourg which had been functioning as an out-station of Calshot while part of the Royal Naval Air Service. Its seaplanes carried out anti-submarine patrols off the French coast and around the Channel Islands until the end of the war and it disbanded on 15 March 1919.

On 12 March 1941 No.243 reformed at Kallang as a fighter squadron for the defence of Singapore. The short-comings of its Buffalos were soon apparent and when Japanese fighters came within range the squadron suffered heavy losses and by the end of January 1942 was operating its surviving aircraft as part of a mixed force, the other Buffalo squadrons being in a similar state. Its identity was gradually lost due to the evacuation of redundant personnel and by the time all fighters were withdrawn from the Singapore airfields, it no longer existed as a unit.

On 1 June 1942 No.243 reformed at Ouston, taking over No.242 Squadron's Spitfires and became operational on the 12th. After defensive duties, it turned its aircraft over to No.232 Squadron at the end of September and in November sailed for North Africa where it became operational again with Spitfires in Algeria in January 1943. For the rest of the Tunisian campaign it flew sweeps and provided escorts for day bombers attacking enemy bases and transport and in June moved to Malta for similar missions over Sicily. A few days after the Allied landings there, No.243 moved into the beach-head, repeating this in September after the Salerno landings. In December 1943 it moved to the Levant and after fully converting to Spitfire IXs left for Corsica in April 1944. Escort missions and ground attack sweeps were flown over northern Italy and southern France and cover provided for the Allied landings on the French Riviera in August before the squadron was again disbanded on 30 September 1944.

No.243 reformed on 15 December 1944 at Morecambe, two days before embarking for Canada where it began train-ing with Dakotas. In January 1945 these began moving across the Pacific to Australia where communications flights began between British bases in the South-West Pacific area, mainly to the British Pacific Fleet bases. By the end of the war the squadron was flying scheduled ser-vices and extended these to Hong Kong on its surrender. A large proportion of the squadron personnel was Australian which was demobilised locally when No.243 disbanded on 15 April 1946.

Squadron bases			
Cherbourg	Aug 1918	Tusciano	13 Sep 1943
	to 15 Mar 1919	Capodichino	11 Oct 1943
Kallang	12 Mar 1941	Gioia del Colle	10 Nov 1943
	to Feb 1942	Kabrit	12 Dec 1943 (A)
Ouston	1 Jun 1942		15 Dec 1943 (G)
Turnhouse	2 Sep 1942	Aleppo	14 Dec 1943 (A)
Left for N. Africa	24 Nov 1942		24 Dec 1943 (G)
Philippeville	7 Dec 1942	Ramat David	31 Jan 1944
Constantine	29 Dec 1942	Alto	2 Apr 1944 (A)
Bone	3 Jan 1943 (A)		8 Apr 1944 (G)
	9 Jan 1943 (G)	Poretta	19 Apr 1944
Tingley	13 Jan 1943	Calenzana	11 Jul 1944
Souk-el-Khemis	28 Jan 1943	Frejus	23 Aug 1944
La Sebala II	16 May 1943	Montelimar	5 Sep 1944
Mateur	25 May 1943	Le Vallon	21 Sep 1944
Hal Far	11 Jun 1943		to 30 Sep 1944
Comiso	14 Jul 1943	Morecambe (2PDC)	
Pachino South	30 Jul 1943		15 Dec 1944
Lentini West	23 Aug 1943	Left for Canada	17 Dec 1944
Panebianco	29 Aug 1943	Dorval	27 Dec 1944
Catania Main	30 Aug 1943	Merryfield (D)	4 Jan 1945
Cassala	2 Sep 1943		to 13 Mar 1945
Falcone	6 Sep 1943	Camden N.S.W.	9 Feb 1945
			to 15 Apr 1946

Aircraft Equipment	Period of service	Representative Serial
Short 184	Aug 1918 – Mar 1919	N2833
Buffalo I	Mar 1941 – Feb 1942	W8237
Spitfire VB	Jun 1942 – Sep 1942	AD316 (SN-H)
Spitfire VB, VC	Jan 1943 – Mar 1944	ER807 (SN-E)
Spitfire IX	Jun 1943 – Sep 1944	JL375 (SN-Z)
Dakota IV	Jan 1945 – Apr 1946	KN350 (VMY-BD)

No. 244 Squadron

No.244 Squadron was formed in August 1918 at Bangor, North Wales, for anti-submarine patrols off the coast of North Wales. It was equipped with D.H.6s which it flew until disbanded on 22 January 1919.

On 1 November 1940 S Squadron at Shaibah was re-designated 244 Squadron, the former having been formed on 21 August 1939, for patrol duties at Habbaniya, moving to Shaibah in September 1940. Equipped with Vincents, it flew patrols until the Iraqi uprising in May 1941 when it took part in bombing attacks on the Iraqi Army. In August it was again operational over Iran, this time on reconnaissance missions. In January 1942 training on Oxfords began in preparation for re-equipment with Blenheims and these began anti-submarine patrols in May, a move being made at the same time to Sharjah. In January 1943 the last Vincent was withdrawn and in February 1944 the first Wellington arrived to begin replacing the Blenheims, this process being completed in April. In March 1944 No.244's base was transferred to Masirah where it remained flying patrols until disbanded on 1 May 1945.

Squadron bases		Sharjah	22 Jan 1942
Bangor	Aug 1918		(det. to May 1942)
	to 22 Jan 1919	Masirah	17 Mar 1944
Shaibah	1 Nov 1940		to 1 May 1945.

Aircraft Equipment	Period of service	Representative Serial
D.H.6	Aug 1918 – Jan 1919	B3021
Vincent	Nov 1940 – Jan 1943	K4121
Blenheim IV	Apr 1942 – Jan 1943	P6931
Blenheim V	Oct 1942 – Apr 1944	BA481 (F)
Wellington XIII	Feb 1944 – May 1945	JA180 (Q)

Hurricane Is, No.245 Squadron

No. 245 Squadron

Badge: In front of a fountain, an eagle volant
Motto: Fugo non fugio (I put to flight, I do not flee)
Name: 'Northern Rhodesia'

No.245 Squadron was formed in August 1918 at Fishguard with Short seaplanes for anti-submarine patrols over the southern half of the Irish Sea. It was disbanded on 19 May 1919.

On 30 October 1939 No.245 reformed at Leconfield with Blenheims as a fighter squadron but in January 1940 received a few Battles for training purposes pending the arrival of Hurricanes in March. In May the squadron's aircraft moved to Hawkinge to help cover the evacuation from Dunkirk and in July went to Northern Ireland for air defence and convoy patrols. It was transferred to southern England in September 1941, and began to fly offensive sweeps over France in addition to defensive tasks. Conversion to Typhoons took place in January 1943, and the squadron joined Second TAF in June on its formation. To prepare the way for the invasion of France, No.245 joined with other squadrons to attack enemy communications and in April 1944 began using rockets as its main weapon. By the end of June it was installed in Normandy attacking enemy tanks and vehicles in support of the army, arriving in

Meteor F.8s, No.245 Squadron

the Netherlands at the beginning of October to fly sweeps over Germany. On 21 March 1945 it occupied its first German base and continued its armed reconnaissance missions until the end of the war. On 10 August 1945 the squadron was disbanded.

On the same day, No.504 Squadron at Colerne was renumbered 245 Squadron which flew Meteors as part of the air defence of the UK till March 1957, when it converted to Hunters. These were flown for only a short time, disbandment coming on 3 June 1957. On 21 August 1958, No.527 Squadron, a Signals Command unit at Watton, was renumbered 245 Squadron, moving a few days later to Tangmere. Here the squadron operated Canberras until renumbered 98 Squadron on 18 April 1963.

Aircraft Equipment	Period of service	Representative Serial
Short 184	Aug 1918 – May 1919	N2908
Blenheim If	Nov 1939 – Mar 1940	L6788
Battle I	Feb 1940 – Mar 1940	P5251
Hurricane I	Mar 1940 – Aug 1941	W9203 (DX-T)
Hurricane IIB	Aug 1941 – Jan 1943	BE496 (MR-M)
Typhoon IB	Jan 1943 – Aug 1945	JR311 (MR-G)
Meteor F.3	Aug 1945 – Mar 1948	EE286 (MR-Q)
Meteor F.4	Nov 1947 – Jun 1950	VT125 (MR-B)
Meteor F.8	Jun 1950 – Mar 1957	WH476 (V)
Hunter F.4	Mar 1957 – Jun 1957	XE686 (Q)
Canberra B.2	Aug 1958 – Apr 1963	WD955

Squadron bases			
Fishguard	Aug 1918 to 19 May 1919	Warmwell	17 Nov 1941
		Chilbolton	23 Nov 1941
Leconfield	30 Oct 1939	Middle Wallop	19 Dec 1941
Drem	12 May 1940	Charmy Down	26 Oct 1942
Hawkinge (D)	28 May 1940 to 5 Jun 1940	Peterhead	29 Jan 1943
		Gravesend	31 Mar 1943
Turnhouse	5 Jun 1940	Fairlop	28 May 1943
Hawkinge (D)	9 Jun 1940 to 1 Jul 1940	Selsey	1 Jun 1943
		Lydd	30 Jun 1943
		Westhampnett	10 Oct 1943
Aldergrove	20 Jul 1940	Holmsley South	1 Apr 1944
Ballyhalbert	14 Jul 1941	Eastchurch	25 Apr 1944
Chilbolton	1 Sep 1941	Holmsley South	30 Apr 1944

Eastchurch	12 May 1944	B.150 Celle	19 Apr 1945
Holmsley South	22 May 1944	B.154 Schleswig	28 May 1945
B.5 Camilly	27 Jun 1944	Warmwell	16 Jun 1945
B.24 St. Andrè de l'Eure		B.154 Schleswig	3 Jul 1945
	28 Aug 1944		to 10 Aug1945
B.24 Beauvais-Tillé	2 Sep 1944	Colerne	10 Aug 1945
B.50 Vitry-en-Artois		Bentwaters	Jun 1946
	4 Sep 1944	Horsham St. Faith	
B.70 Deurne	17 Sep 1944		16 Aug 1946
B.80 Volkel	1 Oct 1944	Stradishall	27 Jun 1955
Warmwell	24 Dec 1944		to 30 Jun 1957
B.80 Volkel	6 Jan 1945	Watton	21 Aug 1958
B.100 Goch	21 Mar 1945	Tangmere	25 Aug 1958
B.110 Achmer	11 Apr 1945		to 18 Apr 1963

No. 246 Squadron

No.246 Squadron was formed in August 1918 from units of the former RNAS station at Seaton Carew on the Durham coast. The seaplane station had an airfield nearby from which coastal patrols were flown, the squadron being the only one to operate Blackburn Kangaroos. It disbanded when the station closed down in May 1919.

On 1 September 1942 No.246 reformed at Bowmore and received Sunderlands. It began anti-submarine patrols on 12 December but was disbanded on 30 April 1943, distributing its aircraft to Nos.228, 330 and 422 Squadrons.

On 11 October 1944 the squadron reformed at Lyneham as a transport unit with Liberators and began operating long-distance services to the Middle and Far East on 19 October. In December No.246 began to receive Yorks and used these at first for carrying VIPs, taking over from the Metropolitan Communications Squadron in February 1945. Some Skymasters were received pending their transfer to No.232 Squadron and at the end of the war the squadron was organised into three flights, one for VIP use, one for cargo

Kangaroo, No.246 Squadron

and one to fly scheduled services to India. In November the VIP flight left the squadron and No.246 became fully equipped with Yorks which it flew on services to India and the Middle East until it merged with No.511 Squadron on 15 October 1946.

Sunderland III, No.246 Squadron

Squadron bases

Seaton Carew	Aug 1918
	to May 1919
Bowmore	1 Sep 1942
	to 30 Apr 1943
Lyneham	11 Oct 1944
Holmsley South	1 Dec 1944
	to 15 Oct 1946

Aircraft Equipment	Period of service	Representative Serial
Short 184	Aug 1918 – May 1919	N2640
Sopwith Baby	Aug 1918 – Oct 1918	
F.E.2b	Aug 1918 – Oct 1918	
Kangaroo	Aug 1918 – May 1919	B9977
Sunderland III	Oct 1942 – Apr 1943	DV980 (G)
Liberators	Oct 1944 – Nov 1945	
e.g. Mk.II, III (FL909), VI (KH169), VII (EW626)		
Halifax III	Nov 1944 – Feb 1945	NA683
York C.1	Dec 1944 – Oct 1946	MW142
Skymaster I	Apr 1945 – Jul 1945	KL977

No. 247 Squadron

Badge: In front of a bezant, a demi-lion erased and crowned holding in the paws a scroll inscribed in Chinese characters 'Chu Feng'
Motto: Rise from the east
Name: 'China-British'

Vampire F.1, No.247 Squadron

No.247 Squadron was formed in August 1918 from units of the former Royal Naval Air Station, Felixstowe, and for the remaining months of the war its flying boats flew patrols over the North Sea. On 22 January 1919 the squadron disbanded.

On 21 July 1940 the Fighter Flight, Sumburgh, was transferred to Roborough for the defence of Plymouth and became 247 Squadron on 1 August. It flew Gladiators on defensive patrols, mainly at night until they were replaced by Hurricanes at the end of the year. Convoy patrols and day and night air defence of the area occupied the squadron until September 1941, when it began intruder missions over north-west France with long-range Hurricane IIBs. It remained in south-west England until September 1942 when it moved to the Midlands and in January 1943 began to convert to Typhoons. Joining the newly-formed Second TAF during the summer of 1943, No.247 took part in sweeps over northern France and in April 1944, took a course in rocket firing in preparation for its army support role during the invasion. On 20 June it began to operate from airstrips in Normandy and followed the breakout to reach the Netherlands by the end of September. Armed reconnaissance sweeps were flown over Germany for the rest of the war, the main targets being enemy transport, railways and barges. On 13 April 1945, the squadron moved into its first German base and it remained in Germany until transferred back to the UK in August to convert to Tempest IIs. It did not have these for long before it was selected to be the first

Vampire squadron in March 1946, and in June No.247 moved to Odiham, its home base for the next eleven years. In May 1951 re-equipment with Meteors began and these gave place to Hunters from June 1955. On 31 December 1957 the squadron was disbanded.

No.247 was reformed on 1 July 1960 at Carnaby as a Bloodhound ground-to-air missile squadron, disbanding on 31 December 1963.

B.86 Helmond	13 Jan 1945	B.156 Luneberg	2 May 1945
Warmwell	21 Feb 1945	B.158 Lubeck	6 May 1945
B.86 Helmond	7 Mar 1945	Chilbolton	20 Aug 1945
B.106 Twente	12 Apr 1945	Odiham	27 Jun 1946
B.112 Hopsten	13 Apr 1945		to 31 Dec 1957
B.120 Langenhagen		Carnaby	1 Jul 1960
	17 Apr 1945		to 31 Dec 1963

Squadron bases

Felixstowe	Aug 1918	Attlebridge	7 Aug 1943
	to 2 Jan 1919	New Romney	13 Aug 1943
Roborough	1 Aug 1940	Merston	11 Oct 1943
St. Eval	10 Feb 1941	Snailwell	3 Oct 1943
Roborough	17 Feb 1941	Merston	5 Nov 1943
Portreath	10 May 1941	Odiham	31 Dec 1943
Exeter (D)	Dec 1941	Merston	13 Jan 1944
	to 17 May 1942	Eastchurch	1 Apr 1944
Exeter	17 May 1942	Hurn	24 Apr 1944
High Ercall	21 Sep 1942	B.6 Coulombs	20 Jun 1944
Middle Wallop	1 Mar 1943	Hurn (A)	23 Jun 1944
Fairlop	5 Apr 1943		to 27 Jun 1944
Gravesend	28 May 1943	B.30 Creton	30 Aug 1944
Bradwell Bay	4 Jun 1943	B.48 Amiens-Glisy	3 Sep 1944
New Romney	10 Jul 1943	B.58 Melsbroek	6 Sep 1944
		B.78 Eindhoven	22 Sep 1944

Aircraft Equipment

Equipment	Period of service	Representative Serial
F.2a	Aug 1918 – Jan 1919	4551
Gladiator II	Aug 1940 – Feb 1941	N5631
Hurricane I	Dec 1940 – Jun 1941	W9270 (HP-Y)
Hurricane IIA, IIB	Jun 1941 – Jan 1942	Z2682 (HP-R)
Hurricane IIC	Jan 1942 – Feb 1943	JS344
Typhoon IB	Jan 1943 – Aug 1945	JP505 (ZY-R)
Tempest II	Aug 1945 – May 1946	MW396 (ZY-T)
Vampire F.1	Mar 1946 – Feb 1949	VF280 (ZY-Y)
Vampire F.3	Oct 1948 – Dec 1949	VF344 (ZY-S)
Vampire FB.5	Dec 1949 – May 1951	VV657 (A)
Meteor F.8	May 1951 – Jun 1955	WH638 (J)
Hunter F.1	Jun 1955 – Jul 1955	WW638 (J)
Hunter F.4	Jul 1955 – Mar 1957	XF320 (R)
Hunter F.6	Mar 1957 – Dec 1957	XF442 (Z)
Bloodhound	Jul 1960 – Dec 1963	–

Blenheim IF, No.248 Squadron

No. 248 Squadron

Badge: A demi-sword in bend partly withdrawn from the scabbard
Motto: Il faut en finir (It is necessary to make an end of it)

No.248 Squadron was formed in August 1918 from the seaplane station at Hornsea Mere and flew coastal patrols off the Yorkshire coast until the end of the war. It was disbanded on 6 March 1919.

On 30 October 1939, No.248 reformed at Hendon with an establishment of eighteen Blenheim Ifs for night defence duties and received its first operational aircraft early in December. Lacking any form of radar, its initial night flying was ineffective and at the end of February 1940 it was transferred to Coastal Command equipped with seven Blenheim IVfs, moving to North Coates and later to Thorney Island and Gosport where it acquired its full number of Blenheims. On 22 May the squadron returned to Fighter Command on its movement to Dyce, a detachment being based at Montrose to extend the coverage of its patrols over the coastal waters of eastern Scotland. On 20 June it was once more transferred to Coastal for reconnaissance flights off the Norwegian coast and attacks on enemy shipping from the Shetlands where it had moved at the end of July. In January 1941 it moved further south to Dyce and flew escort patrols over coastal convoys and reconnaissance missions, using Wick as a detached base. In June 1941 No.248 moved to Bircham Newton to re-equip with Beaufighters and began operations with these on 14 August. Apart from protecting coastal convoys, the Beaufighters were also used for attacks on enemy shipping off the Dutch coast and from September to December a detachment covered the western approaches to the Channel from Cornwall. In February 1942 the squadron returned to Scotland for long-range fighter patrols over the North Sea and at the end of July sixteen of the squadron's aircraft left on the first stage of a flight to Malta all arriving safely by 10 August. After escorting a vital relief convoy to Malta and attacking enemy airfields in Sicily the aircrews returned to the UK leaving their aircraft in Malta, and rejoined the ground echelon at Talbenny which was used as a base for fighter patrols over the Bay of Biscay in support of Coastal's anti-submarine aircraft. In addition, escorts were provided for strike aircraft attacking enemy shipping off the French coast and in December 1943 conversion to Mosquitos began, these being used for fighter-reconnaissance missions. With the elimination of German shipping from the area, No.248 moved to Banff for anti-shipping operations as part of a strike wing for the rest of the war. After flying its last operation on 4 May 1945 the squadron moved to Chivenor in July and was renumbered 36 Squadron on 30 September 1946.

Blenheim IVF, No.248 Squadron

Squadron bases

Hornsea Mere	Aug 1918 to 6 Mar 1919	Sumburgh	30 May 1942
Hendon	30 Oct 1939	Takali	3 Aug 1942 (A)
North Coates	26 Feb 1940	Dyce	5 Aug 1942 (G)
Thorney Island	8 Apr 1940	Talbenny	13 Sep 1942 (R)
Gosport	16 Apr 1940	Pembrey	2 Nov 1942
Dyce	22 May 1940	Talbenny	4 Dec 1942
Sumburgh	31 Jul 1940 (G)	Predannack	18 Jan 1943
	20 Jul 1940 (A)	Portreath	16 Feb 1944
Dyce	6 Jan 1941	Banff	10 Sep 1944
Bircham Newton	21 Jun 1941	Chivenor	19 Jul 1945
Dyce	17 Feb 1942	Thorney Island	31 May 1946 to 30 Sep 1946

Aircraft

Equipment	Period of service	Representative Serial	
Short 184	Aug 1918 – Mar 1919		
Sopwith Baby	Aug 1918 – Nov 1918		
Blenheim If	Dec 1939 – Feb 1940	L1212	
Blenheim IVf	Feb 1940 – Jul 1941	T2131	(WR-P)
Beaufighter Ic	Jul 1941 – Feb 1942	T4774	(WR-M)
Beaufighter VIc	Feb 1942 – Jun 1943	JM331	(WR-X)
Beaufighter X	Jun 1943 – Jan 1944	JM334	
Mosquito VI	Dec 1943 – Sep 1946	LR377	(WR-B)
Mosquito XVIII	Jan 1944 – Feb 1945	MM425	(L)

No. 249 Squadron

Badge: In front of a bezant an elephant passant
Motto: Pugnis et cacibus (With fists and heels)
Name: 'Gold Coast'

No.249 Squadron was formed in August 1918 from the seaplane station at Dundee for coastal patrol duties. A substation was set up at Strathbeg in September and Short 184 seaplanes were flown for the rest of the war, the squadron disbanding on 8 October 1919.

On 16 May 1940, No.249 reformed as a fighter squadron at Church Fenton, initially with Spitfires but after a few weeks re-equipped with Hurricanes. Becoming operational on 3 July, it flew defensive patrols and moved south in August to take part in the Battle of Britain. Offensive missions over France began in December 1940 but in May 1941 No.249 was transferred to Malta by aircraft carrier. There it formed part of the fighter defences, converting to Spitfires in February 1942. Fighter-bomber missions over Sicily began in November 1942 and in October 1943 the squadron moved to Italy. Sweeps were carried out over Albania and Yugoslavia and in September 1944, No.249 converted to Mustangs. In April 1945, it moved to Northern Yugoslavia for a month and after a short period in northern Italy the squadron disbanded on 16 August 1945.

On 23 October 1945, No.500 Squadron at Eastleigh, Kenya, was renumbered 249 Squadron and flew Baltimores for a short time before re-equipping with Mosquitos in February 1946. After taking part in survey flights, No.249 moved to Iraq in June 1946 and became a Tempest fighter squadron. Vampires were received in 1950 and after a period

in Egypt the squadron moved to Jordan and converted to Venoms. In January 1957 it moved to Cyprus and re-equipped with Canberras in September 1957. After twelve years in the area, No.249 disbanded on 24 February 1969.

Squadron bases

Dundee	Aug 1918 to 8 Oct 1919	Canne	15 Jul 1944
		Biferno	Oct 1944
Church Fenton	16 May 1940	Prkos	17 Apr 1945
Leconfield	18 May 1940	Biferno	15 May 1945
Church Fenton	8 July 1940	Brindisi	27 Jun 1945 to 16 Aug 1945
Boscombe Down	14 Aug 1940		
North Weald	1 Sep 1940	Eastleigh	23 Oct 1945
Takali	21 May 1941	Habbaniya	Jun 1946
Qrendi	23 Nov 1942	Deversoir	1 Apr 1949
Hal Far	24 Sep 1943	Amman	1 Jun 1954
Grottaglie	27 Oct 1943	Akrotiri	21 Jan 1957
Brindisi	10 Nov 1943	El Adem	11 Mar 1957
Grottaglie	10 Dec 1943	Akrotiri	15 Oct 1957 to 24 Feb 1969

Aircraft

Equipment	Period of service	Representative Serial	
Short 184	Aug 1918 – Oct 1919	N2794	
Sopwith Baby	Aug 1918 – Sep 1918		
Spitfire I	May 1940 – Jun 1940	K9890	
Hurricane I	Jun 1940 – Feb 1941 May 1941 – Aug 1941	L1832	
Hurricane IIA, IIB	Feb 1941 – Mar 1942		
Spitfire VB, VC	Feb 1942 – Sep 1944	EF608	(GN-B)
Spitfire IX	Jun 1943 – Nov 1943 Apr 1945 – Jun 1945	PT681	(GN-A)
Mustang III	Sep 1944 – Apr 1945 May 1945 – Jun 1945	FB308	
Mustang IV	Jun 1945 – Aug 1945	KM231	
Baltimore IV, V	Oct 1945 – Mar 1946	FW848	
Mosquito FB.26	Mar 1946 – Dec 1946	KA248	
Tempest F.5, F.6	Dec 1946 – Mar 1950	NX200	(GN-F)
Vampire FB.5	Feb 1950 – May 1952	VZ304	(X)
Vampire FB.9	May 1952 – Apr 1954	WR122	(H)
Venom FB.1	Apr 1954 – Nov 1955	WE459	
Venom FB.4	Nov 1955 – Oct 1957	WR531	(R)
Canberra B.2	Sep 1957 – Jan 1960	WK113	
Canberra B.6	Nov 1959 – Oct 1961	WT374	
Canberra B.16	Oct 1961 – Feb 1969	WJ774	

Kittyhawk III, No.250 Squadron

No. 250 Squadron

Badge: A river eagle, standing on a rock
Motto: Close to the sun
Name: 'Sudan'

No.250 was formed in August 1918 at Padstow for coastal reconnaissance duties over the Bristol Channel and its approaches. Equipped with a mixture of D.H.6s and D.H.9s it flew anti-submarine patrols until the Armistice and disbanded on 15 May 1919.

On 1 April 1941 No.250 reformed at Aqir from K Flight and by the end of the month had received enough Tomahawks to become operational on defensive duties in Palestine. In May, a detachment began offensive sweeps over Syria and in June began operations in the Western Desert being withdrawn in February 1942 to defensive duties. After converting to Kittyhawks, it returned to the desert in April as a fighter-bomber unit and provided support for the 8th Army, advancing with it through Libya into Tunisia to end the North African campaign. In July 1943, the squadron flew to Malta to support the landings in Sicily, moving there a few days afterwards. By mid-September, it had occupied airfields in Italy where it spent the rest of the war flying fighter-bomber missions. In August 1945, No.260 Squadron disbanded and transferred its Mustangs to No.250 which flew them until disbanded on 2 January 1947.

Squadron bases

Padstow	Aug 1918	Amriya (D)	11 May 1941
	to 15 May 1919		to 25 May 1941
Aqir	1 Apr 1941	Ikingi Maryut	26 May 1941

Sedadah	17 Jan 1943	Sidi Haneish South	
Bir Dufan Main	19 Jan 1943		13 Jun 1941
Castel Benito	24 Jan 1943	LG.109	8 Nov 1941
El Assa	15 Feb 1943	LG.123	19 Nov 1941
Nefatia Main	8 Mar 1943	LG.122	2 Dec 1941
Medenine Main	21 Mar 1943	LG.123	5 Dec 1941
El Hamma	3 Apr 1943	Tobruk	11 Dec 1941
El Djem	14 Apr 1943	Gazala 3	19 Dec 1941
Kairouan	18 Apr 1943	Msus	27 Dec 1941
Zuara	21 May 1943	Antelat	12 Jan 1942
Hal Far	9 Jul 1943	Msus	21 Jan 1942
Luqa	13 Jul 1943	Mechili	24 Jan 1942
Pachino	18 Jul 1943	Gazala 1	28 Jan 1942
Agnone	5 Aug 1943	Gamil	2 Feb 1942
Grottaglie	16 Sep 1943	LG.12	15 Apr 1942
Bari-Palese	23 Sep 1943	Gambut 1	23 Apr 1942
Foggia Main	3 Oct 1943	Gambut 2	12 Jun 1942
Foggia/Mileni	26 Oct 1943	Sidi Azeiz	17 Jun 1942
Cutella	30 Dec 1943	LG.75	18 Jun 1942
San Angelo	24 May 1944	LG.102	23 Jun 1942
Guidonia	13 Jun 1944	LG.106	27 Jun 1942
Falerium	23 Jun 1944	LG.91	29 Jun 1942
Crete	9 Jul 1944	LG.106	6 Nov 1942
Iesi	26 Aug 1944	LG.101	9 Nov 1942
Fano	18 Nov 1944	LG.76	11 Nov 1942
Cervia	25 Feb 1945	Gambut 1	13 Nov 1942
Lavariano	18 May 1945	Gambut 2	15 Nov 1942
Tissano	22 Jan 1946	Martuba 4	19 Nov 1942
Treviso	23 Sep 1946	Belandah 1	8 Dec 1942
Lavariano	19 Nov 1946	Marble Arch	18 Dec 1942
Treviso	25 Nov 1946	El Chel 2	1 Jan 1943
	to 2 Jan 1947	Hamraiet 3	11 Jan 1943

Aircraft

Equipment	Period of service	Representative Serial
D.H.6	Aug 1918 – May 1919	C5206
D.H.9	Aug 1918 – May 1919	D2963
Tomahawk IIA	Apr 1941 – Apr 1942	AK498 (LD-C)
Hurricane I	Feb 1942 – Apr 1942	V7822
Hurricane IIB	Feb 1942 – Apr 1942	Z3590
Kittyhawk I, II	Apr 1942 – Oct 1942	AL116 (LD-V)
Kittyhawk III	Oct 1942 – Jan 1944	FL904 (LD-C)
Kittyhawk IV	Jan 1944 – Aug 1945	FX616 (LD-S)
Mustang III, IV	Aug 1945 – Jan 1947	FB334

No. 251 Squadron

Badge: A weathercock
Motto: However wind blows

No.251 Squadron was formed in August, 1918 from the former Royal Naval Air Station at Hornsea, Yorkshire. Nos.504, 505 and 506 Flights operated from Atwick, Greenland Top and Owthorne with D.H.6s and carried out coastal anti-submarine patrols for the remainder of the war, being disbanded on 30 June 1919.

On 1 August 1944 No.1407 Flight at Reykjavik was renumbered 251 Squadron for air-sea rescue duties and meteorological flights around Iceland. Its Hudsons included two fitted with airborne lifeboats while a few Ansons were used for local communications flying. In March 1945 conversion to Fortresses began but the Hudsons were not replaced till August when Warwicks were received to supplement the Fortresses. The squadron continued to operate from Iceland until disbanded on 30 October 1945.

Squadron bases

Hornsea	Aug 1918
	to 30 Jun 1919
Reykjavik	1 Aug 1944
	to 30 Oct 1945

Aircraft Equipment	Period of service	Representative Serial
D.H.6	Aug 1918 – Jun 1919	F3393
Hudson III, IIIA	Aug 1944 – Aug 1945	FK743 (AD-L)
Fortress II, IIA	Mar 1945 – Oct 1945	FK210 (AD-W)
Warwick I	Aug 1945 – Oct 1945	HG174
Ventura I	Aug 1944 – Oct 1944	AE720
Anson I	Aug 1944 – Oct·1945	LT199

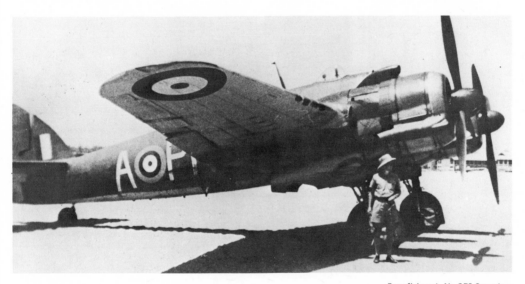

Beaufighter I, No.252 Squadron

No. 252 Squadron

Badge: A Spartan Shield
Motto: With or on

No.252 Squadron was formed in August 1918 from the former RNAS station at Tynemouth and operated three flights of D.H.6s on coastal reconnaissance duties until the end of the war. On 30 Jun 1919 the squadron disbanded.

On 21 November 1940 No.252 reformed at Bircham Newton as the first Coastal Command Beaufighter squadron, receiving its first operational aircraft in December though part of the squadron strength remained Blenheims till April 1941, fully-equipped Coastal Beaufighters having begun to arrive in March. In April, it moved to Northern Ireland for convoy patrols and on 1 May despatched fifteen of its aircraft to Gibraltar en route for hard-pressed Malta. Training and patrols continued from Ulster until all remaining aircraft were passed to 143 Squadron on 15 Jun 1941, leaving the Mediterranean detachment to become the whole squadron. Attacks on enemy shipping and coastal targets in the Eastern Mediterranean from bases in Egypt were carried out in concert with 272 Squadron, under whose wing No.252 operated until becoming independent again on 14 November 1941. After the capture of Libyan airfields early in 1943, the squadron flew anti-shipping sweeps over the waters around Greece and Crete and in February 1945, moved to Greece where, in addition to sweeps over the Aegean and air-sea rescue duties, it supported ground troops against Communist forces attempting to seize the country after the German withdrawal. After their defeat, No.252 remained in Greece until disbanded on 1 December 1946.

Squadron bases

Tynemouth and		Berka III	13 Jan 1943
Seaton Carew (D)	Aug 1918	Magrun	22 Feb 1943
	to 30 Jun 1919	Berka III	5 Aug 1943
Bircham Newton	21 Nov 1940	Lakatamia	23 Sep 1943
Chivenor	1 Dec 1940	LG.91	13 Dec 1943
Aldergrove	3 Apr 1941	Mersa Matruh West	
	to 15 Jun 1941		21 Jan 1944
Luqa (D)	2 May 1941	Gambut	20 Jul 1944
	to 21 May 1941	Mersa Matruh	30 Nov 1944
Heraklion (D)	16 May 1941	Aboukir	6 Feb 1945
	to May 1941	Gianaclis	10 Feb 1945
Abu Sueir (D)	21 May 1941	Hassani	18 Feb 1945
	to 18 Jun 1941	Araxos	28 Aug 1945
Idku	18 Jun 1941		to 1 Dec 1946

Aircraft

Equipment	Period of service	Representative Serial
D.H.6	Aug 1918 – Jun 1919	B3075
Blenheim I	Dec 1940 – Mar 1941	L1279
Blenheim IV	Dec 1940 – Apr 1941	V5741
Beaufighter I	Dec 1940 – Dec 1942	T4665 (PN-D)
Beaufighter VI	Nov 1942 – Jan 1944	EL475 (PN-B)
Beaufighter X	Jan 1944 – Dec 1946	NE319 (J)

Hurricane IIBs, No.253 Squadron

No. 253 Squadron

Badge: The back of a dexter arm embowed fessewise in mogul armour, the head holding an Indian battle axe in bend
Motto: Come one, come all
Name: 'Hyderabad State'

No.253 Squadron was formed in August 1918 at Bembridge, Isle of Wight as a coastal patrol unit. Two flights of seaplanes operated from Bembridge Harbour while two more flights flew from a nearby airfield at Foreland with D.H.6s. After flying anti-submarine patrols until the Armistice, the squadron disbanded on 5 May 1919.

On 30 October 1939, No.253 Squadron reformed at Manston and was originally intended as a shipping protection unit with Blenheims. None were delivered, however, and the squadron began to receive Hurricanes in February 1940 becoming operational on 3 April. In May 1940 one flight was sent to France to reinforce the hard-pressed Hurricane squadrons while the second flight flew daily to French airfields from 17 to 23 May. After re-equipping in Lincolnshire, No.253 took part in the Battle of Britain from the end of August and remained in southern England until January 1941. In February, the squadron moved to

the Orkneys for air defence duties, returning to England in September for convoy patrols off the East Coast. After taking part in the Dieppe raid, No.253 became non-operational in preparation for the invasion of North Africa and arrived in Algeria a few days after the landings. It provided air cover for the army and its supply lines during the Tunisian campaign and after, moving to Italy in October 1943. In February 1944, the squadron arrived in Corsica to undertake escort and anti-shipping missions, returning to Italy in April for similar duties over Yugoslavia. In April 1945, it moved to an airfield captured by Yugoslav partisans near Zadar for the last days of the war. After a period in northern Italy and Austria, the squadron acquired a flight of Spitfire XIs from No.225 Squadron and disbanded on 16 May 1947.

On 18 April 1955, No.253 reformed at Waterbeach as a night fighter squadron with Venoms which it flew until disbanded on 1 September 1957.

Squadron bases

Bembridge and Foreland		Leconfield	3 Jan 1941
	Aug 1918 to 5 May 1919	Skeabrae	10 Feb 1941
Manston	30 Oct 1939	Hibaldstow	21 Sep 1941
Northolt	14 Feb 1940	Friston	14 Jun 1942
Kenley	8 May 1940	Hibaldstow	7 Jul 1942
Kirton-in-Lindsey		Friston (D)	16 Aug 1942
	24 May 1940		to 20 Aug 1942
Turnhouse	21 Jul 1940	Left for N. Africa	Oct 1942
Prestwick	23 Aug 1940	Maison Blanche	13 Nov 1942
Kenley	29 Aug 1940 (A)	Philippeville	21 Nov 1942
	16 Sep 1940 (G)	Setif	1 Jan 1943

Jemappes	15 Feb 1943	Brindisi (D)	6 Sep 1944			
Maison Blanche	13 Mar 1943		to 3 Nov 1944			
Jemappes	Apr 1943	Prkos	5 Apr 1945			
Lampedusa	20 Jun 1943 (G)	Brindisi	16 May 1945			
	23 Jun 1943 (A)	Treviso	27 Jun 1945			
La Sebala I	8 Aug 1943	Zeltweg	23 Sep 1946			
Montecorvino	17 Oct 1943	Treviso	19 Jan 1947			
Capodichino	28 Nov 1943		to 16 May 1947			
Borgo	24 Feb 1944	Waterbeach	18 Apr 1955			
Foggia	30 Apr 1944		to 1 Sep 1957			
Canne	1 Jul 1944					

Aircraft Equipment	Period of service	Representative Serial	
Short 184, 320	Aug 1918 – May 1919	N1613	
D.H.6	Aug 1918 – May 1919		
Battle	Dec 1939 – May 1940	N2252	
Hurricane I	Feb 1940 – Aug 1941	L1982	(SW-B)
Hurricane IIA, IIB	Jul 1941 – Sep 1942	Z3151	
Hurricane IIC	Jan 1942 – Sep 1943	Z3971	(SW-S)
Spitfire VC	Mar 1943 Aug 1943 – Nov 1944	JK868	(SW-K)
Spitfire IX	Sep 1943 – Jun 1944 Nov 1944 – May 1947	PT655	(SW-W)
Spitfire VIII	Nov 1944 – May 1947	JF899	(SW-K)
Spitfire XI	Mar 1947 – May 1947		
Venom NF.2A	Apr 1955 – Sep 1957	WR808	(H)

Beaufighter X, No.254 Squadron

No. 254 Squadron

Badge: A raven, wings endorsed and inverted
Motto: Fljuga vakta ok ljosta (Norse)
(To fly, to watch and to strike)

No.254 Squadron was formed in August 1918 from the coastal reconnaissance station at Prawle Point and flew anti-submarine patrols until the end of the war, disbanding on 22 February 1919.

On 30 October 1939 No.254 reformed at Stradishall as a shipping protection squadron. Equipped with Blenheims, it began convoy patrols over coastal shipping off the East Coast on 29 January 1940. In April 1940, it began reconnaissance missions in addition to its defensive tasks and later provided fighter escorts for anti-shipping raids. In May 1941, the squadron moved to Northern Ireland, returning to Scotland in December where it converted to Beaufighters in June 1942. Torpedo training began in August and in November No.254 joined the strike wing at North Coates for attacks on enemy convoys off the Dutch coast, the first strike taking place on 20 November. It remained at North Coates for the rest of the war and in January 1946, received

a Buckmaster for conversion training in preparation for the arrival of Brigands. These were not taken into service by Coastal Command strike squadrons and No.254 retained Beaufighters until renumbered 42 Squadron on 1 October 1946.

On 1 December 1959, the squadron reformed at Melton Mowbray as a Thor strategic missile unit, disbanding on 23 August 1963.

Squadron bases			
Prawle Point	Aug 1918 to 22 Feb 1919	Dyce	10 Dec 1941
		Carew Cheriton	11 Feb 1942
Stradishall	30 Oct 1939	Dyce	1 Jun 1942
Sutton Bridge	9 Dec 1939	Docking	10 Oct 1942
Bircham Newton	28 Jan 1940	North Coates	7 Nov 1942
Hatston	23 Apr 1940	Chivenor	29 Jun 1945
Sumburgh	16 May 1940	Langham	26 Nov 1945
Dyce	Jul 1940	Thorney Island	6 May 1946 to 1 Oct 1946
Sumburgh	7 Jan 1941		
Aldergrove	29 May 1941	Melton Mowbray	1 Dec 1959 to 23 Aug 1963

Aircraft Equipment	Period of service	Representative Serial	
D.H.6	Aug 1918 – Feb 1919	C5203	
D.H.9	Aug 1918 – Feb 1919	B7666	
Blenheim If	Nov 1939 – Mar 1940	K7065	
Blenheim IV	Mar 1940 – Jul 1942	T1941	(QM-U)
Beaufighter VI	Jun 1942 – Oct 1943	EL290	
Beaufighter X	Oct 1943 – Oct 1946	RD467	(QM-J)
Mosquito XVIII	Apr 1945 – May 1945	PZ300	
Thor	Dec 1959 – Aug 1963	–	

253

No. 255 Squadron

Badge: A panther's face
Motto: Ad auroram
(To the break of dawn)

No.255 Squadron was formed in August 1918 at Pembroke for anti-submarine patrols over St. George's Channel and the approaches to the Bristol Channel. The squadron was disbanded on 14 January 1919.

On 23 November 1940, No.255 reformed at Kirton-in-Lindsey as a night fighter squadron with Defiants. It became operational on 5 January 1941, and received some Hurricanes in March. Conversion to Beaufighters began in July 1941 and the squadron was based for the defence of the Midlands until it left for North Africa in November 1942. During the Tunisian campaign, it provided night defence for Allied bases in Algeria and in August 1943, moved to Sicily. In November, No.255 arrived in Italy and began intruder missions over the Balkans. In January 1945, conversion to Mosquitos began and in September the squadron moved to Malta and thence to Egypt in January 1946. There it disbanded on 30 April 1946.

Squadron bases

Pembroke	Aug 1918	Setif	15 Feb 1943
	to 14 Jan 1919	La Sebala 2	21 May 1943
Kirton-in-Lindsey		Borizzo	17 Aug 1943
	23 Nov 1940	Grottaglie	13 Nov 1943 (A)
Hibaldstow	15 May 1941		21 Nov 1943 (G)
Coltishall	20 Sep 1941	Foggia Main	24 Jan 1944
High Ercall	2 Mar 1942	Rosignano	8 Feb 1945
Honiley	6 Jun 1942	Hal Far	4 Sep 1945 (A)
Left for N. Africa			11 Sep 1945 (G)
	13 Nov 1942	Gianaclis	Jan 1946 (P)
Maison Blanche	15 Nov 1942		to 30 Apr 1946

Aircraft

Equipment	Period of service	Representative Serial
D.H.6	Aug 1918 – Jan 1919	C9415
Defiant I	Nov 1940 – Sep 1941	N3312 (YD-T)
Hurricane I	Mar 1941 – Jul 1941	V7304
Beaufighter II	Jul 1941 – May 1942	R2460 (YD-J)
Beaufighter VI	Mar 1942 – Feb 1945	X8002 (YD-G)
Mosquito XIX	Jan 1945 – Apr 1946	TA408/G (YD-D)
Mosquito NF.30	Jan 1946 – Apr 1946	NT246

Defiant I, No.256 Squadron

No. 256 Squadron

Badge: In front of an anchor, a ferret's head erased
Motto: Addimus vim viribus
(Strength to strength)

No.256 Squadron was formed in August, 1918 at Sea Houses for coastal patrols off the coast of north-east England, being a coastal station already in operation at that time. After the end of the war, the squadron disbanded on 30 June 1919.

On 23 November 1940 No.256 reformed at Catterick as a night fighter squadron with Defiants and became operational over south-west England early in February 1941. In March it moved north to defend Merseyside and in July acquired some Hurricanes. Beaufighters began to arrive in May 1942, and were flown until the squadron was transferred to southern England in April 1943 and converted to Mosquitos. In July 1943, a detachment was sent to Malta to help cover the Allied landings in Sicily and in October the whole squadron moved there. In April 1944 it moved to Algeria where it absorbed the Spitfires of the Gibraltar Defence Flight on 6 May and in August moved to Sardinia, followed a month later by a further move to Italy. Intruder flights over the Balkans began and continued until the end of the war. In September 1945 No.256 moved to Egypt and in addition to its night fighter role also operated a flight of meteorological Mosquitos from April 1946. After moving to Cyprus in July 1946 the squadron disbanded on 12 September 1946.

On 27 November 1952, No.256 reformed at Ahlhorn with Meteor night fighters as part of No.125 Wing for air defence duties in Germany. On 21 January 1959, it was renumbered 11 Squadron.

Squadron bases		Luqa (D)	2 Jul 1943
Sea Houses	Aug 1918	Woodvale	25 Aug 1943
	to 30 Jun 1919	Luqa	14 Oct 1943 (M)
Catterick	23 Nov 1940	La Senia	7 Apr 1944
Pembrey	3 Jan 1941	Reghaia (D)	6 May 1944
Colerne	6 Feb 1941		to 3 Aug 1944
Squires Gate	26 Mar 1941	Alghero (D)	1 Jul 1944
Woodvale	1 Jun 1942		to 15 Aug 1944
Ford	24 Apr 1943	Alghero	15 Aug 1944
		Foggia	22 Sep 1944
		Forli	25 Feb 1945
		Aviano	3 Jun 1945
		El Ballah	12 Sep 1945
		Deversoir	15 Dec 1945
		Nicosia	13 Jul 1946
			to 12 Sep 1946
		Ahlhorn	17 Nov 1952
		Geilenkirchen	12 Feb 1958
			to 21 Jan 1959

Aircraft Equipment	Period of service	Representative Serial
D.H.6	Aug 1918 – Jun 1919	C5173
Defiant I, II	Nov 1940 – May 1942	N3445 (JT-F)
Hurricane I, IIB,	Jul 1941 – May 1942	V7010 (JT-C)
Beaufighter I	May 1942 – Jan 1943	X7845 (JT-G)
Beaufighter VI	Jun 1942 – May 1942	V8501 (JT-R)
Mosquito XII	May 1943 – Sep 1945	HK124 (JT-T)
Mosquito XIII	Feb 1944 – Sep 1945	MM583 (JT-D)
Spitfire VIII, IX	May 1944 – Aug 1944	EN135 (JT-B)
Mosquito IX	Mar 1945 – Aug 1945	LR461
Mosquito VI	Apr 1945 – Oct 1945	RF680 (S)
Mosquito XIX	Sep 1945 – Sep 1946	TA426
Meteor NF.11	Nov 1952 – Jan 1959	WD642 (A)

Hunter F.2s, No.257 Squadron

No. 257 Squadron

Badge: A cinthe sejeant
Motto: Thay myay gyee shin shwe hti (Burmese) (Death or glory)
Name: 'Burma'

No.257 Squadron was formed at Dundee in August 1918, from the former seaplane station built there by the RNAS. It flew anti-submarine patrols off the east coast of Scotland until the end of the war and disbanded on 30 June 1919.

On 17 May 1940 No.257 reformed at Hendon as a fighter squadron. Initially it flew Spitfires but during June exchanged these for Hurricanes, becoming operational on 1 July. The squadron was based in south-east England throughout the Battle of Britain and in March 1941 began taking part in sweeps over France. Night fighter patrols were also flown and in July 1942, No.257 converted to Typhoons which began low-level patrols in September to intercept enemy fighter-bomber raids. Escort missions were also flown and in July 1943, it began offensive operations. The squadron started fighter-bombing sorties in January 1944, and as part of Second TAF moved to France in July to provide air support for the Allied armies. By October, it was based in Belgium for attacks on enemy transport and battlefield targets. On 3 March 1945 No.257 flew its last mission and disbanded on 5 March 1945.

On 1 September 1946, No.257 reformed at Church Fenton as a fighter squadron. Equipped with Meteors, it flew this type until January 1955. Hunters began to arrive in September 1954, the squadron being the first to fly the Sapphire-engined variant. On 29 March 1957 No.257 was disbanded.

On 1 July 1960, the squadron reformed at Warboys as an air defence missile unit, disbanding on 31 December 1963.

Squadron bases		
Dundee	Aug 1918 to 30 Jun 1919	
Hendon	17 May 1940	
Northolt	4 Jul 1940	
Debden	15 Aug 1940	
Martlesham Heath	5 Sep 1940	
North Weald	8 Oct 1940	
Martlesham Heath	7 Nov 1940	
Coltishall	17 Dec 1940	
Honiley	7 Nov 1941	
High Ercall	6 Jun 1942	
Exeter	21 Sep 1942	
Warmwell	8 Jan 1943	
Gravesend	12 Aug 1943	
Warmwell	17 Sep 1943	
Beaulieu	20 Jan 1944	
Tangmere	31 Jan 1944	
Need's Oar Point	10 Apr 1944	
Hurn	2 Jul 1944	
B.3 St. Croix	15 Jul 1944 (A)	
	10 Jul 1944 (G)	
Fairwood Common	11 Aug 1944	
B.3 St. Croix	30 Aug 1944	
B.23 Morainville	6 Sep 1944	
B.51 Lille/Seclin	11 Sep 1944	
B.70 Deurne	2 Oct 1944	
B.89 Mill	8 Feb 1945 to 5 Mar 1945	
Church Fenton	1 Sep 1946	
Horsham St. Faith	15 Apr 1947	
Wattisham	27 Oct 1950 to 29 Mar 1957	
Warboys	1 Jul 1960 to 31 Dec 1963	

Aircraft Equipment	Period of service	Representative Serial
F.2a	Aug 1918 – Jun 1919	N4432
Spitfire I	May 1940 – Jun 1940	P9544
Hurricane I	Jun 1940 – Jul 1941 / Jan 1941 – Jul 1942	V7137 (DT-G)
Hurricane IIA, IIB	May 1941 – Sep 1942	BD729
Hurricane IIC	Apr 1941 – Aug 1941 / Jan 1942 – Sep 1942	Z3088
Spitfire VB	Apr 1942 – May 1942	AB363
Typhoon Ia, Ib	Jul 1942 – Mar 1945	MN598 (FM-P)
Meteor F.3	Sep 1946 – Mar 1948	EE352 (A6-G)
Meteor F.4	Mar 1948 – Oct 1950	VW266 (A6-H)
Meteor F.8	Oct 1950 – Sep 1954	WK943 (N)
Hunter F.2	Sep 1954 – Mar 1957	WN947 (W)
Hunter F.5	Jul 1955 – Mar 1957	WP119 (Q)
Bloodhound I	Jul 1960 – Dec 1963	–

No. 258 Squadron

Badge: In front of wings elevated and conjoined in base, a panther's face

Motto: In medias res (Into the middle of things)

No.258 Squadron was formed in August 1918 at Luce Bay, being the aeroplane unit of the former RNAS airship station at Luce Bay. For the rest of the war, it flew D.H.6s on anti-submarine patrols over the Irish Sea and Firth of Clyde and disbanded on 5 March 1919.

On 20 November 1940, No.258 reformed at Leconfield as a fighter squadron, taking over No.263 Squadron's Hurricanes at Drem on 5 December as its initial equipment. It began flying defensive patrols on 6 January 1941 and moved later in the month to the Isle of Man. The squadron came south in April to fly sweeps over France for a few weeks in May and June, the rest of the time being taken up by patrols over coastal shipping. In October it became non-operational in preparation for a move to the Middle East, the aircrew departing at the end of the month. The outbreak of war in the Far East resulted in No.258 being diverted to Singapore but after only ten days of operations it was withdrawn to less exposed airfields in Sumatra. Following Japanese landings near its airfields, the squadron was evacuated to Java and handed its surviving aircraft over to No.605 Squadron, its remaining personnel leaving for Australia on 23 February 1942.

On 30 March 1942, G Squadron based at Colombo Racecourse was numbered 258 Squadron and its Hurricanes were soon in action during the Japanese carrier strike on Colombo early in April. No further raids took place and in January 1943 the squadron moved to Calcutta and for ten days supplied a detachment for ground-attack sweeps over Burma before returning to Ceylon. In August 1943 it returned to the Burma front and began operations on 1 September. Sweeps and escort missions occupied the squadron until May 1944, when it was withdrawn to re-equip with Thunderbolts. These it took into action for the first time on 7 December and flew ground-attack and escort missions until Jun 1945. It then began training for the invasion of Malaya but the Japanese surrender forestalled this operation and the squadron was disbanded on 31 December 1945.

Squadron bases		
Luce Bay	Aug 1918 to 5 Mar 1919	
Leconfield	20 Nov 1940	
Duxford	30 Nov 1940	
Drem	3 Dec 1940	
Acklington	14 Dec 1940	
Jurby	23 Jan 1941 (G) 1 Feb 1941 (A)	
Valley and Penrhos	18 Apr 1941	
Kenley	21 Apr 1941	
Martlesham Heath	10 Jun 1941	
Debden	3 Oct 1941	
Left for Middle East	30 Oct 1941 (A)	
Seletar	13 Jan 1942 (G)	
Seletar & Kallang	29 Jan 1942 (A)	
Palembang	10 Feb 1942 (A)	
Kemajoran	14 Feb 1942 (A)	
Evacuated	23 Feb 1942	
Colombo Racecourse	30 Mar 1942	
Dum Dum	11 Jan 1943 (A)	
Dambulla	17 Feb 1943 (A)	
Comilla	13 Aug 1843 (G)	
Dohazari	4 Nov 1943	
Chittagong	13 Dec 1943	
Hay	25 Jan 1944	
Hove	30 Jan 1944	
Reindeer	25 Feb 1944	
Arkonam	3 Jun 1944	
Yelahanka	14 Aug 1944	
Arkonam	8 Oct 1944	
Ratnap	26 Nov 1944	
Kyaukpyu	1 May 1945	
Ulunderpet	8 Jun 1945	
Bobbili	21 Aug 1945	
Baigachi	7 Sep 1945	
Zayatkwin	11 Sep 1945	
Kuala Lumpur	25 Sep 1945 to 31 Dec 1945	

Aircraft Equipment	Period of service	Representative Serial
D.H.6	Aug 1918 – Mar 1919	C9452
Hurricane I	Dec 1940 – Apr 1941 / Mar 1942 – Apr 1942	N2493
Hurricane IIA	Apr 1941 – Feb 1942	Z2589
Hurricane IIB	Mar 1942 – Nov 1943	BD701
Hurricane IIC	Nov 1943 – Aug 1944	HV412
Thunderbolt I	Sep 1944 – Jan 1945	HB984 (ZT-S)
Thunderbolt II	Nov 1944 – Dec 1945	KJ366 (ZT-X)

No. 259 Squadron

Badge: On a terrestrial globe an eagle's head erased, facing to the sinister

Motto: Haya ingia napigane (Swahili) (Get in a fight)

No.259 Squadron was formed in August 1918 at Felixstowe when squadron numbers were allotted to sections of the former RNAS stations. It flew flying boats on anti-submarine and reconnaissance sweeps over the North Sea until the Armistice in November 1918, and was disbanded on 13 September 1919.

On 16 February 1943, No.259 reformed at Kipevu in Kenya with Catalinas for anti-submarine patrols over the Indian Ocean. In March 1943, a detachment was sent to Congella, Natal and in June another went to Langebaan in Cape Province until No.262 Squadron was able to take over

256

the area. In May 1943, the bulk of the squadron moved to Congella leaving the squadron headquarters at Kipevu but in September these came together again on a further move to Dar-es-Salaam, Tanganyika, where a flying boat base was established at Kurasini Creek. Some of No.259's boats flew from Masirah and Aden to increase the extent of their patrol area while Tulear in southern Madagascar was also used. On 9 March 1945, the first Sunderland arrived to convert the squadron to this type but a month later these were taken away and No.259 disbanded on 30 April 1945.

Squadron bases

Felixstowe	Aug 1918	
	to 13 Sep 1919	
Kipevu	16 Feb 1943	
Dar-es-Salaam	14 Sep 1943	
	to 30 Mar 1945	

Aircraft

Equipment	Period of service	Representative Serial
F.2a	Aug 1918 – Sep 1919	4543
Catalina Ib	Feb 1943 – Apr 1945	FP281 (G)
Sunderland V	Mar 1945 – Apr 1945	PP159

Kittyhawk IIAs, No.260 Squadron

No. 260 Squadron

Badge: A Morning Star and sword in saltire
Motto: Celer et fortis
(Swift and Strong)

No.260 Squadron was formed in August 1918 at Westward Ho in Devon as a coastal reconnaissance unit and flew anti-submarine patrols with D.H.6s until the Armistice. On 22 February 1919 it was disbanded.

On 22 November 1940, No.260 reformed at Castletown as a fighter squadron and flew Hurricanes on air defence and convoy patrols over the north of Scotland until April 1941, when it moved to Drem to prepare for a move overseas. Early in August, it arrived in Egypt and became operational with Hurricanes on air defence duties in Palestine and Lebanon on August 11. By the end of October it had moved to the Western Desert for ground attack and escort duties. In February 1942, it converted to Kittyhawks which were later used as fighter-bombers in support of the 8th Army. After the Battle of El Alàmein, No.260 moved forward until it reached Tunisia and the end of the war in Africa. Soon after the landings in Sicily in July 1943, the squadron moved into captured airfields on the island to provide fighter-bomber support for the army and by the end of September was based in Italy. In April 1944, it converted to Mustangs and flew fighter-bomber missions over Italy and Yugoslavia for the rest of the war. On 19 August 1945 the squadron was disbanded.

Squadron bases

Westward Ho	Aug 1918		Marble Arch	19 Dec 1942
	to 22 Feb 1919		Gzina	21 Dec 1942
Castletown	22 Nov 1940		Hamraiet 1	1 Jan 1943
Skitten	5 Dec 1940		Hamraiet 3	4 Jan 1943
Castletown	7 Jan 1941		Bir Dufan	12 Jan 1943
Skitten	10 Feb 1941		Sedada	17 Jan 1943
Drem	16 Apr 1941		Bir Dufan	19 Jan 1943
Emb. for Middle East			Castel Benito	23 Jan 1943
	19 May 1941		Sorman	7 Feb 1943
Haifa	10 Aug 1941		El Assa	14 Feb 1943
LG.115	23 Oct 1941		Ben Gardane	2 Mar 1943
LG.109	13 Nov 1941		Nefatia	8 Mar 1943
LG.124	17 Nov 1941		Medenine Main	20 Mar 1943
Sidi Rezegh	9 Dec 1941		El Hamma	3 Apr 1943
Gazala No.2	18 Dec 1941		El Djem	13 Apr 1943
Msus	24 Dec 1941		Kairouan	18 Apr 1943
Antelat	12 Jan 1942		Zuara	19 May 1943
Benina	16 Jan 1942		Luqa	18 Jul 1943
LG.101	1 Feb 1942		Pachino	20 Jul 1943
LG.115	15 Feb 1942		Agnone	4 Aug 1943
Gasr el Arid	10 Mar 1942		Bari	30 Sep 1943
Gambut 2	23 May 1942		Foggia Main	3 Oct 1943
Bir el Beheira	6 Jun 1942		Mileni	26 Oct 1943
LG.76	18 Jun 1942		Cutella	3 Jan 1944
LG.115 & 85	19 Jun 1942		San Angelo	21 May 1944
LG.97	11 Jul 1942		Guidonia	10 Jun 1944
LG.75	6 Nov 1942		Falerium	23 Jun 1944
Sidi Azeiz	10 Nov 1942		Crete	7 Jul 1944
Gambut Main	12 Nov 1942		Iesi	23 Aug 1944
Gazala	15 Nov 1942		Fano	17 Nov 1944
Martuba 4	17 Nov 1942		Cervia	23 Feb 1944
Belandah	10 Dec 1942		Lavariano	18 May 1945
				to 19 Aug 1945

Aircraft

Equipment	Period of service	Representative Serial
D.H.6	Aug 1918 – Feb 1919	C2087
Hurricane I	Nov 1940 – Feb 1942	W9226 (J)
Kittyhawk I, II	Feb 1942 – May 1943	FL233 (HS-O)
Kittyhawk III	Dec 1942 – Apr 1944	FR507 (HS-D)
Mustang III	Apr 1944 – Aug 1945	HB971 (HS-E)
Mustang IV	Jun 1945 – Aug 1945	

No. 261 Squadron

Badge: In front of a sword erect,
the point downwards, a
mullet, the whole in front
of a Maltese Cross
Motto: Semper contendo
(I strive continually)

No.261 Squadron was formed in August 1918 at Felixstowe from Nos.339, 340 and 341 Flights of the former RNAS station. Equipped with F.2a flying boats, it flew patrols over the North Sea until the end of the war. On 13 September 1919 the squadron was disbanded.

On 1 August 1940, the Malta Fighter Flight was re-designated No.261 Squadron and its Hurricanes and Gladiators formed the air defence of Malta until May 1941 when it disbanded. On 12 July 1941, No.127 Squadron at Habbaniya was renumbered 261 Squadron and in August took part in the occupation of Iran. It remained on air defence duties in Palestine and Cyprus until early 1942, when it left to reinforce the air forces in the Far East. The fall of Singapore resulted in its being diverted en route to Ceylon where it arrived in time for the Japanese carrier raids in April. The squadron remained in Ceylon until January 1943, when it moved to the Burma front and began escort and ground-attack missions in February. A year later, No.261 was withdrawn for rest to India and converted to Thunderbolts in June 1944. These it took back into action in Burma on 14 September flying ground-attack and escort sorties until 18 June 1945. It was then withdrawn to prepare for the invasion of Malaya but as the Japanese surrender came before this could be carried out, the squadron was disbanded on 26 September 1945.

Squadron bases

Felixstowe	Aug 1918	Baigachi	7 Feb 1943
	to 13 Sep 1919	Chittagong	21 Jun 1943
Hal Far	1 Aug 1940	Chiringa	23 Oct 1943
	to May 1941	Baigachi	27 Feb 1944
Habbaniya	12 Jul 1941	Alipore	7 Mar 1944
Shaibah	10 Aug 1941	Yelahanka	27 Apr 1944
Mosul	27 Sep 1941	Arkonam	15 Aug 1944
Haifa	1 Jan 1942	Kumbhirgram	2 Sep 1944
St. Jean	8 Jan 1942	Wangjing	22 Nov 1944
Dum Dum	Feb 1942	Myingyang	5 May 1945
China Bay	6 Mar 1942	Tanjore	Jul 1945
Dum Dum	14 Jan 1943		to 26 Sep 1945

Aircraft

Equipment	Period of service	Representative Serial
F.2a	Aug 1918 – Sep 1919	
Sea Gladiator	Aug 1940 – Jan 1941	
	Jul 1941 – Sep 1941	N5519 (R)
Hurricane I	Aug 1940 – May 1941	
	Jul 1941 – Apr 1942	P3731 (J)
Hurricane IIB	Mar 1942 – Nov 1943	BH135 (H)
Hurricane IIC	Oct 1943 – Jun 1944	HW803 (FJ-B)
Thunderbolt I, II	Jun 1944 – Sep 1945	KJ335 (FJ-W)

No. 262 Squadron

No.262 Squadron was formed from a draft of personnel which embarked at Liverpool on 29 September 1942 for South Africa to form the basis of a Catalina squadron. It arrived at Durban on 5 November and moved into its base at Congella a week later. It was not until 21 February 1943, however, that the first of its Catalinas arrived and five days later patrols over the Indian Ocean began. Other Catalinas followed, flying some patrols from Sierra Leone en route, and, to extend the patrol area around the Cape of Good Hope, operations began in October from Langebaan, on the Atlantic coast of Cape Province shortly before overall control of the squadron was transferred from East Africa to the SAAF Coastal Area. South African personnel began to appear in increasing numbers and as the amount of shipping in the approaches to Durban restricted aircraft movements, most of the patrols were flown from Langebaan and St. Lucia, in Zululand. The latter was replaced by a new base at Lake Umsingazi in November 1944 which was used until the squadron, by now manned almost entirely by SAAF personnel, was renumbered 35 Squadron, SAAF on 15 February 1945.

Squadron bases

En route	29 Sep 1942
	to 5 Nov 1942
Congella	12 Nov 1942
	to 15 Feb 1945

Aircraft

Equipment	Period of service	Representative Serial
Catalina Ib	Feb 1943 – Feb 1945	FP307 (F)
Catalina IV	Sep 1944 – Feb 1945	JX353 (B2)

No. 263 Squadron

Badge: A lion rampant, holding
in the fore paws a cross
Motto: Ex ungue leonem
(From his claws one knows
the lion)

No.263 Squadron was formed on 27 September 1918, in southern Italy from the former RNAS station at Otranto and its sub-station at Santa Maria de Leuca. For the rest of the war, it flew anti-submarine patrols over the Straits of Otranto to prevent U-boats passing into the Mediterranean from the Austro-Hungarian ports on the Adriatic. It was disbanded on 16 May 1919.

On 2 October 1939 No.263 reformed at Filton as a fighter squadron. Equipped with Gladiators, it was sent to Norway in April 1940, in an attempt to give air cover for British and Norwegian forces. Operating from a frozen lake, it had all its aircraft rendered unfit for action within three days and returned to the UK to re-equip. In May, the squadron arrived back in Norway, this time further north and flew patrols until the Allied forces were withdrawn from Narvik. Its aircraft embarked on the carrier *Glorious* which was sunk en route to the UK by German surface ships.

On 12 June 1940, ground staff began to arrive at Drem to reform the squadron which was intended to be the first with Whirlwind twin-engined fighters. Some Hurricanes

Gladiator II, No.263 Squadron

were received until these arrived and in November No.263 moved back to south-west England for convoy patrols. In June 1941, offensive sweeps began to be flown and in June 1942, the Whirlwinds were fitted as fighter-bombers for attacks on enemy shipping and airfields. In December 1943, the squadron converted to Typhoons, resuming sweeps on 1 February 1944 and in July replaced its bombs with rockets for close-support duties with the invading Allied armies. No.263 moved to France in August 1944 and flew ground-attack missions for the rest of the war, disbanding on 28 August 1945.

On 29 August 1945, No.616 Squadron at Acklington was renumbered 263 Squadron which flew Meteors as part of the fighter defences of the UK until converted to Hunters in 1955. These remained in service with the squadron until it was renumbered 1 Squadron on 1 July 1958. On 1 June 1959, No.263 reformed at Watton as a Bloodhound surface-to-air missile unit, disbanding on 10 June 1963.

Squadron bases

Otranto	27 Sep 1918	Portreath	18 Mar 1941
	to 16 May 1919	Filton	10 Apr 1941
Filton	2 Oct 1939	Charmy Down	7 Aug 1941
Lesjaskog	24 Apr 1940	Warmwell	19 Dec 1941
Turnhouse	3 May 1940	Charmy Down	23 Dec 1941
Bardufoss	21 May 1940	Colerne	28 Jan 1942
	to 6 Jun 1940	Fairwood Common	
Drem	12 Jun 1940		10 Feb 1942
Grangemouth	28 Jun 1940	Angle	18 Apr 1942
Drem	2 Sep 1940	Colerne	15 Aug 1942
Exeter	28 Nov 1940	Warmwell	13 Sep 1942
St. Eval	24 Feb 1941	Harrowbeer	20 Feb 1943
		Warmwell	15 Mar 1943
Zeals	19 Jun 1943	B.89 Mill	10 Feb 1945
Warmwell	12 Jul 1943	B.105 Drope	16 Apr 1945
Ibsley	5 Dec 1943	B.111 Ahlhorn	30 Apr 1945
Fairwood Common		R.16 Hildesheim	Jun 1945
	5 Jan 1944 (A)		to 28 Aug 1945
Beaulieu	10 Jan 1944 (G)	Acklington	29 Aug 1945
	23 Jan 1944 (A)	Church Fenton	Sep 1945
Warmwell	6 Mar 1944	Boxted	Jun 1946
Harrowbeer	19 Mar 1944	Horsham St. Faith	
Bolt Head	19 Jun 1944		15 Apr 1947
Hurn	10 Jul 1944	Wattisham	27 Oct 1950
Eastchurch	23 Jul 1944	Wymeswold	28 May 1956
B.3 St. Croix	6 Aug 1944	Wattisham	16 Jan 1957
Manston	6 Sep 1944	Stradishall	30 Aug 1957
B.51 Lille/Vendeville			to 1 Jul 1958
	11 Sep 1944	Watton	1 Jun 1959
B.70 Deurne	2 Oct 1944		to 19 Jun 1963
Fairwood Common			
	13 Jan 1945		

Aircraft

Equipment	Period of service	Representative Serial	
Short 184, 320	Sep 1918 – May 1919	N1833	
Sopwith Baby	Sep 1918 – May 1919	N2090	
F.3	Sep 1918 – May 1919		
Gladiator I, II	Oct 1939 – Jun 1940	K7942	(HE-H)
Hurricane I	Jun 1940 – Nov 1940	N2349	(HE-V)
Whirlwind I	Jul 1940 – Dec 1943	P7011	(HE-H)
Typhoon Ib	Dec 1943 – Aug 1945	MN823	(HE-J)
Meteor F.3	Aug 1945 – Mar 1948	EE301	(HE-X)
Meteor F.4	Nov 1947 – Dec 1950	VT168	(HE-E)
Meteor F.8	Oct 1950 – Nov 1954	WA920	(F)
Hunter F.2	Feb 1955 – Oct 1957	WN921	(S)
Hunter F.5	Apr 1955 – Oct 1957	WP108	(T)
Hunter F.6	Oct 1957 – Jul 1958	XE626	(P)
Bloodhound 1	Jun 1959 – Jun 1963	–	

Whirlwind I, No.263 Squadron

Whirlwind I, No.263 Squadron

Defiant Is, No.264 Squadron

No. 264 Squadron

Badge: A helmet
Motto: We defy
Name: 'Madras Presidency'

No.264 Squadron was formed in August 1918, from the seaplane station at Suda Bay, Crete. No.439 Flight at Suda Bay and No.440 Flight at Syra (Siros), 150 miles further north, flew anti-submarine patrols over the shipping routes to Salonika and the Aegean Islands until the end of the war. The squadron disbanded on 1 March 1919.

On 30 October 1939, No.264 reformed at Sutton Bridge as a fighter squadron and received its first Defiant two-seater fighters in December. These it took into action for the first time during the German invasion of the Low Countries in May 1940. The new turret fighters had some initial success but lacked forward-firing armament and manoeuvrability. Losses were heavy in daylight operations and the squadron was switched to night fighting at the end of August where its flexible armament was of more use. Defiants became non-operational on 30 April and were replaced by Mosquitos which were taken into action on 13 June. Intruder missions began in January 1943 from south-west England and a detachment was based at Bradwell Bay for similar sorties across the North Sea until April. In November 1943, No.264 returned to Lincolnshire on defensive patrols and in May 1944, was transferred south to be ready to cover the invasion beaches on D-day and after. The squadron moved to France in August but returned to the UK next month. In January 1945 it rejoined Second TAF for patrols over the Low Countries and intruder missions over Germany for the rest of the war. On 25 August 1945, the squadron was disbanded.

On 20 November 1945 No.125 Squadron at Church Fenton was renumbered 264 Squadron which flew Mosquitos until the end of 1951. They were replaced by Meteors and these remained in service until the squadron was renumbered 33 Squadron on 1 October 1957. On 1 December 1958, the squadron reformed at North Coates as the first Bloodhound surface-to-air missile unit. On 30 November 1962 No.264 was disbanded.

Squadron bases		
Suda Bay	Aug 1918	
	to 1 Mar 1919	
Sutton Bridge	30 Oct 1939	
Martlesham Heath	7 Dec 1939	
Duxford	10 May 1940	
Kirton-in-Lindsey		
	23 Jul 1940	
Hornchurch	22 Aug 1940	
Rochford	27 Aug 1940	
Kirton-in-Lindsey		
	28 Aug 1940	
Rochford	29 Oct 1940	
Debden	27 Nov 1940	
Gravesend	1 Jan 1941	
Biggin Hill	11 Jan 1941	
West Malling	14 Apr 1941	
Colerne	1 May 1942	
Predannack	30 Apr 1943	
Fairwood Common		
	7 Aug 1943	
Coleby Grange	17 Nov 1943	
Church Fenton	19 Dec 1943	
Hartfordbridge	5 May 1944	
Hunsdon	26 Jul 1944	
B.8 Picauville	11 Aug 1944	
B.6 Coulombs	3 Sep 1944	
B.18 Carpiquet	5 Sep 1944	
Predannack	24 Sep 1944	
Colerne	30 Nov 1944	
Odiham	21 Dec 1944	
B.51 Lille/Vendeville		
	8 Jan 1945	
B.77 Gilze-Rijen	26 Apr 1945	
B.108 Rheine	6 May 1945	
B.77 Gilze-Rijen	14 May 1945	
B.106 Twente	6 Jun 1945	
	to 25 Aug 1945	
Church Fenton	20 Nov 1945	
Linton-on-Ouse	22 Jul 1946	
Wittering	20 Apr 1947	
Coltishall	13 Jan 1948	
Linton-on-Ouse	24 Aug 1951	
Middleton St. George		
	1 Mar 1957	
	to 30 Sep 1957	
North Coates	1 Dec 1958	
	to 30 Nov 1962	

Aircraft Equipment	Period of service	Representative Serial
Short 184	Aug 1918 – Mar 1919	N1651
Defiant I	Dec 1939 – Sep 1941	L7029 (PS-Z)
Defiant II	Sep 1941 – Jul 1942	AA420
Mosquito II	May 1942 – Jan 1944	DD636 (PS-D)
Mosquito VI	Jul 1943 – Oct 1943	HX852
Mosquito XIII	Jan 1944 – Aug 1945	MM455 (PS-Q)
Mosquito NF.30	Nov 1945 – Mar 1946	NT440
Mosquito NF.36	Mar 1946 – Feb 1952	RL195 (PS-A)
Meteor NF.11	Dec 1951 – Nov 1954	WD652 (E)
Meteor NF.12	Oct 1954 – Sep 1957	WS604
Meteor NF.14	Oct 1954 – Sep 1957	WS831 (X)
Bloodhound 1	Dec 1958 – Nov 1962	–

No. 265 Squadron

No.265 Squadron was formed in August 1918 from Nos.364, 365 and 366 Flights based at Gibraltar when the former RNAS stations were given squadron numbers. The Short seaplanes and F.3s of the three flights flew anti-submarine patrols over the approaches to the Straits of Gibraltar for the remaining weeks of the war and the squadron disbanded in January 1919.

On 11 March 1943, the troopship *Lancashire* arrived in Mombasa with personnel for the re-formation of No.265 but as no aircraft were available at the time, detachments of the squadron were sent to help other units in Kenya and one went as far as the SAAF depot at Roberts Heights in South Africa. The first Catalina for the squadron left Stranraer on 26 March and proceeded via West Africa to Madagascar where No.265's base was to be set up, arriving on 25 April. Others followed and the first section of the squadron which had arrived at Diego Suarez on 30 March was built up to deal with the whole squadron and this remained the headquarters for the rest of 265's service. The area to be patrolled was vast and to cover it required detachments to be spread at distant places. Kipevu in Kenya was found to be more suitable as a maintenance base than Diego Suarez so a large

section of the squadron was based there from May 1943, while training and patrols were flown from Mombasa. Other patrols started out from Tulear in Southern Madagascar, Mauritius and Pamanza and many ended at different bases than those from which they had set out. In October 1943, patrols over the Red Sea and its approaches were based on Aden and Masirah while in April 1944 the squadron's Catalinas were operating from St. Lucia in the Union of South Africa. On 21 April 1945, the first aircraft left Diego Suarez for Mombasa with stores and personnel, the last patrol having been flown on 12 April and on 30 April 1945, No.265 Squadron disbanded.

Squadron bases

Gibraltar	Aug 1918
	to Jan 1919
Mombasa	11 Mar 1943
Diego Suarez	30 Mar 1943
	to 30 Apr 1945
Numerous detachments (see text).	

Aircraft

Equipment	Period of service	Representative Serial
F.3	Aug 1918 – Jan 1919	
Short 184	Aug 1918 – Jan 1919	
Catalina I, Ib	Apr 1943 – Apr 1945	FP310 (L)

No. 266 Squadron

Badge: A Bateleur Eagle
Motto: Hlabezulu
(The stabber of the sky)
Name: 'Rhodesia'

No.266 Squadron was formed in August 1918, at the seaplane station at Mudros for anti-submarine patrols over the Aegean. On 1 September 1919, the squadron disbanded.

On 30 October 1939, No.266 Squadron reformed at Sutton Bridge and was intended to be a Blenheim squadron. None were received and after training with Battles, it began to receive Spitfires in January 1940. These it took into action for the first time on 2 June over Dunkirk and during August was based in south-east England. Returning to Wittering, the squadron remained in that sector until January 1942, when it began converting to Typhoons; it was May before the last Spitfire was withdrawn. In September No.266 moved to south-west England to counter low-level fighter-bomber attacks and escort other aircraft during raids on the French coast. In March 1944, the squadron joined Second TAF and began ground-attack missions in preparation for the invasion of Europe. In July 1944, it moved to Normandy and until the end of the war was engaged in fighter sweeps over Germany from bases in the Low Countries. On 31 July 1945, the squadron was disbanded.

On 1 September 1946 No.234 Squadron at Boxted was renumbered 266 Squadron and flew Meteors until renumbered 43 Squadron on 11 February 1949. On 14 July 1952, the squadron reformed at Fassberg with Vampire fighter-bombers. These were replaced by Venoms in April 1953, and the squadron disbanded on 15 November 1957.

On 1 December 1959, No.266 reformed at Rattlesden as a Bloodhound surface-to-air missile unit, disbanding on 30 June 1964.

Squadron bases

Mudros	Aug 1918	Hurn	13 Jul 1944
(Skyros (D))	to 1 Sep 1919	B.3 St. Croix	17 Jul 1944
Sutton Bridge	30 Oct 1939	B.23 Morainville	6 Sep 1944
Martlesham Heath	1 Mar 1940	Manston	8 Sep 1944
Wittering	7 Apr 1940 (D)	Tangmere	9 Sep 1944
	14 May 1940 (C)	Manston	10 Sep 1944
Tangmere	9 Aug 1940	B.51 Lille/Vendeville	
Eastleigh	12 Aug 1940		11 Sep 1944
Hornchurch	14 Aug 1940	B.70 Deurne	2 Oct 1944
Wittering	21 Aug 1940	B.89 Mill	8 Feb 1945
Martlesham Heath	28 Sep 1941	B.105 Drope	16 Apr 1945
Wittering	3 Oct 1941	Fairwood Common	
Kings Cliffe	24 Oct 1941		27 Apr 1945
Duxford	29 Jan 1942	B.111 Ahlhorn	4 Jun 1945
Warmwell	21 Sep 1942	R.16 Hildesheim	8 Jun 1945
Exeter	2 Jan 1943		to 31 Jul 1945
Gravesend	7 Sep 1943	Boxted	1 Sep 1946
Exeter	10 Sep 1943	Wattisham	4 Nov 1946
Harrowbeer	21 Sep 1943	Boxted	5 Dec 1946
Bolt Head	7 Mar 1944	Wattisham	4 Jan 1947
Harrowbeer	12 Mar 1944	Tangmere	16 Apr 1947
Acklington	15 Mar 1944	Lubeck	28 Apr 1947
Tangmere	22 Mar 1944	Tangmere	26 Jun 1947
Need's Oar Point	10 Apr 1944		to 11 Feb 1949
Snaith	27 Apr 1944	Fassberg	14 Jul 1952
Need's Oar Point	6 May 1944		to 15 Nov 1957
Eastchurch	29 Jun 1944	Rattlesden	1 Dec 1959
			to 30 Jun 1964

Aircraft

Equipment	Period of service	Representative Serial
Short 184, 320	Aug 1918 – Sep 1919	N1823
Battle	Dec 1939 – Apr 1940	L5348
Spitfire I	Jan 1940 – Sep 1940 Oct 1940 – Apr 1941	N3178 (UO-K)
Spitfire IIA	Sep 1940 – Oct 1940 Mar 1941 – Sep 1941	P8167 (UO-N)
Spitfire VB	Sep 1941 – May 1942	W3834 (UO-P)
Typhoon Ib	Jan 1942 – Jul 1945	MN353 (ZH-J)
Meteor F.3	Sep 1946 – Apr 1948	EE277 (FX-H)
Meteor F.4	Feb 1948 – Feb 1949	VT104 (FX-W)
Vampire FB.5	Jul 1952 – Apr 1953	VZ262 (L-T)
Venom FB.1	Apr 1953 – May 1956	WE457 (A-N)
Venom FB.4	May 1956 – Nov 1957	WR464 (A)
Bloodhound 1	Dec 1959 – Jun 1964	

No. 267 Squadron

Badge: A pegasus
Motto: Sine mora
(Without delay)

No.267 Squadron was formed at Calafrana, Malta, in September 1918, from units based at the seaplane station there. It flew anti-submarine patrols until the Armistice and remained in being as an operational squadron and aircraft holding unit until disbanded on 1 August 1923.

On 19 August 1940 No.267 reformed from the Communications Unit, Heliopolis for local transport duties in Egypt. It used a variety of types for transporting passengers, mail and freight between Egypt and outlying bases. Larger transports were acquired by the end of 1941 and by August 1942, it had standardised on twin-engined transports. Its area of operations extended throughout the Mediterranean area and its role included the movement of personnel and equipment, casualty evacuation and occasional supply-dropping missions to guerilla bands in Italy and the Balkans. In November 1943, No.267 moved to Italy and in February 1945 was transferred to Burma, where it carried supplies during the 14th Army's final offensive that cleared Burma of the Japanese. After a period of general transport duties, the squadron disbanded on 30 June 1946, though it continued operations till 21 July.

On 15 February 1954, No.267 reformed at Kuala Lumpur as a transport support and communications squadron in Malaya. It flew Pioneers, Pembrokes and Dakotas equipped with loud-speakers until renumbered 209 Squadron on 1 November 1958. On 1 November 1962, it reformed at Benson with Argosies for transport duties in No.38 Group, disbanding on 30 June 1970.

Squadron bases

Calafrana	Sep 1918	Mawnybyin	27 Mar 1945
	to 1 Aug 1923	Mingaladon	15 Aug 1945
Heliopolis	19 Aug 1940		to 30 Aug 1946+
Bilbeis	16 Aug 1942	Kuala Lumpur	15 Feb 1954
Marble Arch	8 Jan 1943		to 1 Nov 1958
Cairo West	19 Jan 1943	Benson	1 Nov 1962
Bari	17 Nov 1943		to 30 Jun 1970
Bilaspur	7 Feb 1945	+Disbanded officially	
Tulihal	24 Feb 1945	on 30 June 1946.	

Aircraft Equipment	Period of service	Representative Serial
F.2a	Sep 1918 – Aug 1923	
F.3	Sep 1918 – May 1921	
Fairey IIIC	Dec 1920 – Aug 1923	

Various communications types, e.g.
Anson I (L7992); Magister (P2450); Proctor (P6114); Percival Q-6 (W6085); Hind (K5520); Gull Six (AX698); Lysander I, II (R1987); Simoun (AX676); Gladiator I (K7963); Electra (AX700); Audax (K7525); Wellesley   Aug 1940 – Aug 1942

Lockheed 14, 18	Feb 1941 – Nov 1942	EW977
Hudson III, IV, VI	Aug 1940 – Jul 1943	AE624
Dakota I, III, IV	Aug 1941 – Jun 1946	FD841 (G1)
Pioneer CC.1	Feb 1954 – Nov 1958	XJ451
Pembroke C.1	Sep 1954 – Nov 1958	WV751
Dakota C.3	Mar 1954 – Nov 1958	KP277
Argosy C.1	Nov 1962 – Jun 1970	XR138

Pioneer CC.1, No.267 Squadron

Argosy C.1, No.267 Squadron

No. 268 Squadron

Badge: A swallow soaring,
holding in the claws a
tomahawk
Motto: Adjidaumo
(Chippeway Indian)
(Tail in the air)

No.268 Squadron was formed in August 1918 from the sea-plane station at Calafrana, Malta, for anti-submarine patrols in the Central Mediterranean. On 11 October 1919 it was disbanded.

On 30 September 1940 No.268 reformed at Bury St. Edmunds with Lysanders as an army co-operation squadron and during October absorbed A Flight of No.2 Squadron and B Flight of No.26 Squadron to form its basis. Dawn patrols along the coast of East Anglia began to be flown in order to locate any traces of enemy landings but the Lysander was obsolete for tactical reconnaissance duties and in May 1941 some Tomahawks were received. Though inadequate as a fighter, these could be used for low-level reconnaissance with a greater chance of survival than the multi-purpose Lysanders and in October 1941 missions over northern France began to be flown. In March 1942 Mustangs began to replace both Tomahawks and Lysanders and by August it was fully equipped with Mustangs. Tactical recon-naissance missions increased in numbers and in June 1943 No.268 joined the newly-formed Second TAF in preparation for the invasion of Europe. After being given a course in spotting for naval bombardment in the Clyde, the squadron undertook this task during the landings in Normandy. In July 1944 some Typhoons were added to its strength and in August the squadron moved to France where it provided tactical reconnaissance for the army, arriving in the Low Countries at the end of September. In April 1945 it con-verted to Spitfires and flew reconnaissance and ground attack missions for the remaining weeks of the war, becoming No.16 Squadron on 19 September 1945. On the same day, No.487 Squadron at Cambrai-Epinoy was renumbered 268 Squadron and flew Mosquito fighter-bombers until disbanded on 31 March 1946.

Squadron bases

Calafrana	Aug 1918	Thruxton	15 Oct 1943
	to 11 Oct 1919	Turnhouse	7 Nov 1943
Bury St. Edmunds	30 Sep 1940	North Weald	17 Jan 1944
Snailwell	1 Apr 1941	Llanbedr	7 Feb 1944
West Raynham	20 Jun 1941	North Weald	20 Feb 1944
Barton Bendish	21 Jun 1941	Sawbridgworth	1 Mar 1944
Snailwell	24 Jun 1941	Dundonald	26 Mar 1944
Weston Zoyland	21 Jul 1941	Gatwick	8 Apr 1944
Snailwell	27 Jul 1941	Odiham	27 Jun 1944
Penshurst	4 Aug 1941	B.10 Plumetot	10 Aug 1944
Snailwell	8 Aug 1941	B.4 Beny-sur-Mer	13 Aug 1944
Barton Bendish	28 Sep 1941	B.27 Boisney	1 Sep 1944
Twinwood Farm	30 Sep 1941	B.31 Fresney Folney	
Snailwell	1 Oct 1941		5 Sep 1944
Weston Zoyland	25 Nov 1941	B.43 Fort Rouge	11 Sep 1944
Snailwell	8 Dec 1941	B.61 St. Denis Westrem	
Ibsley (D)	12 Dec 1941		27 Sep 1944
	to Mar 1942	B.70 Deurne	11 Oct 1944
Weston Zoyland	20 May 1942	B.77 Gilze-Rijen	25 Nov 1944
Snailwell	2 Jun 1942	Fairwood Common	
Weston Zoyland	9 Aug 1942		13 Jan 1945
Wing	1 Mar 1943	B.77 Gilze-Rijen	9 Feb 1945
Bottisham	6 Mar 1943	B.89 Mill	8 Mar 1945
Snailwell	10 Mar 1943	B.106 Twente	17 Apr 1945
Odiham	31 May 1943	B.118 Celle	30 May 1945
Tangmere (D)	19 Jun 1943	B.150 Hustedt	18 Jun 1945
	to 3 Jul 1943	B.118 Celle	19 Sep 1945
Funtington	15 Sep 1943	Cambrai-Epinoy	19 Sep 1945
Odiham	8 Oct 1943		to 31 Mar 1946

Aircraft

Equipment	Period of service	Representative Serial
Short 184, 320	Aug 1918 – Oct 1919	8317
Lysander II	Oct 1940 – Apr 1942	L4780
Tomahawk IIA	May 1941 – Aug 1942	AH834
Mustang I, IA	Mar 1942 – Aug 1945	AG466
Mustang II	Nov 1944 – Aug 1945	FR918
Typhoon Ib	Jul 1944 – Dec 1944	JP371
Spitfire XIVB	Apr 1945 – Sep 1945	NH641
Spitfire XIX	Sep 1945	PM577
Mosquito FB.6	Sep 1945 – Mar 1946	LR385

No. 269 Squadron

Badge: An ancient ship in full sail
Motto: Omnia videmus
(We see all things)

No.269 Squadron was formed at Port Said on 6 October 1918 from the seaplane station which had existed since January 1916. It operated seaplanes from the harbour and a flight of B.E.2es and D.H.9s was based ashore. Anti-sub-marine patrols were flown until the Armistice and on 15 September 1919 the seaplanes moved to Alexandria and merged with No.270 Squadron, the landplane flight having been disbanded in March. The squadron continued as No.269 until disbanded on 15 November 1919.

On 7 December 1936 C Flight of No.206 Squadron at Bircham Newton was redesignated 269 Squadron which moved to Abbotsinch at the end of the month with Ansons for coastal reconnaissance duties. Shortly before the out-break of war, the squadron moved to Montrose for patrols off the east coast of Scotland and in October was transferred to Wick. There it converted to Hudsons in April 1940 and after a year of attacks on enemy shipping, took these to Iceland for anti-submarine patrols. It remained there until January 1944, when it returned to the UK to re-equip for air-sea rescue duties. In March 1944 the squadron moved to the Azores, its Hudsons flying out while Spitfires, Martinets and Walruses were flown off an escort carrier to Lagens. For the rest of the war it flew air-sea rescue, meteorological and target-towing sorties and in October 1944 began to receive Warwicks. On 10 March 1946 No.269 disbanded.

The squadron reformed at Ballykelly on 10 March 1952 as a Shackleton maritime reconnaissance unit. On 1 Dec-ember 1958 it was renumbered 210 Squadron. No.269 reformed on 22 July 1959 at Caistor as a Thor strategic missile unit, disbanding again on 24 May 1963.

Squadron bases

Port Said	6 Oct 1918	Abbotsinch	6 Oct 1938
Alexandria	15 Sep 1919	Montrose	25 Aug 1939
	to 15 Nov 1919	Wick	10 Oct 1939
Bircham Newton	7 Dec 1936	Kaldadarnes	12 Apr 1941 (D)
Abbotsinch	30 Dec 1936		31 May 1941 (C)
Eastleigh	17 Jan 1938	Reykjavik	6 Mar 1943
Abbotsinch	24 Mar 1938	Left for UK	3 Jan 1944
Thornaby	29 Sep 1938	Davidstowe Moor	8 Jan 1944

Lagens	8 Mar 1944 to 10 Mar 1946
Ballykelly	10 Mar 1952 to 1 Dec 1958
Caistor	22 Jul 1959 to 24 May 1963

Aircraft Equipment	Period of service	Representative Serial
Short 184	Oct 1918 – Nov 1919	N2915
D.H.9	Oct 1918 – Mar 1919	E8997
B.E.2e	Oct 1918 – Mar 1919	6802
Anson I	Dec 1936 – Jun 1940	N5317 (UA-R)
Hudson I	Jun 1940 – Mar 1941	N7303 (UA-B)

Aircraft Equipment	Period of service	Representative Serial and Code
Hudson III	Mar 1941 – Jul 1945	T9045 (UA-D)
Hudson V	Jan 1944 – Jul 1945	FK737 (UA-C)
Spitfire VB	Feb 1944 – Mar 1946	AD125 (UA-L)
Martinet I	Feb 1944 – Jun 1945	NR488
Walrus I	Feb 1944 – Mar 1946	W2713
Warwick I	Oct 1944 – Mar 1946	BV519 (UA-A)
Shackleton MR.1, MR.1A	Mar 1952 – Dec 1958	VP284 (B-E)
Shackleton MR.2	Apr 1953 – Dec 1958	WL738 (B-K)
Thor	Jul 1959 – May 1963	–

Sopwith Baby, No.270 Squadron

No. 270 Squadron

No.270 Squadron was formed at Alexandria on 6 October 1918 as an anti-submarine patrol unit in No.64 Wing. It had a complement of seaplanes for patrols off the Egyptian coast until the end of the war and on 15 September 1919, merged with No.269 Squadron at Port Said.

On 12 November 1942 No.270 Squadron reformed at Jui, Gambia, for anti-submarine operations off the coast of West Africa. In July 1943 it moved to Nigeria and at the end of the year began to convert to Sunderlands. By May 1944 Catalinas had been completely replaced and the squadron continued its patrols with Sunderlands until the end of the war. On 30 June 1945 the squadron disbanded.

Squadron bases

Alexandria	6 Oct 1918 to 15 Sep 1919
Jui	12 Nov 1942
Apapa	23 Jul 1943 to 30 Jun 1945

Aircraft Equipment	Period of service	Representative Serial
Short 184	Aug 1918 – Sep 1919	N9204
F.3	Mar 1919 – Sep 1919	N4318
Sopwith Baby	Aug 1918 – Apr 1919	N2131
Catalina Ib	Nov 1942 – May 1944	FP225 (G)
Sunderland III	Dec 1943 – Jun 1945	EW109 (Q)

No. 271 Squadron

Badge: A gauntlet holding a cross
Motto: Death and life

No.271 Squadron was formed in September 1918 from elements of the former RNAS station at Otranto in southern Italy. The squadron's seaplanes were part of a force of ships and aircraft guarding the exit from the Adriatic against enemy submarines based at Austro-Hungarian ports breaking out into the Mediterranean. As the war ended a few weeks later, the squadron was disbanded on 9 December 1918.

On 1 May 1940 No.1680 Flight at Doncaster was re-designated 271 Squadron for transport duties. Its main equipment was Harrows, supplemented by a few Bombays and ex-civil airliners, and within a short time the squadron was engaged in evacuating units from France in the face of the German invasion. From the end of June, No.271 was engaged in a lengthy period of transporting ground crews and equipment for squadrons moving base but in January 1941 an additional task was allotted, the maintenance of a regular service with Albatrosses between the UK and Iceland though this was infrequent and dogged by inadequate equipment. Other types were also used in small numbers but major re-equipment came in January 1944, when Dakotas were received and the squadron became an airborne forces unit. Harrows were still retained for ambulance flights

Beaufighter I, No.272 Squadron

and soon after the squadron had supplied twenty-two glider-tugs on D-Day, these began operating casualty evacuation missions from the beachhead. No.271 also supplied aircraft for the Arnhem landings in September 1944 and for the Rhine crossing in March 1945. After losing seven Harrows in the German air attacks on Evère on New Year's Day 1945, the Harrow flight was converted to Dakotas, the last being replaced in May. With the end of the war, the squadron began transport flights to Germany, Italy and Greece which continued until civil airlines were able to operate on European routes. The squadron was renumbered 77 Squadron on 1 December 1946.

Squadron bases

Otranto	Sep 1918		to Jul 1944
	to 9 Dec 1918	Northolt (D)	20 Feb 1945
Doncaster	1 May 1940		to 2 Apr 1945
Down Ampney	29 Feb 1944	Croydon (D)	2 Apr 1945
Doncaster (D)	29 Feb 1944		to 7 Apr 1945
	to 2 Jun 1944	Odiham	30 Aug 1945
Blakehill Farm (D)		Broadwell	5 Oct 1945
	31 May 1944		to 1 Dec 1946

Aircraft

Equipment	Period of service	Representative Serial
F.3	Sep 1918 – Dec 1918	
Short 184	Sep 1918 – Dec 1918	N1395
Harrow I, II	May 1940 – May 1945	K6998 (L)
Bombay I	May 1940 – Jun 1940	L5817
Ford 5-AT-D	May 1940 – Sep 1940	X5000
H.P.42	Jun 1940 – Dec 1940	AS981
Savoia-Marchetti S.73	May 1940 – Jun 1940	OO-AGO
Albatross	Jan 1941 – Apr 1942	AX904 (BJ-W)
Dominie	May 1942 – Jan 1944	X7519
Hudson	Jan 1942 –	
Dakota I	Aug 1943 – Jan 1944	FD904
Dakota III, IV	Jan 1944 – Dec 1946	KG340

No. 272 Squadron

Badge: A man in armour, couped at the shoulders
Motto: On, on!

No.272 Squadron was formed in August 1918 at Machrihanish as a coastal reconnaissance unit and flew anti-submarine patrols over the approaches to the Clyde until the end of the war, disbanding in December 1918.

On 19 November 1940 No.272 reformed at Aldergrove and merged one flight each from Nos.235 and 236 Squadrons to form the basis of the squadron. Its Blenheims began operations on the following day and it flew shipping escort patrols until April 1941, when it converted to Beaufighters, being earmarked for transfer to the Middle East. The first six aircraft left on 24 May and the first squadron aircraft to reach Egypt arrived on 28 May. It set out next day to provide fighter cover for the evacuation of Crete and was joined by others as they arrived in the next few days, the squadron being complete by 1 June. As the only effective long-range fighter squadron in the area, No.272 was active immediately on convoy escort and intruder missions, supplemented by periodic escort duty for other anti-shipping squadrons. Long-range ground attack sorties continued over Egypt and Libya until the squadron was transferred to Malta in November 1942, for similar attacks on Sicily and Tunisia. In September 1943 it moved to Sicily and in February 1944 to Sardinia, using these bases for attacks on the Italian mainland and the coast of southern France. In September 1944 No.272 moved to Italy for attacks around the Adriatic coasts, flying its last operation on 18 April 1945 and disbanding on 30 April 1945.

Squadron bases

Machrihanish	Aug 1918 to Dec 1918	Takali	6 Nov 1942
		Luqa	4 Jun 1943
Aldergrove	19 Nov 1940	Gardabia West	5 Jul 1943
Chivenor	3 Apr 1941	Luqa	17 Jul 1943
Left for M. East		Borizzo	3 Sep 1943
	24 May 1941 (A)	Catania	21 Oct 1943
Abu Sueir	28 May 1941 (A)	Alghero	1 Feb 1944
Idku	14 Jun 1941	Foggia	15 Sep 1944
LG.10	12 Jan 1942	Falconara	20 Mar 1945
Idku	14 Mar 1942		to 30 Apr 1945

Aircraft

Equipment	Period of service	Representative Serial
D.H.6	Aug 1918 – Dec 1918	B2961
Blenheim IV	Nov 1940 – Apr 1941	Z5733
Beaufighter I	Apr 1941 – Jun 1943	T3305 (G)
Beaufighter VI	Nov 1942 – Feb 1944	JL620 (O)
Beaufighter X	Feb 1944 – Apr 1945	LZ121 (J)
Beaufighter XI	Feb 1944 – Aug 1944	JM263 (A)

Spitfire VIII, No.273 Squadron

No. 273 Squadron

No.273 Squadron was formed from Nos.485 and 534 Flights of the former RNAS station at Great Yarmouth in August 1918 and used D.H.4s and B.E.2cs for coastal reconnaissance, supplemented by a few D.H.9As later, while a flight of Camels from Burgh Castle provided protection for the station's reconnaissance aircraft. The squadron was disbanded on 5 July 1919.

On 1 August 1939 No.273 reformed at China Bay, Ceylon, with an establishment of six Vildebeests supplemented by four Seals allotted to the station but flown by No.273. Regular coastal patrols began on 25 August using a Seal seaplane and these were augmented by Vildebeests when the airfield was ready for landplanes on 5 September, the first being flown on 13 September. The lack of enemy activity resulted in anti-aircraft co-operation flights being the main task until the Japanese entered the war. In March 1942 the squadron began to re-equip with Fulmars, (about half of the personnel being naval) and sixteen were on strength when a Japanese carrier force attacked Ceylon on 9 April 1942, one being lost in the defence of the airfield. For the next few days the Fulmars flew reconnaissance sorties looking for enemy ships and then settled back to defensive duties. In August 1942 Hurricanes began to replace the Fulmars and in March 1944 conversion to Spitfires took place. Finally, in July 1944, the squadron was relieved of its defensive role and moved to the Burma front to begin ground attack and escort missions. In February 1945 bombs began to be carried in attacks on Japanese communications targets until the end of the war when the squadron moved to Bangkok and two weeks later to French Indo-China where it disbanded at Saigon on 31 January 1946.

Squadron bases

Great Yarmouth	Aug 1918 to 5 Jul 1919	Chittagong	9 Jul 1944
		Cox's Bazaar	26 Aug 1944
		Maunghnama	31 Dec 1944
China Bay	1 Aug 1939	Kyaukpyu	27 Jan 1945
Katukurunda	18 Jun 1942	Mingaladon	13 May 1945
Ratmalana	1 Sep 1942	Don Muang	11 Sep 1945
China Bay	15 Feb 1943	Tan Son Nhut	23 Sep 1945
Ratmalana	1 Aug 1943		to 31 Jan 1946

Aircraft

Equipment	Period of service	Representative Serial
D.H.4	Aug 1918 – Jul 1919	A8033
D.H.9	Aug 1918 – Jul 1919	D1053
B.E.2c	Aug 1918 – Jan 1919	9973
D.H.9A	Sep 1918 – Jul 1919	
Camel	Aug 1918 – Jul 1919	C68
Vildebeest III	Aug 1939 – Mar 1942	K4160
Seal	Aug 1939 – Mar 1942	K4788
Fulmar II	Mar 1942 – Sep 1942	X8770
Hurricane I	Aug 1942 – Sep 1942	W9296
Hurricane IIB	Aug 1942 – Mar 1944	BG854 (HH-B)
Hurricane IIC	Jan 1944 – Mar 1944	LB672 (L)
Spitfire VIII	Mar 1944 – Jan 1946	LV731 (MS-O)
Spitfire XIV	Nov 1945 – Jan 1946	RN218 (MS-F)

Handley Page V/1500, No.274 Squadron

No. 274 Squadron

Badge: Eight arrows in saltire
Motto: Supero (I overcome)

No.274 Squadron began to form at Seaton Carew in November 1918 a few days before the end of World War One. It was intended to fly D.H.6s on coastal patrol duties but disbanded on June 1919, its number being allotted to a Handley Page V/1500 unit which formed at Bircham Newton on 15 June 1919. After training duties for some months, the four-engined V/1500 was abandoned in favour of smaller twin-engined bombers and the squadron disbanded on 30 January 1920, its personnel passing to the newly-formed No.207 Squadron.

On 19 August 1940, No.274 reformed at Amriya as a fighter squadron and consisted of A Flight with Hurricanes and B Flight with Gladiators; also attached was the French Flight transferred from No.80 Squadron with two Morane 406s and two Potez 63-11s. The latter left on 28 September and during October No.274 became completely equipped with Hurricanes. In December fighter sweeps over the Western Desert began and continued, with short breaks for fighter defence in Egypt, until May 1942, when the squadron's Hurricanes were modified for fighter-bombing duties. It was active in a ground-attack role during the Battle of El Alamein and began moving forward through Libya as the 8th Army captured airfields. After the army reached Tunisia, No.274 was given an air defence role, covering convoys along the Libyan coast, receiving some Spitfires in April 1943, and completely re-equipping with this type shortly after moving to Cyprus in September. In February 1944 the squadron moved to Italy for two months and took part in sweeps over Yugoslavia and Albania before leaving for the UK.

On 24 April 1944 No.274 re-assembled at Hornchurch with Spitfires and began fighter sweeps over northern France in preparation for the invasion of Europe. After covering the Normandy landings, it converted to Tempests in August which it used against flying bombs until their launching sites were captured by the army. At the end of September it joined Second TAF in the Low Countries and flew sweeps over Germany until the end of the war. Early in September 1945 it returned to Warmwell for an arma-

ment training course, leaving its ground echelon in Germany and while so engaged was renumbered 174 Squadron on 7 September 1945.

Squadron bases

Seaton Carew	Nov 1918	LG.89	10 Oct 1942
	to Jun 1919	LG.37	23 Oct 1942
Bircham Newton	15 Jun 1919	LG.104	9 Nov 1942
	to 30 Jan 1920	LG.13	11 Nov 1942
Amriya	19 Aug 1940	Bu Amud	18 Nov 1942
Sidi Haneish South		Martuba 1	27 Nov 1942
	7 Dec 1940	Benina	21 Dec 1942
Gazala	27 Jan 1941	Misurata	20 Jan 1943
Amriya	12 Feb 1941	Mellaha	26 Jan 1943
Sidi Haneish	16 Apr 1941	Derna	9 Aug 1943
Gerawla	17 Apr 1941	Paphos	11 Sep 1943
Amriya	10 Sep 1941	Madna	1 Feb 1944
Sidi Haneish North		Canne	22 Feb 1944
	3 Nov 1941	Emb. for UK	10 Apr 1944
LG.130	13 Nov 1941	Hornchurch	24 Apr 1944
LG.124	20 Nov 1941	Detling	19 May 1944
LG.103	12 Dec 1941	Merston	22 Jun 1944
Msus	23 Dec 1941	Gatwick	28 Jun 1944
El Adem	2 Feb 1942	West Malling	5 Jul 1944
Gasr el Arid	17 Feb 1942	Manston	17 Aug 1944
Gambut 2	22 Feb 1942	Coltishall	20 Sep 1944
Gambut Main	8 Mar 1942	B.70 Deurne	29 Sep 1944
Sidi Haneish	7 Apr 1942	B.82 Grave	2 Oct 1944
Gambut	7 May 1942	B.80 Volkel	7 Oct 1944
LG.07	20 Jun 1942	B.91 Kluis	17 Mar 1945
Sidi Haneish	24 Jun 1942	B.109 Quackenbruck	
LG.92	29 Jun 1942		20 Apr 1945
LG.173	Jul 1942	B.155 Dedelstorf	20 Jun 1945
LG.88	19 Aug 1942	Warmwell (A)	3 Sep 1945
LG.229 (Idku)	9 Sep 1942		to 7 Sep 1945

Aircraft

Equipment	Period of service	Representative Serial	
D.H.6	Nov 1918 – Jun 1919		
V/1500	Jun 1919 – Jan 1920	E8293	
Gladiator II	Aug 1940 – Oct 1940	N5786	
Hurricane I	Aug 1940 – Oct 1941	P2544	(YK-T)
Hurricane IIB, IIC	Oct 1941 – Oct 1943	BE397	(H)
Spitfire VB, VC	Apr 1943 – Apr 1944	JK118	(V)
Spitfire IX	May 1944 – Aug 1944	MH603	(JJ-K)
Tempest V	Aug 1944 – Sep 1945	EJ783	(JJ-N)

Hurricane IIB, No.274 Squadron

Walrus II, No.275 Squadron

No. 275 Squadron

Badge: A walrus' head erased
Motto: Non interibunt
(They shall not perish)

Aircraft Equipment	Period of service	Representative Serial	
Lysander IIIa	Oct 1941 – Aug 1943	V9738	
Walrus I, II	Dec 1941 – Feb 1945	L2207	(PV-Z)
Defiant I, IA	May 1942 – Aug 1943	T3920	
Anson I	Mar 1943 – Aug 1944	EG525	(PV-N)
Spitfire VB	Jan 1943 – Apr 1943	BL468	
	Apr 1944 – Feb 1945	BL294	
Sycamore HR.13, HR.14	Apr 1953 – Sep 1959	XG509	(J)
Whirlwind HAR.4	Mar 1959 – Sep 1959	XJ761	

Bolt Head (D)	18 Oct 1944	Linton-on-Ouse	13 Apr 1953
	to 15 Feb 1945	Thornaby	18 Nov 1954
Harrowbeer	10 Jan 1945	Leconfield	9 Oct 1957
	to 15 Feb 1945		to 1 Sep 1959

Sycamore HR.14, No.275 Squadron

No.275 Squadron was formed at Valley on 15 October 1941 from detachments of Lysanders based at Valley and Andreas for air-sea rescue duties in the Irish Sea area. By the end of the year, it had acquired some Walruses and later Defiants, Spitfires and Ansons. In April 1944 the squadron moved to Warmwell to cover the waters between southern England and Normandy, moving further west after the main battle area moved eastwards. ASR missions continued until the squadron disbanded on 15 February 1945.

On 13 April 1953, No.275 reformed at Linton-on-Ouse as a search and rescue squadron equipped with Sycamores. It provided cover over the North Sea until renumbered 228 Squadron on 1 September 1959.

Squadron bases
Valley	15 Oct 1941	Warmwell	14 Apr 1944
Andreas (D)	30 Nov 1941	Bolt Head	7 Aug 1944
	to 25 Apr 1944	Portreath (D)	7 Aug 1944
Eglinton (D)	30 May 1943		to 15 Feb 1945
	to 14 Apr 1944	Exeter	18 Oct 1944

No. 276 Squadron

Badge: A retriever's head
Motto: Retrieve

No.276 Squadron was formed at Harrowbeer on 21 October 1941, from detachments of air-sea rescue aircraft at Harrowbeer, Roborough, Warmwell, Perranporth and Fairwood Common, its area of operations covering the western end of the English Channel and the Bristol Channel. Defiants and Spitfires were acquired during 1942 for spotting ditched crews and Ansons for dropping dinghies and supplies, Walruses being used for pick-ups. In April 1944 Warwicks equipped for dropping airborne lifeboats were received but these were transferred to No.277 Squadron in November. In August 1944 a detachment moved to Cherbourg and the rest of the squadron joined it in September. By the end of October, its activities had moved eastwards to Belgium where it covered the sea between Flanders and the UK for the rest of the war. In August 1945 it took Walruses to Norway and detachments provided ASR coverage for the waters around Oslo, Kristiansand, Trondheim and Stavanger until November when the squadron returned to the UK to disband on 14 November 1945.

Squadron bases

Harrowbeer	21 Oct 1941	B.61 St. Denis-Westrem	
Warmwell (D)	21 Oct 1941		30 Sep 1944
	to 3 Apr 1944		to 25 Oct 1944
Perranporth (D)	21 Oct 1941	B.63 St. Croix	25 Oct 1944
	to 5 Nov 1941	B.67 Ursel (D)	7 Nov 1944
Fairwood Common (D)			to 15 Dec 1944
	21 Oct 1941	B.83 Knocke-le-Zoute	
	to 24 Apr 1944		11 Dec 1944
Portreath (D)	21 Oct 1941	Andrews Field	8 Jun 1945
	to 3 Apr 1944	Kjevik	23 Aug 1945
Portreath	3 Apr 1944	Sola (D)	23 Aug 1945
A.23 Querqueville (D)			to 24 Sep 1945
	9 Aug 1944	Vaernes	23 Aug 1945
	to 18 Sep 1944		to 20 Sep 1945
A.23 Querqueville	18 Sep 1944	Gardermoen	24 Sep 1945
Portreath (D)	18 Sep 1944	Dunsfold	6 Nov 1945 (G)
	to 31 Oct 1944		10 Nov 1945 (A)
B.48 Amiens-Glisy			to 14 Nov 1945
	30 Sep 1944		

Aircraft Equipment	Period of service	Representative Serial
Lysander IIIA	Oct 1941 – May 1943	V9350 (AQ-K)
Walrus I, II	Oct 1941 – Nov 1945	W3070 (AQ-N)
Defiant I, IA	May 1942 – May 1943	AA404 (VA-P)
Spitfire IIA	Apr 1943 – May 1943	P7366
Spitfire VB	Feb 1942 – Apr 1942	BL495
	Apr 1943 – Jun 1945	EN841 (VA-O)
Anson I	Mar 1943 – May 1944	EG560
Warwick I	Apr 1944 – Oct 1944	BV530

No. 277 Squadron

Badge: A winged hand couped at the wrist clasping a hand rising from water barry waved
Motto: Quaerendo servamus (We save by seeking)

No.277 Squadron was formed on 22 December 1941 at Stapleford Tawney, from air-sea rescue detachments at Martlesham Heath, Hawkinge, Shoreham and Tangmere and its aircraft covered the busy area between south-east England and northern France over which large numbers of RAF fighters and bombers operated. In May 1942 Defiants began to arrive and by the end of the year the squadron had acquired Spitfires for spotting ditched aircrews. From August 1944 No.277's area was extended westwards to Cornwall and in November it received Warwicks from No.276 Squadron. On 15 February 1945 the squadron was disbanded but remained at readiness until 26 February while No.278 Squadron took over its tasks.

Aircraft Equipment	Period of service	Representative Serial
Lysander IIIA	Dec 1941 – Sep 1945	V9431 (BA-S)
Walrus I, II	Dec 1941 – Feb 1945	W3077
Defiant I, IA	May 1942 – May 1943	AA290
Spitfire IIA	Dec 1942 – May 1944	P8030
Spitfire VB	May 1944 – Feb 1945	BM510
Sea Otter II	Nov 1943 – Apr 1944	JM796
Warwick I	Nov 1944 – Feb 1945	HF940

Lysander IIIA, No.277 Squadron

Squadron bases

Stapleford Tawney	
	22 Dec 1941
Shoreham (D)	22 Dec 1941
	to 7 Oct 1944
Hawkinge (D)	22 Dec 1941
	to 5 Oct 1944
Martlesham Heath (D)	
	22 Dec 1941
	to 22 Apr 1944
Gravesend	7 Dec 1942
Shoreham	15 Apr 1944
Warmwell (D)	7 Aug 1944
	to 18 Aug 1944
Hurn (D)	18 Aug 1944
	to 28 Aug 1944
Warmwell (D)	28 Aug 1944
Portreath (D)	1 Nov 1944
	to 15 Feb 1945
Hawkinge	5 Oct 1944
	to 15 Feb 1945

Spitfire IIA, No.278 Squadron

No. 278 Squadron

Badge: In front of a lifebuoy, a
seagull affrontée hovering
Motto: Ex mare ad referiendum
(From out of the sea to
strike again)

No.278 Squadron was formed on 1 October 1941 from
No.3 ASR Flight at Matlask for air-sea rescue duties off the
East Anglian coast. In February 1943 it received Ansons
and by the end of the year had extended its area to include
the north-east of England. In February 1944, it took over
two of No.282 Squadron's detachments in southern Scotland
while other detachments were based in the extreme north,
though in April these were given up and No.278 reverted to
covering East Anglia. Warwicks were received in May 1944,
but in February 1945 the squadron became a Walrus unit
only, operating over the English Channel. On 14 October
1945 No.278 Squadron disbanded.

Squadron bases

Matlask	1 Oct 1941	Peterhead (D)	10 Feb 1944
North Coates (D)	26 Nov 1941		to Apr 1944
	to 12 Jan 1943	Sumburgh (D)	10 Feb 1944
Coltishall	10 Apr 1942		to 20 Apr 1944
Woolsington (D)	6 Oct 1943	Bradwell Bay	21 Apr 1944
	to 10 Dec 1943	Martlesham Heath (D)	
Acklington (D)	10 Dec 1943		21 Apr 1944
	to 19 Dec 1943		to 23 Sep 1944
Hutton Cranswick (D)		Hornchurch (D)	13 Nov 1944
	19 Dec 1943		to 15 Feb 1945
	to 31 Mar 1944	Thorney Island	15 Feb 1945
Ayr (D)	1 Feb 1944	Hawkinge (D)	24 Feb 1945
	to 21 Apr 1944		to 14 Oct 1945
Drem (D)	1 Feb 1944	Beccles (D)	24 Feb 1945
	to 22 Apr 1944		to 14 Oct 1945
Castletown (D)	10 Feb 1944	Exeter (D)	18 Jul 1945
	to 22 Apr 1944		to 14 Oct 1945

Aircraft

Equipment	Period of service	Representative Serial
Lysander IIIA	Oct 1941 – Feb 1943	V9541
Walrus I, II	Oct 1941 – Oct 1945	K8549
Anson I	Feb 1943 – Jul 1944	DG809
Spitfire VB	Apr 1944 – Feb 1945	AD562
Warwick I	May 1944 – Feb 1945	HF968
Sea Otter II	May 1945 – Oct 1945	JM957 (MY-M)

Anson I, No.278 Squadron

Warwick Is, No.279 Squadron

No. 279 Squadron

Badge: Above waves of the sea, nine flashes of lightning
Motto: To see and be seen

No.279 Squadron was formed on 16 November 1941 at Bircham Newton as an air-sea rescue unit. Equipped with Hudsons, it became the first ASR squadron to employ airborne lifeboats and detachments were stationed in south-west England for operations over the Bay of Biscay and the Western Approaches between April 1942 and December 1943. At the end of October 1944 the squadron moved to Thornaby and provided detachments in northern Scotland to cover the activities of strike and patrol squadrons. Hudsons were replaced by Warwicks at the same time and these remained in service until replaced by Lancasters in September 1945. A detachment of these served in Burma from December until the squadron disbanded on 10 March 1946.

Squadron bases
Bircham Newton	16 Nov 1941
Thornaby	31 Oct 1944
Beccles	3 Sep 1945
	to 10 Mar 1946

Aircraft Equipment	Period of service	Representative Serial
Hudson III, V, VI	Nov 1941 – Nov 1944	T9041 (FI-D)
Warwick I	Nov 1944 – Sep 1945	BV288
Hurricane IIC, IV	Apr 1945 – Jun 1945	KZ576
Sea Otter II	Jul 1945 – Sep 1945	JM861
Lancaster ASR.3	Sep 1945 – Mar 1946	SW283

No. 280 Squadron

Badge: In front of a fountain a hand holding a pole, flying therefrom two flags representing the International distress signal 'N.C'
Motto: We shall be there

No.280 Squadron was formed on 10 December 1941 at Thorney Island for air-sea rescue duties. Originally intended to have Hudsons, the squadron moved to Detling with Ansons in February 1942 as the Hudsons were required for other units. In June it began taking part in searches along the coasts of south-east England and East Anglia. In October 1943 No.280 re-equipped with Warwicks which could undertake longer patrols over the North Sea and also carry airborne lifeboats. The squadron continued its rescue role after the end of the war, sending detachments to Cornwall, Northern Ireland, the north of Scotland and Iceland, being disbanded on 21 June 1946.

Squadron bases			
Thorney Island	10 Dec 1941	Langham	6 Sep 1944
Detling	10 Feb 1942	Beccles	30 Oct 1944
Langham	31 Jul 1942	Langham	3 Nov 1945
Bircham Newton	2 Nov 1942	Thornaby	Jan 1946 (P)
Thorney Island	25 Sep 1943		to 21 Jun 1946
Thornaby	20 Oct 1943		
Strubby	1 May 1944		

Post-war detachments based at St. Eval, Thorney Island, Lossiemouth, Aldergrove and Reykjavik.

Aircraft Equipment	Period of service	Representative Serial
Anson I	Feb 1942 – Oct 1943	DG922 (YF-P)
Warwick I	Oct 1943 – Jun 1946	BV304 (YF-F)

No. 281 Squadron

Badge: The head of a St.Bernard's dog affrontee, pendant from the collar a barrel shaped flash

Motto: Volamus servaturi (We fly to save)

No.281 Squadron was formed on 29 March 1942 at Ouston for air-sea rescue duties, initially with Defiants. In February 1943 it added Walrus amphibians and by June had replaced its Defiants with Ansons. On 22 November 1943 the squadron was absorbed by 282 Squadron.

No.281 reformed at Thornaby on the same day with Warwicks for ASR missions and from February 1944 based detachments around the British Isles, moving its base to Tiree at the same time. In February 1945 the squadron moved to Northern Ireland but a detachment remained at Tiree until September. No.281 Squadron disbanded on 24 October 1945.

Squadron bases			
Ouston	29 Mar 1942	Tiree	27 Feb 1944
Woolsington	14 Jun 1943	Mullaghmore	7 Feb 1945
Drem	6 Oct 1943	Limavady	31 Mar 1945
	to 22 Nov 1943	Ballykelly	13 Aug 1945
Thornaby	22 Nov 1943		to 24 Oct 1945

Aircraft Equipment	Period of service	Representative Serial
Defiant I	Apr 1942 – Jun 1943	N3481
Walrus I, II	Feb 1943 – Nov 1943	X1758
Anson I	Apr 1943 – Nov 1943	EG560
Warwick I	Nov 1943 – Oct 1945	BV404 (FA-A4)
Sea Otter II	Apr 1944 – Oct 1945	JM808
Wellington XIV	Sep 1945 – Oct 1945	

Warwick I, No.282 Squadron

No. 282 Squadron

No.282 Squadron was formed on 1 January 1943 at Castletown for air-sea rescue duties in northern Scotland. At first it had only Walrus amphibians but these were supplemented by Ansons in March 1943. In November 1943 it took over No.281 Squadron's detachments at Drem and Ayr and operated around the Scottish coasts until it merged with No.281 Squadron on 31 January 1944.

On 1 February 1944 No.282 reformed at Davidstowe Moor with Warwicks for ASR operations from south-west England. Some amphibians were received in March 1945, and the squadron disbanded on 19 July 1945.

Squadron bases	
Castletown	1 Jan 1943
	to 31 Jan 1944
Davidstowe Moor	1 Feb 1944
St. Eval	19 Sep 1944
	to 19 Jul 1945

Aircraft Equipment	Period of service	Representative Serial
Walrus I, II	Jan 1943 – Jan 1944 Mar 1945 – Jul 1945	L2036 (B4-Q)
Anson I	Mar 1943 – Jan 1944	EG555
Warwick I	Feb 1944 – Jul 1945	HF978 (B4-H)
Sea Otter II	Mar 1945 – Jul 1945	JM745 (B4-T)

No. 283 Squadron

Badge: In front of a Maltese
Cross, a lifebuoy
Motto: Attende et vigila
(Be alert and on guard)

No.283 Squadron began to form in the latter part of February 1943 at the Algiers seaplane station where the early arrivals found two hangars and a slipway available. Personnel continued to arrive during March and April but the Commanding Officer did not arrive until 25 April and this date can be taken to be the effective formation date for the squadron. The first two Walruses of the six on establishment arrived next day and ten days later the squadron moved out to operate its amphibians from land bases. Air-sea rescue missions were flown from North Africa and at the end of August a move was made to Sicily where the Walruses were conveniently placed to answer calls from Allied aircraft operating over Italy from North African bases. Soon detachments were sent to Sardinia and Italy and in December the squadron headquarters moved to Corsica to cover the waters off southern France and northern Italy. In March 1944 Warwicks were received and during the next month the Walruses were passed to 284 Squadron, the squadron moving to Malta where it flew anti-submarine patrols in addition to its ASR role. In October detachments were sent to southern Italy, Greece and Libya while at the end of January 1945, a detachment went to Saki, in the Crimea, to provide ASR facilities for aircraft proceeding to the Yalta Conference. At the end of the war, No.283 remained in Malta until disbanded on 31 March 1946.

Squadron bases			
Algiers	Feb 1943	Palermo	28 Aug 1943
Maison Blanche	6 May 1943	Ajaccio	25 Dec 1943
Tingley	13 May 1943	Borgo	29 Dec 1943
La Sebala	30 May 1943	Hal Far	6 Apr 1944
			to 31 Mar 1946

Aircraft Equipment	Period of service	Representative Serial
Walrus I, II	Apr 1943 – Apr 1944	X9471
Warwick I	Mar 1944 – Mar 1946	BV451 (B)

Walrus I, No.284 Squadron

No. 284 Squadron

Badge: In front of a demi-
fountain, a dolphin
Motto: From the deep

No.284 Squadron was formed on 7 May 1943 from detachments of other air-sea rescue units in the UK and after assembling at Gravesend, moved to Martlesham Heath to prepare for transfer to the Mediterranean. It left during June, the air echelon beginning to fly Walruses from Malta on 12 July while the ground crews arrived in Sicily on 15 August to join the squadron's air party. Rescue missions were flown around the island until November, the squadron headquarters moving to southern Italy at the end of September. Numerous detachments covered the seas traversed by Allied aircraft as far afield as Sardinia, Tunisia and southern France. In March 1944 Warwicks began to arrive and in September 1944 the Walruses were passed to No.293

Squadron and some Hurricanes taken on strength. At the same time headquarters of No.284 moved to Corsica to cover the Western Mediterranean until disbandment on 21 September 1945.

On 15 October 1956 No.284 reformed at Nicosia as a helicopter squadron for rescue and general support suties in Cyprus. On 1 August 1959 it was renumbered 103 Squadron.

Squadron bases

Gravesend	7 May 1943	Bone (D)	15 Sep 1944
Martlesham Heath	17 May 1943		to 14 Nov 1944
Left for Mediterranean		Elmas	17 Sep 1944
	3 Jun 1943 (A)	El Aouina (D)	27 Sep 1944
	16 Jun 1943 (G)		to 28 Jan 1945
Algiers	26 Jun 1943 (G)	Bone	14 Nov 1944
Hal Far	12 Jul 1943 (A)	Elmas (D)	14 Nov 1944
Cassibile	27 Jul 1943 (A)		to 4 Sep 1945
	15 Aug 1943 (G)	Istres (D)	10 Mar 1945
Lentini East	28 Aug 1943		to 20 Sep 1945
Scanzano	25 Sep 1943	Pomigliano (D)	17 Mar 1945
Gioia del Colle	2 Oct 1943		to 13 Apr 1945
Brindisi	15 Nov 1943	Pomigliano	13 Apr 1945
Alghero	14 Mar 1944		to 21 Sep 1945
Ramatuelle (D)	20 Aug 1944	Nicosia	15 Oct 1956
	to 17 Sep 1944 (to 293 Sq.)		to 1 Aug 1959

Sycamore HR.14, No.284 Squadron

Aircraft Equipment	Period of service	Representative Serial	
Walrus I	Jul 1943 — Sep 1944	W3012	(W)
Warwick I	Mar 1944 — Sep 1945	BV460	(L)
Hurricane IIC	Sep 1944 — Mar 1945	HW249	
Sycamore HR.14	Oct 1956 -- Jul 1959	XJ384	
Whirlwind HAR.2	Nov 1956 — Aug 1959	XJ766	

No. 285 Squadron

Badge: In front of a pair of wings elevated and conjoined in base, two bird bolts in saltire

Motto: Respice finem
(Consider the end)

Squadron bases

Wrexham	1 Dec 1941
Honiley	29 Oct 1942
Woodvale	27 Aug 1943
Andover	19 Nov 1944
North Weald	4 Jan 1945
Weston Zoyland	20 Jun 1945
	to 26 Jun 1945

No.285 Squadron was formed at Wrexham on 1 December 1941 from No.9 Group AAC Flight. Equipped initially with Lysanders, Blenheims and Hudsons, it provided aircraft for target towing and simulated attacks to exercise anti-aircraft defences basing various detachments for these purposes at a number of airfields. Defiants, and later Martinets, took over the target-towing duties and Oxfords the bulk of the gunlaying training while some fighter types were used for high speed practice. After several moves of headquarters, the squadron disbanded on 26 June 1945.

Aircraft Equipment	Period of service	Representative Serial
Lysander III, IIIA	Dec 1941 — Jun 1942	V9727
Blenheim I	Dec 1941 — Mar 1942	
Hudson I	Dec 1941 — Mar 1942	V9038
Oxford II	Mar 1942 — Jun 1945	DG156
Defiant I, III	Mar 1942 — Jan 1944	DR882
Martinet I	Jul 1943 — Dec 1943	MS507
Beaufighter I	Sep 1943 — Nov 1944	T4640
Hurricane IIC	Jan 1944 — Jun 1945	LF600
Mustang I	Mar 1945 — Jun 1945	AG366

No. 286 Squadron

Badge: In front of a three-bladed propellor, a grenade fired

Motto: Praesidia nostra exercemus
(We exercise our defences)

Squadron bases

Filton	17 Nov 1941	Locking	10 Oct 1942
Lulsgate Bottom	24 Jan 1942	Weston Zoyland	29 Nov 1943
Colerne	Mar 1942	Culmhead	10 Apr 1944
Lulsgate Bottom	30 Apr 1942	Colerne	20 May 1944
Zeals	26 May 1942	Zeals	28 Jul 1944
Colerne	1 Sep 1942	Weston Zoyland	28 Sep 1944
			to 16 May 1945

No.286 Squadron was formed on 17 November 1941 from No.10 Group AAC Flight at Filton and provided detachments of aircraft at numerous airfields in south-west England for target-towing and gunlaying training for the anti-aircraft defences in the area. On 16 May 1945 the squadron was disbanded.

Aircraft Equipment	Period of service	Representative Serial	
Oxford II	Nov 1941 — May 1945	BG630	
Defiant I, III	Nov 1941 — Jul 1944	AA628	(NW-V)
Master III	Nov 1944 — Mar 1945	W8833	
Hurricane I	Nov 1941 — Jun 1943	AG101	
Hurricane IIC, IV	Apr 1942 — May 1945	PG488	
Martinet I	Jul 1943 — Dec 1944	MS509	

No. 287 Squadron

Badge: A popinjay displayed
perched
Motto: C'est en forgeant (French)
(Practice makes perfect)

Squadron bases			
Croydon	19 Nov 1941	Hornchurch	3 May 1945
North Weald	4 Jul 1944	Bradwell Bay	15 Jun 1945
Gatwick	27 Aug 1944	West Malling	10 Sep 1945
Redhill	20 Jan 1945		to 15 Jun 1946

Aircraft Equipment	Period of service	Representative Serial
Blenheim IV	Nov 1941 – Feb 1942	T2291
Lysander I, III, IIIA	Nov 1941 – May 1942	R1688
Hurricane IIB, IV	Nov 1941 – Feb 1944	W9294
Hudson III	Nov 1941 – Apr 1942	V9160
Master III	Feb 1942 – Sep 1942	W8839
Defiant I, III	Apr 1942 – Oct 1943	DR961
Oxford II	Apr 1942 – Jun 1946	T1005
Martinet I	Sep 1943 – Jun 1946	JN673
Beaufighter I, VI, X	Nov 1944 – Jul 1946	X7626
Tempest V	Nov 1944 – Jun 1945	JN769
Spitfire VB	Nov 1944 – Mar 1944	EN765
Spitfire IX	Nov 1944 – Aug 1945	NH547
Spitfire XVIE	Jun 1945 – Jun 1946	TD132

No.287 Squadron was formed on 19 November 1941 at Croydon from No.11 Group AAC Flight. It provided detachments at numerous airfields in southern England for target-towing and gunlaying exercises until the end of the war and disbanded on 15 June 1946.

No. 288 Squadron

Badge: A stag courant, charged
on the shoulder with a
bezant
Motto: Honour through deeds

No.288 Squadron was formed at Digby on 18 November 1941 from No.12 Group AAC Flight. It provided anti-aircraft co-operation with a variety of aircraft and provided practice for anti-aircraft units in Lincolnshire and Yorkshire for the rest of the war. In May 1945 it re-equipped with Vengeances and was disbanded on 15 June 1946.

On 16 March 1953 the squadron reformed at Middle Wallop with Spitfires to provide target aircraft for training all-weather fighter crews using Brigands of No.288 OCU at Colerne. Balliols replaced the Spitfires after only a few weeks and were flown until the squadron disbanded on 12 September 1957.

Squadron bases			
Digby	18 Nov 1941	Church Fenton	19 Nov 1944
Wellingore	5 Dec 1942	Hutton Cranswick	
Digby	18 Jan 1943		Aug 1945 (P)
Coleby Grange	9 Nov 1943	East Moor	24 May 1946
Digby	25 Nov 1943		to 15 Jun 1956
Collyweston	11 Jan 1944	Middle Wallop	16 Mar 1953
			to 12 Sep 1957

Aircraft Equipment	Period of service	Representative Serial
Blenheim IV	Nov 1941 – Dec 1941	L8837
Lysander II, III	Nov 1941 – Mar 1942	P9060
Hurricane I, IIC	Nov 1941 – 1944	KZ576 (RP-P)
Hudson III	Dec 1941 – Mar 1942	AE606
Defiant I, III	Mar 1942 – Jul 1943	T4069
Oxford I, II	Mar 1942 – May 1945	X6779
Beaufighter VI, X	Mar 1944 – Nov 1944	R2137
Spitfire IX, XVI	1944 – Jun 1946	SL669 (RP-K)
Vengeance II	May 1945 – Jun 1946	HB517 (RP-O)
Spitfire LF.16E	Mar 1953 – Jul 1953	TB549
Balliol T.2	Jun 1953 – Sep 1957	XF931

No. 289 Squadron

No.289 Squadron was formed at Kirknewton on 20 November 1941 as a anti-aircraft co-operation unit from No.13 Group AAC Flight. It stationed detachments at various airfields in southern Scotland and north-east England for co-operation with anti-aircraft batteries in the area until the end of the war. On 26 June 1945 the squadron disbanded.

Squadron bases			
Kirknewton	20 Nov 1941	Eshott	18 May 1945
Turnhouse	20 May 1942	Andover	5 Jun 1945
Acklington	7 May 1945		to 26 Jun 1945

Aircraft Equipment	Period of service	Representative Serial
Blenheim IV	Nov 1941 – Jan 1942	Z5880
Lysander III	Nov 1941 – Mar 1942	T9140
Hudson III	Dec 1941 – Mar 1942	AE505
Hurricane I, IIC, IV	Dec 1941 – Jun 1945	LF628 (YE-S)
Oxford II	Mar 1942 – Jun 1945	LX575
Defiant I, III	Mar 1942 – Jul 1943	DR875
Martinet I	Jun 1943 – Apr 1945	MS513
Vengeance II	Mar 1945 – Jun 1945	FB335
Spitfire XVI	May 1945 – Jun 1945	

No. 290 Squadron

No.290 Squadron was formed at Newtownards from Nos.1617 and 1480 (AAC) Flights on 1 December 1943, for anti-aircraft co-operation duties with the defences of Northern Ireland. A detachment of No.289 Squadron at West Freugh was also absorbed. In August 1944 the squadron moved to Scotland and in January 1945 was sent to Belgium to provide practice for army AA units defending Allied bases in the Low Countries. It remained there until disbanded on 27 October 1945.

Squadron bases			
Newtownards	1 Dec 1943	B.83 Knocke-le-Zoute	
Long Kesh	25 Mar 1944		31 Jan 1945
Turnhouse	28 Aug 1944		to 27 Oct 1945

Aircraft Equipment	Period of service	Representative Serial
Oxford II	Dec 1943 – Oct 1945	HN840
Martinet I	Dec 1943 – Oct 1945	JN581
Hurricane IIC	Dec 1943 – Jan 1945	KZ190
Spitfire VB	Dec 1944 – Oct 1945	BM356

No. 291 Squadron

No.291 Squadron was formed on 1 December 1943 at Hutton Cranswick from Nos.1613, 1629 and 1634 (AAC) Flights. Its main task was to provide target-towing aircraft for anti-aircraft batteries along the East Coast until the end of the war and the squadron disbanded on 26 June 1945.

Squadron bases
Hutton Cranswick 1 Dec 1943
to 26 Jun 1945

Aircraft Equipment	Period of service	Representative Serial
Martinet I	Dec 1943 – Jun 1945	EM616
Hurricane IIC	Mar 1944 – Jun 1945	LF623
Vengeance II	Nov 1944 – Jun 1945	HD442

No. 292 Squadron

No.292 Squadron was formed on 1 February 1944 at Jessore for air-sea rescue duties over the Bay of Bengal, a detachment being based in Ceylon. Initially Walruses were used and in April 1944 were supplemented by Warwicks, but the latter proved unsuitable for tropical conditions and were replaced by Liberators in December. Some Sea Otters were received in November 1944, and as well as carrying out searches over the sea the squadron also covered the coastal area of Burma. In February 1945 the squadron moved to Agartala to be closer to the operational areas as the front line in Burma moved eastwards and it disbanded there on 14 June 1945, its duties being taken over by Nos.1347, 1348 and 1349 Flights operating independently.

Squadron bases
Jessore   1 Feb 1944
Agartala   5 Feb 1945
to 14 Jun 1945

Aircraft Equipment	Period of service	Representative Serial
Walrus I, II	Feb 1944 – Jun 1945	HD808
Warwick I	Apr 1944 – Jun 1945†	HF970 (Q)
Sea Otter	Nov 1944 – Jun 1945	JM766
Liberator VI	Dec 1944 – Jun 1945	KH319 (F)

†Non-operational from December 1944

No. 293 Squadron

Badge: Over waves of the sea, a dexter hand couped at the wrist in bend sinister
Motto: Ex aere salus
(Safety from the air)

On 20 October 1943 ten Warwicks drawn from Nos.283 and 284 Squadrons left the UK for Algeria and on 28 November were redesignated No.293 Squadron at Blida. The squadron began air-sea rescue patrols along the North African coast and in January 1944 began operating detachments in Italy until the squadron headquarters moved there in March. In April 1944 it absorbed several detachments of Walruses from No.283 Squadron and provided air-sea rescue coverage off the Italian coasts until disbanded on 5 April 1946.

Squadron bases
Blida   28 Nov 1943
Bone   1 Dec 1943
Pomigliano   28 Mar 1944
Foggia   21 Mar 1945
Pomigliano   27 Jun 1945
to 5 Apr 1946

Aircraft Equipment	Period of service	Representative Serial
Warwick I	Nov 1943 – Apr 1946	BV315 (ZE-H)
Walrus I, II	Apr 1944 – Apr 1946	Z1813

No. 294 Squadron

Badge: An eagle volant, carrying in the claws a lifebelt
Motto: Vita ex undis abrepta
(Life snatched from the waves)

No.294 Squadron was formed on 24 September 1943 from the Air-sea Rescue Flight at Berka equipped with Wellingtons and Walruses for rescue duties in the Eastern Mediterranean. Detachments were provided in Libya, Cyprus and Palestine and later Greece. In November 1944 Warwicks supplemented the Wellingtons and in addition to ASR missions, the squadron also flew anti-submarine patrols. In June 1945 No.294 moved to Basra and supplied detachments for the Persian Gulf and Arabian Sea areas until disbanded on 8 April 1946.

Wellington XI, No.294 Squadron

Squadron bases
Berka   24 Sep 1943
Amriya South   5 Oct 1943
Idku   29 Mar 1944
Basra   20 Jun 1945
to 8 Apr 1946

Aircraft Equipment	Period of service	Representative Serial
Walrus I	Sep 1943 – Apr 1946	W3050 (G)
Wellington IC	Sep 1943 – May 1944	N2812 (Q)
Wellington XI	Mar 1944 – Nov 1944	MP588 (L)
Wellington XIII	May 1944 – Apr 1946	ME941 (U)
Warwick I	Nov 1944 – Apr 1946	BV966 (B)

Stirling IV, No.295 Squadron

No. 295 Squadron

Badge: A hand manacled and
couped at the wrist
holding a sword in its
scabbard in bend sinister

Motto: In caelo auxilium
(Aid from the skies)

No.295 Squadron was formed at Netheravon on 3 August 1942 as an airborne forces unit and was initially equipped with Whitleys. In November leaflet-dropping flights began over France and in February 1943 Halifaxes were received as additional aircraft. In June 1943 the Halifaxes were engaged in towing gliders to North Africa, a task which continued till September. In October conversion to Albemarles began and these continued supply drops to the resistance forces on France while the squadron trained for its part in the invasion of Europe. On the eve of D-Day, a 295 Squadron aircraft shared with one of 570 Squadron the distinction of dropping the first troops of the invasion force into Normandy; this was followed by twenty-one aircraft of No.295 towing gliders to the landing zones. Nineteen more followed during the day with reinforcements. In September 1944 the squadron sent twenty-two Stirlings towing gliders

to Arnhem followed by seventy-five supply aircraft in the succeeding days, three being lost. The final assault landing was in March 1945, when the Lower Rhine was crossed and a few days after the German surrender twenty-two Stirlings took troops to Norway to disarm the German garrison. A period of trooping duties followed, mainly to the Continent, before the squadron was disbanded on 14 January 1946.

On 1 February 1946 No.295 reformed at Tarrant Rushton as a transport squadron with Halifaxes but disbanded again on 31 March 1946. It reformed at Fairford, again with Halifaxes, on 19 September 1947 as an airborne forces squadron and disbanded finally on 1 October 1948.

Squadron bases

Netheravon	3 Aug 1942	Tarrant Rushton	1 Feb 1946
Holmsley South	1 May 1943		to 31 Mar 1946
Hurn	30 Jun 1943	Fairford	10 Sep 1947
Harwell	14 Mar 1944		to 1 Oct 1948
Rivenhall	7 Oct 1944		
	to 14 Jan 1946		

Aircraft Equipment	Period of service	Representative Serial
Whitley V	Aug 1942 — Nov 1943	EB311
Halifax V	Feb 1943 — Nov 1943	DK130 (PX-EE)
Albemarle I, II	Oct 1943 — Jul 1944	V1749
Stirling IV	Jul 1944 — Jan 1946	LJ652 (8E-X)
Halifax VIII	Feb 1946 — Mar 1946	NA343
Halifax A.9	Sep 1947 — Oct 1948	RT903

No. 296 Squadron

Badge: In front of a sword in pale,
the point downwards,
a scroll

Motto: Prepared for all things

No.296 Squadron was formed at Ringway on 25 January 1942 from the Glider Exercise Unit and took its Hectors and Harts to Netheravon a few days later to tow Hotspurs on training flights. In June 1942 it began to receive Whitleys and in July divided into 296A and 296B Squadron, the former moving to Hurn and becoming the entire squadron on 12 August 1942, when No.296B was redesignated the Glider Pilot Exercise Unit. In October the squadron began leaflet dropping flights over France and in January 1943 began converting to Albemarles. These were flown out to Algeria in June to take part in the airborne landings in Sicily, returning in October to the UK. On the eve of

D-Day, the squadron supplied three pathfinder aircraft followed by eight others with gliders as part of the initial wave of airborne troops. Nineteen more Horsas were towed in on D-Day. At Arnhem twenty-five gliders were towed on the opening day followed by twenty-one more on the following day without loss. Conversion to Halifaxes began at the end of September and supply drops to resistance forces resumed. Thirty Halifaxes took part in the Rhine crossing in March 1945 and at the end of the war troops were flown to Norway and Denmark followed by flights bringing released prisoners-of-war back to the UK. In December 1945 mail flights to India began but the squadron disbanded on 23 January 1946.

Halifax III, No.296 Squadron

Squadron bases

Ringway	25 Jan 1942	Goubrine II	24 Jun 1943
Netheravon	1 Feb 1942	Stoney Cross	25 Jun 1943
Hurn	25 Jul 1942	Hurn	15 Oct 1943
Andover	25 Oct 1942	Brize Norton	14 Mar 1944
Hurn	19 Dec 1942	Earl's Colne	29 Sep 1944
Froha	4 Jun 1943		to 23 Jan 1946

Aircraft

Equipment	Period of service	Representative Serial
Hector	Jan 1942 – Aug 1942	K8146
Hart	Jan 1942 – Aug 1942	K6584
Whitley V	Jun 1942 – Mar 1943	BD493 (XH-J)
Albemarle I, II	Jan 1943 – Sep 1944	P1146
Albemarle V, VI	Sep 1944 – Nov 1944	V1818
Halifax V	Sep 1944 – Mar 1945	LL651
Halifax III	Jan 1945 – Jan 1946	NA668
Halifax VII	Dec 1945 – Jan 1946	PN322

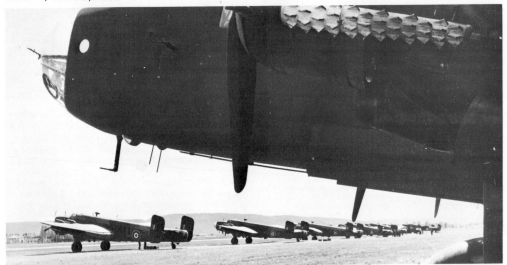

No. 297 Squadron

No.297 Squadron was formed at Netheravon on 22 January 1942 from the Parachute Exercise Squadron and began to receive Whitleys for training paratroops in February. Leaflet-dropping flights began in October and in July 1943 Albemarles were received to supplement the Whitleys. By February 1944 the squadron was completely equipped with Albemarles and these flew supply-dropping flights to resistance forces in France until D-Day. Twenty-four Albemarles took airborne troops to Normandy before the landings and twenty more followed during the day. At Arnhem in September, No.297 towed twenty-eight gliders to the landing zones following next day with twenty-four more. In October the squadron converted to Halifaxes and supplied thirty of these for the airborne part of the Rhine crossing in March 1945. After the end of the war, trooping flights to the Continent began.

Early in 1946, the squadron settled down in the UK as a transport support unit for airborne forces but was reduced to a cadre in September and began converting to Halifax A.9s in January 1947. These were disposed of in October 1948, to allow the crews to convert to Hastings at Dishforth. In December 1948 the squadron detached its converted crews to Schleswigland as part of the force engaged in the Berlin Airlift. The squadron concentrated on delivering coal to the blockaded city until October 1949, when the airlift tailed off after the Russian blockade collapsed. On return flights, the Hastings brought back manufactured goods from Berlin factories. In December 1949 No.297 returned to the UK to be based at Topcliffe which had succeeded Dishforth as the squadron's maintenance base in August 1949, and after a period as an airborne support unit it disbanded on 15 November 1950, most of the crews being transferred to No.24 Squadron at Lyneham.

Squadron bases

Netheravon	22 Jan 1942	Brize Norton	5 Sep 1946
Hurn	5 Jun 1942	Fairford	21 Aug 1947
Thruxton	25 Oct 1942	Dishforth	17 Oct 1948
Stoney Cross	1 Sep 1943	Schleswigland	13 Dec 1948
Brize Norton	14 Mar 1944	Wunstorf	7 Oct 1949
Earl's Colne	30 Sep 1944	Topcliffe	13 Dec 1949
Tarrant Rushton	Mar 1946		to 15 Nov 1950

Aircraft

Equipment	Period of service	Representative Serial
Whitley V	Feb 1942 – Feb 1944	BD872 (L5-S)
Albemarle I, II	Jul 1943 – Oct 1944	P1400 (L5-K)
Albemarle V, VI	Feb 1944 – Dec 1944	V1841 (L5-T)
Halifax III	Oct 1944 – Mar 1946	LK988 (L5-H)
Halifax VII	Dec 1945 – Mar 1947	PN286
Halifax V	Oct 1944 – Dec 1944	LL312
Halifax A.9	Jan 1947 – Oct 1948	RT786
Hastings C.1	Nov 1948 – Nov 1950	TG603 (X)

Halifax III, No.298 Squadron

No. 298 Squadron

Badge: A hand holding a dagger
in bend sinister thrusting
to the dexter
Motto: Silent we strike

No.298 Squadron was formed at Thruxton on 24 August 1942 as an airborne forces unit but after receiving a few Whitleys it was disbanded on 19 October 1942. The squadron reformed at Tarrant Rushton from A Flight of No.295 Squadron with Halifaxes and in February 1944, began supply-dropping flights over France in addition to training for the invasion of Europe. On the eve of D-Day, the squadron sent six aircraft with Horsa gliders to capture the Orne bridges before the main landings and later towed fifteen gliders to the landing zones in Normandy. For the Arnhem landing, the squadron towed thirteen Horsas and seven Hamilcars on the first day, and eight of each on the second. Ten Horsas on the third day took reinforcements to the 1st Airborne Division. For the Rhine crossing, No.298 contributed tugs for twenty-five Horsas and six Hamilcars and after the end of the war took troops to Norway and Denmark. In August 1945 the squadron began flying out to India arriving at Raipur over a period. After a period of general transport duties, it reverted to being an airborne forces squadron in July 1946, and disbanded on 21 December 1946.

Squadron bases

Thruxton	24 Aug 1942	Raipur	Aug 1946 (P)
	to 19 Oct 1942	Digri	9 Dec 1945
Tarrant Rushton	4 Nov 1943	Baroda	20 May 1946
Woodbridge	21 Mar 1945	Mauripur	24 Jul 1946
Tarrant Rushton	24 Mar 1945		to 21 Dec 1946

Aircraft Equipment	Period of service	Representative Serial
Whitley V	Aug 1942 – Oct 1942	EB287
Halifax V	Nov 1943 – Aug 1945	LL224 (8A-A)
Halifax III	Oct 1944 – Aug 1945	NA119 (8A-T)
Halifax VII	Aug 1945 – Dec 1946	PN259 (8T-G)

No. 299 Squadron

No.299 Squadron was formed at Stoney Cross on 4 November 1943 from a nucleus supplied by C Flight of No.297 Squadron. Initially it was equipped with Venturas but in January 1944 replaced these with Stirlings. Training with the airborne forces took up most of the squadron's time but on 5 April No.299 flew its first supply-dropping mission to France with supplies for resistance forces. On D-Day twenty-four Stirlings of the squadron took paratroopers to Normandy before dawn and followed these by sixteen aircraft towing gliders into the dropping zones, losing two aircraft in the process. Supply drops continued until the next major airborne operation, the capture of the bridges at Grave, Nijmegen and Arnhem. Between 17 and 23 September the squadron despatched fifty-four glider tugs (on the first three days) and seventy-two re-supply aircraft to Arnhem, losing five aircraft to concentrated enemy flak in the process. The final airborne landing of the war at Wesel during the Rhine crossing met with little resistance and twenty-nine sorties were flown without loss. In May 1945 airborne troops were taken to Oslo to disarm the German occupation forces and after a period of general transport duties the squadron disbanded on 15 February 1946.

Squadron bases

Stoney Cross	4 Nov 1943
Keevil	15 Mar 1944
Wethersfield	9 Oct 1944
Shepherds Grove	25 Jan 1945
	to 15 Feb 1946

Aircraft Equipment	Period of service	Representative Serial
Ventura I, II	Nov 1943 – Jan 1944	AE733
Stirling IV	Jan 1944 – Feb 1946	LJ891 (5G-D)

No. 300 Squadron

Name: 'Mazowiecki'

No.300 Squadron was formed on 1 July 1940, at Bramcote with Polish personnel as a light bomber squadron equipped with Battles. After only a few operations with these, it moved to Swinderby in August where it converted to a Wellington squadron in October. After taking part in night raids with Wellingtons until March 1944, No.300 re-equipped with Lancasters for the rest of the war. It formed part of the main force of Bomber Command until disbanded on 11 October 1946.

Squadron bases

Bramcote	1 Jul 1940	Hemswell	31 Jan 1943
Swinderby	22 Aug 1940	Ingham	22 Jun 1943
Hemswell	18 Jul 1941	Faldingworth	1 Mar 1944
Ingham	18 May 1942		to 11 Oct 1946

Aircraft

Equipment	Period of service	Representative Serial
Battle I	Jul 1940 – Oct 1940	N2147 (BH-Q)
Wellington IC	Oct 1940 – Dec 1941	R1184 (BH-B)
Wellington IV	Aug 1941 – Jan 1943	Z1320 (BH-K)
Wellington III	Jan 1943 – Apr 1943	Z1661 (BH-Z)
Wellington X	Mar 1943 – Apr 1944	HF598 (BH-M)
Lancaster I, III	Apr 1944 – Oct 1946	JB561 (BH-B)

Warwick III, No.301 Squadron

No. 301 Squadron

Name: 'Pomorski'

No.301 Squadron was formed on 26 July 1940, at Bramcote as a Polish-manned light bomber squadron equipped with Battles. In September it began night attacks on enemy invasion barges in the Channel Ports but began to convert to Wellingtons in October. These became operational before the end of the year and No.301 continued night raids until 31 March 1943, when the squadron was withdrawn from operations and disbanded on 7 April 1943, many of the crews being transferred to No.300 Squadron.

On 7 November 1944, No.301 reformed at Brindisi from No.1586 (Special Duties) Flight. Equipped with Halifaxes and Liberators. it flew supply-dropping missions to Poland, Yugoslavia and northern Italy in support of partisan forces. In March 1945, the personnel of the squadron moved to the UK where they reformed at Blackbushe on 4 April 1945, as a transport unit. During May, Warwicks began to arrive

and in July regular services began to Norway, Italy and Greece. In January 1946 the squadron converted to Halifaxes but in April operational flights ceased and only training sorties were flown thereafter until the squadron was disbanded on 10 December 1946.

Squadron bases

Bramcote	26 Jul 1940	Brindisi	7 Nov 1944
Swinderby	28 Aug 1940	Blackbushe	4 Apr 1945
Hemswell	18 Jul 1941	North Weald	2 Jul 1945
	to 7 Apr 1943	Chedburgh	4 Sep 1945
			to 10 Dec 1946

Aircraft

Equipment	Period of service	Representative Serial
Battle	Jul 1940 – Nov 1940	P6567 (GR-E)
Wellington IC	Oct 1940 – Aug 1941	X9666 (GR-N)
Wellington IV	Aug 1941 – Apr 1943	Z1257 (GR-J)
Halifax II	Nov 1944 – Mar 1945	JP136 (D)
Halifax V	Nov 1944 – Mar 1945	LL118 (C)
Liberator VI	Nov 1944 – Mar 1945	KG994 (R)
Warwick III	May 1945 – Jan 1946	HG275 (GR-S)
Halifax VIII	Jan 1946 – Dec 1946	PP338

No. 302 Squadron

Name: 'Poznanski'

No.302 Squadron was formed on 13 July 1940, with Polish personnel who had escaped from France after the German invasion. It began training with Hurricanes at Leconfield and in mid-October moved to Northolt to take part in the final stages of the Battle of Britain. In May 1941 it moved to the Isle of Man where it was engaged in defensive and convoy protection duties, being transferred to south-west England in August where it re-equipped with Spitfires in October. With these it began to fly offensive sweeps over northern France until February 1943 when it moved to Lincolnshire and Yorkshire for a four-month period of defensive duties. In June it returned south to join Second TAF's sweeps over France. In April 1944, the squadron took up a fighter-bomber role in preparation for the invasion of France and in August moved into the beachhead to provide ground-attack support for the Allied armies in Normandy. After the breakout, it moved forward until based in Belgium by early October. For the rest of the war No.302 flew sweeps over Germany in search of transport and troop targets and at the end of April 1945, occupied its first base in Germany. It remained as part of the occupation forces until disbanded on 18 December 1946.

Spitfire I, No.303 Squadron

Squadron bases

Leconfield	13 Jul 1940	Deanland	1 Apr 1944
Northolt	11 Oct 1940	Southend	12 Apr 1944
Westhampnett	23 Nov 1940	Deanland	14 Apr 1944
Kenley	7 Apr 1941	Chailey	26 Apr 1944
Jurby	29 May 1941	Appledram	28 Jun 1944
Churchstanton	7 Aug 1941	Ford	16 Jul 1944
Warmwell	5 Sep 1941	B.10 Plumetot	3 Aug 1944
Harrowbeer	6 Oct 1941	Fairwood Common	
Warmwell	26 Apr 1942		31 Aug 1944
Heston	7 May 1942	B.51 Lille/Vendeville	
Croydon	30 Jun 1942		16 Sep 1944
Heston	7 Jul 1942	B.70 Deurne	3 Oct 1944
Ipswich	21 Sep 1942	B.61 St. Denis Westrem	
Heston	29 Sep 1942		11 Oct 1944
Kirton-in-Lindsey		B.60 Grimbergen	13 Jan 1945
	2 Feb 1943	B.77 Gilze-Rijen	9 Mar 1945
Hutton Cranswick		B.113 Varrelbusch	
	17 Apr 1943		27 Apr 1945
Heston	1 Jun 1943	B.170 Sylt	27 Aug 1945
Perranporth	20 Jun 1943	B.113 Varrelbusch	
Fairlop	19 Aug 1943		14 Sep 1945
Tangmere	18 Sep 1943	B.111 Ahlhorn	16 Sep 1945
Northolt	21 Sep 1943		to 18 Dec 1946

Aircraft Equipment

Equipment	Period of service	Representative Serial
Hurricane I	Jul 1940 – Mar 1941 May 1941 – Jul 1941	P2752 (WX-R)
Hurricane IIA	Mar 1941 – May 1941	Z2772 (WX-B)
Hurricane IIB	Jul 1941 – Oct 1941	Z5004 (WX-T)
Spitfire VB, VC	Oct 1941 – Sep 1943	W3902 (WX-A)
Spitfire IXC, IXE	Sep 1943 – Feb 1945	MA791 (WX-B)
Spitfire XVI	Feb 1945 – Dec 1946	SM419

No. 303 Squadron

Name: 'Warsaw-Kosciusco'

No.303 Squadron was formed at Northolt on 2 August 1940, with Polish personnel evacuated from France and became operational with Hurricanes before the end of the month. It took part in the Battle of Britain until mid-October when it was withdrawn to Yorkshire for defensive duties. In January 1941 it returned to Northolt to re-equip with Spitfires and began offensive sweeps over France. In July 1941 it moved to Speke for the defence of Merseyside, returning south in October to resume offensive operations. In June 1942, No.303 moved to Lincolnshire and in February 1943, came back to the south for a further period of sweeps. In November 1943, the squadron was transferred to Northern Ireland where it provided protection for shipping arriving in the Clyde and Irish Sea areas. In April 1944 it joined Second TAF in readiness for the landings in Normandy but remained in England, moving to East Anglia to provide fighter escort for Bomber Command raids and carry out armed reconnaissance missions over the Netherlands. In April 1945 No.303 converted to Mustangs but flew only two operations with these before the end of the war. On 26 November 1946, all flying ceased and the squadron disbanded on 11 December 1946.

Squadron bases

Northolt	2 Aug 1940	Heston	8 Apr 1943
Leconfield	11 Oct 1940	Northolt	1 Jun 1943
Northolt	3 Jan 1941	Ballyhalbert	12 Nov 1943
Speke	16 Jul 1941	Horne	30 Apr 1944
Northolt	7 Oct 1941	Westhampnett	18 Jun 1944
Kirton-in-Lindsey		Merston	26 Jun 1944
	16 Jun 1942	Westhampnett	9 Aug 1944
Redhill	15 Aug 1942	Coltishall	25 Sep 1944
Kirton-in-Lindsey		Andrews Field	4 Apr 1945
	20 Aug 1942	Coltishall	16 May 1945
Northolt	2 Feb 1943	Andrews Field	19 Aug 1945
Heston	5 Feb 1943	Turnhouse	28 Nov 1945
Debden	5 Mar 1943	Wick	5 Jan 1946
Heston	12 Mar 1943	Charterhall	6 Mar 1946
Martlesham Heath		Hethel	23 Mar 1946
	26 Mar 1943		to 11 Dec 1946

Aircraft Equipment	Period of service	Representative Serial
Hurricane I	Aug 1940 – Jan 1941	P3120 (RF-D)
Hurricane IIA	Nov 1940 – Jan 1941	
Spitfire I	Jan 1941 – Feb 1941	R6773 (RF-P)
Spitfire IIA	Feb 1941 – Oct 1941	P8073 (RF-Z)
Spitfire VB	Oct 1941 – Jun 1943	W3893 (RF-K)
	Nov 1943 – Jul 1944	AD247 (RF-P)
Spitfire IX	Jun 1943 – Nov 1943	MH777 (RF-N)
	Jul 1944 – Apr 1945	
Spitfire XVI	Feb 1945 – Apr 1945	
Mustang IV	Apr 1945 – Dec 1946	KM112 (PD-D)

No. 304 Squadron

Name: 'Slaski'

No.304 Squadron was formed at Bramcote as a Polish-manned light bomber unit on 22 August 1940, but converted to Wellingtons in November before beginning operations. On 25 April 1941 these flew the first squadron missions and the squadron spent a year with Bomber Command before being transferred to Coastal Command in May 1942. Based on Tiree, it began patrols on 18 May but moved to Pembrokeshire in June and began operating over the Bay of Biscay. Specialised patrol Wellingtons arrived in June 1943. The squadron was based in East Anglia from April until June 1943, flying anti-E-boat patrols over the North Sea and returning to the Bay patrols on arrival in Cornwall. In September 1944, the squadron moved to Benbecula for patrols over the North Atlantic, returning to Cornwall in March 1945. In July No.304 was transferred to Transport Command and received Warwicks. Flights to Italy and Greece began in December 1945 and continued until the squadron converted to Halifaxes in April 1946. These were flown for training purposes until disbandment on 10 December 1946.

Squadron bases

Bramcote	22 Aug 1940	Davidstowe Moor	7 Jun 1943
Syerston	2 Dec 1940	Predannack	13 Dec 1943
Lindholme	19 Jul 1941	Chivenor	19 Feb 1944
Tiree	10 May 1942	Benbecula	21 Sep 1944
Dale	15 Jun 1942	St. Eval	6 Mar 1945
Talbenny	3 Nov 1942	North Weald	10 Jul 1945
Dale	30 Nov 1942	Chedburgh	6 Sep 1945
Docking	2 Apr 1943		to 10 Dec 1946

Aircraft Equipment	Period of service	Representative Serial
Battle	Aug 1940 – Nov 1940	L5522
Wellington IC	Nov 1940 – Jul 1943	R1443
Wellington X	Jun 1943 – Jul 1943	HZ577
Wellington XIII	Jul 1943 – Sep 1943	HZ551
Wellington XIV	Sep 1943 – Jan 1946	HF203 (NZ-J)
Warwick III	Jul 1945 – May 1946	HG332 (QD-U)
Halifax C.8	May 1946 – Dec 1946	PP236

No. 305 Squadron

Name: 'Weilkopolski'

No.305 Squadron was formed at Bramcote on 29 August 1940 as a light bomber unit manned by Polish personnel. It received Battles but two months later converted to Wellingtons for night bombing. Attacks on enemy targets began in April 1941 and were maintained until August 1943 when the squadron was transferred to day bombing. It joined No.2 Group and re-equipped with Mitchells, taking part in its first daylight raid in November 1943. After flying only sixteen missions with Mitchells, the squadron converted to Mosquitos and began low-level attacks on enemy transport targets and airfields in February 1944. These continued for the rest of the war, a move being made to France in November 1944 to shorten the distance between No.305's base and targets in Germany. After the end of the war, the squadron remained with the occupation forces until October 1946 when it returned to the UK and disbanded on 6 January 1947.

Mosquito VI, No.305 Squadron

Squadron bases			
Bramcote	29 Aug 1940	A.27 Cambrai/Epinoy	
Syerston	4 Dec 1940		19 Nov 1944
Lindholme	20 Jul 1941	B.80 Volkel	30 Jul 1945
Hemswell	23 Jul 1942	B.77 Gilze-Rijen	7 Sep 1945
Ingham	22 Jun 1943	B.58 Melsbroek	24 Nov 1945
Swanton Morley	5 Sep 1943	Wahn	11 Mar 1946
Lasham	18 Nov 1943	Faldingworth	Oct 1946 (P)
Harfordbridge	30 Oct 1944		to 6 Jan 1947

Aircraft Equipment	Period of service	Representative Serial
Battle I	Sep 1940 – Nov 1940	L5052
Wellington IC	Nov 1940 – Jul 1941	R1016 (SM-A)
Wellington II	Jul 1941 – Aug 1942	Z8339 (SM-N)
Wellington IV	Aug 1942 – May 1943	R1530 (SM-A)
Wellington X	May 1943 – Sep 1943	HF491
Mitchell II	Sep 1943 – Dec 1943	FV913
Mosquito VI	Dec 1943 – Nov 1946	NS823 (SM-H)

No. 306 Squadron

Name: 'Torunski'

No. 306 Squadron was formed at Church Fenton on 28 August 1940, manned by Polish personnel and equipped with Hurricanes. It became operational on 8 September and moved to Northolt in April 1941 to take part in sweeps over northern France until October when it was allocated to the defence of Merseyside. Spitfires replaced Hurricanes in July 1941 and in December the squadron moved to south-west England to undertake sweeps over north-west France. After a few weeks in Lincolnshire in May 1942, No. 306 was back at Northolt for further sweeps until moving to Yorkshire in March 1943. In August 1943, it came south to join Second TAF's preparations for the invasion of France and in March 1944, converted to Mustangs. With these it helped cover the landings in Normandy but was transferred soon afterwards to combatting flying bombs over south-east England. In October 1944, the squadron moved to East Anglia for bomber escort duties, a task which it carried out till the end of the war. The squadron remained in Fighter Command until disbanded on 6 January 1947.

Squadron bases			
Church Fenton	28 Aug 1940	Heston	21 Sep 1943
Ternhill	7 Nov 1940	Llanbedr	19 Dec 1943
Northolt	3 Apr 1941	Heston	1 Jan 1944
Speke	7 Oct 1941	Llanbedr	15 Mar 1944
Churchstanton	12 Dec 1941	Heston	20 Mar 1944
Kirton-in-Lindsey		Coolham	1 Apr 1944
	3 May 1942	Holmsley South	22 Jun 1944
Northolt	16 Jun 1942	Ford	27 Jun 1944
Hutton Cranswick		Brenzett	9 Jul 1944
	13 Mar 1943	Andrews Field	10 Oct 1944
Catterick	30 May 1943	Coltishall	10 Aug 1945
Gravesend	11 Aug 1943	Fairwood Common	8 Oct 1945
Friston	19 Aug 1943	Coltishall	18 Nov 1945
			to 6 Jan 1947

Aircraft Equipment	Period of service	Representative Serial
Hurricane I	Aug 1940 – Apr 1941	V7118 (UZ-V)
Hurricane IIA	Apr 1941 – Jul 1941	Z2884 (UZ-Z)
Spitfire IIB	Jul 1941 – Dec 1941	P8471 (UZ-J)
Spitfire VB	Dec 1941 – Sep 1942	AB364 (UZ-A)
	Mar 1943 – Mar 1944	EP116 (UZ-L)
Spitfire IX	Sep 1942 – Mar 1943	BS458 (UZ-Z)
Mustang III	Mar 1944 – Jan 1947	FB393 (UZ-U)

No. 307 Squadron

Name: 'Lwowski'

No. 307 Squadron was formed at Kirton-in-Lindsey on 5 September 1940 as a night fighter unit manned by Polish personnel. After training with Defiants, it moved to the Isle of Man and became operational on 8 December. In January 1941 it moved to the mainland to defend Merseyside and at the end of March moved to the south-west. In August 1941 the squadron converted to Beaufighters which it flew until re-equipped with Mosquitos at the end of 1942. In May 1943 No. 307 began flying intruder missions over enemy airfields in France until November when it moved to Scotland. In March 1944 it was transferred to Lincolnshire and began intruder missions over Europe using advanced bases. The squadron's role was changed in January 1945 to bomber support and it moved to East Anglia to accompany Bomber Command's heavy bombers to counter enemy night fighter opposition to their night raids. After the end of the war, it remained in Fighter Command until disbanded on 2 January 1947.

Squadron bases			
Kirton-in-Lindsey	5 Sep 1940	Drem	9 Nov 1943
Jurby	7 Nov 1940	Coleby Grange	2 Mar 1944
Squires Gate	27 Jan 1941	Church Fenton	6 May 1944
Colerne	26 Mar 1941	Castle Camps	27 Jan 1945
Exeter	26 Apr 1941	Coltishall	18 May 1945
Fairwood Common		Horsham St. Faith	
	15 Apr 1943		24 Aug 1945
Predannack	7 Aug 1943		to 2 Jan 1947

Aircraft Equipment	Period of service	Representative Serial
Defiant	Sep 1940 – Aug 1941	N1704
Beaufighter II	Aug 1941 – May 1942	T3035
Beaufighter VI	May 1942 – Feb 1943	X8207
Mosquito II	Dec 1942 – Jan 1945	DZ260 (EW-B)
Mosquito VI	Aug 1943 – Nov 1943	HR141 (EW-P)
Mosquito XII	Jan 1944 – Jan 1945	HK165 (EW-A)
Mosquito 30	Oct 1944 – Nov 1946	RK951 (EW-N)

No. 308 Squadron

Name: 'Krakowski'

No. 308 Squadron was formed on 9 September 1940, at the RAF Polish Depot, Blackpool and moved to Speke on 12 December to begin training. During October, the squadron received Hurricanes and became operational on 12 December. In April 1941 it converted to Spitfires and in June moved to Northolt to undertake bomber escort missions over France. In December it was withdrawn to Lancashire, returning in April 1942, to offensive operations for a year. After defensive duties in Yorkshire between April and September 1943, No. 308 joined Second TAF and began fighter-bomber missions in preparation for the invasion of France. In August 1944 it moved to Normandy to support the Allied armies and moved forward to Belgium early in October. For the rest of the war the squadron carried out offensive sweeps over Germany, attacking enemy transport,

Spitfire IX, No.308 Squadron

airfields and troops movements. After a period with the occupation forces, it disbanded on 18 December 1946.

Squadron bases

Blackpool	9 Sep 1940	Heston	21 Sep 1942
Speke	12 Sep 1940	Northolt	29 Oct 1942
Baginton	25 Sep 1940	Church Fenton	29 Apr 1943
Chilbolton	1 Jun 1941	Hutton Cranswick	5 Jul 1943
Northolt	24 Jun 1941	Friston	7 Sep 1943
Woodvale	12 Dec 1941	Heston	21 Sep 1943
Exeter	1 Apr 1942	Northolt	29 Oct 1943
Hutton Cranswick	7 May 1942	Llanbedr	8 Mar 1944
Redhill	1 Jul 1942	Northolt	15 Mar 1944
Hutton Cranswick	7 Jul 1942	Deanland	1 Apr 1944
Heston	30 Jul 1942	Chailey	26 Apr 1944
Ipswich	1 Sep 1942	Appledram	28 Jun 1944
Ford	16 Jul 1944	B.77 Gilze-Rijen	9 Mar 1945
B.10 Plumetot	3 Aug 1944	B.101 Nordhorn	13 Apr 1945
B.31 Londonières	6 Sep 1944	Fairwood Common	
B.70 Deurne	3 Oct 1944		26 Apr 1945
B.61 St. Denis Westrem		B.113 Varrelbusch	2 Jun 1945
	11 Oct 1944	B.111 Ahlhorn	16 Sep 1945
B.60 Grimbergen	14 Jan 1945		to 18 Dec 1946

Aircraft

Equipment	Period of service	Representative Serial
Hurricane I	Oct 1940 – Apr 1941	P3598
Spitfire I	Apr 1941 – May 1941	X4144
Spitfire IIA, IIB	May 1941 – Sep 1941	P8022 (ZF-L)
Spitfire VB	Sep 1941 – Nov 1943	BL763 (ZF-U)
Spitfire IX	Nov 1943 – Mar 1945	MA299 (ZF-U)
Spitfire XVI	Mar 1945 – Dec 1946	TB896 (ZF-M)

Lysander IIIs, No.309 Squadron

No. 309 Squadron

Name: 'Ziemia Czerwienska'

No.309 Squadron was formed at Abbotsinch on 8 October 1940 as an army co-operation unit for work with the Polish Army in Scotland. It was equipped with Lysanders until March 1943 but Mustangs had been added in July 1942 which, in December, operated from Gatwick on tactical reconnaissance missions over France. In June 1943 the squadron moved to East Anglia and flew shipping reconnaissance off the Dutch and Belgian coasts. In February 1944 the unreliability of the Mustang's Allison engine caused No.309's conversion to Hurricanes and in April it moved back to Scotland for air defence duties. In October 1944 re-equipment with Merlin-powered Mustangs took place and in December the squadron moved to East Anglia to provide escorts for bombers, a task which lasted until the end of the war. It remained in Fighter Command until disbanded on 6 January 1947.

Squadron bases

Abbotsinch	8 Oct 1940	Snailwell	24 Nov 1943
Renfrew	6 Nov 1940	Drem	23 Apr 1944
Dunino	8 May 1941	Peterhead	13 Nov 1944
Findo Gask	25 Nov 1942	Andrews Field	12 Dec 1944
Kirknewton	8 Mar 1943	Coltishall	10 Aug 1945
Snailwell	4 Jun 1943	Bradwell Bay	8 Oct 1945
Wellingore	6 Nov 1943	Coltishall	16 Nov 1945
			to 6 Jan 1947

Aircraft

Equipment	Period of service	Representative Serial
Lysander III, IIIA	Nov 1940 – Mar 1943	T1467
Mustang I, IA	Jul 1942 – Feb 1944	AM221 (WC-A)
Hurricane IV	Feb 1944 – Apr 1944	LE749
Hurricane IIC	Apr 1944 – Jan 1944	PG428 (WC-W)
Mustang III	Oct 1944 – Jan 1947	FX908 (WC-K)

No. 310 Squadron

Badge: In front of a sword erect, a lion rampant queue fourchée
Motto: We fight to rebuild

No.310 Squadron was formed at Duxford on 10 July 1940 with Czechoslovak personnel as a fighter unit. Equipped with Hurricanes, it became operational on 18 August and took part in the Battle of Britain. In February 1941 sweeps over northern France until October when it was allocated moved to Scotland. It was transferred to Cornwall in December and flew defensive patrols till May 1942 when sweeps and bomber escorts were undertaken. In June 1943 No.310 returned to Scotland as part of the defences of Scapa Flow, acquiring some high-altitude Spitfires for this purpose but in September it was back in southern England operating across the Channel. As part of Second TAF, the squadron became a fighter-bomber unit and supported the Allied landings in Normandy. It remained in the UK flying armed reconnaissance sweeps from East Anglia and Kent until the end of the war. In August 1945 the squadron flew to Czechoslovakia where it was formally disbanded as an RAF unit on 15 February 1946.

Squadron bases

Duxford	10 Jul 1940	Hutton Cranswick	21 Feb 1944
Martlesham Heath		Mendlesham	25 Feb 1944
	26 Jun 1941	Southend	28 Mar 1944
Dyce	20 Jul 1941	Appledram	3 Apr 1944
Perranporth	24 Dec 1941	Tangmere	22 Jun 1944
Warmwell	8 Mar 1942	B.10 Plumetot	28 Jun 1944
Perranporth	21 Mar 1942	Tangmere	29 Jun 1944
Exeter	7 May 1942	Lympne	3 Jul 1944
Redhill	16 Aug 1942	Digby	11 Jul 1944
Exeter	20 Aug 1942	North Weald	28 Aug 1944
Castletown	26 Jun 1943	Bradwell Bay	29 Dec 1944
Sumburgh	19 Jul 1943	Manston	27 Feb 1945
Ibsley	19 Sep 1943	R.16 Hildesheim	7 Aug 1945
Mendlesham	19 Feb 1944	Prague	13 Aug 1945
			to 15 Feb 1946

Aircraft

Equipment	Period of service	Representative Serial
Hurricane I	Jul 1940 – Mar 1941	P8809 (NN-T)
Hurricane IIA	Mar 1941 – Dec 1941	Z2488
Spitfire IIA	Oct 1941 – Dec 1941	P8472
Spitfire VB, VC	Nov 1941 – Feb 1944	BL265 (NN-L)
	Jul 1944 – Aug 1944	EE661 (NN-V)
Spitfire VI	Jul 1943 – Sep 1943	BS437
Spitfire IX	Jan 1944 – Jul 1944	BS126 (NN-Z)
	Aug 1944 – Feb 1946	MH999 (NN-G)

No. 311 Squadron

Badge: A thresher and a morning star in saltire, the hafts fracted
Motto: Na mnozstui nehledte (Czech) (Never regard their numbers)

No.311 Squadron was formed at Honington on 29 July 1940 as a Czechoslovak-manned heavy bomber unit. Equipped with Wellingtons, it took part in night raids until transferred to Coastal Command in April 1942. From Northern Ireland it carried out patrols over the Atlantic until transferred to Wales in June. In May 1943 the squadron moved to southern England where it converted to Liberators in July, using these for patrols over the Bay of Biscay until August 1944. It was then transferred to northern Scotland for patrols off

Wellington IC, No.311 Squadron

the Norwegian coast for the rest of the war. In June 1945, No.311 transferred to Transport Command and began flights between the UK and Czechoslovakia. On 15 February 1946 the squadron was disbanded as an RAF unit.

Squadron bases

Honington	29 Jul 1940	Beaulieu	26 May 1943
East Wretham	16 Sep 1940	Predannack	23 Feb 1944
Aldergrove	28 Apr 1942	Tain	7 Aug 1944
Talbenny	12 Jun 1942	Prague	Jun 1945 (P)
			to 15 Feb 1946

Aircraft

Equipment	Period of service	Representative Serial
Wellington IA, IC	Aug 1940 – Jul 1943	P9230 (KX-B)
Liberator V	Jul 1943 – Mar 1945	BZ776 (PP-P)
Liberator VI	Mar 1945 – Feb 1946	KG859

No. 312 Squadron

Badge: A stork volant
Motto: Non multi sed multa
(Not many men but
many deeds)

No.312 Squadron was formed at Duxford on 29 August 1940 with Czechoslovak personnel as a fighter unit. Equipped with Hurricanes, it was sent to Speke to defend Merseyside, coming south in May 1941 for offensive operations until August. Defensive duties occupied the squadron until May 1942 when it began escort missions from south-west England. From June to September 1943 it was based on the Orkneys before joining Second TAF's operations in preparation for the invasion of France. It converted to a fighter-bomber role in April 1944 and supported the landings in Normandy, remaining in the UK after Second TAF moved to France. In July 1944 the squadron moved to East Anglia and undertook long-range escort duties for the rest of the war. In August 1945 No.312 flew home to Czechoslovakia where it was disbanded as an RAF unit on 15 February 1946.

Squadron bases

Duxford	29 Aug 1940	Churchstanton	10 Oct 1942
Speke	26 Sep 1940	Warmwell	20 Feb 1943
Valley	3 Mar 1941	Churchstanton	14 Mar 1943
Jurby	25 Apr 1941	Skeabrae	24 Jun 1943
Kenley	29 May 1941	Ibsley	21 Sep 1943
Martlesham Heath		Llanbedr	2 Dec 1943
	20 Jul 1941	Ibsley	17 Dec 1943
Ayr	19 Aug 1941	Mendlesham	19 Feb 1944
Fairwood Common		Southend	22 Feb 1944
	1 Jan 1942	Mendlesham	3 Mar 1944
Angle	24 Jan 1942	Appledram	4 Apr 1944
Fairwood Common		Tangmere	22 Jun 1944
	18 Apr 1942	B.10 Plumetot	28 Jun 1944
Harrowbeer	2 May 1942	Tangmere	30 Jun 1944
Warmwell	19 May 1942	Lympne	4 Jul 1944
Harrowbeer	31 May 1942	Coltishall	11 Jul 1944
Redhill	1 Jul 1942	North Weald	27 Aug 1944
Harrowbeer	8 Jul 1942	Bradwell Bay	3 Oct 1944
Redhill	16 Aug 1942	Manston	27 Feb 1945
Harrowbeer	20 Aug 1942	Prague	24 Aug 1945
			to 15 Feb 1946

Aircraft

Equipment	Period of service	Representative Serial
Hurricane I	Aug 1940 – May 1941	V6921 (DU-R)
Hurricane IIB	May 1941 – Dec 1941	Z2426
Spitfire IIA	Oct 1941 – Dec 1941	P7444
Spitfire VB, VC	Dec 1941 – Feb 1944	AA911 (DU-D)
Spitfire IX	Jan 1944 – Feb 1946	MH474 (DU-F)

No. 313 Squadron

Badge: A hawk volant, wings elevated and addorsed
Motto: Jeden jestrab mnoho vran rozhan (Czech) (One hawk scatters many crows)

No.313 Squadron was formed at Catterick on 10 May 1941 as the third Czech fighter squadron. Equipped with Spitfires, it moved to Cornwall in August and began to fly defensive patrols and sweeps over France, transferring to the south-east in December 1941 for four months. In June 1943 it moved to northern Scotland for two months, returning south to provide escorts for day bombers over France. As part of Second TAF, it was engaged in preparations for the invasion of France and helped to cover the landings in June 1944. Next month it moved to the Orkneys to protect the fleet base at Scapa Flow. In October, it arrived in East Anglia to fly long-range escort missions in support of Bomber Command's daylight raids but most of its operations were ground-attack sorties over the Netherlands. In August 1945, No.313 left for Czechoslovakia where it was disbanded as an RAF unit on 15 February 1946.

Squadron bases

Catterick	10 May 1941	Ibsley	21 Jan 1944
Leconfield	1 Jul 1941	Mendlesham	19 Feb 1944
Portreath	26 Aug 1941	Southend	14 Mar 1944
Warmwell	25 Nov 1941	Mendlesham	20 Mar 1944
Portreath	30 Nov 1941	Appledram	4 Apr 1944
Hornchurch	15 Dec 1941	Tangmere	22 Jun 1944
Southend	7 Feb 1942	B.10 Plumetot	28 Jun 1944
Hornchurch	6 Mar 1942	Tangmere	29 Jun 1944
Fairlop	30 Apr 1942	Lympne	4 Jul 1944
Churchstanton	8 Jun 1942	Skeabrae	11 Jul 1944
Peterhead	28 Jun 1943	North Weald	4 Oct 1944
Hawkinge	21 Aug 1943	Bradwell Bay	29 Dec 1944
Ibsley	18 Sep 1943	Manston	27 Feb 1945
Woodvale	6 Jan 1944	Prague	24 Aug 1945
Ayr	10 Jan 1944		to 15 Feb 1946

Aircraft

Equipment	Period of service	Representative Serial
Spitfire I	May 1941 – Aug 1941	P9513 (RY-X)
Spitfire IIA	Aug 1941 – Nov 1941	P7660
Spitfire VB, VC	Oct 1941 – Apr 1944	AA881
	Jul 1944 – Oct 1944	EE627
Spitfire VI	Jun 1943 – Jul 1943	BS146
Spitfire VII	Jul 1944 – Aug 1944	MD138
Spitfire IX	Feb 1944 – Jul 1944	MK131 (RY-P)
	Oct 1944 – Feb 1946	NH422 (RY-Y)

No. 315 Squadron

Name: 'Deblinski'

No.315 Squadron was formed at Acklington on 21 January 1941 as a fighter squadron and moved to Speke in mid-March to become operational with Hurricanes in the defence of Merseyside. In July it moved to Northolt and converted to Spitfires, beginning sweeps over northern France. After returning to Lancashire for five months, it resumed offensive operations in September 1942 until withdrawn in June 1943, first to Yorkshire and a month later to Northern Ireland. No.315 joined Second TAF at Heston in November 1943 and converted to Mustangs in March 1944. After covering the landings in Normandy, the squadron was withdrawn from Second TAF to form part of the defences against the flying bombs which had started to arrive in southern England. In October 1944 it moved to East Anglia for long-range escort duties supporting Bomber Command's daylight raids on Germany but a month later was transferred to northern Scotland. From Peterhead, it flew patrols off the Norwegian coast to protect Coastal Command strike wings attacking enemy shipping. In January 1945 it returned

Mustang IIIs, No.315 Squadron

to East Anglia and flew sweeps over the Netherlands for the rest of the war. Remaining in Fighter Command after the end of the war, No.315 disbanded on 14 January 1947.

Aircraft Equipment	Period of service	Representative Serial	
Hurricane I	Feb 1941 – Jul 1941	V6979	(PK-U)
Spitfire IIA	Jul 1941 – Aug 1941	P8503	
Spitfire VB, VC	Aug 1941 – Nov 1942	AB927	
	Jun 1943 – Mar 1944	EP285	(PK-B)
Spitfire IX	Nov 1942 – Jun 1943	EN172	(PK-K)
Mustang III	Mar 1944 – Dec 1946	SR417	(PK-W)

Squadron bases			
Acklington	21 Jan 1941	Holmsley South	26 Jun 1944
Speke	13 Mar 1941	Ford	26 Jun 1944
Northolt	16 Jul 1941	Brenzett	10 Jul 1944
Woodvale	1 Apr 1942	Andrews Field	10 Oct 1944
Northolt	6 Sep 1942	Coltishall	24 Oct 1944
Hutton Cranswick	1 Jun 1943	Peterhead	1 Nov 1944
Ballyhalbert	5 Jul 1943	Andrews Field	15 Jan 1945
Heston	13 Nov 1943	Coltishall	8 Aug 1945
Llanbedr	24 Mar 1944	Fairwood Common	
Heston	28 Mar 1944		19 Nov 1945
Coolham	1 Apr 1944	Coltishall	20 Dec 1945
			to 14 Jan 1947

No. 316 Squadron

Name: 'Warszawski'

No.316 Squadron was formed at Pembrey on 15 February 1941 as a Polish fighter unit equipped with Hurricanes. It was engaged in defensive duties over south-west England until it re-equipped with Hurricane IIs and began sweeps over northern France. In October 1941 the squadron converted to Spitfires and moved to Northolt. After being transferred to Yorkshire at the end of July 1942, No.316 came south again in March 1943 for a further six months of offensive operations. In April 1944 Mustangs were received and the squadron moved to East Anglia for fighter-bomber and escort missions. In July it moved to the south coast to operate against flying bombs before resuming escort duties in October which lasted for the rest of the war. On 11 December 1946 the squadron was disbanded.

Squadron bases			
Pembrey	15 Feb 1941	Friston	11 Jul 1944
Colerne	18 Jun 1941	Coltishall	27 Aug 1944
Churchstanton	2 Aug 1941	Andrews Field	24 Oct 1944
Northolt	12 Dec 1941	Coltishall	16 May 1945
Heston	22 Apr 1942	Andrews Field	10 Aug 1945
Hutton Cranswick	30 Jul 1942	Fairwood Common	
Northolt	12 Mar 1943		17 Sep 1945
Acklington	22 Sep 1943	Andrews Field	5 Oct 1945
Woodvale	16 Feb 1944	Wick	28 Nov 1945
Coltishall	28 Apr 1944	Hethel	15 Mar 1946
West Malling	4 Jul 1944		to 11 Dec 1946

Aircraft Equipment	Period of service	Representative Serial	
Hurricane I	Feb 1941 – Aug 1941	W9233	(SZ-H)
Hurricane IIA, IIB	Aug 1941 – Oct 1941	Z2705	
Spitfire VB, VC	Oct 1941 – Mar 1943	AA847	
	Sep 1943 – Apr 1944	AD562	(SZ-S)
Spitfire IX	Mar 1943 – Sep 1943	LZ989	
Mustang III	Apr 1944 – Nov 1946	FB376	(SZ-Q)

No. 317 Squadron

Name: 'Wilenski'

No.317 Squadron was formed on 22 February 1941 at Acklington as a Polish Hurricane squadron. In June it moved south and began to take part in sweeps and bomber escort missions over France. Converting to Spitfires in October 1941 the squadron joined other Polish squadrons at Northolt in April 1942 but in September was transferred to northern England. In April 1943 it returned south to fly offensive sweeps over northern France and later joined Second TAF preparing for the invasion of Europe. After flying ground-attack missions in support of the landings, No.317 moved to Normandy in August 1944 and by October was based in Belgium. For the rest of the war the squadron flew sweeps over Germany, moving there in April. After a period with the occupation forces, it disbanded on 18 December 1946.

Squadron bases			
Acklington	22 Feb 1941	Kirton-in-Lindsey	13 Feb 1943
Ouston	29 Apr 1941	Martlesham Heath	29 Apr 1943
Colerne	26 Jun 1941	Heston	1 Jun 1943
Fairwood Common	27 Jun 1941	Perranporth	21 Jun 1943
Exeter	21 Jul 1941	Fairlop	21 Aug 1943
Northolt	1 Apr 1942	Northolt	21 Sep 1943
Croydon	30 Jun 1942	Southend	2 Dec 1943
Northolt	7 Jul 1942	Northolt	18 Dec 1943
Woodvale	5 Sep 1942	Deanland	1 Apr 1944
Chailey	26 Apr 1944	B.60 Grimbergen	13 Jan 1945
Appledram	28 Jun 1944	B.77 Gilze-Rijen	9 Mar 1945
Ford	16 Jul 1944	B.101 Nordhorn	13 Apr 1945
B.10 Plumetot	3 Aug 1944	B.113 Varrelbusch	28 Apr 1945
B.31 Londonières	6 Sep 1944	B.111 Ahlhorn	14 Sep 1945
B.51 Lille/Vendeville	10 Sep 1944		to 18 Dec 1946
B.61 St. Denis Westrem	11 Oct 1944		

Aircraft Equipment	Period of service	Representative Serial
Hurricane I	Feb 1941 — Jul 1941	V7339 (JH-X)
Hurricane IIA, IIB	Jul 1941 — Oct 1941	BD719
Spitfire VB	Oct 1941 — Sep 1943	AA762 (JH-W)
Spitfire IX	Sep 1943 — May 1945	MJ551 (JH-A)
Spitfire XVI	May 1945 — Dec 1946	TD128 (JH-M)

No. 318 Squadron

Name: 'Gdanskski'

No.318 Squadron was formed at Detling on 20 March 1943 for tactical reconnaissance duties and received Hurricanes for training purposes. In August the squadron left for the Middle East where it took part in training with the Polish Army before leaving for Italy in April 1944. Now equipped with Spitfires, it flew ground-attack and tactical reconnaissance missions in support of the 8th Army for the rest of the war. In August 1946 the squadron handed over its aircraft and left for the UK where it disbanded on 31 August 1946.

Squadron bases			
Detling	20 Mar 1943	Chiaravalle	24 Aug 1944
Left for Middle East	15 Aug 1943	Piagiolino	31 Aug 1944
		Cassandra	17 Sep 1944
Muqeibila	10 Sep 1943	Rimini	27 Sep 1944
Gaza	12 Oct 1943	Bellaria	7 Nov 1944
LG.207	22 Nov 1943	Forli	4 Dec 1944
Helwan	9 Apr 1944 (A)	La Russia	2 May 1945
Left for Italy	9 Apr 1944 (G)	Treviso	6 May 1945
	23 Apr 1944 (A)	Tissano	14 May 1945
Trigno	1 May 1944	Lavariano	14 Aug 1945
San Vito	17 Jun 1944	Tissano	24 Jan 1946
Tortoretto	26 Jun 1944	Treviso	8 Mar 1946
Fermio	2 Jul 1944	Left for UK	15 Aug 1946
Falconara	30 Jul 1944	Coltishall	19 Aug 1946
			to 31 Aug 1946

Aircraft Equipment	Period of service	Representative Serial
Hurricane I	Apr 1943 — Aug 1943	V6637
Hurricane IIB	Sep 1943 — Feb 1944	
Spitfire VB, VC	Feb 1944 — Mar 1945	EP777
Spitfire IX	Nov 1944 — Aug 1946	TA829

Fokker T-VIIIW, No.320 Squadron

No. 320 Squadron

Badge: In front of a fountain an orange tree fracted and eradicated
Motto: Animo libere dirigimur (We are guided by the mind of liberty)

When the Germans invaded the Netherlands, several seaplanes of the Royal Netherlands Naval Air Service were evacuated to Britain when their home bases became untenable. The most useful of these were the modern Fokker T-VIIIW twin-engined patrol seaplanes which were flown to Pembroke Dock and, on 1 June 1940, formed into No.320 Squadron. For several months the squadron flew patrols until shortage of spares forced the withdrawal of the

Fokkers and their replacement by Ansons, supplemented in October by Hudsons. On 18 January 1941, No.321 Squadron was absorbed and in March 1941, No.320 moved to Scotland for patrols and attacks on enemy shipping in the North Sea. Ansons were retained until October 1941, for traning purposes and in April 1942, the squadron moved to East Anglia. In March 1943 it was transferred to No.2 Group and re-equipped with Mitchells. It began daylight raids on 17 August, attacking enemy communications targets and airfields as part of Second TAF. In October 1944 it moved to Belgium and continued raids until the end of the war, moving to Germany for the last week. On 2 August 1945, No.320 Squadron was transferred to the control of the Royal Netherlands Navy and ceased to be a RAF unit.

Squadron bases			
Pembroke Dock and		Attlebridge	30 Mar 1943
Carew Cheriton	1 Jun 1940	Lasham	30 Aug 1943
Leuchars	20 Mar 1941	Dunsfold	18 Feb 1944
Bircham Newton	20 Apr 1942	B.58 Melsbroek	18 Oct 1944
Methwold	15 Mar 1943	B.110 Achmer	30 Apr 1945
			to 2 Aug 1945

Aircraft Equipment	Period of service	Representative Serial	
Fokker T-VIIIW	Jun 1940 – Sep 1940	AV963	
Anson I	Jun 1940 – Oct 1941	N5202	(TD-E)
Hudson I, II, III	Oct 1940 – Sep 1942	T9339	(TD-C)
Hudson VI	Sep 1942 – Mar 1943	FK402	(TD-R)
Mitchell II	Mar 1943 – Aug 1945	FR143	(NO-A)
Mitchell III	Feb 1945 – Aug 1945	HD358	(NO-J)

No. 321 Squadron

No.321 Squadron was formed on 1 June 1940 at Pembroke Dock with personnel of the Royal Netherlands Naval Air Service. Later in the month it moved to Carew Cheriton and became operational on 28 July 1940. Anti-submarine patrols were flown until the squadron was merged with No.320 Squadron on 18 January 1941.

On 2 March 1942, four Catalinas of the Royal Netherlands Navy arrived at Koggala in Ceylon from Java to escape the Japanese invasion. Patrols over the Indian Ocean were flown and five more Catalinas arrived from Australia at the end of May. The unit was designated No.321 Squadron on 15 August 1942 with headquarters at China Bay, Ceylon, the squadron's base until the end of the war. Detachments were based in South Africa from January to October 1943 and others patrolled the approaches to the Red Sea and Persian Gulf from Masirah and Socotra between September 1943 and December 1944. In December 1944, Liberators began to arrive and in July 1945 No.321's Catalinas and Liberators moved to Cocos Island in preparation for the invasion of Malaya. After the Japanese surrender, relief flights were flown to Java and Sumatra and during October the squadron moved to its new base near Batavia where it passed to the control of the Royal Netherlands Air Force on 8 December 1945.

Squadron bases			
Pembroke Dock	1 Jun 1940	Cocos Island (D)	2 Jul 1945
Carew Cheriton	24 Jun 1940		to 8 Dec 1945
	to 18 Jan 1941	Kemajoran	Oct 1945 (P)
China Bay	15 Aug 1942		to 8 Dec 1945

Aircraft Equipment	Period of service	Representative Serial	
Anson I	Jun 1940 – Jan 1941	N5064	
Catalina II	Aug 1942 – Feb 1945	Y-68	(HH)
Catalina III	Nov 1942 – Dec 1945	Y-82	(QQ)
Catalina V	Apr 1945 – Dec 1945	Y-86	(UU)
Liberator VI	Dec 1944 – Dec 1945	KG852	(A)

No. 322 Squadron

Badge: Perched on a branch, a parrot
Motto: Niet praten maar doen (Dutch) (Actions not words)

No.322 Squadron was formed at Woodvale on 12 June 1943, from No.167 Squadron which had a high proportion of Dutch personnel and was already operational with Spitfire Vs on defensive duties in the Irish Sea area. At the end of December 1943, it moved south to Hawkinge and began flying convoy patrols and sweeps over the Channel for two months before moving to Scotland for tactical training at Ayr. It returned to Hawkinge for a week in March 1944, before joining No.147 Airfield at Acklington and re-equipping with Spitfire XIVs in preparation for the invasion. In April it returned south to attack enemy targets in northern France but soon after the landings it found itself engaged in countering the flying bomb attacks until August, when the capture of their launching sites reduced the menace to mere nuisance raids. The squadron then converted to Spitfire IXs for ground-attack missions over the Low Countries and escort duties with the day bombers, replacing these with Spitfire XVIs in November. In January 1945, the squadron moved to its homeland and began fighter sweeps over the battle areas and northern Germany in search of enemy transport and troops which lasted for the rest of the war. On 7 October 1945, the squadron disbanded in Germany but the number was afterwards revived for a unit of the Royal Netherlands Air Force in recognition of the squadron's wartime record.

Squadron bases			
Woodvale	12 Jun 1943	Fairwood Common	
Llanbedr	15 Nov 1943		10 Oct 1944
Woodvale	30 Nov 1943	Biggin Hill	1 Nov 1944
Hawkinge	31 Dec 1943	B.79 Woensdrecht	3 Jan 1945
Ayr	25 Feb 1944	B.85 Schijndel	21 Feb 1945
Hawkinge	1 Mar 1944	B.106 Twente	18 Apr 1945
Acklington	9 Mar 1944	B.113 Varrelbusch	
Hartfordbridge	23 Apr 1944		30 Apr 1945
West Malling	20 Jun 1944	B.116 Wunstorf	2 Jul 1945
Deanland	21 Jul 1944		to 7 Oct 1945

Aircraft Equipment	Period of service	Representative Serial	
Spitfire VB, VC	Jun 1943 – Mar 1944	EP350	(VL-F)
Spitfire XIV	Mar 1944 – Aug 1944	RB160	(VL-A)
Spitfire IXB	Aug 1944 – Nov 1944	MJ964	(3W-V)
Spitfire XVIE	Nov 1944 – Oct 1945	TB747	(3W-D)

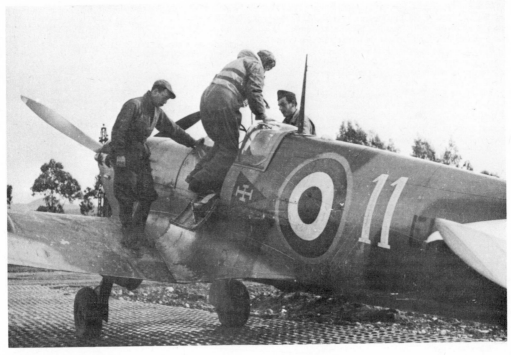

Spitfire VC, No.328 Squadron

No. 326 Squadron
No. 327 Squadron
No. 328 Squadron

Names: No.326 Squadron – G.C.2/7 'Nice'
No.327 Squadron – G.C.1/3 'Corse'
No.328 Squadron – G.C.1/7 'Provence'

Nos.326, 327 and 328 Squadrons were formed on 1 December 1943 by numbering three French fighter squadrons, two in Corsica and one in North Africa for air defence duties. No.328 moved to Corsica to join the other two Spitfire squadrons and as a wing they covered the Allied landings in southern France in August 1944. Early in September, all three moved to France and moved north to Alsace-Lorraine where they flew offensive sweeps over south-west Germany for the rest of the war and supported the French First Army during its advance across the Rhine. In November 1945 the squadrons ceased to be RAF units although in practice they had been acting independently since all RAF units engaged in the invasion of Southern France had been withdrawn to Italy in October 1944.

No.326 Squadron
Squadron bases
Ajaccio/Ghisonaccia
                                1 Dec 1943
Calvi   24 Aug 1944
Le Vallon   3 Sep 1944
Lyon/Bron   7 Sep 1944
Dijon/Longvic   21 Sep 1944
Luxeuil   27 Sep 1944
Colmar   22 Mar 1945
Strasbourg/Entzheim
                                 7 Apr 1945
Grossachsenheim 28 Apr 1945
                              to Nov 1945

No.327 Squadron
Squadron bases
Ajaccio/Campo del Oro
                                1 Dec 1943
Bastia/Borgo   22 Apr 1944
Calvi   23 Aug 1944
Le Vallon   3 Sep 1944
Lyon/Bron   7 Sep 1944
Dijon/Longvic   21 Sep 1944
Luxeuil   27 Sep 1944
Nancy/Essey   Jan 1945
Luxeuil   19 Feb 1945
Colmar   22 Mar 1945
Strasbourg/Entzheim
                                 7 Apr 1945
Stuttgart/Sersheim
                               28 Apr 1945
                              to Nov 1945

No.328 Squadron
Squadron bases
Reghaia   1 Dec 1943
Oran/Taher   Jan 1944
Bastia/Borgo   30 Apr 1944
Campo del Oro   21 Jul 1944
Calvi   23 Aug 1944
Istres   3 Sep 1944
Lyon/Bron   7 Sep 1944
Dijon/Longvic   21 Sep 1944
Luxeuil   21 Feb 1945
Colmar   22 Mar 1945
Strasbourg/Entzheim
                                 7 Apr 1945
Grossachsenheim 27 Apr 1945
                              to Nov 1945

Aircraft Equipment		Period of service	Representative Serial
Spitfire VB/VC	No.326	Dec 1943 – Apr 1944	MA703
	No.327	Dec 1943 – Apr 1944	
	No.328	Dec 1943 – Nov 1944	ER625
Spitfire VIII	No.327	Jul 1944 – Sep 1944	JG749
	No.328	Aug 1944 – Apr 1945	JF296
Spitfire IX	No.326	Dec 1943 – Nov 1945	
	No.327	Dec 1943 – Nov 1945	MA471
	No.328	Dec 1943 – Nov 1945	NH306

No. 329 Squadron

Name: G.C.1/2 'Cigognes'

No.329 Squadron was formed on 5 January 1944 on arrival from North Africa where it had been operating under its Armée de l'Air designation of Groupe de Chasse 1/2. After assembling at Ayr, it moved to Perranporth to begin equipping with Spitfires. Becoming operational on 1 March, the squadron joined No.145 Wing's Free French units on 14 April and provided cover for the landings in Normandy. In August, it moved to France and moved forward into the Low Countries in September. In March 1945, No.329 returned to the UK where it remained until disbanded on 17 December 1945.

Spitfire VC, No.329 Squadron

B.70 Deurne	25 Nov 1944	Dreux	16 Jun 1945
B.85 Schijndel	6 Feb 1945	Harrowbeer	19 Jun 1945
Turnhouse	9 Mar 1945	Fairwood Common	
Skeabrae	3 Apr 1945		14 Jul 1945
Harrowbeer	25 May 1945		to 17 Nov 1945

Squadron bases

Ayr	5 Jan 1944	Selsey	1 Jul 1944
Perranporth	22 Jan 1944	Tangmere	6 Aug 1944
Merston	17 Apr 1944	B.8 Sommervieu	19 Aug 1944
Llanbedr	19 May 1944	B.29 Bernay	3 Sep 1944
Merston	23 May 1944	B.51 Lille/Vendeville	
Funtington	22 Jun 1944		12 Sep 1944
		B.55 Wevelghem	18 Sep 1944

Aircraft

Equipment	Period of service	Representative Serial
Spitfire VB, VC	Feb 1944 — Mar 1944	MH595 (5A-B)
Spitfire IX	Feb 1944 — Nov 1945	PL185 (5A-I)
	Mar 1945 — Nov 1945	
Spitfire XVI	Feb 1945 — Mar 1945	TB388 (5A-H)

Northrop N-3PB, No.330 Squadron

No. 330 Squadron

Badge: In front of a sun in splendour, a Viking's ship in full sail
Motto: Trygg havet (Guarding the seas)

No.330 Squadron was formed on 25 April 1941 from Norwegian naval personnel and on 19 May the freighter *Fjordheim* arrived from Canada with eighteen Northrop N-3PB seaplanes which were erected in a seaplane hangar at Reykjavik. On 2 June the first aircraft was flown and the squadron made its first anti-submarine patrol on 23 June. A detachment was based at Akureyri from July which intercepted two FW 200s engaged in long-range reconnaissance in July 1942. A month earlier, the squadron's first Catalina arrived and patrols were flown by both types until the N-3PBs flew their last operation on 30 December. On 24 January 1943, the squadron left Iceland and arrived at Oban on 28 January where it began to re-equip with Sunderlands. Patrols over the Atlantic occupied No.330 for the rest of the war and soon after the German surrender the squadron moved to Norway where it passed to the control of the Royal Norwegian Air Force on 21 November 1945.

Squadron bases

Reykjavik	25 Jan 1942	Oban	to 31 Mar 1943
Akureyri (D)	20 Jul 1941	Sullom Voe	28 Jan 1943
	to 12 Dec 1941	Stavanger	12 Jul 1943
Budareyri (D)	11 Sep 1941		30 May 1945
			to 21 Nov 1945

Aircraft

Equipment	Period of service	Representative Serial
Northrop N-3PB	Jun 1941 — Jan 1943	No.18 (GS-T)
Catalina III	Jun 1942 — Jan 1943	FP533 (GS-L)
Sunderland II, III	Feb 1943 — Nov 1945	ML824 (WH-Z)

Spitfire VB, No.331 Squadron

No. 331 Squadron

Badge: Two swords in saltire,
enfiled by an amulet
Motto: For Norge (For Norway)

No.331 Squadron was formed on 21 July 1941 at Catterick as a Norwegian-manned fighter unit equipped with Hurricanes. On 15 September it became operational in northern Scotland on defensive duties and converted to Spitfires in November. These it flew south in May 1942 for sweeps over northern France, the first being flown on 6 May. As part of Second TAF, No.331 joined No.132 Wing on 31 March 1944 for the invasion of Europe, moving to Normandy in mid-August for night-bomber sweeps over the battle area. By October, the squadron was based in the Low Countries, flying sweeps over Germany in support of the Allied armies. At the end of April 1945, it moved back to the UK and prepared to move to Norway when the Germans surrendered. After a period at Stavanger, No.331 disbanded on 21 Nov-

ember 1945 as a RAF unit when it passed to the control of the Royal Norwegian Air Force.

Squadron bases

Catterick	21 Jul 1941	Ford	12 Aug 1944
Castletown	21 Aug 1941	B.16 Villons les Buissons	
Skeabrae	21 Sep 1941		20 Aug 1944
North Weald	4 May 1942	B.33 Camp Neuseville	
Manston	30 Jun 1942		1 Sep 1944
North Weald	7 Jul 1942	B.57 Lille/Wambrechies	
Manston	14 Aug 1942		11 Sep 1944
North Weald	20 Aug 1942	Fairwood Common	
Ipswich	7 Sep 1942		19 Sep 1944
North Weald	14 Sep 1942	B.60 Grimbergen	6 Oct 1944
Manston	2 Oct 1942	B.79 Woensdrecht	
North Weald	9 Oct 1942		22 Dec 1944
Llanbedr	5 Jan 1944	B.85 Schijndel	21 Feb 1945
North Weald	21 Jan 1944	Fairwood Common	
Southend	5 Mar 1944		16 Mar 1945
North Weald	13 Mar 1944	B.85 Schijndel	2 Apr 1945
Bognor	31 Mar 1944	B.106 Enschede	18 Apr 1945
Tangmere	22 Jun 1944	Dyce	24 Apr 1945
Funtington	6 Aug 1944	Stavanger	22 May 1945
			to 21 Nov 1945

Aircraft

Equipment	Period of service	Representative Serial	
Hurricane I	Jul 1941 – Aug 1941	V7028	
Hurricane IIB	Aug 1941 – Nov 1941	BD734	(FN-D)
Spitfire IIA	Nov 1941 – Apr 1942	P8190	(FN-F)
Spitfire VB	Mar 1942 – Oct 1942	AR291	(FN-A)
Spitfire IX	Oct 1942 – Nov 1945	PV210	(FN-R)

No. 332 Squadron

Badge: A demi-Norwegian axe
Motto: Samhold i strid
(Together in battle)

No.332 Squadron was formed on 16 January 1942 at Catterick as a Norwegian-manned fighter squadron. Becoming operational with Spitfires on 21 March, the squadron moved south in June and began to fly sweeps over France on 22 June. Based at North Weald, it formed part of a wing with the other Norwegian Spitfire squadron, No.331,

and with it joined Second TAF in No.321 Wing. After providing fighter cover for the Allied landings in France, the squadron moved to Normandy in mid-August 1944. Armed reconnaissance sweeps were flown as the front line advanced into the Netherlands and from captured bases there the squadron carried out attacks on enemy transport and communications targets. At the end of April 1945, No.332 was transferred to Scotland and in May flew to Norway after the German surrender. On 21 September 1945, the squadron was disbanded as a RAF unit and passed to the control of the Royal Norwegian Air Force.

Squadron bases

Catterick	16 Jan 1942	North Weald	27 Mar 1944
North Weald	19 Jun 1942	Bognor	31 Mar 1944
Manston	14 Aug 1942	Tangmere	21 Jun 1944
North Weald	20 Aug 1942	Funtington	6 Aug 1944
Llanbedr	5 Jan 1944	Ford	12 Aug 1944
North Weald	21 Feb 1944	B.16 Villon les Buissons	
Southend	21 Mar 1944		20 Aug 1944

B.33 Camp Neuseville		B.79 Woensdrecht	
	6 Sep 1944		31 Dec 1944
B.57 Lille/Wambrechies		B.85 Schijndel	21 Feb 1945
	11 Sep 1944	B.106 Enschede	18 Apr 1945
B.60 Grimbergen	6 Oct 1944	Dyce	26 Apr 1945
Fairwood Common		Stavanger	22 May 1945
	11 Dec 1944		to 21 Nov 1945

Aircraft Equipment	Period of service	Representative Serial
Spitfire VA, VB	Jan 1942 – Nov 1942 Apr 1943 – Aug 1943	R7022 (AH-F)
Spitfire IX	Nov 1942 – Sep 1945	PL451 (AH-Z)

No. 333 Squadron

Badge: In front of a pair of wings elevated and conjoined in base a Viking ship affrontée

Motto: For Konge, Fedreland og flaggets heder
(For King, country and the honour of the flag)

No.333 Squadron was formed at Leuchars on 10 May 1943 from No.1477 Flight manned by Norwegian personnel. Mosquitos were flown on shipping reconnaissance missions along the Norwegian coast while a flight of Catalinas was based at nearby Woodhaven for patrols to the north of Scotland. Contact was also maintained with resistance forces in Norway by special duties flights which landed men and supplies on the Norwegian coast. In August 1944, the Mosquito flight moved to join a strike wing at Banff, often acting as a pathfinder unit to locate shipping concealed in fjords for other strike squadrons. During June 1945, the squadron moved to Norway and passed to the control of the Royal Norwegian Air Force on 21 November 1945.

Squadron bases

Leuchars	10 May 1943
Woodhaven (D)	10 May 1943
	to Jun 1945
Banff	30 Aug 1944
Stavanger	Jun 1945 (P)
	to 21 Nov 1945

Aircraft Equipment	Period of service	Representative Serial
Mosquito II	May 1943 – Nov 1943	DZ752
Mosquito VI	Nov 1943 – May 1945	HR116 (KK-F)
Catalina IB	May 1943 – Feb 1945	W8424 (KK-B)
Catalina IVA	May 1944 – Nov 1945	JV933 (KK-C)

No. 334 Squadron

No.334 Squadron was formed on 30 May 1945 at Banff from the Mosquito flight of No.333 Squadron soon after the end of the war in Europe. During June it moved to Norway where it passed to the control of the Royal Norwegian Air Force on 21 November 1945.

Squadron bases

Banff	30 May 1945
Stavanger	Jun 1945 (P)
	to 21 Nov 1945

Aircraft Equipment	Period of service	Representative Serial
Mosquito VI	May 1945 – Nov 1945	HR279

No. 335 Squadron

No.335 Squadron was formed on 10 October 1941 at Aqir having originally been intended to become No.361 Squadron, Royal Hellenic Air Force. Equipped with Hurricanes, it was manned by Greek personnel and was engaged in defensive duties until January 1942 when it moved to the Western Desert to fly fighter patrols. In June, it was withdrawn to Egypt and returned in September with Hurricane IIBs for ground-attack and escort missions. After the Battle of El Alamein, the squadron was engaged in shipping protection duties along the Libyan coast until September 1944 when it moved to Italy with Spitfires. After six weeks of sweeps over Albania and Yugoslavia, No.335 moved to Greece in November for sweeps over German-occupied islands in the Aegean and Crete until the end of the war. In September 1945, the squadron moved to Salonika where it disbanded on 31 July 1945.

Squadron bases

Aqir	10 Oct 1941	Mersa Matruh	8 Feb 1943
St. Jean d'Acre	6 Dec 1941	Tocra	12 Feb 1943
Helwan	20 Jan 1942	Benina	29 Jan 1944
El Daba	29 Jan 1942	Tocra	2 Feb 1944
Gerawla	28 May 1942	Bersis	1 Mar 1944
El Daba	21 Jun 1942	Left for Italy	8 Sep 1944 (G)
Idku	29 Jun 1942	Savoia	7 Sep 1944 (A)
Dekheila	8 Aug 1942	Nuova	16 Sep 1944
LG.173	19 Sep 1942	Biferno	4 Oct 1944
LG.85	3 Oct 1942	Left for Greece	2 Nov 1944 (G)
LG.37	23 Oct 1942	Hassani	14 Nov 1944 (A)
LG.13	11 Nov 1942	Sedes	4 Sep 1945
LG.121	18 Nov 1942		to 31 Jul 1945

Aircraft Equipment	Period of service	Representative Serial
Hurricane I	Oct 1941 – Sep 1942	Z4047
Hurricane IIB	Aug 1942 – Oct 1943	BD700
Hurricane IIC	Sep 1943 – Jan 1944	KZ335
Spitfire VB, VC	Dec 1944 – Jul 1946	EE805

No. 336 Squadron

No.336 Squadron was formed on 25 February 1943 at Landing Ground 219 in the Western Desert as the second Greek fighter squadron in the Desert Air Force. It was employed on shipping protection and air defence duties off the Libyan coast until September 1944 when the squadron moved to Italy with No.335. After flying sweeps over the Balkans, both squadrons moved to Greece for attacks on German-held islands in the Aegean. In May 1945, No.336 moved to Salonika where it was disbanded on 31 July 1946.

Squadron bases			
LG.219	25 Feb 1943	Nuova	18 Sep 1944
LG.121	7 Apr 1943	Grottaglie	4 Nov 1944 (A)
El Adem	31 Jan 1944	Hassani	9 Nov 1944 (G)
Bu Amud	5 Mar 1944		14 Nov 1944 (A)
Mersa Matruh	3 Apr 1944	Sedes	16 May 1945 (G)
El Adem	13 Jul 1944		21 May 1945 (A)
Left for Italy	8 Sep 1944 (G)		to 31 Jul 1946

Aircraft Equipment	Period of service	Representative Serial
Hurricane IIC	Feb 1943 — May 1944	HV505
Spitfire VB, VC	Jan 1944 — Jul 1946	JK374

No. 340 Squadron

Name: 'Ile-de-France'

No.340 Squadron was formed on 7 November 1941 at Turnhouse as a Free French fighter squadron equipped with Spitfires. Becoming operational on 29 November, it flew defensive patrols until moving south in April 1942 to begin fighter sweeps over northern France. In March 1943, the squadron was withdrawn for rest and returned to Scotland, moving to south-west England in November for sweeps and anti-shipping operations off Brittany. Joining No.145 Wing of Second TAF in April 1944, No.340 helped to provide fighter cover for the Normandy landings and moved to France in August. After moving forward to Belgium in September, the squadron returned to the UK to fly bomber escort missions, rejoining Second TAF in the Netherlands during February 1945. For the rest of the war, No.340 flew sweeps over Germany and after a short period with the occupation forces was transferred to the control of the Armée de l'Air on 25 November 1945.

Spitfire IX, No.340 Squadron

Spitfire VB, No.340 Squadron

Squadron bases			
Turnhouse	7 Nov 1941	Tangmere	14 Aug 1944
Drem	20 Dec 1941	B.8 Sommervieu	19 Aug 1944
Ayr	29 Dec 1941	B.29 Bernay	2 Sep 1944
Redhill	1 Apr 1942	B.37 Gamaches	10 Sep 1944
Westhampnett	7 Apr 1942	B.51 Lille/Vendeville	
Ipswich	20 Jul 1942		12 Sep 1944
Westhampnett	26 Jul 1942	B.55 Wevelghem	17 Sep 1944
Hornchurch	28 Jul 1942	Biggin Hill	2 Nov 1944
Biggin Hill	23 Sep 1942	Drem	17 Dec 1944
Turnhouse	20 Mar 1943	Turnhouse	31 Jan 1945
Drem	30 Apr 1943	B.85 Schijndel	8 Feb 1945
Ayr (D)	6 Aug 1943	B.105 Drope	16 Apr 1945
	to 28 Sep 1943	A.41 Dreux	16 Jun 1945
Perranporth	9 Nov 1943	B.105 Drope	19 Jun 1945
Merston	17 Apr 1944	B.152 Fassberg	6 Jul 1945
Llanbedr	15 May 1944	Tangmere	3 Sep 1945
Merston	18 May 1944	Warmwell	6 Sep 1945
Funtington	22 Jun 1944	B.152 Fassberg	16 Sep 1945
Selsey	1 Jul 1944		to 25 Nov 1945

Aircraft Equipment	Period of service	Representative Serial
Spitfire IIA	Nov 1941 — Mar 1942	P7829 (GW-C)
Spitfire VB	Mar 1942 — Oct 1942 Mar 1943 — Feb 1944	EN904 (GW-A)
Spitfire IXB	Oct 1942 — Mar 1943 Jan 1944 — Feb 1945	PL427 (GW-W)
Spitfire XVI	Feb 1945 — Nov 1945	TB285 (GW-P)

No. 341 Squadron

Badge: On a hand three crowns of Alsace
Motto: 'Friendship'
Name: G.C.3/2 'Alsace'

No.341 Squadron was formed at Turnhouse on 15 January 1943 from personnel of the Free French Flight which had been operating in the Western Desert. Equipped with Spitfires, it moved to Biggin Hill in March and began to take part in sweeps over France. In October, the squadron moved to Cornwall for similar operations over Brittany, returning in April 1944 to join No.145 Wing. After covering the Allied landings in France in June 1944, No.341 moved to Normandy in August and arrived in Belgium in September.

Armed reconnaissance sweeps over Germany were directed mainly at enemy communications for the rest of the war, apart from a month in Scotland during February 1945. On 7 November 1945 the squadron gave up its aircraft on transfer to Friedrichshaven and on the following day passed to the control of the Armée de l'Air

Squadron bases			
Turnhouse	15 Jan 1943	B.37 Gamaches	10 Sep 1944
Biggin Hill	21 Mar 1943	B.51 Lille/Vendeville	
Perranporth	15 Oct 1943		12 Sep 1944
Merston	17 Apr 1944	B.55 Wevelghem	17 Sep 1944
Funtington	22 Jun 1944	B.70 Deurne	25 Nov 1944
Selsey	1 Jul 1944	Turnhouse	2 Feb 1945
Tangmere	6 Aug 1944	B.85 Schijndel	9 Mar 1945
B.8 Sommervieu	19 Aug 1944	B.105 Drope	16 Apr 1945
B.29 Bernay	2 Sep 1944	B.152 Fassberg	6 Jul 1945
			to 7 Nov 1945

Aircraft Equipment	Period of service	Representative Serial
Spitfire VB	Jan 1943 – Mar 1943 Oct 1943 – Feb 1944	AD244
Spitfire IXB	Mar 1943 – Oct 1943 Feb 1944 – Mar 1945	PT472 (NL-Z)
Spitfire XVI	Mar 1945 – Nov 1945	TB519 (NL-L)

Boston IV, No.342 Squadron

No. 342 Squadron

Badge: On a billet in bend, indented to the base, three alérions
Motto: Nous y sommes (Here we are)
Name: G.B. 1/20 'Lorraine'

No.342 Squadron was formed on 7 April 1943 at West Raynham from personnel of Escadrilles 'Metz' and 'Nancy' transferred from the Middle East, these titles being adopted by A and B Flights respectively. Equipped with Bostons, the squadron began operations on 12 June, flying daylight raids on targets in northern France. Early in 1944, attacks on flying-bomb sites in the Pas-de-Calais began and as the time of the landings in Normandy approached, No.342 took part

in an interdiction campaign to isolate the invasion area from the rest of France. Day and night missions were flown against enemy communications targets until the Allied break-out and in October 1944 the squadron moved to France. Bostons continued to be used until 31 March 1945, Mitchells having begun to arrive as replacements. After moving to the Netherlands, these began tactical bombing on 9 April but on 2 May operations ended. On 2 December 1945, No.342 was transferred to the Armée de l'Air.

Squadron bases			
West Raynham	7 Apr 1943	B.50 Vitry-en-Artois	
Sculthorpe	15 May 1943		17 Oct 1944
Great Massingham	19 Jul 1943	B.77 Gilze-Rijen	22 Apr 1945
Hartfordbridge	6 Sep 1943		to 2 Dec 1945

Aircraft Equipment	Period of service	Representative Serial
Boston IIIA	Apr 1943 – Apr 1945	BZ301 (OA-S)
Boston IV	Aug 1944 – Apr 1945	BZ538 (OA-B)
Mitchell II	Mar 1945 – Dec 1945	FW181 (OA-W)
Mitchell III	Mar 1945 – Dec 1945	KJ729 (OA-S)

No. 343 Squadron
No. 344 Squadron

After the Allied landings in North Africa, a number of Armée de l'Air units based in Algeria and Morocco remained in being and were in most cases re-equipped with British and American aircraft. The majority saw service with North African Tactical or Coastal Air Forces and some were given RAF squadron numbers in the series allotted to Free French units. Two similar squadrons were formed at Dakar under the control of No.295 Wing which was responsible for anti-submarine patrols from West Africa.

Flotille 7E had been flying anti-submarine patrols with a few flying boats which had survived the years of Vichy control and some Sunderlands allotted in July 1943. On 29 November 1943 the unit was given the number '343'

and remained under RAF operational control until the end of the war, reverting to its former status on 27 November 1945. Throughout this period, it flew Sunderlands on anti-submarine and convoy escort missions. No.344 Squadron was its land-based equivalent being equipped with Wellington maritime reconnaissance aircraft. Also based at Dakar it was transferred to French control at the same time as No.343.

Squadron bases
Dakar	29 Nov 1943
	to 27 Nov 1945

Aircraft
Equipment	Period of service	Representative Serial
Sunderland III	Nov 1943 – Nov 1945	JM704 (B)
Wellington XI, XIII	Nov 1943 – Nov 1945	JA567

No. 345 Squadron

Badge: In front of a hurt, a stork volant
Motto: Nil actum credo si quid supersii agendum (I think nothing done if anything remains undone)
Name: G.C. 2/2 'Berry'

No.345 Squadron was formed on 12 February 1944 at Ayr from French personnel transferred from North Africa. Equipped with Spitfires, it moved south to begin operations on 2 May. As part of No.141 Wing of Second TAF, No.345 flew patrols over the Normandy beachhead and in November

moved to Belgium to join No.145 Wing at Wevelghem. For the rest of the war, it was engaged in ground-attack and escort missions over Germany. On 21 November 1945, the squadron passed to the control of the Armée de l'Air.

Squadron bases
Ayr	12 Feb 1944	Fairwood Common	16 Mar 1945
Shoreham	26 Apr 1944	B.85 Schijndel	2 Apr 1945
Deanland	16 Aug 1944	B.105 Drope	17 Apr 1945
Biggin Hill	18 Oct 1944	A.41 Dreux	16 Jun 1945
B.55 Wevelghem	1 Nov 1944	B.105 Drope	19 Jun 1945
B.70 Deurne	25 Nov 1944	B.152 Fassberg	6 Jul 1945
B.85 Schijndel	6 Feb 1945		to 21 Nov 1945

Aircraft
Equipment	Period of service	Representative Serial
Spitfire VB	Mar 1944 – Sep 1944	AA943 (2Y-T)
Spitfire IX	Sep 1944 – Apr 1945	PT913 (2Y-Y)
Spitfire XVI	Apr 1945 – Nov 1945	TB299

Halifax VI, No.346 Squadron

No. 346 Squadron

Name: G.B. 2/23 'Guyenne'

No.346 Squadron was formed at Elvington on 16 May 1944 from French personnel transferred from North Africa. Equipped with Halifaxes, it began taking part in night raids on Germany on 1 June 1944 and remained part of the main force of Bomber Command for the rest of the war. In October 1945, the squadron returned to France and was

transferred to the control of the Armée de l'Air on 27 November 1945.

Squadron bases
Elvington	16 May 1944
	to Oct 1945

Aircraft
Equipment	Period of service	Representative Serial
Halifax V	May 1944 – Jun 1944	LL227 (H7-K)
Halifax III	Jun 1944 – Apr 1945	NA121 (H7-D)
Halifax VI	Mar 1945 – Nov 1945	RG592 (H7-P)

Halifax III, No.347 Squadron

No. 347 Squadron

Name: G.B. 1/25 'Tunisie'

No.347 Squadron was formed on 20 June 1944 at Elvington as the second French heavy bomber squadron in Bomber Command. Equipped with Halifaxes, it began operations on 27 June and took part in the strategic air offensive until the end of the war. In October 1945, it moved to France and passed to the control of the Armée de l'Air on 27 November 1945.

Squadron bases

Elvington	20 Jun 1944
	to Oct 1945

Aircraft Equipment

Aircraft Equipment	Period of service	Representative Serial
Halifax V	Jun 1944 – Jul 1944	LK999 (L8-D)
Halifax III	Jul 1944 – Apr 1945	NA681 (L8-G)
Halifax VI	Mar 1945 – Nov 1945	RG669 (L8-G)

No. 349 Squadron

Badge: Two morning stars in saltire
Motto: Strike hard, strike home

No.349 Squadron was formed on 10 November 1942 at Ikeja in Nigeria as a Belgian-manned fighter squadron for service in the Belgian Congo. After flying Tomahawks for a few months, the squadron's pilots were diverted to ferrying fighters to the Middle East and at the end of May its personnel were transferred to the UK to reform at Wittering with Spitfires on 5 June 1943. Becoming operational on 13 August, it moved south in October and began flying sweeps over France on 24 October. After covering the Normandy landings as part of No.135 Wing, No.349 moved to France in August 1944 for fighter-bomber and escort missions until February 1945 when it returned to the UK to re-equip with Tempests. Conversion was abandoned in April and the squadron moved to the Netherlands to join

132 Wing for the rest of the war, flying armed reconnaissance sweeps over Germany. After a period with the occupation forces, No.349 passed to the control of the Belgian Air Force on 24 October 1946.

Squadron bases

Ikeja	10 Nov 1942	Tangmere	19 Aug 1944
	to May 1943	B.17 Carpiquet	26 Aug 1944
Wittering	5 Jun 1943	B.35 Le Treport	8 Sep 1944
Collyweston	8 Jun 1943	B.53 Merville	12 Sep 1944
Kings Cliffe	29 Jun 1943	B.65 Maldegem	2 Nov 1944
Wellingore	5 Aug 1943	B.77 Gilze-Rijen	13 Jan 1945
Acklington	25 Aug 1943	Predannack	21 Feb 1945
Friston	22 Oct 1943	B.106 Twente	19 Apr 1945
Southend	26 Oct 1943	B.113 Varrelbusch	
Friston	10 Nov 1943		30 Apr 1945
Hornchurch	11 Mar 1944	B.116 Wunstorf	29 Jun 1945
Selsey	11 Apr 1944	B.56 Evère	1 Sep 1945
Coolham	30 Jun 1944	B.116 Wunstorf	4 Sep 1945
Funtington	4 Jul 1944	B.152 Fassberg	29 Nov 1945
Selsey	6 Aug 1944		to 24 Oct 1946

Aircraft Equipment

Aircraft Equipment	Period of service	Representative Serial
Tomahawk I	Jan 1943 – Apr 1943	AH775 (GE-N)
Spitfire VA, VB	Jun 1943 – Feb 1944	BL334 (GE-F)
Spitfire VC	Oct 1943 – Feb 1944	AR490 (GE-A)
Spitfire IX	Feb 1944 – Feb 1945	MK130 (GE-P)
	Apr 1945 – May 1945	
Tempest V	Feb 1945 – Apr 1945	
Spitfire XVI	May 1945 – Oct 1946	TE274 (GE-K)

No. 350 Squadron

Badge: An ancient Belgian warrior's head with helmet

Motto: Belgae gallorum fortissimi (The Belgae, bravest of the Gauls)

Squadron bases

Valley	12 Nov 1941	Hawkinge	1 Oct 1943
Atcham	19 Feb 1942	Southend	13 Oct 1943
Warmwell	5 Apr 1942	Hawkinge	31 Oct 1943
Debden	15 Apr 1942	Hornchurch	30 Dec 1943
Gravesend	30 Jun 1942	Hawkinge	10 Mar 1944
Martlesham Heath	7 Jul 1942	Peterhead	13 Mar 1944
Kenley	16 Jul 1942	Friston	25 Apr 1944
Redhill	31 Jul 1942	Westhampnett	4 Jul 1944
Martlesham Heath	7 Sep 1942	Hawkinge	8 Aug 1944
Redhill	15 Sep 1942	Lympne	29 Sep 1944
Southend	23 Sep 1942	B.56 Evère	3 Dec 1944
Hornchurch	8 Dec 1942	Y.32 As/Ophoven	31 Dec 1944
Heston	1 Mar 1943	B.78 Eindhoven	27 Jan 1945
Debden	5 Mar 1943	Warmwell	24 Mar 1945
Hornchurch	13 Mar 1943	B.78 Eindhoven	2 Apr 1945
Fairlop	15 Mar 1943	B.106 Twente	7 Apr 1945
Acklington	23 Mar 1943	B.118 Celle	16 Apr 1945
Ouston	8 Jun 1943	B.152 Fassberg	6 May 1945
Acklington	20 Jul 1943	B.172 Husum	Jun 1945
Digby	25 Aug 1943	B.116 Wunstorf	Jul 1945
West Malling	7 Sep 1943	B.152 Fassberg	29 Nov 1945
Digby	18 Sep 1943		to 24 Oct 1946

Aircraft Equipment	Period of service	Representative Serial
Spitfire IIA	Nov 1941 – Apr 1942	P8727 (MN-A)
Spitfire VB	Feb 1942 – Dec 1943 Mar 1944 – Jul 1944	BL496 (MN-O)
Spitfire VC	Mar 1944 – Jul 1944	EE613 (MN-E)
Spitfire IX	Dec 1943 – Mar 1944 Jul 1944 – Aug 1944	MK192 (MN-Z)
Spitfire XIV	Aug 1944 – Oct 1946	NH698 (MN-C)
Spitfire XVI	Aug 1946 – Oct 1946	TD325 (MN-M)

No.350 Squadron was formed at Valley on 12 November 1941 as the first Belgian-manned fighter squadron. Equipped with Spitfires, it became operational on defensive duties on 22 December and moved south in April 1942 to begin flying sweeps over northern France. Withdrawn to northern England in March 1943, No.350 resumed offensive operations in October and joined Second TAF in preparation for the invasion of Europe. After covering the Allied landings, the squadron re-equipped with Spitfire XIVs and for the next month was engaged in intercepting flying bombs over southern England. This was followed by sweeps over the Netherlands and in December 1944 the squadron moved to Belgium. Low-level attacks on enemy communications in support of the Allied armies occupied the squadron until the end of the war and after serving with the occupation forces No.350 was transferred to the control of the Belgian Air Force on 15 October 1946.

Spitfire VCs, No.352 Squadron

No. 351 Squadron

No.351 Squadron was formed at Benina, Libya, on 1 July 1944 as a Yugoslav-manned fighter-bomber unit. Equipped with Hurricanes, it moved to Italy to join No.281 Wing of the Balkan Air Force for ground-attack missions in support of Yugoslav partisans. To shorten the range from its mainland base, the squadron normally mounted its sorties from the island of Vis in the Adriatic and in February 1945 began to operate from a captured airfield on the Yugoslav coast. In April the squadron moved to Yugoslavia and was disbanded on 15 June 1945.

Squadron bases

Benina	1 Jul 1944	Prkos	2 Mar 1945 (D)
Canne	22 Sep 1944		5 Apr 1945 (C)
Vis (Det)	18 Oct 1944 to 5 Apr 1945		to 15 Jun 1945

Aircraft Equipment	Period of service	Representative Serial
Hurricane IIC	Jul 1944 – Sep 1944	LB886 (O)
Hurricane IV	Sep 1944 – Jun 1945	LD975 (O)

No. 352 Squadron

No.352 Squadron was formed at Benina on 22 April 1944, the first Yugoslav-manned fighter unit to be formed in the Mediterranean. Equipped with Hurricanes initially, it received Spitfires in June and in August moved to Italy to join No.281 Wing. Escort was provided for fighter-bomber squadrons and No.352 was also engaged in ground-attack missions for the rest of the war, using Vis as an advanced base until 1 January 1945 when the squadron's air echelon became permanently based there. Headquarters remained in Italy until it moved to the Yugoslav mainland to join its air echelon in April 1945 and the squadron disbanded on 15 June 1945.

Squadron bases

Benina	22 Apr 1944	Vis	18 Oct 1944 (D)
Lete	6 May 1944		25 Jan 1945 (A)
Canne	9 Aug 1944	Prkos	12 Apr 1945 to 15 Jun 1945

Aircraft Equipment	Period of service	Representative Serial
Hurricane IIC	Apr 1944 – Jul 1944	KZ449
Spitfire VC	Jun 1944 – Jun 1945	JK604 (C)

No. 353 Squadron

Badge: A Bengal Tiger rampant
Motto: Fear naught in unity

No.353 Squadron was formed at Dum Dum, Calcutta on 1 June 1942, with three Hudsons for general reconnaissance duties. Patrols over the Bay of Bengal began on 13 July and continued until 8 August 1943 after which the squadron moved to Palam to take over the mail runs from 194 Squadron. The Hudsons operated a network of services throughout India and in April 1944, they were supplemented by Dakotas which formed D Flight. In August, five Ansons were taken into use for short-range communications and by October the Hudsons had all been replaced by Dakotas. Expediters took the place of Ansons early in 1945 but by May 1945, the squadron had standardised on Dakotas of which it had twenty-seven on strength during the latter half of the year. Transport duties continued until No.353 disbanded on 1 October 1946.

Squadron bases
Dum Dum   1 Jun 1942
Dhubalia   24 Feb 1943
Tanjore   2 Apr 1943
Palam   24 Aug 1943
             to 1 Oct 1946

Aircraft Equipment	Period of service	Representative Serial
Hudson III	Jun 1942 – Oct 1944	FH373 (Y)
Hudson VI	Oct 1944 – Jul 1944	FK642
Dakota I	Apr 1944 – Sep 1945	FD804
Dakota III	Apr 1944 – Oct 1946	FL509
Anson I, X, XII	Aug 1944 – Jan 1945	NK656
Warwick III	Nov 1944 – Mar 1945	
Expediter II	Jan 1945 – Jul 1945	KN113

No. 354 Squadron

No.354 Squadron was formed on 10 May 1943, at Drigh Road, Karachi, as a general reconnaissance unit but as no aircraft were available at first the personnel were attached to No.320 Maintenance Unit until mid-August when the squadron moved to Cuttack to receive Liberators. The first of these arrived on 28 August and the first patrol was despatched on 22 September. In December 1943, anti-submarine patrols were augmented by attacks on enemy shipping off Burma and both types of operation were continued until the squadron was disbanded on 18 May 1945.

Squadron bases
Drigh Road	10 May 1943	Minneriya	12 Oct 1944
Cuttack	17 Aug 1943	Cuttack	5 Jan 1945†
St. Thomas Mount			to 18 May 1945
	16 Jul 1944	†Move completed on 18 Jan 1945	

Aircraft Equipment	Period of service	Representative Serial
Liberator IIIA	Dec 1943 – Apr 1944	FK227 (T)
Liberator V	Aug 1943 – Aug 1944	BZ805 (V)
Liberator VI	Feb 1944 – May 1945	KG822 (P)

Liberator VI, No.355 Squadron

No. 355 Squadron

Badge: An elephant's head affrontée
Motto: Liberamus per caerula (We liberate through tropical skies)

No.355 Squadron was formed at Salbani, India on 18 August 1943, to be part of No.184 Wing in 221 Group. Towards the end of October, its first Liberators arrived and bombing operations began on 20 November. Attacks on Japanese bases in South-East Asia were maintained until the end of the war and the squadron then began transport and survey duties until disbanded on 31 May 1946.

Squadron bases
Salbani   18 Aug 1943
Digri   3 Jan 1946
Salbani   3 Apr 1946
             to 31 May 1946

Aircraft Equipment	Period of service	Representative Serial
Liberator III	Oct 1943 – Jul 1944	BZ990 (Z)
Liberator VI	Mar 1944 – Sep 1945	KH119 (C)
Liberator VIII	Aug 1945 – May 1946	KP136 (P)

No. 356 Squadron

Badge: A demi-tiger erased
Motto: We bring freedom and
assistance

No.356 Squadron was formed at Salbani, India on 15 January 1944, and a week later its first Liberators began to
arrive. After a period of crew training meteorological
flights began in June and on 27 July the squadron flew its

first bombing mission. Attacks on Japanese bases in Burma,
Sumatra and Malaya were carried out until July 1945,
mining sorties being also flown over enemy harbour approaches. In July 1945, No.356 moved to Cocos Island in
preparation for the invasion of Malaya but the end of the
war came before this could be carried out and after two
months of supply dropping and transport duties, the squadron was disbanded on 15 November 1945.

Squadron bases

Salbani	15 Jan 1944
Cocos Island	22 Jul 1945
	to 15 Nov 1945

Aircraft

Equipment	Period of service	Representative Serial
Liberator VI	Jan 1944 – Nov 1945	KG882 (P)

No. 357 Squadron

Badge: A crocodile
Motto: Mortem hostibus
(We bring death to the
enemy)

No.357 Squadron was formed at Digri, India, on 1 February
1944, from No.1576 (Special Duties) Flight which formed
A Flight of the new squadron. B Flight consisted of four
Catalinas at Redhills Lake, Madras, the squadron establishment having three Liberator IIIs and seven Hudson VIs in
addition.

Initially it used the Hudsons for supply drops to guerilla
forces in Burma while the Liberators and Catalinas undertook long-range flights to Malaya and Sumatra where the
Catalinas landed agents and supplies on the coast. On
21 March 1944, the Catalinas became No.628 Squadron but

the Liberators continued their supply flights until the end
of the war. By January 1945, Dakotas had replaced the
Hudsons and C Flight was formed to operate Lysanders
into strips in enemy-occupied territory, mainly for picking-
up agents and supplying Force 136 operating behind the
Japanese lines. In this respect, No.357 had a comparable
role to Nos.138 and 161 Squadrons in Europe. With the
end of the war, C Flight became the Burma Communications
Squadron on 7 November 1945, and on 15 November 1945,
the squadron was disbanded.

Squadron bases

Digri	1 Feb 1944	Jessore	15 Sep 1944
			to 15 Nov 1945
China Bay (D)	1 Feb 1944	Meiktila (D)	29 Apr 1945
	to Oct 1945		to 26 May 1945
Redhills Lake (D)	1 Feb 1944	Mingaladon (D)	26 May 1945
	to 21 Mar 1944		to 15 Nov 1945

Aircraft

Equipment	Period of service	Representative Serial
Hudson VI	Feb 1944 – Jan 1945	AM949
Liberator III	Feb 1944 – Jan 1945	BZ956 (Z)
Liberator VI	Dec 1944 – Nov 1945	KH320 (D)
Catalina IV	Feb 1944 – Mar 1944	
Dakota IV	Jan 1945 – Nov 1945	KJ924 (K)
Lysander IIIA	Jan 1945 – Nov 1945	V9889 (F)

No. 358 Squadron

Badge: An arm embowed, holding
in the hand a torch
Motto: Alere flamman
(To feed the flame)

No.358 Squadron was formed at Kolar, in India, on 8 November 1944, mainly from personnel of No.1673 Heavy Conversion Unit which had recently disbanded. Sixteen Liberators arrived during the month and crew training began. After moving to Digri in January 1945, the squadron flew its first bombing mission on 13 January when eight aircraft bombed Mandalay. This, however, proved to be the only bombing operation flown as the squadron was then allotted to Special Duties. These consisted of dropping agents and supplies into enemy-occupied territory in the course of which long flights were undertaken. The fact that the first SD operation on 22 January lost three out of eleven aircraft illustrates the hazards of this type of mission when, apart from the distances and weather problems involved, low altitude flights over enemy territory had to be made to locate dropping zones. Such flights continued till the end of the war and after the Japanese surrender supplies were dropped to prisoner-of-war camps in Malaya, Sumatra and Java until an airlift could be arranged to bring the occupants out to Allied bases. On 19 November 1945, the squadron was sent off for disbandment which took place officially two days later.

Squadron bases
Kolar	8 Nov 1944
Digri	3 Jan 1945
Jessore	10 Feb 1945
Bishnupur	19 Nov 1945
	to 21 Nov 1945

Aircraft Equipment	Period of service	Representative Serial
Liberator VI	Nov 1944 – Nov 1945	KH365 (N)

Canberra T.17, No.360 Squadron

No. 360 Squadron
No. 361 Squadron

Badge: In front of a trident erect,
a moth, wings displayed
Motto: Confundemus (We shall
throw into confusion)

No.360 Squadron was formed at Watton on 1 April 1966 with the provisional number of '360' but it was not until 23 September that this was confirmed. Canberra T.4s were flown initially and on 10 October 1966 the squadron took over B Flight of No.97 Squadron. The purpose of No.360 was to create a joint RAF/Royal Navy trials and training unit for electronic counter-measures training and Naval personnel came from No.831 Squadron which was also based at Watton. No.361 Squadron was formed under the control of No.360 on 2 January 1967 until such time as sufficient crews and aircraft were available for deployment to the Far East but No.361 was disbanded on 14 July 1967 and its crews joined No.360.

Specialised ECM-training Canberras began to arrive in the form of Canberra T.17s in December 1966 and in April 1969 the squadron moved to Cottesmore.

Squadron bases
Watton	1 Apr 1966
Cottesmore	21 Apr 1969

Aircraft Equipment	Period of service	Representative Serial
Canberra B.2	Oct 1966 – Aug 1967	WH665
Canberra T.4	Apr 1966 – date	WH839
Canberra B.6	Oct 1966 – Mar 1967	
Canberra T.17	Dec 1966 – date	WK102

Virginia X, No.500 Squadron

No. 500 Squadron

Badge: A horse forcene
Motto: Quo fata vocent
(Whither the fates
may call)
Name: 'County of Kent'

No.500 Squadron was formed at Manston on 16 March 1931 as a Special Reserve Unit. These squadrons consisted of half regular and half reserve personnel for twin-engined units and No.500 was equipped with Virginias on this basis. In October 1932 its establishment was fixed at six (plus two reserve) Virginias and two Avro 504Ks for flying training. On 5 December 1935 No.500 was redesignated a single-engined day bomber squadron in view of the promised complexity of future heavy bombers and doubts as to whether reserve units could cope with them with part-time personnel. Harts arrived in January 1936 and on 25 May 1936 the squadron was transferred from the Special Reserve to the Auxiliary Air Force. In February 1937 Hinds began to replace Harts but on 7 November 1938 the squadron was transferred to Coastal Command and received Ansons in March 1939. Shortly before the outbreak of war, No.500 was mobilised and began flying patrols over the Channel and North Sea. In April 1941 conversion to Blenheims took place and these were used for reconnaissance, patrols and bombing raids on enemy coastal targets. In November 1941 Hudsons were received and in March 1942 the squadron moved to Scotland for patrols over the Atlantic and the approaches to the Clyde and Irish Sea. At the end of August, it moved to Cornwall and in November, soon after the Allied landings, to Algeria, there to fly anti-submarine patrols over the Western Mediterranean. In December 1943 Venturas began to arrive and replaced the Hudsons completely in April 1944. The squadron disbanded on 11 July 1944 and its aircraft were handed over to No.27 (SAAF) Squadron.

Before many of its personnel had left, No.500 reformed on 1 August 1944 at the same base as it had disbanded (La Senia) and moved to Italy later in the month. During September, it received Baltimores and began operations on 10 December. Daylight raids on communications targets occupied the next few months but as the enemy took to moving only at night the squadron's role changed to night interdiction for the rest of the war. In September 1945 No.500 left Italy for Kenya and was renumbered 249 Squadron on 28 September 1945.

On 10 May 1946 the Auxiliary Air Force, was reformed and. No.500 resumed recruiting in Kent, being based at West Malling as a night fighter squadron. Mosquitos arrived in October 1946, but Meteors replaced these from 1948 as the squadron converted to a day fighter role. It flew Meteors until the Royal Auxiliary Air Force squadrons disbanded on 10 March 1957.

Squadron bases

Manston	16 Mar 1931	La Senia	6 Jan 1944
Detling	28 Sep 1938		to 11 Jul 1944
Warmwell	30 Jul 1939	La Senia	1 Aug 1944
Detling	13 Aug 1939	Left for Italy	24 Aug 1944
Bircham Newton	30 May 1941	Pescara	14 Sep 1944
Stornoway	2 Apr 1942	Perugia	15 Oct 1944
St. Eval	31 Aug 1942	Cesenatico	9 Dec 1944
Gibraltar	5 Nov 1942	Villaorba	10 May 1945
Tafaraoui	11 Nov 1942	Eastleigh	28 Sep 1945
Blida	19 Nov 1942	West Malling	10 May 1946
Tafaraoui	3 May 1943		to 10 Mar 1957

Aircraft Equipment	Period of service	Representative Serial	
Virginia X	Mar 1931 – Jan 1936	J7566	(B) 'City of Canterbury'
Hart	Jan 1936 – May 1937	K3018	
Hind	Feb 1937 – Mar 1939	K6700	
Anson I	Mar 1939 – Apr 1941	N5233	(MK-Q)
Blenheim IV	Apr 1941 – Nov 1941	Z6050	
Hudson III, V	Nov 1941 – Apr 1944	FK444	
Ventura V	Dec 1943 – Jul 1944	FP633	(MK-R)
Baltimore IV, V	Sep 1944 – Sep 1945	FA618	(C)
Mosquito NF.30	Apr 1947 – Oct 1948	NT606	(RAA-H)
Meteor F.3	Jul 1948 – Oct 1951	EE420	(RAA-B)
Meteor F.4	Jul 1951 – Feb 1952	VT169	(S7-F)
Meteor F.8	Nov 1951 – Mar 1957	WF714	(K)

302

Vampire F.1, No.501 Squadron

No. 501 Squadron

Badge: A boar's head couped
Motto: Nil time (Fear nothing)
Name: 'City of Bristol' (1930-36)
'County of Gloucester'
(1936-57)

No.501 Squadron was formed at Filton on 14 June 1929 as a Special Reserve unit and began to receive D.H.9As for day bomber duties in March 1930. These were replaced by Wapitis in 1930 and early in 1933, Wallaces came into service. Re-equipped with Harts in July 1936, the squadron had been transferred to the Auxiliary Air Force in May 1936, changing its name to embrace a larger area of recruitment. Hinds were received in March 1938 and at the end of the year No.501 was redesignated a fighter squadron, receiving Hurricanes in March 1939. On the outbreak of World War Two, the squadron flew defensive patrols until the German attack on France in May 1940, when it moved across the Channel to provide fighter cover for the AASF, retiring to Brittany and returning to the UK when France surrendered. No.501 was based in southern England throughout the Battle of Britain and began fighter sweeps over France early in 1941. In April 1941 it converted to Spitfires and moved to Northern Ireland in October 1942. In April 1943 the squadron returned south to fly sweeps and in July 1944, converted to Tempests which it used to catch flying bombs over south England until their launching sites were overrun by the army in September. It then moved to East Anglia for escort missions and for defensive patrols to catch enemy bombers launching flying bombs. On 20 April 1945 the squadron disbanded.

On 10 May 1946 No.501 was reformed as an Auxiliary Air Force fighter squadron at Filton and began local recruiting. In November 1946 Spitfires were received and the Vampires which replaced them began to arrive in February 1949, being flown until disbandment on 10 March 1957.

Squadron bases

Filton	14 Jun 1929	Middle Wallop	10 Oct 1942
Tangmere	28 Nov 1939	Ballyhalbert	19 Oct 1942
Betheniville	10 May 1940	Westhampnett	30 Apr 1943
Anglure	16 May 1940	Martlesham Heath	
Le Mans	2 Jun 1940		17 May 1943
Dinard	11 Jun 1940	Woodvale	5 Jun 1943
Jersey	17 Jun 1940	Westhampnett	12 Jun 1943
Croydon	21 Jun 1940	Hawkinge	21 Jun 1943
Middle Wallop	4 Jul 1940	Southend	21 Jan 1944
Gravesend	25 Jul 1940	Hawkinge	4 Feb 1944
Kenley	10 Sep 1940	Friston	30 Apr 1944
Filton	17 Dec 1940	Westhampnett	2 Jul 1944
Colerne	9 Apr 1941	Manston	2 Aug 1944
Chilbolton	25 Jun 1941	Bradwell Bay	22 Sep 1944
Ibsley	5 Aug 1941	Hunsdon	3 Mar 1945
Tangmere	3 Jul 1942		to 20 Apr 1945
Middle Wallop	24 Aug 1942	Filton	10 May 1946
Hawkinge	8 Oct 1942		to 10 Mar 1957

Aircraft

Equipment	Period of service	Representative Serial	
Avro 504N	Aug 1929 — Mar 1930†	J8689	
D.H.9A	Mar 1930 — Nov 1930		
Wapiti	Sep 1930 — Mar 1933†	K1374	
Wallace I, II	Jan 1933 — Jul 1936	K3672	
Hart	Jul 1936 — Mar 1938	K3869	
Hind	Mar 1938 — Mar 1939†	K5550	
Hurricane I	Mar 1939 — May 1941	L2124	(SD-H)
Spitfire I	Apr 1941 — Jun 1941	X4381	(SD-J)
Spitfire IIA	May 1941 — Sep 1941	P8075	
Spitfire VB, VC	Sep 1941 — Jul 1944	AB402	(SD-K)
Spitfire IX	Nov 1943 — Jul 1944	MH855	(SD-5)
Tempest V	Jul 1944 — Apr 1945	EJ702	(SD-Q)
Spitfire LF.16E	Nov 1946 — Jan 1949	SL541	(RAB-F)
Vampire F.1	Nov 1948 — Jun 1951	TG370	(RAB-O)
Vampire FB.5	Mar 1951 — Mar 1957	VX984	(K)
Vampire FB.9	Feb 1955 — Feb 1957	WR180	

†remained in service for training after replacement as main equipment.

Wallace I, No.502 Squadron

No. 502 Squadron

Badge: A red hand erased
Motto: Nihil timeo
(I fear nothing)
Name: 'Ulster'

No.502 Squadron was formed as a Special Reserve Unit at Aldergrove on 15 May 1925. As a heavy bomber squadron, it began to receive Vimys in June but replaced these by Hyderabads in July 1928. In December 1931 the squadron received Virginias which it gave up in October 1935 on being redesignated a day bomber squadron, re-equipping with Wallaces. These were replaced by Hinds in April 1937 and on 28 November 1938, No.502 was transferred to Coastal Command and converted to Ansons in January 1939. On the outbreak of war, the squadron began patrols off the Irish coast, first with Ansons and then, from October 1940, with Whitleys. In January 1942 the squadron moved to East Anglia, where a maintenance base was set up at Bircham Newton though from February all operations were flown from St. Eval in Cornwall. No.502 pioneered the use of air-to-surface radar and had, on 30 November 1941, made the first successful attack on a U-boat by a Coastal Command aircraft using ASV when U-206 was sunk in the Bay of Biscay. In January 1943 conversion to Halifaxes began, the first patrol by this type being flown on 12 March. In addition to anti-submarine patrols, attacks on enemy shipping off the French coast were made. In September 1944 the squadron moved to Scotland for attacks on enemy shipping off Norway and disbanded on 25 May 1945.

On 10 May 1946 No.502 was reformed as a Mosquito unit of the Auxiliary Air Force and began to form on 17 July. In 1948 it became a day fighter squadron with Spitfires, converting to Vampires in January 1951 and flying this type until disbanded on 10 March 1957.

Squadron bases

Aldergrove	15 May 1925	St. David's	10 Dec 1943
Limavady	27 Jan 1941	Stornoway	11 Sep 1944
Docking	12 Jan 1942		to 25 May 1945
St. Eval	22 Feb 1942	Aldergrove	17 Jul 1946
Holmsley South	2 Mar 1943		to 10 Mar 1957

Aircraft

Equipment	Period of service	Representative Serial	
Vimy	Jun 1925 – Jul 1928	J7247	
Hyderabad	Jul 1928 – Dec 1931	J7742	(2)
Virginia X	Dec 1931 – Oct 1935	K2339	
Wallace II	Oct 1935 – Apr 1937	K6020	
Hind	Apr 1937 – Jan 1939	K6761	
Anson I	Jan 1939 – Oct 1940	N5235	(YG-J)
Whitley V	Oct 1940 – Fev 1942	T4222	(YG-H)
Whitley VII	Feb 1942 – Feb 1943	Z9365	
Halifax II	Jan 1943 – Mar 1945	HR673	
Halifaxx III	Feb 1945 – May 1945	PN399	
Mosquito B.25	Jul 1946 – Dec 1947		
Mosquito NF.30	Dec 1947 – Jun 1949	RK937	
Spitfire F.22	Jun 1948 – Jan 1951	PK567	(RAC-J)
Vampire FB.5	Mar 1951 – Mar 1957	WA292	(V9-D)
Vampire FB.9	Jul 1954 – Mar 1957	WR179	(X)

Virginia X, No.502 Squadron

No. 503 Squadron

Name: 'County of Lincoln'

No.503 Squadron was formed at Waddington on 5 October 1926 as a Special Reserve unit. As a bomber squadron, it was initially equipped with Fawns but received Hyderabad night bombers in 1929, and in 1933, its improved version, the Hinaidi. In October 1935, No.503 became a day bomber squadron and received Wallaces, these being replaced by Harts in June 1936. In 1938, Hinds began to arrive but the squadron disbanded on 1 November 1938, its aircraft and personnel going to No. 616 (South Yorkshire) Squadron which formed on the same day at Doncaster.

Squadron base

Waddington   5 Oct 1926
                to 1 Nov 1938

Aircraft Equipment	Period of service	Representative Serial
Fawn	Oct 1926 – 1929	
Hyderabad	1929 – 1933	J7752
Hinaidi	1933 – Oct 1935	K1909
Wallace II	Oct 1935 – Jun 1936	K5080
Hart	Jun 1936 – Nov 1938	K3023
Hind	1938 – Nov 1938	K6838

No. 504 Squadron

Badge: An oak tree fronted and eradicated
Motto: Vindicat in ventis
(It avenges in the wind)
Name: 'County of Nottingham'

No.504 Squadron was a Special Reserve unit formed at Hucknall on 26 March 1928 as a day bomber squadron equipped with Horsleys. In February 1935 it re-equipped with Wallaces which were replaced by Hinds in May 1937. On 31 October 1938 No.504 became a fighter squadron and received Hurricanes in March 1939. A few days before the outbreak of war, the squadron moved to Digby to fly defensive patrols and in October joined the Debden Sector, using Martlesham Heath as a forward base and alternating between the two airfields at approximately weekly intervals until the Germans invaded France in May 1940. No.504 moved to France for a short period to cover the BEF and at the end of May was sent to the north of Scotland to provide fighter defence for Scapa Flow. In September, it came south again to take part in the latter half of the Battle of Britain and later began flying sweeps over France. A move to Nor-thern Ireland came in August 1941, and after a year on defensive duties the squadron returned to southern England for a period of defensive and offensive operations before going to Scotland in September 1943. The forthcoming invasion of Europe brought the squadron south again to fly sweeps and escort missions and in March 1945 it moved to Colerne to convert to Meteors. On 10 August 1945 it was renumbered 245 Squadron.

On 10 May 1946 No.504 was reformed as a light bomber squadron of the Auxiliary Air Force but flew only training aircraft until redesignated a night fighter unit in April 1947 with Mosquito NF.30s. In May 1948 it received Spitfires to become a day fighter squadron, converting to Meteors in October 1949. No.504 flew this type until disbanded on 10 March 1957.

Hurricane I, No.504 Squadron

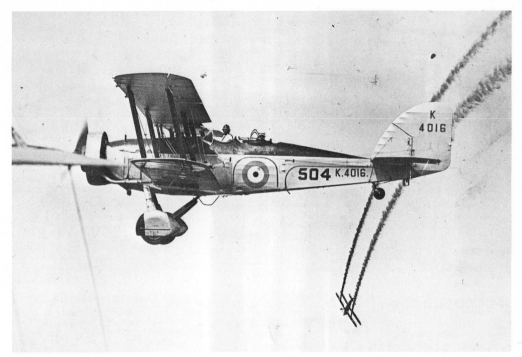

Wallace I, No.504 Squadron

Squadron bases

Hucknall	26 Mar 1928	Kirkistown	22 Jan 1942
Digby	27 Aug 1939	Ballyhalbert	19 Jun 1942
Debden	9 Oct 1939	Middle Wallop	19 Oct 1942
Frequent detachments to		Ibsley	30 Dec 1942
Martlesham Heath		Church Stanton	30 June 1943
Vitry-en-Artois	12 May 1940	Redhill	14 Aug 1943
Lille/Marcq	13 May 1940	Castletown	19 Sep 1943
Norrent Fontes	19 May 1940	Peterhead	18 Oct 1943
Manston	20 May 1940	Hornchurch	19 Jan 1944
Debden	21 May 1940	Digby	30 Apr 1944
Wick	24 May 1940	Detling	11 Jul 1944
Castletown	21 Jun 1940	Manston	13 Aug 1944
Catterick	1 Sep 1940	Hawkinge	25 Feb 1945
Hendon	5 Sep 1940	Colerne	28 Mar 1945
Filton	26 Sep 1940		to 10 Aug 1945
Exeter	26 Sep 1940	Syerston	10 May 1946
Fairwood Common	21 Jul 1941	Hucknall	Nov 1946 (P)
Chilbolton	11 Aug 1941	Wymeswold	2 Apr 1949
Ballyhalbert	26 Aug 1941		to 10 Mar 1957

Aircraft Equipment	Period of service	Representative Serial
Horsley	Oct 1929 – Feb 1934	J8019
Wallace I, II	Feb 1934 – May 1937	K4015
Hind	May 1937 – Mar 1939	K6716
Hurricane I	Mar 1939 – Aug 1941	P3774 (TM-V)
Hurricane IIB	July 1941 – Nov 1941	Z5539
Spitfire IIA, IIB	Oct 1941 – Oct 1942	P8209
Spitfire VB, VC	Jan 1942 – Jan 1944 Mar 1944 – Jul 1944	EE624 (TM-R)
Spitfire VI	Sep 1943 – Nov 1943	BR297
Spitfire IX	Jan 1944 – Mar 1944 July 1944 – Apr 1945	NH587
Meteor III	Apr 1945 – Aug 1945	EE286 (TM-Q)
Mosquito T.3	Apr 1947 – Apr 1947+	VP350
Mosquito NF.30	Apr 1947 – Aug 1948	NT562 (RAD-M)
Spitfire F.22	May 1948 – Oct 1949	PK606 (RAD-G)
Meteor F.4	Oct 1949 – Mar 1952	VZ403 (TM-A)
Meteor F.8	Mar 1952 – Mar 1957	WH310 (J)

+Retained as training equipment after replacement by Mosquito NF.30s

No. 510 Squadron

Squadron base

Hendon	15 Oct 1942
	to 8 Apr 1944

No.510 Squadron was formed at Hendon on 15 October 1942, taking over a miscellany of light transport and communications aircraft formerly operated by No.24 Squadron. It was engaged in communications flying in the UK until redesignated the Metropolitan Communications Squadron on 8 April 1944.

Aircraft

Various types in use at various times e.g.
Spitfire I (R7199), Lysander I (R2635), Tiger Moth II (DE322), Proctor I, III, IV (MX451), Oxford I (L4635), Reliant (W7984), Mohawk III (AR633), Vega Gull (X9391), Hart (K2452), Hornet Moth (W9390), Puss Moth (ES954), Gipsy Moth (MX463), Stampe SV.4B (MX457), Anson I (EG229), Cygnet (HM496), Percival Q.6 (X9363).

No. 511 Squadron

Badge: In front of a compass card, an eagle volante affrontée, the head lowered to the dexter holding in the claws a chain of five links.
Motto: Surely and quickly.

No.511 Squadron was formed at Lyneham on 10 October 1942, from No.1425 Flight which had been operating a service between the UK and Gibraltar with Liberator transports since November 1941. These were supplemented in November 1942 by Albemarles and a detachment based at Gibraltar maintained a link with Malta. On 16 February 1943 C Flight was formed to look after the Albemarles and the squadron had an establishment of twenty-five transport aircraft. In October 1943 a service to India was opened and in November the squadron's first York arrived. A new establishment issued in July 1944 indicated that No.511 was to concentrate only on long-range flights as this allowed for thirteen Yorks for A Flight and twelve Liberators for B Flight, the Dakotas being withdrawn. On 1 October 1944 nine Liberators were handed over to No.246 Squadron and by the end of the year only Yorks remained on strength. Trooping to the Middle and Far East continued until the squadron was disbanded on 7 October 1946.

On 16 October 1946 No.511 reformed, again with Yorks, and took part in the Berlin Airlift before converting to Hastings in 1949. These it flew on Transport Command routes throughout the world until it was renumbered No.36 Squadron on 1 September 1958.

On 15 December 1959 No.511 reformed as the second Britannia squadron in Transport Command, a type which it operated on the trunk routes to the Near and Far East. In June 1970 it moved to Brize Norton to join the other long-range transport squadrons of Air Support Command until disbanded on 6 January 1976.

Squadron bases

Lyneham	10 Oct 1942		to 1 Sep 1958
	to 7 Oct 1946	Lyneham	15 Dec 1959
Lyneham	16 Oct 1946	Brize Norton	16 June 1970
Colerne	1 May 1957		to 6 Jan 1976

Aircraft Equipment	Period of service	Representative Serial
Liberator I, II	Oct 1942 – Jul 1944	AM913
Liberator VII	Jul 1944 – Dec 1944	EW613
Albemarle I, II	Nov 1942 – Mar 1944	P1449
Dakota I, III	Oct 1943 – Jul 1944	FL515
York C.1	Nov 1943 – Sep 1949	MW119
Hastings C.1, C.2	Sep 1949 – Sep 1958	WD488 (JAM)
Britannia C.1, C.2	Dec 1959 – Jan 1976	XM496 Regulus

Britannia C.2, No.511 Squadron

No. 512 Squadron

Badge: In front of a horse's head couped, a sword erect, the point upwards.
Motto: Pegasus militans (Pegasus at war).

No.512 Squadron was formed at Hendon on 18 June 1943 as a transport unit equipped with Dakotas. Flights to Gibraltar and North Africa were carried out until February 1944, when the squadron began training with airborne forces. For some weeks prior to D-Day, unarmed Dakotas carried out leaflet-dropping flights over France and on the day of the landings thirty-two aircraft were despatched with paratroops before dawn followed during the day by seventeen more towing gliders. Casualty evacuation flights from France began soon afterwards and continued for the rest of the war interspersed with general transport duties. During the Arnhem landings, forty-six gliders were towed into the landing zone in the initial two days, followed by twenty-nine resupply missions for the loss of three Dakotas. During the crossing of the Rhine in March 1945, twenty-four aircraft of No.512 towed gliders, losing one in the process. After flying services to the Middle East, the squadron moved to Egypt and, in December, to Italy, operating routes to various points in the Balkans. On 23 February 1946 No.512's aircraft began moving back to the UK and it disbanded on 14 March 1946.

Squadron bases

Hendon	18 June 1943		
Broadwell	14 Feb 1944	Qastina	8 Oct 1945
B.56 Evère	31 Mar 1945	Gianaclis	24 Oct 1945
	to 5 July 1945 (A)	Bari	2 Dec 1945
Holme-in-Spalding Moor			18 Dec 1945 (C)
	6 Aug 1945		to 14 Mar 1946

Aircraft Equipment	Period of service	Representative Serial
Dakota I, III	Jun 1943 – Mar 1946	KG625 (HC-AF)

307

No. 513 Squadron

No.513 Squadron was formed at Witchford on 15 September 1943 as a Stirling unit in Bomber Command, receiving its first aircraft in October. Due to a decision to increase the size of Stirling conversion units, the squadron's aircraft were needed elsewhere and its working-up period was suspended, disbandment taking place on 21 November 1943.

Squadron base

Witchford	15 Sep 1943
	to 21 Nov 1943

Aircraft Equipment	Period of service	Representative Serial
Stirling III	Oct 1943 — Nov 1943	EF200

No. 514 Squadron

Badge: A cloud pierced by a sword.
Motto: Nil obstare potest (Nothing can withstand)

No.514 Squadron was formed at Foulsham on 1 September 1943 in No.3 Group. Equipped with Lancasters, it began operations on 3 November 1943. For the rest of the war, it took part in Bomber Command's strategic bombing of Germany and disbanded on 22 August 1945.

Squadron bases

Foulsham	1 Sep 1943
Waterbeach	23 Nov 1943
	to 22 Aug 1945

Aircraft Equipment	Period of service	Representative Serial
Lancaster II	Sep 1943 — Jun 1943	DS785 (JI-D)
Lancaster I, III	Jun 1944 — Aug 1945	PA186 (A2-G)

No. 515 Squadron

Badge: A gauntlet holding a winged dagger in bend sinister, thrusting to the dexter.
Motto: Celeriter ferite ut hostes nacesit (Strike quickly to kill the enemy).

No.515 Squadron was formed at Northolt on 1 October 1942 from the Defiant Flight. Working with the A & AEE and TRE, Defiants had been fitted with equipment for jamming enemy radar (Operation 'Moonshine'). In June 1943 Beaufighters began to arrive and finally replaced the Defiants in December, the squadron having become non-operational in August. No.100 Group had taken over the task of counter-measures and No.515 joined it in January 1944, converting to Mosquitos in February. Intruder missions began on 5 March, mainly by night, and continued till the end of the war. On 10 June 1945 the squadron disbanded.

Squadron bases

Northolt	1 Oct 1942
Heston	29 Oct 1942
Hunsdon	31 May 1943
Little Snoring	15 Dec 1943
	to 10 June 1945.

Aircraft Equipment	Period of service	Representative Serial
Defiant II	Oct 1942 — Dec 1943	AA575 (P)
Beaufighter II	Jun 1943 — Feb 1944	V8191 (N)
Mosquito II	Feb 1944 — Mar 1944	DD756
Mosquito VI	Mar 1944 — Jun 1945	NS957 (3P-V)

No. 516 Squadron

No.516 Squadron was formed at Dundonald on 28 April 1943 by renumbering No.1441 (Combined Operations) Flight. Its purpose was to provide aircraft for co-operation with Combined Operations training units in western Scotland by carrying out practice attacks on shipping and landing craft, smoke screen laying, gas spraying, low level reconnaissance and demonstrations of aircraft to army units. A mixed establishment of fighters and twin-engined aircraft was used for these tasks until after the invasion of Europe, the requirement for such a unit having declined by the end of the year to an extent that allowed disbandment to take place on 2 December 1944.

Squadron base

Dundonald	28 Apr 1943
	to 2 Dec 1944

Aircraft Equipment	Period of service	Representative Serial
Mustang I	Apr 1943 — Feb 1944	AM236
Lysander II, IIIA	Apr 1943 — Dec 1943	V9311
Anson I	Apr 1943 — Dec 1944	MG858
Blenheim IV	May 1943 — Dec 1944	L9301
Hurricane IIB, IIC	Dec 1943 — Dec 1944	LF534

No. 517 Squadron

Badge: Two cubit arms erased, holding a flash of lightning.
Motto: Non nobis laboramus (We work not for ourselves)

No.517 Squadron was formed from No.1404 (Met) Flight at St. Eval on 11 August 1943. It was intended to be equipped with Halifaxes but until these became available, Hudsons and Hampdens were used for meteorological flights over the Western Approaches. In September 1943 Hudsons were withdrawn and four B-17Fs from the 379th Squadron, USAAF from Little Staughton joined the squadron, flying weather flights until 23 November. The B-17 flights fortunately filled the gap between the withdrawal of the Hampdens and Hudsons from operations in September and the arrival of Halifaxes in November. In November 1943 the squadron moved to Pembrokeshire and in addition to weather flights flew anti-submarine patrols over the Western Approaches, using Tiree as an advanced base for northern sectors. In November 1945 No.517 moved to Devon where it disbanded on 21 June 1946.

Squadron bases			
St. Eval	11 Aug 1943	Brawdy	1 Feb 1944
St. David's	26 Nov 1943	Chivenor	26 Nov 1945
			to 21 June 1946

Aircraft Equipment	Period of service	Representative Serial
Hampden I	Aug 1943 – Oct 1943	AD724
Hudson III	Aug 1943 – Sep 1943	V9123
Halifax V	Nov 1943 – Jun 1946	LL216 (X9-A)
Halifax III	Feb 1945 – Jun 1946	NA231

No. 518 Squadron

Badge: A hand couped at the wrist holding a key the ward uppermost.
Motto: Thaan iuchair againn-ne. (We hold the key)

No.518 Squadron was formed at Stornoway on 9 July 1943 as a meteorological unit equipped with Halifaxes. It moved to Tiree in September and began operational flights on 15 September. These weather flights normally went 700 miles into the Atlantic and from January 1945 carried depth charges in case a U-Boat should be sighted. On 18 September 1945 the squadron moved to Ulster and absorbed the Spitfires and Hurricanes of No.1402 Flight. On 1 October 1946 No.518 became No.202 Squadron.

Squadron bases	
Stornoway	9 Jul 1943
Tiree	25 Sep 1943
Aldergrove	18 Sep 1945
	to 1 Oct 1946

Aircraft Equipment	Period of service	Representative Serial
Halifax V	Jul 1943 – Aug 1945	DG304 (Y5-B)
Halifax III	Mar 1945 – Oct 1946	RG390 (Y5-A1)
Spitfire IX	Sep 1945 – Oct 1946	MB181
Hurricane II	Sep 1945 – Oct 1946	PZ815

No. 519 Squadron

Badge: A polar bear's gamb erased in bend holding a scroll of parchment in front of a flash of lightning.
Motto: Undaunted by weather.

No.519 Squadron was formed at Wick on 15 August 1943 from No.1406 (Met) Flight, taking over the latter's Hampdens and Spitfires. Weather flights were flown over the North Sea and north from Scotland, Hudsons and Venturas soon replacing Hampdens. In November 1944 Fortresses were received for longer-ranged flights and after the end of the war the squadron standardised on Halifaxes. On 31 May 1946 the squadron was disbanded.

Squadron bases	
Wick	15 Aug 1943
Skitten	11 Dec 1943
Wick	29 Nov 1944
Tain	17 Aug 1945
Leuchars	8 Nov 1945
	to 31 May 1946

Aircraft Equipment	Period of service	Representative Serial
Hampden I	Aug 1943 – Oct 1943	P2118 (Z9-D)
Spitfire VI	Aug 1943 – Jan 1945	BR307 (Z9-X)
Hudson III, IIIA	Sep 1943 – Oct 1943 Jul 1944 – Mar 1945	FK744 (Z9-C)
Ventura V	Oct 1943 – Oct 1944	FP583 (Z9-L)
Spitfire VII	Oct 1944 – Dec 1945	MD141
Fortress II	Nov 1944 – Sep 1945	FA703
Halifax III	Aug 1945 – May 1946	NA229

No. 520 Squadron

Badge: A dove holding in the beak an olive branch.
Motto: Tomorrow's weather today.

Aircraft Equipment	Period of service	Representative Serial
Hudson III	Sep 1943 – Mar 1944 Jan 1945 – Oct 1945	FH357
Gladiator II	Sep 1943 – Jun 1944	N5630
Halifax V	Feb 1944 – Jun 1945	LV969 (Z)
Spitfire V	Feb 1944 – Jun 1944	EP412
Hurricane IIC	Jun 1944 – Apr 1946	PZ830 (D)
Martinet I	Sep 1944 – Dec 1945	NR293 (T)
Halifax III	Apr 1945 – Apr 1946	PN190
Warwick I	Aug 1945 – Apr 1946	HG186

Halifax III, No.520 Squadron

No.520 Squadron was formed at Gibraltar on 20 September 1943 from No.1402 Flight for meteorological duties. Initially equipped with Hudsons and Gladiators, it changed this combination to Halifaxes and Spitfires early in 1944. Weather flights were made out into the Atlantic and in September 1944 the squadron took over the Martinets of No.1500 (BAT) Flight for target-towing. Soon after the end of the war, No.520 was given an air-sea rescue role in addition to its meteorological duties and remained in Gibraltar until disbanded on 25 April 1946.

Squadron base	
Gibraltar	20 Sep 1943
	to 25 Apr 1946

Hampden I, No.521 Squadron

No. 521 Squadron

No.521 Squadron was formed at Bircham Newton on 1 August 1942 from No.1401 Flight for meteorological duties over the North Sea and Europe. Hudsons and Blenheims carried out the North Sea flights while Spitfires and Mosquitos were used over enemy territory and Gladiators for local weather flights. On 31 March 1943 the squadron divided into Nos.1401 and 1409 (Met) Flights.

On 1 September 1943 No.521 reformed at Docking with Hampdens, Hudsons and Gladiators. Venturas became the main type by the end of the year and Hurricanes arrived in August 1944 to supplement the old Gladiators which, despite their age, continued to fly sorties until March 1945. Hudsons reappeared in September 1944, as the Venturas were required by other units and in December Fortresses were received to become the only long-range type by the end of the war. In November 1945 the squadron moved to Devon and disbanded on 1 April 1946.

Squadron bases

Bircham Newton	1 Aug 1942
	to 31 Mar 1943
Docking	1 Sep 1943
Langham	30 Oct 1944
Chivenor	3 Nov 1945
	to 1 Apr 1946

Aircraft Equipment	Period of service	Representative Serial
Hudson III	Aug1942 – Mar 1943	FH380
Blenheim IV	Aug 1942 – Mar 1943	V5570
Spitfire V	Aug 1942 – Mar 1943	N2370
Mosquito IV	Aug 1942 – Mar 1943	DZ316
Gladiator II	Aug 1942 – Mar 1943	N2307
Hampden I	Sep 1943 – Dec 1943	L4042
Hudson III, V	Sep 1943 – Jan 1944 Sep 1944 – Mar 1945	FK740
Gladiator II	Sep 1943 – Apr 1945	K7972
Ventura V	Dec 1943 – Oct 1944	FP571
Hurricane II	Aug 1944 – Feb 1946	PZ803
Fortress II	Dec 1944– Feb 1946	FA710
Fortress III	May 1945– Feb 1946	HB786
Halifax III	Dec 1945 – Apr 1946	RG787

No. 524 Squadron

No.524 Squadron was formed at Oban on 20 October 1943 for the purpose of obtaining operational experience with Martin Mariner flying boats. The type was not adopted for RAF service and the squadron disbanded on 7 December 1943.

On 7 April 1944 No.524 reformed at Davidstowe Moor with Wellingtons for patrols against E-boats off the French coast. Once located, these were targets of strike squadrons which worked closely with the Wellingtons though occasionally No.524 took part in bombing attacks on enemy shipping.

In July 1944 it moved to East Anglia for similar operations off the Dutch coast and these continued until the end of the war. On 25 May 1945 the squadron disbanded.

Squadron bases

Oban	20 Oct 1943
	to 7 Dec 1943
Davidstowe Moor	7 Apr 1944
Docking	1 Jul 1944
Bircham Newton	25 Jul 1944
Langham	1 Nov 1944
	to 25 May 1945

Aircraft Equipment	Period of service	Representative Serial
Mariner I	Oct 1943 – Dec 1943	JX105
Wellington XIII	Apr 1944 – Dec 1944	MF320 (C)
Wellington XIV	Dec 1944 – May 1945	NB854 (K)

No. 525 Squadron

Badge: A winged foot enfiled by a chaplet of roses and maple leaves
Motto: Vinciendo vincimus (We link together to conquer)

No.525 Squadron was formed at Weston Zoyland on 2 September 1943 as a transport unit with Warwicks. In November it began flying services to Gibraltar but after a number of accidents to transport Warwicks the type was grounded and No.525 converted to Dakotas. In September 1944 regular flights began to Allied bases in France and Belgium and soon after the end of the war it extended these to the Mediterranean. In March 1946 the squadron took over the mail and newspaper service between the UK and British bases on the Continent which continued until it was renumbered 238 Squadron on 1 December 1946.

Squadron bases

Weston Zoyland	2 Sep 1943
Lyneham	6 Feb 1944
Membury	15 Jul 1945
Abingdon	31 Oct 1946
	to 1 Dec 1946

Aircraft Equipment	Period of service	Representative Serial
Warwick I	Sep 1943 – Sep 1944	BV254
Warwick III	Aug 1944 – Sep 1944	HG219
Dakota III	Jun 1944 – Jul 1945	FD900
Dakota IV	Feb 1945 – Dec 1946	KN432

No. 526 Squadron

No.526 Squadron was formed on 15 June 1943 at Longmans Airport, Inverness for radar calibration duties with Blenheims as its main type. Some Hornet Moths and Oxfords were also used and the squadron provided communications flights with Dominies for units in northern Scotland. All these types were still in service when the squadron was absorbed by 527 Squadron on 1 May 1945.

Squadron base

Inverness	15 Jun 1943
	to 1 May 1945

Aircraft Equipment	Period of service	Representative Serial
Blenheim IV	Jun 1943 – May 1945	Z6166
Hornet Moth	Jun 1943 – May 1945	W5781
Oxford I	Jun 1943 – May 1945	AP482
Dominie I	Aug 1943 – May 1945	X7327

No. 527 Squadron

Badge: In front of a flash of lightning, a crystal.
Motto: Silently we serve.

No.527 Squadron was formed at Castle Camps on 15 June 1943 for radar calibration duties with Blenheims and Hurricanes. The squadron was engaged in calibrating radar stations in southern England and East Anglia and later added Hornet Moths and Spitfires to its strength. On 1 September 1944 it absorbed No.528 Squadron at Digby, adding Oxfords to its establishment and extending its coverage to Lincolnshire. On 1 May 1945 No.526 was similarly taken over and the squadron standardised on Spitfires, Wellingtons, Oxfords and Dominies, the latter being based at Inverness for communications flying. In November 1945 the squadron moved to Watton where it disbanded on 15 April 1946.

On 1 August 1952, N and R Calibration Squadrons of the Central Signal Establishment at Watton were redesignated 527 Squadron. A variety of types were flown until 21 August 1958, when it was renumbered 245 Squadron.

Squadron bases

Castle Camps	15 Jun 1943
Snailwell	28 Feb 1944
Digby	28 Apr 1944
Watton	8 Nov 1945
	to 15 Apr 1946
Watton	1 Aug 1952
	to 21 Aug 1958

Aircraft Equipment	Period of service	Representative Serial
Blenheim IV	Jun 1943 – May 1945	V6262
Hurricane I	Jun 1943 – Apr 1944	P2992
Hurricane IIB	Feb 1944 – Apr 1945	BP672
Hornet Moth	Dec 1943 – Sep 1944	W9391
Spitfire VB	Jul 1944 – Apr 1946	W3129
Oxford II	Sep 1944 – Apr 1946	LX122 (WN-P)
Wellington X	Apr 1945 – Apr 1946	PG371
Dominie I	May 1945 – Apr 1946	HG721
Lincoln B.2	Aug 1952 – Mar 1957	WD141
Canberra B.2	– Aug 1958	
Anson C.19	Aug 1952 – Mar 1957	VL312
Meteor N.F.11	Jun 1953 – Aug 1955	WM184
Varsity T.1	Jan 1954 – Aug 1958	WL678

No. 528 Squadron

No.528 Squadron was formed for calibration duties on 28 June 1943 at Filton with Blenheims and Hornet Moths. In May 1944 it moved to Lincolnshire for similar tasks until disbanded on 1 September 1944 its aircraft and personnel being taken over by No.527 Squadron.

Squadron bases

Filton	28 Jun 1943
Digby	15 May 1944
	to 1 Sep 1944

Aircraft Equipment	Period of service	Representative Serial
Blenheim IV	Jun 1943 – Sep 1944	T2219
Hornet Moth	Jun 1943 – Sep 1944	W5751

No. 529 Squadron

No.529 Squadron was formed at Halton on 15 June 1943 from No.1448 Flight which had been engaged in radar calibration duties with Hornet Moths and Rota autogyros. In August 1944 it changed its base to a field at Crazies Farm, Henley-on-Thames, and continued calibration flights till the end of the war. In May 1945 it became the first RAF squadron to receive a helicopter for operational use when a Hoverfly I was received. On 20 October 1945 the squadron disbanded.

Squadron bases
Halton   15 Jun 1943
Henley-on-Thames 16 Aug 1944
                   to 20 Oct 1945

Aircraft Equipment	Period of service	Representative Serial
Rota I	Jun 1943 — Oct 1945	K4235
Hornet Moth	Jun 1943 — Oct 1945	W5830
Oxford I, II	Sep 1944 — Oct 1945	T1210
Cierva C.40	Jun 1943 — Jul 1944	L7594
Hoverfly I	May 1945 — Oct 1945	KK996

No. 530 Squadron

No.530 Squadron was formed at Hunsdon on 2 September 1942 from No.1451 (Turbinlite) Flight. Turbinlite aircraft were Havocs and Bostons fitted with airborne searchlights which were intended to use radar for intercepting enemy aircraft and, at the right moment, illuminate them for the benefit of accompanying fighters. Hurricanes were supplied when the turbinlite squadrons were formed, their predecessors having flown only the light-equipped aircraft in co-operation with other fighter squadrons. Lack of success and the development of improved airborne radar resulted in the disbandment of turbinlite squadrons on 25 January 1943.

Squadron base
Hunsdon   2 Sep 1942
                  to 25 Jan 1943

Aircraft Equipment	Period of service	Representative Serial
Havoc I, II	Sep 1942 — Jan 1943	AH473
Boston III	Sep 1942 — Jan 1943	W8329
Hurricane IIC	Sep 1942 — Jan 1943	HW130

Boston III, No. 532 Squadron

No. 531 Squadron

No.531 Squadron was formed as a turbinlite squadron on 2 September 1942 from No.1452 Flight at West Malling, disbanding on 25 January 1943.

Squadron bases
West Malling   2 Sep 1942
Debden   2 Oct 1942
West Malling   9 Oct 1942
                  to 25 Jan 1943

Aircraft Equipment	Period of service	Representative Serial
Havoc I, II	Sep 1942 — Jan 1943	AW409
Boston III	Sep 1942 — Jan 1943	W8303
Hurricane IIC	Sep 1942 — Jan 1943	HL605 (A)

No. 532 Squadron

No.532 Squadron was formed on 2 September 1942 at Wittering from No.1453 (Turbinlite) Flight and was disbanded on 25 January 1943.

Squadron bases
Wittering   2 Sep 1942
Hibaldstow   11 Sep 1942
                  to 25 Jan 1943

Aircraft Equipment	Period of service	Representative Serial
Boston III	Sep 1942 — Jan 1943	Z2169
Havoc I, II	Sep 1942 — Jan 1943	AX910
Hurricane IIB, IIC	Sep 1942 — Jan 1943	HL562

No. 533 Squadron

No.533 Squadron was formed at Charmy Down on 2 September 1942 from No.1454 (Turbinlite) Flight and was disbanded on 25 January 1943.

Squadron base
Charmy Down   2 Sep 1942
       to 25 Jan 1943

Aircraft Equipment	Period of service	Representative Serial
Havoc I, II	Sep 1942 – Jan 1943	BJ491
Boston III	Sep 1942 – Jan 1943	AH503
Hurricane IIC	Sep 1942 – Jan 1943	BE514

No. 534 Squadron

No.534 Squadron was formed on 2 September 1942 from No.1455 (Turbinlite) Flight at Tangmere, disbanding on 25 January 1943.

Squadron base
Tangmere   2 Sep 1942
       to 25 Jan 1943

Aircraft Equipment	Period of service	Representative Serial
Havoc I, II	Sep 1942 – Jan 1943	AH450 (A)
Boston III	Sep 1942 – Jan 1943	W8308
Hurricane IIB, IIC, X, XI, XII	Sep 1942 – Jan 1943	BX115

No. 535 Squadron

No.535 Squadron was formed on 2 September 1942 from No.1456 (Turbinlite) Flight at High Ercall, disbanding on 25 January 1943.

Squadron base
High Ercall   2 Sep 1942
       to 25 Jan 1943

Aircraft Equipment	Period of service	Representative Serial
Havoc I	Sep 1942 – Jan 1943	BB907 (B)
Hurricane IIC	Sep 1942 – Jan 1943	

No. 536 Squadron

No.536 Squadron was formed at Predannack from No.1457 (Turbinlite) Flight on 2 September 1942 and was disbanded on 25 January 1943.

Squadron bases
Predannack   2 Sep 1942
Fairwood Common 27 Oct 1944
       to 25 Jan 1943

Aircraft Equipment	Period of service	Representative Serial
Havoc I, II	Sep 1942 – Jan 1943	AH468 (B)
Hurricane IIC	Sep 1942 – Jan 1943	

No. 537 Squadron

No.537 Squadron was formed at Middle Wallop on 2 September 1942 from No.1458 (Turbinlite) Flight and was disbanded on 25 January 1943.

Squadron base
Middle Wallop   2 Sep 1942
       to 25 Jan 1943

Aircraft Equipment	Period of service	Representative Serial
Havoc I, II	Sep 1942 – Jan 1943	BD113
Boston III	Sep 1942 – Jan 1943	Z2160 (O)
Hurricane IIC	Sep 1942 – Jan 1943	BE497

Havoc II, No.538 Squadron

No. 538 Squadron

No.538 Squadron was formed on 2 September 1942 at Hibaldstow from No.1459 (Turbinlite) Flight and was disbanded on 25 January 1943.

Squadron base
Hibaldstow   2 Sep 1942
       to 25 Jan 1943

Aircraft Equipment	Period of service	Representative Serial
Havoc I, II	Sep 1942 – Jan 1943	AH478 (C)
Boston III	Sep 1942 – Jan 1943	W8364 (F)
Hurricane IIC	Sep 1942 – Jan 1943	BP706 (M)

No. 539 Squadron

No.539 Squadron was formed on 2 September 1942 from No.1460 (Turbinlite) Flight at Acklington and was disbanded on 25 January 1943.

Squadron base
Acklington   2 Sep 1942
       to 25 Jan 1943

Aircraft Equipment	Period of service	Representative Serial
Havoc I, II	Sep 1942 – Jan 1943	BJ474
Boston III	Sep 1942 – Jan 1943	Z2185
Hurricane IIC, X	Sep 1942 – Jan 1943	Z3161

No. 540 Squadron

Badge: A mosquito.
Motto: Sine qua non
(Indispensable)

No.540 Squadron was formed on 19 October 1942 at Leuchars from H and L Flights of the Photographic Reconnaissance Unit. The squadron's Mosquitos carried out reconnaissance missions over Norway and based a detachment at Benson for similar flights over France and Italy. From Leuchars, long-range trips were made to German and Polish Baltic ports while another detachment covered southern France and Algeria from Gibraltar in preparation for the landings in North Africa. From February 1944 the squadron was wholly based at Benson and sorties ranged as far afield as Austria and the Canary Islands. At the end of March 1945 No.540 moved to France for the rest of the war, returning to Benson in November where it was disbanded on 30 September 1946.

On 1 December 1947 No.540 reformed at Benson and used its Mosquitos for photographic reconnaissance and survey duties, converting to Canberras at the end of 1952. In March 1953 the squadron moved to Wyton where it was disbanded on 31 March 1956.

Squadron bases

Leuchars	19 Oct 1942		to 30 Sep 1946
Benson	29 Feb 1944	Benson	1 Dec 1947
Coulommiers	29 Mar 1945	Wyton	Mar 1953
Benson	6 Nov 1945		to 31 Mar 1956

Aircraft Equipment	Period of service	Representative Serial
Mosquito IV	Oct 1942 — Sep 1943	W4051
Mosquito VIII	Dec 1942 — Sep 1943	
Mosquito IX	Jul 1943 — Mar 1945	LR415
Mosquito XVI	May 1944 — Sep 1946	MM360
Mosquito VI	Nov 1944 — Jun 1945	RS512 (DH-H)
Mosquito 32	Nov 1944 — Jun 1945	NS588
Mosquito PR.34	Dec 1947 — Dec 1952	RG229
Canberra PR.3	Dec 1952 — Mar 1956	WE136
Canberra PR.7	Sep 1954 — Mar 1956	WH790

No. 541 Squadron

Badge: A bird's eye Speedwell
Motto: Alone above all

No.541 Squadron was formed on 19 October 1942 at Benson from B and F Flights of the Photographic Reconnaissance Unit. Equipped with Spitfires it carried out photographic reconnaissance missions over Europe until the end of the war, some Mustangs being received in June 1944. During 1946 the squadron received some Lancasters for survey work in Africa but disbanded on 30 September 1946, the Lancaster flight becoming No.82 Squadron.

On 1 November 1947 No.541 reformed at Benson with Spitfire PR.19s for photographic reconnaissance duties. In December 1950 these were replaced by Meteors which the squadron took to Germany in June 1951 to reinforce Second TAF, remaining there until disbanded on 6 September 1957.

Squadron bases

Benson	19 Oct 1942
	to 1 Oct 1946
Benson	1 Nov 1947
Buckeburg	7 Jun 1951
Wunstorf	May 1957
	to 6 Sep 1957

Aircraft Equipment	Period of Service	Representative Serial
Spitfire IV, V	Oct 1942 — Jun 1943	R7041
Spitfire IX	Nov 1942 — Jan 1943	BS338
Spitfire XI	Dec 1942 — Oct 1946	EN664 (Q)
Spitfire XIX	May 1944 — Apr 1945	RM637
Mustang III	Jun 1944 — Apr 1945	FX855
Lancaster I	1946 — Sep 1946	TW904
Spitfire PR.19	Nov 1947 — Apr 1951	
Meteor PR.10	Dec 1950 — Sep 1957	VS970

Canberra PR.7, No.542 Squadron

No. 542 Squadron

Badge: Within an orle of seven mullets, a terrestrial globe
Motto: Above all

No.542 Squadron was formed at Benson on 19 October 1942 from A and E Flights of the Photographic Reconnaissance Unit. Using nearby Mount Farm as its operational base for a time, the squadron used Spitfires for photographic reconnaissance missions over Europe until the end of the war. On 27 August 1945 disbandment took place.

On 17 May 1954, No.542 reformed at Wyton with photographic reconnaissance Canberras but disbanded again on 1 October 1955. On 1 November 1955 it reformed from No.1323 Flight at Wyton, moving in the following month to Weston Zoyland to prepare for its detachment to Australia to carry out survey and sampling flights during the nuclear bomb tests in 1956-57. In April 1957 it returned to the UK and was renumbered 21 Squadron on 1 October 1958.

Squadron bases

Benson	19 Oct 1942	Weston Zoyland	15 Dec 1955
	to 27 Aug 1945	Laverton (D)	
Wyton	17 May 1954	Hemswell	1 Apr 1957
	to 1 Oct 1955	Upwood	17 July 1958
Wyton	1 Nov 1955		to 1 Oct 1958

Aircraft Equipment	Period on Service	Representative Serial
Spitfire IV	Oct 1942 — Apr 1945	AB121
Spitfire VII	Nov 1942 — Apr 1943	P9565
Spitfire X	Jul 1944 — Apr 1945	SR398
Spitfire XI	Apr 1943 — Aug 1945	EN424
Spitfire XIX	May 1944 — Apr 1945	RM628
Canberra PR.7	May 1954 — Oct 1955	WH795
Canberra B.2	Nov 1955 — Oct 1958	WJ573
Canberra B.6	Nov 1955 — Oct 1958	WT207

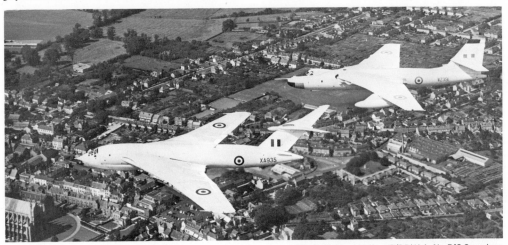

Victor B.1 and Valiant B(PR)K.1, No.543 Squadron

No. 543 Squadron

Badge: A crane's head, the crane carrying an open padlock with key in its beak
Motto: Valiant and vigilant

No.543 Squadron was formed at Benson on 19 October 1943 as a photographic reconnaissance unit equipped with Spitfires. A detachment was stationed at St. Eval in Cornwall for missions over France while the remainder of the squadron was engaged in operational training from Mount Farm, a satellite airfield of Benson, where some Mosquitos were also used for training purposes. No.543 undertook several specialist photographic sorties, including the assessment of the effect of No.617 Squadron's attack on the Ruhr dams and similar missions before and after midget submarines attacked the battleship *Tirpitz* in Altenfjord. In the latter operations, the Spitfires flew from Russian bases. On 18 October 1943 No.543 was disbanded, A Flight being merged with No.541 Squadron and B Flight forming the basis of No.309 Ferry Training Unit.

On 1 July 1955 No.543 reformed at Gaydon and moved to Wyton in November after equipping with Valiants for strategic reconnaissance duties. With the phasing out of the Valiants at the end on 1964, some Victor B.1s were received to bridge the gap until the arrival of the Victor SR.2s. The squadron disbanded on 24 May 1974.

Squadron bases

Benson	19 Oct 1942
	to 18 Oct 1943
Gaydon	1 Jul 1955
Wyton	18 Nov 1955
Honington	23 Mar 1970
Wyton	1 Oct 1970
	to 24 May 1974

Aircraft Equipment	Period of service	Representative Serial
Spitfire IV, V	Oct 1942 — Oct 1943	AA809
Spitfire XI	Sep 1943 — Oct 1943	BS437
Mosquito IV	Jun1943 — Oct 1943	
Valiant B(PR).1	Jul 1955 — Feb 1965	WZ396
Victor B.1	May 1965 — Dec 1965	XA925
Victor SR.2	Dec 1965 — May 1974	XM715

No. 544 Squadron

Badge: A gannet volant, the head lowered
Motto: Quaro (I seek)

No.544 Squadron was formed at Benson on 19 October 1942 with a miscellany of aircraft flown until that date by the Photographic Reconnaissance Unit. Its Spitfires were detached to Gibraltar while Wellingtons experimented with night photography, using this method operationally from December 1942. In March 1943 Mosquitos were received and became the squadron's sole type when B Flight at Gibraltar was transferred to No.541 Squadron. For the rest of the war,

it flew photographic reconnaissance missions over Europe and in February 1945 it operated a courier service for the Yalta conference by flying the first leg from the UK to Italy. In June 1945 survey flights began and continued until the squadron was disbanded on 13 October 1945.

Squadron base
Benson 19 Oct 1942
to 13 Oct 1945

Aircraft Equipment	Period of service	Representative Serial
Spitfire IV	Oct 1942 — Oct 1943	BR666
Wellington IV	Oct 1942 — Mar 1943	Z1418
Anson I	Oct 1942 — Mar 1943	
Maryland I	Oct 1942 — Mar 1943	AR744
Mosquito IV	Mar 1943 — Oct 1943	DZ538
Spitfire IX	Aug 1943 — Oct 1943	
Mosquito IX	Oct 1943 — Mar 1945	MM245
Mosquito XVI	Apr 1944 — Oct 1945	NS633
Mosquito 32	Nov 1944 — Mar 1945	NS587
Mosquito 34	Apr 1945 — Oct 1945	RG179

No. 547 Squadron

Badge: A kingfisher diving
Motto: Celer ad caedendum (Swift to strike)

No.547 Squadron was formed at Holmsley South on 21 October 1942 as a unit of Coastal Command equipped with Wellingtons. Initially it was trained as an anti-shipping squadron equipped for both bombing and torpedo-dropping but in May 1943 it was re-allotted to anti-submarine duties and

began patrols from south-west England in June. At the end of October, crews began conversion to Liberators and patrols over the Bay of Biscay continued with this type. In September 1944 the squadron moved to Scotland where patrols were mixed with attacks on enemy shipping off the Danish and Norwegian coasts until the end of the war. On 4 June 1945 the squadron was disbanded.

Squadron bases

Holmsley South	21 Oct 1942	Davidstowe Moor	31 May 1943
Chivenor	10 Dec 1942	Thorney Island	25 Oct 1943
Tain	18 Jan 1943	St. Eval	10 Jan 1944
Chivenor	31 Mar 1943	Leuchars	28 Sep 1944
			to 4 Jun 1945

Aircraft Equipment	Period of service	Representative Serial
Wellington VIII	Nov 1942 — May 1943	LB118
Wellington XI	Apr 1943 — Nov 1943	HZ359
Wellington XIII	Oct 1943 — Nov 1943	
Liberator V	Oct 1943 — Sep 1944	FL937 (2V-H)
Liberator VI	Jun 1944 — Jun 1945	EW299 (2V-H)
Liberator VIII	Mar 1945 — Jun 1945	KK325

No. 548 Squadron

No.548 Squadron was formed at Lawnton, Queensland, on 15 December 1943 as one of three RAF squadrons based in Australia for air defence duties with Spitfires, the Kittyhawks with which the majority of RAAF squadrons were equipped being inadequate for interception missions. The Spitfire VIIIs to equip the squadron did not arrive till April 1944 and it was mid-June before the squadron reached the Darwin area where the main threat of Japanese air activity existed. A sweep over Selaroe Island, 300 miles north of Darwin was carried out on 5 September 1944 and the airstrip at Cape

Chater in Timor was attacked on 3 June 1945 but these were the only operations carried out before the Japanese surrender. On 9 October 1945 the squadron was disbanded and its personnel returned to the UK.

Squadron bases
Lawnton 15 Dec 1943
Strathpine 19 Jan 1944
Amberley 25 May 1944
Livingstone 15 Jun 1944
Darwin Civil 22 Oct 1944
to 9 Oct 1945

Aircraft Equipment	Period of service	Representative Serial
Spitfire VIII	Apr 1944 — Oct 1945	A58-413 (TS-L)

No. 549 Squadron

No.549 Squadron was formed at Strathpine on 15 December 1943 as a sister unit to No.548 and shared its activities, the third RAF squadron in Australia being No.54 which had been in action in the Darwin area since 1942. Its Spitfires arrived in April 1944 and it moved to Darwin with 548 Squadron in June. It joined No.548 in a sweep on 5 September 1944, and went on its own to Timor on 27 November

1944, but the remainder of its service in Australia was uneventful and it disbanded on 9 October 1945.

Squadron bases
Strathpine 15 Dec 1943
Strauss 16 Jun 1944
Darwin Civil 23 Oct 1944
to 9 Oct 1945

Aircraft Equipment	Period of service	Representative Serial
Spitfire VIII	Apr 1944 — Oct 1945	A58-415

Dakota IIIs, No.575 Squadron

No. 575 Squadron

Badge: A hand couped at the wrist supporting a terrestrial globe
Motto: The air is our path

No.575 Squadron was formed at Hendon on 1 January 1944 from a nucleus supplied by No.512 Squadron. Equipped with Dakotas, it began training with airborne forces for the invasion of Europe and in April began leaflet-dropping flights over France. On D-Day the squadron sent twenty-one aircraft on the initial paradrops and followed later with nineteen glider-towing missions. At Arnhem it provided forty-eight glider-towing aircraft in the first two days of the landings, following these up with thirty-eight re-supply missions. For the Rhine crossing in March 1945, No.575 sent twenty-four aircraft towing gliders. In January 1946 the squadron moved to Italy and flew services to Austria, Roumania, Greece and Bulgaria before being disbanded on 15 August 1946.

Squadron bases
Hendon	1 Feb 1944
Broadwell	14 Feb 1944
Melbourne	5 Aug 1945
Blakehill Farm	16 Nov 1945
Bari	11 Jan 1946
Bari	1 Feb 1946 (C)
	to 15 Aug 1946

Aircraft Equipment	Period of service	Representative Serial
Dakota III	Feb 1944 — Aug 1946	KG630

No. 576 Squadron

Badge: A merlin, wings inverted and addorsed, preying on a serpent
Motto: Carpe diem (Seize the opportunity)

No.576 Squadron was formed on 25 November 1943 from C Flight of No.103 Squadron at Elsham Wolds. It began bombing operations with Lancasters on 2 December and continued this role until the end of the war as part of the main force of Bomber Command. On 13 September 1945 the squadron was disbanded.

Squadron bases
Elsham Wolds	25 Nov 1943
Fiskerton	31 Oct 1944
	to 13 Sep 1945

Aircraft Equipment	Period of service	Representative Serial
Lancaster I, III	Nov 1943 — Sep 1945	PB265 (UL-V2)

No. 577 Squadron

No.577 Squadron was formed at Castle Bromwich on 1 December 1943 from detachments of Nos.6, 7 and 8 Anti-Aircraft Co-operation Units and provided detachments for co-operation with army and naval anti-aircraft guns at many airfields in the Midlands and Wales. Hurricanes and Oxfords formed the mainstay of the squadron during the war, the former being replaced by Spitfires in June 1945, while Vengeances were added for target-towing a month later. On 15 June 1946 the squadron was disbanded.

Squadron base
Castle Bromwich	1 Dec 1943
	to 15 June 1946

Aircraft Equipment	Period of service	Representative Serial
Oxford I	Dec 1943 — Jun 1946	MP408
Hurricane IIC, IV	Dec 1943 — Jul 1945	KZ325
Beaufighter I	Nov 1944 — Jul 1945	V8353
Spitfire VB	Jun 1945 — Jul 1945	AD111
Spitfire XVI	Jun 1945 — Jun 1946	SM391
Vengeance IV	Jul 1945 — Jun 1946	HB428

No. 578 Squadron

No.578 Squadron was formed on 14 January 1944 at Snaith as a heavy bomber squadron in No.4 Group. Equipped with Halifaxes, it began operations on 20 January 1944 and continued till the end of the war. It flew its last operational flight on 13 March 1945 and disbanded on 15 April 1945.

Badge: An arrow in pale, the point
downwards, cleft by
another
Motto: Accuracy

Squadron bases

Snaith	14 Jan 1944
Burn	6 Feb 1944
	to 15 Apr 1945

Aircraft Equipment	Period of service	Representative Serial
Halifax III	Jan 1944 — Apr 1945	MZ527 (LK-D)

No. 582 Squadron

No.582 Squadron was formed on 1 April 1944 at Little Staughton from detachments of Nos.7 and 156 Squadrons. As part of No.8 (Pathfinder) Group, it became operational on 9 April and continued bombing and target marking missions for the rest of the war. On 10 September 1945 the squadron was disbanded.

Badge: On a hurt three mullets in
bend fimbriated
Motto: Praecolamus designantes
(We fly before marking)

Squadron base

Little Staughton	1 Apr 1944
	to 10 Sep 1945

Aircraft Equipment	Period of service	Representative Serial
Lancaster I, III	Apr 1944 — Sep 1945	PB141 (60-F)

No. 587 Squadron

No.587 Squadron was formed at Weston Zoyland on 1 December 1943 from Nos.1600, 1601 and 1625 Flights for anti-aircraft co-operation duties in south-west England and South Wales, using various convenient airfields in the area to base detachments near the batteries they were intended to co-operate with. Henleys, Martinets, Oxfords and Hurricanes formed the initial equipment of the squadron and were later replaced by Spitfires and Vengeances. On 15 June 1946 No.587 was disbanded.

Squadron bases

Weston Zoyland	1 Dec 1943
Culmhead	10 Apr 1944
Weston Zoyland	1 Oct 1944
Tangmere	1 Jun 1946
	to 15 June 1946

Aircraft Equipment	Period of service	Representative Serial
Martinet I	Dec 1943 — Dec 1944	EM412
Henley III	Dec 1943 — May 1944	L3247
Oxford I, II	Dec 1943 — 1944	V4148
Hurricane IIC, IV	Dec 1943 — 1945	LE395
Vengeance IV	Oct 1944 — Jun 1946	HB467
Spitfire XVI	Jul 1945 — Jun 1946	TB304

No. 595 Squadron

No.595 Squadron was formed on 1 December 1943 at Aberporth from Nos.1607, 1608 and 1609 Flights for anti-aircraft co-operation duties in Wales. Various detachments flew Martinets, Henleys, Hurricanes and Oxfords but at the end of 1944 Spitfires and Vengeances also went into service. After the end of the war, the squadron remained in being after most of the other AAC units were disbanded. Flying Spitfires, Martinets and Oxfords, the squadron received Vampires for high-speed co-operation in December 1946, and No.595 operated from South Wales until renumbered 5 Squadron on 11 February 1949.

Squadron bases

Aberporth	1 Dec 1943
Fairwood Common	
	27 Apr 1946
Pembrey	21 Oct 1946
	to 11 Feb 1949

Aircraft Equipment	Period of service	Representative Serial
Henley III	Dec 1943 — Jun 1944	L3258
Hurricane IIC,IV	Dec 1943 — Dec 1944	LB650
Martinet I	Dec 1943 — Feb 1949	HD174
Oxford I, II	Jun 1944 — Feb 1949	EB753
Spitfire VB	Nov 1944 — 1945	BM430
Spitfire IX	Jul 1945	ML185
Spitfire XII	Dec 1944 — Jul 1945	MB848
Spitfire XVI	Sep 1945 — Feb 1949	SL542
Spitfire F.21	Jun 1948 — Feb 1949	
Vampire F.1	Dec 1946 — Oct 1948	VF301

No. 597 Squadron

No.597 Squadron was formed on 10 January 1944 as a transport unit but formation was abandoned on 1 March 1944 before any aircraft had been allotted.

No. 598 Squadron

No.598 Squadron was formed at Peterhead on 1 December 1943 from Nos.1479 and 1632 Flights and a detachment of 289 Squadron at Skeabrae for anti-aircraft co-operation duties in northern Scotland. Detachments were based northwards from Edinburgh to the Shetlands and worked in co-operation with AA batteries and naval craft based on the Forth and Scapa Flow. In March 1945 the squadron was moved to Norfolk and disbanded on 30 April 1945.

Squadron bases

Peterhead	1 Dec 1943
Bircham Newton	12 Mar 1945
	to 30 Apr 1945

Aircraft Equipment	Period of service	Representative Serial
Oxford I, II	Dec 1943 — Apr 1945	HM695
Lysander IIIA	Dec 1943 — 1944	V9818
Martinet I	Dec 1943 — Apr 1945	EM516
Hurricane IIC, IV	Feb 1944 — Apr 1945	LE839

Meteor F.8, No.600 Squadron

No. 600 Squadron

Badge: In front of an increscent, a sword in bend
Motto: Praeter sescentos (More than six hundred)
Name: 'City of London'

No.600 Squadron formed at Northolt on 14 October 1925 as a unit of the Auxiliary Air Force. Equipped with D.H.9As and Avro 504Ns, it was a day bomber squadron until 1934 having received Wapitis in August 1929. These were replaced by Harts in January 1936 pending the arrival of Demon fighters, No.600 having been designated a fighter squadron in July 1934. In April 1937 conversion to Demons was complete and in January 1939 they were replaced by Blenheims. On the outbreak of war day and night patrols were flown, experiments with airborne radar beginning in December 1939. When the Germans invaded Holland, the squadron flew patrols over the Low Countries but in view of the inadequacy of Blenheims for daylight operations, No.600 was allocated to night defence only a few days later. In September 1940 the first Beaufighter was received, conversion being completed early in 1941. In October 1940 the squadron moved to Yorkshire and in March 1941 to south-west England where it remained until September 1942. In November 1942 No.600 moved to North Africa to provide night cover for allied bases and shipping. It moved to Malta in June 1943 and, in September, to Italy where it spent the rest of the war on night defence and intruder missions. Re-equipment with Mosquitos began in January 1945 and on 21 August 1945 the squadron disbanded.

On 10 May 1946 No.600 reformed at Biggin Hill as a day fighter squadron of the Auxiliary Air Force with Spitfires. In 1950 it converted to Meteors and flew these until the Royal Auxiliary Air Force disbanded on 10 March 1957.

Squadron bases

Northolt	14 Oct 1925	Church Fenton	1 Sep 1942
Hendon	18 Jan 1927	Portreath	14 Nov 1942 (A)
Kenley	1 Oct 1938	Blida	18 Nov 1942
Hendon	3 Oct 1938	Maison Blanche	7 Dec 1942
Northolt	25 Aug 1939	Setif	3 Jan 1943
Hornchurch	2 Oct 1939	Luqa	25 Jun 1943
Rochford	16 Oct 1939	Cassibile	26 Jul 1943
Hornchurch	20 Oct 1939	Montecorvino	1 Oct 1943
Manston	27 Dec 1939	Marcianise	2 Feb 1944
Northolt	14 May 1940	La Banca	13 Jun 1944
Manston	20 June 1940	Voltone	19 Jun 1944
Hornchurch	22 Aug 1940	Follonica	5 July 1944
Redhill	12 Sep 1940	Rosignano	28 Jul 1944
Catterick	12 Oct 1940	Falconara	25 Aug 1944
Drem	14 Mar 1941	Cesenatico	15 Dec 1944
Colerne	28 Mar 1941	Campoformido	22 May 1945
Fairwood Common		Aviano	24 Jul 1945
	17 Jun 1941		to 21 Aug 1945
Colerne	27 Jun 1941	Biggin Hill	10 May 1946
Predannack	6 Oct 1941		to 10 Mar 1957

Aircraft Equipment	Period of service	Representative Serial	
D.H.9A	Oct 1925 — Aug 1929	J8184	(B)
Wapiti IIA	Aug 1929 — Jan 1935	K1334	
Hart	Jan 1935 — Apr 1937	K2986	
Demon	Feb 1937 — Feb 1939	K5700	
Blenheim If	Jan 1939 — Feb 1941	L1251	(BQ-Y)
Blenheim IV	Nov 1939 — Apr 1940	P4846	(BQ-W)
Beaufighter I	Sep 1940 — Feb 1942	R2259	(BQ-F)
Beaufighter VI	Feb 1942 — Feb 1945	X8023	(BQ-I)
Mosquito XIX	Jan 1945 — Aug 1945	TA133	(BQ-X)
Spitfire F.14E	Jul 1946 — Jun 1948	TX981	(RAG-X)
Spitfire F.21	Apr 1947 — Nov 1950	LA228	(RAG-N)
Spitfire F.22	Jun 1948 — Apr 1950	PK670	(RAG-X)
Meteor F.4	Mar 1950 — Feb 1952	RA423	(LJ-L)
Meteor F.8	Nov 1951 — Feb 1957	WH281	(V)

Spitfire VC, No.601 Squadron

No. 601 Squadron

Badge: A winged sword.
Motto: None
Name: 'County of London'.

No.601 Squadron was formed at Northolt on 14 October 1925 as a light bomber unit of the Auxiliary Air Force. A nucleus of permanent staff was posted to the squadron and on 4 December the first Auxiliary personnel were enlisted. Flying did not begin till May 1926, and it was the following year before the Avro 504Ks were supplemented by D.H.9A light bombers. In January 1927 the squadron moved to Hendon which was its base till the outbreak of war apart from a few days during the Munich crisis in September 1938. In November 1929 Wapitis began to arrive and a year later had replaced all the D.H.9As. These were in turn replaced by Harts by June 1933 and on 1 July 1934 the squadron was redesignated a fighter unit. The Harts were retained until replaced by Demons in August 1937. In November 1938 No.601 converted to Gauntlet single-seat fighters but in January 1939 began to receive Blenheims. It was with these that fighter patrols began when World War Two broke out

in September 1939 but in March 1940 the squadron had converted to Hurricanes. During the German invasion of France, a detachment operated from French soil for a week followed by defensive duties during the Battle of Britain while based in southern England.

In February 1941 the squadron began taking part in offensive sweeps over northern France which continued till August when re-equipment with Airacobras began. These proved useless and were discarded in favour of Spitfires in March 1942 after only a few minor operations. In April the squadron sailed for the Middle East and re-assembled in Egypt on 25 June. Fighter sweeps over the Western Desert started a few days later and after the rout of the Afrika Korps at El Alamein the squadron moved westwards to Tunisia where it was present at the end of the North African campaign in May 1943. Next month it moved to Malta to cover the Allied landings in Sicily, moving into captured airfields in mid-July. In October No.601 moved to Italy where it spent the rest of the war flying ground-attack missions in support of the Allied armies. On 7 May 1945 it disbanded in northern Italy.

On 10 May 1946 the Auxiliary Air Force was reformed and No.601 began to recruit personnel at Hendon. In December it commenced flying Spitfires but moved to North Weald in March 1949 where it converted to Vampires in December. These it flew until re-equipped with Meteors in August 1952. On 10 March 1957 the Royal Auxiliary Air Force was disbanded and No.601 ceased to exist.

D.H.9A, No.601 Squadron

Blenheim IFs, No.601 Squadron

Squadron bases

Northolt	14 Oct 1925	LG.92	26 Sep 1942
Hendon	15 Jan 1927	LG.21	6 Nov 1942
Biggin Hill	29 Sep 1938	LG.13	9 Nov 1942
Hendon	3 Oct 1938	LG.155	11 Nov 1942
Biggin Hill	2 Sep 1939	Gambut West	13 Nov 1942
Tangmere	29 Dec 1939	Msus	25 Nov 1942
Merville (D)	17 May 1940	El Hasseit	3 Dec 1942
	to 22 May 1940	Melah en Nogra	8 Dec 1942
Middle Wallop	1 Jun 1940	El Merduna 2	21 Dec 1942
Tangmere	17 Jun 1940	El Chel	31 Dec 1942
Debden	19 Aug 1940	Hamraiet	8 Jan 1943
Tangmere	2 Sep 1940	Darragh North	19 Jan 1943
Exeter	7 Sep 1940	Castel Benito	16 Feb 1943
Northolt	17 Dec 1940	Hazbub Main	24 Feb 1943
Manston	1 May 1941	Ben Gardane South	3 Mar 1943
Matlask	2 Jul 1941	Hazbub North	9 Mar 1943
Duxford	16 Aug 1941	Bu Grara	10 Mar 1943
Acaster Malbis	6 Jan 1942	Gabes Main	3 Apr 1943
Digby	25 Mar 1942	La Fauconnerie	11 Apr 1943
Emb.for M.East	10 Apr 1942	Bou Goubrine South	
Ikingi Maryut	18 Jun 1942 (G)		15 Apr 1943
Aboukir	23 Jun 1942 (A)	Hergla North	6 May 1943
LG.13	25 Jun 1942	Ben Gardane	20 May 1943
LG.154	30 Jun 1942	Luqa	15 Jun 1943
LG.85	29 Jul 1942	Pachino	14 Jul 1943
LG.219	4 Aug 1942	Cassibile	17 Jul 1943
Helwan	11 Aug 1942	Lentini West	26 Jul 1943
LG.154	21 Aug 1942	Tortorella	5 Oct 1943

Triolo	18 Oct 1943	Loreto	25 Aug 1944
Canne	26 Nov 1943	Fano	4 Sep 1944
Marcianise	18 Jan 1944	Bellaria	4 Dec 1944
Venafro	23 Apr 1944		to 7 May 1945
Littorio	12 Jun 1944	Hendon	10 May 1946
Fabrico	16 Jun 1944	North Weald	27 Mar 1949
Perugia	3 Jul 1944		to 10 Mar 1957

Aircraft Equipment	Period of service		Representative Serial
Avro 504K, 504N	May 1926 –	1927+	
D.H.9A	Jun 1926 – Oct 1930		J8212
Wapiti IIA, VI	Nov 1929 – Jun 1933		K2238
Hart	Feb 1933 – Aug 1937		K2473
Demon	Aug 1937 – Nov 1938		K5720
Gauntlet II	Nov 1938 – Mar 1939		K7888 (YN-J)
Blenheim IF	Jan 1939 – Mar 1940		L6599
Hurricane I	Mar 1940 – Mar 1941		P3886 (UF-K)
Hurricane IIB	Mar 1941 – Jan 1942		Z2670 (UF-J)
Airacobra I	Aug 1941 – Mar 1942		AH589 (UF-L)
Spitfire VB	Mar 1942 – Apr 1942		BL988
Spitfire VB, VC	May 1942 – Jan 1944		ER220 (UF-V)
Spitfire VIII	Jan 1944 – Jun 1944		JF483 (UF-I)
Spitfire IX	Jun 1944 – May 1945		MK551 (UF-T)
Spitfire LF.16E	Dec 1946 – Dec 1949		SL725 (RAH—Y)
Vampire F.3	Nov 1949 – Sep 1952		VF332 (D)
Meteor F.8	Aug 1952 – Mar 1957		WK745 (H)

+ Retained as basic trainer after supercession by D.H.9A as primary trainer.

Hurricane IIBs, No.601 Squadron

Wapitis IIAs and VI, No.602 Squadron

No. 602 Squadron

Badge: In front of a saltire, a
lion rampant
Motto: Cave leonem cruciatum
(Beware the tormented
lion)
Name: 'City of Glasgow'

No.602 Squadron was formed on 15 September 1925 at
Renfrew as a day bomber unit of the Auxiliary Air Force.
Initially equipped with D.H.9As, it began to replace these
with Fawns on September 1927, though the latter were in
turn replaced by Wapitis in 1929. Harts began to arrive in
February 1934 and the squadron re-equipped with Hinds
in June 1936. On 1 November 1938 No.602 was redesignated an army co-operation squadron but on 14 January
1939 this was changed to become a fighter unit and
Gauntlets were received. These were replaced by Spitfires in
May 1939 and during the early months of the war the
squadron was engaged in intercepting German bombing
raids on Scotland. When the Battle of Britain began, No.602
was still in Scotland, moving south in mid-August and
returning in December. In July 1941 it arrived in south-east
England to take part in sweeps over France for a year before
moving back to Scotland. In January 1943 the squadron
moved to south-west England for convoy protection and
escort missions and in April was part of the first group of
squadrons which were to form the new Second TAF.

After taking part in sweeps over France, it moved back to
Scotland for defensive duties in January 1944, coming south
again in March to begin fighter-bomber missions in preparation for the invasion. By the end of June, No.602 was
operating from airstrips in Normandy and moved forward
with the army to Belgium before returning to the UK in
September to fly sweeps over the Netherlands against V-2
rocket launching sites and transport from East Anglia. It
remained there until disbanded on 15 July 1945.

On 10 May 1946 No.602 reformed as a fighter squadron
of the Auxiliary Air Force at Abbotsinch with Spitfires.
These were replaced by Vampires in 1951 which were
flown until disbandment on 10 March 1957.

Squadron bases			
Renfrew	15 Sep 1925	Bognor	1 Jun 1943
Abbotsinch	20 Jan 1933	Kingsnorth	1 Jul 1943
Grangemouth	7 Oct 1939	Newchurch	13 Aug 1943
Drem	13 Oct 1939	Detling	12 Oct 1943
Dyce	14 Apr 1940	Skeabrae	18 Jan 1944
Drem	28 May 1940	Detling	12 Mar 1944
Westhampnett	13 Aug 1940	Llanbedr	13 Mar 1944
Prestwick	17 Dec 1940	Detling	20 Mar 1944
Ayr	15 Apr 1941	Ford	18 Apr 1944
Kenley	10 Jul 1941	B.11 Longues	25 Jun 1944
Redhill	14 Jan 1942	B.19 Lingevres	13 Aug 1944
Kenley	4 Mar 1942	B.40 Nivillers	2 Sep 1944
Redhill	13 May 1942	B.70 Deurne	17 Sep 1944
Peterhead	17 Jul 1942	Coltishall	29 Sep 1944
Biggin Hill	16 Aug 1942	Matlask	18 Oct 1944
Peterhead	20 Aug 1942	Ludham	23 Feb 1945
Skeabrae	10 Sep 1942	Coltishall	5 Apr 1945
Perranporth	20 Jan 1943		to 15 May 1945
Lasham	14 Apr 1943	Abbotsinch	10 May 1946
Fairlop	29 Apr 1943	Renfrew &	Jul 1949
		Abbotsinch	to Mar 1957

Aircraft Equipment	Period of service	Representative Serial
D.H.9A	Oct 1925 – Jan 1928	H144
Fawn	Sep 1927 – Sep 1929	J7190 (2)
Wapiti IIa	Jul 1929 – Apr 1934	J9860
Hart	Feb 1934 – Jun 1936	K3866
Hind	Jun 1936 – Jan 1939	K5460
Hector	Nov 1938 – Jan 1939	K8100
Gauntlet II	Jan 1939 – May 1939	K7813
Spitfire I	May 1939 – Jun 1941	K9966 (ZT-E)
Spitfire IIA	May 1941 – Jul 1941	P8478
Spitfire VB, VC	Jul 1941 – Oct 1943	AR438 (LO-W)

Aircraft Equipment	Period of service	Representative Serial and Code
Spitfire VI	Sep 1942 – Nov 1942	X4173
Spitfire IX	Oct 1943 – Nov 1944	MJ147 (LO-B)
Spitfire XVI	Nov 1944 – May 1945	SM350 (LO-A)
Spitfire F.14	Jun 1946 – Aug 1947	TX985 (RAI-B)
Spitfire F.21	Apr 1947 – Jan 1951	LA275 (RAI-H)
Spitfire F.22	Jun 1948 – Jan 1951	PK560 (RAI-C)
Vampire F.3	Aug 1953 – Feb 1954	VF335
Vampire FB.5	Jan 1951 – Mar 1957	WA137 (LO-D)
Vampire FB.9	Nov 1954 – Feb 1957	WR261

No. 603 Squadron

Badge: On a rock, a triple towered castle, flying therefrom to the sinister a pennon
Motto: Gin ye daur
(If you dare)
Name: 'City of Edinburgh'

Harts Is, No.603 Squadron

No.603 Squadron was formed on 14 October 1925 at Turnhouse as a day bomber unit of the Auxiliary Air Force. Originally equipped with D.H.9As and using Avro 504Ks for flying training, the squadron re-equipped with Wapitis in 1930, these being replaced by Harts in 1934. On 24 October 1938 No.603 was redesignated a fighter unit and flew Hinds until the arrival of Gladiators at the end of March 1939. Within two weeks of the outbreak of war in September 1939, the squadron began to receive Spitfires and passed on its Gladiators to other squadrons during October. It was operational with Spitfires in time to intercept the first German air raid on the British Isles on 16 October, when it destroyed the first enemy aircraft to be shot down over Britain in the Second World War. It remained on defensive duties in Scotland until the end of August 1940, when it moved to southern England for the remaining months of the Battle of Britain, returning to Scotland at the end of December. In May 1941 the squadron moved south again to take part in sweeps over France until the end of the year. After a further spell in Scotland, No.603 left in April 1942 for the Middle East where its ground echelon arrived early in June. The squadron's aircraft were embarked on the US carrier *Wasp* and flown off to Malta on 20 April to reinforce the fighter defences of the beleaguered island. After nearly four months defending Malta, the remaining pilots and aircraft were absorbed by No.229 Squadron on 3 August 1942.

At the end of June 1942 No.603's ground echelon had moved to Cyprus where they spent six months as a servicing unit before returning to Egypt. In February 1943 Beaufighters and crews arrived to begin convoy patrols and escort missions along the African coast and in August sweeps over German-held islands in the Aegean and off Greece began. Attacks on enemy shipping continued until the lack of targets enabled the squadron to be returned to the UK in December 1944.

On 10 January 1945 No.603 reassembled at Coltishall and, by a curious coincidence, took over the Spitfires of No.229 Squadron and some of its personnel, the same squadron which had absorbed No.603 at Takali in 1942. Fighter-bomber sweeps began in February over the Netherlands and continued till April, when the squadron returned to its home base at Turnhouse for the last days of the war.

On 15 August 1945 the squadron was disbanded.

No.603 reformed as a unit of the Auxiliary Air Force on 10 May 1946 and began recruiting personnel to man a Spitfire squadron. Based at Turnhouse, it flew these until conversion to Vampires in May 1951. By July it was completely equipped and the type was flown until disbandment on 10 March 1957.

Squadron bases

Turnhouse	14 Oct 1925		to 3 Aug 1942
Prestwick	16 Dec 1939	Kasfareet	4 Jun 1942
Dyce & Montrose (D)		Nicosia	28 Jun 1942 (G)
	17 Jan 1940	Kasfareet	21 Dec 1942 (G)
Drem	14 Apr 1940	Edku	25 Jan 1943
Turnhouse	5 May 1940	Misurata West	27 Mar 1943
Hornchurch	27 Aug 1940	Borizzo	4 Sep 1943
Rochford	3 Dec 1940	LG.91	4 Oct 1943
Drem	13 Dec 1940	Gambut 3	11 Oct 1943
Turnhouse	28 Feb 1941		to 26 Dec 1944
Hornchurch	16 May 1941	Coltishall	10 Jan 1945
Rochford	16 Jun 1941	Ludham	24 Feb 1945
Hornchurch	8 Jul 1941	Coltishall	5 Apr 1945
Fairlop	12 Nov 1941	Turnhouse	28 Apr 1945
Dyce	15 Dec 1941	Drem	7 May 1945
Peterhead	14 Mar 1942	Skeabrae	14 Jun 1945
Left for Middle East		Turnhouse	28 Jul 1945
	13 Apr 1942 (G)		to 15 Aug 1945
Takali	20 Apr 1942 (A)	Turnhouse	10 May 1946
			to 10 Mar 1957

Aircraft Equipment	Period of service	Representative Serial
D.H.9A	Oct 1925 – May 1930	
Wapiti IIA	Mar 1930 – Mar 1934	K1136
Hart	Feb 1934 – Feb 1938	K3859
Hind	Feb 1938 – Mar 1939	K6809
Gladiator I	Mar 1939 – Oct 1939	K7931
Spitfire I	Sep 1939 – Nov 1940	L1007 (XT-K)
Spitfire IIA	Oct 1940 – May 1941	P7449
Spitfire VA, VB	May 1941 – Apr 1942	W3111 (XT-O)
Spitfire VC	Apr 1942 – Aug 1942	
Beaufighter I, VI	Feb 1943 – Oct 1943	X7761 (H)
Beaufighter X, XI	Aug 1943 – Dec 1944	LX949 (Z)
Spitfire XVI	Jan 1945 – Aug 1945 Jun 1946 – Jun 1948	SL609 (RAJ-M)
Spitfire F.22	Jun 1948 – Jul 1951	PK341 (XT-G)
Vampire FB.5	May 1951 – Mar 1957	WA398 (M)

Blenheim IFs, No.604 Squadron

No. 604 Squadron

Badge: A seax
Motto: Si vis pacem, para bellum
(If you want peace,
prepare for war).
Name: 'County of Warwick'

Squadron bases			
Hendon	17 Mar 1930	Hurn	2 May 1944
North Weald	29 Sep 1938	Colerne	13 Jun 1944
Hendon	3 Oct 1938	A.8 Picauville	6 Aug 1944
North Weald	2 Sep 1939	B.17 Carpiquet	9 Sep 1944
Northolt	16 Jan 1940	Predannack	24 Sep 1944
Manston	15 May 1940	Odiham	4 Dec 1944
Gravesend	3 Jul 1940	B.51 Lille/Vendeville	
Middle Wallop	26 Jul 1940		31 Dec 1944 (A)
Predannack	7 Dec 1942		5 Jan 1945 (G)
Ford	18 Feb 1943		to 18 Apr 1945
Scorton	24 Apr 1943	Hendon	10 May 1946
Church Fenton	25 Apr 1944	North Weald	28 Mar 1949
			to 10 Mar 1957

Aircraft Equipment	Period of service	Representative Serial	
D.H.9A	Apr 1930 – Sep 1930	J7319	
Wapiti IIA	Jun 1930 – Jun 1935	K1328	
Hart	Sep 1934 – Jun 1935	K3893	
Demon	Jun 1935 – Jan 1939	K4506	
Blenheim If	Jan 1939 – Jan 1941	L8690	(NG-O)
Beaufighter I	Sep 1940 – Apr 1943	R2101	(NG-R)
Beaufighter VI	Apr 1943 – Apr 1944	V8556	(NG-R)
Mosquito XII	Feb 1944 – Sep 1944	HK183	(NG-L)
Mosquito XIII	Apr 1944 – Apr 1945	MM449	(NG-R)
Spitfire LF.16E	Aug 1946 – May 1950	SL681	(RAK-W)
Vampire F.3	Nov 1949 – Sep 1952	VT816	(F)
Meteor F.8	Aug 1952 – Mar 1957	WK737	(K)

No.604 Squadron was formed on 17 March 1930 at Hendon as a day bomber unit of the Auxiliary Air Force. On 2 April it received its first D.H.9As and flew these till the arrival of Wapitis in September 1930. On 23 July 1934 it was redesignated a fighter squadron and received Harts as an interim type pending the delivery of Demon two-seat fighters which arrived in June 1935. Shortly before the outbreak of war, it converted to Blenheims with which it flew defensive patrols and undertook early experiments with airborne radar.

When Germany invaded the Low Countries in May 1940, No.604 flew sweeps over the battle areas but reverted to night patrols in July and became a full-time night fighter squadron. In September Beaufighters began to arrive and by January 1941 the squadron was fully equipped with the type. Early in 1943 the decrease in enemy night raids allowed some Beaufighters to be diverted to intruder operations over the enemy airfields in northern France. Conversion to Mosquitos began in February 1944 and No.604 joined Second TAF to help provide cover for the invasion forces during the Normandy landings. In August 1944 it moved to airfields in Normandy but returned to the UK in September for three months. From January 1945 till it disbanded on 18 April 1945, the squadron was based near Lille to provide night defence for Allied bases in the Low Countries and northern France.

On 10 April 1946 No.604 reformed at Hendon as part of the newly reconstituted Auxiliary Air Force as a fighter squadron. Initially equipped with Spitfires, it converted to jet fighters with the arrival of Vampires in November 1949. These were replaced by Meteors in August 1952 which were flown until the Royal Auxiliary Air Force was disbanded on 10 March 1957.

Demon I, No.604 Squadron

Hart I, No.605 Squadron

No. 605 Squadron

No.605 Squadron was formed on 5 October 1926 at Castle Bromwich as a day bomber unit of the Auxiliary Air Force recruiting in the Birmingham area. Initially equipped with D.H.9As, it received Wapitis in 1930 and Harts in 1934. The latter were replaced by Hinds in 1936 and on 1 January 1939 No.605 was redesignated a fighter squadron and re-equipped with Gladiators. Hurricanes began to arrive a few weeks before the outbreak of World War Two and the squadron took up its war station at Tangmere with a mixture of six Hurricanes and ten Gladiators, completing re-equipment during October. In February 1940 the squadron moved to Scotland but returned south in May to fly patrols over northern France for a week before moving back to Drem. It moved south again in September for the closing stages of the Battle of Britain and in December began escorting bombers over northern France. At the end of March 1941 it moved to the Midlands for day and night defensive patrols and in October was posted overseas. It reached Singapore in January 1942, too late to affect the campaign, and was evacuated to Sumatra on arrival in the area, moving later to Java. There it became caught up in the Japanese invasion and after operating a collection of surviving aircraft was either evacuated in small groups or captured by the Japanese by early March.

A detachment of Hurricanes at Hal Far, Malta, began operating on 10 January 1942 and was presumably part of No.605's air echelon since this number was used on its official reports which end on 27 February 1942. The squadron reformed on 7 June 1942 at Ford as an intruder unit and received Bostons which began operations on 14 July

over enemy airfields in France. In February 1943 it began to receive Mosquitos which it flew on intruder raids for the rest of the war. In March 1945 No.605 moved to Belgium to shorten the range and late in April arrived in the Netherlands where it was renumbered 4 Squadron on 31 August 1945.

No.605 reformed as an Auxiliary Air Force Squadron at Honiley on 10 May 1946 but recruiting was slow and it was not until April 1947 that it received its first operational Mosquito night fighter. A policy change altered the squadron's role to that of a day fighter unit and in July it began to receive Vampires. These it flew until disbanded on 10 March 1957.

Squadron bases

Castle Bromwich	5 Oct 1926	Andir	Feb 1942
Tangmere	27 Aug 1939	Tasik Majala	Mar 1942
Leuchars	11 Feb 1940	Hal Far	10 Jan 1942 (A)
Wick	28 Feb 1940	Takali	12 Feb 1942
Hawkinge	21 May 1940		to 27 Feb 1942 (A)
Drem	28 May 1940	Ford	7 Jun 1942
Croydon	7 Sep 1940	Castle Camps	14 Mar 1943
Martlesham Heath		Bradwell Bay	6 Oct 1943
	26 Feb 1941	Manston	7 Apr 1944
Ternhill	31 Mar 1941	Hartford Bridge	21 Nov 1944
Baginton	31 May 1941	B.71 Coxyde	15 Mar 1945
Honiley	4 Sep 1941	B.80 Volkel	28 Apr 1945
Left for Far East	31 Oct 1941		to 31 Aug 1945
Palembang	Jan 1942	Honiley	10 May 1946
Tijililitan	Jan 1942		to 10 Mar 1957

Aircraft

Equipment	Period of service	Representative Serial
D.H.9A	Oct 1926 – Jun 1930	J8109
Wapiti IIA	Apr 1930 – Dec 1934	J9866
Hart	Oct 1934 – Aug 1936	K2435
Hind	Aug 1936 – Feb 1939	K5467
Gladiator I, II	Feb 1939 – Oct 1939	K7946 (HE-R)
Hurricane I	Aug 1939 – Dec 1940	L2121
Hurricane IIA.	Dec 1940 – Aug 1941	V7055
Hurricane IIB	Aug 1941 – Mar 1942	BD712
Havoc I	Jul 1942 – Oct 1942	AX921
Boston III	Jul 1942 – Mar 1943	AL871 (UP-D)
Mosquito II	Feb 1943 – Jul 1943	DZ760 (UP-K)
Mosquito VI	Jul 1943 – Aug 1945	HJ790 (UP-R)
Mosquito NF.30	Apr 1947 – Jan 1949	MM790 (RAL-F)
Vampire F.1	Jul 1948 – May 1951	TG420 (RAL-F)
Vampire FB.5	Mar 1951 – Mar 1957	WA320 (NR-F)

No. 607 Squadron

Badge: A winged lion salient, the hind legs also winged
Motto: None
Name: 'County of Durham'

No.607 Squadron was formed on 17 March 1930 at Usworth as a day bomber unit of the Auxiliary Air Force. The former landing ground at Hylton used during World War One was in course of preparation as the squadron's base but it was not until September 1932 that any personnel could move to the site. Next month a Gipsy Moth arrived for flying training to commence and in December the first Wapitis were received. These were replaced by Demons, No.608 being redesignated a fighter squadron on 23 September 1937. In December 1938 conversion to Gladiators began and these were taken to France in November 1939 to join the Air Component of the BEF. In March 1940 Hurricanes began to arrive and within a few days of the German invasion in May had completely replaced Gladiators. With its airfields overrun, the squadron moved back to the UK to re-equip and in September moved south to defend southern England during the Battle of Britain. In October No.607 moved to Scotland, returning south in August 1941 for fighter-bomber sweeps, the first taking place on 18 September. In March 1942 the squadron left for India and joined No.166 Wing at Alipore on 25 May. At first engaged in escort and defensive duties, the squadron converted to Spitfires in September 1943 and added ground-attack missions to its role. It flew Spitfires until the end of the Burma campaign, disbanding on 31 July 1945.

On 10 May 1946 No.607 reformed at Ouston as a day fighter squadron of the Auxiliary Air Force. After flying Spitfires for five years, it converted to Vampires and was disbanded on 10 March 1957.

Squadron bases

Usworth	17 Mar 1930	Alipore	25 May 1942
Abbotsinch	12 Aug 1939	Jessore	23 Aug 1942
Usworth	24 Aug 1939	Feni	16 Dec 1942
Acklington	9 Oct 1939	Chittagong	23 Jan 1943
Merville	15 Nov 1939	Alipore	2 Apr 1943
Vitry-en-Artois	13 Dec 1939	Amarda Road	1 Oct 1943
Abbeville	12 Apr 1940	Alipore	15 Oct 1943
Vitry-en-Artois	26 Apr 1940	Ramu	29 Nov 1943
Norrent Fontes	19 May 1940	Nidania	25 Feb 1944
Croydon	22 May 1940 (G)	Rhumkhapalong	21 Mar 1944
Usworth	5 Jun 1940	Wangjing	17 Apr 1944
Tangmere	1 Sep 1940	Imphal Main	27 Apr 1944
Turnhouse	10 Oct 1940	Baigachi	5 Jul 1944
Drem	8 Nov 1940	Sapam	22 Nov 1944
Usworth	12 Dec 1940	Tulihal	13 Dec 1944
Macmerry	16 Jan 1941	Tabingaung	16 Jan 1945
Drem	2 Mar 1941	Dwehla	5 Apr 1945
Skitten	16 Apr 1941	Kwetnge	19 Apr 1945
Castletown	27 Jul 1941	Thedaw	10 May 1945
Martlesham Heath	20 Aug 1941	Mingaladon	14 May 1945
Manston	10 Oct 1941		to 31 Jul 1945
Left for India	21 Mar 1942	Ouston	10 May 1946
			to 10 Mar 1957

Aircraft

Equipment	Period of service	Representative Serial
Wapiti IIA	Dec 1932 – Jan 1937	K1146
Demon	Sep 1936 – Mar 1939	K5735
Gladiator I, II	Dec 1938 – May 1940	K7996
Hurricane I	Mar 1940 – Jun 1941	P2874 (AF-F)
Hurricane IIA, IIB	Jun 1941 – Mar 1942	BE403
Hurricane IIB, IIC	Jun 1942 – Sep 1943	BL880 (AF-B)
Spitfire VC	Sep 1943 – Mar 1944	MA686
Spitfire VIII	Mar 1944 – Jul 1945	MD327 (AF-C)
Spitfire F.14	Nov 1946 – Mar 1949	RM740 (RAN-G)
Spitfire F.22	Jul 1947 – Jun 1951	PK523 (LA-E)
Vampire FB.5	Jun 1951 – Mar 1957	VZ303 (G)
Vampire FB.9	Apr 1956 – Feb 1957	WR266

No. 608 Squadron

Badge: A falcon's leg, belled and fessed
Motto: Omnibus ungulis (With all talons)
Name: 'County of York (North Riding)' later 'North Riding' (from May 1937)

No.608 Squadron was formed on 17 March 1930 at Thornaby as a day bomber unit of the Auxiliary Air Force. Wapitis began to arrive in June 1930 and were replaced by Demons from January 1937, the squadron being redesignated a fighter unit on 5 May 1937. On 20 March 1939 No.608 became a general reconnaissance squadron and re-equipped with Ansons. These began to be replaced by Bothas soon after the outbreak of war and both types flew anti-submarine patrols from Thornaby. Bothas were found to be unsuitable and the squadron reverted to Ansons until March 1941 when Blenheims were received. These were soon replaced by Hudsons and attacks on enemy shipping began. In January 1942 No.608 moved to the North of Scotland for attacks off the Norwegian coast but in October left for North Africa.

By the end of 1942, the squadron was flying anti-submarine patrols over the Western Mediterranean from Algeria, a move being made to Sicily in September for a month before moving on to Italy where the squadron disbanded on 31 July 1944.

On 1 August 1944 No.608 reformed at Downham Market as a Mosquito squadron in No.8 Group and for the rest of the war carried out night attacks on Germany. On 24 August 1945 the squadron was disbanded. It was reformed on 10 May 1946 as an Auxiliary Air Force light bomber unit at Thornaby but did not receive any operational bombers before becoming a night fighter unit with the arrival of Mosquito NF.30s in July 1947. In August 1948 its role was changed to that of a day fighter squadron and it re-equipped with Spitfires. Vampires began to arrive in December 1949 and were flown until disbandment on 10 March 1957.

Squadron bases

Thornaby	17 Mar 1930	Protville	6 Aug 1943
Wick	14 Jan 1942	Borizzo	4 Sep 1943
Sumburgh	5 Aug 1942	Montecorvino	23 Oct 1943 (A)
Gosport	27 Aug 1942		17 Nov 1943 (G)
North Coates	14 Sep 1942	Pomigliano	23 Jun 1944
Left for N.Africa			to 31 July 1944
	29 Oct 1942 (G)	Downham Market	1 Aug 1944
Gibraltar	9 Nov 1942 (A)		to 28 Aug 1945
Blida	14 Nov 1942 (G)	Thornaby	10 May 1946
	17 Dec 1942 (A)		to 10 Mar 1957

Aircraft Equipment	Period of service	Representative Serial		Aircraft Equipment	Period of service	Representative Serial and Code
Wapiti IIA	Jun 1930 – Jan 1937	J9871		Mosquito XVI	Mar 1945 – Aug 1945	RV359 (6T-X)
Demon	Jan 1937 – Mar 1939	K4508		Mosquito NF.30	Jul 1947 – Aug 1948	NT471
Anson I	Mar 1939 – Mar 1941	N5201 (UL-H)		Spitfire F.22	Aug 1948 – Jun 1951	PK407 (RAO-P)
Botha	Oct 1939 – Nov 1940	L6171 (UL-A)		Vampire F.1	Apr 1951 – Jun 1951	TG377
Blenheim IV	Mar 1941 – Jul 1941	Z6043 (UL-H)		Vampire F.3	Dec 1949 – Mar 1954	VT826 (K)
Hudson III, V, VI	Jul 1941 – Jul 1944	AM673 (UL-U)		Vampire FB.5	Mar 1951 – Mar 1957	VZ321 (F)
Mosquito XX	Aug 1944 – Apr 1945	KB265 (6T-F)		Vampire FB.9	Apr 1956 – Feb 1957	WR211
Mosquito 25	Oct 1944 – Apr 1945	KB413 (6T-V)				

Typhoon IB, No.609 Squadron

No. 609 Squadron

Badge: In front of two hunting horns in saltire, a rose
Motto: Tally ho
Name: 'West Riding'

No.609 Squadron was formed on 10 February 1936 at Yeadon as a day bomber unit of the Auxiliary Air Force. It began to receive Harts in June and these were replaced by Hinds before the squadron was redesignated a fighter unit on 8 December 1938. No fighters were received until the the arrival of Spitfires at the end of August 1939, with war only days away. After defensive duties in the north, No.609 moved to south-east England in May 1940, and flew patrols over Dunkirk to cover the evacuation of the BEF. It remained in the south throughout the Battle of Britain and began taking part in offensive sweeps over France in February 1941. In April 1942, Typhoons began to arrive and began operations on 30 June, being used mainly for defensive patrols. Day and night intruder sorties began to be flown in November and on joining Second TAF in March 1944, No.609 adopted rockets as its main weapons. In preparation for the invasion of Europe, the squadron attacked enemy communications and radar stations, moving to Normandy in June to provide the 21st Army Group with air support. After the breakout from the beachhead, the squadron moved forward to the Low Countries and for the rest of the war flew armed reconnaissance sweeps over Germany. On 15 September 1945 the squadron was disbanded.

Reformed as part of the post-war Auxiliary Air Force on 10 May 1946, No.609 was designated as a night fighter squadron. Based at Yeadon, it did not receive an operational aircraft till June 1947 and gave up its Mosquitos in 1948 on becoming a day fighter unit. At the end of 1950 Vampires were received to replace Spitfires and these were flown until disbandment on 10 March 1957.

Squadron bases

Yeadon	10 Feb 1936		Acklington	21 Mar 1944
Catterick	27 Aug 1939		Thorney Island	1 Apr 1944
Acklington	6 Oct 1939		B.2 Bazenville	18 Jun 1944
Drem	17 Oct 1939		Hurn	22 Jun 1944
Northolt	19 May 1940		B.10 Plumetot	1 Jul 1944
Middle Wallop	5 Jul 1940		B.7 Martragny	19 Jul 1944
Warmwell	29 Nov 1940		B.23 Morainville	3 Sep 1944
Biggin Hill	24 Feb 1941		B.35 Baromesnil	6 Sep 1944
Gravesend	27 Jul 1941		B.53 Merville	11 Sep 1944
Biggin Hill	24 Sep 1941		B.67 Ursel	30 Oct 1944
Digby	21 Nov 1941		B.77 Gilze-Rijen	26 Nov 1944
Duxford	30 Mar 1942		A.84 Chièvres	31 Dec 1944
Bourn	26 Aug 1942		B.77 Gilze-Rijen	19 Jan 1945
Duxford	30 Aug 1942		B.91 Kluis	21 Mar 1945
Biggin Hill	18 Sep 1942		B.103 Plantlunne	17 Apr 1945
Manston	2 Nov 1942		B.116 Wunstorf	27 May 1945
Matlask	22 Jul 1943		Lasham	2 Jun 1945
Lympne	18 Aug 1943		Fairwood Common	4 Jun 1945
Manston	14 Dec 1943		Wunstorf	23 Jun 1945
Fairwood Common	6 Feb 1944			to 15 Sep 1945
Manston	20 Feb 1944		Yeadon	10 May 1946
Tangmere	16 Mar 1944		Church Fenton	18 Oct 1950
				to 10 Mar 1957

Aircraft

Aircraft Equipment	Period of service	Representative Serial
Hart	Jun 1936 – Jan 1938	K3011
Hind	Dec 1937 – Sep 1939	K6848
Spitfire I	Aug 1939 – May 1941	R6915 (PR-U)
Spitfire IIA	Feb 1941 – May 1941	P8235 (PR-G)
Spitfire VB, VC	May 1941 – May 1942	W3238 (PR-B)
Typhoon IA, IB	Apr 1942 – Sep 1945	R7708 (PR-V)
Mosquito NF.30	Jun 1947 – Sep 1948	NT568 (RAP-B)
Spitfire LF.16E	Apr 1948 – Feb 1951	SL561 (PR-H)
Vampire FB.5	Nov 1950 – Jan 1951	WA137
Meteor F.8	Jan 1951 – Mar 1957	VZ501 (K)

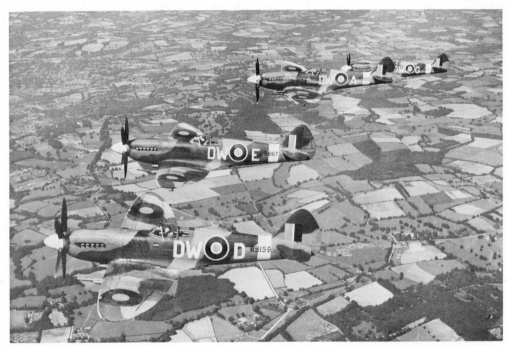

Spitfire XIVs, No.610 Squadron

No. 610 Squadron

Badge: A garb
Motto: Alifero tollitur axe ceres
        (Ceres rising in a winged
        car)
Name: 'County of Chester'

No.610 Squadron was formed at Hooton Park on 10 February 1936 as a day bomber unit of the Auxiliary Air Force. Initially equipped with Harts, it began flying training in May and in May 1938 re-equipped with Hinds. On 1 January 1939 the squadron was redesignated a fighter unit but retained its Hinds in anticipation of the arrival of Defiants. On the outbreak of war it received Hurricanes but by the end of September 1939 had exchanged these for Spitfires, becoming operational on 21 October. When the German offensive opened in May 1940, No.609 moved to Biggin Hill and helped to provide fighter cover for the Dunkirk evacuation beaches and shipping. After taking part in the opening months of the Battle of Britain, the squadron was moved north to rest and re-equip returning south in December to go over to the offensive. After nine months of sweeps and patrols, the squadron returned to Yorkshire for eight months in August 1941, moving to East Anglia in April 1942 for shipping reconnaissance missions. In October 1942 it moved to the North of Scotland, returning south in January 1943. In July 1944 No.610 took its Spitfire XIVs to south-east England to intercept flying bombs for two months. In December the squadron moved to the Continent to join No.127 Wing for sweeps over Germany. It returned to the UK in February 1945 and disbanded on 3 March 1945.

On 10 May 1946 No.610 reformed at Hooton Park as a day fighter squadron of the Auxiliary Air Force. It received Meteors to replace its original Spitfires in April 1951 and flew these until disbanded on 10 March 1957.

Squadron bases

			14 Dec 1943
Hooton Park	10 Feb 1936	Exeter	4 Jan 1944
Wittering	10 Oct 1939	Culmhead	7 Apr 1944
Prestwick	Apr 1940	Fairwood Common	
Biggin Hill	10 May 1940		23 Apr 1944
Gravesend	26 May 1940	Culmhead	30 Apr 1944
Biggin Hill	2 Jul 1940	Bolt Head	16 May 1944
Acklington	13 Sep 1940	Harrowbeer	24 May 1944
Westhampnett	19 Dec 1940	Friston	2 Jul 1944
Leconfield	28 Aug 1941	Lympne	12 Sep 1944
Hutton Cranswick	14 Jan 1942	B.56 Evère	4 Dec 1944
Ludham	4 Apr 1942	Y.32 Ophovon	31 Dec 1944
Castletown	15 Oct 1942	B.78 Eindhoven	27 Jan 1945
Westhampnett	23 Jan 1943	Warmwell	21 Feb 1945
Perranporth	30 Apr 1943		to 3 Mar 1945
Bolt Head	26 Jun 1943	Hooton Park	10 May 1946
Fairwood Common			to 10 Mar 1957

Aircraft Equipment

Aircraft Equipment	Period of service	Representative Serial	
Hart	May 1936 – May 1938	K3881	
Hind	May 1938 – Sep 1939	K6615	
Hurricane I	Sep 1939	L2115	
Spitfire I	Sep 1939 – Feb 1941	L1000	(DW-M)
Spitfire IIA, IIB	Feb 1941 – Jul 1941	P7923	
	Aug 1941 – Nov 1941		
Spitfire VB, VC	Jul 1941 – Aug 1941	BL302	(DW-R)
	Nov 1941 – Mar 1944		
Spitfire XIV	Dec 1943 – Mar 1945	RB167	(DW-E)
Spitfire F.14	Feb 1947 – Feb 1950	NH646	(RAQ-K)
Spitfire F.22	Sep 1949 – Feb 1951	PK511	(DW-N)
Meteor F.4	Apr 1951 – Sep 1951	VT187	(E)
Meteor F.8	Sep 1951 – Mar 1957	WH447	(H)

Meteor F.8s, No.611 Squadron

No. 611 Squadron

Badge: In front of a trident,
a rose
Motto: Beware, beware
Name: 'West Lancashire'

No.611 Squadron was formed on 10 February 1936 at Hendon as a day bomber unit of the Auxiliary Air Force and moved to Speke on 6 May to begin recruiting personnel from Merseyside. Its first Harts arrived in June and were replaced by Hinds in April 1938. On 1 January 1939 the squadron became a fighter unit and received Spitfires in May. After a period of defensive duties on the east coast, it became active in May 1940 over Dunkirk and was based in Lincolnshire during the Battle of Britain. In January 1941 the squadron began taking part in offensive sweeps over France, moving to Scotland in November 1941. It returned south in June 1942 for shipping reconnaissance, escort and defensive missions and after covering the invasion shipping moved to south-west England for a short period. In August 1944 long-range escort missions began to be flown from East Anglia until No.611 moved to the Orkneys in October. After converting to Mustangs, the squadron returned south and began escort duties on 25 March 1945 for the rest of the war. For three months after the end of the war, the squadron was based in northern Scotland where it disbanded on 15 August 1945.

On 10 May 1946 No.611 was reformed at Hooton Park as a day fighter squadron of the Auxiliary Air Force with Spitfires. In 1951 it moved to Woodvale and flew Meteors until disbanded on 10 March 1957.

Squadron bases

Hendon	10 Feb 1936	Coltishall	4 Aug 1943
Speke	6 May 1936	Southend	6 Sep 1943
Duxford	13 Aug 1939	Coltishall	13 Sep 1943
Digby	10 Oct 1939	Ayr	8 Feb 1944
Rochford	14 Dec 1940	Coltishall	19 Feb 1944
Hornchurch	27 Jan 1941	Deanland	29 Apr 1944
Rochford	20 May 1941	Harrowbeer	23 Jun 1944
Hornchurch	16 Jun 1941	Predannack	3 Jul 1944
Drem	13 Nov 1941	Bolt Head	17 Jul 1944
Kenley	3 Jun 1942	Bradwell Bay	30 Aug 1944
Martlesham Heath	13 Jul 1942	Skeabrae	3 Oct 1944
Redhill	20 Jul 1942	Hawkinge	31 Dec 1944
Ipswich	27 Jul 1942	Hunsdon	3 Mar 1945
Redhill	1 Aug 1942	Peterhead	7 May 1945
Biggin Hill	23 Sep 1942		to 15 Aug 1945
Matlask	1 Jul 1943	Hooton Park	10 May 1946
Ludham	31 Jul 1943	Woodvale	14 Jul 1951
			to 10 Mar 1957

Aircraft

Equipment	Period of service	Representative Serial	
Hart	Jun 1936 – Apr 1938	K3817	
Hind	Apr 1938 – Jun 1939	K5500	
Spitfire I	May 1939 – Mar 1941	L1036	(FY-N)
Spitfire IIA, IIB	Aug 1940 – Jun 1941* Nov 1941 – Feb 1942	P7298	
Spitfire VB, VC	Jun 1941 – Nov 1941 Feb 1942 – Jul 1942 Jul 1943 – Jul 1944	P8581	
Spitfire IX	Jul 1942 – Jul 1943 Jul 1944 – Mar 1945	EN562	(FY-B)
Spitfire VII	Oct 1944 – Dec 1944		
Mustang IV	Jan 1945 – Aug 1945	KM132	(FY-S)
Spitfire F.14	Nov 1946 –	MH814	
Spitfire F.22	Jun 1948 – Jun 1951	PK520	(RAR-M)
Meteor F.4	May 1951 – May 1952	VT289	
Meteor F.8	Dec 1951 – Mar 1957	WF741	(E)

*Intermittent until February 1941

No. 612 Squadron

Badge: In front of a trident and a
      harpoon in saltire a thistle
      dipped and leaved
Motto: Vigilando custodimus
      (We stand guard by
      vigilance)
Name: 'County of Aberdeen'

No.612 Squadron was formed at Dyce on 1 June 1937 as an army co-operation unit of the Auxiliary Air Force. At the end of the year it received Hectors but on 1 November 1938 it was redesignated a general reconnaissance squadron, receiving Ansons in July 1939. Hectors were retained until November and the Ansons began coastal patrols on the outbreak of World War Two. In November 1940 conversion to Whitleys began and these flew their first patrols in February 1941, though it was the end of the year before the last Anson left. In December 1941 No.612 moved to Iceland for anti-submarine patrols over the Channel and Bay of Biscay. Some Wellingtons arrived in November and a few operated till January 1943, but it was not until April that conversion was resumed and June before all the Whitleys had been replaced. Patrols over the Bay of Biscay continued till September 1944, apart from a short break in Ulster between January and March 1944. After three months patrolling the Western Approaches, the squadron moved to

East Anglia to fly anti-E-boat patrols off the Dutch coast until the end of the war. On 9 July 1945, the squadron was disbanded.

On 10 May 1946 the Auxiliary Air Force was reformed and No.612 began recruiting at Dyce for personnel to man a fighter squadron. Initially equipped with Spitfires, it converted to Vampires in July 1951, and flew these until the Royal Auxiliary Air Force disbanded on 10 March 1957.

Squadron bases

		Chivenor	1 Dec 1943
Dyce	1 Jun 1937	Limavady	25 Jan 1944 (A)
Wick	1 Apr 1941		28 Jan 1944 (G)
Reykjavik	15 Dec 1941	Chivenor	5 Mar 1944
Thorney Island		Limavady	9 Sep 1944
	18 Aug 1942 (A)	Langham	17 Dec 1944
	26 Aug 1942 (G)		to 9 Jul 1945
Wick	23 Sep 1942	Dyce	10 May 1946
Davidstowe Moor	18 Apr 1943	Edzell	14 Oct 1951
Chivenor	23 May 1943	Dyce	12 Nov 1952
St. Eval	1 Nov 1943		to 10 Mar 1957

Aircraft

Equipment	Period of service	Representative Serial
Tutor	Jun 1937 – Dec 1937*	K6107
Hector	Dec 1937 – Nov 1939	K8104
Anson I	Jul 1939 – Nov 1941	N9722 (WL-H)
Whitley V	Nov 1940 – Dec 1941	P5070 (WL-B)
Whitley VII	Jun 1941 – Jun 1943	Z9376 (WL-M)
Wellington VIII	Nov 1942 – Jan 1943	
Wellington X	Apr 1943 – Jun 1943	
Wellington XIV	Jun 1943 – Jul 1945	NB977 (WL-M)
Spitfire LF.16E	1946 – Jul 1951	SL718 (8W-D)
Spitfire F.14	Apr 1947 – Jul 1951	RM901 (RAS-F
Vampire FB.5	Jul 1951 – Mar 1957	VZ325 (8W-E)

*Afterwards retained as training aircraft

Spitfire F.22, No.613 Squadron

No. 613 Squadron

Badge: In front of two wings
conjoined at base, a
fleur de lys
Motto: Semper parati
(Always ready)
Name: 'City of Manchester'

Squadron bases

Ringway	1 Mar 1939	Wellingore	29 Mar 1943
Odiham	2 Oct 1939	Clifton	28 May 1943
Netherthorpe	29 Jun 1940	Portreath	20 Jun 1943
Firbeck	7 Sep 1940	Snailwell	14 Jul 1943
Doncaster	8 Jul 1941	Lasham	12 Oct 1943
Andover	26 Sep 1941	Swanton Morley	11 Apr 1944
Doncaster	6 Oct 1941	Lasham	24 Apr 1944
Twinwood Farm	11 Apr 1942	Hartfordbridge	30 Oct 1944
Ouston	28 Aug 1942	Cambrai/Epinoy	19 Nov 1944
Wing	1 Mar 1943		to 7 Aug 1945
Bottisham	6 Mar 1943	Ringway	10 May 1946
Ringway	18 Mar 1943		to 10 Mar 1957

Aircraft

Equipment	Period of service	Representative Serial
Hind	May 1939 – Dec 1939	K5490
Hector	Nov 1939 – Jun 1940	K9727
Lysander I, III	Apr 1940 – Apr 1942	P9177
Tomahawk II	Aug 1941 – Apr 1942	AH809
Mustang I	Apr 1942 – Oct 1943	AM209 (SY-Q)
Mosquito VI	Nov 1943 – Aug 1945	LR366 (SY-L)
Spitfire F.14	Feb 1947 – Dec 1948	RM861
Spitfire F.22	Jul 1948 – Mar 1951	PK543 (Q3-F)
Vampire FB.5	Feb 1951 – Mar 1957	WA801 (Q3-A)
Vampire FB.9	Jun 1954 – Mar 1957	WR257

Mosquito FB.6, No.613 Squadron

No.613 Squadron was formed at Ringway on 1 March 1939 as an Auxiliary Air Force army co-operation unit. In May it received Hinds which were still in service at the outbreak or World War Two. Conversion to Hectors began in November 1939 and Lysanders started to arrive in April 1940, both types being used for light bombing and supply dropping missions over France at the end of May. In June No.613 became fully equipped with Lysanders and began coastal patrols, later supplying detachments for air-sea rescue duties. Some Tomahawks were received in August 1941 for tactical reconnaissance training, conversion to Mustangs taking place in April 1942. In December the squadron became operational, flying escort and ground-attack missions in addition to its tactical reconnaissance role. Mosquitos replaced the Mustangs in November 1943 and began fighter-bomber missions at the end of December. In May 1944 night intruder sorties became the squadron's main role and in November No.613 moved to France for the rest of the war. On 7 August it was renumbered 69 Squadron.

On 10 May 1946 No.613 reformed as an Auxiliary Air Force fighter squadron at Ringway, beginning flying in February 1947 with Spitfires. These were replaced by Vampires which were flown until disbandment on 10 March 1957.

Vampire FB.5s, No.614 Squadron

No. 614 Squadron

Badge: On a demi-terrestrial
globe, a dragon passant
Motto: Codaf I geislo (Welsh)
(I rise and search)
Name: 'County of Glamorgan'

No.614 Squadron was formed at Cardiff on 1 June 1937 as an army co-operation unit of the Auxiliary Air Force. Initially equipped with Hinds, it received Hectors by the end of 1937. Shortly after the outbreak of war it began to convert to Lysanders and moved in June 1940 to central Scotland where it began coastal patrols. Training with the army was the main duty of the squadron and in July 1941 it received some Blenheims, re-equipment being completed in January 1942. In support of Bomber Command's 'Thousand Bomber Raids' in May and June 1942, the squadron sent its Blenheims to attack enemy airfields in the Low Countries and in August it laid smoke screens for the landings at Dieppe. In November No.614 moved to North Africa to attack enemy airfields and communications in Tunisia until the end of the campaign in May 1943. It then turned to shipping escort duties in the Western Mediterranean and was disbanded in February 1944.

On 3 March 1944 No.462 Squadron at Celone was renumbered 614 Squadron and its Halifaxes took part in raids on targets in Italy and the Balkans as well as supply-

dropping to partisans. In August 1944 it began to receive Liberators, the Halifaxes finally being withdrawn in March 1945. On 27 July 1945 the squadron was disbanded in Italy.

On 10 May 1946 the Auxiliary Air Force was reformed. No.614 was given Llandow as its base and began recruiting. Spitfires were its initial equipment but in July 1950 the squadron converted to Vampires which were flown until the disbandment of the Royal Auxiliary Air Force on 10 March 1957.

Squadron bases

Cardiff	1 Jun 1937	Oulmene	7 Feb 1943
Odiham	2 Oct 1939	Tafaraoui	22 May 1943
Grangemouth	8 Jun 1940	Borizzo	28 Aug 1943
Macmerry	5 Mar 1941		to Feb 1944
Odiham	27 Sep 1941	Celone	3 Mar 1944
Macmerry	3 Oct 1941	Stornara	10 May 1944
Odiham	26 Aug 1942	Amendola	15 Jul 1944
Portreath	16 Nov 1942		to 27 Jul 1945
Blida	17 Nov 1942	Llandow	10 May 1946
Canrobert	5 Dec 1942		to 10 Mar 1957

Aircraft

Equipment	Period of service	Representative Serial	
Hind	Jun 1937 − 1938	L7238	
Hector	Nov 1937 − Nov 1939	K9779	
Lysander I, II	Nov 1939 − Oct 1940	N1225	
Lysander III	Oct 1940 − Jan 1942	V9583	
Blenheim IV	Jul 1941 − Sep 1942	V5808	
Blenheim V	Aug 1942 − Feb 1944	BA800	(D)
Halifax II	Mar 1944 − Mar 1945	BB446	(T)
Liberator VIII	Aug 1944 − Jul 1945	KH227	
Spitfire LF.16E	Jun 1946 − Jul 1948	SL672	(RAU-T)
Spitfire F.22	Jul 1948 − Jul 1950	PK619	(7A-G)
Vampire F.3	Jul 1950 − Dec 1951	VT867	(V)
Vampire FB.5	Dec 1951 − Mar 1957	WE837	(D)
Vampire FB.9	Feb 1955 − Feb 1956	WR253	(F)

No. 615 Squadron

Badge: On a star of six points, an oak sprig fructed
Motto: Conjunctis viribus (By our united force)
Name: 'County of Surrey'

No.615 Squadron was formed on 1 June 1937 at Kenley as an army co-operation unit of the Auxiliary Air Force. After flying Audaxes and Hectors, it became a fighter squadron on 7 November 1938 and received Gauntlets. These were replaced by Gladiators in May 1939, which the squadron took to France in November 1939 as part of the Air Component of the BEF. In April 1940 conversion to Hurricanes began but ten days after the German offensive in France opened the squadron returned to the UK to re-equip. After taking part in the opening stages of the Battle of Britain, No.615 moved to Scotland at the end of August to rest and re-equip, returning south in October. In February 1941 it began taking part in sweeps over France but moved to North Wales in April for defensive duties. In September it came south again for escort and ground-attack missions, leaving for India in March 1942. Arriving in May, the squadron re-assembled at Jessore by the end of June, moving to the Burma front in December to fly ground-attack and defensive sorties. In May 1943 it retired for re-equipment, receiving Spitfires in October and returning to operations in November. In August 1944 No.615 was withdrawn for defensive patrols around Calcutta, but resumed offensive operations in February being disbanded on 10 June 1945.

On the same day, No.135 Squadron at Vizagapatam was renumbered 615 Squadron. Equipped with Thunderbolts, it was training for the invasion of Malaya until the end of the war and was disbanded on 25 September 1945. On 10 May 1946 No.615 was reformed as a fighter squadron of the Auxiliary Air Force and began to recruit personnel in July. Spitfires began to be flown in October and were replaced by Meteors in 1950. These were flown until the squadron was disbanded on 10 March 1957.

Squadron bases			
Kenley	1 Jun 1937	Jessore	17 Jun 1942 (A)
Old Sarum	29 Aug 1938		22 Jun 1942 (G)
Kenley	4 Sep 1938	Feni	5 Dec 1942
Croydon	2 Sep 1939	Alipore	6 May 1943
Merville	15 Nov 1939	Chittagong	1 Nov 1943
Vitry-en-Artois	13 Dec 1939	Dohazari	13 Dec 1943
Poix	12 Apr 1940	Nazir	25 Feb 1944
Abbeville	27 Apr 1940	Silchar West	19 Mar 1944
Moorseele	16 May 1940	Dergaon	5 May 1944
Kenley	20 May 1940	Palel	23 May 1944
Prestwick	29 Aug 1940	Baigachi	10 Aug 1944
Northolt	10 Oct 1940	Nidania	23 Feb 1945
Kenley	17 Dec 1940	Chharra	15 Apr 1945
Valley	21 Apr 1941	Chakulia	22 May 1945
Manston	11 Sep 1941	Cuttack	29 May 1945
Angle	27 Nov 1941		to 10 Jun 1945
Fairwood Common		Vizagapatam	10 Jun 1945
	24 Jan 1942		to 25 Sep 1945
Left for India	17 Mar 1942	Biggin Hill	10 May 1946
			to 10 Mar 1957

Aircraft Equipment	Period of service	Representative Serial
Audax	Nov 1937 – Mar 1938	K7373
Hector	Dec 1937 – Nov 1938	K7985
Gauntlet II	Nov 1938 – May 1939	K7854 (RR-A)
Gladiator I, II	May 1939 – May 1940	N2304 (KW-R)
Hurricane I	Apr 1940 – Feb 1941	R4194 (KW-P)
	Apr 1941 – Jul 1941	
Hurricane IIA,	Feb 1941 – Apr 1941	Z2703 (KW-M)
Hurricane IIB	Jul 1941 – Mar 1942	BE140
Hurricane IIC	Sep 1941 – Mar 1942	Z3841
	Jun 1942 – Oct 1943	
Spitfire VC	Oct 1943 – Aug 1944	LZ972
Spitfire VIII	Jun 1944 – Jun 1945	MD316
Thunderbolt II	Jun 1945 – Sep 1945	KL856 (KW-D)
Spitfire F.14	Oct 1946 – Jan 1949	NH792 (RAV-W)
Spitfire F.21	Jan 1947 – Jun 1950	LA217 (RAV-J)
Spitfire F.22	Jul 1948 – Sep 1950	PK519 (V6-A)
Meteor F.4	Sep 1950 – Sep 1951	VZ428 (J)
Meteor F.8	Sep 1951 – Mar 1957	WH253 (F)

No. 616 Squadron

Badge: A Yorkshire rose
Motto: Nulla rosa sine spina
(No rose without a thorn)
Name: 'South Yorkshire'

No.616 Squadron was formed on 1 November 1938 at Doncaster and was designated a fighter unit on 15 November. It gave up its Hinds for Gauntlets in January 1939, and from May 1939 had four Battles for training duties in preparation for the arrival of Spitfires. It was not until October that the latter arrived, conversion being completed in November. At the end of May 1940 the squadron began operating over Dunkirk and during the first part of the Battle of Britain it was based in Yorkshire, moving south in mid-August. In April 1941 No.616 began to fly sweeps over France which continued until October. These were resumed in July 1942 with high-altitude Spitfires. From March 1943 onwards, it spent most of its time in south-west England and on 12 July 1944 received the first Meteors to enter squadron service. On 27 July the squadron flew the first operational sortie by a Meteor when it engaged flying bombs launched against southern England. In February 1945 a detachment was sent to Belgium and at the beginning of April the whole squadron moved to the Netherlands, beginning ground-attack missions on 16 April. The war ended a few weeks later and the squadron was disbanded on 29 August 1945.

On 10 May 1946 the squadron was reformed and began to recruit personnel for an Auxiliary Air Force night fighter unit in June. In September 1947 it received operational Mosquitos but was redesignated a day fighter unit in 1948. It began to acquire Meteors in December 1948 and flew this type until disbanded on 10 March 1957.

Squadron bases

Doncaster	1 Nov 1938	Ibsley	18 Mar 1943
Leconfield	23 Oct 1939	Exeter	17 Sep 1943
Catfoss	23 Feb 1940	Fairwood Common	
Leconfield	9 Mar 1940		16 Nov 1943
Rochford	27 May 1940	Exeter	1 Dec 1943
Leconfield	6 Jun 1940	West Malling	18 Mar 1944
Kenley	19 Aug 1940	Fairwood Common	
Coltishall	3 Sep 1940		24 Apr 1944
Kirton-in-Lindsey		Culmhead	16 May 1944
	9 Sep 1940	Manston	21 Jul 1944
Tangmere	26 Feb 1941	Colerne	17 Jan 1945
Westhampnett	9 May 1941	B.58 Melsbroek (D)	
Kirton-in-Lindsey			4 Feb 1945
	6 Oct 1941		to 26 Mar 1945
Kings Cliffe	30 Jan 1942	Andrews Field	28 Feb 1945
West Malling	3 Jul 1942	B.77 Gilze-Rijen	1 Apr 1945
Kenley	8 Jul 1942	B.91 Nijmegen	13 Apr 1945
Great Sampford	29 Jul 1942	B.109 Quackenbruck	
Hawkinge	14 Aug 1942		20 Apr 1945
Great Sampford	20 Aug 1942	B.152 Fassberg	26 Apr 1945
Ipswich	1 Sep 1942	B.156 Luneberg	3 May 1945
Great Sampford	7 Sep 1942	B.158 Lubeck	7 May 1945
Tangmere	23 Sep 1942		to 29 Aug 1945
Westhampnett	29 Oct 1942	Finningley	10 May 1946
Ibsley	2 Jan 1943	Worksop	5 May 1955
Harrowbeer	15 Mar 1943		to 10 Mar 1957

Aircraft Equipment	Period of service	Representative Serial
Hind	Nov 1938 – Jan 1939	L7193
Gauntlet II	Jan 1939 – Nov 1939	K5357
Battle	May 1939 – Nov 1939	N2031
Spitfire I	Oct 1939 – Feb 1941	N3270
Spitfire IIA, IIB	Feb 1941 – Jul 1941 Oct 1941	P7736
Spitfire VB	Jul 1941 – Oct 1942	P8477
Spitfire VI	Apr 1942 – Dec 1943	BS114 (YQ-A)
Spitfire VII	Sep 1943 – Aug 1944	MJ107 (YQ-J)
Meteor I	Jul 1944 – Feb 1945	EE227 (TQ-Y)
Meteor III	Jan 1945 – Aug 1945	EE235 (YQ-H)
Mosquito NF.30	Sep 1947 – Apr 1949	NT590 (RAW-G)
Meteor F.3	Dec 1948 – May 1950	EE348 (RAW-D)
Meteor F.4	Apr 1950 – Dec 1951	RA429 (YQ-H)
Meteor F.8	Dec 1951 – Mar 1957	WK844 (C)

Canberra B.2s, No.617 Squadron

No. 617 Squadron

Badge: On a roundel, a wall in fesse, fracted by three flashes of lightning in pile and issuant from the breach water proper.
Motto: Après moi, le deluge
(After me the flood)

No.617 Squadron was formed on 21 March 1943 at Scampton as a heavy bomber unit. It was primarily intended for one specialised operation, the breaching of the dams which supplied much of the electric power for the German industrial complex in the Ruhr. On 16 May 1943 the squadron's specially-modified Lancasters made a successful attack with the now-famous Wallis 'bouncing bombs' and it was later employed on other operations requiring highly accurate attacks. In adddition, No.617 took part in normal bombing and pathfinding missions. Its modified Lancasters could carry 12,000 and 22,000 lb. bombs which were used against V-bomb bases and the *Tirpitz*. After the German surrender,

the squadron was allocated to 'Tiger Force' and prepared to move to the Far East. It arrived in India in January 1946 returning to the UK in May to occupy its peace-time base at Binbrook. In September 1946 the squadron converted to Lincolns which were replaced in January 1952, when No.617 became the second Canberra squadron. This type equipped the squadron until it disbanded on 15 December 1955, soon after a four-month detachment to Malaya for operations against the Communist guerilla forces.

On 1 May 1958 No.617 reformed at Scampton as a Vulcan squadron of the V-bomber force.

Squadron bases

Scampton	21 Mar 1943	Salbani	Jan 1946 (P)
Coningsby	30 Aug 1943	Binbrook	May 1946 (P)
Woodhall Spa	10 Jan 1944		to 15 Dec 1955
Waddington	17 Jun 1945	Scampton	1 May 1958

Aircraft

Equipment	Period of service	Representative Serial
Lancaster I, III	Mar 1943 – Jun 1945	ED921 (AJ-W)
Lancaster VII	Jun 1945 – Sep 1946	NX783 (KC-G)
Lincoln B.2	Sep 1946 – Jan 1952	SX936 (KC-X)
Canberra B.2	Jan 1952 – Apr 1955	WD997
Canberra B.6	Feb 1955 – Dec 1955	WH955
Vulcan B.1	May 1958 – Jul 1961	XA913
Vulcan B.2	Sep 1961 – date	XL317

Vulcan B.2, No.617 Squadron

No. 618 Squadron

No.618 Squadron was formed on 1 April 1943 at Skitten from detachments of Nos.105 and 139 Squadrons. Its Mosquitos were intended to be the carriers of a variation of the Wallis bomb used with such devastating effect by No.617 Squadron on the Ruhr dams. Code-named 'Highball', the device was a spherical depth charge spun backwards by rockets at about 1000 rpm and was intended to bounce across the sea till it hit a ship to sink alongside. The mining effect of the delayed charge would have probably sunk most warships and the first target was the German Fleet should it emerge into the open sea off Norway. As this did not occur, the squadron never became operational with their new weapon and remained training in Scotland until July 1944, when it was decided to send the unit to the Pacific where suitable targets still existed. After a period of deck-landing training with Barracudas on HMS *Rajah*, the squadron embarked in the escort carriers *Fencer* and *Striker* on 30 October 1944 with twenty-four Mosquito IVs and three Mosquito XVI, the latter for photographic reconnaissance use. Arriving in mid-December in Australia, the aircraft were taken to Fisherman's Bend aircraft factory for assembly and testing and training began at Narromine in February 1945. A detachment was sent to British Pacific Fleet base at Manus in March but difficulties arriving from the use of an RAF unit in areas under the control of the US Navy resulted in No.618 being unable to go into action against Japanese shipping and the squadron was disbanded on 29 June 1945.

Squadron bases

Skitten	1 Apr 1943
Wick	9 Jul 1944
Beccles	21 Aug 1944
Left for Far East	30 Oct 1944
Melbourne	23 Dec 1944
Narromine	7 Feb 1945
	to 29 Jun 1945

Aircraft Equipment	Period of service	Representative Serial
Mosquito IV	Apr 1943 – Jun 1945	DZ537/G
Mosquito VI	Jul 1944 – Oct 1944	PZ274
	Mar 1945 – Jun 1945	HR614
Mosquito XVI	Oct 1944 – Jun 1945	NS577
Beaufighter II	Apr 1943 – Jun 1943	R2458
Barracuda II	Dec 1944	LS704

Lancaster B.1, No.619 Squadron

No. 619 Squadron

No.619 Squadron was formed at Woodhall Spa on 18 April 1943, a nucleus of three crews being supplied by No.97 Squadron. Before the end of the month Lancasters began to arrive and the squadron's first bombing operation took place on 11 June. For the rest of the war it took part in the bomber offensive and disbanded on 18 July 1945.

Squadron bases

Woodhall Spa	18 Apr 1943
Coningsby	9 Jan 1944
Dunholme Lodge	17 Apr 1944
Strubby	28 Sep 1944
Skellingthorpe	30 Jun 1945
	to 18 Jul 1945

Aircraft Equipment	Period of service	Representative Serial
Lancaster I, III	Apr 1943 – Jul 1945	EE111 (PG-S)

No. 620 Squadron

Badge: In front of a demi-
pegasus couped, a flash
of lightning.
Motto: Dona ferentes adsumus
(We are bringing gifts)

No.620 Squadron was formed on 17 June 1943 at Chedburgh as a heavy bomber unit with Stirlings and began operations two days later. It carried out night bombing missions until 19 November 1943, moving a few days later to Leicester East to become an airborne forces squadron. Training in glider-towing and supply dropping was supplemented by operational trips over France to drop supplies to resistance forces which began on 4 February 1944. Early on D-Day, No.620 provided twenty-three Stirlings to drop paratroops in Normandy, following up later with eighteen glider tows. On the opening day of the Arnhem landing, six Stirlings dropped paratroops and nineteen towed gliders into the landing zones, followed by sixty-one supply flights in the course of which five Stirlings were lost. In January 1945 tactical bombing operations began to be flown against major targets behind the German front line and for the last major airborne attack of the war, thirty aircraft towed gliders across the Rhine. Troops were flown to Norway in early May to disarm the German occupation forces shortly before the squadron converted to Halifaxes. In January 1946 No.620 began moving to the Middle East where in June it acquired some Dakotas. On 1 September 1946, the squadron was renumbered 113 Squadron.

Squadron bases

Chedburgh	17 Jun 1943	Aqir	1 Jan 1946
Leicester East	23 Nov 1943		to 14 Jan 1946 (C)
Fairford	18 Mar 1944	Cairo West	3 Mar 1946
Great Dunmow	17 Oct 1944	Aqir	18 Apr 1946
			to 1 Sep 1946

Aircraft

Equipment	Period of service	Representative Serial
Stirling I	Jun 1943 – Aug 1943	BF511
Stirling III	Aug 1943 – Feb 1944	EF442
Stirling IV	Feb 1944 – Jul 1945	LJ970 (QS-S)
Halifax VII	May 1945 – Sep 1946	PP360 (D4-P)
Halifax IX	Aug 1946 – Sep 1946	RT769
Dakota IV	Jun 1946 – Sep 1946	

No. 621 Squadron

No.621 Squadron was formed at Port Reitz, Kenya, on 12 September 1943 as a general reconnaissance unit and began to receive Wellingtons a few days later. On 19 September, a detachment began operating from Mogadishu in the former Italian colony of Somaliland and on 4 November was joined by the squadron headquarters. The squadron's patrol area covered the approaches to the Red Sea and Aden was found to be a more suitable base for the squadron, detachments being based on the Arabian coast and in Somaliland to cover a wider area. Patrols continued till the end of the war when the squadron was moved to Egypt and began converting to Warwicks. These were flown on air-sea rescue duties, being supplemented by Lancasters in April 1946. Conversion to the latter type had just been completed when No.621 was renumbered 18 Squadron on 1 September 1946.

Squadron bases

Port Reitz	12 Sep 1943
Mogadishu	4 Nov 1943
Khormaksar	5 Dec 1943
Mersa Matruh	12 Nov 1945
Aqir	20 Apr 1946
Ein Shemer	6 Jun 1946
	to 1 Sep 1946

Aircraft

Equipment	Period of service	Representative Serial
Wellington XIII, XIV	Sep 1943 – Dec 1945	JA256 (G)
Warwick V	Nov 1945 – Aug 1946	PN817 (V)
Lancaster ASR.3	Apr 1946 – Sep 1946	RF313

No. 622 Squadron

Badge: A long-eared owl volant
affrontée, carrying in the
claws a flash of lightning.
Motto: Bellamus noctu (We make
war by night)

No.622 Squadron was formed on 10 August 1943 at Mildenhall from C Flight of No.15 Squadron. Equipped with Stirlings, it began operations on the same night as forming and converted to Lancasters in December. It formed part of the main force of Bomber Command and took part in attacks on German industry until the end of the war. After a short period of trooping to Italy, the squadron disbanded on 15 August 1945.

On 15 December 1950 No.622 reformed at Blackbushe as the sole transport unit of the Royal Auxiliary Air Force. Equipped with Valettas, it had a nucleus of regular personnel, the balance being supplied mainly by airline personnel from local airlines who in an emergency, would man requisitioned Vikings. Its service career was short and the squadron disbanded on 30 September 1953.

Squadron bases

Mildenhall	10 Aug 1943
	to 15 Aug 1945
Blackbushe	15 Dec 1950
	to 30 Sep 1953

Aircraft

Equipment	Period of service	Representative Serial
Stirling III	Aug 1943 – Dec 1943	EJ113 (GI-Q)
Lancaster I, III	Dec 1943 – Aug 1945	LL782 (GI-H)
Valetta C.1	Dec 1950 – Sep 1953	VL271 (B)

Lancaster B.1, No.622 Squadron

No. 623 Squadron

No.623 Squadron was formed at Downham Market on 10 August 1943, a flight of No.218 Squadron providing the nucleus and the aircraft which flew the squadron's first raid against Germany on the same night. It contributed to Bomber Command's attacks for three months before a decision to increase the size of No.5 Group's conversion units to thirty-seven Stirlings each resulted in the squadron being disbanded on 6 December 1943, and the crews being distributed between Nos.90, 218 and 514 Squadrons.

Squadron base
Downham Market 10 Aug 1943
               to 6 Dec 1943

Aircraft Equipment	Period of service	Representative Serial
Stirling III	Aug 1943 — Dec 1943	EF199 (IC-L)

No. 624 Squadron

No.624 Squadron was formed at Blida, Algeria, on 22 September 1943, from No.1575 (Special Duties) Flight which had been dropping agents and supplies to resistance forces in Italy and southern France. Such duties formed the main task of No.624 with a secondary bombing role when circumstances permitted. With an establishment of eighteen Halifaxes and two Venturas, drops were made over France, Italy, Yugoslavia and Czechoslovakia and early in 1944 the B-17s of the 122nd Squadron, USAAF, were attached for similar missions. Stirlings were added in June 1944, but with southern France and much of Italy in Allied hands by September the squadron was disbanded on 5 September 1944.

On 28 December 1944 No.624 reformed at Grottaglie with Walrus amphibians for mine-spotting duties. Detachments were based around the Italian coast and in Greece for this purpose until the squadron was disbanded on 30 November 1945.

Squadron bases			
Blida	22 Sep 1943	Foggia	21 Feb 1945
Bridisi	Dec 1943 (P)	Falconara	2 May 1945
Blida	15 Feb 1944	Rosignano	9 Jul 1945
	to 5 Sep 1944	Littorio	21 Aug 1945
Grottaglie	28 Dec 1944		to 30 Nov 1945

Aircraft Equipment	Period of service	Representative Serial
Ventura II	Sep 1943 — Oct 1943	AE948
Halifax II	Sep 1943 — Sep 1944	JP159 (Q)
Halifax V	Sep 1943 — Feb 1944	BB433 (K)
Stirling IV	Jun 1944 — Sep 1944	LJ941 (B)
Walrus I	Jan 1945 — Nov 1945	Z1769 (A)

No. 625 Squadron

Badge: Within a circular chain of seven links, a Lancaster rose.
Motto: We avenge

No.625 Squadron was formed on 1 October 1943 at Kelstern from C Flight of No.100 Squadron. Its Lancasters took part in Bomber Command's night offensive against Germany for the rest of the war. After a short period of transport duties when it was engaged in trooping to Italy, the squadron was disbanded on 7 October 1945.

Squadron bases
Kelstern   1 Oct 1943
Scampton   5 Apr 1945
          to 7 Oct 1945

Aircraft Equipment	Period of service	Representative Serial
Lancaster I, III	Oct 1943 — Oct 1945	PD206 (CF-B2)

No. 626 Squadron

Badge: On the waves of the sea, an ancient ship, sails furled, charged on the bow with an eye

Motto: To strive and not to yield

No.626 Squadron was formed at Wickenby on 7 November 1943 from C Flight of No.12 Squadron. Its Lancasters took part in the strategic bomber offensive for the remainder of the war and after a few months on transport duties, the squadron was disbanded on 14 October 1945.

Squadron base

Wickenby	7 Nov 1943
	to 14 Oct 1945

Aircraft Equipment	Period of service	Representative Serial
Lancaster I, III	Nov 1943 — Oct 1945	RA543 (UM-A2)

No. 627 Squadron

Badge: A hawk diving, holding in the beak a firebrand

Motto: At first sight

No.627 Squadron was formed on 12 November 1943 at Oakington from a nucleus supplied by No.139 Squadron. Equipped with Mosquito IVs, it formed part of the Light Night Striking Force which carried out night attacks on Germany to supplement Bomber Command's major raids. In April 1944 it was transferred to No.5 Group and moved to Woodhall Spa and in addition to night raids carried out target marking and photographic reconnaissance, taking part in daylight operations from time to time. On 1 October 1945 the squadron was renumbered 109 Squadron.

Squadron bases

Oakington	12 Nov 1943
Woodhall Spa	15 Apr 1944
	to 30 Sep 1945

Aircraft Equipment	Period of service	Representative Serial
Mosquito IV	Nov 1943 — Sep 1945	DZ442 (AZ-A)
Mosquito XVI	Mar 1945 — Sep 1945	RF444 (AZ-N)
Mosquito XX	Jul 1944 — Sep 1945	KB195 (AZ-B)
Mosquito XXV	Oct 1944 — Sep 1945	KB490 (AZ-Q)

No. 628 Squadron

No.628 Squadron was formed on 21 March 1944, at Redhills Lake, Madras, with Catalinas from a nucleus supplied by B Flight, No.357 Squadron. Although intended for special duties, the squadron spent most of its time on meteorological flights and air-sea rescue missions over the Bay of Bengal and Indian Ocean until disbanded on 1 October 1944.

Squadron base

Redhills Lake	21 Mar 1944
	to 1 Oct 1944

Aircraft Equipment	Period of service	Representative Serial
Catalina Ib	Mar 1944 — Sep 1944	FP225
Catalina IV	Jul 1944 — Sep 1944	

No. 630 Squadron

Badge: On an ogress, a Lancaster rose fimbriated

Motto: Nocturna more (Death by night)

No.630 Squadron was formed on 15 November 1943 at East Kirkby from B Flight of No.57 Squadron. Its Lancasters began operations immediately and for the remainder of the war it took part in the strategic air offensive against Germany. After some transport duties for a few weeks after the end of the war, the squadron disbanded on 18 July 1945.

Squadron base

East Kirkby	15 Nov 1943
	to 18 Jul 1945

Aircraft Equipment	Period of service	Representative Serial
Lancaster I, III	Nov 1943 — Jul 1945	JA872 (LE-N)

No. 631 Squadron

No.631 Squadron was formed on 1 December 1943 at Towyn from Nos.1605 and 1628 Flights with target-towing Henleys for co-operation with the gunnery ranges in Wales. In March 1944 Hurricanes were received for gun-laying practice while Martinets began to replace the Henleys in September 1944. At the end of the war, Vengeances and Spitfires replaced these, the former being in turn replaced by Martinets again in 1947. In August 1948 a few Vampires were received and the squadron was renumbered 20 Squadron on 7 February 1949.

Squadron bases

Towyn	1 Dec 1943
Llanbedr	10 May 1945
	to 7 Feb 1949

Aircraft Equipment	Period of service	Representative Serial
Henley III	Dec 1943 — Feb 1945	L3323
Hurricane IIC	Mar 1944 — Jul 1945	LF910
Martinet I	Sep 1944 — Oct 1944 Jan 1947 — Feb 1949	EM524
Vengeance IV	May 1945 — May 1947	HB426
Spitfire XVI	Jun 1945 — Feb 1949	TE399 (6D-B)
Vampire F.1	Aug 1948 — Feb 1949	TG444

Lancaster B.1, No.635 Squadron

No. 635 Squadron

Badge: In front of a roundel
nebuly, a dexter gauntlet
holding three flashes of
lightning
Motto: Nos ducimus ceteri
secunter (We lead, others
follow)

No.635 Squadron was formed on 20 March 1944 at Downham Market from B Flight, No.35 Squadron and C Flight,

No.97 Squadron. Equipped with Lancasters, the squadron was a pathfinder unit in Bomber Command and took part in the strategic air offensive against Germany until the end of the war. After a period of transport duties it disbanded on 1 September 1945.

Squadron base
Downham Market 20 Mar 1944
to 1 Sep 1945

Aircraft Equipment	Period of service	Representative Serial
Lancaster I, III	Mar 1944 — Sep 1945	ND924 (F2-B)
Lancaster VI	Jul 1945 — Aug 1945	ND418 (F2-Q)

No. 639 Squadron

No.639 Squadron was formed on 1 December 1943 at Cleave from Nos.1602, 1603 and 1604 Flights for anti-aircraft co-operation duties in Cornwall. Hurricanes supplemented the squadron's Henleys in August 1944, and both types remained in service until disbandment on 30 April 1945.

Squadron base
Cleave   1 Dec 1943
to 30 Apr 1945

Aircraft Equipment	Period of service	Representative Serial
Henley III	Dec 1943 — Apr 1945	L3362
Hurricane IV	Aug 1944 — Apr 1945	LD976

Halifax VI, No.640 Squadron

No. 640 Squadron

No.640 Squadron was formed at Leconfield on 7 January 1944 from C Flight of No.158 Squadron. Equipped with Halifaxes, it took part in the bombing offensive against Germany until the end of the war and disbanded on 7 May 1945.

Squadron base
Leconfield   7 Jan 1944
to 7 May 1945

Aircraft Equipment	Period of service	Representative Serial
Halifax III	Jan 1944 — Mar 1945	MZ544 (C8-Z)
Halifax VI	Mar 1945 — May 1945	RG600 (C8-V)

No. 644 Squadron

Badge: In front of an increscent,
a Pegasus rampant
Motto: Dentes draconis serimus
(We sow dragon's teeth)

No.644 Squadron was formed on 23 February 1944 at Tarrant Rushton from a nucleus supplied by No.298 Squadron. Equipped with Halifaxes, it undertook glider-towing exercises in preparation for the invasion of Europe and at the end of March began supply-dropping flights to the Resistance in France. On the morning of D-Day, twenty of the squadron's aircraft towed gliders to Normandy, including three for the first attack on an enemy battery before the main force arrived. At Arnhem, twenty aircraft were provided in the first wave and when supply-dropping in France ended with the liberation of the country, dropping over Norway began. In January 1945 tactical bombing in front of the Allied lines in Germany began and in March thirty aircraft were supplied for the last great airborne operation of the war, the crossing of the Lower Rhine. In May 1945 troops were flown to Norway to help disarm the occupation forces and freed prisoners-of-war were flown back to the UK. After a period of trooping to Italy, Greece and North Africa, the squadron moved to Egypt in November 1945 where it was renumbered 47 Squadron on 1 September 1946.

Squadron bases

Tarrant Rushton	25 Feb 1944
Qastina	Nov 1945 (P)
	to 1 Sep 1946

Aircraft

Equipment	Period of service	Representative Serial
Halifax V	Mar 1944 – Dec 1944	LL402 (9U-F)
Halifax III	Dec 1944 – Nov 1945	NA672 (2P-L)
Halifax VII	Mar 1945 – Sep 1946	NA314 (9U-R)

No. 650 Squadron

No.650 Squadron was formed on 1 December 1943 at Cark from No.1614 Flight and a flight earmarked as D Flight of No.289 Squadron. Equipped with Martinets for target-towing duties, it later added Hurricanes to its strength for gun-laying practice. While primarily engaged in co-operation with batteries on the East coast of the Irish Sea, a detachment was also based in the Humber area in February and March 1945. In November 1944, the squadron moved to Anglesey where it disbanded on 26 June 1945.

Squadron bases

Cark	1 Dec 1943
Bodorgan	18 Nov 1944
	to 26 Jun 1945

Aircraft

Equipment	Period of service	Representative Serial
Martinet I	Dec 1943 – Jun 1945	HN890
Hurricane IV	Apr 1944 – Jun 1945	LE757

Auster IV, No.654 Squadron

Nos. 651 to 666 Squadrons

The numbers 651 to 666 were allotted to a group of air observation post squadrons formed between 1941 and 1945. These units were equipped with light aircraft which were used for artillery observation and liaison duties, replacing larger but more vulnerable aircraft, notably the Lysander. Relying on slow speed and manoeuverability near the ground to evade enemy aircraft. AOP aircraft operated from any suitable field close to the army units which they were supporting. The basic type used was the Auster, based on a civilian two-seat light aircraft, and from the original design was developed a range of improved versions, the last being the Auster AOP.9.

AOP squadrons had a high proportion of their pilots and observers provided by the army and during the time that these units were operated by the RAF they worked closely with the army. On 1 September 1957, the Army Air Corps was formed to take over all aspects of AOP operations, relieving the RAF of its maintenance tasks which constituted the major part of the RAF's connection with AOP squadrons.

Due to the fact that they operated in small detachments from various locations which changed frequently, base lists for AOP squadrons are to little purpose, squadron headquarters being often in farms and villages and serving only as a link between the squadron aircraft. When in action, detachments flew from locations which are, for the most part, now meaningless. For these squadrons, therefore, no base lists have been compiled and only brief narrative of each squadron is given to indicate the areas in which it operated.

No. 651 Squadron

Formed at Old Sarum on 1 August 1941, No.651 went to North Africa with the First Army in November 1942, moving later to Sicily and Italy later in the war. In November 1945, the squadron moved to the Middle East for a period. No.657 Squadron was renumbered 651 on 1 November 1955 at Middle Wallop for its last two years as a RAF unit.

No. 652 Squadron

No.652 was formed at Old Sarum on 1 May 1942 and went to Normandy with the Second Army in June 1944, taking part in the campaign in France, the Low Countries and Germany for the rest of the war. It remained in Germany as part of the occupation forces, later becoming a unit of the Army of the Rhine until absorbed by the Army Air Corps.

No. 653 Squadron

Formed at Old Sarum on 20 June 1942, No.653 landed in Normandy in June 1944 and took part in the advance through the Low Countries to northern Germany where it disbanded on 15 September 1945.

No. 654 Squadron

No.654 formed at Old Sarum on 15 July 1942 and landed in North Africa in December 1942. It moved to Sicily with the Eighth Army in July 1943 and later in the year to Italy where it remained until disbanded on 29 June 1947.

No. 655 Squadron

Formed at Old Sarum on 8 December 1942, No.655 was transferred to North Africa in August 1943 for a period of training before moving to Italy in December. It remained there until disbanded on 31 August 1945.

No. 656 Squadron

No.656 was formed at Westley on 31 December 1942 and left for India in August 1943. It began operations on the India-Burma frontier in January 1944 and in September 1945 moved to Malaya where it disbanded in January 1947. In July 1948, it was reformed at Kuala Lumpur from Nos.1902, 1903 and 1907 Flights and supported the Commonwealth forces in Malaya throughout the Emergency, being absorbed into the Army Air Corps in 1957.

No. 657 Squadron

Formed at Ouston on 31 January 1943, No.657 moved to North Africa in August 1943 and arrived in Italy in February 1944. It remained there until March 1945 when it moved to the Netherlands to support the First Canadian Army. Returning to the UK in November 1945, it co-operated with army units in southern England until renumbered 651 Squadron on 1 November 1955.

No. 658 Squadron

No.658 Squadron was formed at Old Sarum on 30 April 1943 and moved to France in June 1944. After the end of the war in Europe, it returned to the UK and left for India in October 1945, being disbanded on 1 April 1947.

No. 659 Squadron

Formed at Firbeck on 30 April 1943, No.659 Squadron landed in Normandy in June 1944 and spent the rest of the war with 21st Army Group. In October 1945 it left for India and was based on the North-West Frontier until disbanded on 14 August 1947.

No. 660 Squadron

No.660 Squadron was formed at Old Sarum on 31 July 1943 and moved to France in July 1944 to support the 21st Army Group for the rest of the war.

No. 661 Squadron

Formed at Old Sarum on 31 August 1943, No.661 Squadron moved to France in August 1944 to provide support for the First Canadian Army, disbanding on 31 October 1945. On 1 May 1949, No.661 reformed at Kenley as part of the Royal Auxiliary Air Force, disbanding on 10 March 1957.

No. 662 Squadron

No.662 Squadron was formed at Old Sarum on 30 September 1943 and moved to France in June 1944. After supporting 21st Army Group for the rest of the war, the squadron disbanded on 15 December 1945. Reformed as a Royal Auxiliary Air Force unit on 1 February 1949, No.662 had its headquarters at Colerne until disbanded on 10 March 1957.

No. 663 Squadron

Formed at San Basilio in Italy on 14 August 1944, No.663 Squadron was manned by Polish personnel and provided support for the Eighth Army for the rest of the war, disbanding on 4 October 1946. On 1 July 1949, it was reformed at Hooton Park as a Royal Auxiliary Air Force unit, disbanding on 10 March 1957.

No. 664 Squadron

No.664 Squadron was formed at Andover on 9 December 1944 with Canadian personnel and moved to the Netherlands in March 1945. The squadron disbanded on 31 May 1946 and reformed at Hucknall on 1 September 1949 as a Royal Auxiliary Air Force unit, disbanding on 10 March 1957.

No. 665 Squadron

Formed at Andover with Canadian personnel on 22 January 1945, No.665 Squadron moved to the Netherlands in April 1945 to join the First Canadian Army and was disbanded on 10 July 1945.

No. 666 Squadron

No.666 Squadron was formed at Andover on 5 March 1945 with Canadian personnel and moved to the Continent in June, disbanding on 31 October 1945. On 1 May 1949 it was reformed at Perth as part of the Royal Auxiliary Air Force, disbanding on 10 March 1957.

Notes on Aircraft   *Auster AOP.9, No.656 Squadron*

All squadrons used Austers throughout their periods of service. Wartime marks were the Auster I, III, IV and V. After the war the Auster AOP.6 became the standard AOP aircraft and were supplemented by the later AOP.9. In addition, Nos.652, 653, 654 and 656 were initially equipped with Tiger Moth IIs for training. No.657 operated a few Hoverfly I and II helicopters in 1946-47.

No. 667 Squadron

No.667 Squadron was formed on 1 December 1943 at Gosport from Nos.1662 and 1631 Flights with Defiants for target-towing duties. These were supplemented and eventually replaced by Barracudas and Vengeances while Hurricanes and Oxfords were received for gun-laying practice. The Hurricanes were replaced by Spitfires after the end of the war and the squadron co-operated with army and navy batteries and ships until the end of the war, disbanding on 20 December 1945.

Squadron base

Gosport	1 Dec 1943
	to 20 Dec 1945

Aircraft Equipment	Period of service	Representative Serial
Defiant I, III	Dec 1943 – Jan 1945	N1558
Hurricane IIC	Apr 1944 – Aug 1945	P3151
Barracuda II	May 1944 – Jun 1945	BV725
Oxford I	Jun 1944 – Dec 1945	HM706
Vengeance IV	Oct 1944 – Dec 1945	HB512
Spitfire XVI	Jul 1945 – Dec 1945	TB392

Nos. 668 to 673 Squadrons

Six squadrons, numbered 668 to 672, were formed in India for airborne assaults in South-East Asia. Each was to have had an establishment of eighty Hadrians and ten light aircraft and the personnel consisted of RAF pilots surplus to current requirements and pilots from the Glider Pilot Regiment. On 16 November 1944 No.668 formed at Calcutta and No.669 at Bikram followed by No.670 at Fatehjang on 14 December 1944. It was later found that No.669 had been formed at the wrong airfield and since No.671 was due to form there No.669 was renumbered 671 on 31 December. On 1 January 1945 No.669 reformed at Basal where it should have formed in the first place. The three squadrons, Nos.668, 669 and 670, were part of No.343 Wing. A second wing, No.344, comprised Nos.671, 672 and 673 Squadrons. On 16 November 1944, No.672 formed at Bikram where No.673 joined it on 1 January 1945: on the same day No.669 had been renumbered No.671 to complete the wing. Until the end of the war, the squadrons undertook sporadic glider training and courses in jungle warfare but were never used in operations due to the Japanese surrender. On 25 October 1945 Nos.671 and 673 disbanded, followed by Nos.668 and 669 on 10 November. The two remaining squadrons, Nos.670 and 672 disbanded on 1 July 1946.

No.668 Squadron bases

Calcutta	16 Nov 1944
Lalaghat	4 Feb 1945
Belgaum	30 Apr 1945
Fatehjang	28 Jun 1945
Upper Topa Camp	5 Jul 1945
Fatehjang	21 Aug 1945
	to 10 Nov 1945

No.669 Squadron bases

Bikram	16 Nov 1944
	to 31 Dec 1944
Basal	1 Jan 1945
Belgaum	19 Mar 1945
Upper Topa Camp	27 May 1945
Basal	23 Jun 1945
Fatehjang	6 July 1945
	to 10 Nov 1945

No.670 Squadron bases

Fatehjang	14 Dec 1944
Dhamial	30 May 1945
Basal	1 Jun 1945
Upper Topa Camp	23 Jun 1945
Fatehjang	26 Jul 1945
Chaklala	1 Apr 1946
	to 1 July 1946

No.671 Squadron bases

Bikram	1 Jan 1945
Belgaum	9 Feb 1945
Bikram	3 Apr 1945
Kargi Road	26 Aug 1945
	to 25 Oct 1945

No.672 Squadron bases

Bikram	16 Nov 1944
(No personnel till 23 Jan 1945)	
Belgaum	26 Feb 1945
Bikram	30 Apr 1945
Kargi Road	Aug 1945
Fatehjang	19 Nov 1945
Chaklala	1 Apr 1946
	to 1 July 1946

No.673 Squadron bases

Bikram	27 Jan 1945
Belgaum	19 Feb 1945
Bikram	10 Apr 1945
Tilda	26 Aug 1945
Kargi Road	16 Sep 1945
	to 25 Oct 1945

Aircraft Equipment		Period of service	Representative Serial
Hadrian	668 Sqn.	Feb 1945 – Apr 1945	
	669 Sqn.	Nov 1944 – Dec 1944	
		Jun 1945 – Jul 1945	
	670 Sqn.	Jan 1945 – Jun 1945	KH902
	671 Sqn.	Jan 1945 – Aug 1945	
	672 Sqn.	Nov 1944 – Aug 1945	
	673 Sqn.	Jan 1945 – Sep 1945	FR703
Horsa	670 Sqn.	Dec 1945 – Jun 1946	
Tiger	668 Sqn.	Aug 1945 – Nov 1945	DE452
Moth II	669 Sqn.	Jul 1945 – Nov 1945	DE477
	670 Sqn.	Jul 1945 – Jul 1946	NL965
	671 Sqn.	Jan 1945 – Aug 1945	MA936
	672 Sqn.	Nov 1944 – Aug 1945	DE824
	673 Sqn.	Jan 1945 – Sep 1945	NL731

No. 679 Squadron

No.679 Squadron was formed on 1 December 1943 at Ipswich from Nos.1616 and 1627 Flights with Martinets and Hurricanes for anti-aircraft co-operation duties in East Anglia. Barracudas and Vengeances supplemented these later and all four types were in service when the squadron was disbanded on 26 June 1945.

Squadron base

Ipswich   1 Dec 1943
         to 26 Jun 1945

Aircraft

Equipment	Period of service	Representative Serial
Martinet I	Dec 1943 – Jun 1945	HP201
Hurricane IIC, IV	Dec 1943 – Jun 1945	KZ909
Barracuda II	Mar 1944 – Jun 1945	DR154
Vengeance IV	Apr 1945 – Jun 1945	FD315

No. 680 Squadron

No.680 Squadron was formed from A Flight, No.2 Photographic Reconnaissance Unit at Matariya on 1 February 1943. Equipped with Spitfires, Hurricanes and Beaufighters it flew photographic reconnaissance missions over enemy bases in North Africa. It moved forward to Tunisia in April 1943, and extended its activities to Sicily and Sardinia while detachments in Libya and Cyprus kept watch on Greece and Crete. In June, the squadron withdrew its Tunisian-based aircraft to Matariya and concentrated on keeping track of the enemy in the Eastern Mediterranean for a period. In August 1944, a detachment moved to Italy and remained there for a year and after the end of the war other detachments undertook survey work in Iran, Iraq and Palestine. Mosquitos had been added to the squadron strength in February 1944 and in July 1946, it gave up its Spitfires to become wholly equipped with Mosquitos. At the same time it moved to Palestine where it was renumbered 13 Squadron on 1 September 1946.

Squadron bases

LG129 Matariya	1 Feb 1943
Deversoir	25 Feb 1945
Ein Shemer	9 Jul 1946
	to 1 Sep 1946

Squadron detachments

Tunisia	Apr 1943 – Jun 1943
Cyprus	May 1943 – Aug 1944
Italy	Aug 1944 – Aug 1944
Iran	Jun 1945 – Sep 1945
Iraq	Aug 1945 – Sep 1945
Palestine	Sep 1945 – Jan 1946

Aircraft

Equipment	Period of service	Representative Serial
Beaufighter I	Feb 1943 – Mar 1943	T3301
Hurricane I	Feb 1943 – Feb 1944	Z5132
Hurricane IIB	Mar 1943 – Dec 1944	
Spitfire IV, V	Feb 1943 – Jun 1944	BP908
Spitfire XI	Aug 1943 – Jul 1946	MB774
Spitfire VI	Mar 1943 – 1943	
Mosquito XVI	Feb 1944 – Sep 1946	MM291
Mosquito PR.34	Mar 1946 – Sep 1946	RG318

Spitfire XIX, No.681 Squadron

No. 681 Squadron

No.681 Squadron was formed from No.3 Photographic Reconnaissance Unit at Dum Dum on 25 January 1943. Equipped with Spitfires, Hurricanes and Mitchells it flew photographic reconnaissance missions over Burma and Siam. In August 1943, it began to receive Mosquitos but in December standardised on Spitfire XIs. For the rest of the war, it kept watch on enemy ports and railways in South-East Asia and in September 1945, moved to Hong Kong. In December 1945 a detachment began operating in Java while another spent a month in French Indo-China before the squadron changed its base to Seletar in January 1946. A further detachment was based in Siam until April when the squadron left for India. On 1 August 1946, it was renumbered 34 Squadron.

Squadron bases

Dum Dum	25 Jan 1943
Chandina	9 Dec 1943
Dum Dum	31 Jan 1944
Alipore	5 May 1944
Mingaladon	25 May 1945
Kai Tak	27 Sep 1945
Seletar	9 Jan 1946
Palam	3 May 1946
	to 1 Aug 1946

Squadron detachments

Burma	Sep 1945 – Dec 1945
Java	Dec 1945 – Apr 1946
French Indo-China	Dec 1945 – Jan 1946
Siam	Jan 1946 – Apr 1946

Aircraft

Equipment	Period of service	Representative Serials
Spitfire IV	Jan 1943 – Sep 1943	AB319 (J)
Spitfire XI	Sep 1943 – Apr 1946	PL781 (F)
Spitfire XIX	Jul 1945 – Aug 1946	PS918 (Z)
Hurricane IIB	Jan 1943 – Sep 1943	BN224 (V)
B-25B, B-25C	Jan 1943 – Dec 1943	N5-144 (B)
Mosquito II	Sep 1943 – Dec 1943	DZ697
Mosquito VI	Aug 1943 – Dec 1943	HJ759 (W)
Mosquito IX	Sep 1943 – Dec 1943	LR463 (N)

No. 682 Squadron

No.682 Squadron was formed from No.4 Photographic Reconnaissance Unit at Maison Blanche on 1 February 1943, for photographic reconnaissance duties in the Western and Central Mediterranean. After flying missions over Tunisia and Italy from Algeria, it moved to Italy in December 1943 and for the rest of the war based detachments at many airfields in Italy. In September 1944, a detachment was sent to southern France which moved forward behind the Allied armies until it reached Nancy in November where it stayed

until the end of March 1945. On 14 September 1945, the squadron was disbanded having flown Spitfires exclusively throughout its period of service.

Squadron bases

Maison Blanche	1 Feb 1943
La Marsa	6 Jun 1943
San Severo	8 Dec 1943
	to 14 Sep 1945

Aircraft Equipment	Period of service	Representative Serial
Spitfire IV	Feb 1943 – Dec 1943	AB426
Spitfire XI	Feb 1943 – Sep 1945	PL842
Spitfire XIX	Jun 1944 – Sep 1945	RM630

No. 683 Squadron

Badge: In front of a mullet of six points, a telescope in bend
Motto: Nihil nos latet (Nothing remains concealed)

No.683 Squadron was formed from B Flight, No.69 Squadron at Luqa on 8 February 1943, for photographic reconnaissance duties from Malta. Though equipped with Spitfires throughout its period of service, it also had a few Mosquitos for two months in 1943. In November 1943, the squadron moved to Tunisia for a month before being transferred to Italy where it joined No.682 in providing detachments of Spitfires throughout the Allied-occupied section of the country for the rest of the war. In August 1945, it sent a detachment to Greece but was disbanded on 21 September 1945.

On 1 November 1950, No.683 was reformed as a survey unit with Lancasters at Fayid. It provided detachments in Arabia and Africa for air survey purposes and in January 1952 moved to Aden. In May 1952, the squadron moved to Iraq where it was disbanded on 30 November 1953.

Squadron bases

Luqa	8 Feb 1943
El Aouina	22 Nov 1943
San Severo	20 Dec 1943
	to 21 Sep 1945
Fayid	1 Nov 1950
Khormaksar	Jan 1952 (P)
Habbaniya	May 1952 (P)
	to 30 Nov 1953

Aircraft Equipment	Period of service	Representative Serial
Spitfire IV	Feb 1943 – Jul 1943	BS358
Spitfire XI	Apr 1943 – Sep 1945	EN507
Spitfire XIX	Sep 1944 – Sep 1945	RM641
Mosquito IV	May 1943 – Jul 1943	DZ352
Lancaster PR.1	Nov 1950 – Nov 1953	PA394
Valetta C.1	Nov 1950 – Nov 1953	VX498

No. 684 Squadron

Badge: A mask
Motto: Invisus videns (Seeing though unseen)

No.684 Squadron was formed at Dum Dum from a nucleus supplied by No.681 Squadron on 29 September 1943 for photographic reconnaissance duties in South-East Asia. While No.681 operated Spitfires, No.684 provided longer-ranged twin-engined aircraft for missions over Burma, Siam and Malaya. Mosquitos were the main type used but Mitchells were flown until May 1945. A detachment was based in Ceylon in September 1944 which covered the Dutch East Indies until the end of the war and in October 1945 the squadron moved to Saigon. In January 1946, it was transfer-

red to Siam where it carried out survey flights until renumbered 81 Squadron on 1 September 1946.

Squadron bases

Dum Dum	29 Sep 1943
Comilla	9 Dec 1943
Dum Dum	31 Jan 1944
Alipore	5 May 1944
Tan Son Nhut	11 Oct 1945
Don Muang	27 Jan 1946
	to 1 Sep 1946

Squadron detachments
Ceylon Sep 1944 – Oct 1945
Cocos Is. Jun 1945 – Nov 1945
Malaya Nov 1945 – Feb 1946

Aircraft Equipment	Period of service	Representative Serial	
Mosquito II	Sep 1943 – May 1945	DZ696	
Mosquito VI	Sep 1943 – May 1945	HJ759	(W)
Mosquito IX	Oct 1943 – May 1945	LR463	(N)
Mosquito XVI	Feb 1944 – Feb 1946	NS497	(J)
Mosquito PR.34	Jul 1945 – Sep 1946	RG249	(U)
B-25C	Sep 1943 – May 1945	MA957	(Z)
Beaufighter VI, X	Aug 1945 – Oct 1945	EL364	

Vengeance IV, No.691 Squadron

No. 691 Squadron

Badge: In front of a sword and anchor in saltire, a popinjay
Motto: Volamus ut serviamus (We fly to serve)

No.691 Squadron was formed on 1 December 1943 at Roborough from No.1623 Flight for anti-aircraft co-operation duties in South-west England. Initially equipped with Defiants, Hurricanes and Oxfords, it received Barracudas later. At the end of the war, Vengeances, Martinets and Spitfires were taken on strength and the last two, with Oxfords, remained the main equipment of the squadron until it was renumbered

17 Squadron on 11 February 1949.

Squadron bases

Roborough	1 Dec 1943
Harrowbeer	21 Feb 1945
Exeter	1 Aug 1945
Weston Zoyland	29 Apr 1946
Fairwood Common	Jul 1946
Chivenor	4 Oct 1946
	to 11 Feb 1949

Aircraft Equipment	Period of service	Representative Serial
Hurricane I	Dec 1943 — Mar 1944	L1715
Hurricane IIC	Mar 1944 — 1945	LF638
Defiant I, III	Dec 1943 — Apr 1945	V1108
Oxford I	Dec 1943 — Feb 1949	V3385
Barracuda II	Jan 1944 — Mar 1945	DR190
Vengeance IV	Apr 1945 — May 1947	HB322
Martinet I	Aug 1945 — Feb 1949	
Spitfire XVI	Aug 1945 — Feb 1949	TB993
Harvard IIB	Nov 1945 — Feb 1949	KF331

No. 692 Squadron

Badge: In front of a pair of wings conjoined in base, a dagger, point downwards
Motto: Polus dum sidera pascet (So long as the sky shall feed the stars)
Name: 'Fellowship of the Bellows'

No.692 Squadron was formed on 1 January 1944 at Graveley as a light bomber unit in No.8 Group. Equipped with

Mosquitos it formed part of the Light Night Striking Force and was the first squadron to carry 4,000 lb bombs in Mosquitos. After carrying out night raids on Germany for the rest of the war, it disbanded on 20 September 1945.

Squadron bases

Graveley	1 Jan 1944
Gransden Lodge	4 Jun 1945
	to 20 Sep 1945

Aircraft Equipment	Period of service	Representative Serial
Mosquito IV	Jan 1944 — Jun 1944	
Mosquito XVI	Mar 1944 — Sep 1945	MM183 (P3-A)

No. 695 Squadron

Badge: In front of a maunch,
three arms in armour
conjoined

Motto: We exercise their arms

No.695 Squadron was formed on 1 December 1943 at Bircham Newton from Nos.1611 and 1612 Flights for anti-aircraft co-operation duties in East Anglia. Initially, Henleys, Martinets and Lysanders were used for target-towing and Hurricanes for gun-laying practice and by the end of the war the Martinet was the standard target tug. It was then replaced for a period by Vengeances. Spitfires replaced the Hurricanes and in 1946 Oxfords were received. At the end of 1948, target-towing Beaufighters began to arrive but the squadron was renumbered 34 Squadron on 11 February 1949.

Squadron bases

Bircham Newton	1 Dec 1943
Horsham St.Faith	11 Aug 1945
	to 11 Feb 1949

Aircraft Equipment	Period of service	Representative Serial	
Henley III	Dec 1943 – Jun 1944	L5429	
Hurricane IIC	Dec 1943 – Sep 1945	PZ751	(8Q-W)
Lysander I, II	Dec 1943 – Jan 1944	P1725	
Martinet I	Dec 1943 – May 1945	HN862	(8Q-F)
	Dec 1946 – Jan 1949		
Spitfire VB	Sep 1944 – Jul 1945		
Spitfire XVI	Jul 1945 – Feb 1949	TE450	
Vengeance IV	Mar 1945 – May 1947	HB519	(8Q-C)
Oxford I, II	Jun 1946 – Feb 1949		
Harvard IIB	Dec 1946 – Feb 1949	KF155	
Beaufighter TT.10	Dec 1948 – Feb 1949	RD780	

No. 1435 Squadron

No.1435 Squadron was unique among RAF squadrons in that its designation was not officially approved until after the unit had been operating for some time. It began operations as a squadron on 2 August 1942, at Luqa, Malta, with Spitfires and pilots transferred mainly from No.603 Squadron. The number 1435 had been previously used by No.1435 Flight, a night fighter unit also based at Malta, which had been recently disbanded and when a new Spitfire unit was formed it adopted this number. As the new unit was considerably larger than a flight, it became known as 1435 Squadron and this designation was later approved by the Air Ministry.

Operations had begun on 23 July 1942, as a flight and until the end of the year it was engaged in fighter defence duties. In January 1943, it became a fighter-bomber squadron and flew sweeps over Sicily until the Allied landings. In

October 1943, it moved to Italy where it formed part of the Balkan Air Force. Ground attack missions over Albania and Yugoslavia and local air defence occupied the squadron during its stay in southern Italy and in February 1945, it moved north to keep in range of the retreating German forces as they evacuated the Balkans. A detachment was based on the Yugoslav island of Vis in the Adriatic from September 1944 until April 1945, when the squadron was withdrawn from operations. It disbanded on 9 May 1945.

Squadron bases

		Brindisi	3 Jun 1944
Luqa	2 Aug 1942	Grottaglie	2 Jul 1944
Grottaglie	27 Oct 1943	Falconara	13 Feb 1945
Brindisi	9 Nov 1943	Gragnano Camp	26 Apr 1945
Grottaglie	30 May 1944		to 9 May 1945

Aircraft Equipment	Period of service	Representative Serial	
Spitfire VB, VC	Aug 1942 – Nov 1943	BS161	(V-U)
Spitfire VC	May 1944 – Sep 1944	EP332	(V-A)
Spitfire IX	Mar 1943 – Apr 1945	JK531	(V-T)

Equipment Index

AIRACOBRA, Bell
601
ALBACORE, Fairey
119
ALBATROSS, de Havilland
271
ALBEMARLE,
Armstrong-Whitworth
295, 296, 297, 511, 570
ALDERSHOT, Avro
99
ANDOVER, Avro
99
ANDOVER C.1,
Hawker-Siddeley
21, 32, 46, 52, 84
ANSON I, Avro
7, 24, 35, 44, 48, 51, 52,
58, 61, 63, 75, 76, 97,
104, 106, 108, 109, 116,
144, 148, 173, 192, 206,
207, 215, 217, 220, 224,
233, 251, 267, 269, 275,
276, 278, 280, 281, 282,
320, 321, 353, 500, 502,
510, 516, 544, 567, 608,
612
ANSON X, XII, Avro
31, 116, 147, 167, 353
ANSON C.19, Avro
31, 58, 116, 527
ARGOSY,
Armstrong-Whitworth
70, 105, 114, 115, 215,
267
ARGUS, Fairchild
173
ARMSTRONG-WHITWORTH
F.K.3
47, 53
ARMSTRONG-WHITWORTH
F.K.8
2, 10, 17, 35, 47, 50, 55,
82, 98, 142, 150
ATLAS, Armstrong-Whitworth
2, 4, 13, 16, 26, 208
AUDAX, Hawker
2, 4, 5, 13, 16, 20, 24, 26,
28, 52, 61, 63, 77, 105,
114, 144, 146, 148, 173,
208, 211, 226, 237, 267,
615
AUSTER, Taylorcraft
651 to 666 inclusive
AVRO 500
3, 4, 5
AVRO 504, 504A, 504B
1, 3, 5, 9, 12, 19, 23, 24,
25, 29, 53, 54, 55, 57, 62,
64, 65, 66, 67
AVRO 504J, 504K
33, 36, 43, 51, 74, 75, 77,
87, 89, 90, 92, 98, 155,
186, 187, 188, 189, 190,
198, 601
AVRO 504N
501, 601
BABY, Sopwith
219, 229, 246, 248, 249,
270
BALLIOL, Boulton-Paul
288
BALTIMORE, Martin
13, 52, 55, 69, 162, 203,
223, 249, 500
BARRACUDA, Fairey
567, 618, 667, 679, 691

BASSETT, Beagle
26, 32, 207
BATTLE, Fairey
12, 15, 35, 40, 52, 63, 88,
98, 103, 105, 106, 141,
142, 150, 185, 207, 218,
226, 234, 235, 242, 245,
253, 266, 300, 301, 304,
305, 616
B.E.1, Royal Aircraft Factory
2
B.E.2, Royal Aircraft Factory
2, 3, 6
B.E.2a, Royal Aircraft Factory
2, 3, 4, 5, 6, 9, 16, 30
B.E.2b, Royal Aircraft Factory
2, 6, 9, 16, 29, 66, 105
B.E.2c, Royal Aircraft Factory
2, 4, 5, 6, 7, 8, 9, 10, 12,
13, 14, 15, 16, 17, 19, 21,
23, 24, 25, 26, 29, 30, 31,
33, 34, 36, 37, 38, 39, 43,
46, 47, 49, 50, 51, 52, 54,
55, 57, 58, 62, 63, 66, 67,
75, 76, 77, 78, 96, 98, 114,
142, 189, 190, 191, 273
B.E.2d, Royal Aircraft Factory
2, 6, 7, 9, 10, 12, 13, 14,
15, 16, 33, 37, 42, 47, 50,
51, 62, 63, 66, 75, 100,
105, 110, 142
B.E.2e, Royal Aircraft Factory
2, 5, 6, 7, 8, 9, 10, 12, 13,
14, 15, 16, 21, 26, 30, 31,
34, 36, 38, 39, 42, 46, 50,
51, 52, 53, 55, 58, 62, 67,
75, 76, 77, 78, 91, 98, 99,
110, 113, 114, 141, 142,
144, 187, 190, 269
B.E.2f, 2g, Royal Aircraft
Factory
10
B.E.3, Royal Aircraft Factory
3
B.E.4, Royal Aircraft Factory
3
B.E.8, 8a, Royal Aircaft
Factory
1, 2, 3, 5, 6, 9
B.E.12, 12a, 12b,
Royal Aircraft Factory
10, 14, 17, 19, 21, 36, 38,
39, 47, 48, 50, 51, 66, 67,
75, 76, 77, 78, 89, 141,
142, 144
BEAUFIGHTER I, Bristol
25, 29, 46, 68, 69, 89, 141,
143, 153, 173, 176, 219,
235, 236, 248, 252, 256,
272, 285, 577, 600, 603,
604, 680
BEAUFIGHTER II, Bristol
96, 125, 143, 255, 307,
515, 618
BEAUFIGHTER VI, Bristol
27, 29, 46, 68, 89, 96, 108,
125, 141, 144, 153, 176,
177, 219, 227, 235, 236,
248, 252, 254, 255, 256,
272, 287, 288, 307, 600,
603, 604, 684
BEAUFIGHTER X, XI, Bristol
5, 17, 20, 22, 27, 34, 39,
42, 45, 46, 47, 84, 143,
144, 177, 211, 217, 235,
236, 248, 252, 254, 272,
287, 288, 603, 684, 695

BEAUFORT, Bristol
22, 39, 42, 47, 48, 86, 217
BELFAST, Short
53
BELVEDERE, Bristol
26, 66, 72
BEVERLEY, Blackburn
30, 34, 47, 53, 84
BLENHEIM I, Bristol
8, 11, 18, 20, 21, 23, 25,
27, 29, 30, 34, 39, 44, 45,
55, 57, 60, 61, 62, 64, 68,
82, 84, 90, 92, 101, 104,
107, 108, 110, 113, 114,
139, 141, 144, 145, 203,
211, 219, 222, 223, 229,
234, 235, 236, 242, 245,
248, 252, 254, 285, 600,
601, 604
BLENHEIM IV, Bristol
6, 8,, 11, 13, 14, 15, 18,
21, 25, 34, 35, 39, 40, 45,
52, 53, 55, 57, 59, 60, 82,
84, 86, 88, 90, 101, 104,
105, 107, 108, 110, 113,
114, 139, 140, 143, 162,
173, 203, 211, 212, 218,
226, 235, 236, 244, 248,
252, 254, 272, 287, 288,
289, 500, 516, 521, 526,
527, 528, 600, 608, 614
BLENHEIM V, Bristol
8, 13, 18, 34, 42, 113,
114, 139, 162, 244, 614
BLERIOT XI
2, 3, 5, 6, 9, 10, 16, 23, 24
BLOODHOUND, Bristol
25, 41, 62, 85, 94, 112,
141, 222, 242, 247, 257,
263, 264, 266
BOMBAY, Bristol
117, 216, 271
BOSTON I, III, Douglas
18, 23, 88, 107, 114, 173,
223, 226, 342, 530, 531,
532, 533, 534, 537, 538,
539, 605
BOSTON IV, Douglas
13, 18, 55, 88, 114, 342
BOSTON V, Douglas
13, 18, 55, 114
BOTHA, Blackburn
608
BOXKITE, Bristol
3
BREGUET
2, 4
BRIGAND, Bristol
8, 45, 84
BRISTOL F.2B
2, 4, 5, 6, 8, 9, 11, 12, 13,
14, 16, 20, 22, 24, 28, 31,
33, 34, 35, 36, 39, 48, 62,
67, 75, 76, 88, 100, 105,
111, 114, 138, 139, 140,
141, 186, 208
BRISTOL M.1B, M.1C
14, 47, 72, 111, 150
BRISTOL SCOUT
1, 2, 3, 4, 5, 6, 7, 9, 10, 11,
12, 14, 15, 16, 17, 24, 30,
36, 47, 63, 65, 111
BRISTOL TB.75
4
BRITANNIA, Bristol
99, 511

BUCCANEER,
Hawker-Siddeley
12, 15, 16, 208, 216
BUFFALO, Brewster
60, 67, 71, 146, 243
BULLDOG, Bristol
3, 17, 19, 23, 24, 29, 32,
41, 54, 56, 111
CAMEL, Sopwith
3, 17, 28, 37, 43, 44, 46,
47, 50, 51, 54, 61, 65, 66,
70, 71, 73, 75, 78, 80, 81,
89, 94, 112, 139, 143, 150,
151, 152, 155, 187, 188,
189, 198, 201, 203, 204,
208, 209, 210, 213, 219,
220, 222, 225, 230, 233,
273
CANBERRA B.2,
English Electric
6, 9, 10, 12, 15, 18, 21, 27,
32, 35, 40, 44, 45, 50, 51,
57, 59, 61, 73, 76, 85, 90,
97, 98, 100, 101, 102, 103,
104, 109, 115, 139, 149,
151, 192, 199, 207, 245,
249, 360, 361, 527, 542,
617
CANBERRA PR.3,
English Electric
17, 39, 58, 69, 82, 540
CANBERRA T.4,
English Electric
85, 360/361
CANBERRA B.6, B(I).6,
English Electric
6, 9, 12, 21, 76, 100, 101,
109, 139, 213, 249,
360/361, 542, 617
CANBERRA PR.7,
English Electric
13, 17, 31, 39, 58, 80, 81,
82, 540, 542
CANBERRA B(I).8,
English Electric
3, 14, 16, 59, 88
CANBERRA PR.9,
English Electric
13, 39, 58
CANBERRA T.11,
English Electric
85
CANBERRA B.15, E.15,
English Electric
32, 45, 73, 100, 249
CANBERRA B.16,
English Electric
6
CANBERRA T.17,
English Electric
360
CANBERRA TT.18,
English Electric
7
CANBERRA T.19,
English Electric
85, 100
CAPRONI CA.148
117
CATALINA I, Consolidated
119, 190, 191, 202, 205,
209, 210, 212, 240, 259,
262, 265, 270, 333, 628
CATALINA II, Consolidated
209, 210, 240, 321
CATALINA IIIA, Consolidated
119, 321, 330

CATALINA IV, IVa, IVb,
Consolidated
190, 191, 202, 205, 210,
212, 240, 262, 333, 357,
628
CATALINA V, Consolidated
321
CAUDRON G-III
1, 4, 5, 19, 23, 25, 29
CHIPMUNK, de Havilland
114
CIERVA C-40
529
CLEVELAND, Curtiss
24
CLOUD, Saunders-Roe
48
CODY
4
COMET C.2, de Havilland
51, 216
COMET C.4, de Havilland
216
CORONADO, Consolidated
231
CUCKOO, Sopwith
185, 186, 210
CURTISS JN-4
24, 25
CYGNET, General Aircraft
510
DAKOTA I, II, & DC.3,
Douglas
24, 31, 117, 216, 267, 271,
253, 511, 512
DAKOTA III, Douglas
10, 24, 31, 46, 48, 52, 62,
77, 96, 110, 117, 147, 187,
194, 215, 216, 231, 233,
238, 267, 271, 353, 511,
512, 525, 575
DAKOTA IV, Douglas
10, 18, 21, 24, 27, 30, 31,
46, 48, 52, 53, 62, 70, 76,
77, 78, 96, 110, 113, 114,
147, 187, 204, 215, 231,
238, 243, 267, 271, 357,
525, 620
DEFIANT, Boulton-Paul
85, 96, 125, 141, 151, 153,
255, 256, 264, 275, 276,
277, 281, 285, 286, 287,
288, 289, 307, 515, 667,
691
D.H.1A, Airco
14
D.H.2, Airco
5, 14, 17, 24, 29, 32, 41,
47, 111
D.H.4, Airco
18, 25, 27, 30, 49, 55, 57,
63, 97, 98, 110, 117, 122,
124, 125, 202, 205, 211,
212, 217, 223, 224, 226,
227, 273
D.H.5, Airco
24, 32, 41, 64, 65, 68
D.H.6, Airco
67, 99, 105, 110, 144, 187,
190, 236, 244, 250, 251,
252, 253, 254, 255, 256,
258, 260, 272, 274
D.H.9, Airco
17, 27, 47, 49, 55, 98, 99,
103, 104, 105, 107, 108,
109, 110, 117, 119, 120,
121, 122, 123, 124, 125,
126, 127, 128, 129, 130,
132, 137, 142, 144, 186,
202, 206, 211, 212, 218,
219, 221, 223, 224, 226,
227, 233, 250, 254, 269,
273

D.H.9A, Airco
3, 8, 11, 12, 14, 18, 25,
27, 30, 35, 39, 45, 47, 55,
57, 60, 84, 99, 100, 101,
110, 120, 205, 207, 212,
221, 273, 501, 600, 601,
602, 603, 604, 605
D.H.10, 10A AMIENS,
de Havilland
60, 97, 104, 216
D.H.86b, de Havilland
24, 117, 216
DEMON, Hawker
6, 23, 25, 29, 41, 64, 65,
74, 208, 600, 601, 604,
607, 608
DEPERDUSSIN
3
DEVON, de Havilland
31, 207
DOLPHIN, Sopwith
19, 23, 79, 81, 87, 90, 91,
123, 141
DOMINIE & D.H.89A,
de Havilland
24, 173, 271, 526, 527
DOUGLAS DC.2K
31, 117
DRAGON, de Havilland
24
DRAGONFLY, Westland
194
ENSIGN,
Armstrong-Whitworth
24
ENVOY, Airspeed
24
EXPEDITOR, Beech
52, 353
F.2A, Felixstowe
228, 230, 231, 232, 240,
247, 257, 259, 261, 267
F.3, Felixstowe
232, 234, 238, 263, 265,
267, 270, 271
F.5, Felixstowe
230, 231
FAIREY IIIB, IIIC
219, 229, 230, 267
FAIREY IIID
202
FAIREY IIIF
8, 14, 24, 35, 45, 47, 202,
203, 207
FARMAN F.20 (Henry Farman)
2, 5, 6, 10, 24, 26, 30, 31,
32, 64
FARMAN S.7, S.11
(Maurice Farman)
2, 3, 4, 9, 14, 16, 19, 23,
24, 25, 29, 30, 65
FAWN, Fairey
11, 12, 100, 503, 602
F.E.2b, Royal Aircraft Factory
6, 11, 12, 16, 18, 20, 23,
25, 28, 33, 36, 38, 51, 58,
64, 83, 90,, 100, 101,
102, 116, 118, 131, 133,
148, 149, 166, 191, 192
199, 200, 246
F.E.2d, Royal Aircraft Factory
20, 25, 33, 51, 57, 83, 101,
102, 148, 149, 192
F.E.8, Royal Aircraft Factory
5, 29, 40, 41
FLAMINGO, de Havilland
24
FOKKER F.22
24
FOKKER T-VIIIW
320
FORD 5-AT-D
271

FORTRESS I, Boeing
90, 220
FORTRESS II, Boeing
59, 206, 214, 220, 223,
251, 519, 521
FORTRESS III, Boeing
214, 220, 223, 521
FOX, Fairey
12
FULMAR, Fairey
273
FURY I, Hawker
1, 25, 43
FURY II, Hawker
25, 41, 73, 87
GAMECOCK, Gloster
3, 17, 23, 32, 43
GAUNTLET, Gloster
6, 17, 19, 32, 33, 46, 54,
56, 65, 66, 74, 79, 80, 111,
112, 151, 213, 234, 601,
602, 615, 616
GLADIATOR, Gloster
3, 6, 14, 25, 33, 54, 56,
65, 72, 73, 80, 85, 87, 94,
112, 117, 123, 127, 141,
152, 237, 247, 261, 263,
267, 274, 520, 521, 603,
605, 607, 615
GORDON, Fairey
6, 14, 29, 35, 40, 45, 47,
207, 223
GRAHAM-WHITE XV
65
GREBE, GLOSTER
19, 25, 29, 32, 56, 111
GULL, Percival
173, 267
HADRIAN, Waco
668, 669, 670, 671, 672,
673
HALIFAX I, Handley Page
35, 76, 138
HALIFAX II, Handley Page
10, 35, 51, 58, 76, 77, 78,
102, 103, 138, 148, 158,
178, 192, 301, 502, 614,
624
HALIFAX III, Handley Page
10, 35, 51, 48, 76, 77, 78,
96, 102, 158, 171, 187,
190, 192, 199, 246, 296,
297, 298, 346, 347, 502,
517, 518, 519, 520, 521,
578, 640, 644
HALIFAX IV, Handley Page
76, 77, 148, 161, 192, 295,
296, 297, 298, 301, 346,
347, 517, 518, 520, 624,
644
HALIFAX VI, Handley Page
76, 77, 78, 102, 158, 202,
224, 346, 347, 644
HALIFAX VII, Handley Page
47, 190, 295, 296, 297,
298, 620, 644
HALIFAX VIII, Handley Page
113, 301, 304
HALIFAX IX, Handley Page
47, 113, 202, 295, 297, 620
HAMPDEN, Handley Page
7, 44, 49, 50, 61, 76, 83,
97, 106, 144, 185, 207,
517, 519, 521
HANDLEY PAGE O/100
207, 214, 215
HANDLEY PAGE O/400
58, 70, 97, 100, 115, 134,
144, 207, 214, 215, 216
HANDLEY PAGE V/1500
166, 167, 274
HANDLEY PAGE H.P.42
271

HARDY, Hawker
6, 30, 237
HARRIER GR.1, 1A,
Hawker-Siddeley
1, 3, 4, 20
HARROW, Handley Page
37, 75, 93, 115, 214, 215,
271
HART, Hawker
5, 6, 11, 12, 15, 17, 18, 23,
24, 27, 33, 39, 40, 45, 57,
142, 173, 237, 296, 500,
501, 503, 510, 600, 601,
602, 603, 604, 605, 609,
610, 611
HARVARD, North American
1, 20, 41, 691, 695
HASTINGS, Handley Page
24, 36, 47, 48, 53, 70, 97,
99, 114, 151, 202, 242,
297, 511
HAVOC, Douglas
23, 25, 85, 93, 161, 530,
531, 532, 533, 534, 535,
536, 537, 538, 539, 605
HAWKER-SIDDELEY HS.125
32
HECTOR, Hawker
2, 4, 13, 26, 53, 59, 296,
602, 612, 613, 614, 615
HENDON, Fairey
38
HENLEY, Hawker
587, 595, 631, 639, 695
HERCULES, Lockheed
24, 30, 36, 47, 48, 70
HEREFORD, Handley Page
185
HERON, de Havilland
60
HEYFORD, Handley Page
7, 9, 10, 38, 58, 78, 97, 99,
102, 148, 149, 166
HINAIDI, Handley Page
10, 99, 503
HIND, Hawker
12, 15, 18, 21, 24, 34, 40,
44, 49, 50, 52, 57, 62, 63,
82, 83, 88, 90, 98, 103,
104, 106, 107, 108, 110,
113, 114, 139, 142, 185,
211, 218, 267, 500, 501,
502, 503, 504, 602, 603,
605, 609, 610, 611, 613,
614, 616
HORNET, de Havilland
19, 33, 41, 45, 64, 65, 80
HORNET MOTH, de Havilland
24, 116, 510, 526, 527,
528, 529
HORSA, Airspeed
670
HORSLEY, Hawker
11, 33, 36. 100. 504
HOVERFLY, Sikorsky
529, 657
HUDSON I, Lockheed
24, 206, 220, 224, 233,
269, 271, 285, 320, 517
HUDSON II, Lockheed
206, 320
HUDSON III, IIIA, Lockheed
48, 53, 59, 62, 139, 161,
163, 203, 206, 216, 217,
220, 233, 251, 267, 269,
279, 287, 288, 289, 320,
353, 500, 517, 519, 520,
521, 608
HUDSON V, Lockheed
48, 53, 161, 200, 224, 269,
279, 500, 521, 608
HUDSON VI, Lockheed
8, 48, 62, 117, 163, 194,

216, 217, 220, 231, 233,
267, 279, 320, 353, 357,
608
HUNTER F.1, Hawker
43, 54, 222, 247
HUNTER F.2, Hawker
257, 263
HUNTER F.4, Hawker
3, 4, 14, 20, 26, 43, 54, 66,
67, 71, 74, 92, 93, 98, 111,
112, 118, 130, 222, 234,
245, 247
HUNTER F.5, Hawker
1, 34, 41, 56, 208, 257,
263
HUNTER F.6, Hawker
1, 4, 19, 20, 26, 43, 54,
56, 63, 65, 66, 74, 92, 93,
111, 208, 247, 263
HUNTER FGA.9, Hawker
1, 8, 20, 28, 43, 45, 54, 58,
208
HUNTER FR.10, Hawker
2, 4, 8, 79
HURRICANE I, X, Hawker
1, 3, 6, 17, 29, 30, 32, 33,
43, 46, 56, 71, 79, 80, 85,
87, 94, 95, 96, 98, 111,
116, 121, 123, 126, 127,
128, 145, 151, 173, 182,
185, 193, 195, 208, 213,
225, 229, 232, 237, 238,
239, 242, 245, 247, 249,
250, 253, 255, 256, 258,
260, 261, 263, 273, 274,
286, 288, 289, 302, 303,
306, 308, 310, 312, 315,
316, 317, 318, 331, 335,
501, 504, 527, 534, 539,
605, 607, 610, 615, 680,
691
HURRICANE IIA, IIB, Hawker
1, 3, 17, 20, 28, 30, 32, 33,
43, 46, 56, 67, 69, 71, 73,
74, 79, 80, 81, 94, 111,
116, 121, 126, 127, 128,
133, 134, 135, 136, 146,
151, 174, 175, 185, 208,
213, 232, 238, 242, 245,
247, 249, 250, 253, 256,
257, 258, 261, 273, 274,
287, 302, 303, 306, 310,
312, 316, 317, 318, 331,
335, 504, 516, 527, 534,
601, 605, 607, 615, 680,
681
HURRICANE IIC, Hawker
1, 3, 5, 6, 11, 17, 28, 30,
32, 33, 34, 42, 43, 46, 60,
63, 73, 79, 80, 87, 94, 96,
113, 123, 127, 134, 135,
136, 146, 176, 193, 225,
229, 237, 238, 239, 241,
247, 253, 257, 258, 261,
273, 279, 284, 285, 286,
288, 289, 291, 309, 335,
336, 351, 352, 516, 518,
520, 521, 530, 531, 532,
533, 534, 535, 536, 537,
538, 539, 577, 587, 595,
598, 607, 615, 631, 667,
679, 691, 695
HURRICANE IID, Hawker
5, 6, 20, 164, 184, 289
HURRICANE IV, Hawker
6, 20, 42, 63, 137, 164,
184, 186, 279, 286, 287,
309, 351, 567, 577, 587,
595, 598, 639, 650, 679
HYDERABAD, Handley Page
10, 99, 502, 503
IRIS, Blackburn
209

JAGUAR GR.1, British Aero-
space
2, 6, 14, 17, 20, 31, 41, 54
JAVELIN FAW.1, Gloster
46, 87
JAVELIN FAW.2, Gloster
46, 85, 89
JAVELIN FAW.4, Gloster
3, 11, 41, 72, 87, 151
JAVELIN FAW.5, Gloster
5, 11, 41, 72, 87, 151
JAVELIN FAW.6, Gloster
29, 46, 85, 89
JAVELIN FAW.7, Gloster
23, 25, 33, 64
JAVELIN FAW.8, Gloster
41, 85
JAVELIN FAW.9, Gloster
5, 11, 23, 25, 29, 33, 60,
64
JUNKERS Ju 52/3m
173
KANGAROO, Blackburn
246
KITTYHAWK I, Curtiss
94, 112, 250, 260
KITTYHAWK II, Curtiss
250, 260
KITTYHAWK III, Curtiss
112, 250, 260
KITTYHAWK IV, Curtiss
112, 250
LANCASTER I, III, Avro
7, 9, 12, 15, 18, 35, 37,
38, 44, 50, 57, 61, 70, 75,
82, 83, 90, 97, 100, 101,
103, 106, 109, 115, 120,
138, 148, 149, 150, 153,
156, 160, 166, 170, 178,
179, 186, 189, 195, 203,
207, 210, 214, 218, 224,
227, 279, 300, 514, 541,
550, 576, 582, 617, 619,
621, 622, 625, 626, 630,
635, 683
LANCASTER II, Avro
61, 115, 514
LANCASTER VI, Avro
635
LANCASTER VII, Avro
9, 37, 40, 49, 104, 617
LANCASTRIAN, Avro
24, 231, 232
LERWICK, Saunders-Roe
209
LIBERATOR I, Consolidated
120, 160, 511
LIBERATOR II, Consolidated
108, 120, 148, 159, 178,
224, 231, 246, 511
LIBERATOR III, Consolidated
59, 86, 120, 148, 159, 160,
178, 232, 246, 354, 355,
357
LIBERATOR V, Consolidated
53, 59, 86, 120, 160, 200,
224, 311, 354, 547
LIBERATOR VI, Consolidated
8, 37, 40, 53, 70, 99, 102,
104, 148, 159, 160, 178,
200, 203, 206, 215, 220,
223, 232, 246, 292, 301,
311, 321, 354, 355, 356,
357, 358, 547
LIBERATOR VII, Consol-
idated
232, 246, 511
LIBERATOR VIII, Consol-
idated
53, 59, 86, 102, 120, 159,
160, 203, 206, 214, 215,
220, 228, 246, 355, 547,
614

LIBERATOR IX, Consol-
idated
231
LIGHTNING F.1, 1A, English
Electric
56, 74, 111
LIGHTNING F.2, 2A. English
Electric
19, 92
LIGHTNING F.3, English
Electric
23, 29, 56, 74, 111
LIGHTNING F.6, English
Electric
5, 11, 23, 56, 74
LINCOLN, Avro
7, 9, 12, 15, 35, 44, 49, 50,
57, 58, 61, 83, 90, 97, 100,
101, 115, 116, 138, 148,
149, 151, 192, 199, 207,
214, 527, 617
LOCKHEED 10A, 12A
24, 173, 267
LOCKHEED 14
267
LODESTAR, Lockheed
117, 173, 267
LONDON, Saunders-Roe
201, 202, 204, 209, 210,
228, 240
LYSANDER I, Westland
2, 4, 6, 13, 16, 26, 208,
237, 267, 287, 598, 613,
614, 695
LYSANDER II, Westland
2, 4, 6, 13, 16, 20, 26, 28,
173, 208, 225, 231, 237,
239, 241, 267, 268, 288,
516, 614, 695
LYSANDER III, IIIA, Westland
4, 13, 16, 116, 138, 148,
161, 225, 231, 239, 241,
275, 276, 277, 278, 285,
287, 288, 289, 309, 357,
516, 613, 614
MAGISTER, Miles
24, 173, 267
MANCHESTER, Avro
49, 50, 61, 83, 97, 106, 207
MARAUDER, Martin
14, 39
MARINER, Martin
524
MARTINET, Miles
5, 20, 269, 285, 286, 287,
289, 290, 291, 520, 567,
587, 595, 598, 631, 650,
679, 691, 695
MARTINSYDE G-100/102
25, 27, 30, 51, 63, 67, 72,
110, 142
MARTINSYDE S.1
1, 2, 4, 6, 9, 10, 14, 16, 23,
24, 30, 67, 144
MARYLAND, Martin
8, 39, 69, 203, 223, 544
MASTER, Miles
286, 287
MENTOR, Miles
24
METEOR F.1, Gloster
616
METEOR F.3, Gloster
1, 56, 63, 66, 74, 91, 92,
124, 222, 234, 245, 257,
263, 266, 500, 504, 616
METEOR F.4, Gloster
1, 19, 41, 43, 56, 63, 65,
66, 74, 91, 92, 222, 245,
257, 263, 266, 500, 504,
600, 610, 611, 615, 616
METEOR F.8, Gloster
1, 19, 34, 41, 43, 54, 56,

63, 64, 65, 66, 72, 74, 85,
92, 111, 222, 245, 247,
257, 263, 500, 504, 600,
601, 604, 609, 610, 611,
615, 616
METEOR FR.9, Gloster
2, 8, 79, 208, 541
METEOR PR.10, Gloster
2, 13, 81
METEOR NF.11, Gloster
5, 11, 29, 68, 85, 87, 96,
125, 141, 151, 256, 264,
527
METEOR NF.12, Gloster
25, 29, 46, 64, 72, 85, 152,
153, 264
METEOR NF.13, Gloster
39, 219
METEOR NF.14
25, 33, 46, 60, 64, 72, 85,
152, 153, 264
MITCHELL, North American
98, 180, 226, 305, 320,
342, 681, 684
MOHAWK, Curtiss
5, 146, 155, 510
MORANE N
4, 60
MORANE BB
1, 3, 60
MORANE LA PARASOL
1, 3, 60
MOSQUITO I, de Havilland
69
MOSQUITO II, de Havilland
23, 25, 27, 85, 141, 143,
151, 157, 169, 239, 264,
307, 333, 515, 605, 681,
684
MOSQUITO III, de Havilland
169, 504
MOSQUITO IV, de Havilland
105, 109, 139, 192, 521,
540, 543, 544, 618, 627,
683, 692
MOSQUITO VI, de Havilland
4, 8, 11, 14, 18, 21, 22, 23,
25, 27, 29, 36, 39, 45, 47,
69, 82, 84, 89, 107, 110,
114, 141, 143, 151, 157,
162, 169, 211, 235, 239,
248, 256, 264, 268, 305,
307, 333, 515, 540, 605,
618, 681, 684
MOSQUITO VIII, de Havilland
540
MOSQUITO IX, de Havilland
105, 109, 139, 140, 256,
540, 544, 681, 684
MOSQUITO XII, de Havilland
29, 46, 85, 96, 108, 151,
256, 307, 604
MOSQUITO XIII, de Havilland
29, 85, 96, 151, 256, 264,
604
MOSQUITO XV, de Havilland
85
MOSQUITO XVI, de Havilland
4, 14, 69, 81, 98, 105, 109,
128, 139, 140, 163, 176,
180, 192, 540, 544, 571,
608, 618, 627, 680, 684,
692
MOSQUITO XVII, de Havil-
land
25, 68, 85, 125, 219
MOSQUITO XVIII, de Havil-
land
248, 254
MOSQUITO XIX, de Havilland
68, 89, 157, 169, 176, 255,
256, 600

MOSQUITO XX, de Havilland
128, 139, 162, 608, 627
MOSQUITO B.25, de Havilland
128, 139, 142, 162, 163,
502, 608, 627
MOSQUITO FB.26, de Havilland
55, 249
MOSQUITO NF.30, de Havilland
23, 25, 29, 39, 68, 85, 125,
141, 151, 219, 239, 255,
264, 307, 500, 502, 504,
605, 608, 609, 616
MOSQUITO PR.32, de Havilland
540, 544
MOSQUITO PR.34, de Havilland
13, 58, 81, 540, 544, 680,
684
MOSQUITO B.35, de Havilland
14, 58, 98, 109, 139
MOSQUITO NF.36, de Havilland
23, 25, 29, 39, 85, 141,
199, 219, 264
MOTH, de Havilland
24, 173, 510
MUSTANG I, IA, North
American
2, 4, 16, 26, 63, 168, 169,
170, 171, 225, 231, 239,
241, 268, 285, 309, 516,
613
MUSTANG II, North American
2, 225, 268
MUSTANG III, North American
19, 64, 65, 93, 112, 118,
122, 126, 129, 165, 213,
234, 249, 250, 260, 306,
309, 315, 316, 541
MUSTANG IV, North American
19, 64, 65, 112, 118, 122,
126, 154, 213, 234, 249,
250, 260, 303, 611
NEPTUNE, Lockheed
36, 203, 210, 217
NIEUPORT 13
11
NIEUPORT 12 & 14
45, 46, 65
NIEUPORT 17 & 27
1, 14, 17, 29, 40, 60, 67,
111, 150
NIGHTHAWK, Miles
24
NIGHTHAWK, Nieuport
1
NIGHTJAR, Nieuport
203
NIMROD, Hawker-Siddeley
42, 51, 120, 201, 203, 206
NORTHROP N3PB
330
OVERSTRAND, Boulton-Paul
101, 144
OXFORD, Airspeed
1, 5, 17, 20, 24, 41, 116,
173, 192, 285, 286, 287,
288, 289, 290, 510, 526,
527, 529, 567, 577, 587,
595, 598, 667, 691, 695
PANTHER, Parnall
205
PEMBROKE, Percival
21, 60, 81, 152, 207, 267
PERCIVAL Q.6 PETREL
24, 173, 267, 510
PERTH, Blackburn
209

PHANTOM FG.1, McDonnell-
Douglas
43, 111
PHANTOM FGR.2, McDonnell-
Douglas
2, 6, 14, 17, 19, 23, 29, 31,
41, 54, 92, 111
PIONEER, Scottish Aviation
20, 78, 209, 215, 230, 267
PROCTOR, Percival
24, 31, 117, 173, 267, 510
PUMA, Westland
33, 230
PUP, Sopwith
36, 46, 50, 54, 61, 64, 65,
66, 87, 89, 92, 112, 141,
187, 188, 189
PUSS MOTH, de Havilland
510
RANGOON, Short
203, 210
R.E.1, Royal Aircraft Factory
2
R.E.5, Royal Aircraft Factory
2, 6, 7, 9, 12, 16
R.E.7, Royal Aircraft Factory
6, 9, 12, 19, 21, 37, 38,
49, 62
R.E.8, Royal Aircraft Factory
4, 5, 6, 7, 8, 9, 12, 13, 14,
15, 16, 21, 30, 34, 37, 42,
50, 52, 53, 59, 63, 67, 69,
89, 91, 105, 106, 110, 113,
117, 142, 144, 208
RELIANT, Stinson
510
ROC, Blackburn
24, 241
ROTA, Avro
81, 529
SABRE, North American
3, 4, 20, 26, 66, 67, 71, 92,
93, 112, 130, 234
SALAMANDER, Sopwith
86, 96, 157
SARO A.7
209
SAVOIA-MARCHETTI S.73
24, 271
SAVOIA-MARCHETTI S.79K
117
SCAPA, Supermarine
202, 204, 228, 240
SCION, Short
173
S.E.2, Royal Aircraft Factory
3, 5
S.E.5, Royal Aircraft Factory
56, 60
S.E.5A, Royal Aircraft Factory
1, 17, 24, 29, 30, 32, 40,
41, 47, 50, 56, 60, 61, 64,
68, 72, 74, 81, 84, 85, 87,
92, 93, 94, 111, 143, 145,
150
SEAL, Fairey
273
SEA KING HAR.3, Westland
202
SEA OTTER, Supermarine
277, 278, 279, 281, 282,
292
SENTINEL, Stinson
194
SHACKLETON MR.1, Avro
42, 120, 203, 204, 205,
206, 220, 224, 240, 269
SHACKLETON MR.2, AEW.2,
Avro
8, 27, 38, 42, 120, 203,
204, 205, 206, 210, 220,
224, 228, 269,

SHACKLETON MR.3, Avro
42, 120, 201, 203, 206, 220
SHORT 184
202, 219, 229, 235, 237,
238, 239, 240, 241, 242,
243, 245, 246, 248, 249,
253, 263, 264, 265, 266,
268, 269, 270, 271
SHORT 320
253, 263, 266, 268
SHORT R.24/31
209
SHORT S.23/M
119
SHORT S.26/M
119
SIDESTRAND, Boulton-Paul
101
SIMOUN, Caudron
267
SINGAPORE III, Short
203, 205, 209, 210, 228,
230, 240
SISKIN, Armstrong-Whitworth
1, 17, 19, 25, 29, 32, 41,
43, 54, 56, 111
SKYMASTER, Douglas
231, 232, 246
SNIPE, Sopwith
1, 3, 17, 19, 23, 25, 29, 32,
37, 41, 43, 45, 56, 70, 78,
80, 81, 111, 143, 201, 208
SOPWITH 1½-STRUTTER
37, 43, 44, 45, 70, 78
SOUTHAMPTON, Supermarine
201, 203, 204, 205, 209,
210
SPAD VII
17, 19, 23, 30, 63, 72, 92
SPAD XIII
19, 23
SPITFIRE I, Supermarine
19, 41, 54, 64, 65, 66, 72,
74, 92, 111, 122, 123,
124, 129, 131, 132, 152,
212, 222, 234, 238, 249,
257, 266, 303, 308, 313,
501, 510, 602, 603, 609,
610, 611, 616
SPITFIRE II, Supermarine
19, 41, 54, 64, 65, 66, 71,
72, 74, 91, 111, 118, 121,
122, 123, 124, 129, 130,
131, 132, 145, 152, 154,
222, 234, 266, 276, 277,
303, 306, 308, 310, 312,
313, 315, 331, 340, 350,
501, 504, 602, 603, 609,
610, 611, 616
SPITFIRE IV, Supermarine
69, 140, 541, 542, 543,
544, 680, 681, 682, 683
SPITFIRE V, Supermarine
19, 26, 32, 33, 41, 43, 54,
63, 64, 65, 66, 71, 72, 73,
74, 80, 81, 87, 91, 92, 93,
94, 111, 118, 121, 122,
123, 124, 126, 127, 129,
130, 131, 132, 133, 136,
145, 152, 154, 164, 165,
167, 184, 185, 186, 208,
213, 222, 225, 229, 232,
234, 237, 238, 241, 242,
243, 249, 253, 257, 266,
269, 274, 275, 276, 277,
278, 287, 290, 302, 303,
306, 308, 310, 312, 313,
315, 316, 317, 318, 322,
326, 327, 328, 329, 331,
332, 335, 336, 340, 341,
345, 349, 350, 352, 501,
504, 520, 521, 527, 541,
543, 567, 577, 595, 601,

602, 603, 607, 609, 610,
611, 615, 616, 680, 695,
1435
SPITFIRE VI, Supermarine
124, 129, 234, 310, 313,
504, 519, 602, 616, 680
SPITFIRE VII, Supermarine
124, 131, 313, 519, 542,
611, 616
SPITFIRE VIII, Supermarine
17, 20, 28, 32, 43, 54, 67,
73, 81, 87, 92, 94, 131,
132, 136, 145, 152, 153,
154, 155, 185, 208, 238,
241, 253, 256, 273, 327,
328, 548, 549, 601, 607,
615
SPITFIRE IX, Supermarine
1, 6, 19, 28, 32, 33, 43, 56,
64, 65, 66, 72, 74, 80, 81,
87, 91, 92, 93, 94, 111,
118, 122, 124, 126, 127,
129, 130, 131, 132, 133,
145, 152, 153, 154, 164,
165, 183, 185, 208, 213,
222, 225, 229, 232, 234,
237, 238, 241, 242, 243,
249, 253, 256, 274, 287,
288, 302, 303, 306, 308,
310, 312, 313, 315, 316,
317, 318, 322, 326, 327,
328, 329, 331, 332, 340,
341, 345, 349, 350, 501,
504, 518, 541, 544, 595,
601, 602, 611, 1435
SPITFIRE X, Supermarine
542
SPITFIRE XI, Supermarine
2, 4, 16, 26, 140, 253, 541,
542, 543, 680, 681, 682,
683
SPITFIRE XII, Supermarine
41, 91, 595
SPITFIRE XIV, Supermarine
2, 11, 16, 17, 20, 26, 28,
41, 91, 130, 132, 136, 152,
268, 273, 322, 350, 600,
602, 607, 610, 611, 612,
613, 615
SPITFIRE XVI, Supermarine
5, 16, 17, 19, 20, 33, 34,
63, 65, 66, 74, 126, 127,
164, 229, 287, 288, 289,
302, 303, 308, 317, 322,
329, 340, 341, 345, 349,
350, 501, 567, 577, 587,
595, 601, 602, 603, 609,
612, 614, 631, 667, 691,
695
SPITFIRE XVIII, Supermarine
11, 28, 32, 60, 81, 208
SPITFIRE XIX, Supermarine
2, 16, 34, 60, 81, 82, 268,
541, 542, 681, 682, 683
SPITFIRE F.21, Supermarine
1, 41, 91, 122, 595, 600,
602, 615
SPITFIRE F.22, Supermarine
73, 502, 504, 600, 602,
603, 607, 608, 610, 611,
613, 614, 615
SPITFIRE F.24, Supermarine
80
STAMPE SV.4B
510
STIRLING I, Short
7, 15, 75, 90, 149, 214,
218, 620
STIRLING III, Short
7, 15, 75, 90, 149, 161,
171, 196, 199, 214, 218,
513, 620, 622, 623

STIRLING IV, Short
138, 148, 161, 190, 196, 242, 295, 299, 570, 620, 624

STIRLING V, Short
46, 51, 158, 196, 242

STRANRAER, Supermarine
209, 210, 228, 240

SUNDERLAND I, Short
95, 201, 202, 204, 210, 228, 230

SUNDERLAND II, Short
119, 201, 202, 204, 228, 230

SUNDERLAND III, Short
95, 119, 201, 202, 204, 228, 230, 246, 270, 330, 343

SUNDERLAND V, Short
88, 201, 204, 205, 209, 228, 230, 240, 259

SWIFT F.1, F.2, F.4, Supermarine
56

SWIFT FR.5, Supermarine
2, 4, 79

SWORDFISH, Fairey
119, 202

SYCAMORE, Bristol
32, 103, 110, 118, 194, 225, 228, 275, 284

TABLOID, Sopwith
3

TEMPEST F.2, Hawker
5, 16, 20, 26, 30, 33, 54, 152, 183, 247

TEMPEST V, Hawker
3, 16, 33, 56, 80, 174, 222, 274, 287, 349, 501

TEMPEST VI, Hawker
6, 8, 39, 213, 249

THOR, Douglas
77, 82, 97, 98, 102, 104, 106, 107, 113, 130, 142, 144, 150, 218, 220, 223, 226, 240, 254, 269

THUNDERBOLT I, Republic
5, 30, 113, 134, 135, 146, 258, 261

THUNDERBOLT II, Republic
5, 30, 34, 42, 60, 79, 81, 113, 123, 131, 134, 146, 258, 261, 615

TIGER MOTH, de Havilland
24, 27, 52, 81, 116, 510, 652, 653, 654, 656, 668, 669, 670, 671, 672, 673

TOMAHAWK, Curtiss
2, 4, 16, 26, 73, 94, 112, 168, 171, 208, 231, 239, 241, 250, 268, 349, 613

TOMTIT, Hawker
24

TUTOR, Avro
24, 612

TWIN PIONEER, Scottish Aviation
21, 78, 152, 209, 230

TYPHOON, Hawker
1, 3, 4, 56, 137, 164, 168, 174, 175, 181, 182, 183, 184, 186, 193, 195, 197, 198, 245, 247, 257, 263, 266, 268, 609

VALENTIA, Vickers
31, 70, 216

VALETTA, Vickers
30, 48, 52, 70, 78, 84, 110, 114, 115, 204, 216, 233, 622, 683

VALIANT, Vickers
7, 18, 49, 90, 138, 148, 199, 207, 214, 543

VAMPIRE F.1, de Havilland
3, 20, 54, 72, 130, 247, 501, 595, 605, 608, 631

VAMPIRE F.3, de Havilland
5, 20, 32, 54, 72, 73, 247, 601, 602, 604, 608, 614

VAMPIRE FB.5, de Havilland
3, 4, 5, 6, 11, 14, 16, 25, 26, 28, 32, 54, 60, 67, 71, 72, 73, 93, 94, 98, 112, 118, 145, 185, 213, 234, 247, 249, 266, 501, 502, 602, 603, 605, 607, 608, 609, 612, 613, 614

VAMPIRE FB.9, de Havilland
6, 8, 20, 26, 28, 32, 45, 60, 73, 93, 185, 213, 234, 249, 501, 502, 602, 607, 608, 613, 614

VAMPIRE NF.10, de Havilland
23, 25, 151

VARSITY, Vickers
97, 115, 116, 151, 527

VC.10, British Aircraft Corporation
10

VEGA GULL, Percival
24, 510

VENGEANCE, Vultee
45, 82, 84, 110, 288, 289, 291, 567, 577, 587, 631, 667, 679, 691, 695

VENOM FB.1, de Havilland
5, 6, 8, 11, 14, 16, 28, 32, 45, 60, 73, 94, 98, 145, 266

VENOM NF.2, de Havilland
23, 33, 219, 253

VENOM NF.3, de Havilland
23, 89, 125, 141, 151

VENOM FB.4, de Havilland
5, 6, 8, 11, 28, 60, 94, 142, 208, 249, 266

VENTURA, Lockheed
13, 21, 140, 251, 299, 500, 519, 521, 624

VERNON, Vickers
45, 70

VICKERS F.B.5
5, 7, 11, 16, 18, 24, 32, 41

VICKERS FB.19
14, 30, 47, 111, 141

VICTOR B.1, Handley Page
10, 15, 55, 57, 543

VICTOR K.1, Handley Page
55, 57, 214

VICTOR B.2, Handley Page
100, 139

VICTOR SR.2, Handley Page
543

VICTORIA, Vickers
70, 216

VILDEBEEST I, Vickers
22, 100

VILDEBEEST II, Vickers
100

VILDEBEEST III, Vickers
22, 36, 42, 100, 273

VILDEBEEST IV, Vickers
22, 42

VIMY, Vickers
7, 9, 45, 58, 70, 99, 100, 216, 502

VINCENT, Vickers
8, 31, 45, 47, 55, 84, 207, 223, 244

VIRGINIA, Vickers
7, 9, 10, 51, 58, 75, 214, 215, 500, 502

VOISIN
4, 5, 7, 12, 16, 30

VULCAN B.1, Avro
44, 50, 83, 101, 617

VULCAN B.2, Avro
9, 12, 27, 35, 44, 50, 83, 101, 617

WALLACE, Westland
501, 502, 503, 504

WALRUS, Supermarine
89, 269, 275, 276, 277, 278, 281, 282, 283, 284, 292, 294, 624

WALRUS, Westland
3

WAPITI, Westland
5, 11, 20, 24, 27, 28, 30, 31, 39, 55, 60, 84, 501, 600, 601, 602, 603, 604, 605, 607, 608

WARFERRY, Foster-Wickner
24

WARWICK I, II, Vickers
38, 167, 251, 269, 276, 277, 278, 279, 280, 281, 282, 283, 284, 292, 293, 294, 520, 525, 621

WARWICK III, Vickers
167, 301, 304, 353, 525

WARWICK V, Vickers
179

WASHINGTON, Boeing
15, 35, 44, 57, 90, 115, 149, 192, 207

WELLESLEY, Vickers
7, 14, 35, 45, 47, 76, 77, 117, 148, 207, 223, 267

WELLINGTON I, IA, IC, Vickers
9, 15, 36, 37, 38, 40, 57, 69, 70, 75, 93, 99, 101, 103, 108, 109, 115, 148, 149, 150, 156, 162, 192, 214, 215, 221, 294, 300, 301, 304, 305, 311

WELLINGTON II, Vickers
12, 57, 75, 104, 142, 148, 158, 214, 305

WELLINGTON III, Vickers
12, 37, 38, 40, 57, 70, 75, 99, 101, 115, 142, 150, 156, 162, 166, 192, 199, 300

WELLINGTON IV, Vickers
142, 300, 301, 305, 544

WELLINGTON VIII, Vickers
36, 38, 69, 172, 179, 221, 547, 612

WELLINGTON X, Vickers
36, 37, 38, 40, 70, 99, 104, 142, 150, 162, 166, 192, 196, 199, 215, 300, 304, 305, 527, 612

WELLINGTON XI, Vickers
36, 38, 221, 294, 344, 547

WELLINGTON XII, Vickers
36, 172

WELLINGTON XIII, Vickers
8, 36, 38, 69, 203, 221, 244, 294, 304, 344, 524, 547, 621

WELLINGTON XIV, Vickers
14, 36, 38, 172, 179, 281, 304, 524, 612 621

WELLINGTON XVI, Vickers
24, 99, 232, 242

WESSEX, Westland
18, 22, 28, 72, 78

WHIRLWIND I, Westland
137, 263

WHIRLWIND HAR.2, HAR.4, Westland
22, 110, 155, 217, 225, 228, 275, 284

WHIRLWIND HAR.10, Westland
22, 28, 32, 84, 103, 110, 202, 225, 228, 230

WHITLEY I, Armstrong-Whitworth
10, 58, 78, 166

WHITLEY II, Armstrong-Whitworth
7, 51, 58, 97

WHITLEY III, Armstrong-Whitworth
7, 51, 58, 77, 97, 102, 166

WHITLEY IV, Armstrong-Whitworth
10, 51, 78

WHITLEY V, Armstrong-Whitworth
10, 51, 58, 77, 78, 102, 109, 138, 161, 295, 296, 297, 298, 502, 612

WHITLEY VII, Armstrong-Whitworth
53, 58, 502, 612

WOODCOCK, Hawker
3, 17

YORK, Avro
24, 40, 51, 59, 99, 206, 242, 246, 511

355

Index of Locations in United Kingdom

ABBOTSINCH, Renfrew
(7 miles W of Glasgow)
21, 34, 225, 232, 239, 309,
602, 607
ABERPORTH, Cardigan
(5 miles NE of Cardigan)
595
ABINGDON, Berkshire
(5 miles SSW of Oxford)
15, 24, 30, 40, 46, 47, 51,
52, 53, 59, 62, 63, 97, 98,
103, 104, 106, 147, 150,
166, 167, 185, 238, 242,
525
ACASTER MALBIS, Yorkshire
(5 miles S of York)
601
ACKLINGTON, Northumber-
land (8 miles S of Alnwick)
1, 18, 19, 25, 29, 32, 43,
56, 63, 66, 72, 74, 79, 91,
92, 111, 130, 140, 141,
152, 164, 167, 198, 219,
222, 258, 263, 266, 278,
289, 315, 316, 317, 322,
349, 350, 539, 607
ALCONBURY, Huntingdon-
shire (13 miles S of Peterborough)
15, 40, 52, 139, 156
ALDERGROVE, Co.Antrim
(10 miles W of Belfast)
2, 9, 59, 86, 118, 120, 143,
202, 206, 220, 224, 231,
233, 245, 252, 254, 272,
280, 311, 502, 518
ANDOVER, Hampshire
(2½ miles W of Andover)
Alt. Weyhill
2, 9, 11, 12, 13, 16, 21, 44,
53, 59, 63, 81, 82, 101,
103, 104, 105, 106, 107,
116, 119, 142, 148, 169,
170, 207, 214, 215, 225,
285, 289, 296, 613
ANDREAS, Isle of Man
(15 miles N of Douglas)
41, 93, 275
ANDREWS FIELD, Essex
(11 miles N of Chelmsford)
Alt. Great Saling
19, 65, 122, 129, 276, 303,
306, 309, 315, 316, 616
ANGLE, Pembroke
(8 miles W of Pembroke)
32, 152, 263, 312, 615
APPLEDRAM, Sussex
(2 miles SSW of Chichester)
175, 181, 302, 308, 310,
312, 313, 317
ARBROATH, Angus
(15 miles NE of Dundee)
65
ASHFORD, Kent
(3 miles SW of Ashford)
65, 122
ASHINGTON, Northumber-
land (32 miles N of New-
castle)
36
ASTON DOWN, Gloucester-
shire (5 miles SE of Stroud)
Alt. Minchinhampton)
4, 98, 187

ATCHAM, Shropshire
(4 miles E of Shrewsbury)
74, 131, 232, 350
ATTLEBRIDGE, Norfolk
(9 miles NW of Norwich)
88, 247, 320
AYR, Ayrshire
(1 mile NE of Ayr)
Alt. Heathfield
1, 3, 18, 26, 56, 64, 72,
141, 165, 169, 186, 222,
232, 239, 241, 278, 312,
313, 322, 329, 340, 345,
602, 611
BAGINTON, Warwickshire
(3 miles SSE of Coventry)
32, 79, 134, 135, 308, 605
BALDERTON, Nottingham-
shire (3 miles S of Newark)
227
BALDONNEL, Dublin
(9 miles SW of Dublin)
100, 141
BALLYHALBERT, Co.Down
(19 miles ESE of Belfast)
25, 26, 63, 130, 153, 245,
303, 315, 501
BALLYKELLY, Co.London-
derry (14 miles E of Lon-
donderry)
59, 86, 120, 203, 204, 210,
220, 240, 269, 281, 504
BANFF, Banffshire
(4 miles W of Banff)
14, 65, 143, 144, 235, 248,
333, 334
BANGOR, Caernarvonshire
(2 miles E of Bangor)
244
BARDNEY, Lincolnshire
(10 miles E of Lincoln)
9, 106, 189, 227
BARFORD ST. JOHN,
Oxfordshire (4 miles S of
Banbury)
4, 169
BARTON BENDISH, Norfolk
(11 miles SSE of Kings
Lynn)
268
BASSINGBOURN, Cambridge-
shire (11 miles SW of Cambridge)
24', 35, 40, 51, 59, 102,
104, 108, 215, 242
BEAULIEU, Hampshire
(8 miles SSW of South-
ampton)
Alt. Brockenhurst
53, 79, 84, 103, 117, 224,
257, 263,311
BECCLES, Suffolk
(7 miles WSW of Lowestoft)
278, 279, 280, 618
BEKESBOURNE, Kent
(4 miles SE of Canterbury)
2, 50, 56
BEMBRIDGE, Isle of Wight
(4 miles SE of Ryde)
253
BENEBECULA, Outer Heb-
rides (On NW point of
island)
36, 179, 206, 220, 304

BENSON, Oxfordshire
(12 miles SSE of Oxford)
21, 30, 52, 58, 63, 82, 103,
105, 114, 140, 144, 147,
150, 167, 215, 267, 540,
541, 542, 543, 544
BENTWATERS, Suffolk
(12 miles ENE of Ipswich)
Alt. Butley
56, 64, 65, 118, 124, 126,
129, 165, 234, 245
BEVERLEY, Yorkshire
(1 mile W of Beverley)
33, 34, 47, 80, 82
BICESTER, Oxfordshire
(9 miles SW of Bucking-
ham)
2, 5, 12, 33, 48, 90, 100,
101, 104, 108, 116, 118,
142, 144, 217
BIGGIN HILL, Kent
(13 miles SSE of London)
1, 3, 19, 23, 32, 37, 39, 41,
56, 64, 66, 72, 74, 79, 91,
92, 124, 133, 140, 141,
154, 213, 242, 264, 322,
340, 341, 345, 600, 601,
602, 609, 610, 611, 615
BINBROOK, Lincolnshire
(10 miles SW of Grimsby)
5, 9, 11, 12, 50, 64, 85,
101, 109, 139, 142, 617
BIRCHAM NEWTON, Norfolk
(14 miles NE of Kings Lynn)
7, 11, 18, 21, 32, 34, 35,
39, 42, 49, 53, 56, 59, 60,
99, 101, 119, 166, 167,
200, 206, 207, 220, 221,
233, 235, 248, 252, 254,
269, 274, 279, 280, 320,
500, 521, 534, 598, 695
BLACKBUSHE, Hampshire
(10 miles SSE of Reading)
Alt. Hartfordbridge Flats
16, 69, 88, 107, 140, 162,
167, 171, 226, 264, 301,
305, 322, 342, 605, 613,
622
BLAKEHILL FARM, Wiltshire
(7 miles NW of Swindon)
Alt. Cricklade
233, 271, 575
BLANDFORD, Dorset
(RAF Depot only)
26
BLYTON, Lincolnshire
(16 miles NNW of Lincoln)
199
BODNEY, Norfolk
(8 miles N of Thetford)
21, 82
BODORGAN, Anglesey
(12 miles SE of Holyhead)
Alt. Aberffraw
650
BOGNOR, Sussex
(6 miles ESE of Chichester)
19, 66, 122, 331,,332, 602
BOLT HEAD, Devon
(12 miles SW of Dartmouth)
41, 234, 263, 266, 275,
610, 611
BOSCOMBE DOWN, Wiltshire
(7 miles NNE of Salisbury)

9, 10, 35, 42, 51, 56, 58,
78, 88, 97, 109, 150, 166,
214, 217, 218, 224, 249
BOTTESFORD, Leicestershire
(7 miles NW of Grantham)
90, 207
BOTTISHAM, Cambridgeshire
(6 miles E of Cambridge)
2, 4, 168, 169, 241, 268,
613
BOURN, Cambridgeshire
(6 miles W of Cambridge)
15, 97, 101, 105, 162, 609
BOWMORE, Islay
(On Loch Indaal)
119, 246
BOXTED, Essex
(2 miles NE of Colchester)
25, 56, 222, 234, 263, 266
BRACEBRIDGE HEATH,
Lincolnshire (4 miles S of
Lincoln)
121
BRADWELL BAY, Essex
(16 miles NE of Southend)
3, 19, 23, 29, 56, 64, 77,
124, 126, 151, 157, 198,
219, 247, 278, 287, 309,
310, 312, 313, 501, 605,
611
BRAMCOTE, Warwickshire
(7 miles NE of Coventry)
151, 215, 300, 301, 304,
305
BRAMHAM MOOR, Yorkshire
(12 miles SW of York)
33
BRAWDY, Pembrokeshire
(8 miles NW of Haverford-
west)
517
BREIGHTON, Yorkshire
(12 miles SSE of York)
78, 112, 240
BRENZETT, Kent
(10 miles S of Ashford)
122, 129, 306, 315
BRIZE NORTON, Oxfordshire
(14 miles W of Oxford)
10, 24, 53, 99, 115, 296,
297, 511
BROADWELL, Oxfordshire
(16 miles W of Oxford)
10, 76, 271, 512, 575
BROCKWORTH, Gloucester-
shire (4 miles E of Glou-
cester)
Alt. Hucclecote
86, 90
BROOKLANDS, Surrey
(17 miles SW of London)
Alt. Weybridge
1, 8, 9, 10
BUCKMINSTER, Leicester-
shire (8 miles S of Grantham)
38, 90
BURN, Yorkshire
(14 miles S of York)
578
CAISTOR, Lincolnshire
(13 miles WSW of Grimsby)
269

CALSHOT, Hampshire
(8 miles SSE of South-
ampton)
201, 230, 240

CAMBRIDGE, Cambridgeshire
(2 miles E of Cambridge)
Alt. Teversham
16

CARDIFF, Glamorgan
(2 miles E of Cardiff)
Alt. Pengam Moors
614

CAREW CHERITON, Pem-
brokeshire (5 miles E of
Pembroke)
Alt. Pembroke, Milton
236, 254, 320, 321

CARK, Lancashire
(11 miles NW of Lancaster)
Alt. Flookborough
650

CARNABY, Yorkshire
(3 miles SW of Bridlington)
Alt. Bridlington, Lowthorpe
150, 247

CASTLE ARCHDALE, Fer-
managh (11 miles NNW of
Enniskillen)
119, 201, 202, 209, 228,
240

CASTLE BROMWICH,
Warwickshire (6 miles NE
of Birmingham)
9, 19, 34, 38, 54, 55, 71,
115, 132, 577, 605

CASTLE CAMPS, Cambridge-
shire (15 miles SE of Cambridge)
25, 68, 73, 85, 96, 151,
157, 307, 527, 605

CASTLETOWN, Caithness
(7 miles E of Thurso)
3, 17, 54, 66, 118, 123,
124, 131, 167, 213, 232,
260, 278, 282, 310, 331,
504, 607, 610

CATFOSS, Yorkshire
(12 miles NNE of Hull)
42, 97, 100, 226, 616

CATTERICK, Yorkshire
(5 miles SE of Richmond)
17, 26, 41, 53, 54, 63, 64,
68, 76, 115, 118, 122, 127,
130, 131, 134, 145, 219,
222, 256, 306, 313, 331,
332, 504, 600, 609

CATTEWATER   See Mount
Batten

CHAILEY, Sussex
(10 miles NNE of Brighton)
302, 308, 317

CHARMY DOWN, Somerset
(3 miles N of Bath)
87, 125, 137, 234, 245,
263, 533

CHARTERHALL, Ber-
wickshire (15 miles WSW
of Berwick)
130, 165, 303

CHATTIS HILL, Hampshire
(7 miles SSW of Andover)
91, 92, 93

CHEDBURGH, Suffolk
(5 miles SW of Bury St.
Edmunds)
214, 218, 301, 304, 620

CHIDDINGSTONE CAUSE-
WAY, Kent (6 miles NNW
of Tunbridge Wells)
Alt. Penshurst
78

CHILBOLTON, Hampshire
(8 miles NW of Winchester)
26, 54, 174, 183, 184, 238,
245, 247, 308, 501, 504

CHINGFORD, Essex
(8 miles NNE of London)
138, 154

CHIVENOR, Devon
(4 miles W of Barnstaple)
Alt. Braunton
5, 14, 17, 26, 36, 51, 59,
77, 172, 179, 235, 252,
254, 272, 304, 517,
521, 547, 612, 691

CHURCH FENTON, Yorkshire
(10 miles SSW of York)
19, 23, 25, 26, 41, 46, 64,
68, 71, 72, 73, 85, 87, 96,
112, 124, 125, 129, 141,
183, 213, 234, 242, 249,
257, 263, 264, 288, 306,
307, 308, 600, 604, 609

CLEAVE, Cornwall
(5 miles N of Bude)
639

CLIFTON, Yorkshire
(2 miles N of York)
4, 169, 613

COAL ASTON, Yorkshire
(3 miles S of Sheffield)
33

COLEBY GRANGE, Lincoln-
shire (7 miles S of Lincoln)
68, 142, 264, 288, 307

COLERNE, Wiltshire
(3 miles NE of Bath)
19, 24, 29, 36, 74, 87, 89,
114, 118, 124, 125, 131,
137, 151, 165, 175, 183,
184, 219, 245, 256, 263,
264, 286, 307, 316, 317,
501, 504, 511, 600, 604,
616

COLLYWESTON, North-
amptonshire (12 miles WNW
of Peterborough)
Alt. Easton-on-the-Hill
23, 133, 152, 288, 349

COLTISHALL, Norfolk
(9 miles NNE of Norwich)
1, 6, 23, 25, 41, 64, 66, 68,
72, 74, 80, 118, 124, 125,
133, 137, 141, 151, 152,
154, 195, 222, 229, 234,
242, 255, 257, 264, 274,
278, 303, 306, 307, 309,
312, 315, 316, 318, 602,
603, 611, 616

CONINGSBY, Lincolnshire
(10 miles NW of Boston)
6, 9, 12, 15, 23, 29, 35, 40,
44, 45, 54, 57, 59, 61, 83,
97, 106, 109, 111, 139,
149, 617, 619

COOLHAM, Sussex
(6 miles SSW of Horsham)
129, 222, 306, 315, 349

COPMANTHORPE, Yorkshire
(4½ miles S of York)
57, 76

COTTESMORE, Rutland
(13 miles S of Grantham)
9, 10, 12, 15, 35, 44, 49,
57, 98, 106, 115, 149, 185,
207, 360

CRAIL, Fifeshire
(8 miles S of St. Andrews)
104

CRAMLINGTON, North-
umberland (9 miles N of
Newcastle-upon-Tyne)
36, 58, 63

CRANAGE, Cheshire
(9 miles N of Crewe)
96

CRANFIELD, Bedfordshire
(8 miles SW of Bedford)
4, 35, 62, 82, 108, 181,
207, 239

CROFT, Yorkshire
(5 miles S of Darlington)
Alt. Neasham
78

CROUGHTON, Northampton-
shire (9 miles W of Bucking-
ham)
Alt. Brackley
124

CROYDON, Surrey
(11 miles S of London)
Alt. Waddon
1, 2, 3, 17, 32, 41, 72, 84,
92, 111, 116, 145, 147,
207, 271, 287, 302, 307,
501, 605, 607, 615

CULMHEAD, Somerset
(6 miles S of Taunton)
Alt. Churchstanton
66, 126, 131, 154, 165,
234, 286, 302, 306, 312,
313, 316, 504, 587, 610,
616

DALCROSS, Invernessshire
(8 miles NNE of Inverness)
41, 63, 122

DALE, Pembrokeshire
(11 miles W of Pembroke)
304

DALLACHY, Morayshire
(9 miles E of Elgin)
144

DALTON, Yorkshire
(7 miles ENE of Ripon)
102

DAVIDSTOWE MOOR, Corn-
wall (11 miles W of Laun-
ceston)
53, 144, 206, 269, 282,
304, 524, 547, 612

DEANLAND, Sussex
(6 miles E of Lewes)
64, 91, 234, 302, 308, 317,
322, 345, 611

DEBDEN, Essex
(16 miles SSE of Cambridge)
17, 25, 29, 41, 54, 65, 71,
73, 80, 85, 87, 111, 121,
124, 129, 157, 257, 258,
264, 303, 350, 504, 531,
601

DETLING, Kent
(4 miles NE of Maidstone)
1, 4, 26, 50, 53, 59, 80,
118, 124, 132, 143, 165,
184, 229, 235, 239, 274,
280, 318, 500, 504, 567,
602

DIGBY, Lincolnshire
(10 miles SSE of Lincoln)
Alt. Scopwick
2, 11, 19, 25, 29, 46, 55,
56, 73, 79, 92, 111, 121,
151, 167, 198, 203, 209,
210, 213, 222, 229, 242,
288, 310, 350, 504, 527,
528, 601, 609, 611

DISHFORTH, Yorkshire
(5 miles E of Ripon)
10, 30, 47, 51, 78, 215,
230, 297

DOCKING, Norfolk
(14 miles NE of Kings Lynn)
53, 143, 221, 235, 254,
304, 502, 521, 524

DONCASTER, Yorkshire
(1 mile SE of Doncaster)
7, 82, 169, 271, 613, 616

DONIBRISTLE, Fifeshire
(5 miles SE of Dunfermline)
22, 36, 42, 100

DOVER/GUNSTON ROAD,
Kent (1 mile NE of Dover)
3, 4, 6, 9, 15, 27, 49, 50,
58, 110, 218, 233

DOWN AMPNEY, Glouceter-
shire (8 miles NNW of
Swindon)
271

DOWNHAM MARKET,
Norfolk (9 miles S of Kings
Lynn)
214, 218, 571, 608, 623,
635

DREM, East Lothian
(15 miles ENE of Edinburgh)
Alt. Gullane
29, 43, 64, 65, 72, 91, 96,
111, 123, 124, 130, 141,
145, 150, 186, 197, 222,
232, 242, 245, 258, 260,
263, 278, 281, 307, 309,
340, 600, 602, 603, 605,
607, 609, 611

DRIFFIELD, Yorkshire
(2 miles WSW of Great
Driffield)
Alt. Eastburn
33, 51, 58, 75, 77, 88, 97,
98, 102, 104, 158, 196,
202, 213, 215, 217, 219,
346

DUNDEE, Angus
(2 miles E of Dundee)
249, 257

DUNDONALD, Ayrshire
(8 miles N of Ayr)
Alt. Gailes
2, 18, 26, 63, 268, 516

DUNHOLME LODGE, Lin-
colnshire (4 miles N of
Lincoln)
44, 141, 170, 619

DUNINO, Fifeshire
(6 miles SE of St. Andrews)
309

DUNSFOLD, Surrey
(8 miles S of Guildford)
16, 98, 180, 231, 276, 320

DUXFORD, Cambridgeshire
(8 miles S of Cambridge)
4, 8, 19, 29, 46, 56, 64, 65,
66, 67, 72, 80, 91, 92, 111,
119, 123, 124, 129, 133,
165, 169, 181, 195, 222,
242, 258, 264, 266, 310,
312, 601, 609, 611

DYCE, Aberdeenshire
(6 miles NW of Aberdeen)
3, 111, 122, 129, 130, 141,
143, 145, 165, 234, 235,
248, 254, 310, 602, 603,
612

EARL'S COLNE, Essex
(9 miles WNW of Col-
chester)
296, 297

EASTCHURCH, Kent
(12 miles NW of Canterbury)
4, 12, 21, 33, 48, 53, 65,
100, 122, 124, 132, 142,
174, 175, 181, 183, 184,
207, 245, 247, 263, 266

EAST FORTUNE, East
Lothian (3 miles NE of
Haddington)
185

EAST KIRKBY, Lincolnshire
(11 miles N of Boston)
57, 139, 630
EASTLEIGH, Hampshire
(3 miles NE of South-
ampton)
7, 28, 42, 45, 224, 266, 269
EAST MANTON, Wiltshire
26
EAST MOOR, Yorkshire
(7 miles N of York)
158, 288
EAST RETFORD, Notting-
hamshire (6 miles E of
Worksop)
186, 187, 200
EAST WRETHAM, Norfolk
(4 miles NNE of Thetford)
115, 311
EDINBURGH, Midlothian
(Not an airfield)
77
EDZELL, Kincardineshire
(2 miles NE of Edzell)
612
EGLINTON, Co. Londonderry
(6 miles NNE of London-
derry)
41, 133, 134, 152, 275
ELGIN, Morayshire
(2 miles SW of Elgin)
17, 57, 232
ELSHAM WOLDS, Lincoln-
shire (15 miles WNW of
Grimsby)
57, 100, 103, 576
ELVINGTON, Yorkshire
(5 miles SE of York)
77, 346, 347
ESHOTT, Northumberland
(9 miles S of Alnwick)
Alt. Felton
289
EVANTON, Ross & Cromarty
(13 miles N of Inverness)
Alt. Novar
64, 106
EXETER, Devon
(5 miles E of Exeter)
21, 26, 42, 66, 87, 124,
125, 131, 151, 165, 213,
222, 247, 257, 263, 266,
275, 278, 307, 308, 310,
317, 504, 601, 610, 616,
691
FAIRFORD, Gloucestershire
(9 miles N of Swindon)
10, 30, 47, 53, 113, 190,
295, 297, 620
FAIRLOP, Essex
(10 miles NE of London)
19, 64, 65, 81, 122, 154,
164, 182, 193, 195, 239,
245, 247, 302, 313, 317,
350, 602, 603
FAIRWOOD COMMON,
Glamorgan (5 miles W of
Swansea)
33, 41, 66, 68, 79, 118,
124, 125, 127, 132, 164,
183, 193, 197, 198, 222,
257, 263, 264, 266, 268,
276, 302, 306, 307, 308,
312, 315, 316, 317, 322,
329, 331, 332, 504, 536,
595, 600, 609, 610, 615,
616, 691
FALDINGWORTH, Lincoln-
shire (9 miles NNE of
Lincoln)
300, 305

FARNBOROUGH, Hampshire
(2 miles N of Aldershot)
1, 2, 4, 5, 6, 7, 8, 10, 15,
30, 53, 70, 100, 101, 108
FELIXSTOWE, Suffolk
(10 miles SW of Ipswich)
209, 210, 230, 231, 232,
247, 259, 261
FELTHAM, Middlesex
(13 miles WSW of London)
Alt. Hanworth
133, 155
FELTWELL, Norfolk
(11 miles WNW of Thet-
ford)
37, 57, 75, 77, 192, 214
FERMOY, Co. Cork
(19 miles NNE of Cork)
106
FERSFIELD, Norfolk
(17 miles SW of Norwich)
107, 140, 180
FILTON, Gloucestershire
(4 miles N of Bristol)
19, 20, 25, 33, 42, 62, 66,
100, 101, 118, 236, 263,
286, 501, 504, 528
FINDO GASK, Perthshire
(7 miles W of Perth)
309
FINNINGLEY, Yorkshire
(6 miles SE of Doncaster)
7, 12, 18, 76, 77, 98, 101,
102, 106, 616
FIRBECK, Yorkshire
(9 miles S of Doncaster)
613
FISHGUARD, Pembrokeshire
(15 miles WSW of Cardigan)
245
FISKERTON, Lincolnshire
(4 miles E of Lincoln)
49, 150, 576
FOLKINGHAM, Lincolnshire
(9 miles SE of Lincoln)
223
FORD, Sussex
(8 miles W of Chichester)
Alt. Yapton
10, 19, 22, 23, 29, 65, 66,
96, 97, 115, 122, 127, 132,
141, 144, 148, 149, 170,
215, 256, 302, 306, 308,
315, 317, 331, 332, 602,
604, 605
FORELAND, Isle of Wight
(5 miles SE of Ryde)
253
FOULSHAM, Norfolk
(17 miles NW of Norwich)
98, 180, 192, 514
FOWLMERE, Cambridgeshire
(10 miles SSW of Cam-
bridge)
2, 15, 16, 19, 21, 111, 124,
133, 154, 167, 174
FRISTON, Sussex
(4 miles W of Eastbourne)
32, 41, 64, 131, 253, 306,
308, 316, 349, 350, 501,
610
FULBECK, Lincolnshire
(13 miles SSW of Lincoln)
49, 189
FULL SUTTON, Yorkshire
(8 miles E of York)
77, 102, 231
FUNTINGTON, Sussex
(4 miles WNW of Chi-
chester)

4, 19, 33, 65, 66, 122, 127,
164, 183, 198, 222, 268,
329, 331, 332, 340, 341,
349
GAINSBOROUGH, Lincoln-
shire (Not an airfield)
33
GATWICK, Surrey
(6 miles S of Redhill)
2, 4, 18, 19, 26, 53, 57, 63,
65, 80, 98, 116, 141, 168,
171, 175, 183, 229, 239,
274, 287
GAYDON, Warwickshire
(9 miles E of Stratford-on-
Avon)
138, 543
GOLDHANGAR, Essex
(11 miles E of Chelmsford)
37, 74
GOLDINGTON, Bedfordshire
(2 miles E of Bedford)
75
GORMANSTOWN, Co. Neath
(21 miles N of Dublin)
117
GOSPORT, Hampshire
(3 miles W of Portsmouth)
Alt. Fort Grange
3, 8, 13, 14, 17, 22, 23, 28,
29, 40, 41, 42, 45, 48, 56,
78, 79, 86, 88, 100, 186,
210, 233, 248, 608, 667
GRANGEMOUTH, Stirling-
shire (12 miles SE of Stirling)
141, 263, 602, 614
GRANSDEN LODGE, Hunt-
ingdonshire (10 miles W of
Cambridge)
53, 142, 169, 192, 692
GRAVELEY, Huntingdonshire
(5 miles W of Huntingdon)
35, 115, 161, 227, 692
GRAVESEND, Kent
(2 miles SE of Gravesend)
2, 4, 19, 21, 32, 56, 64, 65,
66, 71, 72, 74, 85, 92, 111,
122, 124, 132, 133, 141,
165, 174, 181, 193, 245,
247, 257, 264, 266, 277,
284, 306, 350, 501, 604,
609, 610
GREAT DUNMOW, Essex
(11 miles NE of Harlow)
190, 620
GREAT MASSINGHAM, Nor-
folk (11 miles E of Kings
Lynn)
18, 107, 169, 342
GREAT SAMPFORD, Essex
(7 miles SSW of Haverhill)
65, 133, 616
GREAT YARMOUTH, Nor-
folk (On South Denes, Gt.
Yarmouth)
212, 228, 229, 273
GRIMSBY, Lincolnshire
(5 miles S of Grimsby)
Alt. Waltham
100, 142, 550
GRIMSETTER, Orkney Islands
(4 miles SE of Kirkwall)
129, 132, 234
GROVE, Berkshire
(12 miles SW of Oxford)
174, 184
GUERNSEY, Channel Islands
(3 miles SW of St. Peter
Port)
17

HADLEIGH, Suffolk
(7 miles W of Ipswich)
75
HAINAULT FARM, Essex
(3 miles WNW of Romford)
39, 44, 151, 153
HALTON, Buckinghamshire
(4 miles SE of Aylesbury)
529
HAMWORTHY, Dorset
(4 miles W of Bourne-
mouth)
210
HARLAXTON, Lincolnshire
(2 miles SW of Grantham)
68, 98
HARLING ROAD, Norfolk
(7 miles ENE of Thetford)
75, 88, 94
HARRIETSHAM, Kent
(7 miles E of Maidstone)
50, 78
HARRINGTON, North-
amptonshire (6 miles W of
Kettering)
218
HARROWBEER, Devon
(8 miles N of Plymouth)
1, 26, 64, 126, 130, 131,
175, 183, 193, 263, 266,
275, 276, 302, 312, 329,
610, 611, 616, 691
HARWELL, Berkshire
(11 miles N of Newbury)
75, 105, 107, 148, 215,
226, 295, 570
HATFIELD, Hertfordshire
(4 miles E of St. Albans)
2, 116, 239
HATSTON, Orkney Islands
(2 miles NW of Kirkwall)
254
HAWARDEN, Flintshire
(4 miles W of Chester)
173
HAWKINGE, Kent
(2 miles N of Folkestone)
Alt. Folkestone
1, 2, 3, 4, 16, 17, 25, 26,
38, 41, 56, 65, 66, 79, 83,
91, 120, 124, 132, 234,
245, 277, 278, 313, 322,
350, 501, 504, 567, 605,
611
HELPERBY, Yorkshire
(15 miles NW of York)
76
HEMSWELL, Lincolnshire
(12 miles N of Lincoln)
12, 61, 75, 76, 83, 97, 100,
109, 139, 144, 150, 170,
199, 300, 301, 305, 542
HENDON, Middlesex
(8 miles NNW of London)
24, 116, 248, 257, 504,
510, 512, 575, 600, 601,
604, 611
HENLEY-ON-THAMES, Berk-
shire (7 miles NE of Reading)
529
HENLOW, Bedfordshire
(10 miles SE of Bedford)
19, 23, 43, 80
HESTON, Middlesex
(11 miles W of London)
116, 129, 212, 302, 303,
306, 308, 315, 316, 317,
350, 515
HETHEL, Norfolk
(7 miles SW of Norwich)
65, 126, 303, 316

HIBALDSTOW, Lincolnshire
(8 miles SE of Scunthorpe)
253, 255, 532, 538
HIGH ERCALL, Shropshire
(8 miles ENE of Shrews-
bury)
41, 68, 247, 255, 257, 535
HINGHAM, Norfolk
(13 miles WSW of Norwich)
51, 100, 102
HOLME-IN-SPALDING-
MOOR, Yorkshire
(16 miles SE of York)
76, 101, 512
HOLMSLEY SOUTH, Hamp-
shire (9 miles NE of Bour-
nemouth)
58, 129, 167, 174, 175,
182, 184, 245, 246, 295,
306, 315, 502, 547
HONILEY, Warwickshire
(12 miles SE of Birming-
ham)
32, 91, 96, 130, 135, 219,
234, 255, 257, 285, 605
HONINGTON, Suffolk
(5 miles S of Thetford)
7, 9, 10, 12, 15, 39, 44, 51,
55, 57, 58, 75, 77, 90, 102,
103, 105, 199, 204, 214,
215, 311, 543
HOOTON PARK, Cheshire
(7 miles S of Liverpool)
13, 48, 117, 610, 611
HORNCHURCH, Essex
(12 miles W of London)
19, 39, 41, 54, 64, 65, 66,
74, 78, 80, 81, 92, 111,
116, 122, 129, 132, 154,
189, 222, 229, 239, 264,
266, 274, 278, 287, 313,
340, 349, 350, 504, 567,
600, 603, 611
HORNE, Surrey
(6 miles SE of Redhill)
130, 303
HORNSEA MERE, Yorkshire
(13 miles NE of Hull)
248, 251
HORSHAM ST. FAITH, Nor-
folk (3 miles N of Norwich)
18, 19, 23, 34, 64, 65, 66,
74, 105, 110, 114, 118,
139, 141, 245, 257, 263,
307, 695
HOUNSLOW, Middlesex
(10 miles W of London)
4, 10, 15, 24, 27, 39, 52,
85, 87, 107
HOVE, Sussex
(Not an airfield)
78
HUCKNALL, Nottinghamshire
(5 miles NNW of Notting-
ham)
98, 104, 130, 135, 205,
218, 504
HUGGATE, Yorkshire
(18 miles E of York)
168, 170
HULLAVINGTON, Wiltshire
(5 miles N of Chippenham)
114
HUNSDON, Hertfordshire
(3 miles NW of Harlow)
3, 21, 29, 85, 151, 154,
157, 219, 264, 501, 515,
530, 611
HURN, Hampshire
(5 miles NNE of Bourne-
mouth)
125, 164, 170, 181, 182,

193, 197, 198, 239, 247,
257, 263, 266, 277, 295,
296, 297, 570, 604, 609
HUTTON CRANSWICK,
Yorkshire (15 miles N of
Hull)
1, 19, 26, 91, 124, 129,
168, 170, 195, 234, 278,
288, 291, 302, 306, 308,
310, 315, 316, 610
HYLTON, Durham
(8 miles SE of Newcastle)
36
IBSLEY, Hampshire
(11 miles NNE of Bourne-
mouth)
32, 66, 118, 124, 129, 165,
234, 263, 268, 310, 312,
313, 501, 504, 616
INGHAM, Lincolnshire
(8 miles N of Lincoln)
199, 300, 305
INVERGORDON, Ross &
Cromarty (14 miles N of
Inverness)
201, 209, 210, 228, 240
INVERNESS, Invernesshire
(1 mile N of Inverness)
Alt. Longmans
241, 526
IPSWICH, Suffolk
(2 miles SE of Ipswich)
131, 154, 302, 308, 331,
340, 611, 679
JERSEY, Channel Islands
17
JURBY, Isle of Man
(14 miles N of Douglas)
258, 302, 307, 312
KEEVIL, Wiltshire
(10 miles ESE of Bath)
196, 299
KELSTERN, Lincolnshire
(11 miles SSW of Grimsby)
170, 625
KENLEY, Surrey
(14 miles S of London)
1, 3, 13, 17, 23, 24, 32, 36,
39, 46, 64, 66, 80, 84, 88,
91, 95, 108, 110, 111, 165,
253, 258, 302, 312, 350,
501, 600, 602, 611, 615,
616
KIDLINGTON, Oxfordshire
(6 miles NNW of Oxford)
52, 167
KILLADEAS, Co. Fermanagh
(5 miles NNW of Ennis-
killen)
240
KING'S CLIFFE, North-
amptonshire (10 miles W
of Peterborough)
91, 93, 266, 349, 616
KINGSNORTH, Kent
(3 miles S of Ashford)
19, 65, 122, 184, 602
KINLOSS, Morayshire
(9 miles W of Elgin)
8, 77, 120, 201, 206, 217
KIRKISTOWN, Co. Down
(20 miles SE of Belfast)
504
KIRKNEWTON, Midlothian
(9 miles SW of Edinburgh)
289, 309
KIRMINGTON, Lincolnshire
(12 miles W of Grimsby)
142, 150, 153, 166
KIRTON-IN-LINDSEY, Lin-
colnshire (16 miles N of
Lincoln)

43, 65, 71, 74, 85, 121,
133, 136, 222, 253, 255,
264, 302, 303, 306, 307,
317, 616
KIRTON LINDSEY, Lincoln-
shire (18 miles N of
Lincoln)
33
LAKE DOWN, Wiltshire
(6 miles NNW of Salisbury)
107, 108, 109, 136, 201
LAKENHEATH, Suffolk
(8 miles W of Thetford)
149, 199
LANGAR, Nottinghamshire
(11 miles ESE of Notting-
ham)
207
LANGHAM, Norfolk
(14 miles W of Cromer)
254, 280, 521, 524, 612
LARKHILL, Wiltshire
(9 miles N of Salisbury)
3
LASHAM, Hampshire
(15 miles NE of Winchester)
107, 175, 181, 182, 183,
305, 320, 602, 609, 613
LEADENHAM, Lincolnshire
(11 miles S of Lincoln)
38
LECONFIELD, Yorkshire
(10 miles NNE of Hull)
19, 26, 41, 51, 64, 72, 74,
81, 92, 96, 97, 129, 134,
166, 170, 196, 202, 213,
228, 234, 245, 249, 253,
258, 275, 302, 303, 313,
610, 616, 640
LEEMING, Yorkshire
(11 miles NNW of Hull)
7, 10, 33, 35, 77, 102
LEE-ON-SOLENT, Hampshire
(11 miles SE of South-
ampton)
26, 63
LEICESTER EAST, Leicestershire (4 miles ESE of
Leicester)
190, 196, 620
LEIGHTERTON, Gloucester-
shire (9 miles S of Stroud)
29, 66
LEUCHARS, Fifeshire
(4 miles NW of St.Andrews)
3, 11, 23, 25, 29, 42, 43,
72, 74, 86, 107, 111, 114,
120, 144, 151, 160, 203,
205, 206, 217, 222, 224,
233, 235, 320, 333, 519,
540, 547, 605
LILBOURNE, Northampton-
shire (3 miles E of Rugby)
34, 55, 73, 84
LIMAVADY, Co. Londonderry
(16 miles E of London-
derry)
53, 143, 172, 221, 224,
281, 502, 612
LINDHOLME, Yorkshire
(7 miles ENE of Doncaster)
50, 57, 100, 110, 304, 305.
LINTON-UPON-OUSE, York-
shire (9 miles NW of York)
4, 35, 41, 51, 58, 64, 65,
66, 76, 77, 78, 92, 102,
264, 275
LISSETT, Yorkshire
(7 miles E of Driffield)
158
LITTLE SNORING, Norfolk
(4 miles NE of Fakenham)

23, 115, 141, 169, 515
LITTLE STAUGHTON, Hunt-
ingdonshire (8 miles NNW
of Barmouth)
109, 582
LLANBEDR, Merioneth
(7 miles NNW of Barmouth)
20, 41, 66, 74, 129, 131,
164, 168, 193, 198, 232,
268, 306, 308, 312, 315,
322, 329, 331, 332, 602,
631
LLANDOW, Glamorgan
(14 miles WSW of Cardiff)
614
LOCKING, Somerset
(17 miles SW of Bristol)
286
LONDON COLNEY,
Hertfordshire (4 miles SSE
of St. Albans)
1, 24, 54, 56, 74, 92
LONG KESH, Co. Down
(11 miles WSW of Belfast)
74, 231, 290
LONGTOWN, Cumberland
(8 miles N of Carlisle)
41
LOPCOMBE CORNER,
Wiltshire (8 miles ENE of
Salisbury)
52, 74, 85
LOSSIEMOUTH, Morayshire
(4 miles N of Elgin)
6, 8, 21, 44, 54, 57, 63,
82, 83, 110, 280, 346
LUCE BAY, Wigtown
(4 miles SSE of Stranraer)
258
LUDFORD MAGNA,
Lincolnshire (17 miles NE
of Lincoln)
101, 104
LUDHAM, Norfolk
(12 miles NE of Norwich)
1, 19, 91, 167, 195, 602,
603, 610, 611
LULSGATE BOTTOM,
Somerset (7 miles SW of
Bristol)
286
LYDD, Kent
(16 miles SW of Folkestone)
174, 175, 245
LYMPNE, Kent
(7 miles W of Folkestone)
1, 2, 16, 21, 26, 33, 34, 41,
53, 59, 65, 72, 74, 91, 98,
102, 108, 120, 127, 130,
137, 165, 186, 310, 312,
313, 350, 609, 610
LYNEHAM, Wiltshire
(10 miles WSW of Swindon)
24, 36, 47, 48, 53, 70, 206,
216, 242, 246, 511, 525
MACHRIHANISH,
Argyllshire (4 miles W of
Campbeltown)
65, 272
MACBERRY, East Lothian
(11 miles E of Edinburgh)
13, 63, 225, 607, 614
MAGHABERRY, Co. Antrim
(12 miles SW of Belfast)
231
MANSTON, Kent
(12 miles ENE of
Canterbury)
1, 2, 3, 9, 18, 21, 23, 26,
29, 32, 46, 48, 56, 59, 62,
63, 74, 77, 79, 80, 91, 92,
110, 118, 119, 124, 130,

359

137, 139, 143, 151, 164, 174, 175, 181, 183, 184, 193, 197, 198, 206, 219, 222, 224, 229, 235, 242, 253, 263, 266, 274, 310, 312, 313, 331, 332, 500, 501, 504, 567, 600, 601, 604, 607, 609, 615, 616

MARHAM, Norfolk
(9 miles SE of Kings Lynn)
15, 35, 38, 44, 49, 51, 55, 90, 100, 105, 109, 115, 139, 148, 149, 191, 207, 214, 218, 242

MARTLESHAM HEATH,
Suffolk (5 miles E of
Ipswich)
1, 3, 15, 17, 22, 25, 26, 41, 54, 56, 64, 65, 71, 72, 111, 122, 124, 132, 133, 151, 182, 198, 222, 236, 239, 242, 257, 258, 264, 266, 277, 278, 284, 303, 310, 312, 317, 350, 501, 504, 605, 607, 611

MATLASK, Norfolk
(7 miles SW of Cromer)
3, 19, 56, 65, 72, 122, 137, 195, 222, 229, 278, 601, 602, 609, 611

MATTISHALL, Norfolk
(10 miles W of Norwich)
51

MELBOURNE, Yorkshire
(11 miles SE of York)
10, 575

MELTON MOWBRAY,
Leicestershire (13 miles NE
of Leicester)
38, 254

MEMBURY, Wiltshire
(12 miles NW of Reading)
19, 187, 525

MENDLESHAM, Suffolk
(11 miles N of Ipswich)
310, 312, 313

MEPAL, Cambridgeshire
(5 miles W of Ely)
7, 44, 49, 75, 113

MERRYFIELD, Somerset
(7 miles SE of Taunton)
53, 187, 238, 242, 243

MERSTON, Sussex
(2 miles SE of Chichester)
41, 80, 118, 130, 131, 145, 174, 181, 182, 184, 229, 232, 247, 274, 303, 329, 340, 341

METHERINGHAM,
Lincolnshire (10 miles SE
of Lincoln)
106, 189

METHWOLD, Norfolk
(11 miles NW of Thetford)
21, 57, 149, 207, 214, 218, 320

MIDDLETON ST. GEORGE,
Durham (6 miles E of
Darlington)
33, 76, 78, 92, 264, 608

MIDDLE WALLOP, Hampshire
(5 miles SW of Andover)
16, 19, 23, 32, 56, 93, 125, 151, 164, 169, 182, 234, 236, 238, 245, 247, 288, 501, 504, 537, 601, 604, 609

MILDENHALL, Suffolk
(12 miles NW of Bury St.
Edmunds)
15, 35, 38, 44, 73, 75, 115, 149, 207, 211, 218, 622

MILFIELD, Northumberland
(13 miles SSW of Berwick)
183, 184

MILLTOWN, Morayshire
(4 miles NE of Elgin)
224

MISSON, Yorkshire
(8 miles SE of Doncaster -
not an airfield)
94

MOLESWORTH,
Northamptonshire (11 miles
WNW of Huntingdon)
19, 54, 124, 129, 159, 234

MONTROSE, Angus
(1 mile N of Montrose)
2, 25, 80, 83, 111, 141, 232, 269, 603

MORPETH, Northumberland
(11 miles NNW of Newcastle)
72

MOUNT BATTEN, Devon
(1 mile SE of Plymouth)
Alt. Cattewater
203, 204, 209, 237, 238

MOUNT FARM, Oxfordshire
(7 miles SE of Oxford)
140

MULLAGHMORE,
Co. Londonderry (6 miles
SW of Ballymoney)
281

MULLION, Cornwall
(12 miles SW of Falmouth)
Alt. Predannack
236

NARBOROUGH, Norfolk
(9 miles SE of Kings Lynn)
35, 56, 59, 60, 64, 83, 121

NEED'S OAR POINT,
Hampshire (9 miles S of
Southampton)
193, 197, 257, 266

NETHERAVON, Wiltshire
(13 miles W of Andover)
1, 3, 4, 7, 10, 11, 12, 13, 18, 19, 20, 21, 26, 32, 33, 35, 42, 43, 48, 52, 53, 57, 66, 72, 89, 97, 99, 115, 142, 187, 207, 208, 215, 295, 296, 297

NETHERTHORPE, Yorkshire
(14 miles S of Doncaster)
613

NEWCHURCH, Kent
(7 miles SSE of Ashford)
3, 19, 56, 132, 184, 602

NEW HAGGERSTON,
Northumberland (9 miles
SE of Berwick)
77

NEWHAVEN, Sussex
(9 miles E of Brighton)
242

NEWLYN, Cornwall
(2 miles SSW of Penzance)
235

NEWMARKET HEATH,
Cambridgeshire (10 miles
ENE of Cambridge)
75, 99, 138, 161, 190, 192, 215

NEW ROMNEY, Kent
(10 miles SW of Folkestone)
181, 182, 247

NEWTON, Nottinghamshire
(6 miles ESE of Belfast)
98, 103, 150

NEWTOWNARDS, Co. Down
(10 miles ESE of Belfast)
231, 290

NORTH COATES, Lincolnshire
(10 miles SE of Grimsby)

22, 25, 53, 59, 86, 143, 144, 235, 236, 248, 254, 264, 278, 608

NORTH CREAKE, Norfolk
(6 miles NNW of Fakenham)
171, 199

NORTH KILLINGHOLME,
Lincolnshire (10 miles NW
of Grimsby)
228, 550

NORTH LUFFENHAM,
Rutland (6 miles WSW of
Swaffham)
61, 144

NORTHOLT, Middlesex
(12 miles WNW of London)
1, 4, 12, 16, 18, 23, 24, 25, 32, 41, 43, 52, 65, 74, 92, 111, 124, 140, 207, 213, 229, 253, 257, 271, 302, 303, 306, 308, 315, 316, 317, 515, 600, 601, 604, 609, 615

NORTH PICKEHAM, Norfolk
(2 miles SE of Swaffham)
220

NORTH WEALD, Essex
(4 miles SSE of Harlow)
1, 2, 4, 17, 25, 26, 29, 33, 39, 44, 46, 56, 63, 64, 66, 71, 72, 74, 75, 111, 116, 121, 124, 127, 130, 151, 168, 222, 234, 242, 249, 257, 268, 285, 287, 301, 304, 310, 312, 313, 331, 332, 601, 604

NORWICH, Norfolk
(2 miles NE of Norwich)
Alt. Mousehold
18, 85, 117

NUTTS CORNER, Co. Antrim
(8 miles W of Belfast)
120, 160, 220, 231

OAKINGTON, Cambridgeshire
(5 miles NNW of Cambridge)
7, 10, 27, 30, 46, 86, 100, 101, 206, 218, 242, 571, 627

OBAN, Argyllshire
(On Sound of Kerrera)
209, 210, 228, 330, 524

ODIHAM, Hampshire
(14 miles S of Reading)
2, 4, 13, 18, 26, 33, 46, 53, 54, 59, 63, 66, 72, 96, 130, 168, 170, 171, 174, 175, 182, 184, 225, 230, 233, 239, 247, 264, 268, 271, 604, 613, 614

OKEHAMPTON, Devon
(1 mile NW of
Okehampton)
16

OLD SARUM, Wiltshire
(3 miles N of Salisbury)
Alt. Ford Farm
13, 15, 18, 34, 53, 59, 98, 103, 107, 125, 126, 225, 615

OLD WESTON, Hertfordshire
(5 miles E of Hitchin)
75

OMAGH, Co. Tyrone
105

ORANMORE, Galway
2, 105

ORFORDNESS, Suffolk
(17 miles E of Ipswich)
37

OULTON, Norfolk
(12 miles NNW of Norwich)
18, 21, 88, 114, 139, 214, 223, 236

OUSTON, Durham
(11 miles NW of Newcastle)
72, 81, 122, 131, 198, 232, 242, 243, 281, 317, 350, 607, 613

PADSTOW, Cornwall
(11 miles NNE of Newquay)
250

PEMBREY, Carmarthan
(17 miles WNW of Swansea)
5, 32, 79, 92, 238, 256, 316, 595

PEMBROKE, Pembrokeshire
(5 miles E of Pembroke)
Alt. Carew Cheriton
255

PEMBROKE DOCK,
Pembrokeshire (2 miles
NW of Pembroke)
95, 119, 201, 209, 210, 228, 230, 240, 248, 320, 321

PENRHOS, Caernarvon
(3 miles WSW of Pwllheli)
258

PENSHURST, Kent
(6 miles NNW of Tunbridge
Wells)
268

PENSTON, Midlothian
(12 miles E of Edinburgh)
77

PERRANPORTH, Cornwall
(7 miles SW of Newquay)
19, 65, 66, 130, 132, 183, 234, 276, 302, 310, 317, 329, 340, 341, 602, 610

PETERHEAD, Aberdeenshire
(4 miles W of Peterhead)
19, 26, 63, 65, 118, 122, 129, 132, 164, 165, 234, 245, 278, 309, 313, 315, 350, 504, 598, 602, 603, 611

POCKLINGTON, Yorkshire
(10 miles E of York)
102

POLEBROOK, Northampton-
shire (10 miles SW of
Peterborough)
90, 130

PORTLAND, Dorset
(2 miles S of Weymouth)
241

POTREATH, Cornwall
(12 miles NW of Falmouth)
66, 76, 130, 143, 152, 234, 235, 247, 248, 263, 274, 276, 277, 313, 600, 613, 614

PRAWLE POINT, Devon
(10 miles SSW of Dartmouth)
254

PREDANNACK, Cornwall
(12 miles SW of Falmouth)
1, 33, 64, 141, 151, 165, 179, 183, 222, 234, 248, 264, 304, 307, 311, 349, 536, 600, 604, 611

PRESTWICK, Ayrshire
(3 miles N of Ayr)
102, 141, 253, 602, 603, 610, 615

RATTLESDEN, Suffolk
(8 miles SE of Bury St.
Edmunds)
266

RED BARN, Wiltshire
(On Salisbury Plain)
26

REDHILL, Surrey
(2 miles SE of Redhill)
1, 16, 66, 116, 131, 219,

231, 287, 303, 308, 310,
312, 340, 350, 504, 600,
602, 611
RENDCOMBE, Gloucestershire
(5 miles NNE of Cirencester)
45, 46, 48, 62, 110
RENFREW, Renfrewshire
(6 miles W of Glasgow)
55, 309, 602
RIDGEWELL, Essex
(17 miles NW of Colchester)
90
RINGWAY, Cheshire
(9 miles S of Manchester)
4, 296, 613
RIPON, Yorkshire
(2 miles SE of Ripon)
76, 189
RIVENHALL, Essex
(12 miles W of Colchester)
295, 570
ROBOROUGH, Devon
(8 miles N of Plymouth)
247, 691
RUFFORTH, Yorkshire
(4 miles W of York)
158, 346
ST. ANGELO, Co. Fermanagh
(3 miles N of Enniskillen)
235
ST. DAVIDS, Pembrokeshire
(13 miles SW of Fishguard)
53, 58, 220, 502, 517
ST. EVAL, Cornwall
(6 miles NNE of Newquay)
22, 42, 53, 58, 86, 143,
179, 203, 206, 210, 217,
220, 224, 228, 233, 234,
236, 238, 240, 247, 263,
280, 282, 304, 500, 502,
517, 547, 612
ST. MAWGAN, Cornwall
(4 miles NE of Newquay)
7, 10, 22, 42, 201, 206,
217, 228
SAWBRIDGWORTH,
Hertfordshire (4 miles N of
Harlow)
24, 63, 80, 126, 168, 170,
182, 268
SCAMPTON, Lincolnshire
(6 miles N of Lincoln)
9, 10, 18, 21, 27, 33, 35,
49, 57, 81, 83, 85, 98, 100,
107, 148, 153, 214, 617,
625
SCORTON, Yorkshire
(9 miles SSW of Darlington)
26, 56, 122, 130, 167, 219,
604
SCULTHORPE, Norfolk
(14 miles ENE of Kings
Lynn)
21, 214, 342
SEA HOUSES, Northumber-
land (12 miles N of Alnwick)
256
SEALAND, Flint
(4 miles WNW of Chester)
Alt. South Shotwick
27, 79, 90, 95, 98, 103
SEATON CAREW, Durham
(6 miles NNE of Middles-
brough)
36, 246, 252, 274
SEDGEFORD, Norfolk
(11 miles NNE of Kings
Lynn)
13, 64, 72, 87, 110, 122
SELSEY, Sussex
(4 miles S of Chichester)
33, 65, 74, 222, 245, 329,

340, 341, 349
SHAWBURY, Shropshire
(7 miles NNE of Shrewsbury)
90, 131, 137
SHEPHERD'S GROVE, Suffolk
(9 miles NE of Bury St.
Edmunds)
82, 196, 299
SHERBURN-IN-ELMET,
Yorkshire (11 miles SSW
of York)
46, 121
SHOREHAM, Sussex
(6 miles W of Brighton)
14, 81, 82, 277, 345
SKEABRAE, Orkney Islands
(13 miles NW of Kirkwall)
3, 66, 118, 129, 132, 164,
234, 253, 312, 313, 329,
331, 602, 603, 611
SKELLINGTHORPE,
Lincolnshire (3 miles W of
Lincoln)
50, 61, 619
SKITTEN, Caithness
(4 miles NNW of Wick)
48, 172, 179, 217, 232,
260, 519, 607, 618
SNAILWELL, Cambridgeshire
(13 miles ENE of Cambridge)
56, 137, 152, 168, 170,
181, 182, 183, 184, 247,
268, 309, 527, 613
SNAITH, Yorkshire
(9 miles W of Goole)
51, 150, 578
SOUTH CARLTON,
Lincolnshire (3 miles N of
Lincoln)
25, 57, 66, 96
SOUTHEND, Essex
(2 miles N of Southend)
Alt. Rochford
19, 37, 41, 54, 59, 64, 65,
66, 74, 121, 122, 141, 152,
198, 199, 222, 234, 264,
302, 310, 312, 313, 317,
331, 332, 349, 350, 501,
600, 603, 611, 616
SPEKE, Lancashire
(6 miles SE of Liverpool)
13, 144, 229, 236, 303,
306, 308, 312, 315, 611
SPILSBY, Lincolnshire
(15 miles NNE of Boston)
44, 65, 75, 129, 207
SPITTLEGATE, Lincolnshire
(2 miles SE of Grantham)
Alt. Grantham
29, 39, 43, 70, 83, 100,
106, 113, 211
SQUIRE'S GATE, Lancashire
(3 miles S of Blackpool)
256, 307
STAPLEFORD TAWNEY,
Essex (14 miles NE of
London)
3, 46, 151, 242, 277
STIRLING, Stirlingshire
(1 mile W of Stirling)
Alt. Raploch
43, 63
STONEHENGE, Wiltshire
(8 miles NNW of Salisbury)
97, 108
STONEY CROSS, Hampshire
(11 miles W of Southampton)
26, 46, 175, 232, 239, 242,
296, 297, 299
STORNOWAY, Isle of Lewis
(2 miles E of Stornoway)
48, 58, 500, 502, 518

STOW MARIES, Essex
(9 miles SE of Chelmsford)
37
STRADISHALL, Suffolk
(11 miles SW of Bury St.
Edmunds)
1, 9, 35, 51, 54, 75, 85, 89,
101, 109, 115, 125, 138,
148, 149, 150, 152, 158,
186, 207, 208, 214, 215,
236, 245, 254, 263
STRANRAER, Wigtownshire
(On Loch Ryan)
209, 228, 240
STRUBBY, Lincolnshire
(8 miles SE of Louth)
144, 227, 280, 619
STURGATE, Lincolnshire
(11 miles NNW of Lincoln)
50, 61
SULLOM VOE, Shetland
Islands (10 miles NNW of
Lerwick)
190, 201, 204, 210, 240,
330
SUMBURGH, Shetland Islands
(21 miles S of Lerwick)
3, 48, 66, 125, 129, 143,
144, 232, 234, 235, 248,
254, 310, 608
SUTTON BRIDGE,
Lincolnshire (8 miles W of
Kings Lynn)
73, 254, 264, 266
SWANNINGTON, Norfolk
(9 miles NNW of Norwich)
85, 157, 229
SWANTON MORELY, Norfolk
(15 miles NW of Norwich)
3, 88, 98, 105, 152, 180,
226, 305, 613
SWINDERBY, Lincolnshire
(8 miles SW of Lincoln)
50, 300, 301
SWINGFIELD, Kent
(6 miles WNW of Dover)
119
SYDENHAM, Co. Down
(1 mile E of Belfast)
88, 206
SYERSTON, Nottingham
(5 miles SW of Newark)
49, 61 106, 304, 305, 504
TADCASTER, Yorkshire
(10 miles SW of York)
57, 76, 94
TAIN, Ross & Cromarty
(9 miles NNE of Cromarty)
17, 86, 144, 186, 311, 519,
547
TALBENNY, Pembrokeshire
(10 miles WNW of Pembroke)
248, 304, 311
TALLAGHT, Co. Dublin
(1 mile NW of Tallaght)
117, 141, 149
TANGMERE, Sussex
(3 miles ENE of Chichester)
1, 14, 17, 25, 26, 29, 32,
34, 40, 41, 43, 65, 66, 69,
72, 74, 82, 85, 87, 91, 92,
96, 98, 115, 118, 124, 127,
129, 130, 131, 141, 145,
148, 164, 165, 183, 197,
198, 207, 208, 213, 217,
219, 222, 229, 233, 238,
245, 257, 266, 268, 302,
310, 312, 313, 329, 331,
332, 340, 341, 349, 501,
534, 587, 601, 605, 607,
609, 616
TARRANT RUSHTON, Dorset

(12 miles NW of Bourne-
mouth)
196, 295, 297, 298, 644
TAYPORT, Fifeshire
(2 miles E of Dundee)
210
TEALING, Angus
(4 miles N of Dundee)
63
TELSCOMBE CLIFFS, Sussex
(3 miles W of Newhaven)
78
TEMPSFORD, Bedfordshire
(7 miles E of Bedford)
109, 138, 161
TERNHILL, Shropshire
(14 miles NE of Shrewsbury)
19, 78, 87, 131, 132, 133,
134, 306, 605
THERFIELD, Hertfordshire
(2 miles SW of Royston)
75
THETFORD, Norfolk
(2 miles SE of Thetford)
25, 35, 38, 45, 51, 128,
156
THIRSK, Yorkshire
(9 miles SSE of North-
allerton)
226
THORNABY, Yorkshire
(4 miles S of Middlesbrough)
92, 106, 114, 143, 185,
220, 224, 233, 269, 275,
279, 280, 281, 608
THORNEY ISLAND, Sussex
(8 miles ENE of Portsmouth)
12, 22, 36, 42, 46, 48, 53,
56, 59, 63, 80, 86, 129, 130,
131, 143, 164, 193, 198,
217, 222, 233, 236, 248,
254, 278, 280, 547, 609,
612
THROWLEY, Kent
(13 miles E of Maidstone)
50, 112, 143, 188
THRUXTON, Wiltshire
(6 miles W of Andover)
16, 63, 142, 168, 170, 225,
268, 297, 298
THURLEIGH, Bedfordshire
(7 miles N of Bedford)
160
TILSHEAD, Shropshire
(3 miles W of Larkhill)
Alt. Shrewton
225
TIREE, Hebrides
224, 281, 304, 518
TOPCLIFFE, Yorkshire
(8 miles NE of Rippon)
24, 36, 47, 53, 62, 77,
102, 203, 210, 297
TORQUAY, Devon
(17 miles S of Exeter)
239
TOWYN, Merioneth
(1 mile NW of Towyn)
631
TRESCO, Scilly Isles
234
TUDDENHAM, Suffolk
(8 miles NW of Bury St.
Edmunds)
90, 107, 138, 149, 186, 207
TURNHOUSE, Midlothian
(6 miles W of Edinburgh)
3, 36, 63, 64, 65, 77, 81,
83, 104, 122, 123, 141,
164, 197, 232, 242, 243,
245, 253, 263, 268, 289,
290, 303, 329, 340, 341,

603, 607

TWINWOOD FARM, Bedfordshire (4 miles N of Bedford)
164, 169, 239, 268, 613

TYDD ST. MARY, Lincolnshire (12 miles W of Kings Lynn)
51

TYNEMOUTH, Northumberland (8 miles NE of Newcastle)
252

UPAVON, Wiltshire (14 miles NW of Andover)
3, 9, 17, 54, 73, 85, 87, 230

UPPER HEYFORD, Oxfordshire (13 miles N of Oxford)
7, 10, 18, 33, 34, 40, 57, 58, 76, 81, 99, 105, 108, 113, 122, 123, 157, 158, 215, 218, 226

UPWOOD, Huntingdonshire (10 miles SSE of Peterborough)
7, 18, 21, 35, 40, 49, 50, 52, 61, 63, 72, 76, 90, 102, 105, 139, 148, 156, 190, 191, 214, 542

USWORTH, Co. Durham (7 miles SE of Newcastle)
43, 103, 607

UXBRIDGE, Middlesex (16 miles W of London - not an airfield)
1, 4, 207

VALLEY, Anglesey (6 miles SE of Holyhead)
20, 125, 131, 157, 242, 258, 275, 312, 350, 615

WADDINGTON, Lincolnshire (4 miles S of Lincoln)
9, 12, 21, 23, 27, 44, 49, 50, 57, 61, 82, 83, 88, 97, 100, 101, 110, 123, 142, 203, 204, 207, 503, 617

WALMER, Kent (1 mile S of Deal)
233

WARBOYS, Huntingdonshire (6 miles NE of Huntingdon)
128, 156, 257, 571

WARMWELL, Dorset (5 miles WSW of Dorchester) Alt. Woodsford
2, 3, 19, 41, 56, 63, 66, 79, 80, 118, 130, 137, 152, 164, 174, 175, 181, 182, 184, 217, 234, 245, 247, 257, 263, 266, 274, 275,

276, 277, 302, 310, 312, 313, 340, 350, 500, 609, 610

WATERBEACH, Cambridgeshire (6 miles NNE of Cambridge)
1, 18, 24, 25, 46, 51, 53, 54, 56, 59, 62, 63, 64, 77, 153, 215, 220, 222, 253, 514

WATTISHAM, Suffolk (9 miles WNW of Ipswich)
18, 25, 29, 41, 56, 86, 107, 110, 111, 114, 152, 226, 236, 257, 263, 266

WATTON, Norfolk (11 miles NNE of Thetford)
18, 21, 34, 51, 82, 90, 97, 98, 105, 115, 116, 151, 192, 199, 245, 263, 360, 361, 527

WELLINGORE, Lincolnshire (10 miles S of London)
29, 54, 81, 154, 288, 309, 349, 613

WEST FREUGH, Wigtownshire (4 miles SSE of Stranraer)
63, 130

WESTGATE, Kent (2 miles W of Margate)
219

WESTHAMPNETT, Sussex (2 miles NE of Chichester) Alt. Goodwood
41, 65, 91, 118, 124, 129, 130, 131, 145, 174, 175, 184, 245, 302, 303, 340, 350, 501, 602, 610, 616

WESTLEY, Suffolk (1 mile W of Bury St. Edmunds)
241, 268

WEST MALLING, Kent (5 miles W of Maidstone)
3, 25, 26, 29, 32, 64, 80, 85, 91, 96, 98, 124, 130, 141, 153, 157, 234, 264, 274, 287, 316, 322, 350, 500, 531, 567, 616

WESTON-ON-THE-GREEN, Oxfordshire (8 miles N of Oxford)
2, 18, 90

WESTON ZOYLAND, Somerset (4 miles SE of Bridgwater)
16, 19, 26, 63, 76, 100, 122, 140, 151, 168, 169, 170, 171, 222, 231, 241, 268, 285, 286, 525, 542, 587, 691

WEST RAYNHAM, Norfolk (14 miles NE of Kings Lynn)
1, 4, 18, 41, 54, 76, 85, 90, 101, 114, 139, 141, 180, 239, 268, 342

WESTWARD HO, Devon (9 miles WSW of Barnstaple)
260

WETHERSFIELD, Essex (17 miles N of Chelmsford)
196, 299

WHITEBURN, Berwickshire (12 miles NW of Berwick)
77

WICK, Caithness (1 mile N of Wick)
3, 41, 42, 43, 48, 58, 86, 111, 122, 144, 220, 269, 303, 316, 504, 519, 605, 608, 612, 618

WICKENBY, Lincolnshire (9 miles NE of Lincoln)
12, 109, 626

WIGTOWN, Wigtownshire (1 mile S of Wigtown)
182

WINFIELD, Berwickshire (7 miles WSW of Berwick)
222

WING, Buckinghamshire (6 miles NNE of Aylesbury)
268, 613

WITCHFORD, Cambridgeshire (2 miles SW of Ely)
115, 195, 196, 513

WITTERING, Northamptonshire (10 miles WNW of Peterborough)
1, 7, 19, 23, 25, 32, 38, 40, 41, 45, 49, 56, 58, 61, 68, 74, 76, 100, 118, 138, 139, 141, 151, 152, 213, 219, 229, 230, 264, 266, 349, 532, 610

WOODBRIDGE, Suffolk (10 miles ENE of Ipswich)
298

WOODFORD, Essex (8 miles NE of London — not an airfield)
39

WOODHALL SPA, Lincolnshire (15 miles ESE of Lincoln)
97, 109, 112, 195, 617, 619, 627

WOODHAM MORTIMER, Essex (7 miles E of Chelmsford)

37

WOODHAVEN, Fifeshire (1 mile S of Dundee)
231, 233

WOODVALE, Lancashire (12 miles NNW of Liverpool)
63, 167, 198, 219, 222, 256, 285, 308, 313, 315, 316, 317, 322, 501, 611

WOOLFOX LODGE, Rutland (14 miles S of Grantham)
61, 62, 218

WOOLSINGTON, Northumberland (6 miles NW of Newcastle)
278, 281

WORKSOP, Nottinghamshire (14 miles S of Doncaster)
616

WORTHY DOWN, Hampshire (3 miles N of Winchester)
7, 35, 49, 58, 102, 207, 215

WRATTING COMMON, Cambridgeshire (13 miles SE of Cambridge)
90, 195

WREXHAM, Denbighshire (2 miles NE of Wrexham)
96, 285

WYE, Kent (2 miles NNE of Ashford)
3, 86

WYMESWOLD, Leicestershire (11 miles S of Nottingham)
56, 263, 504

WYTON, Huntingdonshire (3 miles NE of Huntingdon)
13, 15, 26, 39, 40, 44, 46, 51, 57, 58, 65, 81, 82, 83, 89, 90, 93, 104, 108, 109, 114, 117, 128, 130, 138, 139, 156, 163, 211, 540, 542, 543

YATESBURY, Wiltshire (10 miles SW of Swindon)
28, 54, 65, 73

YEADON, Yorkshire (7 miles NW of Leeds)
609

YELLING, Bedfordshire (6 miles NNW of Bedford)
75

YORK, Yorkshire (2 miles N of York)
231

ZEALS, Wiltshire (8 miles NW of Shaftesbury)
66, 118, 132, 174, 182, 184, 263, 286

Index of Overseas Locations

AALBORG, Denmark
69
ABADAN, Iran
74, 123
ABBEVILLE, France
Alt. B.92: Drucat
3, 4, 5, 13, 18, 26, 35, 52,
607, 615
ABEELE, France
4, 5, 6, 8, 10, 29, 32, 41, 53
ABLAINZEVILLE, France
12
ABOUKIR, Egypt
29, 33, 56, 64, 80, 123,
142, 145, 204, 228, 230,
252, 601
ABSCON, France
19, 42, 98
ABU SUEIR, Egypt
6, 13, 37, 40, 46, 70, 89,
104, 145, 208, 213, 214,
216, 252, 272
ACCRA, Gold Coast
82
ACHMER, Germany
Alt. B.110
98, 175, 180, 184, 245, 320
'ACORN' see KALYANPUR
ACROMA, Libya
208
ADEN (see also KHORMAK-
SAR, SHEIKH OTHMAN)
203, 223
AFISSE NORTH, Palestine
242
AFRIKANDA, Russia
144
AFULEH, Palestine
142
AGARTALA, India
5, 17, 27, 31, 60, 62, 117,
155, 194, 216, 292
AGENVILLERS, France
9
AGNONE, Sicily
112, 250, 260
AGRA, India
20, 30
AGRINION, Greece
112, 211
AHLHORN, Germany
Alt. B.111
14, 96, 149, 193, 197,
213, 256, 263, 266, 302,
308, 317
AIRE, France
10
AJACCIO, Corsica
283
AKROTIRI, Cyprus
1, 6, 9, 13, 29, 32, 35, 56,
70, 73, 84, 208, 249
AKUREYRI, Iceland
330
AKYAB, Burma
27, 30, 62, 67, 135, 139,
194, 230
ALEPPO, Syria
232, 243
ALEXANDRIA, Egypt
113, 202, 204, 206, 228,
230, 269, 270
ALGHERO, Sardinia
14, 23, 39, 256, 272, 284
ALGIERS, Algeria (see also
ARZEW, MAISON BLANCHE)
283, 284

ALIMINNI, Italy
224, 225
ALIPORE, India
5, 17, 34, 67, 79, 81, 136,
146, 155, 261, 607, 615,
681, 684
ALLAHABAD, India
34, 97, 110, 177
ALLONVILLE, France
4, 9, 34, 53, 80, 82, 203
ALMAZA, Egypt
45, 78, 216
ALMYROS, Greece
11
ALOR STAR, Malaya
62
ALQUINES, France
41, 98, 149, 206, 215
ALTO, Corsica
154, 232, 242, 243
AMARDA ROAD, India
20, 27, 67, 81, 110, 131,
135, 136, 177, 607
AMBALA, Italy
3, 5, 20, 28, 31, 60, 99,
114
AMBER-KOJ, Greece
17, 47
AMBERLEY, Australia
548
AMBLIE, France
Alt. B.14
132
AMEL EL CHEL, Libya
73
AMENDOLA, Italy
142, 150, 178, 214, 614
AMIENS, France (see also
MONT JOIE)
2, 3, 9
AMIENS GLISY, France
Alt. B.48
16, 69, 87, 137, 140, 181,
182, 219, 247, 276
AMIFONTAINE, France
12
AMMAN, Jordan
14, 32, 33, 249
AMRIYA, Egypt
29, 30, 33, 47, 55, 73,
80, 84, 94, 112, 113, 117,
223, 250, 274, 294
AMSEAT, Libya
55
AMY, France
Alt. Roye
57
ANCONA, Italy
55
ANDIR, Java
Alt Bandoeng
242, 605
ANDRANO, Italy
224
ANGLURE, France
1, 501
ANICHE, France
22, 40, 64
ANTELAT, Libya
33, 94, 112, 229, 238, 250,
260
ANTHENAY, France
52
APAPA, Nigeria
270
APOLLONIA, Libya
94

AQIR, Palestine
6, 11, 32, 37, 45, 55, 70,
74, 80, 84, 113, 147, 159,
160, 208, 211, 215, 250,
335, 620, 621
AQSU, Iraq
208
AQUINO, Italy
208
ARAWALI, India
5
ARAXOS, Greece
32, 252
ARCADE, Italy
66
ARGOS, Greece
80, 113, 139, 208
ARJANA, Tunisia
225, 241
ARKONAM, India
30, 79, 134, 146, 258, 261
ARTINS, France
226
ARZEW, Algeria
210
AS/OPHOVEN, Belgium
Alt. Y.32
41, 130, 350, 610
ASA, Sicily
152, 232, 242
ASANOL, India
28, 45, 60, 62, 82, 113,
136, 215
ASCQ, France
4, 5, 6, 42, 85
ASMARA, Eritrea
47, 163, 237
ASSEVILLERS, France
80, 84
ATHIES, France
9, 24, 46
AUBERCHICOURT, France
203
AUBERIVES-SUR-SUIPPES,
France
88, 218
AUCHEL, France
Alt. Lozinghem
3, 18, 22, 23, 25, 32, 40, 43,
58, 70, 83, 101, 148
AUCHY, France
16
AULNOY, France
5, 11, 42
AULNOYE, France
22, 52, 62, 88, 99
AUTHIE, France
Alt. B.22
26
AUTREVILLE, France
216
AUXI-LE-CHATEAU, France
6, 8, 52, 99, 110
AVESNES-LE-COMTE,
France
12, 43, 54
AVESNES-LE-SEC, France
52
AVIANO, Italy
13, 18, 55, 114, 256, 600
AVRILLY, France
Alt. B.34
168
AZELOT, France
55, 94, 104

BAGHDAD WEST, Iraq

6, 8, 30, 55, 63, 70, 84
BAHEIRA (BIR EL), Libya
260
BAHRAIN see MUHARRAQ
BAIGACHI, India
5, 11, 20, 30, 67, 81, 84,
89, 123, 131, 134, 136,
146, 152, 155, 176, 258,
261, 607, 615
BAILLEUL, France
1, 4, 5, 6, 7, 19, 32, 42, 53,
60, 65, 69
BAIZIEUX, France
4, 18, 23, 24, 46, 56, 60,
68, 73, 201
BALLEROY see LIGNE-
ROLLES
BANCOURT, France
151
BANDOENG see ANDIR
BANGALORE, India
1, 3
BAQUBA, Arabia
30
BARCE, Libya
6, 208
BARDUFOSS, Norway
46, 263
BARENTU, Sudan
237
BARI, Italy
Alt. Palese
112, 117, 208, 250, 260,
267, 512, 575
BARODA, India
298
BAROMESNIL, France
Alt. B.35
164, 183, 198, 222, 609
BASAL, India
31, 194, 215, 669, 670
BASRA, Iraq
8, 30, 45, 63, 72, 203, 294
BASTIA see BORGO and
PORETTA
BATAVIA, Java (see also
KEMAJORAN)
34, 205
BATHURST, Gambia
95, 204
BATTIPAGLIA, Italy
93, 111
BAVAY, France
27, 49, 107
BAVICHOVE, Belgium
39
BAZENVILLE, France
Alt. B.2
174, 609
BEAUREGARD, France
38
BEAUVAIS, France
Alt. A.61, Tille
65, 73, 79, 122, 132, 174,
175, 184, 245
BEAUVOIS, France
25, 27, 32, 49
BEAUVRAIGNES, France
18
BELANDAH, Libya
112, 250, 260
BELGAUM, India
668, 669, 671, 672, 673
BELLARIA, Italy
92, 145, 241, 318, 601
BELLEVILLE FARM, France
32, 80

BELLEVUE (LA), France
8, 11, 18, 32, 35, 48, 49,
59, 60, 62, 73, 80
BEN GARDANE, Tunisia
6, 92, 145, 223, 260, 601
BENINA, Libya
33, 55, 70, 162, 260, 274,
335, 351, 352
BENY-SUR-MER, France
Alt. B.4
2, 4, 268
BERGUES, France
202, 213, 217
BERKA, Libya
14, 38, 55, 227, 237, 252,
294
BERLAIMONT, France
2
BERMUDA
231
BERNAY, France
Alt. B.29
74, 329, 340, 341
BERRY-AU-BAC, France
1, 12, 142
BERSEE, France
88
BERSIS, Libya
33, 89, 108, 134, 237, 335
BERTANGLES, France
3, 6, 9, 11, 16, 18, 21, 22,
23, 24, 48, 52, 54, 65, 82,
84, 85, 209
BERTRY, France
6, 23, 80, 84, 92
BETHENCOURT, France
56, 57, 201
BETHENIVILLE, France
15, 40, 103, 139, 501
BETTONCOURT, France
11, 45, 110
BEUGNATRE, France
59, 60, 201
BEVILLERS, France
102
BHATPARA, India
211
BHOPAL, India
5, 30
BICKENDORF, Germany
7, 12, 18, 25, 29, 43, 49,
59, 70, 79, 84, 149, 206
BIENFAY, France
3
BIFERNO, Italy
13, 39, 55, 213, 223, 227,
249, 335
BIKRAM, India
117, 668, 671, 672, 673
BILASPUR, India
10, 96, 267
BILBEIS, Egypt
117, 162, 267
BIR DUFAN, Libya
73, 112, 250, 260
BIR EL BAHEIRA, Egypt
260
BISHNUPUR, India
358
BISSEGHEM, Belgium
7, 24, 43, 65, 82, 108
BIZERTA, Tunisia
230
BLANGERMONT, France
98
BLIDA, Algeria
13, 14, 18, 23, 36, 114,
142, 150, 293, 500, 600,
608, 614, 624
BOBBILI, India
5, 81, 123, 131, 258
BOFFLES, France

60
BOIRY ST. MARTIN, France
8, 12
BOIS DE ROCHE see CONTE-
VILLE
BOISDINGHEM, France
20, 21, 22, 25, 45, 46, 49,
53, 54, 55, 57, 60, 70, 80,
203, 206
BOISNEY, France
Alt. B.27
2, 4, 268
BOLOGNA, Italy
87, 208, 225
BOMBAY, India
132
BONE, Algeria (see also
TINGLEY)
72, 111, 154, 219, 225,
232, 242, 243, 284, 293
BONNEUIL, France
52, 82
BOOS, France
85, 87
BORGHETTO, Itlay
87, 185
BORGO, Corsica
253, 283, 327, 328
BO RIZZO, Sicily
52, 87, 255, 272, 603, 614
BOU FICHA, Tunisia
225, 241
BOUGE, Belgium
62
BOUGENAIS, France
105
BOU GOUBRINE, Tunisia
6, 92, 145, 296, 601
BOU GRARA, Tunisia
92, 145, 601
BOULOGNE, France
7
BOURLON, France
52
BOUSSIERES, France
87, 210
BOUVINCOURT, France
1, 43, 80, 84
BOUVELLES, France
6, 205
BRAY DUNES, France
43, 52, 54, 65, 92, 204
BRINDISI, Italy
Alt. Campo Casale
18, 32, 55, 73, 112, 114,
148, 213, 223, 249, 253,
284, 301, 624
BRON see LYON/BRON
BROOME, Australia
205
BRUAY, France
3, 16, 18, 23, 35, 40, 46,
54, 71
BRUGES, Belgium
6
BRUGGEN, Germany
2, 14, 17, 20, 31, 67, 71,
80, 87, 112, 130, 213
BRUILLE, France
203, 209
BRUNEI, Borneo
110
BRUYERES, France
57
BRYAS, France
40
BU AMUD, Egypt
6, 11, 14, 55, 73, 80, 89,
94, 123, 134, 229, 238,
274, 336
BUCKEBURG, Germany
2, 79, 541

BUCKHEIM, Germany
7
BUDAREYRI, Iceland
330
BURDINNE, Belgium
88
BURG EL ARAB, Egypt
47, 73, 208
BUSIGNY, France
24, 46
BUTTERWORTH, Malaya
9, 12, 18, 27, 33, 45, 47,
52, 62, 110
CACHY, France
62, 73, 79, 80
CAEN see CARPIQUET
CAFFIERS, France
54
CAGLIARI see ELMAS
CAIRO WEST, Egypt
Alt. LG.224
96, 117, 216, 267, 620
CALAIS, France
9, 66
CALCUTTA, India (see also
DUM DUM)
668
CALDIERO, Italy
34
CALENZANA, Corsica
154, 232, 242, 243
CALVI MAIN, Corsica
43, 72, 93, 111, 326, 327,
328
CAMBRAI/EPINOY, France
Alt. A.75
69, 107, 268, 305, 613
CAMDEN, Australia
243
CAMILLY, France
Alt. B.5
198, 245
CAMPLAIN L'ABBE, France
16, 148
CAMP NEUSEVILLE, France
Alt. B.33
66, 127, 331, 332
CAMPO CASALE see BRIN-
DISI
CAMPO DELL'ORO, Corsica
(see also AJACCIO)
327, 328
CAMPOFORMIDO, Italy
72, 87, 185, 225, 600
CANDAS, France
34
CANNE, Italy
6, 32, 73, 80, 92, 145, 241,
249, 253, 274, 351, 352,
601
CANROBERT, Algeria
13, 18, 114, 614
CAPELLE, France
38, 65, 88, 108, 204
CAPE TOWN, S. Africa
26
CAPODICHINO, Italy
43, 72, 93, 111, 225, 243,
253
CAPPY, France
23, 24, 46
CARNIERES, France
13
CARPIQUET, France
Alt. B.17
33, 222, 264, 349, 604
CARTHAGO, Sudan
47
CARVIN, France
152, 207
CASABLANCA, Morocco

219
CASSALA, Sicily
43, 72, 93, 111, 243
CASSANDRA, Italy
241, 318
CASSIBILE, Italy
92, 145, 284, 600, 601
CASTEL BENITO, Libya
6, 89, 92, 112, 117, 145,
250, 260, 601
CASTIGLIONE, Italy
208
CATANIA, Sicily
43, 87, 117, 229, 243, 272
CATIGNY, France
52, 82, 101
CATILLON, France
101
CAUDRY, France
59
CAWNPORE, India
31
CECINA, Italy
13, 18, 55, 114
CELLE, Germany
Alt. B.118
2, 4, 11, 14, 16, 41, 93, 94,
98, 130, 137, 145, 245,
268, 350
CELONE, Italy
Alt. Foggia No.1
55, 114, 178, 223, 614
CERIGNOLA, Italy
37, 40, 70, 104, 142, 150
CERVIA, Italy
112, 250, 260
CESENATICO, Italy
500, 600
CHAILLY-EN-BRIE, France
27, 98, 107
CHAKLALA, India
5, 62, 99, 215, 670, 672
CHAKRATA, India
34, 159
CHAKULIA, India
30, 42, 135, 615
CHALLERANGE, France
103, 150
CHAMPIEN, France
54, 73, 79, 80, 84
CHANDINA, Italy
62, 113, 681
CHANGI, Singapore
18, 48, 52, 81, 84, 103,
110, 194, 205, 215
CHATEAU BOUGON, France
Alt. Nantes
1, 73, 98, 114, 218
CHATEAU DE WERPPE see
CHOCQUES
CHATEAUDUN, France
1
CHEMY, France
214
CHERBOURG, France
243
CHERIA, Tunisia
40, 104
CHETTINAD, India
11, 20
CHHARRA, India
20, 82, 84, 615
CHIARAVALLE, Italy
241, 318
CHIENGMAI, Thailand
20
CHIEVRES, Belgium
Alt. A.84
164, 183, 198, 609
CHINA BAY, Ceylon
17, 261, 273, 321, 357
CHIPILLY, France

8, 9, 22, 24, 35, 52
CHIRINGA, India
  20, 22, 27, 177, 211, 261
CHITTAGONG, India
  30, 67, 79, 82, 110, 135,
  136, 139, 146, 152, 177,
  258, 261, 273, 607, 615
CHOCQUES, France
Alt. Chateau de Werppe
  4, 10, 16, 42
CHOLAVARUM, India
  5, 11, 27, 34, 45, 47, 60,
  82, 84, 113, 123
CHRISTMAS ISLAND, Pacific
Ocean
  217
CITADEL, France
  52
CLAIRMARAIS, France
  1, 4, 20, 27, 53, 54, 58, 65,
  74, 98, 101, 149, 209
CLARY, France
Alt. Iris Farm
  20, 211
CLAVIER, Belgium
  12
CLERMONT, France
  23, 80
COCOS ISLAND, Indian Ocean
  99, 136, 217, 321, 356
COGNAC, France
  26
COGNELEE (FORT DE),
Belgium
  5, 7, 9, 43, 149
COLMAR, France
  326, 327, 328
COLOMBO, Ceylon
  230
COLOMBO RACECOURSE,
Ceylon
  11, 30, 258
COMILLA, India
  30, 31, 62, 67, 79, 113,
  134, 146, 152, 194, 211,
  238, 258, 684
COMISO, Sicily
  18, 43, 72, 93, 111, 243
COMPIEGNE, France
  3, 4
CONDE VRAUX, France
  1, 15, 114
CONGELLA, Africa
  262
CONSTANTINE, Algeria
  152, 232, 242, 243
CONTEVILLE, France
Alt. Bois de Roche
  24, 41, 49, 54, 65, 84, 205
COUCOU, Belgium
  21, 53, 82
COUDEKERQUE, France
  98, 207, 214, 215
COULOMBS, France
Alt. B.6
  137, 181, 182, 247, 264
COULOMMIERS, France
  2, 3, 4, 540
COURCELLES-LE-COMTE,
France
  12, 15, 59
COX'S BAZAAR, India
  5, 123, 135, 273
COXYDE, Belgium
Alt. B.71
  605
CRAMAILLE, France
  52, 216
CRECY-EN-PONTHIEU,
France
  18, 53, 57, 59
CRETE, Italy

112, 250, 260
CRETON, France
Alt. B.30
  137, 181, 182, 247
CROCHTE, France
  217
CROISETTE, France
  62
CUERNE, France
  74
CUERS/PIERREFEU, France
Alt. Y.13
  237, 238
CUTELLA, Italy
  250, 260
CUTTACK, India
  62, 134, 354, 615

DABA, Egypt
  73, 112, 113, 211, 235
DABAING, Burma
  67
DAKAR, French West Africa
  343, 344
DAKAWA, Tanganyika
  26
DALBUMGARH, India
  28, 42, 45, 131
DAMBULLA, Ceylon
  30, 258
DARDONI, India
  5, 27, 28, 31
DAR-ES-SALAAM,
Tanganyika
  26, 230, 259
DARRAGH, Libya
  601
DARWIN, Australia
  54, 548, 549
DEDELSTORF, Germany
Alt. B.155
  3, 33, 56, 174, 274
DEIR-EL-EELAH, Palestine
  14, 67, 111
DEKHEILA, Egypt
  74, 235
DEOLALI, India
  159
DERGAON, India
  5, 34, 60, 615
DERNA, Libya
  55, 80, 148, 227, 274
DEURNE, Belgium
Alt B.70 Antwerp
  2, 4, 74, 130, 132, 174,
  175, 184, 193, 197, 245,
  257, 263, 266, 268, 274,
  302, 308, 329, 341, 345,
  602
DEVERSOIR, Egypt
  6, 32, 213, 249, 256, 680
DHAMIAL, India
  117, 670
DHIBBAN see HABBANIYA
DHUBALIA, India
  31, 36, 62, 99, 159, 215,
  353
DIEGO SUAREZ, Madagascar
  265
DIEPPE, France
  26
DIGRI, India
  45, 99, 110, 159, 215,
  298, 355, 357, 358
DIJON/LONGVIC, France
  326, 327, 328
DIMAPUR, India
  11, 113
DINARD, France
  501
DINJAN, India
  5, 146

DJEDEIDA, Tunisia
  37, 70
DJIDJELLI, Algeria
  87, 154, 242
DOHAZARI, India
  27, 60, 79, 82, 110, 135,
  258, 615
DON MUANG, Thailand
  Alt. Bangkok
  20, 211, 273, 684
DORVAL, Canada
  231, 243
DOSHAN TAPPEH, Iran
  74, 123
DOUAI, France
  13
DOUBLE MOORINGS, India
  67, 152
DOUR, France
  88
DREUX, France
  329, 340, 345
DRIGH ROAD, India
  31, 60, 84, 160, 354
DRIONVILLE, France
  88, 92, 98, 107
DROGLANDT, France
  5, 6, 7, 10, 15, 21, 28, 32,
  41, 46, 57, 65, 70, 82
DROPE, Germany
Alt. B.105
  74, 197, 263, 266, 340,
  341, 345
DRUCAT see ABBEVILLE
DUM DUM, India
Alt. Calcutta
  5, 45, 52, 60, 62, 113,
  135, 136, 146, 176, 258,
  261, 353, 681, 684
DUREN, Grermany
  12, 59
DWEHLA, Burma
  155, 607

EASTLEIGH, Kenya
  21, 30, 39, 49, 82, 100,
  142, 208, 214, 249, 500
ECHEMINES, France
  12, 73, 105
ECOIVRES, France
  107
ECURY-SUR-COOLE, France
  150
ED DAMER, Sudan
  35, 207
EDINBURGH FIELD,
Trinidad
  53
EDKU see IDKU
EIL, Germany
  43, 84, 92, 208
EINDHOVEN, Netherlands
Alt. B.78
  16, 41, 69, 130, 137, 140,
  168, 181, 182, 247, 350,
  610
EIN SHEMER, Palestine
  6, 13, 18, 32, 37, 38, 178,
  208, 214, 621, 680
EKATERINODAR, Russia
  47
EL ADEM, Libya
  6, 33, 47, 73, 80, 94, 112,
  117, 178, 213, 238, 336
EL AOUINA, Tunisia
  284, 683
EL ARISH, Egypt
  67
EL ASSA, Libya
  73, 112, 250, 260
EL BALLAH, Egypt
  73, 94, 256

EL BASSA, Palestine
  80, 208
EL CHEL, Libya
  92, 145, 250, 601
EL DABA see DABA
EL DJEM, Tunisia
  112, 117, 250, 260
ELEUSIS, Greece
  11, 30, 33, 80, 208
EL FIRDAN, Egypt
  14, 229, 237, 238
EL GAMIL see GAMIL
EL GUBBI, Libya
  6, 55, 73, 80, 208, 223, 238
EL HAMMA, Tunisia
  112, 250, 260
EL HASSEIT, Libya
  92, 601
ELINCOURT, France
  35
EL KHANKA, Egypt
  46, 216
ELLON, France
Alt. B.12
  19, 65, 122
EL MAGRUN, Libya
  37, 70, 227, 252
ELMAS, Sardinia
  284
EL MERDUNA, Libya
  92, 601
EL NOGRA, Libya
  92
ELSENBORN, Germany
  5, 7
EL SIRTAN, Libya
  55
EMERCHICOURT, France
  5, 7
ENFIDAVILLE, Tunisia
  55, 223
ENSCHEDE see TWENTHE
EPISKOPI, Cyprus
  112
ERKOWEIT, Sudan
  45, 47
ERRE, France
  148
ESCAUCOURT, France
  85
ESNES, France
  56
ESQUERDES, France
  70
ESTOURMEL, France
  12
ESTREE BLANCHE, France
  22, 41, 56, 66
ESTREE-LES-CRECY, France
  87
ESTREES-EN-CHAUSSEE,
France
  8, 9, 34, 35, 59, 73, 83, 85,
  92, 207, 208
ETRUN, France
  13
EVERE, Belgium
Alt. B.56
  349, 350, 512, 610

FABRICA, Italy
  92, 145, 601
FALCONARA, Italy
  13, 18, 38, 55, 114, 237,
  241, 272, 318, 600, 624
FALCONE, Sicily
  43, 72, 93, 111, 243
FALERIUM, Italy
  112, 208, 250, 260
FAMECHON, France
  101, 102, 151
FANO, Italy

87, 92, 112, 145, 185, 241,
250, 260, 601
FASSBERG, Germany
Alt B.152
3, 11, 14, 16, 26, 27, 33,
56, 98, 112, 118, 130,
174, 266, 340, 341, 345,
349, 350, 616
FATEHJANG, India
668, 670, 672
FAUQUEMBERGUES, France
58
FAUX-VILLECERF, France
142, 226
FAYID, Egypt
6, 13, 37, 39, 70, 78, 84,
92, 108, 112, 159, 178,
204, 208, 214, 216, 683
FAZILPUR, India
30, 134
FENI, India
Alt. Fenny
5, 11, 30, 82, 113, 123,
146, 177, 211, 607, 615
FERE-EN-TARDENOIS,
France
2, 3, 4, 5
FERMIO, Italy
241, 318
FIENVILLERS, France
1, 6, 11, 15, 19, 21, 23, 27,
41, 42, 43, 45, 53, 54, 55,
57, 60, 70, 101, 201
FILESCAMP, France
46, 60, 203
FISMES, France
52
FLAUMONT, France
80
FLENSBURG, Germany
Alt. B.166
181, 182, 184
FLEZ, France
22, 24, 47, 54, 84
FLORINGHEM, France
2, 21, 88, 103
FOGGIA, Italy
6, 18, 32, 38, 40, 73, 87,
104, 112, 148, 225, 250,
253, 255, 256, 260, 272,
293, 624
FOLLONICA, Italy
225, 600
FONTAINECHAUDE, Tunisia
142, 150
FONTAINE-SUR-MAYE,
France
151
FORLI, Italy
13, 18, 55, 114, 256, 318
FORT DE COGNELEE see
COGNELEE
FORT ROUGE, France
Alt. B.43
2, 4, 268
FORT SANDEMAN, India
5
FOUCAUCOURT, France
8, 73, 85, 208
FOUQUEROLLES, France
32, 43, 73, 80
FOURNEUIL, France
27, 49
FRANCESCO, Italy
225
FRANC WARET, Belgium
107
FRANQUEVILLE, France
83
FREETOWN, Sierra Leone
95
FREJUS, France

Alt. Y.12
154, 232, 242, 243
FRESNOY FOLNEY, France
Alt. B.31
2, 4, 268
FRETNUM, France
218
FROHA, Algeria
296
FROIDMONT, France
21, 64, 74, 209
FUKA, Egypt
18, 33, 45, 55, 80, 223
FYZABAD, India
113

GABES, Tunisia
6, 73, 137, 601
GALORIA, Itlay
225
GAMACHES, France
Alt. B.37 Corroy
74, 340, 341
GAMBUT, Libya
6, 14, 33, 38, 45, 47, 55,
73, 80, 84, 92, 94, 112,
113, 145, 148, 208, 229,
237, 238, 250, 252, 260,
601, 603
GAMIL, Egypt
33, 73, 94, 213, 238, 250
GANNAVARAM, India
22, 217
GARDABIA, Libya
37, 40, 70, 104, 227, 272
GARDERMOEN, Norway
129, 130, 276
GASR-EL-ARID, Libya
73, 94, 260
GASR GARABULLI, Libya
73
GATOW, Germany
3, 80, 174
GAYE, France
73
GAZA, Egypt
33, 80, 208, 318
GAZALA, Libya
33, 55, 73, 80, 94, 112,
229, 238, 250, 260, 274
GEBEIT, Sudan
35, 207
GEILENKIRCHEN, Germany
2, 3, 11, 19, 59, 92, 96,
234, 256
GELA WEST see MONTE
LUNGO
GENECH, France
2, 19
GENEIFA, Egypt
74
GERAWLA, Egypt
Alt. Maaten Gerawla
33, 112, 208, 274, 335
GERBINI, Sicily
18, 23, 126, 223
GERPINNES, Belgium
6, 12, 59
GHEDI, Italy
28
GHISONACCIA, Corsica
326
GIANACLIS, Egypt
38, 39, 47, 148, 252,
255, 512
GIARABUB, Libya
33, 113
GIBRALTAR
Alt. North Front
13, 23, 43, 48, 52, 81, 111,
179, 202, 204, 210, 224,
233, 500, 520, 608

GILZE-RIJEN, Netherlands
Alt. B.77
2, 4, 33, 164, 183, 198,
219, 222, 226, 264, 268,
302, 305, 308, 317, 342,
349, 609, 616
GIOIA DEL COLLE, Italy
81, 92, 145, 152, 154, 232,
242, 243, 284
GLIKI see IMBROS
GLISY see AMIENS
GOCH, Germany
Alt. G.100
174, 175, 184, 245
GONDECOURT, France
6, 88, 108
GORDON'S TREE, Sudan
47, 237
GOUBRINE see BOU
GOUBRINE
GRAND FAIT, France
80
GRAVE, Netherlands
Alt. B.82
80, 130, 274
GRIMBERGEN, Belgium
Alt. B.60
3, 19, 56, 65, 66, 122, 127,
302, 308, 317, 331, 332
GROMBALIA, Tunisia
18, 114
GROSSA, Italy
28, 34, 45, 66, 139
GROSSACHSENHEIM,
Germany
Alt. R.29
328
GROSSETO, Italy
43, 72, 93, 111
GROTTAGLIE, Italy
6, 14, 38, 92, 112, 126,
185, 221, 249, 250, 255,
336, 624
GUIDONIA, Italy
112, 250, 260
GUINDY, India
84
GUTERSLOH, Germany
Alt. Y.99
2, 3, 14, 16, 18, 19, 20, 21,
26, 33, 59, 67, 71, 79, 80,
92, 102, 103, 104, 107,
149, 230
GZINA, Libya
260

HABBANIYA, Iraq
Alt. Dhibban
6, 11, 14, 30, 45, 52, 55,
70, 73, 74, 84, 123, 249,
261, 683
HADERA, Palestine
74, 123
HADITHA, Iraq
127
HAIFA, Palestine
80, 213, 260, 261
HAL FAR, Malta
9, 12, 22, 43, 72, 73, 74,
93, 108, 185, 208, 229,
243, 249, 250, 255, 261,
283, 284, 605
HALF DIE, Gambia
204, 228
HALLUIN, France
41, 70, 74
HAM, France
92
HAMRAIET, Libya
92, 112, 145, 250, 260,
601
HANCOURT, France

23, 101
HANDORF, Germany
Alt. Y.94 Munster
4, 21
HANGELAR, Germany
5, 207
HANI EAST & WEST, Tunisia
40, 104
HARLEBEKE, Belgium
38
HASSANI, Greece
Alt. Kalamaki
13, 18, 38, 39, 55, 73, 94,
108, 112, 221, 252, 335,
336
HASTINGS, Sierra Leone
128
HATHAZARI, India
31, 117, 177
HAUSSIMONT, France
82
HAUTE VISEE, France
101
HAY, India
134, 258
HAZBUB, Tunisia
92, 145, 601
HELIOPOLIS, Egypt
6, 11, 14, 17, 30, 33, 39,
45, 55, 58, 64, 67, 70, 73,
84, 92, 113, 145, 173, 206,
208, 211, 216, 266
HELMOND, Netherlands
Alt. B.86
137, 181, 182, 247
HELWAN, Egypt
6, 8, 11, 18, 29, 33, 39, 45,
47, 55, 70, 74, 80, 112,
134, 142, 145, 206, 211,
318, 335, 601
HERAKLION, Crete
11, 84, 112, 203, 211, 252
HERGLA, Tunisia
92, 145, 601
HERVILLY, France
8, 73
HESDIGNEUL, France
2, 21
HEULE, France
204
HEUMAR, Germany
12, 208
HILDESHEIM, Germany
Alt. R.16
193, 197, 263, 266, 310
HINAIDI, Iraq
1, 6, 8, 30, 45, 55, 70
HMAWBI, Burma
47, 96, 110, 117, 215
HONDSCHOOTE, France
41
HOOG HUIS, France
29
HOPSTEN, Germany
Alt. B.112
3, 56, 80, 137, 181, 182,
247
HOSC RAUI, Libya
178
HOUGES, France
3
HOUSSAY, France
150
'HOVE', Burma
135, 258
HURGHADA, Egypt
127
HURTLEBISE FARM, France
102
HUSTEDT, Germany
Alt. B.150 Scheven
2, 175, 184, 268

366

HUSUM, Germany
Alt. B.172
137, 350

IANNINA, Greece
80, 112
IDKU, Egypt
6, 30, 33, 46, 74, 80, 89,
108, 162, 213, 221, 227,
229, 237, 272, 294, 335,
603
IESI, Italy
13, 112, 250, 260
IKEJA, Nigeria
349
IKINGI MARYUT, Egypt
30, 39, 94, 250, 601
IMBROS, Aegean
Alt. Kephalo
220
IMPHAL, India
11, 28, 81, 152, 155, 194,
607
INCHY, France
3, 60
IRIS FARM see CLARY
ISMAILIA, Egypt
Alt. Moascar
6, 11, 14, 30, 33, 38, 45,
55, 64, 80, 94, 113, 142,
208, 211, 213, 237
ISTRANA, Italy
34, 45
ISTRES, France
284, 328
IWAKUNI, Japan
11, 17, 205
IZEL-LE-HAMEAU, France
1, 5, 11, 13, 18, 22, 23, 29,
32, 45, 52, 58, 59, 60, 64,
84, 94, 100, 101, 102, 203,
209

JALAHALLI, India
42
JAMSHEDPUR, India
20
JANES, Greece
47
JEMAPPES, Algeria
43, 253
JESSORE, India
8, 17, 34, 60, 62, 99, 113,
200, 215, 292, 357, 358,
607, 615
JESWANG, Gambia
200
JEVER, Germany
Alt. B.117
2, 4, 20, 93, 98, 112, 118
JOARI, India
22, 45, 82, 110
JUHU, India
60
JUI, Sierra Leone
95, 204, 270
JUILLY, France
2, 3, 4
JULIS, Palestine
14, 111, 113, 142
JUMCHAR, India
30, 82, 135
JUNCTION STATION,
Palestine
14, 144

K.1, Iraq
208
KABRIT, Egypt
13, 18, 32, 37, 40, 55, 70,
78, 80, 104, 108, 113, 114,
148, 162, 203, 204, 215,
216, 219, 243

KAHE, Tanganyika
26
KAIROUAN, Tunisia
112, 142, 150, 250, 260
KAI TAK, Hong Kong
28, 33, 80, 96, 110, 132,
209, 215, 681
KAJAMALAI, India
5, 20 ,123
KALAFRANA, Malta
Alt. Calafrana
202, 209, 228, 266, 268
KALAMAKI see HASSANI
KALDADARNES, Iceland
98, 269
KALEWA, Burma
60
KALEYMO, Burma
28
KALIDJATI, Java
36, 84, 211
KALLANG, Singapore
11, 27, 31, 39, 48, 67, 110,
152, 155, 215, 243
KALYANPUR, India
Alt. 'Acorn'
17, 20, 110, 155
KAN, Burma
11, 152
KANCHRAPARA, India
27, 79
KANGLA, India
42, 60, 81
KANKESANTURAI, Ceylon
160, 203
KANTARA see QANTARA
KARACHI, India (see also
DRIGH ROAD)
80, 84, 110, 117
KARGI ROAD, India
77, 671, 672, 673
KASFAREET, Egypt
46, 47, 52, 127, 134, 230,
237, 602
KASTRUP, Denmark
Alt. B.160
3, 41, 56, 137, 175, 181,
182, 184
KATUKURUNDA, Ceylon
273
KAZAKLAR, Greece
208
KELANANG, Malaya
11, 17
KEMAJORAN, Java
31, 60, 81, 84, 110, 321
KEPHALO see IMBROS
KERMANSHAH, Iran
237
KHARAGPUR, India
5, 30, 113
KHARTOUM, Sudan
3, 6, 39, 47, 117, 208,
213, 223
KHIRBET DEIRAN, Palestine
113
KHORMAKSAR, Aden
8, 12, 21, 26, 37, 41, 43,
78, 84, 94, 105, 114, 203,
208, 233, 621, 683
KIFRI, Iraq
30
KILIA, Turkey
4
KILID-EL-BAHR, Turkey
4
KILO 8, Egypt
73, 127, 213
KILO 17, Egypt
46, 89
KILO 26, Egypt
6
KILO 143, Egypt

14, 67
KILWA, Tanganyika
26
'KINGS CROSS' see SOUK-
EL-KHEMIS
KINMAGAN, Burma
34, 47, 110, 113
KIPEVU, Kenya
209, 259
KIREC, Greece
150
KIRKUK, Iraq
30, 237
KJEVIK, Norway
130, 276
KLAGENFURT, Austria
43, 72, 93, 111, 225
KLUIS, Netherlands
Alt. B.91
33, 164, 183, 198, 222,
274, 609
KNOCKE-LE-ZOUTE,
Belgium
Alt. B.83
119, 276, 290
KOGGALA, Ceylon
191, 205, 209, 230, 240
KOHAT, India
5, 20, 27, 28, 60
KOKSIJDE see COXYDE
KOLAR, India
82, 110, 358
KORANGI CREEK, India
191, 212
KRENDI see QRENDI
KUALA LUMPUR, Malaya
11, 17, 28, 33, 45, 48, 52,
60, 84, 110, 131, 136,
209, 258, 267
KUANTAN, Malaya
36, 60
KUCHING, Sarawak
110
KUFRA, Egypt
6
KUMBHIRGRAM, India
22, 34, 42, 45, 47, 60, 81,
82, 84, 110, 146, 261
KWA LOKUA, Tanganyika
26
KWETNGE, Burma
34, 113, 155, 607
KYAUKPYU, Burma
5, 31, 117, 123, 134, 258,
273

LANDING GROUNDS IN
WESTERN DESERT
LG.05   18, 30, 213
LG.07   238
LG.08   127
LG.09   11, 37, 148
LG.10   237, 272
LG.12   33, 213, 229, 238,
         250
LG.13   73, 80, 145, 274,
         335, 601
LG.15   14, 145, 238
LG.16   45
LG.18   80
LG.20   127, 213, 238
LG.21   14, 73, 92, 145,
         238, 601
LG.37   80, 127, 274, 335
LG.39   221
LG.75   14, 33, 45, 70, 84,
         213, 237, 250, 260
LG. 76   33, 73, 145, 208,
         213, 250, 260
LG.79   55, 112
LG.81   45
LG.85'   33, 73, 80, 213,
         260, 335, 601

LG.86   39, 55
LG.87   47
LG.88   127, 274
LG.89   6, 47, 73, 127,
         221, 274
LG.90   213
LG.91   6, 52, 112, 162,
         250, 252, 603
LG.92   80, 127, 154, 238,
         274, 601
LG.93   229
LG.95   55
LG.97   260
LG.98   55
LG.99   55
LG.100   55, 208
LG.101   33, 203, 213, 238,
         250, 260
LG.102   30, 80, 229, 250
LG.103   80, 94, 208, 274
LG.104   11, 40, 70, 104, 274
LG.105   128, 238
LG.106   6, 37, 70, 74, 104,
         108, 148, 237, 248,
         250
LG.109   80, 94, 250, 260
LG.110   94
LG.111   80, 229
LG.115   73, 94, 260
LG.116   11, 14, 84, 113
LG.121   30, 80, 134, 238,
         335, 336
LG.122   250
LG.123   229, 238, 250
LG.124   94, 260, 274
LG.125   33
LG.128   80, 237
LG.129   680
LG.130   274
LG.140   37, 70
LG.154   33, 145, 213, 238,
         601
LG.155   73, 145, 213, 238,
         601
LG.167   148
LG.172   6, 33, 127, 213, 238
LG.173   92, 145, 335
LG.175   112
LG.207   318
LG.219   134, 336, 601
LG.222   40, 134
LG.224   14, 37, 39, 70, 104
LG.229   274
LG.237   40, 104, 108, 148
LG.'Y'   237

LAARBRUCH, Germany
2, 3, 5, 15, 16, 31, 68, 69,
79, 80
LA BANCA see NETTUNO
LA BRAYELLE, France
16, 18, 25, 32
LABUAN, Borneo
110, 230
LA FAUCONNERIE, Tunisia
55, 92, 145, 223, 601
LA FERE, France
3, 4
LAGENS, Azores
206, 220, 232, 269
LAGO, Italy
43, 72, 93, 111, 145, 225
LA GORGUE, France
5, 15, 16, 35, 42, 43, 46,
208
LAHAT, Greece
34
LAHORE, India
5, 11, 28, 39, 60, 97, 114,
194
LA HOUSSOYE, France
3, 15, 52, 54, 83, 101

LA JASSE, France
Alt. Y.19
   43, 72, 93, 111
LAKATAMIA, Cyprus
   213, 227, 252
LAKE TIMSAH, Egypt
   230
LALAGHAT, India
   668
LALMAI, India
   11, 117
LA LOUVETERIE, Belgium
   205
LA LOVIE, Belgium
   21, 23, 29, 35, 65, 74
LA MARSA, Tunisia
   682
LAMPEDUSA, Central Mediterranean
   253
LANGENHAGEN, Germany
Alt. B.120
   137, 181, 182, 247
LANKA, India
   5, 11
LARISSA, Greece
   11, 80, 113
LA RUSSIA, Italy
   318
LA SEBALA, Tunisia
   32, 72, 73, 87, 93, 219,
   243, 253, 255, 283, 500
LA SENIA, Algeria
   256
LASHIO, Burma
   17, 28, 45
LA TARGETTE, France
   56, 102, 201
LAVARIANO, Italy
   93, 112, 225, 250, 260,
   318
LAVERTON, Australia
   542
LAVIEVILLE, France
   3, 15, 18, 56
LAWNTON, Australia
   548
LEALVILLIERS, France
   15, 32, 41, 59
LE CATEAU, France
   2, 3, 4
LECHELLE, France
   3, 15, 56
LE CROTOY, France
   6
LEFFRINCKOUCKE, France
   48, 54
LE FRESNEY CAMILLE,
France
Alt. B.5
   175, 184
LE HAMEAU see IZEL-LE-
HAMEAU
LE MANS, France
   17, 501
LEMNOS, Aegean
   226
LENTINI, Sicily
   81, 92, 145, 152, 154,
   232, 242, 243, 284, 601
LE PLANEY, France
   55
LE QUESNOY, France
   11, 57, 107, 149
LES GRANDES CHAPELLES,
France
   88
LESJASKOG, Norway
   263
LE TOUQUET, France
   3, 4, 87
LE TOUQUIN, France

   32, 43, 54, 73, 80
LE TREPORT, France
   33, 349
LE VALLON, France
Alt. Y.18
   154, 242, 243, 326, 327
LEVERANO, Italy
   213
LIETTRES, France
   19, 43, 46, 54, 56, 70, 73,
   80, 84, 151, 203, 210
LIGESCOURT, France
   100, 207
LIGNEROLLES, France
Alt. A.12 Balleroy
   16, 69, 140
LIKUJU, Tanganyika
   26
LIMASSOL, Cyprus
   227
LINGEVRES, France
Alt. B.19
   602
LINSELLES, France
   4, 52, 206
LITTORIO, Italy
Alt. Urbe
   92, 145, 601, 624
LIVINGSTONE, Australia
   54, 548
LONDONIERES, France
Alt. B.31
   308, 317
LONGAVESNES, France
   3, 6, 8, 15, 35, 52, 59
LONGUES, France
Alt. B.11
   132, 602
LORETO, Italy
   87, 92, 145, 185, 601
LOZINGHEM see AUCHEL
LUBECK, Germany
Alt. B.158
   3, 26, 41, 56, 66, 80, 129,
   137, 174, 181, 182, 247,
   266, 616
LUDENDORF, Germany
   9
LUNEBURG, Germany
Alt. B.156
   3, 137, 181, 182, 247, 616
LUQA, Malta
   13, 21, 23, 37, 38, 39, 40,
   69, 92, 104, 105, 107, 108,
   110, 126, 139, 145, 148,
   203, 214, 217, 221, 223,
   227, 250, 252, 256, 260,
   272, 600, 601, 683
LUXEUIL, France
   326, 327, 328
LUXOR, Egypt
   55
LYDDA, Palestine
   14, 33, 134, 211
LYON/BRON, France
   43, 72, 93, 111, 326, 327,
   328
LYON/SATOLAS, France
   225

MAATEN BAGUSH, Egypt
   55, 113, 223
MAATEN GERAWLA see
GERAWLA
MADDALENA, Libya
   112
MADHAIBUNIA, India
   20
MADHAIGANJ, India
   82, 110
MADNA, Italy
   80, 241, 274

MADURA, India
   11, 17, 132, 203
MAFRAQ, Jordan
   6, 32
MAGWE, Burma
   11, 17, 28, 45, 67, 113, 152
MAHARAJPUR, India
Alt. Gwalior
   84
'MAIDA VALE', Burma
Alt. Magwe South
   42, 152
MAISON BLANCHE, Algeria
   32, 43, 72, 81, 93, 111,
   152, 153, 219, 225, 241,
   242, 253, 255, 283, 600,
   682
MAISONCELLE, France
   18, 22, 103, 104, 110
MALDEGHEM, Belgium
Alt. B.65
   33, 222, 349
MALEME, Crete
   30, 33, 208
MALENCOURT, France
   8, 73
MALIGNANO, Italy
   208
MALTA (see also LUQA,
TAKALI, SAFI, QRENDI,
HAL FAR)
   82
MALTEPE, Turkey
   55
MAMFE, Cameroons
   230
MANIPUR ROAD, India
   79, 113
MARAGO OPUNI, Tanganyika
   26
MARAUA, Libya
   6, 55
MARBLE ARCH, Libya
   117, 250, 260, 267
MARCIANISE, Italy
   13, 18, 55, 92, 114, 145,
   600, 601
MARCKE, Belgium
   29, 74
MARCON, Italy
   34
MARCQ, France
   87, 504
MARETZ, France
   6, 208
MARIEUX, France
Alt. Elesmes
   4, 5, 8, 15, 24, 41, 70
MARQUAIN see VILLERS-
LEZ-CAGNICOURT
MARQUISE, France
   85, 110, 149, 151, 216
MARSA GARDANE, Tunisia
   55
MARTRAGNY, France
Alt. B.7
   19, 65, 122, 164, 183, 198,
   609
MARTUBA, Libya
   94, 112, 213, 238, 250,
   260, 274
'MARYLEBONE', Algeria
   242
MASIRAH, Arabia
   244
MATEUR, Tunisia
   43, 72, 93, 111, 243
MATIGNY, France
   7, 23, 24, 52
MAUBEUGE, France
   2, 3, 4, 18, 25, 107, 205,
   206

MAUGHNAMA, Burma
   67, 273
MAUNUBYIN, Burma
   62, 194, 267
MAURIPUR, India
   5, 31, 77, 298
MAZINGARBE, France
   2
MBAGUI, Tanganyika
   26
MBUYINI, Kenya
   26
MECHILI, Libya
   33, 94, 112, 250
MEDAN, Sumatra
   155
MEDENINE MAIN, Tunisia
   55, 112, 223, 250, 260
MEGIDDO, Palestine
   6, 208
MEHARICOURT, France
   18
MEHRABAD, Iran
   74, 123
MEIKTILA, Burma
   17, 28, 34, 42, 79, 113,
   146, 357
MELAH EN NOGRA, Libya
   601
MELBOURNE, Australia
   54
MELLAHA, Libya
   274
MELSBROEK, Belgium
Alt. B.58
   16, 21, 26, 69, 98, 107,
   128, 137, 140, 180, 181,
   182, 245, 305, 320, 616
MELUN, France
   3, 4
MENASTIR, Libya
   45
MENIDI, Greece
Alt. Tatoi
   11, 70, 84, 113, 211
MENIN, Belgium
   10
MERCHIN, France
   54
MERDUMA, Libya
Alt. Bir el Merduma
   73
MERHEIM, Germany
   18, 25, 207
MERSA MATRUH, Egypt
   33, 113, 142, 208, 238,
   252, 335, 336, 621
MERVILLE, France
Alt. B.53
   2, 33, 79, 85, 87, 164, 183,
   198, 222, 349, 601, 607,
   609, 615
MHOW, India
   31
MIANWALI, India
   27, 99
MIHO, Japan
   11
MIKRA BAY, Greece
   17
MILAN, Italy
   28, 34, 66
MILAZZO EAST, Sicily
   81, 152, 154, 225, 242
MILENI, Italy
   112, 250, 260
MILL, Netherlands
Alt. B.89
   2, 4 193, 197, 257, 263,
   266, 268
MINGALADON, Burma

17, 18, 20, 27, 28, 31, 60,
62, 67, 113, 135, 194, 267,
273, 357, 607, 681
MINNERIYA, Ceylon
8, 17, 22, 81, 89, 135, 136,
160, 176, 217, 354
MINNICK, Syria
154
MIRAMSHAH, India
20
MISURATA, Libya
33, 47, 213, 274, 603
MITYLENE, Greece
223
MOASCAR see ISMAILIA
MOGADISHU, Italian Somaliland
213, 621
MOISLAINS, France
6, 20, 35, 107, 205
MOISY, France
88
MOMBASA, Kenya
26, 265
MONASTIR, Tunisia
73, 87
MONCHY-LAGACHE, France
4
MONS-EN-CHAUSSEE,
France
4, 8, 9, 13, 79, 85
MONTECORVINO, Italy
32, 69, 73, 111, 253, 608
MONTELIMAR, France
Alt. Y.21
154, 242, 243
MONTE LUNGO, Sicily
18, 55, 114, 223
MONTICHIARI, Italy
34
MONTIGNY FARM, France
9
MONT JOIE, France
81
MONYWA, Burma
20, 60
MOORSEELE, Belgium
615
MORAINVILLE, France
164, 183, 198, 257, 266,
609
MOREUIL, France
7, 23, 24
MORLANCOURT, France
9
MOROGORO, Tanganyika
26
MORVILLE, Belgium
57, 101
MORY, France
11, 12, 13, 57
MOSCOU FERME, France
218
MOSUL, Iraq
6, 30, 52, 55, 63, 84, 237,
261
MOURMELON-LE-GRAND,
France
88
MOYENVILLE, France
5
MSUS, Libya
33, 92, 94, 112, 145, 229,
238, 250, 260, 601
MTUA, Tanganyika
26
MUDROS, Aegean
144, 221, 223, 266
MUHARRAQ, Bahrain
8, 30, 84, 105, 152, 208
MUQEIBILA, Palestine
Alt. Jenin

123, 154, 318
MURREE, India
31
MUSTABIG, Egypt
67
MYINGYAN, Burma
79, 146, 261

NAIROBI, Kenya (see also
EASTLEIGH)
45, 223, 237
NANCY/ESSEY, France
327
NANTES see CHATEAU
BOUGON
NARROWMINE, Australia
618
NAZIR, India
5, 123, 615
NDOLA, Zambia
29
NEFATIA, Libya
73, 112, 250, 260
NEFZA, Tunisia
43
NEGOMBO, Ceylon
45
NESLE, France
34
NETTUNO, Italy
Alt. La Banca
18, 43, 114, 600
NIAMATA, Greece
113
NICOSIA, Cyprus
1, 6, 29, 32, 43, 56, 70, 74,
80, 84, 103, 114, 208, 213,
256, 284, 603
NIDANIA, India
20, 607, 615
NIJMEGAN, Netherlands
616
NIVELLES, Belgium
Alt. B.75
11, 22, 29, 79, 88, 107, 206
NIVILLERS, France
Alt. B.40
19, 602
NOEUX, France
201
NORDHORN, Germany
Alt. B.101
308, 317
NORRENT FONTES, France
1, 73, 79, 504, 607
NORTH FRONT see GIB-
RALTAR
NUOVA, Italy
335, 336
NURLU, France
9, 34

OCHEY, France
55, 100, 216
OCTEVILLE, France
1, 73
OLDENBURG, Germany
14, 20, 26, 93, 234
OLD LASSITI, Tanganyika
26
ONBAUK, Burma
34, 42, 113
ONDAL, India
34, 110
ONDAW, Burma
34, 42, 113
OOSTHAVEN, Java
205
OPHOVEN see AS
ORCQ, Belgium
40, 203
ORVIETO, Italy

208
OSA, Italy
208
OSSOGNE, France
20
OSTEND, Belgium
6
OTRANTO, Italy (see also
ALIMINNI)
226, 263, 271
OUDEZEELE, France
Alt. Dunkerque
229
OUDNA, Tunisia
40, 104, 142, 150
OULMENE, Algeria
13, 18, 614
OXELAERE, France
8
OZOUER-LE-DOYEN, France
103

PACHINO, Sicily
43, 72, 92, 93, 111, 112,
145, 243, 250, 260, 601
PADOVA, Italy
45
PALAM, India
31, 34, 62, 76, 194, 232,
353, 681
PALATA, Italy
241
PALAZZO, Italy
225
PALEL, India
17, 34, 41, 113, 152, 155,
615
PALEMBANG, Sumatra
27, 34, 62, 84, 211, 232,
242, 258, 605
PALERMO, Sicily
87, 283
PANDAVESWAR, India
99, 110, 215
PANEBIANCO, Sicily
43, 72, 93, 111, 243
PANKHAM FORT, Burma
17
PAPHOS, Cyprus
127, 213, 274
PARACHINAR, India
20, 28
PARAFIELD, Australia
238
PARAMYTHIA, Greece
11, 112, 211
PARASHURAM, India
27, 134
PATENGA, Burma
48, 117, 215
PATHARKUNDI, India
123
PECQ, France
5
PENANG, Malaya
28, 152
PERETOLA, Italy
Alt. Florence
43, 72, 93, 111, 185, 208,
225
PERISTERONA, Cyprus
74, 87
PERONNE, France
7
PERUGIA, Italy
13, 55, 87, 92, 114, 145,
185, 500, 601
PESCARA, Italy
223, 500
PESHAWAR, India
5, 20, 27, 28, 31, 60, 155
PETAH TIQVA, Palestine

6, 14, 32, 208
PETITE SYNTHE, France
49, 65, 85, 87, 211, 218
PETROVSK, Russia
221
PEZARCHES, France
2, 3, 4
PHALEMPIN, France
85
PHAPHAMAU, India
177, 211
PHILIPPEVILLE, Algeria
32, 87, 232, 241, 243, 253
PIAGIOLINO, Italy
241, 318
PICAUVILLE, France
Alt. A.8
264, 604
PIOMBINO, Italy
43, 72, 93, 111
PIZZONE, Italy
226
PLANQUES, France
62
PLANTLUNNE, Germany
Alt. B.103
164, 183, 198, 609
PLIVOT, France
53, 103, 139, 142
PLUMETOT, France
Alt. B.10
2, 33, 184, 198, 268, 302,
308, 310, 312, 313, 317,
609
POGGIA RENATICO, Italy
42
POIX, France
Alt. Croixrault
18, 53, 57, 59, 615
POMIGLIANO, Italy
23, 284, 293, 608
PONTEDERA, Italy
87, 185
POONA, India
5, 10, 76, 232
POPERINGHE, Belgium
4, 19, 29, 65, 70
PORETTA, Corsica
154, 232, 237, 238, 242,
243
PORTO POTENZO, Italy
55
PORT REITZ, Kenya
621
PORT SAID, Egypt
144, 269
PORT SUDAN, Sudan
3, 14
POUAN, France
150
POULAINVILLE, France
8, 35, 46, 52, 201
PRAGUE, Czechoslovakia
310, 311, 312, 313
PREMONT, France
9
PRKOS, Yugoslavia
6, 73, 213, 249, 253, 351,
352
PRONVILLE, France
5, 32
PROTVILLE, Tunisia
13, 14, 39, 47, 52, 111,
144, 152, 154, 232, 242,
608
PROVEN, France
7, 9, 58, 82
PROYART, France
9, 20, 92, 101, 205

QAIYARA, Iraq
14, 237
QANTARA, Egypt

14, 111, 113, 142, 145, 216
QASABA, Egypt
6, 33, 73, 208
QASSASSIN, Egypt
14, 134, 223
QASTINA, Palestine
47, 512, 644
QOTAFIYA, Egypt
45, 211
QRENDI, Malta
185, 229, 249
QUACKENBRUCK, Germany
Alt. B.109
33, 222, 274, 616
QUELMES, France
82, 209
QUERQUEVILLE, France
276
QUETTA, India (see also
SAMUNGLI)
5, 20, 28, 31, 48, 82, 84,
110, 114
QUEVENVILLERS, France
9, 82
QUIEVY, France
60
QUILEN, France
149, 214, 216
QUONSET POINT, United
States
53

RAFA, Egypt
14, 67
RAIPUR, India
238, 298
RAJYESWARPUR, India
42, 155
RAMAT DAVID, Palestine
6, 32, 74, 127, 154, 208,
213, 243
RAMATUELLE, France
43, 72, 93, 111, 225, 284
RAMLEH, Palestine
6, 11, 14, 33, 110, 113,
142, 145, 208, 211
RAMU, Burma
11, 79, 81, 134, 135, 136,
607
RANCHI, India
11, 27, 28, 45, 47, 79, 82,
84, 110, 177, 211
RANEFFE, France
52
RANGOON, Burma
136, 230
RATMALANA, Ceylon
11, 22, 30, 42, 81, 84; 136,
160, 217, 273
RATNAP, Burma
134, 258
RAUDIN, France
73
RAVENNA, Italy
43, 72, 93, 111
RAYAK, Syria
80, 208
RECKEM, France
10, 48, 79
RECQ, France
6
REDHILLS LAKE, India
191, 212, 230, 240, 357,
628
RED ROAD, India
17, 136
REGHAIA, Algeria
32, 36, 39, 153, 256, 328
REGINA, Italy
13, 142, 150
REIMS/CHAMPAGNE, France
73, 105, 226

'REINDEER', Burma
Alt. Ramu
135, 258
RELY, France
42, 54
REMAISNIL, France
11, 62, 73, 80
REUMONT, France
53, 218
REYKJAVIK, Iceland
53, 86, 120, 204, 209,
221, 251, 269, 330, 612
REYVILLE, Tunisia
55, 223
RHEINE, Germany
Alt. B.108
264
RICHMOND, Australia
54
RIMINI, Italy
43, 72, 93, 111, 241, 318
RISALPUR, India
1, 5, 11, 20, 27, 31, 39,
60, 97, 117, 146, 152
RIVOLTO, Italy
39, 43, 72, 93, 111
ROBAT, Aden
12
RONCHIN, France
4, 103
ROSIERES-EN-SANTERRE,
France
21, 57
ROSIGNANO, Italy
237, 255, 600, 624
ROUGEFAY, France
87
ROUVRES, France
73
ROVILLE, France
115, 216
ROYE see AMY
ROZOY-EN-BRIE, France
49
RUISSEAUVILLE, France
25, 27, 32, 73, 98
RUMKHAPALONG, Burma
136, 152, 607
RYES, France
Alt. B.15
193

SACHSENHEIM see GROSS-
ACHSENHEIM
SADAUNG, Burma
28, 155
SAFI, Malta
111, 112, 126
SAINS-LES-PERNES, France
148
ST. ANDRE-AUX-BOIS,
France
6, 21, 27, 35, 55, 57,60,
99, 100, 101, 102
ST. ANDRE DE L'EURE,
France
Alt. B.24
19, 122, 174, 184, 243
ST. CATHARINE, Corsica
237, 238
ST. CROIX, France
Alt. B.3
175, 193, 266, 276
ST. CROIX, Belgium
Alt. B.63
197, 257, 263
ST. DENIS WESTREM,
Belgium
Alt. B.61
2, 4, 268, 276, 302, 308,
317
ST. HONORINE, France

Alt. B.21
168
ST. INGLEVERT, France
21, 97, 100, 115, 214
ST. JEAN D'ACRE, Palestine
47, 80, 127, 147, 159, 213,
261, 335
ST. LEGER, France
18
ST. LUCIEN FERME, France
103, 218
STE. MARIE CAPPEL, France
1, 4, 19, 20, 35, 45, 46, 48,
57, 60, 79, 201, 210
ST. NAZAIRE, France
1
ST. OMER, France
1, 3, 4, 5, 6, 7, 8, 9, 10,
11, 12, 13, 15, 16, 18, 19,
20, 22, 23, 25, 27, 28, 29,
32, 35, 40, 41, 42, 43, 45,
46, 53, 54, 56, 58, 59, 60,
62, 64, 71, 73, 74, 79, 82,
83, 85, 87, 98, 99, 104,
210
ST. POL, France
6, 38
ST. QUENTIN, France
3, 4
ST. THOMAS MOUNT, India
5, 20, 34, 42, 45, 60, 82,
84, 113, 123, 135, 146,
155, 200, 211, 215, 354
SALBANI, India
9, 82, 159, 160, 355, 356,
617
SALERNO, Italy
225
SALON-DE-PROVENCE,
France
225
SALONIKA, Greece
14, 47
SAMARRA, Iraq
63
SAN ANGELO, Italy
112, 208, 250, 260
SAN BASILIO, Italy
663
SAN LUCA, Italy
139
SAN PANCRAZIO, Italy
32
SAN PIETRO, Italy
66
SAN SEVERO, Italy
55, 682, 683
SAN STEPHANO, Italy
17, 25, 56, 207, 208
SAN VITO, Italy
241, 318
SANTA CRUZ, India
203
SANTA LUCA, Italy
34, 42
SANTA PELAGIO, Italy
42, 45
SAPAM, India
5, 11, 17, 20, 136, 155, 607
SARCEDO, Italy
28
SARONA, Palestine
113, 142
SART, Belgium
6, 8
SATOLAS see LYON/
SATOLAS
SAULTAIN, France
42, 64, 209
SAVOIA, Libya
80, 94, 237, 335
SAVY, France

5, 13, 15, 19, 35, 41, 52,
60, 69, 82, 85
SCANZANO, Italy
225, 284
SCARAMANGA, Greece
230
SCHAFFEN, Belgium
Alt. B.64 Diest
41, 130, 168
SCHIJNDEL, Netherlands
Alt. B.85
66, 74, 127, 322, 329, 331,
332, 340, 341, 345
SCHLESWIG(LAND),
Germany
Alt. B.164
26, 47, 53, 56, 175, 181,
182, 184, 245, 297
SECLIN, France
Alt. B.51 Vendeville
2, 21, 53, 74, 85, 87, 193,
197, 257, 263, 264, 266,
302, 317, 329, 340, 341,
604
SECUNDERABAD, India
20
SEDADAH, Libya
250
SEDES, Greece
32, 94, 335, 336
SEK KONG, Hong Kong
28, 45, 80
SELETAR, Singapore
11, 17, 22, 34, 36, 39, 52,
66, 81, 84, 88, 89, 100,
103, 110, 155, 205, 209,
230, 232, 242, 258, 681
SELVIGNY, France
15
SEMBAWANG, Singapore
28, 60, 194
SEMPLAK, Java
62
SENLIS, France
1, 3, 15, 43, 94
SENNAR, Sudan
47
SENON, France
6, 87
SERCHES, France
Alt. Mont de Soissons
52
SERNY, France
18, 22, 25, 27, 32, 38, 41,
46, 62, 83, 88, 92, 102,
103, 148, 208
SERRAGIA, Corsica
237, 238
SERRETELLE, Italy
81, 152, 154, 225, 232, 242
SERRIS, France
2, 3, 4
SETIF, Algeria
18, 87, 114, 242, 253,
255, 600
SFAX, Tunisia
6, 73
SHAIBAH, Iraq
6, 32, 74, 84, 244, 261
SHALLUFA, Egypt
32, 37, 38, 40, 70, 100,
104, 162, 213, 221
SHANDUR, Egypt
6, 39, 47, 73, 108, 127,
134, 147, 160, 178, 213,
221, 223, 237
SHANGHAI, China
2
SHARJAH, Oman
6, 8, 78, 84, 210, 244
SHEIKH OTHMAN, Aden
11, 39, 41, 94, 203

SIDI AHMED, Tunisia
13
SIDI AMOR, Tunisia
13, 39, 47
SIDI AZEIZ, Egypt
33, 112, 208, 223, 238,
250, 260
SIDI BARRANI, Egypt
112, 113, 237
SIDI HANEISH, Egypt
6, 33, 73, 80, 112, 250,
274
SIDI REZEGH, Libya
94, 260
SIGIRIYA, Ceylon
160
SIGONELLA, Sicily
Alt. Gerbini 3
23, 55, 203
SILCHAR, India
34, 60, 211, 615
SIMANGGANG, Borneo
110
SINELLO, Italy
241
SINGAPORE see SELETAR,
TENGAH, CHANGI, KAL-
LANG, SEMBAWANG
SINTHE, Burma
11, 152
SIRTAN, Libya
223
SISTERON, France
Alt. Y.20
43, 72, 93, 111, 225
SKAANLAND, Norway
46
SKYROS, Aegean
266
SOERABAJA, Java
60
SOLA, Norway
Alt. Stavanger
130, 276, 331, 332, 334
SOLUCH, Libya
104
SOMMERVIEU, France
Alt. B.8
74, 164, 168, 329, 340, 341
SONCAMP, France
8, 12, 87
SONGEA, Tanganyika
26
SORMAN, Libya
6, 260
SOUGE, France
12, 103
SOUK-EL-ARBA, Algeria
18, 72, 93, 111, 152, 225,
241
SOUK EL KHEMIS, Tunisia
Alt. 'Kings Cross'
72, 81, 93, 111, 152, 154,
232, 241, 242, 243
SOUSSE, Tunisia
134
SPICH, Germany
7, 11, 22, 62
SPY, Belgium
57
STACEGHEM, Belgium
7, 10
STAHHILLE, Belgium
213
STAVANGER, Norway (see
also SOLA)
330, 333
STAVROS, Aegean
221, 223,
STORNARA, Italy
614
STRASBOURG/ENTZHEIM,

France
326, 327, 328
STRATHPINE, Australia
548, 549
STRAUSS, Australia
549
STREE, Belgium
80, 101, 208
STUTTGART/SERSHEIM,
Germany
327, 328
SUDA BAY, Crete
11, 113, 264
SUEZ, Egypt
8, 55, 142, 145
SUMMIT, Sudan
223
SUNGEI PATANI, Malaya
27
SURCAMPS, France
102
SUZANNE, France
20, 35
SWEVEGHEM, France
21, 53
SYLHET, India
117
SYLT, Germany
Alt. B.170 Westerland
3, 26, 33, 56, 302

T.1, Iraq
127
TABINGAUNG, Burma
17, 155, 607
TAFAROUI, Algeria
500, 614
TAHER, Algeria
87, 154, 328
TAHOUNE GUEMAC, Syria
127
TA KALI, Malta
32, 73, 81, 126, 152, 154,
185, 208, 227, 229, 232,
238, 242, 247, 249, 272,
603, 605
TAKORADI, Gold Coast
73, 82, 110
TAMET, Libya
73, 92
TAMU, Burma
11, 28, 152
TANJORE, India
11, 36, 60, 261, 353
TANK, India
20, 28
TAN SON NHUT, French
Indo-China
273, 684
TANTONVILLE, France
55, 99
TARANTO, Italy
224, 226, 227
TARCIENNE, France
9
TARQUINIA, Italy
13, 18, 34, 43, 55, 72, 93,
111, 114, 225
TASIK MAJALA, Java
605
TATOI see MENIDI
TAUKKYAN, Burma
17, 60
TAVETA, Kenya
26
TEL AVIV, Palestine
6
TELERGMA, Algeria
14
TEMMER, Tunisia
Alt. Kairouan North
37, 70

TEMPLEUX, France
8
TENGAH, Singapore
7, 11, 20, 27, 28, 34, 39,
45, 60, 62, 64, 74, 81, 84,
100, 103, 152, 155
TENNANT, Burma
17, 155
TERRIA, Libya
178
TETEGHEM, France
24, 29, 54, 74, 204, 208,
210
THASOS, Aegean
222
THAZI, Burma
20
THEDAW, Burma
17, 20, 60, 152, 155, 607
THUILLES, Belgium
84, 92, 211
TILDA, India
76, 673
TILLE see BEAUVAIS
TINGLEY, Algeria
32, 43, 81, 87, 154, 232,
242, 243, 283
TISSANO, Italy
43, 72, 87, 93, 111, 112,
225, 250, 318
TJIKAMBER, Java
36
TJIKAMPEH, Java
36
TJILATJAP, Java
205
TJILILITAN, Java
232, 605
TMIMI, Libya
208, 223, 237
TOBRUK, Libya
6, 250
TOCRA, Libya
148, 335
TORTORELLA, Italy
Alt. Foggia No.2
37, 92, 145, 601
TORTORETTO, Italy
241, 318
TOUNGOO, Burma
67, 113, 155
TOUQUIN see LE TOUQUIN
TRAMECOURT, France
208
TRE CANCELLI, Italy
43, 72, 93, 111, 225
TRECON, France
52
TREIZENNES, France
4, 18, 22, 27, 32, 40, 42,
43, 58, 102, 120, 203, 210
TREORSO, Italy
66
TREVISO, Italy
43, 87, 92, 93, 111,
112, 145, 241, 250, 253,
318
TRIGNO, Italy
80, 208, 241, 318
TRIKKALA, Greece
80
TRIOLO, Italy
Alt. Foggia No.7
92, 145, 601
TULIHAL, India
11, 42, 81, 113, 117, 152,
155, 215, 233, 267, 607
TULO, Tanganyika
26
TUSCIANO, Italy
43, 72, 243
TUZ KHURTMATLI, Iraq

30
TWENTHE, Netherlands
Alt. B.106 Enschede
2, 4, 33, 41, 66, 127, 130,
137, 181, 182, 219, 247,
264, 268, 322, 331, 332,
349, 350

UDINE see CAMPOFORMIDO
ULUNDURPET, India
131, 134, 258
UMRITSAR, Sudan
237
UMTALI, Kenya
237
UPPER TOPA, India
667, 668, 669
URSEL, Belgium
Alt. B.67
164, 183, 198, 276, 609
UTIQUE, Tunisia
81

VAENGA, Russia
81, 134, 144
VAERNES, Norway
129, 165, 276
VALHEREUX, France
3, 56
VARRELBUSCH, Germany
Alt. B.113
302, 308, 317, 322, 349
VARSSENAERE, Belgium
202, 217
VASSINCOURT, France
1
VASTO, Italy
112
VAVUNIYA, Ceylon
17, 22, 89, 132, 217
VENAFRO, Italy
92, 145, 208, 601
VENDEVILLE see SECLIN
VERONA, Italy
28, 34, 66
VERT GALAND, France
3, 4, 8, 11, 12, 13, 15, 19,
22, 23, 32, 56, 57, 59, 60,
66, 84, 218
VIEUL AROY, France
2
VIGNACOURT, France
8, 15, 20, 29, 54, 80, 151
VILLAFRANCA, Italy
87, 185, 208, 225
VILLAORBA, Italy
Alt. Rivolto
500
VILLAVERLA, Italy
34, 139
VILLENEUVE-LES-VERTUS,
France
73, 105
VILLERS BOCAGE, France
35
VILLERS-BRETTONEUX,
France
11, 24, 25, 27, 34
VILLERS-FAUX, France
142
VILLERS-LEZ-
CAGNICOURT, France
27, 42, 49, 62, 98
VILLESENEUX, France
53, 100, 216
VILLONS-LES-BUISSONS,
France
Alt. B.16
66, 127, 331, 332
VIS, Adriatic
351, 352
VITRY-EN-ARTOIS, France

88, 151, 174, 175, 184, 226, 245, 342, 504, 607, 615

VIZAGAPATAM, India
5, 30, 81, 84, 136, 615

VOLKEL, Netherlands
3, 41, 56, 80, 174, 175, 184, 245, 274, 305, 605

VOLTONE, Italy
600

WADI GAZOUZA, Sudan
45, 211, 223

WADI HALFA, Sudan
6, 237

WADI NATRUN, Egypt
39, 45, 55

WADI SIRRU, Libya
92, 145

WAGONLIEU, France
12

WAHN, Germany
Alt. B.119
2, 4, 11, 14, 17, 68, 69, 87, 98, 107, 128, 180, 305

WAMBRECHIES, France
Alt. B.57
66, 127, 331, 332

WAMIN, France
80

WANGJING, India
5, 79, 136, 146, 261, 607

WARLOY BAILLON, France
3, 4, 7, 22

WELI SHEIKH NURAN, Palestine
67, 113

WELSCHAP see EINDHOVEN

WEVELGHEM, Belgium
Alt. B.55
74, 329, 340, 341, 345

WHEELER FIELD, Trinidad

53

WILDENRATH, Germany
3, 4, 14, 17, 20, 60, 67, 71, 88, 92

WITHERIES, France
22

WOENSDRECHT, Netherlands
Alt. B.79
66, 127, 322, 331, 332

WORLI, India
152

WUNSTORF, Germany
2, 3, 4, 5, 11, 26, 27, 41, 53, 80, 164, 183, 198, 297, 322, 349, 350, 541, 609

XAFFEVILLERS, France
97, 100, 215

YAZAGYO, Burma
34, 113

YELAHANKA, India
30, 42, 45, 47, 60, 79, 84, 110, 113, 123, 134, 135, 146, 152, 211, 258, 261

YE-U, Burma
28

YUNDUM, Gambia
200

YWADON, Burma
17

ZAYATKWIN, Burma
5, 30, 34, 81, 113, 131, 135, 152, 155, 258

ZEAVIS, France
49

ZELTWEG, Austria
43, 72, 87, 92, 111, 253

ZUARA, Libya
112, 250, 260

Coastal Patrol Flights

August to November 1918

The following flights formed part of Nos.219 to 274 Squadrons when coastal patrol stations were given squadron numbers in August 1918. There were also certain flights outside the squadron organisation and this table is intended to show to which squdrons, if any, numbered flights were allotted. Seaplane flights were normally equipped with Short 184 floatplanes, but Sopwith Babies, Fairey IIIBs, IIICs and Campanias were also in use. Although numbered in the same series as home-based flights, some Mediterranean-based flights were primarily for offensive duties. The force based around Otranto was intended to block the Straits of Otranto to U-boats based on Austro-Hungarian ports on the Adriatic but several squadrons were employed on bombing raids on Albania and Montenegro. Squadrons shown under 'E. Mediterranean' were mobile formations used in the Aegean.

Flight No.	Squadron	Base	Aircraft
300	—	Catfirth	F.3
306	—	Houton Bay	F.2a
307	—	Houton Bay	F.2a
309	—	Stenness	F.3
310	—	Stenness	F.3
311	—	Stenness	F.3
318	257	Dundee	F.2a
319	257	Dundee	F.2a
324	228	Yarmouth	F.2a
325	228	Yarmouth	F.2a
326	228	Yarmouth	F.2a
332	231	Felixstowe	F.2a
337	247	Felixstowe	F.2a
338	247	Felixstowe	F.2a
339	261	Felixstowe	F.2a
340	261	Felixstowe	F.2a
341	261	Felixstowe	F.2a
342	259	Felixstowe	F.2a
343	259	Felixstowe	F.2a
344	259	Felixstowe	F.2a
345	240	Calshot	F.2a
346	240	Calshot	F.2a
347	238	Cattewater	F.3
348	238	Cattewater	F.3
349	238	Cattewater	F.3
350	234	Tresco	F.3
351	234	Tresco	F.3
352	234	Tresco	F.3
353	234	Tresco	F.3
354	270	Alexandria	F.3
355	270	Alexandria	F.3
356	270	Alexandria	F.3
357	271	Taranto	F.3
358	271	Taranto	F.3
359	263	Otranto	F.3
360	267	Malta	F.3
361	267	Malta	F.3
362	267	Malta	F.3
363	267	Malta	F.3
364	265	Gibraltar	F.3
365	265	Gibraltar	F.3
366	265	Gibraltar	F.3
367	271	Taranto	F.3
400	249	Dundee/Strathbeg	Seaplanes
402	246	Seaton Carew	Seaplanes
403	246	Seaton Carew	Seaplanes
404	248	Hornsea Mere/ North Coates	Seaplanes/ DH6 Conv'ted
405	248	Hornsea Mere	Seaplanes
406	219	Westgate	Seaplanes
407	233	Dover	Seaplanes
408	242	Newhaven	Seaplanes
409	242	Newhaven	Seaplanes
410	240	Calshot	Seaplanes
411	240	Calshot	Seaplanes
412	253	Bembridge	Seaplanes
413	253	Bembridge	Seaplanes
416	241	Portland	Seaplanes
417	241	Portland	Seaplanes
418	239	Torquay	Seaplanes
419	239	Torquay	Seaplanes
420	237	Cattewater	Seaplanes
421	237	Cattewater	Seaplanes
422	237	Cattewater	Seaplanes
423	237	Cattewater	Seaplanes
424	235	Newlyn	Seaplanes
425	235	Newlyn	Seaplanes
426	245	Fishguard	Seaplanes
427	245	Fishguard	Seaplanes
428	229	Yarmouth	Seaplanes
429	229	Yarmouth	Seaplanes

430	—	Houton Bay	Seaplanes	501	250	Padstow	D.H.6
431	269	Port Said	Seaplanes	502	260	Westward Ho	D.H.6
432	269	Port Said	Seaplanes	503	260	Westward Ho	D.H.6
433	268	Malta	Seaplanes	504	251	Atwick	D.H.6
434	268	Malta	Seaplanes	505	251	Greenland Top/	D.H.6
435	263	Otranto	Seaplanes			West Ayton	
436	263	Otranto	Seaplanes	506	251	Owthorne	D.H.6
437	266	Mudros	Seaplanes	507	252	Tynemouth	D.H.6
438	266	Skyros	Seaplanes	508	252	Tynemouth	D.H.6
439	264	Suda Bay	Seaplanes	509	252	Seaton Carew	D.H.6
440	264	Syra	Seaplanes	510	251	West Ayton/Redcar	D.H.6
441	263	Sta. Maria de Leuca	Seaplanes	511	253	Foreland	D.H.6
442	219	Westgate	Seaplanes	512	253	Foreland	D.H.6
450	249	Dundee	Seaplanes	513	241	Chickerell	D.H.6
451	246	Seaton Carew	Seaplanes	514	242	Telscombe Cliffs	D.H.6
452	246	Seaton Carew	Seaplanes	515	236	Mullion	D.H.6
453	248	Hornsea	Seaplanes	516	236	Mullion	D.H.6
454	229	Yarmouth	Seaplanes	517	254	Prawle Point	D.H.6
455	229	Yarmouth	Seaplanes	518	254	Prawle Point	D.H.6
470	219	Manston	Camel	519	255	Pembroke	D.H.6
471	233	Walmer	Camel	520	255	Pembroke	D.H.6
472	226	Taranto	D.H.4	521	244	Bangor	D.H.6
473	226	Taranto	D.H.4	522	244	Bangor	D.H.6
474	226	Taranto	D.H.4	523	258	Luce Bay	D.H.6
475	220	E. Mediterranean	Camel	524	258	Luce Bay	D.H.6
476	220	E. Mediterranean	Camel	525	256	Ashington	D.H.6
477	220	E. Mediterranean	Camel	526	256	New Haggerston	D.H.6
478	222	E. Mediterranean	Camel	527	256	Sea Houses	D.H.6
479	222	E. Mediterranean	Camel	528	256	Sea Houses	D.H.6
480	222	E. Mediterranean	Camel	529	258	Luce Bay	D.H.6
481	225	Otranto	Camel	530	244	Bangor	D.H.6
482	225	Otranto	Camel	531	272	Machrihanish	D.H.6
483	225	Otranto	Camel	532	272	Machrihanish	D.H.6
485	273	Burgh Castle	Camel	533	272	Machrihanish	D.H.6
486	273	Burgh Castle	Camel	534	273	Covehithe	D.H.9
487	230	Butley	Camel	550	227	Taranto	Caproni
490	212	Yarmouth	D.H.9	551	227	Taranto	Caproni
491	233	Guston Road	D.H.9	552	221	E. Mediterranean	D.H.9
492	254	Prawle Point	D.H.9	553	221	E. Mediterranean	D.H.9
493	236	Mullion	D.H.9	554	221	E. Mediterranean	D.H.9
494	250	Padstow	D.H.9	555	219	Manston	D.H.9
495	246	Seaton Carew	Kangaroo	556	219	Manston	D.H.9
496	224	Otranto	D.H.4	557	212	Yarmouth	D.H.9
497	224	Otranto	D.H.4	558	212	Yarmouth	D.H.9A
498	224	Otranto	D.H.4	559	223	E. Mediterranean	D.H.9
499	227	Taranto	Caproni	560	223	E. Mediterranean	D.H.9
500	250	Padstow	D.H.6	561	223	E. Mediterranean	D.H.9
				562	—	Malta	D.H.9

Abbreviations found in Squadron Records

AA	Anti-aircraft
AAC(U)	Anti-aircraft co-operation (unit)
A & AEE	Aeroplane & Armament Experimental Establishment
AAF	Auxiliary Air Force (RAF); Army Air Force (US)
AASF	Advanced Air Striking Force (France 1939/40)
ABC	Airborne Cigar (see 'Cigar')
ABDA	American, British, Dutch Australian Command (S.E.Asia 1942)
Abdulla	Homing in on Wurzburg radar emissions
AC	Army Co-operation
ACAS	Assistant Chief of Air Staff
ACH	Advanced Chain Home (Radar stations)
ACI	Air Council Instruction
ACR	Air Control Radar
ADEE	Air Defence Experimental Establishment
ADGB	Air Defence of Great Britain
ADRDE	Air Defence Research and Development Establishment
AEAF	Allied Expeditionary Air Force (Europe 1944-45)
AEF	Allied Expeditionary Force (1944/45)
AES	Air Electronics School
AEW	Airborne Early Warning (Role prefix)
AGS	Air Gunners School
AHB	Air Historical Branch (of Air Ministry)
AHQ	Air Headquarters
AI	Air Interception (airborne radar)
AID	Aeronautical Inspection Department
Alphabet	Operations against flying-bomb carriers (1944-45)
AM	Air Ministry
AMDP	Air Member for Development and Production
AMES	Air Ministry Experimental Station (early radar stations)
AMRE	Air Ministry Research Establishment, Dundee (became TRE)
Anakim	First invasion of Burma from India
ANS	Air Navigation School
Anvil	Landing in Southern France 1944 (became 'Dragoon')
AP	Armour Piercing
APC	Armament Practice Camp
Arabian Nights	Thousand-Bomber Raids on Germany (1942)
ARC	Aeronautical Research Council
Argument	Combined RAF/USAAF offensive against German aircraft industry
Armour	Re-occupation of Hong Kong (1945)
ASR	Air-sea Rescue
ASU	Aircraft Storage Unit
ASV	Air-to-Surface Vessel (Radar equipment)
ASWDU	Air-sea Warfare Development Unit
ATAF	Allied Tactical Air Force
ATFERO	Atlantic Ferry Organisation (became Ferry Command)
ATS	Armament Training Station
B	Bomber (Role prefix)
BABS	Beam Approach Beacon System

BAFF	British Air Forces in France (1939-40)
BAFO	British Air Forces of Occupation
Banquet	Anti-invasion measures using training aircraft
Baytown	Landing by 8th Army in Southern Italy
BAT	Beam Approach Training
BBSU	British Bombing Survey Unit
BC	Bomber Command
BDU	Bombing Development Unit
BEF	British Expeditionary Force
Benedict	Delivery of RAF Hurricane squadrons to N. Russia
B & GS	Bombing and Gunnery School
BMEWS	Ballistic Missile Early Warning Station
BPC	British Purchasing Commision in USA
BSDU	Bomber Support Development Unit
C	Transport (Role prefix)
CAACU	Civilian Anti-aircraft Co-operation Unit
Cabrank	Standing patrols of fighter-bombers on call for tactical support of army units
CAM Ship	Catapult Aircraft Merchant Ship
CANS	Civil Air Navigation School
Catechism	Bomber attacks on *Tirpitz* at Tromso
CBO	Combined Bomber Offensive
CC	Coastal Command
CCDU	Coastal Command Development Unit
CFS	Central Flying School
Channel Stop	Air plan to prevent the passage of German warships from Brest to Germany by day
CHL	Chain Home Low (part of radar defence system)
Cigar	Jamming of German fighter direction radio
Circus	Daylight bomber attacks, heavily escorted by fighters, intended to bring German fighters into action
CIU	Central Interpretation Unit, Medmenham (for photographic reconnaissance interpretation)
CMF	Central Mediterranean Force
COHQ	Combined Operations Headquarters
Colossus	First British airborne operation (against aqueduct in Southern Italy)
Cornet	Raid on Ruhr dams
CRD	Controller of Research & Development
Cromwell	Warning of imminent invasion of UK (1940/41)
Crossbow	Offensive operations against V-weapons
CRO	Civilian Repair Organisation
CSE	Central Signals Establishment
CU	Conversion Unit
DA	Delayed action (bomb)
DAF	Desert Air Force
DAP	Director of Aeroplane Production, Air Ministry
DCAS	Deputy Chief of Air Staff
D/F	Direction Finding
DH	de Havilland (type number prefix originally applied to Aircraft Manufacturing Co. types)
Diver	Flying bomb attacks and defence
Dodge	Repatriation of Commonwealth Forces from

	Mediterranean area
Dracula	Assault on Rangoon
Dragoon	Allied landings in Southern France (August 1944)
D.W.I.	Directional Wireless Installation (actually a device for exploding magnetic mines from aircraft)
Dynamo	Evacuation of the BEF from Dunkerque May-June 1940
DZ	Dropping zone (for parachute troops)
E	Electronics (role prefix)
EAC	Eastern Air Command (in North Africa)
EANS	Empire Air Navigation School
EFTS	Elementary Flying Training School
E & RFTS	Elementary & Reserve Flying Training School
Eureka	Ground transmitter for guiding aircraft to target
E & WS	Electrical and Wireless School
Exodus	Evacuation by air of freed prisoners-of-war
F	Fighter (role prefix); also FAW − All-weather fighter
FAA	Fleet Air Arm
FB	Fighter-bomber (role prefix)
FC	Fighter Command
FEAF	Far East Air Force
FFI	Forces Francaises de l'Interieur ('Maquis')
FFL	Forces Francaises Libres ('Free French')
FGA	Fighter-Ground Attack (role prefix)
Firebrand	Occupation of Corsica (1943)
Firedog	RAF operations during Emergency in Malaya
FIS	Flying Instructors School
FIU	Fighter Interception Unit
Flax	Air patrols to intercept Axis aircraft between Sicily and Tunisia (April 1943)
Flower	Patrol over German night fighter airfields
FR	Fighter-Reconnaissance
Freshman	Glider-borne attack on Vermork heavy water plant in Norway (November 1942)
FTU	Ferry Training Unit
Fuller	Action in Channel against German battle-cruisers (February 1942)
Fullhouse	Fighter operations over France to restrict enemy air and ground movements during invasion of Normandy
Gardening	Minelaying by aircraft
GCA	Ground Controlled Approach
GCI	Ground Control Interception
Gee	Radar navigation aid
Gilbey	Night attacks on enemy shipping off Dutch coast by Coastal Command
Gomorrah	Bomber Command attacks on Hamburg in July and August 1943
Gondola	Coastal Command offensive against U-boats in Bay of Biscay (1943)
Goodwood	Bomber attack on *Tirpitz*
GP	General purpose
GPEU	Glider Pilot Exercise Unit
GR	General Reconnaissance (superceeded by MR); also Ground attack/Reconnaissance (role prefix)
Grand Slam	22,000-lb penetration bomb
Green Bottle	Device carried by Coastal Command aircraft to permit homing on U-boat radar signals
GRU	General Reconnaissance Unit; Gunnery Research Unit
GTS	Glider Training School
H2S	Radar navigation and target identification aid
Habo	Coastal Command night patrol off Normandy coast (1941/42)
Haddock	Bomber Command force for operating against Italy from Southern France (June 1940)
HAR	Helicopter Air Rescue (Role prefix)
HC	Helicopter transport (Role prefix)
HE	High Explosive; Home Establishment (1915/19)
HF	High-altitude fighter (role prefix)
HP	Handley Page
Husky	Invasion of Sicily (July 1943)
IAF	Indian Air Force (later RIAF)
IE	Initial Equipment
IF	Independent Force (1918)
IFF	Identification Friend or Foe
Intruder	Night patrol to attack enemy aircraft on or over their own airfields
IR	Initial reserve
IRBM	Intermediate range ballistic missile
Ironclad	Capture of Diego Suarez, Madagascar (1942)
JCS	Joint Chiefs of Staff
Jim Crow	Channel reconnaissance by Fighter Command
JPRO	Joint Photographic Reconnaissance Organisation
Jubilee	Raid on Dieppe (August 1942)
Ladbroke	Glider attack near Syracuse (July 1943)
Lagoon	Long-range shipping reconnaissance
LAM	Long Aerial Mine (Anti-aircraft mine)
LF	Low-altitude fighter (Role prefix)
LG	Landing ground (normally used in North Africa)
Loran	Long-range navigation system
LR	Long range
LZ	Landing Zone (for gliders)
MAAF	Mediterranean Allied Air Force
MAC	Mediterranean Air Command
MAEE	Marine Aircraft Experimental Establishment
Mandrel	Jamming of German early warning radar
Manna	Dropping of food by Bomber Command over Netherlands (April 1945)
MAP	Ministry of Aircraft Production
Market	Airborne landings to secure bridges between Eindhoven and Arnhem; 'Market Garden' was the landings at Arnhem
Mastiff	Dropping of supplies to and evacuation of Allied prisoners-of-war in Far East
MCS	Metropolitan Communications Squadron
MEAF	Middle East Air Force
Met	Meteorological (Role prefix)
Millenium	Thousand-bomber raid on Cologne (May 1942)
Millenium Two	Similar raid on Bremen (June 1942)
Monica	Radar carried by bombers to give warning of approach of enemy fighters
MOS	Ministry of Supply
MOTU	Maritime Operational Training Unit
MR	Maritime Reconnaissance (Role prefix)

MRU or Moru Mobile Radio Unit
MSFU Merchant Ship Fighter Unit (Catafighters)
MU Maintenance Unit
Mutton Laying aerial minefields in path of enemy bombers

NAAF Northwest African Air Forces
NACAF Northwest African Coastal Air Force
NAPRW Northwest African Photographic Reconnaissance Wing
NASAF Northwest African Strategic Air Force
NATAF Northwest African Tactical Air Force
NATBF Northwest African Tactical Bomber Force
NATCC Northwest African Troop Carrier Command
NATO North Atlantic Treaty Organisation
NEAF Near East Air Force
NEI Netherlands East Indies
Neptune Initial landings in Normandy (June 1944)
NF Night fighter (Role prefix)
Noball V-weapon sites as targets for Allied aircraft
NTU Navigation Training Unit

OAFU Observers Advanced Flying Unit
OANS Observers Air Navigation School
Oboe Blind bombing radar aid
Obviate Attack on *Tirpitz* by Lancasters (October 1944)
Occult Aerial lighthouse
OCU Operational Conversion Unit
ORB Operations Record Book
OTU Operational Training Unit

PAC Parachute & Cable air defence
PAFU Pilots Advanced Flying Unit
Paiforce Persia and Iraq Force
PDC Personnel Dispersal Centre
PDE Projectile Development Establishment
Percussion Coastal Command anti-submarine patrol over Bay of Biscay
PFF Pathfinder Force
Planefare Berlin Airlift
Pointblank Combined RAF/USAAF bomber offensive against Germany
Popular Tactical reconnaissance mission
POW Prisoner-of-War
PPI Plan position indicator (Radar device)
PR Photographic Reconnaissance (Role prefix)
PRU Photographic Reconnaissance Unit

RAAF Royal Australian Air Force
RAE Royal Aircraft Establishment
RAF Royal Aircraft Factory (became RAE); Royal Air Force
RAFFC Royal Air Force Flying College
Ramrod Fighter-bomber operation
R & D Research and Development
Ranger Long-range offensive sortie
RCAF Royal Canadian Air Force
RCM Radio Countermeasures
RDF Radio Direction Finding (original cover name for Radar)
Rebecca Aircraft navigation device working in conjunction with Eureka ground installation
RFC Royal Flying Corps
RFS Reserve Flying School
Rhubarb Short-range day intruder sortie
RIAF Royal Indian Air Force

Ribbon Commonwealth air force of occupation in Japan
RN Royal Navy
RNZAF Royal New Zealand Air Force
Robroy Resupply missions to airborne forces in Normandy
Rodeo Offensive sweeps by fighters
Rover David Attacks on tactical targets by Cabrank aircraft
RP Rocket Projectile
RRE Royal Radar Establishment
RS Reserve Squadron (1915/16)

S Strike (Role prefix)
SAAF South African Air Force
SAM Surface-to-Air Missile
SAP Semi-Armour Piercing
SAS Special Air Service
SASO Senior Air Staff Officer
SBA Standard Beam Approach
SCBS Strike Command Bombing School
SE Servicing Echelon
SEAC South East Asia Command
Serrate Homing device to enable night fighters to track enemy aircraft radar transmissions
SFTS Service Flying Training School
SHAEF Supreme Headquarters Allied Expeditionary Force
Ski Site German flying bomb launching site
SLG Satellite Landing Ground
SM Strategic Missile
SOC Struck off charge
SP Staging Post
SRAF Southern Rhodesian Air Force
SR Strategic Reconnaissance (Role prefix); Stored reserve (part of unit establishment)
Stamina Air supply of Imphal (1944)
STC Strike Command
Strangle Interdiction campaign in Italy (1944)
Swamp Anti-submarine operation in Mediterranean to hunt U-boats to exhaustion by concentrating aircraft in the area of every sighting

T Trainer (Role prefix)
TAF Tactical Air Force
Tallboy 12,000-lb penetration bomb
TB Torpedo bomber
TDS Training Depot Station
TF Torpedo-fighter (Role prefix)
Thursday Chindit operation behind Japanese lines in Burma maintained by air supply
TI Target Indicator
Tonga Airborne landings in Normandy (June 1944)
TRE Telecommunications Research Establishment
TS Training Squadron (1916/19)
TT Target Towing (Role prefix)
Tube Alloys British atomic bomb research prior to transfer to USA

UDF Union Defence Force (South Africa)
UE Unit Equipment
UP Unrotated Projectile (Rocket)
Upkeep Spherical 10,000-lb bomb for attacking dams ('Bouncing Bomb')
USAAF United States Army Air Force (originally Corps)
USATC United States Air Transport Command
USN United States Navy

USSAFE	United States Strategic Air Forces in Europe		
Varsity	Airborne landings across Lower Rhine (March 1945)		
Vegetable	Airborne mines laid at sea		
VHF	Very High Frequency (Radio)		
VIP	Very Important Person		
VLR	Very Long Range		
WAAF	Women's Auxiliary Air Force		
WAC	West Africa Command		
WDU	Wireless Development Unit		
WE	War Establishment		
Window	Strips of tinfoil to confuse enemy radar		
WT	Wireless Telegraphy		
Zipper	Invasion of Malaya (1945)		

Photographic Index

The following list contains photographs provided by sources which supply photographs to the public and gives the reference number of each as shown on the original. The current addresses are given at the end of the table. Those not shown are from private sources and not available for sale.

The first thirteen listed are shown under page numbers, the remainder by squadron numbers. Where more than one photograph appears under a squadron number, these have been numbered 1A, 1B, etc., the sequence being left to right on the page, then top to bottom, as appropriate.

Position and Type		Ref. No.	Source
p.3	Venom NF.3	32918S	Flt
p.4	Buccaneers & Phantoms	TN 6293/170	MoD
p.5	D.H.2s	H.1925	MoD
p.6	Bristol Fighters & Wapitis	H.1085	MoD
p.7	Valentias	H.803	MoD
p.8	Sunderland I	CH 829	IWM
p.9	Hurricane IICs	CH 5485	IWM
p.10	Hastings Met.1	PRB 24287	MoD
p.11	Meteor F.8s	PRB 8616	MoD
p.12	Hastings C.1	PRB 14025	MoD
p.13	Swift FR.5s	PRB 19505	MoD
p.14	Victor/Valiant/Vulcan	PRB 19750	MoD
p.15	Nimrod MR.1		HQ, NEAF
1A	Fury Is	13392	Flt
1B	Harrier GR.1s	700802	HSA
2	Jaguar T.2	1923/1	RAF Germany
3A	Woodcock Is	H.1141	MoD
3B	Hurricane IICs	CH 3496	IWM
4A	Atlas Is	48831	Flt
4B	Audax I	H.227	MoD
5A	Lightning F.3s	T.6258	MoD
6A	Gordon I	H.152	MoD
6B	Demon I	H.225	MoD
6C	Hurricane IVs	CNA 3199	IWM
7A	Stirling Is	CH 5282	IWM
7C	Heyford III	H.1524	MoD
8A	D.H.9As/Nighthawk	138288	MoD
9A	Heyford III	H.747	MoD
9B	Wellington I	CH 2	IWM
11A	Blenheim I	CM 27	IWM
11B	Fawn II	H.1612	MoD
12A	Fox I	H.161	MoD
12B	B.E.2C	H.719	MoD
13A	Audax Is	H.230	MoD
13B	Hector Is	H.651	MoD
14A	Wellesley Is	H.381	MoD
14B	Jaguar GR.1	1596-8	RAF Germany
16	Canberra B(I).8	PRB 19495	MoD
17	Bulldog IIA	H.1077	MoD
18A	Wessex HC.2	PRB 27330	MoD
18B	D.H.4	Q 11674	IWM
19	Lightning F.2A	5842	MoD
20	Harrier GR.1	PRB 2975/64	MoD
21B	Twin Pioneer CC.1	PRB 19663	MoD
22	Beaufort Is	CH 643	IWM
23A	Vampire NF.10s	28084S	Flt
24B	D.H.89A	H.1538	MoD
25A	Javelin FAW.7	PRB 19532	MoD
25B	Blenheim IF	HU 7681	IWM
26A	Atlas I	H.672	MoD
26B	Tomahawk Is	CH 5864	IWM
28B	Audax Is	PC72/119/18	RAFM
29A	S.E.5As	Q 60608	IWM
30A	Hardys	P.127	RAFM
30B	D.H.9A	H.100	MoD
31	Bristol F.2B	H.1886	MoD
32A	Siskin IIIA	Q 69697	IWM
33A	Horsley IIs	H.722	MoD
35	Vulcan B.2	TN 2471	MoD
36A	Horsley IIIs	H.207	MoD
37	Snipe	G.1118	MoD
38	Hendon I	H.176	MoD
40	Wellington IC	CM 1358	IWM
41	Siskin IIIAs	H.1248	MoD
43A	Gamecock I	H.1485	MoD
43C	Phantom FGR.2s	TN 6228/42	MoD
44	Hampden Is	CH 3481	IWM
45	Vengeance IA	PC73/4/763	RAFM
46B	Andover C.1	3004/23	MoD
47B	Beverley C.1s	PRB 54/15	MoD
48A	Cloud I	H.252	MoD
50	B.E.12	H.1949	MoD
51B	Stirling V	CI 1703	IWM
52	Battle I	H.179	MoD
53	Belfast C.1	262/1	MoD
54B	Hunter F.1s	32035S	Flt
57A	Hart Is	H.217	MoD
57B	Victor K.1	TN 6232/49	MoD
58B	Canberra PR.9s	PRB 19714	MoD
60A	D.H.10s	H.1109	MoD
60B	Meteor NF.14s	PC73/4/549	RAFM
61A	Anson I	PC72/55/59	RAFM
61B	Lancaster II	MH 5955	IWM
64	Hornet F.3	PC73/4/423	RAFM
66	Belvedere HC.1	T 5262	MoD
67B	Buffalo Is	K1228	IWM
68	D.H.5	E 1444-1914	IWM
69A	R.E.8	E 1418-1178	IWM
69B	Maryland I	PC73/4/537	RAFM
70	Victoria III	P 491	RAFM
71	Hurricane I	CH 2406	IWM
72B	Gladiator Is	H.192	MoD
73A	Spitfire IX	P.259	RAFM
74B	Lightning F.6	141145	MoD
75	Lincoln B.1	P.421	RAFM
77	Whitley V	C 926	IWM
78	Twin Pioneer CC.1	PRB 18406	MoD
79A	Gauntlet IIs	H.914	MoD

377

No.	Aircraft	Ref	Source
80	Gladiator Is	H.188	MoD
81	Hurricane IIB	CR 39	IWM
83	Lancaster I	H.1566	MoD
84	D.H.9A	H.806	MoD
85A	Hurricane Is	C 1156	IWM
85B	Canberra T.11	T 6274	MoD
86	Beaufort Is	A 9381	IWM
87	Hurricane IICs	CH 6938	IWM
88	Boston IIIs	CH 6184	IWM
89	Beaufighter VI	CF 511	IWM
90	Blenheim Is	H.79	MoD
92	Hunter F.6s	PRB 19329	MoD
94	Hurricane IICs	CM 3654	IWM
98B	Mitchell IIs	CH 12862	IWM
98C	Canberra B.2	TN 6322/48	MoD
99A	Aldershot Is	H.1378	MoD
99B	Hinaidi II	12991	Flt
100	Vildebeest II	H.364	MoD
103	Whirlwind HC.10	K 28427	Westland
105	Blenheim IV	CM 1357	IWM
106	Hampden I	H.2048	MoD
107A	Boston III	PC74/41/1229	RAFM
108	Liberator II	CM 3386	IWM
111A	Lightning F.1As	PRB 21720	MoD
111B	Hunter F.6s	PRB 13314	MoD
112	Kittyhawk IV	CNA 3493	IWM
113	Blenheim Is	CM 106	IWM
119	Swordfish IIIs	PC73/4/722	RAFM
120A	Liberator III	CH 18035	IWM
120B	Shackleton MR.3s	PRB 25976	MoD
128	Hurricane I	CM 2533	IWM
130A	Spitfire XIV	CL 1353	IWM
131	Spitfire VBs	PC74/47/32	RAFM
132	Spitfire XIV	FE 599	IWM
134	Hurricane IIBs	CR 55	IWM
135	Thunderbolt Is	CF 202	IWM
136	Spitfire VIIIs	CF 682	IWM
137	Whirlwind I	18469S	Flt
139	Victor B.2	26626	MoD
141	Venom NF.3	32914	Flt
142	Battle I	C 790	IWM
143	Beaufighter X	CH 17875	IWM
148	Lysander IIIA	NA 25412	IWM
149	Stirling I	CH 5136	IWM
151A	Venom NF.3	PRB 11271	MoD
154	Spitfire VC	CNA 602	IWM
155A	Mohawk IVs	PC73/4/556	RAFM
155B	Whirlwind HC.4s	MAL 82	IWM
160	Liberator II	CM 3063	IWM
164	Typhoon IB	CH 13240	IWM
165	Spitfire VBs	CH 7688	IWM
166	Heyford IIIs	PC73/81/141	RAFM
172	Wellington VIII	PC74/66/194	RAFM
173	Lockheed 12A	P.854	RAFM
174	Hurricane IIBs	CH 5628	IWM
180	Mitchell IIs		Flt
182	Typhoon IB	PC73/59/7	RAFM
183	Typhoon IB	CH 9289	IWM
185	Hurricane IIB	CM 1293	IWM
188	Avro 504Ks	Q 69120	IWM
190	Halifax III	H.1247	MoD
193	Typhoon IB	CH 11393	IWM
197	Typhoon IB	CH 11592	IWM
198	Typhoon IB	CL 472	IWM
199A	Stirling III	CH 12683	IWM
201	Sunderland MR.5s	32862	Flt
203	Nightjars	H.1422	MoD
204	Southampton I	H.657	MoD
205	Singapore III	H.275	MoD
206A	Hudson III	CH 6573	IWM
208A	Bristol Fighters	H.857	MoD
208B	Hunter FGA.9s	PRB 14837	MoD
209A	Singapore III	H.276	MoD
209B	Lerwick I	P.811	RAFM
210A	Rangoon I		Flt
213	Hurricane I	CM 1407	IWM
214	Stirling III	MH 5513	IWM
215	Liberator VI	CI 998	IWM
218	Battle I	C 449	IWM
219	Meteor NF.13	PRB 7919	MoD
220A	Liberator VI	CA 122	IWM
220B	Fortress IIA	CH 11130	IWM
221A	D.H.9	Q 60270	IWM
222	Hunter F.4s	PRB 11260	MoD
223	Baltimore IIIA	CNA 1115	IWM
225	Whirlwind HC.10	T 2881	MoD
226	D.H.9s	H.94	MoD
229	Baby	H.1020	MoD
230B	Pioneer CC.1		Flt
231	Liberator IX	CH 18794	IWM
232	Lancastrian C.2	CH 17061	IWM
233B	Hudson I	CH 989	IWM
235	Blenheim IVFs	CH 2992	IWM
236	Beaufighter X	CH 18538	IWM
237	Hurricane Is	E 11721	IWM
237/8	Short 184s	PC73/113/14	RAFM
240A	Stranraer I	CH 2551	IWM
242	Stirling V	CH 16499	IWM
243	Short 184	Q 68223	IWM
245A	Hurricane Is	CH 2682	IWM
245B	Meteor F.8s	PRB 13234	Mod
246A	Kangaroo	PC73/4/466	RAFM
246B	Sunderland III	CH 10191	IWM
247	Vampire F.1	R 73	MoD
248A	Blenheim IF	MH 165	IWM
248B	Blenheim IVF	MH 42	IWM
250	Kittyhawk IV	CM 3756	IWM
252	Beaufighter I	P.850	RAFM
253	Hurricane IIBs	CH 4391	IWM
256	Defiant I	MH 4532	IWM
257	Hunter F.2s	PRB 9505	MoD
260	Kittyhawk IIAs	CM 4338	IWM
263A	Gladiator II	PC73/91/8	RAFM
263B	Whirlwind I	CH 8392	IWM
264	Defiant Is	CH 880	IWM
267A	F.2A	H.1225	MoD
270	Baby	PC72/153/19	RAFM
272	Beaufighter I	CM 1125	IWM
273	Spitfire VIII	CF 1053	IWM
274A	Handley Page V/1500	H.1561	MoD
275A	Walrus II	PC73/4/821	RAFM
277	Lysander IIIA	CH 7571	IWM
278A	Spitfire IIA	P.362	RAFM
278B	Anson I	P.357	RAFM
279	Warwick Is	CH 18380	IWM
282	Warwick I	PC73/4/826	RAFM
284A	Walrus I	CNA 432	IWM
284B	Sycamore HR.14	CMP 920	IWM
294	Wellington XI	PC73/59/69	RAFM
295	Stirling IV	CH 13857	IWM
296	Halifax III	IWM 16516	IWM
298	Halifax III	C 5458	IWM
303	Spitfire I	CH 2441	IWM
308	Spitfire IX	CL 601	IWM

309	Lysander IIIs	H 17774	IWM
311	Wellington IC	CH 2265	IWM
315	Mustang IIIs	MH 13762	IWM
320	Fokker T-VIIIW	CH 1156	IWM
328	Spitfire VC	Air 714	ECP-Armées
329	Spitfire VC	Air 4174	ECP-Armées
330	Northrop N-3PB	CS 217	IWM
331	Spitfire VB	CH 1512	IWM
340A	Spitfire VB	DG3000	ECP-Armées
340B	Spitfire IX	Air 15141	ECP-Armées
342	Boston IV	Air 4078	ECP-Armées
347	Halifax III	CH 14613	IWM
352	Spitfire VC	CNA 3097	IWM
355	Liberator VI	C 5160	IWM
356	Liberator VI	CI 1548	IWM
360	Canberra T.17	TN 6833/4	MoD
500	Virginia X	H.744	MoD
501	Vampire F.1	X27919	MoD
502A	Wallace I	H.748	MoD
503	Hinaidi		Flt
504A	Hurricane I	H.1995	MoD
532	Boston III	MH 5710	IWM
538	Havoc II	MH 5711	IWM
542	Canberra PR.7	PRB 8328	MoD
543	Victor/Valiant	PRB 17302	MoD
550	Lancaster I	CH 14187	IWM
571	Mosquito XVI	H.1575	MoD
575	Dakota IIIs	CH 18862	IWM
600	Meteor F.8	PRB 5441	MoD
601A	Spitfire VC	H.1414	MoD
601B	D.H.9A	H.580	MoD
601D	Hurricane IIBs	CH 3517	IWM
602	Wapitis	H.1516	MoD
603	Hart Is	H.922	MoD
604A	Blenheim IFs	HU 2303	IWM
605	Hart Is	H.140	MoD
609	Typhoon IB	CH 9822	IWM
610	Spitfire XIVs	CH 13817	IWM
611	Meteor F.8	P.369	RAFM
612	Whitley VIIs	CS 249	IWM
614	Vampire FB.5s	PC74/12/10	IWM

616	Meteor Is	CL 2925	IWM
619	Lancaster I	CH 12350	IWM
635	Lancaster I	BU 5903	IWM
640	Halifax VI	HU 1980	IWM
644	Halifax VII	CL 2632	IWM
654	Auster IV	NA 22489	IWM
681	Spitfire XIX	PC72/32/28	RAFM

Photographic Library Addresses

IWM: Imperial War Museum
Lambeth Road, London SE.1

MoD: Ministry of Defence
Rm.69, Fourth Floor
King Charles Street
London SW.1

RAFM: Royal Air Force Museum
Hendon, London NW9 5LL

Flt: Flight International
Dorset House, Stamford Street
London SE1 9LU

ECP: Etablissement Cinematographique et
Photographique des Armées
Fort d'Ivry
94 Ivry-sur-Seine, France

In addition to the above, we would like to thank the following who have contributed photographs: John A.Bagley, Roy Benwell, Peter Berry, Roger Bishop, D.N.Blades, British Aircraft Corporation, Charles E.Brown, Charles W.Cain, Peter M.Corbell, Clive Davies, D.Dingle, Richard Hadlow, Donald M.Hannah, E.Hayward, Michael J.Hooks, Peter Howard, V. Ferry, R.P.Howard, A.Johnson, M.P.Marsh, K.D.G.Mitchell, the late Peter Moss, D.H.Newton, R.M.Rayner, D.Ricketts, Bruce Rigelsford, D.J.Smith, M.W.Stubbs, W.A.Threadgold, Eric Watts, D.Wylds and Nos.23, 26, 54, 55, 202 and 206 Squadrons and RAF Station, Tengah.